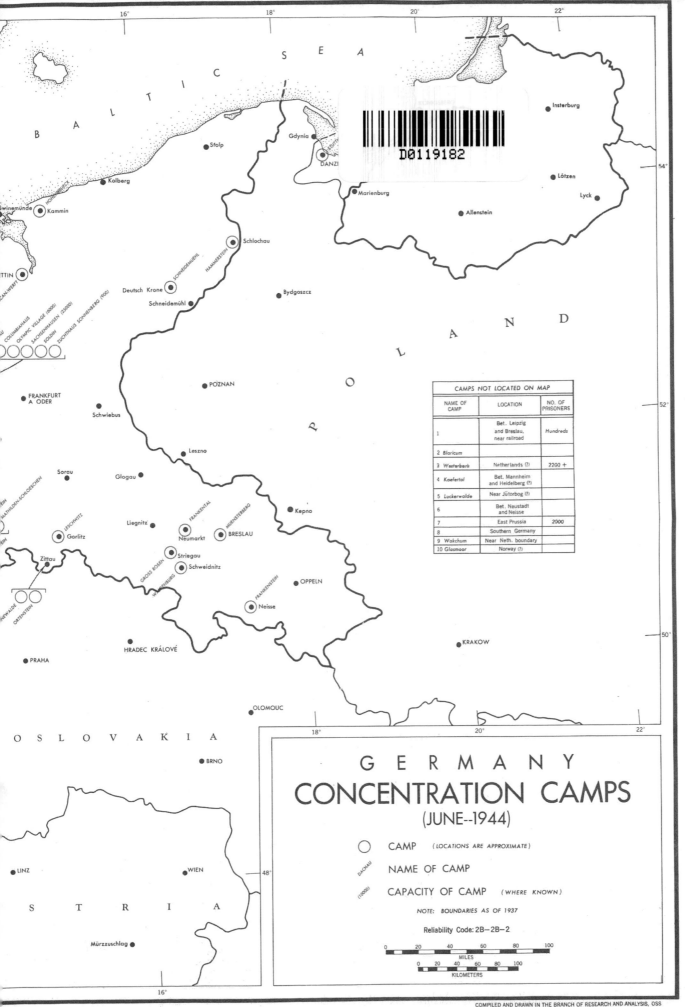

D0119182

G E R M A N Y

CONCENTRATION CAMPS
(JUNE--1944)

○ CAMP *(LOCATIONS ARE APPROXIMATE)*

DACHAU NAME OF CAMP

(1000) CAPACITY OF CAMP *(WHERE KNOWN)*

NOTE: BOUNDARIES AS OF 1937

Reliability Code: 2B—2B—2

0 20 40 60 80 100
MILES

0 20 40 60 80 100
KILOMETERS

CAMPS NOT LOCATED ON MAP		
NAME OF CAMP	LOCATION	NO. OF PRISONERS
1	Bet. Leipzig and Breslau, near railroad	Hundreds
2 Blaricum		
3 Westerbork	Netherlands (?)	2200 +
4 Kaefertal	Bet. Mannheim and Heidelberg (?)	
5 Luckerwalde	Near Jüterbog (?)	
6	Bet. Neustadt and Neisse	
7	East Prussia	2000
8	Southern Germany	
9 Wakchum	Near Neth. boundary	
10 Glasmoor	Norway (?)	

COMPILED AND DRAWN IN THE BRANCH OF RESEARCH AND ANALYSIS, OSS
LITHOGRAPHED IN THE REPRODUCTION BRANCH, OSS

CONFIDENTIAL

Reference Guide to

HOLOCAUST
LITERATURE

St. James Reference Guides

American Literature

English Literature, 3 vols.

French Literature, 2 vols.

Holocaust Literature

Short Fiction

World Literature, 2 vols.

Reference Guide to

HOLOCAUST
LITERATURE

INTRODUCTION BY
JAMES E. YOUNG

EDITOR
THOMAS RIGGS

ST. JAMES PRESS

GALE GROUP
THOMSON LEARNING

Detroit • New York • San Diego • San Francisco
Boston • New Haven, Conn. • Waterville, Maine
London • Munich

STAFF

Thomas Riggs, *Editor*

Mariko Fujinaka, Stephen Meyer, *Associate Editors*

Janice Jorgensen, Sara Olenick, *Contributing Editors*

Robert Rauch, *Senior Line Editor*

Tony Craine, Ellen Finkelstein, Laura Gabler, Joan Hibler, Amy Tao, Amy Tikkanen, *Line Editors*
Erika Fredrickson, Rebecca Stanfel, *Researchers*

Melissa Hill, *Project Coordinator*

Erin Bealmear, Joann Cerrito, Jim Craddock, Stephen Cusack, Miranda H. Ferrara, Kristin Hart,
Margaret Mazurkiewicz, Carol A. Schwartz, Christine Tomassini, Michael J. Tyrkus, *St. James Press Staff*

Peter M. Gareffa, *Managing Editor, St. James Press*

Mary Beth Trimper, *Manager, Composition and Electronic Prepress*
Evi Seoud, *Assistant Manager, Composition Purchasing and Electronic Prepress*
Dorothy Maki, *Manufacturing Manager*
Rhonda Williams, *Buyer*

Cynthia Baldwin, *Senior Art Director*
Barbara J. Yarrow, *Manager, Imaging and Multimedia Content*
Randy Bassett, *Imaging Supervisor*
Christine O'Bryan, *Graphic Specialist*

Library of Congress Catalog Cataloging-in-Publication Data
Reference guide to holocaust literature / introduction by James Young ;
editor, Thomas Riggs.
     p. cm.
Includes bibliographical references and index.
ISBN 1-55862-467-8
    1. Holocaust, Jewish (1939-1945), in literature--Bio-bibliography. I.
Riggs, Thomas, 1963-

PN56.H55 R43 2002
809'.93358--dc21

Printed in the United States of America

St. James Press is an imprint of Gale
Gale and Design is a trademark used herein under license
10 9 8 7 6 5 4 3 2 1

CONTENTS

EDITOR'S NOTE

The *Reference Guide to Holocaust Literature* provides critical coverage of 223 writers and 307 of their works. Almost all the works are novels, short stories, poems, plays, memoirs, and diaries, though a few books in related genres—such as Yaffa Eliach's *Hasidic Tales of the Holocaust,* an oral history—were chosen for their literary merit or other prominence. The earliest work covered in the guide is Lion Feuchtwanger's *The Oppermanns,* published in 1933, the year Adolf Hitler became chancellor of Germany. The most recent book, W.G. Sebald's *Austerlitz,* appeared in 2001.

The 11 distinguished members of our advisory board, headed by Michael Berenbaum, selected the writers featured in this collection. These entrants, about half of whom are living, represent a broad range of nationalities and have published in a variety of languages, though most of the works discussed in this guide are available in English. Of the writers, 130 are classified as western or eastern European, with French, German, and Polish being the most prevalent. The other nationalities with broad representation are American, with 63 writers, and Israeli, with 24. Nationality, however, can be misleading, especially in a community where displacement, isolation, and exile have been common. For example, Rachmil Bryks, a Polish-born author granted U.S. citizenship after the war, wrote not in Polish or English but in Yiddish.

The *Reference Guide to Holocaust Literature* is divided into two sections. The first contains biographical and bibliographic information, as well as brief critical essays, on all 223 writers. Each of these entries has the following organization:

- *Biographical data,* listing, if known, the entrant's nationality, date and place of birth, education, spouse and number of children, career, awards, and, if the entrant is deceased, the death date.

- *Bibliography,* listing the title and date of the entrant's separately published works, including novels, short-story collections, and books of drama, verse, and nonfiction. Edited and translated books are included, as are media adaptations, theatrical activities, and manuscript collections. The bibliography ends with a selected list of critical studies about the author's work.

- *Critical essay on the entrant's work,* written by an established scholar or other qualified reviewer.

The second section has 307 essays, each discussing a work of Holocaust literature by one of the 223 writers. Some writers, such as Aharon Appelfeld, Primo Levi, and Elie Wiesel, have several works represented, though many entrants have just one.

I would like to thank the various people involved in the project, including the 11 advisers, whose suggestions on writers, contributors, and other topics were essential, and the 120 contributors, who spent a great amount of time researching and writing their essays. Because of the primary research done for this book, the *Reference Guide to Holocaust Literature* contains information not available in any other source. Also deserving recognition for its hard work and commitment is the book's staff: Stephen Meyer, who, in addition to many other responsibilities, commissioned writers and corresponded with them; Mariko Fujinaka, who oversaw the compilation of the biographical and bibliographic sections, reviewed text for errors, and headed many day-to-day organizational tasks; Sara Olenick, who helped compile the biographical and bibliographic sections; Janice Jorgensen, who reviewed text for errors; Robert Rauch, who, in addition to editing many of the essays, helped plan and oversee the editing of the text; Tony Craine, Ellen Finkelstein, Laura Gabler, Joan Hibler, Amy Tao, and Amy Tikkanen, who edited essays; Erika Fredrickson and Rebecca Stanfel, whose research for the book was invaluable; and Melissa Hill, who, as project coordinator, handled the many in-house responsibilities, including the proofreading, and patiently helped guide the book to completion.

Finally, I would like to thank the living writers who supplied us with biographical and bibliographic information, as well as the museums, especially the United States Holocaust Memorial Museum, and other organizations that responded to our request for information and advice. I am particularly grateful to Benton Arnovitz, director of academic publications at the United States Holocaust Memorial Museum, whose suggestions at the beginning of the project were indispensable. St. James Press is publishing this guide with the hope of serving the academic field of Holocaust literature, which, through its analysis of texts, helps us critically approach an event so incomprehensible that language itself has proved far from fully representing it.

—Thomas Riggs, *Editor*

ADVISERS

CONTRIBUTORS

Dvir Abramovich
Karen Achberger
Kazimierz Adamczyk
Sandra Alfers

Gregory Baer
Ulrich Baer
Ehrhard Bahr
David Ball
Nicole Ball
Angelika Bammer
Rachel Baum
Samuel I. Bellman
Renate Benson
Michael Berenbaum
Alan L. Berger
Jacqueline Berke
Franz Blaha
Felicity Bloch
Patricia Pollock Brodsky
Sharon Brown
Emily Budick
Steven Dedalus Burch
Andrew Bush

Justin D. Cammy
Grace Connolly Caporino
Steven R. Cerf
Josh Cohen

Tish Dace

Robert Eaglestone
Peter R. Erspamer
Sidra Dekoven Ezrahi

Esther Faye
William R. Fernekes
Jaimey Fischer
Jennifer L. Foray
Richard Freadman

Mila Ganeva
Zev Garber
Piero Garofalo
Stanisław Gawliński
Ellen Gerstle
Simone Gigliotti
Abigail Gillman
Michael S. Glaser
Myrna Goldenberg

Alain Goldshlager
Mark Gruettner
M. Martin Guiney
Stefan Gunther

Jay L. Halio
Marilyn J. Harran
Heather Hathaway
Beth Hawkins
Joanna Hobot
Michael Hoffman
K. Hannah Holtschneider

Radu Ioanid

Manfred Jacobson

Eran Kaplan
Andrzej Karcz
Avi Kay
Cynthia A. Klíma

Lawrence L. Langer
Oliver Leaman
Julian Levinson
Wojciech Ligęza
Mark R. Lindsay
Elizabeth Loentz

Erin McGlothlin
Maryann McLoughlin
Andrew Markus
Alisa Gayle Mayor
Alejandro Meter
Stephen Meyer

Alice Nakhimovsky
Margie Newman
Adam Zachary Newton

Eugene Orenstein
Annamaria Orla-Bukowska
Jan Osborn

Cornelius Partsch
David Patterson
Susan Pentlin
Peter Pierce
Sanford Pinsker
Diane Plotkin
Alan Polak

Judy Rawson
Allan Reid
Paul Reitter
Andrei Rogachevskii
Edgar Rosenberg
Joseph Rosenblum
Alvin H. Rosenfeld
John K. Roth
Judith Ruderman
Susan Russell
Suzanne Rutland

Murray Sachs
Ivan Sanders
Ernestine Schlant
Walter Schmitz
Gerd K. Schneider
Helga Schreckenberger
Olav Schröer
David Scrase
Ziva Shavitsky
Lisa Silverman
R. Clifton Spargo
J.D. Stahl
Rebecca Stanfel
Eric Sterling
Martha Sutro
Christina Svendsen

Margaret Tejerizo
Molly Abel Travis
Richard Tuerk
Maureen Turim

Sue Vice

Hans Wagener
Daniel Walden
Binyomin Weiner
Lenore Weitzman
George R. Wilkes
Ralph G. Williams
Linda M. Woolf

James E. Young
Robert Youngblood

Alexandra Zapruder
Susan Zuccotti

ALPHABETICAL LIST OF WRITERS

Walter Abish
S. Y. Agnon
Ilse Aichinger
Jean Améry
Yehuda Amichai
Robert Antelme
Bruno Apitz
Aharon Appelfeld
Silvano Arieti
Sholem Asch

Ingeborg Bachmann
Mark Baker
Giorgio Bassani
Jurek Becker
Louis Begley
Saul Bellow
Dahn Ben-Amotz
Mary Berg
Thomas Bernhard
Bruno Bettelheim
Abraham Biderman
Halina Birenbaum
Livia E. Bitton-Jackson
Thomas "Toivi" Blatt
Heinrich Böll
Josef Bor
Jorge Luis Borges
Tadeusz Borowski
Bertolt Brecht
Lily Brett
Edith Bruck
Rachmil Bryks

Italo Calvino
Albert Camus
Paul Celan
Arthur A. Cohen
Elie Aron Cohen
Adam Czerniaków

Charlotte Delbo
E. L. Doctorow
Alexander Donat
Emil Dorian
Gerhard Durlacher
Friedrich Dürrenmatt

Marek Edelman
Cordelia Edvardson
Yaffa Eliach
Helen Epstein
Leslie Epstein

Fania Fénelon
Bertha Ferderber-Salz

Lion Feuchtwanger
Jerzy Ficowski
Eva Figes
Ida Fink
Moshe Flinker
Anne Frank
Viktor E. Frankl
Erich Fried
Saul Friedländer
Carl Friedman
Max Frisch
Ladislav Fuks

Romain Gary
Pierre Gascar
Peter Gay
Natalia Ginzburg
Jacob Glatstein
Richard Glazar
Hirsh Glik
Frances Goodrich
Haim Gouri
Chaim Grade
Günter Grass
Uri Zvi Greenberg
David Grossman
Vasily Grossman
Henryk Grynberg
Luba Gurdus

Hans Habe
Albert Hackett
Kitty Hart
Eugene Heimler
John Hersey
William Heyen
Eva Heyman
Wolfgang Hildesheimer
Geoffrey Hill
Etty Hillesum
Edgar Hilsenrath
Rolf Hochhuth
Gert Hofmann

Edmond Jabès

Ka-Tzetnik 135633
Yoram Kaniuk
Chaim A. Kaplan
Yitzhak Katzenelson
Thomas Keneally
Imre Kertész
Heinar Kipphardt
A. M. Klein
Gerda Weissmann Klein
Victor Klemperer

Irena Klepfisz
Ruth Klüger
Wolfgang Koeppen
Sarah Kofman
Eugen Kogon
Gertrud Kolmar
Bernard Kops
Janusz Korczak
Jerzy Kosinski
Abba Kovner
Hanna Krall
Herman Kruk
Jack Kuper
Tony Kushner
Anatoli Kuznetsov

Claude Lanzmann
Barbara Lebow
Isabella Leitner
Olga Lengyel
Denise Levertov
Primo Levi
Meyer Levin
Abraham Lewin
Maria Lewitt
Jakov Lind
Arnošt Lustig

Bernard Malamud
Itzik Manger
Vladka Meed
Aharon Megged
Albert Memmi
Robert Menasse
Arthur Miller
Liana Millu
Czesław Miłosz
Marga Minco
Kazimierz Moczarski
Patrick Modiano
Kadya Molodowsky
Elsa Morante
Filip Müller

Martin Niemöller
Yehuda Nir
Sara Nomberg-Przytyk
Miklos Nyiszli

Krystyn Olszewski
Uri Orlev
Amos Oz
Cynthia Ozick

Dan Pagis
Georges Pérec

Gisella Perl
Harold Pinter
Chaim Potok
Jacques Presser

Miklós Radnóti
Piotr Rawicz
Erich Maria Remarque
Charles Reznikoff
Adrienne Rich
Mordecai Richler
Emmanuel Ringelblum
Philip Roth
Eva Mändlová Roubíčková
David Rousset
Tadeusz Różewicz
Yitskhok Rudashevski
Adolf Rudnicki
Anatolii Rybakov
Jaroslaw Rymkiewicz

Nelly Sachs
Jean-Paul Sartre
Robert Schindel
Bernhard Schlink
André Schwarz-Bart

W. G. Sebald
Mihail Sebastian
Jorge Semprun
Hannah Senesh
Anne Sexton
Martin Sherman
Janusz Nel Siedlecki
Dawid Sierakowiak
Isaac Bashevis Singer
Joshua Sobol
Manès Sperber
Art Spiegelman
George A. Steiner
Jean-François Steiner
Frank Stiffel
Aryeh Lev Stollman
William Styron
Abraham Sutzkever
Erwin Sylvanus
Wladyslaw Szlengel
Wladyslaw Szpilman
Wisława Szymborska

George Tabori
Nechama Tec
Giuliana Tedeschi

D. M. Thomas
Germaine Tillion
Avraham Tory

Leon Uris

Susan Varga
Mark Verstandig
Rudolf Vrba

Edward Lewis Wallant
Jiří Weil
Peter Weiss
Ernst Wiechert
Elie Wiesel
Simon Wiesenthal
Benjamin Wilkomirski
Bogdan Wojdowski

A. B. Yehoshua
Yevgeny Yevtushenko

Arnold Zable
Aaron Zeitlin
Yitzhak ''Antek'' Zuckerman
Stefan Zweig

CHRONOLOGICAL LIST OF WRITERS

(?)–1943	Wladyslaw Szlengel		1911–	Anatolii Rybakov
1878–1942	Janusz Korczak		1911–1977	Hans Habe
1880–1942	Adam Czerniaków		1911–1991	Max Frisch
1880–1942	Chaim A. Kaplan		1911–2000	Wladyslaw Szpilman
1880–1957	Sholem Asch		1912–	Mark Verstandig
1881–1942	Stefan Zweig		1912–1974	Rachmil Bryks
1881–1960	Victor Klemperer		1912–1978	Jean Améry
1884–1958	Lion Feuchtwanger		1912–1990	Adolf Rudnicki
1886–1944	Yitzhak Katzenelson		1912–1991	Edmond Jabès
1887–1950	Ernst Wiechert		1912–1997	David Rousset
1888–1970	S. Y. Agnon		1913–	Abraham Sutzkever
1890–1955	Frances Goodrich		1913–1960	Albert Camus
1891–1970	Nelly Sachs		1913–1985	Charlotte Delbo
1892–1984	Martin Niemöller		1914–	Luba Gurdus
1893–1942	Abraham Lewin		1914–	Liana Millu
1893–1956	Emil Dorian		1914–	George Tabori
1894–1943	Gertrud Kolmar		1914–	Giuliana Tedeschi
1894–1975	Kadya Molodowsky		1914–1943	Etty Hillesum
1894–1976	Charles Reznikoff		1914–1980	Romain Gary
1896–1971	Jacob Glatstein		1914–1981	Silvano Arieti
1897–1944	Herman Kruk		1914–1986	Bernard Malamud
1898–1956	Bertolt Brecht		1914–1993	John Hersey
1898–1970	Erich Maria Remarque		1915–	Arthur Miller
1898–1974	Aaron Zeitlin		1915–	Saul Bellow
1898–1981	Uri Zvi Greenberg		1915–1981	Yitzhak ''Antek'' Zuckerman
1899–1970	Jacques Presser		1915–1996	Sara Nomberg-Przytyk
1899–1986	Jorge Luis Borges		1916–	Frank Stiffel
1900–1944	Emmanuel Ringelblum		1916–1982	Peter Weiss
1900–1959	Jiří Weil		1916–1991	Natalia Ginzburg
1900–1979	Bruno Apitz		1916–1991	Wolfgang Hildesheimer
1900–1995	Albert Hackett		1916–1997	Pierre Gascar
1901–1956	Miklos Nyiszli		1916–2000	Giorgio Bassani
1901–1969	Itzik Manger		1916–2000	Janusz Nel Siedlecki
1902–	Bertha Ferderber-Salz		1917–1985	Heinrich Böll
1903–1987	Eugen Kogon		1917–1985	Erwin Sylvanus
1903–1990	Bruno Bettelheim		1917–1990	Robert Antelme
1904–1991	Isaac Bashevis Singer		1917–2001	Ka-Tzetnik 135633
1905–1964	Vasily Grossman		1918–1983	Fania Fénelon
1905–1980	Jean-Paul Sartre		1918–1985	Elsa Morante
1905–1981	Meyer Levin		1918–1987	Abba Kovner
1905–1983	Alexander Donat		1919–1982	Piotr Rawicz
1905–1984	Manès Sperber		1919–1987	Primo Levi
1905–1997	Viktor E. Frankl		1920–	Aharon Megged
1906–1979	Josef Bor		1920–	Albert Memmi
1906–1996	Wolfgang Koeppen		1920–	Marga Minco
1907–	Germaine Tillion		1920–1970	Paul Celan
1907–1945	Mihail Sebastian		1920–1998	Richard Glazar
1907–1975	Kazimierz Moczarski		1921–	Ilse Aichinger
1907–1988	Gisella Perl		1921–	Ida Fink
1908–	Simon Wiesenthal		1921–	Krystyn Olszewski
1909–1944	Miklós Radnóti		1921–	Eva Mändlová Roubíčková
1909–1972	A. M. Klein		1921–	Tadeusz Różewicz
1909–1993	Elie Aron Cohen		1921–1944	Hannah Senesh
1909–2002	Avraham Tory		1921–1988	Erich Fried
1910–1982	Chaim Grade		1921–1990	Friedrich Dürrenmatt
1911–	Czesław Miłosz		1922–	Marek Edelman

1922–	Eugene Heimler
1922–1944	Hirsh Glik
1922–1951	Tadeusz Borowski
1922–1982	Heinar Kipphardt
1923–	Peter Gay
1923–	Haim Gouri
1923–	Vladka Meed
1923–	Jorge Semprun
1923–	Wisława Szymborska
1923–1985	Italo Calvino
1923–1990	Dahn Ben-Amotz
1923–1994	Ladislav Fuks
1923–1997	Denise Levertov
1924–	Mary Berg
1924–	Abraham Biderman
1924–	Jerzy Ficowski
1924–	Gerda Weissmann Klein
1924–	Isabella Leitner
1924–	Maria Lewitt
1924–	Leon Uris
1924–	Rudolf Vrba
1924–1943	Dawid Sierakowiak
1924–2000	Yehuda Amichai
1925–	Claude Lanzmann
1925–	William Styron
1926–	Kitty Hart
1926–	Edgar Hilsenrath
1926–	Bernard Kops
1926–	Arnošt Lustig
1926–1944	Moshe Flinker
1926–1962	Edward Lewis Wallant
1926–1973	Ingeborg Bachmann
1927–	Thomas "Toivi" Blatt
1927–	Günter Grass
1927–	Jakov Lind
1927–1943	Yitskhok Rudashevski
1928–	Cynthia Ozick
1928–	André Schwarz-Bart
1928–	Elie Wiesel
1928–1974	Anne Sexton
1928–1986	Arthur A. Cohen
1928–1996	Gerhard Durlacher
1929–	Halina Birenbaum
1929–	Cordelia Edvardson
1929–	Imre Kertész
1929–	Chaim Potok
1929–	Adrienne Rich
1929–	George A. Steiner
1929–1945	Anne Frank
1929–1979	Anatoli Kuznetsov
1930–	Yoram Kaniuk
1930–	Yehuda Nir
1930–	Harold Pinter
1930–1986	Dan Pagis
1930–1994	Bogdan Wojdowski
1931–	Walter Abish
1931–	Livia E. Bitton-Jackson
1931–	E. L. Doctorow
1931–	Rolf Hochhuth
1931–	Ruth Klüger

1931–	Uri Orlev
1931–	Nechama Tec
1931–1944	Eva Heyman
1931–1989	Thomas Bernhard
1931–1993	Gert Hofmann
1931–2001	Mordecai Richler
1932–	Aharon Appelfeld
1932–	Edith Bruck
1932–	Eva Figes
1932–	Saul Friedländer
1932–	Geoffrey Hill
1932–	Jack Kuper
1933–	Louis Begley
1933–	Philip Roth
1933–	Yevgeny Yevtushenko
1933–1991	Jerzy Kosinski
1934–1994	Sarah Kofman
1935–	Thomas Keneally
1935–	Jaroslaw Rymkiewicz
1935–	D. M. Thomas
1936–	Henryk Grynberg
1936–	Barbara Lebow
1936–	A. B. Yehoshua
1936–1982	Georges Pérec
1937–	Yaffa Eliach
1937–	Hanna Krall
1937–1997	Jurek Becker
1938–	Leslie Epstein
1938–	Martin Sherman
1938–	Jean-François Steiner
1939–	Amos Oz
1939–	Joshua Sobol
1939–	Binjamin Wilkomirski
1940–	William Heyen
1941–	Irena Klepfisz
1943–	Susan Varga
1944–	Robert Schindel
1944–	Bernhard Schlink
1944–2001	W. G. Sebald
1945–	Patrick Modiano
1946–	Lily Brett
1947–	Helen Epstein
1947–	Arnold Zable
1948–	Art Spiegelman
1952–	Carl Friedman
1954–	David Grossman
1954–	Robert Menasse
1954–	Aryeh Lev Stollman
1956–	Tony Kushner
1959–	Mark Baker

ALPHABETICAL LIST OF WORKS

The Accident, novel by Elie Wiesel, 1961

Adam, play by Joshua Sobol, 1989

Adam Resurrected, novel by Yoram Kaniuk, 1969

All but My Life, memoir by Gerda Weissmann Klein, 1957

And the Sun Kept Shining, memoir by Bertha Ferderber-Salz, 1965

And Where Were You, Adam?, novel by Heinrich Böll, 1951

Andorra: A Play in Twelve Scenes, play by Max Frisch, 1962

The Apprenticeship of Duddy Kravitz, novel by Mordecai Richler, 1959

Ascent to Heaven, novella by Adolf Rudnicki, 1948

Ashes to Ashes, play by Harold Pinter, 1996

At the Mind's Limits: Contemplations by a Survivor on Auschwitz and Its Realities, autobiographical essays by Jean Améry, 1966

Atrocity, novel by Ka-Tzetnik 135633, 1961

Auschwitz: A Doctor's Eyewitness Account, memoir by Miklos Nyiszli, 1947

Auschwitz and After, memoir by Charlotte Delbo, 1970

Auschwitz: True Tales from a Grotesque Land, memoir by Sara Nomberg-Przytyk, 1985

Austerlitz, novel by W.G. Sebald, 2001

The Awful Rowing toward God, poems by Anne Sexton, 1975

Babi Yar: A Documentary Novel, novel by Anatoli Kuznetsov, 1966

''Babii Yar,'' poem by Yevgeny Yevtushenko, 1961

Badenheim 1939, novel by Aharon Appelfeld, 1975

Bent, play by Martin Sherman, 1979

Biedermann and the Fire Raisers: A Morality without a Moral, play by Max Frisch, 1958

Bitter Herbs: A Little Chronicle, novel by Marga Minco, 1957

Blood from the Sky, novel by Piotr Rawicz, 1961

The Book of Questions, miscellany by Edmond Jabès, 1963–73

Bread for the Departed, novel by Bogdan Wojdowski, 1971

A Bright Room Called Day, play by Tony Kushner, 1991

Bronstein's Children, novel by Jurek Becker, 1986

Bruder Eichmann, play by Heinar Kipphardt, 1983

Burned Child Seeks the Fire: Memoir, memoir by Cordelia Edvardson, 1984

The Cannibals, play by George Tabori, 1974

A Canopy in the Desert, poem by Abba Kovner, 1970

A Cat in the Ghetto: Four Novelettes, novelettes by Rachmil Bryks, 1952

Child of the Holocaust, memoir by Jack Kuper, 1967

Child of the Shadows, novel by Henryk Grynberg, 1965

The Chocolate Deal, novella by Haim Gouri, 1964

The Chosen, novel by Chaim Potok, 1967

City of God, novel by E. L. Doctorow, 2000

Clouded Sky, poems by Miklós Radnóti, 1946

Co czytalem umarlym, poems by Wladyslaw Szlengel, 1977

Collected Poems, poems by A. M. Klein, 1974

Collected Poems, poems by Tadeusz Różewicz, 1957

Come Spring: An Autobiographical Novel, novel by Maria Lewitt, 1980

The Condemned of Altona, play by Jean Paul Sartre, 1960

The Conversations with an Executioner, memoir by Kazimierz Moczarski, 1977

Counting My Steps: An Autobiography, memoir by Jakov Lind, 1969

A Cup of Tears: A Diary of the Warsaw Ghetto, diary by Abraham Lewin, 1988

The Dance of Genghis Cohn, novel by Romain Gary, 1967

Dark Soliloquy: The Selected Poems of Gertrud Kolmar, collection of poems by Gertrud Kolmar, 1955

Darkness Casts No Shadow, novel by Arnošt Lustig, 1976

Dawn, novel by Elie Wiesel, 1960

''Death Fugue,'' poem by Paul Celan, 1948

The Death Train: A Personal Account of a Holocaust Survivor, memoir by Luba Krugman Gurdus, 1978

Die Denunziation, novella by Gert Hofmann, 1979

The Deputy, play by Rolf Hochhuth, 1963

''Deutsches Requiem,'' short story by Jorge Luis Borges, 1949

Diamonds of the Night, short stories by Arnošt Lustig, 1958

Diary of a Young Girl, diary by Anne Frank, 1947

The Diary of Anne Frank, play by Frances Goodrich and Albert Hackett, 1956

The Diary of Dawid Sierakowiak: Five Notebooks from the Lodz Ghetto, diary by Dawid Sierakowiak, 1960

The Diary of Eva Heyman: Child of the Holocaust, diary by Eva Heyman, 1964

The Diary of the Vilna Ghetto: June 1941–April 1943, diary by Yitskhok Rudashevski, 1968

Dr. Korczak and the Children, play by Erwin Sylvanus, 1957

Dreams of Anne Frank: A Play for Young People, Play by Bernard Kops, 1993

The Drowned and the Saved, memoir by Primo Levi, 1986

Drowning: Growing up in the Third Reich, memoir by Gerhard Durlacher, 1987

Dry Tears: The Story of a Lost Childhood, memoir by Nechama Tec, 1984

''During the Eichmann Trial,'' poem by Denise Levertov, 1961

''Eastern War Time,'' poem by Adrienne Rich, 1989–90

Eli: A Mystery Play of the Sufferings of Israel, play by Nelly Sachs, 1951

''Eli, the Fanatic,'' short story by Philip Roth, 1959

Elli: Coming of Age in the Holocaust, memoir by Livia E. Bitton-Jackson, 1980

The Emigrants, novel by W.G. Sebald, 1993

Enemies: A Love Story, novel by Isaac Bashevis Singer, 1966

''The English Garden,'' short story by Walter Abish, 1977

Erika: Poems of the Holocaust, poems by William Heyen, 1984

''Errinerungen an Prometheus,'' poem by Robert Schindel, 1964

Di ershte Nakht in Geto, poems by Abraham Sutzkever, 1979

Eva: A Novel of the Holocaust, novel by Meyer Levin, 1959

Exile in the Fatherland: Martin Niemöller's Letters from Moabit Prison, memoir by Martin Niemöller, 1975

Eyewitness Auschwitz: Three Years in the Gas Chambers, memoir by Filip Müller, 1979

The Fall, novel by Albert Camus, 1956

The Fanatic, novel by Meyer Levin, 1964

The Far Euphrates, novel by Aryeh Lev Stollman, 1997

Fateless, novel by Imre Kertész, 1975

Fear and Misery of the Third Reich, play by Bertolt Brecht, 1941

Di Festung, poems by Abraham Sutzkever, 1945

The Fiftieth Gate: A Journey through Memory, memoir by Mark Raphael Baker, 1997

The Final Station: Umschlagplatz, novel by Jaroslaw Marek Rymkiewicz, 1988

Five Chimneys, memoir by Olga Lengyel, 1946

The Forest of the Dead, novel by Ernst Wiechert, 1945

The Forgotten, novel by Elie Wiesel, 1989

Fragments: Memories of a Wartime Childhood, memoir by Binjamin Wilkomirski, 1995

Fragments of Isabella: A Memoir of Auschwitz, memoir by Isabella Leitner, 1978

From the Ashes of Sobibor: A Story of Survival, memoir by Thomas Blatt, 1997

From the Diary of a Snail, novel by Günter Grass, 1972

The Garden of the Finzi-Contini, novel by Giorgio Bassani, 1962

The Gates of the Forest, novel by Elie Wiesel, 1964

Gebürtig, novel by Robert Schindel, 1992

''The German Refugee,'' short story by Bernard Malamud, 1963

Ghetto, play by Joshua Sobol, 1983

Ghetto Diary, diary by Janusz Korczak, 1978

''Ghetto Factory 76: Chemical Waste Conversion,'' poem by Rachmil Bryks, 1967

The Ghetto Fights, memoir by Marek Edelman, 1945

The Ghost Writer, novella by Philip Roth, 1979

Green Aquarium, poems by Abraham Sutzkever, 1972

Hannah Senesh, play by Aharon Megged, 1958

Hannah Senesh: Her Life and Diary, diary by Hannah Senesh, 1966

Hasidic Tales of the Holocaust, oral history by Yaffa Eliach, 1982

Heavy Sand, novel by Anatolii Rybakov, 1978

Heddy and Me, memoir by Susan Varga, 1994

Heldenplatz, play by Thomas Bernhard, 1988

Herod's Children, novel by Ilse Aichinger, 1948

History: A Novel, novel by Elsa Morante, 1974

Holocaust, poem by Charles Reznikoff, 1975

The Holocaust Kingdom, memoir by Alexander Donat, 1965

Hope Is the Last to Die: A Coming of Age under Nazi Terror, memoir by Halina Birenbaum, 1967

House of Dolls, novel by Ka-Tzetnik 135633, 1953

How German Is It, novel by Walter Abish, 1980

Human Behaviour in the Concentration Camp: A Medical and Psychological Study, memoir and study by Elie Aron Cohen, 1952

The Human Species, memoir by Robert Antelme, 1947

I Am Alive!, memoir by Kitty Hart, 1961

I Cannot Forgive, memoir by Rudolf Vrba, 1963

I Keep Recalling: The Holocaust Poems of Jacob Glatstein, poems by Jacob Glatstein, 1993

I Rest My Case, memoir by Mark Verstandig, 1995

I Was a Doctor in Auschwitz, memoir by Gisella Perl, 1948

I Will Bear Witness: A Diary of the Nazi Years, diary by Victor Klemperer, 1995

Ice Fire Water: A Leib Goldkorn Cocktail, novel by Leslie Epstein, 1999

If Not Now, When?, novel by Primo Levi, 1982

The Immortal Bartfuss, novel by Aharon Appelfeld, 1988

In Full View, essays by Lily Brett, 1997

In the Days of Simon Stern, novel by Arthur A. Cohen, 1973

Incident at Vichy, play by Arthur Miller, 1964

The Informed Heart: Autonomy in a Mass Age, memoir and study by Bruno Bettelheim, 1960

An Interrupted Life: The Diaries of Etty Hillesum, 1941–43, diaries of Etty Hillesum, 1981

The Investigation, play by Peter Weiss, 1965

The Island on Bird Street, children's novel by Uri Orlev, 1981

Jacob the Liar, novel by Jurek Becker, 1969

Jakob Littners Aufzeichnungen aus einem Erdloch: Roman, novel by Wolfgang Koeppen, 1948

Jewels and Ashes, memoir by Arnold Zable, 1991

Joel Brand: Die Geschichte eines Geschäfts, play by Heinar Kipphardt, 1965

Journal 1935–1944: The Fascist Years, diary by Mihail Sebastian, 1996

The Journey, novel by Ida Fink, 1990

Jubiläum, play by George Tabori, 1984

Kaddish for a Child Not Born, novel by Imre Kertész, 1990

King of the Jews: A Novel of the Holocaust, novel by Leslie Epstein, 1979

Kol Ha-shirim: ''Aba'', poetry by Dan Pagis, 1991

''The Lady of the Lake,'' short story by Bernard Malamud, 1958

Landscape in Concrete, novel by Jakov Lind, 1963

''Landscape of Screams'', poem by Nelly Sachs, 1957

The Last Jew, play by Yaffa Eliach, 1977

''The Last Mohican,'' short story by Bernard Malamud, 1958

The Last of the Just, novel by André Schwarz-Bart, 1959

''The Lecture,'' short story by Isaac Bashevis Singer, 1967

''The Letter Writer,'' short story by Isaac Bashevis Singer, 1968

Letters from Westerbork, correspondence of Etty Hillesum, 1982

Lieder fun churban 'on lieder fun gloybin, poems by Aaron Zeitlin, 1967

Life and Fate, novel by Vasily Grossman, 1980

Life with a Star, novel by Jiří Weil, 1949

Like a Tear in the Ocean, novels by Manès Sperber, 1951

Literature or Life, memoir by Jorge Semprun, 1994

Little Eden: A Child at War, memoir by Eva Figes, 1978

The Long Voyage, memoir by Jorge Semprun, 1963

The Lost Childhood: A Memoir, memoir by Yehuda Nir, 1989

Malina: A Novel, novel by Ingeborg Bachmann, 1971

The Man from the Other Side, children's novel by Uri Orlev, 1988

Man's Search for Meaning: An Introduction to Logotherapy, memoir and study by Viktor E. Frankl, 1946

Maus—A Survivor's Tale, story by Art Spiegelman, 1986 and 1991

The Messiah of Stockholm, novel by Cynthia Ozick, 1987

Mila 18, novel by Leon Uris, 1961

The Mission, novel by Hans Habe, 1965

Mr. Mani, novel by A. B. Yehoshua, 1990

Mr. Sammler's Planet, novel by Saul Bellow, 1970

Mr. Theodore Mundstock, novel by Ladislav Fuks, 1963

Mutters Courage, play by George Tabori, 1994

My Father's House, novel by Meyer Levin, 1947

My German Question: Growing up in Nazi Berlin, memoir by Peter Gay, 1998

My Hate Song, poem by Itzik Manger, 1961

My Little Sister, poem by Abba Kovner, 1967

My Mother's Sabbath Days, memoir by Chaim Grade, 1958

My Name Is Asher Lev, novel by Chaim Potok, 1972

''My Quarrel with Hersh Rasseyner,'' short story by Chaim Grade, 1982

Naked among Wolves, novel by Bruno Apitz, 1958

The Nazi and the Barber, novel by Edgar Hilsenrath, 1971

Night, novel by Edgar Hilsenrath, 1964

Night, memoir by Elie Wiesel, 1958

Night and Hope, short stories by Arnošt Lustig, 1958

The Night in Lisbon, novel by Erich Maria Remarque, 1961

Night of the Girondists, or *Breaking Point*, novel by Jacques Presser, 1957

Night of the Mist, memoir by Eugene Heimler, 1959

Nightfather, novel by Carl Friedman, 1991

Not of this Time, Not of this Place, novel by Yehuda Amichai, 1963

CHRONOLOGICAL LIST OF WORKS

The Oppermans, novel by Lion Feuchtwanger, 1933

Fear and Misery of the Third Reich, play by Bertolt Brecht, 1941

The World of Yesterday: An Autobiography, memoir by Stefan Zweig, 1941

The Royal Game, novella by Stefan Zweig, 1944

"The Secret Miracle," short story by Jorge Luis Borges, 1944

The Song of the Murdered Jewish People, epic poem by Yitzhak Katzenelson, 1944

Di Festung, poems by Abraham Sutzkever, 1945

The Forest of the Dead, novel by Ernst Wiechert, 1945

The Ghetto Fights, memoir by Marek Edelman, 1945

Ocalenie, poems by Czesław Miłosz, 1945

"One Destiny: An Epistle to the Christians," essay by Sholem Asch, 1945

Warsaw Ghetto: A Diary, diary by Mary Berg, 1945

A World Apart, memoir by David Rousset, 1945

Clouded Sky, poems by Miklós Radnóti, 1946

Five Chimneys, memoir by Olga Lengyel, 1946

Man's Search for Meaning: An Introduction to Logotherapy, memoir and study by Viktor E. Frankl, 1946

The Pianist: The Extraordinary Story of One Man's Survival in Warsaw, 1939–45, memoir by Wladyslaw Szpilman, 1946

The Theory and Practice of Hell: The German Concentration Camps and the System behind Them, memoir and study by Eugen Kogon, 1946

There Is a Place on Earth: A Woman in Birkenau, memoir by Giuliana Tedeschi, 1946

We Were in Auschwitz, memoir by Janusz Nel Siedlecki, Krystyn Olszewski, and Tadeusz Borowski, 1946

Zog Nit Keynmol, poetry by Hirsh Glik, 1946

Auschwitz: A Doctor's Eyewitness Account, memoir by Miklos Nyiszli, 1947

Diary of a Young Girl, diary by Anne Frank, 1947

The Human Species, memoir by Robert Antelme, 1947

My Father's House, novel by Meyer Levin, 1947

"O the Chimneys!," poem by Nelly Sachs, 1947

The Plague, novel by Albert Camus, 1947

Smoke over Birkenau, short stories by Liana Millu, 1947

Sunrise over Hell, novel by Ka-Tzetnik 135633, 1947

Survival in Auschwitz, memoir by Primo Levi, 1947

Ascent to Heaven, novella by Adolf Rudnicki, 1948

"Death Fugue," poem by Paul Celan, 1948

Herod's Children, novel by Ilse Aichinger, 1948

I Was a Doctor in Auschwitz, memoir by Gisella Perl, 1948

Jakob Littners Aufzeichnungen aus einem Erdloch: Roman, novel by Wolfgang Koeppen, 1948

On Both Sides of the Wall, memoir by Vladka Meed, 1948

"Deutsches Requiem," short story by Jorge Luis Borges, 1949

Life with a Star, novel by Jiří Weil, 1949

The Wall, novel by John Hersey, 1950

And Where Were You, Adam?, novel by Heinrich Böll, 1951

Eli: A Mystery Play of the Sufferings of Israel, play by Nelly Sachs, 1951

Like a Tear in the Ocean, novels by Manès Sperber, 1951

The Second Scroll, novel by A.M. Klein, 1951

Streets of the River: The Book of Dirges and Power, poems by Uri Zvi Greenberg, 1951

A Cat in the Ghetto: Four Novelettes, novelettes by Rachmil Bryks, 1952

Human Behaviour in the Concentration Camp: A Medical and Psychological Study, memoir and study by Elie Aron Cohen, 1952

Notes from the Warsaw Ghetto: The Journal of Emmanuel Ringelblum, diary by Emmanuel Ringelblum, 1952

A Plaque on via Mazzini, novel by Giorgio Bassini, 1952

Spark of Life, novel by Erich Maria Remarque, 1952

House of Dolls, novel by Ka-Tzetnik 135633, 1953

Pillar of Salt, novel by Albert Memmi, 1953

The Quarry, novel by Friedrich Dürrenmatt, 1953

The Season of the Dead, novella by Pierre Gascar, 1953

Dark Soliloquy: The Selected Poems of Gertrud Kolmar, collection of poems by Gertrud Kolmar, 1955

"Shibboleth," poem by Paul Celan, 1955

The Diary of Anne Frank, play by Frances Goodrich and Albert Hackett, 1956

The Fall, novel by Albert Camus, 1956

The Path to the Nest of Spiders, novel by Italo Calvino, 1956

All but My Life, memoir by Gerda Weissmann Klein, 1957

Bitter Herbs: A Little Chronicle, novel by Marga Minco, 1957

Collected Poems, poems by Tadeusz Różewicz, 1957

Dr. Korczak and the Children, play by Erwin Sylvanus, 1957

"Landscape of Screams," poem by Nelly Sachs, 1957

Night of the Girondists, or Breaking Point, novel by Jacques Presser, 1957

The Resistible Rise of Arturo Ui, play by Bertolt Brecht, 1957

Biedermann and the Fire Raisers: A Morality without a Moral, play by Max Frisch, 1958

Diamonds of the Night, short stories by Arnošt Lustig, 1958

Hannah Senesh, play by Aharon Megged, 1958

My Mother's Sabbath Days, memoir by Chaim Grade, 1958

Naked among Wolves, novel by Bruno Apitz, 1958

Night, memoir by Elie Wiesel, 1958

Night and Hope, short stories by Arnošt Lustig, 1958

"The Lady of the Lake," short story by Bernard Malamud, 1958

"The Last Mohican," short story by Bernard Malamud, 1958

Who Loves You like This, memoir by Edith Bruck, 1958

Young Moshe's Diary: The Spiritual Torment of a Jewish Boy in Nazi Europe, diary by Moshe Flinker, 1958

The Apprenticeship of Duddy Kravitz, novel by Mordecai Richler, 1959

"Eli, the Fanatic," short story by Philip Roth, 1959

Eva: A Novel of the Holocaust, novel by Meyer Levin, 1959

The Last of the Just, novel by André Schwarz-Bart, 1959

Night of the Mist, memoir by Eugene Heimler, 1959

The Tin Drum, novel by Günter Grass, 1959

"Two Formal Elegies," poems by Geoffrey Hill, 1959

The Condemned of Altona, play by Jean Paul Sartre, 1960

Dawn, novel by Elie Wiesel, 1960

The Diary of Dawid Sierakowiak: Five Notebooks from the Lodz Ghetto, diary by Dawid Sierakowiak, 1960

The Informed Heart: Autonomy in a Mass Age, memoir and study by Bruno Bettelheim, 1960

"Zürich, the Stork Inn," poem by Paul Celan, 1960

The Accident, novel by Elie Wiesel, 1961

The Death Train: A Personal Account of a Holocaust Survivor, memoir by Luba Krugman Gurdus, 1978

Fragments of Isabella: A Memoir of Auschwitz, memoir by Isabella Leitner, 1978

Ghetto Diary, diary by Janusz Korczak, 1978

Heavy Sand, novel by Anatolii Rybakov, 1978

Little Eden: A Child at War, memoir by Eva Figes, 1978

When Memory Comes, memoir by Saul Friedländer, 1978

Bent, play by Martin Sherman, 1979

Die Denunziation, novella by Gert Hofmann, 1979

Di ershte Nakht in Geto, poems by Abraham Sutzkever, 1979

Eyewitness Auschwitz: Three Years in the Gas Chambers, memoir by Filip Müller, 1979

The Ghost Writer, novella by Philip Roth, 1979

King of the Jews: A Novel of the Holocaust, novel by Leslie Epstein, 1979

The Parnas: A Scene from the Holocaust, novel by Silvano Arieti, 1979

The Portage to San Cristóbal of A.H., novel by George Steiner, 1979

Sophie's Choice, novel by William Styron, 1979

The Unloved: From the Diary of Perla S., novel by Arnošt Lustig, 1979

Come Spring: An Autobiographical Novel, novel by Maria Lewitt, 1980

Elli: Coming of Age in the Holocaust, memoir by Livia E. Bitton-Jackson, 1980

How German Is It, novel by Walter Abish, 1980

Life and Fate, novel by Vasily Grossman, 1980

''The Shawl,'' short story by Cynthia Ozick, 1980

What a Beautiful Sunday!, memoir by Jorge Semprun, 1980

An Interrupted Life: The Diaries of Etty Hillesum, 1941–43, diaries of Etty Hillesum, 1981

The Island on Bird Street, children's novel by Uri Orlev, 1981

A Reading of Ashes: Poems, poems by Jerzy Ficowski, 1981

Return to Auschwitz: The Remarkable Story of a Girl Who Survived the Holocaust, memoir by Kitty Hart, 1981

The White Hotel, novel by D.M. Thomas, 1981

Hasidic Tales of the Holocaust, oral history by Yaffa Eliach, 1982

If Not Now, When?, novel by Primo Levi, 1982

Letters from Westerbork, correspondence of Etty Hillesum, 1982

''My Quarrel with Hersh Rasseyner,'' short story by Chaim Grade, 1982

The Quality of Witness: A Romanian Diary 1937–1944, diary by Emil Dorian, 1982

The Retreat, novel by Aharon Appelfeld, 1982

Schindler's List, novel by Thomas Keneally, 1982

Bruder Eichmann, play by Heinar Kipphardt, 1983

Ghetto, play by Joshua Sobol, 1983

''Rosa,'' short story by Cynthia Ozick, 1983

A Scrap of Time and Other Stories, short stories by Ida Fink, 1983

Trost Und Angst: Erzählungen Über Juden Und Nazis, memoirs and poems by Erich Fried, 1983

Tzili: The Story of a Life, novel by Aharon Appelfeld, 1983

Burned Child Seeks the Fire: Memoir, memoir by Cordelia Edvardson, 1984

Dry Tears: The Story of a Lost Childhood, memoir by Nechama Tec, 1984

Erika: Poems of the Holocaust, poems by William Heyen, 1984

Jubiläum, play by George Tabori, 1984

Radical Humanism: Selected Essays, essays by Jean Améry, 1984

The Tale of the Ring: A Kaddish, memoir by Frank Stiffel, 1984

Auschwitz: True Tales from a Grotesque Land, memoir by Sara Nomberg-Przytyk, 1985

Shoah, oral history by Claude Lanzmann, 1985

Stripes in the Sky: A Wartime Memoir, memoir by Gerhard Durlacher, 1985

Zuckerman Bound: A Trilogy and Epilogue, story by Philip Roth, 1985

Bronstein's Children, novel by Jurek Becker, 1986

The Drowned and the Saved, memoir by Primo Levi, 1986

See Under: Love, novel by David Grossman, 1986

Veilchenfeld, novel by Gert Hofmann, 1986

Maus—A Survivor's Tale, story by Art Spiegelman, 1986 and 1991

Drowning: Growing up in the Third Reich, memoir by Gerhard Durlacher, 1987

The Messiah of Stockholm, novel by Cynthia Ozick, 1987

Stifled Words, memoir by Sarah Kofman, 1987

A Cup of Tears: A Diary of the Warsaw Ghetto, diary by Abraham Lewin, 1988

The Final Station: Umschlagplatz, novel by Jaroslaw Marek Rymkiewicz, 1988

Heldenplatz, play by Thomas Bernhard, 1988

The Immortal Bartfuss, novel by Aharon Appelfeld, 1988

The Man from the Other Side, children's novel by Uri Orlev, 1988

Ravensbrück, memoirs by Germaine Tillion, 1988

A Shayna Maidel, play by Barbara Lebow, 1988

Surviving the Holocaust: The Kovno Ghetto Diary, diary by Avraham Tory, 1988

Adam, play by Joshua Sobol, 1989

The Forgotten, novel by Elie Wiesel, 1989

The Lost Childhood: A Memoir, memoir by Yehuda Nir, 1989

''Eastern War Time,'' poem by Adrienne Rich, 1989–90

The Journey, novel by Ida Fink, 1990

Kaddish for a Child Not Born, novel by Imre Kertész, 1990

Mr. Mani, novel by A.B. Yehoshua, 1990

''Di rayze aheym/The journey home,'' poem by Irena Klepfisz, 1990

A Surplus of Memory: Chronicle of the Warsaw Ghetto Uprising, memoir by Yitzhak Zuckerman, 1990

A Bright Room Called Day, play by Tony Kushner, 1991

Jewels and Ashes, memoir by Arnold Zable, 1991

Kol Ha-shirim: ''Aba,'' poetry by Dan Pagis, 1991

Nightfather, novel by Carl Friedman, 1991

Underground, play by Joshua Sobol, 1991

Wartime Lies, novel by Louis Begley, 1991

Wings of Stone, novel by Robert Menasse, 1991

Gebürtig, novel by Robert Schindel, 1992

Still Alive: A Holocaust Girlhood Remembered, memoir by Ruth Klüger, 1992

Trap with a Green Fence: Survival in Treblinka, memoir by Richard Glazar, 1992

Dreams of Anne Frank: A Play for Young People, play by Bernard Kops, 1993

The Emigrants, novel by W.G. Sebald, 1993

I Keep Recalling: The Holocaust Poems of Jacob Glatstein, poems by Jacob Glatstein, 1993

Operation Shylock: A Confession, novel by Philip Roth, 1993

The Shovel and the Loom, novel by Carl Friedman, 1993

Heddy and Me, memoir by Susan Varga, 1994

Literature or Life, memoir by Jorge Semprun, 1994

Mutters Courage, play by George Tabori, 1994

Rue Ordener, Rue Labat, memoir by Sarah Kofman, 1994

Fragments: Memories of a Wartime Childhood, memoir by Binjamin Wilkomirski, 1995

I Rest My Case, memoir by Mark Verstandig, 1995

I Will Bear Witness: A Diary of the Nazi Years, diary by Victor Klemperer, 1995

The Reader, novel by Bernhard Schlink, 1995

The World of My Past, memoir by Abraham Biderman, 1995

Ashes to Ashes, play by Harold Pinter, 1996

Journal 1935–1944: The Fascist Years, diary by Mihail Sebastian, 1996

Traces, short stories by Ida Fink, 1996

The Far Euphrates, novel by Aryeh Lev Stollman, 1997

The Fiftieth Gate: A Journey through Memory, memoir by Mark Raphael Baker, 1997

From the Ashes of Sobibor: A Story of Survival, memoir by Thomas Blatt, 1997

In Full View, essays by Lily Brett, 1997

Where She Came From: A Daughter's Search for Her Mother's History, memoir by Helen Epstein, 1997

My German Question: Growing up in Nazi Berlin, memoir by Peter Gay, 1998

Poems, New and Collected, 1957–1997, poems by Wisława Szymborska, 1998

The Triumph of Love, poems by Geoffrey Hill, 1998

We're Alive and Life Goes On: A Theresienstadt Diary, diary by Eva Roubíčková, 1998

Ice Fire Water: A Leib Goldkorn Cocktail, novel by Leslie Epstein, 1999

Paper Bridges: Selected Poems of Kadya Molodowsky, poems by Kadya Molodowsky, 1999

City of God, novel by E. L. Doctorow, 2000

Austerlitz, novel by W.G. Sebald, 2001

ALPHABETICAL LIST OF WRITERS AND WORKS

INTRODUCTION

Like other literary responses to catastrophe, Holocaust literature necessarily locates the era in a number of national and cultural literary traditions. Even the definition of the Holocaust itself depends on who writes about it, under what conditions, and to which audience. In its broadest sense Holocaust literature consists of all of the literary responses to the destruction of European Jewry and other peoples by the German Nazi state and its collaborators during World War II. As such, it is necessarily an international literature, with works in all of the European languages as well as in Hebrew, Yiddish, and English. In its most expansive definition Holocaust literature thus includes the diaries of victims and memoirs of survivors; chronicles and documents compiled collectively by community groups and assembled in the forms of archives and "memorial books"; novels and short stories on Holocaust-related themes by those who witnessed the destruction as well as by those removed from it; poetry and drama from the concentration camps and ghettos as well as that composed after the war with aspects of the Holocaust as the subject; ballads and songs written both to inspire fighters in the ghettos during the war and to commemorate the Holocaust afterward; and religious responses that relate the events of the Holocaust in the form of traditional Jewish legends and parables. In the 1980s the descendants of Holocaust survivors began to add their own unique voices—as found in the so-called commix and in rock and roll lyrics—to the more traditional literary genres.

Indeed, the very languages in which these works are written determine their shape, content, and preoccupying themes. In choosing to write in Hebrew instead of Yiddish, for example, the ghetto diarists Chaim A. Kaplan and Zelig Kalmanovitsh may not have deliberately chosen every specific allusion and figure in the Hebrew over those used in Emmanuel Ringelblum's Yiddish diary, but they located events within different linguistic realms all the same. Whereas Hebrew tends to recall events in the sanctified context of Scripture and rabbinical disputation, writers in Yiddish often emphasized the details of daily life and its hardships. Conversely, questions of theodicy, covenant, and scriptural antecedent have a lexicon in Hebrew they do not have in Yiddish.

In some cases whether a Holocaust literature even came to exist depended on the national literary traditions of the victims. Because Jewish religious tradition is an essentially literary one, with a 2,500-year-old history of catastrophe responses, remembering the Holocaust in writing assumed something approaching a religious obligation. Both because Jews were the principal racial victims of the Nazis and because their tradition mandated it, Jewish writers have thus accounted for the great majority of the thousands of Holocaust literary works. By contrast, the primarily oral tradition of the tribes of Sinti and Roma (commonly, if somewhat pejoratively, known as Gypsies) practically guaranteed a frightful literary silence on their part. Because their story depended on the voices of the witness-victims themselves, the history of the Gypsies' deportations and mass murder died in the throats of the victims and so remains largely unwritten.

At some point nearly all of the writers of the Holocaust, whether a diarist like Kaplan or memoirists like Elie Wiesel and Primo Levi, have lamented the sheer impossibility of their task: how to describe what seems indescribable. How could they make believable what seemed incredible even to the eyewitnesses? Moreover, many writers have been plagued by the fear that the narrative act itself, with its intrinsic ordering properties, would betray what seemed to be the completely inchoate experience of the ghetto. How was it possible, Kaplan asked, to describe a disorderly thing in an orderly fashion? For writers attempting to leave behind a literature of testimony, questions of how to describe events without distorting them assumed nearly paralyzing significance. In most cases, however, the writers concluded that, as difficult as their literary conundrum seemed, silence was not an alternative. They recognized that without a literature the Holocaust would have been a self-consuming catastrophe, giving the killers a posthumous victory.

Every literary form represents the Holocaust in a slightly different way, each conveying different shades of meaning and a different understanding of the events. Because they were written from within the whirlwind, for example, ghetto and concentration camp diaries suggest themselves rhetorically as literal remnants of the events. At the same time, since they wrote from day to day without knowing their end, the diarists are dependent on readers to complete their stories. For a sense of the chaotic realities facing inmates of the concentrations camps and ghettos, the details of daily life under Nazi siege, and an understanding of how the victims grasped their circumstances at the time, the diaries of writers like Ringelblum, Kaplan, Kalmanovitsh, Moshe Flinker, Anne Frank, Eva Heyman, and others remain invaluable as sources.

By contrast, the hundreds of Holocaust survivor-memoirists necessarily have written with the advantage of hindsight, which has allowed them to know from the beginning of their recollections how it turned out. Although they, like the diarists, have been inspired by the powerful urges to testify to such crimes and to order otherwise inchoate experiences, the memoirists also have had time to meditate on their survival and to reflect on their later lives in the light of their people's destruction. Survivors like Levi and Wiesel were thus able to find and relate the significance of early events in the light of later ones. For this reason the shape of a Holocaust memorist's work may depend as much on the writer's later preoccupations as on the events themselves. The incoherence of events as experienced at the time is often relieved by the much more complete understanding a survivor years later brings to the past. As a result, the versions of survival we find in memoirs are often laced with the foreboding of those who know that the worst was indeed possible.

On the one hand, literary historians agree that it is crucial to distinguish categorically between eyewitness literature, such as the diary and memoir, and the more imaginative realm of novels and short stories. Nevertheless, it has also become clear that the lines between factual and fictional literature of the Holocaust are not always clear and are often blurred by memoirists and novelists alike. A memoir like Wiesel's *Night,* for example, while having a factual basis in the author's actual experiences during the war, also contains both formal elements of the parable and profoundly symbolic imagery. By opening his memoir with the story of Moshe the Beadle, who survived an early mass execution of Jews only to be disbelieved by the other inhabitants of the memoirist's Hungarian shtetl, Wiesel is able parabolically to warn his own audience against disbelieving the harrowing account they are about to read. The facts of the memoir remain true even as their meaning is conveyed in the symbolic imagery of the parable.

Similarly, if toward entirely different ends, Holocaust fiction often borrows heavily from the nonfictional discourse of diaries and memoirs. In particular, what has come to be called the ''documentary fiction'' of the Holocaust continues to raise some of the most troubling critical issues surrounding its incorporation of eyewitness accounts. To what extent, for example, does a documentary novel of the Holocaust such as Anatoli Kuznetsov's *Babi Yar* or John Hersey's *The Wall* document events, and to what extent does it fictionalize them? Because the novel has traditionally sustained a certain fact-fiction ambiguity as part of its discourse, both writers and readers have asked if it is an appropriate form for the representation of true but altogether unbelievable events.

As a result, some Holocaust novelists, like Jean-François Steiner in *Treblinka,* have gone to great lengths to assert an absolute link between their fiction and the historical facts of the Holocaust. Others, like the novelist D.M. Thomas, in reference to his book *The White Hotel,* have claimed on ethical grounds that they have no right to imagine such suffering and therefore have had to rely on the voices of actual witnesses. In both cases it is difficult to know whether such documentary claims are generated by the needs of history or of literature, whereby the claims are fabricated as part of the novels' essential fiction. The problem with these and other documentary novels of the Holocaust is that, by mixing actual events with completely fictional characters, the works, citing literary license, simultaneously relieve themselves of an obligation to historical fact even as they imbue their fiction with the historical authority and pathos of real events.

Other issues in Holocaust fiction emerge in comparisons of the national contexts of such works. For example, in comparing the brilliant short tales of Sara Nomberg-Przytyk with those of Tadeusz Borowski in *This Way for the Gas, Ladies and Gentlemen,* one is struck by the stark differences between their preoccupations, themes, and voices. In her vividly told *Auschwitz: True Tales from a Grotesque Land,* Nomberg-Przytyk brings into sharp relief the unique experiences of women in the concentration camps. She shows the ways in which a woman's history of subjugation provided her with a ready-made literary lexicon for the humiliation and degradation she found at the hands of the Nazis, even as she reflects on her own mixed identity in the camp as a Jewish woman and a Polish socialist. Borowski, on the other hand, was a non-Jewish Pole interned at Auschwitz as a socialist who came to be regarded after the war as one of Poland's greatest young writers. Although his personal conduct in the camp was by all accounts beyond reproach, even at times heroic in his assistance to the harder-pressed Jewish inmates, Borowski uses a fictional narrator who relates the stories through the self-accusing eye of someone seemingly inured to the suffering and death surrounding him. Moreover, because nothing before or after the war seemed to compare to the atrocities he had witnessed in Auschwitz and because he believed no one would comprehend them, Borowski limited his language and metaphors to that of the camp's realities, thus sealing both his and his readers' minds in the concentration camp universe, from which he would allow no literary escape.

Unlike Borowski's mercilessly direct depictions of horror in Auschwitz, other writers such as the Czernowitz-born Israeli novelist and survivor Aharon Appelfeld have eschewed any pretense of documentation for the larger, more universally humane truths of despair, alienation, and hope, which he reveals in lyrically spare tales. In novels such as *Badenheim 1939, The Age of Wonders, Tzili, The Immortal Bartfuss,* and *Katerina,* among a dozen others, Appelfeld hews closely to the details of a war-ravaged childhood even as he explores the souls of those trapped in the times. His stories of an oblivious Jewish community on the eve of annihilation, of children shunted among Carpathian villages, or of the perpetually displaced survivor at home only in a criminal netherworld between the concentration camps and refuge in Israel have been translated into a dozen languages and continue to find a universal resonance among the world's readers.

In the 1960s and early 1970s other Israeli novelists (some of them poets as well), including Yehuda Amichai, Hanoch Bartov, Yoram Kaniuk, and Haim Gouri, were more apt to explore the gap between their identities as Israeli Jews in their own land and their memory of a time when Jews in exile had been destroyed. In the case of Amichai's *Not of This Time, Not of This Place* (1963) and of Gouri's *The Chocolate Deal* (1965), national preoccupations with reparations, archaeology, and a newly found Jewish self-sufficiency provided thematic backdrops for trying to understand what had been lost and just how terrible the destruction had been, despite a new life in Israel. In the *The Brigade* (1965) Bartov similarly probed the Israeli's conflicted impulses toward revenge and rescue by telling the story of a brigade of Palestinian Jews in Germany as part of the Allied occupation forces after the war. Perhaps the richest novel of this time in both spiritual and psychological terms, as well as in its intricate fabular structure, is Kaniuk's *Adam Resurrected* (1971), a devastating tale of a survivor's memory and sanity, the conflation of his past and present as set in an Israeli psychiatric institution.

Later in Israel the survivor-novelist Ida Fink and the postwar-generation essayist and novelist David Grossman have added brilliantly complicating strains to the Holocaust literary canon from two very different perspectives. In her collection of short stories *A Scrap of Time* (1985), Fink distilled the terror and madness of day-to-day life for ordinary, unheroic Jews trying to get by a day at a time in Poland during the war. Rife with quotidian details of individual moments, Fink's stories restored the richness of life lost as it was being pulled apart one strand at a time. And then, rather than attempting to find reassuring meaning in such moments, the narrator herself is always on the verge of unremembering such moments altogether. From a completely different vantage point, David Grossman also made his inability to remember events he never experienced directly the subtext of his enormously ambitious novel *See Under: Love* (1985). Regarded by many as the greatest single work of the postwar generation, Grossman's novel is told through the wildly imaginative eyes of a child desperately trying to penetrate the stories of his parents' generation from ''the land of there''—Europe and the Holocaust—removed in both time and place.

Indeed, the range of possible literary responses to the Holocaust by the descendants of survivors has continued to grow. In an age dominated by popular culture, the children of survivors are as likely to distinguish themselves in the words of rock songs as they are in classical verse. In their recording *Ashes and Dust* the Israeli musicians Yehuda Poliker and Yakov Gilad pair lyrics responding to the Holocaust with haunting instrumentals. Like Poliker and Gilad, the second-generation American novelists Melvin Bukiet and Thane Rosenbaum have made their relationship to Holocaust memory—not the Holocaust as such—the subject of their art.

The treatment of the Holocaust as a vicarious past may have found its most remarkable expression in Art Spiegelman's Pulitzer Prize–winning ''commix'' of the Holocaust, *Maus—A Survivor's Tale.* For as Spiegelman himself has been quick to point out, *Maus* is not about the Holocaust so much as about the survivor's tale itself and the artist-son's recovery of it. Just as his father recalled what had happened to him at the hands of the Nazis, his son Art recalls what happened to him at the hands of his father as well as the effect his father's stories had on him. Although some early reviewers were taken aback by the audacity of representing the Holocaust in cartoons, that Spiegelman chose to render his father's tale of survival in this form is neither surprising nor controversial. After all, as a comics artist and founder of *Raw* magazine, Spiegelman only turned to what has always been his working artistic medium. As for possible objections to folding the deadly high seriousness of the Holocaust into what some would regard as the trivial low seriousness of the comics, Spiegelman has pointed to the ways in which the medium itself has raised—and dismissed—issues of decorum as part of its raison d'être.

That comics would serve such a story so well, however, is startling. Yet Spiegelman seems to have realized that, in order to remain true both to his father's story and to his own experience of it, he would have to remain true to his medium. In doing so, he has also cultivated the unique capacity of the ''commixture'' of image and narrative for telling the double-stranded tale of his father's story and of his own recording of it. Written over a 13-year period between 1978 and 1991, the result is a narrative hybrid echoing with the ambient noise and issues surrounding its telling. It is a continuous narrative rife with the discontinuities of its reception and production, the absolutely authentic voice of Spiegelman's father counterposed to the fabular images of cartoon animals.

The voices of both survivors and the next generation can similarly be heard and seen in dozens of theatrical performances of Holocaust drama staged during and after the war. From the productions of *Brundibar* and *The Emperor of Atlantis* in Theresienstadt, which allegorically portrayed the inmates' relationship to their captors, to Broadway extravaganzas like *The Diary of Anne Frank,* dramatic renderings of the Holocaust shape and transform historical memory and the understanding of events according to the times, places, and cultural contexts surrounding their performances. Given the theater's traditional role as a public stage for contemporary political and social commentary, the searing and often controversial critiques and satires of governments, bystanders, the Church, perpetrators, and even the victims themselves in plays like Rolf Hochhuth's *The Deputy,* Peter Weiss's *The Investigation,* Arthur Miller's *Incident at Vichy,* Joshua Sobol's *Ghetto,* and Martin Sherman's *Bent,* among dozens of other works, cannot be surprising. In many cases theatrical representations of the Holocaust bring into the public eye issues, characters, and moral dilemmas that seem to emanate as much from the preoccupations of contemporary audiences and playwrights as from the events themselves. For unlike other literary media, dramatic representations of the Holocaust on the stage necessarily bring ideas, people, and history to life in the contemporary moment, animated and conditioned as much by the present as by the past.

In his now famous admonition against "poetry after Auschwitz," the Frankfurt School critic Theodor W. Adorno suggested that not only is poetry after Auschwitz barbaric but that it may be immoral to derive the slightest bit of aesthetic pleasure from the suffering of Holocaust victims. Although after he read Paul Celan's masterpiece "Todesfugue" ("Death Fugue"), Adorno later retracted his dictum against such poetry, critical questions over the poetic appropriation of Holocaust imagery persist. To what extent do lineation, rhyme, and meter, for example, distract from and domesticate the brutal facts of the Holocaust? Or to what extent can the aesthetic qualities of poetry and figurative language actually reveal truths—both historical and personal—unavailable to documentary narrative? Through the verse of Celan, Leonie (Nelly) Sachs, Jacob Glatstein, Abraham Sutzkever, Yitzhak Katzenelson, and Dan Pagis, among many others, readers glean insight into both the Holocaust and its devastating effect on the poet's inner life, a kind of knowledge that falls between public and private memory, between communal and personal history.

Had Adorno been aware of the poets writing in Yiddish in the ghettos and concentration camps, he might never have issued his proscription against poetry after Auschwitz. For in poems like Katzenelson's "The Song of the Murdered Jewish People," composed largely in Vittel, a transit camp on the way to Auschwitz, or in Sutzkever's shattering responses to the deaths of his mother and child in the Vilna ghetto, there is no redemption, no consoling beauty to be found. In both cases the poets' Yiddish allows them to invoke biblical precedents, although always for their inadequacy. The language allows the poets to bring their furious debate with God over the meaning of events down to the poet's level, eye to eye, as Glatstein did in poems such as "Dead Men Don't Praise God," "Without Jews," and "My Brother Refugee," written in the United States during the war.

Widely regarded as the single greatest postwar poem in the German language, Celan's "Todesfugue" continues to haunt readers with the imagery and sounds of events irreconcilable to life, unassimilable to memory, and drawn elliptically from the death camps. Born Paul Antschel in Czernowitz in 1920, Celan published the poem first in a Romanian translation (as "Death Tango") in 1947 and prefaced it with a note suggesting that the poem was "built on the evocation of a real fact [that] the condemned were forced to sing nostalgic songs while others dug graves." Its opening lines are repeated in a mind-staggering refrain:

> Black milk of daybreak we drink it at evening
> we drink it at midday and morning we drink it at night
> we drink and we drink

Within 10 years of the publication of the original German version in 1948, the poem had become a national obsession. Committed to memory by schoolchildren, recited endlessly on the radio, reprinted in the mass media, and dissected constantly by critical foes and friends, the poem assumed a life of its own in the former land of the murderers.

Sachs, the other great German-language poet of the Holocaust, won the Nobel Prize for Literature in 1966 (shared with S.Y. Agnon) at least partly for her collection of Holocaust poetry *O the Chimneys* (1967). Born in 1891 in Berlin to an assimilated middle-class Jewish family, Sachs escaped in 1940 to Sweden, where she spent the rest of her life. Unlike Celan, with his elliptical allusions to images of the concentration camps and his implied challenge to a religious understanding of the Holocaust, Sachs attempted to embed the literal fragments of destruction in biblical contexts, drawing as well on the *Zohar* and its cabalistic images of exile. Her poem "O the Chimneys" is thus prefaced by a citation from Job 19:26: "And though after my skin worms destroy this body, yet in my flesh shall I see God." The poem itself begins,

> O the chimneys
> On the ingeniously devised habitations of death
> When Israel's body drifted as smoke
> Through the air—
> Was welcomed by a star, a chimney sweep,
> A star that turned black
> Or was it a ray of sun?

Other poems, such as "Chorus of the Rescued," meditate on the survivors' difficulty in reentering a normal world:

> Lest the song of a bird,

or a pail being filled at the well,
Let our badly sealed pain burst forth again
and carry us away—

In addition to giving a voice to the survivors' return to life, poetry can also articulate the terrible void left in the wake of the victims. "Written in Pencil in the Sealed Railway-Car," a poem written in Hebrew by the Israeli poet Pagis, also born in Czernowitz, is regarded by many as the purest precipitate of silence in poetry:

here in this carload
i am eve
with abel my son
if you see my other son
cain son of man
tell him that i

Perhaps only in poetry can silence be given simultaneous voice and void, can such loss remain so deeply felt and yet unredeemed.

Critical approaches to Holocaust literature have also evolved over the years since the end of the war. Early commentators like A. Alvarez questioned the traditional critic's role as arbiter of good and bad literature or even as a definer of a Holocaust literary canon, which would necessarily exclude too many voices needing to be heard. Others, like Lawrence Langer in his pathbreaking study *The Holocaust and the Literary Imagination* (1976), raised Adorno's early dictum against Holocaust literature only to show how such literature was necessary. Like other early critics of the literature, Langer concentrated on formulating what he called an "aesthetics of atrocity." Through a series of close readings of writers as diverse as Anthony Hecht, Charlotte Delbo, Jorge Semprun, Jerzy Kosinski, Jakov Lind, Ladislav Fuks, and Andre Schwarz-Bart, among others, Langer offered keen insights into how writers sought to express the inexpressible.

In 1980 Alvin Rosenfeld and Sidra Ezrahi offered sustained close readings of still further works in two new critical studies, in which they also reflected on the "problematics of Holocaust literature" as well as on the ethical and literary implications of appropriating the Holocaust through metaphor. In two studies four years later, David Roskies and Alan Mintz located literary responses to the Holocaust in the longer continuum of Jewish responses to catastrophe over the ages, beginning with biblical responses to the destruction of the Temple (as in Lamentations), continuing through the Hebrew chronicles of the Crusader massacres, and including the early twentieth-century pogrom poetry of Chaim Nachman Bialik and Moshe Leyb Halpern, among others. By restoring Yiddish and Hebrew literary responses to the Holocaust to the longer Jewish cultural and religious tradition of which they are necessarily a part, critics like Roskies and Mintz showed how Jewish writers simultaneously invoke and challenge the tradition, relying upon it and expanding it with their own new responses to destruction.

Yet another generation of critics, including Sara Horowitz and the present author, continues to build on this work, to ask not whether such destruction can be represented but how it has been represented   for better or worse and toward what kinds of ends, meanings, and historical interpretations. Rather than weighing "authentic" against "inauthentic" responses, these later critics tend to locate literary responses to the Holocaust within the national communities spawning them and to compare the literary with other kinds of memorial media. In this view neither the Holocaust nor its literature can be reduced to anything approaching an essential truth, work, or canon. This does not mean that there are no ways to judge and evaluate Holocaust literature. But how readers interpret and evaluate this literature, and to what ends, is now also a part of Holocaust literary criticism.

—James E. Young

READING LIST

Anthologies

Ajzensztadt, Amnon. *Endurance: Chronicles of Jewish Resistance.* Oakville, Ontario: Mosaic Press, 1987.

Brown, Jean E., Elaine C. Stephens, and Janet E. Rubin, eds. *Images from the Holocaust: A Literature Anthology.* Lincolnwood, Illinois: NTC Publishing Group, 1997.

Florsheim, Stewart J., ed. *Ghosts of the Holocaust: An Anthology of Poetry by the Second Generation.* Foreword by Gerald Stern. Detroit: Wayne State University Press, 1989.

Forman, Frieda, ed. *Found Treasures: Stories by Yiddish Women Writers.* Introduction by Irena Klepfisz. Toronto: Second Story Press, 1994.

Friedlander, Albert H., ed. *Out of the Whirlwind: A Reader of Holocaust Literature.* Rev. and enl. ed. New York: UAHC Press, 1999.

Friedman, Saul S., ed. *Holocaust Literature: A Handbook of Critical, Historical, and Literary Writings.* Westport, Connecticut: Greenwood Press, 1993.

Fuchs, Elinor, ed. *Plays of the Holocaust: An International Anthology.* New York: Theatre Communications Group, 1987.

Gillon, Adam, ed. *Poems of the Ghetto: A Testament of Lost Men.* New York: Twayne, 1969.

Glatstein, Jacob, Israel Knox, and Samuel Margoshes, eds. *Anthology of Holocaust Literature.* Philadelphia: Jewish Publication Society of America, 1968.

Harshav, Benjamin and Barbara, eds. *American Yiddish Poetry: A Bilingual Anthology.* Translated with the participation of Kathryn Hellerstein, Brian McHale, and Anita Norich. Berkeley: University of California Press, 1986.

Heifetz, Julie. *Oral History and the Holocaust: A Collection of Poems from Interviews with Survivors of the Holocaust.* Oxford and New York: Pergamon Press, 1985.

Howe, Irving, and Eliezer Greenberg, eds. *A Treasury of Yiddish Poetry.* New York: Holt, Rinehart and Winston, 1969.

Langer, Lawrence L., ed. *Art from the Ashes: A Holocaust Anthology.* New York: Oxford University Press, 1995.

Leftwich, Joseph, ed. and trans. *The Golden Peacock: A Worldwide Treasury of Yiddish Poetry.* New York: Thomas Yoseloff, 1961.

Lévy, Isaac Jack, ed. and trans. *And the World Stood Silent: Sephardic Poetry of the Holocaust.* Urbana: University of Illinois Press, 1989.

Mintz, Ruth Finer, ed. and trans. *Modern Hebrew Poetry: A Bilingual Anthology.* Berkeley: University of California Press, 1966.

Ramras-Rauch, Gila, and Joseph Michman-Melkman, eds. *Facing the Holocaust: Selected Israeli Fiction.* Introduction by Gila Ramras-Rauch. Afterword by Gershon Shaked. Philadelphia: Jewish Publication Society, 1985.

Rittner, Carol, and John K. Roth, eds. *Different Voices: Women and the Holocaust.* St. Paul, Minnesota: Paragon House, 1993.

Rochman, Hazel, and Darlene Z. McCampbell, eds. *Bearing Witness: Stories of the Holocaust.* New York: Orchard Books, 1995.

Roth, John K., and Michael Berenbaum, eds. *Holocaust: Religious and Philosophical Implications.* St. Paul, Minnesota: Paragon House, 1989.

Schiff, Hilda, ed. *Holocaust Poetry.* New York: St. Martin's Press, 1995.

Teichman, Milton, and Sharon Leder, eds. *Truth and Lamentation: Stories and Poems on the Holocaust.* Urbana: University of Illinois Press, 1994.

Zych, Adam A., ed. *The Auschwitz Poems: An Anthology.* Oświęcim, Poland: Auschwitz-Birkenau State Museum, 1999.

Bibliographies

Braham, Randolph L. *The Hungarian Jewish Catastrophe: A Selected and Annotated Bibliography.* 2nd ed., rev. and enl. New York: Social Science Monographs and Institute for Holocaust Studies, City University of New York; distributed by Columbia University Press, 1984.

Cargas, Harry J. *The Holocaust: An Annotated Bibliography.* Haverford, Pennsylvania: Catholic Library Association, 1977.

Edelheit, Abraham J. and Hershel. *Bibliography on Holocaust Literature.* Boulder, Colorado: Westview Press, Inc., 1986.

———. *Bibliography on Holocaust Literature: Supplement.* Boulder, Colorado: Westview Press, Inc., 1990.

Laska, Vera. *Nazism, Resistance & Holocaust in World War II: A Bibliography.* Metuchen, New Jersey: Scarecrow Press, 1985.

Sable, Martin H. *Holocaust Studies: A Directory and Bibliography of Bibliographies.* Greenwood, Florida: Penkevill Publishing Company, 1987.

Szonyi, David M., ed. *The Holocaust: An Annotated Bibliography and Resource Guide.* Hoboken, New Jersey: Ktav Publishing House for the National Jewish Resource Center, New York, 1985.

Literary Criticism

Aaron, Frieda W. *Bearing the Unbearable: Yiddish and Polish Poetry in the Ghettos and Concentration Camps.* Foreword by David G. Roskies. Albany: State University of New York Press, 1990.

Aberbach, David. *Surviving Trauma: Loss, Literature, and Psychoanalysis.* New Haven: Yale University Press, 1989.

Adorno, Theodor W. *Negative Dialectics.* Translated by E.B. Ashton. New York: Seabury Press, 1973.

Ahokas, Pirjo, and Martine Chard-Hutchinson, eds. *Reclaiming Memory: American Representations of the Holocaust.* Turku, Finland: University of Turku, School of Art Studies, 1997.

Alexander, Edward. *The Holocaust and the War of Ideas.* New Brunswick, New Jersey: Transaction Publishers, 1994.

———. *The Resonance of Dust: Essays on Holocaust Literature and Jewish Fate.* Columbus: Ohio State University Press, 1979.

Alphen, Ernst van. *Caught by History: Holocaust Effects in Contemporary Art, Literature, and Theory.* Stanford, California: Stanford University Press, 1997.

Alter, Robert. *After the Tradition: Essays on Modern Jewish Writing.* New York: Dutton, 1969.

———. *Defenses of the Imagination: Jewish Writers and Modern Historical Crisis.* Philadelphia: Jewish Publication Society of America, 1977.

Alter, Robert, ed. *Modern Hebrew Literature.* New York: Behrman House, 1975.

Banner, Gillian. *Holocaust Literature: Schulz, Levi, Spiegelman and the Memory of the Offense.* London and Portland, Oregon: Vallentine Mitchell, 2000.

Bauman, Zygmunt. *Modernity and the Holocaust.* Ithaca, New York: Cornell University Press, 1989.

Berger, Alan L., ed. *Bearing Witness to the Holocaust, 1939–1989.* Lewiston, New York: Edwin Mellen Press, 1991.

Berger, Alan L. *Children of Job: American Second-Generation Witnesses to the Holocaust.* Albany: State University of New York Press, 1997.

———. *Crisis and Covenant: The Holocaust in American Jewish Fiction.* Albany: State University of New York Press, 1985.

Berger, James. *After the End: Representations of Post-Apocalypse.* Minneapolis: University of Minnesota Press, 1999.

Bilik, Dorothy Seidman. *Immigrant-Survivors: Post-Holocaust Consciousness in Recent Jewish American Fiction.* Middletown, Connecticut: Wesleyan University Press, 1981.

Blanchot, Maurice. *The Writing of the Disaster.* Translated by Ann Smock. Lincoln: University of Nebraska Press, 1986.

Bosmajian, Hamida. *Metaphors of Evil: Contemporary German Literature and the Shadow of Nazism.* Iowa City: University of Iowa Press, 1979.

———. *Sparing the Child: Grief and the Unspeakable in Youth Literature about Nazism and the Holocaust.* New York: Routledge, 2001.

Braham, Randolph L., ed. *Reflections of the Holocaust in Art and Literature.* Boulder, Colorado: Social Science Monographs; New York: Csengeri Institute for Holocaust Studies, City University of New York; distributed by Columbia University Press, 1990.

Brenner, Rachel Feldhay. *Writing as Resistance: Four Women Confronting the Holocaust: Edith Stein, Simone Weil, Anne Frank, Etty Hillesum.* University Park: Pennsylvania State University Press, 1997.

Caruth, Cathy, ed. *Trauma: Explorations in Memory.* Baltimore: Johns Hopkins University Press, 1995.

Caruth, Cathy. *Unclaimed Experience: Trauma, Narrative, and History.* Baltimore: Johns Hopkins University Press, 1996.

Cernyak-Spatz, Susan E. *German Holocaust Literature.* New York: Peter Lang, 1985.

Cole, Tim. *Selling the Holocaust: From Auschwitz to Schindler: How History Is Bought, Packaged, and Sold.* New York: Routledge, 1999.

Colombat, André Pierre. *The Holocaust in French Film.* Metuchen, New Jersey: Scarecrow Press, 1993.

Des Pres, Terrence. *The Survivor: An Anatomy of Life in the Death Camps.* New York: Oxford University Press, 1976.

Doneson, Judith E. *The Holocaust in American Film.* Philadelphia: Jewish Publication Society, 1987.

Ezrahi, Sidra DeKoven. *Booking Passage: Exile and Homecoming in the Modern Jewish Imagination.* Berkeley: University of California Press, 2000.

———. *By Words Alone: The Holocaust in Literature.* Foreword by Alfred Kazin. Chicago: University of Chicago Press, 1980.

Felman, Shoshana, and Dori Laub. *Testimony: Crises of Witnessing in Literature, Psychoanalysis, and History.* New York: Routledge, 1991.

Fisch, Harold. *A Remembered Future: A Study in Literary Mythology.* Bloomington: Indiana University Press, 1984.

Fischel, Jack, and Sanford Pinsker, eds. *Literature, the Arts, and the Holocaust.* Greenwood, Florida: Penkevill Publishing Company, 1987.

Fishman, Charles M., ed. *Blood to Remember: American Poets on the Holocaust.* Lubbock: Texas Tech University Press, 1991.

Flanzbaum, Hilene, ed. *The Americanization of the Holocaust.* Baltimore: Johns Hopkins University Press, 1999.

Fox, Thomas C. *Stated Memory: East Germany and the Holocaust.* Rochester, New York: Camden House, 1999.

Fridman, Lea Wernick. *Words and Witness: Narrative and Aesthetic Strategies in the Representation of the Holocaust.* Albany: State University of New York Press, 2000.

Fried, Lewis, ed. *Handbook of American-Jewish Literature: An Analytical Guide to Topics, Themes, and Sources.* New York: Greenwood Press, 1988.

Friedlander, Albert H. *Riders towards the Dawn: From Holocaust to Hope.* New York: Continuum, 1994.

———. *A Thread of Gold: Journeys towards Reconciliation.* Translated by John Bowden. London: SCM Press; Philadelphia: Trinity Press International, 1990.

Friedländer, Saul, ed. *Probing the Limits of Representation: Nazism and the "Final Solution."* Cambridge, Massachusetts: Harvard University Press, 1992.

Gilman, Sander L., and Karen Remmler, eds. *Reemerging Jewish Culture in Germany: Life and Literature since 1989.* New York: New York University Press, 1994.

Gilman, Sander L., and Jack Zipes, eds. *Yale Companion to Jewish Writing and Thought in German Culture, 1096–1996.* New Haven: Yale University Press, 1997.

Goodenough, Elizabeth, Mark A. Heberle, and Naomi B. Sokoloff, eds. *Infant Tongues: The Voice of the Child in Literature.* Foreword by Robert Coles. Detroit: Wayne State University Press, 1994.

Gurewitsch, Brana, ed. *Mothers, Sisters, Resisters: Oral Histories of Women Who Survived the Holocaust.* Tuscaloosa: University of Alabama Press, 1998.

Haft, Cynthia J. *The Theme of Nazi Concentration Camps in French Literature.* The Hague: Mouton, 1973.

Halio, Jay L., and Ben Siegel, eds. *Daughters of Valor: Contemporary Jewish American Women Writers.* Newark: University of Delaware Press, 1997.

Halperin, Irving. *Messengers from the Dead: Literature of the Holocaust.* Philadelphia: Westminster Press, 1970.

Hamburger, Michael. *From Prophecy to Exorcism: The Premises of Modern German Literature.* London: Longmans, 1965.

Hartman, Geoffrey H., ed. *Holocaust Remembrance: The Shapes of Memory.* Oxford, England, and Cambridge, Massachusetts: Blackwell, 1994.

Hartman, Geoffrey H. *The Longest Shadow: In the Aftermath of the Holocaust.* Bloomington: Indiana University Press, 1996.

Heinemann, Marlene E. *Gender and Destiny: Women Writers and the Holocaust.* New York: Greenwood Press, 1986.

Hirsch, David H. *The Deconstruction of Literature: Criticism after Auschwitz.* Providence, Rhode Island: Brown University Press; Hanover, New Hampshire: University Press of New England, 1991.

Hoffman, Frederick John. *The Mortal No: Death and the Modern Imagination.* Princeton, New Jersey: Princeton University Press, 1964.

Hook, Elizabeth Snyder. *Family Secrets and the Contemporary German Novel: Literary Explorations in the Aftermath of the Third Reich.* Rochester, New York: Camden House, 2001.

Horowitz, Sara R. *Voicing the Void: Muteness and Memory in Holocaust Fiction.* Albany: State University of New York Press, 1997.

Howe, Irving. *World of Our Fathers*. New York: Harcourt Brace Jovanovich, 1976.

Howe, Irving, and Eliezer Greenberg, eds. *Voices from the Yiddish: Essays, Memoirs, Diaries*. Ann Arbor: University of Michigan Press, 1972.

Huyssen, Andreas. *Twilight Memories: Marking Time in a Culture of Amnesia*. New York: Routledge, 1995.

Insdorf, Annette. *Indelible Shadows: Film and the Holocaust*. New York: Random House, 1983.

Isser, Edward R. *Stages of Annihilation: Theatrical Representations of the Holocaust*. Madison, New Jersey: Fairleigh Dickinson University Press; London and Cranbury, New Jersey: Associated University Presses, 1997.

Jaanus, Maire. *Literature and Negation*. New York: Columbia University Press, 1979.

Kahn, Lothar. *Mirrors of the Jewish Mind: A Gallery of Portraits of European Jewish Writers of Our Time*. New York: Thomas Yoseloff, 1968.

Knopp, Josephine Zadovsky. *The Trial of Judaism in Contemporary Jewish Writing*. Urbana: University of Illinois Press, 1974.

Kohn, Murray J. *The Voice of My Blood Cries Out: The Holocaust As Reflected in Hebrew Poetry*. New York: Shengold Publishers, 1979.

Korman, Gerd, ed. *Hunter and Hunted: Human History of the Holocaust*. New York: Viking Press, 1973.

Kremer, S. Lillian. *Witness through the Imagination: Ozick, Elman, Cohen, Potok, Singer, Epstein, Bellow, Steiner, Wallant, Malamud: Jewish-American Holocaust Literature*. Detroit: Wayne State University Press, 1989.

——. *Women's Holocaust Writing: Memory and Imagination*. Lincoln: University of Nebraska Press, 1999.

Kritzman, Lawrence D., ed. *Auschwitz and After: Race, Culture, and "The Jewish Question" in France*. New York: Routledge, 1995.

LaCapra, Dominick. *History and Memory after Auschwitz*. Ithaca, New York: Cornell University Press, 1998.

——. *Representing the Holocaust: History, Theory, Trauma*. Ithaca, New York: Cornell University Press, 1994.

——. *Writing History, Writing Trauma*. Baltimore: Johns Hopkins University Press, 2001.

Lang, Berel. *The Future of the Holocaust: Between History and Memory*. Ithaca, New York: Cornell University Press, 1999.

——. *Holocaust Representation: Art within the Limits of History and Ethics*. Baltimore: Johns Hopkins University Press, 2000.

Lang, Berel, ed. *Writing and the Holocaust*. New York: Holmes & Meier, 1988.

Langer, Lawrence L. *Admitting the Holocaust: Collected Essays*. New York: Oxford University Press, 1995.

——. *The Age of Atrocity: Death in Modern Literature*. Boston: Beacon Press, 1978.

——. *The Holocaust and the Literary Imagination*. New Haven: Yale University Press, 1975.

——. *Holocaust Testimonies: The Ruins of Memory*. New Haven: Yale University Press, 1991.

——. *Preempting the Holocaust*. New Haven: Yale University Press, 1998.

——. *Versions of Survival: The Holocaust and the Human Spirit*. Albany: State University of New York Press, 1982.

Lazar, Moshe, ed. *The Anxious Subject: Nightmares and Daymares in Literature and Film*. Malibu, California: Undena Publications, 1983.

Leak, Andrew N., and George Paizis, eds. *The Holocaust and the Text: Speaking the Unspeakable*. New York: St. Martin's Press, 2000.

Leftwich, Joseph, ed. and trans. *The Way We Think: A Collection of Essays from the Yiddish*. 2 vols. South Brunswick, New Jersey: Thomas Yoseloff, 1969.

Levin, Meyer. *In Search: An Autobiography*. New York: Horizon Press, 1950.

Lewis, Stephen. *Art out of Agony: The Holocaust Theme in Literature, Sculpture and Film*. Montreal and New York: CBC Enterprises/les Enterprises Radio-Canada, 1984.

Memmi, Albert. *The Liberation of the Jew*. Translated by Judy Hyun. New York: Orion Press, 1966.

Meyer, Michael J., ed. *Literature and Ethnic Discrimination*. Amsterdam and Atlanta, Georgia: Rodopi, 1997.

Milchman, Alan, and Alan Rosenberg, eds. *Postmodernism and the Holocaust*. Amsterdam and Atlanta, Georgia: Rodopi, 1998.

Miłosz, Czesław. *The History of Polish Literature*. New York: MacMillan, 1969.

Mintz, Alan, ed. *The Boom in Contemporary Israeli Fiction*. Hanover, New Hampshire: Brandeis University Press, published by University Press of New England, 1997.

Mintz, Alan. *Hurban: Responses to Catastrophe in Hebrew Literature*. New York: Columbia University Press, 1984.

——. *Popular Culture and the Shaping of Holocaust Memory in America*. Seattle: University of Washington Press, 2001.

Niewyk, Donald L., ed. *Fresh Wounds: Early Narratives of Holocaust Survival*. Chapel Hill: University of North Carolina Press, 1998.

Nochlin, Linda, and Tamar Garb, eds. *The Jew in the Text: Modernity and the Construction of Identity*. London: Thames and Hudson, 1995.

Ofer, Dalia, and Lenore J. Weitzman, eds. *Women in the Holocaust*. New Haven: Yale University Press, 1998.

Ozick, Cynthia. *Metaphor and Memory: Essays*. New York: Alfred A. Knopf, 1989.

Patraka, Vivian M. *Spectacular Suffering: Theatre, Fascism, and the Holocaust*. Bloomington: Indiana University Press, 1999.

Patterson, David. *Along the Edge of Annihilation: The Collapse and Recovery of Life in the Holocaust Diary*. Seattle: University of Washington Press, 1999.

——. *The Shriek of Silence: A Phenomenology of the Holocaust Novel*. Lexington: University Press of Kentucky, 1992.

——. *Sun Turned to Darkness: Memory and Recovery in the Holocaust Memoir*. Syracuse, New York: Syracuse University Press, 1998.

Patterson, David, and Alan L. Berger, eds. *Encyclopedia of Holocaust Literature*. Westport, Connecticut: Greenwood Press, 2002.

Peitsch, Helmut, Charles Burdett, and Claire Gorrara, eds. *European Memories of the Second World War*. New York: Berghahn Books, 1999.

Reiter, Andrea. *Narrating the Holocaust*. Translated by Patrick Camiller. London: Continuum, in association with the European Jewish Publication Society, 2000.

Ricœur, Paul. *The Symbolism of Evil*. Translated by Emerson Buchanan. New York: Harper and Row, 1967.

Rosen, Norma. *Accidents of Influence: Writing as a Woman and a Jew in America*. Albany: State University of New York Press, 1992.

Rosenberg, Alan, James R. Watson, and Detlef Linke, eds. *Contemporary Portrayals of Auschwitz: Philosophical Challenges*. Amherst, New York: Humanity Books, 2000.

Rosenberg, David, ed. *Testimony: Contemporary Writers Make the Holocaust Personal*. New York: Times Books, 1989.

Rosenfeld, Alvin H. *A Double Dying: Reflections on Holocaust Literature*. Bloomington: Indiana University Press, 1980.

———. *Imagining Hitler*. Bloomington: Indiana University Press, 1985.

Rosenfeld, Alvin H., ed. *Thinking about the Holocaust: After Half a Century*. Bloomington: Indiana University Press, 1997.

Roskies, David G. *Against the Apocalypse: Responses to Catastrophe in Modern Jewish Culture*. Cambridge, Massachusetts: Harvard University Press, 1984.

Roskies, David G., ed. *The Literature of Destruction: Jewish Responses to Catastrophe*. Philadelphia: Jewish Publication Society, 1988.

Roth, John K., and Elisabeth Maxwell, eds. *Remembering for the Future: The Holocaust in an Age of Genocide*. 3 vols. New York: Palgrave, 2001.

Rovit, Rebecca, and Alvin Goldfarb, eds. *Theatrical Performance during the Holocaust: Texts, Documents, Memoirs*. Baltimore: Johns Hopkins University Press, 1999.

Rubenstein, Richard L., and John K. Roth. *Approaches to Auschwitz: The Holocaust and Its Legacy*. Atlanta: John Knox Press, 1987.

Santner, Eric L. *Stranded Objects: Mourning, Memory, and Film in Postwar Germany*. Ithaca, New York: Cornell University Press, 1990.

Sartre, Jean-Paul. *What Is Literature?* Translated by Bernard Frechtman. New York: Philosophical Library, 1949.

Schiff, Ellen. *From Stereotype to Metaphor: The Jew in Contemporary Drama*. Albany: State University of New York Press, 1982.

Schlant, Ernestine. *The Language of Silence: West German Literature and the Holocaust*. New York: Leo Baeck Institute, 1997.

Schulman, Elias. *The Holocaust in Yiddish Literature*. New York: Education Department of the Workmen's Circle, 1983.

Schumacher, Claude, ed. *Staging the Holocaust: The Shoah in Drama and Performance*. Cambridge and New York: Cambridge University Press, 1998.

Schwarz, Daniel R. *Imagining the Holocaust*. New York: St. Martin's Press, 1999.

Sicher, Efraim. *Beyond Marginality: Anglo-Jewish Literature after the Holocaust*. Albany: State University of New York Press, 1985.

Sicher, Efraim, ed. *Breaking Crystal: Writing and Memory after Auschwitz*. Urbana: University of Illinois Press, 1998.

Skloot, Robert. *The Darkness We Carry: The Drama of the Holocaust*. Madison: University of Wisconsin Press, 1988.

Skloot, Robert, ed. *The Theatre of the Holocaust*. Madison: University of Wisconsin Press, 1982.

Sliwowska, Wiktoria, ed. *The Last Eyewitnesses: Children of the Holocaust Speak*. Translated by Fay and Julian Bussgang. Postscript by Jerzy Ficowski. Evanston, Illinois: Northwestern University Press, 1998.

Sokoloff, Naomi B. *Imagining the Child in Modern Jewish Fiction*. Baltimore: Johns Hopkins University Press, 1992.

Sokoloff, Naomi B., Anne Lapidus Lerner, and Anita Norich, eds. *Gender and Text in Modern Hebrew and Yiddish Literature*. New York: Jewish Theological Seminary of America; Cambridge, Massachusetts: distributed by Harvard University Press, 1992.

Steiner, George. *Extraterritorial: Papers on Literature and the Language Revolution*. New York: Atheneum, 1971.

———. *In Bluebeards Castle: Some Notes towards the Redefinition of Culture*. New Haven: Yale University Press, 1975.

———. *Language and Silence: Essays on Language, Literature, and the Inhuman*. New York: Atheneum, 1967.

Striar, Marguerite M. *Rage before Pardon: Poets of the World Bearing Witness to the Holocaust*. New York: Continuum, 1996.

Taub, Michael. *Israeli Holocaust Drama*. Syracuse, New York: Syracuse University Press, 1996.

Vanderwal Taylor, Jolanda. *A Family Occupation: Children of the War and the Memory of World War II in Dutch Literature of the 1980s*. Amsterdam: Amsterdam University Press, 1997.

Vice, Sue. *Holocaust Fiction*. London and New York: Routledge, 2000.

Vidal-Naquet, Pierre. *Assassins of Memory: Essays on the Denial of the Holocaust*. Translated and with a foreword by Jeffrey Mehlman. New York: Columbia University Press, 1992.

Wiedmer, Caroline. *The Claims of Memory: Representations of the Holocaust in Contemporary Germany and France*. Ithaca, New York: Cornell University Press, 1999.

Wiesel, Elie. *A Jew Today*. Translated by Marion Wiesel. New York: Random House, 1978.

———. *Legends of Our Time*. Translated by Steven Donadio. New York: Holt, Rinehart and Winston, 1968.

———. *One Generation After*. Translated by Lily Edelman and the author. New York: Random House, 1970.

Young, James E. *The Texture of Memory: Holocaust Memorials and Meaning*. New Haven: Yale University Press, 1993.

———. *Writing and Rewriting the Holocaust: Narrative and the Consequences of Interpretation*. Bloomington: Indiana University Press, 1988.

Yudkin, Leon I., ed. *Hebrew Literature in the Wake of the Holocaust*. Rutherford, New Jersey: Fairleigh Dickinson University Press; London: Associated University Presses, 1993.

Yuter, Alan J. *The Holocaust in Hebrew Literature, from Genocide to Rebirth*. Port Washington, New York: Associated Faculty Press, 1983.

Zapruder, Alexandra. *Salvaged Pages: Young Writers Diaries of the Holocaust*. New Haven: Yale University Press, 2002.

Teaching Guides

Davies, Ian, ed. *Teaching the Holocaust: Educational Dimensions, Principles and Practice*. London: Continuum, 2000.

Garber, Zev, Alan L. Berger, and Richard Libowitz, eds. *Methodology in the Academic Teaching of the Holocaust*. Lanham, Maryland: University Press of America, 1988.

Greenbaum, Beth. *Bearing Witness: Teaching about the Holocaust*. Portsmouth, New Hampshire: Boynton/Cook Publishers-Heinemann, 2001.

Lauckner, Nancy A., and Miriam Jokiniemi, eds. *Shedding Light on the Darkness: A Guide to Teaching the Holocaust*. New York: Berghahn Books, 2000.

Rosen, Philip, and Nina Apfelbaum. *Bearing Witness: A Resource Guide to Literature, Poetry, Art, Music, and Videos by Holocaust Victims and Survivors*. Westport, Connecticut: Greenwood Press, 2001.

Salmons, Paul. *Torn Apart: A Student's Guide to the Holocaust Exhibition*. London: Imperial War Museum, 2000.

Stephens, Elaine C., Jean E. Brown, and Janet E. Rubin. *Learning About—The Holocaust: Literature and Other Resources for*

Young People. North Haven, Connecticut: Library Professional Publications,1995.

Sullivan, Edward T. *The Holocaust in Literature for Youth: A Guide and Resource Book*. Lanham, Maryland: Scarecrow Press, 1999.

Teaching about the Holocaust: A Resource Book for Educators. Washington, D.C.: United States Holocaust Memorial Museum, 2000.

Totten, Samuel. *Holocaust Education: Issues and Approaches*. Boston: Allyn and Bacon, 2002.

Totten, Samuel, ed. *Teaching Holocaust Literature*. Boston: Allyn and Bacon, 2001.

Totten, Samuel, and Stephen Feinberg, eds. *Teaching and Studying the Holocaust*. Foreword by John K. Roth. Boston: Allyn and Bacon, 2001.

WRITERS

A

ABISH, Walter

Nationality: American (originally Austrian: immigrated to the United States, 1956, granted U.S. citizenship, 1960). **Born:** Vienna, 24 December 1931. **Military Service:** Israeli Army: tank corps, 1949–51. **Family:** Married Cecile Gelb. **Career:** Writer-in-residence, Wheaton College, Norton, Massachusetts, Spring 1977; visiting professor, State University of New York, Buffalo, Fall 1977, Yale University, Spring 1985, Brown University, Spring 1986, and Cooper Union, Spring 1987, 1993, and 1994. Lecturer, Columbia University, 1979–88. **Awards:** National Endowment for the Arts fellowship, 1979; C.A.P.S. grant, Guggenheim fellowship, and Pen/Faulkner award, for *How German Is It,* all in 1981; National Endowment for the Arts fellowship, 1985; MacArthur fellowship, 1987–92; American Academy and Institute of Arts & Letters award of merit medal for the novel, 1991; Lila Wallace Reader's Digest fellowship, 1992–95. D.Litt.: State University College, Oneonta, New York, 1996. **Agent:** Donadio & Olson, Inc. Literary Representatives, 121 West 27th Street, Suite 704, New York, New York 10001, U.S.A.

PUBLICATIONS

Novels

Alphabetical Africa. 1974.
How German Is It. 1980.
Eclipse Fever. 1993.

Short Stories

Minds Meet. 1975.
In the Future Perfect. 1977.
99: The New Meaning. 1990.

Poetry

Duel Site. 1970.

*

Critical Studies: ''Present Imperfect: A Note on the Work of Walter Abish'' by Tony Tanner, in *Granta,* Spring 1979, pp. 65–71; ''The Puzzle of Walter Abish: In the Future Perfect,'' in *Sub-Stance,* 27, Fall 1983, pp. 115–24, and ''The New Novel and Television Culture: Reflections on Walter Abish's *How German Is It,*'' in *Fiction International,* 17(1), Spring 1987, pp. 152–64, both by Alain Arias-Misson; ''Walter Abish's Fictions: Perfect Unfamiliarity, Familiar Imperfections'' by Richard Martin, in *Journal of American Studies* (England), 17(2), 1983; pp. 229–41; ''The Disposition of the Familiar (Walter Abish)'' by Regis Durand, in *Delta Magazine* (France), 1983, pp. 73–83; ''Walter Abish's *How German Is It:* Language & the Crisis of Human Behavior'' by Dieter Saalmann, in *Critique,* Spring 1985, pp. 105–21; ''Walter Abish and the Questioning of the Reader'' by Christopher Butler, in *Facing Texts,* edited by Heide Ziegler, 1988; ''Walter Abish's *How German Is It:* Representing the Postmodern'' by Paul Wotipka, in *Contemporary Literature,* 30, Winter 1989, pp. 503–17; ''Walter Abish and the Topographies of Desire'' by Jerry A. Varsava, in *Contingent Meanings, Postmodern Fiction, Mimesis, and the Reader,* 1990; ''Walter Abish's *How German Is It:* Postmodernism and the Past'' by Maarten Van Delden, in *Salmagundi Magazine,* 85/86, Winter/Spring 1990, pp. 172–94; *Novel Arguments: Reading Innovative American Fiction* by Richard Walsh, 1995; ''How Global Is It: Walter Abish and the Fiction of Globalization'' by Thomas Peyser, in *Contemporary Literature,* 40(2), Summer 1999, pp. 240–62.

*   *   *

Walter Abish, best known for his P.E.N./Faulkner-winning *How German Is It* (1980), is the author of three novels, numerous short stories, and a volume of poetry, *Duel Site* (1970). *Alphabetical Africa* (1974), a novel that bears out the Abish entry in *Encyclopaedia Britannica* (''American writer of experimental novels and short stories whose fiction takes as its subject language itself''), consists of 52 chapters—the first chapter contains only words beginning with ''A,'' chapter two adds ''B'' words, and so on through ''Z'' and then back through the alphabet. It also deftly plays with the reader's preconceived notions about Africa and documents the dynamics of linguistic appropriation of a space often considered exotic in the West. *Eclipse Fever* (1993), Abish's most plot-driven novel, combines his continued concern with the representational properties of language with a sophisticated examination of moral and ethical questions: the novel exhorts the reader to think about colonialism; global capitalism; the relation between history and fiction; and identity, both personal and national.

How German Is It displays Abish's dual concern with language and the reality it purports to represent and the ways in which history informs the present. ''The English Garden'' (published in *In the Future Perfect* [1977]), a precursor to *How German Is It,* has an epigraph from John Ashbery's ''The New Spirit,'' which reads, ''[r]emnants of the old atrocity subsist, but they are converted into ingenious shifts in scenery, a sort of

'English Garden' effect, to give the required air of naturalness, pathos and hope.'' Both the short story and the novel reflect how the German present is always pregnant with the past, particularly the Nazi past, and chronicle the various modes of self-delusion post–World War II Germans engaged in to avoid confronting their recent past.

How German Is It is unequivocal about the role the reader has to play in answering the thorny questions associated with how Germany is perceived, how Germany perceives itself, how the past figures in the German present, how Germany chooses to deal with the Holocaust, and how mechanisms of denial and acceptance might manifest themselves. The novel is more interested in posing questions than in providing definitive answers, and readers are left to their own devices regarding the search for meaning underneath the surfaces Abish so detachedly describes. This deferral of meaning on the novel's part does not imply that there exists no meaning at all; it merely points out the need for readers to become acutely aware of the ethical significance of the answers they provide to questions about the Holocaust.

While not overtly about the Holocaust, *How German Is It* acutely registers the event's aftershocks in Germany—a feature that is shared by a number of uncollected short stories that Abish initially intended as a sequel novel (*As If*) to *How German Is It*. ''I Am the Dust Under Your Feet'' (1987) features the dialogue between two German Jews (an art historian and an architect) buried in a mass grave (both were killed during a death march at the end of the war) who try to explain the Germany outside—and their Germany—to a fetus buried with them. The story has a pronounced caustic edge: it indirectly examines the claim German Jews could possibly have to their Germanness when speaking from a mass grave. It also ruminates on the state of contemporary Germany, when in one strand of the story the game warden protecting the plot of land where the mass grave is located is murdered by Turkish poachers—who curse their task of disposing of the body in German. The irony of this situation lies in the game warden's SS past: a representative of Nazi Germany's drive to purify the German body politic is killed by the ''other'' now present in postwar Germany. ''Just When We Believe That Everything Has Changed'' (1985), ''House on Fire'' (1990), ''Is This Really You?'' (1988), and ''Furniture of Desire'' (1989) similarly examine the intellectual and epistemological subterfuges Germans employ in the wake of their most recent past. One typical passage from ''Is This Really You?'' reads:

> By now Selten has reestablished a firm grip on the day-to-day. . . . On weekends it is only thirty minutes by car to the countryside—the vine-covered hills, everything *almost* unchanged. One can visit medieval villages untouched by the war. People still speak the local dialect. One can sit back lazily in the tiny garden of one of the restaurants and drink several glasses of the excellent local white wine. One can, if so moved,

follow with sensuous detachment the outlines of the hills and then, retaining a mental picture of the tenth-century church steeple and the upper section of the archway, the entrance to this tiny community, focus on a cloud or, being alerted by a faint hum, finally locate the origin of the familiar sound, a distant plane, without evincing—and why on earth should one?—the slightest apprehension that the plane might carry a number of those formidable 500-pounders earmarked (that is the nature of paranoia) for this very picturesque spot. In 1943, '44, and '45, life was less predictable.

How German Is It, together with the short stories mentioned, forms a testament to ''the past that will not pass'' and to the specific instantiations of that past in the present, as well as to the *Sinneslücken* (gaps of meaning), both in the transmission of cultural memory and, literally, in the country's rebuilt fabric, created by the deliberate attempts to erase the past from the present. The part of Abish's work that has the Holocaust as its often unarticulated, yet nevertheless present, backdrop is characterized by a narrative approach in which mimeticism is replaced by a network of associative stimuli that evoke a certain picture of Germany and that construct an image of the place. This image has no special claim to representational accuracy but also refuses to relinquish the possibility that this bricolage of signifiers can reveal profound truths.

—Stefan Gunther

See the essays on ''The English Garden'' and *How German Is It*.

AGNON, S(hmuel) Y(osef)

Nationality: Israeli (originally Austro-Hungarian: immigrated to Palestine, 1924). **Born:** Shmuel Yosef Czaczkes, Buczacz, Galicia, 17 July 1888. **Education:** Studied at private schools and briefly at Baron Hirsch School. **Family:** Married Esther Marks in 1919; one son and one daughter. **Career:** Lived in Palestine, 1907–13; first secretary, Jewish Court, Jaffa, and secretary, National Jewish Council; lecturer and tutor in Germany, 1913–24; lived in Jerusalem, 1924–70. Editor, *Jüdisher Verlag,* Berlin, 1913–24. President, Mekitzei Nirdamim (society for the publication of ancient manuscripts), beginning 1950. **Awards:** Bialik prize, 1934, for *Bi-levav yamin;* Hakhnasat Kala, 1937; Ussishkin prize, 1950, for *Tmol shilshom;* Bialik prize, 1954; Israel prize in literature, 1954, 1958; Nobel prize for literature, 1966. Honorary doctorates: Jewish Theological Seminary of America, 1936; Hebrew University, Jerusalem, 1959. Fellow, Bar Ilan University. **Member:** Hebrew Language Academy. **Died:** 17 February 1970.

PUBLICATIONS

Collections

Kol sipurav shel Sh. Y. Agnon (11 vols.). 1931–62.
Selected Stories of S.Y. Agnon, edited by Samuel Leiter (English translations). 1970.
Twenty-One Stories, edited by Nahum N. Glatzer (English translations). 1970.
Takhrikh shel sipurim, compiled by Emunah Yaron. 1984.
Yafo yefat yamim: Leket mi-tokh sipurav shel Sh. Y. Agnon/ Jaffa, Belle of the Seas: Selections from the Works of S.Y. Agnon (Hebrew and English). 1998.

Novels

Ve-hayah he-akov le-mishor. 1912.
Giv 'at ha-hol [The Hill of Sand]. 1919.
Be-sod yesharim [Among the Pious]. 1921.
Me-hamat ha-metsik [From the Wrath of the Oppressor]. 1921.
'Al Kapot ha-Man'ul [Upon the Handles of the Lock]. 1922.
Polin: Sipure agadot [Poland]. 1924.
Ma'aseh rabi Gadiel ha-Tinok [The Tale of Little Reb Gadiel]. 1925.
Agadat ha-sofer. 1929.
Hakhnasat kalah. 1931; as *The Bridal Canopy,* 1937.
Sipur pashut. 1934; as *A Simple Story,* 1985.
Bi-levav yamim. 1935; as *In the Heart of the Seas: A Story of a Journey to the Land of Israel,* 1947.
Ore'ah nata lalun. 1939; as *A Guest for the Night,* 1968.
Tmol shilshom. 1945; as *Only Yesterday,* 2000.
*Shirah.*1971; translated as *Shira,* 1989.
Pithe devarim. 1977.

Short Stories

Ma'aseh ha-meshulah me-erets ha-Kedosha. 1924.
Ma'aseh ha-ez sefer li-yeladim, with Ze'ev Raban, 1925.
Tsipori. 1926.
Sipur ha-shanim ha-tovot/Ma'aseh ha-rav veha-oreah. 1926; one story, ''Tehilla,'' translated in *Tehilla, and Other Israeli Tales,* 1956.
Sipure ahavim. 1930.
Me'az u-me'atah [From Then and from Now]. 1931.
Be-shuvah ve-nahat: Sipure 'agadot. 1935.
Kovets sipurim. 1937.
Mi-dirah le-dirah: Sipur. 1939.
Elu ve-'elu [These and Those]. 1941; section translated as *A Dwelling Place of My People: Sixteen Stories of the Chassidim,* 1983.
Shevuat emunim. 1943; translated as *Betrothed,* in *Two Tales: Betrothed and Edo and Enam,* 1966.
Sipurim ve-agadot. 1944;
Samukh ve-nir'eh: Sipurim 'im sefer ha-ma'asim [Never and Apparent]. 1950.

'Ad henah [Until Now]. 1952.
Al kapoth hamanul. 1953.
Ha-esh ve-ha'etsim. 1962.
A Book That Was Lost and Other Stories, edited by Alan Mintz and Anne Golomb Hoffman. 1995.

Other

Sefer, sofer, ve-sipur: Sipurim 'al sofrim ve-'al sefarim. 1937.
'Al Berl Kazenelson. 1944.
Sifrehem shel Anshe Butshatsh. 1955.
Pen ishon ha-mavet, with Adah Amikhal Yeivin (theater scripts). 1960.
'Al Meshulam Tokhner zal: Devarim le-zikhro. 1966.
Kinot le-Tish'ah be-Av. 1969.
Me-'atsmi el 'atsmi [From Me to Me]. 1976.
Esterlain yekirati: Mikhtavim 684–691 (1924–1931) (correspondence). 1983.
Kurzweil (correspondence). 1987.
Agnon's Aleph Bet: Poems (for children, in Hebrew and English). 1998.

Editor, with Ahron Eliasberg, *Das Buch von den Polnischen Juden.* 1916.
Editor, *Moaus Zur: Ein Chanukkahbuch.* 1918.
Editor, *Yamin noraim.* 1937; as *Days of Awe: Being a Treasury of Traditions, Legends and Learned Commentaries . . . ,* edited by Nahum N. Glatzer, 1948; revised as *Days of Awe: A Treasury of Jewish Wisdom for Reflection, Repentance, and Renewal on the High Holy Days,* 1995.
Editor, *Atem reitem* [Ye Have Seen]. 1959; as *Present at Sinai: The Giving of the Law: Commentaries Selected by S.Y. Agnon,* 1994.
Editor, *Sifreyhem shel Tsadikim.* 1961.

*

Bibliography: *Bibliographiah 'al Shmuel Yosef Agnon ve-Yetsirto* by Johanan Arnon, 1971; *Samuel Joseph Agnon: A Bibliography of His Work in Translation Including Selected Publications about Agnon and His Writing* by Isaac Goldberg, 1996.

Critical Studies: *Dr. Sh. Y. Agnon* by Eliezer Raphael Malachi, 1935; *S.Y. Agnon: The Writer and His Work,* 1966; *Agnon,* 1966; *Shmuel Yosef Agnon,* 1967; *Nostalgia and Nightmare: A Study in the Fiction of S.Y. Agnon* by Arnold J. Band, 1968; *The Fiction of S.Y. Agnon* by Baruch Hochman, 1970; *S.Y. Agnon and the Revival of Modern Hebrew* by Aaron Bar-Adon, 1972; *S.Y. Agnon* by Harold Fisch, 1975; *Irony in the Works of S.Y. Agnon* (dissertation) by Esther Fuchs, Brandeis University, 1980; *The Dream As a Junction of Theme and Characterization in the Psychological Fiction of S.Y. Agnon* (dissertation), University of California Berkeley, 1984, and *Agnon's Art of Indirection: Uncovering Latent Content in the Fiction of S.Y. Agnon,* 1993, both by Nitza Ben-Dov; *Shmuel*

Yosef Agnon: A Revolutionary Traditionalist by Gershon Shaked, 1989; *Between Exile and Return: S.Y. Agnon and the Drama of Writing* by Anne Golomb Hoffman, 1991; *Relations between Jews and Poles in S.Y. Agnon's Work* by Samuel Werses, 1994; *Tradition and Trauma: Studies in the Fiction of S.J. Agnon* by David Patterson, 1994; *Ghetto, Shtetl, or Polis? The Jewish Community in the Writings of Karl Emil Franzos, Sholom Aleichem, and Shemuel Yosef Agnon* by Miriam Roshwald, 1995; *The Centrifugal Novel: S.Y. Agnon's Poetics of Composition* by Stephen Katz, 1999.

* * *

The life of Nobel Prize-winning novelist Shmuel Yosef Agnon could itself be the subject of a grand novel. His biography had four phases: his life among the Galician Jewry in Buczacz, Poland, from his birth in 1888 until 1907; his life in Jaffa, Palestine, as a member of the Second Aliyah (second wave of modern Jewish immigration to Palestine) from 1907 to 1913; his life in Germany from 1913 to 1924; and his life in Jerusalem from 1924 until his death in 1970. These phases in his life were the raw materials for nearly seven decades of panoramic writing on Jewish life.

Agnon began to write at an early age. Between 1903 and 1908 sixty items in Hebrew and Yiddish were published in nine different journals. The promotion of Hebrew language and literature was an important part of the agenda of Zionist groups in Eastern Europe. Agnon published his first Hebraic poems in 1903 at the age of 14. It was already apparent during his adolescence that he would become a writer.

In 1907 Agnon went to Jaffa. Immigration to Jaffa was an important turning point for him. Whereas Buczacz was rural and provincial, Jaffa attracted Eastern European figures of considerable interest during the Second Aliyah, many of whom were spurred to immigration by the pogroms at Kishinev. Six years later, Agnon left Palestine for Germany, where he connected with several leading Jewish intellectuals including Martin Buber, Gershom Scholem, Franz Rosenzweig, and the Zionist thinkers Ahad Ha'am and Natan Birnbaum. He also met the publisher Salman Schocken, who agreed to set him up with a stipend in exchange for the right to publish Agnon's books. In 1924 Agnon returned to Palestine and settled in Jerusalem after his possessions, including his library of rare books and a number of manuscripts in progress, were destroyed in a fire.

Arnold J. Band views Agnon as a rare combination of an observant Jew and an uncompromising artist. His works contain ironies regarding man's relationship with God that are reminiscent of Fyodor Dostoyevsky and Franz Kafka. He is read by some as a pious storyteller and by others as a modern ironist. Gershom Scholem calls this "the dialectics of simplicity."

According to Anne Golomb Hoffman, Agnon thematizes the cultural breakdown of Judaism among the Hasidim in small-town Galicia followed by a Jewish Renaissance motivated by immigration to Palestine/Israel. Agnon writes during the earliest renewal of Hebrew as an active language. His writing bears the impact of the cultural-political upheaval caused by the Holocaust, which manifests itself in a conflict between the sacred and the secular in his writing. The revival of Hebrew constituted the secularization of a language of religious ceremony. Agnon favored a mystical and rabbinic approach to language and writing. Torah is at the mythic center of Agnon's universe.

—Peter R. Erspamer

See the essay on "The Sign."

AICHINGER, Ilse

Nationality: Austrian. **Born:** Vienna, 1 November 1921. **Education:** Studied medicine, University of Vienna, 1946–48. **Family:** Married the poet Günter Eich in 1952 (died 1972); two children. **Career:** Forced work in a pharmacy during World War II; lector, S. Fischer Verlag, 1949–50; assistant to Inge Aicher-Scholl, Ulm Academy for Design, 1950–51; began association with *Gruppe 47,* 1951. **Awards:** Austrian State prize for literature and *Gruppe 47* prize, both in 1952; City of Düsseldorf Immermann prize and City of Bremen prize, both in 1955; Bavarian Academy of Fine Arts prize, 1961, 1991; Anton Wildgans prize, 1969; Nelly Sachs prize, 1971; City of Vienna prize, 1974; City of Dortmund prize, 1975; Trackle prize, 1979; Petrarca prize, 1982; Belgian Europe Festival prize and Weilheim prize, both in 1987; Town of Solothurn prize, 1991; Roswitha medal. **Address:** c/o Fischer Verlag, Postfach 700480, Frankfurt 6000, Germany.

PUBLICATIONS

Collections

Dialoge, Erzahlungen, Gedichte [Dialogues, Short Stories, Poems], edited by Heinz F. Schafroth. 1965.
Ilse Aichinger: Selected Short Stories and Dialogue, edited by James C. Alldridge. 1966.
Ilse Aichinger, edited by James C. Alldridge. 1969.
Gedichte und Prosa [Poems and Prose]. 1983.
Selected Poetry and Prose, edited by Allen H. Chappel. 1983.
Gesammalte Werke [Collected Works] (8 vols.), edited by Richard Reichensperger. 1991.

Novel

Die größere Hoffnung. 1948; as *Herod's Children,* 1963.

Short Stories

Rede unter dem Galgen [Speech under the Gallows]. 1951; as
Der Gefesselte, 1953; as *The Bound Man and Other Stories,*
1955.
Eliza, Eliza. 1965.
Nachricht vom Tag: Erzahlungen [News of the Day: Short
Stories]. 1970.
Schlechte Worter [Bad Words] (includes radio plays). 1976.
Meine Sprache und ich: Erzahlungen [My Language and I:
Stories]. 1978.
Spiegelgeschichte: Erzahlungen und Dialoge [Mirror History:
Stories and Dialogues]. 1979.

Plays

Zu keiner Stunde [Never at Any Time] (dialogues). 1957.
Besuch um Pfarrhaus: Ein Horspiel, Drei Dialoge [A Visit to
the Vicarage: A Radio Play, Three Dialogues. 1961.
Knöpfe [Buttons] (radio play). In *Hörspiele,* 1961.
Auckland: 4 Horspiele (radio plays). 1969.
Weisse Chrysanthemum (radio play). In *Kurzhörspiele,* 1979.

Radio Plays: *Knöpfe,* 1953; *Gare maritime* [Maritime Sta-
tion], 1973; *Belvedere; Weisse Chrysanthemum,* 1979.

Poetry

Verschenkter Rat [Advice Given]. 1978.

Other

Wo ich wohne: Erzahlungen, Gedichte, Dialoge [Where I
Live: Short Stories, Poems, Dialogues]. 1963.
Grimmige Marchen, with Martin Walser, edited by Wolfgang
Mieder. 1986.
Kleist, Moos, Fasane (memoir). 1987.

Editor, *Gedichte,* by Günter Eich. 1973.

*

Critical Studies: ''Who Is the Bound Man?: Towards an
Interpretation of Ilse Aichinger's *Der Gefesselte,*''in *German
Quarterly*, 38, January 1965, and ''The Ambivalent Image in
Aichinger's *Spiegelgeschichte,*'' in *Révue des Langues Vivantes*
(Belgium), 33, 1967, both by Carol Bedwell; ''Ilse Aichinger's
Absurd I'' by Patricia Haas Stanley, in *German Studies
Review*, 2, 1979; ''A Structural Approach to Aichinger's
Spiegelgeschichte'' by Michael R. Ressler, in *Unterrichtspraxis,*
12 (1), 1979, pp. 30–37; ''Aichinger: The Sceptical Narrator''
by Hans Wolfschütz, in *Modern Austrian Writing: Literature
and Society after 1945,* edited by Wolfschütz and Alan Best,
1980; ''Buttons'' by Sabine I. Golz, in *SubStance,* 21(2), 68,
1992, pp. 77–90; ''Winter Answers in the Poetry of Ilse
Aichinger'' by Amanda Ritchie, in *Focus on Literature,* 1(2),
Fall 1994, pp. 111–27; ''Ilse Aichinger: The Poetics of Silence''
by Andrea Reiter, in *Contemporary German Writers, Their
Aesthetics and Their Language,* edited by Arthur Williams,
Stuart Parkes, and Julian Preece, 1996; ''Out from the Shadows!: Ilse Aichinger's Poetic Dreams of the Unfettered Life''
by Edward R. McDonald, in *Out from the Shadows: Essays on
Contemporary Austrian Women Writers and Filmmakers,* ed-
ited by Margarete Lamb Faffelberger, 1997; *Wenn Ihr Nicht
Werdet Wie Die Kinder: The Significance of the Child in the
World-View of Ilse Aichinger* by Catherine Purdie, 1998.

* * *

Ilse Aichinger's first work, the novel *Herod's Children*
(1963; Die größere Hoffnung, 1948), is the only one in her
relatively small literary oeuvre that deals directly with aspects
of the Holocaust. Much of her work, however, is influenced by
events in her early life relating to the persecution of the Jews by
the Nazis and by the hardship and sorrow she and her mother
endured under Austria's Nazi regime. Born to a Jewish mother
and a Gentile father—they divorced in 1927—Aichinger's
grandmother and her mother's siblings were murdered at a
concentration camp in Minsk.

Aichinger began her career as a full-time writer in 1947 and
soon became one of the most important authors of postwar
literature in German. In her early writing Aichinger developed
her own style and imagery; her work has none of the features of
the *Truemmerliteratur* (literature born of the rubble) as created
by Wolfgang Borchert and **Heinrich Boll**, among others, nor
does it fit into any other literary movement in the immediate
post–1945 era. Some of her poems and short stories may be
compared more properly to the work of Franz Kafka, Paul
Celan, and Ingeborg Bachmann.

Herod's Children introduces the topic of death, especially
that of children and young adults, which is a recurrent theme in
Aichinger's work. The death of her grandmother and of her
mother's siblings in the Holocaust haunted Aichinger, mainly
because of the senselessness and brutality—the novel's young
protagonist, Ellen, is torn apart by a grenade; her friend Bibi
who had been hiding for six weeks is found and savagely
beaten by police guards before being deported; and Ellen's
grandmother dies a painful death when she commits suicide by
poison. In Aichinger's later work her preoccupation with death
expresses her criticism of postwar Germany and Austria, still
poisoned by Nazi ideology, and of a society that, when forced
to come to terms with the horrors of the Holocaust, too often
denied it had taken place or attempted to excuse in various
ways its barbarity. Aichinger depicts postwar German society
as dangerously shallow in character, its identity either defined

by outlived traditional values, especially in the relationship between men and women ("Mondgeschichte" ["Moonstory"]), or by its rejection of change and a consequent sterility in every aspect of life ("Seegeister" ["Ghosts on the Lake"]). Society's lack of values and loss of identity is the topic of "Der Gefesselte" ("The Bound Man") and "Seegeister," the story of a woman who will disintegrate if she takes off her sunglasses, which shield her from the reality of life.

In a number of stories where the protagonists—often children—oppose the status quo, they are defeated. The young boy in the story "Das Plakat" ("The Advertisement"), terrified at the stagnation of his life, wants change as does the young girl in the story. Both are run over by a train as they seek death willingly once they realize they are condemned to a life of noncommunication in an adult world devoid of spiritual values. In "Mein Vater aus Stroh" ("My Father of Straw"), the father figure is represented as ineffectual, and his daughter, in a reversal of roles, takes on the task of a nurturing parent. Aichinger suggests that the death of the two children in "Das Plakat"—as well as that of Ellen in *Herod's Children* and her other young protagonists—preserves in some way their innocence and hope for a better life. This seems paradoxical, but it is Aichinger's belief that through death a new language and a world of new values may be created; her literary technique, in part, reflects her transformation of the death-and-resurrection theme. The best example of this is found in "Spiegelgeschichte" ("Story in a Mirror"), in which a young woman who dies from complications following an abortion comes alive at the moment of her burial. An anonymous person tells the woman's life story, and her sterility is underlined through the killing of her unborn child. When the woman reaches babyhood the narrator talks about the difficulty in forgetting how to talk, thus hinting at the necessity of learning a new, more meaningful language. Paradoxically, the moment of the woman's birth coincides with the moment she is pronounced dead by those surrounding her in her death agony. The last words of the story demonstrate the fact, though, that only a few understand this message:

> "'It's the end' say the ones standing behind you, 'she is dead!'"
> "Quiet! Let them talk!"

Shedding the old life, Aichinger suggests, enables one to find new words and new values. Aware, however, of the difficulty in making her solution germane to society's ills, she later developed further in her writings the symbolic and mystical aspects of her style and vision that were already present in *Herod's Children*. Her characters now inhabit a world where the mundane and the logical are subsumed by the magical and the grotesque ("Eliza, Eliza," "Mein gruener Esel" ["My Green Donkey"], "Die Puppe" ["The Doll"], "Die Maus" ["The Mouse"]). In trying to escape the horrors of her youth and the grim reality of a postwar German society still not rid of its Nazi past, Aichinger created so private and personal a literary world that it is esoteric even to those who are her initiates.

—Renate Benson

See the essay on *Herod's Children*.

AMÉRY, Jean

Pseudonym for Hans Mayer. **Nationality:** Austrian. **Born:** Vienna, 31 October 1912. **Education:** Studied philosophy in Vienna. **Career:** Member, Belgian resistance network, during World War II; worked as a journalist following World War II. Traveled to Germany as a lecturer, beginning in 1964. **Awards:** Bavarian Academy of Fine Arts literary prize, 1972; Vienna prize and Lessing prize (Hamburg), both in 1977. **Died:** Suicide, 17 October 1978.

PUBLICATIONS

Collections

Sonderheft Jean Améry. 1978.
Weiterleben, aber wie? Essays 1968–1978, edited by Gisela Lindemann. 1982.
Radical Humanism: Selected Essays. 1984.
Der integrale Humanismus: Zwischen Philosophie und Literatur: Aufsätze und Kritiken eines Lesers, 1966–1978, edited by Helmut Heissenbüttel. 1985.

Novels

Lefeu, oder, der Abbruch: Roman-Essay. 1974.
Charles Bovary, Landarzt. 1978.
Rendezvous in Oudenaarde. 1982.

Other (autobiographical essays)

Jenseits von Schuld und Sühne: Bewältigungsversuche eines Überwältigten. 1966; as *At the Mind's Limits: Contemplations by a Survivor on Auschwitz and Its Realities,* 1980.
Über das Altern: Revolte und Resignation. 1968; as *On Aging: Revolt and Resignation,* 1994.
Widersprüche. 1971.
Unmeisterliche Wanderjahre. 1971.
Hand an sich legen: Diskurs über den Freitod. 1976; as *On Suicide: A Discourse on Voluntary Death,* 1999.

Other (critical essays)

Karrieren und Köpfe: Bildnisse berühmter Zeitgenossen. 1955.
Teenager-Stars; Idole unserer Zeit. 1960.

Im Banne des Jazz: Bildnisse grosser Jazz-Musiker. 1961.
Geburt der Gegenwart: Gestalten und Gestaltungen der westlichen Zivilisation seit Kriegsende. 1961; as *Preface to the Future: Culture in a Consumer Society,* 1964.
Gerhart Hauptmann, der ewige Deutsche. 1963.
Winston S. Churchill: Ein Jahrhundert Zeitgeschichte. 1965.
Über die Tugend der Urbanität, with Friedrich Heer and Wolf Dieter Marsch. 1969.
Ideologie und Motivation. 1973.
Lessingscher Geist und die Welt von heute (originally a speech). 1978.
Örtlichkeiten (originally radio broadcasts).1980.
Bücher aus der Jugend unseres Jahrhunderts. 1981.
Cinéma: Arbeiten zum Film, edited by Joachim Kalka. 1994.
Ressentiments: Rede im Süddeutschen Rundfunk am 7. März 1966 (originally a speech). 1995.

*

Bibliography: ''Jean Améry: Ausgewahlte Bibliographie'' by Friedrich Pfafflin, in *Text Kritik* (Germany), 99, 1988, pp. 70–83.

Critical Studies: ''Tragic Wisdom: Reflections on Gabriel Marcel and Jean Améry'' by William Kluback, in *Journal of Evolutionary Psychology,* 7(3–4), August 1986, pp. 306–21; '''Heimat,' 'Ortlichkeiten,' and Mother-Tongue: The Cases of Jean Améry and Elias Canetti'' by Irene Stocksieker Di Maio, in *Der Begriff ''Heimat'' in der deutschen Gegenwartsliteratur,* edited by Helfried W. Selinger, 1987; ''What the Holocaust Meant in the Thinking of Primo Levi and Jean Améry'' by Alexander Stille, in *Dissent,* 37(3), Summer 1990, pp. 361–66; ''Jean Améry and Austria'' by Ruth Beckermann, in *Insiders and Outsiders: Jewish and Gentile Culture in Germany and Austria,* edited by Dagmar C. G. Lorenz and Gabriele Weinberger, 1994; ''The Passion of Reason: Reflections on Primo Levi and Jean Améry'' by Eugene Goodheart, in *Dissent,* 41(4), Fall 1994, p. 518; ''Homes without Heimats? Jean Améry at the Limits'' by Dan Stone, in *Angelaki* (England), 2(1), 1995, pp. 91–100; ''Wieviel Heimat braucht der Mensch? Aspects of Jewish Self-Determination in the Works of Jean Améry and Primo Levi'' by Karin Lorenz-Lindemann, in *The Jewish Self-Portrait in European and American Literature,* edited by Hans-Jurgen Schrader, Elliott M. Simon, and Charlotte Wardi, 1996.

* * *

Jean Améry first gained recognition in Germany when he began to write explicitly for a German audience in the mid-1960s. Having refused to travel to Germany and write for a German audience since the end of the war, Améry did not begin to write about his experience of the Holocaust until 1964. He read the resulting essays on German radio before they were published as a book (*At the Mind's Limits*). Beginning in 1964 Améry undertook a number of lecturing journeys through Germany. His pen name, Jean Améry, is partly a direct translation of Hans Mayer, Jean being the equivalent of Hans (as well as a reference to Sartre) and Améry a French sounding anagram of Mayer.

Améry's writings are largely reflections on his experiences in the Holocaust and their consequences on his own life and on wider society. He wrote as an intellectual who had been permanently removed from his natural context of life and work. His work is characterized by the dilemma of being rooted in German culture and language and the awareness that this culture and language has disowned him. Most of his published work is autobiographical, having his Holocaust experiences as their underlying theme. Other significant autobiographical publications deal with the issue of aging (*Über das Altern*) and suicide (*Diskurs über den Freitod*).

Améry's German and French intellectual heritage is displayed clearly in his work (frequent quotes and allusions). His style—which features irony, parody, and travesty—is reminiscent of **Tadeusz Borowski.** Améry remained in a permanent exile from the German cultural context, while continuing to write in German. His work should be interpreted as part of the postwar development of German literature as well as of the emerging literature of Holocaust testimonials. Authors such as Alfred Andersch and **Ingeborg Bachmann** responded to his writings in their own work. Améry's writings express the dilemmas of German-Jewish Holocaust survivors whose entire cultural and linguistic tradition before the war was identified with Germany. The violence done to the German language by its misuse during the time of National Socialism and the forced separation of German Jews from this cultural context meant that an assimilated Jew such as Améry, who did not have any Jewish education, was removed from his natural cultural environment without having any other tradition to take its place.

Améry was philosophically indebted to Jean-Paul Sarte's Existentialism, and his interpretation of his Jewishness follows Sarte's views. Améry did not receive a Jewish education, and although he was aware that his family was regarded as Jewish by others, his own Jewishness became significant only with the application of the Nuremberg Laws in his native Austria in 1938. He identifies as Jewish only because he has to, having been robbed of any other positive cultural identification.

Always a keen observer of postwar West Germany, Améry became a political voice in the 1960s. Motivated by Existentialism's political implications, Améry critically examined the politics of the left and far left in 1960s Germany, expressing particular disappointment at the emerging anti-Zionism of the left (1967). Améry supported the State of Israel, convinced of its necessity in a post-Holocaust world, though he did not want to live there himself.

Améry's writings express a sense of abandonment and loss of home. His essay on *Heimat* (Home) is particularly poignant in this respect. After repeated suicide attempts, Amery killed himself in 1978, overdosing on tranquilizers in a Salzburg hotel. He interpreted suicide as a rebellious act of a free person. In contrast to the camps where death was ubiquitous and controlled by the guards, Améry interpreted suicide as an expression of regaining control of one's own life.

As a writer Améry saw himself as a redundant person, his warnings about the anti-Semitic politics of the German left having gone unheard, his "mission" failed (raté). Having begun his career as a writer for a German context in his 50s, he felt that he had come too late. Commentators have repeatedly noted that many German intellectuals appeared to treat Améry as an "institutionalized conscience" and as a "professional Jew," one that could be called on in times of need, but whose message could otherwise go unnoticed.

Améry's writings contain little description of his experiences in the camps. They are instead reflections on the human capability for inhumanity. Guided by the humanistic tradition of the Enlightenment, Améry's voice is an ambiguous and challenging mixture of hope in and despair at humanity.

—K. Hannah Holtschneider

See the essays on *At the Mind's Limits: Contemplations by a Survivor on Auschwitz and Its Realities* and *Radical Humanism: Selected Essays.*

AMICHAI, Yehuda

Nationality: Israeli (originally German: immigrated to Palestine, 1936). **Born:** Würzburg, 1924. **Education:** Studied Biblical texts and Hebrew literature, Hebrew University, Jerusalem. **Military Service:** Jewish Brigade of the British Army, 1942–46; Palmach (later Israeli Defense Forces), 1946–ca. 1948: fought in the Negev during Israel's war of independence; Israeli Army, 1973: involved during the Yom Kippur War. **Career:** Teacher, various secondary schools and colleges. **Awards:** Bialik prize, 1975; Israel prize for poetry, 1982; foreign honorary member, American Academy and Institute of Arts and Letters, 1986. **Died:** September 2000.

PUBLICATIONS

Collections

Collected Poems. 1963.
Shirim 1948–1962. 1963; as *Poems,* 1969.
Selected Poems. 1968.
Selected Works. 1981.
The Early Books of Yehuda Amichai. 1988.
The Selected Poetry of Yehuda Amichai, edited by Chana Bloch and Stephen Mitchell. 1986; revised edition, 1996.

Yehuda Amichai: A Life of Poetry, 1948–1994. 1994.
Selected Poems, edited by Ted Hughes and Daniel Weissbort. 2000.

Poetry

Achshav uve-yamim ha-aharim [Now and in Other Days]. 1955.
Be-merhav shtei tikvot [Two Hopes Away]. 1958.
Ba-gina ha-yziburit [In the Park]. 1958.
Achshav ba-ra'ash [Now in Noise]. 1969.
Now, with David Avidan, Aharon Appelfeld, and Itzhak Orpaz, edited by Gabriel Moked (English translations). 1969.
Ve-lo al manat lizkor [Not to Remember]. 1971.
Songs of Jerusalem and Myself (English translations). 1973.
Me-ahore col ze mistater osher gadol [Behind All This Hides a Great Happiness]. 1974.
Mas'ot Binyamin ha-aharon mi-Tudelah. 1976; translated as *Travels of a Latter-Day Benjamin of Tudela,* 1977; bilingual edition, 1986.
Zeman. 1977; as *Time,* 1979.
Amen (English translations). 1977.
On New Year's Day, Next to a House Being Built (English translation). 1979.
Shalva gedola: shelot u-teshuvot. 1980; as *Great Tranquillity: Questions and Answers,* 1983.
Shire ahavah/Love Poems (Hebrew and English). 1981.
Me-adam atah ve-el adam tashuv [Of Man Thou Art, and Unto Man Shalt Thou Return]. 1985.
Sha'at hesed [Hour of Grace]. 1986.
Shire Yerushalayim/Poems of Jerusalem (Hebrew and English). 1987.
Gam ha-egrof haia pa'am yad ptuha ve-etzbaot. 1990; as *Even a Fist Was Once an Open Palm with Fingers,* 1991.
Nof galui eyinaim/Open Eyed Land (Hebrew, English, and German). 1992.
'Od shire ahavah/More Love Poems (Hebrew and English). 1994.
Achziv, Keisaria ve-ahava ahat achziv/Akhziv Cesarea and One Love (Hebrew and English). 1996.
Exile at Home, with photographs by Frederic Brenner. 1998.
Patuah sagur patuah. 1998; as *Open Closed Open,* 2000.

Novels

Lo me-akhshav, lo mikan. 1963; as *Not of This Time, Not of This Place,* 1968.
Mi itneni malon. 1971.

Short Stories

Ba-ruach ha-nora'ah ha-zot [In This Terrible Wind] 1961; as *The World Is a Room and Other Stories,* 1984.

Plays

Masa le-ninveh. 1962; as *Journey to Nineveh,* 1985.
Pa'amonim ve-rakavot [Bells and Trains] (plays and radio scripts). 1968.
The Day Martin Buber Was Buried: A Radio Play (translation). 1970.

Other

Ha-zanav ha-shamen shel Numa [Numa's Fat Tail] (for children). 1978.

*

Bibliography: *To Commemorate the 70th Birthday of Yehuda Amichai: A Bibliography of His Work in Translation* by Essi Lapon-Kandelshein, edited by Nava Duchovni, 1994.

Critical Studies: "Children and Lovers: On Yehuda Amichai's Poetic Works" by Warren Bargad, in *Midstream,* October 1975; "Israel's Master Poet" by Robert Alter, in *New York Times Magazine,* 8 June 1986; *The Writing of Yehuda Amichai: A Thematic Approach* by Glenda Abramson, 1989, and *The Experienced Soul: Studies in Amichai,* edited by Glenda Abramson, 1997; *Voices of Israel: Essays on and Interviews with Yehuda Amichai, A. B. Yehoshua, T. Carmi, Aharon Appelfeld, and Amos Oz* by Joseph Cohen, 1990; "Poet of Life's Noises: Portrait of Yehuda Amichai" by Rahel Musleah, in *Hadassah Magazine,* 76(9), May 1995; "Wrestling with the Angel of History: The Poetry of Yehuda Amichai" by Chana Bloch, and "Yehuda Amichai: Down to Earth" by Jeredith Merrin, both in *Judaism,* 45(3), Summer 1996; "Eternal Present: Poetic Figuration and Cultural Memory in the Poetry of Yehuda Amichai, Dan Pagis, and Tuvia Rubner" by Amir Eshel, in *Jewish Social Studies,* 7(1), 2000, pp. 141–66.

* * *

Yehuda Amichai, whom Chana Kronfeld called "the most central poet Israeli modernism has produced," was born in Würzburg, Germany, in 1924. His family emigrated to Palestine in 1936, first to Haifa, then to Jerusalem, where the poet lived for most of his life. Amichai served in the British army from 1942 to 1946, and he fought in the Palmach, the commando force of the Haganah, during Israel's war of independence. He studied Bible and Hebrew literature at Hebrew University and then taught in schools and colleges in Jerusalem and abroad for more than 30 years. Amichai's first book of poems appeared in 1955. He went on to publish numerous volumes of poetry, short stories, children's books, and a collection of plays. His poems have been translated into some 40 languages, with numerous collections available in English. Amichai received the Bialik Award in 1975 and the prestigious Israel Prize in 1982, and in 1986 he was named an honorary member of the American Academy of Arts and Sciences. His final book and magnum opus, *Patuach sagur patuach,* appeared in 1998, and an award-winning translation, *Open Closed Open,* was published in 2000, the year of Amichai's death.

Amichai regarded T.S. Eliot, W.H. Auden, Lea Goldberg, and the medieval Hebrew poets as his central influences. As Kronfeld has written in *On the Margins of Modernism,* his poems exhibit "the prototypical traits of Anglo-American modernism, including the difficulty of classical allusion, highly figurative language, and syntactic fragmentation." At the same time, however, Amichai insisted that he was "a man who writes poems" rather than a professional poet, and he was perhaps best known for his antielitist poetic voice and his passion for the quotidian. This ambivalence at the heart of Amichai's poetics also characterized his complex Jewish sensibility. Although the poems are often brashly iconoclastic when treating Jewish themes, they allude frequently to liturgical and scriptural texts, and they engage in midrashic practice as well as theological meditation. Amichai can be compared to the nineteenth-century German Jewish poet Heinrich Heine, whose lyrics remained beholden to the German romantic idiom even as he sought to expose, through hyperbole, mimicry, and irony, the conceits of idealism. Amichai's works are archives of Jewish textual memory; yet the Jewish past they preserve has been deromanticized and refracted through the exquisite prism of his imagination.

In 1959, at the age of 35, Amichai returned to his native Würzburg, a visit recounted in fictionalized form in the novel *Lo me-akhshav, lo mikan (Not of This Time, Not of This Place).* The novel is perhaps Amichai's most extended autobiographical work, although one might also mention the autobiographical epic poem of 1967, "Mas'ot Binyamin ha-aharon mitudela" ("The Travels of the Last Benjamin of Tudela"). Although many poems—above all the love poems and those about his father—address the poet's personal past, one can barely untangle biographical from mythic strains in these texts. The stunning interconnectedness of individual, collective, and transcendent dimensions of existence and, at the same time, of Jewish and universal tropes is a trademark of his oeuvre in its entirety. As Amichai declares in *Open Closed Open,* "Jewish history and world history / grind me between them like two grindstones, sometimes to a powder. And the solar year and the lunar year / get ahead of each other or fall behind, / leaping, they set my life in perpetual motion." Seldom is there an attempt to achieve equilibrium; the poems are intended to unsettle, surprise, and even shock. Likewise, *Not of This Time, Not of This Place,* the poet's early and only novel, reveals that disorientation and dislocation are necessary corollaries of any memory quest.

In her study *The Writing of Yehuda Amichai,* Glenda Abramson is right to observe in the novel a "foretaste and summary" of the central themes and motifs of the lyric oeuvre: memory; desire and love; childhood; war; the landscape and history of Israel and, above all, of Jerusalem; and the exigencies of everyday life, ironically juxtaposed with the quests for meaning, faith, and answers. With regard to diction and style, the novelistic and lyric voices are one and the same. Amichai's characters inhabit the identical linguistic universe as do his lyric selves, a world rife with metaphor and symbolism, in which prose becomes poetry and poetry becomes prose and in which a biblical or liturgical expression is as apropos as any modern turn of phrase.

—Abigail Gillman

See the essay on *Not of This Time, Not of This Place.*

ANTELME, Robert

Nationality: French. **Born:** 1917. **Family:** Married the writer Marguerite Duras in 1939 (divorced). **Career:** Active in the French resistence, 1943–44, arrested and imprisoned in 1944. **Died:** 1990.

PUBLICATION

Memoir

L'Espèce humaine. 1947; as *The Human Species,* 1992.

*

Critical Studies: ''Purity and Danger: Between Hell and Reason'' by Bernard Knox, in *New Republic,* 207(22), 23 November 1992; ''An Introduction to Robert Antelme'' by Kevin C. O'Neill, in *Marguerite Duras Lives On,* edited by Janine Ricouart, 1998.

* * *

Robert Antelme survived imprisonment at Gandersheim, an especially cruel subcamp of Buchenwald, a death march, and finally incarceration at Dachau, where he was liberated. He is best known for his work *The Human Species* (1992; *L'Espèce humaine,* 1947), which tells this story and maintains that the human race is indissolubly one, a point shown by the extremities of the camps. The book was reissued in 1957 as, in France, intellectuals and others began to take more notice of the Holocaust (**André Schwarz-Bart**'s *Le dernier des justes* [1959; *The Last of the Just*] won the Prix Goncourt in 1959, for example). As Dan Stone writes, the ''book, when it finally achieved success at the end of the 1950s, was lauded by the French intellectual establishment (to which, thanks to his marriage to [the avant-garde writer] Marguerite Duras, Antelme had easy access).'' The book was extremely influential to generations of French thinkers.

For French writer and philosopher Maurice Blanchot, in his essay ''The Indestructible,'' Antelme illustrates a basic truth about being. The human subject is reduced to its need, to ''naked life,'' ''human existence . . . lived as lack at the level of need.'' The human becomes an ''egoism without ego'' and alien from his (or her) own self. This most basic level affirms a sacredness to life beyond being human. In turn then, this bears a relation to the act of writing or speaking. Blanchot suggests that it is not simply a question of ''telling the story'' (that is, relating facts) but of speaking, of speaking to another human being. And this is the tension Blanchot finds in *The Human Species*, a book about the way humanity is taken away that is at the same time reasserting humanity; thus, it is ''choking'' or ''stifling'' words. For French writer George Perec, the camps are too distant for non-survivors to talk about. The facts given in memoirs are, for him, too far from any experience of the truth. Yet Antelme's testimony affirms the triumph of the human over the camps; the SS, for Perec, cannot stop history. As in Antelme's testimony, Perec seems to pass over the fate of the Jews, and for some critics his conclusions, influenced by Antelme's memoir, are too glib. For Sarah Kofman, a leading French philosopher, *The Human Species* offers a way to think about the dilemmas of the Holocaust; her book *Smothered Words* (1998) comes from Antleme's account. She suggests that his book does not simply celebrate on ''old-fashioned'' humanism, based on similarities, but rather begins, or is a way of understanding, a new form of humanism that is based not on what people have in common but on differences, on the experience of lacking—a community which has nothing in common.

What is perhaps significant is not merely the influence of *The Human Species* but the sort of influence it has had. By its insistence on survival and in its French national and non-Jewish context, the book, when used to think through the Holocaust, leads to a certain sort of interpretation. For Blanchot it is the reading of the book against its feeling of human survival that is its strength. Overall, however, it shares more with **David Rousset**'s *L'univers concentrationnaire* (1946) and the ability to recuperate the Holocaust into a wider and more extensive narrative (of humanity rather than Marxist revolution) than other survivor narratives.

—Robert Eaglestone

See the essay on *The Human Species.*

APITZ, Bruno

Nationality: German. **Born:** Leipzig, 28 April 1900. **Education:** Studied to be a stamp-cutter, 1914–15. **Family:** Married Marlis Kieckhäfer in 1965; one daughter. **Career:** Joined Worker Education Association (Socialist Worker Youth of the Social Democratic Party), 1914; arrested for anti-war propaganda and imprisoned in Cottbus, 1917–18; worked as a bookstore assistant and actor, Leipzig and Hamburg, 1919–27; theater director, Berlin, 1928–30; chairperson of Leipzig district, Union of Proletarian-Revolutionary Writers, 1930–33; penal servitude in Sachsen and imprisonment in Buchenwald, 1933–45; administrative manager, Leipzig city theatres, 1946; chairman, art and literature trade union, Leipzig, 1951; worked in film in East Berlin, 1952. Beginning in 1955 journalist and novelist. Editor, *Leipziger Volkszeitung,* 1945. **Award:** Honored by the City of Leipzig, 1975. **Died:** 7 April 1979.

PUBLICATIONS

Novels

Nackt unter Wölfen. 1958; as *Naked among Wolves,* 1960.
Der Regenbogen [The Rainbow]. 1976.
Schwelbrand. 1984.

Short Stories

Esther. 1959.

Plays

Screenplay: *Nackt unter Wölfen,* 1963.

Radio Play: *Nackt unter Wölfen,* 1960.

*

Critical Studies: "Survival under Fascism: Deception in Apitz' *Nackt unter Wölfen,* Becker's *Jakob der Lugner,* and Kohlhaase's *Erfindung einer Sprache*" by Helen L. Cafferty, in *West Virginia University Philological Papers,* 30, 1984; *Bruno Apitz, 1900–1979: Biographie, Texte, Bibliographie* by Renate Florstedt, 1990.

* * *

Bruno Apitz began writing at the age of 18 and published his first poems and short stories in newspapers and journals in the 1920s. In 1924, while working as an actor in Leipzig, he wrote his first drama, *Der Mensch im Nacken* ("The Man on Your Tail"). Like the novel *Fleck und Barb, die Unrasierten* ("Fleck and Barb, the Unshaven") and the dramas *Und was sagt ihr dazu?* ("And What Do You Say to That") and *Paradies und gute Erde* ("Paradise and Good Soil") as well as the poems and full-length plays he wrote at the end of the war reflecting his incarceration in the Buchenwald concentration camp, it was never published or performed. A number of short radio plays dealing with his Buchenwald years were broadcast in the postwar years but are now forgotten. It was not until 1958 that Apitz saw success with his novel *Naked among Wolves* (*Nackt unter Wölfen,* 1958), which rapidly became a bestseller in both East and West Germany. The novel was translated into some 30 languages, adapted as a radio play

(1960), and turned into a popular film (1963). Apitz himself wrote both the radio script and the screenplay. In 1959 Apitz published the story *Esther* and in 1976 his autobiographical novel *Der Regenbogen* ("The Rainbow").

Naked among Wolves is one of the first German concentration camp novels and contains much of what Apitz experienced in the eight years (1937–45) he was imprisoned in Buchenwald. A committed communist from his youth on and a member of the Communist Youth Organization from 1920 and the Communist Party of Germany from 1927, he described his political struggles and experiences in his earlier works. These political activities resulted in jail sentences in 1917 and 1918–19 and in lengthy stays in various camps from the very beginning of the Third Reich. Apitz's work accordingly reflects first and foremost his lfe as a socialist in the first half of the twentieth century and not primarily his life during the Holocaust. Buchenwald was not, of course, an extermination camp, but a camp for political prisoners. Jews were, however, sent there and killed from 1938 on, and the Jewish child described in *Naked among Wolves*—who miraculously survives the last weeks of the war in Buchenwald—did in fact exist. This child has symbolic value, however, and is not intended to encapsulate Jewish experience in the Holocaust. Apitz, properly, should be seen as an antifascist writer rather than a writer from, or on, the Holocaust.

—David Scrase

See the essay on *Naked among Wolves.*

APPELFELD, Aharon

Nationality: Israeli (originally Romanian: immigrated to Palestine, 1946). **Born:** Czernovitz, Bukovina, 1932. **Education:** After first grade deported to a concentration camp in Transnistria; Hebrew University, Jerusalem, late 1940s. **Military Service:** Israeli Army. **Family:** Married; two sons and one daughter. **Career:** Liberated by the Russian army, 1944, and worked as a kitchen helper before emigrating. Professor of Hebrew literature, Ben Gurion University of the Negev, Beer Sheva, Israel. Visiting fellowship for Israeli writers, St. Cross College, Oxford University, 1967–68; visiting professor: Boston University, Brandeis University, and Yale University; visiting scholar, Harvard University. **Awards:** Youth Aliyah prize; twice recipient of the Anne Frank Prize; Milo prize; Jerusalem prize; Prime Minister's prize for creative writing, 1969; Brenner prize, 1975; Israel prize, 1983; Present Tense Award for fiction, 1985, for *Tzili: The Story of a Life;* H. H. Wingate literary award, 1987, 1989; National Jewish book award for fiction, Jewish Book Council, 1989, for *The Immortal Bartfuss;* Bialik prize; Harold U. Ribelow prize. **Agent:** Weidenfeld & Nicolson, 91 Clapham High Street, London SW4 7TA, England.

PUBLICATIONS

Novels

Bekumat hakark'a [At Ground Level]. 1968.
Ha-or veha-kutonet [The Skin and the Gown]. 1971.
Ke'ishon h'ayin [As an Apple of His Eye]. 1972.
Shanim vesha'ot [Years and Hours] (two novellas). 1975.
Badenheim 'ir nofesh (novella). 1975; as *Badenheim 1939*, 1980.
Tor hapelaot (novella). 1978; as *The Age of Wonders*, 1981.
Ketonet veha-pasim [The Shirt and the Stripes]. 1983; as *Tzili: The Story of a Life*, 1983.
Michvat ha'or [Searing Light]. 1980.
Ha'pisgah [The Summit]. 1982; as *The Retreat*, 1984.
El eretz hagomé (novella). Translated as *To the Land of the Cattails*, 1986; as *To the Land of the Reeds*, 1987.
Ritspat esh [Tongue of Fire]. 1988.
Bartfus ben ha-almavet (novella). As *The Immortal Bartfuss*, 1988.
Al kol hapesha'im. Translated as *For Every Sin*, 1989.
Ba'et uve'onah achat [At One and the Same Time]. 1985; as *The Healer*, 1990.
Katerinah. 1989; as *Katerina*, 1992.
Mesilat barzel. 1991; as *The Iron Tracks*, 1998.
Ad nefesh. Translated as *Unto the Soul*, 1994.
Laish. 1994.
'Ad she-ya'aleh 'amud ha-shahar [Until the Dawn's Light]. 1995.
Mikhreh ha-kerah [Ice Mine]. 1997.
Timyon [Abyss]. 1993; as *The Conversion*, 1998.
Kol asher ahavti [All That I Have Loved]. 1999.
Masa' el ha-horef [Journey into Winter]. 2000.

Short Stories

Ashan [Smoke]. 1962.
Ba-gai ha-poreh [In the Fertile Valley]. 1963.
Kafor al ha'aretz [Frost on the Land]. 1965.
In The Wilderness. 1965.
Be-komat ha-karka [On the Ground Floor]. 1968.
Now, with David Avidan, Aharon Appelfeld, and Itzhak Orpaz, edited by Gabriel Moked (English translations). 1969.
Hamishah sipurim. 1969.
Adne ha-nahar [Pillars of the River]. 1971.
Keme'ah edim: Mivhar [Like a Hundred Witnesses: A Selection]. 1975.

Other

Masot be-guf rishon [Essays in First-Person]. 1979.
Writing and the Holocaust, edited by Berel Lang. 1988.

Beyond Despair: Three Lectures and a Conversation with Philip Roth (translation). 1994.
Sipur hayim [Story of a Life] (memoir) 1999.

Editor, *Me-'olamo shel Rabi Nahman mi-Braslav*. 1970; as *From the World of Rabbi Nahman of Bratslav*, 1973.

*

Critical Studies: "Tzili: Female Adolescence and the Holocaust in the Fiction of Aharon Appelfeld" by Naomi B. Sokoloff, in *Gender and Text in Modern Hebrew and Yiddish Literature*, edited by Sokoloff, Anne Lapidus Lerner, and Anita Norich, 1992; "Aharon Appelfeld's *For Every Sin*: The Jewish Legacy after the Holocaust" by Avraham Balaban, in *Hebrew Literature in the Wake of the Holocaust*, edited by Leon I. Yudkin, 1993; *Aharon Appelfeld: The Holocaust and Beyond*, 1994, and "Aharon Appelfeld: A Hundred Years of Jewish Solitude," in *World Literature Today*, 72(3), Summer 1998, pp. 493–500, both by Gila Ramras-Rauch; *Foregone Conclusions: Against Apocalyptic History* by Michael André Bernstein, 1994; "Aharon Appelfeld: On the Brink of the Void" by Norma Rosen, in *Congress Monthly*, 61(5), September 1994, p. 8; "Appelfeld and His Times: Transformations of Ahashveros, the Eternal Wandering Jew" by Gershon Shaked, in *Hebrew Studies: A Journal Devoted to Hebrew Language and Literature*, 36, 1995, p. 87–100; "Literature, Ideology, and the Measure of Moral Freedom: The Case of Aharon Appelfeld's *Badenhaim 'ir nofesh*" by Emily Miller Budick, in *Modern Language Quarterly*, 60(2), June 1999, pp. 223–49; "Is Aharon Appelfeld a Holocaust Writer?" by Leon I. Yudkin, in *The Holocaust and the Text: Speaking the Unspeakable*, edited by Andrew Leak and George Paizis, 2000; *Aharon Appelfeld: From Individual Lament to Tribal Eternity* by Yigal Shvartz, 2001.

* * *

Aharon Appelfeld's fiction focuses on the assimilated Jew living in Europe just before the Holocaust or on the Jew in Israel in the years following the catastrophe. His characters, the men, women, and children, are either extensions of Appelfeld himself or reflections of his experiences as a child from a highly assimilated, urbane family. His grandparents, who spoke Yiddish and with whom he was quite close, were very observant, while his parents, to the disappointment of his grandparents, were highly assimilated and spoke German and took pride in German culture. All of his villages are Drajinetz, where he spent most of his eight and a half years before the Nazis occupied Bukovina, and his cities are all Czernovitz, the family's weekend and holiday destination. In a November 1998 *New Yorker* article he described his visit to the tiny village of his childhood, "from which [he] draws and draws, and it seems that there is no end to its waters." His writing is quiet but intense, concise, and controlled, without bitterness or accusation.

Appelfeld's life was transformed in June 1941 when the Germans and the Romanians invaded Bukovina and murdered most of the inhabitants, including his mother and grandmother. He and his father escaped to the Czernovitz ghetto, from which they were later sent to Transnistria to die. He was separated from his father and escaped to the forests, where he lived by instinct, wandering for three years, a frightened but determined young child who survived by running errands for prostitutes and horse thieves. In addition to his mother tongues of German, Yiddish, Ruthenian, and Romanian, he learned to speak the Ukrainian of the Soviet soldiers for whom he became a kitchen worker. In 1946 he went to Italy with a band of children like him and from there boarded an illegal ship to Palestine. All of these experiences found expression in his novels.

Appelfeld's works are about the war, yet none, except for *Tzili: The Story of a Life,* refers to his experiences as a child caught in the Nazi grip. In this, his most autobiographical work, he is indirect and writes in a girl's voice to avoid chronicling his own experiences, thereby sacrificing imagination for reportage. He writes about the victims, seeking to reveal their inner life and the suffering he shares with other survivors. His most enduring influence is Franz Kafka, whose theme of alienation, according to Appelfeld, marked the twentieth century. His mentors in Israel led him to Max Brod, Kafka's close friend, and others who encouraged and supported his writing. Like Kafka, Appelfeld is preoccupied with the isolated individual who is unable to find comfort and validation from society. In his prewar novels his characters are too rational to anticipate the oncoming catastrophe. Often his characters are unaware of their purpose as survivors. They act and react in sincere bewilderment. They are uneasy with themselves or with others and recall their prewar years with embarrassment for their Jewishness and, paradoxically, for their futile attempts at assimilation, when they sought to shed their origins as well as their overt habits. Although he is not observant, his Jewishness is a curious blend of deep spirituality, substantial familiarity with the Torah, and strong memories of the experience of assimilation, strands of which are richly portrayed in his characters.

The winner of the prestigious Israel Prize in 1983 and of numerous other awards since then, Appelfeld has had a distinguished career as a professor of literature at Ben Gurion University, lecturer at Beer Sheva University, and visiting professor in the United States and Europe. Writing in Hebrew, his adopted tongue and his first literary tongue, he works carefully and sparsely, taking about one and a half years to write each novel, which he then puts aside for review four or five years later. In his ironic, wry style, characteristic of his fiction, he has described his 30 books as works about "one hundred years of Jewish loneliness and isolation." He added, "I'm probably among the last living 'Jewish writers,' that is, one who writes for Jews, about Jews." Sincerely modest, he does not comment on his unique place in Jewish literature, although his novels, most of which have been called "small

masterpieces" by the critics, have presented a remarkable and unforgettable portrayal of the impact of the Holocaust on East European Jewry and on postwar Palestine.

—Myrna Goldenberg

See the essays on *Badenheim 1939, The Immortal Bartfuss, The Retreat,* and *Tzili: The Story of a Life.*

ARIETI, Silvano

Nationality: American (originally Italian: immigrated to New York, 1939). **Born:** Pisa, 28 June 1914. **Education:** Lycee Galileo, Pisa, B.A. 1932; University of Pisa, M.D. (summa cum laude) 1938; William Alanson White Institute, New York, 1946–52, diploma in psychoanalysis 1952. **Family:** Married 1) Jane Jaffe, c. 1942, two sons; 2) Marianne Thompson in 1965. **Career:** Fellow in neuropathology, New York State Psychiatric Institute, 1939–41; visiting fellow, primate biology laboratories, Yale University, 1940; resident in psychiatry, Pilgrim State Hospital, West Brentwood, New York, 1941–44; psychiatrist, 1946–52, and faculty member and training analyst, 1962–81, William Alanson White Institute of Psychiatry, New York; practicing psychiatrist and psychoanalyst, specializing in schizophrenia and depression, 1952–81; associate professor of clinical psychiatry, State University of New York Downstate Medical Center, Brooklyn, 1953–61; professor of clinical psychiatry, New York Medical College, 1961–81. Editor, *The World Biennial of Psychiatry and Psychotherapy,* 1971 and 1973; editor, *Journal of the American Academy of Psychoanalysis,* 1973–81. **Awards:** Gold medal award, Milan Group for the Advancement of Psychotherapy, 1964; Frieda Fromm-Reichmann award, American Academy of Psychoanalysis, 1968; National Book Award for science, 1975, for *Interpretation of Schizophrenia;* Sigmund Freud award and Emil A. Gutheil award, both in 1978. **Member:** American Medical Association; American Psychiatric Association; several other American medical, psychiatric, and psychoanalytic organizations. **Died:** 7 August 1981.

PUBLICATIONS

Novel

The Parnas: A Scene from the Holocaust. 1979.

Other (psychology)

Interpretation of Schizophrenia. 1955.
The Intrapsychic Self; Feeling, Cognition, and Creativity in Health and Mental Illness. 1967.
The Will to Be Human. 1972.

Creativity: The Magic Synthesis. 1976.
Psychotherapy of Schizophrenia and Dynamic Cognition. 1976.
Love Can Be Found: A Guide to the Most Desired and Most Elusive Emotion, with James A. Arieti. 1977.
Severe and Mild Depression: The Psychotherapeutic Approach, with Jules Bemporad. 1978; as *Psychotherapy of Severe and Mild Depression,* 1993.
Understanding and Helping the Schizophrenic: A Guide for Family and Friends. 1979.
Abraham and the Contemporary Mind. 1981.

Editor, *American Handbook of Psychiatry* (7 vols.). 1959; revised and expanded, 1974.
Editor, with Gerard Chrzanowski, *New Dimensions in Psychiatry: A World View.* 1975; revised, 1977.

*

Critical Studies: ''Comments on Silvano Arieti: Anti-Psychoanalytic Cultural Forces in the Development of Western Civilization'' by Jerome D. Frank, in *American Journal of Psychotherapy,* 50 (4), Fall 1996, pp. 473–74; Silvano Arieti special section in *Journal of the American Academy of Psychoanalysis,* 27(4), 1999, pp. 541–603; ''Psychoanalysis and the Problem of Evil: Silvano Arieti's *Parnas* and the Holocaust'' by Harvey Peskin, in *Judaism,* 50 (2), 2001, pp. 131–43.

*   *   *

Born in Pisa, Italy, on June 28, 1914, Silvano Arieti was the son of a physician. His father's position made it possible for the young Arieti to have a relatively comfortable upbringing. He attended the medical school at the University of Pisa, from which he graduated summa cum laude with a specialty in neurology and psychiatry. Arieti went on to do an internship, during which time he treated his first psychiatric patient. After completing his internship in 1939, he and his family left for the United States to escape the increasingly oppressive anti-Semitic Fascism that was spreading throughout Italy.

Soon after his arrival in the United States, Arieti obtained an appointment as a fellow in the department of neuropathology at the New York State Psychiatric Institute. From 1941 to 1944 he was a resident at Pilgrim State Hospital in Brentwood, New York. During his residency there he married Jane Jaffe, and they had two sons. In 1946 Arieti took a position at the William Alanson White Institute of Psychiatry in New York City, where he remained until 1952. As a result of his work at the institute, Arieti published his first book, *Interpretation of Schizophrenia,* in 1955. In its second edition (1975) the study book won the National Book Award for science. Among Arieti's other prestigious honors were the 1964 Gold Medal Award for the Advancement of Psychiatry and the Frieda Fromm-Reichmann Award, which he won in 1968 for his contributions to the understanding of schizophrenia.

After the publication of his first book, Arieti became a leader in the field of psychiatry. He was the editor in chief of the *American Handbook of Psychiatry* (1959), the founder of the *Journal of the American Academy of Psychoanalysis*, and the author of numerous volumes. When he wrote his Holocaust novel *The Parnas: A Scene from the Holocaust* (1979), Arieti brought to bear the sum of his professional insight and personal experience.

The title character in *The Parnas* was based on Giuseppe Pardo Roques, the man Arieti most admired as he was growing up in Pisa. Unlike Arieti and his family, Roques was not able to get out of Italy before the Germans arrived, and, along with the other Jews of Pisa, he was murdered in the summer of 1944. A man of great learning and impeccable character, Roques was known for his kindness and generosity. He suffered, however, from a mysterious mental illness that ultimately confined him to his house and made it impossible for him to flee from the Nazis.

During his years of study in Pisa, Arieti dreamed of finding a cure for his elder and mentor. He thus wrote *The Parnas* not only as a tribute to the courage and spirituality of Roques but also as an exploration of the bestial evil that characterized the Holocaust. Arieti's work in psychiatry led him to conclude that mental illness was deeply tied to human spirituality, and in *The Parnas* he makes that point very powerfully. In 1998, 17 years after his death in 1981, an international symposium on the life and work of Arieti was held in Pisa.

—David Patterson

See the essay on *The Parnas: A Scene from the Holocaust.*

ASCH, Sholem

Nationality: American (originally Polish: immigrated to the United States, 1910). **Born:** Kutno, 1 November 1880. **Education:** Studied in Hebrew schools; attended rabbinical college; studied with Isaac Leib Peretz in Warsaw. **Married:** Mathilde Shapiro. **Career:** Worked as a letter writer while in school in Wloclawek; moved to the United States; lived in Poland after World War I and also lived in France before returning to the United States; traveled frequently to Europe and Palestine; moved to Israel, 1954. **Awards:** Polish Republic's Polonia Restituta, 1932; Anisfeld-Wolf book award, 1947, for *East River.* **Died:** 10 August 1957.

PUBLICATIONS

Collections

Children of Abraham: The Short Stories of Sholem Asch. 1942.
Tales of My People. 1948.

From Many Countries; The Collected Short Stories of Sholem Asch. 1958.

Novels

A shtetl [The Village]. 1904.
Reb shloyme nogid: A poeme fun Yudishen leben (prose narrative). 1913.
Motke ganev. 1916; as *Mottke, The Thief,* 1935.
Der veg tsu zikh [The Way to Oneself]. 1917.
Amerike. Translated as *America,* 1918.
Kiddush ha-shem. 1919; as *Kiddush ha-Shem: An Epic of 1648,* 1926.
Di Muter. 1919; as *The Mother,* 1930.
Onkl Mozes. 1918; as *Uncle Moses,* 1920.
Dos bukh fun tsar. 1921.
Toyt urteyl [Death Sentence]. 1926.
Khaym Lederers Tsurikkumen. 1927; as *Chaim Lederer's Return,* in *Three Novels,* 1938.
Erets Yisroel. 1927.
Der mizbeyeh. 1928.
Himel un erd. 1928.
Tsvay veltn. 1928.
Gots gefangene [Prisoners of God]. 1933.
Farn mabul (trilogy). 1934; as *Three Cities,* 1934.
Peterburg [St. Petersburg]. 1934.
Warshe [Warsaw]. 1949.
Moskva [Moscow]. 1935.
*Der thilim yid.*1934; as *Salvation,* 1934.
The War Goes On, 1936; as *The Calf of Paper,* 1936.
Dos gezang fun tol. 1938; as *The Song of the Valley,* 1939.
Three Novels (includes *Uncle Moses; Chaim Lederer's Return; Judge Not*). 1938.
Christological Trilogy:
  Der man fun Notseres. Translated as *The Nazarene,* 1939.
  Der sheliekh. Translated as *The Apostle,* 1943.
  Mary (translation). 1949.
Vos ikh gloyb. Translated as *What I Believe,* 1941; as *My Personal Faith,* 1942.
East River (translation). 1946.
Mosheh. 1951; as *Moses,* 1951.
Grosman un zun. Translated as *A Passage in the Night,* 1953.
Der novi. Translated as *The Prophet,* 1955.

Plays

Meshieh's tsaytn: A kholm fun mayn folk [The Time of the Messiah: A Dream of My People]. 1906.
Got fun nekomeh. 1907; as *God of Vengeance,* 1918.
Mitn shtrom [With the Stream]. 1909.
Amnon un Tamar. 1909.
Um Winter. 1910; as *In Winter,* translated in *Six Plays of the Yiddish Theatre,* edited by Isaac Goldberg, 1916.
Der Zindiger. 1910; as *The Sinner,* translated in *Six Plays of the Yiddish Theatre,* edited by Isaac Goldberg, 1916.

Der Landsman [The Compatriot]. 1911.
Ver iz der tate [Where Is Father] (produced 1918).
Night (translation). 1920.
Di Kishufmakherin fun Kastilien [The Witch of Castile]. 1921.
Yosele [Joseph]. 1921.
Yikhus. 1923.
Bilder un humoresken. 1925.
Shabsay tsevi (produced Romania, 1926); translated as *Sabbatai Zevi,* 1974.
Rebe Doktor Zilber (produced 1927).
Koyln [Coals]. 1928.
Dramatishe shriftn: (Biblishe un historishe dramen). 1928.
Naye Dramen. 1930.
Dramatishe shriftn (includes *Meshiehs tsaytn; Unzer gloybn; A shnirl perl; Der toyter mentsh*). 1931.

Short Stories

Fun eyn kval. 1927.
Naye ertseylungen. 1928.

Other

Mayn rayze iber Shpanyen. 1926.
Mayseh'lekh fun Humesh (for children). Translated as *In the Beginning; Stories from the Bible.* 1935.
Catalog of Hebrew and Yiddish Manuscripts and Books from the Library of Sholem Asch, edited by Leon Nemoy. 1945.
One Destiny: An Epistle to the Christians (translation). 1945.

*

Manuscript Collection: Yale University, New Haven, Connecticut.

Critical Studies: *Nine Yiddish Writers: Critical Appreciations* by Harry Rogoff, 1931; *The Christianity of Sholem Asch: An Appraisal from the Jewish Viewpoint* by Hayim Lieberman, translated by Abraham Burstein, 1953; *The Flowering of Yiddish Literature* by Solomon Liptzin, 1963; *The Controversial Sholem Asch: An Introduction to His Fiction* by Ben Siegel, 1976; "The Jews of East River: Americans Yet Forever Jews" by Amy Alexander, in *Studies in American Jewish Literature,* 5, 1986, pp. 54–60; "The Foreskin of the Heart: Ecumenism in Sholem Asch's Christian Trilogy" by Goldie Morgentaler, in *Prooftexts,* 8(2), May 1988, pp. 219–44; "History and Martyrology Tragedy: The Jewish Experience in Sholem Asch and Andre Schwarz-Bart" by Stanley Brodwin, in *Twentieth Century Literature,* 40(1), Spring 1994, pp. 72–91; "Christianity As a Consistent Area of Investigation in Sholem Asch's Works Prior to *The Nazarene,*" in *Yiddish,* 9(2), 1994, pp. 58–76, "*The Nazarene* As a Jewish Novel," in *Jewish Quarterly,* 41(3), 155, Autumn 1994, pp. 36–39, "Our Secular Jewish Heritage: Sholem Asch Seen Anew," in *Jewish Currents,* 49(7), July 1995, p. 25, and "Abraham Cahan and Sholem Asch," in *Yiddish,* 11(1–2), 1998, pp. 1–17, all by

Hannah Berliner Fischthal; ''Peretz, Asch, and *God of Vengeance*'' by Joseph C. Landis, in *Yiddish,* 10(1), 1995, pp. 5–17; ''Novelizing Myth in Sholem Asch's *Moses*'' by Vladimir Tumanov, in *Yiddish,* 11(1–2), 1998 pp. 162–84; ''Jewish Anxiety in 'Days of Judgement': Community Conflict, Antisemitism, and the God of Vengeance Obscenity Case'' by Harley Erdman, in *Theatre Survey,* 40(1), May 1999, pp. 51–74.

* * *

One of the most popular and prolific Yiddish authors, Sholem Asch sought to use his work to teach that the deaths of victims of anti-Semitic violence were a confirmation of the Jewish mission to witness God's providence and of the need for Christians to free themselves of pagan anti-Judaism. In many respects a traditionalist understanding based on common Jewish responses to the pogroms of Eastern Europe, many of his first literary responses to the Nazi genocide nevertheless provoked outrage in the Jewish world by dint of the language that he used in order to sway his increasingly Christian readership.

In his earliest novels and plays, inspired by the work of Sholom Aleichem, Y.L. Peretz, Mendele Sforim, Maxim Gorky, and Boleslaw Prus, Asch paints a harmonious picture of relations between Jews and Christians in his native Poland. In the trilogy *Three Cities* (1933), for instance, he shows workers of both communities joining a common cause against their enemies, the corrupt and the intolerant. His treatment of what he saw as the common core of the two faiths led him out of the mainstream, prompting him to begin a career-long investigation of their troubled history together (*In the Land of Israel*, 1911). At the center of the conflicts between the two, Asch saw the hand of pagan anti-Judaism, a force that throughout history vainly sought to extinguish the faith of Jews in their God. In *Kiddush Ha-Shem* (1919; ''The Sanctification of the Name''), the Hebrew term for ''martyrdom,'' he hoped to give pogrom victims comfort by drawing parallels with the Jewish martyrs killed by Cossacks in 1648. As he would in his works on the Holocaust, Asch made liberal use of the psalms in evoking a heroic Jewish faith that would not be shaken by adversity or even martyrdom. The play was republished in 1942, when Asch heard the first accounts of the Holocaust to reach the Western public.

Asch built his reputation in the Jewish world on just such affirmations, but his attempt to reach non-Jewish audiences with the same message, immensely successful as it was, met with a barrage of criticism in Jewish communities from the United States to Palestine. When Asch hoped to encourage rapprochement between the Polish government and its Jews in the 1920s and 1930s, he was cast as a traitor and opportunist. When in the 1930s he decided the time had come to tackle the roots of the split between Jews and Christians, he was cast as naïve or, worse, a Christian convert and a missionary. Nevertheless, *Salvation* (*Der Tehilim Yid*, ''The Psalm Jew''), written in the early days of Nazi rule in 1933, contrasted the religiosity of pogrom victims with the Christian leaders who sought their death or conversion. *The War Goes On* (1936) laid the blame for the plight of German Jewry on a Teutonic tendency in German society that was as anti-Christian as it was anti-Semitic. Asch then turned to the stories of Jesus, Paul, and Mary, writing *The Nazarene* (1939), *The Apostle* (1943), and *Mary* (1943) as a broadside against the anti-Judaism that he believed had robbed the two faith communities of their greatest prophet, the Jewish Jesus. Knowing how controversial this would be in both Jewish and Christian communities, Asch still believed it to be his most appropriate, constructive response to the evils of Nazism. In the light of this Christological trilogy, critics came to see even his earlier works as prologues to apostasy.

The bitter disappointment of many Jewish readers with *The Nazarene* and its sequels was heightened by a widespread expectation that Asch would write a novel for and about the victims of the Holocaust, as he had for survivors of the pogroms. Asch instead wrote a series of short stories and articles that transposed the themes of *Kiddush Ha-Shem, Salvation,* and *The Nazarene* onto the Holocaust (*One Destiny, In the Valley of Death, Tales from the Shadow of Death/Tales of My People*). The victims still died with their faith in God intact (as in ''Exalted and Hallowed,'' written in winter 1942 in response to the destruction of the Warsaw Ghetto), heroically unassimilated in a world overrun by a pagan revolt. Distressed beyond words at the disappearance of the Polish-Jewish world he had come from, Asch sought comfort not from the leaders of Jewish community—rationalistic ''Sadducees''— but from the hope that his speeches and novels could stir a new sense of ''messianic'' solidarity among the spiritually inclined of the Jewish and Christian worlds. His impact on the Christian West was enormous. In both style and content, however, his essays were designed to stir resentment amongst the Jewish communities that had once laid such great store in his work, and the Holocaust stories, though not seen as offensive, were never judged among his greatest work.

—George R. Wilkes

See the essay on *One Destiny: An Epistle to the Christians.*

B

BACHMANN, Ingeborg

Pseudonym: Ruth Keller. **Nationality:** Austrian. **Born:** Klagenfurt, 25 June 1926. **Education:** Studied jurisprudence and philosophy in Innsbruck, Graz, and Vienna, 1945–50, University of Vienna, Ph.D. 1950. **Family:** Relationship with Max Frisch, *q.v.,* 1958–early 1960s. **Career:** Correspondent, U.S. Control Commission, Vienna, 1950; writer for the broadcasting group Red/White/Red Radioplays, 1951–53. Lived in Italy, 1953–57. Visiting scholar, Harvard University, 1955; visiting chair of poetics, University of Frankfurt, 1959–60. Traveled to Egypt and the Sudan, mid–1960s; lived between Munich, Berlin, Zürich, and Rome, 1963–73. **Awards:** Gruppe 47 prize, 1953, for *Die gestundete Zeit;* literary prize of the German industry (Stuttgart), 1954; city of Bremen literature prize, 1957; radio play prize of the War Blind, 1959, for *Der gute Gott von Manhattan;* Association of German Critics literary prize, for *Das dreissigste Jahr;* Georg Büchner prize, 1964; Austrian national medal, 1968; Wildgans prize, 1971; Heinrich Böll award, 1983. **Member:** German Academy for Language and Literature, 1957; West Berlin Academy of Arts, literature division, 1964. **Died:** 16 October 1973.

PUBLICATIONS

Collections

Werke, edited by Christine Koschel, Inge von Weidenbaum, and Clemens Münster. 1978.
   Bd. 1. Gedichte, Hörspiele, Libretti, Übersetzungen.
   Bd. 2. Erzählungen.
   Bd. 3. Todesarten: Malina und unvollendete Romane.
   Bd. 4. Essays, Reden, vermischte Schriften, Anhang.
In the Storm of Roses: Selected Poems, edited by Mark Anderson. 1986.
Ausgewählte Werke, edited by Konrad Paul and Sigrid Töpelmann. 1987.
   Bd. 1. Gedichte, Hörspiele, Schriften.
   Bd. 2. Erzählungen.
   Bd. 3. Romane.
Songs in Flight: The Complete Poetry of Ingeborg Bachmann (English and German). 1994.
''Todesarten''-Projekt, edited by Robert Pichl, Monika Albrecht, and Dirk Göttsche. 1995.
   Bd. 1. Todesarten, Ein Ort für Zufalle, Wüstenbuch, Requiem für Fanny Goldmann, Goldmann/Rottwitz-Roman und andere Texte.
   Bd. 2. Das Buch Franza.
   Bd. 3. Malina (2 vols.).

Bd. 4. Der ''Simultan''-Band und andere spät Erzählungen.
Selected Prose and Drama, with Christa Wolf, edited by Patricia A. Herminghouse. 1998.

Novels

Todesarten [Ways of Death] (trilogy):
   Malina. 1971; translated as *Malina: A Novel,* 1990.
   Der Tag des Friedens (fragment of unfinished second novel, *Der Fall Franza*). 1976.
   Requiem für Fanny Goldmann (fragment of unfinished third novel). Published with *Der Fall Franza,* 1979; translated as *The Book of Franza and Requiem for Fanny Goldmann,* 1999.

Short Stories

Das dreissigste Jahr. 1961; as *The Thirtieth Year,* 1964.
Simultan. 1972; as *Three Paths to the Lake,* 1989.
Undine geht: Erzählungen [Undine Departs: Stories]. 1973.
Sämtliche Erzählungen. 1978.
Die Fähre. 1982.

Plays

Der Idiot, adaptation of the novel by Fyodor Dostoevsky (ballet), music by Hans Werner Henze (produced 1952). 1955.
Der gute Gott von Manhattan (radio play). 1958.
Der Prinz von Homburg, adaptation of a play by Heinrich von Kleist (opera libretto), music by Hans Werner Henze (produced 1960). 1960.
Der junge Lord, adaptation of a fable by Wilhelm Hauff (opera libretto), music by Hans Werner Henze (produced 1965). 1965; translated and published as *The Young Milord,* 1966.
Ein Ort für Zufälle. 1965.
Die Hörspiele (includes *Ein Geshäft mit Traumen; Die Zikaden; Der gute Gott von Manhattan*). 1976; as *Three Radio Plays: A Deal in Dreams; The Cicadas; The Good God of Manhattan.* 1998.

Radio Plays: *Ein Geschäft mit Träumen,* 1952; *Herrenhaus,* 1954; *Die Zikaden,* 1955; *Der gute Gott von Manhattan,* 1958.

Poetry

Die gestundete Zeit [Borrowed Time]. 1953.
Anrufung des Grossen Bären [Invocation of the Great Bear]. 1956.

Sämtliche Gedichte. 1983.
Liebe: Dunkler Erdteil. Gedichte aus den Jahren 1942–1967.
1984.
Dass noch tausend und ein Morgen wird. 1986.
Letzte, unveröffentlichte Gedichte Entwürfe und Fassungen,
edited by Hans Höller. 1998.
Ich weiss keine bessere Welt: Unveröffentlichte Gedichte,
edited by Isolde Moser, Heinz Bachmann, and Christian
Moser. 2000.

Other

*Die kritische Aufnahme der Existentialphilosophie Martin
Heideggers* (dissertation). 1950.
Jugend in einer Oesterreichischen Stadt (memoir). 1961.
*Frankfurter Vorlesungen: Probleme zeitgenoessischer
Dichtung.* 1980.
*Die Wahrheit ist dem Menschen zumutbar: Essays, Reden,
kleinere Schriften.* 1981.
Das Honditschkreuz. 1983.
Anrufung der grossen Dichterin (essays). 1984.

Translator, *Gedichte: Italienisch und deutsch,* by Giuseppe
Ungaretti. 1961.

*

Film Adaptations: *Der Fall Franza*, 1986; *Malina,* 1991.

Critical Studies: ''Ingeborg Bachmann's Wortspiele'' by
Gerhard F. Probst, in *Modern Austrian Literature,* 12(3–4),
1979 pp. 325–45; ''The Collected Works of Ingeborg
Bachmann'' by T. J. Casey, in *German Life and Letters*
(England), 34(3), April 1981, pp. 315–36; *Women Writers:
The Divided Self: Analysis of Novels by Christa Wolf, Ingeborg
Bachmann, Doris Lessing and Others* by Inta Ezergailis, 1982;
Ingeborg Bachmann issue of *Modern Austrian Literature,*
18(3–4), 1985; ''Ingeborg Bachmann'' by Juliet Wigmore, in
The Modern German Novel, edited by Keith Bullivant, 1987;
*The Voice of History: An Exegesis of Selected Short Stories
from Ingeborg Bachmann's Das dreissigste Jahr and Simultan
from the Perspective of Austrian History* by Lisa de Serbine
Bahrawy, 1989; *The Image of the Woman in the Works of
Ingeborg Bachmann* by Eckenbert von Redwitz, 1993; ''Writ-
ing on the Border: From Lyric to Language Game in the
Fiction of Ingeborg Bachmann'' by Marjorie Perloff, in *Sul-
fur: Literary Bi-Annual of the Whole Art,* 32, Spring 1993, pp.
162–84; *Understanding Ingeborg Bachmann* by Karen R.
Achberger, 1994; *Waking the Dead: Correspondence between
Walter Benjamin's ''Concept of Remembrance'' and Ingeborg
Bachmann's ''Ways of Dying,''* by Karen Remmler, 1996;
''Reading Ingeborg Bachmann'' by Elizabeth Boa, in *Women's
Writing in German: Feminist Critical Approaches,* edited by
Chris Weedon, 1997; ''Murder and Self-Resuscitation in
Ingeborg Bachmann's *Malina*'' by Margaret McCarthy, in
Out from the Shadows: Essays on Contemporary Austrian

Women Writers and Filmmakers, edited by Margarete Lamb-
Faffelberger, 1997; *Thunder Rumbling at My Heels: Tracing
Ingeborg Bachmann,* edited by Gudrun Brokoph-Mauch, 1998;
*Ingeborg Bachmann's Telling Stories: Fairy Tale Beginnings
and Holocaust Endings* by Kirsten A. Krick-Aigner, 2001.

*   *   *

The work of Ingeborg Bachmann is informed in great part
by the Holocaust. Her writings bear the unmistakable imprint
of her childhood and youth in Carinthia during the seven years
Austrians lived under National Socialism, from the annexation
(Anschluss) in 1938 until the end of World War II in 1945.
These were impressionable years for the young Austrian girl,
daughter of a Carinthian teacher who had already joined the
Nationalist Socialist Party in 1932, at a time when it was still
illegal in Austria. Bachmann was 11 years old when the
National Socialists annexed Austria in the spring of 1938 and
18 years old when they were defeated by the Allied forces in
the spring of 1945. Her writings and interviews bear witness to
the great impact of these two historical moments on her life:
''There was a definite moment that shattered my childhood:
the march of Hitler's troops into Klagenfurt. It was something
so horrible that this day marks the beginning of my memory:
started by a pain inflicted too early, with an intensity that I
perhaps never experienced again later in life. Of course, I
didn't understand all that the way an adult would. But this
enormous brutality that you could sense, this screaming,
singing and marching—the surfacing of my first mortal fear.
An entire army came at that moment into our quiet, peaceful
Carinthia . . .''

The end of the years under the Nazis seems to have been as
exhilarating as the beginning was frightening. Bachmann's
character Franziska Jordan in the novel fragment *The Book of
Franza* remembers ''the most beautiful spring of her life''
when the British occupation forces came to her hometown of
Klagenfurt and she went out to meet them. As an adult, Franza
marries a Viennese psychiatrist and helps him to write a book
on Holocaust survivors, for which he fails to acknowledge her
contributions, however.

Between those two extreme moments of 1938 and 1945 lies
the everyday reality of life under Austrian National Socialism.
In her chilling story ''Youth in an Austrian Town'' (1959)
Bachmann describes the political taboo permeating both public and private life as World War II begins like a force of nature
crashing from without into their peaceful family life: ''The
children sit quietly at the table . . . while thunder rings from the
radio and the voice of the news reporter shoots around the
kitchen like a bolt of lightning.'' A childhood of fearful
obedience is recalled with quiet dispassion. Cruelty is woven
into the fabric of upbringing in this Austrian town. The
children ''are only allowed to whisper and for the rest of their
lives they will never lose the habit of whispering.'' In school
the children are permitted to leave their notebooks and go to
the bunker when the alarm sounds, to save candy for the

wounded, and to knit socks for the soldiers. In ''Among Murderers and Madmen,'' in the same volume, a regular gathering of men in a Viennese pub shows how little has changed since the war and how unwilling these Austrians are to deal openly with their fascist past.

Visions of the Holocaust haunt the narrator's nightmares in the central chapter of Bachmann's only completed novel, *Malina*. Elisabeth Mattrei, the protagonist of Bachmann's last story published during her lifetime, ''Three Paths to the Lake,'' remembers reading **Jean Améry**'s essay ''On Torture,'' although she never mentions him by name, referring only to ''an essay . . . by a man with a French name who was Austrian and lived in Belgium . . . She wanted to write to this man, but she didn't know what to say or why.'' Bachmann's story, as if written in place of Elisabeth's letter, is an ''homage to Améry.''

Jews are among the most important people in Bachmann's life and work. Her diary tells of her ecstatic encounter in June 1945 with an English occupation soldier, Jack Hamesh, who, as the immigrant son of Viennese Jews, was able to interview her in perfect German about her membership in the BDM (Bund Deutscher Mädel, or League of German Girls). They talked endlessly of ''books by Thomas Mann and Stefan Zweig and Schnitzler and Hofmannsthal,'' all authors who had been banned by the Nazis, as he introduced her to many authors she had been kept ignorant of under National Socialism. During this ''most beautiful summer of my life,'' she proudly professed her friendship with this Jew as she walked with him through the streets of her hometown. Bachmann's writings are informed by the work of (mostly Austrian) Jews, from Joseph Roth to Améry, from **Paul Celan**, who was also a close friend, to Hannah Arendt, whom she met in New York in 1962, from Arnold Schoenberg to Gustav Mahler, from Ludwig Wittgenstein and Sigmund Freud to Theodor W. Adorno, Walter Benjamin, and Gershom Scholem. After their meeting in Rome, Scholem sent Bachmann a poem in 1967 with the title ''To Ingeborg Bachmann after Her Visit in the Ghetto of Rome.'' The poem, as if in answer to the description of the ghetto in Bachmann's essay ''What I Saw and Heard in Rome,'' marked the beginning of their dialogue over messianism and forgiveness.

—Karen R. Achberger

See the essay on *Malina: A Novel.*

BAKER, Mark (Raphael)

Nationality: Australian. **Born:** Melbourne, 7 October 1959. **Education:** Melbourne University, B.A. (honors) 1983; Wolfson College, Oxford (fellowship), M.Phil. 1986, D.Phil. 1994. **Career:** Historian, University of Melbourne, 1988–2000. Since 2000 founder and CEO, MindAtlas Pty. Ltd. Founder and editor, *Generation Magazine: Australian Jewish Life,* 1989–2000. Founder, Keshet, Jewish humanitarian relief foundation, 1995. **Awards:** Lady Davis fellowship, 1986–87, and Golda Meir fellowship, 1994–95, both Hebrew University of Jerusalem; New South Wales Premier's award, 1997, for *The Fiftieth Gate.*

PUBLICATIONS

Memoir

The Fiftieth Gate: A Journey through Memory. 1997.

Other

Editor, *Jews, Gardens, God, and Gays: Essays in Honour of John Foster (1944–1994).* 1997.

*   *   *

Coming to mainstream prominence mainly through the publication of his family memoir, *The Fiftieth Gate* (1997), Mark Raphael Baker has enjoyed an esteemed academic career as a historian at the University of Melbourne (1988–2000). The recipient of major international fellowships from Oxford University and the Hebrew University of Jerusalem (Lady Davis Fellowship, 1986–87; Golda Meir Fellowship, 1994–95), Baker conducted research concerning the social history of East European Jewry. His teaching areas have included the Holocaust, comparative genocide, modern Jewish history, and Jewish philosophy. In 1989 Baker founded *Generation Magazine: Australian Jewish Life,* a quarterly devoted to social commentary and artistic pursuits that continued publication until 2000. Baker's outrage at the Rwandan genocide in 1994 was expressed in his establishment in 1995 of Keshet, a Jewish humanitarian relief foundation that aimed to increase public awareness of regional and international atrocities. In early 2000 Baker founded and has remained the chief executive officer of MindAtlas Pty. Ltd., an innovative online repository of knowledge that aims to promote awareness and tolerance of cross-cultural diversity and difference.

Baker was born in 1959 in Melbourne, Australia, which is residence to the largest community of Holocaust survivors per capita outside Israel. Baker is a member of the second generation, the often-applied phrase to children of Holocaust survivors. His parents met in the small community of survivors that gathered mainly in the capital cities of Melbourne and Sydney and married in 1953. As told in *The Fiftieth Gate,* as a teenager he became acculturated to pop-culture references to, rather than discussion of, his parents' traumatic pasts. His parents' difficulty and anxiety in discussing this past was resented by Baker, a recipient of what he viewed as the material overindulgence resulting from the newly found wealth immigrant communities acquired from the industries of property investment and development, clothing, textiles, and manufacturing synonymous with the postwar economic boom of the 1950s.

Baker's adolescence of living privately as a vicarious witness to his parents' pasts is also arguably a metaphor for a larger collective dynamic between silence and speakability of the traumas of Nazi Europe that migrated with survivors into a subterranean Australian historical and social consciousness. Before 1980 the Holocaust was not visibly commemorated or widely spoken about as a public narrative of trauma. There was a wall of silence, if not resistance, to knowledge. Certain international events and trends served as moments in this confrontation with silence, at both the community and national level. In Israel, events included the Adolf Eichmann trial in Jerusalem in 1961, the Six-Day War in June 1967, and the Yom Kippur war in October 1973. Debates over denial and war crimes were taking place, and in 1977 the Office of Special Investigation was established by American President Jimmy Carter, who also sought to make Holocaust memorialization an official program of the U.S. government. The screening of the American television miniseries *Holocaust* in the late 1970s also marked a major watershed in consciousness in both the United States and West Germany. The impact of these events in Australia was not immediate or entirely visible but instead contributed to an already existing but largely community-based culture of Holocaust memories.

In Sydney the Warsaw Ghetto Uprising of April 1943 was commemorated from the late 1940s and was named Solemn Memorial Day in the 1970s. In November 1979 a Holocaust committee under the Jewish Board of Deputies was established, and in 1981 the first major exhibition on the Holocaust attracted some 40,000 people. In May 1982 the Board of Deputies established a separate Holocaust Remembrance Committee, and in May 1983 an Australian Association of Holocaust survivors was formed. Subsequent events included the first International Gathering of Holocaust Survivors in May 1985, the formation of a descendants' group and child survivors, oral testimony projects, teaching kits, websites, the opening of the Sydney Jewish and Holocaust Museum, and school trips to Poland. In Melbourne the visibility of international events also shaped an emerging consciousness, though it was still largely confined to family and community commemorated events, such as the Buchenwald Ball, an annual event attended by survivors and their spouses. In *The Fiftieth Gate* Baker discusses movingly his father's inspired contributions to this gathering.

In Melbourne in particular a literary consciousness was forged through the works of children of survivors rather than from first-generation memories. During the 1980s and 1990s the poetry, short stories, and novels of **Lily Brett** and the

second-generation writing of Arnold Zable, for example, began to push the Holocaust from a concern of survivors, their families, and communities to the mainstream. This literature exposed the legacies of generational transmission and the continuing presence of burdensome and inexplicable memories. The presence of war criminals in Melbourne and Adelaide, the establishment of a government-sponsored Special Investigations Unit, and the publication in 1994 of an anti-Semitic novel about the Holocaust, *The Hand That Signed the Paper,* by Helen Demidenko (who was later exposed as a fraud) all contributed to a greater cultural sensitivity to the Holocaust's intimate and mournful location in the identities of various Jewish communities in Australia.

Through his profile in Jewish community circles, academic career, and occasional journalism in mainstream daily newspapers, Baker has contributed—in a dramatically moving fashion—to the repositioning of the Holocaust as an urgent moral concern in discussions of contemporary genocide, literary hoaxes, historical revisionism, and denial. It would be difficult, therefore, to discuss the passage in historical consciousness of the Holocaust from a location of personal and community memories to a concern that demanded that attention of Australian public and social debate in the past decade without the contribution of Baker's intellectual diversity, luminous output, and significant visibility. *The Fiftieth Gate* contributed immeasurably to that painful but necessary passage.

—Simone Gigliotti

See the essay on *The Fiftieth Gate: A Journey through Memory.*

BASSANI, Giorgio

Pseudonym: Giacomo Marchi. **Nationality:** Italian. **Born:** Bologna, 4 March 1916. **Education:** University of Bologna, 1934–39. **Famiy:** Married Valeria Sinigallia in 1943; two children. **Military Service:** Active in the anti-Fascist resistance during World War II: imprisoned, May–July 1943, forced into hiding, Florence, 1943–45. **Career:** Moved to Rome, 1945. Literature teacher, Naples Naval Institute, and librarian after the war; teacher of theatre history, National Academy of Dramatic Arts, Rome, 1957–67; beginning 1958 editor, Feltrinelli publishing house; collaborated on various periodicals (*Fiera Letteraria, Mondo, Nuovi Argomenti*, and the *Corriere della Sera*) during the 1950s; traveled in North America, 1972–74. Vice president, Radiotelevisione Italiana (RAI), Rome, 1964–65; visiting professor, University of California, Berkeley, 1976. Editor, *Botteghe oscure,* 1948–60, and *Paragone,* 1953–71. **Awards:** Charles Veillon prize in Italian literature, 1955, for *Gli ultimi anni di Clelia Trotti;* Strega prize, 1956, for *Cinque storie ferraresi;* Viareggio prize, 1962, for *Il giardino dei Finzi-Contini;* Campiello prize, 1969, for

L'airone; Nelly Sachs prize, 1969; Premi Roma. **Died:** 13 April 2000.

PUBLICATIONS

Collections

Il romanzo di Ferrara [The Romance of Ferrara] 1974; revised, 1980.
In rima e senza: 1939–1981 [Rhymed and Unrhymed]. 1982.

Novels

Una lapide in Via Mazzini [A Plaque on Via Mazzini] (novella). 1952.
La passeggiata prima di cena [A Stroll before Supper] (novella). 1953.
Gli ultimi anni di Clelia Trotti [The Last Years of Clelia Trotti] (novella) 1955.
Gli occhiali d'oro (novella). 1958; as *The Golden Spectacles,* 1960.
Una notte del '43 [A Night in '43] (novella). 1960.
Il giardino dei Finzi-Contini. 1962; as *The Garden of the Finzi-Contini,* 1965.
Dietro la porta (novella). 1964; as *Behind the Door,* 1972.
L'airone. 1968; as *The Heron,* 1970.

Short Stories

Una citta di pianura (as Giacomo Marchi). 1940.
Cinque storie ferraresi. 1956; as *Dentro le mura,* 1973; translated as *Five Stories of Ferrara,* 1971; revised to include additional stories and published as *Le storie ferraresi,* 1960; translated as *A Prospect of Ferrara,* 1962.
Due novelle. 1965.
L'odore del fieno. 1972; as *The Smell of Hay,* 1975.

Poetry

Storie dei poveri amanti e altri versi [Stories of Poor Lovers and Other Poems]. 1946.
Te lucis ante. 1947.
Un altra liberta [Another Freedom]. 1951.
L'alba ai vetri: Poesie 1942–1950 [Dawn at the Windows] (collection of his first 3 vols. of poetry). 1963.
Epitaffio [Epitaph]. 1974.
In gran segreto [With Great Secrecy]. 1978.
Rolls Royce and Other Poems (selections from *Epitaffio* and *In gran segreto* in English and Italian). 1982.

Other

Le parole preparate, e altri scritti di letteratura [The Prepared Words]. 1966; revised and enlarged as *Di là dal cuore,* 1984.

*

Film Adaptations: *The Garden of the Finzi-Continis,* 1971.

Critical Studies: ''The Storie Ferraresi of Giorgio Bassani'' by Marianne Shapiro, in *Italica,* 49, 1972, pp. 30–48; *Giorgio Bassani* by Giorgio Varanini, 1975; Giorgio Bassani issue of *Canadian Journal of Italian Studies,* 1, Fall/Winter 1977–78; ''The Closed World of Giorgio Bassani,'' in *Italian Culture,* 3, 1981, pp. 103–30, ''Bassani: The Motivation of Language,'' in *Italica,* 62(2), Summer 1985, pp. 116–25, and *The Exile into Eternity: A Study of the Writings of Giorgio Bassani,* 1987, all by Douglas Radcliff-Humstead; ''Visual Memory and the Nature of Epitaph: Bassani's *Epitaffio*'' by Linda Nemerow-Ulman, in *Italian Quarterly,* 27(106), Fall 1986, pp. 33–44; *Vengeance of the Victim: History and Symbol in Giorgio Bassani's Fiction* by Marilyn Schneider, 1986; ''The Trilogy of the Narrator-Protagonist: Anti-Semitism in the Novels of Bassani'' by Judith Kelly, in *Tuttitalia,* 1, June 1990, pp. 33–38; ''Judaism and Manhood in the Novels of Giorgio Bassani'' by Lucienne Kroha, in *The Italian Jewish Experience,* edited by Thomas P. DiNapoli, 2000.

* * *

The Italian novelist **Italo Calvino** said of Giorgio Bassani in 1958: ''All Bassani's fiction has a political message stemming from his fundamental trauma: seeing antisemitic persecution in the middle classes of Ferrara.'' Anti-Semitism is treated in all of Bassani's fiction, but the Holocaust is not. He wrote six books that were incorporated in *The Romance of Ferrara* in 1980. Of these books the Holocaust figures fully in only two: *Five Stories of Ferrara* (1956) and *The Garden of the Finzi-Contini* (1962). The five short stories cover the history of Ferrara and its Jewish community from the mid-nineteenth century until about 1950, a crucial date being the general election of 1948, which marked a new beginning for Italy after World War II.

Ferrara is the setting for all of Bassani's fiction. He grew up there within the Jewish community. His brand of realism requires him to base his narrative in the grid of the streets between the all-enclosing town walls. The reader is treated as an insider, and a map of the city is a useful aid for our understanding of the tales' geography. Ferrara figures much as James Joyce's Dublin and William Faulkner's Jefferson and Yoknapatawpha County figure in their fiction. Not only do the street names recur (such as Via Mazzini in heart of the old ghetto), the characters criss-cross from one story to another and later into the novels. Take the Catholic, left-wing Bottecchiari family for instance. The minority Jewish community—self-made, some wealthy—also has recurring names like the Corcos and the Finzi-Contini. Many are assimilated through marriage. Several were members of the Fascist Party from the first years. Few are aware of the threat.

The point of view of the narrative is that of a member of the Jewish community who grew up through school in Ferrara and university in Bologna, following a career reminiscent of Bassani's. Bassani, however, was not only a Jew but also an antifascist, a member of the moderate Action Party, and he was not only watching out for injustice to the Jews, he had an eye also on the antifascists in prison, among them Partisans who became Communist members of parliament after the 1948 elections. All of this took place in the aftermath of the 1943–45 civil war in the north, which left a brooding sense of injustice.

So if *A Plaque in Via Mazzini* features the one Ferrarese who returns from the Holocaust in the character of Geo Josz, *A Night in '43* bears witness to the unavenged killing of eleven men—two of them Jewish merchants in hiding, three of them lawyers who were members of the Action Party—below the castle walls on the night of 15 December by assorted unknown Fascists after the assassination of the local Fascist Consul. *The Walk before Supper* becomes a Holocaust story because, though it looks back to before the unification of Italy in 1870, we are told in parentheses just near the end that the hero, the famous Dr. Elia Corcos, was "as an old man, ninety, like his father . . . in the crowd of a hundred and eighty-three Jews who were sent to Fo'ssoli and from there deported to Germany." *Lida Mantovani* is more about class and poverty but has a tenuous Jewish theme in that Lida has a child by a maverick Jewish lover, David. *The Last Years of Clelia Trotti* deals with a courageous woman, an old-fashioned socialist, watched by the secret police, who died in prison in 1943 under the German occupation. The point of view is that of Bruno Lattes, an antifascist Jew whose parents are deported to Germany while he escapes to the United States and in 1946 expects to settle there and teach Italian. Clelia Trotti before her capture had imparted to him her political views, some good practical know-how, and her staunch humanitarian conviction.

Bassani saw himself as a historian and had an eye and an ear for the nuances of change from 1938 to 1943 and 1945 to 1947. He was the reader who discovered and launched Tomasi di Lampedusa's *The Leopard* in 1958. In his preface to it he particularly praised it for being a book about "Italy and its history," which had "something essential to say to all of us," something "unusual in the whole range of Italian literature."

His first novel, *The Golden Spectacles* (1958), and his last, *The Heron* (1968), have much in common. Neither is a novel of the Holocaust. Both protagonists are Jewish men suffering from the difficulties of assimilation and both commit suicide, having been disadvantaged by growing anti-Semitism under Fascism in the late thirties. In *The Golden Spectacles* Dr. Fadigati is further excluded because of his homosexuality. He drowns himself in the Po in 1938. In *The Heron* Edgardo Limentani is a rich jewish landowner, assimilated to the extent of having married his Catholic mistress and having a blue-eyed daughter. He had spent time in Switzerland and thus avoided the Holocaust. He shoots himself in 1947. *Behind the Door* (1964) tackles anti-Semitism as it touches the first-person narrator as a schoolboy. The time is 1929–30. The narrator is undergoing the rites of passage to the Liceo, discovering

treachery, and the differences of class, intelligence, sexuality, race, and religion. Bassani is at his best describing the states of mind caused by bullying.

The Smell of Hay (1972) is a collection of short narrative pieces and memoirs. In *More News of Bruno Lattes* we find Bruno in denial of his Jewishness and identifying with his Catholic mother, whose maiden name is Marchi, like Bassani's own mother. The smell of hay comes from the newly mown Jewish cemetery where in 1938 Bruno's uncle's funeral is interrupted by someone outside its walls insisting on singing a love song to an accordion, abetted by a soldier nodding his head to the music.

Such small slights to a sensitive minority are essential to Bassani's observation. His contained rage results in a fiction characterized by melancholy and memory that leaves his reader discomforted but not roused.

—Judy Rawson

See the essays on *The Garden of the Finzi-Contini* and *A Plaque on Via Mazzini*.

BECKER, Jurek

Nationality: German (originally Polish: immigrated to East Berlin, 1945). **Born:** Lodz, 30 September 1937. **Education:** Studied philosophy, Humboldt University of Berlin, 1957–60; studied film, Potsdam-Babelsberg, 1960. **Military Service:** People's Army, 1955–56. **Family:** Married Christine Harsch-Niemeyer in 1986 (second marriage); three children. **Career:** Joined the Socialist Unity party, 1957; expelled from East Germany; 1976; moved to West Berlin, 1979. Wrote television plays and film scripts for the DEFA during the 1960s. Poet-in-residence, Oberlin College, 1978; guest professor, University of Essen, 1979, University of Augsburg, 1981, Cornell University, 1984, University of Texas, Austin, 1987, and Washington University. **Awards:** Charles Veillon prize (Switzerland) and Heinrich Mann prize, both in 1971, for *Jakob der Lügner;* City of Bremen literature prize, 1973, for *Irreführung der Behörden;* Silver Bear for East Germany, Berlin Film Festival, 1974, for the screenplay of *Jacob the Liar;* National prize for literature of the GDR, 1975; Adolf-Grimme prize, 1987, for *Liebling Kreuzberg;* Bavarian TV prize, 1990; Bundesfilmpreis, 1991; Thomas Mann award. **Member:** Berlin Academy of the Arts, 1990. **Died:** 14 March 1997.

PUBLICATIONS

Novels

Jakob der Lügner. 1969; as *Jacob the Liar,* 1975.
Irreführung der Behörden [Confusing the Authorities]. 1973.

Der Boxer [The Boxer]. 1976.
Schlaflose Tage. 1978; as *Sleepless Days*, 1979.
Aller Welt Freund [Everybody's Friend]. 1982.
Bronsteins Kinder. 1986; as *Bronstein's Children*, 1988.
Amanda herzlos. 1992.

Short Stories

Nach der ersten Zukunft [After the First Future]. 1980; translated as a dissertation, 1992.
Five Stories. 1993.

Plays

Screenplays: *Jakob der Lügner,* 1973.

Television plays: *Liebling Kreuzberg* (series), 1986; *Wir sind auch nur ein Volk,* 1994; *Ende des Grössenwahns,* 1996.

Other

Ende des Grössenwahns: Aufsätze, Vorträge. 1996.

*

Film Adaptations: *Jacob the Liar,* 1999.

Bibliography: "Bibliography" by Colin Riordan, in his *Jurek Becker,* 1998.

Critical Studies: "The Treatment of Holocaust Themes in GDR Fiction from the Late 1960s to the Mid-1970s: A Survey" by Nancy Lauckner, in *Studies in GDR Culture and Society,* edited by Margy Gerber, 1981; *The Works of Jurek Becker: A Thematic Analysis* by Susan Martha Johnson, 1988; "Radios and Trees: A Note to Jurek Becker's Ghetto Fiction," in *Germanic Notes,* 19(1–2), 1988, pp. 22–24, and "Jurek Becker's Holocaust Fiction: A Father and Son Survive," in *Critique,* 30(3), Spring 1989, pp. 193–209, both by Russell E. Brown; "Tales and the Telling: The Novels of Jurek Becker" by Martin Kane, in his *Socialism and the Literary Imagination: Essays on East German Writers,* 1991; *Writing As Revenge: Jewish German Identity in Post-Holocaust German Literary Works: Reading Survivor Authors Jurek Becker, Edgar Hilsenrath, and Ruth Klüger* (dissertation) by Jennifer L. Taylor, Cornell University, 1995; "1945 World War II Ends, and Eight-Year-Old Jurek Becker Is Freed from a Concentration Camp and Begins to Learn German" by Frank D. Hirschbach, in *Yale Companion to Jewish Writing and Thought in German Culture, 1096–1996,* edited by Jack Zipes and Sander L. Gilman, 1997; *Jurek Becker,* 1998, *How I Became a German: Jurek Becker's Life in Five Worlds,* 1999, and *Jurek Becker and Cultural Resistance in the German Democratic Republic,* 2001, all by Sander L. Gilman; *Jurek*

Becker, edited by Colin Riordan, 1998; *Jurek Becker: A Jew Who Became a German?* by David Rock, 2000.

*   *   *

Jurek Becker can be defined as an author of the Holocaust on several levels: as a concentration camp survivor, as a teller of stories about the Holocaust, and as an intellectual who struggled with the role of narrative in post-Holocaust Germany. Becker's work is often divided into two categories: "Holocaust" fiction and "political" fiction, with the latter category referring to those texts dealing ostensibly with German social and political developments. Attempts, however, to categorize Becker's texts thusly often fail to recognize that as a part of the postwar German identity, the Holocaust has taken on political dimensions, meaning that politics and the Holocaust are as intertwined in postwar Germany as they are in Becker's fiction.

As a nonnative speaker of German, who learned the language only after the Holocaust when he and his father were reunited and settled in East Berlin, Becker has an interesting relationship to the language. Two specific influences on Becker's language are noteworthy. He has explained that even though he experienced relatively little Jewish culture during his childhood in East Berlin, he was exposed to Jewish storytellers. Critics have noted similarities between Becker's writing and the storytelling styles of Sholem Aliechem and **Isaac Bashevis Singer**, notably the linear nature and distinct vocal quality of his narratives. Becker's language has also been influenced by his work in film. Before turning to literary texts, Becker began his writing career at the East German film studios. After his falling-out with the socialist elite in East Germany and his subsequent move to the West, he also wrote for West German television and films. (Indeed, he achieved his greatest popular recognition with the scripts for the German television series *Liebling Kreuzberg*.) The dialogues and descriptions in Becker's literary texts often contain the type of detail and tone found in television, film, and storytelling. Such influences help explain Becker's ability to write literary texts that are popular and accessible, while still obtaining a level of literary merit worthy of several prestigious literary awards.

The texts commonly grouped together as Becker's Holocaust novels are *Jakob der Lügner* (1969; *Jacob the Liar,* 1975), *Der Boxer* (1976; "The Boxer"), and *Bronsteins Kinder* (1986; *Bronstein's Children,* 1988). At least one of Becker's short stories, "Die Mauer" ("The Wall") in his collection *Nach der ersten Zukunft* (1980; "After the First Future," translated as a dissertation, 1992) can also be included in this category. *Jacob the Liar,* which was originally written as a film script, tells the story of a Jewish resident of a ghetto who brings hope to his fellow Jews with his lies about the imminent approach of the Soviet Army. Its sensitivity, humor, and poetic language make it a rare gem among stories of the Holocaust written in German. *Der Boxer* and *Bronstein's Children* both tell the stories of intergenerational conflicts between Holocaust survivors and their children. Though set at different times, these two later novels reflect the difficulties facing both survivors and other Germans as they deal with the emotional, political, and personal consequences of the Holocaust.

While Becker's ''non-Holocaust'' texts do not deal directly with the Holocaust, their themes have much in common with his Holocaust narratives. These thematic commonalities reflect Becker's ability to place the Holocaust into the context of broader societal debates in postwar and post-Holocaust Germany—debates dealing with issues of history, resistance, truth, guilt, and identity.

Becker rarely provides his readers with answers, and his stories often lack resolution for the characters involved. Becker even goes so far as to provide *Jacob the Liar* with two endings so that readers must choose which to believe. In this way, Becker captures the ambiguity surrounding the Holocaust in Germany during the latter half of the twentieth century. But rather than shutting down debate, this ambiguity has served as an impetus to further discussion about how to deal with Germany's past and, in particular, with the Holocaust.

—Gregory Baer

See the essays on *Bronstein's Children* and *Jacob the Liar*.

BEGLEY, Louis

Nationality: American (originally Polish: immigrated to the United States, 1948, granted U.S. citizenship, 1953). **Born:** Ludwik Begleiter, Stryj, 6 October 1933. **Education:** Harvard University, B.A. (summa cum laude) 1954, LL B (magna cum laude) 1959. **Military Service:** United States Army, 1954–56. **Family:** Married 1) Sally Higginson in 1956 (divorced 1970), two sons and one daughter; 2) Anne Muhlstein Dujarric de la Riviere in 1974. **Career:** Admitted to the Bar of New York State, 1961. Associate, 1959–67, and since 1968 partner, Debevoise & Plimpton, New York. Lecturer on legal topics in the People's Republic China, 1983, 1987, 1988, and 1989; senior visiting lecturer, Wharton School, University of Pennsylvania, Philadelphia, 1985, 1986. **Awards:** *Irish Times*-Aer Lingus international fiction prize, 1991, Ernest Hemingway Foundation award and Prix Medicis Etrange, both in 1992, all for *Wartime Lies;* Harold U. Ribalow prize, 1992; Jeanette Schocken prize and American Academy of Arts and Letters literature award, both in 1995; Konrad-Adenauer-Stiftung literature prize, 2000. Chevalier de l'Ordre des Arts et Lettres, 2000. **Agent:** Georges Borchardt, 136 East 57th Street, New York, New York 10022, U.S.A. **Address:** Debevoise & Plimpton, 875 3rd Avenue, Floor 25, New York, New York 10022, U.S.A.

PUBLICATIONS

Novels

Wartime Lies. 1991.
The Man Who Was Late. 1993.
As Max Saw It. 1994.
About Schmidt. 1996.
Mistler's Exit. 1998.
Schmidt Delivered. 2000.

*

Film Adaptations: *About Schmidt,* 2001.

Critical Studies: ''A Problem of Growth'' by Janet Malcolm, in her *The Purloined Clinic,* 1992; ''An Occupied Gentleman'' by Joan Juliet Buck, in *Vanity Fair,* 56, February 1993, p. 72; ''Childhood Lost: Children's Voices in Holocaust Literature'' by Naomi B. Sokoloff, in *Infant Tongues: The Voice of the Child in Literature,* 1994; ''The Lives of Louis Begley'' by Hal Espen, in *New Yorker,* 30 May 1994 pp. 38–46; ''Fiction in Review'' by Jane Mendelsohn, in *Yale Review,* 83, January 1995, pp. 108–20; ''Louis Begley: Trying to Make Sense of It'' by Victoria N. Alexander, in *Antioch Review,* 55, Summer 1997, pp. 292–304; ''Lost Time: Trauma and Belatedness in Louis Begley's *The Man Who Was Late*'' by Allan Hepburn, in *Contemporary Literature,* 39(3), Fall 1998, pp. 380–404; ''Louis Begley Joins the Firm'' by Steven G. Kellman, in *Hollins Critic,* 36(3), June 1999, pp. 1–11.

*   *   *

Although Louis Begley wrote short stories while a student at Harvard, publishing them in the *Harvard Advocate,* it was not until 1991 that he published his first novel, *Wartime Lies,* and became immediately well known as a Holocaust writer. Begley has since proved to be not merely a Holocaust survivor with one good book in him but a writer of considerable talent who produced no fewer than five novels in the last decade of the twentieth century.

When it appeared, *Wartime Lies* was widely acclaimed as autobiographical. The young hero Maciek and the writer shared the same birth year and were Polish Jews, and both survived in Poland by passing as Christians. Begley himself, however, has always played down the autobiographical element, stressing his need to invent, embellish, and thereby make an interesting and gripping story. His own recollected life would have made for a short and dull book, he insists. It might be added that the recollections of a preadolescent boy would be limited, if not, at times, suspect. There is, however, no doubt that Begley's experiences as a Jewish child who, with his resourceful mother, survived the Holocaust in Poland are essential to his literary work. The novel was nominated for, and received, numerous literary prizes.

In 1993, two years after the appearance of *Wartime Lies*, Begley's second novel appeared. *The Man Who Was Late* is about Ben, a Central European Jew who commits suicide, leaving his friend Jack to sift through notes, letters, and papers and use his own memories of Ben in order to make sense of a life that was clearly full of guilt, depression, loneliness, and regret. How Ben survived in Europe is never revealed. The novel is centered rather on Ben's inability to grasp happiness, enjoy relationships, and lead a meaningful life. As with Joseph Conrad's *Heart of Darkness*, with which it has much in common, Begley's tale underscores the impossibility of truly knowing Ben through the ploy of mixing the two subjectivities of source: on the one hand, there is the information provided and left by Ben himself; on the other hand, there is the information recollected, arranged, and imagined by Jack.

Begley's other novels do not relate to the Holocaust; however, the role of justice and any concomitant rewards for how one leads one's life recurs as a theme in all Begley's work. Why did Maciek survive while others did not? What does one deserve for having led an honest and morally or socially good life? The simple answer is that we do not live in a world that is just or even ordered. We live rather in an irrational universe where human behavior is rewarded capriciously. To explain Begley's preoccupation by ascribing it to survivor's guilt is, however, simplistic. It is, perhaps, a response as much related to elements of existentialism as to anything else.

Begley is, then, not just a Holocaust writer but someone, like **Primo Levi** or **Marga Minco**, who used the experience of the Holocaust to embark on a literary career. His works contain links to that experience but are not wholly dependent on it. It is, however, striking that he seems to have come to literature only after producing his survivor account, which, not untypically for Holocaust survivors, he wrote half a century after his experiences.

—David Scrase

See the essay on *Wartime Lies*.

BELLOW, Saul

Nationality: American. **Born:** Solomon Bellows, Lachine, Quebec, Canada, 10 June 1915. **Education:** University of Chicago, 1933–35; Northwestern University, B.S. (honors) in sociology and anthropology 1937; graduate studies in anthropology, University of Wisconsin, 1937. **Military Service:** Merchant Marines, 1944–45. **Family:** Married 1) Anita Goshkin in 1937 (divorced), one son; 2) Alexandra Tschacbasov in 1956 (divorced), one son; 3) Susan Glassman in 1961 (divorced), one son; 4) Alexandra Ionesco Tuleca in 1974 (divorced); 5) Janis Freedman in 1989, one daughter. **Career:**

Biography writer, WPA Writers' Project; instructor, Pestalozzi-Froebel Teachers College, Chicago, 1938–42; member of editorial department of "Great Books" project, Encyclopedia Britannica, Inc., Chicago, 1943–46; member of English department, 1946, assistant professor of English, 1948–49, and associate professor, 1954–59, University of Minnesota at Minneapolis; Grunier Distinguished Services Professor and member of Committee on Social Thought, 1962–93, and committee chair, 1970–76, University of Chicago. Since 1993 professor of English, Boston University. Visiting lecturer, New York University, 1950–52; creative writing fellow, Princeton University, 1952–53; faculty member, Bard College, 1953–54; visiting professor of English, University of Puerto Rico, Rio Piedras, 1961; celebrity-in-residence, University of Chicago, 1962; lecturer and fellow, Oxford University, Academy for Policy Study, 1966; fellow, Brandford College, Yale University; war correspondent, *Newsday*, 1967. Founder and coeditor, *The Noble Savage*, 1960–62. **Awards:** Guggenheim fellowship in Paris and Rome, 1948; National Institute of Arts and Letters grant, 1952; National Book award, 1954, for *The Adventures of Augie March*, 1965, for *Herzog*, and 1971, for *Mr. Sammler's Planet*; O. Henry Award, 1956, for "The Gonzaga Manuscripts," and 1980, for "A Silver Dish"; Ford grants, 1959 and 1960; Friends of Literature fiction award, 1960; James L. Dow award, 1964; Prix International de Litterature (France), 1965, for *Herzog*; Jewish Heritage award, B'nai B'rith, and Croix de Chevalier (France), both in 1968; Formentor prize, 1970; Pulitzer prize, 1976, for *Humboldt's Gift*; Nobel prize, 1976, for literature; Gold medal, American Academy of Arts and Letters, Emerson-Thoreau medal, American Academy of Arts and Sciences, and Neil Gunn International fellowship, all in 1977; Brandeis University creative arts award, 1978; Malaparte prize for literature (Italy), 1984; National Medal of Arts, 1988; Lifetime Achievement award, National Book Awards, 1990. D.Litt: Northwestern University, 1962, Bard College, 1963, New York University, 1970, Harvard University, 1972, Yale University, 1972, McGill University, 1973, Brandeis University, 1974, Hebrew Union College, 1976, and Trinity College (Dublin), 1976. Commander, Legion of Honour (France), 1983; Commander, Order of Arts and Letters (France), 1985. **Member:** American Academy of Arts and Letters. **Addresses:** Office: 1126 East 59th Street, Chicago, Illinois 60637, U.S.A.; or c/o Boston University, 754 Commonwealth Avenue, Boston, Massachusetts 02215, U.S.A.

PUBLICATIONS

Collections

The Portable Saul Bellow. 1974.
Collected Fiction, edited by Janice Bellow. 2001.

Novels

Dangling Man. 1944.
The Victim. 1947.
The Adventures of Augie March. 1953.
Henderson the Rain King. 1959.
Herzog. 1964; critical edition, 1976.
Mr. Sammler's Planet. 1970.
Humboldt's Gift. 1975.
The Dean's December. 1982.
More Die of Heartbreak. 1987.
A Theft (novella). 1989.
The Bellarosa Connection (novella). 1989.
The Actual (novella). 1997.
Ravelstein. 2000.

Short Stories

Seize the Day, with Three Short Stories and a One-Act Play.
  1956.
Mosby's Memoirs, and Other Stories. 1968.
Him with His Foot in His Mouth, and Other Stories. 1984.
Something to Remember Me By: Three Tales (includes *Something to Remember Me By; A Theft; The Bellarosa Connection*). 1991.

Plays

The Wrecker. In *New World Writing 6,* 1954.
The Last Analysis, a Play (produced New York, 1964). 1965.
Under the Weather (three one-act comedies: *Orange Souffle; A Wren; Out from Under;* produced London and New York, 1966).
Orange Souffle. In *Esquire,* January 1965.
A Wren. In *Esquire,* October 1965.

Other

Like You're Nobody: The Letters of Louis Gallo to Bellow, 1961–1962, plus "Oedipus-Schmoedipus, the Story That Started It All" (letters and short story). 1966.
To Jerusalem and Back: A Personal Account (memoir). 1976.
Nobel Lecture (Stockholm, December 12, 1976). 1977.
It All Adds Up: From the Dim Past to the Uncertain Future: A Nonfiction Collection. 1994.

Editor, *Great Jewish Short Stories.* 1963.

*

Bibliography: *Saul Bellow: A Comprehensive Bibliography* by B. A. Sokoloff and Mark E. Posner, 1971; *Saul Bellow: His Works and His Critics: An Annotated International Bibliography* by Marianne Nault, 1977; *Saul Bellow: A Bibliography of Secondary Sources* by Francine Lercangée, 1977; *Basic Bibliography in English and Chinese for the Study of Saul Bellow* by William Yeh, 1977; *Saul Bellow: An Annotated Bibliography* by Gloria L. Cronin and Blaine H. Hall, 1987.

Manuscript Collection: Regenstein Library, University of Chicago.

Critical Studies: *Saul Bellow* by Earl Rovit, 1967; *The Novels of Saul Bellow; An Introduction* by Keith Michael Opdahl, 1967; *Saul Bellow: A Critical Essay* by Robert Detweiler, 1967; *Saul Bellow: In Defense of Man* by John Jacob Clayton, 1968; *Saul Bellow's Fiction* by Irving Malin, 1969; *Saul Bellow* by Robert R. Dutton, 1971, revised, 1982; *Saul Bellow* by Brigitte Scheer, 1972; "Imagining the Holocaust: *Mr. Sammler's Planet* and Others" by Edward Alexander, in *Judaism,* 22, 1973, pp. 288–300; *Saul Bellow's Enigmatic Laughter* by Sarah Blacher Cohen, 1974; *Saul Bellow: A Collection of Critical Essays,* edited by Earl H. Rovit, 1975; *Critical Essays on Saul Bellow,* edited by Stanley Trachtenberg, 1979; *Saul Bellow* by Malcolm Bradbury, 1982; *Saul Bellow's Moral Vision: A Critical Study of the Jewish Experience* by L. H. Goldman, 1983; *Saul Bellow, Vision and Revision* by Daniel Fuchs, 1984; "The Holocaust in *Mr. Sammler's Planet*" by Lillian S. Kremer, in *Saul Bellow Journal,* 4(1), Fall/Winter 1985, pp. 19–32; *Saul Bellow,* edited by Harold Bloom, 1986; "The Holocaust in the Novels of Saul Bellow" by L. M. Goldman, in *Modern Language Studies,* 16(1), Winter 1986, pp. 71–80; *Saul Bellow in the 1980s: A Collection of Critical Essays,* edited by Gloria L. Cronin and L. H. Goldman, 1989; *Saul Bellow* by Robert F. Kiernan, 1989; *Saul Bellow: Against the Grain* by Ellen Pifer, 1990; *Saul Bellow at Seventy-Five: A Collection of Critical Essays,* edited by Gerhard Bach and Jakob J. Kollhofer, 1991; *Saul Bellow* by Peter Hyland, 1992; *Saul Bellow, A Mosaic,* edited by L. H. Goldman, Gloria L. Cronin, and Ada Aharoni, 1992; *New Essays on Seize the Day,* edited by Michael P. Kramer, 1998; *Bellow: A Biography* by James Atlas, 2000; *Small Planets: Saul Bellow and the Art of Short Fiction,* edited by Gerhard Bach and Gloria L. Cronin, 2000; *A Room of His Own: In Search of the Feminine in the Novels of Saul Bellow* by Gloria L. Cronin, 2001.

* * *

It is difficult to generalize about Saul Bellow's ideas about the Holocaust except to say that he has found it extremely confusing and complicated. As readers would expect from this most cerebral of writers, he tries to examine many points of view about the Holocaust, its survivors, and its aftermath. For example, in his short story "Mosby's Memoirs" (1968) his unlikable protagonist, Willis Mosby, showed during the war great admiration for the Nazis, whom, because of their "managerial revolution," he considered unbeatable, and after the war he argued that "however deplorable the concentration camps had been, they showed at least the rationality of German political ideas." In the work *To Jerusalem and Back* (1976), although the Holocaust is not nearly as central as one might expect, Bellow repeatedly finds himself examining different, even extreme ideas about it, such as that of Prof. Jacob Leib Talmon, who asks Bellow, "Didn't Hitler after all win? As far as the Jews are concerned?" In the same book he seems to conclude that "it is difficult to apply reasonable propositions to the survivors of the Holocaust," and he seems to feel that the same could be said about the Holocaust itself and its aftermath.

Bellow's second novel, *The Victim* (1947), treats Kirby Allbee's persecution of Asa Leventhal in post–World War II New York City. Behind it lie the horrors of the Nazi persecution of the Jews and the death camps. This background makes horrifying a series of incidents that may to an outsider and sometimes even to Leventhal appear trivial. In fact, several critics argue that Bellow agrees with the protagonist of the novel *Herzog* (1964) that all Jews in the post-Holocaust world are "survivors" and that "to realize that you are a survivor is a shock." Still, he ultimately seems puzzled about just where this realization leads.

Artur Sammler, of *Mr. Sammler's Planet* (1970), is a literal survivor of the Holocaust, as is Harry Fonstein of the short novel *The Bellarosa Connection* (1989). Sorella Fonstein is determined that her husband, Harry, have a chance to thank in person Billy Rose, the Broadway impresario, for rescuing him from the Nazis. After the Nazis had confiscated the investments of Harry's father, he died. Harry's sister and her husband hid in the woods but ended up in the death camps. In spite of a poorly constructed orthopedic boot, Harry escaped from Lemberg (Lvov), in the Ukraine, managing to walk with his mother to Italy, where she died. He eventually reached Rome, where he worked as a waiter at a reception for Hitler. Imprisoned in Rome, he risked being deported by the SS. He escaped from the Italian jail, went to Ellis Island, and then was sent to Cuba, thanks to an underground organization Rose had set up. Thus, when Fonstein, who at the time knew no English, heard the name Billy Rose, what he thought was the Bellarosa Connection came into existence. Thanks largely to Rose, "Fonstein had survived the greatest ordeal of Jewish history." After he had married Sorella, he went to the United States, where in time he made a small fortune.

When Harry approaches Rose at Sardi's in New York City, the impresario turns his back on him, and a bouncer leads Harry from the restaurant. Sorella eventually acquires a manuscript by one of Rose's associates, the same person who had met Harry at Ellis Island and had told him that he had to go to Cuba. The manuscript implicates Rose in shady dealings. Sorella meets with Rose, hoping to use the manuscript to get him to receive her husband's thanks. But Rose claims that he does not remember Harry Fonstein and refuses to meet with him. His forgetfulness contrasts with the nameless narrator's memory. The narrator is a relative of Sorella by marriage and the founder of the Mnemosyne Institute, an organization, as the name implies, dedicated to memory. He is in Jerusalem to explore the idea of setting up an Israeli branch when Rose goes there to donate a sculpture garden. It is there Sorella confronts him, but Rose, with justice, tells Sorella, "I did all I could,"

and he adds, "And for that point of time, that's more than most can say."

Both Sorella and the story's narrator are American Jews, and for this reason the narrator feels that, unlike Harry Fonstein, he can never "grasp the real facts" of the case. For the narrator ultimately, and perhaps for Bellow too, even though they may be "survivors," they are non-European Jews and thus did not directly experience the Holocaust and have trouble remembering, much less understanding, it. Like the nameless narrator of *The Bellarosa Connection,* the best such people can do is to try to remember what they learn from others about the horrible things that happened and then to pass the memories on to others.

—Richard Tuerk

See the essay on *Mr. Sammler's Planet.*

BEN-AMOTZ, Dahn

Nationality: Israeli (originally Polish: immigrated to Palestine in the 1930s). **Born:** Mosse Tehilimzeigger, 1923. **Education:** Ben Shemen agricultural school, Palestine. **Military Service:** Palmach during Israel's War of Independence. **Career:** Radio broadcaster, journalist, playwright, and author. Newspaper correspondent, Paris, late 1940s. Traveled to the United States, early 1950s. Helped create *Three Men in a Boat* radio show, Israel. **Died:** 1990.

PUBLICATIONS

Novels

Lizkor lishcoah. 1968; as *To Remember, to Forget,* 1968.
Lo sam zayin [Does Not Give a Damn]. 1973.
Ziyunim zeh lo ha-kol: Roman mafteah le-lo man'ul [Screwing Isn't Everything]. 1979.
Ziyunyune ha-derekh: Roman mafteah le-lo man'ul (sequel to *Ziyunim zeh lo ha-kol*). 1980.

Short Stories

Arba'ah ve-'arba'ah: Sipurim [Four and Four: Stories]. 1950.
Sipurim poh sipurim sham. 1982.

Plays

Tefos kamah she-atah yakhol (Seret-metah-meforash) [Catch As Catch You Can] (screenplay). 1975; as *Mishak yeladim* [Nothing to It], 1982.
Tel-Aviv ha-ketanah: Hizayon [Little Old Tel-Aviv], with Hayim Hefer. 1980.

'Al 'akhbarim va-anashim, with Ehud Manor, adaptation of a novel by John Steinbeck (produced 1990).

Screenplays: *Matsor* [Siege], with Gilberto Tofano, 1968; *Sheloshah yamim ve-yeled,* with Uri Zohar and Amatsia Hiouni, adaptation of a story by A. B. Yehoshua, 1976.

Other

Yalkut ha-kezavim, with Hayim Hefer. 1956.
Mah nishma' [What's New]. 1959.
Ekh la-'asot mah [How to Do What]. 1962.
Milon olami le-'ivrit miduberet [The World Dictionary of Hebrew Slang] (2 vols.), with Netiva Ben-Yehuda. 1972, 1982.
Yofi shel milhamah. 1974.
Keri'ah tamah; Sifrutek [Reflection in Time]. 1974.
Nashim kotvot le-Dan Ben-Amots: Bi-teguvah le-sefer "Ziyunim zeh lo ha-kol," with Varda Rasiel Jackont (correspondence). 1980.
Sipure Abu-Nimer [Stories and Fables from the Arab Folklore]. 1982.
Sefer ha-felots veha-shikhehah, with Donald Wetzel and Martin Riskin. 1985.
Kelil tif'eret ha-melitsah (dictionary and reader of 19th century Hebrew). 1986.
Ten hiyukh: Metav ha-kezavim she-lo hikhzivu ba-'itonut ha-tseva'it, with Ze'ev Anner and Dani Kerman. 1989.

Editor, with Shlomo Shva, *Erets Tsiyon Yerushalayim.* 1973.

Translator, with Amnon Dankner, *'Adif melafefon 'al ha-gever mi-pene she,* by M. L. Brooks. 1985.

*

Critical Study: *Dan Ben Amots: Biyografyah* by Amnon Dankner, 1992.

Theatrical Activities: Actor: Films—*A Streetcar Named Desire,* 1951; *Matsor* [Siege], 1970.

* * *

Writer Moshe Shamir captured the essence of the new sabra culture—the native-born Israelis—in his description of Elik, a Zionist pioneer, as a man who came from the sea. Leaving their roots behind, turning their backs on centuries of Jewish history, the sabras were intended to become the antithesis of the Diaspora Jew. Whereas the latter was perceived by Zionist ideologues as weak and passive, the sabras were envisioned as farmers and warriors, masters of their own historical fate. Dahn Ben-Amotz—writer, journalist, actor, and radio personality—exhibited these traits perhaps more than any other member of his generation.

Born Mosse Tehilimzeigger, Ben-Amotz was sent to Palestine from Poland by his parents during his early teens. In Palestine he attended the Ben Shemen agricultural school,

which was one of the grooming grounds for the emerging Israeli political and military elite. (His counselor was Shimon Peres.) Ben-Amotz soon realized that in order to blend into the new culture, he had to rid himself of any signs of the Diaspora. He changed his name, first to Moshe Shimony and later to Dahn Ben-Amotz, which he felt possessed the right sabra sound. He also reinvented his personal history, claiming to be an orphan with relatives in some of the older Zionist settlements. For years Ben-Amotz would claim that he was a true sabra.

In the 1940s during the fight for Israeli independence, Ben-Amotz served in an elite underground movement, but he spent the years of the War of Independence in Europe as an emissary of the young state. There he discovered another side of Europe—not the home of Diaspora Judaism that he was taught to despise but rather Europe as a cultural center. After the war he served a short stint as a Paris correspondent for Israeli papers, hoping to hone his writing skills in that intellectual hub. This was followed by an extended visit to the United States that included a stay in Hollywood, where he mingled with the likes of Marlon Brando and Shelly Winters, who were captivated by this "noble savage" from the romantic East. (He had a speaking part in *A Streetcar Named Desire.*)

His return to Israel in the 1950s signaled the beginning of Ben-Amotz's rise to prominence in the Israeli cultural arena. He was the driving force behind the creation of the radio show "Three Men in a Boat," a weekly satirical review that became the country's most popular show, and he wrote regularly for Israeli newspapers. As a public personality Ben-Amotz epitomized the sabra ethos of strength and self-confidence. He was one of the leading voices of a new culture that created a vibrant, modern language that turned its back on tradition. This was most evident with the publication in 1972 of his dictionary of Hebrew slang, written with Netiva Ben Yehuda, that gave an official seal of approval to the legitimacy of the sabra way of life.

Ben-Amotz's literature, however, revealed another, more vulnerable, side of sabra culture. His short story "Parents Meeting" (1962), drawing on autobiographical motives, revealed the hardships of the new immigrants in an Israeli boarding school in the pre-state era. In the screenplay for the movie *Siege* (1968) in which he also acted, Ben-Amotz exposed the difficulties that a war widow faces in militaristic Israeli society. And in the novel *Does Not Give a Damn* (1973) he told of the travails of a soldier wounded in battle and his rehabilitation efforts.

While for years Ben-Amotz concealed the truth about his past and presented himself as a native Israeli (in his later years he dressed in an Arab *jalabia* and lived in an old Arab house in Jaffa), in his novel *To Remember, To Forget* (1968) he revealed some autobiographical motifs to which he would admit only much later in life. The novel's protagonist, like Ben-Amotz himself, is a young man who lost his family in the Holocaust and attempted (by changing his name) to re-create himself as a true sabra. The novel was Ben-Amotz's major attempt to deal with the memory of the Holocaust and with the attitudes of Israeli society toward it. In the 1980s Ben-Amotz was diagnosed with cancer. When his disease became known to the public, he also brought to light the truth about his personal history. He made a much-publicized trip to Poland that included a tour of Auschwitz. He told friends that in the visitor's book in Auschwitz he signed under the name Mosse Tehilimzeigger. This was a symbolic gesture that exposed the dual nature of the sabra ethos—repressing the past but at the same time being constantly forced to remember it with all its horrors as an integral part of the collective Jewish experience.

—Eran Kaplan

See the essay on *To Remember, to Forget.*

BERG, Mary

Pseudonym for Miriam Wattenberg. **Nationality:** American (originally Polish: immigrated to the United States, 1944). **Born:** Lodz, Poland, 1924. **Education:** Graduated from a Lodz Gymnasium; attended junior college. **Family:** Married an American-born student, late 1940s. **Career:** Has lived in the United States since the end of World War II. Has worked as an artist. **Award:** First prize for a Winter Relief poster, graphic arts school, Warsaw Ghetto, 1942.

PUBLICATION

Diary

Warsaw Ghetto: A Diary, edited by S. L. Shneidermann. 1945.

* * *

Media Adaptation: *A Bouquet of Violets,* produced Warsaw, 1986, from the diary *Warsaw Ghetto: A Diary.*

Critical Studies: "She Lived in the Warsaw Ghetto: An Interview with Mary Berg" by Esther Elbaum, in *Hadassah Newsletter,* March–April 1945, pp. 20–21; "Diaries of the Holocaust" by Marie Syrkin, in *Midstream,* May 1966, pp. 3–20; *The Case of Hotel Polski* by Abraham Shulman, 1982; *Forgotten Victims: The Abandonment of Americans in Hitler's Camps* by Mitchell G. Bard, 1994; "Holocaust Victims of Privilege" by Susan Pentlin, in *Problems Unique to the Holocaust,* edited by Harry James Cargas, 1999.

* * *

Mary Berg, the author of *Warsaw Ghetto: A Diary* (1945), was born Miriam Wattenberg in 1924 in Lodz, Poland. Her father, Shya, was a prosperous art and antique dealer in the city and belonged to an Orthodox synagogue. Her mother, Lena, a dress designer, was born in the United States to Polish-born parents and had U.S. citizenship; she returned to Poland in 1918. Mary—who had a younger sister, Anna—had only been in the United States once to visit her grandparents.

Berg wrote the first entry in her diary on 10 October 1939, when her father, in spite of the danger, went out on the streets of Warsaw to buy violets for her fifteenth birthday. In the entry she described her family's return to Lodz from summer vacation as war grew imminent in late August. As the Germans neared the city, the family fled to Warsaw on bicycle and foot. They arrived safely and survived the siege of Warsaw. A few weeks later, they returned to Lodz, where they found the family's shop and apartment vandalized.

In Lodz the family realized they had made a mistake returning. Berg's father returned to Warsaw after a neighbor informed on him and then fled to Soviet-occupied Poland. She returned to high school but soon witnessed atrocities. From the apartment window, she saw blood on the pavement as a man was tied to a car driven by Germans and dragged. At school students grew too afraid to come to school. Germans tormented two girlfriends, making them strip and dance. In December Berg returned to Warsaw with her mother and sister.

After her father's return in April, they got an apartment at 41 Sienna Street. They put her mother's calling card on the door to indicate that she was a U.S. citizen, hoping it was a talisman against the frequent German raids. Berg's high school began meeting in secret, and she finished her exams and graduated. She joined the Youth Club of the House Committee in their block of apartments and founded a club with a group of friends from Lodz. They called themselves the Lodz Artistic and began giving shows to raise relief funds. Berg became known as "the American girl" because she preformed American songs.

When the ghetto gates were closed, Berg and her family remained on Sienna Street in an area called the Little Ghetto. Berg's father became a janitor in the building, and the family remained relatively well-off. In early 1941 she registered for a graphics arts class offered by the Judenrat. At first she resisted using "pull" to secure a seat, as there were more than 600 applicants, but she eventually relented. She was horrified with the corruption she saw in the ghetto and torn by moral dilemmas she and her friends faced.

Berg's mother registered with the Gestapo as a U.S. citizen. On 17 July 1942, a few days before the major deportation to Treblinka, Berg and her family left the ghetto with a group of about 700 people who were foreign-born or held foreign passports, and they were interned in the Pawiak Prison. From the prison windows, she could see friends working amidst the abandoned apartments and desperate lines of Jews marching to the deportation site. She learned about Treblinka and the use of gas from another inmate.

The day before the first ghetto uprising on 18 January 1943, the Berg family boarded a train that they feared would head east. To their relief, it traveled west to an internment camp at Vittel in France. There, they lived in resort hotels and were well fed, but they continued to receive mail from desperate friends and family in Warsaw. It was uncertain if Berg would be considered a citizen and allowed to travel to the United States with her family on a prisoner exchange, but finally, on 1 March 1944, they boarded a train bound for Lisbon, Portugal.

They finally arrived in New Jersey on 16 March 1944, on a Swedish exchange ship, the *S.S. Gripsholm.* A young Yiddish journalist, S. L. Shneiderman, met Berg on the dock. He learned she had brought a diary with her. Written in shorthand, it consisted of 12 small spiral notebooks. In the next months Berg worked with Shneiderman, flushing out some details and adding full names to the diary where she had only used initials. It was published in Yiddish, in serialized form, in the fall of 1944 and in English in the *Jewish Contemporary Record.* Her name was shortened to Berg to protect family who might be alive in Poland; an English translation by Norbert Guterman appeared in February 1945.

On 19 April 1944 the Wattenberg family headed the mourners at the Warsaw Synagogue in New York as they marched to city hall commemorating the first anniversary of the Warsaw Ghetto Uprising. Berg gave interviews and appeared on radio programs that spring, but she was also eager to return to life. She entered junior college and continued to develop her work as an artist. She never published her experiences again. Her diary has been republished around the world, but it has not been republished in English. *A Bouquet of Violets,* a play based on the diary, was performed in Warsaw in 1986.

—Susan Lee Pentlin

See the essay on *Warsaw Ghetto: A Diary.*

BERNHARD, Thomas

Nationality: Austrian (originally Dutch: immigrated to Austria, 1932). **Born:** Heerland, 9 February 1931. **Education:** Studied music and acting, Salzburg Mozarteum, 1952–57, degree 1957. **Career:** Grocer's assistant, Salzburg, 1947; contracted tuberculosis and spent two years in convalescence, 1949–51; journalist for the socialist *Demokratisches Volksblatt,* beginning 1952; contributor, *Die Furche* newspaper, 1953–55. Freelance writer beginning 1957. Also worked as a court reporter and librarian. Intermittent travel, to Italy and Yugoslavia, 1953–57, London, 1960, and Poland, 1962–63; settled on a farm in Ohlsdorf an Herzversagen, Upper Austria, 1965. **Awards:** Julius Campe prize, 1964; Bremen prize, 1965; Austrian state prize for literature, 1967; Anton Wildgans prize,

1968; Georg Büchner prize, 1970; Grillparzer prize, 1971; Austrian PEN Club Theodor Csokor prize, 1972; Hannover Dramatists prize and Seguier prize, both in 1974; Austrian Chamber of Commerce literature prize, 1976; Premio Prato, 1982; Premio Modello, 1983; Prix Medicis, 1988. **Member:** Deutsche Akademie für Sprache und Dichtung (withdrew, 1979). **Died:** 12 February 1989.

PUBLICATIONS

Collection

Stücke (4 vols.). 1988.

Novels

Frost. 1963.
Vestörung [Perturbation]. 1967; as *Gargoyles,* 1970.
Das Kalkwerk. 1970; as *The Lime Works,* 1973.
Korrektur. 1975; as *Correction,* 1979.
Ja. 1978; as *Yes,* 1992.
Die Billigesser. 1980; as *The Cheap-Eaters,* 1990.
Beton. 1982; as *Concrete,* 1984.
Wittgenstein's Neffe: Eine Freundschaft. 1982; as *Wittgenstein's Nephew: A Friendship,* 1986.
Die Untergeher. 1983; as *The Loser,* 1991.
Holzfällen. 1984; as *The Woodcutters,* 1987; as *Cutting Timber: An Imitation,* 1988.
Auslöschung: Ein Zerfall. 1986; as *Extinction,* 1995.
Alte Meister. 1988; as *Old Masters: A Comedy,* 1989.
In der Höhe: Rettungsversuch, Unsinn. 1989; as *On the Mountain: Rescue Attempt, Nonsense,* 1991.

Short Stories

Prosa. 1967.
An der Baumgrenze [At the Timberline]. 1969.
Ereignisse [Events]. 1969.
Midland in Stilfs: Drei Erzälungen. 1970.
Der Wetterfleck: Erzälungen. 1976.
Die Erzälungen, edited by Ulrich Greiner. 1979.
Der Stimmenimitator. 1980; as *The Voice Imitator,* 1997.

Plays

Die Rosen der Einöde: Fünf Sätze für Ballet, Stimmen und Orchester (includes *Die Rose*; *Der Kalbskopf*; *Unter den Pflaumenbäumen*; *Phantasie*; *Der Kartenspieler*). 1959.
Unter den Pflaumenbäumen (opera libretto; produced Vienna, 1959). In *Die Rosen der Einöde,* 1959.
Köpfe: Kammeroper (opera libretto), music by Gerhard Lampersberg (produced Maria-Saal, Austria, 1960). 1960.
Der Kartenspieler (opera libretto; produced Berlin, 1967). In *Die Rosen der Einöde,* 1959.

Ein Fest für Boris (produced Hamburg, Germany, 1970). 1970; as *A Party for Boris,* in *Histrionics: Three Plays,* 1990.

Der Italiener [The Italian] (screenplay). 1971.

Der Ignorant und der Wahnsinnige [The Ignoramus and the Madman] (produced Salzburg, 1972). 1972.

Der Kulterer (screenplay). 1974.

Die Jagdgesellschaft [The Hunting Party] (produced Vienna, 1974). 1974.

Die Macht der Gewohnheit: Komödie (produced Salzburg, 1974). 1974; as *The Force of Habit: A Comedy* (produced London, 1976), 1976.

Der Präsident (produced Vienna, 1975). 1975; translated as *The President,* in *Performing Arts Journal,* 1982.

Der Berühmten [The Famous] (produced Vienna, 1976). 1976.

Minetti: ein Portrait des Künstlers als alter Mann (produced Stuttgart, 1976). 1977.

Immanuel Kant (produced Stuttgart, 1978). 1978.

Vor dem Ruhestand: Eine Komödie von deutscher Seele [Before Retirement] (produced Stuttgart, 1979). 1979; as *Eve of Retirement* (produced Minneapolis, 1982), published in *Performing Arts Journal,* 1982.

Der Weltverbesserer [The Worldimprover] (produced Bochum, 1980). 1979.

Am Ziel (produced Salzburg, 1981). 1981.

Über allen Gipfeln ist Ruh: Ein deutscher Dichtertag um 1980. 1981.

Der Schein trügt (produced Bochum, 1984). 1983; as *Appearances Are Deceiving,* in *Theater,* 15, 1983.

Die Stücke, 1969–1981. 1983.

Ritter, Dene, Voss (produced Salzburg, 1986). 1984; translated as *Ritter, Dene, Voss,* in *Histrionics: Three Plays,* 1990.

Der Theatermacher (produced Salzburg, 1986). 1984.

Einfach Kompliziert (produced Berlin, 1986). 1986.

Elisabeth II (produced Berlin, 1989). 1987.

Heldenplatz [Heroes' Square] (produced Vienna, 1988). 1988.

Claus Peymann und Hermann Beil auf der Sulzweise: Nach dem ersten Jahr an der Burg (produced Vienna, 1987). 1987.

Der deutsche Mittagstisch: Dramolette. 1988.

Histrionics: Three Plays (includes *Histrionics*; *Ritter, Dene, Voss*; *A Party for Boris*). 1990.

Claus Peymann kauft sich eine Hose und geht mit mir essen: Drei Dramolette. 1990.

Screenplay: *Der Italiener,* 1971.

Poetry

Auf der Erde und in der Hölle [On Earth and in Hell]. 1957.

In hora mortis [In the Hour of Death]. 1958.

Unter dem Eisen des Mondes [Under the Iron of the Moon]. 1958.

Die Irren; Die Häftlinge. 1962.

Ave Vergil. 1981.

Gesammelte Gedichte [Collected Poems], edited by Volker Bohn. 1991.

Memoirs

Gathering Evidence: A Memoir (5 vols.). 1983.

Die Ursache: Eine Andeutung [Indication of the Cause]. 1975.

Der Keller: Eine Entziehung [The Cellar: An Escape]. 1976.

Der Atem: Eine Entscheidung [Breath: A Decision]. 1978.

Die Kälte: Eine Isolation [In the Cold]. 1981.

Ein Kind [A Child]. 1982.

Other

Amras. 1964.

Ungenach [Trouble]. 1968.

Watten: Ein Nachlass [Mudflats]. 1969.

Gehen. 1971.

Theorie torgesteuerter Entwicklungsprozesse. 1979.

Ein Lesebuch, edited by Raimund Fellinger (selections). 1993.

Thomas Bernhard, Karl Ignaz Hennetmair: Ein Briefwechsel 1965–1974 (correspondence). 1994.

Editor, *Gedichte,* by Christine Lavant. 1987.

*

Film Adaptation: *Der Kulterer* (television), 1973.

Critical Studies: "A Drama of Disease and Derision: The Plays of Thomas Bernhard" by Martin Esslin, in *Modern Drama,* 23(4), January 1981, pp. 367–84; "The Works of Thomas Bernhard: 'Austrian Literature'" by Gerald A. Fetz, in *Modern Austrian Literature,* 17(3–4), 1984, pp. 171–92; Thomas Bernhard issue of *Modern Austrian Literature,* 21(3–4), 1988; *Understanding Thomas Bernhard* by Stephen D. Dowden, 1991; "Thomas Bernhard," in *Partisan Review,* 58, Summer 1991, pp. 493–505, and *Thomas Bernhard: The Making of an Austrian,* 2001, both by Gitta Honegger; Thomas Bernhard section of *Pequod,* 33, 1992, pp. 52–133; *Thomas Bernhard and His Grandfather Johannes Freumbichler: Our Grandfathers Are Our Teachers* by Caroline Markolin, translated by Petra Hartweg, 1993; "Playing It Safe: Historicizing Thomas Bernhard's Jews" by Michael P. Olson, in *Modern Austrian Literature,* 27(3–4), 1994, pp. 37–49; *The Nihilism of Thomas Bernhard: The Portrayal of Existential and Social Problems in His Prose Works* by Charles W. Martin, 1995; "Comitragedies: Thomas Bernhard's Marionette Theater" by Bianca Theisen, in *MLN,* 111, April 1996, pp. 533–59; "Thomas Bernhard, Jews, *Heldenplatz*" by Jeanette R. Malkin, in *Staging the Holocaust: The Shoah in Drama and Performance,* edited by Claude Schumacher, 1998; *The Rhetoric of National Dissent in Thomas Bernhard, Peter Handke, and Elfriede Jelinek* by Matthias Konzett, 2000; *The Novels of Thomas Bernhard:*

Form and Its Function by Jonathan James Long, 2001; "Thomas Bernhard" by Thomas J. Cousineau, in *The Review of Contemporary Fiction*, 21(2), Summer 2001, pp. 41–70.

* * *

In most of his 15 novels, 18 plays, and 6 autobiographical works, Thomas Bernhard investigates the effects of Nazism and the Holocaust on the individual. However, only two of his plays, *Heldenplatz* and *Eve of Retirement*, use the background of the Holocaust as the primary motif.

Bernhard's firsthand experiences with illness, death, Nazism, Catholicism, the educational system, and Austrian culture provided him with the recurrent themes of his life's work. Born to an unwed mother, Bernhard knew early in life what it felt like to be a social outcast. His main authority figure was his grandfather, who displayed the tyrannical behavior of some of his grandson's fictional characters. Bernhard also experienced World War II and recalled seeing corpses on the streets of Salzburg after the bombings. His hatred of Nazis stems in part from the humiliations he suffered at the hand of a Nazi teacher. In addition, after the war he was sent to convalesce at a sanatorium headed by an unrepentant former Nazi who terrified his patients as the schoolmaster had his students. Bernhard's obsession with illness, death, and decay stems also from his loss of good health in his teens when he contracted tuberculosis. Bernhard wrote, "I always take up the subject of those dreadful times, but people just shake their heads. In me these terrible experiences are just as present as if they had been only yesterday." In both *Heldenplatz* and *Eve of Retirement*, Bernhard does not simply refer to the history of the Holocaust, he also voices his fears about contemporary Austrian Nazism.

In *Heldenplatz* the main character, a Jewish professor, has committed suicide after returning to Vienna 50 years after Hitler's takeover only to find it even more anti-Semitic than it was in 1938. His wife is going insane because she can still hear the cheers from the Nazi rally that was held on the main square, Heldenplatz, many years ago. In *Eve of Retirement* two sisters and their brother, a former Nazi, secretly celebrate Heinrich Himmler's birthday and rejoice in the fact that their president is also a former Nazi. The brother dresses up in his SS uniform, while one of the sisters, Clara, an invalid who hates the other two, waits to see if she will have to don a concentration camp uniform as she did the year before. Both plays were written, in part, in response to the election of Kurt Waldheim to the presidency of Austria in 1986. Waldheim, who worked in a concentration camp, at first denied his Nazi past. Later, when the truth was revealed, many Austrians rallied to his defense and elected him.

Bernhard's plays exhibit the influence of the Theatre of the Absurd; they are similar to Samuel Beckett in their grotesque situations (such as the two siblings in *Eve of Retirement*, who sit and thumb through the photo album of the brother's life as a Nazi while they drink champagne and listen to Mozart, and the widow's ability to hear the crowd's cheers from the past in *Heldenplatz*), their repetitious and exaggerated language (such as the long rants in *Heldenplatz*), and their general themes of disease and despair. In addition, like Theatre of the Absurd and the plays of **George Tabori**, Bernhard's plays include black humor.

Like other Austrian writers of the postwar generation (especially Peter Handke and **Paul Celan**), Bernhard was influenced by the speech theories of another Austrian, Ludwig Wittgenstein. Wittgenstein's "speech criticism" involves a skepticism about language's ability to effectively communicate. In *Heldenplatz* the persistent ravings of the professor's brother, Robert, seem so exaggerated that one begins to wonder about their truthfulness. In *Eve of Retirement* Clara, who is bound to a wheelchair, radically disagrees with her Nazi siblings, but she is unable to articulate her views because of the torrents of words spewed at her by her more powerful siblings. Because of his skepticism toward language, Bernhard rejected the documentary mode of the late 1960s in Germany utilized most famously by **Rolf Hochhuth** in *The Deputy* and **Peter Weiss** in *The Investigation*. He wrote instead that "truth itself is quite impossible to communicate." Therefore, Bernhard deals with deliberate distortions in order to shock the audience into trying to figure out the truth for themselves. Moreover, his characters' fate always symbolizes the fate of Austria: his plays are populated with people who are either morally or physically diseased.

Bernhard's recurring themes of disease, death, moral decay, Nazism, suicide, madness, fear, alienation, and the horrible weight of history reveal his moral pessimism. Even though both plays feature characters who radically disagree with the Nazis, their positions are hopeless and helpless. They are driven to suicide, they die, or they simply suffer silently in the face of the horror.

—Susan Russell

See the essay on *Heldenplatz*.

BETTELHEIM, Bruno

Nationality: American (originally Austrian: immigrated to the United States, 1939, granted U.S. citizenship, 1944). **Born:** Vienna, 28 August 1903. **Education:** University of Vienna, 1921–26, 1936–38, Ph.D. in psychology 1938. **Family:** Married 1) Regina Altstadt in 1930 (divorced 1941), one adopted daughter; 2) Gertrud Weinfeld in 1941 (died 1984), two daughters and one son. **Career:** Worked in his family's lumber business, 1926–38; prisoner, Dachau, 1938; research associate, Progressive Education Association, Chicago, 1939–41; associate professor of psychology, Rockford College, Illinois, 1941–44; assistant professor, 1944–47, associate professor, 1947–52, professor of educational psychology,

1952–73, Rouly professor of education and professor of psychology and psychiatry, 1963–73, Stella M. Rowley Distinguished Service Professor of Education, 1973, and director, Sonia Shankman Orthogenic School, 1944–73, University of Chicago. Moved to Palo Alto, California, 1973, and taught at Stanford University. **Awards:** National Book Award and National Book Critics Circle award, both in 1977, for *The Uses of Enchantment: The Meaning and Importance of Fairy Tales;* Goethe medal, 1983. D.H.L.: Cornell University. Fellow, Center for Advanced Studies in the Behavioral Sciences, 1971–72. **Died:** Suicide, 13 March 1990.

PUBLICATIONS

Memoirs

The Informed Heart: Autonomy in a Mass Age. 1960.
A Home for the Heart. 1974.
Surviving, and Other Essays. 1979; as *Surviving the Holocaust,* 1986.

Other (psychology)

Love Is Not Enough: The Treatment of Emotionally Disturbed Children. 1950.
Dynamics of Prejudice: A Psychological and Sociological Study of Veterans, with Morris Janowitz. 1950.
Overcoming Prejudice. 1953.
Symbolic Wounds: Puberty Rites and the Envious Male. 1954; revised edition, 1962.
Truants from Life: The Rehabilitation of Emotionally Disturbed Children. 1955.
Paul and Mary: Two Case Histories from "Truants from Life." 1961.
Dialogues with Mothers. 1962.
Child Guidance: A Community Responsibility (speech). 1962.
Art: As the Measure of Man, with George D. Stoddard and Irwin Edman. 1964.
The Empty Fortress: Infantile Autism and the Birth of the Self. 1967.
The Children of the Dream. 1969.
Obsolete Youth: Toward a Psychograph of Adolescent Rebellion. 1970.
Food to Nurture the Mind (speech). 1970.
Moral Education: Five Lectures, with others. 1970.
The Uses of Enchantment: The Meaning and Importance of Fairy Tales. 1976.
On Learning to Read: The Child's Fascination with Meaning, with Karen Zelan. 1982.
Freud and Man's Soul. 1982.
A Good Enough Parent: A Book on Child-Rearing. 1987.
Janusz Korczak: A Tale for Our Time. 1989.
Freud's Vienna and Other Essays. 1990.
Recollections and Reflections. 1990.

The Art of the Obvious, with Alvin A. Rosenfeld. 1993.

*

Critical Studies: *Psychoanalysis in a Vacuum: Bruno Bettelheim and the Holocaust* by Jacob Robinson, 1970; "Bruno Bettelheim's Uses of Enchantment and Abuses of Scholarship" by Alan Dundes, in *Journal of American Folklore,* 104(411), Winter 1991, pp. 74–83; *Educating the Emotions: Bruno Bettelheim and Psychoanalytic Development,* edited by Nathan M. Szajnberg, 1992; "Bruno Bettelheim" by Karen Zelan, in *Prospects* (Paris, France), 23(1–2), 1993, pp. 85–100; *Bettelheim: A Life and Legacy* by Nina Sutton, translated by David Sharp in collaboration with the author, 1996; "Bruno Bettelheim and the Concentration Camps" by Christian Fleck and Albert Muller, in *Journal of the History of the Behavioral Sciences,* 33(1), 1997, pp. 1–38; *The Creation of Dr. B: A Biography of Bruno Bettelheim* by Richard Pollak, 1997; *Autonomy in the Extreme Situation: Bruno Bettelheim, the Nazi Concentration Camps and the Mass Society* by Paul Marcus, 1999; "Bruno Bettelheim and the Chazon Ish: Toward a New Jewish Psychotherapy" by Raymond S. Solomon, in *Journal of Psychology and Judaism,* 24(3), 2000, pp. 223–31.

Theatrical Activities: Actor: **Film**—*Zelig,* 1983.

*   *   *

Bruno Bettelheim has the distinction of being one of the first writers to bring the horrors of the Nazi concentration camps to world attention. Drawing on his personal experiences in Dachau and Buchenwald, Bettelheim published "Individual and Mass Behavior in Extreme Situations" (1943), in which he analyzes life in the concentration camps. This article brought him international acclaim and propelled his career as a psychoanalyst in the United States. He was appointed to the faculty at the University of Chicago, served as director of the Sonia Shankman Orthogenic School, and published extensively on autism, mentally disturbed children, and appropriate parenting.

Born in Vienna, Austria, in 1903, Bettelheim was arrested and sent to Dachau in 1938. He was later transferred to Buchenwald and upon his release in 1939 emigrated to the United States. Bettelheim spent approximately eight months as a concentration camp prisoner. "Individual and Mass Behavior in Extreme Situations" was published in the *Journal of Abnormal and Social Psychology.* Bettelheim completed the article in 1942, but it was rejected by a variety of psychiatric and psychoanalytic journals. In the article Bettelheim discusses his imprisonment and presents his analysis of the social stratification of the camps, the psychological differentiation between new and old prisoners, the identification of the prisoner with camp hierarchy and the SS, the need for and nature of resistance in the camps, the stages of adaptation to camp life, the role of the concentration camp system in mass behavior both inside and outside the camps, and descriptions of the Musselmen. The article was subsequently reworked and republished over the course of Bettelheim's life and makes up the bulk of chapters four and five of his most cited work on the Holocaust, *The Informed Heart*. It should be noted that while the major analytic themes reappear in varying degrees with each revision, the conclusions are not consistent. It is unclear whether these changes represent Bettelheim's evolution in psychoanalytic thinking or reflect changes to counter criticisms raised by other scholars.

It is difficult to reach conclusions about Bettelheim's motivations based on historical and biographical research. He claimed to have extensive psychoanalytic training prior to his internment in the concentration camps and arrival in the United States. It was later learned, however, that Bettelheim's doctorate was in the area of aesthetics and that he had at best undergone a limited personal analysis. He was not a trained psychoanalyst, and there is no evidence that he even met Sigmund Freud. Biographers conclude that, at best, he exaggerated his research conclusions; at worst, he based his analyses on fabricated data to further his reputation and career. This calls into question all of his research conclusions and writings.

Clearly Bettelheim did not fabricate his time in Dachau and Buchenwald, but questions have been raised about his descriptions of methods and his conclusions. This may well explain why he revised his writings when faced with criticisms from other Holocaust scholars and survivors. It is highly unlikely, considering the nature and function of the concentration camp system, that Bettelheim could have systematically engaged in the sort of empirical research and extensive interviewing of prisoners that he describes in his works. It is more likely that his conclusions were based on more limited conversations and grounded in his own personal perceptions and experiences. It should also be noted that Bettelheim did not experience the most notorious periods of history at either Dachau or Buchenwald, and he never had any experiences in camps designed largely as centers for the annihilation of European Jewry.

While Bettelheim's work has received a high degree of recognition from both the general public and the psychological community, it has been highly criticized by some Holocaust scholars and Holocaust survivors. Most notable is the criticism leveled by Terrence Des Pres in his book *The Survivor* against Bettelheim's description of prisoner behavior as infantile and regressive. Survivors in particular take issue with his simplistic analysis of social stratification in the camps, his description of old and new prisoners, and his erroneous conclusions about prisoner identification with the SS. Bettelheim is accused of either misreading or misrepresenting life and behavior in the Nazi concentration camp. Perhaps the greatest criticism leveled against Bettelheim is that he was anti-Semitic, particularly in his blame of Jews for their own destruction.

—Linda M. Woolf

See the essay on *The Informed Heart*.

BIDERMAN, Abraham (Hersz)

Nationality: Australian (originally Polish: immigrated to Australia, 1949). **Born:** Lodz, 1924. **Family:** One son. **Career:** Prisoner, Lodz Ghetto, 1940–44, Auschwitz, 1944, Althammer, 1944, Dora, and Bergen-Belsen. Worked in the clothing industry, Australia, beginning in 1949. **Awards:** National Biography award and Banjo Patterson award for nonfiction, National Book Council, both in 1996, for *The World of My Past.*

PUBLICATION

Memoir

The World of My Past. 1995.

*   *   *

The Holocaust survivor Abraham Biderman was born in Lodz, Poland, and during his formative childhood years he enjoyed a traditional, close, middle-class lifestyle within an extended family. All of this changed dramatically with the Nazi conquest of Poland in September 1939. He has written a memoir of his experiences in the Lodz ghetto, where he was incarcerated in 1940, before eventually being transported to Auschwitz in August 1944 when the ghetto was liquidated. After spending two months in Auschwitz, he was evacuated to Althammer. From there he was sent to Dora, the underground factory where Wernher von Braun's rockets were built, and finally to Bergen-Belsen, where he spent the last few weeks of the war working as a slave laborer for the infamous SS Lieutenant Colonel Rudolf Hoess, the former commandant of Auschwitz. He was liberated by the British and witnessed Hoess's surrender. Although he was offered the opportunity to emigrate to the United States, he decided to apply to Australia. Sponsored by family friends, he joined a substantial survivor community in Melbourne, which has the largest proportion of Holocaust survivors on a pro rata basis of any place outside Israel, the vast majority from Poland. As with many of his confreres, Biderman went into the *schmatte* (clothing) business and was very successful.

So that his son Simon (named for his grandfather, who perished in Auschwitz) would remember and to explain it to other family members, Biderman decided to write his story. He began in 1985 and produced the major work entitled *The World of My Past*. The book also was written in fulfillment of the last wish of his mother, Fradle—''Remember, remember what they did to us''—as his parents were taken away on their arrival at the station in Auschwitz. In his memoir Biderman describes the scene as follows: ''I stood confused. Although I saw what was taking place around me, my mind could not fully come to grips with the tragedy which was unravelling. My mother, holding on to my father's arm, leaned her head against him as they walked and were herded away with the others. My parents were only in their early forties. I never saw them again.'' Remembering the events of the Holocaust and passing them on to others became his ''eleventh commandment,'' as the Jewish philosopher Emil Fackenheim has called it.

After six years of attempting to find a commercial publisher, Biderman decided in 1995 to self-publish his book, with a print run of about 1,000 copies. The book was selected by the National Book Council for its CUB Banjo Award for nonfiction in 1996 as well as for its biennial biography award. Comparing his difficulties in finding a publisher with **Eli Wiesel**'s in the 1960s, he told Susan Wyndham, a reporter with the *Sydney Morning Herald,* ''Nothing has changed. Holocaust stories were of no interest to the Western world then and they are of no interest today.'' As a result of the work's significant acclaim, however, it was later republished by Random House. This is unusual in publishing and reflects the strength of the memoir.

Biderman's memoir joins a significant body of Holocaust literature produced in Australia, written by survivors and their descendants and also by interested Jewish and non-Jewish scholars and novelists. Many of the writers in these various categories have received prestigious literary awards over the years. They include **Mark Baker**, Lilly Brett, Inga Clendinnen, **Thomas Keneally**, Romana Koval, Serge Liberman, and Arnold Zable. While a significant number of actual survivor testimonies have been published in Australia, Biderman's stands out, however, for receiving an award, since the survivor generation rarely developed sufficient literary skills in English to produce an award-winning publication. Biderman joins his *Landsmann* the poet Jacob Rosenberg in writing about the Lodz ghetto, but Rosenberg's poetry is written in Yiddish, although some has been translated into English.

As a firsthand account of a survivor's experiences in the Lodz ghetto and the extermination camps, Biderman's memoir has come to play an extremely important role within Australian Holocaust literature. Sir Zelman Cowen, the leading Australian Jewish scholar and the former governor-general, has written, ''As do accounts of such writers as **Primo Levi**, Elie Wiesel and Samuel Pisar, so too *The World of My Past* overwhelms me with the tragedy and horror of it all.''

—Suzanne Rutland

See the essay on *The World of My Past.*

BIRENBAUM, Halina

Nationality: Israeli (originally Polish; immigrated to Israel, 1947). **Born:** Warsaw, 15 September 1929. **Family:** Married Chaim Birenbaum; two sons. **Career:** Prisoner, Majdanek, Auschwitz, Ravensbrück, and Neustadt-Glewe, World War II. Author and translator. **Award:** ''Figure of Reconciliation'' award, Polish Council of Christians and Jews, 2001.

PUBLICATIONS

Collection

Sounds of a Guilty Silence: Selected Poems. 1997.

Memoirs

Nadzieja umiera ostatnia. 1967; as *Hope Is the Last to Die: A Personal Documentation of Nazi Terror,* 1971; as *Hope Is the Last to Die: A Coming of Age under Nazi Terror,* 1996.
Powrót do ziemi praojców. 1991.
Kazdy odzyskany dzien: Wspomnienia. 1998.
Wolanie o pamiec. 1999.

Poetry

Nigun penimi. 1985.
Nawet gdy sie smieje. 1990.
Nie o kwiatach. 1993.

Other

Translator, *Asher karati la-metim: Shire geto Varshah* [What I Read to the Deads], by Wladyslaw Szlengel. 1987.

* * *

Halina Birenbaum is a Polish-born Jewish author, poet, and translator best known for *Hope Is the Last To Die* (1967), an autobiographical account of her experiences in the Warsaw Ghetto and a series of concentration camps. Born in Warsaw in 1929, she had her childhood interrupted by the invasion of Poland in 1939. She lived through the initial period of occupation and the establishment of the ghetto, managing with her family, and due primarily to her mother's determination and courage, to avoid being captured and sent to the camps until well into 1942. She was sent first to Majdanek, and then, after surviving a night in the gas chamber only because supplies of gas had run out, she was sent to Auschwitz, then Ravensbrück, and finally Neustadt-Glewe. She lost almost her entire family, including her father; her mother, with whom she was particularly close; one of a pair of brothers; and virtually all other relatives and friends.

All Birenbaum's activities, literary and otherwise, form a coherent whole and serve the same end: promotion of understanding and reconciliation between Jews and especially Poles, but also Germans and others. After liberation she returned to Warsaw and in 1947 emigrated to Israel with a Zionist organization. In Israel she initially devoted herself primarily to being a wife and mother. She relates how, at a time when it was not a common occurrence, she was asked, as a survivor, to speak to a group of Israeli school children about her experiences in the Holocaust. She agreed, somewhat reluctantly, and in the process discovered an ability to communicate with an immediacy and sincerity that she was later able to transform into an equally effective voice on the printed page. Although she had already committed herself to record her experiences in writing, the experience of establishing a connection with the school children motivated and inspired her and helped give shape to her feelings, memories, and beliefs.

Birenbaum's autobiography, as well as her other writings, may be somewhat lacking in artistic sophistication, but it is highly effective and demonstrates clarity of thought, a well-developed vision of the world and human nature, and an expansive and compelling spirituality. Her work is informed not only by a desire to come to terms with the evil she and others experienced but also to proclaim the existence of good as well as a powerful affirmation of hope and faith. She is often compared to or at least grouped with **Anne Frank** and **Hannah Senesh** because of the subject matter and adolescent narrative perspective of her work.

Since the initial publication of *Hope Is the Last To Die* in 1967, Birenbaum has spent her time writing and working with young people in Israel, Poland, and Germany. She has frequently accompanied groups of Israeli youths to Poland, visited elementary schools in Germany, and addressed a variety of formal and informal youth groups in Poland. She has been the subject of two documentary films, one French and one Israeli. She writes in Polish and Hebrew and frequently publishes creative, topical, and reflective pieces in Polish publications. In March 2001 she was awarded the ''Reconciliation Person of the Year'' Award by the Polish Council for Polish-Jewish Dialogue for her ''patient service to the sacred and difficult cause of reconciliation.'' The award was all the more significant in that it was given at a time when the controversy surrounding the ''Jedwabny affair'' was raging in Poland (evidence had surfaced implicating Polish citizens of the town of Jedwabny in executions and other atrocities against Jews for which the Nazis had been held responsible). Birenbaum, while not failing to record acts of perfidy and cowardice on the part not only of Germans but also of Poles and Jews, has gone to great lengths in her writing and public life to point out countless acts of courage and generosity on the part of all groups but perhaps especially of Poles.

—Allan Reid

See the essay on *Hope Is the Last to Die: A Coming of Age under Nazi Terror.*

BITTON-JACKSON, Livia E(lvira)

Also wrote as Livia Elvira Bitton. **Nationality:** American (originally Czechoslovakian: immigrated to the United States,

1951; granted U.S. citizenship, 1956). **Born:** Elli L. Friedman, Somorja, 28 February 1931. **Education:** Brooklyn College, City University of New York, B.A. 1961; New York University, M.A. 1963, Ph.D. in Hebrew culture and Jewish history 1968. **Family:** Married Leonard G. Jackson in 1977; one son and one daughter. **Career:** Associate professor, 1970–71, and dean of students, 1972–75, Academy of Jewish Religion. Since 1980 professor of Hebrew and Judaic studies, Herbert H. Lehman College, City University of New York. Lecturer in Hebrew literature, 1965–68, Hunter College, City University of New York; adjunct assistant professor of Hebrew language and literature, Brooklyn Center of Long Island University, 1965–68; assistant professor of Judaic studies, Brooklyn College, City University of New York, 1972–76; professor of Jewish history, Tel Aviv University, 1980–81. **Awards:** Long Island University outstanding teacher award, 1967; New York University Founder's Day award, for highest bracket of scholastic preferment, 1969; Christopher award, 1981, for *Elli: Coming of Age in the Holocaust;* United Jewish Appeal Eleanor Roosevelt humanitarian award and Jewish Teachers Union Jewish heritage award, both in 1982, for *Elli: Coming of Age in the Holocaust.* **Agent:** Gloria Stern, Gloria Stern Agency, 1230 Park Avenue, New York, New York 10028, U.S.A. **Address:** c/o Department of C.O.G.S., Herbert H. Lehman College, City University of New York, Bronx, New York 10468, U.S.A.

PUBLICATIONS

Memoirs

Elli: Coming of Age in the Holocaust. 1980.
I Have Lived a Thousand Years: Growing Up in the Holocaust (for young adults). 1997.
My Bridges of Hope: Searching for Life and Love after Auschwitz (sequel to *I Have Lived a Thousand Years;* for young adults). 1999.

Other

A Decade of Zionism in Hungary, the Formative Years: The Post-World War I Period: 1918–1928 (as Livia Elvira Bitton). 1968.
The Jewess As a Fictional Sex Symbol. 1973.
Biblical Names of Literary Jewesses (originally a speech). 1973.
Madonna or Courtesan: The Jewish Woman in Christian Literature. 1982.

*

Critical Study: ''Women Writers and the Holocaust: Strategies for Survival'' by Ellen S. Fine, in *Reflections of the*

Holocaust in Art and Literature Social Science Monographs, 1990.

* * *

Livia E. Bitton-Jackson, who was born Elli L. Friedman, endured the Holocaust as a teenager. She was incarcerated with her mother in Auschwitz, Plaszow, Augsburg, and Mühldorf. Along with her mother and her brother, Bubi, she survived the horrors of the concentration camps. After liberation in 1945 she completed high school in a camp for displaced persons and then in 1951 immigrated to the United States. She received a Ph.D. degree in Hebrew culture and Jewish history from New York University and subsequently taught at a number of colleges, including City University of New York, where in 1968 she became professor of Hebraic and Judaic studies at Herbert H. Lehman College. In 1977 she moved to Israel, where she taught at Tel Aviv University. She has received numerous awards and honors, especially for her three volumes of memoirs.

Bitton-Jackson's memoir *Elli: Coming of Age in the Holocaust* was published in 1980 to critical acclaim, winning a number of prestigious awards. Her critical work *Madonna or Courtesan: The Jewish Woman in Christian Literature* was published in 1982. In 1997 she adapted *Elli* for a teenage audience as *I Have Lived a Thousand Years: Growing Up in the Holocaust*, which was chosen as Best Book for Young Adults by the American Library Association and which also won the 1998 Christopher Award.

My Bridges of Hope: Searching for Life and Love after Auschwitz, a sequel to *I Have Lived a Thousand Years,* recounts Bitton-Jackson's life after liberation in 1945 in postwar Europe. Oppressed by the anti-Semitism in Czechoslovakia, the girl and her family decided to immigrate to the United States. While they waited out the six years until they could leave, the courageous young woman rescued Jewish orphans from a Slovakian riot, helped Jews escape to Palestine, and became the head of a Jewish school. In the midst of this she dealt with post-traumatic stress as well as enduring the usual pangs of adolescence and coming to terms with her own identity. In 1951 she and her mother escaped from behind the Iron Curtain. An epilogue of several paragraphs telescopes her life after 1951. As *Kirkus Reviews* said of the sequel, "Interesting and inspiring, this story makes painfully clear how the fight to survive extended well beyond the war years; the discomforts and obstacles the author faced and articulates in such riveting detail will make readers squirm at the security and ease of their own lives."

—Maryann McLoughlin

See the essay on *Elli: Coming of Age in the Holocaust.*

BLATT, Thomas "Toivi"

Nationality: American (originally Polish: immigrated to the United States, 1959). **Born:** Izbica, 15 April 1927. **Education:** Studied journalism in Szczecin. **Family:** Married Dana Blatt. **Career:** Prisoner, Sobibor, World War II. Moved to Santa Barbara, California, and established an electronics business. Lecturer on the Holocaust. Produced two documentary films on the Holocaust. Lives in Bellevue, Washington. **E-mail Address:** Thomasblatt@msn.com.

PUBLICATIONS

Memoir

From the Ashes of Sobibor: A Story of Survival. 1997.

Other

Sobibor: The Forgotten Revolt (historical account). 1995.
Nur Die Schatten Bleiben. 2000.

*

Film Adaptations: *Escape from Sobibor,* 1987.

Theatrical Activities: Actor: **Films**—*Escape from Sobibor,* 1987.

* * *

At Sobibor in Poland at least 250,000 Jews lost their lives. Few survived to tell of the camp; the SS officers and guards who ran it; the men, women, and children who died there; and the heroic revolt of some 500 prisoners—the single most successful revolt staged in any of the camps. Thomas "Toivi" Blatt is one of those few.

In two books, the memoir *From the Ashes of Sobibor: A Story of Survival* (1997) and the historical account *Sobibor: The Forgotten Revolt* (1996), Blatt chronicles the inhuman ordeal of imprisonment within the confines of a death camp—seeing the trains arrive daily with their human cargo destined for the gas chambers, and always wondering if he might be next. Blatt survived because of his remarkable will, ingenuity, and courage, and, quite simply, because he was lucky. Survival endowed him with a staggering responsibility to tell the story that no words can adequately describe. As he writes in the preface to *Sobibor: The Forgotten Revolt* "witnessing genocide is overwhelming: writing about it is soul shattering." Reading these two books is also soul shattering because Blatt brings us inside the deepest circle of hell.

While *Sobibor* is an historical exposition of the camp, describing its construction, the executioners who ran it, and the planning and events of the revolt on 14 October 1943, *From the Ashes of Sobibor* records many of these same events, from the unique perspective of a sixteen-year-old boy who watches his father, mother, and younger brother taken to their deaths.

Blatt's memoir tells of his family's life in Izbica, a small town in eastern Poland, the majority of whose population were Jews. From a quiet town, Izbica is transformed into an over-populated transit center. The Blatt family endures hardship and deprivation. Blatt must grow up quickly. During numerous *Aktions* (Nazi roundups of Jews to be sent to the death camps), Blatt has the responsibility of concealing the family hiding place, a small space built into the attic, before running to seek his own refuge. Eventually his family cannot escape the dragnet. They, too, are seized and sent to Sobibor. If Izbica is purgatory, Sobibor is hell itself.

With luck and ingenuity, Blatt manages to survive, vowing that he will speak on behalf of those who perished. On several occasions he narrowly escapes death. During the revolt, luck alone saves him. But Blatt's luck nearly runs out during his months of hiding. Concealed in a barn under a table covered with hay, Blatt and his two friends spend months in the most wretched of conditions. In the end, the farmer who has harbored them decides that they are a liability. When smothering the boys fails, he shoots them. Wounded in the jaw, Blatt is left for dead. Dazed and bleeding, he escapes when the farmer decides to postpone digging his grave until morning.

In his memoir Blatt tells a remarkable story of survival in terse and restrained language. Witnessing the death of his family and countless others, he refuses to allow himself to be overwhelmed by emotion, knowing that it will cost him his life. The memoir's language bears witness to that decision; feelings are concealed beneath the text. For Blatt, survival required shutting down his emotions, moving through the days without feeling, so that he might endure. In the end, he not only endures but triumphs, fulfilling his vow to witness for his family and the many others who became the ashes of Sobibor.

—Marilyn J. Harran

See the essay on *From the Ashes of Sobibor: A Story of Survival.*

BÖLL, Heinrich (Theodor)

Nationality: German. **Born:** Cologne, 21 December 1917. **Education:** Began apprenticeship to a book dealer, Bonn, 1937–38; briefly studied literature and classical philology at the University of Cologne, 1939, before being drafted into the army. **Military Service:** German Army, 1939–45: wounded in action four times; corporal; prisoner of war, April–September 1945. **Family:** Married Annemarie Cech in 1942; four sons (two deceased). **Career:** Following the war held a variety of odd jobs while writing; worked for the Cologne Bureau of Statistics, 1950–51; full-time writer from 1951; began association with Gruppe 47, 1951. Visiting chair of poetics, University of Frankfurt, 1964. Coeditor, *Labyrinth,* 1960–61, and *L,* from 1976. President, PEN International, 1971–74. **Awards:** Gruppe 47 prize, 1951, for ''The Black Sheep''; Rene Schickele prize, 1952; literary prize of the German industry; Southern German radio prize and Association of German Critics literary prize, both in 1953, for *Mönch and Räuber;* French publishers prize for best foreign novel, 1954, for *Tribune de Paris;* City of Wuppertal Edward von der Heydt prize 1958; North Rheine-Westphalia art prize, 1959; Charles Veillon prize, 1960; city of Cologne literature prize, 1960; Premio d'Isola d'Elba, 1965; Premio Calabria, 1966; Georg Büchner prize, 1967; Nobel prize for literature, 1972; Scottish Arts Council fellowship, 1973; Carl von Ossietzky medal, International League of Human Rights, 1974; first Neil Gunn fellow, Scottish Arts Council, 1974; named honorary member of American Academy of Arts and Letters, and of American National Institute of Art and Literature, both 1974; named honorary citizen of City of Cologne, 1983; honorary title of professor conferred by North Rhine-Westphalia, 1983. D.Litt: Trinity College, University of Dublin; University of Aston; University of Birmingham; and Brunel University, all 1973. **Died:** 16 July 1985.

PUBLICATIONS

Novels

Der Zug war pünktlich (novella). 1949; as *The Train Was on Time,* 1956.
Die schwarzen Schafe. 1951.
Wo warst du, Adam? (novella). 1951; as *Adam, Where Art Thou?,* 1955; as *And Where Were You, Adam?,* 1973.
Nicht nur zur Weihnachtszeit. 1952.
Und sagte kein einziges Wort. 1953; as *Acquainted with the Night,* 1954; as *And Never Said a Word,* 1978.
Haus ohne Hüter. 1954; as *Tomorrow and Yesterday,* 1957; as *The Unguarded House,* 1957.
Das Brot der frühen Jahre. 1955; as *The Bread of Our Early Years,* 1957; as *The Bread of Those Early Years,* 1976.
So ward Abend und Morgen. 1955.
Im Tal der donnernden Hufe. 1957.
Der Mann mit den Messern. 1958.
Der Bahnhof von Zimpren. 1959.
Billard um Halbzehn. 1959; as *Billiards at Half-Past Nine.* 1961.
Als der Krieg ausbrach, Als der Krieg zu Ende war (2 novellas). 1962; as *Absent Without Leave,* 1965.
Ansichten eines Clowns. 1963; as *The Clown,* 1965.
Entferung von der Truppe. 1964.
Ende einer Dienstfahrt. 1966; as *The End of a Mission,* 1967.
Geschichten aus zwölf Jahren. 1969.
Gruppenbild mit Dame. 1971; as *Group Portrait with a Lady,* 1973.

Die verlorene Ehre der Katharina Blum. 1974; as *The Lost Honor of Katharina Blum,* 1975.
Berichte zur Gesinnungslage der Nation. 1975.
Fürsorgliche Belagerung. 1979; as *The Safety Net,* 1982.
Du fährst zu oft nach Heidelberg. 1979.
Das Vermächtnis (novella). 1982; as *A Soldier's Legacy,* 1985.
Frauen vor Flusslandschaft: Roman in Dialogen und Selbstgesprächen. 1985; as *Women in a River Landscape: A Novel in Dialogues and Soliloques,* 1988.
Der Engel schwieg (novella). 1992.

Short Stories

Wanderer, kommst du nach Spa. 1950; as *Traveller, If You Come to Spa,* 1956.
Unberechenbare Gäste: Heitere Erzählungen. 1956.
Doktor Murkes gesammeltes Schweigen und andere Satiren. 1958.
Die Waage der Baleks und andere Erzählungen. 1958.
Absent without Leave and Other Stories. 1965.
Eighteen Stories. 1966.
Children Are Civilians Too. 1970.
Der Mann mit den Messern: Erzählungen (selections). 1972.
Gesammelte Erzählungen (2 vols.). 1981.
Die Verwundung und andere frühe Erzählungen. 1983; as *The Casualty,* 1986.
Der Angriff: Erzählungen 1947–1949. 1983.
Veränderungen in Stäck: Erzählungen 1962–1980. 1984.
Mein trauriges Gesicht: Erzählungen. 1984.
The Stories (selection). 1986.
The Silent Angel. 1995.
The Mad Dog: Stories. 1997.

Plays

Die Brücke von Berczaba (radio play). In *Zauberei auf dem Sender und andere Hörspiele,* 1962.
Der Heilige und der Räuber (radio play). In *Hörspielbuch des Nordwestdeutschen und Süddeutschen Rundfunks 4,* 1953; as *Mönch und Räuber,* in *Erzählungen, Hörspiele, Aufsätz,* 1961.
Ein Tag wie sonst (radio play). 1980.
Zum Tee bei Dr. Borsig (radio play). In *Erzählungen, Hörspiele, Aufsätz,* 1961.
Eine Stunde Aufenthalt (radio play). In *Erzählungen, Hörspiele, Aufsätz,* 1961.
Die Spurlosen (radio play). 1957.
Bilanz (radio play). Published with *Klopfzeichen,* 1961.
Klopfzeichen (radio play). Published with *Bilanz,* 1961.
Ein schluck Erde (produced 1961). 1962.
Zum Tee bei Dr. Borsig (includes *Mönch und Räuber; Eine Stunde Aufenthalt; Bilanz; Die Spurlosen; Klopfzeichen; Sprechanlage; Konzert für Stimmen*). 1964.
Hausfriedensbruch (radio play). 1969.

Aussatz (produced 1970). Published with *Hausfriedensbruch,* 1969.

Radio Plays: *Die Brücke von Berczaba,* 1952; *Ein Tag wie sonst,* 1953; *Der Heilige und der Räuber,* 1953; *Zum Tee bei Dr. Borsig,* 1955; *Anita und das Existenzminimum,* 1955, revised version as *Ich habe nichts gegen Tiere,* 1958; *Die Spurlosen,* 1957; *Bilanz,* 1957; *Eine Stunde Aufenthalt,* 1957; *Die Stunde der Wahrheit,* 1958; *Klopfzeichen,* 1960; *Hausfriedensbruch,* 1969.

Poetry

Gedichte. 1972.

Other

Irisches Tagebuch. 1957; as *Irish Journal,* 1967.
Im Ruhrgebiet. 1958.
Unter Krahnenbäumen. 1958.
Menschen am Rhein. 1960.
Brief an einen jungen Katholiken. 1961.
Erzählungen, Hörspiele, Aufsätz. 1961.
Assisi. 1962.
Hierzulande. 1963.
Frankfurter Vorlesungen. 1966.
Aufsätz, Kritiken, Reden 1952–1967. 1967.
Leben im Zustand de Frevels. 1969.
Neue politische und literarische Schriften. 1973.
Nobel Prize for Literature (lecture). 1973.
Politische Meditationen zu Glück und Vergeblichkeit, with Dorthee Sölle. 1973.
Drei Tage in März, with Christian Linder. 1975.
Der Lorbeer ist immer noch bitter: Literarische Schriften. 1976.
Briefe zur Verteidigung der Republik, with Freimut Duve and Klaus Staeck. 1977.
Einmischung erwünscht: Schriften zur Zeit. 1977.
Werke, edited by Bernd Balzer (10 vols.). 1977–78.
Missing Persons and Other Essays. 1977.
Querschnitte: Aus Interviews, Aufsätzen, und Reden, edited by Viktor Böll and Renate Matthaei. 1977.
Gefahren von falschen Brüdern: Politische Schriften. 1980.
Warum haben wir aufeinander geschossen? with Lew Kopelew. 1981.
Rendevous mit Margaret: Liebesgeschichten. 1981.
Was soll aus dem jungen bloss werden? (memoir). 1981; as *What's to Become of the Boy? or Something to Do with Books,* 1984.
Der Autor ist immer noch versteckt. 1981.
Vermintes Gelände. 1982.
Antikommunismus in Ost und West. 1982.
Ich hau dem Mädche mix jedonn, ich han et bloss ens kräje: Texte, Bilder, Dokumente zur Verteihung des Ehrenbürgerrechts der Stadt Köln, 29 April 1983. 1983.

Ein-und Zusprüche: Schriften, Reden und Prosa 1981–83. 1984.

Weil die Stadt so fremd geworden ist. 1985.

Bild-Bonn-Boenish. 1985.

Die Fähigkeit zu trauern: Schriften und Reden 1983–1985. 1986.

Denken mit Böll. 1986.

Rom auf den ersten Blick: Landschaften, Städte, Reisen. 1987.

Editor, with Erich Kock, *Unfertig ist der Mensch.* 1967.

Edtior, with Freimut Duve und Klaus Staeck, *Verantwortlich für Polen?* 1982.

Translator, with Annemarie Böll:

Kein Name bei den Leuten [No Name in the Street], by Kay Cicellis. 1953.

Ein unordentlicher Mensch, by Adriaan Morriën. 1955.

Tod einer Stadt [Death of a Town], by Kay Cicellis. 1956.

Weihnachtsabend in San Cristobal [The Saintmaker's Christmas Eve], by Paul Horgan. 1956.

Zur Ruhe kam der Baum des Menschen nie [The Tree of Man], by Patrick White. 1957.

Der Teufel in der Wüste [The Devil in the Desert], by Paul Horgan. 1958.

Die Geisel [The Hostage], by Brendan Behan. 1958.

Der Mann von Morgen fruh [The Quare Fellow], by Brendan Behan. 1958.

Ein Wahrer Held [The Playboy of the Western World], by J.M. Synge. 1960.

Die Boot fahren nicht mehr aus [The Islandman], by Tomás O'Crohan. 1960.

Eine Rose zur Weihnachtszeit [One Red Rose for Christmas], by Paul Horgan. 1960.

Der Gehilfe [The Assistant], by Bernard Malamud. 1960.

Kurz vor dem Krieg gegen die Eskimos, by J.D. Salinger. 1961.

Das Zauberfass [The Magic Barrel], by Bernard Malamud. 1962.

Der Fänger im Roggen [The Catcher in the Rye], by J.D. Salinger. 1962.

Ein Gutshaus in Irland [The Big House], by Brendan Behan. Published in *Stücke,* 1962.

Franny und Zooey, by J.D. Salinger. 1963.

Die Insel der Pferde [The Island of Horses], by Eilís Dillon. 1964.

Hebt den Dachbalken hoch, Zimmerleute; Seymour wird vorgestellt [Raise High the Roof Beam, Carpenters; Seymour: An introduction], by J.D. Salinger. 1965.

Caesar und Cleopatra, by G.B. Shaw. 1965.

Der Spanner [The Scarperer], by Brendan Behan. 1966.

Die Insel des grossen John [The Coriander], by Eilís Dillon. 1966.

Das harte Leben [The Hard Life], by Flann O'Brien. 1966.

Neun Erzählungen [Nine Stories], by J.D. Salinger. 1966.

Die schwarzen Füchse [A Family of Foxes], by Eilís Dillon. 1967.

Die Irrfahrt der Santa Maria [The Cruise of the Santa Maria], by Eilís Dillon. 1968.

Die Springflut [The Sea Wall], by Eilís Dillon. 1969.

Seehunde SOS [The Seals], by Eilís Dillon. 1970.

Erwachen in Mississippi [Coming of Age in Mississippi], by Anne Moody. 1970.

Candida, Der Kaiser von Amerika, Mensch und Übermensch [Candida, the King of Amerika, Man and Superman], by G.B. Shaw. 1970.

Handbuch des Revolutionärs, by G.B. Shaw. 1972.

*

Bibliography: *Heinrich Böll in America 1954–1970* by Ray Lewis White, 1979.

Critical Studies: *Böll, Teller of Tales: A Study of His Works and Characters* by Wilhelm Johannes Schwartz, 1969; *A Student's Guide to Böll* by Enid Macpherson, 1972; *Heinrich Böll: Withdrawal and Re-Emergence,* 1973, and *Heinrich Böll: A German for His Time,* 1986, both by J.H. Reid; *The Major Works of Böll: A Critical Commentary* by Erhard Friedrichsmeyer, 1974; *The Writer and Society: Studies in the Fiction of Günter Grass and Heinrich Böll* by Charlotte W. Ghurye, 1976; *The Imagery in Heinrich Böll's Novels* by Thor Prodaniuk, 1979; *Heinrich Böll,* 1981, and *Understanding Heinrich Böll,* 1992, both by Robert C. Conard; *Heinrich Böll* by Klaus Schröter, 1982; *Heinrich Böll: On His Death: Selected Obituaries and the Last Interview,* translated by Patricia Crampton, 1985; *Heinrich Böll and the Challenge of Literature* by Michael Butler, 1988; *The Woman As Survivor: The Evolution of the Female Figure in the Works of Heinrich Böll* by Aleidine Kramer Moeller, 1991; *The Narrative Fiction of Heinrich Böll: Social Conscience and Literary Achievement,* edited by Michael Butler, 1994; *Heinrich Böll: Forty Years of Criticism* Reinhard K. Zachau, 1994; *On the Rationality of Poetry: Heinrich Böll's Aesthetic Thinking* by Frank Finlay, 1996.

* * *

Heinrich Böll's considerable literary output embraces almost 40 years, from 1947 to his death in 1985. He began writing in 1936, but nothing of his early works was published. After the war, Böll and Wolfgang Borchert, among others, created what was termed *Truemmerliteratur* ("literature born of the rubble"), a realistic portrayal of war. Their view, shared by most post 1945 European writers and philosophers, differed considerably from the Expressionists' belief during and after World War I in the regeneration of mankind. In contrast, World War II and especially the Holocaust led to a lack of belief in any new, positive values; consequently, the new Weltanschauung was born of a pessimism that was close at times to nihilism.

With the exception of the short novel *Wo warst du, Adam? (And Where Were You, Adam?),* Böll's postwar literature

(1947–52) consists of short stories almost all of which deal with aspects of the war. With the exception of the story ''Todesursache: Hakennase'' (''Cause of Death: Hooked Nose''), Böll does not deal explicitly with the Holocaust. Generally, his approach is indirect, revealed through the reactions of his protagonists to their war experiences. As in *And Where Were You, Adam?*, Böll's protagonists are never heroes; they have no control over their lives at the front, and they all suffer mentally or physically from the effects of the war and anti-Semitism. In these stories, Böll attacks the lie of Nazi propaganda that glorified war. His method is often to concentrate on the fate of a single character in order to intensify his condemnation of the brutality and absurdity of war. One of the best examples is the title story of the collection *Wanderer kommst du nach Spa . . .* (''Stranger, Bear Word to the Spartans We . . .''). A young, wounded soldier is brought into a high school that has been transformed into an army hospital. The story is in form of a soliloquy narrated by the young man. He realizes that it is his own school that he had left only three months earlier when forced to join the army. Having lost both arms and a leg he is now dying in his school which once promoted traditional values of higher learning symbolized by the paintings and busts of classical and historical figures, and by the unfinished quotation about Spartan bravery at the battle of Thermopylae written on the blackboard by the young soldier when he was still a student. Böll's cynicism, marked by sadness, is directed against these classical values which have been rendered meaningless by the reality of the Nazi regime. The atmosphere of destruction, and the stark description of mutilation and pain are typical of Böll's war literature.

Böll's later stories of this period, although still influenced by the war, are more critical of contemporary German society which reveals itself as predominantly materialistically oriented and unwilling to give up its Nazi past and admit its guilt. ''Nicht nur zur Weihnachtszeit'' (''Christmas Not Just Once a Year'') is on the surface a hilariously funny story about the author's aunt having seemingly gone mad because of her concern about the risk to her Christmas tree's ornaments arising from the bombing of the city. To restore the aunt's sanity the family resorts to year-round Christmas trees and celebrations. The aunt does not notice that in the course of the years the family members are replaced by paid actors and wax dolls. Böll begins to develop his new technique of social criticism with this work. While the story about the aunt is quite absurd, the reflections on most of the other family members are factual and point to the major problem of postwar German society: namely, that the war for the majority of Germans was nothing but an interruption of their former life style which was, and is again, dominated by materialism.

After 1952 Böll turned primarily to the novel form, where he continued to depict the ills of German society as he saw them: corruption among politicians and the clergy in *Und sagte kein einziges Wort* (1953; *And Never Said a Word*) and

Germans' love of authority, their petit-bourgeois attitude, and hypocritical and unscrupulous character in *Billard um halb zehn* (1959; *Billiards at Half-Past Nine)* and *Ansichten eines Clowns* (1963; *The Clown*). He felt all of these contributed to the rise of Nazism, the war, and the Holocaust. The award of the Nobel Prize for Literature in 1972 recognized Böll's important contribution to literature and the courage displayed in his lifelong critique of contemporary German culture and mores.

—Renate Benson

See the essay on *And Where Were You, Adam?*

BOR, Josef

Nationality: Czechoslovakian. **Born:** Josef Bondy, Ostrava, Austria-Hungary, 2 July 1906. **Education:** Graduate of the University of Brno, 1929. **Family:** First wife and two children killed in Terezín; married second wife (died) after World War II, two children. **Career:** Prisoner, Terezín and Buchenwald, World War II. Lawyer. Foreign minister, Czech government, after World War II. Traveled across Europe lecturing on the Holocaust. **Died:** 1979.

PUBLICATIONS

Memoir

Terezínské rekviem. 1963; as *The Terezín Requiem,* 1963.

Novel

Opuštená panenka [The Derelict Doll]. 1961.

Plays

Ten třetí [The Third Man] (produced 1978).

Television Play: *Appassionata.*

Screenplay: *Terezin Requiem.*

Radio Play: *Ten třetí,* 1979.

Other

Editor, with Rudolf Iltis and František Gotlieb, *Zivot a odkaz,* by Richard Feder. 1973.

* * *

Although the name Josef Bor does not appear in many Czech lexicons of twentieth-century Czech literature, his contribution to literature of the Holocaust is significant and certainly worthy of mention. He was born Josef Bondy in Ostrava in 1906 and spent his working life as a lawyer. He and his family were transported to Terezín and later to Buchenwald, where his wife and two children were killed. He returned alone to Prague, where he became foreign minister and worked in the Czech government under Ladislav Svoboda. He remarried and had two children with his second wife. It was not until he was more than 50 years old that he began to write. Bor's work can be contrasted with that of F.E. Kraus; however, Bor attempts to dig psychologically deeper and does not point accusatory fingers in his works but rather tries to show the value of a person's being in the face of deadly danger (*Literatura s hvězdou Davidovou*). In *O městu ve tvaru hvězdy* M. Valtrová describes Bor as ''belonging to those authors whose work whips unexpectedly like a flame.'' His first work, *Opuštěná panenka* (''The Derelict Doll,'' 1961), has an autobiographical subtext and presents the fate of three generations of an extended Jewish family interned in Terezín and later in the death camps. The doll is symbolic for the suffering and loss of human dignity in the camps. In *Věstník: Židovských náboženských obcí v Československu* it is stated that in this work, ''We see the ghetto from two sides: on one side there is suffering, which the superman has wrought for his victim; on the other, there is cultural life, brotherhood, and resistance.''

It was at the urging of friends that Bor penned *Terezínské rekviem* (*The Terezín Requiem*), and this work belongs among the best of Holocaust remembrance. The study of Giuseppe Verdi's *Requiem* was a great joke for Adolf Eichmann, who laughed when he heard that Jews would be singing a Catholic opera. The musical and ideological version of the requiem, however, was reworked by Director Raphael Schächter, who made the words ''Libera me!'' (''Set me free!'') the key phrase that escaped the comprehension of the Nazis in the audience.

In later years Bor became interested in the reconciliation between Jews and Christians. He began to do biblical research and investigated various historical sources for more writing material. He lectured at the Jewish Town Hall and the Hus House in Prague. He also spoke to Unitarian groups. He traveled to Berlin, Vienna, and various parts of East Germany to relate his experiences and make amends with Christian groups. The Berlin religious community, in cooperation with Bor and Aktion Sühnezeichen (Operation Mark of Atonement), created a mimeograph called *Propheten und ihr Gott* (''Prophets and Their God''), which remains unpublished. In this work Bor investigates the questions as to why a people of Johann Wolfgang von Goethe, Immanuel Kant, and Ludwig van Beethoven were hypnotized by a regime of such immense cruelty. In his essay *Standortsbestimmung zum Jüdisch-Christlichen Dialog,* Bor asks, ''Why do great masses of Christians react so differently in history when it has to do with the Jews?''

Bor's play *Ten třetí* (*Der Dritte* in German, ''The Third Man'' in English) is an attempt to come to terms with the Holocaust and represents the way history could have been had the Jews not been forced to take the blood of Christ upon themselves. His son stated in the foreword to *Der Dritte* that ''Josef Bor's search for the causes of the Jewish tragedy and the roots of anti-Semitism led him to the beginnings of Christianity.'' Bor lived to see the German world premiere performance of this play. At this 1978 performance he spoke to the young performers and told them, as translated from the foreward of *Der Dritte,* ''It was for me one of the biggest surprises of my life. I just cannot ignore what this performance of my drama means. The youth from Odenwald are performing my play, hence, I have become one of them. It is the first time in history, as far as I know, that a Passion play, as it no doubt will be understood by the Christian audience, by a Jewish author will be performed. That is a big step toward reconciliation between Christians and Jews and with one of their own: Jesus himself. This shows that the greatness of Jesus does not change, be it godly or human, even if one accepts that he was not deceived by Judas, that the Jews did not condemn Him, and that they [the Jews] did not take His blood upon themselves.'' Bor unfortunately did not live to hear the radio play of ''The Third Man'' produced by the BBC. He died in 1979 and was buried next to his second wife. There is a memorial at his grave site to his first wife and two children.

—Cynthia A. Klíma

See the essay on *The Terezín Requiem.*

BORGES, Jorge Luis

Nationality: Argentine. **Born:** Buenos Aires, 24 August 1899. **Education:** College Calvin, Geneva, Switzerland, 1914–18; also studied at Cambridge University, England, and in Buenos Aires. **Family:** Married 1) Elsa Astete Millán in 1967 (divorced 1970); 2) María Kodama in 1986. **Career:** Moved with his family to Geneva, Switzerland, 1914; lived in Spain with his family and associated with Andalusian poet Rafael Cansinos-Asséns and with a new literary circle, the Ultraists, 1919–21; returned to Buenos Aires with his family and associated with the poet Macedonio Fernandéz and his literary circle; cofounder, *Prisma* (Ultraist magazine); cofounder and editor, *Proa,* 1924–26, and *Sur,* 1931; columnist, *El Hogar* weekly, Buenos Aires, 1936–39; literary advisor, Emecé Editores, Buenos Aires; municipal librarian, Buenos Aires, 1937–46; state poultry inspector, 1946; teacher of English literature at several private institutions and lecturer in Argentina and Uruguay, 1946–55; director, National Library, Buenos Aires, 1955–73; professor of English and U.S. literature, University of Buenos

Aires, 1956–70. Norton professor of poetry, Harvard University, 1967–68; visiting lecturer, University of Texas, 1961–62, University of Oklahoma, 1969, University of New Hampshire, 1972, and Dickinson College, 1983. President, Argentine Writers Society, 1950–53. **Awards:** Buenos Aires municipal literary prize, 1928, for *El idioma de los argentinos;* Argentine Writers Society prize, 1945, for *Ficciones, 1935–1944;* National prize for literature, for *El Aleph;* International Congress of Publishers prize (shared with Samuel Beckett), 1961; Fondo de les Artes, 1963; Ingram Merrill Foundation award, 1966; Bienal Foundation Matarazzo Sobrinho Inter-American literary prize, 1970; Jerusalem prize, 1971; Alfonso Reyes prize (Mexico), 1973; Government of Chile Bernando O'Higgins prize, 1976; French Academy gold medal, 1979; Miguel de Cervantes award (Spain) and Balzan prize (Italy), both 1980; Ollin Yoliztli prize (Mexico), 1981; Ingersoll Foundation and Rockford Institute T.S. Eliot award for creative writing, 1983; Menendez Pelayo University gold medal (Spain), 1983; National Book Critics Circle award for criticism, 1999, for *Selected Non-Fictions.* Honorary degrees: University of Cuyo, Argentina, 1956; University of the Andes, Colombia, 1963; Oxford University, 1970; University of Jerusalem, 1971; Columbia University, 1971; Michigan State University, 1972; University of Chile, 1976; University of Cincinnati, 1976. Honorary Fellow, Modern Language Association (U.S.), 1961; Commandeur de l'Ordre des Lettres et des Arts (France), 1962; Order of Merit, Italy, 1968; Order of Merit, Federal Republic of Germany, 1979; Icelandic Falcon Cross, 1979; Honorary K.B.E. (Knight Commander, order of the British Empire). **Member:** Argentine National Academy; Uruguayan Academy of Letters. **Died:** 14 June 1986.

PUBLICATIONS

Collection

Obras completas, edited by José Edmundo Clemente (10 vols.). 1953–60; in one volume, 1974.

Short Stories

Historia univeral de la infamia. 1935; as *A Universal History of Infamy,* 1971.
El jardín de senderos que se bifurcan [Garden of the Forking Paths]. 1941.
Seis problemas para Isidro Parodi, with Adolfo Bioy Casares, 1942; as *Six Problems for Don Isidro Parodi,* 1983.
Ficciones, 1935–1944. 1944; revised edition, 1956; translated as *Ficciones,* 1962; as *Fictions,* 1965.
Dos fantasías memorables, with Casares, under joint pseudonym H. Bustos Domecq. 1946.
El aleph. 1949; as *The Aleph and Other Stories, 1933–1969,* 1970.
La muerte y la brújula. 1951.

La hermana de Eloísa [Eloisa's Sister], with Luisa Mercedes Levinson. 1955.
Labyrinths: Selected Stories and Other Writings, edited by Donald A. Yates and James E. Irby. 1962; revised edition, 1964.
Cronicas de Bustos Domecq, with Casares. 1967; as *Chronicles of Bustos Domecq,* 1979.
El informe de Brodie. 1970; as *Dr. Brodie's Report,* 1971.
El matrero. 1970.
El congreso. 1971; as *The Congress,* 1974; as *The Congress of the World,* 1981.
El libro de arena. 1975; as *The Book of Sand,* 1977.
Nuevos cuentos de Bustos Domecq, with Casares. 1977.

Novel

Un modelo para la muerte, with Adolfo Bioy Casares. 1946.

Poetry

Fervor de Buenos Aires [Passion for Buenos Aires]. 1923.
Luna de enfrente [Moon across the way]. 1925.
Cuaderno San Martín [San Martin Copybook]. 1929.
Poemas 1923–1943. 1943.
Poemas 1923–1958. 1958.
El hacedor. 1960; as *The Dreamtigers,* 1963.
Obra poética 1923–1964. 1964.
Para las seis cuerdas. 1965; revised edition, 1970.
Obra poética 1923–1967. 1967.
Nueva antología personal. 1968.
Obra poética (5 vols.). 1969–72.
Elogio de la sombra. 1969; as *In Praise of Darkness,* 1974.
El otro, el mismo. 1969.
El oro de los tigres. 1972; as *The Gold of the Tigers: Selected Later Poems,* 1979.
Selected Poems 1923–1967, edited by Norman Thomas di Giovanni. 1972.
La rosa profundo. 1975.
La moneda de hierro. 1976.
Historia de la noche. 1977.
Poemas 1919–1922. 1978.
Obra poética 1923–1976. 1978.
La cifra. 1981.
Antología poética. 1981.

Play

Screenplay: *Los orilleros; El paraíso de los creyentes,* with Adolfo Bioy Casares, 1955.

Other

Inquisiciones [Inquisitions] (essays). 1925.
El tamaño de mi esperanza [The Measure of My Hope] (essays). 1926.

El idioma de los argentinos [The Language of the Argentines] (essays). 1928; revised edition, as *El lenguaje de Buenos Aires,* with José Edmundo Clemente, 1963.

Figari (essays). 1930.

Discusión. 1932.

Las Kennigar (essays). 1933.

Historia de la eternidad [History of Eternity] (essays). 1936; revised edition, 1953.

Nueva refutación del tiempo [New Refutation of Time] (essays). 1947.

Aspectos de la literatura gauchesca (essays). 1950.

Antiguas literaturas germánicas, with Delia Ingenieros (essays). 1951; revised edition, with Maria Esther Vázquez, as *Literaturas germánicas medievales,* 1966.

Otras inquisiciones (essays). 1952; as *Other Inquisitions 1937–1952,* 1964.

El Martín Fierro, with Margarita Guerrero (essays). 1953.

Leopoldo Lugones, with Bettina Edelberg (essays). 1955.

Manual de zoología fantástica, with Guerrero (essays). 1957; revised edition, as *El libro de los seres imaginarios,* 1967; translated as *The Imaginary Zoo,* 1969; revised edition, as *The Book of Imaginary Beings,* 1969.

Antología personal. 1961; as *A Personal Anthology,* edited by Anthony Kerrigan, 1968.

The Spanish Language in South America: A Literary Problem; El Gaucho Martín Fierro (lectures). 1964.

Introducción a la literatura inglesa, with Vázquez. 1965; as *An Introduction to English Literature,* 1974.

Introducción a la literatura nortamericana, with Esther Zemborain de Torres. 1967; as *An Introduction to American Literature,* 1971.

Nueva antología personal. 1968.

Borges on Writing, edited by Norman Thomas di Giovanni, Daniel Halpern, and Frank MacShane. 1973.

Prólogos. 1975.

Qué es el budismo? [What Is Buddhism?], with Alicia Jurado. 1976.

Libros de sueños. 1976.

Adrogué. 1977.

Borges oral (lectures). 1979.

Prosa completa (2 vols.). 1980.

Siete noches (essays). 1980; as *Seven Nights,* 1984.

Nueve ensayos dantescos [New Dante Essays]. 1982.

Atlas, with María Komada. 1985; translated as *Atlas,* 1985.

Los conjurados. 1986.

Biblioteca personal: Prólogos. 1988.

Editor, with Pedro Henriques Urena, *Antología clasica de la literatura Argentina.* 1937.

Editor, with Silvina Ocampo and Adolfo Bioy Casares, *Antología de la literatura fantástica.* 1940; as *The Book of Fantasy,* 1988.

Editor, with Ocampo and Casares, *Antología poética Argentina.* 1941.

Editor, with Casares, *Los mejores cuentos policiales* (2 vols.). 1943–51.

Editor, with Silvina Bullrich Palenque, *El Campadrito: Su destino, sus barrios, su música.* 1945.

Editor, with Casares, *Prosa y verso,* by Francisco de Quevedo. 1948.

Editor and translator, with Casares, *Poesía gauchesca* (2 vols.). 1955.

Editor, with with Casares, *Cuentos breves y extraordinarios.* 1955; as *Extraordinary Tales,* 1971.

Editor, with Casares, *Libro del cielo y del infierno.* 1960.

Editor, *Paulino Lucero, Aniceto y gallo, Santos Vega,* by Hilario Ascasubi. 1960.

Editor, *Macedonia Fernández* (selection). 1961.

Editor, *Páginas de historia y de autobiografía,* by Edward Gibbon. 1961.

Editor, *Versos,* by Evaristo Carriego. 1963.

Editor, with María Komada, *Breve antología anglosanjona.* 1978.

Editor, *Micromegas,* by Voltaire. 1979.

Editor, *Cuentistas y pintores argentinos.* 1985.

Translator, *La metamorfosis,* by Kafka. 1938.

Translator, *Bartleby,* by Herman Melville. 1944.

Translator, *De los héroes; Hombres representativos,* by Carlyle and Emerson. 1949.

*

Bibliography: *Borges: An Annotated Primary and Secondary Bibliography* by David William Foster, 1984; *The Literary Universe of Borges: An Index to References and Illusions to Persons, Titles, and Places in His Writing* by Daniel Balderston, 1986.

Critical Studies: *Borges, The Labyrinth Maker* by Ana María Barrenchea, edited and translated by Robert Lima, 1965; *The Narrow Act: Borges' Art of Allusion* by Ronald J. Christ, 1969; *The Mythmaker: A Study of Motif and Symbol in the Short Stories of Borges* by Carter Wheelock, 1969; *Borges,* 1970, and *Borges Revisited,* 1991, both by Martin S. Stabb; *The Cardinal Points of Borges,* edited by Lowell Dunham and Ivor Ivask, 1971; *Borges* by J.M. Cohen, 1973; *Prose for Borges,* edited by Charles Newman and Mary Kinzie, 1974; *Tongues of Fallen Angels: Conversations with Borges* by Selden Roman, 1974; *Borges: Ficciones* by Donald Leslie Shaw, 1976; *Paper Tigers: The Ideal Fictions of Borges* by John Sturrock, 1977; *Borges: Sources and Illumination* by Giovanna De Garayalde, 1978; *Borges: A Literary Biography* by Emir Rodríguez Monegal, 1978; *Borges* by George R. McMurray, 1980; *Borges and His Fiction: A Guide to His Mind and Art* by Gene H. Bell-Villada, 1981, revised edition, 1999; *Borges at Eighty: Conversations,* edited by William Barnstone, 1982; *The Prose of Borges: Existentialism and the Dynamics of Surprise,* 1984, and *The Meaning of Experience in the Prose of Borges,* 1988, both by Ion Tudro Agheana; *Borges,* edited by Harold Bloom,

1986; *The Poetry and the Poetics of Borges* by Paul Cheselka, 1987; *The Emperor's Kites: A Morphology of Borges's Tales* by Mary Lusky Friedman, 1987; *Critical Essays on Borges*, edited by Jaime Alazraki, 1987; *Borges and the Kaballah* by Jaime Alazraki, 1988; *In Memory of Borges,* edited by Norman Thomas di Giovanni, 1988; *Borges and His Successors: The Borges Impact on Literature and the Arts,* edited by Edna Aizenberg, 1990; *Borges: A Study of the Short Fiction* by Naomi Lindstrom, 1990; *A Dictionary of Borges* by Evelyn Fishburne, 1990; *Jorge Luis Borges: A Writer on the Edge* by Beatriz Sarlo Sabajanes, 1993; *Readers and Labyrinths: Detective Fiction in Borges, Bustos Domeq, and Eco* by Jorge Hernández Martín, 1995; *The Man in the Mirror of the Book: A Life of Jorge Borges* by James Woodall, 1996; *Nightglow: Borges' Poetics of Blindness* by Florence L. Yudin, 1997; *The Secret of Borges: A Psychoanalytic Inquiry into His Work* by Julio Woscoboinik, translated by Dora Carlisky Pozzi, 1998; *Humor in Borges* by René de Costa, 2000.

* * *

Over the course of the years literary and cultural critics have warned about politicizing Jorge Luis Borges's oeuvre. It has been suggested time after time that Borges's fiction is both apolitical and ahistorical. Those who defend this position have suggested that Borges was never interested in local color but rather universal topics. Others have accused him of withdrawing from the reality of his country and the rest of the world and hiding in a world of fantasy, dreams, and intellectual games. A closer look at Borges's life and work will show a lesser known aspect of the writer's political views and his strong commitment and determination to fight injustice and oppression both in his native Argentina and abroad.

Born in Buenos Aires in 1899, a descendant of patrician Argentines and English immigrants, Borges was raised in a bilingual home. In fact, his very language was English. From early on his father inculcated in him a passion for reading and philosophy. Georgie—as he was known to his family and close friends—was intrigued early on by texts like the Hebrew Bible and the writings of Baruch Spinoza. In 1914 Borges traveled with his family to Europe for the first time and was caught in the middle of World War I. At school in Switzerland he befriended two Jewish boys with whom he shared typical adolescent experiences and a wide array of literary readings. During that time Borges became interested in the German language and read Heinrich Heine's *Lyrisches Intermezzo*. It is through the German language that the young Borges became interested in everything Jewish. The simplicity of the lexicon in Heine's text allowed the young Borges to become quite familiar with the language and opened up to him the world of German literature and Jewish culture. It was his reading of the German best-seller of the time, Gustav Meyrink's *The Golem* (1915), that augmented Borges's fascination with Jewish mysticism and the cabala. Borges's fascination with Jewish thought led him to explore the writings of Martin Buber, Fritz Mauthner, Franz Kafka, and Max Brod, among others.

Back in Argentina after a relatively brief stay in Spain, Borges became a part of the leading intellectual circles in Buenos Aires. He befriended several distinguished Argentine Jewish writers, including Alberto Gerchunoff, Cesar Tiempo, and Carlos Grunberg, and printed some of his works in Manuel Gleizer's press. (Gleizer was one of the first Jewish publishers in the country.) Borges's permanent contact with Argentina's largely cosmopolitan Jewish community thus became apparent in both his poetry and his fiction.

In 1934 the journal *Crisol,* a right-wing periodical, published an offensive and highly anti-Semitic diatribe accusing Borges of "hiding" his Jewish identity and trying to "cover-up" his Jewish past. This prompted Borges to reply with an article of his own that was published in *El Hogar,* a magazine for which he was the editor of a literary section. He entitled the piece "Yo, judío" ("I, the Jew"). In it Borges "thanked" the magazine for considering him to be a member of such a privileged group and toyed with the possibility that his mother's family may have indeed descended from *conversos*. If up until that time Borges had been driven to write on Jewish topics by positive ideals, in the years that followed his interests in Jewish culture were to be fueled by the ever-increasing waves of anti-Semitism, the rise of Nazism, and, ultimately, the Holocaust.

During World War II Borges wrote several passionate articles against the Nazi regime, which he saw as a threat not only to Germany but to all Western civilization. In the 1940s he wrote two short stories in which he explicitly condemned Germany's expansionist objectives and its Nazi ideology. In "The Secret Miracle" (*Ficciones,* 1944) and "Deutsches Requiem" (*El aleph,* 1949) Borges probes the limits of representation and brings to the surface fundamental issues for the understanding of the Holocaust.

—Alejandro Meter

See the essays on "Deutsches Requiem" and "The Secret Miracle."

BOROWSKI, Tadeusz

Nationality: Polish. **Born:** Żytomierz, Ukraine, 12 November 1922; lived in Warsaw after 1932. **Education:** Taught by Franciscan monks; Warsaw University. **Career:** Worked as a night watchman; worked as a hospital orderly while imprisoned in Auschwitz and Dachau, 1943–45; political journalist, Warsaw, 1946–51. **Died:** Suicide, July 1951.

PUBLICATIONS

Collection

Utwory zebrane [Collected Works] (5 vols.). 1954.

Memoir

Byliśmy w Oświęcimiu, with Janusz Nel Siedlecki and Krystyn Olszewski. 1946; as *We Were in Auschwitz,* 2000.

Short Stories

Kamienny swiat [World of Stone]. 1948.
Pożegnanie z Marią [Farewell to Maria]. 1949.
Opowiadania z ksiazek i z gazet. 1949.
Czerwony maj. 1953.
Wybór opowiadaŃ. 1959.
This Way for the Gas, Ladies and Gentlemen, and Other Stories (selections from *Kamienny swiat* and *Pożegnanie z Marią*). 1967.
Opowiadania wybrane. 1971.
DzieŃ na Harmenzach. 1978.

Poetry

Gdziekolwiek ziemia [Wherever the Earth]. 1942.
Imiona nurtu [The Names of the Current]. 1945.
Poszukiwania [Tracing], with Krystyn Olszewski. 1945.
Poezje wybrane. 1971.
Poezje. 1972.
Selected Poems. 1990.

Other

Pewien zolnierz. 1947.
Na przedpolu; artykuly i reportae (political science). 1952.
Proza z lat 1948–1952. 1954.
Wiersze. 1968.
Wspomnienia, wiersze, opowiadania (reminiscences, verse, and stories). 1977.
Rozmowa z przyjacielem: Wiersze, with Tadeusz Drewnowski (correspondence). 1999.

*

Film Adaptations: *Landscape after a Battle,* from the short story, ''Bitwa pod Grunwaldem.''

Critical Studies: ''A Discovery of Tragedy (The Incomplete Account of Tadeusz Borowski)'' by Andrzej Wirth, in *Polish Review,* 12(3), 1967, pp. 43–52; ''Tadeusz Borowski: A European Education'' by Jan Kott, in *The Theatre of Essence and Other Essays,* 1984; ''When the Earth Is No Longer a Dream and Cannot be Dreamed through to the End'' by Jan Walc, in *Polish Review,* 32(2), 1987, pp. 181–94; ''Beyond Self: A Lesson from the Concentration Camps'' by Piotr Kuhiwczak, in *Canadian Review of Comparative Literature/ Revue Canadienne de Litterature Comparee,* 19(3), September 1992, pp. 395–405; ''Images of the Jew Focused on in the Translated Polish Works of Tadeusz Borowski, Jerzy Andrzejewski, and Czeslaw Milosz'' by Harriet L. Parmet, in *Shofar,* 18(3), Spring 2000, pp. 13–26; *Suffering Witness: The Quandary of Responsibility after the Irreparable* by James Hatley, 2000.

* * *

At 20 Tadeusz Borowski became a prisoner at Auschwitz; he wrote his best stories before he was 23. Liberated from the Dachau-Allach camp, he returned to Poland, and within several years he published his collections of stories, *Farewell to Maria* and *The World of Stone*, as well as two social-realist works and a number of articles. His writing was deeply controversial. The values of his literary world were noticed, but he suffered merciless attacks—first from Catholic circles and later from Communist ones. The former accused him of amorality and nihilism, the latter of writing pessimistic stories that did not fit with the obligatory optimism of Stalinism.

Borowski's writing was shocking for literary critics and readers not prepared to accept the cruel truth of Auschwitz. He revealed a world where nobody was innocent. In the camp the price for one's survival was the life of a fellow prisoner. Auschwitz is shown as a profit-bringing enterprise, with no mention of heroism or religious faith. The prisoners are cunning people who trade and make deals.

Long before Hannah Arendt Borowski spoke of the triviality of evil. He did not demonize the Germans; he portrayed them as officials rather than butchers. He showed people enslaved by starvation and the looming presence of death, reduced to being objects or beasts of burden. A young Auschwitz prisoner points to the destructive power of hope, which helped to lead people to gas chambers.

This world is described by Tadek, a narrator who closely resembles Borowski. Tadek belongs to a group of privileged prisoners who are not hungry and are well acquainted with the rules of the survival ''game.'' In Auschwitz he sees the essence of European civilization in which there were always lords and slaves.

This picture of Auschwitz evoked objections. Reality and artistic creation were often mistaken, and Borowski was accused of immoral behavior in the camp. Certainly the camp experience determined his vision, and none of his stories on other subjects attained an artistic level equal to those in which he showed what the camp really was. For Borowski the camp was a model of a totalitarian society, a direct consequence of

Nazism and a product of European civilization. Thus, the camp civilization became the most essential issue.

Borowski focused on the camp phenomenon three times. In 1946 he published *We Were in Auschwitz* with **Janusz Nel-Siedlecki** and **Krystyn Olszewski.** After his return to Poland he published a collection of stories that included ''A Day at Harmenz'' and ''This Way for the Gas, Ladies and Gentlemen.'' He added three new stories: ''Farewell to Maria,'' ''The Death of an Insurgent,'' and ''The Battle of Tannenberg,'' all with a common narrator. The first tells about the time preceding his arrest, the second about the Dachau-Allach camp, and the third about the period after the liberation. The judgement criterion is the camp. The pre-Auschwitz and post-Auschwitz worlds are described in the same terms.

Borowski resumed the issue of the camp in 1948 in *The World of Stone*, his defense against the attacks of Catholic and Marxist critics. Although Borowski referred to camp life, the thematic range of the stories is wider, and he exposed and condemned evil also in the post-war reality. He adopted a different form of writing, using utmost condensation of images that pertain to single motifs or events. The stories, however, do not make a uniform whole, and the evil described is not equal. Sometimes its manifestations are negligible, evoking accusations of all-present pessimism and nihilism.

Borowski's writing concerning the camp belongs to classical works of this genre, and there are many splendid critical works on it (by **Czeslaw Milosz,** Tadeusz Drewnowski, Andrzej Werner, and Zygmunt Ziatek), yet it still evokes diverse opinions and arguments. That Borowski joined the Communist Party and sided in his writing with the new totalitarian ideology is variously perceived. The opinions concerning the artistic values of his prose related to the camp are divergent. Questions arise concerning the status and the psychological portrait of the narrator, the distance between narrator and writer, the reporting or the parabolic construction of the stories, and the author's involvement in the evaluation of the presented world. It seems that to some extent all opinions are legitimate, while the discrepancies between them result from the attempt to find a common denominator for several stories, while in fact in each of them a separate literary strategy is employed.

An important issue was raised by **Henryk Grynberg** in ''*Holocaust w literaturze polskiej*'' in *Prawda nieartystyczna* (1984), who accused Borowski of universalizing the Shoah theme. By seeking reference to Auschwitz in ancient civilization or in the medieval visions of doomsday Borowski describes a concentration camp, not an extermination camp, which is beyond comparison.

Nevertheless, despite the universalization of the Auschwitz experience, Borowski's writing is a Holocaust testimony in which the difference between the fate of the Aryans and of the Jews is clearly marked. ''Auschwitz, Our Home'' is an attempt to re-create the writer's letters to his fiancée, Maria Rundo.

The narrator is a student, a humanist who has just come to Auschwitz, which he treats as an intellectual challenge and seeks a proper form of describing it. He writes letters to console his girlfriend; they seem to be a continuation of conversations from before their arrest. The next stories, which are directly concerned with the Holocaust, are ''The People Who Walked On'' and ''This Way for the Gas, Ladies and Gentlemen.'' They deal with extermination and record the changes in the author's psyche. The first is a testimony of intellectual helplessness in the face of the extermination of hundreds of thousands of Hungarian Jews. Here we can read his famous sentence that is a harbinger of his laconic, cold, and precise manner: ''Between two throw-ins in a soccer game, right behind my back, three thousand people had been put to death.'' It is the ''Canada'' perspective and the perspective of the Sonderkomando in Auschwitz-Birkenau that allows the Auschwitz I camp to be called ''our home'', since at the threshold of a gas chamber there is no difference between it and the normal world.

—Kazimierz Adamczyk

See the essays on *This Way for the Gas, Ladies and Gentlemen* and *We Were in Auschwitz.*

(FRIEDRICH) BRECHT, (Eugen) Bertolt

Nationality: German. **Born:** Eugen Berthold Friedrich Brecht, Augsburg, 10 February 1898. **Education:** Studied medicine at the University of Munich, 1917–21. **Family:** Married 1) Marianne Zoff in 1922 (divorced 1927), one daughter; 2) Helene Weigel in 1929, one son and one daughter; one son with Paula Banholzer. **Career:** Worked as an orderly in an Augsburg hospital, 1918; dramaturg, Munich Kammerspiele, 1923–24, Deutsches Theater, Berlin, 1924–33; went into exile in Denmark, 1933–39, Sweden, 1939–41, the United States, 1941–47, and Switzerland, 1947–48; lived in East Berlin beginning 1949. Editor, with Lion Feuchtwanger and Willi Bredel, *Das Wort*, 1936–39; founder, with Helene Weigel, Berliner Ensemble, 1949. **Awards:** Kleist prize, 1922; first prize, *Berliner Illustrierte Zeitung*, 1928, for short story ''Die Bestie''; Stalin peace prize, 1954. **Died:** 14 August 1956.

PUBLICATIONS

Collections

Versuche (15 vols.). 1930–57.
Gesammelte Werke (2 vols.). 1938.

Stücke [Plays] (14 vols.). 1960.

Schriften zum Theater [Writings on Theatre] (7 vols.). 1963.

Gedichte [Poems] (9 vols.). 1964.

Prosa [Narrative Prose] (5 vols.). 1965.

Schriften zur Literatur und Kunst [Writings on Literature and Art] (3 vols.). 1966.

Schriften zur Politik und Gesellschaft [Writings on Politics and Society] (1 vol.). 1967.

Bertolt Brecht, Gesammelte Werke, edited by Elisabeth Hauptmann (9 vols.). 1967; First three vols. translated as *Collected Plays,* edited by John Willett and Ralph Manheim, 1971; vol. 4 translated as *Poems 1913–1956,* 1976; vol. 5 translated as *Short Stories 1921–1946,* 1983.

Plays

Warren Hastings, Gouverneur von Indien: Schauspiel in vier Akten und einem Vorspiel, with Lion Feuchtwanger. 1916; as *Kalkutta, 4. Mai: Drei Akte Kolonialgeschichte,* 1925; translated as *Warren Hastings,* in *Two Anglo-Saxon Plays,* 1928.

Trommeln in der Nacht (produced Munich, 1922). 1922; revised version, in *Stücke 1,* 1955; translated as *Drums in the Night,* and published in *Jungle of Cities and Other Plays,* 1966.

Baal (produced Leipzig, 1923). 1922; revised version produced Berlin, 1926, published in *Stücke 1,* 1955; translated and published in *Baal; A Man's a Man; The Elephant Calf,* 1964.

Im Dickicht der Städte (produced Munich, 1923); revised version (produced Darmstadt, 1927). 1927; translated as *In the Jungle of Cities,* in *Seven Plays,* 1961.

Pastor Ephraim Magnus, with Arnolt Bronnen, adaptation of the work by Hans Henry Jahn (produced 1923).

Leben Eduards des Zweiten von England, with Lion Feuchtwanger, adaptation of *Edward II* by Christopher Marlowe (produced Munich, 1924). 1924; translated as *Edward II,* 1966.

Die Hochzeit (produced Frankfurt, 1926). As *Die Kleinbürgerhochzeit,* in *Stücke 13,* 1966; translated as *A Respectable Wedding,* in *Collected Plays 1,* 1970.

Mann ist Mann, with others (produced Darmstadt, 1926); revised version (produced Berlin, 1931). 1927; revised version, in *Stücke 2,* 1957; translated as *Man Equals Man,* in *Seven Plays,* 1961; as *A Man's a Man,* in *Baal; A Man's a Man; The Elephant Calf,* 1964.

Das Elefantkalb. Published with *Mann ist Mann,* 1927; translated as *The Elephant Calf,* in *Wake,* Autumn 1949; (in book form) in *Baal; A Man's a Man; The Elephant Calf,* 1964.

Die Dreigroschenoper, adaptation of *Beggar's Opera* by John Gay (opera libretto), music by Kurt Weill (produced Berlin, 1928). 1929; translated as *The Threepenny Opera,* in *From the Modern Repertoire,* edited by Eric Bentley, 1949.

Happy End, with Elizabeth Hauptmann (produced Berlin, 1929), music by Kurt Weill. Translated as *Happy End,* 1982.

Lindberghflug, with Elizabeth Hauptmann (produced Baden-Baden, 1929), music by Kurt Weill. 1929; retitled *Der Ozeanflug.*

Aufstieg und Fall der Stadt Mahagonny (opera libretto), music by Kurt Weill (produced Leipzig, 1930). Translated as *The Rise and Fall of the City of Mahagonny,* 1976.

Das Badener Lehrstück vom Einverständnis (opera libretto), music by Paul Hindemith (produced Baden-Baden, 1929). In *Versuche 2,* 1930; translated in *Harvard Advocate,* 134(4), February 1951.

Der Jasager, adaptation of Arthur Waley's translation of the Japanese play *Taniko* (opera libretto), music by Kurt Weill (produced Berlin, 1930). In *Versuche 4,* 1931; translated in *Accent,* 7(2), 1946; (in book form) as *He Who Said Yes; He Who Said No,* in *The Measures Taken and Other Lehrstücke,* 1977.

Die Massnahme (opera libretto), music by Hanns Eisler (produced Berlin, 1930). In *Versuche 4,* 1931; translated as *The Measures Taken,* in *Colorado Review,* 1(1), Winter 1956–57; (in book form) in *The Measures Taken and Other Lehrstücke,* 1977.

Die heilige Johanna der Schlachthöfe (opera libretto), music by Paul Dessau (produced Hamburg, 1959). In *Versuche 5,* 1932; translated as *St. Joan of the Stockyards,* in *From the Modern Repertoire,* edited by Eric Bentley, 1949.

Die Mutter, adaptation of the novel by Maxim Gorky (opera libretto), music by Hanns Eisler (produced Berlin, 1932). In *Versuche 7,* 1932; revised version in *Gesammelte Werke 2,* 1938; translated as *The Mother,* 1965.

Die sieben Todsünden der Kleinbürger (opera libretto), music by Kurt Weill (produced Champs-Élysées, France, 1933). 1959; translated as *The Seven Deadly Sins of the Petty Bourgeoisie,* in *Tulane Drama Review,* 6(1), 1961.

Die Rundköpfe und die Spitzköpfe (opera libretto), music by Hanns Eisler (produced Copenhagen, 1934). In *Gesammelte Werke 2,* 1938; translated in *International Literature* (Moscow), 5, 1937; (in book form) as *Roundheads and Peakheads,* in *Jungle of Cities and Other Plays,* 1966.

Die Gewehre der Frau Carrar (produced Paris, 1937). In *Gesammelte Werke 2,* 1938; translated in *Theatre Workshop,* April–June, 1938; (in book form) as *The Guns of Carrar,* 1971; as *Señora Carrar's Rifles,* in *Collected Plays 4, iii,* 1983.

Furcht und Elend des Dritten Reiches (produced Paris, 1938). As *Deutschland: Ein Greuelmärchen* (13-scene version), 1941, 1944 (24-scene version); translated as *Fear and Misery in the Third Reich* (12-scene version), 1944; as *The*

Private Life of the Master Race (17-scene version), 1944; as *Fear and Misery of the Third Reich* (24-scene version), in *Collected Plays 4, iii*, 1983.

Die Ausnahme und die Regel (produced Palestine, 1938). In *Gesammelte Werke 2*, 1938; translated as *The Exception and the Rule*, in *Chrysalis*, 11–12, 1954; (in book form) in *The Jewish Wife and Other Short Plays*, 1965.

Die Horatier und die Kuratier (produced 1958). In *Gesammelte Werke 2*, 1938; translated as *The Horatians and the Curatians*, in *Accent*, 7(1), Autumn 1947.

Mutter Courage und ihre Kinder (produced Zurich, 1941; revised version, Berlin, 1949). In *Versuche 9*, 1949; revised edition, 1950; translated as *Mother Courage and Her Children*, 1941.

Der gute Mensch von Setzuan (produced Zurich, 1943). In *Versuche 12*, 1953; revised edition, 1958; translated as *The Good Woman of Setzuan*, in *Parables for the Theatre*, 1948; as *The Good Person of Setzuan*, in *Plays 2*, 1962.

Leben des Galilei, with Charles Laughton (produced Los Angeles, 1947). In *From the Modern Repertoire, Series 2*, edited by Eric Bentley, 1953; as *Life of Galileo*, in *Collected Plays 5, i*, 1980.

Der kaukasische Kreidekreis (produced Northfield, Minnesota, 1948). In *Two Parables for the Theatre*, 1948.

Herr Puntila und sein Knecht Matti (produced Zurich, 1948). In Finnish translation, 1946; in *Versuche 10*, 1950; translated as *Mr. Puntila and His Man Matti*, in *Collected Plays 6, iii*, 1977.

Die Antigone des Sophokles, adaptation of Hölderlin's translation of Sophocles' play (produced Chur, Switzerland, 1948). As *Antigonemodell*, 1949; revised edition, 1955; translated as *Antigone*, 1989.

Der Hofmeister, adaptation of the play by J. M. R. Lenz (produced Berlin, 1950). In *Versuche 11*, 1951; translated as *The Tutor*, in *Collected Plays 9*, 1973.

Herrnburger Bericht (opera libretto), music by Paul Dessau (produced Berlin, 1951). 1951.

Das Verhör des Lukullus, adaptation of his own radio play (opera libretto), music by Paul Dessau (produced Berlin, 1951), subsequently retitled *Die Verurteilung des Lukullus*. 1951.

Der Prozess der Jeanne d'Arc zu Rouen 1431, adaptation of his own radio play (produced Berlin, 1952). In *Stücke 12*, 1959; translated as *The Trial of Joan of Arc*, in *Collected Plays 9*, 1973.

Don Juan, adaptation of a work by Molière (produced Berlin, 1953). In *Stücke 12*, 1959; translated as *Don Juan*, in *Collected Plays 9*, 1973.

Der Gesichte des Simone Machard, with Lion Feuchtwanger (produced Frankfurt, 1957). In *Sinn und Form*, 5–6, 1956; (in book form) in *Stücke 9*, 1957; translated as *The Visions of Simone Machard*, 1965.

Die Tage des Kommune (opera libretto), music by Hanns Eisler (produced East Germany, 1956). In *Versuche 15* and *Stücke 10*, both 1957; translated as *The Days of the Commune*, in *Dunster Drama Review*, 10(2), 1971; (in book form) 1978.

Pauken und Trompeten, adaptation of a play by Farquhar (produced 1956). In *Stücke 12*, 1959; translated as *Trumpets and Drums*, in *Collected Plays 9*, 1973.

Der aufhaltsame Aufstieg des Arturo Ui (produced Stuttgart, 1958). In *Sinn und Form: Zweites Sonderheft Bertolt Brecht*, 1957; (in book form) in *Stücke 9*, 1957; translated as *The Resistible Rise of Arturo Ui*, in *Collected Plays 6, ii*, 1976.

Schweyk im zweiten Weltkrieg (opera libretto), music by Hanns Eisler (produced Warsaw, 1957). In *Stücke 10*, 1957; translated as *Schweyk in the Second World War*, in *Collected Plays 7*, 1976.

Coriolan, adaptation of a play by William Shakespeare (produced Frankfurt, 1962). In *Stücke 11*, 1959; translated as *Coriolanus*, in *Collected Plays 9*, 1973.

Der Bettler oder der tote Hund. In *Stücke 13*, 1966; translated as *The Beggar or the Dead Dog*, in *Collected Plays 1*, 1970.

Er treibt den Teufel aus. In *Stücke 13*, 1966; translated as *Driving Out a Devil*, in *Collected Plays 1*, 1970.

Lux in Tenebris. In *Stücke 13*, 1966; translated as *Lux in Tenebris*, in *Collected Plays 1*, 1970.

Der Fischzug. In *Stücke 13*, 1966; translated as *The Catch*, in *Collected Plays 1*, 1970.

Was kostet das Eisen (produced Stockholm, 1939). In *Stücke 13*, 1966.

Dansen. In *Stücke 13*, 1966.

Turandot; oder, Der Kongress der Weisswäscher (opera libretto), music by Hanns Eisler. 1967.

Radio Plays: *Berliner Requiem*, 1929; *Die heilige Johanna der Schlachthöfe*, 1932.

Poetry

Taschenpostille: Mit Anleitung, Gesangsnoten und einem Anhang. 1926.

Hauspostille: Mit Anleitung, Gesangsnoten und einem Anhang. 1927; as *Manual of Piety: A Bilingual Edition*, 1966.

Lieder, Gedichte, Chöre, music by Hanns Eisler. 1934.

Svendborger Gedichte; Deutsche Kriegsfibel; Chroniken: Deutsche Satiren für den deutschen Freiheitssender. 1939.

Selected Poems. 1947.

Hundert Gedichte, 1918–1950. 1951.

Buckower Elegien [Buckow Elegies]. 1953.

Gedichte. 1955.

Gedichte und Lieder. 1956.

Selected Poems. 1959.

Ausgewählte Gedichte. 1960.

Poems on the Theatre. 1961.
Selected Poems. 1965.
Liebesgedichte. 1966.
Gedichte für Städtebewohner. 1980.
Gedichte aus dem Nachlass, 1913–1956. 1982.

Novel

Dreigroschenroman. 1934; as *A Penny for the Poor,* 1937; as
    Threepenny Novel, 1956.

Other

Kalendergeschichten. 1948; as *Tales from the Calendar,* 1961.
Offener Brief an die deutschen Künstler und Schriftsteller.
    1951.
*Die Erziehung der Hirse, Nach dem Bericht von G. Frisch:
    Der Mann, der das Unmögliche wahr gemacht hat.* 1951.
An meine Landsleute. 1951.
Kriegsfibel. 1955.
Lieder und Gesänge. 1957.
Die Geschäfte des Herrn Julius Caesar: Romanfragment.
    1957.
Geschichten vom Herrn Keuner. 1958.
Brecht: Ein Lesebuch für unsere Zeit, edited by Elizabeth
    Hauptmann and Benno Slupianek. 1958.
Bertolt Brecht in Selbstzeugnissen und Bilddokumenten, ed-
    ited by Paul Raabe. 1959.
*Kleines Organon für das Theater: Mit einem "Nachtrag zum
    Kleinen Organon."* 1960; as "A Short Organum for the
    Theatre" in *Brecht on Theatre,* 1964.
Flüchtlingsgespräche. 1961.
Helene Weigel, Actress: A Book of Photographs (translation).
    1961.
Gespräch auf der Probe. 1961.
Dialoge aus dem Messingkauf. 1964.
Über Lyrik. 1964.
Ein Kinderbuch (for children). 1965.
Me-ti; Buch der Wendungen-Fragment. 1965.
Über Klassiker. 1965.
Über Theater. 1966.
Kühle Wampe: Protokoll des Films und Materialien. 1969.
Politische Schriften. 1970.
Über den Beruf des Schauspielers. 1970.
Über experimentelles Theater. 1970.
Brecht Fibel. 1970.
Herr Bertolt Brecht sagt. 1970.
*Über die irdische Liebe und andere gewisse Welträtsel in
    Liedern und Balladen.* 1971.
Über Politik auf dem Theater. 1971.
Über Politik und Kunst. 1971.
Über Realismus. 1971.

Arbeitsjournal 1938 bis 1955 (3 vols.). 1973.
Der Tui-Roman: Fragment. 1973.
*Tagebücher 1920–1922: Autobiographische Aufzeichnungen
    1920–1954.* 1975; as *Diaries 1920–1922,* 1979.
Brecht in Gespräch. 1975.
*Und der Haifisch, der hat Zähne: Die grossen Songs und
    Kleinen Lieder.* 1977.
Ein gemeiner Kerl: Geschichten. 1978.
Der Städtebauer: Geschichten und Anekdoten 1919–1956.
    1978.
Nordseekrabben. 1979.
Briefe. 1981; as *Brecht Letters,* 1989.
Ich leb so gern. 1982.
Über die bildenden Künste. 1983.
Brecht-Journal. 1983.
Fragen an Brecht. 1987.
Bertolt Brecht Journals. 1993.
Bad Time for Poetry: 152 Poems and Songs. 1995.

*

Film Adaptation: *Die Dreigroschenoper,* 1931.

Bibliography: *Brecht-Bibliographie* by Gerhard Nellhaus, in
first Bertolt Brecht issue of *Sinn und Form* (East Germany),
1949; *Bertolt Brecht-Bibliographie* by Walter Nubel, in second Bertolt Brecht issue of *Sinn und Form,* 1957; *Bertolt-
Brecht-Bibliographie* by Klaus-Dietrich Petersen, 1968; "A
Selected Brecht Bibliography" by Darko Suvin, Max Spalter,
and Richard Schotter, in *The Drama Review,* 12(2), 1968, pp.
156–69; *Bibliographie Bertolt Brecht* by Gerhard Seidel and
Gisela Kuntze, 1975; *Twentieth-Century Theatre: Bertolt
Brecht: Annotated Bibliography* by Mark Russell, 2000.

Critical Studies: *The Theatre of Bertolt Brecht* by John
Willett, 1959; *Brecht: A Choice of Evils,* 1959, revised as
Brecht: The Man and His Work, 1971, and *Bertolt Brecht,*
1969, both by Martin Esslin; *Brecht; A Collection of Critical
Essays,* edited by Peter Demetz, 1962; *The Art of Bertolt
Brecht* by Walter Weideli, translated by Daniel Russell, 1963;
Bertolt Brecht: His Life, His Art and His Times by Frederic
Ewen, 1967; *Brecht's Tradition* by Max Spalter, 1967; *Bertolt
Brecht; The Despair and the Polemic* by Charles R. Lyons,
1968; *The Case against Bertolt Brecht, with Arguments Drawn
from His Life of Galileo* by Gerhard Szczesny, translated by
Alexander Gode, 1969; *Theatre of War; Comments on 32
Occassions,* 1972, *The Brecht Commentaries, 1943–1980,*
1981, and *The Brecht Memoir,* 1985, all by Eric Bentley;
Essays on Brecht: Theater and Politics, edited by Siegfried
Mews and Herbert Knust, 1974; *Bertolt Brecht* by Claude Hill,
1975; *Brecht, A Biography* by Klaus Völker, translated by
John Nowell, 1978; *Towards Utopia: A Study of Brecht* by
Keith A. Dickson, 1978; *Bertolt Brecht in America* by James
K. Lyon, 1980; *Brecht in Perspective,* edited by Graham

Bartram and Anthony Waine, 1982; *Brecht in Exile* by Bruce Cook, 1983; *Brecht in Context: Comparative Approaches* by John Willett, 1984; *Critical Essays on Bertolt Brecht,* 1989, and *A Bertolt Brecht Reference Companion,* 1997; both edited by Siegfried Mews; *The Cambridge Companion to Brecht* by Peter Thomson and Glendyr Sacks, 1994; *Brecht for Beginners* by Michael Thoss, 1994; *Brecht and Company: Sex, Politics, and the Making of the Modern Drama* by John, Fuegi, 1994; Giles, *Bertolt Brecht: Centenary Essays* edited by Steve and Rodney Livingstone, 1998.

Theatrical Activities: Director: several of his own plays.

* * *

Neither the gradual exclusion of the Jews from the German polity in the 1930s nor the Holocaust play a significant part in Bertolt Brecht's opus. One of the rare comments on the subject appears in a 1942 journal entry and focuses on the psychological function of racist ideology: "Nor is anti-semitism something that makes no sense, even if it is abominable. The nation was dealing with a spectre there. The bourgeoisie, which had never achieved power, thereby created a feeling of nationhood." Brecht's analysis of national Socialism derives primarily from a Marxist position. In his view the fascist dictatorship did not constitute a historical aberration but rather a "consistent" stage of late capitalism, logical in its brutality and its imperialist aggression. The notion that anti-Semitism was merely a symptom of the bourgeoisie's self-delusional weakness, limited to that particular class, as the above statement seems to imply, and, therefore, on a certain level, a given, may have drawn Brecht away from a direct confrontation with the Nazi program of genocide. While he devoted much of his career to exposing the horrors of fascism, both its victims and the heroic resistance fighters in his works tend to be marked by their class status. As a result his treatment of Nazism fell in line with one of the foundational myths of the German Democratic Republic, which pronounced itself "the winner of history" and the true home of the anti-fascist, Communist exiles. Although Brecht chose to settle in East Berlin after the war, his relationship with the Stalinist regime of the GDR until his death in 1956 was far from harmonious.

In the mid-1920s Brecht moved from Bavaria to Berlin, the mecca of German theater. He began to study the writings of Karl Marx and set out to formulate a sharp critique of contemporaneous theatrical practice. The centerpiece of his theory of the epic theater, the *Verfremdungseffekt* ("alienation effect"), is both a formal device and a philosophical principle designed to disrupt a "culinary" or empathetic reception of the action presented on the stage. Brecht intended to raise the spectators' level of critical-social consciousness and to enable them see the all-too-familiar world in an estranging manner. In 1931 Brecht and the composer Kurt Weill landed a spectacular and enigmatic hit with *The Threepenny Opera*, depicting bourgeois society as a criminal organization. Reflective of a growing commitment to communism and to revolutionary activism, Brecht wrote the *Lehrstück* ("play for learning") *The Measures Taken* with a new collaborator, Hanns Eisler. Because the play provided a coldly rational lesson in how to subordinate emotion to party discipline, it later became a matter of inquiry for the House Committee on Un-American Activities.

On 28 February 1933, a day after the Reichstag fire, Brecht and his family fled Germany. Throughout the many hardships of exile in Denmark, Sweden, Finland, and the United States, he tirelessly attacked the "house-painter" Hitler, whom he begrudgingly recognized as a "cunning" and "original" politician. Aside from his Marxist critique Brecht showed a keen interest in the ideological facade of Nazism and in the regime's ability to mobilize the masses through propaganda and theatrical spectacle. The parable play *Roundheads and Pointed Heads* (1934) suggests that the capitalists allowed the Nazis to foment anti-Semitism merely as a diversionary tactic obscuring the fact that the real social divisions were between the exploiters and the exploited. *Señora Carrar's Rifles* (1937) is set in Spain at the time of the Civil War and depicts the exemplary decision of a simple woman to take up arms and join the resistance against General Franco. The motivation for doing so, however, is personal revenge, not a political commitment. In *Fear and Misery of the Third Reich* (1938) Brecht brings out a sense of the futility of action and of the pervasive distrust of others in the experience of ordinary people. In a scene entitled "The Jewish Wife" a woman's insightful critique of the regime remains a private matter. Having decided to emigrate, she anxiously informs her friends and her self-deceiving husband that she is going away "for a time."

Brecht never criticized Joseph Stalin publicly, but his decision not to move from Finland to the nearby Soviet Union may have been motivated by the differences between the epic theater and the doctrine of social realism, which demanded a strictly mimetic representation of reality and an optimistic message. After his arrival in California in July 1941 Brecht revisited an older project, *Schweyk in the Second World War,* and turned it into an anti-fascist vehicle. Set in occupied Prague and on the Russian front, the play ridicules Hitler and other Nazi leaders and predicts their demise. Though mostly unsuccessful in Hollywood, Brecht was involved in one notable film project, Fritz Lang's *Hangmen also Die*. The film was a fictional account of the assassination by Czech resistance fighters of Reinhard Heydrich, the ruthless deputy Reich protector of Nazi-occupied Bohemia-Moravia.

—Cornelius Partsch

See the essays on *Fear and Misery in the Third Reich* and *The Resistible Rise of Arturo Ui.*

BRETT, Lily

Nationality: American (originally Australian: immigrated to the United States, 1989). **Born:** A displaced person's camp in Germany, 5 September 1946; lived in Australia from 1948. **Family:** Married David Rankin in 1981; three children. **Career:** Music journalist, *Go-Set* (Australia), mid-1960s. **Awards:** Mattara poetry prize, 1986, for *Poland;* C.J. Dennis prize for poetry, Victorian Premier's Literary Awards, 1987, for *The Auschwitz Poems;* Steele Rudd award, 1992, for *What God Wants;* New South Wales Premier's award for fiction, 1995, for *Just Like That;* Commonwealth Writers' prize, 2000, for *Too Many Men.*

PUBLICATIONS

Poetry

The Auschwitz Poems. 1986.
Poland and Other Poems. 1987.
After the War: Poems. 1990.
Unintended Consequences. 1992.
In Her Strapless Dresses. 1994.
Mud in My Tears. 1997.

Novels

Just Like That. 1994.
Too Many Men. 1999.

Short Stories

Collected Stories. 1999.
Things Could Be Worse. 1990.
What God Wants. 1992.

Other

In Full View (essays). 1997.
New York (collection of newspaper columns).2001.

* * *

Lily Brett is at the forefront of an increasing number of Australian descendants of Jewish Holocaust survivors who have felt the need to write about the anguish of having been born after the war to parents traumatized by their experiences during that time. What distinguishes Brett's work is that it encompasses a range of writing—poetry, short stories, novels, and autobiographical essays—all of which in some way grappling with her parents' experiences of the Holocaust as well as

testifying to the legacy of its continuing effects on her. Of all the writing being produced by other Australian children of survivors, hers has gained the most international recognition, most recently in Germany and Austria. Some of her work has been awarded important Australian literary prizes, the most notable being *The Auschwitz Poems* (awarded the Victorian Premier's Literary Awards C.J. Dennis prize for poetry in 1987) and her novel *Just Like That,* which was awarded the New South Wales Premier's award for fiction in 1995. Her novel *Too Many Men* was also short-listed for the Miles Franklin award, Australia's premier literary award.

Like many of the new second generation writers, Brett was only able to begin to articulate a desire to know about the Holocaust, about what had happened to her parents, to the rest of her extended family and to Jews more generally, when she was approaching middle age. It was only then that she was able to look at what had been impossible to face before. And what she has discovered through her writing are the many ways in which the effects of the Holocaust's devastation of her parents' lives, and in particular her mother's, were transmitted to her as their daughter. It would not be too far-fetched to say, then, that the writing that came out of that desire to finally confront the horror that had indelibly marked her (especially her body), and whose effects she had known or registered in less conscious ways throughout her childhood, functions simultaneously as a memorialization of her parents' traumas and losses and as a way of working through the demons of the horror, anxiety, and guilt that stalked her as a child and arguably have continued to do so as an adult. It would also not be stretching the point too much to suggest that Brett's writing (as well as, significantly, the prizes she has been awarded for it) functions moreover as the belated gift of a daughter to a mother: a replacement for the prize that was irremediably denied her mother when the Nazis marched into Lodz in 1939—a university education and a professional career—and a replacement for the prizes that Brett had refused to her mother throughout her childhood and adolescence—the successful education and career that her mother had wanted for her daughter.

Such complex and awful complicity with the Holocaust's devastation of the lives of their parents is a theme that reverberates in the works of many of the second generation. What is most noticeable in Brett's literary relation to the Holocaust, however, is the extent to which she (perhaps no more than others) appears to be captivated and captured by that event. Given that so many of the same Holocaust themes and scenes are repeated in Brett's writing, it seems that her writing serves also to keep her fixated on and fascinated by the Holocaust, so that she can remain, like her heroine Esther in *Just Like That,* ''ablaze with Hitler and concentration camps and what happened to the Jews.''

—Esther Faye

See the essay on *In Full View.*

BRUCK, Edith

Pseudonym for Edith Steinschreiber. **Nationality:** Italian (originally Hungarian: immigrated to Italy, 1954). **Born:** Tiszakarad, 3 May 1932. **Family:** Married Nelo Risi. **Career:** Lives in Rome and works for RAI (Italian Radio and Broadcasting Company).

PUBLICATIONS

Memoir

Chi ti ama così. 1958; as *Who Loves You Like This,* 2001.

Novels

Andremo in città. 1962.
Le sacre nozze [The Sacred Nuptials]. 1969.
Due stanze vuote. 1974.
Transit. 1978.
Mio splendido disastro. 1979.
Lettera alla madre. 1988.
Nuda proprietà. 1993.
L'attrice. 1995.
Il silenzio degli amanti. 1997.
Signora Auschwitz. 1999.

Poetry

Il tatuaggio. 1975.
In difesa del padre. 1980.
Monologo. 1990.
Itinerario/Útirány: Poesie scelte. 1998.

*

Film Adaptations: *Andremo in città,* 1966.

Critical Studies: "An Interview with Edith Bruck" by Brenda S. Webster, in *13th Moon,* 11(1–2), 1993, pp. 170–75; "Strategies for Remembering: Auschwitz, Mother, and Writing in Edith Bruck" by Adalgisa Giorgio, in *European Memories of the Second World War,* edited by Helmut Peitsch, Charles Burdett, and Claire Gorrara, 1999.

Theatrical Activities: Director: **Films**—*Improvviso,* 1979; *Un altare per la patria,* 1986; *Un altare per la madre,* 1987.

* * *

Edith Bruck's first book, *Who Loves You Like This* (published as *Chi ti ama così* in 1958), is a memoir that was inspired by the irrepressibility of her near-death experience in being deported to the concentration camps at the age of 12 and by the resultant obligation to bear witness to it. She chose the literary genre of the memoir because at the time she could not reduce her life to fiction. Her later works, however, including novels and poetry, also comment on her concentration-camp experience.

Bruck particularly thematizes the Auschwitz experience in her novel *Lettera alla madre* (1988). The narrator of the novel is the letter writer, Katia, a survivor of Auschwitz. The addressee of the letter, Katia's mother, died in the gas chambers along with several of Katia's siblings. Katia's letter is a desperate attempt to form a dialogue with her deceased mother, with whom she had a love/hate relationship. The mother was a strict orthodox Jew, while Katia is a religiously nonobservant Jew. The narrator regrets the fact that no true dialogue can take place but tries to content herself with an imaginary dialogue.

The letter itself is a combination of autobiographical reminiscences and a thematization of intergenerational conflict as well as a poignant lament over the Holocaust from the viewpoint of an eyewitness. Portions of the novel may have been influenced by the 1987 suicide of the preeminent Holocaust survivor and author **Primo Levi**, who publicly endorsed Bruck's literary career.

The continued desire for a dialogue with the murdered mother is also thematized in Bruck's poem "Impression" (1993):

> Last night in bed / with my eyes closed, / The cats far away in the darkness, / I felt a hand on my forehead, a gesture / somewhere between blessing and consolation / I didn't know who it belonged to / but such wholeness came over me / that I smiled there, alone, / the way a contented child might smile in a dream / Only on waking did I think of the hand / of my mother, long dead

Both the novel and the poem express that Bruck's mother, who died during the Holocaust, is still a major part of Bruck's life, 50 years after her death.

In the poem "Survivors" (1993), Bruck alludes to the irrepressibility of the Holocaust experience, which traumatizes its victims for the rest of their lives:

> With us survivors / you have to tread softly: an offhand, / everyday look connects itself / to other terrible looks. / Each pain is part of the one single pain / that pulses all the time in our blood.

Like the German-Swedish poet **Nelly Sachs**, she pleads for humans everywhere to recognize the vulnerability of the Holocaust survivors, who will never fully recover from what they experienced. Later in the poem, she refers to the phenomenon known as survivor's guilt:

> We are not like others / We survived for others, in place of others / The life we remember, the life / we must remember in order to live / is not our own / Leave us in peace. We are not alone.

Bruck posits that those who survived the cruel agony of the concentration camps have a moral obligation to remember those who did not survive, such as her mother.

—Peter R. Erspamer

See the essay on *Who Loves You Like This.*

BRYKS, Rachmil

Nationality: American (originally Polish: immigrated to the United States, 1949, granted U.S. citizenship, 1953). **Born:** Scarzisk, 18 April 1912. **Family:** Married Irene Wolf in 1946; two daughters. **Career:** Worked for Development Corp. for Israel, New York, 1960–73. Member of cultural branch of Workmen's Circle and Independent Katzetnik Organization (for survivors of concentration camps). **Agent:** Sanford J. Greenburger Associates, Inc., 825 Third Avenue, New York, New York 10022, U.S.A. **Died:** 1974.

PUBLICATIONS

Novels

Der kaiser in geto [The King in the Ghetto]. 1961.
Di papirene kroyn [The Paper Crown] (sequel to *Der kaiser in geto*). 1969.
Di antloyfers [The Fugitive]. 1975.

Short Stories

Kiddush Hashem. 1952; as *A Cat in the Ghetto: Four Novelettes,* 1959.
Di vos zaynen nisht gibliben [Those Who Did Not Survive]. 1972.

Poetry

Yung grin mai [Young Green May]. 1939.
Geto fabrik 76/Ghetto Factory 76: Chemical Waste Conversion (Yiddish and English). 1967.

*

Film Adaptations: *A Cat in the Ghetto,* 1970.

* * *

Rachmil Bryks was born in Scarzisk, Poland. The son of orthodox parents, Bryks developed his interest in poetry and story writing at a very young age. His first book of poems, *Young Green May,* was published in 1939. Although shortly thereafter forced into the Lodz ghetto, Bryks continued to write until he was deported to Auschwitz. His caustic descriptions of the Lodz ghetto almost cost him his life, but he was rescued by his cohorts in the ghetto. Most of his family members were murdered during the Holocaust, and one of his surviving brothers was shot by Polish nationalists shortly after the war. Years of slave labor took their toll on Bryks's health, but after liberation he began to write of the Holocaust. Professor Irving Howe, in the preface to Bryks's *A Cat in the Ghetto*, stated of Bryks's work that "what Rachmil Bryks deals with is not 'mere' literature but the most terrible event in modern life, perhaps the most terrible event of all human history." In the preface to Bryks's *Kiddush Hashem*, S. Morris Engel, who has translated many of Bryks's works from their original Yiddish into English, referred to Bryks's work as "not just a *bukh* [book], but rather as *sefer*, or holy writings."

Kiddush Hashem was published in 1959 and contains the novelettes *A Cat in the Ghetto* as well as *Kiddush Hashem*. *Kiddush Hashem* tells of the hope and desire that fill the minds of those being transported in a crowded train to what they hope will be just a labor camp in Vienna. Instead, the trickery and deceit of the Nazis is revealed to the Jews when they arrive at Auschwitz. Husbands and wives are brutally separated, infants are snatched from their mothers, and Dr. Mengele immediately commences with his selections. Bryks's descriptions of the horrors are explicit and vivid. He does not cut corners in his graphic depictions of the torture inflicted upon the inmates. Hope, however, does not die easily among the inmates of the camp. Engel relates that "they [the Nazis] failed ultimately in the spiritual plane where they hoped to pull down their victims to their depths of depravity."

Bryks has only recently been recognized as a Holocaust writer, thanks to his daughters' immense effort in educating the public on their father's work and life. They have continued to lecture in Israel and Bryks's works are slowly being translated into many other languages, such as German, Swedish, Hebrew, and Polish. Some of his works have been adapted into radio plays and theatrical performances. *A Cat in the Ghetto* became a film in 1970. Bryks's work can be compared to that of **Arnošt Lustig** and **Elie Wiesel.**

In the introduction to *A Cat in the Ghetto*, Sol Liptzin perhaps says it best when describing Bryks's work: "The reader of Rachmil Bryks will not easily forget. The images he conjures up and the scenes of horror and heroism he depicts will linger on in the memory for a long, long time and will stimulate the thinking of Jews about their tomorrow no less than about their yesteryear."

—Cynthia A. Klíma

See the essays on *A Cat in the Ghetto: Four Novelettes* and *Ghetto Factory 76: Chemical Waste Conversion.*

C

CALVINO, Italo

Nationality: Italian (originally Cuban: immigrated to Italy, 1925). **Born:** Santiago de las Vegas, 15 October 1923. **Education:** Studied agronomy, 1941, and literature, 1945–47, University of Turin, graduated 1947. **Military Service:** Conscripted into Young Facists, 1940; Italian Resistance, 1943–45. **Family:** Married Esther Judith "Chichita" Singer in 1964; one daughter. **Career:** Member of editorial staff, Einaudi, Turin, 1947–48, and again beginning 1950; member of staff, *L'Unita*, 1948–50; co-editor, *Il Menabò*, Milan, 1959–66. **Awards:** Riccione prize, 1947; Premio de l'Unita prize, 1947; Saint-Vincent prize, 1952; Viareggio prize, 1957; Bagutta prize, 1959; Veillon prize, 1963; Feltrinelli prize, 1972; Austrian state prize for European literature, 1976; Nice Festival prize, 1982. **Member:** American Academy (honorary), 1975. **Died:** 20 September 1985.

PUBLICATIONS

Collection

Romanzi e Racconti, edited by Claudio Milanini. 1992.

Novels

Il sentiero dei nidi di ragno. 1947; as *The Path to Nest of Spiders*, 1956; printed with preface by author, 1964.
I nostri antenati (trilogy). 1960; as *Our Ancestors*, 1980.
  Il visconte dimezzato. 1952; as *The Cloven Viscount*, published with *The Non-Existent Knight*, 1962.
  Il barone rampante. 1957; as *The Baron in the Trees*, 1959.
  Il cavaliere inesistente. 1959; as *The Non-Existent Knight*, published with *The Cloven Viscount*, 1962.
La giornata d'uno scrutatore. 1963.

Short Stories

Ultimo viene il corvo. 1949; as *Adam, One Afternoon, and Other Stories*, 1957.
Fiabe italiane: Raccolte della tradizione popolare durante gli ultimi cento anni e transcritte in lingua dai vari dialette. 1956; as *Italian Fables*, 1959; as *Italian Folk Tales*, 1975; as *Italian Folktales*, 1980.
I racconti. 1958.
Marcovaldo; ovvero, Le stagioni in città. 1963; as *Marcovaldo; or, The Seasons in the City*, 1983.
La nuvola di smog e La formica argentina. 1965.
Le cosmicomiche. 1965; as *Cosmicomics*, 1968.

Ti con zero. 1967; as *T Zero*, 1969; as *Time and the Hunter*, 1970.
Gli amori difficili. 1970; as *Difficult Loves*, 1984.
The Watcher and Other Stories. 1971.
Le città invisibili. 1972; as *Invisible Cities*, 1974.
Il castello dei destini incrociati. 1974; as *The Castle of Crossed Destinies*, 1977.
Se una notte d'inverno un viaggiatore. 1979; as *If on a Winter's Night a Traveler*, 1981.
Palomar. 1983; as *Mr. Palomar*, 1985.
Sotto il sole giaguaro. 1986; as *Under the Jaguar Tree*, 1988.
La Strada di San Giovanni. 1990; as *The Road to San Giovanni*, 1993.

Also author of *The Crow Comes Last* and *L'entrata in guerra* [The Entry into War].

Play

Un re in ascolto [The King Listens] (opera libretto), music by Luciano Berio. 1984.

Other

Una pietra sopra: Discorsi di letteratura e società. 1980.
Collezione di sabbia: Emblemi bizzarri e inquietanti del nostro passato e del nostro futuro gli oggetti raccontano il mondo. 1984.
The Uses of Literature. 1985.
The Literature Machine. 1987.
Six Memos for the Next Millennium (lectures). 1988.
Perchè leggere i classici (essays). 1992.

Editor, *Poesie edite e inedite*, by Cesare Pavese. 1962.
Editor, *Vittorini: Progettazione e letteratura*. 1968.

*

Critical Studies: *Calvino: A Reappraisal and an Appreciation of the Trilogy* by J. R. Woodhouse, 1968; *Calvino, Writer and Critic* by JoAnn Cannon, 1981; "Calvino" by Richard Andrews, in *Writers and Society in Contemporary Italy*, edited by Michael Caesar and Peter Hainsworth, 1984; *Italo Calvino* issue of *The Review of Contemporary Fiction*, 6(2), Summer 1986; *Italo Calvino*, edited by Harold Bloom, 1988; *Calvino and the Age of Neorealism: Fables of Estrangement* by Lucia Re, 1990; *Calvino: A San Remo* by Piero Ferrara, 1991; *Understanding Italo Calvino* by Beno Weiss, 1993; *Italo Calvino: Eros and Language* by Tommasina Gabriele, 1994; *Italo Calvino* by Martin McLaughlin, 1997; *Italo Calvino: A*

Journey Toward Postmodernism by Constance Markey, 1999; *Italo Calvino and the Landscape of Childhood* by Claudia Nocentini, 2000; *Painting with Words, Writing with Pictures: Word and Image in the Work of Italo Calvino* by Franco Ricci, 2001.

*   *   *

Italo Calvino rarely grappled with the Holocaust directly in his writings, but he was nevertheless deeply marked by the events of World War II and by his own anti-Nazi activities. He was conscripted by the army of the fascist puppet state the Republic of Salo but fled the draft. Instead, he joined the Italian Resistance movement, even though his parents were taken hostage by the Nazis and imprisoned as a gesture of retaliation. Calvino's experiences as a Garibaldi partisan from 1944 to 1945 were crucial to the development of his political and moral beliefs. They also formed the basis for his first novel, *The Path to the Nest of Spiders,* considered a ground-breaking example of neo-realist literature in Italian and a strong voice in the country's post-war attempts at coming to terms with the war and Benito Mussolini's term in power.

This novel belongs to the earliest cycle in Calvino's output, a period from 1945 to 1949 in which he wrote highly realistic, concretely imagined stories set during the war and influenced by the staccato style of Ernest Hemingway's *Hills Like White Elephants*, which made a strong impression on him as a young man. Calvino was already well known when he published it; he was first brought to the public eye by the short story collection *The Crow Comes Last,* which won the Premio de l'Unita prize in 1947. These stories, as well as the semi-autobiographical *L'entrata in guerra* ("The Entry into War"), contain numerous elements that Calvino would later rework in his acclaimed *The Path to the Nest of Spiders*. Many of the characters are the same—the small boy as narrator, the pedantic Marxist partisan cook, the sadistic young men fascinated more by weapons than by a cause. Both are set in the poverty-stricken towns of northern Italy, where the mostly Communist partisans compete with the black shirt brigades for supporters, and the general populace often seems confused about the difference between the two sides. Calvino portrays men at a stage before they have reached the full political consciousness necessary for commitment to an abstract cause. Although Calvino is certainly on the side of the partisans in this novel, he differs from other wartime novelists such as Elio Vittorini and Marcello Venturi in that he realizes that the struggle is more complex than a Manichean battle between good and evil. By recognizing the flaws of the partisans as well as their heroism and enthusiasm, he arrives at a portrait that is at once more interesting and more real.

The Holocaust is absent from most of Calvino's fiction, particularly the immediate post-war works. His portrayals of Nazi officers and conscripted German sailors emphasize their alienness to local characters and local politics. They are ignored or exploited, fought against or used as allies, but their ideology appears absurd, and despite their authority they are turned into pawns of local power struggles. Calvino came to grips privately with the horror of the Holocaust and the anti-Semitism that existed in Italian as well as German society. He was a great friend and admirer of Primo Levi, the Italian writer interned in Auschwitz, and wrote several prefaces to Levi's work.

The main importance of the writing from Calvino's early period is the key role it played in the development of the neo-realist novel in contemporary European literature. Like the films of Rossellini and de Sica, the early stories presented a new realism of content (in contrast to the realism of nine-teenth-century novels or the censured fiction under fascism), a new realism of style (implying a more authentic representation of popular Italian, including dialect and regionalisms), and a socio-political message influenced by Marxism. Calvino's lengthy and witty 1964 preface to *The Path to the Nest of Spiders* is perhaps the best introduction to his wartime writings and to his place in the neo-realist movement, which he calls "the anonymous voice of the age," even though the preface is written from the perspective of a much older man looking back critically at his youth. By 1964 Calvino had already turned away from neo-realism in order to write fantastical, playful, and decidedly postmodern fictions such as *Invisible Cities, Cosmicomics,* and *If on a Winter's Night a Traveler,* the works for which he is justly most famous. Whatever technical fire-works his early post-war fiction may lack, however, they are skilled and seamless evocations, simultaneously the most historical and the most personal stories of Calvino's career.

—Christina Svendsen

See the essay on *The Path to the Nest of Spiders.*

CAMUS, Albert

Nationality: French. **Born** Mondovi, Algeria, 7 November 1913. **Education:** University of Algiers, graduated 1936. **Family:** Married 1) Simone Hié in 1933 (divorced); 2) Francine Faure in 1940, twin son and daughter. **Career:** Worked as a meteorologist, ship-broker's clerk, automobile parts salesman, clerk in the automobile registry division of the prefecture, actor and amateur theatre producer, Algiers, 1935–39; member of the Communist party, 1935–39; staff member, *Alger-Républicain,* Algiers, 1938–39; editor, *Soir-Républicain,* Algiers, 1939–40; sub-editor for layout, *Paris-Soir,* 1940; teacher, Oran, Algeria, 1940–42; convalescent in central France, 1942–43; joined resistance in Lyons region, 1943; journalist, Paris, 1943–45. Reader and editor of Espoir series, Gallimard Publishers, Paris, 1943–60. Co-founding editor, *Combat,* 1945–47. **Awards:** Critics prize (France), 1947; Nobel prize for literature, 1957. **Died:** 4 January 1960.

PUBLICATIONS

Collections

Complete Fiction. 1960.
Théâtre, récits, nouvelles; Essais, edited by Roger Quilliot (2 vols.). 1962–65.
Collected Plays. 1965.
Oeuvres complètes (5 vols.). 1983.

Novels

L'Étranger. 1942; as *The Stranger,* 1946; as *The Outsider,* 1946.
La Peste. 1947; as *The Plague,* 1948.
La Chute. 1956; as *The Fall,* 1957.
La Mort heureuse. 1971; as *A Happy Death,* 1972.

Short Stories

L'Exil et le royaume. 1957; as *Exile and the Kingdom,* 1958.

Plays

Le Malentendu (produced 1944). Published with *Caligula,* 1944; translated as *Cross Purpose* and published with *Caligula,* 1948.
Caligula (produced 1945). Published with *Le Malentendu,* 1944; translated as *Caligula* and published with *Cross Purpose,* 1948.
L'État de siège (produced 1948). 1948; as *State of Siege,* in *Caligula and Three Other Plays,* 1958.
Les Justes (produced 1949). 1950; as *The Just Assassins,* in *Caligula and Three Other Plays,* 1958; as *The Just,* 1965.
La Dévotion à la croix, adaptation of a play by Calderón (produced 1953). 1953.
Les Esprits, adaptation of a work by Pierre de Larivey (produced 1953). 1953.
Un Cas intéressant, adaptation of a work by Dino Buzzati (produced 1955). 1955.
Requiem pour une nonne, adaptation of a work by William Faulkner (produced 1956). 1956.
Le Chevalier d'Olmedo, adaptation of the play by Lope de Vega (produced 1957). 1957.
Caligula and Three Other Plays (includes *Caligula; Cross Purpose; State of Seige; The Just Assassins*). 1958.
Les Possédés, adaptation of a novel by Fyodor Dostoevsky (produced 1959). 1959; as *The Possessed,* 1960.

Other

L'Envers et L'endroit. 1937.
Noces. 1939.

Le Mythe de Sisyphe. 1942; as *The Myth of Sisyphus and Other Essays,* 1955.
Lettres à un ami allemand. 1945.
L'Existence. 1945.
Le Minotaure; ou La Halte d'Oran. 1950.
Actuelles 1–3: Chroniques 1944–1948, Chroniques 1948–1953, Chronique algérienne 1939–1958 (3 vols.). 1950–58.
L'Homme révolté. 1951; as *The Rebel: An Essay on Man in Revolt,* 1953.
L'Été. 1954.
Réflexions sur la guillotine, in *Réflexions sur la peine capitale,* with Arthur Koestler. 1957; as *Reflections on the Guillotine,* 1960.
Discours de Suède. 1958; as *Speech of Acceptance upon the Award of the Nobel Prize for Literature,* 1958.
Resistance, Rebellion, and Death (selection). 1960.
Méditation sur le théâtre et la vie. 1961.
Carnets: Mai 1935–février 1942. 1962; translated as *Carnets 1935–1942,* 1963; as *Notebooks 1935–1942,* 1963.
Lettre à Bernanos. 1963.
Carnets Janvier 1942–mars 1951. 1964; as *Notebooks 1942–1951,* 1965.
Lyrical and Critical (essays), edited by Philip Thody. 1967.
Le Combat d'Albert Camus, edited by Norman Stokle. 1970.
Selected Essays and Notebooks, edited by Philip Thody. 1970.
Le premier Camus. 1973; as *Youthful Writings,* 1977.
Journaux de voyage, edited by Roger Quilliot. 1978; as *American Journals,* 1987.
Fragments d'un combat 1938–1940: Alger-Républicain, Le Soir-Républicain, edited by Jacqueline Lévi-Valensi and André Abbou. 1978.
Correspondance 1932–1960, with Jean Grenier, edited by Marguerite Dobrenn. 1981.
Selected Political Writings, edited by Jonathan King. 1981.
Oeuvre fermée, oeuvrete, edited by Raymond Gay-Croisier and Jacqueline Lévi-Valensi. 1985.
Carnets: Mars 1951–décembre 1959. 1989.

*

Bibliography: *Camus: A Bibliography* by Robert F. Roeming, 1968; and subsequent editions by Raymond Gay-Croisier, in *A Critical Bibliography of French Literature 6,* 1980; *Camus in English: An Annotated Bibliography of Camus's Contributions to English and American Periodicals and Newspapers* by Peter C. Hoy, second edition, 1971; *Camus, A Bibliography* by Robert F. Roeming, 1993.

Critical Studies: *Camus: A Study of His Work,* 1957, *Camus, 1913–1960: A Biographical Study,* 1962, and *Camus,* 1989, all by Philip Thody; *Camus* by Germaine Brée, 1959, revised edition, 1972; *Camus: A Collection of Critical Essays,* edited by Germaine Brée, 1962; *Camus: The Artist in the Arena* by Emmett Parker, 1965; *Camus* by Philip H. Rhein, 1969; revised edition, 1989; *Camus* by Conor Cruise O'Brien, 1970;

The Theatre of Camus by Edward Freeman, 1971; *Camus: The Invincible Summer* by Albert Maquet, 1972; *The Unique Creation of Camus* by Donald Lazere, 1973; *Camus: A Biography* by Herbert R. Lottman, 1979; *Camus's Imperial Vision* by Anthony Rizzuto, 1981; *Camus: A Critical Study of His Life and Work,* 1982, and *Camus: The Stranger,* 1988, both by Patrick McCarthy; *Exiles and Strangers: A Reading of Camus's Exile and the Kingdom* by Elaine Showalter, 1984; *Exile and the Kingdom: A Political Rereading of Camus* by Susan Tarrow, 1985; *The Ethical Pragmatism of Camus: Two Studies in the History of Ideas* by Dean Vasil, 1985; *Beyond Absurdity: The Philosophy of Camus* by Robert C. Trundle, 1987; *Camus: A Critical Examination* by David Sprintzen, 1988; *Camus and Indian Thought* by Sharad Chaedra, 1989; *Understanding Camus* by David R. Ellison, 1990; *Camus's L'Estranger: Fifty Years On,* edited by Adele King, 1992; *Tragic Lucidity: Discourse of Recuperation in Unamuno and Camus* by Keith W. Hansen, 1993; *Arendt, Camus, and Modern Rebellion* by Jeffrey C. Isaac, 1994; *Albert Camus: The Thinker, the Artist, the Man* by Eric S. Bonner, 1996; *Albert Camus: A Life* by Oliver Todd and Benjamin Ivry, 1997; *Albert Camus, Marguerite Duras, and the Legacy of Mourning* by Michelle Beauclair, 1998.

* * *

Born in Algeria of a French father and a Spanish mother, Albert Camus grew up in a working-class suburb of Algiers, in relative poverty and without his father, killed in World War I when Albert was a year old. The tuberculosis Camus contracted at 17 affected his health permanently yet also heightened his pleasure in nature—the sun, sand, and sea—and strengthened his will to live. The scholarship that enabled him to study at the University of Algiers literally changed his life by inspiring his passion for moral philosophy. That passion issued in a didactic impulse to include a humane moral wisdom in everything he ever wrote, whether fiction, drama, essay, or political journalism.

In his early twenties Camus the polemical journalist espoused radical politics, demanding justice for the poor and politically oppressed. Camus the budding author and moralist, on the other hand, emphasized an existential dilemma: the tragic paradox that humans have the capacity to imagine an ideal life but are thwarted in achieving their ideal by their inherently limited powers and their mortality. This dilemma constituted the most bleakly pessimistic moral philosophy Camus ever adopted, since it expressed resignation both to human frailty and to the chilling indifference of the universe to human concerns. Not surprisingly, the novel Camus worked on in those years, but never published, depicted the hero's search for a happy death rather than a happy life.

The outbreak of World War II in September 1939 had the unexpected effect of turning Camus's attention from death to life. In 1940 he left Algeria to work for a Paris newspaper, and

a year later, back in Algeria, he totally recast that early novel about death, turning it instead into a morality tale confronting conventional and unconventional life views. Suggestively renamed *The Stranger,* it appeared in 1942 and quickly became Camus's first literary success.

Late in 1942 Camus decided that, with his worsening tuberculosis, he would fare better in the healthy mountain air of central France, which was then unoccupied territory. He worked there in quiet isolation, undisturbed by the war, except for one anxious period when he was cut off from all communication with his family because North Africa had been successfully invaded by the Allies. Before long he began to make trips to Paris to maintain contact with his publisher and with friends, especially those involved in the resistance. Out of sympathy with their cause, he joined the resistance himself and began to contribute inspirational articles to the resistance newspaper, *Combat.* As the war wound down, he decided he must take his place in the Paris literary world, and he arranged for his wife and children in Algeria to join him in Paris.

His new life in the capital began auspiciously, with the acclaimed publication, in 1947, of what is still regarded as his finest novel, *The Plague.* Its success, however, left him totally unprepared for the hard times ahead. When two of his plays, staged in 1948 and 1949, and a political tract called *The Rebel,* published in 1951, were all poorly received by the critics, the vulnerably sensitive Camus became depressed and spent the next three years trying to break a severe case of writer's block. During those three bleak years he made an ill-advised journalistic attempt to intervene in the violent civil war in Algeria, which had begun in 1952. Adopting the moral high ground, he urged calm, reason, and conciliation, but his words fell on deaf ears. Both sides had already hardened their positions and become hopelessly polarized.

Valiantly struggling for self-renewal and vindication, Camus first vented his anger against his critics in 1956 with a witty, but ambiguous, satirical novel called *The Fall.* He then restored his dignity, with respect to the Algerian tragedy, in 1957, with a volume of six exemplary short stories under the title *Exile and the Kingdom.* He was rewarded with the Nobel Prize for Literature later that same year. No one could have suspected at the time, however, that the honor would mark the end of his literary career. On 4 January 1960 the mortality Camus had long decried caught up with him in the absurd form of a fatal automobile accident, of which he was an innocent victim.

Camus was perhaps the most impressive French literary talent of his generation, widely admired in the 1940s and 1950s as a hero of the resistance, a model for the younger generation, an outspoken defender of the oppressed, and a guardian of the moral conscience of Europe.

—Murray Sachs

See the essays on *The Fall* and *The Plague.*

CELAN, Paul

Pseudonym for Paul Antschel. **Nationality:** Romanian. **Born:** Czernovitz, Bukoviana, 23 November 1920. **Education:** Studied medicine, École Préparatoire de Médecine, Tours, France, 1938; studied German philology and literature, Licence des Lettres, Paris, 1950. **Family:** Married Gisele de Lestrange in 1952; two sons (one deceased). **Career:** Forced laborer in Southern Moldovia during World War II; worked as a psychiatric field surgeon after the war; moved to Bucharest, 1945, and worked as a translator of Russian literature and a reader in a publishing house; lived in Vienna, December 1947 to July 1948; moved to Paris, 1948; reader, German language and literature, Ecole Normale Superior, Sorbonne University of Paris, 1959–70. **Awards:** City of Bremen literary prize, 1958; Georg Büchner prize, 1960. **Died:** Suicide, April, 1970.

PUBLICATIONS

Collections:

Gedichte: Eine Auswahl [Poems: A Selection]. 1959.
Ausgewählte Gedichte: Zwei Reden. 1968.
Ausgewählte Gedichte. 1970.
Selected Poems. 1972.
Gedichte (2 vols.). 1975.
Paul Celan: Prose Writings and Selected Poems. 1977.
Paul Celan: Poems. 1980; revised and enlarged as *Poems of Paul Celan*, 1988; revised and enlarged, 1995.
Gesammelte Werke (5 vols.). 1983.
65 Poems. 1985.
Gedichte: 1938–1944. 1985.
Last Poems. 1986.
Collected Prose. 1986.
Das Frühwerk, edited by Barbara Wiedemann. 1987.
Paul Celan: Die Gedichte aus dem Nachlass, edited by Bertrand Badiou, Jean-Claude Rambach, and Barbara Wiedemann. 1997.
A Voice: Translations of Paul Celan. 1998.
Glottal Stop: 101 Poems. 2000.
Selected Poems and Prose of Paul Celan. 2001.

Poetry

Der Sand aus den Urnen. 1948.
Mohn und Gedächtnis [Poppy and Memory]. 1952.
Von Schwelle zu Schwelle [From Threshold to Threshold]. 1955.
Sprachgitter [Language Grid]. 1959; as *Speech-Grille and Selected Poems*, 1971.
Die Niemandsrose [The Nobody Rose]. 1963.
Schwarzmaut. 1969.
Atemkristall. 1965; as *Breath Crystal*, 1976.
Atemwende. 1967; as *Breathturn*, 1995.

Fadensonnen. 1968; as *Threadsuns*, 2000.
Lichtzwang. 1970.
Schneepart. 1971.
Zeitgehöft. 1976.
Todesfuge (reprint of a poem in *Mohn und Gedächtnis*). 1984.

Other

Edgar Jené und der traum vom traume [Edgar Jené and the Dream of the Dream]. 1948.
Ansprache bei Verleihung des Bremen Literatur-Preises an Paul Celan (acceptance speech for City of Bremen literary prize). 1958.
Der Meridian (acceptance speech for Georg Büchner prize, Darmstadt, October 22, 1960). 1961; as *The Meridian*, 1977.
Paul Celan, Nelly Sachs: Correspondence, edited by Barbara Wiedemann. 1995.

Translator, *Un erou al timpului nostru*, by Mikhail Lermontov. 1946.
Translator, *Wie Man wünsche beim Schwanz packt: Ein Drama in sechs Akten*, by Pablo Picasso. 1954.
Translator, *Hier irrt Maigret: Kriminalroman*, by Georges Simenon. 1955.
Translator, *Maigret und die schrecklichen Kinder: Kriminalroman*, by Georges Simenon. 1955.
Translator, *Die Zwölf*, by Aleksandr Aleksandrovich Blok. 1958.
Translator, *Gedichte*, by Osip Mandelstam. 1959.
Translator, *Drei russische Dichter: Alexander Block, Ossip Mandelstamm, Sergej Jessenin.* 1963.
Translator, with Adelheid Christoph and Rainer Kirsch, *Gedichte*, by Sergei Aleksandrovich Esenin. 1965.
Translator, *Einundzwanzig Sonette*, by William Shakespeare. 1967.

*

Bibliography: ''Bibliographie zu Paul Celan: Werke und Sekundärliteratur,'' in *Zeitschrift für Kulturaustausch*, 3(32), 1982, pp. 245–87; ''Bibliographie zu Paul Celan,'' in *Text + Kritik*, 53/54 July, 1984, pp. 100–49 (second, enlarged edition), both by Christiane Heuline; *Paul Celan Bibliographie* by Christiane Bohrer, 1989; *Paul Celan: Ein Bibliographie* by Jerry Glenn, 1989; *Paul Celan: A Bibliography of English-Language Primary and Secondary Literature 1955–1996* by Jerry Glenn, 1997; *Paul Celan: Die Zweite Bibliographie* by Jerry Glenn and Jeffrey D. Todd, 1998.

Critical Studies: *Paul Celan* by Jerry Glenn, 1973; Paul Celan section, edited by Jerry Glenn, in *Sulfur*, 11, 1984, pp. 5–99; ''Paul Celan: The Strain of Jewishness,'' in *Commentary*, 79, April 1985, pp. 44–55, and *Paul Celan: Poet, Survivor, Jew*, 1995, both by John Felstiner; *Argumentum e Silentio*, edited by Amy D. Colin, 1986; *Paul Celan: A Biography of His Youth* by

Israel Chalfen, translated by Maximilian Bleyleben, 1991; *Paul Celan: Holograms of Darkness* by Amy D. Colin, 1991; *Holocaust Visions: Surrealism and Existentialism in the Poetry of Paul Celan* by Clarise Samuels, 1993; "The Problem of Language and National Identity for Holocaust Poet, Paul Celan" by James M. Van der Laan, in *History of European Ideas,* 16(1–3), January 1993, pp. 207–21; *Word Traces: Readings of Paul Celan,* edited by Aris Fioretos, 1994; *Pathways to Paul Celan: A History of Critical Responses As a Chorus of Discordant Voices* by Bianca Rosenthal, 1995; *The Early Poetry of Paul Celan: In the Beginning Was the Word* by Adrian Del Caro, 1997; "Language and the Holocaust: Reflections on the Poetry of Paul Celan" by Emery George, in *Michigan Quarterly Review,* 36(1), Winter 1997, pp. 475–83; "Writing after/about Auschwitz: Paul Celan" by Peter Horn, in *Pretexts* (South Africa), 6(2), November 1997, pp. 159–65; "Paul Celan: Poet of the Shoah" by Alain Suied, translated by Steve Light, in *New Literary History,* 30(1), Winter 1999, pp. 217–19.

*   *   *

Paul Celan is widely considered the most ambitious and complex author to write poetry after Auschwitz. His international reputation results principally from his early poem "Todesfuge" (1948; "Death Fugue," 1967). After that poem's publication, Celan abandoned most direct references to the Holocaust and wrote increasingly abstract lyric verse in German, the language taught to him by his mother and spoken by her murderers. In much of his later work, specifically in the volumes *Sprachgitter* (1959, "Language Grid") and *Atemwende* (1967; "Breathturn," 1995), he investigates the capacity of language to express a traumatic and fundamentally inaccessible reality and the capacity of German in particular to permit testimony to German crimes and Jewish suffering. For Celan the Holocaust was not a topic to be selected or dismissed; it unavoidably cast its shadow on all of postwar culture and existence. He considered poetry—after Auschwitz and because of Auschwitz—to have become more fragile and, by necessity, more prone to take risks in its search to convey irremediable loss.

Celan was born Paul Antschel, the only child of assimilated Jewish parents in Czernowitz, Romania. After the Nazis' invasion of his native country, he was forced to work in a labor camp, while his parents were deported to concentration camps where his father perished under uncertain circumstances, and his mother was fatally shot by the Germans. When Soviet troops occupied Czernowitz in 1944, Celan moved via Budapest and Vienna to Paris.

While an astute observer of politics, Celan insisted that the Holocaust needed to be considered in other terms. Invoking ethical considerations, he regarded it primarily as a breach in human relations. For this reason, he stressed the dialogic nature of poetry in opposition to a tradition of German verse

that he nonetheless acknowledged as formative. He insisted that any attentive reader could understand his poems, in spite of their appearance of hermetism. In response to criticism, he defended the opacity and difficulty of his later work as necessary to address the reality of the Holocaust and what he considered the discouraging persistence of anti-Semitism, the denial of responsibility, and a generally repressive politics in postwar Europe. Beginning with the collection *Die Niemandsrose* (1963; "The Nobody Rose") dedicated to the poet Osip Mandelstam, Celan identified himself increasingly as a Jewish poet and added to his sources in German culture and French modernism further references to Jewish mysticism and Jewish precursors—gleaned primarily from readings in adulthood. In his correspondence, he insisted that anti-Semitism is a form of anti-humanism. His complicated relation to the German language and his German readership found poignant expression in an ultimately ineffective confrontation (chronicled in the poem "Todtnauberg") with Martin Heidegger, the philosopher who had been a Nazi party member and whose work Celan nonetheless greatly admired.

In speeches delivered upon receiving several prestigious literary awards, Celan stressed his belief in the survival of the German language as a means to access even extreme reality. At the same time, his poems syntactically and semantically pry open this language to reveal overlooked or repressed signification, and to expose what he considered its potential for inauthentic speech. In the important "Straitening" (1959), Celan strikingly interlaces the search for the traces of annihilation at the sites of Nazi crimes with a dissection of German words and sentences. Celan further inserts references to the nuclear attacks on Hiroshima and Nagasaki into this poem to compel his readers to reflect on the relation between different modes of mass destruction. Much of Celan's poetry of the 1960s is written under the impact of severe mental suffering that resulted in suicide attempts, forced hospitalization, medication, and the separation from his wife and son, whose lives he had threatened. Poetry became for Celan a means of survival, allowing him to design a "search for reality" which increasingly eluded him. Whether his mental illness and eventual suicide were direct results of his experiences and losses under the Nazis remains open for debate.

Celan's work offers a plethora of syntactically compacted terms that refer, often obliquely, to Jewish culture, Eastern European sites, acts of testimony, and graphic images of suffering. Since these references are so tightly embedded in a linguistic context that is often far removed from the Holocaust, critics disagree whether they can be interpreted as Holocaust references or whether they signal the difficulty of having unambiguous references to what Celan ultimately considered an incomprehensible event. Recent critics largely reject a reading of Celan's oeuvre as exclusively Holocaust-themed. In light of the publication of Celan's correspondence with his wife and friends, postwar events such as an unfounded but highly publicized plagiarism charge in the 1960s (which Celan attributed largely to anti-Semitism) are now considered equally important factors shaping his work.

—Ulrich Baer

See the essays on ''Death Fugue,'' ''Shibboleth,'' and ''Zürich, the Stork Inn.''

COHEN, Arthur A(llen)

Nationality: American. **Born:** New York City, 25 June 1928. **Education:** Friends Seminary, New York, 1941–44; University of Chicago, B.A. 1946, M.A. 1949, further graduate study, 1949–50; Jewish Theological Seminary of America, 1950–52. **Family:** Married Elaine Firstenberg Lustig in 1956; one daughter. **Career:** Founder, with Cecil Hemley, and managing director, Noonday Press, 1951–55; founder and president, Meridian Books, 1955–60; vice president, World Publishing Co., 1960–61; director of religion department, 1961–64, and editor-in-chief and vice-president of general books division, 1964–68, Holt, Rinehart & Winston, Inc.; managing editor, Viking Press, Inc., 1968–75; founder, with Elaine Lustig, and president, Ex Libris (rare books), 1974–86. Visiting lecturer, Brown University, 1972, and Jewish Institute of Religion, 1977; Tisch Lecturer in Judaic Theology, Brown University, 1979. Consultant, Fund for the Republic ''Religion and the Free Society'' project, 1956–59; member, 1983–86, and chairman of the board, 1985–86, YIVO Institute for Jewish Research; member of advisory board, Institute for Advanced Judaic Studies, Brandeis University. **Awards:** Edgar Lewis Wallant prize, 1973, for *In the Days of Simon Stern;* Jewish Book Council national Jewish book award in fiction, 1984, and William and Janice Epstein award, 1985, both for *An Admirable Woman;* George Wittenborn memorial award, 1986, for *Herbert Bayer: The Complete Works.* **Died:** 31 October 1986.

PUBLICATIONS

Collection

An Arthur A. Cohen Reader: Selected Fiction and Writings on Judaism, Theology, Literature, and Culture, edited by David Stern and Paul Mendes-Flohr. 1998.

Novels

The Carpenter Years. 1967.
In the Days of Simon Stern. 1973.
A Hero in His Time. 1976.
Acts of Theft. 1980.
An Admirable Woman. 1983.
Artists & Enemies: Three Novellas. 1987.

Other

Martin Buber. 1958.
The Natural and the Supernatural Jew: An Historical and Theological Introduction. 1962; revised, 1979.
The Communism of Mao Tse-Tung. 1964.
The Myth of the Judeo-Christian Tradition. 1970.
A People Apart: Hasidism in America, with photos by Philip Garvin. 1970.
If Not Now, When? Conversations between Mordecai M. Kaplan and Arthur A. Cohen. 1970.
Osip Emilevich Mandelstam: An Essay in Antiphon. 1974.
Sonia Delaunay. 1975.
The Tremendum: A Theological Interpretation of the Holocaust. 1981.
The American Imagination after the War: Notes on the Novel, Jews and Hope. 1981.
Herbert Bayer: The Complete Works. 1984.

Editor, with Marvin Halverson, *A Handbook of Christian Theology; Definition Essays on Concepts and Movements of Thought in Contemporary Protestantism.* 1958.
Editor, *The Anatomy of Faith: Theological Essays of Milton Steinberg.* 1960.
Editor, *Humanistic Education and Western Civilization: Essays in Honor of Robert Maynard Hutchins.* 1964.
Editor, *Arguments and Doctrines: A Reader of Jewish Thinking in the Aftermath of the Holocaust.* 1970.
Editor, *The New Art of Color: The Writings of Robert and Sonia Delaunay.* 1978.
Editor, *The Jew: Essays from Martin Buber's Journal ''Der Jude.''* 1980.
Editor, with Paul Mendes-Flohr, *Contemporary Jewish Religious Thought: Original Essays on Critical Concepts, Movements, and Beliefs.* 1987.

*

Critical Studies: *Crisis and Covenant: The Holocaust in American Jewish Fiction* by Alan L. Berger, 1985; *Witness through the Imagination: Jewish American Holocaust Literature* by Lillian S. Kremer, 1989.

* * *

Arthur A. Cohen was a challenging and wide-ranging thinker who set for himself the task of formulating a Jewish theology for the postwar world. Chief among his concerns was the question of the theological implications of the Holocaust. Beginning with a series of analytical books and essays on modern Jewish thought and Jewish and Christian theology, he turned his energies to literary fiction in the late 1960s, producing a ''messianic epic'' (*In the Days of Simon Stern*) alongside a series of novellas. He also produced a powerful meditation on the Holocaust and the problem of evil, *The Tremendum,* which is perhaps the best known of his entire opus. All of

Cohen's varied works are characterized by an elegant and occasionally recondite writing style and by a common set of concerns, foremost among them the possibility of Jewish faith in the contemporary world. Other recurrent themes are the theological incommensurability of Christianity and Judaism, the redemptive vision at the core of Judaism, and the significance for contemporary Jews of the work of Franz Rosenzweig. As the scholar David Stern has noted, Cohen may be situated amongst a generation of Jewish thinkers that emerged on the American scene in the postwar years, a group that included Eugene Borowitz, Emil Fackenheim, Will Herberg, Steven Schwartzchild, and Joseph Soloveitchik. These figures shared an overall distrust of cultural liberalism, and they opened their work in different ways to the influences of European existentialism.

In *The Tremendum*, a ''theological interpretation of the Holocaust,'' Cohen asserts that the Holocaust represents an unprecedented manifestation of absolute evil. As such, it fundamentally alters the terms of God's relationship to the Jewish people. Unlike the destruction of the Temples or the expulsion from Spain, the Holocaust cannot be explained as divine retribution; traditional Jewish theodicies do not suffice. In their place Cohen calls for a recognition that normal time can open onto ''the abyss,'' a dimension in which intelligible causality is interrupted and the provenance of God gives way to that of ''infinitized man.'' Cohen's neologism for the Holocaust, *the Tremendum*, recasts the central idea of the nineteenth-century German theologian Rudolf Otto. Otto contends that God's presence manifests itself to humans as a *mysterium tremendum*, an unfathomable or terrifying mystery. By contrast, Cohen identifies the Holocaust as a manifestation of sheer terror without the accompanying mystery of God's presence.

Cohen proposes that Jews must come to regard *the Tremendum* in the same way that the Passover *Haggadah* has instructed them to consider the exodus from Egypt—namely as a decisive moment in their own experience of God. ''I was really, even if not literally present in Egypt,'' he writes, ''and really if not literally, present at Sinai. . . . No less is it the case that the death camps account my presence really.'' Having drawn this analogy Cohen asserts that contemporary Jews have an obligation to hear the witness as though they were also witnesses. For Cohen, then, the Holocaust represents a challenge to traditional conceptions of the Jewish God, but a challenge that can be met. ''The God of Israel is worth the undertaking,'' he asserts. ''And the time is now to build again upon the wreckage of previous understandings.'' When he describes this project of ''building again,'' Cohen emphasizes that the new understanding of God will differ from the old, specifically with reference to the question of power. Cohen describes a God with limited control over the world. ''The God who will endure,'' he writes, ''may well prove to be less imperious and authoritarian, but may gain in credibility and truth what he has lost in unconditional absoluteness.'' Cohen's

God will endure, that is, though not in the guise of the proverbial omniscient and omnipotent father.

Cohen's longest and most celebrated work of fiction, *In the Days of Simon Stern*, also deals with the question of post-Holocaust faith. Written from the perspective of a blind, oracular narrator named Nathan, it recounts the emergence of the Messiah during the 1940s in New York. When the messianic figure Simon Stern receives news of the death camps, he determines that ''now is the time to begin the work of redemption.'' He travels to Europe and retrieves a group of Holocaust survivors, whom he houses in a version of Solomon's Temple—rebuilt on Manhattan's Lower East side. The messianic project self-destructs, but, as the novel's narrator assures us, the Messiah himself has escaped and is now at large in the world. The novel is at once playful and profoundly serious in its declaration of faith in Judaism's redemptive mission. One of its many running themes concerns the difference between the genre of Greek tragedy, with its doctrine of the implacability of fate, and a ''messianic epic,'' with its insistence that human history remains open to the incursion of the divine.

—Julian Levinson

See the essay on *In the Days of Simon Stern.*

COHEN, Elie Aron

Nationality: Dutch. **Born:** Groningen, 16 July 1909. **Education:** University of Groningen, M.D. 1935; University of Utrecht, D.Med. Science 1952; University of Leiden, specialist youth doctor. **Family:** Married 1) Aaltje van der Wonde in 1936 (died 1943), one son (deceased); 2) Marguerite Herrmann in 1947, one son and one daughter. **Career:** Physician in general practice, Aduard, 1935–41. Prisoner, Amersfoort, Westerbork, and Auschwitz, World War II. Physician, Arnhem, 1947–66; school physician, Arnhem, 1966–74; psychotherapist, Arnhem, 1974–93. **Award:** Officier in Orde van Oranje Nassau, 1974. **Agent:** Julian Bach Jr., 3 East 48th Street, New York, New York, U.S.A. **Died:** 22 October 1993.

PUBLICATIONS

Memoir

De afgrond: Een egodocument. 1972; as *The Abyss: A Confession,* 1973.

Other

Het Duitse concentratiekamp; Een Medische en Psychologische studie (dissertation; memoir and study). 1954; as *Human*

Behavior in the Concentration Camp: A Medical and Psychological Study, 1988.

* * *

Elie Aron Cohen had been a general practitioner in Aduard, a village west of Groningen, in The Netherlands, from 1935 until 1 May 1941, when Jews were forbidden by the Germans to practice medicine. Arrested on 13 August 1942, he was taken first to the Amersfoort prison and concentration camp in Holland, then to the Westerbork transit camp, and finally to Auschwitz. He worked as a doctor in these camps until 18 January 1945, when he, along with the other prisoners, was forced to evacuate Auschwitz and proceed on the death march to Mauthausen. From there he was taken to two labor camps in Austria, Melk and then Ebensee, where he was freed by American forces on 6 May 1945. His book *The Abyss: A Confession* is an autobiographical account of his experiences.

The Abyss is completely different from Cohen's only other book, *Human Behaviour in the Concentration Camp: A Medical and Psychological Study,* written as his dissertation for a doctoral degree. *The Abyss* is a personal narrative, written in a natural, conversational tone, in which the author describes his functions as a camp physician and readily confesses what he perceives to be his own failings. It grew out of interviews he gave to a Dutch weekly. Although there are countless first-person narratives about life in the concentration camps, in *The Abyss,* which Cohen calls "an admonitory monument," his goal is to warn the reader of the depths to which humans are capable of descending when they are demoralized and driven by extreme hunger. *Human Behaviour in the Concentration Camp,* on the other hand, is a well-researched academic study of human nature, from which Cohen withholds any personal feelings. It was originally written at the University of Utrecht in 1952 and published in Dutch in 1954. In 1988 it was translated and published in The Netherlands, London, Stockholm, New York, and Tokyo.

There are many books in which the author attempts to provide insight into the psychology of Hitler, for example, Rudolph Binion's *Hitler among the Germans,* which examines the psychodynamics of his rise and fall, Ian Kershaw's *Hitler: 1889–1936,* or Ron Rosenbaum's *Explaining Hitler.* Other works, such as Detlev J.K. Peukert's *Inside Nazi Germany: Conformity, Opposition and Racism in Everyday Life* and Daniel Goldhagen's *Hitler's Willing Executioners,* analyze both the German people's blind devotion and their opposition to their führer. Many others deal with the psychology of the SS, for example, Heinz Höhne in *The Order of the Death's Head* or Willi Frischauer in *Himmler: The Evil Genius of the Third Reich,* to name but two. Hannah Arendt, in *Eichmann in Jerusalem: A Report of the Banality of Evil,* provides a frightening insight into Adolf Eichmannn, who did not recognize his behavior as anything but blind obedience to the state, and the prison psychologist G.M. Gilbert, in his book *Nuremberg Diary,* writes about his interviews with those who were put on trial after the war. There are also many books and articles about the prisoners in the camps.

None of these works, however, uses Freudian psychoanalytic ideas to attempt to explain the forces that influenced the behavior of the prisoners or of the SS. Although he was neither a psychologist nor a psychiatrist, Cohen does employ Freudian thought, and in this way his two books are unique. They provide a different kind of insight into human behavior during the Holocaust.

After receiving his doctorate on 11 March 1952, Cohen resumed the general practice of medicine and worked as a school physician in Arnhem. He later contributed several articles to journals and newspapers about what he called "post-concentration camp syndrome."

—Diane Plotkin

See the essay on *Human Behavior in the Concentration Camp: A Medical and Psychological Study.*

CZERNIAKÓW, Adam

Nationality: Polish. **Born:** Warsaw, 1880. **Education:** Studied chemistry at Warsaw Polytechnic. **Family:** Married Dr. Felicja Czerniaków. **Career:** Teacher and engineer. City counselor, Warsaw; senator, Polish Parliament. Also worked as a journalist. Cofounder, Union of Jewish Craftsmen, Poland; member, Jewish Engineers Association. Chairman, Warsaw Jewish Council, Warsaw Ghetto, 1939–42. **Died:** Suicide, 23 July 1942.

PUBLICATION

Diary

The Warsaw Diary of Adam Czerniaków, edited by Raul Hilberg. 1979 (originally published in Hebrew translation, 1968).

*

Critical Study: "Adam Czerniakow and His Times" by Joseph L. Lichten, in *Polish Review,* 29(1–2), 1984, pp. 71–89.

* * *

Adam Czerniaków, as the Judenrat president in the Warsaw Ghetto, was the leader of the largest Jewish community during the Holocaust. The Germans appointed him to that office on 4 October 1939. Earlier, on 23 September, before the defeat of Warsaw, its mayor, Stefan Starzynski, appointed him the chairman of the Jewish Council. That fact was of significance for Czerniaków's attitude. In his diary he did not refer to the Judenrat. He felt obliged to perform the role entrusted to him by the mayor of Warsaw and history.

Czerniaków's diary has a special place among more than 100 memoirs of the Warsaw Jews. It was written by a man who daily met the Germans enforcing Hitler's policy toward the Jews. His diary is a precious source of information about the Warsaw Ghetto. He commenced writing it on 6 September 1939. The final note is dated 23 July 1942, several hours before swallowing cyanide. Two farewell letters were found on his desk—one to his wife, the other to the Jewish Council Executive.

Czerniaków belonged to the Jewish middle class assimilated to Polish culture. Born in Warsaw in 1880, he completed his academic technical education in Warsaw and Dresden. In independent Poland he actively participated in the social and political life. He was a cofounder of the Union of Jewish Craftsmen in Poland, a member of the Jewish Engineers Association, a city counselor in Warsaw, and a senator of the Polish Parliament elected in the complementary election. As a journalist he wrote of issues pertaining to education, science, and culture. He was also a pedagogue. Though in favor of Jewish assimilation, he publicly criticized the discriminating policy of the Polish government.

Czerniaków perceived his function as a historic mission. His convictions stemmed from positivistic ideology. Thus he was committed to the protection of Jewish people, and he felt that he was their true leader. In his contacts with the Germans he behaved with dignity, and in the times of extermination he led a daily struggle for survival of as many Jews as possible. The only fighting method available to him was appealing to German officials. He attempted to delay the establishment of the ghetto. He applied for releasing prisoners and hostages and organized the education and social welfare systems and the health service, and he supported the ghetto's cultural and religious life and obtained help for the poor and sick. He collected the imposed contributions, but he negotiated for them to be diminished. He organized the Jewish police that was subject to him; however, they were not only responsible for maintaining the order in the ghetto but also for fulfilling German orders and conducting the selections for the labor camps.

The Judenrat president was well aware of his ambivalent function. The refusal to perform it would mean death. He was on duty, like a captain of a ship, and in that behavior he saw sense and honor. In his struggle he had a series of minor victories, but in the face of the final catastrophe they were insignificant. Forced to give a direct order of sending the orphaned children to Treblinka, he chose death. It confirmed not only his fidelity to his convictions but also the bankruptcy of his earlier efforts and positivistic ideas.

The leader of the Warsaw Ghetto was not a naive person. His diary reflects his growing awareness of the approaching catastrophe. Yet for a long time in his rationalistic mind he would not admit the possibility of murdering hundreds of thousands of people exclusively on racial grounds, and against the logic of the war, since the Jews were the cheapest labor force.

Czerniaków's suicide, committed at the beginning of the largest extermination wave, stirred the Jews of Warsaw and evoked many spontaneous comments and later interpretations. **Marek Edelman,** the only living leader of the Warsaw Ghetto Uprising, wrote after the war that instead of committing ''private suicide'' Czerniaków should have called the Jews of Warsaw to resistance, making them fully aware of the significance of the conducted deportations. Yitzhak Katznelson, a poet, saw Czerniaków's suicide as ''a sign of his desire to free himself of guilt feelings, to expiate a sin weighed on his conscience,'' according to the introduction by J. Kermisz to *The Warsaw Diary of Adam Czerniaków* (1982).

Undoubtedly, that act determines the perception of Czerniaków's choices and of his entire activity as the leader of the Jewish community. Reading the diary is crucial for understanding his motives and the sense of his suicide. The two farewell letters constitute a particular form of conclusion for that diary. He wrote to his wife that he could not sign the order to send the Jewish orphans to Treblinka. In the other letter, to the Jewish Council Executive, he wrote: ''I can no longer bear all this. My act will show everyone the right thing to do.''

—Kazimierz Adamczyk

See the essay on *The Warsaw Diary of Adam Czerniaków.*

D

DELBO, Charlotte

Nationality: French. **Born:** Vigneux sur Seine, 10 August 1913. **Family:** Married Georges Dudach (died 1942). **Career:** Assistant to Louis Jouvet (actor and theater director); worked for the United Nations; assistant to philosopher Henri Lefèvre. Editor, *Cahiers de la Jeunesse*. **Died:** 1 March 1985.

PUBLICATIONS

Memoirs

Auschwitz et après (trilogy). 1970; as *Auschwitz and After*, 1995.
    Aucun de nous ne reviendra. 1965; as *None of Us Will Return*, 1968.
    Une connaissance inutile [Useless Knowledge]. 1970.
    Mesure de nos jours [Measure of Our Days]. 1971.

Plays

La Sentence. 1972.
Qui rapportera ces paroles? 1974; as *Who Will Carry the Word?* in *The Theatre of the Holocaust*, edited by Robert Skloot, 1982.
Maria Lusitania; Le coup d'état. 1975.

Other

Les Belles Lettres. 1961.
Le Convoi du 24 janvier. 1965; as *Convoy to Auschwitz: Women of the French Resistance*, 1997.
La Théorie et la pratique, dialogue imaginaire mais non tout à fait apocryphe entre Herbert Marcuse et Henri Lefebvre. 1969.
Spectres, mes compagnons [Phantoms, My Companions]. 1977.
Le Mémoire et les jours. 1985; as *Days and Memory*, 1990.

*

Critical Studies: "Literature, the Exile's Agent of Survival: Alexander Solzhenitsyn and Charlotte Delbo," in *Mosaic* (Canada), 9(1), 1975, pp. 1–17, "Charlotte Delbo, a Woman/Book," in *Faith of a (Woman) Writer*, edited by Alice Kessler-Harris and William McBrien, 1988, and "The Triple Courage of Charlotte Delbo," in *The Massachusetts Review*, 41(4), 2001, pp. 483–97, all by Rosette C. Lamont; "Art and Testimony: The Representation of Historical Horror in Literary Works by Piotr Rawicz and Charlotte Delbo" by Lea Fridman Hamaoui, in *Cardozo Studies in Law and Literature*, 3(2), Fall 1991, pp. 243–59; "From Sight to Insight: The Legacy of Charlotte Delbo" by Lawrence L. Langer, in *Contemporary French Civilization*, 18(1), Spring 1994, p. 64; "Charlotte Delbo: Theatre as a Means of Survival" by Claude Schumacher, in his *Staging the Holocaust: The Shoah in Drama and Performance*, 1998; "Memory and Language: The Example of Charlotte Delbo," in *Journal of the Institute of Romance Studies*, 6, 1999, and *A Literary Analysis of Charlotte Delbo's Concentration Camp Re-Presentation*, 2000, both by Nicole Thatcher; "Body, Trauma, and the Rituals of Memory: Charlotte Delbo and Ruth Klüger" by Karein K. Goertz, in *Shaping Losses: Cultural Memory and the Holocaust*, edited by Julia Epstein and Lori Hope Lefkovitz, 2001.

* * *

Charlotte Delbo's style is taut and factual and marked by restraint of the highest degree. Delbo was motivated by the desire to let the world know what had happened in the camps, and yet her work is marked by the feeling that anyone who was not there could not really understand. The only way to get them to grasp what went on was to describe the camps in as calm and matter-of-fact a manner as possible. This was important, she argued, because what had happened was not so much evil as inconceivable, and the inconceivable cannot really be grasped in language. Some of her prose is not completely descriptive of external events but is more reflective; she contemplates what is taking place and what has taken place in the past, as though weighing what is happening in the scales of justice and finding it wanting. Her reaction is not rage but resignation, yet not a resignation that is equivalent to acceptance. It is a kind of puzzled resignation that people can behave so cruelly to each other and also admiration at the occasional acts of nobility that manage to exist within the context of the Holocaust.

Delbo interposes poetry occasionally with prose, and the poems provide her with a space in which she can be more openly emotional. This is an opportunity she readily accepts. There are not many poems in her books of prose, but they play an important role: the contrast between their display of passion and the apparent coolness of the prose is an important aspect of her style. The balance is well judged. There are just enough poems to provide the reader with evidence of the moral outrage and anguish of the author but not so much as to betray the principle that in describing the indescribable one has to steer close to the facts throughout and not go beyond them. Without the poems the reader might feel that the unremittingly descriptive style is meant to be ironic. Delbo desires to represent in her work her feeling that she really belonged with the dead, and, although in fact she survived, she really died, so there is a detachment in her prose that is the detachment of someone not really living in the contemporary world. She is both there and somewhere else, and this leads to a degree of detachment in her work, a feature not untypical of many writers who experienced the Holocaust personally.

Another aspect of Delbo's style is the absence of religious imagery or the idea of being part of a tradition of suffering and persecution. Delbo was not Jewish and was sent to the camps as a result of her opposition to German control of France and also due to the important role her husband played in the resistance. There was nothing in her cultural background to prepare her for what was being done to her or to others. This perhaps made her even cooler in her account of the camps, since her persecution along with that of so many others came out of the blue and could only be described, not explained.

—Oliver Leaman

See the essay on *Auschwitz and After*.

DOCTOROW, E(dgar) L(aurence)

Nationality: American. **Born:** New York City, 6 January 1931. **Education:** Kenyon College, Gambier, Ohio, B.A. (honors) in philosophy 1952; Columbia University, graduate study in English drama, 1952–53. **Military Service:** United States Army: served in the Signal Corps, 1953–55. **Family:** Married Helen Esther Setzer in 1954; two daughters and one son. **Career:** Desk clerk, La Guardia Airport, New York, 1955–56; script reader, Columbia Pictures Industries, Inc., New York, 1956–58; senior editor, New American Library, New York, 1959–64; editor-in-chief, 1964–69, and vice president and publisher, 1968–69, Dial Press, New York; faculty member, Sarah Lawrence College, Bronxville, 1971–78. Since 1982 professor, New York University. Writer-in-residence, University of California, Irvine, 1969–70; creative writing fellow, Yale School of Drama, 1974–75; visiting professor, University of Utah, 1975; visiting senior fellow, Princeton University, 1980–81. **Awards:** Guggenheim fellowship, 1973; Creative Artists Service fellow, 1973–74; National Book Critics Circle award and American Academy of Arts and Letters award, both in 1976, for *Ragtime;* National Book Critics Circle award, 1982, for *Loon Lake,* and 1989, for *Billy Bathgate;* National Book award, 1986, for *World's Fair;* Edith Wharton Citation of Merit for fiction and New York State Author, both 1989–91; PEN/Faulkner award and William Dean Howells medal, American Academy of Arts and Letters, both 1990, for *Billy Bathgate;* National Humanities medal, 1998; Commonwealth award, 2000. D.H.L.: Kenyon College, 1976, Brandeis University, 1989. D.Litt.: Hobart and William Smith College, 1979. **Member:** American Academy and National Institute of Arts and Letters, 1984. **Agent:** Amanda Urban, International Creative Management, 40 West 57th Street, New York, New

York 10019, U.S.A. **Address:** c/o Random House Inc., 201 East 50th Street, New York, New York 10022, U.S.A.

PUBLICATIONS

Novels

Welcome to Hard Times. 1960; as *Bad Man from Bodie,* 1961.
Big As Life. 1966.
The Book of Daniel. 1971.
Ragtime. 1975.
Loon Lake. 1980.
World's Fair. 1985.
Billy Bathgate. 1989.
Three Complete Novels. 1984.
The Waterworks. 1994.
City of God. 2000.

Short Stories

Lives of the Poets: Six Stories and a Novella. 1984.

Plays

Drinks before Dinner (produced New York, 1978). 1979.

Screenplay: *Daniel,* 1983.

Other

Jack London, Hemingway, and the Constitution: Selected Essays, 1977–1992. 1993.

Editor, with Katrina Kenison, *The Best American Short Stories 2000.* 2000.

*

Film Adaptations: *Welcome to Hard Times,* 1967, 1991; *Ragtime,* 1981; *Daniel,* 1983, from the novel *The Book of Daniel; Billy Bathgate,* 1991.

Bibliography: *E. L. Doctorow: An Annotated Bibliography* by Michelle M. Tokarczyk, 1988.

Critical Studies: "Marching Backward into the Future: Progress As Illusion in Doctorow's Novels" by David Emblidge, in *Southwest Review,* Autumn 1977, pp. 397–409; "Women and Tragic Destiny in Doctorow's *The Book of Daniel*" by Mildred Culp, and "Doctorow's *The Book of Daniel:* All in the Family" by Robert Forrey, both in *Studies in American Jewish Literature,* 2, 1982, pp. 155–73; *E. L. Doctorow: Essays and Conversations,* edited by Richard Trenner, 1983; *E. L. Doctorow* by Paul Levine, 1985; "E. L. Doctorow's 'Jewish' Radicalism" by Carol Iannone, in *Commentary,* 81(3), March 1986, pp. 53–56; "From the Lion's Den: Survivors in E. L. Doctorow's

The Book of Daniel," in *Critique,* 29(1), Fall 1987, pp. 3–15, and *E. L. Doctorow's Skeptical Commitment,* 2000, both by Michelle M. Tokarczyk; *E. L. Doctorow: A Democracy of Perception: A Symposium with and on E. L. Doctorow,* edited by Herwig Friedl and Dieter Schulz, 1988; *E. L. Doctorow* by Carol C. Harter and James R. Thompson, 1990; *E. L. Doctorow* by John Parks, 1991; *Models of Misrepresentation: On the Fiction of E. L. Doctorow,* 1991, and *Conversations with E. L. Doctorow,* 1999, both by Christopher Morris; *Understanding E. L. Doctorow* by Douglas Fowler, 1992; *Fiction As False Document: The Reception of E. L. Doctorow in the Postmodern Age* by John Williams, 1996; "'The Jews,' Ragtime, and the Politics of Silence" by Michelle Persell, in *Literature and Psychology,* 43(4), 1997, pp. 1–15; *Critical Essays on E. L. Doctorow,* edited by Ben Siegel, 2000.

* * *

In his *Newsweek* magazine article, "A Vision of the American Zion," E. L. Doctorow rejoiced at the nomination of Sen. Joe Lieberman for U.S. vice president, crediting Lieberman's religion, or the rectitude of character that he traces to that religion, as the basis of his electability. Ruminating on anti-Semitism and the achievements of certain prominent Jews, Doctorow asked, "when did I stop writing about Jewish history and start writing about American history?" He rejected the otherness stigma of American Jews in "national life," including "national elective office." Hence, Jewish history and American history should be compatible ideas. Some Doctorow novels have offered a blending of Americana with the Jewish experience—*The Book of Daniel* (1971), portions of *Ragtime* (1975), *World's Fair* (1985), and especially *City of God* (2000). It is doubtful, however, that Jewish history and American history—considering the outcome of the 2000 presidential election—will have as close a link as suggested by Doctorow in his *Newsweek* article. But his religious flight of fancy in *City of God,* wherein a large cross is mysteriously stolen from an Episcopal church in New York City and inexplicably deposited on the roof of a building that houses a small synagogue, suggests in a remarkable way— through the Holocaust—the confluence of Jewish history with American history.

City of God is at once a critique of contemporary Christianity and contemporary Judaism. Christianity is faulted directly for not recognizing the immense scale of the Holocaust and therefore not doing nearly enough to make commensurate amends. Judaism is faulted for not evolving theologically and in practice—though, as *City of God* brings out, the universe has been evolving ever since the big bang, a "revelation" about the Judaeo-Christian religious systems may be evolving, and even God may be evolving. But this double-edged critique is background for Doctorow's grand effort at consciousness-raising, giving readers a detailed, indelible account of the Holocaust's horrors. Everett, the scriptwriter whose experiences, thoughts, and readings are so integral to the book,

recasts and rewrites the narrative of a Jewish boy's survival in an Eastern European Nazi death camp, which is told to him by a young woman rabbi (daughter of a Holocaust survivor who originally provided the account). Everett sets the ghetto in Kovno, Lithuania, instead of in the actual Polish village of her father's story, and the woman recognizes his background source as the Kovno ghetto described in **Avraham Tory**'s diary. When she questions him about it, he admits his heavy reliance on that material.

Surviving the Holocaust: The Kovno Ghetto Diary (1990), by Tory (translated by Jerzy Michalowicz), offered Doctorow a sizable body of Holocaust material that he could draw on directly and apply indirectly to structure the plot of his fragmented antinovel. In summer 1941 the German forces, moving through the Baltic region, established a local authority, known as an "Elders Council," in each ghetto they encountered, wherein Jewish "leaders" would collaborate with Nazi delegates (in anticipation of the Final Solution). In the Kovno ghetto Tory, a young lawyer and secretary to the council who had access to Nazi and Jewish leaders alike, secretly began to compile a collection of the council's transactions and relations with the German oppressors. Into this resource went his own descriptions and records of events, Nazi documents of all kinds, and whatever else he could obtain to preserve what was happening to the Kovno Jews. Tory hid the remarkable diary collection, which was subsequently traced and recovered. Doctorow, using the history as well as the contents of the diary, makes the search for the hidden (but lost) archive of the Kovno ghetto victims a minor mystery.

Appearing in *New Yorker* magazine, Doctorow's story "A House on the Plains" is a narrative by the son of a psychopathic mother who, in the early 1900s, successfully carried out an elaborate program of deceit, trickery, fraud, and serial murder in Illinois. Luring men (mostly unwitting Scandinavians) to their death for their money, she also murdered her three adopted children for their life insurance and burned down her mortgaged farmhouse to destroy the evidence. The story contains echoes and distorted elements of the Holocaust and its aftermath, including false identities, the idea of "inferior" Nordic men, destruction by fire of incriminating evidence, and the killer's escape to a new land and new identity.

—Samuel I. Bellman

See the essay on *City of God.*

DONAT, Alexander

Nationality: American (originally Polish; immigrated to the United States, 1946). **Born:** Michael Berg, Warsaw, 1905. **Family:** Married Lena; one son. **Career:** Journalist; worked for a tailor and a printer. Founder, Waldon Press, New York, 1949. **Died:** 1983.

PUBLICATIONS

Memoir

The Holocaust Kingdom: A Memoir. 1965.

Other

Jewish Resistence. 1964.
Neopalimaia kupina: Evreiskie siuzhety v russkoi poezii; antologiia. 1973.

Editor, *The Death Camp Treblinka: A Documentary.* 1979.

*

Critical Study: "Alexander Donat" by Myra Alperson, in *Jewish Profiles: Great Jewish Personalities and Institutions of the Twentieth Century,* edited by Murray Polner, 1991.

*   *   *

Alexander Donat, the author of the memoir *The Holocaust Kingdom* (1965), was born Michael Berg in 1905 in Warsaw, where his father had lived since the turn of the century. In October 1944, when Berg was a prisoner in the concentration camp at Vaihingen, a transport was being prepared to leave. Berg exchanged his name with a certain Alexander Donat, so that he, Berg, could be placed on the transport. Soon after, the new Alexander Donat left Vaihingen with his new name, and the one who remained behind as Michael Berg was sent to Kochendorf, where the Nazis murdered him. Thus, the new Donat survived to remember the one who died bearing his original name.

By the time the Germans invaded Poland on September 1, 1939, Berg had become an accomplished journalist living in Warsaw with his wife, Lena, and their two-year-old son. After the Germans took Warsaw in September 1939, however, he had to support his family by other means. When the occupying forces began hunting down journalists and other members of the intelligentsia, Berg fled the city. On January 2, 1940, he returned to Warsaw to be with his family. Once the ghetto was sealed, he attempted to obtain work with the Jewish Council, but to no avail. He eventually found a job in a tailor shop. After surviving the deportations of July–September 1942, Berg and his wife entrusted their son to a family of Polish Catholics, who managed to get the five-year-old child out of the ghetto in February 1943. The boy's parents remained in the ghetto and lived through the Warsaw Ghetto Uprising in the spring of 1943, only to be sent to Majdanek.

Once he was in Majdanek, Berg's skills as a printer saved his life, for in June he was transferred to a printing factory in Radom. In July 1944 the inmates of Majdanek were forced to march to Radom to escape the advancing Soviet army; in Radom, Berg joined them for their march to Lodz. Before they made it to Lodz, however, they were placed on a train destined for the camp at Vaihingen, where Berg became Donat. From Vaihingen, the new Donat went on to survive other camps, including Auschwitz and Dachau. His wife was also sent to Auschwitz and from there was transported to Oskar Schindler's factory in Czechoslovakia. Donat was liberated on April 29, 1945, by the Americans while being transported from Dachau to yet another camp.

When Donat and his wife were reunited with their son, Wlodek, shortly after the war, they discovered that the Catholic family had exercised a certain influence over the little boy. He told them that he wanted nothing to do with them because they were Jews who had killed his Lord Jesus Christ. Nevertheless, in April 1946 Donat, his wife, and their son immigrated to the United States, where he went into the printing business. His son, then called William, graduated from Colgate University and went on to have a family of his own. In addition to writing his memoir, Donat edited an important volume entitled *The Death Camp Treblinka* (1979). He died in 1983.

—David Patterson

See the essay on *The Holocaust Kingdom.*

DORIAN, Emil

Nationality: Romanian. **Born:** Bucharest, 1893. **Education:** Attended medical school, ca. 1916. **Military Service:** Physician during World War I. **Family:** Married Paula Fränkel; two daughters. **Career:** Physician and writer. Secretary general, Jewish Community of Bucharest, following World War II; director, Documentary Archives of the Federation of Jewish Communities of Romania, following World War II. **Died:** 1956.

PUBLICATION

Diary

The Quality of Witness: A Romanian Diary, 1937–1944, edited by Marguerite Dorian. 1982; published in Romanian as *Jurnal din vremur de prigoanæa,* 1996.

Novels

Conversations with My Horse. 1928.
Profeti si paiate. 1920; as *Prophets and Clowns.* 1930.
The Poison. 1939.

Critical Study: "The Victim as Eyewitness: Jewish Intellectual Diaries During the Antonescu Period" by Leon Volovici, in *The Destruction of Romanian and Ukrainian Jews During the Antonescu Era,* edited by Randolph L. Braham, 1997.

* * *

Early in his publishing career the child born to Herman and Ernestina Lustig in 1893 took the pen name Emil Dorian. He grew up in his native Bucharest at a time when the Jews of Romania had not yet been granted citizenship. Therefore, if Jews wanted to attend public schools, they had to pay exorbitant fees. Because his father earned only a modest income as a German language teacher, Dorian was forced to attend the newly founded Jewish schools, where he received something less than a traditional Jewish education. By the time he graduated from high school in 1910, he was already a published poet and an avid student of literature. He enrolled in medical school and was in the last month of his studies when Romania entered World War I in the summer of 1916. Dorian was sent to the Moldavian front to serve as a physician, an experience that later formed the basis for *Conversations with My Horse* (1928), his dark satire on war. Soon after the end of the war he married Paula Fränkel, with whom he had two daughters.

By the mid-1920s Dorian had become a poet whose work was widely known for its pacifist views and its eloquent expression of love for humankind. And yet the more he devoted his thinking and writing to themes of social justice, the greater his impatience and exasperation, which ultimately turned into despair. Among his works are several volumes of poetry, novels, essays on popular topics in medicine, and numerous articles on Romanian and Jewish life. Two of his novels—*Prophets and Clowns* (1930) and *The Poison* (1939)—are on specifically Jewish themes. The first is a critique of the Jewish and Gentile Romanian bourgeoisie, and the second is an intense analysis of Romanian anti-Semitism. Dorian also published translations of works by Heinrich Heine and Eliezer Steinberg's Yiddish fables, all the while operating a medical practice from an office in his home.

In 1937 Dorian began keeping a daily account of his life in Romania, which he maintained until his death a generation later. The entries from the first seven years of his diary form his *Jurnal din vremur de prigoanæa,* the Holocaust diary that was published in Romania in 1996, 14 years after the English edition, *The Quality of Witness: A Romanian Diary 1937–1944,* appeared in 1982. Because he successfully avoided being sent to a concentration camp or being deported to Transnistria, Dorian was able to chronicle one of the most violent periods in Romanian history. During the years he kept his Holocaust diary he also completed a three-volume anthology of Yiddish poetry in translation, and scattered among the entries describing the devastation of Jewish life and European culture one

finds progress reports on his *Anthology of Yiddish Literature,* a project that became all the more dear to him as European Jewry was being wiped out.

After the war Dorian held two important positions in the Romanian Jewish community. He served as secretary general of the Jewish Community of Bucharest and later was the director of the Documentary Archives of the Federation of Jewish Communities of Romania. Because of what he viewed as the collapse of the moral fiber of Romanian society, however, he resigned from both positions. When Dorian died in 1956, it was perhaps due as much to disillusionment and a broken heart as to any other cause.

—David Patterson

See the essay on *The Quality of Witness: A Romanian Diary, 1937–1944.*

DURLACHER, Gerhard (Leopold)

Nationality: Dutch (originally German: immigrated to The Netherlands, 1937, granted Dutch citizenship, 1953). **Born:** Baden-Baden, 10 July 1928. **Education:** Koninklijke H.B.S., Apeldoorn, Netherlands, 1945–47; studied medicine at the University of Utrecht, 1948–54; University of Amsterdam, 1955–65, Ph.D. in Sociology 1965. **Family:** Married Anneke Sasburg in 1959; three daughters. **Career:** Wiardi Beckmann Foundation, 1962–63; professor, University of Amsterdam, 1965–83. Traveled to Yad Vashem to meet fellow survivors of Camp BIIB at Auschwitz-Birkenau, 1983, to the United States to interview other survivors, 1986, and to the reunion of camp survivors, Beit Terezin, Israel, 1990. **Awards:** Anne Frank award, for *Drenkeling,* and AKO prize for literature, for *Quarantaine,* both in 1994. Honorary doctorate, University of Amsterdam. **Died:** July 1996

PUBLICATIONS

Collection

Verzameld werk. 1997.

Memoirs

Strepen aus de hemel: Oorlogsherinneringen. 1985; as *Stripes in the Sky: A Wartime Memoir,* 1991.
Drenkeling kinderjaren in het derde rijk. 1987; as *Drowning: Growing Up in the Third Reich,* 1993.
De zoektocht. 1991; as *The Search,* 1998.
Quarantaine. 1993.
Niet verstaan. 1995.

*

Film Adaptations: *Laatste getuigen* [Last Witness], 1991, from the work, *De zoektocht.*

* * *

Gerhard Durlacher grew up in the German town of Baden-Baden and lived through the initial years of Nazi rule in that town. In his memoir *Drowning: Growing Up in the Third Reich* he describes 1 April 1933: "We push our way to the front through the crowd of onlookers. Some of them look at us with puzzlement, others passively or with consternation. But there are also those among them who grin as though the spectacle gives them pleasure. Mr. Kindler from the clothing store around the corner is among them. With legs apart and hands on hips, he stands in the front row, the red swastika badge gleaming on his leather jacket. Brawny men in brown uniforms are standing on both sides of the entrance with revolvers strapped to their shoulders and shining black boots on their legs, immovable as statues. Lanky youths, a good bit taller than I, yell out slogans, while older people in shabby clothes murmur either in agreement or shaking their heads. 'Don't buy from Jews, they are your misfortune,' and 'The Jews are dragging down the German people. Germans defend yourselves.' The big display windows are scribbled over with Stars of David in dripping chalk . . . ''

Drowning is a small collection of various remembrances from Durlacher's childhood, before his family fled to what they hoped was safety in Holland. They were ultimately deported to Auschwitz-Birkenau in 1942. *Drowning* was published subsequent to Durlacher's first memoir, *Stripes in the Sky,* in which he described his experiences in Auschwitz-Birkenau from 1942 to the end of the war.

In spite of the scars of the concentration camp, Durlacher was able, in the final ten years of his life, to write about what had formerly been inexpressible to him. According to him his memories came back after reading two books in the early 1980s: Martin Gilbert's *Auschwitz and the Allies* and Walter Laqueur's *The Terrible Secret.* Both books attempt to investigate why the Allied forces ignored pleas for help after the true purpose of concentration camps became known. Durlacher agrees with Laqueur's conclusion, which focuses on the nature of belief and the way in which some horrifying atrocities are so numbing that they are impossible to accept. In *Stripes in the Sky* Durlacher attempts directly to discover why the fate of European Jews was so persistently ignored.

Durlacher was one of 89 boys at Auschwitz who were selected by Dr. Josef Mengele to postpone their entrance to the gas chamber. Mengele doubtlessly had plans for these boys; the war's end came before he could enact them. Durlacher was one of the camp's few survivors to be liberated, in critically ill condition, by the Russians. After the war he eventually made his way to Holland, went to university, married a non-Jew, and became a sociology professor. He had three daughters. His final book, *The Search,* chronicles his efforts to find the survivors of the original 89 "Birkenau boys" and to go back with them to the camp. He died in 1996.

—Martha Sutro

See the essays on *Drowning: Growing Up in the Third Reich* and *Stripes in the Sky: A Wartime Memoir.*

DÜRRENMATT, Friedrich

Nationality: Swiss. **Born:** Konolfingen, 5 January 1921. **Education:** University of Zurich, 1941–42; University of Bern, 1942. **Family:** Married 1) Lotti Geissler in 1946 (died 1983), one son and two daughters; 2) Charlotte Kerr in 1984. **Career:** Drama critic, *Die Weltwoche,* Zurich, 1951–53; codirector, Basler Theater, 1968–69; co-owner, *Züricher Sonntags-Journal,* 1969–71. Writer-in-residence, University of Southern California, Los Angeles, 1981; traveled to Greece and South America, 1983–84, and to Egypt, 1985. **Awards:** City of Bern drama prize, 1948, for *Es steht geschrieben;* City of Bern literature prize, 1954, for *Ein Engel kommt nach Babylon;* radio play prize of the War Blind, 1957, for *Die Panne;* Prix Italia, RAI, 1958, for *Abendstunde im Spätherbst;* Preis zur Förderung des Bernischen Schrifttums, 1959, for *Das Versprechen;* Schiller prize, Mannheim, 1959, for *Grieche sucht Griechin;* New York Drama Critics Circle award for best foreign play, 1959, for *The Visit;* Grillparzer prize, Austria, 1968, for *Der Besuch der alten Dame;* Grosser Schiller-Preis, Schweizer Stiftung, 1969, for *Die Physiker;* Canton of Bern Grosser Literaturpreis, 1969; International Writers prize, Welsh Arts Council, University of Wales, 1976; Buber-Rosenzweig medal, 1977; City of Bern literature prize, 1979; Austrian State award, 1983; Carl Zuckmayer medal, Rhineland Palatinate, 1984; Bavarian literature prize, 1985. Honorary degrees: Temple University, 1969; Hebrew University, 1977; University of Nice, 1977; University of Neuchâtel, 1981. **Died:** Neuchâtel, 14 December 1990.

PUBLICATIONS

Collections

Werkausgabe in dreissig Bänden (30 vols.). 1980.
Gesammelte Werke, edited by Franz Josef Görtz (7 vols.). 1988.

Plays

Es steht geschrieben [It Is Written] (produced Zurich, 1947). 1947; revised version, as *Der Wiedertäufer* [The Anabaptists] (produced Zurich, 1967), 1967.

Der Blinde [The Blind Man] (produced Basel, Switzerland, 1948). 1947; revised edition, 1965.

Romulus der Grosse (produced Basel, 1949). 1957; revised version (produced Zurich, 1957), 1964; translated as *Romulus the Great* and published with *An Angel Comes to Babylon,* 1957.

Die Ehe des Herrn Mississippi (produced Munich, 1952). 1952; as *Fools Are Passing Through* (produced New York, 1958); as *The Marriage of Mr. Mississippi* (produced London, 1959), published with *Problems of the Theatre,* 1964.

Herkules und der Stall des Augias: Mit Randnotizen eines Kugelschreibers (radio play). 1954; as *Herkules und der Stall des Augias* (stage play version of the radio play; produced Zurich, 1963), 1963; as *Hercules and the Augean Stables,* 1963.

Ein Engel kommt nach Babylon (produced Munich, 1953). 1954; revised version (produced Zurich, 1957), 1957; translated as *An Angel Comes to Babylon* (produced California, 1962), and published with *Romulus the Great,* 1957.

Der Besuch der alten Dame (produced Zurich, 1956). 1956; as *The Visit* (produced New York, 1958), 1956.

Nächtliches gespräch mit einem verachteten Menschen: Ein Kurs für Zeitgenossen (radio play). 1957; as *Conversation at Night with a Despised Character: A Curriculum for Our Times,* 1957.

Das Unternehmen der Wega (radio play). 1958; as *The Mission of the Vega,* 1962.

Der Prozess um des Esels Schatten [The Trial of the Ass's Shadow] (radio play). 1958.

Stranitzky und der Nationalheld [Stranitzky and the National Hero] (radio play). 1959.

Abendstunde im Spätherbst (radio play). 1959; as *Episode on an Autumn Evening,* 1959; as *Incident at Twilight,* in *Postwar German Theatre,* 1968.

Frank der Fünfte: Oper einer Privatbank [Frank the Fifth: Opera of a Private Bank], music by Paul Burkhard (produced Zurich, 1959). 1960; revised edition, 1964.

Der Doppelgänger (radio play). 1960.

Die Panne, adaptation from his novel (radio play). 1961.

Die Physiker (produced Zurich, 1962). 1962; as *The Physicists* (produced New York, 1964), 1964.

Der Meteor (produced Zurich, 1966). 1966; as *The Meteor,* 1973.

König Johann, adaptation of a work by William Shakespeare (produced Basel, 1968). 1968.

Play Strindberg: Totentanz nach August Strindberg (produced Basel, 1969). 1969; as *Play Strindberg* (produced New York, 1971), published as *Play Strindberg: The Dance of Death Choreographed,* 1973.

Göthes Urfaust: Ergänzt durch das Buch von Doktor Faustus aus dem Jahre 1589, adaptation of a work by Johann Wolfgang von Goethe (produced Zurich, 1970). 1980.

Porträt eines Planeten [Portrait of a Planet] (produced Dusseldorf, 1970). 1971.

Titus Andronicus: Eine Komödie nach Shakespeare, adaptation of a work by William Shakespeare (produced Dusseldorf, 1970). 1970.

Der Mitmacher. 1976.

Die Frist (produced Zurich, 1977). 1977.

Die Panne [The Breakdown], adaptation of his own novel. 1979.

Achterloo (produced Zurich, 1983). 1983.

Radio Plays: *Der Prozess um des Esels Schatten,* 1951; *Stranitzky und der Nationalheld,* 1952; *Nächtliches Gespräch mit einem verachteten Menschen,* 1952; *Herkules und der Stall des Augias,* 1954; *Das Unternehmen der Wega,* 1954; *Die Panne,* 1956; *Abendstunde im Spätherbst,* 1958; *Der Doppelgänger,* 1961.

Screenplays: *Es geschah am heiligen Tag* (It Happened in Broad Daylight), 1960; *Die Ehe des Herrn Mississippi,* 1961; *Der Besuch der alten Dame,* 1963.

Novels

Pilatus (novella). 1949.

Der Nihilist (novella). 1950; as *Die Falle,* in *Die Stadt: Prosa I–IV,* 1952.

Der Tunnel (novella). In *Die Stadt: Prosa I–IV,* 1952.

Das Bild des Sisyphos (novella). 1952.

Der Richter und sein Henker. 1952; as *The Judge and His Hangman,* 1954; as *End of the Game,* 1955.

Der Verdacht. 1953; as *The Quarry,* 1961.

Grieche sucht Griechin. 1955; as *Once a Greek . . . ,* 1965.

Die Panne [The Breakdown]. 1956; as *Traps,* 1960; as *A Dangerous Game,* 1960.

Das Versprechen: Requiem auf den Kriminalroman. 1958; as *The Pledge,* 1959.

Der Sturz (novella). 1971.

Justiz. 1985; as *The Execution of Justice,* 1989.

Minotaurus: Eine Ballade. 1985.

Der Auftraug; Oder, Vom Beobachten des Beobachters der Beobachter. 1986; as *The Assignment: Or, On the Observing of the Observer of the Observers,* 1988.

Short Stories

Die Stadt: Prosa I–IV. 1952.

Der Hund; Der Tunnel; Die Panne: Erzählungen (vol. 20 of *Werkausgabe in dreissig Bänden*). 1980.

Grieche sucht Griechin; Mister X macht Ferien; Nachrichten über den Stand des Zeitungswesens in der Steinzeit: Grotesken (vol. 21 of *Werkausgabe in dreissig Bänden*). 1980.

Der Sturz; Abu Chanifa und Anan ben David; Smithy; Das Sterben der Pythia: Erzählungen (vol. 23 of *Werkausgabe in dreissig Bänden*).

Other

Theaterprobleme (essay). 1954; as *Problems of the Theatre*, with the play, *The Marriage of Mr. Mississippi*, 1958; as *Problems of the Theatre*, 1964.

Friedrich Schiller: Eine Rede (acceptance speech). 1960.

Der Rest ist Dank: Zwei Reden, with Werner Weber (acceptance speech). 1961.

Die Heimat im Plakat: Ein Buch für Schweizer Kinder (satirical drawings). 1963.

Monstervortrag über Gerechtigkeit und Recht nebst einem helvetischen Zwischenspiel: Eine kleine Dramaturgie der Politik (lecture). 1966; translated in *Plays and Essays*, 1982.

Theater-Schriften und Reden (essays and speeches), edited by Elisabeth Brock Sulzer:

Vol. 1: *Theater-Schriften und Reden.* 1966.

Vol. 2: *Dramaturgisches und Kritisches.* 1972.

Vol. 3: *Writings on Theatre and Drama* (translated selections from *Theater-Schriften und Reden* and *Dramaturgisches und Kritisches*). 1976.

Sätze aus Amerika (travel book). 1970.

Zusammenhänge: Essay über Israel: Eine Konzeption. 1976.

Gespräch mit Heinz Ludwig Arnold. 1976.

Lesebuch. 1978.

Albert Einstein: Ein Vortrag (lecture). 1979.

Theater: Essays, Gedichte und Reden (vol. 24 of *Werkausgabe in dreissig Bänden*). 1980.

Kritik: Kritiken und Zeichnungen (vol. 25 of *Werkausgabe in dreissig Bänden*). 1980.

Literatur und Kunst: Essays, Gedichte und Reden (vol. 26 of *Werkausgabe in dreissig Bänden*). 1980.

Philosophie und Naturwissenschaft: Essays, Gedichte und Reden (vol. 27 of *Werkausgabe in dreissig Bänden*). 1980.

Politik: Essays, Gedichte und Reden (vol. 28 of *Werkausgabe in dreissig Bänden*). 1980.

Plays and Essays (includes *Romulus the Great; The Visit; 21 Points to The Physicists; The Judge and His Hangman; Problems of the Theater; A Monster Lecture on Justice and Law Together with a Helvetian Interlude*), edited by Volkmar Sander. 1982.

Rollenspiele: Protokoll einer fiktiven Inszenierung und Achterloo III, with Charlotte Kerr. 1986.

*

Film Adaptations: *The Judge and His Hangman* (television), 1957; *Fools Are Passing Through,* 1961; *The Visit,* 1964; *The Deadly Game* (television), 1982, from the novel, *Die Panne; The Pledge,* 2001.

Bibliography: *A Bibliography of Four Contemporary German-Swiss Authors: Friedrich Dürrenmatt, Max Frisch, Robert Walser, Albin Zollinger* by Elly Wilbert-Collins, 1967; *Friedrich Dürrenmatt: Bibliographie* by Johannes Hansel, 1968; *Friedrich Dürrenmatt; A Bibliography* by Regina Lawler, 1968; "Durrenmatt: A Bibliography" by Peter Gontrum, in *West Coast Review,* 4(3), 1970, pp. 25–32, 37–44.

Critical Studies: *The Playwrights Speak,* edited by Walter Wager, 1967; *Friedrich Dürrenmatt* by Murray B. Peppard, 1969; *Friedrich Dürrenmatt* by Armin Arnold, translated by Sheila Johnson, 1972; *To Heaven and Back: The New Morality in the Plays of Friedrich Dürrenmatt* by Kurt J. Fickert, 1972; *Dürrenmatt: A Study in Plays, Prose, Theory* by Timo Tiusanen, 1977; *Dürrenmatt: A Study of His Plays* by Urs Jenny, translated by Keith Hamnett and Hugh Rorrison, with additional material by Kenneth S. Whitton, 1978; *Friedrich Dürrenmatt: A Collection of Critical Essays,* edited by Bodo Fritzen and Heimy F. Taylor, 1979; *The Theatre of Friedrich Dürrenmatt: A Study in the Possibility of Freedom,* 1980, and *Dürrenmatt: Reinterpretation in Retrospect,* 1990, both by Kenneth S. Whitton; *Play Dürrenmatt,* edited by Moshe Lazar, 1983; *Friedrich Dürrenmatt: The Happy Pessimist,* 1997; *Understanding Friedrich Dürrenmatt* by Roger Alan Crockett, 1998.

*　*　*

Swiss dramatist Friedrich Dürrenmatt (1921–90) was born in Konolfingen in Bern canton and died in Neuchâtel. The son of a Protestant minister, he haphazardly pursued literary, philosophical, and scientific studies at both Basel and Zürich universities before devoting himself to full-time writing. In particular his readings in **Bertolt Brecht**'s epic theater and Thornton Wilder's metaphysical comedies proved decisive in his becoming a playwright. Throughout his career Dürrenmatt wrote prose fiction and critical essays, in addition to his world-renowned dramas.

Only one of his fictional works, the detective novel *Der Verdacht* (1953; *The Quarry,* 1962), deals directly with the Holocaust. Here a Bern police superintendent, with the help of a Jewish Holocaust survivor, pursues a notorious Nazi physician who operated without anesthetics on his victims in the camps. The novel's reflections on the potency of evil anticipate many of the central concerns of Dürrenmatt's mature dramas.

In his two most famous plays, the grotesque comedies *Der Besuch der alten Dame* (1956; *The Visit,* 1958) and *Die Physiker* (1962; *The Physicists,* 1964), Dürrenmatt leaves behind his earlier historically metaphysical costume dramas and treats Holocaust-related issues, but without actually setting them in World War II. He strongly felt that a stage setting of Auschwitz itself would reveal that art is weaker than reality. As Lawrence Langer has observed: "Dürrenmatt knew that there are ways of bringing Auschwitz to the audience without bringing Auschwitz directly to the audience, not by ignoring the horrors of the gas chamber and the crematorium but by inventing situations equally gruesome, reported with remorseless exactitude, but only peripherally—if at all—identifiable with the events of the Holocaust."

Clearly the town of Güllen (meaning "liquid manure" in Swiss dialect) in *The Visit* and the insane asylum in *The Physicists* are effective settings for the atrocities of an angst-ridden post-Holocaust world. The perverted mass behavior governed by a distortion of justice in the former play and the anxieties about the future of a world without meaning or life in the latter one reveal Dürrenmatt's fears unleashed by World War II. In *The Visit* (subtitled *a Tragic Comedy*) the myriad characters representing all walks of life, from religion to medicine and education to commerce, become accomplices out of greed in the murder of a defenseless victim; castrated toadies and an ever-increasing number of spineless townspeople wearing yellow shoes evoke Holocaust resonances. In *The Physicists,* paradoxically, the more the scientists recuse themselves from bellicose governmental agencies, the greater the chances that a nuclear holocaust might be unleashed by the power-hungry director of their mental institution.

In his longest essay on drama, "Theaterprobleme" (1954; "Problems of the Theater," 1964), the playwright explains his attraction to the grotesque as a moral comedic force. Revealing that he considers Napoleon to be European history's last tragic figure, Dürrenmatt claims that the disappearance of concreteness and immanence in modern life make tragedy impossible. Thus the twentieth century, although characterized by such "world butchers with slaughtering machines" as Hitler and Stalin, was essentially a nontragic age. Black comedy, with all of its distancing devices, was the only suitable medium for exploring impersonal bureaucracy and the disappearance of direct individual responsibility. In an ever-increasingly anonymous statistical world, Dürrenmatt saw it as his mission to create a stage-worthy grotesque comedic genre of critique. As he states, in this age "Creon's secretaries deal with Antigone's case." After Strindberg and Shakespeare adaptations in the late 1960s and '70s, Dürrenmatt fell silent as a dramatist.

Despite the social satirical critique that characterizes Dürrenmatt's oeuvre, there are moments at the end of his important works where the main characters voice deep personal insights into their conduct. The most famous of these takes place in *The Visit* when Alfred Ill deeply regrets his own complicity in the mistreatment of Claire Zachanassian 45 years before. In *The Quarry* such a moment is Holocaust-specific. Gulliver, the Jewish survivor and helper of the police superintendent, defends his murder of the notorious camp physician: "We as individuals cannot save this world, that would be as hopeless a task as that of poor Sisyphus . . . We can help only in single instances, not in the whole—the limitation of the poor Jew Gulliver, the limitation of all people. Therefore, we ought not to try to save the world but to get through it—that is the only true adventure that remains for us at this late hour."

—Steven R. Cerf

See the essay on *The Quarry*.

E

EDELMAN, Marek

Nationality: Polish. **Born:** Homel, Belarus, 1922. **Family:** Married Alina Margolis; one daughter and one son. **Career:** Cardiologist, Pirogów Hospital, Lodz. Activist, Jewish Labor Bund; cofounder, Jewish Fighting Organization, 1942; co-leader, Warsaw Ghetto Uprising, 1943; activist, *Komitet Obrony Robotników* (Workers Defense Committee), 1976–80; member, trade union Solidarity, 1980–89. **Awards:** White Eagle Order, 1998; honorary citizen of Lodz, 2000. Honorary doctorates: Yale University, New Haven, Connecticut; Université Libre, Brussels, Belgium.

PUBLICATION

Memoir

Getto walczy: Udzial Bundu w obronie getta warszawskiego. 1945; as *The Ghetto Fights,* 1946.

*

Critical Studies: *Shielding the Flame: An Intimate Conversation with Dr. Marek Edelman, the Last Surviving Leader of the Warsaw Ghetto Uprising* by Hanna Krall, 1986; "The Curious Case of Marek Edelman," in *Commentary,* 83, March 1987, pp. 66–69, and "Poles, Jews, and History," in *What Is the Use of Jewish History,* 1992, both by Lucy S. Dawidowicz.

* * *

Marek Edelman, a heart surgeon and the last living leader of the Warsaw Ghetto Uprising, was born in 1922. During the war he was an activist of the bund and one of the organizers of the Jewish Fighting Organization. After the death of Mordechaj Anielewicz Edelman became the commander of the ghetto uprising. After the fall of the uprising, together with a few fighters he managed to get through canals to the "Aryan side," where he hid with the help of the members of the underground Polish Socialist Party. In 1944 he also fought in the Warsaw Uprising. After the war he moved to Lodz. He became involved in the fight for the human rights that were abandoned in socialist Poland. From 1976 to 1980 he was a member of *Komitet Obrony Robotników* (Workers Defense Committee) and then of the independent trade union Solidarity. In 1989 he participated in the negotiations of the opposition with the government, the Round Table talks, preceding the structural changes in Poland. In 1998 he was honored with the White Eagle Order, the highest Polish order.

Edelman is not a writer. Notwithstanding, in 1946 he decided to play the role of a witness and a memory keeper and started writing a book devoted to the martyrdom and the uprising of the Warsaw Jews entitled *The Ghetto Fights.* Edelman's war experience and the reflections on it also became the theme of *Shielding the Flame,* a book written by Hanna Krall based on interviews. In both these narratives as well as in Edelman's interviews he emphasizes that "one should always be on the side of the hurt and the weak, one should engage oneself in difficult and dangerous matters." The author warns against giving in to fanaticism and ideologies that activate the evil side of man and make him stop treating homicide as a terrible thing. In his memoirs and relations Edelman does not aspire to being called a hero. That title is reserved for his dead companions.

Edelman wrote about the need to be constantly engaged in the fate of the world in his letter to the leaders of NATO in which he called the war in Kosovo the first war declared in the defense of man. Bill Clinton cited these words in his speech for the 50th anniversary of NATO.

—Joanna Hobot

See the essay on *The Ghetto Fights.*

EDVARDSON, Cordelia (Maria Sara)

Pseudonym: Maria Heller. **Nationality:** Israeli (originally German: immigrated to Sweden after World War II and to Israel in the 1970s). **Born:** Berlin, 1929; daughter of the writer Elisabeth Langgässer. **Career:** Since 1974 Middle East correspondent, *Svenska Dagebladt* (Stockholm). **Awards:** Geschwister-Scholl Prize, 1986, for German translation of *Bränt barn söker sig till elden.*

PUBLICATIONS

Memoirs

Om jag glömmer dig . . .: En invandrares dagbok från Israel. 1976.
Bränt barn söker sig till elden. 1984; as *Burned Child Seeks the Fire,* 1997.

Novel

Viska det till vinden [Whisper It to the Wind]. 1988.

Poetry

Så kom jag till Kartago (as Maria Heller). 1958.
Jerusalems leende. 1991.

Other

Kärlekens vittne. 1963.
Till kvinna född. 1967.
Miriam bor i en kibbutz (for children). 1969; as *Miriam Lives in a Kibbutz,* 1970.
Du har varit nära. 1971.
Två rum i Jerusalem. 1978.

*

Critical Studies: ''Remembered Literature in the Camps: The Cases of Jean Améry, Primo Levi, Ruth Klüger, Cordelia Edvardson, and Nico Rost'' by Petra S. Fiero, in *Germanic Notes and Reviews,* 28(1), Spring 1997, pp. 3–11; ''Jewish Women Authors and the Exile Experience: Claire Goll, Veza Canetti, Else Lasker-Schuler, Nelly Sachs, Cordelia Edvardson'' by Dagmar C. G. Lorenz, in *German Life and Letters* (England), 51(2), April 1998, pp. 225–39; ''Reconstructing Mother—The Myth and the Real: Autobiographical Texts by Elisabeth Langgässer and Cordelia Edvardson'' by Helga Kraft, in *Facing Fascism and Confronting the Past: German Women Writers from Weimar to the Present,* edited by Elke P. Frederiksen and Martha Kaarsberg Wallach, 2000.

* * *

Cordelia Edvardson's mother, Elisabeth Langgässer (1899–1950), was a prominent German novelist and poet and the illegitimate child of a Roman Catholic mother and a Jewish father. Edvardson was also an illegitimate child, and her father was also Jewish. Growing up in Berlin, Edvardson always felt different, out of place. After the Nuremberg laws of 1935, this feeling increased more and more as the laws and decrees against Jews were enforced. Langgässer and her gentile husband, Cordelia's stepfather, did their best to alleviate the hurt and growing danger and to protect her. Finally, as Berlin was being steadily emptied of its Jews, they managed to find Cordelia adoptive parents who were Spanish. Thus, acquiring a Spanish passport, Edvardson seemed safe from further persecution. It soon proved otherwise, and she was categorized as a *Volljüdin* (''full Jew'') and subjected to separation from her parents, forced labor, and then, in 1944, deportation. She survived Theresienstadt, Auschwitz, and further evacuations.

After liberation she was taken to Sweden to recuperate from the starvation, sickness, and maltreatment of these years. Her experiences, and the difficult path to an acceptance of the Jewish identity forced upon her, form the background to her work. Scorched by them—the title of her memoir, *Burned Child Seeks the Fire,* eloquently underscores the trauma—she proved willing to subject herself a second time to the metaphysical fires that aided her in the process of accepting her Jewish identity.

Her transformation did not take place rapidly or smoothly. She was not a survivor who sought to forget her experiences, form a new life, and act as if all could be forgotten. On the contrary, in the immediate postwar period she refused to accept the advice of well-meaning Swedish caregivers that her ordeal was over and should be forgotten. Instead she sought out those who encouraged her to talk about her hurt and who were willing to listen and to try to understand. The role of Israel and the Six-Day War, which she covered as a Swedish journalist, was crucial in her development. Forced to become a Jew, she was now fully and deeply Jewish. In 1974 she relocated to Israel.

Her work *Burned Child Seeks the Fire* traces this development and provides a penetrating examination not only of the events in her personal life that helped form her character and her psyche but also of the political events of the time and their impact on her. The memoir, as is so often the case with survivors, came late, some 40 years after the horror. However, this indicates the length of the process rather than any attempt to forget.

Burned Child Seeks the Fire appeared in Swedish in 1984 and won its author the Geschwister-Scholl Prize when it appeared in German two years later. It was published in English in 1997. The work concentrates largely on her own personal development and ultimate transformation, and thus brings up the complicated relationship with her mother (both beloved and hated). Left hanging along with this complex topic is her relationship with the Germany that, like her, sought to evolve and transform itself after the Third Reich—especially, of course, with regard to Jews. Edvardson's relationship with this Germany is the subject of her 1988 book, *Viska det till vinden* (''Whisper It to the Wind'').

Edvardson, a journalist by profession, is a gifted writer, whose penetrating self-scrutiny and deep examination of the Third Reich as it pertained to her locates her in the very top rank of Holocaust writers. Her work is not simply a factual description of what she experienced in her formative years but an impressive psychological self-study, which gives an accurate picture of the dark years in which the Jews of Europe were murdered.

—David Scrase

See the essay on *Burned Child Seeks the Fire: Memoir.*

ELIACH, Yaffa

Nationality: American (originally Russian: immigrated to Palestine, 1946, to the United States, 1954). **Born:** Yaffa Sonensohn, Vilna, 31 May 1937. **Education:** Brooklyn College, New York, 1957–69, B.A. 1967, M.A. 1969; City University of New York, 1969–73, Ph.D. in Russian intellectual history 1973. **Family:** Married David Eliach in 1953; one son and one daughter. **Career:** Since 1969 professor of history and literature, Department of Judaic Studies, Brooklyn College. Drama director, Camp Massad, Pocono Mountains, Pennsylvania, 1954–80; founder and volunteer director, Center for Holocaust Studies, Brooklyn, 1974–90; since 1999 founder and president, Shtetl Foundation, New York. Lecturer. **Awards:** Woodrow Wilson dissertation fellowship, 1971–72; Myrtle Wreath award for humanitarian activities (with Joseph Papp), 1979; Christopher award, 1982, for *Hasidic Tales of the Holocaust;* Guggenheim fellowship and Louis E. Yavner award, both in 1987; Women's Branch of the Orthodox Jewish Congregation of America's "Distinguished Woman of Achievement," 1989; AMIT Women's Rambam award, 1990; award of accomplishment, 1994, and National Holocaust Education award, 1995, Union of Orthodox Jewish Congregations; CBS-TV "Woman of the Year," 1995; Brooklyn College Alumna of the Year award, 1998; Eternal Flame award, 1999. Honorary doctorates: Yeshiva University, New York; Spertus College, Chicago. **Agent:** Miriam Altshuler, 53 Old Post Road, Red Hook, New York 12571, U.S.A.

PUBLICATIONS

Memoir (and history)

There Once Was a World: A 900-Year Chronicle of the Shtetl of Eishyshok. 1998.

Play

The Last Jew: A Play in Four Acts, with Uri Assaf (produced Tel-Aviv, 1975). 1977.

Poetry

Eshet ha-dayag [The Fisherman's Wife]. 1965.

Other

Jewish Hasidim, Russian Sectarian Non-conformists in the Ukraine, 1700–1760 (dissertation). 1973.
Hasidic Tales of the Holocaust (history). 1982.
We Were Children Just Like You (photo history). 1990.
The Shtetl Children (photo history). 2001.

Editor, with Brana Gurewitsch, *The Liberators: Eyewitness Accounts of the Liberation of Concentration Camps: Oral History Testimonies of American Liberators from the Archives of the Center for Holocaust Studies.* 1981.

Contributor to encyclopedias.

*

Film Adaptations: *There Once Was a Town* (documentary), 2000, from *There Once Was a World: A 900-Year Chronicle of the Shtetl of Eishyshok.*

Critical Study: "Collector of Souls: Y. Eliach's Tower of Faces Honoring Jews of Ejszyszki, Poland at the Holocaust Memorial Museum" by Marjorie Rosen, in *People Weekly,* 41, 17 January 1994, pp. 36–39.

* * *

Yaffa Eliach was born in the town of Eisysky, near Vilna, Poland (now Lithuania). A survivor of the Holocaust, she has dedicated her life to Holocaust studies. She was a member of President Jimmy Carter's Commission on the Holocaust in 1978–79 and accompanied his fact-finding mission to Eastern Europe in 1979. She founded and served as director of the Center for Holocaust Studies in Brooklyn, New York. She has contributed to *Encyclopedia Judaica, The Women's Studies Encyclopedia,* and *The Encyclopedia of Hasidism.* She has been a frequent lecturer at numerous conferences and educational venues and has appeared on television several times in documentaries and interviews. In the *Observer* (London) Eliach stated, "I feel my generation . . . is the last link with the Holocaust." In the *Jerusalem Post* Eliach stated, "Don't teach about dead Jews; bring the Jews back to life." She has devoted a major part of her life to education on the Holocaust, and she has been especially adept at educating children and teachers on Holocaust.

Eliach's personal experience as a survivor of the Holocaust lends to her firsthand knowledge of the struggle to survive and the aftermath of this great tragedy. During a two-day period in 1941 more than 5,000 Jews of her shtetl of Eisyshok were massacred by the German army. Only 720 Jews survived, with Eliach's family being among them. She relates her harrowing experience in *Once There Was a World: A 900-Year Chronicle of the Shtetl of Eisyshok* (1998). She recounts the vivid, colorful religious life of her shtetl, whose inhabitants were so well-treated by the German army during World War I that they saw no reason to fear the Germans in 1941. This work is not without controversy, for Polish groups have greatly criticized Eliach's treatment of the Poles in these memoirs. In memory of her village, however, Eliach created the *Tower of Life,* a permanent exhibit for the U.S. Holocaust Museum in Washington, D.C.

Eliach has devoted herself to the preservation of memory of the Holocaust. Through her literature and her historical documentation she has sought to provide a Jewish viewpoint on the

Holocaust—specifically a perspective from a survivor's vantage point. She has also preserved her memories (via lecture) on video and audiocassettes. In *Life of the U.S. Holocaust Museum* Eliach speaks of her creation of the *Tower of Life* and her motivation for its development. In *On the Threshold between Personal and Collective Memory* Eliach discusses the lack of ability of Jews to keep personal records of their suffering during the Shoah; therefore, she concludes, there is a need to rely on one's personal memory and to combine it into collective memory in order to avoid a repetition of history. She relates her experiences during the Holocaust in the audio recording *The Mystery of Good and Evil* and emphasizes the necessity of educating children on preventing such horrors in the future. A documentary entitled *There Once Was a Town* is based on her chronicle of Eisyshok and is narrated by Ed Asner, a descendant of Eisyshok families. She is a pioneer in Jewish women's studies, and as Helen Epstein states in *The International Research Institute on Jewish Women,* "There Once Was a World" is not only encyclopedic in scope, but mainstreams the life of women—rebbetzins, traveling peddlers, seamstresses, bath house attendants, child brides, mothers-in-law—in a way that was not possible before the advent of Jewish studies." Eliach has also built a replica of her shtetl Eisyshok in Israel, complete with synogogue and an immense learning center on shtetl life.

Eliach's relentless effort to recount her life and the lives of others has provided much material used in courses on the Holocaust. Her desire to preserve memory has made her one of the foremost contributors to Holocaust documentation.

—Cynthia A. Klíma

See the essays on *Hasidic Tales of the Holocaust* and *The Last Jew.*

EPSTEIN, Helen

Nationality: American (originally Czechoslovakian: immigrated to the United States, 1948; U.S. citizenship, 1954). **Born:** Prague, 27 November 1947. **Education:** Hunter College High School, New York; Hebrew University, Jerusalem, B.A. in musicology 1970; Columbia University, master's degree in journalism 1971. **Family:** Married Patrick Mehr in 1983; two sons. **Career:** Freelance cultural journalist in New York City for publications, including *New York Magazine, ARTNews, Esquire,* and the *New York Times;* professor of journalism, 1974–86, and director of undergraduate program, 1979–86, New York University; faculty member, Prague Summer Seminars, Charles University, and affiliate, Hadassah International Research Institute on Jewish Women, Brandeis University; lives in Cambridge, Massachusetts and lectures on family history and the psychological effects of war-related

trauma. Represented the United States, Centenary Conference of Nobel Peace Prize Writers, Norway, 2001. **Agent:** Jim Brown, 25 West 43rd St., New York, NY 10012, U.S.A.

PUBLICATIONS

Memoir

Where She Came From: A Daughter's Search for Her Mother's History. 1997.

Other

Children of the Holocaust: Conversations with Sons and Daughters of Survivors. 1979.
The Companies She Keeps: Tina Packer Builds a Theater. 1985.
Music Talks: Conversations with Musicians (profiles of classical musicians). 1987.
Joe Papp: An American Life (biography). 1994.

Translator, with Franci Epstein, *Under a Cruel Star: A Life in Prague, 1941–1968,* by Heda M. Kovály. 1986.

*

Critical Studies: "For the Holocaust 'Second Generation,' an Artistic Quest" by Dinitia Smith, in *New York Times* (*Late New York Edition*), 23 December 1997, p. E1; "Traumatic Memory and American Jewish Writers: One Generation after the Holocaust" by Janet Burstein, in *Yiddish,* 11(3–4), 1999; pp. 188–97; "Letters from Helen Epstein and Arnold Birenbaum," in *The New York Review of Books,* 46(15), 1999, p. 50.

*   *   *

Helen Epstein is the author of two highly significant second generation works. Her book *Children of the Holocaust: Conversations with Sons and Daughters of Survivors* (1979) made a singular contribution in raising public consciousness about the existence of a group, international in composition, with a distinct angle of vision concerning the Shoah. This book illuminates many second generation issues, including the transmission of trauma, the fact that the most important event in the lives of children of survivors occurred before they were born, and how the second generation works through its awesome legacy. Nearly 20 years passed before the appearance of *Where She Came From: A Daughter's Search for Her Mother's History* (1997). Epstein notes that the first book "is about rupture. The second, about connection." Moreover, she and her mother translated Czechoslovakian writer Heda Kovály's prizewinning memoir *Under a Cruel Star: A Life in Prague 1941–1968* (1986). Each of these books has been translated into several languages.

Born in Prague in 1947, Epstein, who was brought to America as a young child, is the eldest of three children and the only daughter of Kurt and Frances (Franzi). Her parents survived Theresienstadt, Auschwitz, and Bergen-Belsen. Kurt was a member of Czechoslovakia's Olympic water polo team. Franzi was a dressmaker fluent in several languages.

The multilingual Epstein is a professional journalist who began her writing career by describing the Soviet invasion of Czechoslovakia while still a student at Hebrew University. In addition to her works on the Holocaust, she has written other books, including *The Companies She Keeps* (1985), *Music Talks* (1987), and *Joe Papp: An American Life* (1994). She is the first woman to have received tenure in New York University's Department of Journalism. Epstein also worked as a freelance cultural reporter for the Sunday *New York Times,* where her 1979 article on children of survivors was published, after the author persuaded the editors that there was in fact a second generation phenomenon. Her book *Children of the Holocaust* has been termed a "turning point in the evolution of children of survivors as a communal, emotional, and political entity."

Epstein articulates what many in the second generation feel but have not yet publicly expressed. For example, referring to her Holocaust legacy, she writes of an "iron box" that lay buried deep inside her. This box contained "slippery, combustible things more secret than sex and more dangerous than any shadow or ghost." Words were inadequate to describe its contents. Furthermore, Epstein writes powerfully about the lack of extended family among daughters and sons of survivors, noting that her family tree "had been burnt to a stump." *Children of the Holocaust* is, on one level, the author's attempt to discover her nonbiological family—other children of survivors who have their own version of her iron box. She correctly surmises that there is "an invisible, silent family scattered about the world." Consequently Epstein set out to interview second generation members in Australia, Canada, Israel, and the United States.

Epstein brings great psychological insight, historical research, and personal experience to bear in writing *Children of the Holocaust.* She identifies the presence of Holocaust imagery in the lives of the second generation. For example, she writes of imagining the Seventh Avenue local subway being transformed into a "train of cattle cars on its way to Poland." Acknowledging the incredible strength and support of her family, especially Franzi's resourcefulness, the author also writes of the ambiguity of Jewish identity among the community of secular refugees in which she was raised. For instance, while the Holocaust "had become the touchstone of [the survivors'] identities as Jews and . . . a touchstone for their children as well, it provided no structure, no clue to a way of life."

Epstein skillfully and with great passion describes the dilemma of many in the second generation. She writes of feeling the necessity of suppressing feelings of anger toward her parents. Moreover, the author identifies a common phenomenon among her peers. At times, she notes, "my life seemed to be not my own. Hundreds of people lived through me, lives that had been cut short in the war." Consequently her murdered grandmothers, for whom she is named, lived through her. This is both a blessing and a burden, as it is an enormous encumbrance on the second generation, in effect robbing many of the "carelessness of childhood." Thus, for the second generation the issue is not failing to remember that this generation is the "answer" to the Holocaust in the eyes of their parents. But the second generation has its own mission. "We need," writes Epstein, "to learn how to translate our consciousness of evil, our skepticism, our sense of outrage into constructive action."

The author has lived in Massachusetts with her husband and their two children. She has been a member of the Prague Summer Seminars at Charles University and has lectured throughout America and abroad on the second generation, on long-term psychological effects of trauma, and on family history. In 2001 she represented the United States at the Centenary Conference of Nobel Peace Prize Writers in Norway.

—Alan L. Berger

See the essay on *Where She Came From: A Daughter's Search for Her Mother's History.*

EPSTEIN, Leslie

Nationality: American. **Born:** Los Angeles, 4 May 1938. **Education:** Yale College, New Haven, Connecticut, 1956–60, B.A. (summa cum laude) 1960; Merton College, Oxford (Rhodes scholar), 1960–62, Dip. Anthro. 1962; University of California, Los Angeles, M.A. in theatre arts 1963; Yale Drama School, Yale University, New Haven, Connecticut, D.F.A. 1976. **Family:** Married Ilene Epstein in 1969; one daughter and two sons. **Career:** Lecturer and professor, Queens College, City University of New York, 1965–68. Since 1978 professor of English and director of graduate creative writing program, Boston University. Visiting professor, Lane College, Summer 1964, Silliman College, Spring 1972; Fulbright research fellow, Groningen University, Netherlands, 1972–73; visiting professor, Johns Hopkins University, Spring 1977. **Awards:** Samuel Goldwyn Creative Writing award, University of California, Los Angeles, 1963; Lemist Esler fellowship, Yale Drama School, 1963–65; award, 1969, and fellowship grant, 1972, 1981–82, National Endowment for the Arts; Playboy editors' award for non-fiction, 1971; City University of New York research grant, 1972; New York State Council on the Arts fellowship, 1976; Guggenheim fellowship, 1977–78; American Academy and Institute of Arts and Letters award, 1977; Ingram Merill Foundation grants, 1981 and 1982; Boston University Kahn prize. **Member:** American Academy of

Rhodes Scholars. **Agent:** Lane Zachary, 1776 Broadway, Ste. 1405, New York, NY 10019, U.S.A.

PUBLICATIONS

Novels

P.D. Kimerakov. 1975.
King of the Jews: A Novel of the Holocaust. 1979; as *The Elder,* 1979.
Regina. 1982.
Pinto and Sons. 1990.
Pandaemonium. 1997.
Ice Fire Water: A Leib Goldkorn Cocktail. 1999.

Short Stories

The Steinway Quintet Plus Four. 1976.
Goldkorn Tales. 1985.

*

Critical Studies: ''American Authors and Ghetto Kings: Challenges and Perplexities'' by Ellen Schiff, in *America and the Holocaust,* edited by Sanford Finsker and Jack Fishcel, 1984; ''Even the Smallest Position'' by Frederick Busch, in *The Georgia Review,* 38(3), Fall 1984, pp. 525–41; ''King of the Jews Reconsidered'' by Irene C. Goldman, in *Midstream,* 32(4), April 1986, pp. 56–58; ''Power and Powerlessness in the Judenrat: Chairman M. C. Rumkowski As King of the Jews'' by Sidney Krome, in *West Virginia University Philological Papers,* 38, 1992, pp. 258–69; ''The Fantastic in Holocaust Literature: Writing and Unwriting the Unbearable'' by Michael Yogev, in *Journal of the Fantastic in the Arts,* 5,(2), 18, 1993, pp. 32–49; ''An Interview with Leslie Epstein'' by Mark Brownlow, in *Agni,* 39, 1994, pp. 64–82; '''Emotion Recollected in Tranquillity?' Representing the Holocaust in Fiction'' by Rudiger Kunow, in *Emotion in Postmodernism,* edited by Gerhard Hoffmann and Alfred Hornung, 1997.

* * *

Hollywood is the world's dream factory, a place where myths are manufactured and the imagination often seems to outstrip reality. Leslie Epstein knows this milieu with an intimacy few contemporary writers can match. As the son of Philip Epstein and the nephew of Julius Epstein—screenwriters who coauthored *Casablanca*—he watched the studio crowd parade into the family living room from a unique vantage point—upstairs and in p.j.'s.

If Hollywood contributed to Epstein's Sunset Boulevard street smarts, his years at Yale (1956–1960) added a significant measure of academic anchoring. That he was awarded a Rhodes scholarship after graduation suggests how intellectually accomplished the young Epstein was. What the formula leaves out, however, is how provocative and daring Epstein could be as a creative writer. His natural inclination is to link lighthearted humor with weighty subjects, and this is especially so when the Holocaust occupies a central place in his narratives.

According to Epstein, the worst crime that one writing about the Holocaust can commit is sentimentality. Overly pious writers sacrifice the essentials of good fiction and in the process do no favor either to a better understanding of the Holocaust (if such an ''understanding'' is, indeed, possible) or to fiction itself. Instead, Epstein sneaks up on the Holocaust from an oblique angle, always insisting that understatement will be more effective than overt preaching.

Writing in the pages of the *New York Times Book Review,* Katha Politt declares that ''if writers got gold stars for the risks they took, Leslie Epstein would get a handful.'' Whether the subject is Cold War politics (*P.D. Kimerakov*) or the remnants of Old World Jewish culture adrift in the violent, drug-ridden world of the contemporary Lower East Side (the Golkorn series), Epstein brings a satirical wit to all that his fictive eye imagines. The yoking of disparate elements is his trademark, one that often divides critics into those who applaud his ambition and those who wish he would write more traditional narratives.

It is, however, with his novels that center on the Holocaust—directly focusing on the concentration camp world of *King of the Jews* (1979) or indirectly evoking the Holocaust through an elaborately constructed metaphor of a Western shoot-out in *Pandaemonum* (1997)—that the reader sees Epstein's abiding concern with the twentieth century's most horrific crime. Rightly or wrongly, trivialization is the charge that has dogged his works. To write Holocaust fiction has, to some, always seemed a contradiction in terms, but his novels present the moral/intellectual dilemmas that embroil ordinary characters placed in extraordinary circumstances. What might have been an unmitigated disaster in less skillful hands becomes novels with equal measures of daring and honesty.

Epstein, particularly in *King of the Jews,* pioneered the very possibility of Holocaust fiction by Jewish-American authors. He often paid dearly for not maintaining a respectful silence, but his novels probe what it was like to live at a time when no decision, no action, could have made a difference. His mordant humor became a way of turning these doomed lives into something approaching myth. In this sense, the very contemporary Epstein relies on the much older traditions of Yiddish storytelling and the complicated ways that a bittersweet humor can become simultaneously a shield and a weapon.

—Sanford Pinsker

See the essays on *Ice Fire Water: A Leib Goldkorn Cocktail* and *King of the Jews: A Novel of the Holocaust.*

F

FÉNELON, Fania

Nationality: French. **Born:** Fania Goldstein, Paris, 2 September 1918. **Education:** Paris Conservatory of Music, 1934. **Career:** Professional singer, piano and voice teacher. Member, French resistance, 1940–43; prisoner, Birkenau and Bergen-Belsen, World War II; conductor, women's orchestra, while imprisoned in Birkenau, 1944–45. **Awards:** First prize in piano, Paris Conservatory of Music, 1934. Legion of Honor. **Agent:** Opera Mundi, 100 Avenue Raymond Poincare, 75016 Paris, France. **Died:** 19 December 1983.

PUBLICATION

Memoir

Sursis pour l'orchestre, with Marcelle Routier. 1976; as *Playing for Time,* 1977; as *Musicians of Auschwitz,* 1977.

*

Film Adaptations: *Playing for Time* (television), 1980.

*   *   *

Fania Fénelon, a Parisian cabaret singer, was arrested and sent to Birkenau for being half-Jewish and for helping the resistance by serving as a courier and allowing resistance members to sleep in her apartment. In her riveting memoir, *Playing for Time,* she remarked that no five minutes in Auschwitz-Birkenau were the same. Her life there was constantly in a state of flux, from the beginning of her internment to her ascension as a prisoner with some privileges as a member of the women's orchestra to being shipped to Bergen-Belsen to being rescued by the English as she lay dying of typhus.

Fénelon's autobiography, which was transformed into a movie by Arthur Miller and starred Vanessa Redgrave, is a significant Holocaust memoir. It is a testament to the indomitable spirit and stamina of Holocaust survivors, who remained strong emotionally because they possessed the will to survive. Fénelon became an unofficial leader of the Jewish women who performed in the only all-female orchestra in the concentration camps, guiding the other women morally and emotionally. For instance, she helped fellow prisoner Clara, risking her life by agreeing to join the orchestra only if Clara could also. She also offered guidance to Clara when she discerned that Clara's obsession with food was corrupting her morally, inducing her to sell her body.

Fénelon's account is very detailed, perhaps because the horrors to which she was an eyewitness were so shocking that they remained frozen indelibly in her mind, even decades later. Although many years passed from the atrocities of Auschwitz-Birkenau to the writing her autobiography, her descriptions are so lucid that it sometimes seems as if the events occurred more recently. One example is her vivid depiction of the escape, capture, and death of Mala and Edek, lovers in Auschwitz-Birkenau. Fénelon called Mala a legend, and Little Irene, another orchestra member, labeled her their hope of salvation. Mala enjoyed special privileges because of her role as an interpreter and her vibrant spirit; she and Edek managed to escape the camp with false papers she obtained, with Edek wearing an SS uniform and Mala in men's clothing. Fénelon's longing for freedom is apparent in the passage in which she relishes vicariously their liberty. When Mala was captured by a Gestapo agent in a cafe, Edek allowed himself to be taken prisoner also, not wanting to survive without her. Although the Nazi officers could have killed Mala and Edek on the spot, they chose to return them to Auschwitz-Birkenau. Fénelon observes that the Nazis made a big spectacle of the escape and the capture, forcing the other prisoners to stand in line during a long roll call because of the escape and later forcing them to watch the murders of Mala and Edek. Fénelon effectively undercuts the intentions of the Nazi officers who demand that the prisoners observe the killings; she points out that Mala and Edek, having been returned to the concentration camp, actually inspired them to be strong: Mala stated to the prisoners, ''Revolt! Rise up! There are thousands of you. Attack them—they're cowards and even if you're killed, anything's better than this, at least you'll die free! Revolt!'' Fénelon also points out that although the Nazi soldiers wanted to kill Mala in front of the prisoners, she slashed her wrist with a razor—an act of defiance against the Nazis by attempting to control her own destiny.

Fénelon's memoirs manifest the learning process that a prisoner underwent after arriving in the camps. She and Clara were relieved upon their arrival at Auschwitz-Birkenau because they spotted the Red Cross trucks and thus believed that they would be well treated. Fénelon even tried unsuccessfully to get a ride in one of them so that she did not have to walk to the barracks. Her attitude changed, however, when she discovered shortly thereafter that the Red Cross trucks were a ruse to lull the Jews into a false sense of hope—and to prevent them from panicking—and that these trucks transported Jews to the crematoria.

Fénelon's autobiography is informative and demonstrates how music kept her alive, both physically and emotionally. The author points out clearly a telling irony that she observed in Auschwitz-Birkenau: the Nazis maintained a love of culture and spared some Jews simply to entertain them, yet they mercilessly and cruelly destroyed millions of innocent people.

—Eric Sterling

See the essay on *Playing for Time*.

FERDERBER-SALZ, Bertha

Nationality: American (originally Austrian: immigrated to the United States after World War II). **Born:** Bertha Frost, Kolbuszowa, 1902. **Family:** Married 1) first husband in 1929 (died), two daughters; 2) David Salz in 1948. **Career:** Bookkeeper, ca. 1920s. Prisoner, concentration camps, World War II. Contributor to Yiddish periodicals; lecturer on the Holocaust; volunteer, Center for Holocaust Studies. **Award:** Medal, Center for Holocaust Studies, 1985.

PUBLICATION

Memoir

Un di zun hot geshaynt. 1965; as *And the Sun Kept Shining,* 1980.

* * *

Bertha Ferderber- (actually Verderber) Salz was born Bertha Frost in 1902 in the small Galician town Kolbuszowa. During World War I her family moved to Austria where she learned German, a skill that proved useful during the Holocaust. At age 16 Ferderber-Salz moved to Kraków to attend a high school with a business focus. She worked as a bookkeeper until her marriage in 1929. Following the Nazi occupation of Poland, Ferderber-Salz first hid out in the country with her children and only joined her husband in the Kraków ghetto after securing a hiding place for her young daughters with a Polish woman. From the ghetto Ferderber-Salz was moved to various concentration camps: first Plaszow, where her husband was sentenced to death because of his poor health, then Auschwitz, and finally Bergen-Belsen. After the camp's liberation by the British troops, Ferderber-Salz had to battle to regain guardianship of her children as well as of her two surviving nephews. Ensuing her futile search for more surviving members of her once large family, Ferderber-Salz and her two daughters immigrated to the United States, making their home in New York City. In 1948 she married David Salz, a childhood friend who had immigrated to the United States in 1916. Ferderber-Salz lectured tirelessly about the Holocaust and its legacy at various schools, primarily at Brooklyn College. She also volunteered at the Center for Holocaust

Studies, translating the testimonies of Holocaust survivors into English. In 1985 the center awarded her a medal for her efforts.

According to her daughter, Rachel Garfunkel, Ferderber-Salz's literary career arose from necessity. Still ailing as a result from her incarceration in the camps, she was not able to work immediately after her arrival in the United States. In order to support herself and her two daughters, she began to submit autobiographical as well as fictional stories to various Yiddish language newspapers and magazines. In 1965 Menorah Publishing in Tel Aviv published her autobiographical novel *And the Sun Kept Shining* in the original Yiddish. It was subsequently translated into Hebrew and because of its success turned into a play. In 1980 the English translation of the work was published in the United States.

And the Sun Kept Shining—the title refers to the world's indifference to the suffering of the Jewish people at the hand of the Nazis—places Ferderber-Salz's personal experiences in the larger context of the persecution of the Polish Jewish population. Clearly meant as a testimony to the victims of the Holocaust, the work celebrates their courage in the face of unspeakable suffering and their refusal to abandon their faith or human dignity that ultimately allows them to triumph over their dehumanized torturers. Ferderber-Salz tells her story in a factual and straightforward manner that emphasizes content over formal or aesthetic concerns. The contrast between the enormity of the events and the restrained way in which they are narrated as well as Ferderber-Salz's own courage and resilience shown throughout the story rank the book among the most successful personal narratives of a Holocaust survivor.

—Helga Schreckenberger

See the essay on *And the Sun Kept Shining*.

FEUCHTWANGER, Lion

Pseudonym: J. L. Wetcheek. **Nationality:** German; lived in exile in France, 1933–40, and the United States beginning in 1940. **Born:** Munich, 7 July 1884. **Education:** Studied philosophy, literature, and language at Berlin University; Munich University, Ph.D. in literature 1907. **Military Service:** Served briefly in the German Army during World War I (discharged for medical reasons). **Family:** Married Marta Loffler in 1912; one daughter (deceased). **Career:** Drama critic, *Die Schaubühne,* 1908–11; full-time writer. **Died:** 21 December 1958.

PUBLICATIONS

Collections

Gesammelte Werke [Collected Works]. 1933–54.
Gesammelte Werke in Einzelausgaben. 1959.

Novels

Der tönerne Gott: Roman [The God of Clay]. 1910.

Thomas Wendt: Ein dramatischer Roman. 1920.

Die hässliche Herzogin Margarete Maultasch: Roman. 1923; as *The Ugly Duchess*, 1927.

Jud Süss: Roman. 1925; as *Power*, 1926; as *Jew Suess*, 1926.

Wartesaal-Trilogie (Waiting Room Trilogy):

   Erfolg: Drei Jahre Geschichte einer Provinz (2 vols.). 1930; as *Success: Three Years History of a Province*, 1930.

   Die Geschwister Oppermann. 1933; as *The Oppermanns*, 1933.

   Exil: Roman. 1940; as *Paris Gazette*, 1940.

Josephus Trilogie:

   Der jüdische Krieg (trilogy). 1932; as *Josephus*, 1932.

   Die Söhne: Roman. 1935; as *The Jew of Rome*, 1935.

   Der Tag wird kommen. 1945; as *Josephus and the Emperor*, 1942; as *The Day Will Come*, 1942.

Der falsche Nero: Roman. 1936; as *The Pretender*, 1937.

Die Brüder Lautensack. 1944; as *Double, Double, Toil and Trouble*, 1943; as *The Lautensack Brothers*, 1944.

Simone: Roman. 1944; as *Simone*, 1944.

Waffen für Amerika [Arms for America]. 1947; as *Die Füchse im Weinberg* [Foxes in the Vineyard] (2 volumes), 1948; as *Proud Destiny*, 1947.

Goya oder der arge Weg der Erkenntnis. 1951; as *This Is the Hour*, 1951.

Narrenweisheit, oder Tod und Verklärung des Jean-Jacques Rousseau. 1952; as *Tis Folly to Be Wise; or, Death and Transfiguration of Jean-Jacques Rousseau*, 1953.

Die Jüdin von Toledo: Roman. 1955; as *Spanische Ballade*, 1955; as *Raquel, the Jewess of Toledo*, 1956.

Jefta und seine Tochter: Roman. 1957; as *Jefta and His Daughter*, 1958.

Das Haus der Desdemona, oder Grösse und Grenzen historischer Dichtung (unfinished), edited by Fritz Zschech. 1961; as *The House of Desdemona; or, The Laurels and Limitations of Historical Fiction*, 1963.

Plays

Die Einsamen: Zwei Skizzen. 1903.

Kleine Dramen: Joel; König Saul; Das Weib des Urias; Der arme Heinrich; Donna Bianca; Die Braut von Korinth (2 vols.). 1905–06.

Der Fetisch: Schauspiel. 1907.

Ein' feste Burg ist unser Gott: Volksstück, adaptation of a work by Arthur Müller. 1911.

Julia Farnese: Ein Trauerspiel in drei Akten. 1915.

Warren Hastings, Gouverneur von Indien: Schauspiel in vier Akten und einem Vorspiel, with Bertolt Brecht. 1916; as *Kalkutta, 4. Mai: Drei Akte Kolonialgeschichte*, 1927.

Pierrots Herrentraum: Eine Pantomine in fünf Bildern, music by A. Hartmann-Trepka. 1916.

Vasantasema: Ein Schauspiel in drei Akten: Nach dem Indischen des Königs Sudraka. 1916.

Der König und die Tanzerin: Ein Spiel in vier Akten: Nach dem Indischen des Kalidasa. 1917.

Friede: Ein burleskes Spiel: Nach den "Acharneern" und der "Eirene" des Aristophanes. 1918.

Appius und Virginia: Trauerspiel. 1918.

Jud Süss: Schauspiel. 1918.

Die Kriegsgefangenen: Ein Schauspiel in fünf Akten [The Prisoners of War]. 1919.

Der Amerikaner oder die entzauberte Stadt: Eine melancholische Komödie. 1921.

Der Frauenverkäufer: Ein Spiel in drei Akten nach Calderon. 1923.

Der holländische Kaufmann: Schauspiel. 1923.

Leben Eduards des Zweiten von England, with Bertolt Brecht, adaptation of *Edward II* by Christopher Marlowe (produced Munich, 1924). 1924; translated as *Edward II*, 1966.

Hill: Komödie in vier Akten 1925; as *Wird Hill amnestiert?* 1927.

Two Anglo-Saxon Plays: Oil Islands; Warren Hastings. 1928.

Three Plays: Prisoners of War; 1918; The Dutch Merchant. 1934.

Wahn oder der Teufel in Boston: Ein Stück in drei Akten, edited by E. Gottlieb and F. Guggenheim. 1948.

Die Witwe Capet: Ein Stück in Drei Akten. 1956; as *The Widow Capet*, 1956.

Die Gesichte der Simone Marcard, with Bertolt Brecht. 1957; as The Visions of Simone Marchard, 1965.

Short Stories

PEP: J. L. Wetcheeks amerikanisches Liederbuch (as J. L. Wetcheek). 1928; as *PEP: J. L. Wetcheek's American Songbook*, 1929.

Marianne in Indien und sieben andere Erzählungen. 1934; as *Marianne in India*, 1935; as *Little Tales*, 1935.

Venedig (Texas) und vierzehn andere Erzählungen. 1946.

Odysseus und die Schweine und zwölf andere Erzählungen. 1950; as *Odysseus and the Swine, and Other Stories*, 1949.

Other

Heinrich Heines Fragment: "Der Rabbi von Bacharach": Eine kritische Studie (dissertation). 1907.

Die Aufgabe des Judentums, with Arnold Zweig. 1933.

Moskau 1937: Ein Reisebericht für meine Freunde. 1937; as *Moscow 1937: A Visit Described for My Friends*, 1937.

Unholdes Frankreich: Meine Erlebnisse unter der Regierung Petain. 1942; as *Der Teufel in Frankreich*; as *The Devil in France*, 1941.

Centum Opuscula: Eine Auswahl (essays). 1956.

Translator, *Die Perser*, by Aeschylus. 1915.

*

Film Adaptations: *Jud Süss,* 1934; *Die Geschwister Oppermann* (television), 1986.

Bibliography: *A Bibliography of Lion Feuchtwanger's Major Works in German* (dissertation) by Gertrude Goetz, University of Southern California, 1971; *A Bibliography of Lion Feuchtwanger's Works in English Translation* (dissertation) by Herta Maria Klopp Keilbach, University of Southern California, 1973; "Bibliographie zu Lion Feuchtwanger" by Wolfgang Müller-Funk, in *Text + Kritik,* 79/80, 1983, pp. 133–45.

Manuscript Collection: Feuchtwanger Memorial Library in Doheny Memorial Library, University of Southern California, Los Angeles.

Critical Studies: *Lion Feuchtwanger: The Man, His Ideas, His Work,* edited by John M. Spalek, 1972; *Insight and Action: The Life and Work of Lion Feuchtwanger,* 1975, and "Lion Feuchtwanger: The Hazards of Exile," in *Exile: The Writer's Experience,* edited by John M. Spalek and Robert F. Bell, 1982, both by Lothar Kahn; "An Ancient and Modern Identity Crisis: Lion Feuchtwanger's 'Josephus' Trilogy" by Marc L. Raphael, in *Judaism: A Quarterly Journal of Jewish Life and Thought,* 21, 1972, pp. 409–14; "Double, Double, Toil and Trouble: Kritisches zu Lion Feuchtwangers Roman *Die Bruder Lautensack*" by Sigrid Schneider, in *MLN,* 95, 1980, pp. 641–54; *Lion Feuchtwanger's Erfolg, a "Grossstadt" Novel* by Judith Wessler, 1989; "In Buddha's Footsteps: Feuchtwanger's *Jud Süss,* Walther Rathenau, and the Path to the Soul" by William Small, in *German Studies Review,* 12(3), October 1989, pp. 469–85; "The Case of the Well-Crafted Novel: Lion Feuchtwanger's 'Goya'" by Jost Hermand, translated by James Steakley, in *High and Low Cultures: German Attempts at Mediation,* edited by Hermand and Reinhold Grimm, 1994; "Warren Hastings in the Drama of Lion Feuchtwanger and Bertolt Brecht: Contexts and Connections" by T. H. Bowyer, in *Comparative Drama,* 31(3), Fall 1997, pp. 394–413; "Mapping the Other: Lion Feuchtwanger's Topographies of the Orient" by Paul Levesque, in *The German Quarterly,* 71(2), Spring 1998, pp. 145–65; *God and Judaism in the Lives and Works of Beer-Hofmann and Feuchtwanger* 1998; *Lion Feuchtwanger: A Bibliographic Handbook* (vol. 2) by Sandra H. Hawrylchak and John M. Spalek, 1998.

* * *

The early work of Munich-born Lion Feuchtwanger, son of a well-to-do Jewish margarine manufacturer, deals with the contemplative wisdom of the Eastern versus the Western (Nietzschean) philosophy of action. Prime examples for this theme are his drama *Warren Hastings* (1916), which was later reworked, together with **Bertolt Brecht**, into *Kalkutta, 4. Mai* (1927), and his drama about the German November Revolution of 1918, *Thomas Wendt* (1920). The theme of contemplation versus action, materialism versus spirituality, was initially continued in Feuchtwanger's most important works, his historical novels.

For Feuchtwanger the historical novel, which for him includes works that deal with the recent past or with problems of the present, should not merely depict life and events of the past, but rather it should deal with problems and issues of the present in historical garb. Through his historical novels he wants to gain insights from history for the present and the future. Historical facts are a mere means for him to gain distance from the present, thus gaining a better perspective. His almost Hegelian underlying philosophy is that the course of history is marked by progress of humanity toward a society governed by reason, even if here and there reason suffers a temporary defeat and the development seems to be going backward a step or two.

Adhering to this theory, Feuchtwanger wrote *The Ugly Duchess* (1923), in which the fourteenth-century duchess Margarethe of Tyrol tries in vain to cope with her physical ugliness by shrewdly reigning her country. In his perhaps biggest international success, *Power* (1925), the eighteenth-century "Court Jew" Süss-Oppenheimer undergoes an inner development from a life of frantic activity to an attitude of contemplation and acceptance of his fate.

As a witness of power politics of the Weimar Republic and the rise of National Socialism, Feuchtwanger felt impelled to deal with the politics of his own times. He earned the Nazis' hate by publishing *Success: Three Years History of a Province* (1930), a novel about the reactionary politics in Bavaria from 1921 to 1924 and Hitler's failed putsch of 1923. The next novel of what he later referred to as his Waiting Room Trilogy was *The Oppermanns* (1933). The novel deals with the persecution of Jews shortly before and after the Nazis' accession to power. In the third volume, *Paris Gazette* (1940), he deals with the fate of the German exiles in France. As a whole, the Waiting Room Trilogy may be considered Feuchtwanger's contribution to the German intellectuals' fight against Hitler. Other novels, such as the historical satire *The Pretender* (1936), *Double, Double, Toil and Trouble* (*The Lautensack Brothers,* 1943), and a novel about French resistance and collaboration, *Simone* (1944), were less successful in dealing with the Third Reich.

In 1936, during his exile in France—he had left Germany in 1933—Feuchtwanger visited the Soviet Union and published a disturbing defense of the Soviet system in his report *Moscow 1937: A Visit Described for My Friends.* In 1940 he had experienced internment in France, as he reports in detail in *The Devil in France* (1942).

The progress of reason in history is the theme of his novels dealing with the time before and after the French Revolution: *Proud Destiny* (1947) is a novel about the writer, businessman, and politician Beaumarchais and Benjamin Franklin, the American envoy in Paris. Since in October 1940 Feuchtwanger had come to America, ultimately settling in Pacific Palisades,

California, the book may be considered an homage to the United States. *This Is the Hour* (1951) is about the development of Spanish artist Francisco de Goya's career, from his early work as a conventional court painter to the political responsibility he later demonstrated in his social-critical *Caprichos*. In *Tis Folly to Be Wise; or, Death and Transfiguration of Jean-Jacques Rousseau* (1952) Feuchtwanger writes about the last weeks of the French philosopher's life and the effect of his ideals on the French as well as on the American Revolution.

Throughout his career Feuchtwanger was drawn to the theme of Jewishness. In his Josephus Trilogy (*Josephus,* 1932; *The Jew of Rome,* 1935; and *Josephus and the Emperor,* or *The Day Will Come,* 1942) he deals with the theme of nationalism versus cosmopolitanism by describing the development of Flavius Josephus, a Jewish historian of the first century A.D. Toward the end of his life he took up the theme of Jewishness by writing about the beautiful *Raquel, the Jewess of Toledo* (1955), who for seven years was able to prevent Alfonso VIII of Castile from going to war against the Moors. In *Jefta and His Daughter* (1957) he wrote about a character from the Old Testament who kept his promise to God and sacrificed his own daughter.

Feuchtwanger explicitly dealt with the Holocaust only in *The Oppermanns.* But in dealing with the fate of the Jews in history and the development of National Socialism in Germany, he made an important contribution to our understanding of this dark period of German history.

—Hans Wagener

See the essay on *The Oppermanns.*

FICOWSKI, Jerzy

Nationality: Polish. **Born:** Warsaw, 4 September 1924. **Education:** Studied sociology and philosophy at the University of Warsaw, 1946–50. **Military Service:** Polish underground Home Army during World War II; fought in the Warsaw Uprising, 1944; imprisoned, 1944–45. **Family:** Married 1) Wanda Komala in 1951 (divorced), two daughters; 2) married Elzbieta Bussold in 1968, one daughter. **Career:** Traveled with Gypsy caravans, 1948–50; worked with Mazowsze (Polish national song and dance ensemble), 1951. **Awards:** Polish PEN Club award, 1977, for translation work; Poets' and Painters' Press award (London), 1981; Alfred Jurzykowski Foundation award (New York), 1984; K. Tzetnik award in Holocaust literature (Jerusalem), 1986; Jan Karski award, YIVO Institute, 1994; Sejny Borderlands award, 1999. **Member:** Stowarzyszenie Pisarzy Polskich (Polish Writers' Association).

PUBLICATIONS

Poetry

Olowiana zolnierze [Tin Soldiers]. 1948.
*Zwierzenia.*1952.
Popolsku. 1955.
Wiersze wybrane (selections). 1956.
Moje strony świata [My Parts of the World]. 1957.
Makowskie bajki, with Tadeusza Makowskiego. 1959.
Amulety i definicje [Amulets and Definitions]. 1960.
Pismo obrazkowe. 1962.
Maciupinka. 1968.
Ptak poza ptakiem. 1968.
Wiersze niektóre [Some Poems]. 1971.
Odczytanie popiołów. 1979; as *A Reading of Ashes: Poems,* 1981.
Smierc jednorozca [Death of a Unicorn]. 1981.
Errata: wiersze. 1981.
Gryps i Errata [A Coded Message and an Erratum]. 1982.
Poezje wybrane (selections). 1982.
Wskazówki dla poczatkujacych zegarów: Wybór poezji 1945–1985 (selections). 1993.
Inicjal. 1994.

Short Stories

Czekanie na sen psa [Waiting for the Dog to Fall Asleep]. 1970.

Other

Cyganie polscy. 1953; as *Cyganie na polskich drogach,* 1965; as *The Gypsies in Poland: History and Customs,* 1989.
Wspominki starowarszawskie: Karty z raptularza. 1959.
Galazka z drzewa slonca (folklore). 1961; selections translated as *Sisters of the Bird and Other Gypsy Tales,* 1976.
Denerwujek (poetry for children). 1961.
Kolorowy kalendarzyk (poetry for children). 1964.
Regiony wielkiej herezji; Szkice o zyciu i twórczosci Brunona Schulza. 1967.
Maciupinka (poetry for children). 1968.
Tecza na niedziele (for children). 1971.
Demony cudzego strachu: Wspominki cyganskie. 1986.
Okolice sklepów cynamonowych: szkice, przyczynki, impresje (on Bruno Schulz). 1986.
Wisla wpadla do Baltyku (for children). 1987.
List do Marc Chagalla. 1988.
Cyganie w Polsce: Dzieje i obyczaje. 1989.
Pod berlem krola pikowego: Sekrety cyga 'nskich wrozb. 1990.
Witold Wojtkiewicz (biography). 1996.
Bajedy z augustowskich lasów. 1998.
Wszystko to czego nie wiem. 1999.

Editor, *Druga jesien*. 1973.
Editor, *Bruno Schulz, Ksiega listów* (correspondence). 1975.
Editor, *Bruno Schulz, Listy, fragmenty: Wspomnienia o pisarzu* (correspondence). 1984.
Editor, *Xiega balwochwalcza*, by Bruno Schulz. 1988; as *The Book of Idolatry*, 1988.
Editor, *Letters and Drawings of Bruno Schulz*. 1990.
Editor, *Bruno Schulz: Ilustracje do wlasnych utworów*. 1992.
Editor, *Republika marzen: Utwory rozproszone, opowiadania, fragmenty, eseje, rysunki*. 1993.
Editor, *Z listów odnalezionych* (correspondence). 1993.
Editor, *The Collected Works of Bruno Schulz*. 1998.

Translator, *Piesn o zamordowanym zydowskim narodzie* [Song of the Murdered Jewish Nation], by Yitzhak Katzenelson. 1983.
Translator, *Piesni (Papušakre gila); wiersze w jezyku cyganskim*, by Papusza. 1956.
Translator, *Piesni mówione*, by Papusza. 1973.
Translator, *Lesie, ojcze mój*, by Papusza. 1990.

*

Critical Study: ''Jerzy Ficowski's Notes from Prison'' by J. Frank Corliss Jr. and Grazyna Sandel, in *Cross Currents*, 3, 1984, pp. 245–58.

*   *   *

In the work of Jerzy Ficowski the issue of the Holocaust belongs to a larger whole. The unsubmissive writer, whose writing used to be forbidden by official censorship, speaks up about the injustice suffered by the representatives of national minorities and also tries to preserve the heritage of the multicultural Second Republic of Poland (1918–39). He voices his determined protest against extermination as well as against all forms of persecutions and of destroying human dignity. The inconceivable crimes committed during World War II led to the collapse of the order of the world in which various ethnic communities used to coexist in harmony. The ghastly heritage of intolerance also loomed over the postwar reality. In Ficowski's writing the same fundamental objection also concerns the oblivion to the fate of the Jews, Ukrainians, and Gypsies. In moral terms those crimes have not been paid for sufficiently. In one case history is the source of threat. On the one hand, in a series of drastic images, Ficowski uncovers the truth about the twentieth-century history, but on the other he embarks on a search for a poetic Arcadia.

Ficowski focuses on the Holocaust issue both in his poetry and in prose. Particularly worth noticing are his two short stories ''Osada przejezdna'' (''A Settlement on the Way'') and ''Że głupi i że Abraham'' (''Not Only Stupid, But Also an Abraham'') from the volume entitled *Czekanie na sen psa* (*Waiting for the Dog to Fall Asleep*). In the former the narrator speaks of a village appearing in a glimpse in which the dead (victims of extermination) spend their vacations. The topography of that place is precarious and the status of that ephemeral world is unclear. The phantasms connected with the childhood memories appear in a dream aura. The construction of time and space, as well as the language of metaphors and discursive comments, makes it possible to juxtapose that eminent short story with Bruno Schultz's prose. In ''Not Only Stupid, But Also an Abraham'' the mad protagonist enthusiastically welcomes the deportation of the Jews to the execution place that he perceives as a journey to the Promised Land. In the face of the crime that achieves unification through death the categories of wisdom and stupidity are no longer valid. This work also constitutes a penetrating study of fear and uncertainty.

In Ficowski's volume entitled *Odczytanie popiołów* (1979; *A Reading of Ashes*) the poem ''List do Marc Chagalla'' (''A Letter to Marc Chagall'') has a prominent place. It has been translated into many languages. It was written in the years 1950–56. Published in the *Po prostu* weekly, it was also reprinted in two other collections—*Moje strony świata* (1957; *My Parts of the World*) and *Wiersze niektóre* (1971; *Some Poems*). It also had two special bibliophile editions—in French and in Polish—illustrated by Chagall himself. The French painter and Polish poet exchanged some letters in connection with the poem. In ''A Letter to Marc Chagall'' Ficowski includes some excerpts from a book by Maria Hochberg-Mariańska and Noe Grüss, *Dzieci oskarżają* (1947; *The Children Accuse*). In the introduction he writes: ''No word of poetry is capable of matching the shocking power of children's statements.''

A splendid sequel to *A Reading of Ashes* is the series of poems in the collection *Gryps i Errata* (*A Coded Message and an Erratum*)—poems from the years 1968–80, published in 1982. The dialogue with the dead is particularly worth noticing. The erratum is nothing else but the correction of the state of consciousness. Ficowski touches upon the issue of the painful memory—the posthumous scream of the dead comes to us from the pages covered with writing (the poem entitled ''Archiwum Ringelbluma [Oneg Szabat],'' or ''Ringelblum Archive [Oneg Shabath]''). Bitter irony points to a relationship between the practice of covering people's corpses with newspapers and a contemporary newspaper whose purpose is to cover ''the truth lying on its back'' (''Z prasoznawstwa'' [''Of the Press Studies'']). The disappearance of the traces of the Jews in small Polish towns is paralleled by the erosion of hope (''Kolejka'' [''A Line'']). The psychical comfort of the deliberate ignorance of the Holocaust is decidedly condemned (''Tomasze'' [''Thomases'']). The events connected with the forced exodus of the meritorious people of Jewish descent from the People's Republic of Poland are the subject matter of the poem entitled ''Dworzec Gdański 1968'' (''Gdański Railway Station 1968'').

—Wojciech Ligęza

See the essay on *A Reading of Ashes: Poems*.

FIGES, Eva

Nationality: British (originally German: immigrated to England, 1939). **Born:** Eva Unger, Berlin, 15 April 1932. **Education:** Kingsbury Grammar School, 1943–50; Queen Mary College, University of London, 1950–53; B.A. (honors) in English 1953. **Family:** Married John George Figes in 1954 (divorced 1963); one daughter and one son. **Career:** Editor, Longmans, Green & Co., Ltd., London, 1955–57, Weidenfeld & Nicolson, Ltd., London, 1962–63, and Blackie & Son, Ltd., London, 1964–67. Since 1987 co-editor, Macmillan Women Writers series. Writer-in-residence, Brunel University, 1977–79. **Awards:** *Guardian* fiction prize, 1967, for *Winter Journey;* C. Day Lewis fellowship, 1973; Arts Council fellowship, 1977–79; Society of Authors traveling scholarship, 1988. Fellow, Queen Mary and Westfield College, 1990. **Agents:** Rogers, Coleridge & White, Ltd., 20 Powis Mews, London W11 1JN, England; Elaine Markson, 64 Greenwich Avenue, New York, New York 10011, U.S.A.

PUBLICATIONS

Novels

Equinox. 1966.
Winter Journey. 1967.
Konek Landing. 1969.
Days. 1974.
B. 1976.
Nelly's Version. 1977.
Waking. 1981.
Light. 1983.
The Seven Ages. 1986 or 1987.
Ghosts. 1988.
The Tree of Knowledge. 1990.
The Tenancy. 1993.
The Knot. 1996.

Memoir

Little Eden: A Child at War. 1978.

Plays

Radio Plays: *Time Regained,* 1980; *Dialogue between Friends,* 1982; *Punch-Flame and Pigeon-Breast,* 1983; *The True Tale of Margery Kempe,* 1985.

Television Play: *Days,* 1981, from her own novel.

Other

The Banger (for children). 1968.
Patriarchal Attitudes: Women in Society. 1970; revised edition, 1986.

Scribble Sam: A Story (for children). 1971.
Tradition and Social Evolution. 1976.
Sex and Subterfuge: Women Writers to 1850. 1982.

Editor, with Abigail Mozley and Dinah Livingstone, *Women Their World.* 1980.
Editor, *Women's Letters in Wartime (1450–1945).* 1993.

Translator, *The Gadarene Club,* by Martin Walser. 1960; as *Marriage in Phillipsburg,* 1961.
Translator, *The Musicians of Bremen: Retold* (for children). 1967.
Translator, *He and I and the Elephants,* by Bernhard Grzimek. 1967.
Translator, *Little Fadette,* by George Sand. 1967.
Translator, *The Old Car,* by Elisabeth Borchers. 1967.
Translator, *A Family Failure,* by Renate Rasp. 1970.
Translator, *The Deathbringer,* by Manfred von Conta. 1971.

*

Critical Studies: *Structures of Identity: A Reading of the Self-Provoking Fiction of Christine Brooke-Rose, Brian Stanley Johnson, Eva Figes, and Paul West* (dissertation) by Brian Gerard MacLaughlin, Pennsylvania State University, 1981; by Michele Field, in *Publishers Weekly,* 231, 16 January 1987, pp. 56–57; ''Childhood and Self in Eva Figes' *Little Eden*'' by Aranzazu Usandizaga, in *BELLS* (Spain), 1, 1989, pp. 207–14; *Women Writers Talk: Interviews with 10 Women Writers* by Olga Kenyon, 1990; '''A Piece of Shrapnel Lodges in My Flesh, and When It Moves, I Write': The Fiction of Eva Figes'' by Anna Maria Stuby, in *Anglistik & Englischunterricht* (Germany), 60, 1997, pp. 113–27.

* * *

Eva Figes is one of Great Britain's most prolific contemporary female writers. Her publications include more than a dozen novels, an autobiographical work, children's books, and literary translations, as well as works of nonfiction. Figes became best known for her groundbreaking feminist work *Patriarchal Attitudes* (1970), a thoroughly researched examination of the ideology underlying male-female relationships. Other nonfiction works include *Tradition and Social Evolution* (1976), *Sex and Subterfuge: Women Writers to 1850* (1982), and the anthology *Women's Letters in Wartime (1450–1945),* which she edited in 1993. All of her nonfiction works are characterized by an interdisciplinary approach that combines historical, psychological, cultural, and biographical perspectives. Figes's position as a feminist is also reflected in her fiction. Her protagonists are predominantly females whose isolation, despair, or illnesses often reflect their restricted social space and male-dominated existence. While this is particularly true of the early works *Equinox* (1966), *Days*

(1974), and *Waking* (1981), later novels such as *Ghosts* (1988), *The Tree of Knowledge* (1990), and *The Tenancy* (1993) demonstrate similar preoccupations.

Figes's early novels have been well received, and she won the prestigious *Guardian* Fiction Prize in 1967 for her novel *Winter Journey*. Her readership, however, has remained small due to her experimental and aesthetically challenging style of writing, which reflects the acknowledged influence of Franz Kafka and Virginia Woolf, both of whom resisted narrative coherence in their fiction. In addition, her literary exploration of the inner realm of consciousness, of multiple selves, and of the impossibility of unmediated access to reality, combined with her preoccupation with the problems of representation and the relativity of knowledge, in particular historical knowledge (a theme the author foregrounds especially in *The Tree of Knowledge*), have led critics to see Figes as a precursor of postmodernism. The metafictionality of her novel *B* (1976), about a writer who loses control over his life when "reality" and "fiction" change place, or the appropriation of the conventions of the gothic novel in *Tenancy* (1993), to depict isolation and urban dread, support such an association.

In an article for the *Observer* from 11 June 1978, the author relates her rejection of the aesthetic traditions prevalent in postwar British writing to her personal history as a German refugee from the Holocaust, which instilled in her a sense of statelessness that precludes any notion of political or aesthetic continuity. Figes was born Eva Unger on 15 April 1932 in Berlin, the oldest child of an upper–middle class, assimilated Jewish family. In 1939 she and her family made a late, lucky escape from Germany after her father had been released from Dachau. Her autobiographical work *Little Eden: A Child at War* (1978) relates the experiences of Figes's early years in England, culminating in her understanding of the political reality of Nazi Germany and the Holocaust, which she had escaped but which had led to the nearly complete destruction of European Jewry. The earlier novel *Konek Landing* (1969) can be seen as Figes's literary attempt to come to terms with her understanding of the Holocaust. Stephan Konek, the male protagonist of this complex experimental work, struggles to remember the past, which leads him to a series of nightmarish encounters with other victims and perpetrators. Although the Holocaust is not featured directly in Figes's other novels, the recurring themes of alienation, exclusion, marginalization of the "other," guilt, and separation suggest its underlying impact on the author's entire body of work. The author herself acknowledged this impact in her article in the *Observer:* "A piece of shrapnel lodges in my flesh, and when it moves, I write."

—Helga Schreckenberger

See the essay on *Little Eden: A Child at War.*

FINK, Ida

Nationality: Israeli (originally Polish: immigrated to Israel, 1957). **Born:** Zbaraż, 11 January 1921. **Education:** Studied music at a conservatory in Lvov, 1938–41. **Married:** Bruno Fink in 1948; one daughter. **Career:** Documentary work, Yad Vashem Institute, Tel-Aviv; music librarian, Goethe Institute, Tel-Aviv, 1972–83. Since 1983 freelance writer in Holon. **Awards:** Anne Frank prize in literature, 1985, and PEN/Book-of-the-Month Club translation prize, for *Skrawek czasu;* Jacob Buchman memorial prize, Yad Vashem, 1995.

PUBLICATIONS

Short Stories

Skrawek czasu. 1983; as *A Scrap of Time and Other Stories,* 1987; revised edition, 1995.
Slady. 1996; as *Traces,* 1997.

Novel

Podróż. 1990; as *The Journey,* 1992.

*

Critical Study: "Trusting the Words: Paradoxes of Ida Fink" by Marek Wilczynski, in *Modern Language Studies,* 24(4), 1994, pp. 25–38.

* * *

Born in Zbaraż, Poland, in 1921, a survivor of what a character in one of her stories calls "the Hitler time," Ida Fink is one of the most important and powerful writers to come out of the Holocaust. She stands alongside such powerful and established writers as **Elie Wiesel, Primo Levi,** and **Charlotte Delbo.** Her style is gently and distinctively lyrical, restrained, and understated; her approach to the subject of the Holocaust is markedly different from that of the other writers to whom she bears comparison. Whereas they portray the horrors of life—and death—in the concentration camps, where bestiality was the order of the day, Fink portrays another heart of darkness located on the periphery of the Holocaust. It is here that ordinary men, women, and children—more than three million Polish Jews inhabiting the small towns and villages of Poland—are trying, with mounting despair and desperation, to deal with a terror so grimly threatening and grotesque that it strains credibility. It is here—as in Auschwitz—in a pastoral setting of lush green orchards, carefully tended gardens, and deep forests, that sadistic and satanic atrocities are being committed. Babies are snatched from their parents and shot, neighbors betray neighbors for small rewards, and whole towns are rounded up as targets of an action (a new euphemism for mass murder).

Fink was confined to the ghetto until 1942. She spent the remaining war years in hiding and on the run, with the help of false identity papers certifying that she was Aryan. In 1957 she immigrated to Israel, where, switching from the musical study she had begun in Poland, she became a journalist. Her first volume of short stories was published, initially in Polish as *Skawek Czasu* (1983), then in English as *A Scrap of Time* (1987). She had waited more than 10 years before beginning to write: "Subconsciously," she explained in an interview, "I needed distance. I was afraid to touch these things with words. I thought one should speak about this in a quiet voice." This "quiet voice," almost a whisper, would become the corner-stone of her style. "She chose to whisper," as one reviewer noted, "and her soft whisper breaks your heart."

Based almost entirely on her own experiences and those of family and friends, her stories provide a uniquely intimate and chilling picture of the everyday comings and goings of Polish Jews, trapped but nonetheless frantically trying to escape total extermination. Alas, most did not, but those who did are tenderly memorialized, though never sentimentalized, in the 22 brief but all who tried haunting stories included in this collection. It won a series of awards, including the first Anne Frank Prize in Literature in 1985 and the PEN/Book-of-the-Month Club Translation Prize.

In 1990 Fink published *Podróż* (*The Journey,* 1992), a novel based on her own experiences during the war when she managed, with her false documents, to serve as a volunteer laborer in Germany. Only through great "cleverness and luck," as she points out in the novel, was it possible to survive daily life under the very nose of the enemy, surrounded as well by indifferent if not hostile bystanders. In 1996 *Slady* (*Traces,* 1997) appeared, a volume of 18 short stories representing a continuation of her portrait of Jewish life and death in occupied Poland. These three relatively brief texts, taken together, constitute the thin but deeply impressive canon of Fink. In 1995 she was awarded the Jacob Buchman Memorial Prize at a ceremony that took place at Israel's Yad Vashem shrine. The citation reads: "The theme of survival burns like fire within Ida Fink. She has succeeded in treating her subject with sensitivity, understanding, [and a] brilliant creative ability. The enormous talent she reveals in her work places her among the foremost authors of Holocaust literature."

In one interview Fink emphasized that it is not profitable, or even sensible to say, as some do, that the Holocaust reveals behavior so beyond human norms that it might as well have occurred on another planet. Not at all, she insists: "It happened on our planet, in the world of reality. I describe the simple person in this situation. My heroes live in fear and despair, witnessing death day and night, and yet [they] struggle to survive."

It is only in our own witnessing of this struggle, as Fink depicts it in her stunning vignettes, that we can begin to connect with the Holocaust as it went on—incredibly and horrifically—day after day for six years. To learn what happened in the Holocaust, we must read history. But for those who want to feel the Holocaust "on the pulse" (as Coleridge said of literature in general), it is equally important that we read the stories of Ida Fink.

—Jacqueline Berke

See the essays on *The Journey, A Scrap of Time and Other Stories,* and *Traces.*

FLINKER, Moshe (Zev)

Nationality: Dutch. **Born:** The Hague, 9 October 1926. **Died:** Murdered, Auschwitz, 1944.

PUBLICATION

Diary

Hana'ar Moshe: Yoman shel Moshe Flinker. 1958; as *Young Moshe's Diary: The Spiritual Torment of a Jewish Boy in Nazi Europe,* 1971.

* * *

Born in The Hague on 9 October 1926, Moshe Zev Flinker was known to be a bright student both at the public school he attended and in the Jewish studies he pursued with a private tutor. He had a particular facility with languages—he studied eight foreign tongues—and soon mastered Hebrew, the language in which he kept a diary. His studies came to an end, however, when Holland surrendered to the German juggernaut on 15 May 1940. The occupying forces quickly implemented the anti-Semitic policies that had forced the German Jews out of any "legitimate" presence in life. Compelled to wear the yellow star, Jewish professionals such as doctors and lawyers could have only Jewish patients and clients, a point that was soon meaningless since all Jews had to deposit their money in a German bank.

On 14 July 1942, the Nazis began rounding up Jews and sending them to Westerbork for deportation to Auschwitz. As the deportations were getting under way, the boy's father, Eliezer Flinker, a Polish-born businessman, moved the family from German-occupied Holland to German-occupied Belgium. A wealthy man, Flinker managed to hide enough money to enable his family to make their escape. Thus, in the summer of 1942 he, his wife, and their five daughters and two sons settled in Brussels. He obtained a so-called Aryan permit to move into an apartment, and he successfully bribed his way into having the permit extended several times.

Meanwhile, the young boy followed the news of the war and prepared himself for an eventual future in the Jewish state that he believed was about to be reborn. He began studying Arabic, for example, so that one day he could become a diplomat for peace in the new land. He and his family remained relatively safe until 7 April 1944, the eve of Passover. On that day, as the household was preparing for the Passover seder, a Jewish informer led local Gestapo agents to the Flinkers' apartment. Since the Flinker family was orthodox in its life-style, with matzos stacked on the seder table and kosher meat in the kitchen, they were not able to hide from the Germans the fact that they were Jews. The entire family was arrested that evening and sent to Auschwitz.

Although Moshe Flinker's five sisters and younger brother survived, he and his parents were murdered. After the war came to an end, his sisters returned to the apartment where the family had lived in Brussels. In the basement of the apartment building they found three notebooks in which their brother had kept his diary. From those notebooks *Hana'ar Moshe: Yoman shel Moshe Flinker* was published in 1958; the English translation, *Young Moshe's Diary,* appeared in 1971. His diary demonstrates that during the war the teenager was keenly aware of what was taking place. Not only did he know about the systematic deportation of the Jews to the east but he also knew the murderous aim of the deportation. The diary also demonstrates a deeply rooted identification with the Jews and a profound sense of the historical import of the events transpiring around him. Indeed, he saw in the Holocaust an event of biblical significance to the Jews and to the world, something that would bring the world to the threshold of the messianic age. As for Moshe Flinker it brought him only to the threshold of a gas chamber.

—David Patterson

See the essay on *Young Moshe's Diary.*

FRANK, Anne(lies) (Marie)

Nationality: German (fled with her family to the Netherlands, 1933). **Born:** Frankfurt, 12 June 1929. **Died:** Typhus, Bergen-Belsen, March 1945.

PUBLICATIONS

Diary

Het achterhuis. 1947; as *Diary of a Young Girl,* 1952; revised editions, as *Anne Frank: The Diary of a Young Girl,* 1967, *The Diary of Anne Frank: The Critical Edition,* edited by David Barnouw and Gerrold van der Stroom, 1989, and *The Diary of Anne Frank: The Definitive Edition,* edited by Otto Frank and Mirjam Pressler, 1995.

Other

The Works of Anne Frank. 1959.
Tales from the House Behind: Fables, Personal Reminiscences, and Short Stories (translated from the original manuscript, *Verhalen rondom het achterhuis*). 1962; as *Anne Frank's Tales from the Secret Annex,* 1983.

*

Film Adaptation: *The Diary of Anne Frank,* 1959.

Critical Studies: *Anne Frank: A Portrait in Courage* by Ernst Schnabel, translated by Richard and Clara Winston, 1958, as *Footsteps of Anne Frank,* 1959; *A Tribute to Anne Frank,* edited by Anna G. Steenmeijer, 1970; *The Last Seven Months of Anne Frank* by Willy Lindwer, translated by Alison Meersschaert, 1991; *Anne Frank in the World: Essays and Reflections,* edited by Carol Ann Rittner, 1998; *Anne Frank: The Biography* by Melissa Müller, translated by Rita and Robert Kimber, 1998; *Anne Frank and Etty Hillesum: Inscribing Spirituality and Sexuality* by Denise de Costa, translated by Mischa F. C. Hoynick and Robert E. Chesal, 1998; *A Scholarly Look at The Diary of Anne Frank,* edited by Harold Bloom, 1999; *Anne Frank: Reflections on Her Life and Legacy,* edited by Hyman Aaron Enzer and Sandra Solotaroff-Enzer, 2000.

*   *   *

Anne Frank is arguably the most famous author on the Holocaust. *Diary of a Young Girl* (1947) is enormously popular worldwide and has garnered a wide variety of readers from schoolchildren to university academics. People who wish to learn about the Holocaust often turn to either Anne's diary or **Elie Wiesel**'s *Night*. The diary's unique appeal stems from its manifestation of Anne's innocence, frankness, and precociousness, as well as the tragic nature of her ultimate fate. In the diary's third entry, she mentions that she wants to divulge in writing what lies deep within her heart. The secret nature of her diary permitted her to write frankly and describe events faithfully. Because she protected the identity of those whom she wrote about, she was able to write truthfully and without fear of reproach. Thus, the Van Pels became the Van Daans, and Fritz Pfeffer was transformed into Mr. Dussel (which translates into English as "Mr. Dope"). As an adolescent, Anne is perhaps too young to worry about being so tactful. She includes information about sexuality, her strong feelings for Peter, and her anger toward her mother—sections of the diary that her father felt it appropriate to censor when it was published in 1947.

Furthermore, unlike most other diaries and accounts of the Shoah, Anne's work possesses a sense of immediacy because she wrote as events were happening, not years later upon reflection. For example, in her 29 July 1943 entry, Anne castigates Mrs. Van Daan for her selfishness, pushiness, pessimism, coquetry, and numerous other faults; but, as an addendum, she adds, "Will the reader take into consideration that when this story was written the writer had not cooled down from her fury!'' Here, Anne admits a lack of reflection, which is actually refreshing, for it renders the entry genuine, immediate, and heartfelt.

From the diary, the reader learns how Anne and the other inhabitants of the annex deal with their confinement. Mr. Van Daan smokes, while Mrs. Van Daan complains, fights with her husband and others, and flirts with Mr. Frank. Margot studies intensely, while Mr. Dussel reads, studies Spanish (he was considering moving to South America after the war), and thinks of his lover Charlotte. Anne and Peter turn to each other. Furthermore, the diary illustrates that Jews in hiding employed humor as a defense mechanism, as when Mr. Dussel arrives in the annex. Anne informs him that only civilized languages are allowed to be spoken in the annex—and that does not include German. This joke of Anne's demonstrates how she is able to release tension by mocking her oppressor.

The diary exists in more than one version; Anne heard on the British radio on 28 March 1944 that war diaries would be collected, and subsequently started to revise her work. She unequivocally states her desire to be a writer and wonders whether her writing will be good enough for her to write professionally. She discusses the quality of her stories, fables, and essays, which Miep Gies found and collected along with the diary; this collection, originally published in Dutch in 1949, is called *Tales from the Secret Annex* (1962; also known as *Tales from the House Behind*). In her 4 April 1944 diary entry, Anne reflects upon her writing and judges ''Eva's Dream'' to be her best fable. The works in the collection clearly relate to the situation in which Anne is immersed while in hiding. *Tales from the Secret Annex* is a popular book, although not as widely known or read as Anne's diary.

Anne's diary demonstrates the writer's self-consciousness and her awareness of herself as an author. She writes not only for herself but also for future readers who want to know more about her life in hiding and about the Holocaust. Her diary is fascinating because it shows readers what some Jews in hiding knew about the war effort and the Holocaust, as well as how they coped with their precarious situation. The reader also gains insight into how a teenage girl felt about leaving behind her friends and all that she had—to be confined in a small space with adults, many of whom were rude and condescending to her and treated her like a child—during a time in which she was changing and transforming into a young woman. Anne considers the years in the annex pivotal and significant. In her 4 April 1944 entry, Anne Frank writes that she wants to have a more fulfilling and valuable life than that of her mother or Mrs. Van Daan. It thus should not be surprising to the readers that in the same entry, she continues, ''I want to go on living even after my death!'' And she has.

—Eric Sterling

See the essay on *Diary of a Young Girl.*

FRANKL, Viktor E(mil)

Nationality: Austrian. **Born:** Vienna, 26 March 1905. **Education:** University of Vienna, M.D. 1930, Ph.D. 1949. **Family:** Married 1) Mathilde Grosser in 1941 (died 1945); 2) Eleonore Katharina Schwindt in 1947, one daughter. **Career:** Director of neurology department, Rothschild Hospital, Vienna, 1940–42; director of neurology department, Poliklinik Hospital, 1946–70; beginning 1947 professor of neurology and psychiatry, University of Vienna; beginning 1970 distinguished professor of logotherapy, U.S. International University. Visiting professor, Harvard University, 1961, Southern Methodist University, 1961, 1966, Stanford University, 1971–72, and Duquesne University, 1972; guest lecturer at more than a hundred colleges and universities in the United States as well as in Australia, Asia, and Africa. **Awards:** Austrian State Prize for Public Education, 1956; honors from Religion in Education Foundation, 1960, and Indianapolis Pastoral Counseling Center; founders award, West Virginia Wesleyan College, 1968; Austrian Cross of Honor first class for science and art, 1969; distinguished lecturer award, Washington College, 1970; City of Vienna prize for scientific achievement, 1970; honorary citizen of Austin, Texas, 1976; Quest Medal, St. Edward's University, 1976; plaque of appreciation, University of the Philippines and University of Santo Tomas, 1976; American Psychiatric Association Oskar Pfister prize. Honorary degrees (selection): LL. D., Loyola University and Edgecliff College, both in 1970; D.H.L., Rockford College, 1972. **Died:** 2 September 1997.

PUBLICATIONS

Memoir

Was nicht in meinen Büchern steht: Lebenserinnerungen. 1995; as *Viktor Frankl—Recollections: An Autobiography,* 1997.

Play

Synchronisation in Buchenwald: A Metaphysical Conference (translation of the 1945 original). 1978.

Other (psychology)

Ärztliche Seelsorge. 1946; as *The Doctor and the Soul: An Introduction to Logotherapy,* 1955; revised edition, as *The Doctor and the Soul: From Psychotherapy to Logotherapy,* 1965.
Ein Psycholog erlebt das Konzentrationslager. 1946; as *From Death-Camp to Existentialism: A Psychiatrist's Path to a New Therapy,* 1959; revised edition, as *Man's Search for Meaning: An Introduction to Logotherapy,* 1963.

Trotzdem Ja zum Leben sagen: Drei Vorträge. 1946.

Die Psychotherapie in der Praxis: Eine kasuistische Einführung für Ärzte. 1947.

Die Existenzanalyse und die Probleme der Zeit. 1947.

Zeit und Verantwortung. 1947.

Der umbewusste Gott. 1948; as *The Unconscious God: Psychotherapy and Theology,* 1975; revised edition, as *Man's Search for Ultimate Meaning,* 1997.

Der unbedingte Mensch: Metaklinische Vorlesungen. 1949.

Homo patiens: Versuch einer Pathodizee. 1950.

Logos und Existenz. Drei Vorträge. 1951.

Die Psychotherapie im Alltag: Sieben Radiovorträge. 1952.

Pathologie des Zeitgeistes: Rundfunkvorträge über Seelenheilkunde. 1955; as *Psychotherapie für jedermann,* 1971; as *Psychotherapie für den Laien,* 1971.

Theorie und Therapie der Neurosen; Einführung in Logotherapie und Existenzanalyse. 1956.

Das Menschenbild der Seelenheilkunde: Drei Vorlesungen zur Kritik des dynamischen Psychologismus. 1959; as *Der Mensch auf der Suche nach Sinn: Zur Rehumanisierung der Psychotherapie,* 1972.

Psychotherapy and Existentialism: Selected Papers on Logotherapy, with James C. Crumbaugh, Hans O. Gerz, and Leonard T. Maholick. 1967; revised edition, 1973.

The Will to Meaning: Foundations and Applications to Logotherapy. 1969; revised edition, 1988.

Der Wille zum Sinn: Ausgewählte Vorträge über Logotherapie. 1972.

Anthropologische Grundlagen der Psychotherapie. 1975.

Das Leiden am sinnlosen Leben: Psychotherapie für heute. 1977.

The Unheard Cry for Meaning: Psychotherapy and Humanism. 1978.

Der Mensch vor der Frage nach dem Sinn: Eine Auswahl aus dem Gesamtwerk. 1979.

Logotherapie und Existenzanalyse: Texte aus fünf Jahrzehnten. 1987; revised edition, as *Texte aus sechs Jahrzehnten,* 1994.

Editor, with Victor E. Freiherr Gebsattel and J.H. Schultz, *Handbuch der Neurosenlehre und Psychotherapie* (5 volumes). 1957–61.

*

Film Adaptation: *Frankl and the Search for Meaning,* 1973.

Audiocassette Adaptation: *Meaninglessness: Today's Dilemma,* 1971.

Critical Studies: *The Pursuit of Meaning: Logotherapy Applied to Life* by Joseph B. Fabry, 1968, revised edition, as *The Pursuit of Meaning: Viktor Frankl, Logotheraphy, and Life,* 1980; *Viktor E. Frankl: Life with Meaning* by William Blair

Gould, 1993; ''Meaning and Love in Viktor Frankl's Writing: Reports from the Holocaust'' by J.B. Gerwood, in *Psychol Rep (Psychological Reports),* December 1994, 75(3), pt. 1, pp. 1075–81; ''The Missing Pieces of the Puzzle: A Reflection on the Odd Career of Viktor Frankl,'' in *Journal of Contemporary History,* 35(2), 2000, pp. 281–306, and ''Viktor Frankl and the Genesis of the Third Viennese School of Psychotherapy,'' in *The Psychoanalytic Review,* 88(2), 2001, pp. 311–34, both by Timothy Pytell; *When Life Calls Out to Us: The Love and Lifework of Viktor and Elly Frankl* by Haddon Klingberg, 2001.

* * *

Viktor E. Frankl is known both as an eminent psychoanalyst and a highly prolific writer. Frankl's articles and books concern logotherapy, an area of existential analysis that he pioneered and through which he successfully bridged the gap between psychology, philosophy, and religion. His writings, however, extend beyond general explication of theoretical ideas and case studies. In essence all of his writings are autobiographical. Through his writings one can trace the developing threads of his beliefs, ideas, and personal growth over time. The Holocaust clearly had a major impact on Frankl's development as a person and as an analyst. One can get an intimate glimpse into this development by reading his book *Man's Search for Meaning.*

Man's Search for Meaning is undoubtedly Frankl's best known work. At the time of Frankl's death the book had been translated into more than two dozen languages and had sold more than 10 million copies. In this text Frankl provides a moving account of his experiences in the concentration camps of Nazi-occupied Europe and an introduction to logotherapy. His basic ideas, while shaped by the Holocaust and his experiences in the camps, can be found in his early writings and presentations. While still a teen Frankl gave a public lecture on the meaning of life, began publishing in psychoanalytic journals, and established professional relationships with Sigmund Freud and Alfred Adler. Frankl's publications and professional relations continued during his early twenties with work focusing on the interrelationship between psychotherapy and philosophy, meaning and values, and logotherapy. Thus, while many consider *Man's Search for Meaning* as Frankl's beginning work, it represents rather an extension of his previous writings. Clearly his experiences during the Holocaust further shaped his ideas, but these ideas did not evolve solely from this time.

Frankl was already an experienced and highly respected doctor of neurology and psychiatry at the time of the Anschluss, the annexation of Austria into Nazi Germany. So well known and respected was Frankl that he was granted an immigration visa to the United States. Frankl chose, however, to let his immigration visa go unused rather than leave his aging parents. He continued his professional activities until he and his family were deported to Theresienstadt in 1942. Prior to his deportation he served as director of the Neurological Department of the Rothschild Hospital. In that capacity he routinely falsified diagnosis in an effort to protect his patients from the Nazi policies concerning euthanasia of the mentally ill. His actions exemplified the values apparent in his later writings.

Prior to his initial deportation in 1942 Frankl had begun work on his first book, *The Doctor and the Soul*. Unfortunately the manuscript was destroyed upon his arrival at Auschwitz. From initial deportation until liberation Frankl was interned in four camps: Theresienstadt, Auschwitz, and two subcamps of Dachau—Kaufering and Tuerkheim. Frankl's experiences in these camps confirmed and solidified his existential beliefs and ideas. As Gordon Allport wrote in his preface to *Man's Search for Meaning*: "Frankl is fond of quoting Nietzsche, saying, 'He who has a why to live can bear with almost any how.'" Prior to his liberation Frankl was struck with typhoid fever and worked to avoid falling into a fatal sleep by attempting to reconstruct his manuscript. Over a period of nine days in 1946 Frankl dictated the entire text of *Ein Psycholog erlebt das Konzentrationslager*, a work translated into English as *Man's Search for Meaning*. It should also be noted that upon liberation Frankl discovered that his wife, whom he married shortly before deportation in 1942, his parents, and his brother were all killed during the Holocaust.

While receiving critical acclaim Frankl's writings and response to the Holocaust have not escaped criticism. Frankl avoided the word Jew and references to himself as a Jew in *Man's Search for Meaning*. He preferred to focus on the actions of individuals as opposed to the actions and status of particular groups. Frankl's focus is problematic for those who define the Holocaust principally as the intentional destruction of European Jewry as well as for those who characterize the Holocaust as a unique form of inexplicable evil. Frankl also was criticized for holding a position of reconciliation following the Holocaust, a position that he exemplified through his own return to native Vienna following liberation.

Man's Search for Meaning is part of an extensive collection of writings by Frankl. If he had elected to leave Austria following the Anschluss, he would still have made significant contributions to psychology and psychoanalysis by bridging the gap between the psychological and the spiritual. *Man's Search for Meaning* not only makes a significant contribution to this body of literature but perhaps more importantly increases our understanding of life in the Nazi concentration camps and the value of finding life's meaning even during suffering.

—Linda M. Woolf

See the essay on *Man's Search for Meaning: An Introduction to Logotherapy*.

FRIED, Erich

Nationality: British and Austrian (originally Austrian: immigrated to England, 1938, granted British citizenship, 1949; regained Austrian citizenship, 1982). **Born:** Vienna, 6 May 1921. **Education:** State schools in Vienna. **Family:** Married 1) Maria Marburg in 1944 (divorced 1952), one son; 2) Nan Spence-Eichner in 1952 (divorced 1965), one son and one daughter; 3) Katherine Boswell in 1965, one daughter and two sons. **Career:** Child actor, Vienna, 1926–27; chemist, United Dairies; librarian and glass-factory worker, London, 1938–46; worked for the Jewish Refugee Committee, London, 1939; editor, *Neue Auslese*, English Central Office of Information, London, 1946–49; co-editor, *Blick in die Welt*, London, 1949–50; part-time work for the British Broadcasting Corporation (BBC), London, 1950–52; translator, German language division, BBC, London, 1952–68. Beginning of association with Gruppe 47, 1963. **Awards:** Co-recipient, Schiller-Gedächtnispreises des Landes Baden-Württemberg, 1965; Österreichischer Würdigungspreis für Literatur, 1973; International Publishers' prize, 1977, for *Hundert Gedichte ohne Vaterland;* City of Vienna prize for literature, 1980; Bremen literary award, 1983; Vienna golden decoration, 1985; Austrian state prize and Carl-von-Ossietzky medal, both in 1986; Georg Büchner prize, 1987. Honorary degree: University of Osnabrück, 1988. **Died:** 22 November 1988.

PUBLICATIONS

Collection

Gesammelte Werke, in 4 Bänden [Collected Works in 4 Volumes], edited by Volker Kaukoreit and Klaus Wagenbach. 1993.

Poetry

Deutschland [Germany]. 1944.
Österreich [Austria]. 1945.
Gedichte. 1958.
Reich der Steine [Realm of Stones]. 1963.
Überlegungen [Reflections]. 1964.
Warngedichte [Poems of Warning]. 1964.
Und Vietnam und . . . [And Vietnam and . . .]. 1966.
Anfechtungen [Arguments]. 1967.
Zeitfragen. 1968.
Last Honours [German and English]. 1968.
Befreiung von der Flucht [Deliverance from Flight]. 1968; revised edition, 1983.
Die Beine der grösseren Lügen [The Legs of the Bigger Lies]. 1969.
On Pain of Seeing. 1969.
Unter Nebenfeinden. 1970.

Aufforderung zur Unruhe: Ausgewählte Gedichte. 1972.
Die Freiheit den Mund aufzumachen. 1972.
Gegengift. 1974.
Höre, Israel! 1974; revised edition, 1983.
Kampf ohne Engel. 1976.
Die bunten Getüme. 1977.
So kam ich unter die Deutschen. 1977.
Hundert Gedichte ohne Vaterland. 1978; as *One Hundred Poems without a Country,* 1978.
Liebesgedichte [Love Poetry]. 1979.
Lebensschatten. 1981.
Zur Zeit und zur Unzeit. 1981.
Das Missverständnis. 1982.
Das Nahe suchen. 1982.
Es ist was es ist: Liebesgedichte, Angstgedichte, Zorngedichte. 1983.
Trost und Angst: Erzählungen über Juden und Nazis [Consolation and Anxiety: Stories about Jews and Nazis] (selection of short memoirs and poems). 1983.
Beunruhigungen. 1984.
Um Klarheit. 1985.
In die Sinne einradiert. 1985.
Von Bis nach Seit: Gedichte aus den Jahren 1945–1958. 1985.
Frühe Gedichte [Early Poems]. 1986.
Wächst das Rettende auch?: Gedichte für den Frieden, with Claudia Hahm and David Fried. 1986.
Unverwundenes: Liebe, Trauer, Widersprüche: Gedichte. 1988.
Gründe: Gesammelte Gedichte, edited by Klaus Wagenbach. 1989.
Einbruch der Wirklichkeit: Verstreute Gedichte 1927–1988 (selections), edited by Volker Kaukoreit. 1991.
Love Poems (selections from *Liebesgedichte* and *Es ist was es ist* in German and English). 1991.

Novels

Ein Soldat und ein Mädchen [A Soldier and a Girl]. 1960.
Kinder und Narren [Children and Fools]. 1965.

Short Stories

Fast alles Mögliche. 1975.
Das Unmass aller Dinge. 1982.

Plays

Unter dem Milchwald, adaptation of a work by Dylan Thomas (produced Berlin, 1956).
Ein Sommernachtstraum, adaptation of a work by William Shakespeare (produced Bremen, 1963).
Arden muss sterben (opera libretto), music by Alexander Göhr (produced Hamburg, 1967).1967; as *Arden Must Die,* 1967.
Und alle seine Mörder. 1984.

Radio Plays: *Unter dem Milchwald* (adaptation), 1954; *Izanagi und Izanami,* 1960; *Die Expedition,* 1962; *Indizienbeweise,* 1966; *Welch Licht scheint dort,* 1980.

Other

Intellektuelle und Sozialismus, with Paul A. Baran and Gaston Salvatore (essays and lectures). 1968.
Ich grenz noch an ein Wort und an ein andres Land: Über Ingeborg Bachmann; Erinnerung, einige Anmerkungen zu ihrem Gedicht "Böhmen liegt am Meer" und ein Nachruf (essay). 1983.
Und nicht taub und stumpf werden: Unrecht, Widerstand, und Protest. 1984.
Kalender für den Frieden 1985, with David Fried and Pavel Uttitz. 1984.
Die da reden gegen Vernichtung: Psychologie, bildende Kunst und Dichtung gegen den Krieg, with Alfred Hrdlicka and Erwin Ringel, edited by Alexander Klauser, Judith Klauser, and Michael Lewin. 1986.
Mitunter sogar Lachen: Zwischenfälle und Erinnerungen. 1986.
Die Umrisse meiner Liebe: Lyrik, Erzählung, Essay, edited by Ingeborg Quaas. 1986.
Nicht verdrängen, nicht gewöhnen: Texte zum Thema Österreich, edited by Michael Lewin. 1987.
Gedanken in und an Deutschland: Essays und Reden, edited by Michael Lewin. 1988.
Von der Nachfolge dieses jungen Menschen, der nie mehr alt wird, with Herbert Heckmann und Volker Kaukoreit. 1988.
Misstrauen lernen: Prosa, Lyrik, Aufsätze, Reden, edited by Ingeborg Quaas. 1989.
Anfragen und Nachreden: Politische Texte, edited by Volker Kaukoreit. 1994.
Die Muse hat Kanten: Aufsätze und Reden zur Literatur, edited by Volker Kaukoreit. 1995.

Editor and translator, *Der Stern, der tat sie lenken.* 1966.
Editor, with Helga M. Novak and Peter-Paul Zahl, *Am Beispiel Peter-Paul Zahl.* 1976.

Translator, *Am frühen Morgen: Autobiographisches, Radio-Essays, Gedichte und Prosa,* by Dylan Thomas. 1957.
Translator, *Unter dem Milchwald,* by Dylan Thomas. 1958.
Translator, *Ein verdienter Staatsmann,* by Thomas Stearns Eliot. 1959.
Der verbindliche Liebhaber, by Graham Greene. 1960.
Die Bacchantinnen, by Euripides. 1960.
Ein Sommernachtstraum, by William Shakespeare. 1964.
Lysistrata, by Aristophanes. 1985.

*

Critical Studies: "Erich Fried: Poetry and Politics" by Rex Last, in *Modern Austrian Writing: Literature and Society after 1945,* edited by Alan Best and Hans Wolfschutz, 1980; "From

Solipsism to Engagement: The Development of Erich Fried As a Political Poet'' by Martin Kane, in *Forum for Modern Language Studies* (England), 21(2), April 1985, pp. 151–69; ''Erich Fried's *Ein Soldat und ein Madchen*'' by Ilse Newbery, in *German Life and Letters* (England), 42(1), October 1988, pp. 46–59; ''In the Dark: Erich Fried's Portrayal of Austria,'' in *German Life and Letters,* 45(3), 1992, pp. 230–33, ''Between Austrian Centre and Free German League of Culture: Erich Fried's Literary Beginnings in London,'' in *New German Studies* (England), 17(2), 1992/1993, pp. 109–31, *Erich Fried: A Writer without a Country,* 1996, '''Das grosse Turnierfeld, auf dem sie sich versuchen': Erich Fried's Work for German Radio,'' in *German Life and Letters,* 51(1), January 1998, pp. 121–46, and ''Erich Fried-Language and Heimat,'' in *German-Speaking Exiles in Great Britain,* edited by Ian Wallace, 1999, all by Steven W. Lawrie; ''. . . und . . . Fried . . . und . . . : The Poetry of Erich Fried and the Structure of Contemporaneity'' by Nora M. Alter, in *Studies in 20th Century Literature,* 21, Winter 1997, pp. 79–109.

* * *

Erich Fried is primarily known for his poetry that addresses various political and social matters. As a young child, he began to show his interest in political issues, and this interest mounted as the social and political situation in Austria began to deteriorate for the Jews. He witnessed the killing of 83 people on Bloody Friday in Vienna. His father was kicked to death during an interrogation, and his mother served 13 months in prison. He left at age 17 for London and took up life as a translator for the BBC and as a writer. Fried's translations of over 20 Shakespearean plays continue to be the standard edition in the German language today.

Fried's profound gift for language gained prominence in the 1940s. He published his first work entitled *Deutschland* (''Germany'') in 1944. His poetry uses very few words, yet he manipulates word order and uses double meanings to create a puzzle of words that evoke deep contemplation at the end. It is in poetry that Fried revealed his most profound thoughts on the direction of mankind and man's treatment of man. Rex Last stated of Fried in his essay ''Erich Fried: Poetry and Politics,'' that ''the negative elements in his work form an essential part of his world view, and his provocations derive directly from his keen, almost ruthless intelligence and penetrating insight into any situation to which he directs his attention.''

In 1960 Fried published his work *Ein Soldat und ein Mädchen* (''A Soldier and a Girl''), a novel which centers on a Jewish GI who meets a woman, Helga, who was in charge of a Nazi camp. She has been condemned to death but wants to make her final act an act of love with a man, and the man she has chosen is the Jewish GI. Indeed, this is a bizarre twist in the novel and their behavior is something that Fried used as a symbolic gesture of reconciliation between two factions that hated one another. This is not an unusual thematic technique when considering Fried—his work evokes thought from the reader; it asks questions; it offers no solutions but instead presents awkward and seemingly impossible situations that the reader must sort and ponder.

Fried was an optimist, though to many this would not seem to be the case. As a prolific poet, his ability to weave his work at such high rates of speed is mind-boggling. He had intense hopes that his poems would make people think of their actions and their own emotions. His work *Trost und Angst: Erzählungen über Juden und Nazis* (''Consolation and Anxiety: Stories about Jews and Nazis'') presents poetry and short stories about his experiences as a young man in Vienna at the onset of World War II. He addresses his native Austrians and the Germans in ''Volksgenossen, deutsche Männer und Frauen!'' (''Fellow Countrymen, German Men and Women'') and begs them to come to their senses. In the afterword of the work, he states, ''I have personally experienced everything that has been reported in these stories.'' He does not allow his readers to forget that it was not only Jews who were murdered in the Holocaust but also Gypsies and innocent Germans. He addresses the neo-Nazi issue in Europe as well, blaming miserable family circumstances that have led children to give themselves over to deceitful ideas.

Throughout all of his works, Fried never lets us forget that there are good and bad people, that much can be solved via dialogue, and that hatred can disappear if we take time to understand one another. He sees the Holocaust as an expression of hatred between people that never knew one another. As a Jew, he remained an outsider due to his expressive voice against Zionism, which he perceived as another form of dehumanization that was ignored by the rest of the world. He maintains that, ''Humanism and struggle against injustice and war, I believe, belong together today as they did then.''

He remained an activist against all that he perceived as unjust, and he protested wars and dehumanizing efforts that were financed by the industrialized world. Even though he himself was a socialist, he protested the Soviet invasion of Hungary in 1956 and supported the Czechs and Slovaks during the Prague Spring of 1968. Wherever there was a small voice of protest, Fried was ready to lend a hand with a loudspeaker of poetic support and personal participation. He is considered to be one of the most avid and passionate poets and novelists of the twentieth century.

—Cynthia A. Klíma

See the essay on *Trost und Angst: Erzählungen über Juden und Nazis.*

FRIEDLÄNDER, Saul

Nationality: Israeli: grew up in hiding in France; lived in Israel after World War II; studied in Europe. **Born:** Pavel

Friedländer, 11 October, 1932, Prague, Czechoslovakia. **Education:** Institut d'études Politiques, Paris, graduated 1955; Graduate Institute of International Studies, Geneva, Switzerland, Ph.D. in history, 1963. **Military Service:** Israeli Defense Forces, 1951–53. **Family:** Married Meiry Hagith in 1959; three children. **Career:** Secretary to the president, World Zionist Organization, 1958–60; head of scientific department, Israeli Ministry of Defense, 1960–61; associate professor and professor of contemporary history, Graduate Institute of International Studies, Geneva, 1964–88; professor and chairman of department of international relations, Hebrew University, Jerusalem, 1969–75; since 1975 Maxwell Cummings Chair of European History, Tel Aviv University; 1939 Club chair in Holocaust Studies, University of California, Los Angeles. Founder and editor-in-chief, *History & Memory.* **Awards:** Israel Prize for history, 1983; John D. and Catherine T. MacArthur Foundation fellowship, 1999. **Address:** University of California, Department of History, 6265 Bunche Hall, Los Angeles, CA 90095–1473, U.S.A.

PUBLICATIONS

Memoir

Quand vient le souvenir. 1978; as *When Memory Comes,* 1979.

Other

Le Role du facteur americain dans la politique etrangere et militaire de l'Allemagne: Septembre 1939–Decembre 1941. 1963.
Hitler et les Etats-Unis, 1938–1941. 1963; as *Prelude to Downfall: Hitler and the United States, 1939–1941,* 1967.
Pie XII et le IIIe Reich Documents. 1964; as *Pius XII and the Third Reich: A Documentation,* 1966.
Kurt Gerstein ou l'Ambiguite du bien. 1967; as *Kurt Gerstein: The Ambiguity of Good,* 1969; as *Counterfeit Nazi: The Ambiguity of Good,* 1969.
Reflexions sur l'avenir d'Israel. 1969.
L'Antisemitisme nazi: Histoire d'une psychose collective. 1971.
Arabes et Israeliens, with Mahmoud Hussein. Translated as *Arabs and Israelis: A Dialogue,* 1975.
Histoire et psychoanalyse: Essai sur les possibilites et les limites de la psychohistoire. 1975; as *History and Psychoanalysis: An Inquiry into the Possibilities and Limits of Psychohistory,* 1978.
Some Aspects of the Historical Significance of the Holocaust. 1977.
A Conflict of Memories?: The New German Debates about the "Final Solution." 1987.
Reflections on Nazism: An Essay on Death and Kitsch. 1993.
Memory, History, and the Extermination of the Jews of Europe. 1993.

The Jews in European History: Seven Lectures, with Christ Meier, Amos Funkenstein, and Eberhard Jackel, edited by Wolfgang Beck. 1994.
Nazi Germany and the Jews: Volume 1, The Years of Persecution, 1933–1939. 1997.

Editor, with others, *Visions of Apocalypse: End or Rebirth?* 1984.
Editor, *Probing the Limits of Representation: Nazism and the "Final Solution."* 1992.

*

Critical Studies: *Fictions in Autobiography: Studies in the Art of Self-Invention* by Paul John Eakin, 1985; "Holocaust and Autobiography: Wiesel, Friedlander, Pisar" by Joseph Sungolowsky, in *Reflections of the Holocaust in Art and Literature,* 1990; "Heinrich Böll, Primo Levi, and Saul Friedlander: Protrayals of Self and History" by Kathy Rugoff, in *Connecticut Review,* 13(1), Spring 1991, pp. 41–49; "Cultural Multiplicity in Two Modern Autobiographies: Friedlander's *When Memory Comes* and Dinesen's *Out of Africa*" by John Burt Foster, Jr., in *Southern Humanities Review,* 29(3), Summer 1995, pp. 205–18; "Forming the Holocaust" by Irene Tucker, in *Poetics Today,* 17(2), Summer 1996, pp. 241–52; *Passing into History: Nazism and the Holocaust beyond Memory: In Honor of Saul Friedländer on His Sixty-Fifth Birthday,* edited by Gulie Ne'eman Arad, 1997; "*Nazi Germany and the Jews:* Reflections on a Beginning, a Middle, and an Open End" by Gulie Ne'eman Arad, in *History & Memory: Studies in Representations of the Past,* 9(1–2), Fall 1997, pp. 409–33; "Towards the Final Solution" by Gordon Alexander Craig, in his *Politics and Culture in Modern Germany,* 1999; *Rethinking the Holocaust* by Yehuda Bauer, 2001.

* * *

Saul Friedländer is one of the most significant historians of the Holocaust. He has written some of the major works on the Holocaust, including *Nazi Germany and the Jews: Vol. 1, The Years of Persecution, 1933–1939* (1997); *Prelude to Downfall: Hitler and the United States 1939–1941* (1967); and *Pius XII and the Third Reich* (1966). But more than this he has also been one of the most significant thinkers about the Holocaust, meditating on issues such as the relationship between memory and history (in *Memory, History, and the Extermination of the Jews of Europe* [1993]); representation and Holocaust (see *Probing the Limits of Representation: Nazism and the "Final Solution"* [1992], which he edited); and the "logic" and presentation of Nazism (*Reflections of Nazism: An Essay on Kitsch and Death* [1993]). There is almost no area of Holocaust scholarship in which Friedänder has not made a significant intervention. A good overview of his work can be found in a special double issue of the journal *History and Memory* that was dedicated to him in 1997.

One of Friedländer's many intellectual strengths is his ability to see and to make connections and to refuse the clean distinctions that others are happy to accept unquestioningly. For example, rather than accepting a simple distinction or opposition between history and memory, he argues that the memory, both private and public, and historiography are "intertwinned and interrelated." Thus, his work shuttles between memory and history. On the one hand he argues for the "most rigorous requirements of scholarship"; on the other— and at the same time—he is aware of the "inadequacy of traditional historiographical representation." This is the inexorable bind that dealing with "the unmasterable past" of the Holocaust creates.

In his *Reflections on Nazism* he follows this line of argument. He suggests that any analysis of Nazism based on solely "political, economic and social" factors is not enough and that it is the "re-evocation and reinterpretation" of the past in art, literature, and film, for example, that "helps us better to understand the past itself." Following this line of analysis he suggests that the phenomenon of kitsch—the "pinnacle of good taste in the absence of taste"—illuminates Nazism as "the anti-modern face of modernity." Nazism is the contradictory combination of the way in which the "kitsch vision reinforces the aesthetic criteria of a submissive mass" and, opposed to this, the "unfathomable world of myths"—it sums up both the fear of transgression of the law and the aspiration for total power, the ultimate transgression of the law.

Friedländer's position on the difficulties and dangers of representing the Holocaust reflects this, too. On the one hand, in an extremely interesting and powerful exchange of letters with the German historian Martin Brozat after the *Historikerstreit*, Friedlander argues against the "normalisation" of Holocaust history; on the other hand, he argues that while historical representations are not enough, because of the obligation to bear witness (and the Nazi attempt to prevent such bearing witness), the "record should not be distorted or banalised by grossly inadequate representations." What is needed, he writes in an influential article ("Trauma, Transference and 'Working Through"), is a "simultaneous acceptance of two contradictory moves: the search for ever-closer historical linkages and the avoidance of a naïve historical positivism leading to simplistic and self-assured historical narrations." In his memoir he began to develop these ideas in a literary way.

—Robert Eaglestone

See the essay on *When Memory Comes.*

FRIEDMAN, Carl

Nationality: Dutch. **Born:** Caroline Friedman, Eindhoven, 29 April 1952. **Career:** Worked as a translator in Antwerp, Belgium. Journalist, Amsterdam. **Address:** c/o Persea Books, 171 Madison Avenue, New York, New York 10016, U.S.A.

PUBLICATIONS

Novels

Tralievader. 1991; as *Nightfather,* 1994.
Twee koffers vol [Two Suitcases Full]. 1993; as *The Shovel and the Loom,* 1996.

Short Stories

De grauwe minnaar: Verhalen. 1996; as *The Gray Lover: Three Stories,* 1998.

*

Film Adaptations: *Nightfather,* 1995; *Left Luggage,* 1998, from the novel *The Shovel and the Loom.*

* * *

Carl Friedman has written two novels concerning the Holocaust, *Nightfather* (1994) and *The Shovel and the Loom* (1996), both translated from the Dutch. The protagonist of each novel is, like Friedman herself, a daughter of Holocaust survivors who struggles to make sense of life after the Holocaust.

Friedman's work is part of a growing body of literature written by the sons and daughters of Holocaust survivors. While some second-generation writers, such as **Art Spiegelman** and **Helen Epstein**, chronicle their parents' experiences in nonfiction works, Friedman confronts the Holocaust in novel form. Her novels share many of the same themes of other second-generation fiction: the relationship between parent and child, the emotions of the second generation, the impossibility of fully comprehending the horror of the Holocaust. What distinguish Friedman's novels from other second-generation literature are their form and the distinctiveness of their voice.

Both *Nightfather* and *The Shovel and the Loom* are short and intense novels, whose simplicity in form belies the sophistication of their concerns. They provide emotional snapshots, moments of connection and confusion taken from the lives of their protagonists. Their plots are simple, but the issues they raise are complex and compelling, a combination that makes these novels particularly suitable for classroom study.

Both of Friedman's novels feature protagonists at significant moments in their development. The daughter of *Nightfather* is a young schoolgirl just beginning to make sense of her family's difference from other families. *The Shovel and the Loom* features a woman of 20 just beginning her adult life. Friedman creates her protagonists in moments of flux, as they work to articulate who they are and how the Holocaust affects their identities. By emphasizing the ways in which her characters wrestle with the legacy of the Holocaust, Friedman invites the reader to engage in a similar struggle. Thus, while Friedman's novels feature the children of Holocaust survivors, the concerns they raise are clearly relevant to a broader post-Holocaust audience.

This helps to explain how Friedman avoids turning her protagonists' questions into pathologies. The daughters grapple, but they are not plagued; neither wishes for different parents. This is a significant accomplishment on the part of the author, for it is difficult to acknowledge the enormous pain of the Holocaust, passed down between generations, without portraying the second generation as wounded and in need of repair. Indeed, other second-generation protagonists, such as those in the works of Thane Rosenbaum and J.J. Steinfeld, often seem much more tormented. Friedman's novels sound a different emotional key, one that suggests that the children of Holocaust survivors bear a crucial knowledge about the world. Her characters carry an understanding of the fragility of life and a concern for evil and goodness that is not shared by others. In Friedman's work the pathology lies with the world that created the Holocaust and that continues to fail in its efforts to come to terms with what happened.

Friedman thereby presents the second generation as vital witnesses to the Holocaust. While the term "witness" is generally used to describe Holocaust survivors, Friedman's fiction reveals that the second generation too has a story to tell. Both parent and child are witnesses, albeit to a different experience. The survivors' stories are never eclipsed in these works, nor are their stories simply carried by the second generation. Rather, each generation is affected by the experiences of the other. Focusing on the children of survivors, Friedman's novels ask what it means to live after the destruction in a world that has largely moved on. There may be no question more important for the reader to face.

—Rachel N. Baum

See the essays on *Nightfather* and *The Shovel and the Loom*.

FRISCH, Max (Rudolf)

Nationality: Swiss. **Born:** Zurich, 15 May 1911. **Education:** Studied Germanistics, University of Zurich, 1930–33; Federal Institute of Technology, Zurich, diploma in architecture 1940. **Military Service:** Swiss Army, 1939–45. **Family:** Married 1) Gertrud Anna Constance von Meyenburg in 1942 (divorced 1959), two daughters and two sons; 2) Marianne Öllers in 1968 (divorced). **Career:** Freelance journalist for various Swiss and German newspapers, including *Neue Zürcher Zeitung* and *Frankfurter Zeitung*, beginning 1933; architect, Zurich, 1942–54. Full-time writer, 1955–1991. **Awards:** Conrad Ferdinand Meyer prize; Rockefeller Foundation drama grant, 1951; Raabe prize, 1954; Schleussner Schüller radio play prize, 1955; Georg

Büchner prize, Veillon prize, and city of Zurich literature prize, all in 1958; Northrhine-Westphalia literature prize, 1963; city of Jerusalem prize and Schiller prize (Baden-Wurttemberg), both in 1965; Schiller prize (Zurich), 1974; German Book Trade peace prize, 1976; Modern Language Association of America commonwealth award and International Neustadt prize for literature, University of Oklahoma, both in 1986; Heine prize (Düsseldorf), 1989. Honorary degrees: Philipps University, Marburg, West Germany, 1963; Bard College, New York, 1980; City University of New York, 1982; Technische Universität, Berlin, 1987. Commandeur de l'Ordre des Arts et des Lettres, 1985. **Member:** Deutsche Akademie für Sprache und Dichtung; Akademie der Künste; American Academy and Institute of Arts and Letters (honorary); American Academy of Arts and Sciences (honorary). **Died:** 4 April 1991.

PUBLICATIONS

Collections

Stücke [Plays] (2 vols.):
  Stücke 1: Santa Cruz; Nun singen sie wieder; Die Chinesische Mauer; Als der Krieg zu Ende war; Graf Öderland. 1962.
  Stücke 2: Don Juan oder Die Liebe zur Geometrie; Biedermann und die Brandstifter; Die grosse Wut des Philipp Hotz; Andorra. 1962.
Gesammelte Werke in zeitlicher Folge (7 vols.):
  Bd.1.1931–1944: Kleine Prosaschriften; Blätter aus dem Brotsack; Jürg Reinhart; Die Schwierigen, oder, J'adore ce qui me brûle; Bin: oder, Die Reise nach Peking. 1976.
  Bd. 2. 1944–1949: Santa Cruz; Nun singen sie wieder; Die Chinesische Mauer; Als der Krieg zu Ende war; Kleine Prosaschriften; Tagebuch 1946–1949. 1976.
  Bd. 3. 1949–1956: Graf Öderland; Don Juan: oder, Die Liebe zur Geometrie; Kleine Prosaschriften; Der Laie und die Architektur Achtung; Die Schweiz; Stiller; Rip van Winkle. 1976.
  Bd. 4. 1957–1963: Homo faber; Kleine Prosaschriften; Herr Biedermann und die Brandstifter; Biedermann und die Brandstifter; Mit einem Nachapiwl; Die grosse Wut des Philipp Hotz; Andorra. 1976.
  Bd. 5. 1964–1967: Mein Name sei Gantenbein; Kleine Prosaschriften; Zürich-Transit; Biografie, ein Spiel. 1976.
  Bd. 6. 1968–1975: Tagebuch 1966–1971; Wilhelm Tell für die Schule; Kleine Prosaschriften; Dienstbüchlein; Montauk. 1976.
  Bd. 7. 1976–1985: Kleine Prosaschriften; Triptychor; Der Mensch erscheint in Holoz an; Blaubart. 1986.

Plays

Nun singen sie wieder: Versuch eines Requiems (produced Zurich, 1945). 1946; as *Now They Sing Again: Attempt of a*

Requiem, in *Contemporary German Theatre*, edited by Michael Roloff, 1972.

Santa Cruz: Eine Romanz (produced Zurich, 1946). 1946.

Die chinesische Mauer: Eine Farce (produced Zurich, 1946). 1947; revised edition, 1972; as *The Chinese Wall*, 1961.

Als der Kriege zu Ende war: Schauspiel (produced Zurich, 1948). 1949; as *When the War Was Over*, in *Three Plays*, 1967.

Graf Öderland: Ein Spiel in Zehn Bildern [Count Öderland: A Play in Ten Scenes] (produced Zurich, 1951). 1951; as *Count Öderland*, in *Three Plays*, 1962; revised edition, 1963; as *A Public Prosecutor Is Sick of It All* (produced Washington D.C., 1973).

Don Juan; oder, die Liebe zur Geometrie: Eine Komödie in fünf Akten (produced Zurich, 1953). 1953; as *Don Juan; or, The Love of Geometry: A Comedy in Five Acts*, in *Three Plays*, 1967.

Biedermann und die Brandstifter: Eine Lehrstück ohne Lehre, mit einem Nachspiel (produced Zurich, 1958). 1958; as *The Fire Raisers* (produced London, 1961), published as *Biedermann and the Fire Raisers: A Morality without a Moral*, 1962; as *Biedermann and the Firebugs: A Learning Play without a Lesson*, 1963.

Die grosse Wut des Philipp Hotz (produced Zurich, 1958). 1958; as *The Great Fury of Philipp Hotz* (produced 1969), published as *Philipp Hotz's Fury*, in *Esquire*, October, 1962, in book form, in *Three Plays*, 1967.

Andorra: Stück in zwölf Bildern (produced Zurich, 1961). 1962; translated as *Andorra: A Play in Twelve Scenes* (produced New York, 1963), in *Three Plays*, 1962.

Zurich-Transit: Skizze eines Films (television play). 1966.

Biografie: Ein Spiel (produced Zurich, 1968). 1967; revised edition, 1968; as *Biography: A Game*, 1969.

Rip van Winkle: Hörspiel (radio play). 1969.

Triptychon: Drei szenische Bilder. 1978; as *Triptych: Three Scenic Panels*, 1981.

Radio Plays: *Rip van Winkle*, 1953; *Herr Biedermann und die Brandstifter*, 1953; *Herr Quixote*, 1955; *Eine Lanze fur die Freiheit*, 1955; *Andorra*, 1959.

Television Play: *Zurich-Transit*, 1966.

Novels

Jürg Reinhart: Eine sommerliche Schicksalsfahrt. 1934; revised edition, as *J'adore ce qui me brule; oder, Die Schwierigen: Roman*, 1943, 2nd revised edition, as *Die Schwierigen; oder, J'adore ce qui me brule*, 1957.

Antwort aus der Stille: Eine Erzählung aus den Bergen [Answer out of the Silence: A Tale from the Mountains]. 1937.

Bin; oder, Die Reise nach Peking [Am; or, the Trip to Peking]. 1945.

Stiller. 1954; as *I'm Not Stiller*, 1958.

Homo Faber: Ein Bericht. 1957; as *Homo Faber: A Report*, 1959.

Meine Name sei Gantenbein. 1964; as *A Wilderness of Mirrors*, 1965.

Montauk: Eine Erzählung. 1975; translated as *Montauk*, 1976.

Der Mensch erscheint im Holozän: Eine Erzählung. 1979; as *Man in the Holocene: A Story*, 1980.

Blaubart: Eine Erzählung. 1982; as *Bluebeard*, 1984.

Other

Geschrieben im Grenzdienst 1939. 1940.

Blätter aus dem Brotsack [Pages from the Knapsack] (diary). 1940.

Marion und die Marionetten: Ein Fragment. 1946.

Das Tagebuch mit Marion [Diary with Marion]. 1947; revised edition, as *Tagebuch, 1946–1949*, 1950; as *Sketchbook, 1946–49*, 1977.

Achtung, die Schweiz: Ein Gespräch über unsere Lage und ein Vorschlag zur Tat, with Lucius Burckhardt and Markus Kutter. 1956.

Die Neue Stadt: Beiträge zur Diskussion, with Lucius Burckhardt and Markus Kutter. 1956.

Ausgewählte Prosa, edited by Stanley Corngold. 1961.

Öffentlichkeit als Partner (essays). 1967.

Erinnerungen an Brecht. 1968.

Dramaturgisches: Ein Briefwechsel mit Walter Höllerer. 1969.

Der Mensch zwischen Selbstentfremdung und Selbstverwirklichung, with Rudolf Immig. 1970.

Glück: Eine Erzählung. 1971.

Wilhelm Tell für die Schule. 1971.

Tagebuch, 1966–71.1972; as *Sketchbook, 1966–71*, 1974.

Dienstbuchlein. 1974.

Stich-Worte. 1975.

Zwei Reden zum Friedenspreis des Deutschen Buchhandels 1976. 1976.

Erzählende Prosa, 1939–1979. 1981.

Forderungen des Tages. 1983.

*

Film Adaptation: *Voyager*, 1991, from the novel *Homo Faber*.

Bibliography: *A Bibliography of Four Contemporary German-Swiss Authors: Friedrich Dürrenmatt, Max Frisch, Robert Walser, Albin Zollinger* by Elly Wilbert-Collins, 1967; ''Bibliographie zu Max Frisch'' by Thomas Beckermann, in *Text + Kritik* (Germany), 47–48, 1975, pp. 88–98; ''Max Frisch Bibliography'' by Gerhard F. Probst, in his *Perspectives on Max Frisch*, 1982.

Critical Studies: ''Max Frisch: Moralist without a Moral'' by Theodore Ziolkowski, in *Yale French Studies*, 29, 1962, pp. 132–41; *Max Frisch* by Ulrich Weisstein, 1967; *Max Frisch* by Carol Petersen, translated by Charlotte La Rue, 1972; *The Novels of Max Frisch*, 1976, and *The Plays of Max Frisch*, 1985, both by Michael Butler; *The Dramatic Works of Max*

Frisch by Gertrud Bauer Pickar, 1977; *Max Frisch, His Work and Its Swiss Background* by Malcolm Pender, 1979; "*Montauk:* The Invention of the Max Frisch" by Timothy Shipe, in *Critique,* 22(3), 1981, pp. 55–70; *Perspectives on Max Frisch,* edited by Gerhard F. Probst and Jay F. Bodine, 1982; "Max Frisch Revisited: *Blaubart*" by Alfred D. White, in *Monatshefte fur Deutschen Unterricht, Deutsche Sprache und Literatur,* 78(4), Winter 1986, pp. 456–67; *Life As a Man: Contemporary Male-Female Relationships in the Novels of Max Frisch* by Claus Reschke, 1990; *Understanding Max Frisch* by Wulf Köpke, 1991; "Max Frisch: The Courage of Failure" by Victor Brombert, in *Raritan,* 13(2), Fall 1993, pp. 9–32; *Max Frisch, the Reluctant Modernist* by Alfred D. White, 1995; "'Insanity in the Darkness': Anti-Semitic Stereotypes and Jewish Identity in Max Frisch's *Andorra* and Arthur Miller's *Focus*" by Ladislaus Lob, in *Modern Language Review* (England), 92(3), July 1997, pp. 545–58; "'Das Vorhandensein einer andern Welt': Max Frisch, the Second World War and Morality in German-Swiss Writing" by Malcolm Pender, in *The Writers' Morality/Die Moral der Schriftsteller,* edited by Ronald Speirs, 2000.

*   *   *

Max Frisch, the author of *Andorra, Biedermann and the Firebugs* (U.K. title, *Biedermann and the Fire Raisers*) and *Now They Sing Again,* was born on 15 May 1911 in Zurich, Switzerland, and died there on 4 April 1991. As a German-Swiss dramatist and novelist, he is one of the most respected writers in German-speaking countries. Frisch's life was characterized by frequent travels; he finally settled in Berzona, a Swiss canton of Ticino.

Just as Frisch moved around the world, he explored many areas as he sought to establish himself professionally. He began studying literature and history at the University of Zurich in 1930 but left the university after the death of his father in 1933. Subsequently, he supported himself as a freelance journalist and architect and later returned to writing full time. In his literary productions he tried varied genres, including diaries, dramatized lyrical poetry, plays of social criticism, allegorical plays, prose investigating the dichotomous nature of the individual, literary and political essays, and parable plays castigating anti-Semitism. Like Frisch, his characters are wanderers. In the novel *Homo Faber,* Walter Faber, a 50-year-old UNESCO engineer, moves from New York to Venezuela, back to New York, then to Paris, Italy, Germany, Athens, and other regions of the world. These frequent moves seem to reflect structurally the search for self-identity, a theme that also appears in Frisch's novels *Stiller* and *A Wilderness of Mirrors* and in his stage play *Andorra.*

Frisch's plays are didactic, just like those written by **Bertolt Brecht,** with whom he is sometimes compared. Unlike Brecht,

however, Frisch was more pessimistic in his belief that mankind is capable of learning from previous mistakes. The inability to change is the central theme in *Biography: A Game,* in which the protagonist, a famous middle-aged professor, is given a chance to modify his biography, but the alterations he makes are only minimal and he, and his fate, remain essentially the same. This "recurrence of the same" is also apparent in his allegorical play *The Chinese Wall.* Of the three dramatic unities—plot, time, and place—only that of the basic underlying idea stays the same, since the action spans more than 2,000 years in different countries and regions. The central figure, however, the weak modern intellectual, remains just as ineffective when it comes to controlling dictatorial governments, torture, war, and mass killings. Frisch uses the figure of the ineffectual intellectual in many of his plays: in *Biedermann and the Firebugs* the warning of the Ph.D. that the world is on the verge of being destroyed is drowned out by the sirens, and the professor in *Now They Sing Again,* as well as the teacher in *Andorra,* demonstrate the futility of humanistic thinking and humanistic values.

In his *Questionnaire 1987* (translated by Rolf Kieser), Frisch's pessimism is starkly apparent. Since mankind has developed the technical means to realize the apocalypse, he asks, "Can you imagine that the human spirit we have trained is programmed for self-destruction of the species?" This leads him to the question, "What, except for wishful thinking, speaks against it?" Frisch does not answer this question, just as he does not offer a solution to the pressing existential problems of modern time, which include violence, prejudice, dictatorships, genocide, and anti-Semitism. When once criticized by students at the University of Zurich in this regard, Frisch, in "Café Odeon" (from his *Sketchbook 1946–1949*), referred to Henrik Ibsen, who once said that he was there to ask questions, not to answer them: "As a playwright I should consider I had done my duty if I succeeded in a play of mine in putting a question in such a way that from then on the members of the audience were unable to live without an answer. But it must be their answer, their own, which they can provide only in the framework of their own lives." In this sense Frisch can be compared to Sisyphus in Albert Camus's *Myth of Sisyphus,* who rolls the stone to the mountain top, being well aware that the stone does not stay put but keeps falling down. Frisch, just like Sisyphus, never gave up asking his contemporaries uncomfortable questions, and in this sense he was a true educator, albeit a pessimistic one since he believed that mankind did not learn much from past experiences, including the Holocaust.

—Gerd K. Schneider

See the essays on *Andorra: A Play in Twelve Scenes, Now They Sing Again: Attempt of a Requiem,* and *Biedermann and the Firebugs: A Morality without a Moral.*

FUKS, Ladislav

Nationality: Czech. **Born:** Prague, 24 September 1923. **Education:** Charles University, Ph.D. 1949. **Career:** Clerk, Bela pod Bezdezem paper mill, Czechoslovakia, 1950–52; associated with Prague Paper Mills, 1952–55, the State Institute for Preservation of Historic Monuments, Prague, 1956–59, and the National Gallery, Prague, 1959–62; beginning 1963 full-time writer and lecturer on anti-Semitism and Czech literature. **Awards:** Czechoslovak award of the year for literature, 1963, 1966, 1968, and 1974; artist of merit, 1978; honored for distinction for reconstruction services, 1983. **Died:** 19 August 1994.

PUBLICATIONS

Novels

Variace pro temnou strunu [Variations for a Sombre String]. 1966.
Pan Theodor Mundstock. 1963; as *Mr. Theodore Mundstock,* 1968.
Mysi Natalie Mooshabrove [Mice of Natalia Mooshaber]. 1970.
Pribeh kriminalniho rady [Story of a Chief Detective Inspector]. 1971.
Neboztici na bale [The Deceaseds at the Ball]. 1972.
Pasacek z doliny [A Little Horseman from the Dale]. 1977.
Kristalovy pantoflicek [A Little Crystallier Slipper]. 1978.
Obraz Martina Blaskowitze [The Picture of Martin Blaskowitz]. 1980.
Vevodkyne a kucharka [The Duchess and the Cook]. 1983.
Spalovac mrtvol. 1967; as *The Cremator,* 1984.
Cesta do zaslibene zeme: A jine povidky. 1991.

Short Stories

Mi cernovlasi bratri [My Dark-Haired Brothers]. 1964.
Smrt morcete [Death of a Guinea Pig]. 1969.
Osloveni z tmy [A Voice from the Darkness]. 1972.
Navrat z zitneho pole [Return from the Rye Field]. 1974.

Other

Zamek Kynzvart: Historie a pritomnost [The Kynzvart Chateaux: History and Presence]. 1958.
Let, myslenko na zlatych kridlech vanku. 1994.
Moje zrcadlo: Vzpominky, dojmy, ohlednuti. 1995.

*

Media Adaptations: *The Cremator; Story of a Chief Detective Inspector; A Little Horseman from the Dale; The Deceaseds at the Ball* (Czech television); *My Dark-Haired Brothers* (Czech television); *Mr. Theodore Mundstock, Mr. Theodor* (opera), 1984, both from the novel *Mr. Theodore Mundstock.*

Critical Studies: "Some Contemporary Czech Prose Writers" by Josef Skvorecky, in *Novel,* 4, 1970, pp. 5–13; "Mythic and Modern Elements in the Art of Ladislav Fuks: Natalia Mooshaber's Mice" by Thomas G. Winner, in *Fiction and Drama in Eastern and Southeastern Europe: Evolution and Experiment in the Postwar Period,* edited by Henrik Birnbaum and Thomas Eekman, 1980; *The Jews in the Works of Ladislav Fuks* by Sonia I. Kanikova, 1988.

* * *

Ladislav Fuks is an author who is not well known outside his native Czechoslovakia, but not because he was not prolific. It was the political times that caused many of his works simply not to gain the recognition they deserved. In the 1950s the Communist resistance against fascists was stressed in public school education in Czechoslovakia. The fact that many of the Czech victims were Jewish was not mentioned, and the information was swept into a corner and largely ignored until the turbulent 1960s. It was especially the early half of the 1960s that brought to light many of the atrocities that were committed against Czech Jews, and in these highly charged times students became very interested in learning about a history of which they were largely ignorant. Joseph Stalin was dead, and the floodgates of curiosity and experimentation began to open.

This was precisely the time Fuks became active as a writer and screenwriter. Surprisingly, although he wrote many works that encompassed Jewish themes, Fuks himself was not Jewish. His understanding of Jewish life and suffering stemmed from his personal observations during the occupation and his loss of many Jewish friends. Shortly before his death, he told *Contemporary Authors* about his reasons for writing on Jewish themes: "My creation has been influenced by my experiences and life under Nazi occupation, during which I lost a great many of my Jewish friends. In my work, I often reach up for horror or absurdity—but it is always functional, never self-purposeful."

Fuks's works are often psychological, sometimes filled with horror, and full of twists. He was a contemporary of Ivan Klíma, **Arnošt Lustig**, and **Jiří Weil**. His novel *Pan Theodor Mundstock* (*Mr. Theodore Mundstock*) can be classified with Lustig's *Darkness Casts No Shadow,* Klíma's *Láska a smetí* (*Love and Garbage*), and Weil's *Život s hvězdou* (*Life with a Star*). All of these works deal both with the psychological dilemmas the characters in the works face and with the effect on the reader, who finds himself connected to each character's fate.

Fuks was an active participant in the Czech new wave cinema. *Mr. Theodore Mundstock* was directed as a film by Juraj Herz, and several of Fuks's other works, including *Spalovač mrtvol* (*The Cremator*) and *Mí černovlasí bratri* (*My*

Dark-Haired Brothers), were also adapted for film or television. *The Cremator* became one of the leading art house films of the Czech new wave and won many international awards. It was not without controversy, for it was distributed in 1969, after the Soviet invasion. Thus, the film's content was deemed to be rather suspicious by government censors. The work shows how ideology converts an eccentric crematory worker, Pan Kopfrklingl, into a man capable of extreme cruelty. Under Nazi duress he becomes an informant and executioner for the Gestapo. *My Dark-Haired Brothers* tells the story of five schoolmates, three of whom are Jewish, during the time of the occupation. The richest of the three refuses to see the dangers that surround him.

In 1984 Leoš Faltus wrote and produced the opera *Mr. Theodor,* which was based on motifs by Fuks. The opera was awarded several prizes. *Mr. Theodore Mundstock* has also been performed as a play in French by the director Bruno Boeglin.

Despite his popularity, Fuks's life took on a rather surreal ending. According to the journalist Olga Švadlenová, he was living as a derelict, without friends or contacts with the outside world. He died in his apartment in Prague on 19 August 1994. No one knew of his death for two days.

—Cynthia A. Klíma

See the essay on *Mr. Theodore Mundstock.*

G

GARY, Romain

Pseudonyms: Émile Agar; Fosco Sinibaldi. **Nationality:** French. **Born:** Romain Kacew, Vilna, Lithuania, 8 May 1914. **Education:** Studied law in Aix-en-Provence and Paris. **Military Service:** French Air Corps: Salon Flying School, shooting instructor, 1938; Free French Forces, 1940–44. **Family:** Married 1) Lesley Blanch in 1944 (divorced 1952); 2) the actress Jean Seberg in 1962 (divorced 1970), one daughter (deceased) and one son. **Career:** Writer, *Vogue;* Secretary and adviser, French embassies, Sofia, Bulgaria, and Bern, Switzerland; spokesman, United Nations, 1952–56; Chargé d'Affaires, La Paz, Bolivia; Consul General of France, Los Angeles, 1956–60; traveled and wrote for American journals. **Awards:** Prix des Critiques, 1945, for *Éducation européenne*; Prix Goncourt, 1956, for *Racines du ciel*, 1975, for *La Vie devant soi*. **Died:** Suicide, 2 December 1980.

PUBLICATIONS

Novels

Forest of Anger. 1944; as *Éducation européenne,* 1945; revised edition, as *Nothing Important Ever Dies,* 1960; as *A European Education,* 1960.
Le Grand Vestiaire. 1948; as *The Company of Men,* 1950.
Les Coleurs du jour. 1952; as *The Colors of the Day,* 1953.
Racines du ciel. 1956; as *The Roots of Heaven,* 1958.
Lady L. 1958.
The Talent Scout. 1961; as *Les Mangeurs d'étoiles,* 1966.
The Ski Bum. 1965.
La Danse de Gengis Cohn. 1967; as *The Dance of Genghis Cohn,* 1968.
La Tête coupable. 1968; as *The Guilty Head,* 1969.
Adieu Gary Cooper. 1969.
Chien blanc. 1970; as *White Dog,* 1970.
Europa. 1972; translated as *Europa,* 1978.
Les Enchanteurs. 1973; as *The Enchanters,* 1975.
The Gasp. 1973.
Gros-câlin (as Émile Agar). 1974.
Les Têtes de Stéphanie. 1974; as *Direct Flight to Allah,* 1975.
Au-delà de cette limite votre ticket n'est plus valable. 1975; as *Your Ticket Is No Longer Valid,* 1977; as *The Way Out,* 1977.
La Vie devant soi (as Émile Agar). 1975; as *Momo,* 1978; as *Madame Rosa,* 1979; as *The Life before Us,* 1986.
Pseudo (as Émile Agar). 1976.
Clair de femme. 1977.
Charge d'âme. 1977.

Les Clowns lyriques. 1979.
L'Angoisse du roi Salomon (as Émile Agar). 1979; as *King Solomon,* 1983.
Les Cerfs-volants [The Kites]. 1980.
L'Homme à la colombe (as Fosco Sinibaldi). 1984.

Short Stories

Gloire à nos illustres pionniers. 1962; as *Hissing Tales,* 1964.

Plays

Johnnie Cœur. 1961.
La Bonne Moitié. 1979.

Memoir

La Promesse de l'aube. 1960; as *The Promise at Dawn,* 1961.

Other

Tulipe. 1946.
Pour sgnarelle (essay). 1965.
Les Trésors de la mer Rouge. 1971.
La Nuit sera calme, with François Bondy. 1974.
Vie et mort d'Emile Ajar. 1981.

*

Film Adaptations: *Roots of Heaven,* 1958; *The Man Who Understood Women,* 1959, from the novel *Les Coleurs du jour; Lady L,* 1965; *Oiseaux vont mourir au Pérou,* 1968 (as *Birds in Peru,* 1968); *Promise at Dawn,* 1970 (as *La Promesse de l'aube,* 1970); *The Ski Bum,* 1971 (as *Point Zero,* 1971); *La Vie devant soi,* 1977 (as *A Life Ahead,* 1977, and *Madame Rosa,* 1978); *Clair de femme,* 1979 (as *Womanlight,* 1979); *Your Ticket Is No Longer Valid,* 1981 (as *Finishing Touch,* 1981, and *A Slow Descent into Hell,* 1981); *White Dog,* 1982; *Genghis Cohn,* 1993, from the novel *La Danse de Gengis Cohn; Les Faussaires,* 1994 (as *The Imposters,* 1994), from the novel *La Tête coupable.*

Critical Studies: Romain Gary issue of *Livres de France* (France), 18(3), March 1967; ''Romain Gary and the End of an Old Dream'' by Frederic C. Gray, in *Proceedings: Pacific Northwest Conference on Foreign Languages*, edited by Walter C. Kraft, 1973; ''The Art of Survival: Romain Gary's *The Dance of Genghis Cohn,''* in *Modern Language Studies,* 10(3), 1980, pp. 76–87; ''On the Death of a Friend: Romain

Gary'' by Francois Bondy, in *Encounter* (England), 57(2), August 1981, p. 33–34; ''A Man and His Double'' by Francois Bondy, in *Encounter,* 57(4), October 1981, p. 42–43; ''The Symbolic Imagination of Romain Gary'' by Jane McKee, in *The Maynooth Review/Reiviu Mha Nuad* (Ireland), 6(2), May 1982, pp. 60–71; ''Emile Ajar Demystified'' by Bette H. Lustig, in *The French Review: Journal of the American Association of Teachers of French,* 57(2), December 1983, pp. 203–12; ''Gary-Ajar and the Rhetoric of Non-Communication'' by Leroy T. Day, in *The French Review,* 65(1), October 1991, pp. 75–83; ''Romain Gary: Last Judgement Questionnaire'' by Nancy Huston, in *Brick*, 47, Winter 1993, pp. 28–34; ''On the Holocaust Comedies of 'Emile Ajar''' by Jeffrey Mehlman, in *Auschwitz and After: Race, Culture, and 'the Jewish Question' in France,* edited by Lawrence D. Kritzman, 1994; ''The Labor of Love'' by Tzvetan Todorov, in *Partisan Review,* 64(3), Summer 1997, pp. 375–83; ''Romain Gary: A Foreign Body in French Literature'' by Nancy Huston, in *Suleiman*, edited by Susan Rubin, 1998.

Theatrical Activities: Director: **Films**—*Oiseaux vont mourir au Pérou,* 1968; *Kill!* 1971.

* * *

Romain Gary was a fighter pilot, diplomat, novelist, and filmmaker, and his life and literature tantalized French society from 1945 until his suicide in 1980. Before 1965 he wrote neither on the Holocaust nor about any subject surrounding his own Jewish identity. When Jewish themes finally began to emerge in his writing, they developed in tandem with an increasingly evident sense of alienation and depression. Nevertheless, *La Danse de Genghis Cohn* (1967) and subsequent novels presented defiant explorations of the author's faith in humanity. Beyond his sense of isolation as a Jew, Gary continued to identify European, and specifically German, culture with respect for the rights and integrity of the individual.

Gary's earlier works, notably *L'Education européenne*, *Les Couleurs du jour,* and *Les Racines du ciel,* met with instant acclaim. His heroes were artfully developed through the tragicomic situations Europeans had faced in wartime and in the years that followed. Typically an ''ordinary'' man or woman living in extraordinary times, the bold partisan and the poor refugee alike could be the subject of Gary's eloquent and witty examinations of the Western civilization that had survived the challenge mounted by the fascist armies. In the first postwar years Gary, like others of his generation, wrote as if the new Europe had learned through its suffering to be cosmopolitan and inclusive. The problems of negotiating different national or ethnic memories of the war years did not receive attention, and the appearance of evidently Jewish characters in *L'Education européenne* was not accompanied by comment on their identity or on the distinctive situations they encountered as Jews. In *La Promesse de l'aube,* an account of his childhood, Gary gave no attention to the Jewish cultures he experienced in

Vilna and Warsaw, and the happy life he painted appeared as if untainted by anti-Semitism. In subsequent years Gary would consistently refer to a mixed Russian, Cossack, Jewish and Tatar heritage, which only obscured the extent to which his Jewishness had affected his early years in Russia and as a refugee in Lithuania and Poland. A life of moving among societies in which anti-Semitism was still more or less accepted gave him reason to prefer the interesting cosmopolitan identity he was often charged with creating himself.

La Danse de Genghis Cohn was the first work to signal Gary's growing critique of European culture and politics, themes he developed further in subsequent novels, for example, in *Europa* and *The Gasp*. Throughout his literary career Gary nevertheless maintained that liberal European ideals represented the benchmark for a humane society and that war and genocide had only underlined the need to explore Western concepts of enlightenment and human rights with greater precision.

Gary's turn to writing about Jews was partly influenced by his experience in the United States, where **William Styron**, author of *Sophie's Choice,* was a longtime companion, but the timing of the shift in his works appears to have been more directly related to his return to Europe. Like many Jewish intellectuals in Europe and America, Gary was disturbed by the resurgence of anti-Semitic violence and then by anti-Zionist politics in Europe in the 1960s. At the time of the appearance of *Genghis Cohn,* he revisited Warsaw, touring the site of the former ghetto. Gary then rounded on his wartime hero, Charles de Gaulle, when on the outbreak of the Six-Day War in 1967 the president broke off military ties with Israel, speaking of the ''arrogance'' of the Jews. While Gary argued that the Holocaust had shown that Jews needed a homeland in Israel, his response to Israel was also far from uncritical. There was, he maintained, a nationalist and ''racist'' extreme in Israel that he had no desire to excuse. Personally, he once commented, he would prefer to live in Italy rather than Israel. The ''Jewish shift'' in Gary's novels, from the time of *Genghis Cohn,* correspondingly turned on the life of Jews marked by pressures similar to those he had faced in the Diaspora: multicultural, the Jews were also frequently conscious of the limits with which the societies they lived in could accept them.

Writing on Jewish subjects late in life under the pseudonym Emil Ajar, Gary created Jewish characters that were, like the author himself, aging and alienated. The Jewish novels are those in which Gary made his sense of alienation from high society most evident, a trend that was heightened in his last works. He felt no compunction about refusing literary honors he felt morally compromising, notably the Prix Paul Morand of the Académie Française, named after a literary rival and wartime supporter of the Pétain regime. Gary's personal crises were often tied to his work, and scholars have continued to debate whether his obsession with pseudonyms and the continual re-creation of his public persona should be connected with his suicide in 1980. Like Hemingway, Gary shot himself in a dressing gown, leaving his partner to discover his body and a brief suicide note.

—George R.Wilkes

See the essay on *The Dance of Genghis Cohn.*

GASCAR, Pierre

Nationality: French. **Born:** Pierre Fournier, Paris, 1916. **Career:** Prisoner, German prison camps, World War II. Worked as a journalist and book critic. **Awards:** Prix Goncourt, 1953, for *Les Bêtes;* Grand Prix de Litterature, 1969; Prix Roger Caillois, 1994. **Died:** February 1997.

PUBLICATIONS

Novels

Les Meubles. 1949.
Le Visage clos. 1951.
Les Bêtes, suivi de le temps des morts. 1953; as *Beasts and Men,* 1956.
La Graine. 1955; as *Seed,* 1959.
L'Herbe des rues. 1956.
La Barre de corail: Suivi de Les aveugles de Saint-Xavier. 1958; as *The Coral Barrier,* 1961.
Le Fugitif. 1961; as *The Fugitive,* 1964.
Le Meilleur de la vie. 1964; as *The Best Years,* 1967.
Les Charmes. 1965.
Le Présage. 1972.
Les Sources. 1975.

Short Stories

Les Femmes. 1955; with *Soleils: Récits,* as *Women and the Sun,* 1965.
Soleils: Récits. 1960; with *Les Femmes,* as *Women and the Sun,* 1965.
Les Moutons de feu. 1963; as *Lambs of Fire,* 1965.
Auto. 1967.
Le Gros Chêne. 1977.
Le Fortin: Nouvelles. 1983.
Pour le dire avec des fleurs. 1988.

Play

Les Pas perdus. 1958.

Memoirs

Terres de mémoire: Gascogne, Guyenne, Quercy, Périgord noir. 1980.

Le Temps des morts: Le Rêve russe [The Season of the Dead: The Russian Dream]. 1998.

Other

Aujourd'hui la Chine (travel essay). 1955.
Voyage chez les vivants (travel essay). 1958.
Le Feu mal éteint; Nazis, fascistes, racistes se regroupent dans le monde et préparent leur jour J (as Pierre Fournier). 1961.
Luc Simon: 28 novembre 1962–12 janvier 1963. 1962.
Chambord. 1962.
Vertiges du présent, ce difficile accord avec le monde. 1962.
Normandie (nonfiction). 1962.
Saint-Marc (photo essay). 1964.
Normandie (photo history). 1967.
Histoire de la captivité des Français en Allemagne (1939–1945). 1967.
L'Or (history). 1968.
Chimères (essays). 1969.
Rimbaud et la Commune. 1971.
L'Arche. 1971.
Les Bouchers (history). 1973.
Quartier latin. 1973.
L'Homme et l'animal. 1974.
Dans la forêt humaine. 1976.
Charles VI: Le Bal des ardents (biography). 1977.
Toffoli: Ou, La force du destin (biography). 1979.
Un Jardin de curé (nonfiction). 1979.
L'Ombre de Robespierre (biography). 1979.
Le Boulevard du crime (history). 1980.
Les Secrets de Maître Bernard: Bernard Palissy et son temps (biography). 1980.
Le Règne végétal. 1981.
Gérard de Nerval et son temps (biography). 1981.
Buffon (biography). 1983.
Le Diable à Paris. 1984.
Humboldt l'explorateur (biography). 1985.
Du côté de chez Monsieur Pasteur (biography). 1986.
L'Ange gardien. 1987.
Montesquieu (biography). 1989.
Album les écrivains de la révolution (photo history). 1989.
Portraits et souvenirs (literary criticism). 1991.
La Friche. 1993.
Gascogne (history). 1998.
Le Transsibérien: Récit (narration). 1998.
Aïssé: Récit (narration). 1998.

*

Critical Studies: ''The Concentrationary World of Pierre Gascar'' by Chester Obuchowski, in *French Review,* 34, 1961, pp. 327–35; ''The Metamorphoses of Animals and Men in Gascar's *Les Betes*'' by Judith L. Radke, in *The French Review,* 39, 1965, p. 85–91; ''The Grammar of Water, the

Syntax of Fire'' by Nancy Willard, in *Chicago Review*, 22, 1971, pp. 104–18.

* * *

In reference to his origins in the region of Gascony in southern France, Pierre Fournier changed his last name to Gascar when he became a published author in the years following World War II. The name suggests the simple, rustic flavor for which his writing was to become known. Gascar is known primarily as an author of short fiction, a far less popular genre in France than in the English-speaking world, but he also published novels, plays, and assorted nonfiction. He is not especially known as a writer on the Holocaust, but the novella *The Season of the Dead* from 1953, featuring a narrator who witnesses the deportation of Jews from the vantage point of his prisoner-of-war camp, is one of his best-known works. In 1998, shortly after his death, a memoir of the real-life war experiences upon which his story was based appeared under the title *The Season of the Dead: The Russian Dream*. It can be argued that several of his other early works are poetic treatments of certain aspects of World War II, including the Holocaust.

In the 1998, autobiographical version of *The Season of the Dead*, Gascar relates his experience with left-wing politics in the 1930s and his sympathy for the Soviet Union, which had already started to cool by the time the war began. Captured on the front during the 1940 invasion of France, he was to spend the rest of the war in German prison camps. After two failed escape attempts, he was transferred, along with other refractory French prisoners of war, to a remote camp outside the town of Rawa-Ruska, then in the Polish province of Galicia (now part of Ukraine). Both the 1953 and the 1998 versions develop in detail the following true circumstances. On their way from the train station to the camp, the prisoners noticed members of the local Jewish population from the white armbands with blue Stars of David that the Germans forced them to wear. During the years Gascar spent in the camp, he could see the Jews from afar, especially those who were pressed into work crews by the occupiers. When the Jewish population from areas east of Rawa-Ruska began to be deported to concentration camps, the trains stopped there on the way. The prisoner-of-war camp was close to the railway depot, and the prisoners could hear the cries of the victims from the cattle cars. At first the Jews of Rawa-Ruska were not included in these deportations, which made Gascar wonder if they enjoyed some sort of protection. Any such illusion was destroyed, however, when he and the other prisoners discovered one day that all of the Jews in the area had disappeared. Not long afterward, the camp was liberated by the Soviet army, and Gascar gradually found his way back to France. The 1953 novella uses the Holocaust as its main plot device, while the 1998 memoir, although it gives even more details about Gascar's perspective on the Holocaust than does the story, is far more wide-ranging in scope. For example, it provides an unrelated analysis of

Soviet history and ideology, which explains the subtitle, *The Russian Dream*.

Gascar earned his living as a journalist and book critic while working on the stories that would eventually appear under the title *Les Bêtes* in 1953 and in English translation in 1956 as *Beasts and Men. Le Temps des morts* (*The Season of the Dead*) was published the same year in a combined volume with the collection of stories, a fact that brings out subtle thematic and stylistic links between the two. While *The Season of the Dead* deals explicitly with the Holocaust, his other stories from that time can be seen as allegories of the dehumanizing power of war. All of them can be said to define the concept of the ''concentrationary world'' that he discovered as a prisoner of war and witness to the Holocaust. (The term comes from Chester Obuchowski's 1961 article in *French Review* titled ''The Concentrationary World of Pierre Gascar.'') Whether they are about the psychosis of a man charged with herding horses during a war (''The Horses'') or the training of dogs to attack humans in a postwar French military camp in Germany (''The Dogs''), stories in this early collection draw upon concentration camp imagery to show the fragility of the boundaries separating humans from animals.

The rest of Gascar's large subsequent output rarely makes reference to his war experiences. One of several possible exceptions is *Les Femmes* (1955; *Women and the Sun*, 1964), a collection of stories that further develop the dark theme of captivity and escape characterizing his early work. Although he continued to be known as a writer with an ability to give voice to the nonhuman in an often unsettling manner, earning the label ''kafkaesque,'' his fiction progressively took on a more hopeful cast as he matured.

—M. Martin Guiney

See the essay on *The Season of the Dead*.

GAY, Peter (Jack)

Nationality: American (originally German: immigrated to Cuba, 1939, the United States, 1941, granted U.S. citizenship, 1946). **Born:** Peter Joachim Fröhlich, Berlin, 20 June 1923. **Education:** University of Denver, B.A. 1946; Columbia University, New York, M.A. 1947, Ph.D. 1951; psychoanalytic training at Western New England Institute for Psychoanalysis, 1976–83. **Family:** Married Ruth Slotkin in 1959; three stepdaughters. **Career:** Instructor and assistant professor of government, 1947–56, associate professor, 1956–62, and professor of history, 1962–69, Columbia University; professor of comparative and intellectual European history, 1969, Durfee Professor of History, 1970–84, and Sterling Professor of History, 1984, Yale University, New Haven, Connecticut. Visiting fellow, Institute for Advanced Study, Berlin, 1984.

Awards: Frederic G. Melcher book award, 1967, for *The Party of Humanity: Essays in the Enlightenment;* National Book Award, 1967, for *The Enlightenment: An Interpretation,* Volume I: *The Rise of Modern Paganism;* Guggenheim fellow, 1967–68, and 1976–77; Phi Beta Kappa Ralph Waldo Emerson award, 1969, for *Weimar Culture: The Outsider As Insider; Los Angeles Times* book prize nomination, 1984, for *The Bourgeois Experience: Victoria to Freud,* Volume 1: *Education of the Senses;* Amsterdam prize for history, 1991; Geschwister-Scholl-Preis (Germany), 1999. D.H.L.: University of Denver, 1970; University of Maryland, 1979; Hebrew Union College, 1983; Clark University, 1985; Suffolk University, 1987; Tufts University, 1988. Alfred Hodder Jr. fellow, Princeton University, 1955–56; fellow, American Council of Learned Societies, 1959–60; fellow, Center for Advanced Study in the Behavioral Sciences, 1962–63; overseas fellow, Churchill College, Cambridge University, 1970–71; fellow, Rockefeller Foundation, 1979–80.

PUBLICATIONS

Memoir

My German Question: Growing up in Nazi Berlin. 1998.

Other

The Dilemma of Democratic Socialism: Eduard Bernstein's Challenge to Marx. 1952.
Voltaire's Politics: The Poet As Realist. 1959.
The Party of Humanity: Essays in the French Enlightenment. 1964.
Age of Enlightenment, with Time-Life Books. 1966.
The Loss of Mastery: Puritan Historians in Colonial America. 1966.
The Enlightenment: An Interpretation (2 vols.). 1966.
　The Enlightenment: An Interpretation: The Rise of Modern Paganism. 1966.
　The Enlightenment: An Interpretation: The Science of Freedom. 1969.
Weimar Culture: The Outsider As Insider. 1968.
The Bridge of Criticism: Dialogues among Lucian, Erasmus, and Voltaire on the Enlightenment On History and Hope, Imagination and Reason, Constraint and Freedom and on Its Meaning for Our Time. 1970.
The Berlin-Jewish Spirit, A Dogma in Search of Some Doubts. 1972.
Modern Europe, with Robert K. Webb (2 vols.). 1973.
Style in History. 1974.
Art and Act: On Causes in History: Manet, Gropius, Mondrian. 1976.
Freud, Jews and Other Germans: Masters and Victims in Modernist Culture. 1978.

The Bourgeois Experience: Victoria to Freud (5 vols.). 1984.
　Education of the Senses. 1984.
　The Tender Passion. 1986.
　The Cultivation of Hatred. 1993.
　The Naked Heart. 1995.
　Pleasure Wars. 1998.
Freud for Historians. 1985.
A Godless Jew: Freud, Atheism, and the Making of Psychoanalysis. 1987.
Freud: A Life for Our Time. 1988.
Reading Freud: Explorations & Entertainments. 1990.
Mozart. 1999.
Moritz Frohlich-Morris Gay: A German Refugee in the United States. 1999.
Schnitzler's Century: The Making of Middle-Class Culture, 1815–1914. 2001.

Editor and translator, *The Question of Jean Jacques Rousseau,* by Ernst Cassirer. 1954.
Editor and translator, *Philosophical Dictionary,* by Francois Marie Arouet de Voltaire (2 vols.). 1962.
Editor and translator, *Candide,* by Voltaire (bilingual edition). 1963.
Editor, *John Locke on Education,* by John Locke. 1964.
Editor, *Deism: An Anthology.* 1968.
Editor, with John Arthur Garraty, *The Columbia History of the World.* 1971; as *A History of the World,* 1972.
Editor, with Gerald J. Cavanaugh and Victor G. Wexler, *Historians at Work* (4 vols.). 1972.
Editor, *Eighteenth Century Studies: Presented to Arthur M. Wilson.* 1972.
Editor, *The Enlightenment: A Comprehensive Anthology.* 1973; revised edition, 1985.
Editor, *A Freud Reader.* 1989.

Translator, *Dictionnaire philosophique* by Voltaire. 1953.

*

Critical Studies: "In Bed with the Victorians: Views of P. Gay" by Noel Gilroy Annan, in *The New York Review of Books,* 33, 20 November 1986, pp. 8–9; "Putting Freud on the Couch, Historian Peter Gay Finds a Genius Whose Stature Time Cannot Shrink" by Eric Levin, in *People Weekly,* 29, 6 June 1988, p. 101–02; "Two Jews: Freud and Gay" by Benjamin Goodnick, in *Judaism,* 38, Winter 1989, pp. 103–11.

* * *

　Born Peter Joachim Fröhlich on 20 June 1923 in Berlin, Peter Gay narrowly escaped the Holocaust, sailing to Cuba with his parents on the *Iberia* in April 1939. In January 1941 the family arrived in Key West, Florida, and in 1943 they officially changed their names to Gay, the English translation of Fröhlich. At the University of Denver, from which Gay graduated in 1946, the future historian developed an interest in the eighteenth-century philosopher David Hume and the Enlightenment. Gay's first book, however, was his Columbia University dissertation about the German socialist political philosopher Eduard Bernstein, which appeared in 1952 as *The Dilemma of Democratic Socialism.*

In 1953 Gay returned to the eighteenth century with a translation of Voltaire's *Dictionnaire philosophique,* and in 1959 he published *Voltaire's Politics: The Poet As Realist.* His translation of *Candide* followed in 1963, and *The Party of Humanity: Essays in the French Enlightenment* in 1964. The latter won the Frederic G. Melcher Award in 1967. In that same year Gay received a National Book Award for *The Rise of Modern Paganism* (1966), the first of his two-volume *The Enlightenment: An Interpretation.* Here he examined the origins of eighteenth-century secular thought, which he traced to classical ideas. In *The Science of Freedom* (1969) Gay placed eighteenth-century intellectuals within their historical context. While working on the Enlightenment, he also published *A Loss of Mastery: Puritan Historians in Colonial America* (1966), in which he criticized William Bradford, Cotton Mather, and Jonathan Edwards for their lack of objectivity, a quality Gay has repeatedly insisted is necessary for the student of history. His four lectures at Columbia, where he was then teaching, became *Weimar Culture: The Outsider As Insider* (1968), winner of Phi Beta Kappa's 1969 Ralph Waldo Emerson Award.

Freud, Jews, and Other Germans (1978) continued Gay's exploration of late nineteenth- and early twentieth-century German history. He maintained that German Jews were not necessary supporters of modernism and that modernism itself was not as antibourgeois or as antirational as many had claimed. In the mid-1970s he enrolled in the New England Institute for Psychoanalysis to learn more about Sigmund Freud and psychology. In *Freud for Historians* (1985) Gay argued that historians should apply psychological methods to their study of the past. Further studies of Freud followed, including *A Godless Jew: Freud, Atheism, and the Making of Psychoanalysis* (1987), *Freud: A Life for Our Time* (1988), and *Reading Freud* (1990).

Along with his biography of Freud, Gay's most enduring legacy is likely to be his five-volume *The Bourgeois Experience: Victoria to Freud* (1984–97). Drawing on a wealth of primary material, this work overturned many previously held views about the late nineteenth century. Other works that drew on this theme are *The Education of the Senses* (1984), which rejected the equation of Victorian age with sexual prudery, and *Pleasure Wars* (1997), in which Gay demonstrated that the bourgeois, far from being philistine, patronized the arts, including avant-garde painting.

In a 1985 interview Gay said, "I wanted to understand how ideas arose and what they meant in their whole context."

Whether looking at culture or the psyche, Gay has fulfilled that goal in his elegantly written books.

—Joseph Rosenblum

See the essay on *My German Question: Growing up in Nazi Berlin.*

GINZBURG, Natalia

Pseudonym: Alessandra Tournimparte. **Nationality:** Italian. **Born:** Natalia Levi, Palermo, 14 July 1916. **Education:** University of Turin, 1935. **Family:** Married 1) Leone Ginzburg in 1938 (died 1944), two daughters; 2) Gabriele Baldini in 1950 (died 1969). **Career:** Editorial consultant, Einaudi Publishing Company, Rome, 1944, and Turin, 1945–49; worked in the publishing business during the 1950s; lived in London, 1959–61; elected to the Italian parliament as independent left-wing deputy, 1983. **Awards:** Viareggio prize, 1957, for *Valentino;* Strega prize, 1964, for *Lessico famigliare;* Marzotto prize for European drama, 1968, for *The Advertisement;* Milan Club Degli Editori award, 1969; Bagutto award, 1984; Ernest Hemingway prize, 1985. **Died:** 7 October 1991.

PUBLICATIONS

Collection

Opere [Works]:
  Opere: Volume primo. 1986.
  Opere: Volume secondo. 1987.

Novels

La strada che va in citta (as Alessandra Tournimparte). 1942; with additional stories, as *La strada che va in città, e altri racconti,* 1945; first edition translated as *The Road to the City: Two Novelettes,* 1949.
E stato cosi [The Dry Heart]. 1947.
Valentino (novella). 1951; translated as *Valentino* and published with *Sagittarius* as *Valentino and Sagittarius: Two Novellas,* 1987.
Tutti i nostri ieri. 1952; as *A Light for Fools,* 1956; as *Dead Yesterdays,* 1956; as *All Our Yesterdays,* 1985.
Sagittario (novella). 1957; translated as *Sagittarius* and published with *Valentino* as *Valentino and Sagittarius: Two Novellas,* 1987.
Le voci della sera. 1961; as *Voices in the Evening,* 1963.
Lessico famigliare. 1963; as *Family Sayings,* 1967; as *What We Used to Say,* 1997.

Cinque romanzi brevi (selections). 1964; with additional stories, as *Cinque romanzi brevi, e altri racconti,* 1993; first edition translated as *Valentino and Sagittarius: Two Novellas,* 1987.
Caro Michele. 1973; as *No Way,* 1974; as *Dear Michael,* 1975.
Famiglia (two novellas). 1977; as *Family: Two Novellas,* 1988.
La citte e la casa. 1984; as *The City and the House,* 1986.

Plays

Ti ho sposato per allegria [I Married You for the Fun of It]. 1966.
L'inserzione; translated as *The Advertisement* (produced London, 1968). 1969.
Paese di mare e altre commedie. 1973.
L'intervista: Commedia in tre atti. 1989.

Other

Romanzi del 900, with Giansiro Ferrata. 1956.
La famiglia Manzoni (biography). 1983; as *The Manzoni Family,* 1987.
Le piccole virtu (essays). 1962; as *The Little Virtues,* 1985.
Mai devi domandarmi (essays). 1970; as *Never Must You Ask Me,* 1973.
Vita immaginaria (essays). 1974.
Serena Cruz, o la vera giustizia [Serena Cruz, or True Justice]. 1990.

*

Bibliography: "A Bibliography of the Writings of Natalia Ginzburg" by Cathe Giffuni, in *Bulletin of Bibliography,* 50(2), June 1993, pp. 139–44.

Critical Studies: *Women in Modern Italian Literature: Four Studies Based on the Work of Grazia Deledda, Alba De Céspedes, Natalia Ginzburg, and Dacia Maraini* by Bruce Merry, 1990; *Natalia Ginzburg: Human Relationships in a Changing World* by Alan Bullock, 1991; "Natalia Ginzburg," in *Salmagundi,* 96, Fall 1992, pp. 52–167; "Natalia Ginzburg: Bonded and Separating Narrator-Daughters and the Maternal in *Sagittario*" by Teresa L. Picarazzi, in *Nemla Italian Studies,* 17, 1993, pp. 91–105; "Anchoring Natalia Ginzburg" by Wallis Wilde-Menozzi, in *Kenyon Review,* 16(1), Winter 1994, pp. 115–30; "Silent Witness: Memory and Omission in Natalia Ginzburg's *Family Sayings*" by Judith Woolf, in *Cambridge Quarterly* (England), 25(3), 1996, pp. 243–62; "Racial Laws and Internment in Natalia Ginzburg's *La strada che va in citta* and *Tutti i nostri ieri*" by Claudia Nocentini, in *The Italian Jewish Experience,* edited by Thomas P. DiNapoli, 2000; *Natalia Ginzburg: A Biography* by Maja Pflug, translated by Sian Williams, 2000; *Natalia Ginzburg: A Voice of the*

Twentieth Century, edited by Angela M. Jeannet and Giuliana Sanguinetti Katz, 2000.

*   *   *

Born Natalia Levi in Palermo, Sicily, in 1916, where her father taught anatomy at the university, the future Natalia Ginzburg grew up in the geographic and cultural antipode of Turin. Her family had moved to the northern Italian city, a city with a significant Jewish population (home also to the two important and nonrelated Jewish Italian authors, Carlo and **Primo Levi,** as it was to Cesare Pavese, who was later to be an important coeditor with Ginzburg at the prestigious publishing house of Giulio Einaudi), because her father had been offered a professorship at that prestigious and progressive university. Natalia grew up in a secular and nonobservant home, but their being Jewish, according to the Fascist racial laws of 1938, would have a profound effect on the male members of her family and on the life of her husband Leone, with Antonio Gramsci one of the most active and renowned anti-Fascist Italian intellectuals.

In the year the racial laws were promulgated Natalia met and married Leone Ginzburg, a Jewish Russian who had spent the summers of his youth in Italy (it has just recently been learned that he was the illegitimate child of his Russian mother and her Italian lover) and, after completing his university studies, was offered a lectureship in Russian literature at the University of Turin. Because Leone refused to swear allegiance to Fascism and because he was a non-Italian, he was dismissed from his lectureship. Following his dismissal, Leone began his activity as writer for and editor of anti-Fascist publications, which generated his reputation and kept him under the perpetual watch of the Fascists. With Italy's declaration of war on France and Great Britain, Leone was picked up by the Fascist police and sent into internal exile (as was Carlo Levi, who used his exile experiences in his classic novel *Cristo si è fermato a Eboli* [*Christ Stopped at Eboli*]) to a village in the then backward south—in Leone's case to the central province of the Abruzzi east of Rome, in Levi's case to Basilicata in the instep of "the boot of Italy."

Natalia, now a mother of two daughters, joined her husband in exile and made transmogrified autobiographical use of their life in the Abruzzi for her wartime novel *Tutti i nostri ieri* ("All Our Yesterdays"). Though their life was harsh and poor and the region was fairly Fascist, the inhabitants of the region expected the area to improve under the Fascist government, and the Ginzburg family managed to survive at the common village level and to be fairly well accepted in their village of Pizzoli, not far from the capital of L'Aquila. Natalia repaid the sympathy shown to her, her husband, and her family in *Tutti i nostri ieri,* which she published under her married name. (She had already, because of the racial laws, published two books under a pseudonym.) Criticism has been leveled against Natalia for using the Ginzburg family name rather than her maiden name because she remarried after Leone's death and because of his high martyr status as anti-Fascist. *Tutti i nostri ieri* is the only novel (in the second of the three parts) in which World War II figures in Natalia's writing. In the sober, seemingly unemotional realism she became famous for, she renders a gripping portrait of a human configuration of Jews, Fascist and non-Fascist Italians, and an initially sympathetic young German soldier in the small Abruzzi town in which the second part of her novel takes place. Things will turn tragic when the young German discovers that a Jew is being hidden in the house that is the setting for the book (human life in the interiors of homes is one of the distinctive qualities of Natalia's writing). The German returns to being a Wehrmacht soldier and is unwillingly killed, and the event is used by the Germans to execute a number of male civilian "enemies." Typical of her sober acceptance of death, Natalia, a narrator, does not shed emotional tears over the execution in *Tutti i nostri ieri* but moves the novel along to the ensuing series of events.

Leone becomes a heroic anti-Fascist martyr by leaving the relative security of the village of his exile in the Abruzzi and returning to Rome after the deposition of Benito Mussolini in order to resume his anti-Fascist publishing. Natalia and her two daughters followed Leone to Rome, ironically being offered passage and being driven to the outskirts of the city by retreating German soldiers after their defeat at Monte Cassino en route to occupy Rome. Leone's printing shop in Rome was discovered three weeks after his resumption of publishing, and he was taken to the infamous Regina Coeli prison. Natalia never saw Leone again and only later learned the circumstances of his death from a fellow prisoner. After initial beatings by Italian Fascists, Leone was turned over to the Gestapo and tortured. He was found dead in his cell in 1944, tragically not long before the German retreat from Rome.

After the armistice between the Germans and the Allies, Natalia returned home to Turin—indirectly via Florence because of the military situation—and began her work as editor at the head office of the Einaudi publishing house. In 1950 she married her second husband, Gabriele Baldini, a professor of English at the University of Trieste. He continued to teach in Trieste, and she lived and worked in Turin.

When, in 1950, her husband was offered a professorship in Rome, Natalia joined Baldini to live and work in the Rome office of Einaudi. In 1959 Baldini was appointed director of the Italian Cultural Institute in London, so Natalia lived with him there for two years, returning to Rome in 1961 and spending the remainder of her life in the capital. Baldini died in 1969, leaving Natalia a widow for the second time.

Natalia not only continued to publish a series of novels after her first one in 1942 but she also became the successful author of quite a few light theater pieces as well as an essayist. She became active in politics mostly because political figures urged her to because of her fame as a writer and because of her well-known work on behalf of and advocacy for the rights of abused, orphaned, and neglected children. She allowed herself to be a candidate for a coalition of independent left-wing

parties and served two terms in the Italian Parliament. Held in high esteem after her terms in Parliament and for her prize-winning and popular novels translated into many languages, she was sought out by interviewers and called on by writers from abroad. She died relatively peacefully, a very public figure, in Rome in 1991.

—Robert B. Youngblood

See the essay on *What We Used to Say.*

GLATSTEIN, Jacob

Nationality: American (originally Polish: immigrated to the United States, 1914). **Born:** Lublin, 20 August 1896. **Education:** Studied law, New York University, 1918. **Career:** Worked as a literary critic, journalist, and editor. Member, Inzikhistn (introspectivist) group of poets. **Died:** 19 November 1971.

PUBLICATIONS

Poetry

Yankev Glatshteyn. 1921.
Fraye Ferzn. 1926.
Kredos. 1929.
Yidishtaytshn. 1937.
Gedenklider [In Remembrance]. 1943.
Shtralendike Yidn [Radiating Jews]. 1946.
Dem Taatns Shotn [Father's Shadow]. 1953.
Fun mayn gantser mi [Of All My Labor]. 1956.
Di Freyd fun Yidisn Vort [Joy of the Yiddish Word]. 1961.
Mi-kol 'amali: Shirim u-fo'emot. 1964.
A Yid fun Lublin [A Jew from Lublin]. 1966.
Kh'tu dermonen. 1967.
Poems (English translations). 1970.
Gezangen fun rekhts tsu links [Songs from Right to Left]. 1971.
The Selected Poems of Jacob Glatstein (English translations). 1972.
Selected Poems of Yankev Glatshteyn (English translations). 1987.
I Keep Recalling: The Holocaust Poems of Jacob Glatstein (English translations). 1993.

Novels

Ven Yash iz Geforen [When Yash Went Forth]. 1938; as *Homeward Bound,* 1969.
Ven Yash iz Gekumen [When Yash Arrived]. 1940; as *Homecoming at Twilight,* 1962.

Emil un Karl (for children). 1940.

Play

Di Purim gvardye. 1930.

Other

Lider. 1921.
In tokh genumen: Eseyen (essays). 1947.
Oyf greyte temes. 1967.
In der velt mit Yidish: Eseyen (essays). 1972.

Editor, *Finf un zibetsik yor yidishe prese in Amerike, 1870–1945* [75 Years of the Yiddish Press in the United States, 1870–1945]. 1945.
Editor, *Mit mayne fartogbikher: In tokh genumen, 1958–1962.* 1963.
Editor, with Israel Knox and Samuel Margoshes, *Anthology of Holocaust Literature.* 1973.

*

Critical Study: "Jacob Glatstein: The Literary Uses of Jewishness" by Chana Bloch, in *Judaism,* XIV, Fall 1965, pp. 414–31.

*   *   *

Yiddish poet and writer Jacob Glatstein was born in Lublin, Poland, in 1896 and migrated to America in 1914. Four years later, at the age of 22, he studied law at New York University but never completed his degree probably due to his preoccupation with Yiddish writing. He was a core member of the Inzikhistn (Introspectivist) group, which sought to modernize Yiddish poetry. In 1920 the Yiddish poets Aaron Glants-Leyeles and N.B. Minkoff launched the Yiddish magazine *In Zikh* and published the anthology *In Zikh: A Zamlung Introspektive Lider.* The beliefs, ethos, and poetics of the Inzikhistn are contained in these publications. Noteworthy is the acceptance of free verse, suggestion and association in lieu of structured patterns and imposed ideology. The objective is to release the poet's full emotional response to everyday events far and near. Glatstein's first book of verse, *Yankev Glatshteyn* (1921), influenced by theories of self-analysis and individualism, expresses the emotion and thought of the individual in a modern metropolis. And it does so in the fullness of the Introspectivist charge of "individuality in everything and introspection in everything."

From his earliest poems onward Glatstein showed himself to be an Inzikhist with an individuality. Though he accepted the Introspectivist perspective that the medium not the subject makes a Yiddish poem Jewish, he ventured out on his own and resolved to be a rugged individualist. The title of his first book suggests this, and names of his second and third books of

verse, *Fraye Ferzn* (1926) and *Kredos* (1929), confirm it. Cosmopolitanism infused with sentiments of Jewish tradition were dominant in his poetry. This was to change dramatically, however, with a visit to his birthplace in 1934, a year after Hitler's rise to power and several years before the outbreak of World War II. His autobiographical travel narratives, *Ven Yash iz Geforen* (1938; "When Yash Went Forth"; an earlier version was serialized in *In Zikh*) and *Ven Yash iz Gekumen* (1940; "When Yash Arrived"), speak of the impending doom of European Jewry and the life-effecting changes it wrought to Glatstein, who saw himself as a free American artist now transformed to a marked Jew. This transformation from Lublin and back, drawing from Jewish tradition and made somber by the worsening state of interwar Jewry, became the hallmark of Glatstein's Holocaust poems.

Glatstein was the author of numerous books of poetry, novels, and essays. His poetry has been translated into English, Hebrew, Russian, Spanish, and French and has been included in a number of anthologies. His volumes of poetry include *Shtralendike Yidn* (1946; "Radiating Jews"), *Dem Taatns Shotn* (1953; "Father's Shadow"), *Di Freyd fun Yidisn Vort* (1961; "Joy of the Yiddish Word"), and *A Yid fun Lublin* (1966; "A Jew from Lublin"). An exemplary poet and essayist, he also excelled as a literary critic, columnist, editor, and publicist. He was a quintessential Introspectivist whose skill and talent in multiple genres cast a long shadow on twentieth-century Jewish writing. He died of a heart attack in Queens, New York, at the age of 75.

—Zev Garber

See the essay on *I Keep Recalling: The Holocaust Poems of Jacob Glatstein.*

GLAZAR, Richard

Nationality: Swiss (originally Czechoslovakian). **Born:** Prague, 1920. **Education:** Studied in Prague, London, and Paris, mid-1940s; degree in economics. **Family:** Married; two children. **Career:** Interned, 1942, and escaped, 1943, Treblinka death camp. Lived in Czechoslovakia, 1950s and 1960s; fled to Switzerland after the Soviet invasion, 1968. Worked as an engineer in Bern, Switzerland, until 1995. Returned to Prague, 1995. **Died:** Suicide, 1998.

PUBLICATION

Memoir

Die Falle mit dem grünen Zaun: Überleben in Treblinka. 1992; as *Trap with a Green Fence: Survival in Treblinka,* 1995.

* * *

Richard Glazar was born in Prague in 1920. The son of an officer in the Austrian army who had been wounded in World War I, he grew up speaking both German and Czech in a secular humanistic Jewish home. In 1939, after the Germans occupied Czechoslovakia, Glazar's parents helped him escape to a remote rural Czech town where he kept a low profile—not registered as a Jew—while doing farm chores. In early September 1942 he was deported to the Theresienstadt ghetto. A month later he was transferred to the Treblinka death camp. After being held there for 10 months as one of a thousand *Arbeitsjuden* (work Jews), Glazar was one of the few to escape during the prisoner uprising on 2 August. He fled across Poland with a fellow inmate, Karel Unger, whom he had already befriended in Theresienstadt. The two eventually settled in Mannheim, Germany, where, under assumed names, they passed themselves off until the end of the war as Gentile Czech workers belonging to the Todt Organization.

Beginning in 1945 Glazar studied in Prague, London, and Paris and earned an economics degree. In the early 1950s, during the Stalinist era in Czechoslovakia, he was arrested because of his nonconformist political views and forced once again to do manual labor, this time in a steel plant, from 1951 to 1953. With the liberalizing of the Czechoslovak government in the 1960s, Glazar's personal and professional situation increasingly improved. After the Soviet invasion of 1968, however, he fled with his wife and two children to Switzerland. Upon his retirement from an engineering firm in Bern in 1995, he moved back to Prague, where he committed suicide in 1998.

Earlier, in 1957, Glazar returned to Treblinka for the first time after the war on a business trip. As one of only 54 eyewitnesses, Glazar testified at the trials of the Nazi officials in charge of Treblinka in Düsseldorf in 1963 and 1971. The author of an invaluable memoir, *Die Falle mit dem grünen Zaun: Überleben in Treblinka* (1992; *Trap with a Green Fence: Survival in Treblinka,* 1995), Glazar also made major contributions to two important Holocaust-related works: Gitta Sereny's study *Into That Darkness* (1974) and **Claude Lanzmann**'s film *Shoah* (1985). In his writings and interviews Glazar confessed that, together with his outer coolness and his close, mutually supportive friendship with the other inmates in his unit, luck played a major role in his survival. He had arrived at Treblinka exactly when the guards desperately needed another slave laborer to sort victims' clothing. Had he stepped off the train at any other time, he probably would have been gassed along with most of the others in his transport.

Sereny characterizes him as "the most credible of witnesses" who survived Treblinka. In the chapter she accords him exclusively, Glazar succinctly describes the four successive phases of operation in Treblinka's history: (1) the fledgling first stage under Dr. Eberl through much of 1942, before Franz Stangl, the later commandant and organizing force, came on the scene in September; (2) Stangl's first months (September through December 1942), a period in which the duties of the work Jews, who were assigned to sort and pack the goods confiscated from the gas chamber's victims, had not yet been clearly organized; (3) the first half of 1943, when there was a "terrible kind of community" between "the murderers" in charge of the camp and the work Jews, with each of these groups literally dependent on the efficient mass murder of incoming transports for their own survival—although the labor was backbreaking, goods could be stolen and exchanged with the SS and Ukrainian guards, allowing Glazar and his fellow inmates, at times, to be among the best-fed and best-dressed victims of Nazi oppression; (4) the final unraveling culminating in the armed inmate uprising of 2 August during which each of the German camp officials, aware of the approaching Soviet army, became increasingly terrified of the consequences of his individual genocidal acts.

Glazar is also featured in Claude Lanzmann's *Shoah,* in which he provides detailed and vivid testimony about his incarceration in Treblinka, covering his arrival, his daily life as a work Jew, and the organizing of the 1943 uprising. In one of the most effective examples of armed insurrection carried out by Nazi prisoners, the inmates permanently shut down the largest Nazi camp devoted exclusively to extermination, a site where close to 900,000 Jews had been exterminated. Glazar's extended interviews with Lanzmann are no less evocative and precise than his written memoirs.

—Steven R. Cerf

See the essay on *Trap with a Green Fence: Survival in Treblinka.*

GLIK, Hirsh

Nationality: Russian. **Born:** Vilna, Lithuania, 1922. **Education:** Apprenticed in the paper business. **Career:** Worked in a hardware store; member, Young Vilna group of poets; editor and publisher, *Yungvald,* periodical of Young Vilna group; composed poems/songs of resistance, Vilna ghetto, early 1940s; forced to work in Estonian labor camps, c. 1941–43. **Died:** Presumed murdered, victim of the Holocaust, 1944.

PUBLICATIONS

Poetry

Zog nit keynmol az du geyst dem letsten veg/Song of the Jewish Partisans in the Battle of the Ghetto, music by Dmitri and Daniel Pokrass (score). 1946; as *The Hymn of Jewish Resistance,* 1972.

Lider un poemes. 1953.

* * *

Best known for his lyrics to the famous partisan song "Zog Nit Keynmol," the Lithuanian poet Hirsh Glik was a prominent poet and lyricist in the Vilna ghetto and related camps prior to his death in 1944. Born in Vilna in 1922, Glik was a member of the Young Vilna group of poets whose membership included Leyzer Volk, Chaim Grade, and Abraham Sutzkever. Writing in Yiddish, the Young Vilna poets were influenced by contemporary social issues (anti-Semitism, poverty) as well as deep connections to Jewish tradition, which were particularly strong in the city known as "the Jerusalem of Lithuania." Before the outbreak of World War II Glik had edited and published four issues of *Yungvald* (Young Forest), a periodical of the Young Vilna poets group.

Following the German conquest of Lithuania in 1941 Glik and his father were interned in the Vilna ghetto. Later relocated to the forced labor camp of Biala Vaka outside of Vilna, Glik continued to author poetry and song lyrics, and in 1943 he was sent back to the Vilna ghetto upon the liquidation of the forced labor camp. An active supporter of Jewish partisan activities, Glik emphasized in his poetry and song lyrics heroism as a source of identity and the strength of the Jewish community during times of adversity. Indicative of his works during the Holocaust are the lyrics to three songs: "Zog Nit Keynmol" ("Never Say That You Have Reached the Final Road"), "Shtil Di Nakht" ("The Silent Night Was Filled with Stars"), and "Dos Zangl" ("The Cornstalk"). In "Zog Nit Keynmol" and "Shtil Ki Nakht" Glik's lyrics represent Jewish partisans as fearless and determined, knowing that despite the dangers and risks they might encounter, their efforts eventually will lead to victory, such as in this excerpt from Shtil Ki Nakht: "Encouraged by her triumph in the battle, / For our free nation yet to come." "Dos Zangl," likely created in the Biala Vaka labor camp prior to its liquidation in 1943, looks to the future in a different way. A tender lyric about two young lovers whose separation will not weaken their affection for one another, "Dos Zangl" incorporates wedding rituals to emphasize the continuity of Jewish life despite the horrors of the Holocaust: "And the trees between them, too, stand like a wedding canopy." Although frequently ill Glik continued to write poetry and lyrics until the liquidation of the Vilna ghetto in October 1943. Later transferred to the Goldfeld labor camp in Estonia by the Germans, he escaped in 1944 but was not heard from again.

In the broader context of Holocaust literature Glik's work can be seen as an effort to sustain Jewish culture in the face of catastrophe while inspiring the Jewish community to rise up against oppression. Placing Glik's output within the historic development of Jewish poetry, more often than not his works represent a poetic tradition describing the struggles that Jews have endured as a minority group in predominantly Christian

and Muslim societies. Less prominent in Glik's poetry, but still evident, are the symbols, rituals, and customs of Jewish life that must be maintained if Judaism is to survive in a hostile and changing world.

—William R. Fernekes

See the essay on *Zog nit keynmol.*

GOODRICH, Frances and HACKETT, Albert

Nationality: American. **GOODRICH, Frances. Born:** Belleville, New Jersey, 21 December 1890. **Education:** Vassar College, graduated 1912; New York School of Social Work, 1912–13. **Family:** Married 1) Robert Ames in 1917 (divorced 1923); 2) Henrik Willem Van Loon in 1927 (divorced 1930); 3) Albert Hackett in 1931. **Career:** Actress in stage productions, including *Coming Out of the Kitchen,* 1916; writer for Paramount, 1943–46, and Metro-Goldwyn-Mayer, 1948. **Died:** 19 January 1984. **HACKETT, Albert. Born:** Albert Maurice Hackett, New York, 16 February 1900. **Family:** Married 1) Frances Goodrich in 1931 (died 1984); 2) Gisele Svetlik in 1985. **Career:** Playwright, screenwriter, and actor. Appeared in films, including *Black Fear,* 1915, *The Venus Model,* 1918, *Coming Out of the Kitchen,* 1919, *Anne of Green Gables,* 1919, *Molly O',* 1921, *The Good-Bad Wife,* 1921, *The Country Flapper,* 1922, *The Darling of the Rich,* 1922, and *Whoopee!,* 1930. **Awards, with Goodrich:** Academy Award nominations, Academy of Motion Picture Arts and Sciences, 1934, for *The Thin Man,* 1935, for *Ah, Wilderness!,* 1950, for *Father of the Bride,* and 1954, for *Seven Brides for Seven Brothers;* Writers Guild awards, 1948, for *Easter Parade,* 1951, for *Father's Little Dividend,* and 1954, for *Seven Brides for Seven Brothers;* award for best American play, New York Drama Critics' Circle, Antoinette Perry award, best dramatic author, and Pulitzer prize for drama, Columbia University Graduate School of Journalism, all 1956, all for *The Diary of Anne Frank;* Writers Guild award, 1959, for *The Diary of Anne Frank.* **Died:** 16 March 1995.

PUBLICATIONS

Plays

Up Pops the Devil (produced New York, 1930). 1933.
Bridal Wise (produced New York, 1932).
Western Union, Please (produced 1939). As *Western Union, Please: A Comedy in Three Acts,* 1942.

The Great Big Doorstep (produced New York, 1942). 1943.
The Diary of Anne Frank: Dramatized by Frances Goodrich and Albert Hackett, adaptation of *Diary of a Young Girl* by Anne Frank (produced New York, 1955). 1956.
It's a Wonderful Life: Screenplay, with Frank Capra. 1986.

Screenplays: *Up Pops the Devil,* 1931; *The Secret of Madame Blanche,* 1933; *Penthouse,* with Leon Gordon and Hugo Butler, 1933; *Fugitive Lovers,* with George B. Seitz, 1934; *The Thin Man,* adaptation of the novel by Dashiell Hammett, 1934; *Chained,* 1934; *Hide-Out,* 1934; *Naughty Marietta* (musical; songs by Victor Herbert), with John Lee Mahin, 1935; *Ah, Wilderness!,* adaptation of the play by Eugene O'Neill, 1935; *Rose Marie,* with Alice Duer Miller, 1936; *Small Town Girl,* with Mahin and Edith Fitzgerald, 1936; *After the Thin Man,* adaptation of fiction by Hammett, 1936; *The Firefly,* 1937; *Thanks for the Memory,* 1938; *Another Thin Man,* adaptation of fiction by Hammett, 1939; *Society Lawyer,* 1939; *Doctors at War* (short film), 1943; *Lady in the Dark,* adaptation of a Broadway show by Moss Hart, 1944; *The Hitler Gang,* 1944; *The Virginian,* adaptation of the novel by Owen Wister, 1946; *It's a Wonderful Life,* with Frank Capra, adaptation of a story by Philip Van Doren Stern, 1946; *The Pirate* (musical; songs by Cole Porter), adaptation of the play by S. N. Behrman, 1948; *Summer Holiday* (musical), adaptation of *Ah, Wilderness!* by Eugene O'Neill, 1948; *Easter Parade* (musical; songs by Irving Berlin), with Sidney Sheldon, 1948; *In the Good Old Summertime* (musical), adapted from the film *The Shop around the Corner,* 1949; *Father of the Bride,* adaptation of the novel by Edward Streeter, 1950; *Father's Little Dividend,* 1951; *Too Young to Kiss,* 1951; *Give a Girl a Break* (musical; songs by Ira Gershwin and Burton Lane), 1954; *Seven Brides for Seven Brothers* (musical; songs by Johnny Mercer and Gene DePaul), with Dorothy Kingsley, adaptation of ''The Sobbin' Women'' by Stephen Vincent Benet, 1954; *The Long, Long Trailer,* 1954; *Gaby,* adapted from the film *Waterloo Bridge,* 1956; *A Certain Smile,* adaptation of the novella by Francoise Sagan, 1958; *The Diary of Anne Frank,* 1959; *Five Finger Exercise,* adaptation of the play by Peter Schaffer, 1962.

*

Media Adaptations: *Seven Brides for Seven Brothers,* adapted for Broadway and for television; *Society Lawyer,* 1939, remake of *Penthouse; Father of the Bride,* 1991, remake of the original; *Father of the Bride Part II,* 1995, remake of *Father's Little Dividend; The Diary of Anne Frank,* 1980, adapted for the stage, 1997.

Critical Studies: *Backstory: Interviews with Screenwriters of Hollywood's Golden Age* by Patrick McGilligan, 1986; *The Real Nick and Nora: Frances Goodrich and Albert Hackett,* *Writers of Stage and Screen Classics* by David L. Goodrich, 2001.

* * *

Frances Goodrich and Albert Hackett's play *The Diary of Anne Frank,* an adaptation of the famous diary, was first produced on Broadway in 1955 and won the Pulitzer Prize. Goodrich and Hackett, a husband-and-wife MGM screenwriting team, had earlier smash hits such as *Father of the Bride* and *It's a Wonderful Life.* Previously, however, they had not written about the Holocaust. Their play, although a huge success, proved to be very controversial and was part of a bitter legal dispute that also involved Otto Frank (**Anne Frank**'s father), novelist **Meyer Levin**, and playwright Lillian Hellman. In fact, Levin sued Otto Frank and producer Kermit Bloomgarden on various charges, including plagiarism because the content of Goodrich and Hackett's play was similar to his earlier drama (Levin blamed Frank and Bloomgarden). A jury decided that Frank should pay Levin $50,000 in damages, but after the verdict was thrown out, Frank paid Levin $15,000 for his rights to the play (one of the conditions of the settlement being that Levin could not legally stage his drama anywhere in the world), although it is worth pointing out that similarities between the two plays were inevitable because Levin and the Goodrich-Hackett team obviously used the same source—Anne's diary.

Levin was one of the first people to discern the great potential of the diary, and he brought it to the attention of the American public with his brilliant and laudatory review that appeared on the cover of the *New York Times Book Review.* The diary became hugely successful in part because he championed it tirelessly and monomaniacally. Inspired by the diary and perhaps feeling a bond with Anne Frank (Levin was present at the liberation of Bergen-Belsen, where she had died of typhus a month earlier), Levin convinced Otto Frank to let him write the play based on Anne's diary. Frank agreed but changed his mind after important drama producers and playwrights panned the draft. On Lillian Hellman's suggestion, Goodrich and Hackett were chosen. Goodrich and Hackett immediately immersed themselves in learning about the Holocaust and visited the secret annex where Anne had written the diary. They also met with Hellman for help. Despite Levin's numerous attempts, through lawsuits and the media, to stop Goodrich and Hackett's version from appearing onstage, the play was produced after much revision and a total of eight drafts, and it proved to be enormously successful.

Levin objected to the Goodrich and Hackett version because he considered it too commercial and universal and thought that it thus was not true to the diary and Anne's feelings. He correctly pointed out that Goodrich and Hackett had omitted almost all references to Judaism. In order to appeal to a wide variety of audiences, this play about the Holocaust contains virtually no references to Anne as a Jew, although many comments about her Jewish faith appear in her diary. In their play Goodrich and Hackett transform Anne into an everyman figure, someone to whom everyone can relate. Even Hanukkah is portrayed as a day of presents, not unlike Christmas. There is no parallel made to the persecution of Jews by the Greeks, and the subsequent deliverance, that is part of the Hanukkah story. **Cynthia Ozick** claims that Goodrich and Hackett, like Otto Frank, wanted the play to be accessible to everyone, a story to which they could relate and a story that would not offend anyone. Levin believed that such a story was then not truly about the Holocaust or the persecution of Jews and thus was a violation of the diary and Anne's thoughts.

Levin also did not approve of the humor in the play. Goodrich and Hackett's play contains much humor and thus was not as somber and intense as Levin's version. Goodrich and Hackett wanted people to enjoy the play and have fun, not to leave the theater feeling depressed. But the diary is about the Holocaust and thus, opined Levin, sad thoughts should be expected. Levin emphasized Anne's statements in the diary about the persecution of Jews while Goodrich and Hackett ignored these remarks, focusing instead on the growing romantic relationship between Anne and Peter as well as the bickering that involved the Van Daans and others. Although Levin believed that Goodrich and Hackett's version stripped the diary of its Jewishness and was a cheap commercial vehicle, it can also be asserted that the poignancy and tragedy of their play is understated, that audience members feel great sadness when Anne and the others in the secret annex are arrested (although no Nazi ever appears onstage). One of the last lines of Goodrich and Hackett's play, and arguably the most quoted line, is Anne's last words in the drama: "In spite of everything, I still believe that people are really good at heart." Thus, the play concludes on an optimistic note that Otto Frank, Goodrich, and Hackett desired. This line, however, is taken out of context from the diary and is actually part of a longer speech in which Anne claims to feel the suffering of millions. The diary entry itself is therefore somewhat pessimistic and bleak, not optimistic; detractors of Goodrich and Hackett's play suggest that such selective quoting from the diary distorts what Anne Frank really wrote and believed. Perhaps Goodrich and Hackett's attempts to universalize the plight of Anne Frank and to make the audience feel optimistic misrepresents Anne Frank's meaning, but perhaps these attempts have helped make *The Diary of Anne Frank* one of the most successful dramas in the world.

—Eric Sterling

See the essay on *The Diary of Anne Frank.*

GOURI, Haim

Nationality: Israeli. **Born:** Tel-Aviv, 9 October 1923. **Education:** Hebrew University, Jerusalem, 1950–52, B.A. 1952;

Sorbonne University, Paris, 1953. **Military Service:** Palmach (later Israeli Defense Forces), 1941–49: worked in Hungary, Austria, and Czechoslovakia among Jews who survived the Holocaust, Summer 1947; Israel's War of Independence: infantry officer, Negev Brigade; Israeli Defense Forces: reserve officer, Six-Day War, 1967, and officer, armored regiment in the Sinai, Yom Kippur War, 1973. **Family:** Married in 1952; three daughters. **Career:** Columnist, *La Merchav,* 1954–70. Since 1970 senior writer, *Davar.* Writer-in-residence, Hebrew University, Jerusalem, 1993; visiting professor, Hebrew College, Boston, 1998. Created, with others, documentary film trilogy about the Holocaust, 1974–83. **Awards:** Usishkin prize, 1963, for *Flowers of Fire;* Sokolov prize, 1964, for *Facing the Glass Cage;* Bialik prize, 1975, for *Gehazi's Visions;* Israel Composers' and Writers' Association prize, 1979; Israel prize for poetry, 1988; Neuman prize, 1994, for *The One Who Comes after Me;* Municipality of Jerusalem Uri Zvi Greenberg award, 1998, for body of poetry. D.Litt.: Ben-Gurion University of the Negev, 1999. **Member:** Hebrew Writers' Association. **Agent:** Hayim Goldgraber & Associates, P.O. Box 600443, Newtonville, Massachusetts 02460, U.S.A.

PUBLICATIONS

Collections

'Ad kav nesher, 1949–1975. 1975.
Various Poems, with Stanley F. Chyet. 1985.
Heshbon 'over: Mivhar shirim, 1945–1987 [Selected Poems, 1945–1987]. 1988.
Words in My Lovesick Blood/Milim be-dami ha-holeh ahavah, edited by Stanley F. Chyet (English and Hebrew). 1996.
Ha-Shirim [Collected Poems]. 1998.

Poetry

Pirhe esh [Flowers of Fire]. 1949.
'Ad 'alot ha-shahar [Until Dawn]. 1950.
Shire hotam [Sealed Poems]. 1954.
Shoshanat ruhot [The Wind Rose]. 1960.
Tenuah le-maga [Movement to Touch]. 1968.
Mar'ot Gehazi [Gehazi's Visions]. 1974.
Ayumah [Fearsome]. 1979.
Mahberot Elul [Notebooks of Elul]. 1985.
Ha-Ba aharai [The One Who Came after Me]. 1994.

Novels

'Iskat ha-shokolad (novella). 1964; as *The Chocolate Deal,* 1968.

''Ha-Sefer ha-meshuga''' [''The Crazy Book'']. 1971.
Ha-Hakirah: Sipur Re'u'el [The Investigation: Reuel]. 1980.

Short Stories

Dapim yerushalmiyim. 1958.
Mi makir et Yosef G'? [Who Knows Joseph G?]. 1980.
Reshimot mi-bet ha-yayin [Notes from the Tavern]. 1991.

Other

Mul ta ha-zekhukhit: Mishpat Yerushalayim [The Glass Booth:
    The Jerusalem Trial]. 1962.
*Ahad 'asar sipure ahavah: Sheloshim shanah la-'aliyat 11 ha-
    yishuvim ba-Negev.* 1976.
Jericho/Yeriho (English and Hebrew). 1983.

*

Critical Study: ''From the Naive to the Nostalgic in the
Poetry of Haim Gouri'' by Reuven Shoham, in *Prooftexts*,
18(1), January 1998, pp. 19–43.

Theatrical Activities: Director: Documentary Films—*The
81st Blow; The Last Sea, 1945–1948,* 1979; *Pi ha-mered/Fire
in the Ashes,* 1986.

* * *

It is without question that Haim Gouri's Holocaust canon
represents one of the capstone achievements in the response of
modern Hebrew poetry to the European calamity. One of the
first to tackle in verse the horrendous crimes, the native born
Gouri was a member of the Palmach, the commando unit of the
Jewish Defense Forces, from 1941 to 1949, later serving as an
officer in the 1948 war of liberation. In 1947 the Israel prize
laureate (1988) was sent by the Haganah to Europe to assist in
the smuggling of Holocaust survivors from displaced persons camps into Palestine. In this connection it is noteworthy that this deep change was reflected in the author's
semiautobiographical book *The Investigation: Reuel* (1980), a
clear case of art imitating life. Framed through the perspective
of the author's alter ego, the book tells the dramatic story of a
young *Sabre* who is plunged into war-torn Europe and his life-
altering encounters with the survivors that immediately shake
his Zionist ethos to its foundations.

Central to any elaboration is the realization that more than
anything else it was this distressing encounter with the remnants of the Shoah that transformed Gouri, stirring his soul and
rupturing the patina of the Holocaust myth held by his generation and the stereotypic picture eclipsing public perception as
promoted by the state. As should be made clear, since that day

Gouri, the paragon of the culture of memory, has been resolute
in repudiating any attempt to erase the experiential damage
and trauma, although he possesses no intimate knowledge and
has lost no relatives to the Final Solution, integrating and
expounding upon the pain of the victims through a continual
remembrance and reiteration of that loss. Most important,
Gouri's work exemplifies an attempt to undermine and
deconstruct predominant Israeli national assumptions about
the polarization between Israeli nature and Jewish nature and
to correct the blinkered vision that the Jews of Europe went
like sheep to the slaughter or, worse, were actually responsible
for their own fate. In his monumental and best-known poem
Inheritance (1960), for example, Gouri uses the *Akedah* narrative as an all-purpose metaphor for the fate of the Jewish
people, who, in contrast to the biblical Isaac, are left with a
knife embedded in their heart. In a nod to Job, Gouri revolts
against the God who has turned away from his children.

The poet's engagement with the Holocaust has taken the
form of various collections, including *Flowers of Fire* (1949),
Until Dawn (1950), *The Wind Rose* (1960), and *The Notebooks
of Elul* (1985), that declaim explicitly that memory and its
preservation have not dimmed and are aflame with empathy
and identification. Towering above the poems is a sense of the
great pain of Jewish history embodied in the lingering echoes
of the dead that permeates the entire fabric. Gouri deploys a
contemporary young hero, à la Joseph Campbell, who roams
through post-Nazi Europe. Journeying through this Dantean
hell, he encounters the blazing hate of the murderers and the
collaborators that still reverberates through this foreign land
that now encases within its midst the footprints of the past. The
poet's thematic matrix foregrounds the cities, rivers, churches,
and wintry snow of Europe that epitomize the terrible desolation and agony that still studs this landscape. The young
protagonist walking among the ruins of his people writhes in
pain as he is led by an unnamed figure on a nighttime stroll
through the historical sites where human life was trampled and
the dead are buried. In one sequence the poet feels guilty for his
inability to rescue his brethren, and in another he meets ''little
cotty,'' a mysterious lass who personifies the collective horror
felt within by the survivors.

In addition, Gouri has penned *The Glass Booth* (1962), a
groundbreaking account of the Adolf Eichmann trial, flowing
from his coverage of the event. He has also written and
produced a triumvirate series of documentaries about the
Holocaust—*The 81st Blow, The Last Sea,* and *Fire in the
Ashes*—that are part of his mission to drive back the obscuring
clouds of silence and refusal to allow the disaster to disappear
into the mist. Likewise, he is the author of *The Chocolate Deal*
(1964), an exquisitely crafted novella overflowing with
symbology and metaphor exploring the aftershocks that reverberate through the lives of two emotionally crippled survivors.

—Dvir Abramovich

See the essay on *The Chocolate Deal.*

GRADE, Chaim

Nationality: Russian. **Born:** Vilna, Lithuania, 1910 (immigrated to the United States, 1948, naturalized citizen, 1960). **Family:** Married (wife died in the Holocaust). **Career:** Writer and journalist. Member, Young Vilna writers' group, 1930s. **Awards:** William and Janice Epstein Fiction award, Jewish Book Council of the National Jewish Welfare Board, 1968, for *The Well;* Remembrance award, World Federation of Bergen-Belsen Associations, 1969, for *The Seven Little Lanes;* American Academy for Jewish Research award; B'nai B'rith award for excellence; Jewish Heritage award for excellence in literature, 1976; Jewish Book award for fiction, Jewish Book Council, 1978, for *The Yeshiva.* D.H.L.: Jewish Theological Seminary, 1961, and Union College, 1972. **Died:** 26 June 1982.

PUBLICATIONS

Novels

Ha-Anuga. 1962; as *The Agunah,* 1974.
The Well (translation of *Der brunem*). 1967.
Tsemah Atlas (2 vols.). 1968; as *The Yeshiva,* 1976 (vol. 1), 1977 (vol. 2).
Milhemet ha yetser [The Moralists]. 1970.
Rabbis and Wives (English translation). 1982.
The Sacred and the Profane (English translation). 1997.

Short Stories

The Seven Little Lanes (English translation). 1972.
Di kloyz un di gas [Synagogue and Street]. 1974.

Poetry

Yo [Yes]. 1936.
Mussernikes. 1939.
Farwaksene vegn [Dangerous Paths]. 1947.
Oyf di khurves [On the Ruins]. 1947.
Der mamme's tsavue [The Mother's Will]. 1949.
Shain fun farlorene shtern [The Light of Extinguished Stars]. 1950.

Memoir

Der mames shabosim. 1958; as *My Mother's Sabbath Days,* 1986.

Other

Dereth [Generations]. 1945.
Peletim [The Refugees]. 1947.

Der shulhoyf [The Synagogue Courtyard]. 1958.
Der mentsh fun fayer [The Man of Fire]. 1962.
Oyf mayn veg tsu dir [On My Way to You]. 1969.
Der shtumer minzen [The Silent Minzen]. 1976.

*

Film Adaptation: *The Quarrel,* 1991, from the short story ''My Quarrel with Hersh Rasseyner.''

Critical Study: *Havayah ve-shivrah 'al-pi yetsirato ba-prozah shel Hayim Gradeh* (dissertation) by Chana Stohrer, Bar-llan University, 1999.

*   *   *

The Holocaust looms large in the work of Yiddish writer Chaim Grade. Although only some of Grade's poetry and fiction directly address it, much of his work exists in reaction to the events of that period. His early work, particularly his poetry, mourns the loss of his family and friends to the Nazi death machine. In pieces such as *The Yeshiva* and *Der mames shabosim (My Mother's Sabbath Days),* on the other hand, Grade turns to his experiences in pre-war Lithuania. Rather than focus on the tragedy that befell Lithuanian Jewry, works such as these recall the intense intellectual and moral debates that defined that community in its prime. Although he has often been compared to the popular Jewish writer **Isaac Bashevis Singer,** Grade never wrote for a mainstream audience. His work is dense and philosophical, often difficult for non-Jews to grasp. At its core Grade's work struggles with the question of what it means to be Jewish—both before and after the cataclysm of the Holocaust.

Grade was born in Vilna, Lithuania, in 1910. After his father, a Hebrew teacher, died when Grade was a young boy, his mother worked at a fruit stand to provide her son with a traditional education. Grade attended several yeshivot and studied under Rabbi Avraham-Shaye Karelitz, a proponent of the mussar movement. The mussarists, an ascetic, ethical-religious sect of Judaism, sought to breathe new life into what they viewed as stultified religious practice. They aimed to develop in their students a moral religious personality, often through close observation and ascetic self-abnegation. When he was twenty-two, however, Grade abandoned his religious studies in favor of writing poetry. He was drawn to the Young Vilna, a group of artists who strove to forge a vital and modern Yiddish literature. In 1936 Grade published *Yo*, his first book of poetry. Three years later he completed the long narrative poem *Mussarniks*, which introduced the themes to which he would return in much of his later work. Through the autobiographical protagonist, Chaim Vilner, Grade dramatized the events that had pushed him away from the yeshiva. Vilner is caught between the rigid mussar traditions and the allure of the modern world.

Grade survived the Holocaust by escaping to the Soviet Union in 1941, but his wife, mother, and most of his yeshiva and literary friends were murdered. Grade's first work published after the war, a series of poems entitled *Mit Dayn Guf oyn Mayne Hent* (*With Your Body in My Hands*), was dedicated to his wife. In these poems Grade cast his personal love and loss in terms of a national identity, mourning those who perished and describing the survivors in an effort to confront the tragedy that had befallen the Jewish people.

For the most part Grade turned away from poetry and toward fiction after *Mit Dayn Guf oyn Mayne Hent*. After moving from the Soviet Union to Paris in 1946 and then to the United States in 1948, Grade published the short story "My Quarrel with Hersh Rasseyner." The story portrays two Holocaust survivors—Chaim Vilner, the same character who appeared in *Mussarniks*, and another yeshiva student—who are accidentally reunited in a Paris metro station in 1948. The old acquaintances pick up an intellectual debate that the Holocaust had interrupted. Vilner is a secular Jewish writer who had lost his religious faith in God long ago; Hersh Rasseyner is a mussarist teacher who runs a yeshiva for orphans. As the men spend the day together, alternating between mourning their common losses and debating their diametrically opposed views of God and the world, it becomes clear that the Holocaust did not stifle either man's appetite for life. The experience of the Holocaust only reinforced the teacher's faith in God and the writer's faith in himself. In "My Quarrel" Grade also made it clear that, even in the wake of the mass destruction of European Jewry, the dialogue over Jewish identity—and particularly the question about what can be considered a Jewish way of life—needed to be resumed.

"My Quarrel" also indicated that Grade's feelings toward pre-war Lithuania had changed radically since the Holocaust. This shift was again on display in *The Yeshiva*, Grade's masterful two-volume novel set in pre-war Poland. In this work Grade again recreated the yeshivas of his youth. Rather than simply rebel against the mussars as he did in *Mussarniks*, though, the character Chaim Vilner (making another appearance in Grade's work) finds a path between secularism and the repressive mussarist worldview. Vilner becomes a follower of Reb Avraham-Shaye (a fictional recreation of Grade's own childhood teacher), who brings harmony to the two main characters. Similarly in *Der mames shabosim*, Grade recalled—and mourned—the world of his childhood. The intensity with which Grade addressed religious debates marks most of his works.

Grade's literary method and views on human existence were unique. He was one of very few novelists who chose the internal world of Jewish scholarship as their subject. But to say that Grade is an intellectual writer is not to imply that his work is not personal—or profound. The intense ethical debates that

frame much of his fiction mirrored Grade's own intellectual and spiritual struggle; the pre-war eastern European milieu that leaps off the pages of his novels was also Grade's own. By focusing on Jewish scholarship Grade did not turn his back on the events of the Holocaust or seek to retire to a Lithuania of sepia-tinted memory. Instead, he emphasized that Jewish intellectual discourse could continue in the wake of the Holocaust—and, indeed, that it must.

—Rebecca Stanfel

See the essays on *My Mother's Sabbath Days* and "My Quarrel with Hersh Rasseyner."

GRASS, Günter (Wilhelm)

Pseudonym: Artur Knoff. **Nationality:** German. **Born:** Danzig, 16 October 1927. **Education:** Danzig Volksschule and Gymnasium; stonemason's apprentice, Düsseldorf, 1947–48; studied sculpture and painting, Düsseldorf Academy of Art, 1948–52, and Berlin Academy of Fine Arts, 1953–56. **Military Service:** Joined the Hitler Youth, 1930s; German military, 1943–46: wounded in action, 1945, prisoner of war, Marienbad, Czechoslovakia, released 1946. **Family:** Married 1) Anna Margareta Schwartz in 1954 (divorced 1978), three sons and one daughter; 2) Ute Grunert in 1979. **Career:** Worked at a variety of jobs after the war while in school, including on farms, in a potash mine, as a dealer in the black market, as a tombstone cutter, and as a drummer in a jazz band, 1946–56; member, Gruppe 47, beginning in 1955; sculptor and writer, Paris, 1956–60. Party member, 1982–93, and campaign worker, 1965, 1968, 1972, 1987, and 1998, Social Democratic Party (SPD). Lived in Calcutta, India, 1987–88. Since 1976 cofounder and coeditor, *L.* President, Berlin Academy of Fine Arts, 1983–86. **Awards:** Suddeutscher Rund Funk Lyrikpreis, 1955; Gruppe 47 prize, 1958; City of Bremen prize, 1959; German Critics prize, 1960; Foreign book prize (France), 1962; Georg Büchner prize, 1965; Fontaine prize, 1968; Heuss prize, 1969; Mondello prize (Palermo) and Carl von Ossiersky medal, both in 1977; International literary award, Viareggio-Versilia prize, and Majkowski medal, all in 1978; Vienna literature prize, 1980; Feltrinelli prize, 1982; Leonhard Frank Ring, 1988; Karel Capek prize (Czech Republic), 1994; Nobel prize for literature, 1999. Honorary degrees: Kenyon College, 1965; Harvard University, 1976; University of Poznan, 1990; University of Gdansk, 1993; Free University Berlin, 1999. **Member:** American Academy of Arts and Sciences (honorary member).

PUBLICATIONS

Collections

Gesammelte Gedichte. 1971.
Zeichnen und Schreiben: Das bildnerische Werk des Schriftstellers Günter Grass, edited by Anselm Dreher (2 vols.). 1982; as *Graphics and Writing,* 1983.
Bd. 1: Zeichnungen und Texte 1954–1977 [Vol. 1: Drawings and Words 1954–1977]. 1982.
Bd. 2: Radierungen und Texte 1972–1982 [Vol. 2: Etchings and Words 1972–1982]. 1984.

Novels

Die Blechtrommel. 1959, as *The Tin Drum,* 1961.
Katz und Maus. 1961; as *Cat and Mouse,* 1963.
Hundejahre, 1963. as *Dog Years,* 1965.
Örtlich betäubt. 1969; as *Local Anaesthetic,* 1970.
Aus dem Tagebuch einer Schnecke. 1972, as *From the Diary of a Snail,* 1973.
Mariazuehren. 1973; as *Inmarypraise,* 1974.
Der Butt. 1977, as *The Flounder,* 1978.
Das Treffen in Telgte. 1979, as *The Meeting at Telgte,* 1979.
Kopfgeburten; Oder die Deutschen sterben aus. 1980; as *Headbirths; or the Germans are Dying Out,* 1982.
Die Rättin. 1986; as *The Rat,* 1986.
Unkenrufe. 1992; as *The Call of the Toad,* 1992.
Ein weites Feld. 1995; as *Too Far Afield,* 2000.

Plays

Stoffreste (ballet), music by Aribert Reimann (produced Essen, 1957). 1960.
Hochwasser [Flood] (produced Frankfurt, 1957). 1963; in *Four Plays,* 1967.
Onkel, Onkel (produced Cologne, 1958). 1965; in *Four Plays,* 1967.
Fünf Köche (ballet; produced Bonn, 1959).
Zweiunddreissig Zähne (produced 1959.)
Beritten hin und zuruck (produced Frankfurt, 1959). As *Rocking Back and Forth,* 1968.
Noch zehn Minuten bis Buffalo [Only Ten Minutes to Buffalo] (produced Bochum, 1959). Published with *Hochwasser,* 1967; in *Four Plays,* 1967.
Die bösen Köche (produced Berlin, 1961). 1957; as *The Wicked Cooks,* 1964.
Goldmäulchen (produced Munich, 1963).
Die Plebejer proben den Aufstand: Ein deutsches Trauerspiel (produced Berlin, 1966). 1965; as *The Plebeians Rehearse the Uprising: A German Tragedy,* 1966.
Four Plays (includes *Flood; Onkel, Onkel; Only Ten Minutes to Buffalo; The Wicked Cooks*). 1967.
Davor, adaptation of the novel (produced Berlin, 1969). 1973; as *Max: A Play,* 1972.

Die Vogel Scheuchen (ballet; produced Berlin, 1970).

Screenplays: *Katz und Maus,* 1967, *Die Blechtrommel,* 1979.

Radio Plays: *Noch zehn Minuten nach Buffalo,* 1962; *Eine offentliche Diskussion,* 1963; *Die Plebejer proben den Aufstand,* 1966; *Hochwasser,* 1977.

Poetry

Die Vorzuge der Windhuhner [The Advantages of Windfowl]. 1956.
Gleisdreieck [Rail Triangle]. 1960.
Selected Poems (English and German). 1966.
Gedichte. 1967.
Ausgefragt: Gedichte und Zeichnungen [Questioned]. 1967; as *New Poems,* 1968.
Poems of Günter Grass. 1969.
Liebe gepruft: Sieben Gedichte mit sieben Radierungen. 1974.
Mit Sophie in die Pilze gegangen. 1976.
In the Egg and Other Poems (includes poems from *Selected Poems* and *New Poems*). 1977.
Kinderlied: Poems and Etchings (English and German). 1982.
Ach, Butt, dein Mächen geht böse aus: Gedichte und Radierungen. 1983.
Gedichte und Kurzprosa, edited by Anita Overwien-Neuhaus and Volker Neuhaus. 1987.
Die Gedichte 1955–1986. 1988.
Tierschutz. 1990.
Novemberland: Selected Poems, 1956–1993 (English and German). 1996.

Short Story

Mein Jahrhundert. 1999; as *My Century,* 1999.

Other

Die Ballerina. 1963.
Über das Selbstverständliche. 1968; as *Speak Out! Speeches, Open Letters, Commentaries,* 1969.
Über meinen Lehrer Döblin, und andere Vorträge. 1968.
Briefe über die Grenze, with Pavel Kohout. 1968.
Dokumente zur politischen Wirkung. 1971.
Der Bürger und seine Stimme (essays and speeches). 1974.
Denkzettel: Politische Reden und Aufsätze 1965–1976. 1978.
Aufsätze zur literatur. 1980.
Wiederstand lernen. 1984.
On Writing and Politics 1967–1983. 1985.
Meine grüne Wiese: Kurzprosa [My Green Meadow: Short Prose]. 1987.
Zunge zeigen. 1988; as *Show Your Tongue,* 1989.
Deutscher lastenausgleich: Wider das dumpfe Einheitsgebot: Reden und Gespräche. 1990; as *Two States—One Nation,* 1990.

Ein Schnäppchen namens DDR: Letzte Reden vom Glockengeläut. 1990.

Gegen die verstreichende Zeit: Reden, Aufsätze, und Gespräche, 1989–1991. 1991.

Meine grüne Wiese: Geschichten und Zeichnungen [My Green Meadow: Stories and Drawings]. 1992.

Cat and Mouse and Other Writings, edited by A. Leslie Willson. 1994.

Die deutschen und ihre Dichter. 1995.

Meine grüne Wiese: Kurzprosa und Geschichten [My Green Meadow: Short Prose and Stories] 1997.

Fundsachen für Nichtleser. 1997.

Fünf Jahrzehnte: Ein Werkstattbericht, edited by G. Fritze Margull. 2001.

*

Film Adaptations: *Katz und Maus,* 1966; *Die Blechtrommel,* 1979 (as *Le Tambour,* 1979, and *Tin Drum,* 1979); *Die Rättin* (television), 1997.

Bibliography: *Günter Grass: A Bibliography, 1955–1975* by Patrick O'Neill, 1976.

Critical Studies: *Günter Grass: A Critical Essay* by Norris Wilson Yates, 1967; *Günter Grass* by W. Gordon Cunliffe, 1969; *Günter Grass* by Kurt Lothar Tank, 1969; *Günter Grass* by Iréne Leonard, 1974; *Günter Grass' The Tin Drum: A Critical Commentary* by John D. Simons, 1974; *Günter Grass* by Keith Miles, 1975; *The 'Danzig trilogy' of Günter Grass: A Study of The Tin Drum, Cat and Mouse, and Dog Years* by John Reddick, 1975; *Günter Grass: Wort, Zahl, Gott* by Michael Harscheidt, 1976; *Günter Grass: The Literature of Politics* by A.V. Subiotto, 1978; *Günter Grass: The Writer in a Pluralist Society* by Michael Hollington, 1980; *Günter Grass in America: The Early Years* by Ray Lewis White, 1981; *Adventures of a Flounder: Critical Essays on Günter Grass' Der Butt,* edited by Gertrud Bauer Pickar, 1982; *The Narrative Works of Günter Grass: A Critical Interpretation,* 1982, and *Günter Grass: Katz und Maus,* 1992, both by Noel Thomas; *"The Fisherman and His Wife": Günter Grass's The Flounder in Critical Perspective,* edited by Siegfried Mews, 1983; *Günter Grass* by Richard H. Lawson, 1985; *Günter Grass* by Ronald Hayman, 1985; *Critical Essays on Günter Grass,* edited by Patrick O'Neill, 1987; *Understanding Günter Grass* by Alan Frank Keele, 1988; *Günter Grass His Critics* by Siegfried Mews, 1996; *Günter Grass' "ein weites feld" and the German Democratic Republic* by Hans-Dieter Senff, 1998; *Metaphors in Grass' Die Blechtrommel* by Antoinette T. Delaney, 1999; *Günter Grass Revisited* by Patrick O'Neill, 1999; *A Study of the Life and Works of Günter Grass* by Julian Preece, 2000.

*   *   *

The German writer and artist Günter Grass has published numerous works of literature as well as collections of essays, commentaries, letters, speeches, interviews, and paintings and drawings. He has been the winner of major awards, including the Nobel Prize for Literature in 1999. He was made an honorary member of the American Academy of Arts and Sciences, served as the president of the Berlin Academy of Arts (1983–86), and received honorary doctorates from Kenyon College (1965), Harvard University (1976), and the universities of Poznan (1990) and Gdansk (1993) in Poland.

Grass's first novel, *Die Blechtrommel* (*The Tin Drum*), published in 1959, has become one of the best-known works of world literature. In 1961 he published *Katz und Maus* (*Cat and Mouse*), followed by *Hundejahre* (*Dog Years*) in 1963. This so-called Danzig Trilogy deals with the problems of *Vergangenheitsbewältigung,* that is, the coming to terms with the Nazi past and its heinous crimes against the Jewish and Polish people. Grass's readers have sometimes called him—without his approval—the "conscience of the nation."

In 1969 Grass published *Örtlich betäubt* (*Local Anaesthetic*), a book that criticized the fanatic Nazi past as well as the radical elements in some ideologies of the 1960s. He documented a politically active period in his campaign novel *Aus dem Tagebuch einer Schnecke* (*From the Diary of a Snail*). Published in 1972, the book reflected Grass's sympathy for the Social Democratic Party (SPD) under Willy Brandt (1913–92), who became one of his best friends. The novel also retraces the horrible fate of the Jews from Danzig (now Gdansk). Five years later, in 1977, there appeared the epic novel *Der Butt* (*The Flounder*), a satirical account of the war between the sexes. A fictitious meeting between German baroque poets is the setting for *Das Treffen in Telgte* (*Meeting at Telgte*), published in 1979. Grass's concept of a *Kulturnation,* that is, the premise that cultural heritage determines national identity, emerged in this work. The following year his novel *Kopfgeburten* (*Headbirths*) signified the beginning of a new phase, sometimes referred to as Grass's "Orwellian decade." Other literary and artistic creations during the 1980s included *Die Rättin* (1986; *The Rat*), *Zunge zeigen* (1988; *Show Your Tongue*), and *Totes Holz* (1990; *Dead Wood*).

Global problems such as the nuclear arms race, the growth of population in developing countries, and the alarming increase in environmental pollution have been among the most important issues for Grass. *The Rat* explores these issues in depth, and the author demonstrates the urgency of a higher ethical standard in dealing with modern global crises. Trips to India and China, as well as publications by Brandt and the Club of Rome, strongly influenced his reflections on the struggles of the Third World in *The Flounder, Headbirths, The Rat,* and *Show Your Tongue.* The last is a travelogue in which drawings of "pavement dwellers" accompany a literary account of the lives of people who have little hope.

In *Unkenrufe* (1992; *The Call of the Toad*) Grass went beyond the bleak imagery of the 1980s, with German-Polish relations and the reunification of Germany forming the fabric for a fictive love story. *Ein weites Feld* (1995; *Wide Field*), which was torn apart by critics, contrasts writing and politics. Leading up to its publication, Grass wrote a number of essays and made public appearances against the efforts at German reunification. *Mein Jahrhundert* (1999; *My Century*), which portrays the twentieth century in chronological order, is written from a personal point of view.

Grass's works have been both applauded and criticized. Nevertheless, they have always been noticed, especially in times when not very many people wanted to hear or read about the German past of National Socialism and the Holocaust. Grass's international fame has been underscored by the Nobel Prize and the fact that all of his works have been translated into English.

—Mark Gruettner

See the essays on *From the Diary of a Snail* and *The Tin Drum.*

GREENBERG, Uri Zvi

Nationality: Ukrainian. **Born:** Bialykamien, Ukraine, 17 October 1898. **Military Service:** Austrian army, 1915–17; deserted, 1917. Fought with guerrilla groups seeking to establish an independent Jewish nation in Palestine, 1940s. **Career:** Lived in Warsaw and Berlin; moved to Palestine, 1924; worked for the Revisionist movement, Warsaw, 1929–39. Contributor, *Davar,* newspaper of the Labor Party; Revisionist party representative, Zionist Congresses, Poland; active in right-wing politics. Member, Israeli parliament, one term. **Award:** Israel prize, 1957. **Died:** 8 May 1981.

PUBLICATIONS

Collections

Kol ketavav (15 vols.). 1990.
Ma'amarim. 2001.

Poetry

Ergits oyf felder. 1915.
In tsaytens roysh. 1919.
Farnakhtengold. 1921.
Mefisto. 1921.
Emah gedolah ve-yareah. 1925.
Ha-Gavrut ha-'olah. 1926.
Hazon ehad ha-ligyonot. 1927.
Anakre'on 'al kotev ha-'itsavon 11 sha'are shir. 1928.
Kelev bayit. 1929.
Ezor magen u-ne'um ben ha-dam. 1929.
Sefer ha-kitrug veha-emunah. 1936.
Yerushalayim shel matah. As *Jerusalem,* 1939.

Rehovot hanahar: Sefer ha'iliyot yehakoah. 1951; as *Streets of the River: The Book of Dirges and Power,* in *Anthology of Modern Hebrew Poetry,* 1966.
The Mercy of Sorrow (English translations). 1965.
Mivhar mi-shirav. 1968.
Albatros. 1977.
Undzere oyseyes glien. 1978.

Other

Krig oyf dem erd. 1923.
Kelape tish'im ve-tish'ah. 1928.
Ha-Don, with Peretz Hirschbein. 1931.
The Truth about Revisionism, with Eliezer Livneh, Aba Ahimeir, and Vladimir Jabotinsky. 1935.
Uri Tsevi Grinberg bi-melot lo shemonim. 1977.

*

Critical Studies: "The Tenth Muse—A Programatic Term in Uri Zvi Grinberg's Poetry and Journalism," in *Chulyot,* 1, 1993, pp. 124–47, and "The Albatrosses of Young Yiddish Poetry: Uri Zvi Grinberg's Albatros," in *Prooftexts,* 15, 1995, pp. 89–108, both by A. Lipsker; "Uri Zvi Greenberg between Isaiah and Plato" by Dr. Pinhas Ginossar, in *Hamatkonet Vehadmut,* edited by H. Weiss, 2000; "Poetry and History: The Case of U.Z. Greenberg" by Yehuda Friedlander, in *Israel Affairs,* 7(7), 2001.

* * *

Although he did not experience the systematic destruction of European Jewry directly, having escaped Poland in 1930 for Palestine, Uri Zvi Greenberg's personal catastrophe carved deep cicatrices in the young poet's soul and led him to plunge his own autobiographical and psychological waters to sculpt characters and tales based on his own "heart of darkness." In *Streets of the River* the prophet-poet stirs the bleakest depths of his seared soul and unveils a magisterial, philosophical treatise that renders the Holocaust in an inventive, outstanding fashion. It is noteworthy that Greenberg, a scion of a Galician Hassidic family, was au courant with the traditional Jewish model of liturgy (*kinah*) based upon the Book of Lamentations, which depicts, among others, the fall of Jerusalem and the exile to Babylon. Yet, Greenberg felt the need to partly jettison the fettering canonical shackles of the past in his search to craft and evoke the vast dehumanization and murder, as well as his personal grief. As a result, his *ars poetica* was a braiding of German expressionism and the ancient paradigms of Hebrew poetry, thus creating a whirlpool of rasping invectives, abrupt shifts in tone and tempo, and apocalyptic visions reminiscent of Jeremiah and the Midrashim.

It is also significant that as a soldier in the Austrian army in the years 1915–17, Greenberg was witness to the brutal

121

pogroms that took place in Poland. These seismic events ruptured the core of Jewish society and created an aperture from which it never recovered. It is not too much to say that the waves of anti-Semitic attacks deeply affected the young poet and left an indelible imprint upon his work that would become an exemplar of secular national sorrow. What's more, Greenberg's recurring frustration and anger were amplified by the fact that his warnings of an impending apocalypse were not given any credence by the sanguine populace but rather rejected as fanciful, adding to his rage. It followed that Greenberg would proclaim himself as the castigating oracle, the only one capable of recording and wrestling with this traumatic and terrible calamity.

The cycle of poems is typically infused with an extreme, violent polemic against the pillaging gentiles, freighted by manifold exclamation marks, stirring metaphors, epic images, and free, lengthy verse. And while Greenberg promotes the poetic persona à la Walt Whitman, the emphasis is often on the national myth and the collective memory of the Jewish disaster. Often is the case that Greenberg, with a nod to the early Hebrew poets, references quintessential Jewish symbols such as the family at the Sabbath table while at the same time accentuating his own voice as a metonymy for the whole people. As a matter of fact, Greenberg frequently describes the unspeakable slaughter through the mourning of his own family, affirming the individual voice and stressing the universality of the pain. In doing so the reader is positioned and is imperceptibly co-opted into imaginatively identifying with the experience from which they were excluded. It is thus not surprising that in the immediate aftermath of the Holocaust, given the paucity of Hebrew narratives responding to the mind-numbing terror, Greenberg's poetry was used by the state in Yom Ha'shoah commemorations and gradually assumed center stage in the nascent Israeli state's official position toward the remembering of the Holocaust.

—Dvir Abramovich

See the essay on *Streets of the River: The Book of Dirges and Power.*

GROSSMAN, David

Nationality: Israeli. **Born:** Jerusalem, 25 January 1954. **Education:** Hebrew University, B.A. in philosophy and theater 1976. **Family:** Married Michal; two sons. **Career:** Writer. Also worked as a journalist, Kol Israel (Israeli Radio); contributor to periodicals, including *Koteret Rashit.* **Awards:** Ministry of Education prize for children's literature (Israel), 1983, for *Du-krav;* Prime Minister's prize for Hebrew literature, 1984; Israeli Publisher's Association prize for best novel,

1985, for *Hiyukh ha-gedi;* Vallombrosa prize (Italy), 1989; Nelly Sachs prize (Germany), 1992. **Agent:** Deborah Harris, The Harris/Elon Agency, P.O. Box 4143, Jerusalem 91041, Israel.

PUBLICATIONS

Novels

Hiyukh ha-gedi. 1983; as *The Smile of the Lamb,* 1990.
'Ayen 'erekh-ahavah. 1986; as *See Under: Love,* 1989.
Sefer hadikduk hapnimi. 1992; as *The Book of Internal Grammar,* 1994.
Yesh yeladim zig-zag. 1994; as *The Zigzag Kid,* 1997.
She-tihi li ha-sakin. 1998; as *Be My Knife,* 2002.

Short Stories

Ratz [The Jogger]. 1983..

Play

Gan Riki: Mahazeh bi-shete ma 'arakhot. 1988; as *Riki's Kindergarten.*

Other

Ha-Zeman ha-tsahov (nonfiction). 1987; as *The Yellow Wind,* 1988.
Hanochachim hanifkadim (nonfiction). 1992; as *Sleeping on a Wire: Conversations with Palestinians in Israel,* 1993.

Other (for children)

Du-krav. 1984; as *Duel,* 1998.
Itamar metayel 'al kirot. 1986.
Ach chadash l'gamrei. 1986.
Itamar pogesh arnav. 1988.
Itamar mikhtav. 1988.
Itamar ye 'koval ha 'ksamin ha 'shachor. 1992.
Sefer ha-siim shel Fozz. 1994.
Hayo haytem shnei kofim. 1996.
Misheu larutz ito. 2000.

*

Critical Studies: "Interview with David Grossman" by Elena Lappin, in *Jewish Quarterly,* 41(4), Winter 1994, p. 26; *The Project of Expression in Modernist Literature and Music: David Fogel, Arnold Schoenberg, David Grossman* (dissertation) by Eric Stephen Zakim, University of California, Berkeley, 1996; "David Grossman: Language and Self-Discovery" by Kurt Kreiler, in *World Press Review,* 47(11), 2000, p. 13;

''Assassinations: Opposing Views by Amos Oz and David Grossman,'' in *Time,* 20 September 2001.

* * *

Born in Jerusalem in 1954 to working-class parents, David Grossman is the preeminent Joseph figure to the three generations of Israeli writers preceding him. As lineal heir to a modernist Hebrew literary tradition as well as self-conscious sojourner in the ''Egypt'' of international postmodernism, he has assumed the mantle of state-generation forebears like **Amos Oz** and **A.B. Yehoshua**, while at the same time pushing Israeli literature metaphorically *hutz l'aretz,* beyond the established borders of homeland. His ascendancy is notable as much for its celerity as its diversity, his output being a many-colored coat. After a first, unremarkable collection of short fiction, *The Jogger,* the novels *The Smile of the Lamb, See Under: Love, The Book of Intimate Grammar, The Zigzag Kid,* and *Be My Knife* followed in quick succession to increasing acclaim.

Soon after it was translated, *See Under: Love* (1989) was classed by reviewers with William Faulkner's *The Sound and the Fury,* **Gunter Grass**'s *The Tim Drum,* Gabriel García Márquez's *One Hundred Years of Solitude,* and Salman Rushdie's *Midnight Children.* Absent the always-invidious nature of such comparisons, what prompts them in this case is the sheer prodigality of Grossman's world making. Through a fierce inventiveness and their fidelity to a preadult world of interior consciousness, *See Under: Love, The Book of Intimate Grammar* (1994), and *The Zigzag Kid* (1997) stake the kind of Joycean claims for which the only analogue (and precedent) in modern Jewish literature is the American Henry Roth's *Call It Sleep.* Not surprisingly perhaps, Grossman has also penned 10 books of children's fiction and as a child himself acted on Israeli radio, with a knack for mimicry.

Thus beyond an almost obligatory play with narrative form (a postmodern given), like Roth, Grossman has an astonishing ear for dialect and register, from the anachronistic ''formulation'' Hebrew at the end of *See Under: Love* to the macaronics of the early 1960s immigrant Israelis' Yiddish-Polish and Hebrew vernacular in *The Book of Intimate Grammar.* Indeed it is in his Bakhtinian generosity to characters' idiolects—what might be called an ethic of voice—that Grossman chiefly excels, rivaling the elder Yehoshua's achievement in *Mr. Mani. The Smile of the Lamb* (1990), Grossman's first novel, while it may overreach, sets the precedent for vocally differentiated speech style and mental landscapes of the ''other'' by alternating four narratives in four voices: a Sephardi, a Polish survivor, a female psychotherapist, and an iconic Arab named Khilmi who converses with children in an ''infant tongue.''

If the figure of Khilmi is something of an allegorical misfire—Irving Howe called him a heavy-handed Karataev to the novel's Pierre Bezhukhov—the novel itself takes on the freighted and immediately contemporary matter of the Palestinian-Israeli conflict. Similarly *See Under: Love,* for all its sui generis formal daring, takes on two standing taboos in Israeli culture: the Holocaust as the representational property of its survivors and their legatees (Grossman is neither), and as material fact not scrim for elaborate fictionalization. Yet both these novels connect Grossman with Israeli authors of an earlier generation like Oz and Yehoshua as well as writers of many a contemporary national literature in their resolute foregrounding of collective experience. Where *The Smile of the Lamb* is a young novelist's first book and *See Under: Love* is held hostage to its composite structure and occasional ostentation, *The Book of Intimate Grammar* signifies that rare triumph, not a forging of a national conscience yet created, but a hammering of it as already owned and incandescent, in a tense its main character, Aron, calls ''the present continuous.'' Its setting is the Six-Day War of 1967, yet its thrust is deeply cultural rather than political critique in an obvious sense, which attests to Grossman's distinctive brand of humanism.

In the course of writing fiction Grossman also published *The Yellow Wind* (1988) and *Sleeping on a Wire* (1993), interviews with, respectively, West Bank Palestinians and settlers, and Arab Israelis. Tapping into his journalistic roots (he has hosted an early-morning radio show for many years) and capitalizing on his knowledge of Arabic, these books manifest Grossman's equally important public persona as organic intellectual, one who hammers at the forge of his nation's conscience in clear and indeed controversial view. *See Under: Love,* however, remains Grossman's towering accomplishment thus far, not only for its purely novelistic virtues but because of its fatidic weight and its therapeutic heralding of his countrymen and women into a *lieu de mémoire*—the place of the Shoah in Israel's psychocultural life—that it had hitherto either repressed or held at a near distance. In keeping with the model of the biblical Joseph, Grossman's novel ensures that the bones of an abandoned generation will be brought back to the Land of Israel to be remembered and claimed anew.

—Adam Zachary Newton

See the essay on *See Under: Love.*

GROSSMAN, Vasily (Semenovich)

Nationality: Russian. **Born:** Berdichev, Ukraine, ca. 12 December 1905. **Education:** Moscow University (now Moscow M. V. Lomonosov State University), 1924–29, degree in chemistry 1929. **Family:** Married 1) Anna Petrovna Matsuk in 1928 (divorced), one daughter; 2) Olga Mikhailovna. **Career:** Industrial safety engineer and chemical engineer, Donbass mines, until 1932; professional writer, 1932–64. World War II correspondent, *Krasnaya zvezda* newspaper, Moscow, 1941–45;

contributor of sketches and short stories to periodicals, including *Krasnaya zvezda, Literaturnaya gazeta,* and *Novy mir.* **Award:** Received Banner of Labor decoration for his writings, 1955. **Died:** 14 September 1964.

PUBLICATIONS

Novels

Glück auf. 1934.
Stepan Kolchugin. 1937.
Yunost Kolchugina. 1939; as *Kolchugin's Youth,* 1946.
Narod bessmerten. 1942; as *The People Are Immortal,* 1943; as *No Beautiful Nights,* 1944.
Za pravoe delo. 1955.
Vse techet. 1970; as *Forever Flowing,* 1972.
Zhizn' i sud'ba. 1980; as *Life and Fate,* 1985.
The Sistine Madonna. 1989.

Short Stories

Staryi uchitel'. 1962.
Osenniaia buria. 1965.
Dobro vam! 1967.

Play

Esli verit' pifagoreitsam [If You Believe the Pythagoreans]. 1946.

Other

Rasskazy. 1937.
Stalingrad: Sentyabr' 1942–yanvar' 1943 [Stalingrad: September 1942–January 1943]. 1943.
With the Red Army in Poland and Byelorussia (First Byelorussian Front, June–July, 1944 (English translation). 1945.
Gody voiny. 1946; as *The Years of War (1941–1945),* 1946.
Povesti i rasskazy. 1950.
Povesti, rasskazy, ocherki. 1958.
Na evreiskie temy: Izbrannoe v dvukh tomakh. 1985.

Editor, with Ilya Ehrenburg, *Chernaia kniga: O zlodeiskom povsemestnom ubiistve evreev nemetsko-fashistskimi zakhvachikami vo vremenno-okkupirovannykh raionakh Sovetskogo Soiuza i v lageriakh unichtozheniia Pol'shi vo vremia voiny 1941–1945.* 1980; as *The Black Book: The Ruthless Murder of Jews by German-Fascist Invaders throughout the Temporarily Occupied Regions of the Soviet Union and in the Death Camps of Poland during the War of 1941–1945,* 1981.

*

Critical Studies: *Stalingrad Vasiliia Grossmana* by Semen Lipkin, 1986; *The Bones of Berdichev—The Life and Fate of Vasily Grossman* by John and Carol Garrard, 1996.

* * *

Soviet Ukrainian Jewish writer Vasily Semenovich Grossman, one of the greatest chroniclers of the Holocaust, was born, it is believed, in the Ukrainian town of Berdichev. Although Berdichev, situated to the west of Kiev, was significant for the invading German armies because of its strategically placed rail and road links, its much greater importance lay in the fact that it was known as the Jewish capital of the area, having been a crucial center of Judaism and retaining at the time of the Nazi invasion a population that was more than 50 percent ethnically Jewish. The town fell completely into German hands on 17 July 1941; witnesses, however, confirm that the mass extermination of the Jewish population of Berdichev commenced some 10 days earlier.

The precise place and date (probably 12 December 1905) of Grossman's birth cannot be documented with exact certainty, given the fact that no birth certificate has been traced; from photographs, letters, and other family evidence, however, it can be assumed that Grossman spent a significant part of his youth in Berdichev and that he retained a profound impression of the town as is demonstrated, for example, in certain of his fictional works and other writings. Grossman's parents were Jews, although they did not practice their faith. Grossman himself was never a practicing Jew; his own first name was Iosif, Vasily being an adopted name—and in a stark autobiographical note, written in 1947, Grossman remarks that his father, Semyon Osipovich, had been a chemical engineer and that his mother, Yekaterina Savelievna, had taught French. He also adds the date of his mother's death, 1941, mentioning briefly that she had perished in the Nazi-occupied territory of Berdichev. It is not known if Grossman's parents were married; he spent most of his early years in his mother's care and formed a great emotional attachment to her, together with enormous admiration for her personal qualities of dignity, courage, and generosity. Grossman, however, also maintained excellent communication with his father as is clearly revealed from their correspondence that lasted up to the latter's death in 1956. Until the end of his own life Grossman carried an enormous burden of guilt for having failed to act at a critical time in order to facilitate his mother's exit from Berdichev, where she died on 15 September 1941, one of the many victims executed in cold blood and thrown into a pit by the Germans. Grossman's subsequent bravery during the time spent with the Red Army at the front from 1941 to 1945 and especially his great valor and integrity while acting as war correspondent during the Battle of Stalingrad could be interpreted as his attempt to expiate in some way his sense of blame for his mother's death.

It was during his years as a chemistry student at Moscow University (1924–29) that Grossman began to feel drawn to literature. His early first marriage to Anna Petrovna Matsuk (Galya) in 1928 was not a success, but Grossman's only child, his daughter Yekaterina (Katya), was born in January 1930. Katya was, in fact, brought up by Grossman's mother. Grossman's second wife, Olga Mikhailovna, the former wife of Boris Andreyevich Guber, did not in later years provide Grossman with the spiritual help and comfort he needed; these qualities he was to find in his relationship with Yekaterina Vasilievna, wife of the poet Nikolai Zabolotsky, and it was to her that he entrusted important materials for safekeeping at the end of his life.

On graduation from Moscow University Grossman worked as an analyst in the Donbass mines until 1932. From these harsh experiences he created his early prose work *Glück auf* in 1934. Two further collections of stories then swiftly appeared, *Happiness* and *Four Days*. In 1937 Grossman joined the Writers' Union, and he spent the next three years working on a long novel, very much in the socialist realist mode, entitled *Stepan Kolchugin*. Grossman began forging his literary career during the years of the imposition of strict controls on writers, the so-called great terror and the purges, and, although he survived physically, events surrounding him and the fates of friends and family had an enormous impact upon him. His first truly successful short prose work, *The People Are Immortal*, was based on what he had witnessed at the front in 1941; Grossman's reputation as a writer, however, was firmly established by his war reporting from the Battle of Stalingrad. Some of these articles appeared in *Pravda*.

From 1946 until his death in 1964 Grossman himself was to suffer greatly at the hands of the Soviet literary establishment, many of his works being labeled as anti-Soviet. His only play, for example, *If You Believe the Pythagoreans,* which had been written before the war, was denounced, and the publication in 1952 of *For a Just Cause,* the first part of a long novel dealing with the Battle of Stalingrad, made matters even worse. It is likely that Grossman was only "saved" by Joseph Stalin's death in 1953. In the last 10 years of his life Grossman wrote *Life and Fate,* the sequel to *For a Just Cause,* and *Forever Flowing,* his powerful and insightful analysis of Vladimir Lenin and Leninism. The manuscript of *Life and Fate* was seized and "arrested" in February 1961 by the KGB and at a subsequent interview with Mikhail Andreyevich Suslov, chief ideologist of the Party, Grossman was told that the novel would see publication "only after 250 years." The novel was, in fact, smuggled abroad and published in Switzerland in 1980. *Forever Flowing* appeared in West Germany in 1970.

Grossman was little known to later Soviet and to Western readers before his main works were published (and others republished) during the glasnost years. Although his three long novels bear witness most eloquently to the atrocities of both Adolf Hitler's Germany and Stalin's Russia, many of his deeply held beliefs and his attempts to come to terms with the

horrors he witnessed are poignantly expressed in a much shorter work, *The Sistine Madonna,* written in 1955 and not published until 1989.

—Margaret Tejerizo

See the essay on *Life and Fate.*

GRYNBERG, Henryk

Nationality: Polish. **Born:** Warsaw, 4 July 1936. **Education:** University of Warsaw, M.A. in journalism 1959; University of California, Los Angeles, 1969–71, M.A. in Russian literature 1971. **Family:** Married 1) Ruth Maria Meyers in 1964 (divorced 1966); 2) Krystyna Walczak in 1967, one daughter. **Career:** Actor and translator, Jewish State Theatre, Warsaw, 1959–67; secretary, Union of Workers of Culture and Art, 1966–67. Defected to the United States, 1967. Teaching assistant, Russian language and literature, University of California, Los Angeles, c. 1971; worked for the U.S. Information Agency and Voice of America, c. 1971–91. Also contributor and translator from English to Polish, *Kultura* (Paris), *Wiadomosci* (London), and *America Illustrated.* **Awards:** Annual literary prize, Koscielski Foundation, Switzerland, 1966, for *Zydowska wonja;* Tadeusz Borowski fellowship, Poland, 1966.

PUBLICATIONS

Novels

Zydowska wonja (novella). 1965; as *Child of the Shadows,* 1969.
Zwyciestow. 1969; as *The Victory.* 1993.
Zycie ideologiczine [Ideological Life]. 1975; with *Zycie osobiste,* 1992.
Zycie osobiste [Personal Life] (sequel to *Zycie ideologiczine*). 1979; with *Zycie ideologiczine,* 1992.
Zycie codzienne i artystyczne [Everyday and Artistic Life]. 1980.
Kadisz. 1987.

Short Stories

Ekipa "Antygona" [The Antigona Crew]. 1963.
Szkice Rodzinne [Family Sketches]. 1989.
Drohobycz, Drohobycz. 1997.
Ojczyzna [Motherland]. 1999.

Poetry

Swieto kamieni. 1964.
Antynostalgia [Anti-Nostalgia]. 1971.
Wiersze z Ameryki [Poems from America]. 1980.

Wrocilem: Wiersze Wybrane z lat 1964–1989 [I Have Returned: Poems 1964–1989]. 1991.
Rysuje w Pamieci [Sketching in Memory]. 1995.

Plays

Pamietnik Marii Koper [Maria Koper's Diary]. 1993.
Kronika [A Chronicle]. 1994.

Other

Wsord nieobecnych. 1983.
Prawda nieartystyczna [The Nonartistic Truth] (essays). 1984.
Pomnik nad Potomakiem. 1989.
Zwyciestwo. 1990.
Dziedzictwo. 1993.
Dzieci Syjonu. 1994; as *Children of Zion,* 1997.
Yalde Tsiyon: Derekh ha-tela'ot shel yalde Teheran. 1995.
Memorbuch. 2000.
Ida Kaminska (1899–1980): Grande Dame of the Yiddish Theater, with Krystyna Fisher and Michael Steinlauf. 2001.

*

Critical Studies: *Polish Writing Today,* edited by W. Weiniewska, 1967; *Henryk Grynberg* by Justyna Sobolewska, 2000.

* * *

World War II put an end to the happy childhood of Henryk Grynberg, who was three when Germans came to his native village in northeastern Poland and eight when he and his mother were rescued by the Red Army entering that region. Of his very large family only three people survived the Shoah: the writer and his mother, thanks to their "Aryan papers," and his uncle Aron, who many years later in Israel verified the author's knowledge about his family. Most of the writer's relatives died in Treblinka, and his father was murdered by a Polish bandit several months before the end of the war. Grynberg has no memory of the pre-catastrophe world. The Shoah is the world of his childhood memories, and this is the source of the power of expression in his writing. His basic creative method is that of talking about the Shoah in the most common manner. This is a counterworld described in a simple, sparse language. The artistic effect consists of the hiatus between the subject matter and the language. The writer gives up the literariness involving the decorum, which can be noticed in his debut collection of short stories, *The Antigona Crew,* in favor of the informative function. He also focuses on the composition of his works, using paradoxes, unexpected points, and rhetoric devices. "The Grave" is an example. This is the story of a Jew who avoided execution by escaping from the very brink of his grave. After the war he regularly comes to the spot of the

might-have-been execution: "This is the only family grave . . . it is good to have a grave to look after, especially that it is my grave." The writer perceives himself as a calm chronicler of the genocide history. The Holocaust seen from the perspective of personal experience and later as a fragment of the history of European anti-Semitism is the main theme of his writing.

Another traumatic experience was the contact with post-Shoah anti-Semitism during the liberation and in Communist Poland. The censorship, the growing atmosphere of state anti-Semitism, and the impossibility of artistic expression of the truth were the reasons for his emigration. In 1967 he went to California, where his mother and stepfather lived. In America Grynberg continued writing in Polish, and his works were published by Polish immigration circles.

Apart from the Holocaust evidence and the diagnosis of anti-Semitism the identity problem is another crucial theme of Grynberg's prose and poetry. All other trends of his writing are connected with it. This is the history of a false identity—the life with the Aryan papers, the denial of Jewishness, the acceptance of the identity imposed and defined by anti-Semites. On the opposite pole we have the conscious identification, the free choice of being a Jew, and the acceptance of all the ethical obligations resulting from that fact. This evolution of Grynberg's characters and literary narrators does not always parallel the evolution of the author's awareness. The crucial moment for him was when he joined Ida Kaminska's Jewish Theater in Warsaw, which was the starting point of his literary career.

The narrator of his prose and the persona of his poetry usually bear the author's features. Memory, honesty, and compassion are the elements determining his attitude toward the described world. For the truth's sake he gives more details of his family's fate during the Shoah. After the downfall of Communism he visits Poland and solves the mystery of his father's death. In *The Heritage,* consisting of the conversations with the inhabitants of his native neighborhood, he gives the name of the murderer and closes the autobiographical elements in his writing.

From then on Grynberg described the fates of others, recreating them on the basis of notes, old documents, and memoirs. Such is the nature of *Maria Koper's Diary, A Chronicle,* a play about the Lodz ghetto; *The Cabaret on the Other Side,* a play about Wladyslaw Szlengel's cabaret in the Warsaw ghetto; *Children of Zion,* a novel about the fates of Jewish children who survived the Holocaust in the lagers of communist Russia; and *The Memorbuch,* a literary presentation of the life of Adam Bromberg, a Polish Communist from before the war who survived in Russia, was an official publisher in Poland, emigrated in 1968, and died in Sweden. These works should be perceived as the fulfillment of the duty toward the Jewish nation, which is to be understood as identification with its fate and suffering and the obligation to express the essence of its history.

The latter of the enumerated books by Grynberg, *The Memorbuch,* is an extensive work. Bromberg's recollections intermingle with the minutes from the Polish parliamentary sessions before the war, which are the documents of anti-Semitism in the late 1930s. There are also some encyclopedic entries providing information on Jewish history, primarily on persecutions by the Christians in all places connected with Bromberg's life. The author intended to make *The Memorbuch* a voice concerning European or Christian anti-Semitism, which created the basis for the Holocaust through preaching hatred. It is also a story of the expulsion of the Jews from Poland in March 1968 by the Communist authorities and the passive acceptance of the Polish society. Therefore anti-Semitism is an open and eternal problem, and the memory of persecutions constitutes the obligation and the sense of writing.

Grynberg is also the author of seven books of poetry in which the dominating elements are the Holocaust and the identity problem. The perception of the Shoah in verse leads to an even more condensed dimension, and it unites the individual pain with the perspective of the contention with God, which is so characteristic of Jewish culture.

—Kazimierz Adamczyk

See the essays on *Child of the Shadows* and *The Victory.*

GURDUS, Luba (Krugman)

Nationality: American (originally Polish: immigrated to the United States, 1948, naturalized U.S. citizen, 1956). **Born:** Luba Krugman, Bialystok, 1 August 1914. **Education:** School of Applied Art, Berlin; Academy of Fine Arts, Warsaw, B.A. 1939; Institute of Fine Arts, New York University, M.A. 1952, Ph.D. in art history 1962. **Family:** Married John Gurdus in 1935; one son (deceased). **Career:** Illustrator, Bluszcz Publications, Warsaw, 1934–36, and Yedioth Aharenot, Tel-Aviv, 1947–48; director of art research, French & Co., New York, 1956–68; art researcher and historian, Frick Art Reference Library, 1968–78. Since 1978 writer and art historian. Has held memberships in several organizations related to art and the Holocaust. **Award:** Louis E. Yavner Citizen award, 1986.

PUBLICATIONS

Memoirs

They Didn't Live to See (portfolio of lithographic reproductions). 1949.
The Death Train: A Personal Account of a Holocaust Survivor. 1978.

Poetry

Painful Echoes: Poems of the Holocaust. 1985.

Other

The Self-Portrait in French Painting from Neo-Classicism to Realism (dissertation). 1966.

*

Critical Study: *Luba Krugman Gurdus: An Artist's Holocaust Remembrance* (thesis) by Maureen M. Schurr, University of Louisville, 1996.

* * *

Luba Krugman Gurdus was trained at the School of Applied Art in Berlin and at the Warsaw Academy of Fine Arts before World War II, and she received a doctorate in art history from the Institute of Fine Arts of New York University in 1962. Although Gurdus's doctoral studies concentrated on French self-portraiture, her work as a writer, an artist, and a teacher was devoted almost in its entirety to the Holocaust.

Gurdus's drawings and paintings based on her experience of the Holocaust have been exhibited in both Israel and the United States and are included in the permanent collections at Yad Vashem and elsewhere. Her artwork also forms an integral part of each of her three major publications on the Holocaust. *They Didn't Live to See* is a portfolio of 16 lithographic reproductions, predominantly scenes in Majdanek, where Gurdus succeeded in passing among the Polish prisoners. Both the book of poetry *Painful Echoes: Poems of the Holocaust* and the memoir *The Death Train: A Personal Account of a Holocaust Survivor* interweave the author's illustrations with her text. This combination of plastic and written expression by the same artist is unusual among Holocaust testimonies. Hence, in seeking to situate Gurdus's work in the broader literature, one would tend to look in separate directions: to memoirs, especially of Jewish women from Poland (for example, **Gerda Weissmann Klein** or Liliana Zuker-Bujanowska), and to artwork such as the drawings of Birkenau by Halina Olomucki. The fellow Polish Jew and Holocaust victim Bruno Schulz was also an illustrator of his own literary works, although his drawings and writing are markedly different from those of Gurdus.

Gurdus's three principal publications—the portfolio, the collection of poetry, and the memoir—tell and retell her story from the vantage points of different media and genres, overlapping at some points and supplementing one another at others. They form a single, composite whole. Thus, for instance, several of the lithographs from *They Didn't Live to See* reappear, with variants in some cases, as illustrations in the other two books. Likewise, some episodes narrated in *The Death Train* are recounted in the poems of *Painful Echoes,* as in "The Cause of Evil Is the Jew," in which Polish looters blame the brawling that breaks out among them on the supposed corrupting influence of the money of the deported Jews. But the full force of Gurdus's testimony is best registered by setting the several versions together. In the course of the release of Gurdus and her family from their first deportation at Zwierzyniec, for example, the constraints of a personal account in the memoir cannot help but focus attention on their momentary good fortune. The greater flexibility of the lyric, however, allows Gurdus to enlarge the story by aligning her perspective with that of the immediate victims of the same scene, which she does in "Deportation to Belzec" and which concludes, "*We* were driven to Belzec / For the torture of the gas" (italics added). So, too, her son's view of the "death train" itself, which is crucial to the memoir, gains an important antecedent when it is conjoined to the boy's toy train in the poem "Corner" and its corresponding illustration. (See also the reproduction of the boy's own drawing.) Finally, Gurdus brings *The Death Train* to an abrupt end at the moment when, looking out the window with her sister, Mira, as the Russian troops enter Warsaw, they witness the scene the other family members "didn't live to see." Thus, the closing words of the memoir also serve as the title of the portfolio.

They Come and Go, the 12th lithograph in the portfolio, carries the testimony a step further by depicting Jewish women from Majdanek on the streets of Lublin following liberation. The aimlessness of the title is captured in the friezelike composition in which the women march with no goal in view. Nevertheless, neither Gurdus's work nor her life concluded on this note of purposelessness. Instead, the leading woman of the image becomes the point of departure for the culminating prospect of *Painful Echoes*. There, in the illustration *A Dream...* a similar figure in the foreground stands in close association with the barbed wire of the camps, but the group of refugee women now walk toward the rising sun, whose rays are crowned with the word Israel, in keeping with the corresponding poem, "Ode to Homeland." This more hopeful outlook marks the trajectory of Gurdus's own postwar life, which was dedicated to education, that is, a leading forth from the darkness of the Holocaust.

—Andrew Bush

See the essay on *The Death Train: A Personal Account of a Holocaust Survivor.*

H

HABE, Hans

Pseudonym for János Békessy; pseudonym adopted, 1930, legalized, 1955. **Nationality:** Hungarian. **Born:** Budapest, 12 February 1911. **Military Service:** French Army, 1939–40; United States Army, 1942–46: major; Bronze Star. **Education:** University of Heidelberg; University of Vienna, 1929–30. **Family:** Married 1) Margit Bloch in 1931; 2) Erika Lewy in 1934; 3) Eleanor Close in 1942, one son; 4) Ali Ghito in 1947; 5) Eloise Hardt in 1948, one daughter (deceased); 6) Licci Balla in 1958. **Career:** Editor, *Wiener Sonn and Montagszeitung,* Vienna, 1929–33; editor-in-chief, *Der Morgen,* Vienna, 1934–36; League of Nations correspondent, Geneva, Switzerland, *Prager Tageblatt,* Prague; writer and lecturer, United States, 1941–42; editor-in-chief of 18 U.S.-edited German language newspapers, occupied Germany, 1945–46; founder and editor-in-chief, *Müencher Illustrierte* and *Echo der Woche,* Munich, Germany, 1949–51; writer, 1952–77. Also contributor to anthologies, author of syndicated column, "Outside USA," and weekly columnist, *Kölnische Rundschau* (Cologne, Germany), and *Welt am Sonntag* (Hamburg, Germany). Member of board of governors, Haifa University, 1971. **Awards:** Croix de Guerre de Luxembourg; named Great Knight of Mark Twain, *Mark Twain Journal;* Jerusalem Medal, city of Jerusalem; Boston University fellow, 1966; Herzl Prize of Israel, 1972; Grand Cross of Merit from West Germany; Konrad Adenauer prize for literature, 1977. **Member:** Authors Council of West Germany; Journalist Association of Israel. **Died:** 29 September 1977.

PUBLICATIONS

Novels

Drei üeber die Grenze. 1936; as *Three over the Frontier,* 1939.
Eine Zeit bricht zusammen [A World Crumbles]. 1938.
Zu spat? 1939; as *Sixteen Days,* 1939.
A Thousand Shall Fall (autobiographical; English translation). 1941; revised German edition, as *Ob Tausend fallen,* 1961.
Kathrine (English translation). 1943.
Aftermath (English translation). 1947.
Walk in Darkness (English translation). 1948.
Black Earth (English translation). 1952.
Off Limits: Roman der Besatzung Deutschlands. 1955; as *Off Limits: A Novel of Occupied Germany,* 1956; as *Off Limits,* 1957.
Im Namen des Teufels. 1956; as *The Devil's Agent,* 1958.
Die Rote Sichel. 1959.
Ilona. 1960; as *Ilona,* 1961.

Die Tarnowska. 1962; as *The Countess,* 1963.
Die Weissen und die schwarzen Engel [The White and the Black Angels]: *Die Mission.* 1965; as *The Mission,* 1966.
Christoph und sein Vater. 1966; as *Christopher and His Father,* 1967.
Das Netz (third edition). 1969; as *The Poisoned Stream,* 1969.
Palazzo. 1975; as *Palazzo,* 1977.
Staub im September. 1976.

Other

Our Love Affair with Germany (nonfiction). 1953.
Ich stelle mich: Meine Lebensgeschichte. 1954; as *All My Sins: An Autobiography,* 1957.
Der Tod in Texas: Eine amerikanische Tragödie (nonfiction). 1964; as *The Wounded Land: Journey through a Divided America,* 1964.
Meine Herren Geschworenen: Zehn grosse Gerichtsfälle aus der Geschichte des Verbrechens (nonfiction). 1964; as *Gentlemen of the Jury: Unusual and Outstanding European Murder Trials,* 1967.
Im Jahre Null: Ein Beitrag zur Geschichte der deutschen Presse. 1966.
Wien, so wie es war (photographic book). 1969.
Wie einst David: Entscheidung in Israel (nonfiction). 1971; as *Proud Zion,* 1973.
Erfahrungen (philosophical memoirs). 1973.
Leben fuer den Journalismus (nonfiction). 1976.

*

Film Adaptation: *Die Mission,* 1967.

Critical Studies: "Hans Habe" by Robert C. Jespersen, in *Deutsche Exilliteratur seit 1933,* 1976; "'Gute Europaer in Amerikas Uniform': Hans Habe und Stefan Heym in der Psychological Warfare" by Reinhard K. Zachau, in *World War II and the Exiles: A Literary Response,* edited by Helmut F. Pfanner, 1991.

* * *

Hans Habe was the pseudonym of János Békessy, who was born on 12 February 1911 in Budapest. He was the son of the scandalous journalist and newspaper publisher Imre Békessy. Hans lived in Vienna until 1926, when Karl Kraus initiated an extortion scandal against his father. The son studied German language and literature at Heidelberg and found his first position as a reporter for newspapers in Vienna. He edited army newspapers and sympathized temporarily with the Austrian fascists. His early career was quite successful, and he was the first to discover Adolf Hitler's origins and real name, Schicklgruber. Beginning in 1934, Habe was the League of Nations correspondent for the *Neue Wiener Journal* and the *Prager Tageblatt.* In 1936 he published *Drei über die Grenze* (*Three over the Frontier*), described as an "exile novel of a nonexile." Expatriated from Austria, Habe served as a volunteer in the French army in 1939–40, became a German POW, and in 1940 escaped to the United States. His successful war novel *A Thousand Shall Fall* (*Ob Tausend fallen*) was published in the United States in 1941.

After being trained as a defense officer in the U.S. Army, Habe was promoted to major and was assigned to serve as a member of the American committee to establish a democratic press in defeated Germany. His most important achievement was the founding of the Munich newspaper *Die Neue Zeitung.* In his not entirely reliable report *Im Jahre Null: Ein Beitrag zur Geschichte der deutschen Presse* (1966), on the history of the German press, he characterized the attitude of the American occupying forces as "anti-German" and "pro-Russian" and claimed to have repeatedly warned the United States of the communist danger.

Habe published successfully as a novelist in the United States, with his works reflecting his personal experiences. The novel *Aftermath* (1948) portrays the end of the war and postwar period and criticizes the emancipated American woman. *Off Limits* (1954) relates stories surrounding the American occupation of Germany. *Black Earth* (1952) depicts the fight of farmers in Hungary against the Soviet influence on domestic agricultural policies.

In 1946 Habe moved to Hollywood and then, in 1951, to Ascona, Switzerland. His attempt to publish the magazines *Neue Münchner Illustrierte* and *Echo der Woche* in Munich failed, and Habe's journalistic career ended in 1954. With more than 40 publications to his credit, however, Habe established a reputation as a best-selling novelist. From the 1960s on, calling himself an "extremist of the center," he openly opposed left-wing and liberal authors such as **Max Frisch** and **Rolf Hochhuth** in *Welt am Sonntag.* In the same vein he argued against the antireader and antimoral avant-garde, the *nouveau roman,* and the so-called nonrepresentational novel. Throughout his career he remained a pugnacious defender of his own interests and opinions. He sued the magazine *Stern* in 1952 for the publication of details of his private life, and he brought politically motivated suits against others, for example, in the charges made against **Friedrich Dürrenmatt** in 1972. Habe died on 29 September 1977 in Locarno, Switzerland.

—Walter Schmitz

See the essay on *The Mission.*

HART (MOXON), Kitty

Nationality: Polish. **Born:** Bielsko, 1 December 1926. **Education:** Gymnasium Notre Dame, diploma in radiology. **Family:** Married Randolph Hart in 1949; two sons. **Career:** Prisoner, Auschwitz, 1943–44; forced laborer, 1944–45. Moved to England, 1946. Radiographer, hospitals in Birmingham, England, and in private practice. Principal and narrator, documentary film *Return to Auschwitz,* Yorkshire Television, 1978; technical adviser to film director Alan Pakula for *Sophie's Choice,* 1982. **Awards:** Prix Futura and Commonwealth award, both for documentary film *Return to Auschwitz.*

PUBLICATIONS

Memoirs

I Am Alive! 1961.
Return to Auschwitz: The Remarkable Story of a Girl Who Survived the Holocaust. 1981.

*

Theatrical Activities: Actor: **Documentary Film—***Return to Auschwitz* (also known as *Kitty—Return to Auschwitz*), 1979.

* * *

In his study *Perpetrators Victims Bystanders,* Raul Hilberg describes some of the attributes that aided survival during the Holocaust. Among them were youth and physical fitness as well as a "psychological profile" that included realism, rapid decision making, and tenacious holding on to life. Kitty Hart possessed many such qualities. A swimming champion and lover of sports, she was 12 in 1939, when World War II started. Hiding with her mother before being captured by the Nazis, she taught herself to be alert. Later, in Auschwitz and on the death marches, she showed daring and initiative. In addition, she formed a mutually supportive "unit" with her mother and with other "Auschwitz girls." After the war, she settled in England and became a radiographer.

The story of Hart and her mother's survival is told in *I Am Alive!* (1961), one of the earliest camp accounts written in English. Written for her sons, it is very clear and straightforward and begins before the war and ends just after their liberation. Twenty years later Hart was the subject of a prize-winning documentary from Yorkshire TV, "Return to Auschwitz" (1979; also known as "Kitty—Return to Auschwitz"), which covers her first journey to Auschwitz after the war. Hart is accompanied by her son David, and she tries to explain the full horror of what she and his grandmother had experienced. She also wrote a book by the same name, and it tells much the same story but also covers the postwar period.

It is written with the remarkable candour of her first memoir: "I was soon to discover that everybody in England would be talking about personal war experiences for months, even years. . . . But we, who had been pursued over Europe by the mutual enemy, and come close to extermination at the hand of that enemy, were not supposed to embarrass people by saying a word." This sort of English response to the Holocaust is also discussed by Anne Karpf in *The War After*. Hart—after her initial recovery and establishment in England, and at first encouraged by an American friend, Nancie Beg—told and continues to tell the story of her time in Auschwitz.

It is a sign of her courage that Hart became a vocal Holocaust survivor, telling her story in public for more than 20 years and opposing racism and anti-Semitism. She has been particularly active in schools and concerned with education (in her accounts, she stresses that her school years were stolen by the Nazis). She is a "high profile" survivor in the United Kingdom—she was even mentioned in Hansard (the record of government debates) in 1990 and has given evidence in trials in Germany (for example, at the trial of Gottfried Weise ["William Tell"], an SS officer at Auschwitz). She is unsparing of the Nazis and of any hypocrisy associated with the Holocaust. The Allied powers and what she sees as their past and contemporary indifference also have been a target of her work.

At the end of the documentary Hart makes an odd remark on which she later reflects: "I declared that I thought the experience had been worthwhile." But, as she writes, this is not at all what she meant. Instead she was expressing a thought that other survivors have expressed: "If such a terrible thing had to happen, or was allowed to happen through human negligence and human wickedness, then personally I would sooner have gone through it than not gone through it." This reflection also demonstrates her courage.

—Robert Eaglestone

See the essays on *I Am Alive!* and *Return to Auschwitz: The Remarkable Story of a Girl Who Survived the Holocaust.*

HEIMLER, Eugene

Nationality: Hungarian. **Born:** Szombathely, 27 March 1922. **Education:** Academy of Social Science, Budapest, diploma in social science 1947; London School of Economics; Manchester University, diploma in psychiatric social work 1953; University of London. **Family:** First wife killed at Auschwitz; married Livia Salgo in 1946, one son and one daughter. **Career:** Prisoner, German concentration camps, World War II. Journalist, Hungary, following World War II. Moved to England, 1947. Psychiatric social worker, London, 1953–60; psychiatric social work organizer, 1960–65; director, Hounslow Project, England, beginning in 1965. Since 1970 professor of human social functioning, University of Calgary, Alberta, Canada. Director of community care course, University of London, 1960–80; speaker on mental health, U.S. tour, 1964; consultant to World Health Organization and to United States government, 1964; adviser to ministry of social security of England, 1965–67. Also contributor to newspapers and professional journals. Affiliated with Heimler Foundation, Buckinghamshire, England.

PUBLICATIONS

Poetry

Eternal Dawn. 1939.
Confession to the World. 1943.

Memoirs

Night of the Mist. 1959.
A Link in the Chain. 1962.

Other

Prison. 1964.
Mental Illness and Social Work. 1967.
Survival in Society. 1975.
The Storm: The Tragedy of Sinai. 1976.
The Healing Echo. 1985.

Editor, *Resistance against Tyranny: A Symposium.* 1966.

*   *   *

Eugene Heimler belonged to a distinguished group of Holocaust survivors who gained international fame when they published their memoirs and also when they engaged in high-profile humanitarian causes. Born in 1922 in the little town of Szombathely in western Hungary and educated at the Jewish Gymnasium in Budapest, Heimler spent the last year of the war (between the summer of 1944 and May 1945) as a prisoner in the camps of Auschwitz, Buchenwald, Tröglitz, and Berga-Elster. After the war he returned briefly to Hungary, and, as new forms of anti-Semitism and tyranny forced him to emigrate, he made England his new homeland.

Heimler's first major work (if one does not count his two poetry books that came out in 1939 and 1943), *Night of the Mist,* translated from Hungarian and published in English in 1959, has brought its author enormous popularity. It is often mentioned in one breath with and compared to **Primo Levi**'s *Survival in Auschwitz,* **Elie Wiesel**'s *Night,* Micheline Maurel's

An Ordinary Camp, and **Viktor E. Frankl**'s *Man's Search for Meaning.* With these other autobiographical works it shares some common rhetorical strategies employed by the narrators in order to transcend the physical and mental abuse to which they were subjected. While describing an environment where the prisoners' acts, behavior, and identity are totally controlled by the oppressors, Heimler, like other Holocaust survivors, adopts what some scholars have called a symbolic and mystical ''purpose-centered orientation'' that enables him to redefine and thereby cope with the situation in the camps. Heimler defines two types of survivors: those who believed that their unwavering faith in God had protected them and those who were able to find a ''personal meaning in living.'' He found himself in the second category and admits that the task of ''chronicler of our times,'' ''an eye witness and writer without a pen'' in the hell of Auschwitz, has become a bridge between his past dreams of becoming a poet and his future, post-Holocaust life.

Although he is most famous for the memoir *Night of the Mist,* in the years after World War II Heimler also made a name for himself as a poet, writer, journalist, social worker, and political activist who relied on his own experiences during the Holocaust to develop methods of coping with various other forms of personal crisis, social discrimination, and political oppression. His second memoir, *A Link in the Chain* (1962), is a revealing, unusually sincere and very detailed account of his life in the immediate postwar years up until 1960, a period in which the Holocaust survivor struggled to adjust to life after the trauma, to life in a new land speaking a new language. Upon returning to his hometown in western Hungary in 1945, he became a journalist and began to write regularly on the persecution and mass murder of Jews in Hungary of the most recent past. As a result of his articles, however, he received numerous abusive and threatening letters whose content was openly nationalistic and anti-Semitic. When Heimler published an article on the British general election in 1945, he was accused of high treason by the attorney general (the same person on whose order Heimler's father had been deported in 1943) and was arrested.

In the course of the year after his release from prison, the rise of nationalism and the imminent Stalinist terror forced him to leave his beloved Hungary. After 1947 Heimler studied at the London School of Economics and Manchester University and became a psychiatric social worker. Similarly to another famous survivor, the Austrian psychiatrist Victor E. Frankl, Heimler was able to draw upon his camp experiences in the process of creating his own methods of autogenic therapy called Human Social Functioning. Numerous English psychiatrists and counselors have been taught and trained in the Heimler Interview Technique and in Heimler's methods. Heimler was engaged in a variety of local community care projects as well as international human rights projects. He edited the 1966 symposium *Resistance against Tyranny,* to which he contributed a thoughtful essay on Jewish resistance

before and during the Holocaust, and he was also known for his studies on social work in prisons as documented in his 1963 essay ''Children of Auschwitz'' (included in the volume *Prison* edited by George Mikes). Heimler's book *Mental Illness and Social Work* (1967) still remains a standard work in its field.

—Mila Ganeva

See the essay on *Night of the Mist.*

HERSEY, John (Richard)

Nationality: American. **Born:** Tientsin, China, 17 June 1914. **Education:** Yale University, B.A. 1936; Clare College, Cambridge University, 1936–37. **Family:** Married 1) Frances Ann Cannon in 1940 (divorced 1958), four children; 2) Barbara Day Addams Kaufman in 1958, one daughter. **Career:** Private secretary, driver, and factotum for Sinclair Lewis, summer, 1937; writer, editor, and correspondent, *Time* magazine, 1937–44; editor and correspondent, *Life* magazine, 1944–45. Fellow, Berkeley College, 1950–65, master, 1965–70, and fellow, 1965–93, Pierson College, all Yale University; writer-in-residence, American Academy in Rome, 1970–71; adjunct professor of English, 1970–84, and professor emeritus, 1984–93, Yale University. Writer for *New Yorker* and other magazines, 1945–93. Chairman, Connecticut Volunteers for Stevenson, 1952; member of Adlai Stevenson's campaign staff, 1956. Editor and director of writers' co-operative magazine, *'47.* Member of Westport, Connecticut School Study Council, 1945–50, of Westport Board of Education, 1950–52, of Yale University Council Committee on the Humanities, 1951–56, of Fairfield, Connecticut Citizens School Study Council, 1952–56, of National Citizens' Commission for the Public Schools, 1954–56; consultant, Fund for the Advancement of Education, 1954–56; chairman, Connecticut Committee for the Gifted, 1954–57; member of Board of Trustees, Putney School, 1953–56; delegate to White House Conference on Education, 1955; trustee, National Citizens' Council for the Public Schools, 1956–58; member, visiting committee, Harvard Graduate School of Education, 1960–65; member, Loeb Theater Center, 1980–93; member, 1959–61, and chairman, 1964–69, Yale University Council Committee on Yale College; trustee, National Committee for Support of the Public Schools, 1962–68. **Awards:** Pulitzer prize, 1945, for *A Bell for Adano;* Anisfield-Wolf award and Jewish Book Council of America Daroff Memorial fiction award, both in 1950, and Sidney Hillman Foundation award, 1951, all for *The Wall;* Yale University Howland medal, 1952; National Association of Independent Schools award, 1957, for *A Single Pebble;* Tuition Plan award, 1961; Sarah Josepha Hale award, 1963.

M.A.: Yale University, 1947; D.H.L.: Dropsie College, 1950; New School for Social Research, 1950; Syracuse University, 1983; LL D: Washington and Jefferson College, 1950; D.Litt.: Wesleyan University, 1954; Bridgeport University, 1959; Clarkson College of Technology, 1972; University of New Haven, 1975; Yale University, 1984; Monmouth College, 1985; William and Mary College, 1987; Albertus Magnus College, 1988. Honorary fellow, Clare College, Cambridge University, 1967. **Member:** National Institute of Arts and Letters; American Academy of Arts and Letters (secretary, 1961–78, chancellor, 1981–84); American Academy of Arts and Sciences; Authors League of America; Authors Guild. **Died:** 23 March 1993.

PUBLICATIONS

Novels

A Bell for Adano. 1944.
The Wall. 1950.
The Marmot Drive. 1953.
A Single Pebble. 1956.
The War Lover. 1959.
The Child Buyer. 1960.
White Lotus. 1965.
Too Far to Walk. 1966.
Under the Eye of the Storm. 1967.
The Conspiracy. 1972.
My Petition for More Space. 1974.
The Walnut Door. 1977.
The Call: An American Missionary in China. 1985.
Antonietta. 1991.

Short Stories

Fling and Other Stories. 1990.
Key West Tales. 1994.

Other

Men on Bataan. 1942.
Into the Valley: A Skirmish of the Marines. 1943.
Hiroshima. 1946.
Here to Stay: Studies on Human Tenacity. 1962.
The Algiers Motel Incident. 1968.
Letter to the Alumni. 1970.
The President. 1975.
Aspects of the Presidency: Truman and Ford in Office. 1980.
Blues. 1987.
Life Sketches. 1989.

Editor, *Ralph Ellison: A Collection of Critical Essays.* 1973.
Editor, *The Writer's Craft.* 1974.

*

Film Adaptations: *A Bell for Adano,* 1945; *The War Lover,* 1962; *The Wall* (television), 1982.

Bibliography: *John Hersey and James Agee: A Reference Guide* by Nancy Lyman Huse, 1978.

Critical Studies: *John Hersey,* 1967, and *John Hersey Revisited,* 1991, both by David Sanders; ''A Definition of Modern Nihilism: Hersey's *The War Lover*'' by Robert N. Hudspeth, in *University Review,* 35, 1969, pp. 243–49; ''The Wall: John Hersey's Interpretation of the Ghetto Experience'' by Michael Haltresht, in *Notes on Contemporary Literature,* 2(1), 1972, pp. 10–11; *The Survival Tales of John Hersey* by Nancy Lyman Huse, 1983; ''Confucianism, Christianity, and Social Change in John Hersey's *The Call*'' by John T. Dorsey, in *Tamkang Review* (Taiwan), 18(1–4), Autumn/Summer, 1987–88, pp. 323–31; ''Dirty Hands, Bloody Hands: Commitment in John Hersey's *The Conspiracy*'' by Peter G. Christensen, in *Classical and Modern Literature,* 12(4), Summer 1992, pp. 375–87; ''From Yellow Peril to Japanese Wasteland: John Hersey's *Hiroshima*'' by Patrick B. Sharp, in *Twentieth Century Literature,* 46(4), Winter 2000, pp. 434–52.

* * *

The American novelist John Hersey was born in China in 1914 to Protestant missionary parents. A graduate of Yale University, he spent a year at Clare College, Cambridge, studying eighteenth-century English literature before beginning a career as a journalist. Hersey worked as Sinclair Lewis's secretary during the summer of 1937 before he joined the staff of *Time* magazine that fall. During World War II the precocious Hersey was a correspondent for *Time* (1939–45) and *Life* (1942–45) in China, the South Pacific, the Mediterranean theater, and Moscow. While at *Time,* he worked under Henry Luce, whose parents had been evangelistic Presbyterian missionaries also based in China. Some of Hersey's wartime correspondence was published as *Men on Bataan* (1942) and *Into the Valley* (1943). During a period of three weeks in 1943, Hersey drafted his first novel, *A Bell for Adano,* published early in 1944. Set in a small Sicilian town after the Germans were defeated there, the story concerns the conflict between a humane American major, in charge of the occupying forces, who is determined to replace a village bell that had been melted down for armaments, and a bombastic autocrat modeled on General George Patton. *A Bell for Adano* won the Pulitzer Prize for Fiction on 8 May 1945 (V-E Day), was turned into a stage play, and then made into a motion picture.

At the end of the war, while he was stationed in Moscow, Hersey was taken with Soviet journalists to the ruins of recently liberated ghettos in Warsaw, Lodz, and Tallinn (Estonia) as well as to a detention camp at Klooga, Estonia. These experiences touched him deeply, leading him to an overriding concern with wartime disaster and atrocity. In 1945–46 Hersey was assigned by *Life* and the *New Yorker* to travel in China and Japan. The book that resulted from his travels, *Hiroshima* (1946), is the one readers have come to know best. First published on 31 August 1946 as a long essay in the *New Yorker*—which devoted its entire issue to Hersey's account—*Hiroshima* was published in book form that October. Having interviewed about 30 survivors of the atom bomb attack, Hershey chose to focus on six Hiroshima residents, starting with a separate account of where each was when the explosion occurred and then describing their activities during the following days. The book's detached, matter-of-fact voice highlights the horrors of the story. In 1985 Hersey wrote a long article for the *New Yorker* on the 40th anniversary of the bombing, in which he followed up on each of his survivor-subjects, four of whom were still alive. Later editions of *Hiroshima* include this severe new chapter as an "Aftermath."

During the next three years Hersey conducted the massive research needed to write *The Wall,* his one novel devoted completely to the Holocaust. At the time there was no overall history of the Holocaust and little writing in English on the Warsaw Ghetto. Much testimony had, however, been published in both Yiddish and Polish, neither of which Hersey could read. To remedy this, he hired two research assistants who read their translations aloud into a wire recorder. (One of them, Lucy Davidowicz, became a well-known Holocaust historian.) Using the device of the "buried manuscript," Hersey constructed a narrative situation similar to the creation of the Oneg Shabbat archive in Warsaw under the direction of the historian **Emmanuel Ringelblum**.

The narrative of *The Wall* covers the period from shortly after the German occupation of Poland: the construction of the wall that created the terribly crowded ghetto, the building of a team that organized resistance to the Nazis, and finally the historic Warsaw Ghetto revolt, in which a group of well-organized but minimally armed fighters held off the Nazis for more than six weeks. That Hersey's characters are based primarily on the survivors gives the novel a more positive spin than a focus on victimhood might have done. The narrative voice, Noach Levinson, writes in much the way Hersey did in *Hiroshima,* and his characters—both major and minor—linger in the mind. *The Wall* was turned into a play by Millard Lampell, and it ran on Broadway, with George C. Scott playing the lead role of Dolek Berson.

Hersey's career after 1950 was long and productive, although none of his later works achieved the recognition or commercial success of his earlier books. Among the best-known later works were *A Single Pebble* (1956), *The War Lover* (1959), *The Child Buyer* (1960), *White Lotus* (1965), *The Algiers Motel Incident* (1968), and *The Call* (1985). None of these works deals with the Holocaust.

Hersey was active throughout his career in the American Academy of Arts and Letters and in writers' organizations. He spent five years as the master of Pierson College, Yale University (1965–70), and also served as adjunct professor of English at Yale (1970–84), during which time he taught two writing seminars each year, one in fiction and one in journalism. Hersey died in 1993.

—Michael Hoffman

See the essay on *The Wall.*

HEYEN, William

Nationality: American. **Born:** Brooklyn, New York, 1 November 1940. **Education:** State University of New York, Brockport, B.S. in education 1961; Ohio University, Athens, M.A. in English 1963, Ph.D. in English 1967. **Family:** Married Hannelore Greiner in 1962; one daughter and one son. **Career:** English professor, 1967–2000, and since 2000 professor emeritus, State University of New York, Brockport. English teacher, Springville Junior High School, New York, 1961–62; graduate assistant and teaching fellow, Ohio University, 1963–67; English teacher, State University of New York, Cortland, 1963–65; senior Fulbright lecturer, Hannover University, Germany, 1971–72; visiting professor, University of Hawaii, Manoa, Spring 1985. Has taught several short poetry workshops at Hofstra University, Southampton College, and the Chautauqua Institution, 1981–96. **Awards:** Borestone Mountain Poetry prize, 1965; Creative Writing fellowships, National Endowment for the Arts, 1973–74 and 1984–85; American Library Association "notable American book of 1974," for *Noise in the Trees; Ontario Review* poetry prize and State University of New York Brockport outstanding alumni award, both in 1977; John Simon Guggenheim Foundation fellowship, 1977–78; *Poetry* magazine's Eunice Tietjens memorial award, 1978; Witter Bynner prize, American Academy and Institute of Arts & Letters, and Ohio University Alumni Association medal of merit, both in 1982; *Booklist* "outstanding book of 1984," for *The Generation of 2000;* New York Foundation for the Arts, 1984–85; State University of New York alumni honor roll appointment, 1995; Lillian Fairchild memorial award, 1996, and National Small Press book award for poetry, 1997, both for *Crazy Horse in Stillness.*

PUBLICATIONS

Poetry

Depth of Field: Poems. 1970.
Noise in the Trees: Poems and a Memoir. 1974.
The Swastika Poems. 1977.
Long Island Light: Poems and a Memoir. 1979.
The City Parables. 1980.
Lord Dragonfly: Five Sequences. 1981.

Erika: Poems of the Holocaust. 1984.
The Chestnut Rain: A Poem. 1986.
Brockport, New York: Beginning with "And." 1988.
Falling from Heaven: Holocaust Poems of a Jew and a Gentile, with Louis David Brodsky. 1991.
Pterodactyl Rose: Poems of Ecology. 1991.
Ribbons: The Gulf War—A Poem. 1991.
The Host: Selected Poems 1965–1990. 1994.
Crazy Horse in Stillness: Poems. 1996.
Diana, Charles, & the Queen. 1998.

Novel

Vic Holyfield and the Class of 1957: A Romance. 1986.

Memoir

With Me Far Away: A Memoir. 1994.

Other

Pig Notes & Dumb Music: Prose on Poetry. 1998.

Editor, *A Profile of Theodore Roethke* (anthology). 1971.
Editor, *American Poets in 1976* (anthology). 1976.
Editor, *The Generation of 2000; Contemporary American Poets* (anthology). 1984.

*

Critical Studies: "Chapter and Verse" by Stanley Plumly, in *American Poetry Review,* 7(1), January/February 1978; "Animate Mystique: The Dialectic of William Heyen's Poems" by Kenneth MacLean, "William Heyen: The Pure Serene of Memory in One Man" by Vince Clemente, "From Sight to Silence: The Process of William Heyen's Poetry" by Cis Stefanik, and "William Heyen's 'Boys of Piston, Girls of Gear': A Field Guide to the Human in *XVII Machines*" by Ernest Stefanik, all in *Manassas Review,* I(3–4), Summer 1978; "One Man's Music" by Dave Smith, in *American Poetry Review,* 9(2), March/April 1980, pp. 40–43; "The Harvest of the Quiet Eye" by Michael McFee, in *Parnassus,* 10(1), Spring/Summer 1982, pp. 153–71; "William Heyen" by John Drury, in *Critical Survey of Poetry,* edited by Frank N. Magill, 1983; "The Poem as a Reservoir for Grief" by Tess Gallagher, in *American Poetry Review,* 13(4), July/August 1984, pp. 7–11; "Poetry of Light/Century of Darkness" by Robert Morgan, in *Parnassus,* Spring/Summer 1986, pp. 230–36; "William Heyen's Obsessive Ghosts: *Erika* and the Holocaust" by Norbert Krapf, in *Holocaust and Genocide Studies,* 2(1), 1987, pp. 165–69; "Through the Sharpness of Distance: American Poets and the Holocaust" by Charles Fishman, in *Poetry Pilot of the Academy of American Poets,* May 1990, pp.5–12; "William Heyen: Heartwood and Witness Power" by David Watson, and "Heyen's Cryptic Ark" by Max Westler, both in *Black Dirt,* I, Spring/Summer 1998;

The Terror of Our Days: Four American Poets Respond to the Holocaust by Harriet L. Parmet, 2001.

* * *

"We often get to where we are through blunder, naivete, intuition, luck, rather than through lucid planning," said William Heyen in a conversation on his writing talent sponsored by Brockport Writers Forum, SUNY College at Brockport, New York (March, 1978). Nonetheless, Heyen's impulsive muse inspires his hidden self waiting to come forth or be healed. So his early books of poetry reflect personal meditation, a poet's commune with nature. Many of his Holocaust poems are driven by an emotional flow and quest for an American identity of German parentage. His venture into "the aesthetics of the Holocaust" is bold, creative, and imaginative. His lines portray the agony from the abyss from the view of the victim and demonstrate the true intent of T.W. Adorno's oft-quoted proposition, "to write poetry after Auschwitz is barbaric." Notably, his critical poems on Vietnam and the Gulf War *cum* Holocaust art help us preserve memory, a first step to repentance and restoring the flaws of history.

Heyen's writing includes poetry, critical prose, and stories. He is the author of many books of poetry, and his individual poems have appeared in more than two hundred different periodicals and more than a hundred anthologies. His books of poetry include *Depth of a Field* (1970), in reverence of nature; *Noise in the Trees* (1974) and *Long Island Night* (1979), "lifestudies" steeped in remembrance of boyhood experiences; *The Chestnut Rain* (1986), an epic on the plight of the American farmer, America's involvement in Vietnam, and more, a blight on America's chestnut trees, symbol of America's idyllic past and innocence; *Pterodactyl Rose: Poems of Ecology* (1991), poems of sadness and anger that call for action against universal acts of ecocide that threaten the biosphere in which we live; *Ribbons: The Gulf War* (1991), a self-seeking and self-demanding war poem that deconstructs Operation Desert Storm; and *Crazy Horse in Stillness* (1996), which engages the legendary enmity between Sioux leader Crazy Horse and army General George Custer. In sum, his themes include nature and Earth, beginnings and death, the self and the other, history and war, memory and remembrance.

"The purpose of poetry," Heyen once said, "is to help us live our lives." This may explain Heyen's fondness for reading poems from his Long Island childhood in poetry readings. But the poet is haunted by the Third Reich and World War II and the awareness of two paternal uncles and a father-in-law, a Nazi captain, who died in defense of Germany. He grapples with how to reconcile idyllic childhood memories of "soulful" Long Island ponds with the hard reality that "people of my own blood flushed the ashes of millions of people into the pond at Auschwitz." This and other imponderables are flushed out in his volumes of Holocaust poetry: *The Swastika Poems* (1977), *Erika: Poems of the Holocaust* (1984; reissued in

1991), and *Falling from Heaven* (with Louis Daniel Brodsky, 1991). Collectively these writings provide a forum for the author's thoughts and feelings about the Shoah, which are presented in kaleidoscopic and surrealistic fashion. Heyen's Holocaust poems reveal an accomplished poet whose journey to hell and back encompass both unspeakable evil and courageous hope.

—Zev Garber

See the essay on *Erika: Poems of the Holocaust.*

HEYMAN, Eva

Nationality: Hungarian. **Born:** Nagyvárad, 13 February 1931. **Career:** Forced to live in the Nagyvárad ghetto, 1944; sent to Auschwitz. **Died:** Murdered, Auschwitz, 17 October 1944.

PUBLICATION

Diary

Yomanah shel Evah Hayman, edited by Yehudah Marton. 1964; as *The Diary of Eva Heyman,* 1974; as *The Diary of Eva Heyman: Child of the Holocaust,* 1988.

*   *   *

The young diarist Eva Heyman began writing in her journal on her thirteenth birthday in Nagyvárad in northern Transylvania (the modern Oradea, Romania). Though she often addressed her diary, calling it "dear, sweet little diary" (much like **Anne Frank**, who called her diary "Kitty"), Eva never explicitly stated what had prompted her to begin writing. Her social and familial milieu, however, may shed some light on the matter. Her parents divorced when she was a child, leaving Eva in the care of her maternal grandparents and her Austrian governess. Eva's father, Bela Heyman, was an architect, who lived not far from her in Nagyvárad, but rarely saw his daughter. Her mother, Agi, married the well-known Hungarian writer Bela Zsolt and lived in Budapest. Wrapped up in a world of intellectuals, writers, and artists, Eva's mother rarely went to Nagyvárad to spend time with her daughter.

Eva was an only child surrounded by adults and, to a degree, neglected by her own parents. In her diary, she wrote frankly about the pain her parents' divorce had caused her, the jealousy she felt for her mother's second husband, and her own insecurity about her mother's love. In this context, the diary must be seen as much more than just a place to put down her thoughts. The warmth and affection with which she addressed it, and her treatment of it as a beloved friend suggests that she wrote, at least in part, to find some companionship and solace in what must have been a lonely and confusing world.

While there is little question that Eva wrote a diary, there is some question about the authenticity of the 1947 published Hungarian edition, upon which the English version was based. In the last entry of her diary, faced with imminent deportation from the Nagyvárad ghetto, Eva wrote that she was rushing to see Mariska Szabo, the family's Christian cook. Eva apparently entrusted the diary to her, for it was Mariska who returned the diary to Eva's mother after the war. Agi and her second husband had managed to escape the Nagyvárad ghetto without Eva, ultimately making their way to safety in Switzerland.

Agi's closest friend told Judah Marton (who wrote the introduction to the English edition of the diary) that she had heard about the existence of the diary immediately after liberation and that Agi planned to publish it. In his introduction, Marton reminds the reader that Bela Zsolt was a well-known writer, that Agi was "an intellectual with a literary bent," and that the diary was in their possession for several years before it was published. The implication is that Eva's mother—who was plagued with guilt for having left her daughter in the ghetto—wanted to publish the diary in order to preserve her daughter's memory. He further suggests that given Zsolt's literary inclinations, the diary could have been edited or changed.

Although Marton ultimately dismisses these doubts, a careful reading of the text itself reveals inconsistencies. Eva appears to have begun the diary long before the first entry in the published edition. She wrote, "Dear little diary, you were already around by the time they carried Uncle Bela off to the Ukraine . . ." This event occurred in the summer of 1942, a year and a half before the first published entry. On 5 May 1944, Eva wrote, "Dear diary, now you aren't at 3 Istvan Gyongyosi Street—that is, at home—any more, not even at Aniko's, nor at Tusnad, nor at Lake Batalon, nor in Budapest, places you've been with me too before, but in the Ghetto." In the published edition, the only two places in which Eva had her diary were at home and at her friend Aniko's. This would further suggest that the diary existed for several years before the first published entry of 13 February 1944.

Aside from these relatively concrete matters, there are many places where the language doesn't flow, where the text is contrived, or where the sequence or location of a story doesn't read smoothly or fit naturally with the surrounding text. While these are not explicit inconsistencies, they do substantiate the possibility that Eva's mother edited the diary and included information she felt was important, intending to keep the tone consistent but leaving clues to the changes.

The original diary was lost sometime after the first edition of the diary was published in Hungarian, rendering the matter inconclusive. It seems likely that Eva Heyman did keep a diary and that she did record in it not only her thoughts and feelings but also her observations and experiences of the German onslaught in Nagyvárad. It also seems likely that her mother,

Agi, strengthened what might have seemed like a thin or weak text in order to ensure that her daughter's life would be remembered. Though this matter is unlikely to ever be completely resolved, Eva's diary nevertheless stands as a poignant and vivid record of the sudden and violent German onslaught that decimated Hungarian Jewry. Its vivid details about each stage in the German attack provide a unique window into the last months of the life of a young girl enduring and ultimately succumbing to the Nazi menace.

—Alexandra Zapruder

See the essay on *The Diary of Eva Heyman: Child of the Holocaust.*

HILDESHEIMER, Wolfgang

Nationality: German. **Born:** Hamburg, 9 December 1916. **Education:** Studied carpentry in Palestine; London Central School of Arts and Crafts, 1937–39. **Career:** Moved to England, 1933, then to Palestine, 1935. English teacher, British Council, Palestine, 1939; British intelligence officer, Jerusalem, 1943–46; German-English translator, Nuremberg war trials, 1946. Returned to Germany, 1949; moved to Switzerland, 1957. Also worked as an artist. **Awards:** Bremen literature prize and Georg Büchner prize, both in 1966. **Died:** 21 August 1991.

PUBLICATIONS

Collections

Theaterstücke; Über das absurde Theater (includes *Pastorale*; *Neufassung*; *Die Verspätung*; *Nachtstück*; *Die Rede Über das absurde Theater*). 1976.
Hörspiele (includes *Das Opfer Helena*; *Herrn Walsers Raben*; *Unter der Erde*; *Monolog*). 1976.
The Collected Stories of Wolfgang Hildesheimer. 1987.
Die Theaterstücke (includes *Der Drachenthron*; *Die Herren der Welt*; *Pastorale oder Die Zeit für Kakao*; *Landschaft mit Figuren*; *Die Uhren*; *Der schiefe Turm von Pisa*; *Das Opfer Helena*; *Die Verspätung*; *Nachtstück*; *Mary Stuart*), edited by Volker Jehle. 1989.
Gesammelte Werke in sieben Bänden, edited by Christiaan Lucas Hart Nibbrig und Volker Jehle. 1991.
    Bd. 1. Erzählende Prosa. 1991.
    Bd. 2. Monologische Prosa. 1991.
    Bd. 3. Essayistische Prosa. 1991.
    Bd. 4. Biographische Prosa. 1991.
    Bd. 5. Hörspiele. 1991.
    Bd. 6. Theaterstücke. 1991.
    Bd. 7. Vermischte Schriften. 1991.

Novels

Paradiesvögel [Birds of Paradise]. 1954.
Nachtstück [Nocturne]. 1963.
Monolog [Monologue]. 1964.
Tynset (monologue). 1965.
Masante (monologue). 1973.
Marbot: Eine Biographie. 1981; translated as *Marbot: A Biography,* 1983.

Plays

Das Ende einer Welt: Funk-Oper (opera libretto), music by Hans Werner Henze. 1953.
Die Eroberung der Prinzessin Turandot. 1954.
Der Drachenthron: Komödie in drei Akten. 1955.
Begegnung im Balkanexpress. 1956.
Spiele in denen es dunkel wird. 1958.
Pastorale. In *Deutsches Theater der Gegenwart,* edited by Karlheinz Braun, 1960.
Herrn Walsers Raben. 1960.
Die Verspätung: Ein Stück in zwei Teilen. 1961.
Das Opfer Helena: Eine Komödie in zwei Teilen. 1961.
Vergebliche Aufzeichnungen: Nachtstück. 1962; as *Nightpiece,* 1968.
Herrn Walsers Raben. Unter der Erde. Zwei Hörspiele (two radio plays). 1964.
An den Ufern der Plotinitza, with *Begegnung im Balkanexpress.* (two radio plays). 1968.
Mary Stuart eine historische Szene. 1970; translated as *Mary Stuart,* in *Scripts 3,* 1972.
Hauskauf: Hörspiel (radio play). 1974.
Biosphärenklänge: E. Hörspiel (radio play). 1977.

Short Stories

Lieblose Legenden [Loveless Legends]. 1952; translated as *Lieblose Legenden,* 1983.
Ich trage eine Eule nach Athen, with Paul Flora. 1956.

Other

Betrachtungen über Mozart. 1963.
Wer war Mozart?: Becketts Spiel: Über das absurde Theater. 1966.
Frankfurter Vorlesungen. 1967.
Interpretationen. James Joyce. Georg Büchner. Zwei Frankfurter Vorlesungen. 1969.
Zeiten in Cornwall. Mit 6 Zeichnungen des Autors. 1971.
Mozart (biography). 1977; translated as *Mozart,* 1982.

Was Waschbären alles machen, with Rebecca Berlinger (for children). 1979.

Exerzitien mit Papst Johannes: Vergebliche Aufzeichnungen. 1979.

Wolfgang Amadeus Mozart, Idomeneo, 1781–1981: Essays, Forschungsberichte, Katalog. 1981.

Mitteilungen an Max über den Stand der Dinge und anderes. 1983.

Das Ende der Fiktionen: Reden aus fünfundzwanzig Jahren. 1984.

The Jewishness of Mr. Bloom/Das Jüdische an Mr. Bloom (English and German). 1984.

Der ferne Bach: Eine Rede (speech). 1985.

Nachlese. 1987.

Klage und Anklage. 1989.

Was ist eigentlich ein Escoutadou?: Briefe mit Zeichnungen an Julie (Hildesheimer's correspondence). 1996.

Schule des Sehens: Kunstbetrachtungen, edited by Salman Ansari. 1996.

Briefe, edited by Silvia Hildesheimer and Dietmar Pleyer (Hildesheimer's correspondence). 1999.

Editor, *Mozart Briefe* (correspondence). 1975.

Editor, with Vittorio Sereni, *Enrico Della Torre.* 1980.

Translator, *Nachtgewächs,* by Djuna Barnes. 1959.

Translator, *Die Lästerschule: Lustspiel in zehn Bildern,* by Richard Brinsley Sheridan, 1962.

Translator, *Eine Harfe ohne Saiten* [Unstrung Harp], by Edward Gorey. 1963.

Translator, *Das Geheimnis der Ottomane: Ein pornographisches Werk,* by Edward Gorey. 1964.

Translator, *Die heilige Johanna: Dramatische Chronik in sechs Szenen und einem Epilog,* by Bernard Shaw, 1965.

Translator, *Das unglückselige Kind* [The Hapless Child], by Edward Gorey. 1967.

Translator, *Helden* [Arms and the Man], by Bernard Shaw. 1969.

Translator, *Anna Livia Plurabelle,* by James Joyce. 1970.

Translator, *Aktion "Djungel": Bericht aus Malaya,* by F. Spencer Chapman. 1971.

Translator, *Die heilige Johanna: Dramatische Chronik in sechs Szenen und einem Epilog,* by Bernard Shaw. 1971.

Translator, with Hans Manz, Fridolin Tschudi, and Dieter E. Zimmer, *Der zweifelhafte Gast: Elf merkwürdige Geschichten,* by Edward Gorey. 1973.

Translator, *Der Lauf der Welt: Eine lieblose Komödie* [Way of the World], by William Congreve. 1989.

*

Bibliography: *Wolfgang Hildesheimer: Eine Bibliographie* by Volker Jehle. 1984.

Critical Studies: ''Guilt in Absurdity: Wolfgang Hildesheimer's *Tynset*'' by Giles R. Hoyt, in *Seminar,* 14, 1978, pp. 133–40;

Wolfgang Hildesheimer's Tynset, 1978, ''Wolfgang Hildesheimer's Mary Stuart: Language Run Riot,'' in *Germanic Review,* 54, 1979, pp. 110–14, ''Wolfgang Hildesheimer's *Das Opfer Helena:* Another Triumph of the 'They,''' in *Pen to Performance,* edited by Karelisa V. Hartigan, 1983, *The Realm of Possibilities: Wolfgang Hildesheimer's Non-Traditional Non-Fictional Prose,* 1988, and *Wolfgang Hildesheimer and His Critics,* 1993, all by Patricia Haas Stanley; ''Wolfgang Hildesheimer and the German-Jewish Experience: Reflections on *Tynset* and *Masante*'' by Henry A. Lea, in *Monatshefte,* 71, 1979, pp. 19–28; ''Self Defeating Satire? On the Function of the Implied Reader in Wolfgang Hildesheimer's *Lieblose Legenden*'' by Roderick H. Watt, in *Forum for Modern Language Studies* (England), 19(1), January 1983, pp. 58–74; ''Mozart: A Case Study in Logocentric Repression'' by Katherine Arens, in *Comparative Literature Studies,* 23(2), Summer 1986, pp. 141–69; ''Typically Hildesheimer: A German Adaptation of Richard Brinsley Sheridan's *The School for Scandal*'' by Elizabeth Petuchowski, in *Exile and Enlightenment: Studies in German and Comparative Literature,* edited by Uwe Faulhaber, Jerry Glenn, Edward P. Harris, and Hans-Georg Richert, 1987; ''Authenticity as Mask: Wolfgang Hildesheimer's *Marbot*'' by Käte Hamburger, in *Neverending Stories: Toward a Critical Narratology,* edited by Ann Clark Fehn, Ingeborg Hoesterey, and Maria M. Tatar, 1992; ''History As Biography As Fiction: Wolfgang Hildesheimer's *Marbot: Eine Biography,*'' in *Continuities in Contemporary German-Language Literature,* edited by Arthur Williams, Stuart Parkes, and Julian Preece, 1998, and ''Time and Narrative: Wolfgang Hildesheimer's *Tynset* and *Masante,*'' in *German Life and Letters,* 52(4), 1999, pp. 457–74, both by Jonathan Long.

* * *

Wolfgang Hildesheimer was born in Hamburg in 1916. His paternal grandfather, a rabbi, came from a long line of Berlin rabbis; his mother's assimilationist family were art lovers and bookstore owners. He moved to England in 1933 to complete his education before emigrating to Palestine with his Zionist parents in 1935, where he studied to become a carpenter and took courses in drawing and interior design. From 1937 until 1939 he studied at the London Central School of Arts and Crafts. In 1939, with the outbreak of World War II, he returned to Palestine and taught English at the British Council. From 1943 to 1946 he served as a British intelligence officer in Jerusalem, and in 1946 he became a simultaneous German-English translator at the Nuremberg war trials. In addition, he edited the final report of the proceedings. In 1949 he moved to Ambach, West Germany, and worked chiefly as an artist, and in 1953 he settled in Munich, becoming active as a writer. In 1957 he moved to Switzerland, where he spent his remaining years.

During the three years of translating in Nuremberg, Hildesheimer turned to his graphic artwork to escape the harrowing images that accosted him during the trials. He called this artwork *Gegentherapie,* a "therapy to counter" the inhumanity described during the proceedings. In 1950 he became an author by chance, as one day, feeling that it was too cold to paint, he instead put pen to paper for prose.

Hildesheimer's subsequent career as an imaginative writer can be divided into three distinct periods: (1) humorously absurdist, (2) dark and Holocaust related, and (3) focused on the role of the imaginative artist and society. The first stage, from 1950 to 1954, contained his collection of short stories *Lieblose Legenden* (1952; "Loveless Legends") and the novel *Paradiesvögel* (1954; "Birds of Paradise"). In both works humorously alienated characters talk past one another and suddenly find themselves in absurd situations for which they find no solution. Concluding catastrophes anticipate the devastating themes of Hildesheimer's middle period.

Clearly influenced by his Nuremberg experiences, ensuing bouts of depression, and Djuna Barnes's free-associative, stream-of-consciousness poetic novel *Nightwood* (1937), which he translated in 1959, Hildesheimer turned to the setting of the sleepless night for his own imaginative works of the early 1960s. This second stage, from *Nachtstück* (1963; "Nocturne") to *Monolog* (1964; "Monologue") culminated in his novelistic masterpiece *Tynset* (1965).

In an interview given in 1978, Hildesheimer looked back at the delay between the Nuremberg trials and the interior nature of his imaginative writing specifically dealing with the Holocaust: "I was first confronted with all of those frightening terms relating to racism and Anti-Semitism . . . as a simultaneous translator: as this history, both systematic and schematic, which I had only heard about through reports and rumors . . . was being unfolded. The history of the Holocaust was horrific but it belonged to the past and coming to terms with it was not *my* task. The question of personal or collective guilt I left to my sub-conscious to deal with and waited for an inner decision."

As Peter Demetz has commented, Hildesheimer's humorous earlier works now gave way to "a more piercing vision of culture as a recurrent nightmare" that deprived sensitive individuals of their sleep. These works deal with a nighttime in which the protagonists cannot sleep because of the horrors that obsess them. In these years he was artistically adapting his repressed memories from the Nuremberg trials, and the works clearly show individuals unable to direct their own lives in a world offering neither outer nor inner security. A direct reference to the murder of two-thirds of European Jewry in the Holocaust is contained in his play *Monolog* when a character laments, "A Jewish form of comfort and consolation does not appear to exist . . . or, there are no Jews any more, that's really it, or at least not enough of them, to make their type of comfort and solace count." Although not a practicing Jew, Hildesheimer deeply felt his Jewish roots, stating in an interview, "I am not exclusively anchored in or governed by my Judaism; however, I feel Jewish."

In his last literary period Hildesheimer penned the novel *Masante* (1973) and the biography *Mozart* (1977). During the final decade of his life (he died in 1991), he returned almost exclusively to his graphic work, leaving the hundred or so poems of his very last years unpublished.

—Steven R. Cerf

See the essay on *Tynset.*

HILL, Geoffrey (William)

Nationality: British. **Born:** Bromsgrove, Worcestershire, 18 June 1932. **Education:** Keble College, Oxford University, B.A. 1953, M.A. 1959. **Family:** Married 1) Nancy Whittaker in 1956 (divorced), three sons and one daughter; 2) Alice Goodman in 1987, one daughter. **Career:** Member, English department, 1954, and professor of English Literature, 1976–80, University of Leeds; lecturer in English and fellow, Emmanuel College, Cambridge University, 1981–88. Since 1988 professor of literature and religion, Boston University. Visiting lecturer, University of Michigan, Ann Arbor, 1959–60, and University of Ibadan, Nigeria, 1967; Churchill fellow, University of Bristol, 1980; Clark Lecturer, Trinity College, Cambridge University, 1986. **Awards:** Eric Gregory award, 1961, for *For the Unfallen;* Hawthornden pize, 1969, and Geoffrey Faber memorial prize, 1970, both for *King Log;* Whitbread award, 1971, Alice Hunt Bartlett award, 1971, and Heinemann award, 1972, all for *Mercian Hymns;* Duff Cooper memorial prize, 1979, for *Tenebrae;* American Academy Russell Loines award, 1983; Ingram Merrill Foundation award, 1985. D.Litt.: University of Leeds, 1988. Honorary fellow, Keble College, Oxford University, 1981, and Emmanuel College, Cambridge University, 1990. Fellow, Royal Society of Literature, 1972. **Address:** The University Professor Program, Boston University, 745 Commonwealth Avenue, Boston, Massachusetts 02215, U.S.A.

PUBLICATIONS

Poetry

For the Unfallen: Poems 1952–1958. 1959.
Preghiere. 1964.
Penguin Modern Poets 8, with Edwin Brock and Stevie Smith. 1966.
King Log. 1968.
Mercian Hymns. 1971.
Somewhere Is Such a Kingdom: Poems 1952–1971. 1975.
Tenebrae. 1978.
The Mystery of the Charity of Charles Péguy. 1983.
Collected Poems. 1985.
New and Collected Poems, 1952–1992. 1994.

Canaan. 1996.
The Triumph of Love. 1998.

Play

Brand, adaptation of the play by Henrik Ibsen (produced London, 1978). 1978; revised edition, 1981.

Other

The Lords of Limit: Essays on Literature and Ideas. 1984.
The Enemy's Country: Words, Contexture, and Other Circumstances of Language. 1991.

*

Critical Studies: "Speaking of the Holocaust: The Poetry of Geoffrey Hill" by Igor Webb, in *University of Denver Quarterly,* 12(1), 1977, pp. 114–25; *Geoffrey Hill and "The Tongue's Atrocities",* 1978, and *The Force of Poetry,* 1984, both by Christopher Ricks; Geoffrey Hill issue of *Agenda* (London), 17(1), 1979; *Inhabited Voices: Myth and History in the Poetry of Geoffrey Hill, Seamus Heaney, and George Mackay Brown* by David Annwn, 1984; Geoffrey Hill issue of *Agenda,* 23, Autumn/Winter 1985–86; *Geoffrey Hill: Essays on His Work,* edited by Peter Robinson, 1985; *Geoffrey Hill,* edited by Harold Bloom, 1986; *The Poetry of Geoffrey Hill* by Henry Hart, 1986; *The Uncommon Tongue: The Poetry and Criticism of Geoffrey Hill* by Vincent B. Sherry, 1987; *Passionate Intelligence: The Poetry of Geoffrey Hill* by E.M. Knottenbelt, 1990; *An Introduction to Geoffrey Hill* by William Stanley Milne, 1998.

* * *

Born in 1932, the English poet Geoffrey Hill lost the innocence of childhood and came into the consciousness of the horrors that humans are both subject to and capable of when he viewed photographs and newsreels of Nazi concentration camps. Although the Holocaust is central to Hill's conception of atrocity, he is a martyrologist who ranges across vast expanses of history to address the sufferings of many victims. Implicitly agreeing with the claim of the Frankfurt school theorist Theodor Adorno that culture and barbarism go hand in hand and taking up the challenge of Adorno's charge that to write poetry after Auschwitz is barbarous, Hill fully explores the relationship between cultural tradition and human suffering.

Hill is considered by many critics to be the most important British poet of his generation, following in the tradition of the great philosophical and mystical poets Blake, Shelley, Yeats, and Eliot. Compared with more prolific contemporaries such as Ted Hughes and Seamus Heaney, Hill has produced a small oeuvre. Although only a handful of poems from his eight slim volumes deal directly with the Holocaust, they are arresting and memorable addresses. Hill's style is difficult, marked by extreme compression at the level of word and line, symbolism

based on historically arcane if not private meanings, complex irony (including self-irony), and an ambivalence of tone that at times defies interpretation. Readers who persist, however, find that their effort is repaid in poems that are painfully honest, intellectually profound, and shot through with moral urgency.

In Hill's first volume of poetry, *For the Unfallen* (1959), one can find compressed into the 16 lines of "Of Commerce and Society" those features that would come to characterize his method and his major themes, including the Holocaust:

> Statesmen have known visions. And, not alone,
> Artistic men prod dead men from their stone:
> Some of us have heard the dead speak:
> The dead are my obsession this week
> But may be lifted away. In summer
> Thunder may strike, or, as a tremor
> Of remote adjustment, pass on the far side
> From us: however deified and defied
> By those it does strike. Many have died.
>   Auschwitz,
> Its furnace chambers and lime pits
> Half-erased, is half-dead; a fable
> Unbelievable in fatted marble.
> There is, at times, some need to demonstrate
> Jehovah's touchy methods that create
> The connoisseur of blood, the smitten man.
> At times it seems not common to explain.

There is the masterful shaping of language, for example, in the lines "a fable / Unbelievable in fatted marble," with the word "fable" opened up and redistributed in "unbelievable" and "fatted marble." One discerns Hill's self-irony in "The dead are my obsession this week" as well as his interrogation of aesthetic motivation in "Artistic men prod dead men from their stone." In the last stanza he meditates on the enigma of God's ways, an open-ended question that appears throughout his work.

In his poem "History as Poetry" Hill describes poetry as conveying through "the tongue's atrocities" the secrets and truth of "the speechless dead." Throughout his work there echoes the plea that historical memory be kept alive in a culture that has relentlessly commodified sentiment and sensationalized and flattened history into entertainment, rendering futile the power of witness. Even the most fiercely honest literary works are in constant danger of being co-opted and trivialized. A complex of recurring themes in Hill's poetry concerns the limitations of imagination, the equivocation of language, and the failure of communication. His poetics is marked by skepticism and despair, giving rise to a sustained self-interrogation, as he maintains a vigilant watch against the effects of a catharsis that would let the poet and the reader off lightly. The following lines from his poem "Annunciations" warn of the real possibility of such escapism through the blandishments of poetry:

Such precious things put down
And the flesh eased through
   turbulence, the soul
Purples itself; each eye squats full and mild
While all who attend to fiddle or to harp
For betterment, flavour their decent mouths
With goblets of the sweetest sacrifice.

Literature about the Holocaust always faces the danger of becoming a ''precious thing'' that satiates the reader's emotions with poetic ''turbulence'' until the eye ''squats full and mild.'' Hill refuses to allow his readers to push away from the poetic plate feeling sated and relieved. Near the end of his volume *Triumph of Love* he defines poetry as ''a sad and angry consolation'' (CXLVIII). By extension, Hill has claimed that a poetic offering should never be enough. For those readers who have found his poetry to be constantly bracing, profound, even prophetic, his offering has been substantial.

—Molly Abel Travis

See the essays on ''September Song,'' *Triumph of Love,* and ''Two Formal Elegies.''

HILLESUM, Etty

Nationality: Dutch. **Born:** Middelburg, 15 January 1914. **Education:** Studied law, psychology, and Slavic languages and literature, University of Amsterdam, Ph.D. **Career:** Volunteer special assistant, Jewish Council, Westerbork concentration camp, 1942; prisoner, Westerbork and Auschwitz. **Died:** Murdered, Auschwitz, November 1943.

PUBLICATIONS

Diary

Het vestoorde leven: Dagboek van Etty Hillesum, 1941–1943, edited by J.G. Gaarlandt. 1981; as *An Interrupted Life: The Diaries of Etty Hillesum, 1941–43,* 1983; as *Etty: A Diary, 1941–1943,* 1983.

Other

Het denkende hart van de barak: Brieven van Etty Hillesum (letters). 1982; as *Letters from Westerbork,* 1986.

*

Critical Studies: ''Etty Hillesum: A Story of Spiritual Growth'' by Irving Halperin, in *Reflections of the Holocaust in Art and Literature,* edited by Randolph L. Braham, 1990; *Dark Night Spirituality: Thomas Merton, Dietrich Bonhoeffer, Etty Hillesum: Contemplation and the New Paradigm* by Peter King, 1995; *Writing As Resistance: Four Women Confronting the Holocaust: Edith Stein, Simone Weil, Anne Frank, Etty Hillesum* by Rachel Feldhay Brenner, 1997; *Anne Frank and Etty Hillesum: Inscribing Spirituality and Sexuality* by Denise de Costa, translated by Mischa F. C. Hoynick and Robert E. Chesal, 1998; ''Holocaust Chronicle, Spiritual Autobiography, Portrait of an Artist, Novel in the Making: Reading the Abridged Diary of Etty Hillesum'' by Anna Makkonen, in *Biography,* 22(2), Spring 1999, pp. 237–61; *The Uses of Darkness: Women's Underworld Journeys, Ancient and Modern* by Laurie Brands Gagné, 2000.

*   *   *

Etty Hillesum studied law, psychology, and Slavic languages and literature at the University of Amsterdam, where she received her doctorate. She was interned in the concentration camps of Westerbork and Auschwitz, and she died at Auschwitz in 1943 at the age of 29.

One of the most important analyses of the work of Etty Hillesum has been that of Rachel Feldhay Brenner in her book *Writing as Resistance: Four Women Confronting the Holocaust* (1997). Brenner makes reference to how Hillesum defied the terror of the Holocaust and exhibited spiritual resistance in her determination to survive the dehumanization of the concentration camps.

Brenner examines the impact of the Holocaust on Hillesum's religio-moral outlook. Although she was a committed member of the Jewish community, Hillesum did not feel a need to establish close ties with Judaism in a religious sense. Nonetheless she was aware that her Jewish identity made her a target of the Final Solution. She acknowledged her Jewishness and openly empathized with the suffering that befell the Jewish people. Her discourse with God draws on ecumenical theology, stressing the universalist values of the Enlightenment era, and is accordingly a mixture of Judaism and Christianity.

Hillesum saw Gentile society as her natural environment with her faith in the brotherhood of all human beings. Her diary and her correspondence reveal a persistent faith in the ethics of the humanistic ideal.

Brenner views Hillesum's voluntary service as a special assistant to the Jewish Council in the concentration camp of Westerbork as being reminiscent of Bernard Rieux's voluntary service in Albert Camus's novel *The Plague.* (Camus had in fact meant for his novel about bubonic plague to be an allegory for Nazism.) Hillesum's writing of diaries and correspondence that bear witness to important historical events vis-à-vis the Holocaust was motivated by a desire to maintain dignity and self-respect in an age of crisis.

Before the Holocaust Hillesum had been preoccupied with an intellectual, spiritual, and personal development that Brenner describes as ''ethical self-actualization.'' In the end it meant serving humanity with a total disregard for the self, when Hillesum voluntarily chose to go to Westerbork as a social worker.

—Peter R. Erspamer

See the essays on *An Interrupted Life: The Diaries of Etty Hillesum, 1941–43* and *Letters from Westerbork.*

HILSENRATH, Edgar

Nationality: American (originally German: immigrated to the United States, 1951, granted U.S. citizenship, 1958). **Born:** Leipzig, 2 April 1926. **Education:** Completed primary and secondary school in Germany. **Family:** Married Marianne Boehme. **Career:** Moved to Bukovina (now Romania and Ukraine) as a child; imprisoned in the Moghilev-Podelsk (Romania) ghetto and held in a Russian forced labor camp during World War II; worked at several odd jobs in Palestine, 1945–47; reunited with his family, France, 1947; lived in New York and worked as a writer, 1951–75. Moved to Berlin, 1975. **Awards:** Alfred Döblin prize, 1989, for *Das Märchan vom letzten Gedanken;* Hans Sahl prize, 1998. **Agent:** Maximilian Becker, 115 East 82nd Street, New York, New York 10028, U.S.A.

PUBLICATIONS

Novels

Nacht. 1964; as *Night,* 1966.
Der Nazi und der Friseur. 1977; as *The Nazi and the Barber,* 1971; as *The Nazi Who Lived As a Jew,* 1977.
Gib acht, Genosse Mandelbaum. 1979.
Bronskys Geständnis. 1982.
Zibulsky, oder, Antenne im Bauch. 1983.
Das Märchan vom letzten Gedanken. 1989; as *The Story of the Last Thought,* 1990.
Moskauer Orgasmus. 1992.
Jossel Wassermanns Heimkehr. 1993.
Die Abenteur des Ruben Jablonski: Ein autobiographischer Roman. 1997.

*

Critical Studies: *Memories of the Holocaust: Edgar Hilsenrath and the Fiction of Genocide,* 1982, and "Memories of the Holocaust: Edgar Hilsenrath and the Fiction of Genocide," in *Deutsche Vierteljahrsschrift für Literaturwissenschaft und Geistesgeschichte* (Germany), 56(2), June 1982, pp. 277–89, both by Peter Stenberg; "Social Darwinism in Edgar Hilsenrath's Ghetto Novel *Nacht,*" in *Insiders and Outsiders: Jewish and Gentile Culture in Germany and Austria,* edited by Dagmar C.G. Lorenz and Gabriele Weinberger, 1994, and

"History, Identity, and the Body in Edgar Hilsenrath's *The Story of the Last Thought,*" in *Transforming the Center, Eroding the Margins: Essays on Ethnic and Cultural Boundaries in German-Speaking Countries,* edited by Dagmar C.G. Lorenz and Renate S. Posthofen, 1998, both by Lorenz; "Writing As Revenge: Reading Edgar Hilsenrath's *Der Nazi und der Friseur* As a Shoah Survivor's Fantasy" by Jennifer L. Taylor, in *History of European Ideas,* 20(1–3), January 1995, pp. 439–44; "Autobiography and the Fiction of the I: Edgar Hilsenrath" by Bianca Rosenthal, in *The Fiction of the I: Contemporary Austrian Writers and Autobiography,* edited by Nicholas J. Meyerhofer, 1999.

*   *   *

Having survived an episode of the Nazi persecution of European Jewry unfamiliar to many, Edgar Hilsenrath has employed his fiction to tell the story of this forgotten side of the Holocaust and to delve into territory that few other writers have dared to explore. In his unique approach to his subjects and in the unusually humorous tone of much of his writing, he has broken taboos and opened up new possibilities for understanding the dynamics of guilt, victimization, and identity in the context of the Holocaust—all in ways that have subjected him to both praise and controversy.

Hilsenrath has always identified with the German language and German culture. After a youth spent in the eastern German cities of Leipzig and Halle, he escaped Nazi persecution of the Jews with his mother and younger brother and moved to his maternal grandmother's home in Bukovina, located in present-day Romania and Ukraine. After being subjected to the oppressive race laws in Germany, Hilsenrath found a home in the multiethnic region. As a German speaker he spoke the language that was both the administrative language and the common means of communication. As a Jew he was a member of one of the largest groups in the population. Hilsenrath ironically felt like more of a real German in Bukovina than he had in Germany and later described his life in Bukovina as ideal. Tragically this ideal was short-lived.

As World War II progressed the region came under Nazi and fascist Romanian control, and Hilsenrath and other Jews in the area were deported to camps and ghettos. In 1941 Hilsenrath and his family were sent to the ghetto in Ukrainian Moghilev-Podelsk, where they survived until 1945. After the war Hilsenrath moved first to Palestine, then to France, and after that to the United States, before finally returning in 1975 to Germany, where he settled in Berlin. Thomas Kraft writes that in almost all of Hilsenrath's texts, as varied as they may be, the painful experiences of an author in exile are reflected, sometimes directly and sometimes indirectly. Kraft detects a restless driving force, propelled by the traumatic experiences of being uprooted by the terror of the Holocaust—a force that can find balance and peace only in literary expression.

Indeed, in his attempt to find wholeness in his post-Holocaust existence, Hilsenrath has staunchly maintained his use of German in his literary production, though others in his situation had begun writing in other languages. He also returns again and again to his idyllic youth in Bukovina, using it as a setting for works like *Nacht* (1964; *Night,* 1966) and *Gib acht, Genosse Mandelbaum* (1979), and creating characters in *Jossel Wassermans Heimkehr* (1993) and *Der Nazi und der Friseur* (1977; *The Nazi and the Barber,* 1971) who have their roots in the region.

Yet Hilsenrath is not an idealist and does not live in the past. His writing clearly reflects his desire to engage the post-Holocaust reality in which he works in a very direct and sometimes even confrontational way. Hilsenrath's writing was initially so controversial that it went almost entirely unnoticed in Germany. After an initial printing in 1964 of about one thousand copies, his first novel, *Nacht,* was not reprinted. Critics have indicated that his portrayal of the Jews in the text was not in line with the wave of post-Holocaust philo-Semitism prevalent in Germany at the time. In spite of low sales in Germany, translations of Hilsenrath's first novels into English, French, and Italian sold more than a million copies. German audiences finally appeared ready to accept Hilsenrath's work when, in 1977, his second novel, *Der Nazi und der Friseur,* was published. This text, too, was criticized for its portrayal of Holocaust victims and perpetrators, in particular for Hilsenrath's refusal to draw distinct lines between the two groups and for his use of satire and humor in a German novel about the Holocaust and the founding of Israel.

Hilsenrath has remained uncompromising in his writing, refusing to change his style or his approach in the face of criticism or ideological objections. In his 1982 novel, *Bronskys Geständnis,* the title character, the author of a novel much like Hilsenrath's *Nacht,* corrects an interviewer who calls his novel a ''book about the Jewish Ghetto.'' It is, Bronsky informs him, a ''book against violence and inhumanity.'' Indeed, these are Hilsenrath's main themes. Whether he is using humor, satire, or stark realism, Hilsenrath finds creative and unusual ways in his writing to force readers to reexamine their assumptions about the massacre of European Jews by the Nazis, the Armenians' genocide at the hands of the Turks, and German Jewish identity politics in the post-Holocaust world.

—Gregory Baer

See the essays on *Night* and *The Nazi and the Barber.*

HOCHHUTH, Rolf

Nationality: German. **Born:** Eschwege, 1 April 1931. **Education:** Studied bookkeeping at a vocational school; universities of Marburg, Munich, and Heidelberg, 1952–55. **Family:** Married Marianne Heinemann in 1957 (divorced 1972); two sons. **Career:** City-hall runner for the first postwar mayor of Eschwege, his uncle; publisher, reader, and editor, C. Bertelsmann, Gütersloh, Westphalia, beginning in 1955; assistant director and playwright, Municipal Theatre, Basel, Switzerland, 1963. **Awards:** Gerhart Hauptmann prize, 1962, and Berliner Kunstpreis, 1963, both for *Der Stellvertreter;* Young Generation prize, 1963; Melcher prize, 1965; Basel Art prize, 1976; Geschwister-Scholl prize and Stadt Munchen und des Verbandes Bayerischer Verlager prize, both in 1980; Lessing prize, 1981.

PUBLICATIONS

Plays

Der Stellvertreter: Ein christliches Trauerspiel (produced West Berlin, 1963). 1963; as *The Deputy* (produced New York, 1964), published as *The Representative,* 1963; as *The Deputy,* 1964.

Soldaten, Nekrolog auf Genf: Tragödie (produced West Berlin, 1967). 1967; as *Soldiers* (produced Toronto, Ontario, and New York, 1968), published as *Soldiers: An Obituary for Geneva,* 1968.

Guerillas: Tragödie in fünf Akten (produced Stuttgart, West Germany, 1970). 1970.

Die Hebamme: Komödie [The Midwife] (produced 1972). 1971.

Lysistrate und die NATO: Komödie Mit e. Studie: Frauen und Mütter, Bachofen und Germaine Greer [Lysistrata and NATO] (produced 1974). 1973.

Tod eines Jägers [Death of a Hunter]. 1976.

Juristen: Drei Akte für sieben Spieler. 1979.

Arztinnen: 5 Akte. 1980.

Judith (produced Glasgow, Scotland, 1984).

Unbefleckte Empfangnis: Ein Kreidekreis [Immaculate Conception: A Chalk Circle] (produced Berlin, 1989).

Sommer 14: Ein Totentanz [Summer 14] (produced Vienna, 1990).

Alle Dramen [All dramas] (2 vols.). 1991.

Novel

Eine Liebe in Deutschland. 1978; as *A German Love Story,* 1980.

Short Stories

Atlantik-Novelle: Erzählungen und Gedichte. 1985.

Other

Krieg und Klassenkrieg [War and Class War] (essays). 1971.

Zwischenspiel in Baden-Baden. 1974.

Die Berliner Antigone: Prosa und Verse [The Berlin Antigone] (novella). 1975.

Tell '38. 1979; translated as *Tell '38,* 1984.

Spitze des Eisbergs: Ein Reader. 1982.

Rauber-Rede: 3 deutsche Vorwurfe: Schiller/Lessing/ Geschwister Scholl. 1982.

Schwarze Segal: Essays und Gedichte. 1986.

Tater und Denker: Profile und Probleme von Casar bis Junger: Essays. 1987.

War hier Europa? Reden, Gedichte, Essays. 1987.

Alan Turing: Erzählung. 1987.

Menzel: Maler des licts. 1991.

Von Syrakus aus gesehen, gedacht, erzählt. 1991.

Tell gegen Hitler: Historische studien. 1992.

Wessis in Weimar: Szenen aus einem besetzten land. 1993.

Julia oder der weg zur macht: Erzeahlung. 1994.

Effis nacht: Monolog. 1996.

Und Brecht sah das tragische nicht: Pleadoyers, Polimiken, Profile. 1996.

Editor, *Sämtliche Werke, und eine Auswahl der Skizzen und Gemälde,* by Wilhelm Busch:

  Und die Moral von der Geschicht. Eingeleitet mit dem Essay von Theodor Heuss aus der Biographie Die grossen Deutschen. 1959.

  Was beliebt ist auch erlaubt. 1960.

Editor, *Lustige Streiche in Versen und Farben,* by Wilhelm Busch. 1960.

Editor, *Sämtliche Bildergeschichten mit 3380 Zichnungen und Fachsimilies,* by Wilhelm Busch. 1961.

Editor, *Liebe in unserer Zeit: Sechzehn Erzählungen* (2 vols.). 1961.

Editor, *Am grauen Meer,* by Theodor Storm Mosaik. 1962.

Editor, *Die Deutschen,* by Otto Flake. 1962.

Editor, *Dichter und Herrscher,* by Thomas Mann. 1963.

Editor, *Die grossen Meister: Deutsche Erzähler des 20. Jahrhunderts* (2 vols.). 1964.

Editor, *Des Lebens Uberfluss.* 1969.

Editor, *Ruhm und Ehre.* 1970.

Editor, with Hans-Heinrich Koch, *Kaisers Zeiten: Bilder einer Epoche,* by Oscar Tellgmann. 1973.

*

Film Adaptation: *The Investigation,* 1965, from the play *The Deputy.*

Bibliography: "Auswahlbibliographie zu Rolf Hochhuth" by Gunter Peters, in *Text + Kritik* (Germany), 58, 1978, pp. 62–65.

Critical Studies: *Pope Pius XII and the Jews, an Answer to Hochhuth's Play Der Stellvertreter (The Deputy)* by Desmond Fisher, 1963; *The Storm over The Deputy,* edited by Eric Bentley, 1964; *The Deputy Reader: Studies in Moral Responsibility,* edited by Dolores Barracano Schmidt and Earl Robert Schmidt, 1965; *Rolf Huchhuth* by Rainer Taëni, translated by R.W. Last, 1977; *Rolf Hochhuth* by Margaret E. Ward, 1977; "The Apostate Ethic: The Alternative to Faith in Hochhuth's

Der Stellvertreter" by E. Elaine Murdaugh, in *Seminar* (Canada), 15, 1979, pp. 275–89; "American Mythologies: Rolf Hochhuth's Plays *Guerillas, Tod eines Jagers,* and *Judith*" by Manfred Durzak, in *Amerika! New Images in German Literature,* edited by Heinz D. Osterle, 1989; "'Was von Bismarck ubrigblieb...': Rolf Hochhuth and the German Question" by Lucinda Rennison, in *The New Germany: Literature and Society after Unification,* edited by Osman Durrani, Colin Good, and Kevin Hilliard, 1995.

* * *

Since the staging of Rolf Hochhuth's first play, *Der Stellvertreter* (1963; *The Deputy*), the Nazi years have been central to much of his work. Hochhuth's dramas nevertheless moved away from the Holocaust to deal with other aspects of the Nazi regime or with other episodes in the history of state violence in twentieth-century Europe. These plays have made him one of the most influential playwrights in postwar Germany, though *The Deputy* remains his best-known production.

By 1972 Hochhuth's *Deputy* had been produced in 26 countries, inspiring a wave of documentary or factual dramas on similar subjects on both sides of the Atlantic, notably *The Investigation* (1965) by **Peter Weiss** and a string of plays in America focused on the Vietnam War. When *The Deputy* was first staged, the government of Konrad Adenauer was increasingly under fire for its attitude to the resurgence of swastika daubings in the Federal Republic and for the continued employment of former Nazi officials in important positions, some of whom were discussed in the play. The first productions of *The Deputy* thus fell on fertile soil in Germany, some saying that they contributed to the defeat of the Adenauer administration in elections the following year. Hochhuth became a celebrated figure on the German left and was able to devote himself to writing full-time (he had worked in a bookstore and a publishing house).

The product of 10 years of meticulous research, *The Deputy* was widely construed primarily as an attack on the Catholic Church (Hochhuth being a Protestant with radical political leanings). The play met with a fierce reaction from the Catholic hierarchy, already engaged in a heated internal battle over Catholic responses to anti-Semitism, and there were attempts to have the play banned. From the time of the heady debates on the subject at the Second Vatican Council (1962–65), church leaders have cited *The Deputy* as a prime example of the modernist tendency that sought to use the Holocaust as a weapon against the Catholic Church. In interviews at the time, Hochhuth appeared more moderate than his critics cast him, focusing exclusively on the choices made by Pope Pius XII during the commission of the Nazis' Final Solution. One byproduct of the debate over *The Deputy* was the strengthening of voices critical of the pope within the Jewish world, where most Jewish observers had until then lavished praise on Pius XII for his quiet efforts to rescue Jews during the Holocaust.

Hochhuth's second play, *Soldaten, Nekrolog auf Genf* (1967; *Soldiers*, 1968), implicated Britain's wartime Prime Minister Winston Churchill in the firebombing of civilian targets in Germany during World War II. The play was banned in England, where the bombing of Dresden, Hamburg, and other cities was officially cast as part of a military campaign and where the reputation of Churchill, his funeral having brought the country to a standstill in 1965, was still unimpeachable. The ban was subsequently rescinded, but Hochhuth had reaffirmed his own reputation for hitting out against crimes against humanity committed in the course of war.

With *Juristen* (1979; *Jurists*) Hochhuth returned to the Nazi theme, turning a spotlight on the former Nazi judges still employed in postwar Germany. Once more Hochhuth hit home, provoking the resignation of the head of the government of one of West Germany's largest states, Baden-Württemberg. In other plays at the time, Hochhuth turned to issues relating to Germany's responsibility for the two world wars and the responsibility of its leaders for the division of the country into two states, East and West Germany, after 1945. He has lived most of his working life in Switzerland, a choice that reflects his alienation from the West German state created in the wake of the collapse of the Nazi regime.

The contemporary style and political edge of Hochhuth's plays jostle with a profound attachment to the theater of the German Enlightenment (Aufklärung). *The Deputy,* in particular, betrays Hochhuth's attachment to the liberal agenda of Schiller, according to whom an individual is ultimately responsible for his or her actions. Hochhuth's depiction of the Holocaust turns essentially on the decision of some individuals to oppose the Nazis' anti-Jewish policy and by contrast the motivations that prevented others from doing the same. Hochhuth's indictment of the German elite for a succession of moral failures over the course of the twentieth century speaks not of a rejection of any particular form of German nationalism or statist ideology. Instead the theme linking *The Deputy* and his other historical plays is his insistence on the responsibility of individuals in every historic situation to summon the courage to stand out against inhumanity.

—George R. Wilkes

See the essay on *The Deputy.*

HOFMANN, Gert

Nationality: German. **Born:** Limbach, 29 January 1931. **Education:** University of Freiburg/Breisgau, Ph.D. 1957. **Career:** Taught at various universities after leaving East Germany in the 1950s; lecturer in modern German literature, University of Edinburgh, Scotland, 1965–68; returned to Germany in the 1980s. **Awards:** Harkness award, 1965; Radio

Prague International Radio Play prize, 1968; Yugoslavian Radio prize, 1973; Ingeborg Bachmann prize, 1979; Prix Italia, 1980; Alfred Döblin prize, 1982, for *The Spectacle at the Tower.* **Died:** July 1993.

PUBLICATIONS

Novels

Die Denunziation [The Denunciation] (novella). 1979.
Die Fistelstimme. 1980.
Auf dem Turm. 1982; as *The Spectacle at the Tower,* 1984.
Unsere Eroberung. 1984; as *Our Conquest,* 1985.
Der Blindensturz. 1985; as *The Parable of the Blind,* 1986.
Veilchenfeld. 1986.
Die Weltmaschine. 1986.
Unsere Vergesslichkeit. 1987.
Vor der Regenzeit. 1988; as *Before the Rainy Season,* 1991.
Der Kinoerzähler. 1990; as *The Film Explainer,* 1995.
Das Glück. 1992.
Die kleine Stechardin. 1994.

Short Stories

Gespräch über Balzacs Pferd (includes ''Die Rückkehr des verlorenen Jakob Michael Reinhold Lenz nach Riga''; ''Casanova und die Figurantin''; ''Gespräch über Balzacs Pferd''; Der Austritt des Dichters Robert Walser aus dem Literarischen Verein''). 1981; as *Balzac's Horse and Other Stories,* 1988.
Fuhlrotts Vergesslichkeit; Portrait eines uns bekannten Kopfes: Erzählungen. 1981.
Tolstois Kopf: Erzählungen. 1991.

Plays

Der Bürgermeister. 1963; as *The Burgomaster,* 1968.
Kündigungen (includes *Unser Mann in Madras*; *Tod in Miami*). 1968; *Unser Mann in Madras* translated as *Our Man in Madras,* in *Plays in One Act,* edited by Daniel Halpern, 1991.
Die Überflutung: 4 Hörspiele (radio plays: includes *Autorengespräch*; *Schmährede des alten B. auf seinen Sohn*; *Der lange Marsch*; *Die Überflutung*). 1981.

Other

Dionysos Archemythos: Hölderlins transzendentale Poiesis (dissertation). 1996.

*

Critical Studies: '''Ein hoffnungsloser Moralist': Some Observations on the Narrative World of Gert Hofmann'' by Michael Butler, in *German Life and Letters* (England), 47(3), July

1994, pp. 375–84; ''Gert Hofmann's *Die Denunziation*,'' in *German Studies Review*, 19(3), October 1996, pp. 415–32, and *The Language of Silence: West German Literature and the Holocaust*, 1999, both by Ernestine Schlant; *Semiotic Discourses and the Production of Literary Texts: Joseph Roth, Ernst Jünger, Gert Hofmann* (dissertation) by Christoph Prang, University of North Carolina, 1998; '''Das war schon einmal da, wie Langweilig!'?: 'Hörspiel' and Narrative in the Work of Gert Hofmann (1931–1993)'' by Debbie Pinfold, in *German Life and Letters*, 52(4), 1999, pp. 475–89.

* * *

Born in 1931, Gert Hofmann belonged to a generation of postwar German writers who grew up during the Nazi period and, because of their age, were spared direct participation in the war at the fronts or in the concentration camps. Yet as children, Hofmann and his contemporaries were inadvertently witnesses to various horrors, from denunciations, murder, and suicides to ostracism and persecution that affected mostly Jews but also members of their own families. As with Christa Wolf's 1976 novel *Kindheitsmuster,* a major part of Hofmann's literary work was focused intensely on buried childhood memories of life in the family and in his hometown between the late 1930s and 1945. Many of his novels not only dwell upon dramatic events dating to these years but also reflect on the very process of unearthing and reassessing the bits and pieces of memories. In his work the author reveals the cognitive, psychological, and aesthetic problems associated with the endeavor to retrieve the past.

Hofmann started in the 1960s as an author of radio dramas and as a playwright for television, but his indisputable literary breakthrough came in 1979 with the publication of the novella *Die Denunziation* (''The Denunciation''). *Die Denunziation* marked the beginning of his serious interest in the subject of the Holocaust and the German Nazi past. Hofmann surprised the public with the originality of his selection of historical themes as well as with the rich palette of narrative techniques and strategies. Characteristic of Hofmann's prose are the peculiar restlessness and unreliability of the narrative voice. The narrator switches perspectives, cruises freely between past and present, and often shades into an unidentifiable presence as if to underscore the idea that the ''truth'' about the past has become practically inaccessible.

Most of Hofmann's works touching upon themes of persecution, racism, and murder during the Nazi period are set in the microworld of a sleepy provincial town in Germany. Often the author uses his own birthplace in Saxony, Limbach, as the background for the historical events. With almost ethnographic accuracy Hofmann describes the life of the family—with its predictable dynamics, power plays, and idiosyncracies—set

within a small network of friends, neighbors, and relatives. Yet at the same time, he transforms the family into the stage where private attitudes, petty habits, and routine behavior resound with the big moral dilemmas of the time and can be fatally related to ruptures and tragedies of historic proportions. In *Die Denunziation,* for example, it is the Hecht family that disintegrates in the most dramatic way after an anonymous betrayer reports the half-Jewish tailor L. Silberstein to the authorities. After Silberstein is rounded up in 1944, his wife commits suicide, and thereupon the mother of the Hecht family drowns herself, the father is sent to the retreating Eastern Front, where he is killed, and the twin brothers, Karl and Wilhelm Hecht, are separated for life at age 14.

In other short novels, such as *Unsere Eroberung* (1984; *Our Conquest*) and *Veilchenfeld* (1986), the narrator's voice assumes the identity and naive directness of children who have inadvertently become witnesses to historical tragedies. Sent on an errand on 8 May 1945, two brothers from *Unsere Eroberung* run into various adults whom the children suspect of participation in unimaginable horrors. It is again a child, their cousin Edgar, who unearths the nasty truth, namely that a Czech slave laborer has been murdered in the family factory. In the novel *Velichenfeld* the complex conjunction between the quiet and unremarkable everyday life of the small community of Limbach and the cruel political persecution of its only Jewish member, Professor Veilchenfeld, in the course of 1938 is seen again through the eyes of a child.

The theme of the Nazi past is handled with subtlety and humor in Hofmann's most overtly autobiographical text, *Der Kinoerzähler* (1990; ''The Film Explainer''). Once again, the book presents a meticulous study of one community's petty quarrels surrounding the ''Aryanization'' of a Jewish-owned cinema, and it goes on to reveal the subtle mechanisms leading to collaboration in the horrors of Nazism.

Hofmann's approach to the Holocaust and the Nazi past lacks the self-righteous pathos of other contemporaries who became known as the creators of the so-called *Väterliteratur.* While these authors have explored the past of their authoritarian parents only to assess the psychological injuries that were sustained, Hofmann is interested in the broader impact of the atrocities of the Holocaust, on Germans and Jews as well. In his works he manages to maintain a masterful balance between realistic autobiographical details and a modernist sense of rupture, incompleteness, and the impossibility of a consistent account of the experience. At the same time, his novels avoid the traps of sentimentality and philo-Semitism and offer no ready condemnations or absolutions.

—Mila Ganeva

See the essays on *Die Denunziation* and *Veilchenfeld.*

J

JABÈS, Edmond

Nationality: French (originally Egyptian: immigrated to France, 1957, granted French citizenship, 1967). **Born:** Cairo, 16 April 1912. **Education:** College Saint-Jean Baptiste de la Salle and Lycee Francais du Caire, both during the 1920s; Sorbonne University of Paris, 1930–31. **Family:** Married Arlette Sarah Cohen in 1935; two children. **Career:** Lived in exile in Paris, beginning in 1957. **Awards:** Prix des Critiques, Editions du Pavois, 1970, for *Elya;* Prix des Arts, des Lettres, et des Sciences, Foundation for French Judaism, 1982, for entire body of work; Pasolini prize, 1983, for *The Book of Questions;* Citadella Eurotechnic prize, 1987; French Ministry of Culture grand prize in poetry, 1987. Officer of the French Legion of Honor and Commander of Arts and Letters. **Died:** 2 January 1991.

PUBLICATIONS

Poetry

Chansons pour le repas de l'ogre [Songs for the Ogre's Meal]. 1947.
Trois Filles de mon quartier [Three Girls of My Quarter]. 1948.
La Clef de voute [The Key of the Vault]. 1950.
Je batis ma demeure: Poems, 1943–1957 [I Built My House: Poems, 1943–1957]. 1959; revised edition, 1975; selections translated as *A Share of Ink*, 1979.
Le Livre des questions [The Book of Questions]:
  Vol. I: *Le Livre des questions.* 1963; as *The Book of Questions,* 1976.
  Vol. II: *Le Livre de Yukel.* 1964; as *The Book of Yukel* and published with *Return to the Book* (vol. III), 1978.
  Vol. III: *Le Retour au livre.* 1965; as *Return to the Book* and published with *The Book of Yukel* (vol. II), 1978.
  Vol. IV: *Yael.* 1967; translated as *Yael* and published with *Elya* (vol. V) and *Aely* (vol. VI), 1983.
  Vol. V: *Elya.* 1969; translated as *Elya* and published with *Yael* (vol. IV) and *Aely* (vol. VI), 1983.
  Vol. VI: *Aely.* 1972; translated as *Aely* and published with *Yael* (vol. IV) and *Elya* (vol. V), 1983.
  Vol. VII: *El; ou, Le Dernier Livre.* 1973; as *El; or, The Last Book,* 1984.
La Memoire et la main [The Memory and the Hand]. 1974–89.
Ca suit son cours [It Follows Its Course]. 1975.
Le Livre des ressemblances [The Book of Resemblances]:
  Vol. I: *Le Livre des ressemblances.* 1976; as *The Book of Resemblances,* 1990.

  Vol. II: *Le Soupcon, le desert.* 1978; as *Intimations, the Desert,* 1991.
  Vol. III: *L'Ineffacable, l'inapercu.* 1980; as *The Ineffaceable, the Unperceived,* 1992.
Recit. 1981.
Le Petit Livre de la subversion hors de soupcon. 1982; as *The Little Book of Unsuspected Subversion,* 1996.
Le Livre du dialogue. 1984; as *The Book of Dialogue,* 1986.
Le Parcours. 1985.
Le Livre du partage. 1987; as *The Book of Shares,* 1989.
If There Were Anywhere but Desert: The Selected Poems of Edmond Jabès (French and English). 1988.
Le Seuil, le sable: Poésies complètes 1943–1988. 1990.
Le Livre de l'hospitalité. 1991.
From the Book to the Book: An Edmond Jabès Reader (selections). 1991.
Désir d'un commencement; Angoisse d'une seule fin. 1991; as *Desire for a Beginning; Dread of One Single End,* 2001.
Petites poésies jours de pluie et de soleil (for children). 1991.

Other

Preface aux lettres de Max Jacob a Edmond Jabes [Introduction to Max Jacob's Letters to Edmond Jabès]. 1945.
Le Livre des Marges:
  Le Livre des Marges. 1975; as *The Book of Margins,* 1993.
  Dans la double dependance du dit. 1984.
  Bâtir au quotidien. 1997.
Du desert au livre: Entretiens avec Marcel Cohen (interview). 1980; as *From the Desert to the Book,* 1990.
Un Etranger avec, sous le bras, un livre de petit format (aphorisms and reflections). 1989; as *A Foreigner Carrying in the Crook of His Arm a Tiny Book,* 1993.
L'Enfer de Dante. 1987.
La Memoire des mots: Comment je lis Paul Celan/ Worterinnerung: Wie ich Paul Celan lese (French and German). 1990.
Un Regard. 1992.
Cela a eu lieu. 1993.
Les Deux Livres; Suivi de, Aigle et chouette. 1995.

*

Bibliography: *Edmond Jabès Bibliography,* edited by Anthony Rudolph, 1974; *Edmond Jabès: ''Du blanc des mots et du noir des signes'': First Notes of a Bibliographer,* 1993, *Edmond Jabès: ''Du blanc des mots et du noir des signes'': A Preliminary Record of the Printed Books,* 1998, revised edition, 2001, and ''Addenda and Corrigenda to the Bibliography of Edmond Jabès, Together with Lists of Fugitive Works in Journals and

Books,'' in *Australian Journal of French Studies,* 37(2), 2000, p. 253, all by Roger Eliot Stoddard.

Critical Studies: *The Sin of the Book: Edmond Jabès,* edited by Eric Gould, 1985; *Questioning Edmond Jabès* by Warren F. Motte Jr., 1990; ''Edmond Jabes and the Poetry of the Jewish Unhappy Consciousness'' by Joseph G. Kronick, in *MLN,* 106(5), December 1991, pp. 967–96; ''Edmond Jabès: Sill and Sand'' by Mary Ann Caws, in *French Poetry Since the War: The Poetics of Presence and Passage,* edited by Richard Stamelman, 1992; ''Edmond Jabes and the Wound of Writing: The Traces of Auschwitz,'' in *Orbis Litterarum* (Denmark), 49(5), 1994, pp. 293–306, and *Lévinas, Blanchot, Jabès: Figures of Estrangement,* 1997, both by Gary D. Mole; ''The Writing of Catastrophe: Jewish Memory and the Poetics of the Book in Edmond Jabès'' by Richard Stamelman, in *Auschwitz and After: Race, Culture, and ''the Jewish Question'' in France,* edited by Lawrence D. Kritzman, 1994; *Edmond Jabès, the Poetry of the Nomad* by William Kluback, 1998; '''Sharing the Unshareable': Jabes, Deconstruction, and the Thought of the 'Jews''' by Joan Brandt, in *Borders, Exiles, Diasporas,* edited by Elazar Barkan and Marie-Denise Shelton, 1998.

* * *

Edmond Jabès, born in Cairo in 1912, is a poet of exile, wandering, loss, and silence. A French-speaking Italian Jew, Jabès lived the experience of an outsider from childhood, disconnected from his Arab environment by both his religion and his language. Early on he began a correspondence with Max Jacob, who eventually became his literary and spiritual mentor. Although close to the surrealists, Jabès never officially adhered to the group. In 1957 he was exiled by Nasser and elected to live in Paris, leaving everything behind him including his family library. In Paris he published his first book of poetry and aphorisms, *I Built My House* (1959). He went on to write more than two dozen books before his death in 1991. His main works are *The Book of Questions* (1963–73), *The Book of Resemblances* (1976–80), and *The Memory and the Hand* (1974–89).

Jabès's experience of literal and psychic exile is the foundation for his global interrogation of the world and, more specifically, of the inability of language to represent the world. He finds an answer in the rich silence of the desert as well as in ''The Book,'' the only place to which he can belong. Jabès's questioning of language and his obsession with ''The Letter''

connect him to a deeply rooted Judaic tradition and quest. Like music formed from the silence between notes, Jabès's deepest poetry is found in the silence of his suspended sentences and thoughts: ''Any commentary is first a commentary of silence.''

For Jabès the exile must be understood as the opposite of what he calls ''The Being'' and, as such, can only try to give expression to emptiness through the fullness of language. But this is an impossible task. The limitless cannot be expressed with a limited tool; Jabès can only suggest, in a paradoxical way, the existence of the nonexistent: silence becomes a language. In that sense the Jewish experience of wandering the earth is parallel to the wandering of language in its attempt at meaning: ''Faced with the impossibility of writing that paralyzes any writer and the impossibility of being Jewish that, for two thousand years, has torn the people of that name, the writer chooses to write and the Jew to survive.''

With an economy of means similar to the Japanese haiku, Jabès evokes the deepest experiences of the human condition. His sense of being *deraciné* (uprooted) allows him to express a universal experience of solitude and a desire for connection. This cruel perception of the solitude of the human condition gives a unique tone to his poetry—a poetry that suggests more than says, evokes more than describes—and inspires in the reader a consideration of his or her own experience of the existential loneliness we all share. Although a committed Jew, Jabès is open to a larger understanding of spirituality that touches on the universal. Jabès conceives of everything in an inverse way, however, and agrees with the Isaac Luria notion of *tzimtzum,* the fact that, to allow man to live, God retires from the world. Indeed, according to Jabès, if God withdraws from the world, is absent, then man's need for God becomes ever greater.

Jabès's paradoxical reading of the world leads us to a revision of our perceptions and indicates that the true life may be found in a new contemplation of ''The Letter.'' ''The Book'' becomes ''The Book of Life'' in an inverted way— ''God as extreme name of the abyss; Jew as a figure of exile, wandering, strangeness, and separation, which is also the writer's condition.'' Thus, to Adorno, who claims that after Auschwitz one cannot write poetry, Jabès gives the following answer: ''Yes, one can. And furthermore, one has to. One has to write out of that break, out of the unceasingly revived wound.''

—Alain Goldschlager

See the essay on *The Book of Questions.*

K

Ka-Tzetnik 135633

Pseudonym for Yehiel Denur. **Nationality:** Israeli (originally Polish: immigrated to Israel after World War II). **Born:** Yehiel Finer, 1917; took name Denur after moving to Israel. **Education:** Studied the Hebrew classics at a traditional Yeshiva in Lublin. **Family:** Married Nina Asherman. **Career:** Auschwitz survivor; writer; founder, with his wife, Israeli Movement for Arab-Jewish Cooperation (nonpolitical, grass roots organization), 1965. **Agent:** Curtis Brown Ltd., 10 Astor Place, New York, New York 10003, U.S.A. **Died:** 17 July 2001.

PUBLICATIONS

Novels

Salamandra. 1947; as *Sunrise over Hell,* 1977.
Beit ha-bubot. 1953; as *House of Dolls,* 1955.
Ha-shaon [The Clock]. 1960; as *Star Eternal,* 1971.
Karu lo Piepel [They Called Him Piepel]. 1961; as *Piepel,* 1961; as *Atrocity,* 1963; as *Moni: A Novel of Auschwitz,* 1987.
Ka-hol me-effer [The Phoenix Land]. 1966; as *Phoenix over the Galilee,* 1969; as *House of Love,* 1971.
Ha-nidon le-hayim. 1969.
Ahavah bi-lehavot. 1976.
Ha-dim'ah. 1978.
Daniyelah. 1980.
Nakam. 1981.
Di shevu'eh [The Vow]. 1982.
Hibute ahavah, 1984.
ha-'Imut. 1989.

Memoir

Tsofen: Edma': Masa ha-gar'in shel Oshvits. 1987; as *Shivitti: A Vision,* 1989.

*

Critical Studies: *The Holocaust Experience As Mirrored in the Literary Testimony of Ka-tzetnik* (dissertation) by Lea Leibowitz, University of the Witwatersrand, Johannesburg, South Africa, 1988; "Red Fire upon Black Fire: Hebrew in the Holocaust Novels of K. Tsetnik" by Howard Needler, in *Writing and the Holocaust,* edited by Berel Lang, 1988; "Memory in the Work of Yehiel Dinur (Ka-Tzetnik 135633)" by William D. Brierley, in *Hebrew Literature in the Wake of the Holocaust,* edited by Leon I. Yudkin, 1993; *A Phoenix from the Ashes: A Biographical Study of the Life of the Israeli Writer and Holocaust Survivor Yehiel De-Nur* by Gila Ackerman, 1994; "Kitsch and Sadism in Ka-Tzetnik's Other Planet: Israeli Youth Imagine the Holocaust" by Omer Bartov, in *Jewish Social Studies,* 3(2), Winter 1997, pp. 42–76.

* * *

The powerful literary forays of Yehiel Finer (later Yehiel Dinur), who spent two years in the Nazi death camp of Auschwitz, can be accurately described as profound fictionalized chronicles of hell, as stories related by a man who was able to transmit the shattering truth without once lessening its true dimensions. Publishing under the pen name Ka-Tzetnik (or K. Zetnik) 135633, Dinur took the moniker from the German abbreviation KZ (*Konzentrationslager*) for concentration camp inmate, stating, "I must carry this name as long as the world will not awaken after the crucifying of the nation to erase this evil, as humanity has risen after the crucifixion of one man." And on another occasion he observed, "It does not matter that I, Yehiel Dinur, pass away. The most significant fact is that K. Zetnik will stay alive." To be sure, the pseudonym further reinforced the anonymity and seclusion the author chose to embrace for many years until his death in 2001, while at the same time ironically pointing up the obliteration of identity and individuality the Nazis sought to achieve. Besides the pseudonym, the fact that the author adopted the name Dinur, which in Aramaic means "of fire," after settling in Palestine, clearly attests to the motif of transformation through the inferno that constituted a central pillar in his oeuvre.

In 1961 Dinur was summoned, along with hundreds of other survivors, by state prosecutor Gideon Hausner to give evidence at the trial of Adolf Eichmann. It was not surprising that Dinur's submergence within the reality of the Holocaust was so intense, so unforgettable, that, upon seeing the face of the architect of the Final Solution in the glass booth, he fainted, overwhelmed by the blackening, nightmarish images of what he had lived through. Before he collapsed, this is how Dinur described Auschwitz on the witness stand:

> The time there is not a concept as it is here in our planet. Every fraction of a second passed there was at a different rate of time. And the inhabitants of that planet had no names. They had no parents, and they had no children. They were not clothed as we are clothed here. They were not born there and they did not conceive there. They breathed and lived according to different laws of nature. They did not live according to the laws of this world of ours, and they did not die . . .

Time and again, Dinur's confronting novels, which were some of the first to tackle the descent into "planet Auschwitz," as he called it, present and bear witness to the years he and his fellow captives endured, singularly focused on the gleaming monstrosity of the German guards. Gripped mercilessly by his concentrationary experience, Dinur said that his inability to unearth the right registers and words to document the past resulted in exhaustion and breakdown. For the most part his semiautobiographical novels are graphically disturbing confessional pieces that allow the stunned reader an unmediated and acutely faithful glimpse into the eye of the storm, into the irrational nature of evil that shaped the author's life forever. Infused with a narratorial and stylistic obsession for outlining the violence, perversion, and bestiality of the Nazi criminals writ large, fueled by an abrasive reverence for an exact transcription of the abominable, the painful episodes are informed by the despair attendant on daily life in the camps, the raging insanity of evil, and the fevered attempt to maintain, among the fire of the ovens, one's dimming humanity and compassion.

The strong emphasis on authenticity and naturalism is evinced and underlined by Dinur's own commentary on his role: "I do not regard myself as a writer of literature. My writings are the chronicles of the planet Auschwitz." In essence, the thematic quilt of his sextet of novels titled *Salamander: A Chronicle of a Jewish Family in the Twentieth Century* shimmers with a rasping objectivity that primarily dwells on the complete brutality and physical torture perpetrated upon the prisoners, the sexual exploitation and the total dehumanization that was carved into the charred soul of the Jews. Accordingly, in *Sunrise over Hell* (1947), *House of Dolls* (1953), *Star Eternal* (1960), and *Atrocity* (1961), among others, the absurd and insane universe of the Shoah is spotlighted through the figure of Harry Preleshnik, who, as the author's alter ego, witnesses and reports on the ugliness and misery embodied in the surreal and, at times, supernatural reality of Auschwitz. Concomitantly, the prose is often deliriously frenzied, slipping into over-the-top stylized kitsch and sadism, as Omer Bartov has said.

Unable to exorcize the demons of the past, the former inmate, numbed and tormented by post-traumatic syndrome, was so haunted and besieged by the burden of memory that he considered all his prewar output and life as nonexistent. As a matter of fact, he retrieved several of his early works from the Library of Congress, the New York Public Library, and the Hebrew University Library and subsequently tore them to shreds. It has been noted that, while in the nascent days of Israeli statehood, the author's books were treated as pornography by teenage readers who were titillated by the remarkably explicit portrayals of sexual abuse, his corpus is now studied in Israeli high schools and by Israeli Defense Force soldiers. It is of particular salience that the inclusion of his writing in the educational syllabus flowed from the writer's particular wish that his royalties be directed to funding the teaching of the

Holocaust, reflecting his deep concern that memory of the event be preserved. Incredulously, despite the hobbling, unyielding evil he saw, Dinur's vision of life was not entirely that of a broken man. Rather, in later novels such as *Phoenix over the Galilee* (1966), for instance, he conveyed the message of universal peace and encouraged common dialogue and understanding between the warring Jews and Arabs.

—Dvir Abramovich

See the essays on *Atrocity, House of Dolls, Star Eternal,* and *Sunrise over Hell.*

KANIUK, Yoram

Nationality: Israeli. **Born:** Tel-Aviv, 1930. **Military Service:** Palmach (Zionist forces) during Israel's War of Independence, 1948. **Career:** Lived in New York City and worked as an artist during the 1950s; began writing in the 1960s. Theatre and film critic, *Davar* and *Lamerhave.* **Awards:** Bialik prize; Prix de Droits del'Homme (Paris), 1997; President's prize (Israel), 1998; Prix Mediterranee Etranger, 2000, for *Exodus: The Odyssey of a Commander.*

PUBLICATIONS

Novels

The Acrophile (translation). 1961.
Ha-yored le-ma'lah. 1963.
Himmo melekh yerushalaim. 1966; as *Himmo, King of Jerusalem,* 1969.
Adam ben kelev [Son of Dog]. 1969; as *Adam Resurrected,* 1971.
Susets. 1973; as *Rockinghorse,* 1977.
Ha-sipur al doda shlomtsion ha-gedola. 1975; as *The Story of Aunt Shlomzion the Great,* 1979.
Hayehudi ha'ahron [The Last Jew]. 1982.
Aravi tov. 1983; as *Confessions of a Good Arab,* 1984.
Bito. 1987; as *His Daughter,* 1988.
Ahavat David [The Second Book of David]. 1990.
Post-mortem. 1992.
Taigerhil [Tigerhill]. 1995.
Od sipur ahavah [Another Love Story]. 1996.
Nevelot-ha-sipur ha-amiti [Bastards, the Real Story]. 1997.

Short Stories

Mot ha-avir [Death of a Donkey]. 1973.
Afar ve-teshukah [Soil and Desire]. 1975.
Laila al hof im tranzistor [A Night on the Beach]. 1979.
Kemo sipurim. 1983.

Arba sipurim ve-shir [Four Stories and a Poem]. 1985.
Sipurei sof shavua [Weekend Stories]. 1986.

Other

Mi-metulah li-Nyu York (for children). 1963.
Ha-bavit she-bo metim ha-jukim mi-seivah tovah [The House
     Where the Cockroaches Lived to a Ripe Old Age] (for
     children). 1976.
Ha-ganav ha-nadiv [A Generous Thief] (for children). 1980.
Wasserman (for children). 1988.
Yovi, haluk nahal ve-ha-pil [Job, Pebble and the Elephant] (for
     children). 1993.
Ha-saga shel mefaked ha-exodus. 1999; as *Commander of the
     Exodus,* 1999.

*

Film Adaptations: *Rockinghorse; The Vulture,* 1982, from
the novel, *The Last Jew; Himmo, King of Jerusalem,* 1987.

Critical Studies: *Encounters with Israeli Authors,* 1982, and
"Native Israeli Literature and the Spectre of Jewish History"
(interview), in *Modern Hebrew Literature,* (Israel), 8(1–2),
Fall/Winter 1982–83, pp. 60–65, both by Ester Fuchs; "Ambi-
tions and Obsessions" by Jeffrey M. Green, in *Modern Hebrew
Literature,* 9(3–4), Spring/Summer 1984, pp. 61–66; "Rochelle
Furstenberg Interviews Yoram Kaniuk: Profile of a Tel Aviv
Writer" by Rochelle Furstenberg, in *Modern Hebrew Litera-
ture,* 2, Spring 1989; pp. 4–6; "The Bride of the Dead:
Phallocentrism and War in *Himmo, King of Jerusalem*" by
Yosefa Loshitzky, in *Literature/Film Quarterly,* 21(3), 1993,
pp. 218–29; "Fact and Fiction by Yoram Kaniuk" by Leo
Haber, in *Midstream,* 46(8), 1 December 2000, p. 33.

* * *

Despite never having experienced the Holocaust personally, Yoram Kaniuk has been hailed as one of the most
important Hebrew writers of the Holocaust. While working as
a sailor on a migrant ship and meeting Holocaust refugees after
1948, the Holocaust became an obsession for the author.
Although he never lived in the concentration camps, Kaniuk
felt as though he had survived the Holocaust in a kind of
assumed biographical identity. Many of his works revolve
around the Holocaust as well as other events in Jewish history
concerned with the meaning of the settlement of Israel after the
Holocaust and containing often grotesque descriptions of the
pathos of the Holocaust juxtaposed with an absurd form of
nation building in Israel.

Since the 1950s a change had occurred in Hebrew literature
as attitude shifted away from the Zionist narrative featuring
heroic Sabras and pioneers to more ambiguous protagonists in
the story of Jewish life in the postwar era. Hebrew literature
also delivered an ambiguous view of the Holocaust and
Germany and the roles these play in Israeli and Jewish life. The

main body of work that contrasted the paradigmatic, traditional literature at this time was postrealistic Hebrew literature,
created by writers who were born in the 1930s and '40s and
who made their mark in the mid-'50s. Kaniuk is one such
author, alongside Binyamin Tamuz, Yizhak Orpaz, Yehuda
Amichai, Nissim Aloni, Amalia Kahana-Carmon, and, more
broadly, Yaakov Shabtai and A.B. Yehoshua. Events such as
the arrival of the first survivors of the Holocaust in Israel in the
late 1940s and early '50s, the Adolf Eichmann trial in 1961,
and the Six-Day War shaped the development of Kaniuk and
these other authors. These events released new literary forms
and subjects as well as new styles and characters that moved
away from realistic literary tradition.

Kaniuk deals with the new uprooted characters who do not
fit into the Zionist model of building and renewal of the nation;
characters who belong to the lumpen strata that are personified
in some of Kaniuk's works as Holocaust survivors on the verge
of lunacy. In speaking about his obsession with the Holocaust,
Kaniuk stated in an interview, "If literature is something
through which the absurd becomes legitimate, my writing
legitimises my attempt to convey the horror I did not experience physically" and that "black humour is the only viable
response to the absurd," shedding light on some of the literary
techniques Kaniuk deploys in dealing with the Holocaust in
his stories.

Kaniuk's works are imbued with sadness but are still
dominated by an optimistic air. Rather than lamenting on the
loss in the form of a nostalgic elegy, Kaniuk writes satirical
stories that poignantly question the validity of normative
attitudes toward the Holocaust. He and his fellow writers drew
characters and perspectives that had previously been relegated
to the periphery of Jewish experience as seen in Hebrew
literature to the center stage. Implied in Kaniuk's literary
treatment of the Holocaust is a belief that the elements that
were lost in the creation of a new state must be revisited. The
old Jew and the Diaspora experience parallel the aspects of
human existence that do not receive adequate attention; the
animalistic side of all humans, the brutal side, the madness that
in turn defines sanity—these are the elements that must be
given a voice so as to comprehend the events that shape not
only the Jewish identity but also human existence.

—Ziva Shavitsky

See the essay on *Adam Resurrected.*

KAPLAN, Chaim A(ron)

Nationality: Polish. **Born:** Horodyszcze, White Russia (now
Belarus), 1880. **Education:** Institute for Jewish teachers,
Vilna. **Career:** Founder, teacher, and principal, Hebrew ele-
mentary school, Warsaw; wrote for Hebrew and Yiddish

periodicals. **Died:** Presumed murdered, victim of the Holocaust, late 1942 or early 1943.

PUBLICATIONS

Diary

Scroll of Agony: The Warsaw Diary of Chaim A. Kaplan, edited and translated by Abraham I. Katsh. 1999 (originally published in English in 1965).

Other

Sefat 'ami (Hebrew grammar). 1917.
Dikduk ha-lashon ve-shimushah (Hebrew grammar). 1925.
Ketov ka-halakhah! Sefer le-h'atakot ule-hakra'ot sistematiyot, kurs-shimushi male ve-shalem shel ha-ortografiyah ha-'ivrit (Hebrew grammar). 1926.
Hagadah shel Pesah: Iberzetst Yiddish (Jewish liturgy). 1926.
Pezurai; Mehkarim, reshimot u-felyetonim. 1900–1936. 1937.

*

Critical Study: "Beyond Silence and Denial: The Warsaw Diary of Chaim Kaplan" by Frank Graziano, in *The Polish Review,* 29(1–2), 1984, pp. 91–96.

* * *

Chaim Aron Kaplan was born in 1880 in Horodyszcze in White Russia (now Belarus). After Talmudic studies he entered an institute for Jewish teachers in Vilna. He spent most of his adult life in Warsaw, where he founded and became the principal of a Hebrew elementary school. His publications included a Hebrew grammar book, essays on the Hebrew language and Jewish education, and textbooks for children dealing with Jewish history and tradition.

In 1933 Kaplan began to keep a diary in Hebrew. From September 1939, during the period of the war, the occupation, and the ghetto, his diary ceased to be a personal document and was transformed into what was to become an invaluable contribution to the history of the time. Kaplan chose to stay in the Warsaw Ghetto, although his contacts in the United States and Palestine might, in 1941, have secured him an exit visa. On 26 July 1942, he described recording the terrible events in the Warsaw Ghetto as "a historical mission which must not be abandoned." This motivation for keeping the diary in ever-deteriorating circumstances is described by Kaplan as early as 16 January 1940, before the establishment of the ghetto: "I sense within me the magnitude of this hour, and my responsibility toward it, and I have an inner awareness that I am fulfilling a national obligation, a historic obligation that I am not free to relinquish. My words are not rewritten; momentary reflexes shape them. Perhaps their value lies in this. Be that as it may, I am sure that Providence sent me to fulfill this mission. My record will serve as source material for the future historian."

The importance of the diary to Kaplan grew as time passed, and by 13 November 1941, it had assumed such a central role in his existence that he wrote a rare personal note: "This journal is my life, my friend and ally. I would be lost without it. I pour my innermost thoughts and feelings into it, and this brings relief. When my nerves are taut and my blood is boiling, when I am full of bitterness at my helplessness, I drag myself to my diary and at once I am enveloped by a wave of creative inspiration . . . . Let it be edited at some future time—as it may be. The important thing is that in keeping this diary I find spiritual rest. That is enough for me."

Kaplan's final entry, recorded in the evening hours of August 4, 1942, concludes with the words "If my life ends—what will become of my diary?" Although Kaplan could not save himself or his wife—they are believed to have been murdered in Treblinka in December 1942 or January 1943—he managed to transfer his diary to the "Aryan" part of Warsaw.

In late 1942 Kaplan gave the diary to a Jewish friend named Rubinsztejn, who was working as a forced laborer outside the ghetto. Rubinsztejn smuggled the notebooks used by Kaplan to record his diary out of the ghetto singly and passed them on to a Pole named Wladyslaw Wojcek. Wojcek subsequently emigrated to the United States and sold the notebooks to the Jewish Cultural Foundation Library at New York University. The first English-language edition of the diary was published in 1965, and a Hebrew edition was published in 1966. A 1999 English edition included additional portions of the diary that were not available in 1965.

—Alan Polak

See the essay on *Scroll of Agony: The Warsaw Diary of Chaim A. Kaplan.*

KATZENELSON, Yitzhak

Nationality: Polish. **Born:** 1886. **Family:** Married Hannah (murdered, Treblinka, 1942); three sons (deceased). **Career:** Founder, Hebrew school in Lodz. Member, partisan organization Dror, Warsaw Ghetto, World War II; prisoner, Nazi camp, Vittel, France, 1943, then Auschwitz. **Died:** Murdered, Auschwitz, May 1944.

PUBLICATIONS

Poetry

Shirim le-yalde Yisra'el. 1907.
Dos vayse leben: Ertsehlungen un bilder. 1908.
Bi-gevulot Lita, po'emah. 1908.
Ha-To'eh: Mahazeh be-ma'arakhah ahat. 1910.
Sihot. 1910.

Dimdumim: Shirim. 1910.

Anu hayyim u-metim: dramah lirit bi-sheloshah perakim. 1912.

Fatima: Dramatishe poema in dray akten. 1919.

Hizkiyah ba'al ha-halomot sipur. 1920.

Mahmadim: Kovets sipurim shirim agadot u-mahazot. 1923.

Dos lid funem oysgehargetn Yidishn folk. 1944; as *The Song of the Murdered Jewish People,* edited by Shlomo Derech, 1980.

Yesh li shir, l'ildi Yisrael. 1954.

Ba-halom uve-hakits: Sipurim li-yeladim. 1955.

Piesn o zamordowanym zydowskim narodzie. 1982.

Plays

Bahurim: komedye, eyn akt. 1900.

Dekadent: komedye eyn akt. 1908.

Karikaturen: Drame in dray akten. 1909.

Mekhirat Yosef: Deramah bi-sheloshah aktim. 1910.

Ha-Ma'gal: Komedyah be-shalosh ma'arakhot. 1911.

Ahashverosh melekh tipesh: Komedyah be-haruzim be-ma'arakhah ahat. 1920.

Be-vet ha-mishneh: Mahazeh. 1919.

Ha-Hashmona'im: Mahazeh. 1920.

Ha-Skvit ha-yoter tsa'ir: Mahazeh. 1920.

Ha-Hashmonayim mahazeh. 1920.

Letsane Purim: Mahazeh. 1920.

Mekhirat Yosef: Mahazeh. 1920.

Halomot: Mahazeh. 1920.

Ha-Navi: hizayon be-shalosh ma'arakhot. 1922.

Unzere noente bakante: Lirishe drame in dray teyl. 1922.

Kohah shel manginah mahazeh. 1925.

'Al nahares Bovel: Biblishe tragedye in fir aktn. 1967.

Mahazot Tanakhiyim. 1983.

Short Stories

Taltalim. 1919.

Hizkiyah ba'al ha-halomot: Sipur. 1920.

Zarah shomer Shabat: Agadah. 1920.

Novel

Nitsanim. 1900.

Diary

Pinkas Vitel. 1964; as *Vittel Diary,* 1972.

Other

Yalde ha-perahim: agadah li-khvod Shevu'ot (for children). N.d.

Shirim le-yalde Yisra'el (for children). 1912.

Gezang un shpiel: Di ershte shpiel- un lieder-zamlung far Yudishe kinder (for children). 1920.

Gan-yeladim: Kovets shalem shel shirim frebeliyim ve-shirei-'am le-mishak u- lesha'ashu'im (for children). 1920.

Le-ma'an ha-gedolim, with Yitshak Berkman (Hebrew grammar). 1920.

Tal boker. Sefer 1: Mikra'ah 'Ivrit ahare ha-alef-bet, with Yitshak Berkman (Hebrew grammar). 1920.

Shimush ha-lashon: Hu helek shelishi le-sifre ha-dikduk, with Yitshak Berkman (Hebrew grammar). 1921.

Ha-Dikduk: 'Arukh be-shitah kalah (Hebrew grammar). 1921.

Mahatalot: Kovets-hatulim metsuyar, 'arukh be-safah kalah ve-nohah li-yeladim (for children). 1921.

Mayn Idish bukh (Yiddish grammar). 1923.

Tsafririm sefer limud u-mikra 'im mahlakah le-'avodot bi-khetav, with Yitshak Berkman (Hebrew grammar). 1925.

Sefer limud ve-mikra 'im mahlekah le-'avodot bi-khetav, with Yitshak Berkman (Hebrew grammar). 1927.

Ketavim aharonim: 703–704. 1947.

* * *

Yitzhak Katzenelson is considered one of the primary literary witnesses of the Holocaust, a poet in the company of **Paul Celan, Nelly Sachs, Primo Levi, Elie Wiesel,** and—before them—Chaim Nachman Bialik, the poet of the 1903 Kishinev pogrom. In contrast to these fellow poet-witnesses, however, Katzenelson does not write from the perspective of the survivor looking back. Rather, he writes from within the flaming epicenter of the *Hurban* itself. His most famous work, the epic poem *The Song of the Murdered Jewish People* (*Dos lid fun oysgehargetn Yidishn folk*), as well as his more personal record of the times and the events to which he has been witness, his *Vittel Diary,* were written between May 1943 and January 1944 in Vittel, France, where Katzenelson, under the assumed identity of a Honduran national, was interned in the Nazi camp for enemy aliens. In late April 1944, however, Katzenelson, along with most of his fellow Jewish inmates from Vittel, including his eldest son, Zvi, was sent to Auschwitz, via Drancy. He died in Auschwitz in early May, shortly after his arrival. His wife, Hannah, and their two younger sons, Ben-Zion and Benjamin, had perished in Treblinka two years earlier.

Katzenelson wrote in Hebrew and in Yiddish. To his Eastern European contemporaries before the war, he was known as a prolific writer of popular poems, stories, children's songs, and plays. Of particular significance is the importance of his work in the establishment of Hebrew as a vernacular language within the literary culture of Eastern European Jewry. Born into a family of rabbis and Hebrew scholars, and growing up in a household in which Hebrew was introduced as the family language, Katzenelson devoted much of his work as a writer and educator to the goal of establishing Hebrew as the foundational language of Jewish secular—not just religious—culture. He founded and directed a progressive, coeducational

Hebrew school in Lodz; his wife was the school librarian. What they needed were Hebrew texts, and many of Katzenelson's early works were produced in direct response to that need. His first collection of Hebrew poems was published in Warsaw in 1910, and the famous Habima theater company performed his play *Anu chajim umetim* (''We Live and We Die'') as their first play in Hebrew.

After the outbreak of the war and the German occupation of Lodz, Katzenelson and his family fled to Warsaw. In the Warsaw Ghetto, where he became an active member of the partisan organization Dror, he continued his practice of writing for use and from need, producing (often pseudonymously) occasional pieces that were performed in the ghetto and disseminated through the underground press. He also taught Hebrew. But the Holocaust that was to change his world forever also changed his language. For, after having devoted most of his career as a writer and educator to the development of a vernacular Hebrew, in response to the destruction of the world of Eastern European Jewry, Katzenelson shifted his literary language to the traditional vernacular of Eastern Europe's Jews: Yiddish. Moreover, as if to emphasize the local roots of this language, Katzenelson wrote *The Song of the Murdered Jewish People,* his last great work, not only in Yiddish but in a markedly un-Hebraic Yiddish. His final work thus pays homage not to the language of the prophets but to the language of the common people of a world in the process of being destroyed. Hebrew (the language in which Katzenelson still wrote privately, including his *Vittel Diary*) receded to the space of a personal culture, the trace of a dream for the future that the present had curtailed.

—Angelika Bammer

See the essays on *The Song of the Murdered Jewish People* and *Vittel Diary.*

KENEALLY, Thomas

Nationality: Australian. **Born:** Sydney, 7 October 1935. **Education:** St. Patrick's College, New South Wales. **Military Service:** Australian Citizens Military Forces. **Family:** Married Judith Martin in 1965; two daughters. **Career:** High school teacher, Sydney, 1960–64; lecturer in drama, University of New England, New South Wales, 1968–70; visiting professor, 1985, and distinguished professor, 1991–95, University of California, Irvine; distinguished professor, New York University, 1991–95. Member of Australia-China Council, 1978–88; advisor, Australian Constitutional Committee, 1985–88; member of Literary Arts Board of Australia, 1985–88; chair, 1991–93, and since 1994 director, Australian Republican Movement. **Awards:** Miles Franklin award, 1967, 1968; Captain Cook Bi-Centenary prize, 1970; Royal Society of Literature Heinemann award, 1973, for *The Chant of Jimmie*

Blacksmith; American Library Association notable book citation, 1980, for *Confederates;* Booker McConnell prize for fiction and *Los Angeles Times* fiction prize, both in 1982, for *Schindler's List.* Fellow, American Academy of Arts and Sciences. Officer, Order of Australia. **Member:** Australian Society of Authors (chair, 1987–90); National Book Council of Australia (president, 1985–90). **Agent:** International Creative Management, West 57th Street, New York, New York 10019, U.S.A.

PUBLICATIONS

Novels

The Place at Whitton. 1964.
The Fear. 1965.
Bring Larks and Heroes. 1967.
Three Cheers for the Paraclete. 1968.
The Survivor. 1969.
A Dutiful Daughter. 1971.
The Chant of Jimmie Blacksmith. 1972.
Blood Red, Sister Rose: A Novel of the Maid of New Orleans. 1974.
Gossip from the Forest. 1975.
Moses the Lawgiver. 1975.
Season in Purgatory. 1976.
A Victim of the Aurora. 1977.
Passenger. 1979.
Confederates. 1979.
The Cut-Rate Kingdom. 1980.
Bullie's House. 1981.
Schindler's Ark. 1982; as *Schindler's List,* 1982.
A Family Madness. 1985.
The Playmaker. 1987.
To Asmara: A Novel of Africa. 1989; as *Towards Asmara,* 1989.
By the Line. 1989.
Flying Hero Class. 1991.
Woman of the Inner Sea. 1992.
Jacko the Great Intruder. 1994.
A River Town. 1995.
Bettany's Book. 1998.

Plays

Halloran's Little Boat (produced Sydney, 1966). 1975.
Childermass (produced Sydney, 1968).
An Awful Rose (produced Sydney, 1972).

Television Play: *Essington,* 1974.

Other

Ned Kelly and the City of the Bees (for children). 1978.
Outback. 1983.

Australia. 1987.
With Yellow Shoes. 1992.
Now and in Time to Be: Ireland & the Irish. 1992.
The Place Where Souls Are Born: A Journey into the South-west. 1992; as *The Place Where Souls Are Born: A Journey into the American Southwest,* 1992.
Memoirs from a Young Republic. 1993.
Homebush Boy: A Memoir. 1995.
The Great Shame: And the Triumph of the Irish in the English-Speaking World. 1998.

*

Film Adaptation: *Schindler's List,* 1993.

Bibliography: "Thomas Keneally: An Annotated, Secondary Bibliography, 1979–1984" by Janice Chernekoff, in *Bulletin of Bibliography,* 43(4), December 1986, pp. 221–27.

Critical Studies: "Out of Context: A Study of Thomas Keneally's Novels" by Robert Burns, in *Australian Literary Studies* (Australia), 4, 1969, pp. 31–48; "Purpose and the Racial Outsider: Burn and The Chant of Jimmie Blacksmith" by Helen Daniel, in *Southerly* (Australia), 38, 1978, pp. 25–43; "Thomas Keneally: A Checklist" by Marianne Ehrhardt, in *Australian Literary Studies,* 9, 1979, pp. 98–117; "Thomas Keneally and 'the Special Agonies of Being a Woman' by Shirley Walker, in her *Who Is She?,* 1983; "The Ned Kelly of Cracow: Keneally's *Schindler's Ark*" by Michael Hollington, in *Meanjin* (Australia), 42(1), March 1983, pp. 42–46; "'White Ravens' in a World of Violence: German Connections in Thomas Keneally's Fiction" by Irmtraud Petersson, in *Australian Literary Studies,* 14(2), October 1989, pp. 160–73; "'Poor Simulacra': Images of Hunger, the Politics of Aid and Keneally's *Towards Asmara*" by David Kennedy, in *Mosaic* (Canada), 24(3–4), Summer/Fall 1991, pp. 179–89; *Thomas Keneally* by Peter Quartermaine, 1991; *Australian Melodramas: Thomas Keneally's Fiction* by Peter Pierce, 1995; "The Economies of *Schindler's List*" by Kirby Farrell, in *Arizona Quarterly,* 52(1), Spring 1996, pp. 163–88.

* * *

Schindler's List (first published in 1982 as *Schindler's Ark*) has been Australian author Thomas Keneally's best-selling novel. Moreover, no other Booker Prize-winning book has sold so many copies. If this is his only novel, among a couple of dozen, to deal directly with the Holocaust, many of its themes had been rehearsed and would later be reexamined elsewhere in his fiction. For Keneally war has been a perennial incitement of his imagination, particularly in respect to its rending of families and its shaping and deformation of the memories of nations. He has been drawn especially to what might be best regarded as civil wars: the Hundred Years' War (in *Blood Red, Sister Rose,* 1974), the American Civil War (in *Confederates,* 1979), the armistice dealings after World War I

(in *Gossip from the Forest,* 1975), and the Eritrean war of independence (in *Towards Asmara,* 1989).

Keneally writes of the bitter partisan struggle inside the Yugoslav theater of World War II in *Season in Purgatory* (1976), of the Australian homefront in that conflict in *The Fear* (1965) and *The Cut-Rate Kingdom* (1980), and of the long-delayed, destructive consequences of that war for Belorussian emigrants to Australia in *A Family Madness* (1985). About how he came to write *Schindler's List* we have a beguiling story of origins: the chance encounter in 1980 in a Los Angeles luggage shop run by Leopold Pfefferberg, one of the Schindler survivors, and the writer's immediate sense that here was a compelling tale suitable not only for his craft but also for the special bent of his compassion. Nevertheless, a commentator in the *Spectator* in 1994 would lament that it was Keneally who "walked into that leathergoods store" rather than "a humble news reporter" and that, in consequence, the issue was a novel.

The Holocaust story that Keneally came upon was breathtakingly unlikely: how a German entrepreneur and bon vivant saved more than 1,000 Jews by sheltering them as employees in his factory. But the story also accorded with crucial intuitions of his fiction—his analysis of stereotyping (here of Jews as supposedly doomed and designated victims) and of how stereotypes can be manipulated and resisted, as well as surrendered to, fatally. In the Schindler character Keneally created a compassionate renegade. Unlike a number of Keneally's protagonists, Schindler does not give in to coercive institutions; he subverts them from within. The hero as lovable rogue is given fuller play than in any of Keneally's other novels.

In *Schindler's List* Keneally focuses his attention once again on victims and victimization, on those who seem marked or feel themselves to be for malign attention and those—like some of the Germans in the novel—whose warped emotional needs lead them to relish the persecutor's role. In the grand-scale melodrama by which Keneally's fiction may best be characterized, the most powerful theme is dispossession: loss of life, property, selfhood. Nowhere is this toll more agonizingly exacted or resourcefully resisted than in his novel of the Holocaust.

Whether *Schindler's List* was a novel at all bedevilled the Booker judges. In the end Keneally was seen as having deployed the skills of his fictive craft in the interests of a work at once compassionate, astonishing, and surprising in its content and compass. Director Steven Spielberg's version of the novel would receive some harsh criticism (as well as approbation)—for example, from the self-interested **Claude Lanzmann** in *Le Monde* (3 March 1994). The director of the Holocaust film *Shoah* called Spielberg's effort "kitsch melodrama."

In the Australian literary scene Keneally—as a former Catholic seminarian—might appear an unusual figure to write of the Holocaust. It has typically and predictably been the province of Jewish authors such as Arnold Zable and Lily Brett (whose especial concern has been with survivor guilt). Yet his omnivorous embrace of moments of historical calamity and his probing of them for the hope that can be found in the worst of times makes Keneally's project in *Schindler's List* a signal, unrepeated, distinguished part of his oeuvre.

—Peter Pierce

See the essay on *Schindler's List*.

KERTÉSZ, Imre

Nationality: Hungarian. **Born:** Budapest, 9 November 1929. **Military Service:** Compulsory army service, 1951–53. **Career:** Journalist, *Világosság* (daily paper), 1949–51; worked as a freelance writer and translator after 1953. **Awards:** Brandenburg literary award, 1995; Darmstadt Academy Gundolf prize, Leipzig book prize for European Understanding, and Jeanette Schocken prize, all in 1997; World literature prize, 2000.

PUBLICATIONS

Novels

Sorstalanság. 1975; as *Fateless,* 1992.
A nyomkereso [Looking for Traces]. 1977.
Kudarc [Failure]. 1988.
Kaddis a meg nem született gyermekért. 1990; as *Kaddish for a Child Not Born,* 1997.
Jegyzokönyv, with Peter Esterhazy. 1993.
Valaki más: A változás krónikája [I, Another]. 1997.

Other

Az angol lobogó [The English Flag] (narrations). 1991.
Gályanapló (dialogue). 1992.
A holocaust mint kultúra: Három eloadás [The Holocaust As Culture: Three Lectures]. 1993.
A gondolatnyi csend, amíg a kivégzoosztag újratölt [A Thought-Long Silence While the Execution Squad Is Reloading] (monologue and dialogues). 1998.

*

Critical Study: "A Trilogy of Fatelessness" by Zotan Andras Ban, in *The New Hungarian Quarterly,* 32(124), Winter 1991, pp. 36–41.

*   *   *

Imre Kertész is often thought of as a one-book writer. He was 46 years old when in 1975 that book, the novel *Sorstalanság*

(*Fateless,* 1992), was published. Although he has added a few more volumes to his oeuvre since then, it is *Fateless* that remains his best-known, most frequently translated and commented-on work—this in spite of the fact that when it first appeared it was barely noticed and for years thereafter attracted relatively few readers. By the 1980s, however, their numbers grew, and after the fall of communism and the appearance of German and American editions of the work, a new, younger readership began to appreciate the book's style and spirit, realizing that it is not just another Holocaust novel.

Born in Budapest in 1929 into a thoroughly assimilated Hungarian Jewish family, Kertész spent his 15th year in Auschwitz and various other concentration camps, and these experiences form the basis of his first book. In his comments on the work Kertész has nevertheless stressed that *Fateless* is not a personal reminiscence but a work of fiction, one that clearly draws on his Auschwitz memories as well as his predicament as a survivor who stayed in the country from where he had been hauled away during the war.

Kertész, too, became fateless, like his 14-year-old hero, George Köves, who in the camps realizes that he has nothing in common with fellow Jews, especially the religious, for whom he is no Jew because he speaks not a word of Yiddish, while feeling odd about his Hungarian identity, too, since Hungarians do not want him either. Though he stayed in Hungary after the war, Kertész never really fit in. Haunted by the memory of Auschwitz and detesting the new totalitarianism that changed life yet again in the country, he remained for years on the fringes of literary life, working as a hack journalist and writing lyrics for forgettable musicals, while all along preparing to write the book of his life. Kertész is mindful to this day of the ambiguousness of his situation. Auschwitz turned him into a Jew, though in a very specific, limited sense. "I am one who is persecuted as a Jew, but I am not a Jew," he wrote in his diary as recently as the early 1990s.

The two novels that followed *Fateless*—*Kudarc* (1988; "Failure") and *Kaddis a meg nem született gyermekért* (1990; *Kaddish for a Child Not Born,* 1997)—are also full of autobiographical elements and present acutely self-conscious, tortured characters who cannot come to terms with the past and are incapable of having satisfying personal relationships in the present. *Failure* is about a novelist in the throes of a creative crisis. The first part is taken up with a description of an agonizing preparatory process: a writer trying to get down to business; while the second part is the result of his labors: an eerie, Kafkaesque evocation of a city that looks and sounds suspiciously like Kertész's native Budapest during the Stalinist 1950s. The narrator of the novel-within-the-novel is the same writer we met in the first part, who finds himself inexplicably transported back in time. After undergoing a series of bizarre experiences, he learns a great deal about suffering but not enough about the meaning of suffering. In *Kaddish* we meet a middle-aged survivor of Auschwitz who in an anguished *récit* tries to explain to a friend why he couldn't bring himself to fathering a child in post-Holocaust Eastern Europe. Needless to say, Kertész himself does not have a child of his own.

All of Kertész's fictional works are the painful and risky literary undertakings of a writer who turns the material of his own life into serious fiction. The result is stirring and also disquieting, because for his characters transforming lived reality into words on paper is invariably an obsessive rather than a redemptive act.

Kertész writes grim novels, yet the grimness is tempered by satire and irony. Behind a prose that often seems self-consciously formal and fastidious, there are glimmers of subtle humor. Kertész does believe that evil can be confronted with a smile, even a grin. It's interesting to note that while he considers Steven Spielberg's *Schindler's List* cinematic kitsch, he has found Roberto Benigni's *Life Is Beautiful* a Holocaust parable after his own heart. In the final analysis, however, it is Kertész's uncompromising moral and intellectual seriousness and his philosophical bent that evoke admiration and interest. Indeed, all of his writings, including diaries and essays, several volumes of which appeared in the 1990s, have philosophical underpinnings. (After he had had it with literary day labor, Kertész turned to translating, and he has had a distinguished career as a literary translator, producing Hungarian versions of works by Nietzsche, Wittgenstein, and Freud, among many others.)

Kertész may seem like a one-book, or rather a one-theme, writer, but he has delved into the moral ramifications of the Holocaust with such merciless honesty and inexorable logic that along the way he has illuminated other seminal events of the twentieth century.

—Ivan Sanders

See the essays on *Fateless* and *Kaddish for a Child Not Born.*

KIPPHARDT, Heinar

Nationality: German. **Born:** Heinrich Mauritius Kipphardt, Heidersdorf, Upper Silesia, 8 March 1922. **Education:** Studied medicine, 1941–42; Medical Academy, Düsseldorf, 1945–47, M.D. 1950. **Military Service:** Drafted into the German army: served on the Russian front, 1942–44; deserted, 1945; worked as doctor in an American hospital. **Family:** Married 1) Lore Hannen in 1943 (divorced), one daughter and

one son; 2) Pia Pavel in 1971 (with whom he had lived since 1963), two sons previous to marriage. **Career:** Psychiatric assistant, Krefeld and Düsseldorf, 1947–49; psychiatric assistant, Charite Neurological Clinic, East Berlin, 1949; literary adviser and chief dramatist, Deutsches Theater, East Berlin, 1950–59; moved back to West Germany and started writing full time, 1959; chief dramatist, Kammerspiele (Intimate Theatre), Munich, 1970–71; visiting artist, Hamburg, 1977. **Awards:** East German national prize, 1953; Schiller Memorial prize, 1962; Gerhart Hauptmann prize, 1964; Adolf Grimme prize, 1965; German Academy of Representational Arts television prize, 1975; Society of German Doctors film prize and Prix Italia, both in 1976; Bremen literature prize, 1977. **Died:** 18 November 1982.

PUBLICATIONS

Collections

Stücke [Plays]:
> *Stücke 1* (includes *Shakespeare dringend gesucht; Die Stühle des Herrn Szmil; In der Sache J. Robert Oppenheimer*). 1973.
> *Stücke 2* (includes *Joel Brand: Die Geschichte eines Geschäfts; Die Nacht in der Chef geschlachtet wurde; Die Soldaten; Sedanfeier*). 1974.
Theaterstücke: Eine Auswahl (includes *Der Hund des Generals; In der Sache J. Robert Oppenheimer; Joel Brand; Die Soldaten; Die Nacht, in der der Chef geschlachtet wurde; März, Ein Künstlerleben*). 1982.

Plays

Entscheidungen (produced East Berlin, 1952).
Shakespeare dringend gesucht: Ein satirisches Lustspiel in drei Akten [Shakespeare Urgently Sought: A Satirical Comedy in Three Acts] (produced East Berlin, 1953). 1954.
Der Aufstieg des Alois Piontek: Eine tragikomische Farce [The Rise of Alois Piontek: A Tragicomic Farce] (produced East Berlin, 1956). 1956.
Esel schreien im Dunkeln [Donkeys Bray in the Dark]. 1958.
Die Stühle des Herrn Szmil [Mr. Szmil's Chairs], adaptation of a novel by Ilia Ilf and Evgenii Petrov (produced Wuppertal, 1961). In *Junges deutsches Theater von heute,* edited by Joachim Schondorff, 1961.
Der Hund des Generals [The General's Dog] (produced Munich, 1962). 1963.
In der Sache J. Robert Oppenheimer (television play). 1964.
In der Sache J. Robert Oppenheimer (produced West Berlin, 1964). 1966; as *In the Matter of J. Robert Oppenheimer* (produced Los Angeles, 1968; New York, 1969), 1967.
Joel Brand: Die Geschichte eines Geschäfts [Joel Brand: The Story of a Business Transaction] (produced Munich, 1965). 1965.

Die Nacht, in der Chef geschlachtet wurde [The Night the Boss Was Slaughtered] (produced Stuttgart, 1967). In *Stücke 2,* 1974.

Die Soldaten [The Soldiers], adaptation of a play by Jacob Michael Reinhold Lenz (produced Düsseldorf, 1968). 1968.

Sedanfeier: Montage aus Materialien des 70er Krieges (produced Munich, 1970). In *Stücke 2,* 1974.

Leben des schizophrenen Dichters, Alexander März [Life of the Schizophrenic Poet, Alexander Marz] (television play). 1976.

März, ein Kunstlerleben, adaptation of his novel and television play (produced Düsseldorf, 1980). 1980.

Bruder Eichmann [Brother Eichmann] (produced Munich, 1983). 1983.

Television Plays: *Bartleby,* 1963, from the work by Hermann Melville; *In der Sache J. Robert Oppenheimer,* 1964; *Der Hund des Generals,* 1964; *Die Geschichte von Joel Brand,* 1964; *Leben des schizophrenen Dichters Alexander März,* 1975; *Die Soldaten,* 1977; *In der Sache J. Robert Oppenheimer* (new version), 1981.

Novel

März. 1976.

Short Stories

Die Ganovenfresse: Zwei Erzählungen [The Ganoven Mouth: Two Stories]. 1966.

Mann des Tages und andere Erzählungen [The Man of the Day and Other Stories]. 1977.

Poetry

Angelsbrucker Notizen: Gedichte [Notes from Angelsbruck: Poems]. 1977.

Umgang mit Paradiesen: Gesammelte Gedichte. 1990.

Other

Traumprotokolle. 1981.

Essays, Briefe, Entwürfe:
   Schreibt die Wahrheit 1949–64. 1989.
   Ruckediguh, Blut ist im Schuh 1964–82. 1989.
Die Tugend der Kannibalen: Gesammelte Prosa. 1990.

Editor, with Ewald Dede, *Aus Liebe zu Deutschland: Satiren auf Franz Josef Strauss.* 1980.

Editor, with Roman Ritter, *Vom deutschen Herbst zum bleichen deutschen Winter: Ein Lesebuch zum Modell Deutschland.* 1981.

Translator, *Und im Licht mein Herz,* by Nazim Hikmet. 1971.

*

Critical Studies: ''The Appeal of the Executive: Adolf Eichmann on the Stage'' by Anat Feinberg, in *Monatshefte fur Deutschen Unterricht, Deutsche Sprache und Literatur,* 78(2), Summer 1986, pp. 203–14; '''Reportagen der Innenwelt': The Example of Heinar Kipphardt's *Marz*'' by Carol Poore, in *German Quarterly,* 60(2), Spring 1987, pp. 193–204; ''Vergangenheitsbewaltigung through Analogy: Heinar Kipphardt's Last Play *Bruder Eichmann*'' by Glenn R. Cuomo, in *Germanic Review,* 64(2), Spring 1989, pp. 58–66; ''Heinar Kipphardt, *Robert Oppenheimer* and *Bruder Eichmann:* Two Plays in Search of a Political Answer'' by Carl Steiner, in *Amerika! New Images in German Literature,* edited by Heinz D. Osterle, 1989; ''Heinar Kipphardt's *Brother Eichmann*'' by Alexander Stillmark, in *Staging the Holocaust: The Shoah in Drama and Performance,* edited by Claude Schumacher, 1998; ''Documentation and Its Discontents: The Case of Heinar Kipphardt'' by David Barnett, in *Forum for Modern Language Studies* (England), 37(3), 2001, pp. 272–85.

* * *

In 1933, when Heinar Kipphardt was 11 years old, his father, a Silesian dentist, was sentenced to five years in the Dürrgoy concentration camp near Breslau for his passionately anti-Nazi views. Given the anarchy loosed upon the land just then, there may not be anything unusual in the picture of the pale, frightened boy who watched his father's internment and of the young man who seven years later saw action in the German army, by then in full retreat before the Russian advance. Both experiences must have left a profound impression on Kipphardt, whose politics were more radically left wing than his father's had been and whose first major play, *Der Hund des Generals* (1962), deals with the butcheries committed by the generals against infantrymen.

Kipphardt studied philosophy and medicine in Düsseldorf. After the war he practiced as an M.D. in Düsseldorf and East Berlin (his novel *März* is a highly sophisticated study of schizophrenia) before he took up the post of dramaturgic adviser to the Deutsches Theater in East Berlin. In 1961 he settled in Munich. His best-known drama, *In der Sache J. Robert Oppenheimer,* appeared in 1964. Although the subject of the play, Oppenheimer's trial and the revocation of his security clearance (a subject **Erich Maria Remarque** had briefly flirted with), lay 10 ten years in the past, the miasmic McCarthy atmosphere had yet to evaporate, and the wrangling about the building of the hydrogen bomb inspired a spate of related dramas. Kipphardt died in 1982 at the age of 60 and thus barely escaped the fog bombs that exploded after the curtain came down on *Bruder Eichmann* in January 1983.

Kipphardt's name is invariably linked with the names of **Rolf Hochhuth** and **Peter Weiss** as one of the triple pillars of what is called "documentary drama," a genre godfathered by Erwin Piscator and **Bertolt Brecht**. The genre barely flourished outside Germany and barely outlived the 1960s. (*Bruder Eichmann* is the one latecomer, but Kipphardt had already toyed with the subject some 20 years earlier.) Despite the methods of alienation that Brecht passed on to his disciples, his most influential docudrama is arguably also his most Aristotelian: the series of 24 one-acters entitled *Furcht und Elend im Dritten Reich* (1938). (It was misleadingly translated as *The Private Life of the Master Race*; the French title, *Scènes de la vie Hitlérienne,* is much the most apt.) Both Hochhuth's and Weiss's best-known docudramas—Hochhuth's sensationally successful *The Deputy* (1963) and Weiss's *The Investigation* (1965)—take *la vie Hitlérienne,* specifically the Holocaust, for their subject. Of Kipphardt's half dozen best docudramas, two—*Joel Brand* (1964) and *Bruder Eichmann*—deal with the genocide of the Jews; in effect, both look at Eichmann from different perspectives: the desk murderer at 38 and at 54.

Brecht notes that he "based [*Furcht und Elend*] on eyewitness reports and newspaper accounts." This essentially is the stuff of which docudrama is made. Unlike historical playwrights, who within certain limits are free to deal with their subjects pretty much as they please, the docudramatists, dealing with recent or nearly contemporary events, have to assume that their audiences have been brought close enough to the subject by the mass media to keep the playwrights from "cheating." The use of television interviews, film clips, and liberally cribbed speeches, which showcase the factuality of the event, is a staple of docudrama. "You can't write a play about Hitler or Trotsky or Auschwitz or Churchill," Kipphardt told an interviewer in 1967, "without taking all our communication lines into account: our contemporaries are informed in ways that differ from Shakespeare's or Goethe's sources of information." A historical playwright like Goethe had little use for historical accuracy: "[the poet's] business," he claimed, "is to present his paradigmatic ethical world and to this end he confers on historical persons the honor of lending their names to his figures." It would not occur to anyone to ask fresh questions about the way Goethe manipulates his Egmonts and Tassos.

The docudramatist evidently has no such license. At best he can modify his character just sufficiently to suit his thesis, as Kipphardt revamped Oppenheimer and Avner Less (*Bruder Eichmann*). It is significant that both Oppenheimer and Less vehemently objected to what they regarded as Kipphardt's quantum leaps. Nor would it have occurred to Goethe to write *Torquato Tasso* to teach his contemporaries a lesson to be taken home and applied. For Kipphardt and his ilk such lessons are absolutely germane to docudrama: "The dramatist doesn't merely want to describe an historical event; he wants to rescue

from the historical happening its significance for our own time." Hence, the docudramatist alerts spectators not only to the events as they unfold on the stage but also to all of the consequences, dangers, and uncertainties that lie in ambush for them today. Docudrama is both educational and cautionary. It acts as a sociopolitical SOS.

—Edgar Rosenberg

See the essays on *Bruder Eichmann* and *Joel Brand: Die Geschichte eines Geschäfts.*

KLEIN, A(braham) M(oses)

Nationality: Canadian (originally Russian: immigrated to Canada, 1910). **Born:** Ratno, Ukraine, 14 February 1909. **Education:** Studied classics and political science at McGill University, Montreal (cofounder, *The McGilliad*), 1926–30, B.A. 1930 (associated with the "Montreal Group" of poets and writers); University of Montreal, law degree 1933. **Family:** Married Bessie Kozlov in 1935; two sons and one daughter. **Career:** Lawyer, Montreal, 1933–56, and Rouyn, Quebec, 1937–38. Contributor and editor, *Judaean* (Canadian Young Judea), and educational director, Canadian Young Judea, while a student; president, Canadian Young Judea, ca. 1934. Associate director, Zionist Organization of Canada and editor, *The Canadian Zionist,* 1936; cofounder and partner of a law firm; member of public relations staff, Samuel Bronfman, Montreal, 1939–55; associated with the Preview group of Montreal poets, 1940s; lecturer in poetry, McGill University, 1945–48; active in Canadian socialist party politics, 1945, 1949. Contributor and editor, *Canadian Jewish Chronicle,* late 1920s to 1955. **Awards:** Edward Bland fellowship, 1947; Governor General's medal for poetry, 1949, for *The Rocking Chair and Other Poems;* Quebec literary prize and Kovner memorial award, both in 1952; Royal Society of Canada Lorne Pierce gold medal, 1957. **Died:** 20 August 1972.

PUBLICATIONS

Poetry

Hath Not a Jew. 1940.
The Hitleriad. 1944.
Poems: The Psalter of Avram Haktani. 1944; as *Poems,* 1944.
Seven Poems. 1947.
The Rocking Chair and Other Poems. 1948.
Collected Poems, edited by Miriam Waddington. 1974.
A.M. Klein: Complete Poems, edited by Zailig Pollock:

Vol. 1: *Original Poems, 1926–1934.* 1990.
Vol. 2: *Original Poems, 1937–1955 and Poetry Translations.* 1990.
Doctor Dwarf and Other Poems for Children, edited by Mary Alice Downie and Barbara Robertson. 1990.
Selected Poems, edited by Usher Caplan, Seymour Mayne, and Zailig Pollock. 1997.
A Rich Garland: Poems for A.M. Klein (selections), edited by Seymour Mayne and B. Glen Rotchin. 1999.

Novel

The Second Scroll. 1951.

Short Stories

A.M. Klein: Short Stories, edited by M. W. Steinberg. 1983.

Other

A Shout in the Street: An Analysis of the Second Chapter of Joyce's Ulysses. 1952.
Beyond Sambation: Selected Essays and Editorials, 1928–1955, edited by M. W. Steinberg and Usher Caplan. 1983.
A.M. Klein: Literary Essays and Reviews, edited by M. W. Steinberg and Usher Caplan. 1987.
Notebooks: Selections from the A.M. Klein Papers, edited by Zailig Pollock and Usher Caplan. 1994.

Translator, *Of Jewish Music, Ancient and Modern* by Israel Rabinovich. 1952.

*

Bibliography: *A.M. Klein: An Annotated Bibliography* by Zailig Pollock, Usher Caplan, and Linda Rozmovits, 1993.

Critical Studies: *A.M. Klein,* edited by Tom Marshall, 1970; *A.M. Klein,* 1970, and *Folklore in the Poetry of A.M. Klein,* 1981, both by Miriam Waddington; *In Search of Jerusalem: Religion and Ethics in the Writings of A.M. Klein* by Gretl K. Fischer, 1975; *The A.M. Klein Symposium,* edited by Seymour Mayne, 1975; ''A.M. Klein: Portrait of the Poet As Jew'' by Esther Safer Fisher, in *Canadian Literature,* 79, 1978, pp. 121–27; *Like One That Dreamed: A Portrait of A.M. Klein* by Usher Caplan, 1982; *Tapestry for Designs: Judaic Allusions in The Second Scroll and The Collected Poems of A.M. Klein* by Solomon J. Spiro, 1984; A.M. Klein issue of *Journal of Canadian Studies,* 19(2), Summer 1984; ''A.M. Klein and Mordecai Richler: Canadian Responses to the Holocaust,'' in *Journal of Canadian Studies,* 24, Summer 1989, pp. 65–77, and *A.M. Klein, the Father of Canadian Jewish Literature: Essays in the Poetics of Humanistic Passion,* 1990, both by Rachel Feldhay Brenner; *A.M. Klein and His Works* by Noreen Golfman, 1990; *A.M. Klein: The Story of a Poet* by Zailig Pollock, 1994; *Aught from Naught: A.M. Klein's The Second Scroll* by Roger Hyman, 1999; ''Pan-Semitism in A.M. Klein's 'The Three Judgements''' by Feisal G. Mohamed, in *Essays on Canadian Writing,* 72, Winter 2000, pp. 93–108.

*   *   *

Primarily known as one of Canada's most gifted poets, Montreal author A.M. Klein was also a brilliantly imaginative and versatile man of letters. Forced by illness to end his career in 1955, Klein had by then accumulated a remarkably extensive legacy, consisting of novels, short stories, plays, critical essays, book reviews, and translations, in addition to his four published volumes of finely crafted poetry.

Klein's achievements as a writer were realized despite the demanding public life he led, simultaneously with his personal writing career, in the service of his Montreal community. For 20 years he was an active partner in the law firm he helped found, and for 16 of those years he also served as editor of the weekly *Canadian Jewish Chronicle.* For many years he was speechwriter and public relations consultant to the head of the Canadian Jewish Congress, and he himself often represented the Congress, giving speeches across Canada and the United States. For three happy years, after World War II, Klein enjoyed a visiting appointment as professor of poetry in the English Department of his alma mater, McGill University. While he found it relaxing, he was typically conscientious in the preparation of his carefully researched lectures.

The frantic pace and pressure of his double life, as public servant and private writer, exacted a fearful toll on Klein's health and contributed to the disabling breakdown that forced him, reluctantly, to give up permanently all of his activities, both public and private, in 1955 and to live thereafter in quiet retirement until his death in 1972. Nevertheless, Klein always maintained that he had no choice but to live as he did. Deeply ingrained in him was the dual obligation to serve his community actively, in whatever ways he could, and to share with others the advantages his education had given him. This latter obligation inspired him to become a writer, using his own fascination with language as the ideal means of reaching the widest possible audience with the fruits of his learning.

Klein's passionate interest in language, in his youth, was powerfully stimulated by what he viewed as his good fortune: to be growing up in the language-rich city of Montreal. When he entered McGill University in 1927, he was already fluent in four languages—Yiddish, Hebrew, English and French—and had done advanced work in Latin and Greek. The high standard of elegant expression in English, as taught in Montreal's public schools, held a special appeal for him, and he found, in the English Bible and in Shakespeare, admirable models of fine writing, which he resolved to emulate. Thus the heady ambition to become a writer was already burning within him as a McGill undergraduate, and during those years he devoted more and more of his time to writing, succeeding in getting a few of his own poems published in small magazines and in founding, with a friend, a student literary magazine.

For purely economic reasons Klein went directly from McGill to law school, but in his own mind he was committed to what he considered to be his true calling: becoming a writer. Throughout the 1930s, despite the demands of his public life, Klein made time almost every day to experiment with different modes and forms of literary expression and to explore the creative potential in a variety of themes and topics. He became a man obsessed with the power of language and of the written word. Increasingly, also, he found the focus of his writing shifting from aesthetic considerations to the desire to highlight Jewish themes, using the linguistic elegance of English to help preserve and celebrate traditional Jewish values. Noting the consequences of Hitler's rise to power in Germany in 1933, he feared that the cultural traditions of his people, which gave so much meaning to his life, were again in danger of extinction, as had so often occurred in Jewish history. His new obsession became the defense and preservation of those values, through the powers of literary art. His collection of poems on Jewish themes, *Hath Not A Jew* (1940), and his angry polemical poem, *The Hitleriad* (1944), were the direct products of this new obsession.

Once the horrors of the Nazi concentration camps began to filter out, near the end of World War II, Klein's instinctive response was to confront directly, in his poems of that period, the painful implications of the Holocaust. In his last publication, a powerfully moving poetic novel called *The Second Scroll* (1951), Klein became the first Canadian author to describe, in detail, the most inhuman abuses of the camps, yet he also managed to close on a note of triumph by depicting the founding of the state of Israel in 1948 as the latest miracle of Jewish survival and as a joyous vindication of Zionism's redemptive power.

—Murray Sachs

See the essays on *Collected Poems* and *The Second Scroll.*

KLEIN, Gerda Weissmann

Nationality: American (originally Polish: immigrated to the United States after World War II). **Born:** Bielitz (now Bieklsko), 8 May 1924. **Family:** Married Kurt Klein in 1947; two daughters and one son. **Career:** Writer and lecturer. Prisoner, German labor camps, 1942–45. Columnist, ''Stories for Young Readers,'' *Buffalo Sunday News.* Founder and honorary chairman of civic, educational, and philanthropic organizations, including Blue Rose Foundation, Silver Circle at Rosary Hill College (now Daemon College), and Gerda and Kurt Klein Foundation. Member of the board of directors, United Jewish Appeal and Holocaust Commission. **Awards:** Woman of the Year award, Council of Jewish Women, 1974; Humanitaria Citation, Trocaire College; special award for Year of the Child, D'Youville College. D.H.L.: Rosary Hill College (now Daemon College) and Our Lady of Holy Cross College, both 1974. **Agent:** St. Martin's Press, 175 Fifth Avenue, New York, New York 10010, U.S.A.

PUBLICATIONS

Memoir

All but My Life. 1957; expanded edition, 1995.

Other

A Passion for Sharing: The Life of Edith Rosenwald Stern. 1984.
The Hours After: Letters of Love and Longing in the War's Aftermath, with Kurt Klein. 2000.

Other (for children)

The Blue Rose. 1974.
Promise of a New Spring: The Holocaust and Renewal. 1981.
Peregrinations: Adventures with the Green Parrot. 1986.

*

Film Adaptations: *One Survivor Remembers,* 1995, from the memoir *All but My Life.*

* * *

Gerda Weissmann Klein was fifteen years old when the Nazis invaded her town of Bielsko, Poland. Her memoir *All but My Life* is a classic of Holocaust literature and was the basis for the Academy Award-winning best documentary short *One Survivor Remembers.* In 2001 the book entered its forty-eighth printing. It is an extraordinary account of one teenager's struggle to survive and retain her humanity through deportation, slave labor, and a winter death march. It is a remarkable testimony to the sustaining power of family, friendship, loyalty, and love.

Gerda's first heartbreaking loss was that of her beloved older brother Artur, who was sent to a forced labor camp soon after the Germans occupied Bielsko. Then, on 28 June 1942, Gerda's father was taken from the family and sent to a concentration camp. The very next day she was separated from her mother and transported to a series of forced labor camps. Although her parents and brother were taken from her, their spirit continued to guide and sustain her. When tempted to commit suicide and end her suffering, she remembered the vow she has made to her father never to end her life. Her mother's last words, ''Be strong,'' sustained her, as did the occasional scribbled note she received from her brother. None of them survived.

Her memoir is also a testament to the power of friendship. Four girls—Gerda, Ilse, Suse, and Liesel—join together in friendship. Gerda makes a wager with Suse that the war will end in six months—their bet is a quart of strawberries with whipped cream. Suse did not live to collect the bet, dying at the very moment of liberation.

In the end, all that was left to Gerda Weissmann was her life. Liberated in Volary, Czechoslovakia, on 7 May 1945, a day before her twenty-first birthday, she weighed only 68 pounds. Kurt Klein, the young American army lieutenant who liberated her, saw more than an emaciated survivor; he saw a young woman whose luminous humanity endowed her with remarkable beauty. Gerda shared a special bond with her liberator, for he too is Jewish and had experienced tremendous loss. After fleeing to the United States in 1937, he waged a fruitless battle to save his parents. He later discovered that his parents, like Gerda's, had died in Auschwitz.

Although Klein was soon reassigned, he and Gerda shared a bond that neither time nor distance could disrupt. They eloquently describe the story of their growing love in *The Hours After: Letters of Love and Longing in War's Aftermath* (2000), based on the year-long exchange of letters following their first meeting. Their letters are a testimony to the healing power of love as they share their memories of their families and their dreams for the future. Married in Paris in June 1946, the Kleins have dedicated their lives to Holocaust education and to furthering human rights.

In *Promise of a New Spring: The Holocaust and Renewal* (1981), a book for children, Gerda Klein translates the experience of loss into imagery a child can understand. Even as a devastating fire may destroy a forest, sparing only a few trees, so the Holocaust destroyed the Jews, leaving only a few survivors in the winter of their lives to tell the history of that time to the young—those who are in the spring of their lives.

—Marilyn J. Harran

See the essay on *All but My Life*.

KLEMPERER, Victor

Nationality: German. **Born:** Landsberg-on-the-Warthe, Brandenburg, 1881. **Education:** Ph.D. **Military Service:** Germany Army during World War I: Distinguished Service Medal. **Family:** Married Eva Schlemmer. **Career:** Professor, historian, journalist, and film critic. Worked as a freelance writer and journalist prior to World War I; professor of Romance languages and literature, Dresden University of Technology, 1920–35, fired for being Jewish, reinstated in his position after World War II. **Awards:** Geschwister Scholl prize for civic courage (posthumous); National Book Critics Circle award

nomination, 2001, for Volume II of *I Will Bear Witness: A Diary of the Nazi Years, 1942–45*.

PUBLICATIONS

Diaries

Ich will Zeugnis ablegen bis zum letzten: Tagebücher 1933–1941, edited by Walter Nowojski. 1995; as *I Will Bear Witness: A Diary of the Nazi Years 1933–1941*, 1998.

Ich will Zeugnis ablegen bis zum letzten: Tagebücher 1942–1945, edited by Walter Nowojski. 1995; as *I Will Bear Witness: A Diary of the Nazi Years 1942–45*, 1999.

Zwiespältiger denn je: Dresdner Tagebuch 1945, Juni bis Dezember. 1995; as *Und so ist alles schwankend: Tagebücher Juni bis Dezember 1945*, edited by Günter Jäckel, 1996.

Leben sammeln, nicht fragen wozu und warum: Tagebücher 1918–1924, edited by Walter Nowojski. 1996.

Leben sammeln, nicht fragen wozu und warum: Tagebücher 1925–1932, edited by Walter Nowojski. 1996.

So sitze ich denn zwischen allen Stühlen: Tagebücher 1945–1949, edited by Walter Nowojski. 1999.

So sitze ich denn zwischen allen Stühlen: Tagebücher 1950–1959, edited by Walter Nowojski. 1999.

Other

Talmud-Sprüche. 1906.
Adolf Wilbrandt, eine Studie über seine Werke. 1907.
Paul Heyse. 1907.
Prinz Emel von Schönaich-Carolath. 1908.
Paul Lindau. 1909.
Deutsche Zeitdichtung von den Freiheitskriegen bis zur Reichsgründung. 1911.
Die Zeitromane Friedrich Spielhagens und ihre Wurzeln. 1913.
Montesquieu (2 vols.). 1914.
Einführung in das mittelfranzösische; Texte und Erläuterungen für die Zeit vom XIII. bis zum XVII. Jahrhundert. 1921.
Die moderne französische Prosa (1870–1920): Studie und erläuterte Texte. 1923.
Die romanischen Literaturen von der Renaissance bis zur französischen Revolution, with Helmut Hatzfeld and Fritz Neubert. 1924.
Die moderne französische Literatur und die deutsche Schule; Drei Vorträge. 1925.
Romanische Sonderart: Geistesgeschichtliche Studien. 1926.
Stücke und Studien zur modernen französischen Prosa. 1926.
Die moderne französische Lyrik von 1870 bis zur Gegenwart, Studie und erläuterte Texte. 1929.
Idealistische Literaturgeschichte; grundsätzliche und anwendende Studien. 1929.
Pierre Corneille. 1933.
LTI; notizbuch eines philologen. 1947; annotated edition, with Roderick H. Watt, 1997; as *The Language of the Third*

Reich: LTI, lingua tertii imperii; A Philologist's Notebook, 1999.

Delilles "Gärten": Ein Mosaikbild des 18. Jahrhunderts. 1954.

Zur gegenwärtigen Sprachsituation in Deutschland; Vortrag, gehalten im Klub der Kulturschaffenden, Berlin. 1954.

Vor 33 nach 45: Gesammelte Aufsätze. 1956.

Geschichte der französischen Literatur im 19. und 20. Jahrhundert, 1800–1925. 1956.

Der Alte und der neue Humanismus. 1956.

Die moderne französische Lyrik (Dekadenz, Symbolismus, Neuromantik) Studie und kommentierte Texte. 1957.

Curriculum vitae: Erinnerungen eines Philologen: 1881–1918, edited by Walter Nowojski. 1989.

Editor, with Eugen Lerch, *Idealistische Neuphilologie; Festschrift für Karl Vossler zum 6. September 1922.* 1922.

Editor, with Julius Wahle, *Vom Geiste neuer Literaturforschung: Festschrift für Oskar Walzel.* 1924.

Editor and translator, with Eva Klemperer, *Novellen,* by Guy de Maupassant. 1950.

Editor and translator, *Wahrhaftige Geschichte,* by Baron de Charles de Secondat Montesquieu. 1954.

*

Film Adaptation: *I Will Bear Witness* (television), 1999.

Critical Studies: "Victor Klemperer (1881–1960): Reflections on His 'Third Reich' Diaries" by Hans Reiss, in *German Life and Letters* (England), 51(1), January 1998; pp. 65–92; "Victor Klemperer's 'Sprache des vierten Reiches': LTILQI?" by Roderick H. Watt, in *German Life and Letters,* 51(3), July 1998, pp. 360–71; "Prussianism, Nazism, and Romanticism in the Thought of Victor Klemperer" by Lawrence Birken, in *The German Quarterly,* 72(1), Winter 1999, pp. 33–43; "From the Forgotten Everyday-Life of Tyranny: The Diaries of Victor Klemperer" by Vanessa Agnew, translated by Susanne Zur Nieden, in *Marginal Voices, Marginal Forms: Diaries in European Literature and History,* edited by Rachel Langford and Russell West, 1999; "What Victor Klemperer Saw" by Daniel Johnson, in *Commentary,* 109(6), June 2000, pp. 44–50; "Diary of a Tightrope Walker: Victor Klemperer and His Posterity" by Katie Trumpener, in *Modernism/Modernity,* 7(3), September 2000, pp. 487–507; *Scholem, Arendt, Klemperer: Intimate Chronicles in Turbulent Times* by Steven E. Aschheim, 2001.

* * *

Victor Klemperer was born in 1881, the son of a reformed rabbi. He grew up in Berlin. By Klemperer's own admission he was daunted by the precocity of his older brothers, one of whom eventually became a distinguished professor of medicine at Harvard. The result was that Klemperer's own career got off to a slow start. As a young man, in fact, he held several jobs that had nothing to do with Romance literature, which would become his field. In 1913 Klemperer completed his *Habilitationschrift* on Montesquieu while working as a cultural journalist.

Klemperer soon got sidetracked again. He volunteered for military service in 1915 and fought on the Western Front. And so by the time his academic career began in earnest, Klemperer, who had converted to Protestantism and married a non-Jew, was a veteran and almost 40 years old. His new confessional status helped him attain a professorship at the Technical University in Dresden. His military service and marriage helped him keep it—at least for a while—after the Nazi policy of cultural coordination (*Gleichschaltung*) had gone into effect. More important, Klemperer's marriage saved him from being deported.

Klemperer lost his academic post in 1935. For the next six years he continued to lead a life of bourgeois material comfort, however, even as he experienced terrible psychic duress. Not only could he have been interned for keeping the secret diary that brought him posthumous fame, *I Will Bear Witness* (1998; the abridged German edition, *Ich will Zeugnis ablegen bis zum letzten,* appeared in 1995), but also he and his wife, Eva, were hypochondriacs. Klemperer seems to have felt that his heart was not equal to the strain that had been imposed on it and that he soon would die. Eva suffered from fits of hysteria. Yet Klemperer continued to work, on the diaries and also on various scholarly projects.

In 1941 his situation changed dramatically. He and Eva were forced to move into a "Jew House," and he no longer could use the university library. Like almost everyone else in Dresden, the Klemperers had to scrounge for food. And both he and Eva were repeatedly beaten by the Gestapo. Scholarly work became impossible. But Klemperer did not give up the diaries, smuggling them in a Greek dictionary to a friend's house for safekeeping. In the diaries Klemperer reveals himself to be a relentless critic of Nazi culture and of everyone complicitous with it and also to be a great believer in humanist values, even in the face of so much inhumanity. After the war his resilience persisted. He enjoyed a successful career as a Romanist in East Germany, holding several chairs and publishing widely until his death in 1960. This constellation of characteristics won Klemperer many admirers, including some of the leading lights of Holocaust studies—for example, the historians Gordon Craig and **Saul Friedländer**. And in Germany *I Will Bear Witness* was made into a reverential, multipart television film, which aired, to mixed reviews, in 1999.

But as another eminent historian—István Deák—has pointed out, Klemperer did not only heroically record the complexities of the Holocaust, such as the diverse attitudes of Germans toward Jews, he also embodied its complexities. For Klemperer was both a great humanist and an arch misanthrope. He risked his life for posterity by keepings his diaries. Yet he gratuitously named by name the non-Jews who helped him, thereby needlessly subjecting them to great risk. And Klemperer was more than ungrateful toward the people he relied on most. He actually seemed to exult in their demise. That Klemperer acknowledged his vanity and pettiness does little to make these characteristics more attractive. Klemperer was very well informed about the fate of European Jewry. Nonetheless, throughout the war he criticized German Jews for giving up cosmopolitan German values and regressing into ghetto behavior. And for all his fulminations about the treachery of German intellectuals and about how severely they should be punished, Klemperer after the war quietly worked alongside former Nazis. He leaves us brave and precise testimony—and a number of difficult questions.

—Paul Reitter

See the essay on *I Will Bear Witness: A Diary of the Nazi Years.*

KLEPFISZ, Irena

Nationality: American (originally Polish: immigrated to Sweden, 1946, the United States, 1949). **Born:** Warsaw, 1941. **Education:** City College of New York, B.A. and M.A.; University of Chicago, Ph.D. in English literature; post-doctoral fellow, Max Weinreich Center for Jewish Studies, YIVO Institute for Jewish Research, New York. **Career:** Translator-in-residence, YIVO, late 1980s; teacher of creative writing and women's studies, Vermont College; professor of women's studies and Jewish studies, Michigan State University, Lansing; professor of Jewish women's studies, Barnard College. Has also taught at Columbia University, Long Island University, Brooklyn College, State University of New York at Albany, Hamilton College, University of California, Wake Forest University, and Centre College in Kentucky. Founding editor, *Conditions,* 1976–81; editorial consultant, *Bridges: A Journal for Jewish Feminists and Their Friends.* Executive director, New Jewish Agenda, 1990–92.

PUBLICATIONS

Poetry

Periods of Stress. 1975.
Keeper of Accounts. 1982.
A Few Words in the Mother Tongue: Poems Selected and New (1971–1990). 1990.

Other

Why Children? 1980.
Different Enclosures: The Poetry and Prose of Irena Klepfisz. 1985.
Dreams of an Insomniac: Jewish Feminist Essays, Speeches and Diatribes. 1990.

Editor, with Melanie Kaye-Kantrowitz, *The Tribe of Dina: A Jewish Woman's Anthology.* 1989.
Editor, with Rita Falbel and Donna Nevel, *Jewish Women's Call for Peace: A Handbook for Jewish Women on the Israeli/Palestinian Conflict.* 1990.

*

Critical Studies: "Stepmother Tongues," in *Tikkun,* 5(5), September/October 1990, and "History Stops for No One," in *What Is Found There: Notebooks on Poetry and Politics,* 1993, both by Adrienne Rich; *Irena Klepfisz: A Life in Print: The Early Years, 1975–1992* (dissertation) by Esther Helfgott, University of Washington, 1994; "Irena Klepfisz's 'Fradel Schtok' and the Language of Hyphenated Identity" by Gisela Ecker, in *Anglistik & Englischunterricht* (Germany), 53, 1994, pp. 129–39; "The End of Exile: Jewish Identity and Its Diasporic Poetics" by Maeera Y. Shreiber, in *PMLA,* 113(2), March 1998, pp. 273–87; "Pedagogy and the Mother Tongue: Irena Klepfisz's 'Di rayze aheym/The Journey Home'" by Laurence Roth, in *Symposium,* 52(4), Winter 1999, pp. 269–78.

*   *   *

Irena Klepfisz has resisted the classification of her work as either lesbian/feminist or Holocaust/Jewish poetry, explaining in her book *Dreams of an Insomniac,* "I write as much out of a Jewish consciousness as I do out of a lesbian/feminist consciousness. They are both always there, no matter what topic I might be working on. They are embedded in my writing, embedded and enmeshed to the point that they are not necessarily distinguishable as discrete elements. They merge and blur, for in many ways they are the same . . . Alienated. Threatened. Un-American. Individual. Defiant. To me they are ever present." Her Holocaust poetry has not been informed exclusively by her experiences as a child survivor but by the experience of multiple marginalizations (as an unwed, childless Jewish woman; as a lesbian feminist; and as an immigrant and nonnative speaker of English).

Throughout her career Klepfisz has struggled with the label Holocaust poet. After her friend and fellow child survivor Elza's suicide, Klepfisz spent six years writing almost exclusively about the Holocaust, in Elza's voice. Klepfisz felt that she never had this poetry "completely under control." In the 1970s she developed her own "identifiable voice" and progressed beyond poetry as therapy, continuing to worry, however, that her work was dominated by the Holocaust (poems from this period include "death camp," "herr captain," and "about my father"). Klepfisz maintained that the commercialization of the Holocaust (the "Holocaust of American Big Business. The Holocaust of glamour. Of movie stars. TV stations. Of sloppy books that sell millions of copies.") had eroded the meaning of the word Holocaust in America and robbed her "of the possibility of really mourning the losses of [her] life, of even defining them or articulating them properly.

How can [she] say to people that for the survivors . . . the Holocaust never ended?'' Therefore, the majority of Klepfisz's Holocaust poems (exceptions include ''death camp,'' in which the poem's I recounts her own death by gas chamber) focus not on the events of the Holocaust but on its legacy, its ever-presentness in the daily life of survivors. Her early poem ''The Widow and Daughter'' portrays Klepfisz's mother as a survivor not only of the Holocaust but also of motherhood, widowhood, and New York City. The missing father/husband, killed in the Warsaw Ghetto Uprising, haunts mother and daughter, ''press[ing] himself between them . . . forcing them to remember . . . when they sat down to eat they could taste his ashes.'' Two other poems, ''Searching for My Father's Body'' and ''About My Father'' address the void created by the narrator's absent father, revealing her obsession with collecting facts about her father, whom she does not remember, with accounts of his death, and with finding his grave. By dedicating her poem ''*Bashert*'' (''destined'') to ''those who died because . . .'' and ''those who survived because . . .'' and listing the accidents that resulted in either life or death, Klepfisz has underscored the highly individual experiences of both survivors and victims. The poem's four first-person, prose-style cantos recall stations and episodes of the narrator's life, ending in Cherry Plain, where the narrator concludes that she has become ''a keeper of accounts,'' keeping track not of money, as her ''despised ancestors'' but of ''past and present. Pain and pleasure. Living and surviving. Resistance and capitualation. Will and circumstances. Between life and death.''

When she came out as a lesbian, Klepfisz initially felt unwelcome in the secular Yiddish community in which she had grown up. While the labor movement and the Holocaust had sensitized progressive secular Jews to multiple forms of oppression, they remained blind to the oppression of homosexuals despite the striking similarities between Jewish and gay experience. Klepfisz was equally uncomfortable presenting her Holocaust poems in the lesbian community, which she believed was guilty of ''anti-Semitism by omission.'' Although she withdrew from the Jewish community at this juncture, her poetry continued to be ''very Jewish.'' ''From the Monkey House and Other Cages,'' for example, which is written from the perspective of female monkeys born and raised in a zoo, is a ''direct outgrowth of [her] Holocaust literature.''

Increasing anti-Semitism caused by Israel's invasion of Lebanon in 1982 prompted Klepfisz's return to Jewish themes and the Holocaust in her poetry. During a 1987 trip to Israel, Klepfisz met with Palestinian women in East Jerusalem to discuss the Israeli occupation of the West Bank and Gaza. Her poem ''East Jerusalem, 1987'' conveys her solidarity with Palestinian women, which is rooted in her own experience as a survivor, ''We understand we remember history and understand it all . . . If I forget thee . . . may I forget my own past my pain the depth of my sorrows.'' A year later she helped found the Jewish Women's Committee to End the Occupation. Klepfisz has continued to support the Palestinian cause despite

charges of Jewish self-hatred and fueling anti-Semitism, believing that passivity and indifference amount to collaboration and that defending the persecuted, whether Jewish or not, was the best way to honor Holocaust victims, survivors, and the Jewish resistance. In a July 2001 interview with Matthew Rothschild in *Progressive*, Klepfisz explained Jews' unwillingness to criticize Israel's actions: ''Many Jews cannot see themselves as oppressors. They see themselves as victims and say that we can't compare the Holocaust to anything, we can't compare Israel's actions to any other country's actions.''

—Elizabeth Loentz

See the essay on ''*Di rayze aheym/*The journey home.''

KLÜGER, Ruth

Nationality: American (originally Austrian: immigrated to the United States, 1947, granted U.S. citizenship, 1953). **Born:** Vienna, 30 October 1931. **Education:** Hunter College, New York, 1948–50, B.A. 1950; University of California, Berkeley, 1951–53, 1963–65, M.A. 1953, Ph.D. 1967. **Family:** Married W.T. Angress in 1953 (divorced 1963). **Career:** Professor, Case Western Reserve University, Cleveland, Ohio, University of Kansas, Lawrence, and University of Virginia, Charlottesville, 1963–76, University of California, Irvine, 1976–80, and Princeton University, New Jersey, 1980–86. Since 1986 professor emerita, University of California, Irvine. **Awards:** Johann-Jakob-Christoph von Grimmelshausen prize, 1993, Heinrich Heine prize, 1997, and Thomas Mann prize of the city of Lübeck, 1999, all for *weiter leben;* Niedersachsen literature prize and Marie Luise Kaschnitz prize, both in 1994; Andreas Gryphious prize, 1996;

PUBLICATIONS

Memoir

weiter leben: Eine Jugend. 1992; revised as *Still Alive: A Holocaust Girlhood Remembered,* 2001.

Other

The Development of the German Epigram in the 17th Century (dissertation). 1967.
The Early German Epigram: A Study in Baroque Poetry. 1971.
Katastrophen: Über deutsche Literatur [Catastrophes: On German Literature] (essays). 1994.
Frauen lesen anders [Women Read Differently] (essays). 1996.
Knigges ''Umgang mit Menschen'' (lecture). 1996.
Von hoher und niederer Literatur [Of High and Low Literatures] (three lectures). 1996.

Dichter und Historiker: Fakten und Fiktionen [Poets and Historians: Facts and Fictions] (lecture). 2000.

Editor, *Salomon Hermann von Mosenthal: Erzählungen aus dem jüdischen Familienleben* [Salomon Hermann von Mosenthal: Tales from Jewish Family Life]. 1996.

Editor, *Else Lasker-Schüler: In Theben geboren. Gedichte* [Else Lasker-Schüler: Born in Thebes. Poetry]. 1998.

*

Critical Studies: "Memory and Criticism: Ruth Kluger's *weiter leben*" by Dagmar C.G. Lorenz, in *Women in German Yearbook: Feminist Studies in German Literature and Culture,* 9, 1993, pp. 207–24; *Writing as Revenge: Jewish German Identity in Post-Holocaust German Literary Works: Reading Survivor Authors Jurek Becker, Edgar Hilsenrath, and Ruth Klüger* (dissertation), Cornell University, 1995, and "Ruth Kluger's *weiter leben: Eine Jugend:* A Jewish Woman's 'Letter to Her Mother,'" in *Out from the Shadows: Essays on Contemporary Austrian Women Writers and Filmmakers,* edited by Margarete Lamb-Faffelberger, 1997, both by Jennifer L. Taylor; "Between the Extreme and the Everyday: Ruth Kluger's Traumatic Realism" by Michael Rothberg, in *A/B: Auto/Biography Studies,* 14(1), Summer 1999, pp. 93–107; "'Der Richtige Riecher': The Reconfiguration of Jewish and Austrian Identities" by Lisa Silverman, in *The German Quarterly,* 72(3), 1999, pp. 252–64.

* * *

Ruth Klüger, professor emerita of German literature at the University of California at Irvine, did not reflect upon the Holocaust in her scholarly work until the early 1990s. Born in Vienna in 1931, she immigrated to the United States after the war and received a Ph.D. from the University of California at Berkeley in 1967. She was known foremost as a literary scholar of the Early Modern Period (Baroque poetry, in particular) and of eighteenth- and nineteenth-century German literature, focusing on such prominent writers as Gotthold Ephraim Lessing, Heinrich von Kleist, and Adalbert Stifter. She also explored feminist issues such as gender-specific interpretations of texts and representations of femininity in popular culture, which resulted in the book *Frauen lesen anders* ("Women Read Differently").

It was with her autobiography *weiter leben* that her personal experience with the Holocaust was revealed to the public. The work, translated into English and revised as *Still Alive: A Holocaust Girlhood Remembered,* was first published in Germany in 1992 and became a literary success. Germany's leading literary critic Marcel Reich-Ranicki, who has hosted the popular television show *The Literary Quartet,* called it one of the best books to appear in Germany in the 1990s. *weiter leben* earned Klüger numerous prizes, among them the distinguished Johann-Jakob-Christoph von Grimmelshausen prize

in 1993, the Heinrich Heine prize in 1997, and the Thomas-Mann prize in 1999. She also partook in the 1996 television production *Reisen ins Leben-Weiterleben nach einer Kindheit in Auschwitz* ("Journeys into Life: Continuing to Live after a Childhood in Auschwitz").

In various ways *weiter leben* represents an exception in German and international Holocaust literature. As the German title and its English translation indicate, Klüger recounts not only her childhood in Vienna and her imprisonment in Theresienstadt, Auschwitz, and Christianstadt but also her experiences in postwar Germany and as an immigrant in the United States. The continuation of her account into the present and the coupling of her recollections with frank and critical commentary on such issues as memory, language, literature, and religion make *weiter leben* an unusual, even unconventional, Holocaust autobiography.

In the 1990s Klüger's scholarly work also turned toward the Holocaust, anti-Semitism, and German-Jewish writers. In the 1991 article entitled "Dichten über die Shoah. Zum Problem des literarischen Umgangs mit dem Massenmord" ("Writing about the Shoah: The Problem of Representing Mass Murder in Literature"), she raised questions about how the Holocaust can be written. *Katastrophen: Über deutsche Literatur* (1994; "Catastrophes: On German Literature") examines anti-Semitism in German literature, and in *Von hoher und niedriger Literatur* (1996; "Of High and Low Literatures") Klüger investigated the relationship between kitsch, memory, and representations of the Holocaust. The intersection between literature and history is examined in her book *Dichter und Historiker: Fakten und Fiktionen* (2000; "Poets and Historians: Facts and Fictions"). In addition to these publications, she edited *Salomon Hermann von Mosenthal: Erzählungen aus dem jüdischen Familienleben* (1996; "Salomon Hermann von Mosenthal: Tales from Jewish Family Life") and a book on the German-Jewish poet Else Lasker-Schüler entitled *Else Lasker-Schüler: In Theben geboren. Gedichte* (1998; "Else Lasker-Schüler: Born in Thebes. Poetry").

—Sandra Alfers

See the essay on *Still Alive: A Holocaust Girlhood Remembered.*

KOEPPEN, Wolfgang

Nationality: German. **Born:** Greifswald, 23 June 1906. **Career:** Actor, volunteer director, and dramaturgist, Wurzburg, Germany, 1926–27; editor and theater critic, *Berliner Borsen Courier,* Berlin, 1931–33; went into exile in Holland, 1934–38; scriptwriter for various German film studios, 1938–45; program director, South German Broadcasting Network, Munich, ca. 1950s. **Awards:** Georg Büchner prize, German Academy in Darmstadt, 1962; literature prize, Bavarian Academy of the

Arts, 1965; Immermann prize, City of Düsseldorf, 1967; Andreas Gryphius prize, Artists' Guild, 1971; elected honorary Stadtschreiber (city writer), city of Bergen-Enkheim, 1974–75; Munich Kulturpreis, 1982; Arno Schmidt Preis, 1984. Honorary doctorate: Greifswald University, 1990. Honorary citizen, City of Greifswald, 1994. **Died:** 15 March 1996.

PUBLICATIONS

Collection

Gesammelte Werke in sechs Bänden (6 vols.). 1986.

Novels

Eine unglückliche Liebe [An Unhappy Love]. 1934.
Die Mauer schwankt [The Wall Is Shaking]. 1935; as *Die Pflicht*, 1939.
Jakob Littners Aufzeichnungen aus einem Erdloch: Roman. 1948.
Tauben im Gras. 1951; as *Pigeons on the Grass*, 1988.
Das Treibhaus. 1953; as *The Hothouse*, 2001.
Der Tod in Rom. 1954; as *Death in Rome: A Novel*, 1956; as *Death in Rome*, 1992.

Short Stories

Romanisches Café: Erzählende Prosa. 1972.

Poetry

Erleben und Streben: Dichtungen. 1929.

Other

Nach Rußland und anderswohin: Empfindsame Reisen. 1958.
Amerikafahrt. 1958.
New York: Mit einem autobiographischen Nachwort. 1959.
Reisen nach Frankreich. 1961.
Jugend [Youth] (autobiographical piece). 1976.
Morgenrot. 1978.
Die elenden Skribenten [The Miserable Scribblers] (essays and criticism). 1981.
Ich bin gern in Venedig warum. 1994.

*

Critical Studies: "Wolfgang Koeppen and the Human Condition" by S. Craven, in *German Life and Letters* (London), 29, 1976, pp. 201–15; "Mélancholy and Enchantment: Wolfgang Koeppen's Anamnesis" by Dagmar Barnouw, in *Mosaic*, 14(3), Summer 1981, pp. 31–48; *Art and Politics in Wolfgang Koeppen's Postwar Trilogy* by Richard L. Gunn, 1983; *The Transformation of Failure: A Critical Analysis of Character Presentation in the Novels of Wolfgang Koeppen* by Carole Hanbridge, 1983; "From a Death in Venice to a Death in Rome: On Wolfgang Koeppen's Critical Ironization of Thomas Mann" by John Pizer, in *Germanic Review*, 68(3), Summer 1993, pp. 98–107; *Chaos, Control, and Consistency: The Narrative Vision of Wolfgang Koeppen*, 1993, and "The Author As Victim: Wolfgang Koeppen, *Jakob Littners Aufzeichnungen aus einem Erdloch*," in *Modern Language Review*, 92(4), 1997, both by David Basker; "Wolfgang Koeppen and the Bridge of Memory," in *German Life and Letters,* 52(1), 1999, and "Border Negotiations in the Works of Wolfgang Koeppen," in *Modern Language Review*, 95(3), 2000, both by Simon Ward.

* * *

Wolfgang Koeppen, born in 1906 in Greifswald, Germany, began his literary career in the late 1920s as a modern writer within the boundaries of the culture of the Weimar Republic. He was the feature editor of the *Berliner Börsen Courier* from 1931 to 1933. His first two novels, *Eine unglückliche Liebe* (1934) and *Die Mauer schwankt* (1935), were written in emulation of the so-called classical modernity of the turn of the century. Both can be considered as replies to works of the Mann brothers, namely, Heinrich Mann's *Die Jagd nach Liebe* ("The Pursuit of Love") and Thomas Mann's *Der Tod in Venedig (Death in Venice)*. *Die Mauer schwankt,* however, also takes the conservative stylistic turn that was characteristic of nonfascist German literature of the time. In 1934, after a short phase of enthusiasm for the new movement developing in Germany, Koeppen voluntarily went into exile in Holland. In 1938 material necessity drove him back to Germany, and he lived there under difficult circumstances until the end of the war.

In the 1950s Koeppen published the trilogy of works that established his reputation. *Tauben im Gras* (1951; *Pigeons on the Grass,* 1988) shows the fate of people in postwar Munich on a day in 1948 through the characters of the "nigger soldier" Odysseus Cotton, the German writer Philipp, and the celebrated Anglo-Saxon author Edwin. On this day each will become a victim of the still violent society. In *Das Treibhaus* (1953; "The Hothouse") Koeppen portrays the death of the former exile Keetenheuve. As an intellectual and a Social Democrat in the parliament, Keetenheuve recognizes his position as an outsider in Bonn, the provisional capital of the German "restoration" period of the 1950s. The novel ends with his suicide.

The third novel in the trilogy is *Der Tod in Rom* (1954; *Death in Rome*, 1956), a parody of Mann's novella *Death in Venice*. The book gives a caricature of the German nationalistic artist and satirizes the German yearning for Italian culture, which had earlier been perverted by the alliance with the fascist rule of Mussolini. According to Ernestine Schlant in *The Language of Silence,* the character Ilse Kürenberg is "a Jewish protagonist who was driven into exile and who is marked by the Holocaust" and as such belongs to the outsiders. She is shot to death by a former Nazi general, Judejahn, who is now training Arab fighters against Israel. Schlant says that ''Ilse's death is a bitterly ironic comment on the unrepentant fanaticism of Nazi racists, and it also expresses Koeppen's refusal to engage in philo-Semitic amends.'' Those of the younger generation who admit to German guilt are marginalized in this society as well. Adolf, a priest, and Siegfried, an avant-garde composer, are both outside the genealogical line; their lives are dignified but sterile. Bold in its subject matter and dedicated to modernity in its form, Koeppen's trilogy shows the collapse of Western culture and the bankruptcy of its models for explaining the world in the face of wordless brutality. In characters such as Philipp, Keetenheuve and Siegfried, the novels also reflect Koeppen's own desperate role as an artist and intellectual.

Koeppen never completed another novel. He did, however, publish travel writings and later, in an effort to resolve his writer's trauma, the autobiographical fragment *Jugend* (1976). According to Martin Hielscher in *Zitierte Moderne: Poetische Erfahrung und Reflexion in Wolfgang Koeppens Nachkriegsromanen und in ''Jugend,''* this latter work is an apocalyptic ''lament for both the socially destroyed life and the already lost aesthetic existence, embedded in the lament for the lost paradise.'' Koeppen searches for elements of guilt in twentieth-century Germany, and the narrator finds himself in a paradoxical situation as both an ''offender'' and a ''victim'': '' . . . I am Cain, however, I am also Abel.'' In 1948 *Jakob Littners Aufzeichnungen aus einem Erdloch*, a work the critic Bernhard Fetz called a ''substitute for the novel about his own history of the Third Reich,'' was published under Koeppen's name. As a representative of outsiders, Koeppen can justly be considered one of the best-known postwar German authors.

—Walter Schmitz

See the essay on *Jakob Littners Aufzeichnungen aus einem Erdloch*.

KOFMAN, Sarah

Nationality: French. **Born:** 14 September 1934. **Education:** Sorbonne University, Paris. **Career:** Professor of philosophy, Saint-Sernin College, Toulouse, 1960–63, and Claude-Monet College, Paris, 1963–70; lecturer and professor, Sorbonne University, Paris, 1971–90. **Died:** Suicide, 15 October 1994.

PUBLICATIONS

Memoir

Paroles suffoquées. 1987; as *Stifled Words*, 1998.
Rue Ordener, Rue Labat. 1994; translated as *Rue Ordener, Rue Labat*, 1996.

Other (philosophy)

L'Enfance de l'art: Une Interprétation de l'esthétique freudienne. 1970; as *The Childhood of Art: An Interpretation of Freud's Aesthetics,* 1988.
Nietzsche et la métaphore. 1972; as *Nietzsche and Metaphor,* 1993.
Camera obscura, de l'idéologie. 1973; as *Camera Obscura of Ideology,* 1998.
Quatre romans analytiques. 1974; as *Freud and Fiction,* 1990.
Aberrations: Le Devenir-femme d'Auguste Comte. 1978.
Nietzsche et la scène philosophique. 1979.
L'Énigme de la femme: La Femme dans les textes de Freud. 1980; as *The Enigma of Woman: Woman in Freud's Writings,* 1985.
Un Métier impossible: Lecture de ''constructions en analyse.'' 1983.
Mélancolie de l'art. 1985.
Pourquoi rit-on?: Freud et le mot d'esprit. 1986.
Socrate(s). 1989; as *Socrates: Fictions of a Philosopher,* 1998.
Séductions: De Sartre à Héraclite. 1990.
''Il n'y a que le premier pas qui coûte'': Freud et la spéculation. 1991.
Explosion. 1992.
De l'Ecce homo de Nietzsche. 1992; as *Explosion I,* 1999.
Explosion II: Les enfants de Nietzsche. 1993.
Le Mépris des juifs: Nietzsche, les juifs, l'antisémitisme. 1994.
L'Imposture de la beauté et autres textes. 1995.

Other (literary criticism)

Autobiogriffures. 1976; as *Autobiogriffures: Du chat Murr d'Hoffmann,* 1984.
Nerval: Le Charme de la répétition: Lecture de Sylvie. 1979.
Le Respect des femmes: (Kant et Rousseau). 1981.
Comment s'en sortir? 1983.
Lectures de Derrida. 1984.
Conversions: Le Marchand de Venise sous le signe de Saturne. 1987.
Don Juan, ou, le refus de la dette, with Jean-Yves Masson. 1991.

*

Bibliography: ''Sarah Kofman: Bibliography, 1963–1998,'' in *Enigmas: Essays on Sarah Kofman,* edited by Penelope Deutscher and Kelly Oliver, 1999.

Critical Studies: ''Sarah Kofman'' by Janice Orion, in *Shifting Scenes: Interviews on Women, Writing, and Politics in Post-68 France,* edited by Alice A. Jardine and Anne M. Menke, 1991; ''Response to Sarah Kofman'' by Judith Butler, in *Compar(a)ison* (Switzerland), 1(1), 1993, pp. 27–32; ''Double Whaam! Sarah Kofman on *Ecce Homo*'' by Duncan Large, in *German Life and Letters* (England), 48(4), 1995, pp. 441–62;

''Sarah Kofman's *Paroles suffoquees:* Autobiography, History, and Writing after Auschwitz'' by Madeline Dobie, in *French Forum,* 22(3), September 1997, pp. 319–41; *Sarah Kofman* by Françoise Collin and Françoise Proust, 1997; *Enigmas: Essays on Sarah Kofman,* edited by Penelope Deutscher and Kelly Oliver, 1999; ''Pardon? Sarah Kofman and Jacques Derrida (On Mourning, Debt, and Seven Friendships)'' by Penelope Deutscher, in *Journal of the British Society of Phenomenology,* 31(1), 2000, pp. 21–35; ''Of Footnotes and Fathers: Reading Irigaray with Kofman'' by Ranita Chatteriee, in *Psychoanalyses/Feminisms,* edited by Peter L. Rudnytsky and Andrew M. Gordon, 2000; ''Sarah Kofman's *Rue Ordener, Rue Labat* and Autobiography'' by Caroline Sheaffer-Jones in *Australian Journal of French Studies,* 37(1), January/April 2000, pp. 91–104; ''Conversion and Oral Assimilation in Sarah Kofman'' by Nicole Fermon, in *College Literature,* 28(1), Winter 2001, p. 155.

* * *

Sarah Kofman is most celebrated as a philosopher in the European tradition. A professor of philosophy at the Sorbonne in Paris, she was of a standing with thinkers such as Jacques Derrida, Jean-Luc Nancy, and Phillipe Lacoue-Labarthe and was one of the first commentators on deconstruction and on the French intellectual phenomenological heritage. Her work, philosophically inspired most clearly by Friedrich Nietzsche and Sigmund Freud, covered a range of issues and thinkers but perhaps was most focused on issues of gender and thought and on art and on the relationship between literature and philosophy. For example, her book *Socrates: Fictions of a Philosopher* looks at the way Plato, Søren Kierkegaard, and Nietzsche created a ''fictional'' character for Socrates as a central part of their philosophical work.

Kofman's own philosophical work seems to avoid discussion of the war and the Holocaust. In part this avoidance can be put down to the more general reluctance of survivors to speak about the Holocaust and to her own experiences of French anti-Semitism and postwar resettlement, which are detailed in her memoir. She writes in *Rue Ordener, Rue Labat,* however, that all of her works—more than 20 books on philosophical, theoretical, and psychoanalytic subjects—may have been the ''detours required to bring me to write about 'that,''' the ''that'' being the effect of the Nazis on her own life, specifically the deportation and murder of her father. With this in mind, it is possible to see her work—about the silence of women in Freud or about the stories philosophers tell to fill gaps in knowledge—as being concerned centrally with detours, gaps, and avoidances. It is as if it were, in fact, all about ''that,'' her founding prephilosophical experience of the Holocaust.

Of Kofman's works that more directly discuss the Holocaust there are two autobiographical fragments (''Damned Food'' and ''Nightmare: At the Margins of Medieval Studies''), a meditation titled *Paroles suffoquées (Stifled Words),*

and a full memoir, *Rue Ordener, Rue Labat.* The last two of these works were inspired by the experience of the loss of her father, a Parisian rabbi deported to Drancy and then Auschwitz in July 1942. They were also inspired by her need to continue to go over, to speak about and bear witness to, the Holocaust without end. It was for her a subject that could never be exhausted.

Kofman, along with many other major figures in French philosophy, Jewish (Derrida, Emmanuel Levinas, Alain Finkielkraut) and non-Jewish (Maurice Blanchot, Jean-Francois Lyotard), was greatly influenced both directly and indirectly by the thought of Martin Heidegger. Before the war Heidegger was a member of the Nazi party and after the war made no direct comment on the Holocaust. Yet, as Elaine Marks writes of these French thinkers in *Auschwitz and After,* ''it is those texts . . . where Heidegger's thought and poetic style are most recognisable, which, through metaphoric indirection, produce an effect of horror and silence acceptable, to my expectations, at least, of writing 'after Auschwitz.''' The style of thought opened by Heidegger and transformed by Derrida, Levinas, Kofman, and others seems to have offered a rich vein of reflection on the Holocaust.

—Robert Eaglestone

See the essays on *Rue Ordener, Rue Labat* and *Stifled Words.*

KOGON, Eugen

Nationality: Austrian. **Born:** 1903. **Education:** Studied under Othmar Spann. **Career:** Arrested in Austria for opposing the Nazis, 1937, 1938; prisoner, Buchenwald concentration camp, 1939. Professor of political science, University of Munich and University of Marburg, 1951–68. Founder and publisher, with Walter Dirks, *Frankfurter Hefte.* **Award:** Buber-Rosenzweig medal, German Coordinating Committee for Jewish-Christian Relations, 1980. **Died:** 1987.

PUBLICATIONS

Collection

Gesammelte Schriften [Collected Works], edited by Michael Kogon and Gottfried Erb:
  Ideologie und Praxis der Unmenschlichkeit: Erfahrungen mit dem Nationalsozialismus. 1995.
  Europäische Visonen. 1995.
  Die restaurative Republik: Zur Geschichte der Bundesrepublik Deutschland. 1996.
  Liebe und tu, was du willst: Reflexionen eines Christen. 1996.
  Die reformierte Gesellschaft. 1997.

"Dieses merkwürdige, wichtige Leben": *Begegnungen.* 1997.

Bedingungen der Humanität. 1998.

Die Idee des Christlichen Ständestaates: Frühe Schriften 1921–1940. 1999.

Other

Der SS-Staat: Das System de Deutschen Konzentrationslager (memoir and study). 1946; as *The SS State: The System of German Concentration Camps,* 1946, as *The Theory and Practice of Hell: The German Concentration Camps and the System behind Them,* 1950.

Die Wissenschaft im Rahmen der politische Bildung. Vorträge, gehalten vom 16. bis 18. März 1950 in Berlin auf der Tagung der Deutschen Hochschule für Politik, with Alfred Weber (lecture). 1950.

Die Rolle der Arbeiterbewegung in der Kultur einer humanitären Welt. 1963.

Die unvollendete Erneuerung. 1964.

Freiheit in Gesellschaft, with Johannes Baptist Metz, Rudolf Pesch, and Adolf Exeler. 1971.

Wladimir Iljitsch Lenin. Ein Biograph. Essay. 1971.

Die Stunde der Ingenieure: Technologische Intelligenz und Politik. 1976.

Ökologische Zwischenbilanz. 1981.

Eugen Kogon—Ein politischer Publizist in Hessen: Essays, Aufsätze, Reden zwischen 1946 und 1982, edited by Hubert Habicht. 1982.

Editor, with Heinz Winfried Sabais, *Der Mensch und seine Meinung.* 1961.

Editor, with Hermann Langbein and Adalbert Rückerl, *Nationalsozialistische Massentötungen durch Giftgas: Eine Dokumentation.* 1983; as *Nazi Mass Murder: A Documentary History of the Use of Poison Gas,* 1993.

* * *

Journalist by profession, economist and sociologist by training, Austrian-born Eugen Kogon was catapulted into the forefront of postwar German politics by his report on the concentration camp system, published as *Der SS-Staat* ("The SS State," 1946; *The Theory and Practice of Hell,* 1950). A Catholic actively opposed to the Nazis, Kogon was arrested in 1937 and again in 1938 when the Nazis took power in Austria. Transferred to the Buchenwald concentration camp in 1939, he worked as a clerk in the hospital and witnessed the medical experiments on prisoners conducted there. *Der SS-Staat* also made Kogon into one of the best-known survivors of the concentration camps in postwar Germany.

Kogon wrote *Der SS-Staat* on the basis of his report on Buchenwald for the Allies, commissioned in April 1945 after the liberation of the camp. Completed in less than four weeks, Kogon was assisted in his inquiries by a team of former camp inmates, heavily weighted toward the communists, and by a team of German-speaking intelligence officers from the U.S. Army. This was the first constraint on his work, since the communists had been the most influential—and the most compromised—group of prisoners in Buchenwald. The original report was not published, though selected portions were used in the Nuremberg war trials. As a result, the precise accusations contained in the interviews appended to Kogon's text were lost to students of the Holocaust until the 1980s. In this context still, a few dozen prisoners who read the work testified that it was thoroughly objective. The report had achieved this impression of objectivity by sidestepping the difficult subject of the complicity between political prisoners and the concentration camp regime. Only by the time of the publication of *Der SS-Staat* was Kogon able to write more freely about the relationship between the SS and the prisoner population, with a candor that makes his testimony particularly valuable. Nonetheless, Kogon's protected position within the inmate hierarchy is suggested by the anecdotes that appear throughout SS-Staat. Acknowledging the special fate of the Jews, Kogon still focused on the political prisoners, whose determined opposition to the Nazis made them primary actors in camp life. For Kogon and the politicals he worked with, the camp experience was first and foremost a struggle of will against the corruption and brutality of the SS rather than the life of suffering, death, and helpless degradation that appears more frequently in Jewish accounts.

From his earliest days in prison in Vienna, Kogon wrote sketches for essays on postwar planning. After the war his experiences at the hands of the Nazis were a leitmotiv in his passionate appeals for peace and reconciliation in Western Europe. In *Theory and Practice of Hell* Kogon argued that European states had to unite in order to prevent a return to the brutal dictatorship that had turned Europe into a kind of concentration camp. He became the academic coordinator of the European Committee for Research into the Causes and Consequences of the Second World War in Luxembourg, and his work as chair of the campaigning group Europa Union sealed his reputation as one of the leaders of the movement that created the European Communities in the 1950s. Kogon also believed Germany bore a responsibility to combat anti-Semitic violence and prejudice, and for his work in this area, particularly in founding the journal *Frankfurter Hefte,* he was awarded the Buber-Rosenzweig Medal of the German Coordinating Committee for Jewish-Christian Relations in 1980. He himself was disappointed, however, with the limited impact of the journal in educating Germans about current developments touching on their recent past—it was, he felt, too academic.

From 1946 Kogon published a series of articles on the concentration camps and on other aspects of the Nazi regime, a number of which were published posthumously in *Ideologie und Praxis der Unmenschlichkeit* (1995). As he acknowledged in *Der SS-Staat,* one of the main flaws in his report was the lack of information he had available covering the mass murder of the Jews. Kogon wrote repeatedly in the *Frankfurter Hefte* about the repressed consciousness of the German public during the Nazi era of what had happened in the concentration camps, particularly to the Jews. In 1954 he wrote of his personal recollections of the screams of Jews in prison in Vienna following the November pogrom of 1938 (*Kristallnacht*). His articles on the concentration camp system now began to cover the larger death camps as well, and Kogon ultimately edited a collection of academic essays, *Nazi Mass Murder: A Documentary History of the Use of Poison Gas* (1983). His last publication was an article, ''Das Ende der Konzentrationslager'' (1985; ''The End of the Concentration Camp''), suggesting on the basis of the use of the camps after the war that in some senses the camp system continued to serve as an instrument of or model for social control in the postwar world.

Since 1978 Kogon had been working on a second monograph on the Nazi system. He died before completing it, delaying the project for years. In his son's view Kogon's reluctance to press ahead with the task was due in part to his conviction that the lessons of what was merely the first genocidal regime no longer commanded the attention they once had. He also believed that the atrocities of the Nazi regime could not provide any basis for humane social thought, hinting throughout his work at his personal faith, which remained unshaken.

—George R. Wilkes

See the essay on *The Theory and Practice of Hell: The German Concentration Camps and the System behind Them.*

KOLMAR, Gertrud

Pseudonym for Gertrude Chodziesner. **Nationality:** German. **Born:** Berlin, 10 December 1894; cousin of Walter Benjamin. **Education:** Obtained diploma to teach English and French. **Career:** Language teacher in private homes, primarily in Berlin and Hamburg, beginning in 1919. **Died:** Presumed murdered, Auschwitz, 1943.

PUBLICATIONS

Collections

Selected Poems of Gertrud Kolmar. 1970.
Weibliches Bildnis: Sämtliche Gedichte. 1980.

Poetry

Gedichte . . . 1917.
Welten. 1947.
Das lyrische Werk. 1955; as *Dark Soliloquy: The Selected Poems of Gertrud Kolmar,* 1975.

Tag- und Tierträume: Gedichte von Gertrud Kolmar. 1963.
Die Kerze von Arras: Ausgewählte Gedichte. 1968.
Das Wort der Stummen: Nachgelassene Gedichte. 1978.
Frühe Gedichte: (1917–22); Wort der Stummen: (1933). 1980.
Gedichte. 1983.

Novels

Eine Mutter. 1978; translated as *A Jewish Mother from Berlin* and published with *Susanna,* 1997.
Susanna (novella). 1993; translated as *Susanna* and published with *A Jewish Mother from Berlin,* 1997.

Other

Briefe an die Schwester Hilde (1938–1943) (correspondence). 1970.

*

Critical Studies: ''The Poetry of Gertrud Kolmar'' by Erika Langman, in *Seminar,* 14, 1978, pp. 117–32; ''Gertrud Kolmar: An Appraisal'' by Michael C. Eben, in *German Life and Letters,* 37(3), April 1984, pp. 196–210; ''The Unspoken Bond: Else Lasker-Schuler and Gertrud Kolmar in Their Historical and Cultural Context,'' in *Seminar,* 29(4), November 1993, pp. 349–69, and ''More Than Metaphors: Animals, Gender, and Jewish Identity in Gertrud Kolmar,'' in *Transforming the Center, Eroding the Margins: Essays on Ethnic and Cultural Boundaries in German-Speaking Countries,* edited by Dagmar C.G. Lorenz and Renate S. Posthofen, 1998, both by Dagmar C.G. Lorenz; ''Gertrud Kolmar (1894–1943): German-Jewish Poetess'' by Brigitte M. Goldstein, in *Modern Judaism,* 15, October 1995, pp. 265–77; ''1932 Gertrud Kolmar Completes Her Poetry Cycle *Weibliches Bildnis* and Thus Reshapes Her Identity As a Jewish Woman Poet'' by John Bormanis, in *Yale Companion to Jewish Writing and Thought in German Culture, 1096–1996,* edited by Sander L. Gilman and Zack Zipes, 1997; ''Reconsidering Gertrud Kolmar through the Cycle 'German Sea,''' in *Transforming the Center, Eroding the Margins: Essays on Ethnic and Cultural Boundaries in German-Speaking Countries,* edited by Dagmar C.G. Lorenz and Renate S. Posthofen, 1998, and ''Gertrud Kolmar (1894–1943) Germany,'' in *Women Writers in German-Speaking Countries: A Bio-Bibliographical Critical Sourcebook,* edited by Elke P. Frederiksen and Elizabeth G. Ametsbichler, 1998, both by Monika Shafi; ''Narrative Witnessing As Memory Work: Reading Gertrud Kolmar's *A Jewish Mother*'' by Irene Kacandes, in *Acts of Memory: Cultural Recall in the Present,* edited by Mieke Bal, Jonathan Crewe, and Leo Spitzer, 1999.

* * *

Gertrud Kolmar, who has been frequently compared to Else Lasker-Schüler and Nobel Prize winner **Nelly Sachs,** is not generally characterized as a writer of Holocaust literature. There were no extant mentions of death camps in surviving works or letters—perhaps because she knew that these would not pass censorship, perhaps because she did not know the full extent of the Final Solution until she was deported in February 1943 to Auschwitz, where she presumably died soon after arrival. Her poem cycle *Words of the Silent* was written in September and October 1933. These poems chronicle her experience of the early days of National Socialism in Germany and exhibit an extensive knowledge of the conditions in the early concentration camps and "special prisons" in the Berlin vicinity in 1933, as well as Kolmar's uncanny foresight of events to come.

Kolmar's relatives could not convince her to leave Germany, but not because she was blind to the danger of staying. Her attempts to save her literary works, entrusting multiple copies to relatives who did emigrate, suggest that she was cognizant of her situation. The last major work saved was *Susanna,* a novella written during 1940–41, whose narrator is a Jewish governess waiting for an affidavit that will permit her to emigrate. Kolmar remained in Germany partly to care for her ailing, elderly father, but primarily out of the sense that this was her destiny as a Jew and it would be weakness to try to deny or escape it. After Jewish emigration was forbidden in 1941, Kolmar wrote to a relative: "No matter what comes, I will not despair or be unhappy, because I know that I am travelling the path that is my destiny. So many of us have taken this road over the centuries, why should I want to take a different one?" (all translations by Elizabeth Loentz). For Kolmar submission was empowering: "I will submit to my destiny, be it high as a tower, dark and threatening as a cloud . . . I know that I haven't lived as I should and have always been ready to atone. I will accept all suffering as just penance, and bear it without complaint, realizing that it is part of me, that I was born to bear it, and that I am capable of bearing it" (letter to Hilde, 15 December 1942). The problematic notion expressed here, that anti-Semitism and Nazi persecution were just punishment for an individual's or collective sins, was tempered in Kolmar's poems. In the "Jewish Mother," the child suffers innocently. The sins he bears are those of his oppressors, hypocrites, who "nod to what the preacher says, and then go out and kick this soul like an animal." The poem "We Jews" rewards innocents' suffering with the promise of justice in the future, "Cast yourselves among the lowly, be weak, embrace your suffering. Until some day your weary walking shoes will walk on the necks of the mighty."

While the above-mentioned poems address the Jewish situation in particular, other poems in the cycle convey Kolmar's solidarity with other persecuted groups. The lyrical I of "The Abused" is a (Christian-raised) atheist, socialist male. Numerous poems rely heavily on Christian imagery. In "In the Camp" Christ is ever-present, wordlessly dragging his cross to the place of execution. In the ironically titled "Anno Domini 1933" Christ appears, visibly Jewish, to indict "Christian" Germans for poisoning their children with hate. The accused reject his warnings: "You dress up like Jesus Christ, but you're just a Jewish communist." The poem concludes with an analogy between Christ's crucifixion and the persecution of Jews in the "Third, Christian-German Reich."

A common theme of several poems in "Words of the Silent" is the dehumanization of victims of Nazi oppression. In "The Jewish Mother" the child is "kicked like an animal." In "The Prisoners" the prisoners are "like livestock" waiting for the knife. They are without heart or soul, "only bodies," "only names." It should be noted that Kolmar did not subscribe to a hierarchy that valued human over animal life. Being soul-less is not an attribute of animals but of animals that have been robbed of their souls by humans. As the woman in "The Jewish Mother" chastises, "Well-meaning people don't kick animals." Identification with animals and human outcasts is a common theme throughout Kolmar's oeuvre, especially in the poem cycles "Image of a Woman" and "Animal Dreams" and in *Susanna,* whose title figure is considered deranged in large part because she lives in a rich fantasy world that does not distinguish between animals and humans.

In "To the Prisoners" and "We Jews" Kolmar explores the poet's responsibility to combat injustice. This role requires strong empathy with the persecuted. In "To the Prisoners" the poet "I" exclaims, "Oh, I should be with you, crawling on wet stone, cramped, beaten, hungry, lice-ridden, bound in iron shackles." As someone who knows their suffering, the poet must be their voice, and "raise [her] voice like a glowing torch in the dark desert of the world: Justice! Justice! Justice!" ("We Jews"). Kolmar knew that this role was a perilous one. The poet "I" of "To the Prisoners" is certain that she will become one of them, "Because if they find this page, they will arrest me."

—Elizabeth Loentz

See the essay on *Dark Soliloquy: The Selected Poems of Gertrud Kolmar.*

KOPS, Bernard

Nationality: British. **Born:** London, 28 November 1926. **Education:** London elementary schools to age 13. **Family:** Married Erica Gordon in 1956; four children. **Career:** Held various odd jobs, including docker, chef, salesman, waiter, lift man, and barrow boy, 1945–58; resident dramatist, Bristol Old Vic Theatre, 1959. Writer-in-residence, London Borough of

Hounslow, 1980–82; lecturer in drama, Spiro Institute, 1985–86, Surrey, Ealing, and Inner London education authorities, 1989–90, and City Literary Institute, London, 1991. **Awards:** Arts Council bursary 1957, 1979, and 1985; C. Day Lewis fellowship, 1981–83; London Fringe award, 1993, for *Dreams of Anne Frank*. **Agent:** John Rush, Sheil Land Associates, 43 Doughty Street, London WC1 N2LF, England.

PUBLICATIONS

Plays

The Hamlet of Stepney Green: A (Sad) Comedy in Three Acts (produced Oxford, London, and New York, 1958). 1959.
Goodbye, World (produced Guildford, Surrey, 1959).
Change for the Angel (produced London, 1960).
The Dream of Peter Mann (produced Edinburgh, Scotland, 1960). 1960.
Stray Cats and Empty Bottles (produced Cambridge, 1961; London, 1967).
Enter Solly Gold (produced Wellingborough, Northamptonshire, 1962; London, 1970). In *Satan, Socialites, and Solly Gold: Three New Plays from England*, 1961.
Four Plays (includes *The Hamlet of Stepney Green*; *Enter Solly Gold*; *Home Sweet Honeycomb* [radio play]; *The Lemmings* [radio play]). 1964.
The Boy Who Wouldn't Play Jesus (for children; produced London, 1965). 1965.
David, It Is Getting Dark (produced 1966).
It's a Lovely Day Tomorrow, with John Goldschmidt (produced London, 1976).
More Out Than In (produced London, 1980).
Ezra (produced London, 1981). In *Plays* (vol. 1), 1999.
Simon at Midnight (produced London, 1985).
Kafe Kropotkin (produced England, 1988).
Some of These Days (produced London, 1990). As *Sophie! Last of the Red Hot Mamas* (produced London, 1990).
Moss (produced London, 1991).
Androcles and the Lion, adaptation (for children; produced London, 1992).
Who Shall I Be Tomorrow? (for children; produced London, 1992). In *Plays* (vol. 3), 2001.
Playing Sinatra: A Play (produced England, 1992). 1992.
Dreams of Anne Frank: A Play for Young People (produced England, 1992). 1993.
Call in the Night (produced England, 1995). In *Plays* (vol. 2), 1999.
Plays (3 vols.): Playing Sinatra; The Hamlet of Stepney Green; Ezra. 1999.
Dreams of Anne Frank; On Margate Sands; Call in the Night. 2000.

The Dream of Peter Mann; Enter Solly Gold; Who Shall I Be Tomorrow? 2001.

Radio Plays: *Home Sweet Honeycomb*, 1962; *The Lemmings*, 1963; *Born in Israel*, 1963; *The Dark Ages*, 1964; *Israel: The Immigrant*, 1964; *Bournemouth Nights*, 1979; *I Grow Old, I Grow Old*, 1979; *Over the Rainbow*, 1980; *Simon at Midnight*, 1982; *Trotsky Was My Father*, 1984; *More Out Than In*, 1985; *Kafe Kropotkin*, 1988; *Colour Blind*, 1989; *Congress in Manchester*, 1990; *The Ghost Child*, 1990; *Soho Nights*, 1990; *Sailing with Homer*, 1994.

Television Plays: *I Want to Go Home*, 1963; *The Lost Years of Brian Hooper*, 1967; *Alexander the Greatest*, 1971; *Just One Kid*, 1974; *Why the Geese Shrieked* and *The Boy Philosopher*, 1974, from stories by Isaac Bashevis Singer; *It's a Lovely Day Tomorrow*, with John Goldschmidt, 1975; *Moss*, 1975; *Rocky Marciano Is Dead*, 1976; *Night Kids*, 1983; *The Survivor*, 1991.

Novels

Awake for Mourning. 1958.
Motorbike. 1962.
Yes from No-Man's Land. 1965.
The Dissent of Dominick Shapiro. 1967.
By the Waters of Whitechapel. 1969.
The Passionate Past of Gloria Gaye. 1971.
Settle Down Simon Katz. 1973.
Partners. 1975.
On Margate Sands. 1978.

Poetry

Poems. 1955.
Poems and Songs. 1958.
An Anemone for Antigone. 1959.
Erica I Want to Read You Something. 1966.
For the Record. 1971.
Barricades in West Hampstead. 1988.
Grandchildren, and Other Poems. 2000.

Other

The World Is a Wedding (autobiography). 1963.
Neither Your Honey nor Your Sting: An Offbeat History of the Jews. 1985.
Shalom Bomb: Scenes from My Life (autobiography). 2000.

Editor, *Poetry Hounslow*. 1981.

*

Critical Studies: *The Idea of Commitment in Recent British Drama* (dissertation) by John Malcolm Page, University of

California, Riverside, 1966; "British Playwrights in the Early Thermonuclear Era" by Charles A. Carpenter, in his *Dramatists and the Bomb*, 1999.

* * *

Playwright and writer Bernard Kops began writing in the 1950s and was part of a group of writers known as the Angry Young Men, intellectuals who had lived through the Depression and World War II England. His plays and prose center on protesting the politics of the day and prejudice. Kops's own life of poverty in the East End London Jewish ghetto of Stepney Green has had a profound affect on his style and themes. In his works he is quite adept at bringing forth dreams that he must have had while growing up. The way in which he is able to blend dreams with reality has fueled his efforts to create plays for children, namely *Dreams of Anne Frank, Who Shall I Be Tomorrow?*, and *The Boy Who Would Not Play Jesus*. It was precisely his own miserable childhood that has enabled him to relate well to younger audiences.

Kops spent his teenage years hearing about the horrors committed against Jews during World War II. In fact, one of his Dutch cousins returned alive from Bergen-Belsen and the stories related were indeed terrifying to the Kops family. Kops himself had personal experience with anti-Semitism, having endured jobs where anti-Semitic behavior was common and accepted. He heard people screaming anti-Semitic slogans at Eddie Cantor and Sophie Tucker. In his biography, *The World Is a Wedding*, Kops unashamedly describes his past and the impoverished Jewish life he led. His personal life as a young adult was not short of adventure. Kops experimented with drugs, joined a traveling theatrical troupe, and even spent time in a psychiatric hospital. With his play *The Hamlet of Stepney Green*, Kops comes full circle with his life and returns to that which he knows best—East London Jewish life. Kops has faced up to the reality of his childhood and in it he has found a wealth of material. Combining memory and Shakespeare, Kops has created a modern-day Jewish play that seems to be a catharsis for him. Kops later began to see theater as a tool, as an educational forum to fight against social and racial prejudice, and as a way to lead, not follow, society. In his essay "The Young Writer and the Theater," Kops warns other playwrights that, "The greatest danger of all is that you might lose touch with your own background, the one that you drew your inspiration from and now you live in an intellectual no-man's land where writers get their ideas second hand from one another." Kops has great admiration for **Bertolt Brecht,** and this is evident in his own plays where he uses many songs and music to tie scenes and ideas together. Plays such as *Mother Courage and Her Children* (*Mutter Courage und Ihre Kinder*) or *The Three-Penny Opera* (*Die Dreigroschenoper*) are Brecht plays that can be compared to the issues Kops addresses and

the style that he uses in his own plays. The Czech playwright Karel Capek and theater of the 1920s also had an influence on Kops.

In his play *Enter Solly Gold* Kops confronts the hatred for the Jews, especially those who made it big after the Depression and were comfortably set up in the 1960s. In the novel *Yes from No-Man's Land* (1965), Kops spans almost the entire Jewish experience, which runs from the Holocaust to Israel to the question of intermarriage. It is important to note that although Kops did not have personal experience with the Holocaust, it left an impression upon him that was very deep. While Jews in the East were struggling against Adolf Hitler, Kops was fighting his own war at home in London. He overcame a difficult childhood and lived in fear during the bombings of London. He personally experienced Jews being blamed for everything from the death of Jesus Christ to World War II. Yet he prevailed, and his amazing background has become the source of the pain and the laughter that come through in his works. His love for theater has stemmed from a Jewish background that was unstable yet provided Kops with an energy and enthusiasm for life. In his essay "A Very Unangry Young Man: Back Toward the Epic," Kops states, "I want to work in the theatre and for the theatre—committed to this most exciting arena where I must fight like hell and dream of heaven—fight so that continuously I am assured that life in all its aspects is preferable to and defeats death."

—Cynthia A. Klíma

See the essay on *Dreams of Anne Frank: A Play for Young People*.

KORCZAK, Janusz

Pseudonym for Henryk Goldszmit. **Nationality:** Polish. **Born:** Warsaw, 1878. **Education:** Medical school, Warsaw, M.D. **Military Service:** Russian army: doctor on a hospital train in China during Russo-Japanese War, 1905–06, doctor, served on Eastern Front during World War I. Polish army, Polish-Soviet War of 1920. **Career:** Doctor in a Jewish children's hospital in Warsaw, 1904–05, and 1907–10; counselor in summer camps for boys, 1907–10; founder, with Maryna Falska, of a public orphanage for Christian children in Warsaw, 1918–36. Founder, with Stefania Wilczynska, and director, Orphan Home for Jewish Children, Warsaw, 1911–42. Lecturer, Free Polish University and Jewish teachers' institute; host of radio shows during the 1930s; non-Zionist representative to Palestine, Jewish Agency, 1934–36. **Awards:** Poland Academy of Literature golden laurel award, 1937; UNESCO declared 1978–79 the Year of Korczak to coincide with the celebration of the Year of the Child. **Died:** Murdered, Treblinka, 1942.

PUBLICATIONS

Collection

Dziela (10 vols.). 1992–95.

Diary

Ghetto Diary (translation of *Pamietnik z getta*). 1978; as *The Warsaw Ghetto Memoir of Janus Korczak,* 1978; as *The Ghetto Years, 1939–1942,* 1980.

Novel

Dziecko salonu. 1906.

Short Stories

Tajemniczy przyjaciel [Mysterious Friend]. 1957.

Other

Dzieci ulicy: Powiesc Janusza Korczaka. 1901.
Koszalki opalki. 1905.
Slawa: Opowiesc. 1913.
Bobo. 1914.
Józki, Jaski i Franki [Joes, Johns, and Franks] (for children). 1922.
Król Macius na wyspie bezludnej: Powiesc [King Matt on the Desert Island] (for children). 1923.
Bankructwo malego dzeka; Powiesc [Children of the Street] (for children). 1924.
Momenty wychowawcze [Moments of Educational Observation]. 1924.
Król Macius Pierwszy: Powiesc (for children). 1925; as *Matthew, the Young King,* 1945; as *King Matthew the First,* 1986.
Jak kochac dziecko [How to Love a Child] (2 vols.). 1929.
Moski, Joski i Srule (for children). 1934.
Na koloniach letnich. 1946.
Wybór pism (4 vols.). 1957–58; selections translated as *Selected Works of Janusz Korczak,* 1967.
Wybor pism pedagogicznych [Selected Writings on Education] (2 vols.) 1957.
Prawo dziecka do szacunku. 1958; translated with *Kiedy znów bede maly* and published as *When I Am Little Again; and The Child's Right to Respect,* 1991.
Kajtus czarodziej (for children). 1960.
Kiedy znów bede maly. 1961; translated with *Prawo dziecka do szacunku* and published as *When I Am Little Again; and The Child's Right to Respect,* 1991.
Maly czlowiek [Little Man] (photography). 1965.
Fragmenty utworów, with Danuta Stepniewska (for children). 1978.

Pisma wybrane (4 vols.). 1978.
Mysl pedagogiczna Janusza Korczaka: Nowe zródla (selections). 1983.
Mysli (selections). 1987.
Listy i rozmyslania palestynskie (correspondence). 1999.
A Voice for the Child: The Inspirational Words of Janusz Korczak (selections), edited by Sandra Joseph. 1999.

*

Film Adaptation: *Król Macius I,* 1958.

Bibliography: *Janusz Korczak Bibliography* by Joseph J. Buckley, 1976.

Critical Studies: *The Life of Janusz Korczak* by Hanna Olczak, translated by Romauld Jan Kruk and Harold Gresswell, 1965; *The King of Children: A Biography of Janusz Korczak* by Betty Jean Lifton, 1988; *Father of the Orphans; The Story of Janusz Korczak* by Mark Bernheim, 1989; "Janusz Korczak: A Tale for Our Time" by Bruno Bettelheim, in his *Freud's Vienna and Other Essays,* 1990; "Janusz Korczak: Child Advocate Supreme," in *Childhood Education,* 69(1), Fall 1992, pp. 29–31, and "Janusz Korczak and the Jewish Connection: Two Accounts from the Warsaw Ghetto," in *Midstream,* 45(3), 1 April 1999, p. 11, both by Edwin P. Kulawiec; *The Gate of Light: Janusz Korczak, the Educator and Writer Who Overcame the Holocaust* by Adir Cohen, 1994; "Meaningful Encounter and Creative Dialogue: The Pedagogy of Janusz Korczak" by Joop W. A. Berding, in *Journal of Thought,* 30(4), Winter 1995, p. 23.

*   *   *

Janusz Korczak was born Henryk Goldszmidt in 1878 to a wealthy, assimilated family of Warsaw Jews. His memories of his father, however, were largely the memories of a man wracked with mental illness and confined to a hospital cell, an image that would haunt Korczak throughout his life. His familiarity with his father's suffering led him to the realization that all of humanity is "under siege," as he put it. With this realization Korczak resolved to devote his life to "the world's oldest proletariat," namely, children. And the most downtrodden of the children were the orphans.

Thus, from early adulthood, when he became a pediatrician, Korczak devoted his time and energy to alleviating the plight of homeless orphans and other underprivileged children. After writing several provocative works on the horrific state of poverty-stricken children—including *Children of the Street* (1901) and *A Child of the Salon* (1906)—Korczak was appointed head of a Jewish orphanage in Warsaw in 1911. With the exception of his service as a medical officer in World War I, he retained this position for the rest of his life. During the 30-year period he spent at the orphanage Korczak became an internationally known advocate for children, based on his success there and on his numerous writings. He was invited to serve as a lecturer at the Free Polish University and at the Jewish teachers' institute, and his voice became a familiar one on the Polish airwaves as he made appearances on the radio on behalf of his cause.

In the 1930s, with the rise of Nazism in Germany and anti-Semitism in Poland, Korczak's Jewish identity assumed greater and greater depth. After taking on the role of Poland's non-Zionist representative to the Jewish Agency, in 1934 and 1936 he traveled to Palestine, where he met with many of his former pupils. He spent time at the kibbutz Ein Charod and was impressed by the educational and social philosophy of the kibbutz movement. Korczak wanted to settle in Israel, but, faithful to the children in his orphanage, he remained in Warsaw.

With the storm brewing in Europe, Korczak felt that he could not abandon the children. The Nazis forced the orphanage to move into the Warsaw Ghetto in 1940. (The Gestapo officer assigned to supervise the children's home had been a pediatrician himself in civilian life.) As the Nazi oppression grew more and more severe, Korczak looked more and more to his Jewish identity. He worked to save many children from the deadly ghetto streets, and he was quite successful. In the summer of 1942, however, the Nazis ordered him to have the children of the orphanage report for deportation on 5 August 1942. In order to allay the children's fears as long as possible, Korczak told them that they were going on a picnic in the country.

''Promise me you will sing,'' he enjoined them on the day he and his assistant led the orderly procession of 200 orphans to the deportation site. And sing they did. Because of the doctor's fame, the Nazis offered Korczak a last-minute opportunity to escape death. He refused, however, choosing to go with his children to Treblinka so that he could comfort them to the end.

—David Patterson

See the essay on *Ghetto Diary*.

KOSINSKI, Jerzy (Nikodem)

Pseudonym: Joseph Novak. **Nationality:** American (originally Polish: immigrated to the United States, 1957, granted U.S. citizenship, 1965). **Born:** Lodz, 14 June 1933. **Education:** University of Lodz, B.A. 1950, M.A. in history 1953, M.A. in political science 1955; Polish Academy of Sciences, Warsaw, 1955–57; Columbia University, 1958–63, Ph.D. candidate in sociology; New School for Social Research, graduate study, 1962–66. **Family:** Married 1) Mary Hayward Weir in 1962 (died 1968); 2) Katherina von Fraunhofer in 1987. **Career:** Ski instructor, Zakopane, Poland, winters, 1950–56; assistant professor (aspirant) of sociology, Polish Academy of

Sciences, 1955–57; researcher, Lomonosov University, Moscow, 1957. After first arriving in the United States, worked as a paint scraper on excursion-line boats, a truck driver, chauffeur, and cinema projectionist. Resident fellow in English, Center for Advanced Studies, Wesleyan University, 1967–68; visiting lecturer in English and resident senior fellow of the Council of Humanities, Princeton University, 1969–70; professor of English and resident fellow, Davenport College and School of Drama, 1970–73, and fellow, Timothy Dwight College, 1986–91, both Yale University. Actor in a 1981 film; photographer. **Awards:** Ford Foundation fellowship, 1958–60; Prix du Meilleur Livre Etranger (France), 1966, for *The Painted Bird;* Guggenheim fellowship in creative writing, 1967–68; National Book Award, 1969, for *Steps;* National Institute of Arts and Letters and the American Academy of Arts and Letters award in literature, 1970; John Golden fellowship in playwriting, 1970–72; Brith Sholom humanitarian freedom award, 1974; American Civil Liberties Union First Amendment award, 1978; best screenplay of the year award, Writers Guild of America, 1979, and British Academy of Film and Television Arts, 1981, both for *Being There;* Polonia Media National Achievement Perspectives award, 1980; Spertus College of Judaica international award, 1982; Harry Edmonds life achievement award, International House, 1990. Honorary degrees: Albion College, 1988; State University of New York, 1989. **Died:** Suicide, 3 May 1991.

PUBLICATIONS

Novels

The Painted Bird, abridged edition. 1965; complete edition, 1970; revised edition, 1976.
Steps. 1968.
Being There. 1971.
The Devil Tree. 1973; revised edition, 1981.
Cockpit. 1975.
Blind Date. 1977.
Passion Play. 1979.
Pinball. 1982.
The Hermit of 69th Street: The Working Papers of Norbert Kosky. 1988.

Plays

Screenplays: *Being There,* adaptation of his novel, 1977; *Passion Play,* 1982.

Other

The Future Is Ours, Comrade: Conversations with the Russians (as Joseph Novak). 1960.
No Third Path: A Study of Collective Behavior (as Joseph Novak). 1962.

Notes of the Author on *The Painted Bird*. 1965; in *Passing By: Selected Essays, 1962–1991*, 1992.

Art of the Self: Essays à Propos *Steps*. 1969; in *Passing By: Selected Essays, 1962–1991*, 1992.

Passing By: Selected Essays, 1962–1991. 1992.

Conversations with Jerzy Kosinski, edited by Tom Teicholz. 1993.

Editor, *Socjologia Amerykanska: Wybor Prac, 1950–1960* [American Sociology: Translations of Selected Works, 1950–1960]. 1958.

*

Film Adaptation: *Being There*, 1979.

Bibliography: *John Barth, Jerzy Kosinski, and Thomas Pynchon: A Reference Guide* by Thomas P. Walsh and Cameron Northouse, 1977; "The Great Jerzy Kosinski Press War: A Bibliography" by Jerome Klinkowitz and Daniel J. Cahill, in *Missouri Review*, 6(3), Summer 1983, pp. 171–75; *Jerzy Kosinski: An Annotated Bibliography* by Gloria L. Cronin and Blaine H. Hall, 1991.

Critical Studies: *In the Singer's Temple: The Romance of Terror and Jerzy Kosinski* by Jack Hicks, 1981; *Jerzy Kosinski: Literary Alarmclock* by Byron L. Sherwin, 1981; *The Fiction of Jerzy Kosinski* by Daniel Cahill, 1982; *Jerzy Kosinski* by Norman Lavers, 1982; "Jerzy Kosinski's *The Painted Bird* As Holocaust Literature" by Yasuro Hidesaki, in *Kyushu American Literature* (Japan), 26, October 1985, pp. 37–46; *Plays of Passion, Games of Chance: Jerzy Kosinski and His Fiction* by Barbara Tepa Lupack, 1988; *Words in Search of Victims: The Achievement of Jerzy Kosinski* by Paul R. Lilly, Jr., 1988; Jerzy Kosinski issue of *Notes on Contemporary Literature*, 19(2), March 1989; *Jerzy Kosinski, The Literature of Violation* by Welch D. Everman, 1991; *Jerzy Kosinski: A Biography* by James Park Sloan, 1996; *Jerzy Kosinski: Man and Work at the Crossroads of Cultures*, edited by Agnieszka Salska and Marek Jedlianski, 1997; *Critical Essays on Jerzy Kosinski*, edited by Barbara Tepa Lupack, 1998.

* * *

Born in 1933, Jerzy Kosinski was the only son of Moses and Elizbieta Lewinkopf. He and his family left their native Lodz in 1939 before the formation of its notorious ghetto the following year. They lived, first, in Sandomierz and, from 1942 on, in the village of Dabrowa Rzecycka, where their main task was survival. They managed this through the protection of sympathetic Poles, by staying out of German-occupied Poland, by keeping out of sight, and by changing their name to the very Polish Kosinski. From the age of six to twelve the young Jerzy was asked to deny his name and his Jewish heritage and to serve as an altar boy in the local church. Perhaps this practice of living under an assumed identity helped him to imagine a life more interesting than the one he was forced to lead. After the war, in May 1947, the family finally returned to Lodz.

Kosinski was educated there at both the secondary level and at the University of Lodz, where he took a degree in sociology. He continued at Lodz into graduate study, where he took master's degrees in sociology and history. In late December 1957 Kosinski went to New York City to begin doctoral work in sociology at Columbia University. He lived in New York for the rest of his life, marrying twice and becoming an American citizen in 1965.

Kosinski's first two books were works of sociology and political science written under the name of Joseph Novak. The texts contain compendia of Kosinski's research for his Ph.D. thesis, as well as vivid accounts of his travel in the Soviet Union. They were written mostly in Polish and translated by someone who never received formal credit for doing so. Kosinski's English was not yet good enough for writing a book, and his heavily accented speech and uncertain command of English grammar remained issues throughout his career.

As progress on his thesis stalled, Kosinski began to write tales apparently inspired by his life in Poland during the war. He had for years entertained listeners with such stories, and it was these narratives that his audiences took to be accurate accounts of Kosinski's fantastic survival. *The Painted Bird*, written with the unidentified editorial help of someone who could turn Kosinski's storytelling gifts into compelling English, was his first novel. It was mostly received with high praise as a contribution to Holocaust literature as well as a philosophical novel with roots in existentialism. But there was also controversy. The opening lines suggest an autobiographical account of how a small boy wandered through the countryside of an unidentified European country, having terrifying encounters with brutal peasants. But there were some readers who knew that Kosinski and his family had lived through the war in comparative safety. While some readers took the book's events too literally, it was clear to others that its horrifying images and surreal scenes came more from Kosinski's nightmarish imagination than from his actual experiences. Polish critics, reading the book in English, claimed that Kosinski had slandered the Polish people. His publisher, Houghton Mifflin, had insisted that Kosinski choose to call his narrative either fiction or autobiography, and Kosinski had opted to call it "essentially a literary work." This allowed most readers to treat *The Painted Bird* as a product of the imagination, freeing the author from the accusation of lying about his past. This episodic, vividly imagistic narrative sold well, particularly in paperback. Although clearly a Holocaust novel, it contains no concentration camps, German soldiers appear infrequently, and there is only an occasional train carrying Jewish prisoners. Responding to various concerns that had arisen about his book, Kosinski wrote a pamphlet entitled "Notes of the Author on *The Painted Bird*," which he published himself, in an attempt to justify what he had written and to establish himself as a serious writer of fiction.

Steps (1968), Kosinski's next novel, received the National Book Award. It contains fewer references to the Holocaust than its predecessor, and its episodic structure is more terse and detached. *Steps* takes place in a post-Holocaust world in which the ''death of God'' has sanctioned all behavior, a world in which victims seek revenge on their enemies. The narrative voice belongs to a grown-up version of the boy from *The Painted Bird,* and the two settings include the peasant countryside already noted and an economically advanced country much like the United States.

In 1982 the *Village Voice* published a devastating exposé of Kosinski, accusing him of not actually writing his own works, of making up stories about his past, of sexual adventuring, and of relentlessly seeking celebrity. He never really got over this blow to his work and prestige. *The Hermit of 69th Street* (1989) was Kosinski's final attempt to justify his career and his methods, and it is the only one of his remaining novels that contains extensive references to the Holocaust. In it Kosinski justified himself to his Polish critics by claiming Poland's historical sympathies with the Jews, and he explored his newfound feelings of connectedness to his Jewish heritage, which he had denied or ignored throughout much of his life. The novel was not a critical success, however, and it sold poorly. On 3 May 1991 Kosinski took his own life through an overdose of alcohol and barbiturates.

—Michael Hoffman

See the essays on *The Painted Bird,* ''Notes of the Author on *The Painted Bird,*'' and *Steps.*

KOVNER, Abba

Nationality: Israeli (originally Russian: immigrated to Palestine, 1945). **Born:** Sevastopol, 14 March 1918. **Education:** Hebrew secondary school, Vilna. **Family:** Married Vitka Kempner; one son. **Military Service:** Fought in Israel's war of independence, 1948. **Career:** Member, Ha-Shomer ha-Tsa'ir (Zionist youth movement); coleader, Fareinikte Partisaner Organizatzie (F.P.O.); cofounder, Beriha (underground organization to smuggle Jews out of Europe); moved to Palestine after World War II and joined Kibbutz Ein ha-Horesh; cofounder, *Yalkut Moreshet* (journal on the Holocaust), 1963. **Award:** Israel prize in literature, 1970. **Died:** September 1987.

PUBLICATIONS

Collections

Selected Poems: Abba Kovner and Nelly Sachs. 1971.
A Canopy in the Desert: Selected Poems. 1973.

My Little Sister and Selected Poems, 1965–1985. 1986.
Megilot ha-'edut. 1993; as *Scrolls of Testimony,* 2001.
Kol shire Aba Kovner. 1996.

Poetry

'Ad-lo-or: Po'emah partizanit [While Still There Is Night]. 1947.
Peridah meha-darom: Po'emah [Farewell to the South]. 1949.
Admat ha-hol: Po'emah [Earth of Sand, a Poem]. 1961.
Mi-kol ha-ahavot. 1965.
Ahoti ketanah. 1967; as *My Little Sister,* in *My Little Sister and Selected Poems, 1965–1985,* 1986.
Peridah meha-darom: Po'emah. 1969.
Feridah me-ha-darom: Po'emah. 1969.
Hupah ba-midbar. 1970; as *A Canopy in the Desert,* in *A Canopy in the Desert: Selected Poems,* 1973.
Ha-Sefer ha-katan. 1972.
Lahakat ha-ketser mofi'ah 'al Har-Gerizim: Po'emah. 1972.
Tatspiyot [Observations]. 1977.
El [To]. 1980.
Shirat Rozah. 1987.
Slon Ketering: Po'emah. 1987.

Novel

Panim el panim [Face to Face]. 1953.

Memoir

Yom zeh: megilat 'edut. 1962.

Other

The Tree of Life: A Scroll of Testimony on the Fifteenth Anniversary of Israel's Independence: Presented for Recital. 1961.
Der boym fun lebn: Edus megile: Tsum fuftsntn yortog zint dem antshteyn fun Medines-Yisroel. 1963.
This Day: Testimonial Scroll: Presented for Recitation. 1964.
Hupah ba-midbar. 1970.
Rising Night after Night (cantata libretto). 1976.
Megilot ha-esh: Umah 'omedet 'al nafshah: 52 parashot ke-neged 52 shevu'ot ha-shanah/The Scrolls of Fire: A Nation Fighting for Its Life: Fifty-two Chapters of Jewish Maryology (in Hebrew and English). 1981.
'Al ha-gesher ha-tsar: masot be-'al peh [On the Narrow Bridge] (essays). 1981.
Masa' el erets ha-milim: Po'emon: Ve-hu sipurshir le-yeled 'im dimyon [A Journey to the Land of Words] (for children). 1981.

Ha-Mal'akh ha-katan, Mikha'el [Michael, the Little Angel] (for children). 1989.

Mashehu 'al livyetanim [About the Whales] (for children). 1989.

Le-'akev et ha-keri'ah [Beyond Mourning] (letters). 1998.

Editor, with Pesell Freedberg, *Painters in the Kibbutz* (in Hebrew and English). 1961.

Editor, *Rekviyem le-Terezyenshtadt,* by Josef Bor. 1965.

Editor, with Berta Hazan, *Yaldut ba'ah ba-esh: Yeladim be-milhemet sheshet ha-yamim.* 1968; as *Childhood under Fire: Stories, Poems, and Drawings by Children during the Six Days War,* 1968.

Editor, with Hana Volavkova, *Tsiyurim ve-shirim shel yalde geto Terezinshtadt 1942–1944.* 1966; as *I Never Saw Another Butterfly: Children's Drawings and Poems from Terezín Concentration Camp, 1942–1944,* 1978.

*

Critical Studies: "Fantastic Elements in Holocaust Poetry: Abba Kovner's 'Ahoti Ktanah'" by Carl Schaffer, in *The Poetic Fantastic: Studies in an Evolving Genre,* edited by Patrick D. Murphy and Vernon Ross Hyles, 1989; "Abba Kovner: The Rent Canopy and the Cleft Covenant" by Eli Pfefferkorn, in *Modern Language Studies,* 24(4), Fall 1994, pp. 11–24; "The Sheliah Tsibur as a Poetic Persona: Abba Kovner's Self-Portrait," in *Prooftexts,* 15(3), September 1995, pp. 227–47, "Paradise Betrayed: Or, the Betrayal of Paradise: Vilna As Memory in Abba Kovner's Poetry," in *Hebrew Studies,* 37, 1996, pp. 83–98, and "'Meteor-Yid': Abba Kovner's Poetic Confrontation with Jewish History," in *Judaism,* 48(1), Winter 1999, pp. 35–48, all by Zvia Ben-Yoseph Ginor; "Intertextual Relations and Their Rhetorical Significance in Abba Kovner's Daf Kravi" by Reuven Shoham, in *Hebrew Studies,* 37, 1996, pp. 99–118; *Ghetto in Flames: The Struggle and Destruction of the Jews in Vilna in the Holocaust* by Yitzhak Arad, 1980; *The Avengers: A Jewish War Story* by Rich Cohen, 2000.

*   *   *

Abba Kovner's Holocaust poetry emanates from his own personal experience. He witnessed the events that propelled him to fight as a partisan in the forests of Lithuania. His literature rests on realistic foundations but grows beyond the boundaries of realistic fiction. His works are multifarious, interwoven with a surreal subreality of sorts, one that is haunted with nightmares of the Holocaust. In one of the final interviews given by the poet, he stated that poetry is "a request for pardon for what we do in our lives, and for what was done to us." He wrote lengthy narrative poems, weaving a dense tapestry of hard images and austere settings. In his poems Kovner seeks the meaning and significance of the suffering experienced by the people of Vilna. The city is never named but remains paramount in the memory of the Holocaust as contained in his poems.

Commonly referred to as a "poet-warrior," Kovner expresses in his work the polarities typical of the Holocaust experience and the body of literature it has generated. For instance, his poems often express the pain of memory and the force of life and of continuous survival. Thematic duality also dominates his poetry—voice and silence, love and death, light and darkness all emerge simultaneously from his work. Furthermore, his poetry expresses the tension between the poet's own view of the past and the wider perception of it as a sickness. Kovner often sets himself apart from implied others—often the reading audience—echoing the feeling of isolation caused by his experience and the gap between his own perceived reality and that of others. Apart from the tension between one's own version of history and that which belongs to the public, Kovner's poems also convey the vulnerability of the poet and survivor who intimates his own perspective. The poet expresses the torn state of his soul through a vast lexicon of personal codes and metaphors.

Kovner's body of work was rejected by the contemporary mainstream literary culture. His works loosely follow Russian symbolism, taking on the form of long, epic narrative poems. Kovner was writing at a time when Hebrew literature was becoming more streamlined, focusing on the public and concrete local reality of the young state, rather than the individual. In addition, idiosyncratic experiences of the Diaspora had already been relegated as irrelevant to modern Jewish experience. Thus, Kovner's work stood out as deviating somewhat from literary traditions and from the Holocaust literature that came to represent the Holocaust experience as though the Jewish nation had been led "like lambs to the slaughter." He protested against this slogan as early as his time as a partisan fighter in Vilna and continued to express his resentment for this perception in his poetry.

It is important to mention Kovner's own ambiguity about the genre "Holocaust poetry," in which his work was often placed. It was his belief that the work he created was within the realm of modern Israeli and the Jewish experience, implying that the Holocaust must not be treated as a closed book, a separate segment of Jewish history and identity. In a letter to his daughter he wrote that the genre title "is loaded with a negative meaning, denoting one who is enclosed in the experiences of the past, in the atrocities, who clings to them obsessively without the ability to turn his face to the here and the now, to life and not to death." Kovner's Holocaust is a personal interpretation of Jewish history, and the poems he prolifically wrote about it are personal in form, language, and content.

—Ziva Shavitsky

See the essays on *A Canopy in the Desert* and *My Little Sister.*

KRALL, Hanna

Nationality: Polish. **Born:** Warsaw, 20 May 1937. **Education:** Studied journalism at Warsaw University. **Career:** Reporter, *Zycie Warszawy,* 1957–66; editor, *Polityka,* 1966–81; literary consultant, *Tor* film studio, 1981–87. Also contributed to *Gazeta Wyborcza,* ca. 1980s. **Awards:** Solidarnosc prize, 1985; *Odra* magazine award and Polish literary PEN club prize, both in 1989; German Academic Exchange Service scholarship for study in Berlin, 1992; Jeanette Schocken prize and Bremerhaven citizen prize for literature, both in 1993; Polish Culture Foundation prize, 1999; Leipzig book prize for European understanding, 2000, for *Tam juz nie ma zadnej rzeki.*

PUBLICATIONS

Novels

Sublokatorka. 1985; as *The Subtenant* (published with *To Outwit God*), 1992.
Okna [Windows]. 1987.

Short Stories (narrations)

Trudnosci ze wstawaniem: Reportaze; Okna: Powiesc. 1990.
Dowodny na istnienie, 1995; as *Dowody na istnienie/Proofs of Existence* (Hebrew and English). 1995.

Play

Przypadek i inne teksty, with Krzysztof Kieslowski (screenplay). 1998.

Other

Na wchód od Arbatu. 1972.
Syberia, kraj ogromnych mozliwosci, with Zygmunt Szeliga and Maciej Ilowiecki. 1974.
Zdazyc przed Panem Bogiem (interview). 1977; as *Shielding the Flame: An Intimate Conversation with Dr. Marek Edelman, the Last Surviving Leader of the Warsaw Ghetto Uprising,* 1986; as *To Outwit God* (published with *The Subtenant*), 1992.
Dojrzalosc dostepna dla wszystkich. 1977.
Szesc odcieni bieli [Six Shades of White]. 1978.
Hipnoza [Hypnosis]. 1989.
Wybór wierszy (1976–1989), with Aleksander Rozenfeld and Julian Kornhauser. 1990.
Taniec na cudzym weselu. 1994.
Co sie stalo z nasza bajka? [What Happened to Our Fairy Tale?]. 1994.

Tam juz nie ma zadnej rzeki [There Is No River There Anymore]. 1998.

*

Film Adaptations: *Krotki dzien pracy* [Short Working Day], 1981, from the story, *Widok z okna na pierwszym pietrze.*

Critical Study: ''Poland's Best and Brightest: Staff of Liberal Weekly *Polityka*'' by Lawrence Weschler, in *Harper's,* 271, December 1985, p. 60–61.

* * *

Of Jewish descent, Hanna Krall was born in Warsaw in 1937 and survived the German occupation during World War II in a hiding place provided by a Polish family. After studying journalism at Warsaw University, she worked as an editor for the newspaper *Zycie Warsawy.* In 1966 she became editor of the magazine *Polityka,* and in 1969 she began working as a correspondent in the Soviet Union. Her first compilation of reports, *Na wchód od Arbatu* (''East of Arbat''), which appeared in 1972, dealt with numerous aspects of Soviet daily life. In December 1981, after martial law went in effect, she left *Polityka* in order to work as a literary consultant for the film production company Tor, where she stayed until 1987. During this time she also became one of the leading journalists of *Gazeta Wyborcza.* Her reports always search for the impact of history on individual life, and she has received several awards, including the Underground Award of Solidarity in 1985.

In 1977 Krall published *Zdazyc przed Panem Bogiem,* which was published in English as *Shielding the Flame* in 1986 and which she rewrote as a drama in 1980. As in other works, the literary technique of combining fiction and documentary, novel and report, is a characteristic of her so-called fictional autobiography, *Sublokatorka* (1985; *The Subtenant,* 1992). Taking the perspective of a Polish girl, Maria, she tells the experiences of Marta, a Jewish girl her own age. With the help of Maria's family, Marta remains in hiding during World War II. The contrast between the characters of the two girls is fascinating, but their relationship has its difficulties. The narrator develops a theory of symbolic colors in which white stands for heroism, beauty, and courage, while black is connected with degradation, humility, and suffering. The author avoids a black-and-white portrayal, however, in favor of an emphasis, as the critic Lothar Baier has put it, on the ''Clair-obscur, which surrounds Krall's image of the Polish.'' The disintegration of society remains part of Jewish identity in postwar Poland: ''You may belong to us. But only in our fear and degradation when we all are being shot.''

Krall's journalism, compiled in the volumes *Hipnoza* (1989), *Taniec na cudzym weselu* (1994), and *Tam juz nie ma zadnej rzeki* (1998), remains true to these same topics: the hard task of survival, the *syndrom ocalonych* (survival syndrome)—as one of the pieces in *Hipnoza* is titled—the fate of the Jews in Poland both during and after the war, and the difficult relation of Jews to Poland itself. In *Dowodny na istnienie* (1995; *Proofs of Existence,* 1995), she writes, ''Such things happen . . . searching for identity, one's roots . . .'' Inspired by research on Martin Buber, Krall has turned increasingly toward the reconstruction of the world of extinct eastern European Jews, the world of the shtetl and the religiosity of Hasidism. She also looks, however, for the ''constructions of identity'' of the survivors. ''Dibbu,'' included in *Proofs of Existence,* draws a line from Hasidism to religious searching within the American student movement: ''The way to God, on which [Rabbi Zalman Schachter] led the rebellious Jews of Philadelphia and San Francisco, went through Lezajsk, Kock, and Izbica Lubelska''—places connected to the Jewish tradition of eastern Poland. In ''Decyzja'' (''Decision''), from *Tam juz nie ma zadnej rzeki,* Krall generalizes the search for identity on the part of all marginalized peoples. For example, she investigates the ways in which homosexuals understand themselves as persecuted: ''When asked about an association between AIDS and the concentration camps of the war, they answer: discrimination and hate.'' According to Krall, however, their chosen, stage-managed deaths and their ''liturgy of disappearance'' end in kitsch.

Krall's texts search for authentic experience. As the critic Elsbeth Wolffheim has said, ''Her materials are actual events, verifiable historical occurrences . . . Her sources are newspapers, interviews with survivors of the concentration camps, reports of witnesses, and scientific research on the Holocaust.'' Krall herself has said, ''Everything I write about has actually happened. The people I write about have actually existed and are as such co-authors of my books.'' *Tam juz nie ma zadnej rzeki* begins with a text entitled ''Literatura Factu,'' in which she carries on a dialogue with the audience: ''Tell me something, I said,'' and ''At the end of each meeting with my audience I say: tell stories!'' ''Pola,'' included in the same book, deals with an operation of a Hamburg police battalion in Józefów and is a search for a dialogue with historiography, particularly with Daniel Goldhagen. Yet because of Krall's specific writing strategy, which fragments simple history and dissolves time, the actual topics of her books remain recollection and the search for truth.

—Walter Schmitz

See the essay on *Shielding the Flame: An Intimate Conversation with Dr. Marek Edelman, the Last Surviving Leader of the Warsaw Ghetto Uprising.*

KRUK, Herman (Hersh)

Nationality: Polish. **Born:** Plock, 19 September 1897. **Military Service:** Polish Army. **Career:** Involved with the Social Democracy of the Kingdom of Poland and Lithuania and Polish Socialist Party, ca. 1915; left the Communist Party and joined the Jewish Labor Bund, 1920. Founder and secretary, cultural department, National Council of Jewish Trade Unions, Warsaw; secretary, *Yugntbund,* youth organization of the bund, 1925; director, Grosser Library, Warsaw, 1930; head, ''Library Center,'' *Kultur-lige,* ca. 1930; director, *Kultur-lige,* 1936; journalist for the bund's press. Escaped to Vilna, Lithuania, following the German attack on Warsaw. Restored and managed Strashun Library, Vilna, 1941–42; first chairman, underground committee of the bund, Vilna, ca. 1941; vice-chairman, Union of Writers and Artist, Vilna, ca. 1941; coerced by a Nazi agency to manage the Jewish library collections of Vilna for transport to Germany, 1942. Editor, *Byuletin fun biblyotekntsenter,* ''Library Center,'' *Kultur-lige.* **Died:** Murdered, victim of the Holocaust, 1944.

PUBLICATION

Diary

Togbuch fun Vilner Geto [Diary of the Vilna Ghetto]. 1961.

*

Critical Studies: *Guardians of a Tragic Heritage: Reminiscences and Observations of an Eyewitness* by Dina Abramowicz, 1999; *Holocaust Chronicles: Individualizing the Holocaust through Diaries and Other Contemporaneous Personal Accounts* by Robert Moses Shapiro, 1999; *The Holocaust and the Book: Destruction and Preservation,* edited by Jonathan Rose, 2001.

*   *   *

Herman (Hersh) Kruk was born in Plock, in Russian Poland, on 19 September 1897. He was the eldest of three siblings who survived to adulthood. His younger brother, later known as Pinkhes Shvarts (Pinkhos Schwartz), was a prominent member of the Jewish Labor Bund and a journalist, writer, and cultural activist. When he was 17, Kruk lost his father and had to take on the full responsibilities of an adult, aiding his mother in support of the family.

Kruk was greatly affected by the cataclysmic events of World War I. Jewish social and political life, which had been repressed under the czarist regime, developed rapidly during the German occupation. Kruk read extensively and was strongly influenced by a number of the social, political, and cultural currents of the time. He was active for a while in Zionist circles. A permanent influence was his deep love of modern Yiddish literature, which developed in his youth. At the time his spiritual home was the Hazomir Library, founded in Plock during the Russian Revolution of 1905. It was a center of activity for the Jewish nationalist and socialist parties.

Kruk was drawn into the socialist movement in 1915, at the age of 18. When he began to read the Jewish Labor Bund's *Lebns-fragn,* he became an ardent enthusiast of Vladimir

Medem and of the bund's program of national cultural autonomy for the Jews. At the same time Kruk joined a mixed Jewish and Polish circle of the Social Democracy of the Kingdom of Poland and Lithuania (SDKPiL) and attended meetings of a workers' club of the left wing of the Polish Socialist Party (PPS Lewica). Thus, his loyalties were divided between the modern, secular Jewish cultural nationalism of Hazomir and the revolutionary Marxist wing of Polish socialism. Under the impact of the Bolshevik Revolution in Russia and of the revolution in Germany, the SDKPiL and the PPS Lewica united to form the Polish Communist Party, in which Kruk became a militant activist.

Kruk was drafted into the Polish army and, under great risk, conducted revolutionary propaganda in the ranks of the military. He soon developed serious doubts concerning the Bolshevik suppression of the other socialist parties in Soviet Russia, however, and he was deeply troubled by the communists' preference for assimilation as the solution to the Jewish question. During his military service in Warsaw he was drawn to the Jewish Labor Bund, in which his younger brother was active, and to his first love, modern Yiddish culture, which was growing by leaps and bounds in education, literature, the press, the theater, and other forms. Kruk quit the Communist Party and joined the bund in 1920. He cast off his leftist orientation, became an implacable opponent of communism, and identified with the right wing of social democracy. After completing his military service Kruk settled in Warsaw.

All his life Kruk was a zealous autodidact. Having rejected communism, he came to the conclusion that the working class had no better weapon in its struggle than the acquisition of education and knowledge. Kruk found his niche in the educational and cultural work of the Jewish Labor Bund. He took the initiative to found the cultural department of the National Council of Jewish Trade Unions in Warsaw and was not only its official secretary but also its most dynamic activist. Again thanks to his initiative, the cultural department of the Yugntbund-Tsukunft, the youth organization of the bund, was created in 1925, and he headed it as secretary. Around 1930 the Bundist Grosser Library was transferred to the Kultur-lige (Cultural League), and Kruk was appointed the library's director. He transformed the Grosser Library into the largest and most popular Jewish library in Warsaw, building up its collection to some 30,000 books. He also headed the Library Center of the Kultur-lige, which offered instruction in library science to some 400 affiliated Jewish libraries in the cities and towns of Poland. He edited the center's monthly *Byuletin fun biblyotekn-tsenter,* published several brochures in Yiddish and Polish on library science, and published many articles, in both professional journals and general periodicals, about Yiddish books, library science, the dissemination of culture, and other subjects. Kruk took over the leadership of the Kultur-lige in 1936. He also worked as a journalist for the bund's press.

At the outset of World War II, Kruk left Warsaw and managed to make his way to Vilna, which the Soviets had temporarily turned over to an independent Lithuania. There he kept his first Yiddish diary, now in the archives of the YIVO Institute for Jewish Research, about his wanderings as a war refugee. Upon the Soviet annexation of Lithuania, he was forced to remain in Vilna. When Germany invaded the Soviet Union, Kruk decided not to attempt to flee but to remain in Vilna to record the martyrdom of its Jewish community in a diary and to share its fate. He restored the library of the Hevrah Mefitsei Haskalah, was first chairman of the underground committee of the Jewish Labor Bund, and became vice chairman of the ghetto's Union of Writers and Artists. In 1942 the Nazis ordered Kruk to assemble a staff of ghetto Jews under his direction to work for Einsatzstab Rosenberg. Their task was to sort and pack the books, manuscripts, and other cultural treasures of Vilna Jewry, first and foremost of the YIVO Institute, to be sent to Germany or pulped in Vilna. Kruk and others hid as many of the valuable items as they could. During the final liquidation of the Vilna ghetto, on 23–24 September 1943, he was deported to the slave labor camp of Klooga in Estonia, where he continued to keep a diary. Part of this diary survived and was published in Hebrew translation by the Moreshet Institute in Israel. Kruk was murdered in the camp of Lagedi, in Estonia, on the night of 18 September 1944, just before the German retreat.

—Eugene Orenstein

See the essay on *Togbuch fun Vilner Geto.*

KUPER, Jack

Nationality: Canadian (originally Polish: immigrated to Canada, 1948). **Born:** Jankel Kuperblum, Zyrardow, 16 April 1932. **Education:** Studied graphic arts at Central Tech, Toronto, Ontario. **Family:** Married Terrye Lee Swadron in 1955; two daughters and two sons. **Career:** Graphic artist, playwright, and actor, 1952–63, and graphic design animation and still photography supervisor, 1963–66, Canadian Broadcasting Corporation; radio-TV director, Goodis, Goldberg, Soren Advertising, 1966–67; chief film director, Robert Lawrence Productions Ltd., 1967–68; creative director, Kenyon and Eckhardt Advertising, 1968–70. Since 1971 president and director, Kuper Productions Ltd. **Awards:** Best supporting actor, Dominion Drama Festival, 1952; Art Directors Club of Montreal award, 1964; Canadian art director of the year, 1965; Graphica award, 1966; Hollywood Radio and Television Society international broadcasting award, 1968; Canadian Radio Commercial Festival award, 1968; Graphica certificate, 1968, 1969; Canadian Television Commercials Festival award, 1980, 1982; National Education Film and Video Festival Gold Apple (United States), 1992; Columbus International Film and Video Festival Bronze award, 1992; Academy of Canadian Cinema and Television Gemini award, 1992, for *A Day in the Warsaw*

Ghetto: A Birthday Trip in Hell, 1997, for *Who Was Jerzy Kosinski?;* American Film and Video Festival Red Ribbon, 1993; Atlanta Film and Video Festival honorable mention, 1993; Jewish book award for Holocaust literature, 1995, for *After the Smoke Cleared;* National Education Film and Video Festival Bronze Apple, 1996. **Agent:** Beverley Slopen, 131 Bloor Street West, Suite 711, Toronto, Ontario M5S 1S3, Canada.

PUBLICATIONS

Memoirs

Child of the Holocaust. 1967.
After the Smoke Cleared. 1994.

Plays

Sun in My Eyes (produced Toronto, 1961).

Screenplays: *Disguise,* 1987; *Who Was Jerzy Kosinski?* (documentary), 1995; *Children of the Storm* (documentary), 2000; *The Fear of Felix Nussbaum* (documentary), 2000.

Television Plays: *On a Streetcar,* 1955; *Street Music,* 1956; *Lost in a Crowd,* 1957; *Two from King Street,* 1959; *Girl in the Window,* 1959; *It Happened in Kensington Market,* 1959; *The Man in the Railway Station,* 1959; *Sun in My Eyes,* 1960; *The Police* (adaptation), 1961; *Search for an Enemy,* 1961; *The Wounded Soldier,* 1962; *The Magician of Lublin* (adaptation), 1962; *Dawn* (adaptation), 1963; *Neon Dreams,* 1963.

Radio Plays: *Street Music,* 1959; *The Last Warm Day,* 1959; *Bontsha the Silent* (adaptation), 1960; *The Palace,* 1960.

*

Theatrical Activities: Director: Television—*Run!* 1962; *It's a Big Wide Wonderful World,* 1962; *Dawn,* 1963; *I've Got My Eye on You,* 1963; *Mehane Yehuda,* 1971; *A Day in the Warsaw Ghetto: A Birthday Trip in Hell,* 1991; *Shtetl,* 1995. **Documentary Films**—his own screenplays.

*   *   *

When Jack Kuper's autobiographical work, *Child of the Holocaust,* was published in 1967, it was the first Holocaust-related memoir to be published en masse in North America. In a conversation with the author, Kuper recalled the difficulty he experienced in finding a publishing house for the book. Typical of the period, agents and publishers informed him that the World War II was history and the subject matter of the book had little—if any—relevance for the 1960s. Further, he was advised to try to put the suffering he described "behind him and try to get on with his life."

The Polish-born Kuper, however, was hardly "living in the past." By the time that *Child of the Holocaust* was being offered for publication, Kuper had made a name for himself in the Canadian Broadcasting Corporation, where he had evolved from a graphic artist into a playwright and award-winning actor. In addition, Kuper had received international honors for his role as director of the 1962 film *Run,* which parodied the destructive tendencies that modern society holds for those driven to succeed at any cost.

Kuper's sensitivity to the crises that modern man created for himself may be seen as related to his own childhood experiences in which survival and not material success was an immediate and all-encompassing concern. Indeed, it was perhaps his personal success that led Kuper to redouble his efforts to publish the memories he jotted down in Yiddish in 1946. As Kuper himself is aware, it is the unaffected and direct style of the 15-year-old orphaned immigrant boy that is the secret of the success of *Child of the Holocaust.* The book, which has been compared to both *Anne Frank: The Diary of A Young Girl* and **Jerzy Kosinski**'s *The Painted Bird,* has subsequently been in publication for more than three decades. It has appeared in five languages and is part of the curriculum on the Holocaust in schools in Canada, the United States, and Italy.

In 1971 Kuper established his own production company, which has produced both commercials and documentary films. It is through these films that Kuper has continued to explore the meaning of the Holocaust and its impact on his own life. Among the Holocaust-related films that Kuper has produced are *A Day in the Warsaw Ghetto: A Birthday Trip in Hell, The Fear of Felix Nussbaum,* and *Children of the Storm.* The latter film traces the life stories of the Jewish Holocaust orphans (among them Kuper himself) who came to Canada in 1947.

Committed to do more than "show the nasty Nazis" as nonhuman creatures, Kuper has endeavored to reflect the complexity of the Holocaust experience and its consequences. Through his literary and cinema work he has caused individuals to consider the forces that lead ordinary people to do remarkable good and horrible evil as well as the consequences of the above.

Critical of both the commercialization of the Holocaust and of what he saw as the excessive showmanship of institutions such as Yad Vashem, Kuper has been hopeful that in his quiet understatement he will allow people to approach the Holocaust experience with the respect and reverence that he himself has for the memory of the Holocaust and its victims.

—Avi Kay

See the essay on *Child of the Holocaust.*

KUSHNER, Tony

Nationality: American. **Born:** New York City, 16 July 1956; grew up in Louisiana. **Education:** Columbia University, B.A. 1978; New York University, M.F.A. in directing 1984. **Career:** United Nations switchboard operator, Plaza Hotel, New York, 1979–85; member, Heat & Light Co., Inc., theatre company, 1980s; assistant director, St. Louis Repertory Theatre, 1985–86; artistic director, New York Theatre Workshop, 1987–88; beginning 1989 guest artist, New York University Graduate Theatre Program, Yale University, and Princeton University; director of literary services, Theatre Communication Group, New York, 1990–91; playwright-in-residence, Juilliard School of Drama, New York, 1990–92. **Awards:** National Endowment for the Arts directing fellowship, 1985, 1987, and 1993; Princess Grace award, 1986; New York State Council for the Arts playwriting fellowship, 1987; Arts Council of Great Britain John Whiting award, 1990; Kennedy Center/American Express Fund for New American Plays awards, 1990 and 1992; National Arts Club Kesserling award, Will Glickman playwriting prize, and London *Evening Standard* award, all in 1992; Pulitzer Prize for drama, Antoinette Perry award for best play, and New York Drama Critics Circle award for best new play, all in 1993, for *Millennium Approaches,* part one of *Angels in America;* American Academy of Arts and Letters award, 1994; Antoinette Perry award for best play, 1994, for *Perestroika,* part two of *Angels in America;* Lambda Lesbian and Gay Drama award, 1996, for *Thinking about the Longstanding Problems of Virtue and Happiness: Essays, a Play, Two Poems, and a Prayer.* **Agent:** Joyce Ketay, 334 West 89th Street, New York, New York 10024, U.S.A. **Address:** Office: Walter Kerr Theatre, 225 West 48th Street, New York, New York 10036, U.S.A.

PUBLICATIONS

Plays

Yes, Yes, No, No (for children; produced St. Louis, Missouri, 1985). In *Three Plays for Young Audiences,* 1987.
A Bright Room Called Day (produced New York, 1985). 1991.
Stella, adaptation of the play by Johann Wolfgang von Goethe (produced New York, 1987).
The Illusion, adaptation of the play by Pierre Corneille (produced New York, 1988; revised version, produced Hartford, Connecticut, 1990). 1991.
Widows, with Ariel Dorfman, adaptation of the work by Dorfman (produced Los Angeles, 1991).
Angels in America: A Gay Fantasia on National Themes, Part One: Millennium Approaches (produced San Francisco, 1991). 1993.
Angels in America: A Gay Fantasia on National Themes, Part Two: Perestroika (produced New York, 1992). 1994.

Slavs! (Thinking about the Longstanding Problems of Virtue and Happiness). 1995.
A Dybbuk, or between Two Worlds, adaptation of Joachim Neugroschel's translation of the play by S. Ansky (produced New York, 1997). 1997.
The Good Person of Szechuan, adaptation of the play by Bertolt Brecht. 1997.
Henry Box Brown, or the Mirror of Slavery (produced London, 1998).
Hydriotaphia (produced New York, 1998). In *Death & Taxes: Hydriotaphia, and Other Plays,* 2000.
Death & Taxes: Hydriotaphia, and Other Plays. 2000.
Homebody/Kabul (produced New York, 2001).

Other

A Meditation from Angels in America. 1994.
Thinking about the Longstanding Problems of Virtue and Happiness: Essays, a Play, Two Poems, and a Prayer. 1995.
Tony Kushner in Conversation, edited by Robert Vorlicky. 1997.

*

Critical Studies: *Essays on Kushner's Angels,* edited by Per K. Brask, 1995; "'The Angels of Fructification': Tennessee Williams, Tony Kushner, and Images of Homosexuality on the American Stage," in *Mississippi Quarterly,* 49(1), Winter 1995–96, pp. 13–32, and *The Theater of Tony Kushner: Living Past Hope,* 2001, both by James Fisher; "Angels in America: Tony Kushner's Theses on the Philosophy of History" by Charles McNulty, in *Modern Drama,* 39, Spring 1996, pp. 84–96; *Approaching the Millennium: Essays on Angels in America* by Deborah R. Geis and Steven F. Kruger, 1997; "Angels, Monsters, and Jews: Intersections of Queer and Jewish Identity in Kushner's *Angels in America*" by Jonathan Freedman, in *PMLA,* 113, January 1998, pp. 90–102.

*   *   *

Tony Kushner was born in 1956 in New York City and raised in Lake Charles, Louisiana, where his father ran the family lumberyard. Both of his parents were classical musicians. He attended Columbia University as an undergraduate, studying medieval literature before attending New York University as a directing student. He was a member of the Heat & Light Co., Inc., a theater company in New York City in the 1980s.

Kushner's major plays include *Stella* (1985), a children's play adapted from Goethe's 1775 prose drama; *The Illusion* (1988), an adaptation from Pierre Corneille; and *Windows* (1991), an adaptation cowritten with Ariel Dorfman. Though critically unsuccessful, the 1991 New York production of *A Bright Room Called Day* nonetheless led to a commission from San Francisco's Eureka Theatre that developed into his acclaimed masterpiece *Angels in America: A Gay Fantasia on National Themes* (1992). Winning near universal acclaim, it went on to win the Pulitzer Prize, two Tony awards for best play (for *Millennium Approaches,* Part One, and *Perestroika,* Part Two), and a host of other awards. Since then, Kushner has produced *Slavs! (Thinking about the Longstanding Problems of Virtue and Happiness)* (1994), constructed from material discarded from earlier drafts of *Angels in America* and which addresses the collapse of Soviet socialism. Other works are *Hydriotaphia* (written in 1988 and produced in 1998), which presents Sir Thomas Browne, an early historical English capitalist, on his deathbed reviewing his life, and well-received adaptations of Solomon Ansky's *The Dybbuk* and **Bertolt Brecht**'s *A Good Person of Setzuan,* as well as his play *Homebody/Kabul* (2001).

Kushner's plays are straightforwardly political. He has identified himself as a socialist, a position that at the end of the twentieth century in America marginalized him even more than his open homosexuality. For Kushner the current embrace of the capitalist ethic by American middle-class society was nothing less than a repudiation of the ideals for equality and social justice that propelled America from Franklin Roosevelt's New Deal through Lyndon Johnson's Great Society. During those 30 years America appeared to be on the cusp of becoming a genuinely progressive nation. But after the ousting of Richard Nixon and the onset of economic inflation in the 1970s, the Right made deep inroads into the American political landscape, inroads that would have seemed unlikely in the more liberal 1960s. But with the Ronald Reagan/George Bush administrations, bit by bit social programs became dismantled and diluted as the Left, both Old and New, appeared to lose its voice and become complicit in the Right's victory.

The Holocaust did not exterminate Jews alone, and homosexuals and Communists were also among those condemned. As a Jew, a homosexual, and a socialist, Kushner was well positioned to analyze how the voices of each group have been silenced in other communities. His commitment to political and social activism has continued to lead him to protest the moral bankruptcy he sees as pervading American society, as well as to celebrate the moral, artistic, and intellectual achievements of each group. Though Kushner has cautioned his audience/readers not to despair and even to exult in the resistance offered by these groups, his message is perhaps best articulated by Zillah, his paranoid conscience in *A Bright Room Called Day,* when she advises the audience not to sleep too soundly and to listen to its nightmares.

—Steven Dedalus Burch

See the essay on *A Bright Room Called Day.*

KUZNETSOV, Anatoli

Nationality: Russian (defected to England, 1966). **Born:** Kiev, Ukraine, 18 August 1929. **Career:** Wrote for newspapers; associated with construction of the Dnieper River hydroelectric project; worked as a laborer in Siberia. **Died:** 13 June 1979.

PUBLICATIONS

Novel (autobiographical)

Babii Iar: Roman-dokument. 1966; as *Babi Yar: A Documentary Novel,* 1966; as *Babi Yar: A Document in the Form of a Novel,* 1970.

Other

Prodolzhenie legendy; zapiski molodogo cheloveka: Povest. 1957; as *Sequel to a Legend: From the Diary of a Young Man,* 1959; as *The Journey,* 1984.
Selenga: Rasskazy. 1961.
U sebia doma. 1964.
Ogon: Roman. 1969.

*

Critical Study: ''*The White Hotel:* D.M. Thomas's Considerable Debt to Anatoli Kuznetsov and *Babi Yar*'' by Lady Falls Brown, in *South Central Review: The Journal of the South Central Modern Language Association,* 2(2), Summer 1985, pp. 60–79.

* * *

Anatoli Kuznetsov made an important contribution to the literature and knowledge of the Holocaust primarily through *Babi Yar,* which he described as a documentary in the form of a novel. Although most of his previous fictional works were on completely different subjects and later he focused on political commentary, the content and history of the publication of *Babi Yar* in essence became the keynote of Kuznetsov's life and works.

Kuznetsov, a non-Jewish Ukrainian, worked as a professional writer for much of his life. He wrote for newspapers while he was taking part in the construction of the Dnieper River hydroelectric project; he was also a laborer in Siberia. His early novels focus on problems in the lives of construction workers and on the process of growing to adulthood. Kuznetsov gained recognition in the Soviet Union in particular for *Sequel to a Legend* (1957), which was one of the earliest works of the genre of "youth stories" that became popular in the Soviet Union at that time. Other works by Kuznetsov deal with similar subjects, including *Selenga*.

Kuznetsov wrote the novel *Babi Yar* (1966, expanded version published 1970) based on his experiences from ages 12 to 14, when the Nazis occupied Kiev from fall 1941 to fall 1943. Even during the occupation period he was writing some notes for the book, which dealt with the massacre and mass burial of nearly the entire Jewish population of Kiev at the Babi Yar ravine during the beginning of the occupation, as well as with the hardships suffered by the average civilians in Kiev at that time. Although Soviet censorship had greatly affected his previous works as well, the extremely censored publication of *Babi Yar* in a serialized version in the journal *Yunost'* (Youth) was one of the major factors that influenced his decision to defect to Great Britain in 1969. At that time Kuznetsov was at the height of his reputation in the Soviet literary establishment as a member of the editorial board of *Yunost'*, but claiming that the censored publication of his work had eliminated nearly half of what he had wished to say, Kuznetsov sewed 35-millimeter negatives of his writings into the lining of his clothing when he defected so that he could republish the works outside the Soviet Union. Under the pen name of A. Anatolii, he published an expanded version of *Babi Yar*, and critics in the Soviet Union promptly declared him a traitor.

In both its censored and uncensored versions, *Babi Yar* brought recognition to Kuznetsov inside and outside the Soviet Union because of its revelation of the full impact of the Nazi occupation of Kiev and other parts of Ukraine to the world. Although Ilya Ehrenburg's work *The Storm* in 1948 had depicted the Nazi occupation graphically, until the 1960s the Soviet government had not officially recognized the massacre of Jews and other citizens at Babi Yar with any type of memorial. Kuznetsov's novel, along with **Yevgeny Yevtushenko**'s poem "Babii Yar" (1961) and Dmitri Shostakovich's choral *13th Symphony* (1962), expanded awareness of the massacre and helped to provide a clear picture of the atrocities taking place in areas beyond central Europe. Furthermore, Kuznetsov's point of view as a non-Jew is vital for placing the massacre at Babi Yar into the context of the continuing repression that affected nearly all citizens of the Soviet Union, whether by Nazis or by the Soviet government itself. Just as Yevtushenko's poem stresses the common humanity and dignity of the Jewish people and other citizens who were murdered at Babi Yar, Kuznetsov's work emphasizes the ways that both Jewish people and non-Jews in Kiev and elsewhere in the Soviet Union are linked together through their common experiences and relations as friends and neighbors. He writes that in essence only the "nationality" designation in their identification documents indicated any difference, and even this was arbitrary and questionable, for in many cases Russians, Ukrainians, Jews, and other nationalities in Soviet society were all intermixed. Kuznetsov rightly fears that the whole world can become a Babi Yar unless all people know of what has happened, for nobody of any nationality is immune to the chaos, horror, and senselessness of war and genocide.

—Alisa Gayle Mayor

See the essay on *Babi Yar*.

L

LANZMANN, Claude

Nationality: French. **Born:** Paris, 27 November 1925. **Education:** Earned an undergraduate degree in literature and a postgraduate diploma in philosophy. **Career:** Lecturer, Freie University, Berlin, 1948–49; worked as a journalist until 1970; Since 1970 filmmaker. Since 1952 various levels of involvement with *Le Temps modernes*. **Awards:** Ph.D. Honoris Causa, Hebrew University, Jerusalem. Officer Legion d'Honneur (France); Commandeur National Order of Merit (France).

PUBLICATIONS

Film Texts

Shoah. 1985; translated as *Shoah: An Oral History of the Holocaust: The Complete Text of the Film,* 1985; revised as *Shoah: The Complete Text of the Acclaimed Holocaust Film,* 1995.
Un Vivant qui passe: Auschwitz 1943–Theresienstadt 1944. 1997.

Other

Editor, *L'Oiseau n'a plus d'ailes: Les lettres.* 1974; as *The Bird Has No Wings: Letters of Peter Schwiefert,* 1976.
Editor, *Ruin's Traces: Young People's Diaries of the Holocaust.* 2002.

*

Critical Studies: "The Writing of the Holocaust: Claude Lanzmann's *Shoah*" by Jill Robbins, in *Prooftexts: A Journal of Jewish Literary History,* 7(3), September 1987, pp. 249–58; "In an Era of Testimony: Claude Lanzmann's *Shoah*" by Shoshana Felman, in *Yale French Studies,* 79, 1991, pp. 39–81; "Claude Lanzmann and the IDF" by Hillel Halkin, in *Commentary,* 99(6), June 1995, pp. 49–51; "Reflections on Claude Lanzmann's *Shoah*" by Jacob Howland, in *Proteus: A Journal of Ideas,* 12(2), Fall 1995, pp. 42–46; "The Obscenity of Understanding: An Evening with Claude Lanzmann," in *Trauma: Explorations in Memory,* edited by Cathy Caruth, 1995; "Lanzmann's *Shoah*: 'Here There Is No Why'" by Dominick LaCapra, in *Critical Inquiry,* 23(2), Winter 1997, pp. 231–69.

Theatrical Activities: Producer: **Films**—*Pourquoi Israel (Why Israel),* 1972; *Shoah,* 1985; *Tsahal: Tsava Haganah Leisrael (Israeli Defense Forces),* 1994; *Un Vivant qui passe (A Visitor from the Living),* 1997; *Sobibor, 14 octobre 1943, 16 heures (Sobibor, October 14, 1943, 4PM),* 2001.

* * *

Journalist and filmmaker Claude Lanzmann is the writer and director of one of the most acclaimed films ever made on the Holocaust, the nine-and-a-half-hour *Shoah* (1985). Since *Shoah* Lanzmann has continued to make films, publish, and lecture on both the Holocaust and other topics (including, especially, Israel). His prolific productivity has made him one of the most highly regarded voices on the Holocaust and modern Jewish identity. Much of his work is based on, and elaborates, the research for *Shoah,* mostly interviews amounting to more than 350 hours of film footage (with transcripts of them running more than 6,000 pages). In his films Lanzmann had developed a new cinematic language: his films have been based entirely on present-day interviews and have avoided any archival footage or photographs. They instead intercut eyewitness accounts with shots of present-day locations, a deliberate rumination on the relationship between past and present as well as between seeing, understanding, and memory.

Lanzmann was born in 1925 in Paris, to an assimilated Jewish family that made little of its religious origins. At age 17 he joined the French resistance against German occupation and served in Clermont-Ferrand, the small town immortalized in Marcel Ophüls's *The Sorrow and the Pity.* After the war he spent two years in Germany, the first one in Tübingen, where he worked on a thesis on the German philosopher Gottfried Wilhelm Leibniz. In the second year he lectured at the Free University of Berlin on French culture and anti-Semitism (the lectures on the latter topic were stopped by the commandant of the French military government as too political). An associate and friend of Jean-Paul Sartre and Simone de Beauvoir, he has long edited the journal *Les Temps modernes,* which Sartre and de Beauvoir founded; written widely for the news media; and made five films: *Why Israel* (1972; *Pourquoi Israel*), *Shoah* (1985), *Tsahal* (1994), *A Visitor from the Living* (1997; *Un Vivant qui passe*), and *Sobibor, October 14, 1943, 4PM* (2001; *Sobibor, 14 octobre 1943, 16 heures*).

In the early 1970s Lanzmann deplored the turn against Israel by many French intellectuals, including many in Lanzmann's own professional and social circles. *Why Israel* was his response and first film, a three-and-a-half-hour examination of Israeli society that was never released in the United States. After this first effort friends in Israel suggested that

Lanzmann make a film about the Holocaust, an idea that initially mystified him. But he spent the next 11 years researching and interviewing for *Shoah*, which premiered to critical acclaim in 1985. Critics have regarded the film as a cinematic masterpiece and as an indispensable work on the Holocaust.

Lanzmann has considered *Why Israel, Shoah,* and his third film, the five-hour *Tsahal,* a trilogy about "Jewish destiny in more than half a century." *Tsahal* (the Hebrew acronym for the Israeli defense forces) concerns militarism and its role in Israeli identity. The film begins with recollections of the 1973 war by many prominent Israeli officials and includes testimony, reminisces, and advice on the ethos of the military. The second half of the film examines the social and psychological costs of militarism and occupation and interviews various (mostly Jewish) critics of Israel's security methods, including David Grossman and Amos Oz.

In his fourth film, *A Visitor from the Living,* Lanzmann returned to the material he amassed in the research for *Shoah.* The film offers a single, 65-minute interview with Maurice Rossel, who, at 25, had been part of an International Red Cross mission to the "model camp" of Theresienstadt, now in the Czech Republic. Rossel signed off on an infamous report that underscored the amenities of the camp, fabricated by the Nazis for the visit. Unlike *Shoah,* the film does not cut to present-day images of what was once Theresienstadt; instead, the camera remains in the interview for the entire hour. As in *Shoah,* Lanzmann's interview technique proves critical, as he coaxes Rossel into such a convinced defense of his report that Rossel insists he would sign it again, even with the knowledge of the actual business of the camp.

In his film *Sobibor, October 14, 1943, 4PM* (2001), Lanzmann once again mines the footage he shot in making *Shoah* to elaborate on an element touched upon in the earlier film: an uprising and breakout in the Sobibor camp in 1943. The title refers to the time and place of a successful uprising of allegedly "inferior" Jewish prisoners against their "master-race" captors. The Jewish inmates, led by a Jewish Soviet officer, killed enough of their guards with knives and axes to make a dash for the surrounding forest. After the uprising the Nazis closed the camp and tried to eradicate all references to it. The film deploys a similar technique to that in *Shoah*: it combines an interview in the present (with Yehuda Lerner, interviewed in Jerusalem in 1979) with present-day images. In the film Lanzmann dismantled two common assumptions about the Holocaust: that Jewish prisoners had no idea of what awaited them in such camps and that they passively accepted the fate handed to them by the Nazis.

—Jaimey Fisher

See the essay on *Shoah.*

LEBOW, Barbara

Nationality: American. **Born:** Brooklyn, New York, 1 May 1936. **Education:** Vassar College, Poughkepsie, New York, B.A. 1958. **Family:** Three sons. **Career:** Moved to Atlanta, Georgia, 1962; self-employed since beginning association with Academy Theatre in 1964. Playwright-in-residence, Goodmon Scholar, Peace College Theater, Raleigh, North Carolina, 1996; playwright-in-residence, Alabama Shakespeare Festival, Montgomery, 1998–2000. Participates in community outreach programs that produce plays with prison inmates, the homeless, addicts in rehabilitation, the elderly, and the disabled. **Awards:** Atlanta Mayor's fellowship in the arts, 1986; Georgia Governor's award in the arts, 1988; Guggenheim fellowship, 1997. **Agent:** Mary Harden, Harden-Curtis Associates, 850 7th Avenue, Suite 404, New York, NY 10019, U.S.A. **Address:** c/o Academy Theatre, 501 Means St., Atlanta, GA 30318, U.S.A.

PUBLICATIONS

Plays

Little Joe Monaghan (produced 1981). 1995.
A Shayna Maidel (produced Atlanta, 1985). 1988.
The Adventures of Homer McGundy (produced Atlanta, 1985).
Cyparis (produced Atlanta, 1987).
The Keepers (produced Atlanta, 1988). 1995.
Trains (produced Atlanta, 1990).
Tiny Tim Is Dead (produced Atlanta, 1991). 1993.
Lurleen (produced Montgomery, Alabama, 1999).
The Empress of Eden (produced Seattle, 1999).
The Left Hand Singing (produced Little Rock, Arkansas, 2001).

Also author of unpublished plays *Night Witch* (with Frank Wittow) and *Homunculus of Córdoba.*

*

Film Adaptations: *Miss Rose White,* 1991, from the play *A Shayna Maidel.*

Critical Studies: "Toward a Feminist Perspective in American Holocaust Drama" by E.R. Isser, in *Studies-in-the-Humanities,* 17(2), December 1990, pp. 139–48; "'Alive Still, in You': Memory and Silence in *A Shayna Maidel*" by Bette Mandl, in *Staging Difference: Cultural Pluralism in American Theatre and Drama,* edited by Marc Maufort, 1995.

*   *   *

Barbara Lebow has written plays that concern anti-Semitism and, in particular, the Holocaust. The theme of anti-Semitism is significant in Lebow's work because the playwright has written much about the dangers of stereotyping and prejudice. Her unpublished play *Night Witch,* coauthored by Frank Wittow, dramatizes the shocking story of Leo Frank, a Jewish business-man in Georgia who was lynched by an angry anti-Semitic mob in 1915. Frank (named Aaron Gold in Lebow's drama) was falsely accused of murdering a teenage Christian girl and was convicted—merely because he was Jewish. Lebow, as well as historians, point out that the charges and the lynching emanated from anti-Semitism and that Frank was clearly innocent. In Lebow's unpublished play *Homunculus of Córdoba,* a mystical drama set in A.D. 973, the Jewish physician Isaac Ibn Ibrahim is persecuted by Muslims and Christians because of his religion. Furthermore, the decadence of the Nazis serves as a theme in Lebow's unpublished drama *Empress of Eden,* which is based on a true story concerning Nazis who left Germany for the Galapagos Islands shortly before World War II began.

Lebow's most famous play (dramatized in many countries) is *A Shayna Maidel*—the story of two sisters separated by the Holocaust. Rose has enjoyed a sheltered and uneventful life while Lusia has survived Auschwitz but has lost her baby and mother—and is looking for her husband, Duvid. *A Shayna Maidel,* set in 1946, juxtaposes the two sisters as they bond together. Many of Lebow's plays contain characters who are polar opposites and who serve as foils to one another. Lusia maintains her European customs while Rose has shed hers and has become Americanized, which is apparent in her name change—from Rayzel Weiss to Rose White. The play is poignant and touching, manifesting the sensitivity that is evident in Lebow's works. Furthermore, the dialect and dialogue are outstanding, demonstrating Lebow's excellent ear for dialogue and accents.

A Shayna Maidel contains two other themes that pervade the work of Lebow—survival and family. In this drama these two themes are intermingled. The play begins with a scene concerning survival—the birth of Mordechai (the father of Lusia and Rose) during a pogrom in Poland. In the play Rose escapes her feelings of guilt by distancing herself emotionally from her Jewish heritage, changing her name, assuming American customs, and abandoning some aspects of her culture (Mordechai berates her for not keeping kosher). Rose's method of survival resembles Lusia's in that it is psychological. Throughout *A Shayna Maidel* Lusia has flashbacks, or memories. Lebow often employed stories told through memory in her work; it is an effective way for the dramatist to present the plot and to portray how characters feel and react to past events. In *A Shayna Maidel* Lusia relives the past, such as when she struggled in vain to convince her mother to escape Poland for New York City; both mother and daughter unfortunately refused to escape without the other (one had to remain with Lusia's baby, who was not permitted to accompany them). Lusia constantly remembers the past, but Rose has virtually no knowledge of her past—until Lusia's arrival. With Lusia's

help Rose learns about the recent history of her family. She receives from Mordechai a letter, written to her by her mother and dated 4 June 1942. The father has refrained for four years from giving this precious and moving letter to Rose because he thought that it would upset her and because he felt guilty about failing to save his family. Because of his pride, Mordechai had refused to borrow the money necessary to pay for his wife and daughter to come to New York—and then subsequent emigration by Polish Jews was prohibited.

Lebow's drama portrays the importance of family. The family is divided emotionally partly because they were separated physically. Mordechai had taken Rose to New York, but Lusia had remained with her mother in Poland after the girl contracted scarlet fever and became too sick to travel. This seemingly temporary physical distance becomes permanent when the mother and daughter are prevented from leaving Poland. The Weiss family becomes fragmented. Mordechai refuses to talk to Rose about his wife and daughter in Poland and neglects to give Rose the letter from her mother—and her baby spoon that represents the bond between them, the mother's love and caring for her young daughter whom she would never see again. Rose's decision to inscribe a number on her arm represents not only her guilt for enjoying a pleasant life while her mother and niece perished and her sister suffered but also her desire to forge a bond with her sister, for them to be a family again. This is important because earlier in the drama, Rose felt uncomfortable around Lusia and did not want to share her apartment with her.

Lebow's play deals with the aftermath of the Holocaust. Mordechai attempts to redeem himself for failing to bring over his wife and daughter by locating Duvid, reuniting the man with Lusia. Mordechai says that he hopes that they have another baby soon (their daughter, Sprinze, died in Auschwitz) and then a *bris* (circumcision). The play concludes with a restoration of the family and hope for the future.

—Eric Sterling

See the essay on *A Shayna Maidel.*

LEITNER, Isabella

Nationality: American (originally Hungarian: immigrated to the United States, 1945). **Born:** Isabella Katz, Kisvarda, 28 May 1924. **Family:** Married Irving A. Leitner, 1956; two sons. **Career:** Worked in advertising, animation, and the motion picture industry. Lives in New York and lectures on her experiences as a Holocaust survivor. Vice president, American Gathering and Federation of Jewish Holocaust Survivors; since 1973 board member, Juvenile Diabetes Foundation.

PUBLICATIONS

Memoirs

Fragments of Isabella: A Memoir of Auschwitz. 1978.
Saving the Fragments: From Auschwitz to New York. 1985.
Isabella: From Auschwitz to Freedom. 1994.

Other

The Big Lie: A True Story (for children). 1992.

*

Media Adaptations: *Fragments of Isabella* (film), 1989; *Fragments of Isabella* (stage play), produced St. Petersburg, 1993.

Critical Study: '''What Happened'? The Holocaust Memoirs of Isabella Leitner'' by Adrienne Kertzer, in *Transcending Boundaries: Writing for a Dual Audience of Children and Adults,* edited by Sandra L. Beckett, 1999.

*   *   *

Isabella Leitner was born Isabella Katz on 28 May 1924 in the Hungarian town of Kisvárda. Located near the Czech border, Kisvárda had a population of about 20,000, of whom 4,000 were Jews. With four sisters and one brother, Isabella came from a long line of Hasidic rabbis and had a religious upbringing. Her father was a dealer in wine and spirits and had lived all of his life in the anti-Semitic atmosphere of Hungary. As the vicious tide of Nazism continued to rise throughout the 1930s, he was astute enough to see what was coming. Thus, in 1939 he went to the United States to obtain immigration documents for his wife and six children. He tried for months and then for years to obtain the papers necessary to save his family, but it was to no avail. Once Hungary declared war on the United States on 8 December 1941, it was too late for him to return home, and he spent the war in the United States.

On 29 May 1944 Isabella and her family were swept up in the storm of the deportation of the Hungarian Jews. They arrived in Auschwitz on 31 May. Her mother and youngest sister, Potyo, were sent immediately to the gas chambers, leaving Isabella, Chicha, Rachel, Cipi, and their brother Philip. Except for Cipi, the oldest sister, who was murdered in Bergen-Belsen, all survived. In November 1944 Isabella was transferred to Birnbaumel. After being liberated by the Soviets on 25 January 1945, Isabella and her two sisters made their way to Odessa. They convinced the authorities that their father was alive and living in United States, and they were able to obtain passage on a ship. On 8 May 1945, the day the war in Europe ended, Isabella and her two remaining sisters became the first survivors of Auschwitz to set foot on American soil. Some days later the three sisters were reunited with her father,

who was now a book dealer. Their brother Philip did not reach the United States until six months later.

In 1956 Isabella married Irving A. Leitner, a veteran of World War II whom she had met in upstate New York, and they had two sons. Leitner, a writer and editor, worked with his wife in editing her memoirs. Her first book, *Fragments of Isabella,* was first published in 1978 and met with high critical acclaim. In 1989 the Irish producer Michael Scott and the director Ronan O'Leary made the memoir into what became an award-winning film. In 1985 she published a sequel to the memoir, titled *Saving the Fragments: From Auschwitz to New York.* Her husband's stage production of *Fragments of Isabella* had its premiere in St. Petersburg in 1993, and in 1994 the husband-and-wife team combined the first two works, as well as additional material, into a single volume under the title *Isabella: From Auschwitz to Freedom.*

Living in New York, Leitner has been active not only in efforts to preserve the memory of the victims of the Holocaust but also in numerous community service activities.

—David Patterson

See the essay on *Fragments of Isabella: A Memoir of Auschwitz.*

LENGYEL, Olga

Nationality: American (originally Romanian; immigrated to the United States after World War II). **Born:** Transylvania. **Education:** Studied medicine in Transylvania. **Family:** Married Miklos Lengyel (deceased); two sons (deceased). **Career:** Worked as a surgical assistant in Cluj, Transylvania, before World War II; founder and director of an organization in New York that educates about the Holocaust.

PUBLICATION

Memoir

Souvenirs de l'au-delà. 1946; as *Five Chimneys,* 1947.

*   *   *

Olga Lengyel, a university educated medical assistant from Cluj in Transylvania, was deported in 1944. She survived Auschwitz and a death march. Her narrative, first published in English in 1947, is a frank and terrible account of the death camp.

Perhaps the most significant theme in Lengyel's memoir is the way in which the Nazis ''wanted to infect us with their own Nazi morals. In most cases, they succeeded.'' ''Perhaps,'' she says, "the greatest crime these 'supermen' committed against us was their campaign, often successful, to turn us into monstrous beasts ourselves." The memoir reveals moments where inmates have either refused to be degraded morally or have been degraded by the camp experience. In a way that parallels **Primo Levi**'s celebrated discussion of the "gray zone," Lengyel is forgiving of some behavior because of the circumstances and lays the blame solidly with the captors.

One of the reasons that her memoir has attracted attention is that, like **Charlotte Delbo**'s account, it offers a female perspective on the Holocaust. Scholars have discussed the particular horrors that women faced in the Holocaust: in her study Myrna Goldenberg suggests that women showed a strong concern for each other, depended on each other, and were able to adapt what she names "homemaking skills" into coping skills. She also stresses, however, the vulnerability of women, especially to rape and the fear of rape. Lengyel's account is a good example of this. In addition to these issues, Lengyel also discusses the way women acted with babies in the camp and how sex became a commodity to trade and organize in Auschwitz. She also relates the way the SS, especially Irma Griese, degraded the prisoners sexually and in other ways. To limit this testimony to a woman's view, however, would be wrong. Instead, it is clear that this woman's testimony reveals things about Auschwitz that a male testimony cannot, just as a male testimony reveals parts of the experience unavailable to woman survivors: to read Levi, for example, after reading Lengyel, is to be aware that you are reading a testimony from a male perspective. In agreement with Lawrence Langer's discussion of this issue, this is not to set up a "hierarchy of suffering" but to say, after Goldenberg, that women suffered "different horrors within the same hell."

Unlike some memoirs published soon after the war, Lengyel's has no political ax to wield: she writes that she is "neither a political scientist nor an economist. I am a woman who suffered, lost her husband, parents, children and friends. I know the world must share the guilt collectively." Because of the few who resisted and did not become beasts, she writes that she has "not entirely lost her faith in mankind." Her memoir, however, is candid, bleak, and unsparing. Albert Einstein wrote to Lengyel to commend her: "Thank you for your very frank, very well written book. You have done a real service by letting the ones who are now silent and most forgotten speak."

—Robert Eaglestone

See the essay on *Five Chimneys.*

LEVERTOV, Denise

Nationality: American (originally British: immigrated to the United States, 1948, naturalized citizen, 1955). **Born:** Ilford, Essex, 24 October 1923. **Education:** Privately educated; also studied ballet. **Family:** Married the writer Mitchell Goodman in 1947 (divorced 1972); one son. **Career:** Worked in several London hospitals during World War II; worked in an antique store and bookstore, London, 1946; teacher of poetry craft, Young Men and Women's Christian Assocation (YM-YWCA), New York, 1964; professor, Tufts University, Medford, Massachusetts, 1973–79; professor emeritus of English, Stanford University, California, beginning in 1981. Visiting lecturer, Drew University, Madison, New Jersey, 1965; writer-in-residence, City College of the City University of New York, 1965–66; visiting lecturer, Vassar College, Poughkeepsie, New York, 1966–67; visiting professor, University of California, Berkeley, 1969; visiting professor and poet-in-residence, Massachusetts Institute of Technology, Cambridge, 1969–70; visiting professor, Kirkland College, Clinton, New York, 1970–71; Elliston Lecturer, University of Cincinnati, Ohio, 1973; Fannie Hurst Professor (poet-in-residence), Brandeis University, Waltham, Massachusetts, 1981–83. Poetry editor, *Nation,* 1961–62, and *Mother Jones,* 1976–78. Also contributor to poetry anthologies. Co-initiator, Writers and Artists Protest against the War in Vietnam, 1965; active in the antinuclear movement. **Awards:** Bess Hokin prize from *Poetry,* 1959, for poem "With Eyes at the Back of Our Heads"; Longview award, 1961; Guggenheim fellowship, 1962; Harriet Monroe memorial prize, 1964; Inez Boulton prize, 1964; American Academy and Institute of Arts and Letters grant, 1965; Morton Dauwen Zabel memorial prize from *Poetry,* 1965; Lenore Marshall Poetry prize, 1976; Elmer Holmes Bobst award in poetry, 1983; Shelley memorial award, Poetry Society of America, 1984; National Endowment for the Arts senior fellowship, 1990; Robert Frost medal, 1990; Lannan award, 1993. D.Litt.: Colby College, 1970, University of Cincinnati, 1973, Bates College, 1984, Saint Lawrence University, 1984, Allegheny College, 1987, St. Michael's College, 1987, Massachusetts College of Art, 1989, University of Santa Clara, 1993. **Member:** American Academy and Institute of Arts and Letters. **Died:** 20 December 1997.

PUBLICATIONS

Poetry

The Double Image. 1946.
Here and Now. 1957.
Overland to the Islands. 1958.
Five Poems. 1958.
With Eyes at the Back of Our Heads. 1959.
The Jacob's Ladder. 1961.
O Taste and SEE: New Poems. 1964.
City Psalm. 1964.
Psalm Concerning the Castle. 1966.
The Sorrow Dance. 1967.
Penguin Modern Poets 9, with Kenneth Rexroth and William Carlos Williams. 1967.

A Tree Telling of Orpheus. 1968.
A Marigold from North Vietnam. 1968.
Three Poems. 1968.
The Cold Spring and Other Poems. 1969.
Embroideries. 1969.
Relearning the Alphabet. 1970.
Summer Poems 1969. 1970.
A New Year's Garland for My Students, MIT 1969–1970. 1970.
To Stay Alive. 1971.
Footprints. 1972.
The Freeing of the Dust. 1975.
Chekhov on the West Heath. 1977.
Modulations for Solo Voice. 1977.
Life in the Forest. 1978.
Collected Earlier Poems, 1940–1960. 1979.
Pig Dreams: Scenes from the Life of Sylvia. 1981.
Wanderer's Daysong. 1981.
Candles in Babylon. 1982.
Poems, 1960–1967. 1983.
Oblique Prayers: New Poems with Fourteen Translations from Jean Joubert. 1984.
El Salvador: Requiem and Invocation. 1984.
The Menaced World. 1984.
Selected Poems. 1986.
Breathing the Water. 1987.
Poems, 1968–1972. 1987.
A Door in the Hive. 1989.
Evening Train. 1992.
Sands of the Well. 1996.
Batterers. 1996.
The Life around Us: Selected Poems on Nature. 1997.
The Stream and the Sapphire: Selected Poems on Religious Themes. 1997.
This Great Unknowing: Last Poems. 1999.

Recordings: *Today's Poets 3,* with others; *The Acolyte,* 1985.

Short Story

In the Night: A Story. 1968.

Other

The Poet in the World (essays). 1973.
Light up the Cave (essays). 1981.
Lake, Mountain, Moon. 1990.
New & Selected Essays. 1992.
Tesserae: Memories and Suppositions (autobiographical essays). 1995.
Conversations with Denise Levertov, edited by Jewel Spears Brooker. 1998.
The Letters of Denise Levertov and William Carlos Williams, edited by Christopher MacGowan. 1998.

Editor and translator, with Edward C. Dimock, Jr., *In Praise of Krishna: Songs from the Bengali.* 1967.
Editor, *Out of the War Shadow: An Anthology of Current Poetry.* 1967.

Translator, with others, *Selected Writings,* by Jules Supervielle. 1968.
Translator, *Selected Poems,* by Eugene Guillevic. 1969.
Translator, with others, *Poets of Bulgaria,* edited by William Meredith. 1985.
Translator, *Black Iris,* by Jean Joubert. 1988.
Translator, *White Owl and Blue Mouse,* by Jean Joubert. 1990.

*

Bibliographies: *A Bibliography of Denise Levertov* by Robert A. Wilson, 1972; *Denise Levertov: An Annotated Primary and Secondary Bibliography* by Liana Sakelliou-Schulz, 1989.

Manuscript Collections: Green Library, Stanford University, Sanford, California; Humanities Research Center, University of Texas, Austin; Washington University, St. Louis, Missouri; Indiana University, Bloomington; Fales Library, New York University, New York; Beinecke Library, Yale University, New Haven, Connecticut; Brown University, Providence, Rhode Island; University of Connecticut, Storrs; Columbia University, New York; State University of New York, Stony Brook.

Critical Studies: *Denise Levertov* by Linda W. Wagner, 1967; *Denise Levertov: In Her Own Province,* edited by Linda W. Wagner, 1979; *The Imagination's Tongue: Denise Levertov's Poetic* by William Slaughter, 1981; *Understanding Denise Levertov* by Harry Marten, 1988; *Critical Essays on Denise Levertov,* edited by Linda W. Wagner-Martin, 1990; *Denise Levertov: The Poetry of Engagement* by Audrey T. Rodgers, 1993; *Denise Levertov: Selected Criticism,* edited by Albert Gelpi, 1993; *Poetics of the Feminine: Authority and Literary Tradition in William Carlos Williams, Mina Loy, Denise Levertov, and Kathleen Fraser* by Lina A. Kinnahan, 1994.

*   *   *

Denise Levertov was a daughter of Paul Levertoff, a Russian Jew who converted to Christianity and became an Anglican clergyman, and Beatrice Spooner-Jones, a Welshwoman. Both sides of her family were very important to her and helped construct her personality, her views on spiritual and political issues, and her method of creating poetry. Her father, who had been an Orthodox Jewish rabbi of Hasidic heritage, taught her a great deal about Judaism, specifically Hasidism and mysticism, as well as about Christianity. Levertov was, for instance, clearly influenced by Martin Buber's *Tales of the Hasidism: The Early Masters.* The poet's mother endowed her with a love of history. Levertov's poem "During the Eichmann Trial" suggests to readers that she realized that the trial of Adolf Eichmann was history in progress, that the event possessed historical—as well as spiritual—significance. Her poem "Illustrious Ancestors" points to an ancestor—Rabbi Shneur Zalman, the famous *rav* of northern White Russia (now Belarus) who taught the importance of listening, observation, and communication, all of which proved important in Levertov's poetry.

Levertov was profoundly affected by the outbreak of World War II. She aspired to be a ballet dancer, but at the onset of war altered her plans. In an essay with Sybil Estess, which is an important source of biographical information on Levertov, she mentioned that she became a member of the "land army," working on a farm in order to avoid the draft. (In England there was conscription of women.) She later studied to become a nurse but quit because she did not like the pressure of having to take the nursing exam. Levertov has said that she heard the bombing in London and still remembers it vividly. She has recalled England as a drab place because of the war and its destruction. When the war began, she had already been writing poetry. Nonetheless, in her poetry of the time she barely alludes to the devastation of the war or to the Holocaust. (She has referred to the poetry being written in England during this period as "new romanticism" and has claimed that it was rather poor.) Levertov has said that, although she was keenly aware of it, she did not experience anti-Semitism personally. In the interview with Estess she confessed that the war was not the subject of her poetry at the time because she was too immature as a person and as a poet to write about such an overwhelming topic. She wrote her first political poem, "During the Eichmann Trial," long after the war had ended.

Although Levertov was living in England, not Germany, and was merely nine years old when Adolf Hitler assumed power, she was keenly aware of the evil nature of the German leader and of the dangers of Nazism. Her parents sheltered German and Austrian refugees in their home, and she knew of the concentration camps. Her parents took in *Mischlinge* (those of mixed marriages in which one member was Jewish, the other not), in part because they could relate to the situation, Levertov's mother being Roman Catholic and her father a Jew who had converted to Christianity. Levertov's parents primarily took in people who had been raised as, and who thought of themselves as, Christians but who were nonetheless persecuted by the Nazis.

"During the Eichmann Trial," from Levertov's collection of poetry entitled *The Jacob's Ladder,* embodies the author's belief that the poet is endowed with a responsibility to write about ethical and social problems and situations. The poem is considered to be her first political poem. The tone that pervades the tripartite poem is intense, passionate, and emotional, illustrating that the trial was quite significant to Levertov. The poet employs several references to the eye and employs the pronoun "I," suggesting that those following the trial—and reading "During the Eichmann Trial"—need to look not only

at Eichmann but also within. Levertov uses the word "we" in the subheading for the first section ("When We Look Up") to suggest that looking within is essential for everyone, including Jews and even herself. The word "when" implies that the poet considers such introspection to be rare, not an everyday occurrence.

According to Levertov's poem, the actions of the Nazis manifested a moral and social breakdown in humanity, not merely within the ranks of the Nazi regime. The guilty included not only the perpetrators but also the bystanders: those who witnessed the atrocities but refused to look within, those who refused to help because they perceived the Jews, but not themselves, as the victims. Levertov suggests that, if a segment of the human population was targeted and attacked, all of humanity was victimized. Just as the poet reconciles her interest in Judaism and Christianity, she attempts to reconcile all people rather than demarcating human beings into various classifications. She also refuses to demonize Eichmann. Unlike other Holocaust writers who have characterized Eichmann as a monster, Levertov believes that he was merely a human being, amoral but nevertheless a person like anyone else. Human beings who fail to look within and see themselves tend to consider those people unlike themselves to be "the other" and consequently lose their ability to empathize and sympathize with them. When people consider others to be alien and inferior, it becomes easier to commit atrocities or to refrain from helping the victims.

—Eric Sterling

See the essay on "During the Eichmann Trial."

LEVI, Primo

Pseudonym: Damiano Malabaila. **Nationality:** Italian. **Born:** Turin, 31 July 1919. **Education:** University of Turin, 1937–41, B.S. in chemistry (summa cum laude) 1941. **Family:** Married Lucia Morpurgo in 1947; one daughter and one son. **Career:** Worked under a false name as a chemist in northern Italy, 1941–43; partisan, Italian resistance, 1943; betrayed by informer and captured, 1943; worked in a rubber factory while imprisoned in Auschwitz, 1944–45; technical executive, SIVA (paints, enamels, synthetic resins), Settimo, 1948–77. **Awards:** Campiello literary prize (Venice), 1963, for *La tregua,* and 1982, for *Se non ora, quando?;* Bagutta literary prize (Milan), 1967, for *Storie naturali;* Prato prize for resistance, 1975; Strega literary prize (Rome), 1979, for *La chiave a stella;* Viareggio literary prize, 1982, for *Se non ora, quando?;* corecipient, with Saul Bellow, Kenneth B. Smilen fiction award from the Jewish Museum in New York, 1985; Present Tense/Joel H. Cavior literary award, 1986, for *The Periodic Table.* **Died:** Probably suicide, 11 April 1987.

PUBLICATIONS

Collections

Opere (3 vols.):
   Volume primo: Se questo è un uomo; La tregua; Il sistema
      periodico; I sommersi e i salvati. 1987.
   Volume secondo: Romanzi e poesie. 1988.
   Volume terzo: Racconti e saggi. 1990.
Opere (2 vols.), edited by Marco Belpoliti. 1997.

Memoirs

Se questo è un uomo. 1947; as If This Is a Man, 1959; as
   Survival in Auschwitz, 1986.
La tregua. 1963; as The Reawakening, 1965; as The Truce: A
   Survivor's Journey Home from Auschwitz, 1965.
Il sistema periodico. 1975; as The Periodic Table, 1984.
Lilít, e altri racconti. 1981; as Moments of Reprieve, 1986.
I sommersi e i salvati. 1986; as The Drowned and the Saved,
   1988.

Novels

La chiave a stella. 1978; as The Monkey's Wrench, 1986.
Se non ora, quando? 1982; as If Not Now, When?, 1985.

Short Stories

Storie naturali (as Damiano Malabaila). 1966.
Vizio di forma. 1971.
The Sixth Day and Other Tales. 1990.

Poetry

L'osteria di Brema. 1975; translated as Shema, 1976.
Ad ora incerta. 1984.
The Collected Poems of Primo Levi. 1988.

Play

Intervista Aziendale, with Carlo Quartucci (radio play). 1968.

Other

Abruzzo forte e gentile: Impressioni d'occhio e di cuore, edited
   by Virgilio Orsini. 1976.
La ricerca delle radici: Antologia personale 1981; as The
   Search for Roots: A Personal Anthology, 2001.
Dialogo, with Tullio Regge. 1984; translated as Dialogo,
   1989; as Conversations, 1989.
L'ultimo natale di guerra. 1984.
L'altrui mestiere (essays). 1985; as Other People's Trades,
   1989.

Racconti e saggi. 1986; revised edition, as Il fabbricante di
   specchi: racconti e saggi, 1997; as The Mirror Maker:
   Short Stories and Essays, 1989.

Translator, Il processo, by Franz Kafka. 1983.

*

Bibliography: "An English Bibliography of the Writings of
Primo Levi" by Cathe Giffuni, in Bulletin of Bibliography,
50(3), September 1993, pp. 213–21.

Critical Studies: Conversations with Primo Levi by Ferdinando
Camon, translated by John Shepley, 1989; At an Uncertain
Hour: Primo Levi's War against Oblivion by Anthony Rudolf,
1990; A Dante of Our Time: Primo Levi and Auschwitz by Risa
B. Sodi, 1990; Reason and Light: Essays on Primo Levi, edited
by Susan Tarrow, 1990; Understanding Primo Levi by Nicho-
las Patruno, 1995; Primo Levi: Bridges of Knowledge by
Mirna Cicioni, 1995; Primo Levi: Tragedy of an Optimist by
Myriam Anissimov, translated by Steve Cox, 1999; "Primo
Levi, Witness: Symposium," in Judaism, 48(1), Winter 1999,
pp. 49–83; Holocaust Literature: Schulz, Levi, Spiegelman
and the Memory of the Offence by Gillian Banner, 2000; Primo
Levi and the Politics of Survival by Frederic D. Homer, 2001;
The Voice of Memory: Interviews, 1961–1987, edited by
Marco Belpoliti and Robert Gordon, translated by Gordon,
2001; Memory and Mastery: Primo Levi As Writer and Wit-
ness, edited by Roberta S. Kremer, 2001.

* * *

Primo Levi is one of the greatest of the writers of witness to
Shoah; the range of his work, its literary quality, and especially
his astonishing inventiveness with form also make him one of
the major Italian writers of the twentieth century.

His works from beginning to end focus insistently on the
issue of communication. The challenges to communication
within Auschwitz—and about Auschwitz after the liberation
of the camp—provide him the basis for a fundamental investigation of the possibilities and limitations of human language as
an accurate vehicle of meaning. He conceived the project of
writing about the experience of the camp while still in Auschwitz.
Fiercely committed to accuracy, he deployed in the task of
writing not only his astonishing memory—he claims and
displays virtually total recall—but notes that he made at the
risk of his life while still in Auschwitz. Already aware of the
suppression of truth that the Nazis intended and the massive
destruction of records as the camps were abandoned by the
Germans, aware too of the strain on "normal" canons of
credibility that the story of the camps would involve, Levi
insists in his preface to his first book (Survival in Auschwitz)
that "none of the facts [that he reports] is invented."

Levi was fundamental in conceiving and developing the
literature of witness. He produced writings of this category

over the course of his career, most taking the form of narratives. His style is by purpose and habit strikingly lucid in denotation and restrained in tone. He was a chemist committed to using language in ways that are clear, direct, and controlled. He also believed that if people interested in communicating about the experience and meaning of the disaster addressed one another out of the waves of anger and guilt roused by the events, they would drown one another in the tides of their emotions. He therefore purposed to write in a restrained style in order to open up a space for quiet thought and conversation about the implications of those events for our self-understanding as humans. Critics, especially those who read his work in translations, which necessarily miss the subtle play of tones—particularly irony and understatement—that characterizes his writings, often remark with surprise that he could write about events and experiences that horrific so unemotionally, dispassionately, and objectively. But restraint, not lack of emotional response, is what is at stake. Certain phrases, even in the prose works, do display in a flash the depth of the emotions he personally feels, from profound anger, to disgust, to sad and castigating dismissal of disclaimers of responsibility on the part of those who committed or allowed the atrocities. His verse, comprising some 80 poems, of which he says that he composed in verse only to say things he could not say in prose, contains passages of more overt immense anger, as well as passages of great sorrow and compassion. The restraint in the prose writings was tactical, vicarious, in the service of effective communication and thought—and arguably cost him enormously. He believed firmly that Shoah was not just a Jewish disaster but a disaster for and of all humankind and that all have a duty to consider and be responsible for the lessons to be drawn from it. Called by **Jean Améry** once ''the forgiver,'' Levi was anything but sentimental. He believed that forgiveness was a moral impertinence without remorse and a change in life in those who did wrong, and he did not see that those who did the wrong were in fact asking forgiveness.

The first two of his writings were first-person narratives, memoirs of and reflections on the experience of the camp and of the journey home to Torino. Levi was a master of choosing exemplary instances of human response to the pressure of the camps and characteristically renders these in studied pairs or triplets. His ability to present an anecdote that opens on a whole world of moral complexity or fixes subtly a personality or an attitude is virtually without parallel. One of the features that makes his work a challenge, though enormously evocative and insightful, is that experience at times is expressed through allusion to works read in the course of his own education or later in life. Dante, for example, is often a point of reference, and some of Levi's stylistic traits show the impact of *The Divine Comedy*. His literary references are always self-aware and carefully chosen and crafted, however, and mark not only literary indebtedness but, at times, moral distance. In perhaps the most strikingly profound of all his chapters, ''The Canto of Ulysses,'' Dante's poem plays a central part, but one in which, while implying the greatness of the poem and the ways in which it configures Italian identity, he at the same time suggests the negative implications for a Jew of that poem's conception of God and the relations of that concept with the historical experience of Shoah.

Levi was deeply aware of the complex relations between fact, truth, and fiction and was scrupulous in notifying his reader when a work of his should be read as fact and when not. One of the century's most subtle and effective explorations of the art of speaking and the art of listening is one of his works of ''fiction,'' *The Monkey's Wrench*. The concerns of communication after and about Auschwitz are present sustainedly, even if subtly, in this work that fractures Levi's own voice into two, those of himself and an alter ego, Faussone. Levi refused, as a witness, to be boxed—by doubters and, finally, by those who had committed the atrocities—into writing only works of ''fact.'' One of the most striking of his works, *If Not Now, When?* is openly a sort of historical novel. He knew the conditions generally of resistance in Russia and the Jews' place in that resistance, he knew stories. But he was not a witness personally. Because no one was telling that story, however, its truth was being lost, and Levi openly dared to write fiction on this subject in order to tell that truth. He refused, in short, to defer to the cynical question ''If Levi could write such compellingly plausible fiction as a work of witness, might he not have been fabricating in works in which he claimed to be reporting facts—things which 'have been'?''

In his last great work of witness, *The Drowned and the Saved,* he reversed the balance between narrative and analysis characteristic of his earlier works and wrote what is mostly an intense, solemn, and brilliant analysis of major issues arising from the experience of the disaster, infixing illustrative narrative as he felt that to be effective and helpful.

Levi was emphatic in his insistence that with scrupulous attention and honest intention, humans can communicate effectively about experience. He was dedicated to the notion that we must try to deploy our understanding and good will to try to avoid a repetition   in some form, with some people, in some way—of the disaster, a possibility, as he thought, that always threatens if we do not guard our laws, our customs, our speech. The danger is that they may become the means to the outworking of the maxim that he thinks is deep in many people and many nations: ''every stranger is an enemy.'' When that maxim, he believed, becomes the major premise of a social syllogism of fear and hatred, at the end of that logical chain lies the Lager. An atheist (''There is Auschwitz, hence there cannot be God. I do not find a solution to the dilemma. I look for it, but I do not find it.''), he was, as best understood, neither an optimist nor a pessimist. Perhaps the best image for his view of the world, in light of the crematoria of Auschwitz, is that his view is binocular: through one lens he sees the possibility of the world as one of warmth, home, friends, peace; through the other he sees the world of the lords of death. The world itself is neither possibility by nature or in itself. The bridge between the two lenses would then be human choice—the will to decency or to malice. He writes in order to give testimony to the reality of the world of the lords of death and to urge that we through understanding try to create a world of decency and respect.

Aside from his primary works of witness, his novels, short stories, and verse, he wrote a large number of occasional pieces as a columnist for the Torinese newspaper *La stampa*. These are characteristically marked by the huge and curious range of a never-resting intelligence, by a mordant if gentle irony, a delicious wit, and, along with a deep note of sadness, a will to cheer.

—Ralph G. Williams

See the essays on *The Drowned and the Saved, If Not Now, When?, The Periodic Table, The Reawakening,* and *Survival in Auschwitz.*

LEVIN, Meyer

Nationality: American. **Born:** Chicago, 8 October 1905. **Education:** University of Chicago (founder, with John Gunther, *Circle*), 1921–24, Ph.D. 1924; studied art, Académie Moderne, Paris, 1925. **Military Service:** United States Army Psychological Warfare Division, France, during World War II. **Family:** Married 1) Mabel Schamp Foy in 1935 (divorced 1944), one daughter; 2) Tereska Szwarc in 1948, two sons. **Career:** Reporter, feature writer, and columnist, *Chicago Daily News,* 1922–29; moved to Palestine and lived on a kibbutz, beginning in 1928; opened an experimental marionette theater in Chicago and taught puppetry, New School for Social Research, New York City, 1930s; associate editor, *Esquire,* Chicago, 1933–39; war correspondent during the Spanish Civil War; worked for the U.S. Office of War Information and as a war correspondent for the Overseas News Agency and the Jewish Telegraphic Agency during World War II. **Awards:** Jewish Book Council of America William and Janice Epstein fiction award and Harry and Ethel Daroff fiction award, both in 1966, for *The Stronghold;* Jewish Book Council of America Isaac Siegel memorial juvenile award and Charles and Bertie Schwartz juvenile book award, both in 1967, for *The Story of Israel;* honored, World Federation of Bergen/Belsen Associations, 1969. **Died:** 9 July 1981.

PUBLICATIONS

Novels

Reporter. 1929.
Frankie and Johnnie: A Love Story. 1930; revised edition, as *The Young Lovers,* 1952.
Yehuda. 1931.

The New Bridge. 1933.
Old Bunch. 1937.
Citizens. 1940.
My Father's House. 1947.
Compulsion. 1956.
Eva: A Novel of the Holocaust. 1959.
The Fanatic. 1964.
The Stronghold. 1965.
Gore and Igor: An Extravaganza. 1968.
The Settlers. 1972.
The Spell of Time: A Tale of Love in Jerusalem. 1974.
The Harvest. 1978.
The Architect. 1981.

Plays

The Good Old Days (produced Paris, 1951).
Anne Frank (produced Israeli Soldiers Theatre, 1966; Brandeis University, 1972). 1957.
Compulsion, based on his novel (produced New York, 1957). 1958.

Screenplays: *My Father's House,* 1947; *The Illegals,* 1948; *Mountain of Moses,* 1968; *The Falashas,* 1970; *The Unafraid,* 1978.

Other

The Golden Mountain (folk tales). 1932; as *Classic Hassidic Tales,* 1966.
If I Forget Thee: A Picture Story of Modern Palestine (synopsis of his screenplay, *My Father's House*). 1947.
In Search (autobiography). 1950.
The Story of the Synagogue, with Toby K. Kurzband (for children). 1957.
The Story of the Jewish Way of Life, with Kurzband (for children). 1959.
God and the Story of Judaism, with Dorothy K. Kripke (for children). 1962.
The Haggadah Retold. 1968; as *An Israel Haggadah for Passover,* 1970; revised edition, 1977.
Beginnings in Jewish Philosophy. 1971.
The Obsession (autobiography). 1973.

Editor and translator, *Selections from the Kibbutz Buchenwald Diary.* 1946.
Editor, *Diary,* by David S. Kogan. 1955.
Editor, *Golden Egg,* by Arthur D. Goldhaft. 1957.
Editor, with Charles Angoff, *The Rise of American Jewish Literature.* 1970.

Translator, *Tales of My People,* by Sholem Asch. 1948.
Translator, *Women's Barracks,* by Tereska Torres. 1950.
Translator, *Not Yet,* by Torres. 1957.
Translator, *The Dangerous Games,* by Torres. 1957.
Translator, *The Golden Cage,* by Torres. 1959.

Translator, *The Only Reason,* by Torres. 1961.

*

Film Adaptation: *Compulsion,* 1959.

Critical Studies: *Meyer Levin: Fifty Years in Writing,* 1973; "The Haunting of Meyer Levin" by Benno Weiser Varon, in *Midstream,* 22, 1976, pp. 7–23; *The Literary Achievement of Meyer Levin* (dissertation) by Gary Bossin, Kent State University, Ohio, 1980; *Meyer Levin,* 1982, and "The Ghetto and Beyond: First-Generation American-Jewish Autobiography and Cultural History," in *Multicultural Autobiography: American Lives,* edited by James Robert Payne, 1992, both by Steven Joel Rubin; "Meyer Levin's *The Old Bunch:* Children of the Immigrants" by Leslie Field, in *Yiddish,* 6(4), 1987, pp. 73–86; *An Obsession with Anne Frank: Meyer Levin and The Diary* by Lawrence Graver, 1995; *The Stolen Legacy of Anne Frank: Meyer Levin, Lillian Hellman, and the Staging of the Diary* by Ralph Melnick, 1997; *Audacious Pilgrim: The Story of Meyer Levin: A Biography* by Martin Litvin, 1999.

*   *   *

In his own estimation Meyer Levin's career was a testament to the divided sensibility of the Jewish American writer, who must struggle to reconcile his cultural identity as a Jew with his participation in American ideology. Throughout his career Levin was quick to understand—in the eyes of his many critics, far too quick to understand—the obstacles he encountered in the publishing world or the disdain with which some of his books were received as owing to a larger American cultural discomfort with Jewish identity. Even before he became involved in an infamous legal fight over the suppression of his preliminary dramatization of Anne Frank's *Diary of a Young Girl,* Levin perceived himself to have been several times the victim of an implicit censoring of Jewish identity. Never himself an observant Jew, Levin was focused mostly on the cultural dimension of Jewish identity. Having defined himself as a leftist progressive in the Roosevelt New Deal era, Levin's discomfort with the Marxist left stemmed from the inhospitality in such circles to particularist models of ethnic identity. Although his experiences during two trips to Palestine in the 1920s informed the novel *Yehuda* (1931) and a collection of Hasidic tales called *The Golden Mountain* (1932), his first two novels, *Reporter* (1929) and *Frankie and Johnnie* (1930), had been works of American social realism indebted to his work as a journalist in Chicago. Much as Ludwig Lewisohn had begun late in his career to write alternately and differently for the American and Jewish public, Levin's early works also seem written for two distinct audiences. Arguably, however, in his best work the two are held in tension, as was the case with the commercially successful *Old Bunch* (1937), a novel in which Levin explores the lives of a circle of Jewish friends from the west side of Chicago and traces each character's more or less successful assimilation into the currents of contemporary American society.

In later years Levin would himself rehearse and lament a perception about his career that he had begun as a promising social realist novelist and gone astray when he started to treat too explicitly Jewish themes. It is hardly an overstatement to say that Levin's encounter with the Holocaust galvanized the Jewish identity of his authorial voice. If one were to choose a single Jewish American author who seems most defined by Holocaust consciousness, it would have to be Meyer Levin. No fewer than seven of his post-World War II authorial projects treat the Holocaust either as central subject or as central to the book's construct of Jewish identity. Having worked as a correspondent in Spain alongside a number of other American writers (including Ernest Hemingway) who explicitly sided with the losing anti-Fascist cause, Levin desperately wanted to be useful in the American fight against Nazism. To this end he signed on with the Office of War Information in 1941 to create and produce documentary films and later got himself assigned as a war correspondent to cover the final Allied campaign. As a consequence of his desire to be present at the American front, Levin witnessed firsthand the liberation of the camps and tried there to gather the stories and names of the Jewish victims of the Nazis. After the war Levin wrote and produced a film about the illegal emigration to Palestine of a group of Holocaust survivors, which he quickly turned into a novel by the same name. As the first of his Holocaust works, *My Father's House* (1947) begins aboard an illegal emigration ship offering brief life histories of several survivors and then follows in particular the life of a boy whose desperate search to find a father and family killed by the Nazis causes him to resist incorporation into the Zionist dream. The boy and novel are delivered from this recusant Holocaust memory only through the device of the boy's mental breakdown brought on by extreme grief, as the boy symbolically regresses to a younger age in order to be reborn a child of the emergent Jewish homeland.

Soon after this, while working for the Haganah as a filmmaker and helping to promote the illegal emigration of Jews to Palestine, Levin began and completed an autobiography he would self-publish several years later in France. *In Search* (1950) chronicles Levin's struggle to become an authentically Jewish writer, and at the literal and spiritual center of the book is his encounter with the Holocaust. As Levin recounts his work as a reporter interviewing survivors of the Nazi genocide and trying to bring out the Jewish perspective of the tragedy in dispatches that were picked up here and there by smaller American papers, he names and explores questions of survivor guilt; he also details rifts in the Jewish community over questions of collaboration in order to suggest the long reckoning with this terrible history that will have to take place within the Jewish community. Shortly after the publication of his autobiography, Levin read Anne Frank's *Diary* in French and believed he had found the document that would bring the Holocaust home to the rest of the world. Initially humbled by the burden of witness, Levin had predicted in his autobiography that a teller would have to arise from the ruins of the European Jewish community to get the story across. Confident that Anne was that voice, Levin befriended Otto Frank and began almost immediately to help him seek an American publisher for the *Diary*. He acted for a time as the book's unofficial agent in America, and his review in the *New York Times Book Review* helped make it an overnight success. For his services Levin was promised first rights at a dramatic adaptation. But after positive preliminary readings of his work, his script was suddenly dropped for commercial reasons, and Levin responded with a public campaign in the press, in the Jewish community, and in the world of letters to protest the censorship of his voice. Before the play became a hit in the fall of 1955, Levin filed suit against Otto Frank and the play's then producer, Cheryl Crawford, although the case would not come to trial for several years. Levin argued that his play had been dropped because it was too Jewish and that his ideas for the dramatization had been appropriated. A jury decided in Levin's favor on the second point, although the verdict was put aside by the judge.

What is perhaps most significant about Levin's suit is that it proves a symbolic site for the conflicting imperatives of cultural memory of the Holocaust in America, with Anne Frank made a symbol of the universalizing patterns of Holocaust memory in the 1950s. In trying to challenge his audience with a slightly more contentious mode of remembrance, Levin had depicted an Anne who interpreted her plight in terms of her Jewish identity. The legal controversy over the *Diary* would eventually yield two books, a fictional roman à clef called *The Fanatic* (1964) and a memoir called *The Obsession* (1973), in which Levin laid bare the wrong that had been done both to him and to Anne as a de-Judaized Holocaust victim. These books bore the memory of Levin's attempt to win the conscience of an American public. In the midst of the controversy he had written the novel for which he is most remembered, the best-seller *Compulsion* (1956), which like his 1940 labor novel, *Citizens,* was an example of documentary fiction. For this fictional rendering of the Leopold–Loeb murder case, Levin drew from his past experiences reporting the trial and from interviews with the imprisoned Leopold. Following the success of *Compulsion* Levin spent much of the latter half of his career in Israel. Of his other two Holocaust novels, *Eva* (1959), based on his interviews with a survivor, allows Levin to offer a parable against integrationist or assimilationist models of cultural identity as he retells a woman survivor's story of passing among Nazis while yet remaining true to her Jewish identity. In *The Stronghold* (1965) Levin developed a fictional scenario about the last days of the war, in which a group of mythic European statesmen are forced to confront a war criminal modeled on Adolf Eichmann and thus to wrestle in advance with the memory of their own complicity in anti-Semitism and the difficult memory the Holocaust will pose to all European nationalisms. As these two novels treat Holocaust history and memory in the European and Israeli contexts, they give evidence of the author's having solved his own transnationalist dilemma by removing himself imaginatively

from the American context, and most of his later writings might as well be termed Israeli as American fiction.

—R. Clifton Spargo

See the essays on *Eva: A Novel of the Holocaust, The Fanatic, My Father's House,* and *The Stronghold.*

LEWIN, Abraham

Nationality: Polish. **Born:** Warsaw, 1893. **Family:** Married Luba Hotner (died 1942); one daughter (deceased). **Career:** Teacher, Yehudia Girls' School, Warsaw. Associated with Emmanuel Ringelblum. **Died:** Murdered, victim of the Holocaust, ca. 1942.

PUBLICATIONS

Diary

A Cup of Tears: A Diary of the Warsaw Ghetto, edited by Antony Polonsky. 1988.

Other

Kantonistn: vegn der Yidisher rekrutshine in Rusland in di tsaytn fun Tsar Nikolay dem ershtn, 1827–1856. 1934.

* * *

Abraham Lewin was a teacher at the Yehudia secondary school for Jewish girls in Warsaw, where **Emmanuel Ringelblum** was also a member of the faculty. In addition to teaching Hebrew in the interwar period, Lewin authored a historical study in Yiddish, *The Cantonists* (1934), concerning the conscription of Jews into the Russian army in the nineteenth century. Personally acquainted, then, with Lewin's dedication to Jewish education and to his intellectual accomplishments, and no doubt familiar with his role as a Zionist organizer, Ringelblum included Lewin in the directorate of Oneg Shabbes, the archival project for documenting the experience of the Warsaw Ghetto. Lewin's principal contribution to that effort is *A Cup of Tears: A Diary of the Warsaw Ghetto* (1988), covering the period from 26 March 1942 to 16 January 1943. The extant text is written in two parts, the first in Yiddish and the second in Hebrew, drawing upon the command of both languages that he had demonstrated in his professional activities. It is presumed that Lewin died shortly after the final diary entry in the course of the renewal of the major deportations.

Two of the hidden deposits of Oneg Shabbes archives, including Lewin's diary, were recovered after the war, and there exists, moreover, a substantial literature of diaries and memoirs from other sources in the Warsaw Ghetto. Lewin's professional formation would link him to the educator **Chaim A. Kaplan**, for instance, but the latter's diary, *Scroll of Agony* (1965), is a text of extended personal reflection and lamentation. Lewin's sparer account is more closely related to Ringelblum's own diary, *Notes from the Warsaw Ghetto* (1958), and *The Warsaw Diary of Adam Czerniakow* (1979) in that all three grow out of institutional concerns—the aims of Oneg Shabbes, on the one hand, and **Adam Czerniaków**'s work as chairman of the Jewish Council, on the other. Hence, like Ringelblum and, to a lesser degree, Czerniaków, Lewin tends to efface his personal experiences.

Nevertheless, Lewin's writing may be distinguished from their diaries by a certain intimacy of tone. Whereas Ringelblum and Czerniaków concentrate on social structures in the Warsaw Ghetto, Lewin is, above all, an avid listener to and moving recorder of individual tales of suffering. One might compare, for instance, the entries related to 10 June 1942—a date to be "writ large, in bloody letters, in the history of the Warsaw Ghetto," according to Ringelblum. As is his custom, Ringelblum provides an explanatory frame: "Apparently, there was a decision to liquidate . . . smuggling" and "It would seem that the general plan is to exterminate the Jews in the larger cities of Poland through a policy of systematic starvation." Between these remarks the account is by no means dispassionate, but the description remains generalized: "Dozens of smugglers were liquidated that night, in the usual way." Indeed, the only figure singled out by Ringelblum is an especially murderous Nazi guard who had earned the name of Frankenstein.

Czerniaków, for his part, moves the scene to the offices of Nazi power, where, from his point of view, the real battle for the survival of the Warsaw Ghetto was fought. He notes on 10 June, "At the Gestapo I raised the question of the 'Frankenstein' who keeps shooting people every day at one of the gates." But on 11 June, the day following the events that Ringelblum considered so noteworthy, Czerniaków comments, palliatingly, "There is restlessness in the ghetto because of the daily shootings of smugglers as well as of law-abiding pedestrians by elements not readily identifiable," amidst other concerns.

In contrast to Czerniaków, Lewin focuses starkly on the brutality; but he also differs from Ringelblum in that he highlights the drama by employing a literary structure. As is often the case, Lewin's account, although highly condensed, forms a complete story in miniature, with an introductory scene, a sudden climax, and a narrative denouement ("When silence fell, we saw a man . . ."). Like the others, Lewin notes the actions of the murderer, but his attention focuses on the victims. Presented at first as "a young Christian" and "a Jewish woman"—that is, in the anonymity they would have borne in the eyes of the killer—Lewin characteristically adds what information he can, giving them the life, in literature at least, that Frankenstein had taken away: "The Jewish woman was 27 years old and her name was Liman. Before the war the Limans had a fruit store. . . . The Christian who was killed was supplying them with goods." Throughout *A Cup of Tears*

Lewin is the determined researcher into and often the lucid teller of such personalized tales, writing his diary at street level, near at hand to the dying and the dead.

—Andrew Bush

See the essay on *A Cup of Tears: A Diary of the Warsaw Ghetto.*

LEWITT, Maria

Nationality: Australian (originally Polish: immigrated to Australia, 1949). **Born:** Maria Markus, Lodz, 1924. **Family:** Married Julian Lewitt, ca. 1944; two sons. **Career:** Worked on a poultry farm and as a seamstress and machinist, Australia. Cofounded and operated several businesses, including a bakery and a milk bar. **Awards:** Alan Marshall award, 1978, for *Come Spring;* Ethnic Affairs Commission award, 1986, for *No Snow in December.*

PUBLICATIONS

Novels

Come Spring: An Autobiographical Novel. 1980.
No Snow in December: An Autobiographical Novel. 1985.

Other

Just Call Me Bob. 1976.
Grandmother's Yarn (for children). 1985.

*

Critical Studies: "Triumphantly Living" by Nancy Keesing, in *Overland* (Australia), 103, July 1986, p. 75–76; "Survival and Exile in Maria Lewitt's *Come Spring* and *No Snow in December*" by Susan Ballyn, in *Commonwealth Essays and Studies* (France), 12(1), Autumn 1989, pp. 73–80.

* * *

Maria Markus was born in 1924 in Lodz, Poland, the younger daughter of a prosperous middle-class Jewish family. Her paternal grandparents immigrated to Lodz from Lithuania in the mid-nineteenth century. Her father, Borys, qualified in Leipzig as a chartered accountant and subsequently managed a family-owned textile factory. He met her mother, Lydia, while on business in Moscow during the Bolshevik Revolution.

Lydia Wagin's father was an officer in the Imperial Russian Army. Though she converted to Judaism, she remained Russian to the core. Maria's autobiographical Holocaust novel, *Come Spring,* depicts her mother as a spirited woman who saved her daughters and other Jewish relatives and friends.

Maria and her older sister, Eugenia, grew up in a cultured home with books, music, and governesses to look after them. Most of the pupils at the private high school they attended were Jewish. Even in her sheltered existence, Maria was exposed to rising anti-Semitism during the interwar years, which took the form of street demonstrations, poster and leaflet campaigns, economic boycotts, and unfettered public and private displays of prejudice. In September 1939 her father joined in the defense of Warsaw against the German invasion. Shortly after his return to Lodz, he was beaten to death in his own home by a soldier in the SS.

When Lodz, renamed Litzmannstadt, was incorporated into the German Reich, Lydia fled with her daughters to Warsaw. Maria's novel describes the increasingly wretched conditions in the Warsaw Ghetto from 1940 to 1941. In 1941 her mother's sister, who was married to a Polish aristocrat, helped to get them an apartment outside the ghetto. They stayed in Warsaw until they were threatened by *szmalcowniki,* thugs whose occupation was blackmailing and denouncing hidden Jews. They were forced to move to her aunt's isolated village home outside Warsaw. Maria's uncle was a proud, eccentric, and impoverished aristocrat who detested Jews but could not condone murder. For two years, while dying of cancer, he sheltered his wife's family and turned a blind eye to four other extended family members who were hidden in his cellar.

A romance blossomed between Maria and one of the family group hidden in the cellar. Julian Lewitt was the son of her father's business partner. They married after the war, and their son Joe was born in 1945. Their wartime dream had been to leave Poland and Europe. In 1947 they reluctantly separated from their decimated family, joining the general exodus of surviving Jews after the Kielce pogrom of 1946. The Lewitts landed in Melbourne, Australia, in January 1949, after a year in Paris, where their infant son was treated for tuberculosis.

They initially lived and worked with the relatives who sponsored them on their poultry farm in Reservoir, a northern outer suburb of Melbourne. Julian, who had qualified as a textile engineer in Bradford before the war, took factory jobs. Maria finished garments by hand and later worked as a machinist while she looked after her young son at home. Despite the uncongenial work, they regarded Australia as a land of opportunity and freedom. They later started small business ventures, beginning with a milk bar and then a cake shop. Their younger son Michael was born in 1953.

Apart from the separation from her beloved family, the greatest grief Maria experienced in migrating was her exile from her native language and literature, which she could not share with her children. She had grown up with the classics, especially Leo Tolstoy, Anton Chekhov, and the Polish writers Julian Tuwim and Stefan Zeromski. She recalls scribbling even before she learned to write. When she was fed up working as a machinist, she scribbled notes on garment labels. During the war she kept a diary and risked denunciation during weekly trips to change library books. She learned English from her

son's schoolbooks, graduating to works she had already read in Polish translation, such as the plays of George Bernard Shaw and the novels of John Galsworthy, Pearl S. Buck, and some French authors.

In the 1960s Maria enrolled in creative writing classes at Monash University. She was commended for short stories about her wartime experiences that were also short-listed for a number of prizes. Overcoming her anxiety about her inadequate English, she began her autobiographical novel, *Come Spring,* which won the Alan Marshall award in 1978. It was published in Australia in 1980 and in the United States in 1982.

Preceding *Schindler's List, Come Spring* was one of the first books to raise awareness of the Holocaust in Australia. Maria made a conscious effort to preserve its authenticity as testimony by restricting herself to the experiences and limited understanding of her adolescent protagonist, Irina, who, like Maria herself, is only 15 when the war begins.

Maria's second novel, *No Snow in December* (1985), focuses on the core themes of migration, the pain of displacement, and the loss of language, status, and self-worth balanced against the gains of political freedom, tolerance, material prosperity, a good education, and a future for one's children. Although she has not written much poetry, her poem "Smugglers" is used for educational purposes; its powerful yet easily grasped central metaphor is the hidden "baggage" of the past imported by immigrants.

—Felicity Bloch

See the essay on *Come Spring: An Autobiographical Novel.*

LIND, Jakov

Pseudonym for Heinz Landwirth. **Nationality:** Austrian. **Born:** Vienna, 10 February 1927; took name Jakov Chaklan in Palestine after World War II. **Education:** Academy of Dramatic Art, Vienna. **Family:** Married Faith Henry in 1955 (divorced), two children. **Career:** Fled Germany to the Netherlands in 1938, fled back to Germany in 1943 with false identity papers and worked as a deckhand on a river barge; immigrated to Palestine after World War II and worked as a laborer, actor, and editor; since 1956 has lived mainly in London. Writer-in-residence, Long Island University Brooklyn Center, 1966–67.

PUBLICATIONS

Novels

Landschaft in Beton. 1963; as *Landscape in Concrete,* 1966.
Eine bessere Welt. 1966; as *Ergo,* 1966.
Travels to the Enu: The Story of a Shipwreck (novella). 1982.

The Inventor. 1987.

Memoirs

Counting My Steps: An Autobiography. 1969.
The Trip to Jerusalem. 1972.
Numbers: A Further Autobiography. 1973.
Crossing: The Discovery of Two Islands. 1991.

Short Stories

Eine Seele aus Holz. 1962; as *Soul of Wood and Other Stories,*
   1964.
Der Ofen: Eine Erzählung und sieben Legenden. 1973; as *The
   Stove: Short Stories,* 1983.

Plays

Anna Laub (radio play). 1965.
Die Heiden: Spiek in 3 Akten or *Das Sterben der Silberfüchse*
   (radio play). 1965.
The Silver Foxes Are Dead, and Other Plays (English transla-
   tions, includes the radio plays *The Silver Foxes Are Dead;
   Anna Laub; Hunger; Fear*). 1968.
Angst und Hunger: Zwei Hörspiele [Fear and Hunger: Two
   Radio Plays]. 1968.
Ergo, from his novel (produced New York, 1968). 1968.

*

Critical Studies: ''Jakov Lind: Writer at Crossroads'' by
Stella P. Rosenfeld, in *Modern Austrian Literature: Journal of the International Arthur Schnitzler Research Association,* 4(4), 1971, pp. 42–47; ''Conscience and Cannibals: An
Essay on Two Exemplary Tales: 'Soul of Wood' and 'The
Pawnbroker''' by Stephen Karpowitz, in *Psychoanalytic Review,* 64, 1977, pp. 41–62; ''Jakov Lind's War: Guilt and
Identity in the Autobiographical Works and Early Stories''
by Kathleen Thorpe, in *Acta Germanica: Jahrbuch des
Germanistenverbandes im sudlichen Afrika* (Germany), 23,
1995, pp. 107–15; *Jakov Lind: The Cosmopolitan Austrian,*
2000, and *Writing after Hitler: The Work of Jakov Lind,* 2001,
both edited by Edward Timms, Andrea Hammel and Silke
Hassler.

* * *

Jakov Lind was born in Vienna, Austria, the only son of a
Jewish family of Eastern European descent. In 1938 a refugee
organization brought him and his sister to The Netherlands,
where they stayed with various foster families. Following the
German occupation of The Netherlands in 1942, Lind was
moved to the Amsterdam ghetto. He escaped deportation and,
after assuming the identity of a fictitious young Dutchman, hid
out in Nazi Germany. There he first worked as a sailor on a
large Rhine barge and later as an assistant to the director of a

metallurgical institute. After the war Lind joined his family in
Palestine, where he worked at various jobs including construction worker, photographer, and air traffic controller for the
new Israeli air force. In 1950 Lind returned to Austria to study
directing for a semester at the Reinhardt-Institute. After short
stays in Paris, Amsterdam, and Copenhagen, Lind settled in
London in 1954. His literary output includes novels, short
stories, autobiographical works, and plays for theater and
radio. In addition to his work as a writer, Lind has directed
films. He is also an accomplished painter whose work has been
exhibited in Europe and the United States.

Lind's literary work clearly shows the imprint of his
traumatic experiences during the Holocaust. Nazi terror, war,
and survival emerge as central themes especially in his early
writings, which include the prose collection *Soul of Wood*
(1962) and the novels *Landscape in Concrete* (1963) and *Ergo*
(1966). Set during the Nazi period, these texts examine human
behavior in the face of life-threatening circumstances. Through
the use of the literary grotesque, Lind creates an absurd,
nightmarish, and unpredictable world in which fear and guilt
are the primary human experiences.

His preoccupation with his own personal history remains
evident in Lind's later works. His autobiography *Counting My
Steps* (1969) recounts his childhood in Vienna, the years in The
Netherlands, and his fight for survival in Nazi Germany. The
author poignantly reveals loss of identity, cultural alienation,
and survivor guilt as the price of survival. The exploration of
what it means to be Jewish underlies Lind's text *The Trip to
Jerusalem* (1972). In this work, written in the style of New
Journalism, Lind describes his experiences, observations, and
impressions during a four-week trip to Israel. His solidarity
with the country does not prohibit a critical depiction that is
accompanied by a critical examination of the self. In 1973 Lind
published the second installment of his autobiography, entitled
Numbers: A Further Autobiography. A chronological continuation of *Counting My Steps,* the work covers Lind's return
to Europe and his time in Austria. While focusing on day-to-
day encounters, the author relives essential experiences of his
past as he tries to come to terms with fascism. The third
installment of his autobiography, *Crossing: The Discovery of
Two Islands,* appeared in 1991. The work describes Lind's life
in England, his marriage to Faith Henry, and his emerging
career as a writer. As with his previous autobiographical
works, *Crossing* testifies to Lind's continuing preoccupation
with fascism and his own role as a survivor of the Holocaust.

Lind published three literary texts between the second and
third installments of his autobiography. The first, a prose
collection entitled *The Stove,* appeared in 1973, in German,
although it was originally written in English. The rich symbolism of the stories, and in particular of the title story about a
stove business that evokes associations with Auschwitz, allows them to be read on multiple levels. After a nine-year
hiatus, Lind published his novel *Travels to the Enu* in 1982. In
this satiric adventure-travel novel, the protagonist, a writer

named Orlando, is confronted with two types of society, one violent and totalitarian, the other exotic and utopian. The exotic world turns out to be just a mirror image of the unsatisfying reality that had prompted Orlando's trip. In the many discursive passages that interrupt the novel's turbulent story line, Orlando reflects critically on societal structures, war, and disarmament. *The Inventor* (1987) is an epistolary novel. It tells the story of the Jewish brothers Emmanuel and Boris Borovsky. While Boris's letters document his deteriorating marriage, Emmanuel's relate his difficulties finding financial supporters for his invention. In ways similar to his early texts, Lind here creates an absurd world and ironically undermines any ideological or metaphysical construct.

While Anglo-American critics, who have compared him to Franz Kafka and Samuel Beckett, have responded very positively to Lind, his reception in German-speaking countries, where criticism has focused on Lind's unorthodox use of the German language, has been mixed. Starting with his autobiography *Counting My Steps,* however, Lind has chosen to write in English. Thus, it seems probable that the uncomfortable subject matter of his literary works as well as the fact that they defy easy labeling or categorization also account for his ambivalent reception by the German-speaking world.

—Helga Schreckenberger

See the essays on *Counting My Steps: An Autobiography, Landscape in Concrete,* and ''Soul of Wood.''

LUSTIG, Arnošt

Nationality: American (originally Czechoslovak: immigrated to the United States, 1970). **Born:** Prague, 21 December 1926. **Education:** College of Political and Social Sciences, Prague, M.A. 1951, Ing. Degree 1954. **Family:** Married Vera Weislitz in 1949; one son and one daughter. **Career:** Prisoner, Theresienstadt (Terezín), Auschwitz, and Buchenwald concentration camps, World War II. Arab-Israeli war correspondent, Radio Prague, 1948–49; correspondent in Europe, Asia, and North America, Czechoslovak Radio Corp., 1950–68; screenwriter, Barrandov Film Studios, Prague, 1960–68; writer, Israel, 1968–69; screenwriter, Jadran Film Studio, Zagreb, Yugoslavia, 1969–70; member, International Writers Program, 1970–71, and visiting lecturer, 1971–72, University of Iowa, Iowa City. Since 1973 professor of literature, American University, Washington, D.C. Head of the Czechoslovak film delegation to the San Sebastian Film Festival, 1968; member of the jury, Karlovy Vary International Film Festival, 1968; visiting professor, Drake University, 1972–73. Editor, *Mlady svet* magazine, 1958–60. **Awards:** First prize, Mlada Fronta publishing house, 1962, for *Diamonds of the Night;* best short story, University of Melbourne, 1962, for ''Lemon''; first prize, Czechoslovak Radio Corp., 1966, for radio play *Prague Crossroads;* first prize, Monte Carlo Film Festival, 1966, for television film *A Prayer for Katerina Horovitzova;* Klement Gotwald State prize, 1967, nomination for National book award, 1974, and B'nai B'rith award, 1974, all for *A Prayer for Katerina Horovitzova;* first prize, Czechoslovak Radio Corp., 1967, for radio play *A Man the Size of a Postage Stamp;* second prize, San Sebastian Film Festival, 1968, for *Dita Saxova;* Jewish National book award, 1980, for *Dita Saxova,* and 1987, for *The Unloved: From the Diary of Perla S.;* Emmy award, outstanding screenplay, 1985, for documentary *Precious Legacy.* D.H.L.: Spertus College, 1986. **Member:** Authors Guild; Authors League of America. **Address:** Office: Department of Literature, American University, Washington, D.C. 20016, U.S.A.

PUBLICATIONS

Collection

Children of the Holocaust: The Collected Works of Arnost Lustig. 1976.

Novels

Muj znamy Vili Feld. 1949.
Dita Saxova. 1962; as *Dita Sax,* 1966.
Modlitba pro Katerinu Horovitzovou. 1964; as *A Prayer for Katerina Horovitzova,* 1973.
Darkness Casts No Shadow (English translation). 1976.
Z deniku sedmnactilete Perly Sch. 1979; as *The Unloved: From the Diary of Perla S.,* 1985.
Indecent Dreams (three novellas). 1988.

Short Stories

Noc a nadeje. 1958; as *Night and Hope,* 1989.
Demanty noci. 1958; as *Diamonds of the Night,* 1986.
Street of Lost Brothers. 1990.

Plays

Screenplays: *Transport from Paradise,* adaptation of *Night and Hope,* 1963; *Diamonds of the Night,* adaptation of *Darkness Casts No Shadow,* 1964; *Dita Saxova,* 1968.

Television Plays: *The Blue Day,* 1960; *A Prayer for Katerina Horovitzova,* 1965; *Terezin,* with Ernest Pendrell, 1965; *Stolen Childhood,* 1966.

Other

Ulice ztracenych bratri. 1949.
Nikoho neponizis. 1963.
Bile brizy na podzim. 1966.
Horka vune mandli. 1968.

Milacek. 1969.
Tma nema stin. 1991.
Velka trojka, with Milan Kundera and Josef Skvorecky. 1991.
Colette. 1992.
Tanga. 1993.
Green Eyes. 1995.

*

Film Adaptations: *Transport from Paradise,* from the story *Night and Hope,* 1963; *Diamonds of the Night,* from the novel *Darkness Casts No Shadow,* 1964; *Dita Saxova,* 1968.

* * *

Arnošt Lustig was born in 1926 in Prague. He is a survivor of Theresienstadt (Terezín), Auschwitz, and Buchenwald concentration camps. He escaped a transport to Dachau when his train was mistaken for a munitions train and bombed. Lustig returned to Prague and participated in the anti-Nazi uprisings in 1945. It is from those past experiences that Lustig drew his inspiration for novels and short stories. Because Lustig was just a teenager when he was sent to the Theresienstadt ghetto with his mother (his father perished in the gas chambers), writing has become a form of catharsis for him. His works frequently portray women and children who often do not survive the war. Though the fate of many of his characters is known, there remains a thread of optimism that runs through his works, leaving the reader to feel that mankind and humanism will prevail in the end. His observation of human behavior can be compared to the writings of **Elie Wiesel,** most notably Wiesel's highly praised *Night.* Both authors were masters at describing the intimate thoughts, mental state, and emotions of their characters.

Although Lustig wrote of situations that occurred during the Holocaust, he did not consider himself to be a Holocaust writer but rather a writer who expressed his true convictions about history and human character. Indeed, as a man with little formal education, Lustig admitted that everything he learned of man, he learned in the camps. When questioned about his knowledge of human fate in an interview with Rob Trucks in the *New England Review,* Lustig stated, ''It was a university about man that I couldn't have learned better. I learned about goodness, about evil, about the character of man, about the possibilities of man, about the weaknesses of man . . . So with very little exaggeration, I can say that everything I learned about man, or the character of man, about the fate of man, I learned in the camps, until I was seventeen years old.''

Lustig also became a driving force behind Czech New Wave cinema, whose artists include Miloš Forman, Ján Kadár, Elmar Klos, Vera Chytilová, Jan Němec, and Jiří Menzel.

Examples of work from the Czech New Wave, such as *The Firemen's Ball* (directed by Forman) and *Closely Watched Trains* (directed by Menzel), have subjects that vary from lyrically haunting to tragicomical. Although Czech New Wave films have various themes, humanism is certainly the thread that binds all of them together. For example, in *Closely Watched Trains* a young soldier has just come to realize that life is beautiful, only to die in the end. This theme is similar to Lustig's short story ''Stephen and Anne,'' as two young lovers discover love when it is too late. Many of Lustig's works, most notably *Darkness Casts No Shadow* (under the title *Diamonds of the Night*) and *Transport from Paradise,* have been turned into movies by New Wave directors, while his short story ''A Man the Size of a Postage Stamp'' has been broadcast as a radio play. With the fall of Communism, the tradition of the Czech New Wave has been resurrected by new directors, most recently Jan Hřebejk, who directed the Academy Award–nominated film *Musíme si pomáhat,* or *Divided We Fall,* which depicts a Jew being hidden by Christian friends during World War II. The film blends both comedy and tragedy in true Czech New Wave fashion. The contrast of life with death in Lustig's stories and Czech New Wave motifs are also reminiscent of Franz Kafka, whose literature is filled with sudden twists, turns, and twofold meanings, concluding with dark fates for the characters. Lustig's *Transport from Paradise* is one such illustration. In it the Nazis create a false atmosphere for the Red Cross's visit to Theresienstadt. The ghetto is temporarily transformed into a clean and efficient model camp for the observers, a pseudo-paradise, but the observers' departure marks the immediate transport of the camp's inhabitants to Auschwitz.

It is from Czech literature, the Holocaust, and World War II that Lustig created his characters, who represented for him the true inner strength and actual beauty of man. It is said that ''We are only limited by our own perception of ourselves,'' and Lustig's characters are indeed just ordinary people confronting unspeakable circumstances, yet they manage to exert incredible strength to overcome Nazi evil. Seemingly small situations have great significance—for example, a young boy throws a crust at a dying old woman and strikes her in the side, as seen in the short story ''The Children.'' A simple loaf of bread thus becomes as symbolic of death as it does of life.

Lustig has continued to enjoy a renaissance in the Czech Republic since restrictions have been lifted and his books are now more readily available.

—Cynthia A. Klíma

See the essays on *A Prayer for Katerina Horovitzova, Night and Hope, Diamonds of the Night, Darkness Casts No Shadow,* and *The Unloved.*

M

MALAMUD, Bernard

Nationality: American. **Born:** Brooklyn, New York, 26 April 1914. **Education:** Erasmus Hall High School, New York; City College of New York, 1932–36, B.A. 1936; Columbia University, New York, 1937–38, M.A. 1942. **Family:** Married Ann de Chiara in 1945; one son and one daughter. **Career:** Teacher, New York high schools, 1940–49; instructor and associate professor of English, Oregon State University, Corvallis, 1949–61. Member, division of languages and literature, Bennington College, Vermont, 1961–86. Visiting lecturer, Harvard University, 1966–68. President, PEN American Center, 1979–81. **Awards:** Rosenthal award and Daroff award, both in 1958; Ford fellowship, 1959, 1960; National Book award, 1959, 1967; Pulitzer prize, 1967; O. Henry award, 1969, 1973; Jewish Heritage award, 1977; Vermont Council on the Arts award, 1979; Brandeis University creative arts award, 1981; Bobst award and American Academy gold medal, both in 1983; Mondello prize (Italy), 1985. **Member:** American Academy, 1964; American Academy of Arts and Sciences, 1967. **Died:** 18 March 1986.

PUBLICATIONS

Collection

The Complete Stories. 1997.

Novels

The Natural. 1952.
The Assistant. 1957.
A New Life. 1961.
The Fixer. 1966.
Pictures of Fidelman: An Exhibition. 1969.
The Tenants. 1971.
Dubin's Lives. 1979.
God's Grace. 1982.

Short Stories

The Magic Barrel. 1958.
Idiots First. 1963.
Rembrandt's Hat. 1973.
Two Fables. 1978.
The Stories. 1983.
The People, and Uncollected Short Stories, edited by Robert Giroux. 1990.

Other

A Malamud Reader. 1967.
Conversations with Malamud, edited by Lawrence Lasher. 1991.
Talking Horse: Bernard Malamud on Life and Work. 1996.

*

Film Adaptations: *The Fixer,* 1968; *The Angel Levine,* 1970, from the short story; *The Natural,* 1984.

Bibliography: *Malamud: An Annotated Checklist,* 1969, and *Malamud: A Descriptive Bibliography,* 1991, both by Rita N. Kosofsky; *Malamud: A Reference Guide* by Joel Salzburg, 1985.

Critical Studies: *Bernard Malamud* by Sidney Richman, 1967; *Bernard Malamud and Philip Roth: A Critical Essay* by Glenn Meeter, 1968; *Bernard Malamud and the Critics,* 1970, and *Bernard Malamud: A Collection of Critical Essays,* 1975, both edited by Leslie A. and Joyce W. Field; *Art and Idea in the Novels of Bernard Malamud* by Robert Ducharme, 1974; *The Fiction of Bernard Malamud,* edited by Richard Astro and Jackson J. Benson, 1977; *Rebels and Victims: The Fiction of Richard Wright and Bernard Malamud,* 1979, and *The Magic Worlds of Bernard Malamud,* 2001, both by Evelyn Gross Avery; *Bernard Malamud* by Sheldon J. Hershinow, 1980; *The Good Man's Dilemma: Social Criticism in the Fiction of Bernard Malamud* by Iska Alter, 1981; *Theme of Compassion in the Novels of Bernard Malamud* by M. Rajagopalachari, 1988; *Bernard Malamud: A Study of the Short Fiction* by Robert Solotaroff, 1989; *Bernard Malamud Revisited* by Edward A. Abramson, 1993; *The Short Stories of Bernard Malamud: In Search of Jewish Post-Immigrant Identity* by Begoña Sío-Casteñeira, 1998.

* * *

Bernard Malamud is not the sort of writer one thinks of as deeply interested in the Holocaust. His first novel, *The Natural,* was a baseball story without a Jew in it. But the Holocaust nonetheless makes its appearance in a number of ways in his fiction, especially in several of his short stories, such as ''The Last Mohican'' and ''The Lady of the Lake,'' that deal with Holocaust survivors in Italy. And if we connect a virulent anti-Semitism with the Holocaust, which was its major cause, then in his novels, pre-eminently *The Fixer,* which is a fictionalized version of the infamous Bailiss case in nineteenth-century Russia, the Holocaust is also, if indirectly, present.

In these ways Malamud is similar to **Isaac Bashevis Singer**, who escaped the Holocaust by emigrating from Poland well before the Nazi invasion but whose writing is filled with people and events that predate and thereby recall the world the Holocaust destroyed. Not only in "The German Refugee" but also in other stories, as in "The First Seven Years" (in *The Magic Barrel*), Malamud portrays people like Singer's, who speak English with Yiddish or German accents and are themselves recent immigrants to the United States. These first-generation Americans, as with Singer's prewar characters, remind us, too, of the world that was lost. Their care-worn visages and deep sadness also resemble the characteristics of Holocaust survivors.

In several of his stories Malamud uses the Holocaust subtly to suggest the theme of responsibility and human compassion. Occasionally it is invoked directly, as in "The Last Mohican," when Fidelman comes across a cemetery in Rome where one of the tombstones bears an inscription mourning the death of a person's father in Auschwitz at the hands of the Nazis. Or in "The Lady of the Lake," where it is not until the end that we discover that the young woman Freeman née Levin loves and wishes to marry is a Holocaust survivor. But more often it is submerged, as in "The Loan," where loaves of bread burn in the oven and appear as "charred corpses," victims in their way of a failure of compassion.

In the last novel published before his death, *God's Grace*, Malamud depicts the aftermath of a holocaust more terrible and devastating than that of World War II but occasioned by the same basic hatreds and viciousness that caused the earlier one. A nuclear war destroys all of humankind except for Calvin Cohen, a Jewish-American scientist who escapes destruction because he is at the bottom of the sea engaged in research. When he surfaces and sees what has happened, he tries to create an Edenic life on an island, teaching a group of chimpanzees how to speak and to behave in a humane manner. A humanist and an optimist, he works hard and lovingly with his little band to instill in them a kind of civility as well as filial devotion. But the basic drives of envy and jealousy that infect some of them are too strong for the Judeo-Christian commandments Cohen tries to get them to follow, and just as at the end of *The Tenants*, an earlier novel dealing with the difficulties of African-American and Jewish-American rapprochement, the novel ends in slaughter.

Malamud's moralizing could hardly be clearer. As another writer once proclaimed, "We must love one another, or die." Without human compassion and understanding we are all doomed.

—Jay L. Halio

See the essays on "The German Refugee," "The Lady of the Lake," and "The Last Mohican."

MANGER, Itzik

Nationality: Israeli (originally Romanian: immigrated to England after World War II, the United States, 1951, and Israel, 1967). **Born:** Chernovitsy, Romania, 30 May 1901. **Education:** Worked in the shop of his father, a tailor. **Family:** Married Genia Nadir. **Career:** Lived between Bucharest, Warsaw, and Bukovina, 1919–29; wrote lyrics for musicals, 1930s; fled from the Nazis to Paris, 1939; met Margaret D. Waterhouse in England; wrote for American periodicals, 1951–67. **Award:** Itzik Manger prize for Yiddish literature, 1968. **Died:** 21 February 1969.

PUBLICATIONS

Collections

Medresh Itsik (includes *Humesh lider; Megileh-lider*). 1951.
Noente geshtaltn un andere shriftn [Collected Prose Works]. 1961.
Oysgeklibene shriftn: Lider, proze, eseyen, memaurn, edited by Shemuél Rozshanski. 1970.
Ballads of Itzik Manger. 1978.
Shriftn in proze [Prose Works]. 1980.

Poetry

Shtern oyf'n dakh: Lid un balade. 1929.
Lamtern in vint: Lid un balade. 1933.
Humesh lider. 1935.
Felker zingen. 1936.
Megileh-lider. 1936.
Demerung in shpigl: Lid un balade. 1937.
Velvl Zbarzsher shraybt briv tsu Malkeh'le der sheyner. 1937.
Volkens ibern dakh: Lid un balade [Clouds over the Roof: Songs and Ballads]. 1942.
Der shnayder-gezeln Note Manger zingt [The Tailor-Lad Nota Manger Sings]. 1948.
Lid un balade [Song and Ballade]. 1952.
Shtern in shtoyb [Stars in the Dust]. 1967.
The Ballad of the Man Who Reached from Grey to Blue. 1981.
Abishag Writes a Letter Home. 1981.
By the Road There's a Tree. 1981.
The Ballad of the Old Soldier. 1981.
My Grandmother's Flowers. 1981.
A Dark Hand. 1981.
Night Prayer. 1981.

Novel

Di vunderlekhe lebnsbashraybung fun Shmuel Aba Abervo: dos bukh fun Ganeydn. 1939; as *The Book of Paradise: The Wonderful Adventures of Shmuel-Aba Abervo,* 1965.

Short Stories

Noente geshtaltn. 1938.

Plays

Hotsmakh shpil: A Goldfadn-motiv in 3 aktn [Hotsmach Play: Comedy in Three Acts]. 1947.
The Megilla of Itzik Manger, music by Dov Seltzer (produced Tel-Aviv, 1967).

Other

Yidisher teater in Eyrope tsvishn beyde velt-milkhomes: Materialn tsu der geshikhte fun yidishn teater [Jewish Theater between the Two World Wars], with Jonas Turkow and Moses Perenson. 1968.
Shtrikh'n tsum portret fun Itsik Manger (correspondence). 1976.

*

Film Adaptations: *Der purimshpiler: The Jester,* 1937; *The Bent Tree,* 1980.

Bibliography: *Itzik Manger* by Ephim H. Jeshurin, 1961.

Critical Studies: *Poetic and Linguistic Symbiotic Phenomena in Itzik Manger's Biblical Poetry* (dissertation) by Yosi Gamzu, University of Texas, 1976; ''The Last of the Purim Players: Itzik Manger'' by David G. Roskies, in *Prooftexts,* 13(3), September, 1993, pp. 211–35; *Tradition and Innovation in the Ballads of Itsik Manger* (dissertation) by Helen Beer, Oxford University, 1998.

* * *

Considered one of the most prolific Yiddish poets, Itzik Manger was born in 1901 in Chernovitsy, Romania (now Chernivtsi, Ukraine). In 1921 Manger published his first poem, ''Ballad of a Streetwalker.'' In the 1930s he wrote the lyrics for the Warsaw musical production of Sholem Aleichem's novel *Wandering Stars* as well as the lyrics for the first Yiddish film musical, *Yiddle with His Fiddle,* which starred Molly Picon. His popularity as a poet brought him the opportunity to write for several Yiddish theater productions in Warsaw in the 1930s. Manger's best-known series of poems for the theater, ''Songs from the Book of Esther,'' was staged 30 years later on Broadway as *The Megillah of Itzik Manger.* His biblical poetry also served as the basis for the hit musical *Songs of Paradise* produced by Joseph Papp at the New York Shakespeare Festival. His biggest success was with Nathan Alterman's Hebrew version of Samuel Gronemann's *The King and the Cobbler* in the 1960s.

Yiddish literature, deprived of its audience and its practitioners by the forces of history, lives largely in the works of writers such as Manger. His work combines a cosmopolitan sophistication with an equally strong sense of folk identity. Literary craftsmanship meant seeing traditional stories as relics; the process involved rediscovering and then refashioning them. In their re-creations they endure as original folk tales. Manger's career was profoundly shaped by the Holocaust. He chose to write in the ballad form, looking to such characters as wedding jesters for inspiration and charmingly retelling the Bible as ''a Yiddish folk epic to outlast the living folk, the living language, the living landscape.'' His biblical dramas were written in both Hebrew and Yiddish.

During World War II the racial laws in Romania caused Yiddish theater to cease functioning. Nonetheless, a number of Jewish actors who had been deported to Transnistria organized evenings of Yiddish theater in the lagers of Vapniarka, Jmerinka, and Moghilev. Simultaneously in Bucharest, Jewish actors organized in synagogues from 1940 until 1944, under the pretext of holding commemorations. These events allowed them to produce dramas and festivals devoted to Jewish writers; they staged fragments of plays and gave poetry readings. Although the audiences did not dare to applaud, they shouted the toast *L'chaim* at the end of each number. During the years of the ruthless Iron Guard and fascist terror, under the nose of the political police, the lofty human ideas of the classics of Yiddish literature were spread—in Romanian. Jewish theater was not allowed until after the war.

Before World War II there had been five Yiddish theaters in Romania—two in Bucharest, two in Chernovitsy, and one in Yassy. In 1948 the first state theaters were set up, among which was the Jewish State Theatre of Bucharest. Performances were again in Yiddish. Under the Communist regime (1948–89) the repertoires were heavily censored. In 1972 the Jewish State Theatre of Bucharest toured the United States and Canada with great success.

Manger's place in the cultural history of the Jews was recognized by Golda Meir in 1969 when she established the first annual Manger Prize for Yiddish Literature. His writing, which spanned poetry, essays, cultural history, rabbinic writings, politics, and fiction, occupies a central place in Jewish literary identity. His work is included in the *Unesco Anthology of World Poetry, The Treasure of Yiddish Stories,* and *The Treasure of Yiddish Poetry.*

—Martha Sutro

See the essay on ''My Hate Song.''

MEED, Vladka

Nationality: American (originally Polish: immigrated to the United States, 1946). **Born:** Fajga Peltel, Warsaw, 1923.

Family: Married Benjamin Meed. **Career:** Member, Zydowska Organazcja Bojowa (Jewish Fighting Organization), during World War II. Director, weekly radio program, Jewish Labor Committee Yiddish Culture Department; chairman, culture committee of the American Gathering of Jewish Holocaust Survivors; vice president, Jewish Labor Committee. Since 1984 founder and executive director, teachers' training program on Holocaust and Jewish resistance. Contributor to *Forverts* magazine, ca. 1946. **Awards:** Warsaw Ghetto Resistance Organization award, 1973; Morim award of the Jewish Teachers' Association, 1989; Hadassah Henrietta Szold award and Elie Wiesel Remembrance award, both in 1993. D.H.L.: Hebrew Union College, New York, 1998.

PUBLICATION

Memoir

Fun beyde zaytn geto-moyer. 1948; as *On Both Sides of the Wall,* 1971.

*   *   *

Vladka Meed, author of *On Both Sides of the Wall,* was born Fajga Peltel, the oldest of three children of Hanna and Shlomo Peltel. She was the only member of the family to have survived the Holocaust. She was 17 when the German army entered Warsaw and was a member of the Jewish underground resistance from the first days of the occupation. She took the name Vladka when she was smuggled into the "Aryan" side of Warsaw under the name Wladyslawa Kowalska, a false identity obtained from an old Polish passport.

Activism was central to the girl's life from a very early age. Her father, a salesman, was a member of the Jewish Labor Bund, a mass organization in czarist Russia and interwar Poland that sought to transform the lives of the Jewish working poor through socialist organizing and secular Yiddish culture. The bund played a key role in the resistance; many members of the Zydowska Organazcja Bojowa (Jewish Fighting Organization) were from its ranks. She attended the primary school of the Jewish Labor Bund starting at the age of six. Although her family spoke Yiddish in their home, the girl spoke fluent Polish, which she learned in the bundist school. Her command of Polish was a key factor in her survival and her ability to "pass" on the Aryan side.

Vladka married Benjamin Meed, born Miedzyrzecki, who was one of four children of an observant Jewish family. He had been her closest friend on the Aryan side and was also active in the resistance. They married in Warsaw after the Red Army had entered the city. The Meeds arrived in New York City in May 1946, and shortly after their arrival she conducted a speaking tour sponsored by the bund. She also began writing for the Yiddish-language publication *Forverts.* She published 27 articles about her experience in the ghetto at a time,

according to Meed, when "people did not want to know about the Holocaust." *Forverts* and the Workmen's Circle, a Jewish fraternal organization that many survivors joined upon arriving in the United States, encouraged Meed to write a book based on her series of articles in *Forverts.*

Meed's book was published first in Yiddish in 1948 by the Workmen's Circle. In the introduction **Elie Wiesel** describes it as "the first authentic document to reach the free world about the uprising and the destruction of the Warsaw ghetto, or about the Holocaust in general." The book was translated first into Hebrew and then into Spanish. It was published in English translation in 1971 under the title *On Both Sides of the Wall.* Before her arrival in the United States, Meed had never thought of herself as a writer, nor had it ever occurred to her while she was in the ghetto that she would write her memoirs. She has explained simply, "It wasn't a time for writing."

Meed and her husband have been active in Holocaust education and in advocating for survivors. She has served as vice president of the Jewish Labor Committee and has held the culture chair of the American Gathering of Holocaust Survivors. In 1981 the American Gathering of Holocaust Survivors established a national registry to help survivors search for relatives and friends. This registry, now located in the U.S. Holocaust Memorial Museum, is named in honor of Benjamin and Vladka Meed. She has also received an honorary degree from the Hebrew Union College-Jewish Institute of Religion in New York for her unique contribution to human understanding and her ethical beliefs. She was the creator of and has headed the Holocaust and Jewish Resistance Teacher Training Program.

—Margie Newman

See the essay on *On Both Sides of the Wall.*

MEGGED, Aharon

Nationality: Israeli. **Born:** Wloclawcek, Poland, 10 August 1920. **Education:** Attended high school in Palestine (now Israel), 1933–37. **Family:** Married Eda Zirlin in 1944; two sons. **Career:** Member of a kibbutz in Sdot-Yam, Israel, 1938–50; cultural attache, Israeli Embassy, London, 1968–71. Since 1971 columnist, *Davar* newspaper, Tel-Aviv. Writer-in-residence, Haifa University and Oxford University. Editor, *Massa* newspaper, Tel-Aviv, 1952–55; literary editor, *Lamerchav* newspaper, Tel-Aviv, 1955–68. **Awards:** Ussishkin prize, 1955, for *Hedva and I*, and 1966, for *Living on the Dead*; Brenner prize, 1957, for *Israel Haverim*; Shlonsky prize, 1963, for *ha-Brikha*; Bialik prize, 1973, for *Makhbarot Evyatar* and *Al Etzim ve-avanim*; Fichman prize, 1973, for *Asahel.* **Member:** Academy of Hebrew Language, 1980; National Arts

Council; Israeli Writer's Association. **Agent:** Gloria Stern Literary Agency, 1230 Park Avenue, New York, New York 10028, U.S.A. **Address:** Office: c/o *Davar,* Shenkin, Tel-Aviv, Israel.

PUBLICATIONS

Novels

Harkhek ha-arava [Far in the Wasteland]. 1951.
Yad va-Shem [The Name]. 1955.
Mikreh ha-kssil. 1960; as *Fortunes of a Fool,* 1962.
Ha-brikha [The Escape] (novellas). 1962.
Ha-hai' al ha-met. 1965; as *The Living on the Dead,* 1970.
Ha-Khayim ha-Ktzarim. 1971; as *The Short Life,* 1980.
Makhbarot Evyatar [Evyatar's Notebooks]. 1973.
Al etzim ve-avanim [Of Trees and Stones]. 1973.
Ha-ataleph [The Bat]. 1975.
Heinz u'vno ve harnack ha'raah [Heinz, His Son and the Evil Spirit]. 1976.
Masah be-Av [Journey in the Month of Av]. 1980.
The First Sin. 1982.
Asahel. 1982.
Ha-gamal ha-meofef ve-dabeshet ha-zahav [The Flying Camel and the Golden Hump]. 1982.
Ma-aseh meguneh [Indecent Act] (novellas). 1986.
Foiglman. 1988.
Yom ha-or shel Anat [Anat's Day of Illumination]. 1992.
Ga'aguim le-Olga [Longing for Olga]. 1994.
Avel [Iniquity]. 1996.
Duda'im min ha'Aretz ha-Kedoshah [Mandrakes from the Holy Land]. 1998.

Short Stories

Ru'akh yamin [Spirit of the Seas]. 1950.
Israel haverim [Israeli Folk]. 1955.
Ha-yom ha-sheni [The Second Day]. 1967.
Khatzot ha-yom [Midday]. 1973.
Mivhar sipurim [Selected Stories]. 1989.

Plays

Incubator on the Rocks (produced Tel-Aviv, 1950).
Hannah Senesh (produced Tel-Aviv, 1952). 1958.
Hedvah ve-ani (produced Tel-Aviv, 1955). 1954; as *Hedva and I: A Play in Two Acts,* 1957.
Ba-derech le-Eilat [On the Road to Eilat] (produced Tel-Aviv, 1955).
I Like Mike (produced Tel-Aviv, 1960).
Tit for Tat (produced Tel-Aviv, 1960).
Be-reshit [Genesis] (produced Tel-Aviv, 1965). 1989.
Ha-ona ha-boeret [The Burning Season]. 1967.

Ha-onah ha-boeret [The High Season] (produced Tel-Aviv, 1968). 1968.

Other

Masah ha-yeladim la-Aretz ha-Muvtahat [The Children's Journey to the Promised Land]. 1984.
Ezor ha-ra'ash [The Turbulent Zone] (essays). 1985.
Shulhan ha-ketivah [The Writing Desk] (essays). 1989.

Other (for children)

El ha-yeladim be-Teiman [To the Children in Yemen]. 1946.
Ahavat neurim [Young Love]. 1980.
Nadav ve-imo [Nadav and His Mother]. 1988.

*

Critical Studies: "Arabs and Other Problems—A Conversation with Aharon Megged" by Paul Giniewski, in *Midstream,* 45(3), 1 April 1999, p. 29; "Patterns of Failed Return in Aharon Megged's Work: Revisiting the Jewish-Christian Nexus" by Stanley Nash, in *Modern Judaism,* 19(3), 1999, pp. 277–92.

* * *

Aharon Megged is often characterized as representative of the Palmach generation of the late 1940s and early '50s in Israel, for whom sabras were heroic and without blemish. He has frequently written in a realistic style about heroes of one kind or another, but his later works are much more critical of the stereotype of the Israeli as the pioneer and of the Zionist project as a whole. The contrast between kibbutz idealism and the materialism of the city is a frequent theme throughout his work, and in his later books he problematizes life in Israel far more thoroughly. Over the years Megged has become more critical and satirical, and he has used relationships between people as a literary device to represent society as a whole. A particular issue with which he likes to deal is the conflict between the generations in Israel, in particular as this reflects their differing attitudes to life in the Diaspora and to the Holocaust. In "Yad va-Shem" (1955; "The Name") the young couple Yehuda and Raya wish to give their newborn a thoroughly Israeli and sabra name, while Grandfather Zisskind wishes to call the child Mendele to commemorate the grandchild murdered by the Nazis. He wants to commemorate the link between the family and its Jewish past in Europe, while the parents reject this in favor of an entirely new name that represents a break with the past. Megged implies that this decision is both mean-spirited and shallow as well as historically false. In a significant passage Raya cries for the child as though he were entirely alone, an orphan, an indication of the essential impossibility of a complete break from one's past.

One of the most interesting of Megged's works is one that does not mention the Holocaust but which in fact is highly relevant to it. *The Living on the Dead* (1970; *Ha-hai 'al ha-met*) is about a modern Israeli (of the 1960s) relating to the earlier heroic past of the pioneering generation that constructed the country and defeated its many enemies. The main character in the book is an author who is commissioned to write about one of the main heroes of the past but cannot complete the project. The author increasingly feels that the past is suffocating him, interfering with his ability to determine how his life should be. The work raises the question of whether it is possible for Israeli culture to establish a new and individual voice given the omnipresence of the drama and tragedy of the recent historical past. It also emerges that the hero has done a number of things that cannot be admired and that have been ignored. The implications are obvious—the Holocaust was such a momentous past event that it can smother later generations and the attempt to depict it aesthetically and historically should be regarded as potentially dangerous and only undertaken with considerable caution. In addition, when one looks closely at the past all sorts of unpleasant features emerge, and there is no reason to think that Jewish protagonists in the Holocaust would always be revealed to have acted well. The play *The Burning Season* (1967; *Ha-ona ha-boeret*) also represents most of the Jews in Europe during the Holocaust as passive. A more nuanced account is provided in *The Children's Journey to the Promised Land* (1984; *Masa ha-yeladim la-Aretz ha-Muvtahat*), which describes the journey of 800 Jewish children to Israel from Italy, their rehabilitation, and the support of the Italian people. The role of three Jewish soldiers is described in detail.

Megged is a prolific author, and it is not surprising that his output contains not just one view of the past, particularly in regard to the Holocaust. In some ways his varying attitudes to the Holocaust represent well the range of views which exist in Israeli literature.

—Oliver Leaman

See the essay on *Hannah Senesh*.

MEMMI, Albert

Nationality: Tunisian. **Born:** Tunis, 15 December 1920. **Education:** University of Algiers, license in philosophy 1943; Sorbonne, University of Paris, D.Litt. 1970. **Family:** Married Germaine Dubach; two sons and one daughter. **Career:** High school teacher of philosophy, Tunis, 1953–56; director, Center of Educational Research, Tunis, 1953–57; researcher, National Center of Scientific Research, Paris, 1958–60; assistant professor, 1959–66, and professor of social psychology, 1966–70, Sorbonne, University of Paris. Since 1970 professor of sociology, University of Paris, Nanterre. Conference director, 1958, and director of department of social sciences, 1975–78, School of Higher Studies in Social Sciences; Walker Ames Professor,

University of Seattle, 1972. Contributor, *L'Action* newspaper, Tunis, 1950s. **Awards:** Prix Carthage (Tunis), 1953; Prix Feneon (Paris), 1954; Prix Simba (Rome). Commander of Ordre de Nichan Iftikhar (Tunisia); Chevalier de la Legion d'Honneur; Officier of Tunisian Republic; Officier des Arts et des Lettres; Officier des Palmes Academiques. **Member:** Société des Gens de Lettres; Academie des Sciences d'Outremer. **Address:** Office: University of Paris, 92 Nanterre, France.

PUBLICATIONS

Novels

Le Statue du sel. 1953; as *Pillar of Salt,* 1955.
Agar. 1955; as *Strangers,* 1958.
Le Scorpion ou la confession imaginaire. 1969; as *The Scorpion or the Imaginary Confession,* 1971.
Le Desert: Ou, la vie et les aventures de Jubair Ouali El-Mammi. 1977.
Le Pharaoh. 1988.

Poetry

Le Mirliton du ciel. 1989.

Other

Portrait du colonisé [Portrait of the Colonizer].1956.
Portrait du colonisateur [Portrait of the Colonized]. 1957.
Portrait d'un Juif. 1962; as *Portrait of a Jew,* 1962.
La Libération d'un Juif. 1962; as *The Liberation of a Jew,* 1966.
La Poésie algérienne de 1830 a nos jours: approches socio-historiques. 1963.
Les Francais et la racisme, with Paul Hassan Maucorps. 1965.
Ecole pratique des hautes études. 1965.
L'Homme dominé (essays). 1968; as *Dominated Man: Notes towards a Portrait,* 1968.
Juifs et Arabes. 1974; as *Jews and Arabs,* 1975.
Albert Memmi: Un entretien avec Robert Davies suivi d'itineraire de l'expérience vecue a la théorie de la domination. 1975.
La Terre interieure entretiens avec Victor Malka. 1976.
La Dependance: Esquisse pour un portrait du dépendant. 1979; as *Dependence,* 1983.
La Racisme. 1982.
L'Ecriture colorée. 1986.

Editor, *Anthologie des ecrivains maghrebins d'expression francaise* (2 vols.). 1964; revised edition, 1965.

*

Critical Studies: ''Works in Progress/Albert Memmi'' by Harold Flender, in *Intellectual Digest,* 3(4), December 1972, pp. 6–14; "Du scorpion au Désert: Albert Memmi Revisited" by Isaac Yetiv, in *Studies in Twentieth Century Literature,* 7(1), 1982, pp. 77–87; *Albert Memmi* by Judith Roumani, 1987; *Albert Cohen, Albert Memmi, and Elie Wiesel and the Dilemma of Jewish Identity in French Literature and Culture* (dissertation) by Hélène Golencer Schroeter, University of Utah, 1989; "Albert Memmi and Alain Finkielkraut: Two Discourses on French Jewish Identity" by Judith Morganroth-Schneider, in *Romanic Review,* 81(1), January 1990; "Irreconcilable Differences" by Gary Wilder, in *Transition,* 71, 1996; "Oppression, Liberation, and Narcissism: A Jungian Psychopolitical Analysis of the Ideas of Albert Memmi" by Lawrence R. Alschuler, in *Alternatives,* 21(4), 1996.

* * *

Albert Memmi was born in 1920 in the Jewish ghetto of Tunis, the son of a poor saddler-cum-leather worker. A gifted student, he received grants and awards that allowed him, first, to go to the Lycée Carnot and, later, to study philosophy at the University of Algiers. In 1943 he was deported to a labor camp, but he escaped and after the war completed his studies in philosophy at the Sorbonne in Paris. In the early 1950s he returned to Tunisia, where he wrote the literary page for *L'Action,* the first Tunisian daily, and became the director of the Center for Child Psychology. In 1956 Tunisia became a Muslim state, and 95 percent of the Jewish population left, including Memmi. Back in Paris, he published two major texts, written in 1956 and 1957, that brought him to the attention of the world: *Portrait du colonisé* (*Portrait of the Colonized*) and *Portrait du colonisateur* (*Portrait of the Colonizer*). Together they are a methodical survey of the always corrupting relationship between the colonized and the colonizer. These were followed in 1962 by *Portrait d'un Juif* and in 1973 by *L'Homme dominé* (*Dominated Man*), which bears the clarifying subtitle *The Black, the Colonized, the Jew, the Proletariat, the Woman, the Servant, and Racism.* These texts became the starting and reference point for a reflection on colonization so deeply needed during the many political movements of decolonization in the 1960s and 1970s. In Paris, Memmi became professor of social psychiatry at the École Pratique des Hautes Études and director of the collection Domaine Maghrébin for the publisher Maspero.

Memmi published extensively as a novelist (*Pillar of Salt, Agar, The Scorpio, The Desert, The Pharaoh*), as a social and political analyst, and as a thinker. Taking the example of his own experience, so delicately described in *Pillar of Salt,* he describes how colonization is not simply a political state but also an internalized means of seeing and living the social experience. He was the first to recognize and denounce racial and ethnic policies in the terms of the political and sociological views of the second half of the twentieth century. He did this by analyzing the life experiences of those imposing and those suffering racism. His psychosociological views made the experience of racism vivid to a Western world often at a loss to understand the painful reality of its "civilizing mission" in the Third World.

Memmi experienced all of the forms of rejection and racism, individual and social, about which he wrote. A Jew raised in an Arab environment, he embraced classical French and Western culture only to be betrayed by the French political system. Poor, he was seen as an outcast by bourgeois Jews and Christians. Living the experience of the colonized, he came to understand the plight of oppressed nations. His education built an unbreakable wall between himself and his family, and his humanism built a wall between himself and other Jews. All of these experiences of rejection give his literary and scientific texts a unique depth.

Memmi's books were an attempt to understand his own life. As he said, "In the novel, I describe my life; in the essays, I try to understand it." Thus, his works are to be taken as a totality, each text mirroring another. His existence and his books were marked by a search for identity and self-justification. His constant return to his origins rooted him deeply in the context of the Maghreb and in Judaism, while never explaining his experience totally. Indeed, he transcended his own experience and projected a universal perspective on the cruel exploitation of the minority and the weak. He succeeded at transforming his own specific and local experience into a blueprint for universal understanding.

Deeply humanist, Memmi affirmed his position as a Jew without religious belief or practice. He found in his respect for the other, including believers, the ultimate sign of tolerance, although it is seldom returned by believers.

—Alain Goldschlager

See the essay on *Pillar of Salt.*

MENASSE, Robert

Nationality: Austrian. **Born:** Vienna, 21 June 1954. **Education:** Studied literature, philosophy, and political science at universities in Vienna, Salzburg, and Messina, Ph.D. 1980. **Career:** Cofounder, *Zentralorgan herumstreunender Germanisten* (student magazine), 1979; guest assistant, Institute for Literary Theory, University of São Paulo, 1981–88. Since 1988 freelance writer. Writer-in-residence, Amsterdam, 1999. **Awards:** City of Vienna prize for literature, 1989; Heimito-von-Doderer prize of the Niederösterreichischen Society for Art and Culture, 1990; Hans Erich Nossack prize and Theodor-Körner-Stiftungsfonds prize for literature, both in 1992; Elias-Canetti scholarship, 1992–93; German Academic Exchange Service scholarship for study in Berlin, City of Marburg literary award, Alexander Sacher Masoch literary award, and Federal Ministry of Instruction and Art prize, all in 1994; City of Pirmasens Hugo Ball prize, 1996; Austrian state prize for Kulturpublizistik, 1998; Johann Jacob Christoph von Grimmelshausen prize, 1999.

PUBLICATIONS

Novels

Trilogie der Entgeisterung [Trilogy of the Breakdown of Spirit]:
   Sinnliche Gewissheit [Sense Certainty]. 1988.
   Selige Zeiten, brüchige Welt. 1991; as *Wings of Stone,* 2000.
   Schubumkehr [Reverse Thrust]. 1995.
Die Vertreibung aus der Hölle [Expulsion from Hell]. 2001.

Other

Die sozialpartnerschaftliche Ästhetik: Essays zum österreichischen Geist [The Aesthetics of Social Partnership]. 1990.
Das Land ohne Eigenschaften: Essay zur österreichischen Identität [The Land without Qualities] 1992.
Phänomenologie der Entgeisterung: Geschichte des verschwindenden Wissens (philosophy). 1995.
Hysterien und andere historische Irrtümer. 1996.
Überbau und Underground: Die sozialpartnerschaftliche Ästhetik : Essays zum österreichischen Geist. 1997.
Die letzte Märchenprinzessin, with Elisabeth and Eva Menasse (for children). 1997.
Der mächtigste Mann, with Elisabeth and Eva Menasse (caricature of President Bill Clinton). 1998.
Dummheit ist machbar: Begleitende Essays zum Stillstand der Republik. 1999.
Erklär mir Österreich: Essays zur österreichischen Geschichte [Explain Austria to Me]. 2000.

Translator, *Das Fest,* by Ivan Angelo. 1992.

*

Critical Studies: "The Fragmentation of Totality in Robert Menasse's *Selige Zeiten, brüchige Welt*" by Peter Arnds, and "Of Inclusions and Exclusions: Austrian Identity Reconsidered" by Renate S. Posthofen, both in *Transforming the Center, Eroding the Margins: Essays on Ethnic and Cultural Boundaries in German-Speaking Countries,* edited by Posthofen and Dagmar C.G. Lorenz, 1998; "On Despotic Mothers and Dethroned Patriarchs: Barbara Frischmuth's *Über die Verhältnisse* and Robert Menasse's *Selige Zeiten, brüchige Welt*" by Peter Arnds, in *Barbara Frischmuth in Contemporary Context,* edited by Renate S. Posthofen, 1999; "Robert Menasse's Concept of Anti-Heimat Literature" by Michael P.

Olson, in *Austria in Literature,* edited by Donald G. Daviau, 2000.

*   *   *

Born in Vienna in 1954, Robert Menasse belongs to the generation of Jewish writers whose parents fled Austria and Germany during the Nazi period and then returned in the late 1940s and '50s to resume their interrupted lives. Like many of this "second generation" of German and Austrian Jewish writers (**Robert Schindel,** Barbara Honigmann, Maxim Biller), Menasse has not written about the events of the Holocaust directly but rather addressed their residues in postwar and contemporary Austrian politics and culture. Unlike Schindel, however, for whom the Holocaust operates as a tangible point of reference for the contemporary relationships between Jewish and non-Jewish Austrians, Menasse investigates Nazi persecution only from the periphery, from the perspective of forced exile, and even this experience remains an often indirect and implicit theme in his fictional work. Indeed, his work rarely directly refers to the events in Europe between 1933 and 1945, and thus the Holocaust as a catastrophic event functions as an elusive force that informs his writing above all through its absence.

Menasse's oeuvre consists of novels, essays, and philosophical writings. In several volumes of essays published during the 1990s—*Die sozialpartnerschaftliche Ästhetik* (1990; "The Aesthetics of Social Partnership"), *Das Land ohne Eigenschaften* (1992; "The Land without Qualities"), and *Erklär mir Österreich* (2000; "Explain Austria to Me")—he investigates the literature and the political discourse of Austria's Second Republic, revealing an Austrian cultural identity founded simultaneously on the repression of its involvement in the Nazi persecution of the European Jews and on an obsession with fantasies of its own victimization under "foreign" occupation by the National Socialists. According to Menasse, Austrian society is caught in a schizophrenic holding pattern of "either-or," oscillating between the periodic acknowledgement of its role as perpetrator and the retreat into the attitude of victim.

Menasse is perhaps best known for his novelistic work, which includes *Trilogie der Entgeisterung* ("Trilogy of the Breakdown of Spirit," referring to G.W.F. Hegel's *Phenomenology of Spirit*), published between 1988 and 1995, and *Die Vertreibung aus der Hölle* (2001; "Expulsion from Hell"). The novels of the trilogy, *Sinnliche Gewissheit* (1988; "Sense Certainty"), *Selige Zeiten, brüchige Welt* (1991; *Wings of Stone,* 2000), and *Schubumkehr* (1995; "Reverse Thrust"), center on the lives of three characters among whom the narrative perspective alternates. The protagonist of the first and third novels is the Austrian expatriate Roman Gilanian, who meets the Austrian-Jewish characters Leo Singer and Judith Katz in a bar in São Paulo. The second novel of the series explores Leo and Judith's stories from the beginning of their relationship in Vienna until Judith's death in São Paulo 18 years later.

A major leitmotiv in *Trilogie der Entgeisterung* is the notion of homelessness and exile; for Leo and Judith, the children of Jewish refugees who fled to Brazil in the late 1930s and, in the case of Leo's parents, who eventually returned to Austria, home cannot be found in Austria or Brazil. Alienated from Austria by both their Jewishness and the legacy of Austrian persecution in their families and seen as foreigners by the Brazilian natives, both characters are caught in a no-man's land between cultures and identities. In the third novel, which critics have described as an *anti-Heimatroman* (a critique of the Austrian/German genre of "homeland literature"), Roman returns in 1989 to an unknown and unrecognizable Austria caught between its repressed fascist past and the beginning of the "end" of history with the fall of the Iron Curtain. All three characters vacillate between the two geographical poles of their experience, searching but never finding a center point at which they would be able to ground their identities.

In addition to highlighting the problems of disconnected Jewish identity after 1945, Menasse's novels participate in a larger discourse on fascism and the Holocaust by making implicit comparisons between the Nazi period and other totalitarian regimes. In the trilogy readers can recognize the similarities between the Nazi rise to power in Germany and the Brazilian military coup of 1964; Judith witnesses the sudden disappearance of opponents after the coup, and Leo is banned from teaching at Brazilian universities after the student riots of 1968. *Die Vertreibung aus der Hölle* presents two stories of persecution and expulsion, separated by several centuries. Juxtaposed with the story of Manoel, a Jew threatened by the Inquisition in seventeenth-century Portugal, is that of Victor, whose father was forced to flee his native Austria after the *Anschluss* (the annexation of Austria by Germany in 1938). In this novel, as with all of Menasse's work, the protagonists do not themselves experience the sites of suffering, neither in the Inquisition nor in the Holocaust. By avoiding reference to the particular moment of violent persecution, however, Menasse is able to draw parallels between the modi operandi of oppressive regimes and at the same time to insist on the uniqueness of the individual experience.

—Erin McGlothlin

See the essay on *Wings of Stone*.

MILLER, Arthur

Nationality: American. **Born:** New York, 17 October 1915. **Education:** University of Michigan, A.B. 1938. **Family:** Married 1) Mary Grace Slattery in 1940 (divorced 1956), one daughter and one son; 2) Marilyn Monroe in 1956 (divorced 1961); 3) Ingeborg Morath in 1962, one daughter and one son. **Career:** Since 1938 writer, and since 1944 dramatist and essayist. Associate, Federal Theater Project, 1938; writer of radio plays, 1939–44. Contributor to periodicals, including *Esquire, Atlantic, New York Times,* and *Theatre Arts.* Also worked in an automobile parts warehouse, at the Brooklyn Naval Yard, and in a box factory. Resident lecturer, University of Michigan, 1973–74. **Awards:** Avery Hopwood awards, University of Michigan, 1936, for *Honors at Dawn,* and 1937, for *No Villain: They Too Arise;* Bureau of New Plays prize, Theatre Guild of New York, 1938; Theatre Guild National prize, 1944, for *The Man Who Had All the Luck;* Drama Critics Circle awards, 1947, for *All My Sons,* and 1949, for *Death of a Salesman;* Antoinette Perry awards, 1947, for *All My Sons,* 1949, for *Death of a Salesman,* and 1953, for *The Crucible;* Donaldson awards, 1947, for *All My Sons,* 1949, for *Death of a Salesman,* and 1953, for *The Crucible;* Pulitzer prize for drama, 1949, for *Death of a Salesman;* National Association of Independent Schools award, 1954; Obie award, *Village Voice,* 1958, for *The Crucible;* American Academy of Arts and Letters gold medal, 1959; Anglo-American award, 1966; Emmy award, National Academy of Television Arts and Sciences, 1967, for *Death of a Salesman;* Brandeis University creative arts award, 1969; George Foster Peabody award, 1981, for *Playing for Time;* John F. Kennedy award for lifetime achievement, 1984; Algur Meadows award, 1991; medal for Distinguished Contribution to American Letters, National Book Foundation, 2001. L.H.D.: University of Michigan, 1956, and Carnegie-Mellon University, 1970. **Member:** Dramatists' Guild; Authors League of America; National Institute of Arts and Letters. **Agent:** c/o International Creative Management, 40 West 57th Street, New York, New York 10019, U.S.A.

PUBLICATIONS

Collections

Arthur Miller's Collected Plays (includes *All My Sons*; *Death of a Salesman*; *The Crucible*; *A Memory of Two Mondays*; *A View from the Bridge*). 1957.
The Portable Arthur Miller, edited by Harold Clurman (includes *Death of a Salesman*; *The Crucible*; *Incident at Vichy*; *The Price*; *The Misfits*; *Fame*; *In Russia*). 1971.
Collected Plays. 1980.
The Portable Arthur Miller, edited by C. Bigsby. 1995.

Plays

Honors at Dawn (produced Ann Arbor, Michigan, 1936).
No Villian: They Too Arise (produced Ann Arbor, Michigan, 1937).
The Man Who Had All the Luck (produced New York, 1944).
All My Sons (produced New York, 1947). 1947.

Death of a Salesman (produced New York, 1949). 1949; as *Death of a Salesman: Text and Criticism,* 1977.

An Enemy of the People, adaptation of the novel by Henrik Ibsen (produced New York, 1950). 1951.

The Crucible (produced New York, 1953). 1953; as *The Crucible: Text and Criticism,* 1977; as *The Crucible: A Play in Four Acts,* 1995.

A View from the Bridge (produced with *A Memory of Two Mondays,* New York, 1955), with *A Memory of Two Mondays.* 1955; published separately, 1956; revised version (produced New York, 1965), 1956.

A Memory of Two Mondays (produced with *A View from the Bridge,* New York, 1955), with *A View from the Bridge.* 1955; published separately, 1956.

After the Fall (produced New York, 1964). 1964.

Incident at Vichy (produced New York, 1964). 1965.

The Price (produced New York, 1968). 1968.

The Creation of the World and Other Business (produced New York, 1972). 1972.

Up from Paradise, musical version of *The Creation of the World and Other Business,* music by Stanley Silverman (produced Ann Arbor, Michigan, 1974; New York, 1983). 1978.

The Archbishop's Ceiling (produced Washington, D.C., 1977). 1976.

The American Clock (produced Charleston, South Carolina, 1980; New York, 1980). 1980.

The Misfits: An Original Screenplay Directed by John Huston. 1982.

Elegy for a Lady [and] *Some Kind of Love Story* (produced as *Two-Way Mirror,* New Haven, Connecticut, 1983). Published separately, 1984.

Playing for Time, stage adaption of his screenplay (produced England, 1986). 1985.

Danger: Memory! Two Plays: "I Can't Remember Anything" and "Clara" (produced New York, 1987). 1987.

The Golden Years. 1990.

The Last Yankee. 1991.

The Ride Down Mt. Morgan. 1992.

Broken Glass. 1994.

The Crucible: Screenplay. 1996.

Screenplays: *The Story of G.I. Joe,* with others, 1945; *The Crucible,* 1958; *The Misfits,* 1960; *The Price,* 1969; *The Hook,* 1975; *Playing for Time,* 1980; *Everybody Wins,* 1990.

Television Play: *Fame,* 1978.

Novels

Focus. 1945.

The Misfits (novella). 1961; with additional selections as *"The Misfits" and Other Stories,* 1987.

Jane's Blanket (for children). 1963.

Homely Girl, A Life. 1992; as *Plain Girl: A Life,* 1995.

Short Stories

I Don't Need You Anymore. 1967.
"The Misfits" and Other Stories. 1987.

Other

Situation Normal (reportage on the army). 1944.
In Russia, with photographs by Inge Morath. 1969.
In the Country, with photographs by Morath. 1977.
The Theatre Essays of Arthur Miller, edited by Robert A. Martin. 1978; revised edition, 1996.
Chinese Encounters, with photographs by Morath. 1979.
Salesman in Beijing, with photographs by Morath. 1984.
Timebends: A Life (autobiography). 1987.
Inge Morath: Portraits, with others. 1999.
Mr. Peters' Connections. 1999.
Echoes Down the Corridor: Collected Essays, 1947–1999, edited by S. Centola. 2000.

*

Film Adaptations: *All My Sons,* 1948, 1987; *Death of a Salesman,* 1951, 1985; *The Crucible* (also known as *The Witches of Salem*), 1958, 1996; *A View from the Bridge,* 1962; *The Price,* 1969; *After the Fall,* 1969; *Playing for Time,* 1980; *Focus,* 2001.

Critical Studies: *Arthur Miller: Dramatist* by Edward Murray, 1967; *Arthur Miller: A Collection of Critical Essays,* edited by Robert W. Corrigan, 1969; *Psychology and Arthur Miller* by Richard Evans, 1969; *Arthur Miller: Portrait of a Playwright* by Benjamin Nelson, 1970; *Arthur Miller* by S. K. Bhatia, 1985; *Conversations with Arthur Miller,* edited by Matthew Charles Roudane, 1987; *Arthur Miller's Death of a Salesman"* and *Arthur Miller's "The Crucible,"* both by Harold Bloom, both 1996; *Arthur Miller* by Neil Carson, 1982; *Arthur Miller in Conversation* by Steve Centola, 1993; *The Achievement of Arthur Miller: New Essays,* edited by Steve Centola, 1995; *Understanding Arthur Miller* by Alice Griffin, 1996.

* * *

Arthur Miller, the dean of American playwrights, was born 17 October 1915 in New York City. He grew up in Harlem and Brooklyn, a product of the Great Depression in America and of World War II, and was hailed as one of the century's greatest playwrights when *Death of a Salesman* triumphantly premiered on Broadway in 1949. Miller critically and artistically has from the beginning of his career been linked to the works of Henrik Ibsen. Like Ibsen, Miller has long been obsessed with the notion of individual and collective guilt, of the relationship of the individual to society, and of the necessity of moral action, even at the cost of one's physical destruction.

While all his plays question public and private guilt and innocence, Miller only directly addresses the Holocaust in four works, from his middle and late periods. In the earliest of these, his autobiographical play *After the Fall,* the watchtower of a concentration camp hovers over the entire action of the play, a looming shadow over the life and consciousness of the protagonist Quentin that cannot be dismissed. Following such earlier plays as *All My Sons, Death of a Salesman,* and *The Crucible,* where people were asked, ordered, pressured, and even threatened by their community's social structures to deny, repudiate, or corrupt their individual identities and their moral sense, this looming shadow metaphorically creates an even greater resonance, especially as Miller has frequently been critically attacked for seeming to forsake his Jewish identity in his earlier plays.

Incident at Vichy, re-creating the southern French community that shamefully rounded up its Jewish population in willful collaboration with its German occupiers, presents a panoply of Jewish characters robbed of any agency or voice, desperately seeking any answers or repudiation of the inescapable yet unbelievable horrors that await them. *Playing for Time,* a critically acclaimed television adaptation of the memoirs of survivor **Fania Fenelon,** plunges the viewer into the physical and moral abyss of the camps. Here Miller acknowledges that survival was accomplished less by one's character than by chance and that, without a voice or an ability to affect an action, the moral obligation comes from the act of remembering the past. His last Holocaust play, *Broken Glass,* though generally well received, is a less successful and frankly problematic play about a middle-aged Jewish-American woman's obsession in 1938 with the virulent anti-Semitism sweeping Germany, an obsession that culminates in her becoming physically paralyzed by the news. As in such early plays as *Death of a Salesman* and *The Crucible,* here the issue surrounds the denial of identity, specifically that of her husband's Jewishness as a successful executive in a WASP Wall Street firm. Here the obviousness of Sylvia's symbolic paralysis detracts from rather than illuminates the drama Miller has constructed as Sylvia ultimately overcomes her paralysis as her husband approaches his own death. Yet seriously flawed as *Broken Glass* may be, Miller's consistent and passionate advocacy for the individual's need and responsibility to connect and to remain connected to the world remains bracingly intact.

Miller's troubled and troubling examinations of mid to late twentieth-century American life and its responses to the Holocaust have brought up and continue to engage with many of the issues that we are grappling with in the early years of the new millennium. If the Holocaust has forever cast humanity as either victims, perpetrators, or bystanders, then Miller's concentration on them and how they respond to the central moral issues of our day becomes essential reading and performing.

—Steven Dedalus Burch

See the essay on *Incident at Vichy.*

MILLU, Liana

Nationality: Italian. **Born:** Pisa, 1914. **Career:** Journalist before World War II; Partisan, arrested in Venice and deported to Auschwitz/Birkenau, 1944; worked as a teacher, journalist, and lecturer after the war. **Address:** Office: Via Trento, Genoa, Italy 16145.

PUBLICATIONS

Short Stories

Il fumo di Birkenau. 1947; as *Smoke over Birkenau,* 1991.

Novel (autobiographical)

I ponti di Schwerin [The Bridges of Schwerin] 1978.

Other

Dalla Liguria ai campi di sterminio, with Rosario Fucile. 1980.
La camicia di Josepha: Racconti. 1988.
Dopo il fumo: Sono il n. A 5384 di Auschwitz Birkenau. 1999.

*

Critical Study: "Many Bridges to Cross: Sex and Sexuality in Liana Millu's Holocaust Fiction" by Risa Sodi, in *Nemla Italian Studies,* 21, 1997, pp. 157–78.

*   *   *

Born into a Jewish family in Pisa, Italy, Liana Millu was just 24 when Italian Prime Minister Benito Mussolini issued his first racial decrees in September 1938. Along with all other Jewish professors, instructors, and students in public schools throughout the country, she was promptly dismissed from the elementary school where she had found her first teaching position. She worked as a private tutor with an affluent Tuscan family for a short time, as was permitted by the new laws because the family was Jewish. In 1940 she moved to Genoa. There she published her first short stories under a false name, since the anti-Jewish laws prevented her literary works from being distributed or sold in Italy.

Mussolini declared war on the Allies on 10 June 1940. During the three-year period when their country was an independent partner of the Third Reich, Italian Jews were persecuted and harassed while Jewish refugees were often interned, but there were no deportations from Italy. The situation changed in 1943 when Marshal Pietro Badoglio, who had replaced Mussolini as prime minister in July, arranged an armistice with the Allies, which was announced on 8 September. The Germans immediately occupied Italy, reinstated Mussolini, and proceeded to arrest and deport as many Jews as they could find. Along with thousands of Italian non-Jews and a disproportionately high number of Italian and foreign Jews, Millu joined the resistance. She was arrested in Venice in 1944 and deported to Auschwitz-Birkenau. When most of those prisoners who had survived the gas chambers, hard labor, epidemics, and starvation rations were evacuated from the camp in January 1945 to prevent their liberation by the approaching Russian army, she was transferred to a succession of camps in Germany. She was finally liberated from a camp at Malkov, near Stettin, in May. She was so sick and weak that she spent three months in a hospital before returning to Italy in August 1945.

The main body of Millu's literary work revolves around her personal experiences as a Jewish deportee, Auschwitz-Birkenau slave laborer, and Holocaust survivor. Soon after her return to Italy, she wrote and published several stories and articles about the death camps. Her most famous work, *Il fumo di Birkenau* (*Smoke over Birkenau*, 1991), was published by La Prora in Milan in 1947 and republished by Mondadori in 1957 and La Giuntina in 1986. It has been translated into German, English, Dutch, and Norwegian. Another book, a novel entitled *I ponti di Schwerin* ("The Bridges of Schwerin"), appeared in Italy in 1978, was reissued in 1994, and has been translated into German. Somewhat like **Primo Levi**'s *La tregua* (1963; *The Reawakening,* 1965), *I ponti di Schwerin* describes a concentration camp survivor's harrowing journey home through wartorn, lawless, and chaotic Germany and the difficulties and despair of adjusting to "normal" civilian life in Italy after the Holocaust. In addition, Millu has written many other Holocaust testimonies, articles, stories, and even works of theater for young people.

Millu's work has often been compared to that of Levi. Like Levi, she has written in a lean, stark style, capturing the agony and desolation of the Holocaust simply by telling the stories of her characters. Unlike Levi, however, her characters are usually women. Her presentation of the special circumstances and sufferings of female victims is unsurpassed in Holocaust literature. Women in deportation are seduced, raped, lured into prostitution, torn from their husbands and children, and forced to undergo abortions. They are deprived of the minimal means of maintaining their self-respect as women—they have no mirrors, combs, soap, soft fabrics, pretty ribbons, or handkerchiefs. They yearn for the domestic niceties of home. In the camps they work as hard as the men and are just as cruel to each other. They are also occasionally kind and gentle. They are women in extremis, but Millu renders them profoundly moving and human.

—Susan Zuccotti

See the essay on *Smoke over Birkenau.*

MIŁOSZ, Czesław

Pseudonym: J. Syruc. **Nationality:** American (originally Polish: immigrated to the United States, 1960; US citizenship, 1970). **Born:** Szetejnie, Lithuania, 30 June 1911. **Education:** University of Stephan Batory, M. Juris 1934. **Career:** Programmer, Polish National Radio, 1935–39; worked for the Polish Resistance during World War II; cultural attache, Polish Embassy, Paris, 1946–50; freelance writer in Paris, 1951–60. Visiting lecturer, 1960–61, professor of Slavic languages and literature, 1961–78, and since 1978 professor emeritus, University of California, Berkeley. **Awards:** Prix Litteraire Europeen, 1953, for *La Prise du pouvoir;* Marian Kister literary award, 1967; Jurzykowski Foundation award for creative work, 1968; Institute for Creative Arts fellow, 1968; Polish PEN award for poetry translation, 1974; Wandycz award, 1974; Guggenheim fellow, 1976; Neustadt international prize for literature, 1978; University of California university citation, 1978; Zygmunt Hertz literary award, 1979; Nobel Prize for literature, 1980; Bay Area Book Reviewers Association poetry prize, 1986, for *The Separate Notebooks;* Robert Kirsch award for poetry and National Medal of Arts, both in 1990. D.Litt.: University of Michigan, 1977. Other honorary degrees: Catholic University, Lublin, 1981; Brandeis University, 1983. **Address:** Office: Department of Slavic Languages and Literatures, University of California, 5416 Dwinelle Hall, Berkeley, CA 94720, U.S.A.

PUBLICATIONS

Collection

Dziela zbiorowe [Collected Works]. 1980.

Poetry

Poemat o czasie zastyglym [Poem of the Frozen Time]. 1933.
Trzy zimy [Three Winters]. 1936.
Wiersze [Poems] (as J. Syruc). 1940.
Ocalenie [Salvation]. 1945.
Swiatlo dzienne [Daylight]. 1953.
Trak tat poetycki [Treatise on Poetry]. 1957.
Kontynenty [Continents]. 1958.
Krol Popiel i inne wiersze [King Popiel and Other Poems]. 1962.
Gucio zaczarowany [Bobo's Metamorphosis]. 1965.
Lied vom Weltende [A Song for the End of the World]. 1967.
Wiersze [Poems]. 1969.
Miasto bez imienia [City without a Name]. 1969.
Selected Poems. 1973; revised edition, 1981.
Gdzie wschodzi slonce i kedy zapada [From Where the Sun Rises to Where It Sets]. 1974.
Utwory poetyckie [Selected Poems]. 1976.

Bells in Winter. 1978.
Hymn O Perle [Hymn to the Pearl]. 1982.
The Separate Notebooks. 1984.
Unattainable Earth (selections in English). 1986.
The Collected Poems, 1931–1987. 1988.
The World. 1989.
Provinces: Poems, 1987–1991. 1991.
Facing the River: New Poems. 1995.
Swiat: Poema naiwne. 1999.

Novels

La Prise du pouvoir (French translation of original manuscript). 1953; as *The Seizure of Power,* 1955; as *The Usurpers,* 1955.
Dolina Issy. 1955; as *The Issa Valley,* 1981.

Other

Zniewolony umysl. 1953; as *The Captive Mind,* 1953.
Rodzinna Europa. 1959; as *Native Realm: A Search for Self-Definition,* 1968.
Czlowiek wsrod skorpionow: Studium o Stanislawie Brzozowskim [A Man among Scorpions: A Study of St. Brzozowski]. 1962.
The History of Polish Literature. 1969; revised edition, 1983.
Widzenia and Zatoka San Francisco. 1969; as *Visions from San Francisco Bay,* 1982.
Prywatne obowiazki [Private Obligations] (essays). 1972.
Moj wiek: Pamietnik nowiony [My Century: An Oral Diary] (interview with Alexander Wat), edited by Lidia Ciolkoszowa (2 vols.). 1977.
Emperor of the Earth: Modes of Eccentric Vision. 1977.
Ziemia Ulro. 1977; as *The Land of Ulro,* 1984.
Ogrod nauk [The Garden of Knowledge]. 1980.
Nobel Lecture. 1981.
The Witness of Poetry. 1983.
The Rising of the Sun. 1985.
Beginning with My Streets: Essays and Recollections. 1992.
A Year of the Hunter. 1994.
Legendy nowoczesno'sci: eseje okupacyjne. 1996.
Szukanie ojczyzny. 1996.
Traktat moralny: traktat poetycki (interviews). 1996.
Striving towards Being: The Letters of Thomas Merton and Czeslaw Milosz, edited by Robert Faggen. 1997.
Czycie na wyspach (essays). 1997.
Piesek przydroczny. 1997; as *Roadside Dog,* 1999.
Dar = Gabe. 1998.
Inne abecadlo. 1998.
Zaraz po wojnie: korespondenczja z pisarzami 1945–1950 (correspondence). 1998.
Milosz's A B C's. 2001.

Editor, *Antologia poezji spolecznej,* with Zbigniew Folejewski [Anthology of Social Poetry]. 1933.
Editor, *Piesn niepodlegla* [Invincible Song] (resistance poetry). 1942.
Editor and translator, *Drogami Kleski,* by Jacques Maritain. 1942.
Editor and translator, *Praca i jej gorycze* [Work and Its Discontents], by Daniel Bell. 1957.
Editor and translator, *Wybor pism* [Selected Works], by Simone Weil. 1958.
Editor and translator, *Kultura masowa* [Mass Culture]. 1959.
Editor and translator, *Wegry* [Hungary]. 1960.
Editor and translator, *Postwar Polish Poetry: An Anthology.* 1965; revised edition, 1983.
Editor, *Lettres inedites de O. V. de L. Milosz a Christian Gauss* (correspondence). 1976.
Editor, with Drenka Willen, *A Book of Luminous Things: An International Anthology of Poetry.* 1996.

Translator, with Peter Dale Scott, *Selected Poems,* by Zbigniew Herbert. 1968.
Translator, *Mediterranean Poems,* by Alexander Wat. 1977.
Translator, *Ewangelia wedlug sw. Marka* [The Gospel According to St. Mark]. 1978.
Translator, *Ksiega Hioba* [The Book of Job]. 1980.

*

Bibliography: *Czeslaw Milosz: An International Bibliography 1930–80* by Rimma Volynska-Bogert and Wojciech Zaleswski, 1983.

Critical Studies: *Czeslaw Milosz and the Insufficiency of Lyric* by Donald Davie, 1986; *Conversations with Czeslaw Milosz* by Ewa Czarnecha and Aleksander Fiut, translated by Richard Lourie, 1987; *Between Anxiety and Hope: The Poetry and Writing of Czeslaw Milosz,* edited by Edward Mozejko, 1988; *"Down a Spiral Staircase, Never-Ending": Motion As Design in the Writing of Czeslaw Milosz* by Judith Ann Dompkowski, 1990; *The Eternal Moment: The Poetry of Czeslaw Milosz* by Aleksander Fiut, edited by Theodosia S. Robertson, 1990; *The Poet's Work: An Introduction to Czeslaw Milosz* by Leonard Nathan and Arthur Quinn, 1991; *Czeslaw Milosz: A Stockholm Conference, September 9–11, 1991,* edited by Nils Ake Nilsson, 1992; *Dynamics of Being, Space, and Time in the Poetry of Czeslaw Milosz and John Ashbery* by Barbara Malinowska, 1997.

* * *

Poet, novelist, essayist, translator, historian, and critic of literature and culture, Czesław Miłosz is one of Poland's greatest writers and one of the major figures of world literature, "perhaps the greatest," in the opinion of Joseph Brodsky.

The 1980 Nobel Prize for literature is only one of many indications of his achievement and acclaim. He has occasionally been described as a ''poet of the Holocaust,'' although that designation is at least debatable. The Holocaust figures explicitly in a small group of poems he wrote in Warsaw during and shortly after the occupation, and he has addressed it—controversially—in a handful of articles and interviews and in brief references scattered in other writings.

Miłosz was born to a cultured family in a Polish area of Russian-held Lithuania in 1911, studied law in Vilnius and on a government scholarship in France, and began writing early amid the rich literary atmosphere of interwar Poland. He was a central figure in the ''second avant-garde'' in the 1930s. In 1940 he managed to escape to Warsaw after the Soviet Union occupied now independent Lithuania. He spent the period of the occupation in Warsaw in the shadow of the ghetto. Although he was not involved in the resistance militarily (and he has been almost scornful of the pointless bravado of some who were involved), he did participate in such things as underground publishing. He underwent a significant transformation at this time, and his sense of self, of history, of poetry, and of reality were irrevocably altered, as seen in the poem ''Dedication'': ''What is poetry which does not save / Nations or people? / . . . That I wanted good poetry without knowing it, / That I discovered, late, its salutary aim, / In this and only this I find salvation.'' His collection of poems entitled *Ocalenie* (''Salvation''), published in 1945 and the only volume of his work to appear in postwar Poland until 1980, contains poems written during the occupation and stands out as one of his finest accomplishments.

Miłosz initially accepted the new postwar regime, having long held strong left-wing views, and served briefly as a diplomat after the war. For complex reasons, but triggered by the imposition of socialist realism in 1949, he rejected the new People's Poland in favor of exile. He became one of the leading critics of communism and analyzed its excesses and shortcomings with remarkable perspicacity. Most notably his first major prose publication, *The Captive Mind* (1953), addresses the difficulties faced by writers and other intellectuals under the Soviet system. From 1951 to 1961 he lived in France, where he wrote and translated extensively and was involved in the émigré literary and cultural journal *Kultura.* In 1961 he immigrated to the United States, where he had been offered a position at the University of California at Berkeley teaching Polish and Slavic Literatures. He remained there until the 1990s, when he moved back to Poland after changing conditions made that possible.

His literary output has been continuous and substantial. Since the 1930s he has regularly published volumes of poetry, novels, and nonfiction, and he has written a wide range of essays on cultural, literary, political, philosophical, and religious topics. He has translated extensively into Polish and English, from T.S. Eliot to Shakespeare, from Job and the Psalms to Maritain, and he has translated many of his own works. He also wrote a superb history of Polish literature.

Unlike so many of his generation who either perished as members of the resistance or, like **Borowski** or **Różewicz**, whose writings were motivated and characterized by the Holocaust, there are few straightforward references to it in Miłosz's prolific output. Arguably only a handful of poems in *Ocalenie* refer explicitly to the Holocaust, yet there is a sense, however elusive, that his writing and, indeed, his entire world view, have been powerfully influenced by his experiences from that period. His tacit refusal to apply standard formulas, or even to dwell expressly on it, has earned him accusations from some quarters of a sort of dismissive equanimity or at least ambivalence, which he has, in turn, rebutted. This debate was carried out somewhat sporadically from the 1950s to the 1990s and in such disparate publications as *Problems of Communism* and *Tikkun.*

There is a curious disjuncture between what his poetry seems to say on the subject and what these publicistic writings state explicitly, especially on the question of shared blame. While the relevant poems from *Ocalenie* imply a sense of complicity, not only of the lyrical subject and the author, but of all of Western civilization (''What will I tell him, I, a Jew of the New Testament''), his more rationalized, nonliterary pronouncements cautiously but distinctly reject that position—or so it seems. He is, in fact, refusing to accept specific accusations that Christianity and/or Polish culture are inherently anti-Semitic. In his poetry about the Holocaust he is addressing, among other things, the accelerating increase in the tendency of Western civilization to both produce and tolerate such large-scale evil and of indifference to, or toleration of, it.

Miłosz both poet and thinker is enormously complex and defies encapsulation, but his work is clearly imbued with a deeply rooted spirituality and historically grounded humanism.

—Allan Reid

See the essay on *Ocalenie.*

MINCO, Marga

Pseudonym for Sara Menco. **Nationality:** Dutch. **Born:** Ginneken, 31 March 1920. **Family:** Married Bert Voeten in 1945 (died 1992); two daughters. **Career:** Lives and works in Amsterdam. **Awards:** Mutator prize, 1957, for *Het adres;* Vijverberg prize, 1958, and Multatuli prize, both for *Het bittere Kruid;* Mutator prize, for *De andere kant;* Annie Romein prize, 1999.

PUBLICATIONS

Collection

Verzamelde verhalen 1951–1981. 1982.

Novels

Het adres: 3 bekroonde novellen, with Ingeborg Rutgers and
    Auke Jelsma. 1957.
Het bittere Kruid: Een kleine Kroniek. 1957; as *Bitter Herbs: A
    Little Chronicle,* 1960.
Het huis hiernaast. 1965.
Terugkeer. 1966.
Een leeg huis. 1966; as *An Empty House,* 1990.
De dag, dat mijn zuster trouwde. 1970.
Meneer Frits en andere verhalen uit de vijftiger jaren. 1974.
De val. 1983; as *The Fall,* 1990.
De glazen brug. 1986; as *The Glass Bridge,* 1988.
De zon is maar een zeepbel, twaalf droomverslagen. 1990.
Nagelaten dagen [The Days They Left Behind]. 1997.

Short Stories

De andere kant. 1959; as *The Other Side,* 1994.

Other

Editor, *Moderne joodse verhalen* (anthology). 1965.
Kijk 'ns in de la (for children). 1974.
Editor, *Onder onze ogen verhalen over de oorlog* (anthology).
    1995.

*

Critical Studies: "Marga Minco, *Het bittere Kruid:* Ironie en
tragielk" by Luc Renders, in *Klasgids: By die Studie van die
Afrikaanse Taal en Letterkunde* (South Africa), 12(4), 1977,
pp. 9–15; "*Het bittere Kruid* by Marga Minco: Paradise Lost:
Paradise Regained" by A. van den Hoven, in *Canadian
Journal of Netherlandic Studies/Revue Canadienne d'Etudes
Neerlandaises,* 8–9(2–1), Fall 1987/Spring 1988, pp. 92–96;
"Bitter Herbs, Empty Houses, Traps, and False Identities: The
(Post)-War World of Marga Minco" by Jolanda Vanderwal
Taylor, in *Canadian Journal of Netherlandic Studies/Revue
Canadienne d'Etudes Neerlandaises,* 17(1–2), Spring/Fall 1996,
pp. 184–89.

* * *

Almost everything Marga Minco has written is, to a greater
or lesser degree, marked by her experiences as a Jew in The
Netherlands during the German occupation (1940–45). Born
in 1920 with the name Sara Menco, she was the youngest child
in an Orthodox Jewish family. As a young journalist she
distanced herself from Orthodoxy and developed a sturdy

independence that helped her survive by passing, with her blue
eyes and dyed-blond hair, as a Christian. She was the only
member of her immediate family to survive.

Minco's first book, *Bitter Herbs* (1960; *Het bittere Kruid,*
1957), describes through the eyes of an adolescent how her
family, failing to see clearly and act resolutely against impending arrest and deportation, is deported and never returns. The
young heroine, however, whose real name the reader never
learns, manages to survive through the help of the Dutch
resistance, living in numerous safe houses with false papers
until liberation in April 1945. *Bitter Herbs* (the reference is to
the unleavened bread and bitter herbs that are eaten to remind
one of the Exodus from Egypt) was an instant success, earning
several literary prizes, including the Vijverberg Prize in 1958.
A Little Chronicle, as it is subtitled, was quickly translated into
many languages.

A second book, *The Other Side* (1994; *De andere kant,*
1959), was intended to show that Minco could write on topics
other than the recent war, occupation, and persecution of the
Dutch Jews. It has the distinctly existentialist tone shared by
much European literature of the 1950s and, despite her intention, contains material that pertains to the war and to anti-
Semitism. The alienation common to much existentialist literature is also, of course, the experience of the Jew in The
Netherlands and is central to the life of the lonely protagonist
of the eight loosely connected stories of the book. *The Other
Side* received the Mutator Prize.

The novel *An Empty House* (1990; *Een leeg huis,* 1966) also
relies to a great extent on Minco's experiences underground in
Amsterdam. Set in the immediate postwar years, it centers on
two women who were in hiding and meet once more. Through
their reminiscences, they exemplify and illustrate the different
ways of responding to the harrowing past. *The Fall* (1990; *De
val,* 1983) also makes use of reminiscence and, especially,
flashbacks. It relates how an 85-year-old survivor plans a
birthday party, only to fall into street excavations and die.
Forty years earlier a fall had prevented her from being caught
in a roundup, and she had thus managed to avoid deportation
and death. *The Glass Bridge* (1988; *De glazen brug,* 1986) is
likewise set in the aftermath of the war and occupation.

If the war, the occupation, and the fate of the Dutch Jews are
central thematically and characterize much of Minco's work,
her terse, sober, and almost jerky language and syntax characterize her literary style. Her novels consist of short, crisp,
Hemingwayesque sentences. There are frequent flashbacks,
which prevent any chronological linearity and which keep the
reader in suspense and require care and concentration if one is
not to become confused or even baffled.

Minco is one of The Netherland's most popular writers. Her
books reveal not only what Dutch Jews faced once the Germans overran the country in May 1940 and what one was
forced to do in order to survive but also how a survivor needed
to come to terms with the past following liberation in April

1945. Nearly 90 percent of the approximately 140,000 Dutch Jews were deported and murdered. Those who survived relied on help from the Dutch, especially from the Dutch underground, as well as on their own resourcefulness and good luck. *The Diary of Anne Frank* is, to be sure, the best-known account of years spent in hiding before deportation and death. Minco's works provide another picture with different emphases. A cub journalist at age 18 before the war, Minco was destined to be a writer, and she has proven to be a first-class author. Her life determined that she also become a Holocaust writer, but the Holocaust did not make her a writer as, perhaps, it did of others such as **Primo Levi**. Like those of Levi or **Elie Wiesel,** her works excel as literature and do not depend on the Holocaust alone for their effect.

—David Scrase

See the essay on *Bitter Herbs: A Little Chronicle.*

MOCZARSKI, Kazimierz

Nationality: Polish. **Born:** 1907. **Education:** University of Paris, degree in law 1932. **Military Service:** Armia Krajowa (Polish underground) during World War II. **Career:** Worked as a journalist and for the Polish State administration before World War II; head, investigative division, District Board of the Underground Struggle of Warsaw, c. 1944; head, Home Army Information and Propaganda Bureau; imprisoned, 1945–56; journalist, beginning in 1956. Involved with Polish Journalistic Association and Democratic Party, beginning in 1956. Editor, *Problemy Alkoholizmu* (Warsaw). **Died:** 1975.

PUBLICATIONS

Memoirs

Rozmowy z katem. 1977; as *The Conversations with an Executioner,* edited by Mariana Fitzpatrick, 1981.
Zapiski, with Andrzej Krzysztof Kunert. 1990.

Other

Alkohol w kulturze i obyczaju, with Jana Górskiego. 1972.
Po powstaniu. 1980.

* * *

Kazimierz Moczarski is the author of a book entitled *The Conversations with an Executioner.* It is a record of his conversations with Jurgen Stroop, an SS general, the liquidator of the Warsaw Ghetto in 1943 and the person responsible for sending the Jews of Greece to Auschwitz. Moczarski was sentenced by a Stalinist court to death, and in 1949, while awaiting his execution, he spent 225 days in a cell of the Mokotov prison with a German war criminal whose execution Moczarski had been preparing during the war pursuant to the death sentence passed by the Polish underground movement.

Moczarski was born in 1907 in Warsaw. He graduated from the law department in 1932. He also studied journalism and international relations at the Institute des Etudes Internationales at the Law Department of the University of Paris. Before the war he worked for the Polish State administration and as a journalist. The analytical mind of a lawyer and the cognitive passion of a journalist were later reflected in his famous book.

From the earliest months of the German occupation Moczarski was connected with the Polish Home Army, subject to the Polish Government-in-Exile in London. He worked for the Home Army Information and Propaganda Bureau. From January 1944 he was the head of the investigative division in the District Board of the Underground Struggle of Warsaw. Therefore, he was in charge of the investigations conducted against the traitors of the Polish nation, and he passed death sentences. During the 63 days of the Warsaw Ghetto Uprising, he was the head of the Home Army Information and Propaganda Bureau. After the coming of the Red Army, he was active in the underground movement until the day of its formal dissolution by the government in London.

Moczarski was arrested and imprisoned on 11 August 1945. In January 1946 the Communists sentenced him to 10 years in prison. Amnesty brought him mitigation to five years, and he was conditionally set free. The Supreme Court, however, declared the mitigation void, and he was imprisoned for five years. In November 1948 a new investigation was instituted against him, and 49 torture methods were used on him. From 2 March to 11 November 1949 he was imprisoned in one cell with Stroop. On 18 November 1952 a Communist court sentenced Moczarski to death pursuant to a decree on punishing the traitors of the Polish nation and the Nazi criminals. In October 1953 the Supreme Court changed the penalty to life imprisonment. In April 1956 he was released from prison, and on 11 December he was completely rehabilitated. After beginning a normal life Moczarski resumed journalism and was involved in the activity of the Polish Journalistic Association as well as in political activity as a member of the Democratic Party. In both those organizations he was, among others, a vice president of the members' arbitration organ.

The work of his life—*The Conversations with an Executioner*—is one of the most important nonfiction books in Polish literature. As a prisoner who shared the cell with Stroop, Moczarski decided to write a book in order to answer the question concerning the historical, psychological, and sociological mechanism that made some Germans form a group of slaughterers who governed the Reich and attempted to introduce their *Ordnung* in Europe and in the world. Another unrevealed intention of the author was to reach the Polish audience, in spite of the censorship, and accuse the totalitarian

Communist system of its crimes committed on the Polish patriots from the Home Army.

A well-known part of the book deals with the murder of 70,000 Polish Jews during the liquidation of the Warsaw Ghetto in 1943. That genocide brought Stroop Nazi distinctions and a promotion. Moczarski encouraged Stroop to enunciation in order to hear his story and to understand his mentality.

The basic issue in this report is the question of Stroop's sincerity. The author insists that spending many months together in one prison cell makes people sincere. Moczarski thinks that to a considerable extent Stroop showed his real face. Before writing the book he additionally confronted the information obtained from him with other sources.

Moczarski was a witness of the extermination of the Warsaw Jews. As a soldier and a member of the Home Army Information and Propaganda Bureau he met many people who analyzed the situation of the Polish Jews and were involved in helping them. In his book, written in the 1970s, Moczarski remains nobly faithful to his conspiratorial function and— what has not been stressed by the critics—he slightly idealizes the Polish-Jewish relationships during the war. But the latter are not the crucial issue of the book, which is a significant testimony of the times of the Nazi and Stalinist totalitarianism.

—Kazimierz Adamczyk

See the essay on *The Conversations with an Executioner.*

MODIANO, Patrick (Jean)

Nationality: French. **Born:** Boulogne-Billancourt, 30 July 1945. **Family:** Married Dominique Zehrfuss in 1970; two daughters. **Career:** Since 1968 novelist. **Awards:** Prix Roger Nimier, 1968, and Prix Felix Feneon, 1969, both for *La Place de l'étoile;* Grand Prix Roman, L'Academie Francaise, 1972, for *Les Boulevards de ceinture;* Prix Goncourt, 1978, for *Rue des boutiques obscures;* Prix de Monaco, 1984. **Agent:** Beaume, 3 quai Malaquias, 75006 Paris, France.

PUBLICATIONS

Novels

Occupation Trilogy:
    La Place de l'étoile. 1968.
    La Ronde de nuit. 1969; as *Night Rounds,* 1971.
    Les Boulevards de ceinture. 1972; as *Ring Roads,* 1974.
Villa Triste. 1975; as *Villa Triste,* 1977.
Livret de famille [Family Book]. 1977.
Rue des boutiques obscures. 1978; as *Missing Person,* 1980.
Une Jeunesse [A Youth]. 1981.
Memory Lane. 1981.

De si braves garçons [Such Good Boys]. 1982.
Poupée blonde [Blonde Doll]. 1983.
Quartier perdu. 1985.
Dimanches d'août. 1986.
Une Aventure de Choura, illustrated by Dominique Zehrfuss (for children). 1986.
Une Fiancée pour Choura, illustrated by Zehrfuss (for children). 1987.
Remise de peine. 1988.
Catherine Certitude. 1988.
Vestiaire de l'enfance. 1989.
Voyage de noces: Roman. 1990; as *Honeymoon,* 1995.
Fleurs de ruine. 1991.
Un Cirque passé: Roman. 1992.
Chien de printemps: Roman. 1993.
Du plus loin de l'oubli: Roman. 1996.
Des Inconnues. 1999.

Plays

La Polka (produced Paris, 1974).
Lacombe Lucien, with Louis Malle (screenplay). 1974; translated as *Lacombe Lucien,* 1975.

Screenplays: *Lacombe Lucien,* with Louis Malle, 1974; *Une Jeunesse,* 1981; *Le Fils de Gascogne,* 1995.

Other

Interrogatoire par Patrick Modiano suivi de il fait beau, allons au cimetiere, with Emmanuel Berl. 1976.
Dora Bruder. 1997.
Out of the Dark. 1998.

*

Film Adaptations: *Une Jeunesse,* 1981; *Le Parfum d'Yvonne,* from the novel *Villa Triste,* 1994.

Critical Studies: ''Modiano, Agent Double'' by Jacques Bersani, in *Nouvelle Revue Française,* 298, November 1977, pp. 78–84; ''Re-Membering Modiano, or Something Happened'' by Gerlad Prince, in *Sub-Stance,* 49, 1986, pp. 35–43; *The Anguish of the Marginal Hero in the Novels of Patrick Modiano* (dissertation) by Katheryn Lee Wright, Indiana University, 1987; *I Call Myself the Other: The Quest for Identity in the First Nine Novels of Patrick Modiano* (dissertation) by Deborah Scott Alden, University of Connecticut, 1989; ''Patrick Modiano: A French Jew?'' by Ora Avni, in *Yale French Studies,* 85, 1994; *Shaping the Novel: Textual Interplay in the Fiction of Malraux, Hebert, and Modiano* by Constantina Mitchell and Paul Raymond Cote, 1996; *Patrick Modiano,* 1996, and *Patrick Modiano,* 2000, both by Alan Morris; *Rewriting the Past: Memory, History and Narration in the Novels of Patrick Modiano* by William VanderWolk, 1997; *Paradigms of Memory: The Occupation and Other Histories* *in the Novels of Patrick Modiano* by Martine Guyot-Bender and William VanderWolk, 1998.

* * *

In May 1968, when his peers were busy shaking the foundations of Charles de Gaulle's Fifth Republic, 23-year-old Patrick Modiano published *La Place de l'étoile*. This novel was the writer's first journey into the period of the Nazi occupation of France and its corollary: collaboration. The early 1940s had not yet been probed by historians: the myth of France united behind de Gaulle still reigned. The people who had enforced laws eliminating Jews from civil life, those who had turned them in, and the French police, which arrested and helped deport a quarter of France's 300,000 Jews, were still around. The period was still taboo, too recent and too shameful to be exhumed.

Thus, far from the preoccupations of his generation, Modiano was the first to venture into that history. Among French writers born just after the war, he was the only one for whom the occupation played such a major role. At the source of his creative vision was his personal history. In a 1981 interview with J.L. Ezine in *Les Ecrivains sur la sellette,* he stated: "Like all people without roots or country, I'm obsessed with my prehistory. And my prehistory is the shameful, murky period of the Occupation: I've always felt, for obscure family reasons, that I was born of that nightmare. . . . This is where I come from."

Modiano's prehistory is his father, Albert, an Egyptian Jew who lived in occupied Paris illegally, and a gentile Belgian actress who had low-level jobs with a German film company. Albert never registered as a Jew, never wore the star. He seemed to have been a go-between for people who supplied goods to the Nazis and some black market thugs controlled by the Gestapo. Arrested twice, he avoided deportation through the intervention of one of his sleazy business connections. His son hardly knew him; their relationship was troubled. The man disappeared from his life at the end of his adolescence without having explained how he saved himself from the fate of his fellow Jews. The arrest of the father haunts Modiano—an episode in six novels, a primal scene, poignant and shameful, for it exposes the identity of the father both as Jew and as traitor. It also poses the painful problem of the writer's origins.

Most of Modiano's weary, solitary narrator-protagonists, often writers themselves, suffer from a lack of certainty about who they are and from an obscure feeling of anxiety and guilt. (Almost all the novels are written in the first person, a narrative device that allows Modiano to blend autobiography and fiction.) They must elucidate the mystery of their origins so they can go on with their lives. They embark on a difficult, hazardous voyage into their own uncertain memory and the memories of other shadowy characters in the hope of shedding some light on unresolved events of their past and the remote, obscure past of their fathers. The search usually takes the form of an investigation: the narrator turns detective in order to track down the past. Old photographs, magazines, obsolete phone books, municipal records, police files, or maps might yield clues about some long disappeared character who holds the key to the narrator's past. (In *Rue des boutiques obscures* the amnesiac protagonist has even lost his name.) He wanders through the nocturnal, empty streets of Paris. From cafés to hotel bars, Paris triggers childhood memory fragments. It is also the scene of the crimes that occurred in his "prehistory." Even in novels not directly set in the occupation as the first and second trilogies are, this melancholic, ambulatory quest invariably leads to some shady character associated with the criminal collaborators of that era. But it is too late: many never paid for their crimes, the past remains blurry, the quest leads nowhere.

In an interview from 2001, Modiano said, "I feel like I've been writing the same book for over thirty years. . . . The twenty books I published separately seem to form . . . one single book." Indeed, the repetitive, obsessive nature of his work is striking. Similar plots, same places, protagonists with the same names and floating identities, recurrent characters with odd, cosmopolitan names, recurring episodes and themes: remembrance, amnesia, the destructive past, guilt—all themes linked to Modiano's heritage. Narrative discontinuity, fragmentation, lack of closure, constant shift between past and present, the narrator's uncertainties, suppositions, and interrogations that may never be answered are ways of rendering the difficulties of retrieving the past, of accessing knowledge.

Only in *Dora Bruder,* the last book of the second trilogy, is the Holocaust the whole focus of the work. There the fictional story of the young heroine acquires a haunting reality. Little by little her fate becomes the fate of the Jews of France. By recalling with historical precision their elimination from society, the roundups, the names and crimes of the perpetrators, the places in occupied Paris that led to Drancy, from where they would be deported to Auschwitz, her story becomes history. Modiano bears witness and becomes the guardian of memory.

—Nicole Ball

See the essay on the Occupation Trilogy.

MOLODOWSKY, Kadya

Nationality: American (originally Russian, grew up in Poland: immigrated to the United States, 1935). **Born:** Bereza Kartuska, 1894. **Family:** Married Simche Lev. **Career:** Teacher, Yiddish Primary schools, Warsaw; wrote for the Yiddish Press in New York; lived briefly in Israel in the early 1950s writing and editing Yiddish publications. Founder and editor, *Svive,* New York. **Award:** Itzik Manger prize for Yiddish literature, 1971. **Died:** 1975.

PUBLICATIONS

Collection

Paper Bridges: Selected Poems of Kadya Molodowsky, edited by Kathryn Hellerstein. 1999.

Poetry

[Maselhach] Der goi fun di kartofl [etc.]. N.d.
Cheszwendike necht. 1927.
Heshvndike nekht. 1927.
Kheshvandike nekht. 1927.
Dzshike gas. 1933.
Freydke. 1935.
In land fun mayn gebeyn. 1937.
Der melekh David aleyn iz geblibn [Only King David Remained]. 1946.
In Yerusholayim kumen malokhim [Angels Are Coming to Jerusalem]. 1952.
Lider fun hurbn: 700–705. 1962.
Likht fun Dornboym [Lights of the Thorn Bush]. 1965.

Plays

A mantel fun a tunkeln gevantl. In *Fir instsenirungen,* edited by Aaron Jacob Krisofsky, 1936.
Der golem. In *Fir instsenirungen,* edited by Aaron Jacob Krisofsky, 1936.
Ale fentster tsu der zun: Shpil in elf bilder. 1938.
Nokhn got fun midbar: Drame fun idishn lebn in 16tn yorhundert [After the God of the Desert]. 1949.

Novel

Baym toyer [At the Gate]. 1967.

Short Stories

A shtub mit zibn fentster [A House with Seven Windows]. 1957.

Other

Mayselekh (for children). 1931.
A mayse mit a balye: A mantl fun a tunklen gevantl (for children). 1931.
Afn barg (for children). 1938.
Fun Lublin bis Neue-York: tog-bukh fun Rivkah Zilberg [From Lublin to New York: Diary of Rivke Zylberg]. 1942.
Oif di vegen fun Zion [On the Roads of Zion] (for children). 1957.
Martsepanes: Mayselekh un lider far kinder un yugnt [Marzipans: Poems and Stories for Children and Youth]. 1970.

*

Critical Studies: "Encountering the Matriarchy: Kadye Molodowsky's Women's Songs," translated by F. Pczenick, in *Yiddish,* 7(2–3), 1988, pp. 170–87; "Hebraisms As Metaphor in Kadya Molodowsky's 'Froyen-lider I'" by Kathryn Hellerstein, in *The Uses of Adversity: Failure and Accommodation in Reader Response,* edited by Ellen Spolsky, 1990; "Kadye Molodowsky's 'Froyen Lider' ('Women's Songs')" by Sheva Zucker, in *Yiddish,* 9(2), 1994, pp. 44–51.

* * *

In 1928, in the final stanza of a poem from *Dzshike Gas* entitled "A Letter," Kadya Molodowsky writes:

> And say if it's no harmless quirk, quiet whim:
> On the sunniest day, I recall the abyss
> Patiently waiting for me to come,
> Even at the sunniest noontime, like this.

It is this sense of impending doom, this commitment to rendering the abyss that haunts the seemingly peaceful that perhaps best identifies Molodowsky as a Holocaust poet. Though she had already been in the United States for several years (having emigrated from Poland in 1935) when, in 1943, she heard "the bitter news about the *khurbm polyn,*" as quoted in Kathryn Hellerstein's introduction to *Paper Bridges,* she had long before been using her poetry as a vehicle for social and political change, as a mirror for the grinding poverty and desolation of Polish Jewry that preceded the annihilation of this segment of the world—Molodowsky's world—by the Nazis.

Molodowsky's work might be situated at the crossroads of a number of competing influences. Her work is at once deeply religious and highly suspect of the constraints that traditional Judaism places upon its observers, particularly women. Her "Women-Poems," for instance, highlight the *agunah,* a figure of abandonment, loss, and perpetually deferred desire. A figure that also inhabits the landscape—literally and metaphorically—of **S.Y. Agnon**'s tales (and which he claims as his namesake), the *agunah* in Molodowsky's poetry is an almost ghostly creature, foretelling by her own anguish the deeper spiritual, psychological, and physical torment that is to come. Like Scholem Aleichem, Isaac Loeb Peretz, and **Isaac Bashevis Singer,** however, Molodowsky also uses her work to paint portraits of a living, vibrant world, the world of the shtetl, a world steeped in tradition; she breathes life into a community, a culture, on the brink of annihilation and in so doing defiantly rejects the forces that set out to erase this world.

Like **Nelly Sachs** and **Paul Celan,** Molodowsky wrestles with the burden of tradition in a post-Holocaust world, using her poetry to enact a theological revaluation of sorts. The covenantal structure is, for her, implicated in and immensely damaged by the Holocaust; at the same time it becomes a crucial and necessary structure for the revaluation process for the poetic *tikkun* that is to follow. Like Celan and Sachs, her quest for a language that will not violate its object necessitates a return to traditional forms and symbols; this return involves a reworking and rethinking of scripture, a Midrashic encounter of sorts that imbues these textual moments with immediacy and urgency.

In Molodowsky's poetry, as in the poetry of Celan and **Dan Pagis,** language is forced to undergo its own revaluation; language is not only the vehicle for but also the object of a poetic encounter that aims for an almost visceral binding of self to other. This "new" language, the language that "went through . . . the thousand darknesses of death bringing speech . . . enriched by it all," as Celan argues in his Bremen Preis speech, binds past to future, does not overcome the past (as in the sense of *Vergangenheitsbewältigung*), but confronts it, starkly, unflinchingly, and painfully. This confrontation becomes most explicit and deliberate, most self-conscious, in Molodowsky's final volumes of poetry, *Der melekh dovid aleyn iz geblibn* and *Likht fun dornboym*. "My Language" from *Likht fun dornboym,* for instance, describes a language that slips closer to silence, that suspects its own incapacity for expression at the same time that it responds to the imperative to bear witness:

> For this much grief
> The spoken word
> Or silenced word
> Will not suffice.
> There lives in me
> A language, white,
> A word that I
> Have never sealed.
> Speechless, dumb,
> Not formed from words,
> My white language,
> My utterance, voice,
> Assaults my soul.

Language is depicted here as insufficient and intensely private, open, unending, but violent in its refusal to take on form. Even as it strains toward the listening, reading other, it fears it will miss its mark.

Thus the communicative gesture of Molodowsky's poetry is often met by frustration; this very gesture names alienation, solitude, as the given condition even as it attempts to overcome this condition. The act of writing expresses for Molodowsky, as it does for **Elie Wiesel,** a commitment to the process of renewal, a commitment to try to find words for the unspeakable, a commitment to build a relation in the space of absence. According to Hellerstein, such a commitment betrays an implicit hope, perhaps become explicit in her continued evocation of the Paper Bridge, which will carry us, tradition claims, into paradise when the Messiah comes. But, like the paper out of which this bridge is constructed, this is a fragile and precarious hope, alternatingly nourished and broken by the starkness of despair.

—Beth Hawkins

See the essay on *Paper Bridges: Selected Poems of Kadya Molodowsky.*

MORANTE, Elsa

Nationality: Italian. **Born:** Rome, 18 August 1918. **Family:** Married the writer Alberto Moravia in 1941 (separated 1962). **Career:** Writer. **Awards:** Viareggio prize, 1948, for *Menzogne e sortilegio;* Strega prize, 1966, for *L'isola di Arturo;* Prix Medicis Etranger, 1985, for *Aracoeli.* **Died:** 25 November 1985.

PUBLICATIONS

Collection

Elsa Morante. Opere (2 vols.). 1988 (vol. 1), 1990 (vol. 2).

Novels

Menzogne e sortilegio. 1948; abridged and translated edition, as *House of Liars,* 1950.
L'isola di Arturo. 1957; as *Arturo's Island,* 1959.
La storia: Romanzo. 1974; as *History: A Novel,* 1977.
Aracoeli. 1982; as *Aracoeli,* 1984.

Short Stories

Le bellisime avventure di Cateri dalla trecciolina [The Marvelous Adventures of Cathy Pigtail] (for children). 1941; revised and enlarged edition, as *Le straordinarie avventure di Caterina,* 1959.
Lo scialle andaluso [The Andalusian Shawl]. 1963.
Il mondo salvato dai ragazzini e altri poemi [The World Saved by the Little Children]. 1968.

Poetry

Alibi. 1958.

Other

Il gioco segreto [The Secret Game] (essays). 1941.
Botteghe oscure. 1958.

Diario 1938, edited by Alba Andreini. 1989.

Translator, *Il libro degli appunti.* 1945.
Translator, *Il meglio di Katherine Mansfield.* 1957.

*

Critical Studies: "Elsa Morante" by Michel David, in *Le Monde,* 13 April 1968; "Elsa Morante" by Michael Caesar, in *Writers and Society in Contemporary Italy,* edited by Caesar and Peter Hainsworth, 1986, pp. 211–13; "The Textualization of a Female I. Elsa Morante's *Menzogna e sortilegio*" by Valeria Finucci, in *Italica,* 4, 1988, pp. 308–23; "Illusion and Literature in Morante's *L'isola di Arturo*" by Luisa Guy, in *Italica,* 1988, pp. 144–53; "Elsa Morante's *Aracoeli:* The End of a Journey" by Rocco Capozzi, in *Donna,* edited by Ada Testaferri, 1989, pp. 47–58; "The Bewitched Mirror: Imagination and Narration in Elsa Morante" by Sharon Wood, in *Modern Language Review,* April 1991, pp. 310–21; "Elsa Morante and the Adventure of Caterina" by J. Cavallo, in *Forum Italicum,* 28(1), Spring 1994, p. 71; *The Theme of Childhood in Elsa Morante* by Grace Zlobnicki Kalay, 1996.

*   *   *

From 1965 until her death 20 years later, Elsa Morante refused to discuss details about herself, insisting that she had already written her life into her books. This imbrication of fact and fiction is perhaps the only recurring element in an otherwise diverse narrative production. While she misrepresented many of her experiences, these fabrications, deceptions, myths, and alibis construct necessary illusions for both the writer and her characters.

Despite Morante's various assertions to the contrary, she was born in Rome on 18 August 1912. Her mother, Irma Poggibonzi, a schoolteacher of Jewish descent, was married to Augusto Morante. When Elsa was in her teens she learned that he could not have children and that Francesco Lo Monaco was her biological father. The family lived in the Roman working-class district of Testaccio where Morante had homeschooling until the age of 10. In November 1936 she met the writer Alberto Moravia, whom she married in a Catholic ceremony on 14 April 1941. In September 1943 Moravia heard that there was an order for his arrest, so the couple took refuge for a year in Ciociaria, a mountainous region south of Rome. Morante recalls this experience in her third novel, *La Storia. Romanzo* (1974; *History: A Novel,* 1977). Although they remained married Morante and Moravia separated permanently in 1962. She died in Rome on 25 November 1985.

Morante's writing is fiercely independent of contemporary narrative trends and formulates a distinct expression in Italian literary historiography. Her first novel, *Menzogna e sortilegio* (1948; *The House of Liars,* 1950), which won the Viareggio Prize and brought the author critical acclaim, introduces the themes of memory and childhood—the latter interpreted as a

trauma of rejection. Lies and deceit sustain familial relations in a story that spans three generations in Sicily. Similar anxieties are explored in the story "Lo scialle andaluso" (The Andalusian Shawl, 1951), which recounts a son's love-hate relationship with his mother. In her second novel, *L'isola di Arturo* (1957; *Arturo's Island,* 1959), winner of the Strega Prize, the boy Arturo is able to delude himself through self-deception and imaginary tales that his frequently absent father is some sort of hero until maturation prevents Arturo from sustaining the illusion. Morante's collection of 16 poems, *Alibi* (1959; "Alibis"), expands upon this autobiographical material and stipulates fabrication as a necessary condition for life. *Aracoeli* (1982; *Aracoeli,* 1984), her fourth and final novel and winner of the Prix Medicis, reiterates the trauma of rejection through a symbolic journey of desecration.

The Holocaust and Jewish identity assume a prominent position in *History: A Novel,* which engages in a polemical representation of history and fiction. The narrative recounts the period between January 1941 and the summer of 1947, and many of its fictional episodes are derived from Morante's wartime experiences. The text formally juxtaposes history and fiction by introducing each chapter with a descriptive chronicle of the historical events that took place in the time frame covered by the narrative. History—the term is capitalized throughout the text—is presented as sequential acts of persecution, genocide, and violence upon the innocent. Fiction, then, in Morante's exposition must assume responsibility for giving a voice to the stories that History has silenced.

History recounts the experiences of Ida Ramundo and her children. Ida is a half-Jewish widowed schoolteacher who refutes her Semitic origins. A German soldier rapes her, and from this act of violence Useppe is born. The deportation of the Jews and the destruction of the Roman ghetto are recurring themes in the novel. In October 1943 Ida and Useppe are at the Tiburtina Station and witness hundreds of Jews boarding windowless cattle cars to German concentration camps. Later, in one of the narrative's most powerful scenes, Ida is drawn back to the deserted ghetto and hears the voices of the dead. Throughout the narrative Jews are symbolic of the sacrifice of humanity to History, while the Holocaust is the ultimate manifestation of History's violence. In the midst of this devastation, Ida rediscovers an emotive bond between herself and her Jewish identity, but this consolatory moment is overwhelmed by the desecration that leaves nothing in its wake. Following the death of Useppe, Ida goes mad and remains institutionalized until her death.

History occupies a distinctive position within Italian literary representations of the Holocaust that situate it alongside other singular works such as Arnaldo Momigliano's *Pagine ebraiche* (1987; "Jewish Papers") and **Giuliana Tedeschi**'s *Questo povero corpo* (1946; "This Poor Body"). While it sold nearly a million copies in its first year of publication, the novel's representation of History's scandals through micro-histories ignited an ideological polemic that engaged the

Italian left for the better part of 1974 and brought the Holocaust to the forefront of historicist debates.

—Piero Garofalo

See the essay on *History: A Novel.*

MÜLLER, Filip

Nationality: Czechoslovakian. **Career:** Prisoner, Auschwitz, 1942–44. **Award:** International League against Racism and Anti-Semitism prize, 1980, for *Eyewitness Auschwitz: Three Years in the Gas Chambers.*

PUBLICATION

Memoir

Sonderbehandlung: Drei Jahre in den Krematorien und Gaskammern von Auschwitz, with Helmut Freitag. 1979; translated as *Eyewitness Auschwitz: Three Years in the Gas Chambers,* edited by Susanne Flatauer, 1979 (first published as *The Death Factory,* 1966); as *Auschwitz Inferno: The Testimony of a Sonderkommando,* 1979.

* * *

Filip Müller's bleak testimony *Eyewitness Auschwitz: Three Years in the Gas Chambers* is his account of his time in the *Sonderkommando,* the special squads that dealt with the processing, murder, and disposal of the bodies of the victims of the Nazis. These units have attracted a great deal of attention, yet there are few survivors and accounts (another is Rebecca Camhi Fromer, *The Holocaust Odysseys of Daniel Bennahmias, Sonderkommando,* 1993). **Primo Levi,** in his essay "The Gray Zone" from *The Drowned and the Saved,* writes: "Conceiving and organising the squads was National Socialism's most demonic crime. Behind the pragmatic aspect . . . other more subtle aspects can be conceived. This institution represented an attempt to shift onto others—specifically the victims—the burden of guilt, so that they were deprived even the solace of innocence . . . the existence of the squads had a meaning, contained a message; 'We, the master race, are your destroyers, but you are no better then we are; if we so wish and we do

so wish, we can destroy not only your bodies but also your souls, just as we have destroyed ours.'" Müller's unsparing and unhistrionic account is exactly a description of this. The SS men and the *kapos* are hated, but there is a strange, foul, and unwilling complicity between them, as the SS force the "crematory ravens" to do their bidding. Müller's account is spare: a simple report, with little speculation, almost as if the terrible nature of his forced duties made wider reflection impossible.

Müller came to Auschwitz on the first Slovak transport on 20 April 1942. By incredible chance and through his own tenacity and initiative, he managed to survive the camps. The origin of Müller's account was a report he wrote in 1945 or '46, which was then published 20 years later in 1966 as *The Death Factory.* It was then reworked, with a literary collaborator and a translator, into the text *Eyewitness Auschwitz* in 1979. The historian Yehuda Bauer writes in the introduction of the U.S. edition that since Müller "published his memoir in the 70s, we have learned a great deal about Auschwitz, so that we now know that there are inaccuracies in some of his statistics and diagrams as presented here." In her 1999 book *Reading the Holocaust,* Inga Clendinnen goes further: "I suspect the collaborator's hand in the use of the convention of dramatic direct-direct speech reportage from long public speeches by the SS and . . . for the responses by their victims." More than this, she writes that she would challenge the few stories she finds uplifting—"scenes of defiance and/or faith," such as Müller's telling of the well-known dancer story of the shooting of SS man Schillinger—"on the grounds of implausibility." For Clendinnen the question is "is it believable? . . . the critical evaluation of texts (may I accept this? must I reject that?) stands at the heart of the historical enterprise." Passing over debates on the normalization of history—such as the debate between Martin Brozat and **Saul Friedländer**—she reads this text passing over its affective content.

Müller's account is supported in **Rudolf Vrba**'s *I Cannot Forgive.* Müller is also one of the witnesses in **Claude Lanzmann**'s film *Shoah.* The account Müller offers is one of pain and suffering, sparingly told. It is made especially acute because of his position in the special squads, a victim first and foremost, but in an agonizing position of being able to watch other victims.

—Robert Eaglestone

See the essay on *Eyewitness Auschwitz: Three Years in the Gas Chambers.*

N

NIEMÖLLER, Martin

Nationality: German. **Born:** Lippstadt, Westphalia, 14 January 1892. **Education:** Studied theology. **Military Service:** German Navy, beginning in 1910: midshipman, submarine commander during World War I. **Family:** Married Else (died 1961). **Career:** Lutheran minister, beginning in 1924. Pastor, St. Ann's parish in the Dahlem, 1931; organizer, Pfarrernotbund (Pastors' Emergency League, an anti-Nazi group of clergy), 1933; suspended from preaching, 1934; arrested by the Gestapo for treason, 1937; prisoner, Sachsenhausen and Dachau concentration camps, 1937–45. President, office for foreign relations, Evangelical Church, 1945–56; president, Church province of Hesse and Nassau, 1947–64; cofounder, Bekennende Kirche (Confessing Church); cofounder and president, 1961–68, World Council of Churches; participant, Stuttgart Declaration of Guilt. Also promoter of world peace. **Awards:** Lenin Peace prize, 1967; West German Grand Cross of Merit, 1971. **Died:** 6 March 1984.

PUBLICATIONS

Memoirs

Vom U-Boot zur Kanzel [From U-Boat to Pulpit]. 1933; revised edition, as *From U-Boat to Concentration Camp*, 1939.
Martin Niemöller: Briefe aus der Gefangenschaft Moabit [Letters from Moabit Prison]. 1975; as *Exile in the Fatherland: Martin Niemöller's Letters from Moabit Prison*, 1986.

Other

Martin Niemöller und sein Bekenntnis. 1938.
Dennoch getrost (sermons). 1939.
Martin Niemöller über die deutsche Schuld, Not und Hoffnung. 1946.
Zur gegenwärtigen Lage der evangelischen Christenheit. 1946.
Das Aufgebrochene Tor: Predigten und Andachten gefangener Pfarrer im Konzentrationslager Dachau (sermons). 1946.
Die Aufgabe der evangelischen Kirche in Deutschland. 1953.
Können wir noch etwas tun zur friedlichen Wiedervereinigung unseres Volkes? 1955.
Martin Niemöller Reden 1955–1957. 1957.
Reden, 1945–1954. 1958.
Reden, 1958–1961. 1961.
Eine Welt oder keine Welt; Reden, 1961–1963. 1964.

Facing Jesus Christ: Martin Niemöller and Carson Blake Discuss the Mission of the Church, with Eugene Carson Blake. 1965.
Reden, Predigten, Denkanstösse, 1964–1976. 1977.
Was würde Jesus dazu sagen?: Reden, Predigten, Aufsätze 1937 bis 1980. 1980.
Martin Niemöller: Festschrift zum 90. 1982.
Martin Niemöller: Ein Lesebuch. 1987.
Erkundung gegen den Strom: 1952, with Jan Niemöller. 1988.

*

Critical Studies: *Martin Niemöller: The Bible in Dachau* by Jennie Rowena Batten, 1951; *God Is My Fuehrer: A Dramatic Interpretation of the Life of Martin Niemöller* by Gordon C. Bennett, 1970; *Martin Niemöller, 1892–1984* by James Bentley, 1984; "Memories of Martin Niemöller" by Ewart E. Turner, in *Christian Century*, 101, 25 April 1984, pp. 445–46; "The Political Theology of Martin Niemöller" by John S. Conway, in *German Studies Review*, 9(3), October 1986; *Remembrance and Recollection: Essays on the Centennial Year of Martin Niemöller and Reinhold Niebuhr, and the Fiftieth Year of the Wannsee Conference* by Hubert G. Locke and Marcia Sachs Littell, 1996; *Martin Niemöller* by Matthias Schreiber, 1997.

* * *

Martin Niemöller, German Lutheran pastor and a founder of the anti-Nazi Bekennende Kirche (Confessing Church), part of the larger Lutheran and Reformed Church of Germany, was born in 1892 to Pastor Heinrich and Paula Niemöller in Lippstadt, Westphalia. Niemöller was raised in a strong Reformed tradition ("All my ancestors were Reformed") and in German nationalism, which left an indelible mark on his life. His patriotism and love of the sea motivated him to join the Kaiser's navy in 1910. He enlisted as an officer-cadet and served his country heroically as a German naval lieutenant and U-boat commander during the First World War. After the war he studied theology in Münster and was ordained by the Rt. Rev. Dr. Simon in 1924. Unable to find a pulpit position to his liking, he worked at social services for the Inner Mission in Westphalia, where he was not entirely satisfied, and in 1931 he accepted the position of third pastor of the historical St. Ann's parish in the Dahlem ("settlement on the mountain") suburb of Berlin. In spite of his nonpolitical Christian calling, ex-naval officer Niemöller never forgot nor forgave Germany's humiliation at the hands of the Allies and the imposed Treaty of Versailles, which, he believed, reduced Germany to occupied territory. With this in mind, he wrote his memoirs of the

First World War, *Vom U-Boot zur Kanzel* (1933; "From U-Boat to Pulpit"), in part to replace Germany's traumatic defeat and fragmentation by a program of national unity inspired by the duty of honor and the fatherland. At the end of his reminiscence, he saw hope from the "years of darkness" of the Weimar Republic in Adolf Hitler's National Socialist Party.

But Niemöller's support for Hitler (since 1923) was to end abruptly and permanently. Soon after Hitler ascended to power, Niemöller became disillusioned with the Nazi state sterilization law (25 July 1933), racial theories, and Nazification of the Protestant churches. On 21 September 1933 he and others protested the infamous Aryan paragraph of the church synod of Brandenburg, and two weeks later he organized the Pfarrernotbund (Pastors' Emergency League) to protect Lutheran pastors from the police. In 1934 he was one of the original organizers of the Barmen Synod, which produced the theological basis for the Confessing Church, and whose leadership he assumed in 1937. On 27 June 1937 he preached his last sermon at his church in Dahlem, and a few days later, on 1 July, he was arrested for his anti-Hitler sermons and incarcerated at Moabit prison. After eight months of imprisonment, he was acquitted of treason but was immediately seized by the Gestapo and placed in "protective custody" first at Sachsenhausen and later at Dachau. He was liberated by the Allied troops in early 1945.

After the war Niemöller became an adamant pacifist who opposed nuclear weapons and German rearmament. He advocated a reunited Germany and sought contacts in Eastern Europe. For these efforts he was awarded the Lenin Peace prize in 1967 and the West German Grand Cross of Merit in 1971. He is best known, however, for his resistance against Hitler and his advocacy of reconciliation, including his participation in the meeting that produced the *Stuttgarter Schuldbekenntnis* (19 October 1945; "Stuttgart Confession of Guilt"), acknowledging the German people's collective guilt for the Holocaust, as well as his election as one of the six presidents of the World Council of Churches, the ecumenical body of mainline Protestant denominations.

—Zev Garber

See the essay on *Exile in the Fatherland: Martin Niemöller's Letters from Moabit Prison*.

NIR, Yehuda

Nationality: American (originally Polish: immigrated to Palestine after World War II and later to the United States). **Born:** Lvov, 31 March 1930. **Education:** Hebrew University, Jerusalem, 1951–58, M.D. 1958. **Military Service:** Polish Home Army during the Warsaw Uprising of 1944; Israeli Army during the War of Independence, 1948. **Family:** Married

Bonnie Maslin in 1973; three sons and one daughter. **Career:** Head of child psychiatry, Memorial Sloan-Kettering Cancer Center; psychologist, private practice, New York. Since 1979 associate professor of psychology, Cornell University Medical College, Ithaca, New York.

PUBLICATIONS

Memoir

The Lost Childhood: A Memoir. 1989.

Other

Loving Men for All the Right Reasons, with Bonnie Maslin. 1982; as *Patterns of Heartbreak: How to Stop Finding Mr. Wrong,* 1992; as *How to Get Married One Year from Today: Advice on Romance for Men and Women,* 1994.
Not Quite Paradise: Making Marriage Work, with Bonnie Maslin. 1987.

*

Critical Study: "Yehuda Nir," in *Sh'ma,* 25(481), 11 November 1994.

* * *

Yehuda Nir was nine years old when the Germans overran his half of Poland in 1939, signaling the start of World War II. Three weeks later the Soviets entered Lvov and annexed it to the Soviet Union. Yehuda's father's prosperous business was nationalized. The swift change of status for his family culminated two years later when Yehuda witnessed his father being marched away never to be seen again.

These events marked the beginning of a six-year ordeal where Yehuda would survive by living on the run with his mother and sister, using his wits and a finely honed instinct to avoid detection as a Jew. Posing as Catholics, with forged baptismal certificates, the trio managed to elude deportation, flee the ghetto, and eventually depart for Warsaw, where their anonymity saved them. Dyeing his hair, concealing his circumcision, and wearing a Hitler Youth uniform were only some of the ruses Nir engaged to survive. But the sheer nerve, quick wit, and chameleon-like changes left an imprint on the man who went on to live by an existentialist creed that impelled him to act whenever justice was threatened.

After the war Nir lived in Palestine, where he completed his high-school equivalency requirements. Later he went to Vienna to medical school. He also studied medicine in Jerusalem, and after his marriage he moved with his wife to Philadelphia in 1959 to complete his studies. He finished his training with a residency in child psychiatry at Mt. Sinai Hospital in New York and has since made his home in Manhattan.

Nir has been a practicing psychiatrist in Manhattan, where he has also taught psychiatry at Cornell University Medical College. Special areas of his practice include treating post-traumatic stress disorder and treating children. With his second wife, Bonnie Maslin, a psychologist, he has written self-help books.

Nir's smiling eyes and rapid-fire speech reveal only a fragment of the persona who is utterly action oriented. When Israel was attacked on Yom Kippur in 1973, he postponed his second wedding for three weeks, flying to Israel to serve as an army doctor working in a 24-hour clinic treating trauma survivors. When President Reagan went to a Bitburg cemetery where SS were buried, Nir flew to Germany with 30 people to protest the president's actions. Years later, when he donated 10,000 copies of his book to every high school in Holland, he was challenged by the Dutch Secretary of Education, who questioned his inclusion of Samuel Beckett's lines as an epigraph in his Holocaust memoir, *The Lost Childhood:* "Let me say before I go any further that I forgive nobody. / I wish them all an atrocious life and then the fires and ice / of hell and in the execrable generations to come . . ." Nir countered by saying: "Maybe if young people take action, then they can create a world in which forgiveness is possible. My goal is to disrupt the couch potato so that young people will educate themselves and not be passive, but rather to choose action when they see injustice." Nir has made time to travel around the country speaking to young people about his Holocaust experience. Students are drawn to him because his message is authentic and intrepid.

His Holocaust memoir is so compelling that it attracted the attention of a composer and librettist, who teamed up to write an opera based on *The Lost Childhood.* Produced by the American Opera Projects, it was a work in progress as of 2001. Gottfried Wagner, great-grandson of the composer and a friend of Nir's, chose to direct the opera of the same title. Their friendship has been based on a spirit of openness, exemplified in Nir's correspondence with Wagner: "You say that you have been crucified on the history of Germany, and I believe you. You don't even ask for forgiveness—all you want is to engage in dialogue to understand what has happened, how it happened, and to ask whether it is possible to prevent it from happening again. You are a German who can help create a world in which we, the Jews, can contemplate forgiveness."

An avid opera fan, Nir has favored this genre because its power allows him to disappear into that sublime world of art. Given the severity of his life, it is no coincidence that this survivor has lived by the belief that avenging an evil is a righteous act, a vendetta, a word he pronounces in a perfect and resolute pitch.

—Grace Connolly Caporino

See the essay on *The Lost Childhood.*

NOMBERG-PRZYTYK, Sara

Nationality: Polish. **Born:** Lublin, 10 September 1915. **Education:** University of Warsaw. **Family:** Married Andrzej Przytyk; two sons. **Career:** Teacher, Białystok, before World War II. Lived in the Białystok ghetto, 1941–43; prisoner, Stutthof and Auschwitz. Worked as a journalist, Lublin, after World War II. Forced to leave Poland, 1968; moved to Israel, 1968–75, then Canada, 1975–96. **Died:** 1996.

PUBLICATIONS

Memoirs

Kolumny Samsona [The Columns of Samson]. 1966.
Auschwitz: True Tales from a Grotesque Land, edited by Eli Pfefferkorn and David H. Hirsch. 1985.

* * *

Born in Lublin, Poland, on 10 September 1915, Sara Nomberg grew up in a Hasidic family. Her grandfather was renowned throughout Poland as a Talmudist and for several years was the headmaster of a yeshiva in Warsaw. He later moved to a small town near Lublin, where he served as the rabbi for the community. Many of her other relatives were also rabbis. Living in the Jewish area of Lublin, she came to know the meaning of poverty at an early age. The sight of Jewish children dying of malnutrition and of Jewish women growing old before their time made a deep impression upon her. Her experience of Polish anti-Semitism was equally powerful, and she came to associate Jewish poverty with Polish anti-Semitism.

Nomberg attended gymnasium in Lublin and then enrolled at the University of Warsaw. While living in Warsaw, her strong sense of social justice led her to become involved in the communist movement; she simply could not see how the religious tradition of her upbringing had made life any better for the Jews and others suffering from injustice. As a result of her political activities, she was incarcerated for five years as a political prisoner. When Germany invaded Poland in 1939, she fled to the Soviet-occupied East, to Białystok, where she had taught school before the war. Shortly after Germany's move against the Soviets on 22 June 1941, she was rounded up with the rest of the Jews of Białystok and confined to a ghetto. She remained in the Białystok ghetto until August 1943; when the ghetto was liquidated, she was sent to the concentration camp at Stutthof. On 13 January 1944 she was transported from Stutthof to Auschwitz.

With the help of fellow communists, Nomberg managed to get assigned to work in the infirmary in Auschwitz. There she came to know the Angel of Death, Josef Mengele, well. In January 1945, as the Russians approached Auschwitz, she was sent with hundreds of others on the death march to Ravensbrück. From Ravensbrück she was transported to Rostock. On 1 May

1945, the Germans fled from the Soviets, who were advancing on Rostock, and she was free.

After her liberation Nomberg returned to Lublin. There she married a magistrate by the name of Andrzej Przytyk and worked as a journalist until October 1968, when she was forced to leave Poland. Before leaving, however, Nomberg-Przytyk had written two books. The first was *Kolumny Samsona* (*The Pillars of Samson*), which was published in Poland in 1966; it relates the story of the Białystok ghetto up to the time of its liquidation. Her second book was the volume for which she is best known, *Auschwitz: True Tales from a Grotesque Land* (1985), translated from an unpublished Polish manuscript titled *Lydzi w Oswiecim*. She had an offer to publish her Holocaust memoir in Poland on the condition that she remove all references to Jews, but she refused.

When she was forced to leave Poland in 1968, Nomberg-Przytyk went to Israel, where she placed the manuscript of her unpublished work in the care of the archives at Yad Vashem. In 1975 she left Israel to settle in Canada with her two sons. She died in Canada in 1996.

—David Patterson

See the essay on *Auschwitz: True Tales from a Grotesque Land.*

NYISZLI, Miklos

Nationality: Romanian. **Born:** 1901. **Education:** University of Breslau, Germany. **Family:** Married (died); one daughter (deceased). **Career:** Physician, Oradea-Naeyvaad; prisoner and physician, Auschwitz, 1944–45. **Died:** 1956.

PUBLICATION

Memoir

Dr. Mengele boncolóorvosa voltam az auschwitzi krematóri-umban. 1947; as *Auschwitz: A Doctor's Eyewitness Account.* 1960.

* * *

Romanian physician Miklos Nyiszli, Auschwitz prisoner A 8450, completed his memoir of Auschwitz soon after the war. *Auschwitz: A Doctor's Eyewitness Account,* the only work he published about his experiences, provides extraordinary insight into daily life within the deepest circle of hell, the gas chambers and crematoriums of Auschwitz-Birkenau.

Upon his arrival in Auschwitz in May 1944, Nyiszli responded to the Nazi call for physicians who were trained in Germany and skilled in forensic pathology. Forced to prove his credentials, Nyiszli succeeded in pleasing his Nazi boss, Josef Mengele, an accomplishment that allowed him to live under far better conditions than most prisoners but that tried him in different ways. Nyiszli's memoir is an objective account of months spent laboring in the service of Mengele, as well as caring for the *Sonderkommando* workers of the crematoriums.

Nyiszli's dispassionate descriptions only serve to amplify the horror. In one heart-wrenching episode Nyiszli tells how he lied to a father and son as he examined them, comforting them rather than telling them that they would soon be sent to the gas chamber. The next time he sees them they are dead, and he must cook their bodies so that their skeletons can be sent as research specimens to Berlin.

A less expert physician might not have met the demands that Mengele put upon him, but Nyiszli had been exceptionally well trained, including a period of study at the German University of Breslau. His professional credentials, his ability to perform what was required of him, and his knowledge of German, sometimes exceeding in fluency that of his captors, seems to have earned their grudging respect, or so Nyiszli convinced himself. It is on this point that **Bruno Bettelheim** challenged Nyiszli in the preface to the 1960 edition of his book, suggesting that he chose preservation of life over preservation of his soul, fooling himself into believing he was still a physician when he was merely a tool in the hands of the criminal doctors of Auschwitz.

Yet, within the limited means available to him, Nyiszli tried to do what he could, first to save his own wife and daughter, then to help other inmates. His access to a pharmacy that equaled the "best stocked drugstore in Berlin" enabled him to give medicines and vitamins to needy prisoners. The tasks he performed seared his soul, and he sought refuge each night in sleeping pills. He was haunted by his choices, such as his refusal to give poison to *Sonderkommando* members who wished to commit suicide.

Nyiszli's book is especially important for its description of the revolt by the 12th *Sonderkommando*. Most of the men died, and only Nyiszli and his medical colleagues were spared. But the men succeeded in destroying one crematorium and damaging another, halting at least briefly the assembly line of death.

In January 1945 Nyiszli was sent to Mauthausen, then to Melk on the Danube, and finally to Ebensee, where he was liberated on 5 May 1945. Some weeks later he was reunited with his wife and daughter who had survived Bergen-Belsen. Nyiszli's knowledge of the inner workings of the Birkenau factory of death made him a crucial witness in the war crimes trials in Nuremberg, at which he testified in October 1947.

In the closing words of his memoir, Nyiszli vowed that he would never hold a scalpel again. It was the Nazis who forced him to turn an instrument of healing into a tool of death.

—Marilyn J. Harran

See the essay on *Auschwitz: A Doctor's Eyewitness Account.*

O

OLSZEWSKI, Krystyn

Nationality: Polish. **Born:** Warsaw, 1921. **Education:** Studied architecture at Warsaw Polytechnics, after World War II. **Career:** Political prisoner in Auschwitz, Pawiak, Gross Rosen, Buchenwald, and Dachau during World War II. Returned to Poland after the war. General designer of urban planning, Warsaw, Baghdad, Singapore, 1964–81. Lecturer, Warsaw Polytechnics.

PUBLICATIONS

Memoir

Byliśmy w Oświęcimiu, with Tadeusz Borowski and Janusz Nel Siedlecki. 1946; as *We Were in Auschwitz,* 2000.

*

Critical Studies: "When the Earth Is No Longer a Dream and Cannot be Dreamed through to the End" by Jan Walc, in *Polish Review,* 32(2), 1987, pp. 181–94; "Beyond Self: A Lesson from the Concentration Camps" by Piotr Kuhiwczak, in *Canadian Review of Comparative Literature/Revue Canadienne de Litterature Comparee,* 19(3), September 1992, pp. 395–405; *Suffering Witness: The Quandary of Responsibility after the Irreparable* by James Hatley, 2000.

* * *

Krystyn Olszewski—Auschwitz prisoner number 75817—is one of the coauthors of the book *We Were in Auschwitz* (2000), which was originally published in Munich in 1946 as *Byliśmy w Oswiecimiu.* The publication is considered to be one of the most important literary testimonies of the concentration camp and the Holocaust.

Olszewski was born in Warsaw in 1921, and thus he belongs to the generation that reached its intellectual maturity in the years of World War II. He was a prisoner of Pawiak, Auschwitz, Gross Rosen, Buchenwald, and Dachau. **Tadeusz Borowski** also belonged to that generation. The clash between their youthful idealism and the cruel truth of what it means to be a man discovered in concentration camps is for them a source of judgment of the world and of the literary shape of *We Were in Auschwitz.*

According to Borowski's testimony, which was written down by Professor Tadeusz Mikulski, Olszewski is the author of two short stories. They are "I Fear the Night" and "The Fifth Hundred." Two other stories told by him were used by Borowski as the material for two more short stories. Earlier, in 1945, Olszewski and Borowski together published a pair of poems under the title *Tracing.* Its value is purely documentary.

The friendship with Borowski, as well as with **Janusz Nel Siedlecki,** the third coauthor of *We Were in Auschwitz,* decided Olszewski's place in the history of literature. That place was confirmed by his participation in the creation of that book. On the copy of *We Were in Auschwitz* that he donated to Borowski he wrote: "To Tadeusz, in memory of our common work on something which we together started and which he finished. Krystyn."

After his return to communist Poland, Olszewski studied and graduated from the Warsaw Polytechnics, and he became an architect. In the years 1964–81 he was subsequently the general designer of the general urban planning of Warsaw, Baghdad and Singapore. He became a United Nations expert and a lecturer at the Warsaw Polytechnics.

—Kazimierz Adamczyk

See the essay on *We Were in Auschwitz.*

ORLEV, Uri

Nationality: Israeli (originally Polish: immigrated to Israel, 1945). **Born:** Jerzy Henryk Orlowski, Warsaw, 24 February 1931. **Education:** Kibbutz high school. **Military Service:** Israeli Army, 1950–52. **Family:** Married 1) Erela Navin in 1956 (divorced 1962), one daughter; 2) Ya'ara Shalev in 1964, one daughter and two sons. **Career:** Prisoner, Bergen-Belsen, 1943–45. Worked on a cattle ranch at a kibbutz before moving to Jerusalem in 1962. **Awards:** Awards from Israeli Broadcast Authorities, 1966, 1970, 1975, 1979, and 1991; Youth Alia prize, 1966, for *The Last Summer Vacation;* Prime Minister prize (Israel), 1972 and 1989; Mildred L. Batchelder award and Sydney Taylor book award, both in 1985, for *The Island on Bird Street;* Janusz Korczak literary prize (Poland), 1990; Mildred L. Batchelder award, 1991, and National Jewish Book Council award (New York), 1992, both for *The Man from the Other Side;* Annual Book Parade prize (Israel), 1995, for *Lydia, Queen of Palestine;* Mildred L. Batchelder award, 1996, for *The Lady with the Hat;* Hans Christian Andersen award, 1996; Ministry of Education Zeew prize, 1997, for *The Sandgame.* **Member:** Hebrew Writers Association; Israeli Translators Association; International Board on Books for Young People. **Agent:** Nili Cohen, Institute for the Translation of Hebrew Literature, P.O. Box 10051, Ramat Gan 52001,

Israel. **Address:** c/o Keter Publishing House, P.O. Box 7145, Jerusalem 91071, Israel.

PUBLICATIONS

Novels

Hayale-'oferet. 1956; as *The Lead Soldiers,* 1979.
'Ad mahar [Till Tomorrow]. 1958.

Novels (for young adults)

Kasheh le-hiyot aryeh [It's Hard to Be a Lion]. 1979.
Ha-I bi-rehov ha-tsiporim. 1981; as *The Island on Bird Street,* 1984.
Keter ha-drakon [The Dragon's Crown]. 1984.
Ha-Ish min ha-tsad ha-aher. 1988; as *The Man from the Other Side,* 1991.
Ha-Geveret 'im ha-migba'at. 1990; as *The Lady with the Hat,* 1995.
Lidyah, malkat Erets Yisra'el. 1991; as *Lydia, Queen of Palestine,* 1993.
Mishak ha-hol. 1996; as *The Sandgame,* 1999.
Shirat ha-livyatanim [Song of the Whales]. 1997.
Ruts yeled, ruts [Run Boy, Run]. 2001.

Novels (for children)

Hayat ha-hoshekh [The Beast of Darkness]. 1976.
Ketanah-gedolah [The Big Little Girl]. 1977.
Meshaga'at pilim [Hole in the Head]. 1977.
Mahashavot tsehorayim [Noon Thoughts]. 1978.
Si'aminah veha-hatulim shel Yemin Mosheh. 1979.
Hultsat ha-aryeh [The Lion Shirt]. 1979; as *A Lion for Michael,* 2000.
Ha-Mabul ha-shahor [The Black Cloud], with Yiftah Alon. 1979.
Ma'ase be-manoah she-hif'il et ha-moah [How Mr. Cork Made the Brain Work]. 1979.
Motsets ha-mazal [The Good Luck Pacifier]. 1980.
Savta soreget [Granny Knits]. 1981.
Rosh ha-'ir ten la-shir [Mr. Mayer, Let Us Sing]. 1981.
Ah boger [Big Brother]. 1983.
Masa'le-gil arba' [How to Be Four]. 1985.
Hafifat rosh. 1986; as *Hairy Tuesday,* 1999.
Ketsitsah meha-tsohorayim [A Mouthful of Meatball]. 1995.
Rehoke mishpahah [Last of Kin]. 1996.

Short Stories

Hufshat ha-kayits ha-ahronah: Sipurim [The Last Summer Vacation]. 1968.

Short Stories (for children)

Tor ha-kenafayim [The Wings Turn]. 1981.
Ha-Mishpahah ha-nodedet [The Wandering Family]. 1997.

Poetry (for children)

'Al tsad sem'ol [On the Wrong Side of the Bed]. 1985.

Plays

Television Plays: *Who Will Ring First?* (for children), 1979; *The Dream of the Chinese Crown Prince,* 1991.

Other

Editor, with Tsofiyah Shiber, *Ha-Tafkid he-'atsuv shel ha-ti'ud: yoman mahbo* [Sad Task of Documentation], by Salek Perehodnik. 1993.

Translator, *Ba-yeshimon uva-'aravah,* by Henryk Sienkiewicz. 1982.
Translator, *Peshitat ha-regel shel g'ek ha-katan,* by Janusz Korczak. 1985.
Translator, *Kaitush ha-mekhashef,* by Janusz Korczak. 1987.
Translator, *Hazarah meha-kokhavim,* by Stanislav Lem. 1988.
Translator, *Yomane kokhavim,* by Stanislav Lem. 1990.
Translator, *Ha-shed meha-shevi'it,* by Kornel Makuszynski. 1990.
Translator, *Masa' be-siman kelev,* by Kornel Makuszynski. 2000.

*

Film Adaptations: *The Island on Bird Street,* 1996.

Critical Studies: ''Survival! Polish Children during World War II'' by Marilyn Fain Apseloff, in *Visions of War: World War II in Popular Literature and Culture,* edited by M. Paul Holsinger and Mary Anne Schofield, 1992; ''Author Spotlight: Uri Orlev,'' in *Bookbird,* 31(3), September 1993, p. 39; ''Childhood Lost: Children's Voices in Holocaust Literature'' by Naomi B. Sokoloff, in *Infant Tongues: The Voice of the Child in Literature,* 1994; ''Telling the Life Story of Death'' by Nava Semel, in *Modern Hebrew Literature* (Israel), 20–21, 1998, pp. 18–22.

*   *   *

''I don't wish to finish with the Holocaust,'' Uri Orlev once said, ''because what other people call the Holocaust was, for me, my childhood.'' Orlev is an accomplished author of two children's novels about the experiences of boys surviving the Holocaust in Poland. He was born as Jerzy Orlowski in Warsaw in 1931. His father, a physician and an officer in the Polish Army, was taken prisoner on the Russian front when World War II broke out. After the Nazis killed his mother, his aunt Stefania cared for Uri and his younger brother and eventually smuggled them out of the ghetto. They were sent to Bergen-Belsen in 1943 with their aunt and were liberated by the 9th U.S. Army in April 1945.

After the war Orlev and his brother went to a kibbutz in what is now Israel. Orlev completed his education and worked on the kibbutz cattle farm. Eventually he left the kibbutz for Jerusalem, where he has lived with his second wife and four children. In *The Sandgame* Orlev writes, ''When I was a child we played a game called 'How Many Children Will You Have?' Usually, it was played in a sandbox. One child took a handful of sand, tossed it in the air, and flipped his hand over so that the back of it faced up. As some of the falling sand settled there, he announced: 'So many children will you have!' ... The sand thrower tossed the sand into the air again, flipped his hand palm-side up, and called out as the sand fell: 'This many will die in the forest!' He was referring to the grains that missed his hand and dropped to the ground. That happened to most of them. A smaller number fell into his open palm. And so he kept tossing the remaining sand into the air, catching it now on the back of his hand and now in his palm while announcing: 'This many will be run over!' 'This many will die of the plague!''' This was Orlev's metaphor for explaining to his son how it was with the Germans. ''They kept throwing us into the air and great numbers of us died, but my brother and I landed safely each time.''

In his novels for children and young people, skillfully translated into English by Hillel Halkin, Orlev fictionalizes his experiences in the Warsaw Ghetto. He tells stories that resemble his own but that are truthful and believable inventions, based on history and personal experience, not literal retellings of his life.

One of Orlev's great gifts is telling history in clear and direct words to young readers. In *The Sandgame* he writes, ''We might have survived the war in the ghetto if the Germans hadn't begun to evacuate it. Starting in the summer of 1942, thousands of Jews were taken every day and sent in trains for 'resettlement.' You might think that this was the Germans' idea of a sick joke, but they weren't trying to be funny. They were simply trying to hide what they were doing from their victims and from history. ... Within three months the population of the ghetto shrank from half of a million to fifty or sixty thousand.'' His mother and his aunt were employed in a factory with about a thousand workers. ''The only salary, of course, was the right to stay alive. The factory was in a converted apartment building and we lived in the building next to it, which was the only inhabited house for blocks around. It was like living on a little island in a strange, silent sea of death.''

This idea of living on an island is the central metaphor of *The Island on Bird Street,* which recounts the story of Alex, a Jewish boy who survives for months waiting for his father alone in an abandoned building in the ghetto. In *The Man from the Other Side* Orlev tells the story of 14-year-old Marek, who accompanies his Polish stepfather as they smuggle supplies into the ghetto through the sewers.

A central theme in Orlev's books is the maturing relationship of a boy with his father or with a man who becomes a father to the boy. In his memoirs Orlev talks about his ''adventures'' during the war: ''I thought of myself as the hero of a thriller who had to survive until the happy ending on the book's last page, no matter who else was killed in it, because he was the main character.'' Thus, his tone is one of heroism and adventure, even when the events he describes are horrifying. This approach allows him to keep horror and despair at bay and to tell his stories to young readers with honesty but also with hope.

—J.D. Stahl

See the essays on *The Island on Bird Street* and *The Man from the Other Side.*

OZ, Amos

Nationality: Israeli. **Born:** Amos Klausner, Jerusalem, 4 May 1939. **Education:** Hebrew University, Jerusalem, B.A. in Hebrew literature and philosophy 1965; St. Cross College, Oxford University, M.A. 1970. **Military Service:** Israeli Army, 1957–60; fought as reserve soldier in tank corps in Sinai, 1967, in Golan Heights, 1973. **Family:** Married Nily Zuckerman in 1960; two daughters and one son. **Career:** Since 1986 professor and Agnon Chair of Hebrew Literature, Ben Gurion University of the Negev, Beer Sheva, Israel. Visiting fellow, St. Cross College, Oxford University, 1969–70; writer-in-residence, Hebrew University of Jerusalem, 1975 and 1990, University of California, Berkeley, 1980, Colorado College, 1984–85, Boston University, 1987, Princeton University, 1997, and St. Anne's College, Oxford University, 1998. Editor, *Siach lochamium;* contributor to various periodicals, including *Davar* (Israel), *Encounter,* and *Partisan Review.* Since 1977 cofounder and representative, Shalom Achshav (Peace Now). Member, Kibbutz Hulda, beginning in 1954. **Awards:** Holon prize for literature, 1965; Israel-American Cultural Foundation award, 1968; B'nai B'rith literary award, 1973; Brenner prize, 1976, for *The Hill of Evil Counsel;* Ze'ev award for children's books, 1978; Bernstein prize, 1983; Bialik prize, 1986; Prix Fémina Étranger, 1988, for *Black Box;* Wingate prize, 1988; German Publishers Association international peace prize, 1992; Israel prize in literature, 1998. Honorary doctorates: Hebrew Union College, 1988; Western New England College, 1988; Tel Aviv University, 1992. Chevalier de l'Ordre des Arts et des Lettres, 1984; French Cross of the Knight of the Légion d'Honneur, 1997. **Member:** Academy of the Hebrew Language, 1991. **Agent:** Mrs. D. Owen, 28 Narrow Street, London E.14, England. **Address:** c/o Ben Gurion University of the Negev, Beer Sheva, Israel.

PUBLICATIONS

Novels

Makom aher. 1966; as *Elsewhere, Perhaps,* 1973.
Mikha'el sheli. 1968; as *My Michael,* 1972.
'Ad mavet (two novellas). 1971; as *Unto Death,* 1975.
La-ga'at ba-mayim, la-ga'at ba-ruah. 1973; as *Touch the Water, Touch the Wind,* 1974.
Har ha-'etsah ha-ra'ah: Sheloshah sipurim (three novellas). 1976; as *The Hill of Evil Counsel,* 1978.
Menuhah nekhonah. 1982; as *A Perfect Peace,* 1985.
Kufsah shehorah. 1986; as *Black Box,* 1988.
La-da'at Ishah. 1989; as *To Know a Woman,* 1991.
Ha-matsav ha-shelishi [The Third Condition]. 1991; as *Fima,* 1993.
Al tagidi lailah. 1994; as *Don't Call It Night,* 1995.
Panter ba-martef. 1995; as *Panther in the Basement,* 1997.
Oto ha-yam. 1999; as *The Same Sea,* 2001.

Short Stories

Anashim aherim: Mivhar [Different People]. 1974.
Artsot ha-tan: Sipurim. 1965; as *Where the Jackals Howl and Other Stories,* 1981.

Other

Soumchi (for children). 1978; translated as *Soumchi,* 1980.
Be-or ha-tekhelet ha-'azah: ma'amarim u-reshimot. 1979; as *Under This Blazing Light: Essays,* 1995.
Poh va-sham be-Erets-Yisra'el bi-setav 1982 (essays). 1983; as *In the Land of Israel,* 1983.
Mi-mordot ha-Levanon: ma'amarim u-reshimot (essays). 1987; as *The Slopes of Lebanon,* 1989.
Shetikat ha-shamayim: 'Agnon mishtomem 'al Elohim (literary criticism). 1993; as *The Silence of Heaven: Agnon's Fear of God,* 2000.
Israel, Palestine, and Peace: Essays. 1994.
Mathilim sipur. 1996; as *The Story Begins: Essays on Literature,* 1999.
Kol ha-tikvot: Mahashavot 'al zehut Yisra'elit [All Our Hopes] (essays). 1998.

Editor, with Richard Flantz, and author of introduction, *Until Daybreak: Stories from the Kibbutz.* 1984.

*

Film Adaptations: *Michael Sheli,* 1975 (as *My Michael,* 1975), from the novel *Mikha'el Sheli; Kufsah shehorah* (Black Box), 1994.

Bibliography: *'Amos 'Oz—bibliyografyah, 1953–1981: 'Im mivhar hashlamot 'ad kayits 1983* by Joseph Jerushalmi, 1984; *'Amos 'Oz—bibliyografyah: La-shanim 1984–1996* by Ruti Kalman, 1998.

Critical Studies: "The Jackal and the Other Place: The Stories of Oz" by Leon I. Yudkin, in *Journal of Semitic Studies* (England), 23, 1978, pp. 330–42; "On Oz: Under the Blazing Light" by Dov Vardi, in *Modern Hebrew Literature* (Israel), 5(4), 1979, pp. 37–40; "The Beast Within: Women in Amos Oz's Early Fiction," in *Modern Judaism,* 4(3), October 1984, pp. 311–21, and *Israeli Mythogynies: Women in Contemporary Hebrew Fiction,* 1987, both by Esther Fuchs; "Amos Oz in Arad: A Profile" by Shuli Barzilai, in *Southern Humanities Review,* 21(1), Winter 1987; *Voices of Israel, Essays on and Interviews with Yehuda Amichai, A. B. Yehoshua, T. Carmi, Aharon Applefeld, and Amos Oz* by Joseph Cohen, 1990; "Language and Reality in the Prose of Amos Oz," in *Modern Language Studies,* 20(2), Spring 1990, pp. 79–97, and *Between God and Beast: An Examination of Amos Oz's Prose,* 1993, both by Avraham Balaban; "Portrait: Amos Oz, Israel's Willful Conscience," in *U.S. News & World Report,* 110(14), 15 April 1991; "Amos Oz" by Eleanor Wachtel, in *Queen's Quarterly* (Canada), 98(2), Summer 1991; *The Tensions between Zionism's Messianism and Liberal Humanitarianism in the Works of Amos Oz* (dissertation) by Emily Dembitz Katz, Hampshire College, 1992; "Amos Oz and Izhak Ben Ner: The Image of Woman in Literary Works, and as Transvalued in Film Adaptations" by Nurith Gertz, in *Israeli Writers Consider the "Outsider,"* edited by Leon I. Yudkin, 1993; "The Epistolary Politics of Amos Oz's *Black Box*" by Joshua M. Getz and Thomas O. Beebee, in *Prooftexts,* 18(1), January 1998, pp. 45–65; *Amos Oz Writing the Israeli Paradox* by Rebecca Steffens and others, 2000.

*   *   *

One of Israel's most popular writers and a major figure in contemporary Hebrew culture, Amos Oz is a member of what is often referred to as the state generation of writers (*Dor Hamedinah*). This is the second generation of native-born Israeli writers (**A.B. Yehoshua** is another), who began to write and publish in the late 1950s and the early 1960s and who continue to dominate Israeli literature. In many ways Oz typifies the transition from mid-twentieth century to contemporary Hebrew writing. Born in Jerusalem in 1939 and a member of the kibbutz Hulda from 1954, Oz grew up against the backdrop of the early ideals of the Jewish *yishuv* (settlement) in Palestine and the nascent post-1948 state. Informing both the public consciousness and the literature was the figure of the new Hebrew in his new/ancient homeland. Indeed, the literature was intended not only to reflect this new reality but also to help create it. Therefore, Hebrew writing from the early decades of the twentieth century through the late 1950s directly repudiated diasporic (European) Jewish history. It laid to rest the old Jewish victim and replaced him with the independent warrior-farmer who worked the land, battled its enemies, and built the new Jewish nation. This nation, it was expected, would realize the aspirations for a communal, national existence for Jews without reverting to outmoded traditions of religious belief and worship. The gender bias of the pronoun ''him'' in the above description is intended. This was a fiction written primarily by men, and it concerned itself largely with heroic males involved in traditional areas of male endeavor in a world defined by public rather than by private action. Oz's name, meaning ''potency'' or ''vigor,'' is itself a reflection of these tendencies within the prestate and early state period. Oz replaced his father's diasporic name, Klausner, marking the son's shift into Israeli/Hebrew heroism.

Born before the war of independence, Oz, like others of his generation, imbibed these national goals as expressed in the press, in the ideology of the youth movement, and in the budding literature. Coming to his maturity after the establishment of the state of Israel, however, Oz did not experience nationhood as an event still to be achieved, as sufficiently precarious so as to require constant protection by its defenders and constructors. Furthermore, he lived through the series of both dramatic and mundane events that marked the transformation from *yishuv* to statehood. This included the influx of Jewish refugees and survivors from decimated Europe, who represented just that population of old Jews that the state of Israel had imagined itself as replacing. It was the Adolf Eichmann trial in the early 1960s that put the Holocaust center stage in the national consciousness and made it available as a subject for Israeli fiction, a fact that was reinforced, albeit also transformed, by the Six-Day War. This war had seemed to many a second Auschwitz in the making. That Israel achieved a stunning victory defused some of the shame attached to the Diaspora. It also inaugurated the new reality of a politically and territorially powerful Jewish state, presumably even less in need of being defended by its contemporary population and perhaps requiring just the opposite of the old heroic stance, the recovery of some of the traditional European principles of Jewish humanism and humility.

Like other writers of his generation, Oz simultaneously participated in the national myths of the first half of the twentieth century and stepped back from them as the new reality of Israel asserted itself. In particular he rejected the nationalistic goals of a politically motivated fiction intended to realize an as yet unattained Zionist ideal and began to return Hebrew literature to its nineteenth-century origins in the more fraught and personal experience of individuals caught in the crosscurrents of, on the one hand, national aspirations and events and, on the other, private emotions and desires. These were the issues that had also characterized Hebrew literature (the writings of Joseph Haim Brenner, for example) during the early decades of the prestate *yishuv*. Thus, the bulk of Oz's writings, including his single Holocaust text, *Touch the Water, Touch the Wind,* published in Hebrew in 1973 and in an English translation by Nicholas de Lange in 1974, are

withdrawals from the didacticism and straightforward social realism of the more popular Israeli fiction of the 1930s and 1940s. Instead, his writings evoke impressionistically, sometimes surrealistically, the inner dynamics of the human mind and heart as his protagonists, often autobiographically informed, strive toward a heroism that can never be realized and that, could it be attained, would likely be barren or, worse, psychologically and ethically oppressive. For as Oz suggests in his more political writings (*In the Land of Israel,* for example), not only have the internal dynamics of Jewish reality changed since the inception of the state, so, too, have Israel's international relations, including, especially after 1967, its relations with its Palestinian neighbors. The pursuit of peace both as a legacy of the Jews' European past and as a response to its immediately political present is a leitmotif of many of Oz's fictional works, including *Touch the Water, Touch the Wind.*

—Emily Budick

See the essay on *Touch the Water, Touch the Wind.*

OZICK, Cynthia

Nationality: American. **Born:** New York City, 17 April 1928. **Education:** New York University, B.A. (cum laude) in English 1949 (Phi Beta Kappa); Ohio State University, Columbus, M.A. 1951. **Family:** Married Bernard Hallote in 1952; one daughter. **Career:** English instructor, New York University, 1964–65; Stolnitz Lecturer, Indiana University, Bloomington, 1972; distinguished artist-in-residence, City University of New York, 1982; Phi Beta Kappa Orator, Harvard University, 1985. **Awards:** National Endowment for the Arts fellowship, 1968; Wallant award and B'nai B'rith award, both in 1972; Jewish Book Council Epstein award, 1972, 1977; American Academy award, 1973; Hadassah Myrtle Wreath award, 1974; Lamport prize, 1980; Guggenheim fellowship, 1982; Strauss Living award, 1983; Rea short story award, 1986. Honorary doctorates: Yeshiva University, New York, 1984; Hebrew Union College, Cincinnati, 1984; Williams College, Williamstown, Massachusetts, 1986; Hunter College, New York, 1987; Jewish Theological Seminary, New York, 1988; Adelphi University, Garden City, New York, 1988; State University of New York, 1989; Brandeis University, Waltham, Massachusetts, 1990; Bard College, Annandale-on-Hudson, New York, 1991; Spertus College, 1991; Skidmore College, 1992; Seton Hall University, 1999; Rutgers University, 1999; University of North Carolina, 2000. **Address:** Office: c/o Alfred A. Knopf, 201 E. 50th Street, New York, New York 10022–7703, U.S.A.

PUBLICATIONS

Collection

A Cynthia Ozick Reader. 1996.

Novels

Trust. 1966.
The Cannibal Galaxy. 1983.
The Messiah of Stockholm. 1987.
The Puttermesser Papers. 1997.

Short Stories

The Pagan Rabbi and Other Stories. 1971.
Bloodshed and Three Novellas. 1976.
Levitation: Five Fictions. 1982.
The Shawl: A Story and a Novella. 1989; "The Shawl" originally published in *New Yorker,* 1980.

Poetry

Epodes: First Poems. 1992.

Play

Blue Light (produced New York, 1994).

Other

Art and Ardor (essays). 1983.
Metaphor and Memory (essays). 1989.
What Henry James Knew and Other Essays on Writers. 1993.
Fame and Folly: Essays. 1996.
Quarrel & Quandary: Essays. 2000.

Editor, *The Best American Essays 1998.* 1998.

*

Bibliography: "A Bibliography of Writings by Ozick" by Susan Currier and Daniel J. Cahill, in *Texas Studies in Literature and Language,* Summer 1983.

Critical Studies: *Cynthia Ozick,* edited by Harold Bloom, 1986; *The World of Cynthia Ozick,* edited by Daniel Waldon, 1987; *The Uncompromising Fictions of Ozick* by Sanford Pinsker, 1987; *Cynthia Ozick* by Joseph Lowin, 1988; *Understanding Cynthia Ozick,* 1991, and "A Postcolonial Jew: Cynthia Ozick's Holocaust Survivor," in *SPAN* (Australia), 36, October 1993, pp. 436–43, both by Lawrence S. Friedman; *Cynthia Ozick's Fiction: Tradition and Invention* by Elaine M. Kauvar, 1993; *Cynthia Ozick's Comic Art: From Levity to Liturgy* by Sarah Blacher Cohen, 1994; *Greek Mind/Jewish Soul: The Conflicted Art of Cynthia Ozick* by Victor H.

Strandberg, 1994; "Do We Not Know the Meaning of Aesthetic Gratification?: Cynthia Ozick's 'The Shawl,' the Akedah, and the Ethics of Holocaust Literary Aesthetics" by Joseph Alkana, in *MFS,* 43(4), Winter 1997, pp. 963–90; "'And Here (Their) Troubles Began': The Legacy of the Holocaust in the Writing of Cynthia Ozick, Art Spiegelman, and Philip Roth" by Sophia Lehmann, in *CLIO,* 28(1), Fall 1998, pp. 29–52.

*   *   *

Cynthia Ozick belongs at the forefront of a group of postwar Jewish American writers (including Hugh Nissenson and **Arthur A. Cohen**) who have discovered in the religious traditions of Judaism a conceptual underpinning for their art. Her literary project may thus be distinguished from that of writers like **Saul Bellow** and **Philip Roth**, who often write about an ethnic Jewish milieu without explicitly engaging with the moral and theological basis of Judaism itself. Employing a range of literary modes—including the novel, the short story, and the personal and critical essay—Ozick's writings frequently move toward the form of the parable. Her recurrent theme is the clash between ethical outlooks, often characterized as a moral or Judaic outlook confronting an aesthetic or Hellenic one. Another abiding theme in her work is the problem of responding to the Holocaust, and the figures that emerge as heroes in her writings are often characterized as witnesses to the destruction of European Jewry.

At the center of Ozick's writing is her conception of Judaism. This conception depends more upon an overall ethical and ideological orientation than upon the specifics of ritual practice. In particular she emphasizes the second commandment, the ban on idol worship. In an essay entitled "Literature as Idol: Harold Bloom" she writes, "The single most useful, and possibly the most usefully succinct, description of a Jew—as defined theologically, can be rendered negatively: a Jew is someone who shuns idols." For Ozick an idol is not merely a plastic form of a god; she extends the category to include any product of the human imagination that comes to be worshiped in and for itself. What makes an idol so dangerous, according to Ozick, is its ability to demand complete submission, eliminating human compassion and obscuring a proper view of history. She maintains that even literature, when conceived of in purely aesthetic terms, has a tendency to become an idol.

Many of Ozick's essays, including the manifesto-like "Towards a New Yiddish," reach toward a definition of a specifically Jewish literature. The mark of such a literature, in Ozick's view, is that it "passionately wallow[s] in the human reality; it will be touched by the covenant." Jewish literature, she contends, resists becoming an idol by insistently turning toward the world in a gesture of moral judgment. As she writes in the preface to *Bloodshed and Three Novellas* (1976), "I believe that stories ought to judge and interpret the world." Interestingly Ozick writes in a style that is highly ornate, elegant, and, indeed, literary. Thus it may be said that the style of her writing stands in tension with its ethical commitment. Ozick herself has hinted at this dualism in her work, asserting in an interview that she has "two heads: one that writes the fiction, the other that writes the essays."

Beginning with her very first prose work, a long novel entitled *Trust* (1966), the Holocaust has figured as a crucial point of reference. Her fiction is populated by characters who strive to retain the memory of the Holocaust amidst forces of forgetfulness. In *Trust* Enoch's work as a tabulator of death camp victims leads him back to Jewishness. He is contrasted with the anti-Semitic Allegra, who screams "the concentration camps are all over!" In "Envy, or Yiddish in America," the Yiddish poet Edelshtein desperately seeks a translator into English, asserting that "whoever forgets Yiddish courts amnesia of history." Also Ozick often uses the figure of a Holocaust survivor to articulate the moral truth of a story. In "Bloodshed" a Hasidic rabbi who survived Buchenwald impugns the assimilated Bleilip for surrendering to an "unearned" despair. In "The Pagan Rabbi" Sheindel, who was born in a concentration camp, represents a keeper of the faith while her husband, Kornfeld, worships nature, abandons his Jewish faith, and ends up taking his life. About Sheindel Ozick writes that she "had no mother to show, she had no father to show, but she had, extraordinarily, God to show."

Ozick's overall treatment of the Holocaust is informed by the Hellenic/Jewish antimony that underpins her writings. For Ozick the Hellenic outlook leads to an indifference, if not downright hostility, to history and the claims of memory. By contrast the Jewish outlook attends to what Ozick calls "the voice of the Lord of History." Yet much of Ozick's work complicates any simple alignment between memory and Jewish anti-idolatry on the one hand and forgetting and Hellenic aestheticism on the other. In *The Messiah of Stockholm* (1987) the worshiper of art, Lars, strives to recover the writings of Jewish writer Bruno Schulz, who was killed by the Nazis, and in "Rosa" the eponymous protagonist, a lover of Greek culture, keeps alive the memory of her daughter, who died in a concentration camp. In these works it turns out that the characters with a heightened aesthetic imagination are precisely the ones who avoid the amnesia of the surrounding world. Finally Ozick's work suggests that art and Holocaust memory are not necessarily antithetical even though their proper alignment requires a complicated balancing act.

—Julian Levinson

See the essays on *The Messiah of Stockholm,* "Rosa," and "The Shawl."

P

PAGIS, Dan

Nationality: Israeli (originally Romanian: immigrated to Palestine, 1946). **Born:** Radautz, Bukovina, 16 October 1930. **Education:** Hebrew University, Jerusalem, Ph.D. in medieval Hebrew poetry. **Family:** Married; one daughter and one son. **Career:** Prisoner, concentration camp, Transnistria, 1941–44. Teacher, kibbutz school; professor, medieval Hebrew literature, Hebrew University, Jerusalem. Also taught at Harvard University and University of California, Berkeley. **Died:** 1986.

PUBLICATIONS

Collections

Poems. 1972.
Selected Poems of T. Carmi and Dan Pagis. 1976.
Points of Departure. 1981.
Variable Directions: The Selected Poetry of Dan Pagis. 1989; as *The Selected Poetry of Dan Pagis,* 1996.
Kol ha-shirim: "Aba" (pirke prozah) [Collected Poems and Father (Prose Passages)]. 1991.

Poetry

She'on ha-tsel [The Shadow Dial]. 1959.
Shahut me'uheret: Shirim. 1964.
Gilgul: Shirim [Transformation]. 1970.
Moah: Shirim [Brain]. 1975.
Shenem 'asar panim [Synonyms]. 1982.
Milim nirdafot: Shirim [Twelve Faces]. 1984.
Shirim aharonim [Last Poems], edited by Shimon Sandbank. 1987.

Other

Shire ha-hol shel Mosheh Ibn 'Ezra [The Secular Poems of Moses Ibn Ezra] (dissertation). 1967.
Shirat ha-hol ve-torat ha-shir le-Mosheh Ibn 'Ezra u-vene doro [Secular Poetry and Poetic Theory, Moses Ibn Ezra and His Contemporaries] (literary criticism). 1970.
Ha-Betsah she-hithapsah (for children). 1973.
Hidush u-masoret be-shirat-ha-hol ha-'Ivrit, Sefarad ve-Italyah [Change and Tradition in the Secular Poetry, Spain and Italy]. 1976.
Ke-hut ha-shani: Shire ahavah 'Ivriyim mi-Sefarad, Italyah, Turkiyah ve-Teman [Scarlet Thread]. 1978.
Al sod hatum: Le-toldot ha-hidah ha-'Ivrit be-Italyah uve-Holand [Secret Sealed] (literary criticism). 1986.

Hebrew Poetry of the Middle Ages and the Renaissance. 1991.

Editor, *Ha-Kad ha-'atik,* by Ludwig Strauss. 1960; with Gad Ulman as *Ha-Kad ha-'atik: Agadot,* 1986.
Editor, *Kol ha-shirim,* by David Vogel. 1966.
Editor, *Shire Levi Ibn al-Tab'an* [The Poems of Levi Iban al-Tabban]. 1967.
Editor, *Torat ha-shirah ha-Sefaradit* [Introduction to the Hebrew Poetry of the Spanish Period], by David Yellin. 1972.
Editor, with Heinrich Brody, *Shire ha-hol* [Secular Poems], by Moses Ibn Ezra. 1977.
Editor, with Ezra Fleischer, *Kitve Profesor Hayim Shirman (1904–1981): Reshimah bibliyografit.* 1982; as *A Bibliography of the Writings of Prof. Jefim (Haim) Schirmann (1904–1981)* 1983.

Translator, *Hitbonenut be-tahrite gulgolet ha-pil me-et Henri Mur bi-Yerushalayim bi-zeman ha-milhamah* [Looking at Henry Moore's Elephant Skull Etchings in Jerusalem during the War], by Shirley Kaufman. 1980.

*

Critical Studies: "The Confines of Language and Beyond: Avner Treinen and Dan Pagis" by Alex Zehavi, in *Modern Hebrew Literature* (Israel), 9(1–2), Fall/Winter 1983, pp. 70–78; "Transformations: Holocaust Poems in Dan Pagis' *Gilgul*" by Naomi Sokoloff, in *Hebrew Annual Review,* 8, 1984, pp. 215–40; "Time Denatured into Meaning: New Worlds and Renewed Themes in the Poetry of Dan Pagis" by Tamar Yacobi, in *Style,* 22(1), Spring 1988, pp. 93–115; "The Gilgul of Dan Pagis: Myth, History, Silence" by John Felstiner, in *Translation Review,* 32–33, 1990, pp. 8–11; "Dan Pagis—Out of Line. A Poetics of Decomposition," in *Prooftexts,* 10(2), May 1990, pp. 335–63, "Seeking the Meridian: The Reconstitution of Space and Audience in the Poetry of Paul Celan and Dan Pagis," in *Religion and the Authority of the Past,* edited by Tobin Siebers, 1993, and "Dan Pagis and the Prosaics of Memory," in *Holocaust Remembrance: The Shapes of Memory,* edited by Geoffrey Hartman, 1994, all by Sidra DeKoven Ezrahi; "Poetry Chronicle: Dan Pagis, Robert Hass" by Charles Berger, in *Raritan,* 10(1), Summer 1990, p. 126; "Footprints, Traces, Remnants: The Operations of Memory in Dan Pagis' 'Aqebot'" by Wendy Zierler, in *Judaism,* 41(4), Fall 1992, pp. 316–33; "Scripture in a Sealed Railway-Car: A Poem of Dan Pagis" by Karl A. Plank, in *Literature and Theology* (England), 7(4), December 1993, pp. 354–64; *Return and Gestures in the Poetic Language of Dan Pagis* (dissertation) by Robert Karl Baruch, University of California, Los Angeles, 1994; "Dan Pagis and the Poetry of Displacement" by Robert Alter, in *Judaism,* 45(4), Fall 1996, pp.

399–402; "Eternal Present: Poetic Figuration and Cultural Memory in the Poetry of Yehuda Amichai, Dan Pagis, and Tuvia Rubner" by Amir Eshel, in *Jewish Social Studies,* 7(1), 2000, pp. 141–66.

* * *

Dan Pagis, poet and scholar, was born in 1930 in Radautz, a small town in Bukovina some 30 miles from Czernowicz. While politically a part of Romania, the Bukovina of Pagis's childhood remained in ethnic and cultural terms a provincial outpost of the defunct Austro-Hungarian Empire. Bukovinian peasants were Ukrainian, while the Jewish middle class, to which Pagis belonged, was linguistically and culturally German. When Pagis was four years old, his father left for Palestine and his mother died, the first of several shifts and losses that would punctuate his early life. This first shift was a comfortable one. Pagis was brought up by his maternal grandmother and grandfather, a sugar merchant, whom he loved: "Grandpa masquerades as an ordinary sugar merchant. Actually he is an emperor hidden from the eyes of men, tolerant and enlightened." His grandfather's study is the backdrop for a number of poems that evoke a science-minded child setting off from that protected library on imaginative astronomical journeys.

That world was shattered in October 1941 when Pagis was deported along with the rest of Bukovinian Jewry. He found himself in a concentration camp (not a death camp) in Transnistria, where he remained for three years. His grandparents died there. In later life he almost never spoke about the experience, not even writing about it until his second volume of poems. There he describes his own escape in a characteristically elliptical way: "the rain stole across some border / so did I." Survival is presented as a kind of cosmic accident: "It's true, I was a mistake, I was forgotten / in the sealed car, my body tied up / in the sack of life." His poems present him as a surprised and lonely observer of his own cutoff lives, both the one that went before and the one that came after.

Pagis reached Palestine in 1946. Hebrew was new to him, and his mastery of it puts him—along with his friend and contemporary **Aharon Appelfeld**—in that rare group of writers who achieve greatness in a language they learned as adolescents. Pagis went on to earn a doctorate in medieval Hebrew poetry, becoming a professor at Hebrew University and the author of a number of important studies on the secular poetry of Spain and surrounding areas. His own poetry, which mixes religious allusions with everyday speech, can be said to draw on his academic background, but it is just as much the poetry of a survivor looking back or the poetry of a twentieth-century man looking at ordinary surroundings in unusual ways.

Pagis published five books during his lifetime: *The Shadow Dial* (1959), *Transformation* (1970), *Brain* (1975), *Synonyms* (1982), and *Twelve Faces* (1984). *Last Poems* came out in 1987, a year after his early death from cancer. *Collected Poems* appeared in 1991. Translator Stephen Mitchell has provided two excellent English-language anthologies: *Points of Departure* (1981) and *The Selected Poetry of Dan Pagis* (1989). The translations used here are from one or the other of these books.

Perhaps the most characteristic feature of Pagis's poems is their assumption of surprising and revealing perspectives. Sometimes the view is evolutionary (imagining the human condition from a sped-up temporal perspective) and sometimes astronomical (imagining the world as it might look from some vantage point way outside). In some poems inanimate objects or even parts of the body are given limited but poignant aspects of being. So in the poem "Balloons," balloons have balloon-sized souls and suffer balloon-like deaths; in "Twelve Faces of the Emerald," the emerald contemplates itself with philosophical coldness (and some characteristic Pagis irony).

Irony or playfulness imbues many poems whose subjects are serious or even painful. In the poem "Brain," Brain's spiritual revelations are tempered by references to his own limitations, which he does not see; his flights of intellect are made just a little absurd when contrasted to his actual and not very awesome physical presence. The poem "End of the Questionnaire" is about awakening from death—and filling out a questionnaire about housing. The strangeness of the linkage makes it unclear whether this poem is a dark one (because the questions emphasize physical death) or light (because there is something out there after all).

Lack of understanding is a commonplace in Pagis's poems. In the poem "Brothers," one of several about the story of Abel and Cain, Cain the murderer is at the mercy of forces he cannot control. He is surprised by what he has done and deserves the protection that he receives. In another poem on biblical themes Job is distinguished not for his understanding but precisely for its opposite: he fails to see that he has in fact won his argument with God. Brain also tries valiantly to understand but learns mostly to avoid the entrapment of thought.

Pagis's perspective on the human condition can be mordant. The ape-hero of "The Readiness," waiting to evolve, commences like a boastfully confident émigré; evolution's doubtful achievement is a human with suit and cigarette, seated "in perfect readiness for the invention of chess." But with all the qualifications and contradictions, his is a world that honors above all the human capacity for abstract thought. Among Pagis's most striking poems are those about physics and physicists. In the poem "Point of Departure" the bookish child makes an easy flight into a world without gravity and also without harm. While in much of Pagis's work references to a disappearing past are anguished references to the Holocaust, in this poem the surroundings of his European childhood dissolve painlessly: "I fly so fast that I'm motionless / and leave behind me / the transparent wake of the past."

—Alice Nakhimovsky

See the essay on *Kol ha-shirim: "Aba" (pirke prozah).*

PÉREC, Georges

Nationality: French. **Born:** Paris, 7 March 1936. **Education:** Claude Bernard College, Paris, and Geoffroy-Saint-Hilaire College, D'Etampes, 1946–54. **Military Service:** 1958–59. **Family:** Married Paulette Pétras in 1960. **Career:** *La Ligne Générale,* 1959–63; *Cause Commune,* 1972–73. **Member:** OuLiPo (*Ouvroir de Littérature Potentielle;* Workshop of Potential Literature), Paris. **Awards:** Renaudot prize, 1965; Médicis prize, 1980. **Died:** 3 March 1982.

PUBLICATIONS

Collections

Georges Perec: Les Choses, espèces d'espaces: Résumé analytique, commentaire critique, documents complémentaires, edited by Martine Schneider. 1991.
Three by Perec. 1996.
Species of Spaces and Other Pieces, edited by John Sturrock. 1997.

Novels

Les Choses; Une histoire des années soixante. 1965; as *Les Choses; A Story of the Sixties,* 1968; as *Things; A Story of the Sixties,* 1990.
Quel petit vélo à guidon chromé au fond de la cour? 1966.
Un Homme qui dort. 1967.
La Disparition. 1969; as *A Void,* 1994.
Les Revenentes. 1972.
W, ou, le souvenir d'enfance (autobiographical novel). 1975; as *W, or the Memory of Childhood,* 1988.
Je me souviens: Les Choses communes I. 1978.
''53 jours.'' 1989; as *''53 Days,''* edited by Harry Mathews and Jacques Roubaud, 1992.

Short Stories

La Vie, mode d'emploi. 1978; as *Life, a User's Manual,* 1987.
Le Voyage d'hiver. 1993; as *The Winter Journey,* 1995.

Poetry

Trompe l'œil. 1978.
La Clôture: Et autres poèmes. 1980.
Ulcérations: Un jeu d'intérieur sur un texte de Georges Pérec; Conception typographique Alain Roger. 1986.
Cantatrix sopranica L. et autres écrits scientifiques (in French and English) 1991.

Beaux présents, belles absentes. 1994.

Plays

Théâtre. 1, la poche parmentier: Précédé de l'augmentation. 1981.

Other

Petit traité invitant à la découverte de l'art subtil du go, with Pierre Lusson, and Jacques Roubaud. 1969.
La Boutique obscure; 124 rêves. 1973.
Espèces d'espaces. 1974.
Tentative d'épuisement d'un lieu parisien. 1975.
Alphabets: Cent soixante-seize onzains hétérogrammatiques. 1976.
Les Mots croisés (crossword puzzles). 1979.
Un Cabinet d'amateur: Histoire d'un tableau. 1979.
Récits d'Ellis Island: Histoires d'errance et d'espoir, with Robert Bobert. 1980; as *Ellis Island,* 1995.
Cocktail queneau. 1982.
Penser, classer. 1985.
Les Mots croisés II (crossword puzzles). 1986.
Vœux. 1989; as *A Little Illustrated Alphabet Primer,* 1996.
Entretien (avec Gabriel Simony) (interview). 1989.
Je suis né. 1990.
Perec/rinations (crossword puzzles). 1997.
Jeux intéressants (word games). 1997.
Cher, très cher, admirable et charmant ami: Correspondence, Georges Perec-Jacques Lederer (1956–1961). 1997.
Nouveaux jeux intéressants (word games). 1998.

Translator, *Le Naufrage du stade Odradek* [The Sinking of the Odradek Stadium], by Harry Mathews. 1989.

＊

Film Adaptations: *A Man Who Sleeps,* 1974.

Critical Studies: ''Georges Perec'' by Harry Mathews, in *Grand Street,* 3(1), Autumn 1983, pp. 136–45; *The Poetics of Experiment: A Study of the Work of Georges Perec,* 1984, and ''Georges Perec and the Broken Book,'' in *Auschwitz and After: Race, Culture, and 'the Jewish Question' in France,* edited by Lawrence D. Kritzman, both by Warren F. Motte 1994; ''Literary Quotations in Perec's *La Vie mode d'emploi,*'' in *French Studies,* 41(2), April 1987, pp. 181–94, and *Georges Perec: A Life in Words,* 1993, both by David Bellos; *Georges Perec, Traces of His Passage* by Paul Schwartz, 1988; Georges Perec and Felipe Alfau issue of *Review of Contemporary Fiction,* Spring 1993; ''Masculine/Feminine: Georges Perec's Narrative of the Missing One'' by Stella Behar, in *Neophilologus* (Netherlands), 79(3), July 1995 July, pp. 409–19; ''Puzzles and Lists: Georges Perec's *Un Homme qui dort*" by Chris Andrews, in *MLN,* 111(4), September 1996, pp. 775–96; ''An Auto-bio-graphy: *W, ou, le souvenir d'enfance* or the Space of the Double Cover'' by Michel Sirvent, in *Sites,* 1(2), Fall 1997, pp. 461–80; ''Georges Perec, *W, ou, le souvenir d'enfance*'' by Joyce Block Lazarus, in *Strangers and Sojourners,* 1999; ''Georges Perec on Ellis Island'' by Dan Stone, in *Jewish Quarterly,* 47(2), Summer 2000, p. 37; ''Dreaming the Self, Writing the Dream: The Subject in the Dream-Narratives of Georges Perec'' by David Gascoigne, in *Subject Matters: Subject and Self in French Literature from Descartes to the Present,* edited by Paul Gifford and Johnnie Gratton, 2000.

* * *

By the time of his premature death in 1982, Georges Pérec had established himself as one of the most important and restlessly innovative writers of the French postwar period. Taken as a whole, his corpus reads as an ongoing and ever-changing experiment with literary language. In novels, essays, poetry, drama, and screenplays as well as more eclectic writerly exercises—fragmentary memoirs, crosswords, palindromes, and other word games—he dazzles his readers with his apparently effortless mastery of language and its possibilities.

Pérec's restless experimentalism as a writer, however, is indissociable from his biography. Born in Paris in 1936 to Jewish parents, he was raised from the age of six by his non-Jewish uncle and aunt in rural France after his father's death in combat and his mother's deportation to Auschwitz. These skeletal facts help make sense of the obsessive play with gaps, fragmentation, and absence that pervades each of his twenty very different books; the trauma of irretrievable loss that shapes his childhood finds itself expressed in his very mode of writing.

Pérec found a channel for his writerly obsessions in his membership of OuLiPo (*Ouvroir de Littérature Potentielle; Workshop of Potential Literature*), a Paris-based international group of writers founded in 1960 by Raymond Queneau and François LeLionnais. The guiding strategy of OuLiPo is ''writing under constraint,'' an exercise whereby literature is subjected to arbitrary disciplines imported from, for example, mathematics, logic, or chess. Amongst the most famous and substantial products of this strategy is Pérec's extraordinary ''lipogrammatic'' novel of 1969, *La Disparation*. A lipogram is a text in which one or more letters is prohibited from appearing. In *La Disparation* the prohibited letter is perhaps the most daunting of all: *e.* Its ''story'' mimes this strategy, telling of the disappearance of a man named Anton Voyl (translated as Anton Vowl in Gilbert Adair's ingenious English translation, *A Void*) and his friends' vain attempts to find him.

As many of his critics have noted, it is impossible to avoid reading into this dazzlingly sustained (the novel is around 300 pages long) experiment in linguistic absence the traumatic familial absence that shaped his life. There is little in the way of direct reference to or narration of the Holocaust in Pérec, yet its memory insinuates itself into the very texture of his writing. While he alludes to the Nazi genocide in *Récits d'Ellis Island* (*Ellis Island*) and *Espèces d'espaces* (*Species of Space*) and interweaves some Holocaust-related stories into the intricate narrative patchwork that makes up perhaps his most famous novel, *La Vie mode d'emploi* (*Life: A User's Manual*), it is the formal patterning more than any content of his writing that registers the memory of trauma most potently. In the structural lacunae of his texts, Pérec demonstrates the impossibility of representing that trauma directly.

This is the case even for the text that confronts the Holocaust and its effect on his life most explicitly: his 1975 book *W, ou le souvenir d'enfance* (*W, or the Memory of Childhood*). Interweaving autobiography and fiction, the book is a painstaking demonstration of the Holocaust's stubborn resistance to conventional narration or representation. If the book is unique in his corpus for the relative directness with which it addresses his traumatic history, it is characteristic in its thoroughgoing refusal of a representational aesthetic.

—Josh Cohen

See the essay on *W, or the Memory of Childhood.*

PERL, Gisella

Nationality: American (originally Romanian: immigrated to the United States, 1947, granted U.S. citizenship). **Born:** 1907. **Family:** Married (died); one son (deceased) and one daughter. **Career:** Gynecologist and director of hospital, Sighet, Hungary (now Romania). Prisoner and camp physician, Auschwitz-Birkenau, 1944–45; prisoner, Bergen-Belsen, 1945. Physician, New York, 1947–79. Moved to Jerusalem, 1979. Volunteer consultant in gynecology, Shaare Zedek Hospital, Jerusalem, beginning in 1979. **Died:** 1988.

PUBLICATION

Memoir

I Was a Doctor in Auschwitz. 1948.

* * *

Gisella Perl was trained as a gynecologist and obstetrician. With her surgeon husband, she operated a hospital in Sighet,

Hungary (now Romania). As wife, mother, and physician, Perl enjoyed a successful and rewarding life. All of that changed when the Nazis invaded Hungary in 1944. Forced from their home, Perl, her parents, husband, and son were sent first to the ghetto and then to Auschwitz-Birkenau. Her daughter, Gabriella, was hidden by non-Jews and survived the war.

Perl recorded her experiences in a brief memoir, *I Was a Doctor in Auschwitz* (1948). Most of the memoir focuses upon Perl's time as camp gynecologist in Birkenau. The book also recounts Perl's struggle to survive after she was taken from Birkenau, finally arriving at that most horrible of destinations, Bergen-Belsen, where the Nazis dumped thousands with neither food nor shelter.

Perl wrote only one book about her Holocaust experiences, but in this single small work she created an unforgettable portrait of women's suffering and courage. In a series of interlocking episodes, Perl describes a world where three uncooked potatoes are worth a bag of diamonds; where a piece of string to tie one's shoes can mean the difference between life and death; and where telling a Nazi guard that one is pregnant is a death sentence. It is a world where trying to maintain a semblance of human decency—cutting off a piece of cloth from the camp uniform to cleanse oneself from the latrine—is considered a crime.

Perl describes a world gone mad, where she feels compelled secretly to kill newborn babies in order to save the lives of their mothers, for if a pregnancy were discovered, both mother and child would be killed. It is a world of unfathomable cruelty and extraordinary compassion, a world where Perl and her nine women colleagues at Birkenau, doctors and nurses, band together as sisters, committed to one another and to the more than 30,000 women within their care.

As the Russians drew close to Auschwitz, Josef Mengele, the camp physician, tore Perl away from her "camp sisters." She was sent first to Berlin, then to a labor camp near Hamburg, and lastly to Bergen-Belsen, where she survived in the midst of mountains of corpses until she was liberated by the British army in April 1945. In yet another cruel twist, liberation brought Perl to new depths of suffering, for it was only then that she learned that her husband and son, along with her parents, had perished. Overwhelmed by despair, Perl sought to end her life. She was pulled back from the brink only by the loving care of a young Catholic priest whose compassion and kindness served as the antidote for the poison she had taken.

Dr. Perl came to the United States in 1947 as an "Ambassador of the Six Million," as she called herself, speaking to physicians and nurses about her experiences. The following year, in which *I Was a Doctor in Auschwitz* was published, she was granted citizenship by a special act of Congress. She opened a practice in New York City, where she became an expert in the treatment of infertility and delivered 3,000 babies, many to women for whom she had cared in Auschwitz and Bergen-Belsen. In 1979 she moved to Jerusalem, fulfilling a vow she had made to her father as the family was being deported to Auschwitz. She spent her final years as a volunteer consultant in gynecology to Shaare Zedek Hospital.

—Marilyn J. Harran

See the essay on *I Was a Doctor in Auschwitz.*

PINTER, Harold

Nationality: British. **Born:** Hackney, London, 10 October 1930. **Education:** Royal Academy of Dramatic Art, 1948. **Military Service:** Conscientious objector. **Family:** Married 1) Vivien Merchant in 1956 (divorced 1980), one son; 2) Lady Antonia Fraser in 1980. **Career:** Poet and playwright. Has worked as a waiter, National Liberal Club; dishwasher; and salesman. Actor, using stage name David Baron, 1948–58, performing with Shakespearean repertory company, Ireland, 1950–52, with Bournemouth Repertory Company and other repertory companies, 1952–58. Since 1970 director of plays, and since 1973 associate director, National Theatre, London. **Awards:** *Evening Standard* drama award, 1961, and Newspaper Guild of New York award, 1962, both for *The Caretaker;* Italia prize for television play, 1963, for *The Lover;* two Screenwriters Guild awards, for television play and for screenplay, both 1963; New York Film Critics award, 1964, for *The Servant;* British Film Academy award, 1965 and 1971; New York Drama Critics Circle award, Whitbread Anglo-American Theater award, and Antoinette Perry award, all 1967, all for *The Homecoming;* Shakespeare prize, Hamburg, West Germany (now Germany), 1970; Writers Guild award, 1971; Best New Play award, *Plays & Players,* 1971, and Antoinette Perry award nomination, 1972, both for *Old Times;* Austrian State prize in literature, 1973; New York Drama Critics Circle award, 1980; Pirandello prize, 1980; Common Wealth award, Bank of Delaware, 1981; Elmer Holmes Bobst award for arts and letters, 1985, for drama; David Cohen British Literature prize, 1995. Honorary degrees from many institutions in the United Kingdom and the United States, including University of Reading, 1970, University of Birmingham, 1971, University of Glasgow, 1974, University of East Anglia, 1974, University of Stirling, 1979, Brown University, 1982, University of Hull, 1986, University of Sussex, 1990, University of East London, 1994, University of Sofia (Bulgaria), 1995, and an honorary fellowship from Queen Mary College, 1987. Commander, Order of the British Empire, 1966. **Member:** League of Dramatists; Modern Language Association (honorary fellow). **Agent:** Judy Daish Associates, 2 St. Charles Place, London W10 6EG, England.

Collections

The Birthday Party and Other Plays (includes *The Birthday Party; The Room; The Dumb Waiter*). 1960; as *The Birthday Party and The Room*, 1961.

A Slight Ache and Other Plays (includes *A Slight Ache; A Night Out; The Dwarfs; Trouble in the Works; The Black and White; Request Stop; Last to Go; Applicant*). 1961.

The Caretaker and The Dumb Waiter. 1961.

Three Plays: A Slight Ache, The Collection, The Dwarfs. 1962.

The Collection and The Lover (includes a prose piece, *The Examination*). 1963.

The Dwarfs and Eight Review Sketches (includes *The Dwarfs; Trouble in the Works; The Black and White; Request Stop; Last to Go; Applicant; Interview; That's All; That's Your Trouble*). 1965.

Tea Party and Other Plays (includes *Tea Party; The Basement; Night School*). 1967.

The Lover, Tea Party, The Basement: Two Plays and a Film Script. 1967.

A Night Out, Night School, Revue Sketches: Early Plays. 1968.

Landscape and Silence (includes *Landscape; Silence; Night*). 1969.

Five Screenplays (includes *Accident; The Caretaker; The Pumpkin Eater; The Quiller Memorandum; The Servant*). 1971; revised edition, omitting *The Caretaker* and including *The Go-Between,* 1971.

Plays (4 vols.). 1976–81; as *Complete Works,* 1977–81.

The French Lieutenant's Woman and Other Screenplays (includes *The French Lieutenant's Woman; Langrishe; Go Down; The Last Tycoon*). 1982.

Other Places: Three Plays (includes *A Kind of Alaska; Victoria Station; Family Voices*). 1983.

Plays

The Room (produced Bristol, England, 1957; with *The Dumb Waiter,* London, 1960; San Francisco, 1960; with *A Slight Ache,* New York, 1964).

The Birthday Party: A Play in Three Acts (produced Cambridge, England, 1958; New York, 1967). 1959; second revised edition, 1981.

The Dumb Waiter (produced in German translation, Frankfurt-am-Main, Germany, 1959; with *The Room,* London, 1960; with *The Collection,* New York, 1962).

Trouble in the Works [and] *The Black and White* (produced as part of *One to Another,* Hammersmith, England, 1959; London, 1959).

Request Stop, Last to Go, Special Offer, [and] *Getting Acquainted* (produced as part of *Pieces of Eight,* London, 1959).

The Caretaker: A Play in Three Acts (produced London, 1960; New Haven, Connecticut, 1961; New York, 1961). 1960.

A Night Out (produced London, 1961).

A Slight Ache (London, 1961; with *The Room,* New York, 1964).

The Collection (produced London, 1962; with *The Dumb Waiter,* New York, 1962).

The Dwarfs (produced with *The Lover,* London, 1963; with *The Dumb Waiter,* New York, 1974). 1990.

The Lover (produced with *The Dwarfs,* London, 1963; New York, 1964).

The Homecoming: A Play in Two Acts (produced Cardiff, Wales, England, 1965; London, 1965; New York, 1967). 1965; revised edition, 1968.

Tea Party (produced with *The Basement,* New York, 1968). 1965.

The Basement (produced with *Tea Party,* New York, 1968).

Landscape (radio play). 1968.

Night (produced as part of *We Who Are about To . . .* , London, 1969).

Landscape [and] *Silence* (produced London, 1969; New York, 1970).

Sketches (produced New York, 1969).

Old Times (produced London, 1971; New York, 1971). 1971.

Monologue (television play). 1973.

No Man's Land (produced London, 1975). 1975.

Betrayal (produced London, 1978; New York, 1980). 1978; revised edition, 1980.

Other Pinter Pauses (revue; produced New York, 1979).

The Hothouse (produced London, 1980; New York, 1982). 1980; revised edition, 1982.

Family Voices: A Play for Radio (produced London, 1981). 1981.

The French Lieutenant's Woman (screenplay). As *The French Lieutenant's Woman: A Screenplay,* 1981.

A Kind of Alaska: A Play (produced London, 1982). 1981.

Victoria Station. 1982.

Other Places (triple bill, includes *Family Voices, A Kind of Alaska,* and *Victoria Station;* produced London, 1982). 1982; revised edition, omitting *Family Voices* and including *One for the Road,* 1983 (produced New York, 1984; London, 1985).

Precisely (sketch; produced as part of *The Big One,* London, 1983).

One for the Road: A Play (produced Hammersmith, 1984). 1984; revised edition, 1985.

Mountain Language (produced London, 1988; with *The Birthday Party,* New York, 1989). 1988.

Party Time & The New World Order. 1993.

Moonlight: A Play. 1993.

Ashes to Ashes. 1996.

Celebration (produced with *The Room,* New York, 2001).

Screenplays: *The Servant,* 1963; *The Guest,* adaptation of his *The Caretaker,* 1964; *The Pumpkin Eater,* 1964; *The Quiller Memorandum,* 1967; *Accident,* 1967; *The Birthday Party,* 1968; *The Go-Between,* 1971; *The Homecoming,* 1971; *The Last Tycoon,* 1975; *The French Lieutenant's Woman,* 1981; *Betrayal,* 1983; *Turtle Diary,* 1986; *The Handmaid's Tale,* adaptation of the novel by Margaret Atwood, 1990; *Lolita,* 1997. Also adapted Fred Uhlman's novel *Reunion,* 1989.

Television Plays: *Night School,* 1960; *The Collection,* 1961; *The Lover,* 1963; *Tea Party,* 1965; *The Basement,* 1967; *Pinter People,* 1968; *Monologue,* 1973.

Radio Plays: *A Slight Ache,* 1959; *A Night Out,* 1960; *The Dwarfs,* 1960; *Dialogue for Three,* 1964; *That's Your Trouble,* 1964; *That's All,* 1964; *Applicant,* 1964; *Interview,* 1964; *Landscape,* 1968; *Family Voices: A Play for Radio,* 1981.

Poetry

Poems. 1968.
Poems and Prose 1949–1977. 1978; revised edition, as *Collected Poems and Prose,* 1986.
I Know the Place: Poems. 1979.
Ten Early Poems. 1990.
Collected Poems and Prose. 1996.

Other

The Compartment, with Samuel Beckett and Eugene Ionesco (unreleased screenplay). Published in *Project 1,* 1963.
Mac. 1968.
The Proust Screenplay: A la recherche du temps perdu, with Joseph Losey and Barbara Bray. 1978.
The Heat of the Day. 1989.
Various Voices: Prose, Poetry, Politics. 1998.

Editor, with John Fuller and Peter Redgrove, *New Poems 1967: A P.E.N. Anthology.* 1968.
Editor, with Geoffrey Godbert and Anthony Astbury, *A Hundred Poems by a Hundred Poets: An Anthology.* 1986.
Editor, with Godbert and Astbury, *Ninety-Nine Poems in Translation: An Anthology.* 1994.

*

Bibliography: *Harold Pinter: An Annotated Bibliography* by Steven H. Gale, 1978.

Critical Studies: *Harold Pinter* by Walter Kerr, 1967; "'. . . Apart from the Known and the Unknown': The Unreconciled Worlds of Harold Pinter's Characters" by Francis Gillen, in *Arizona Quarterly,* 26(1), Spring 1970, pp. 17–24; "Harold Pinter: Action and Control: *The Homecoming and Other Plays*" by John Russell Brown, in his *Theatre Language: A Study of Arden, Osborne, Pinter and Wesker,* 1972; "Who Can Afford to Live in the Past?: *The Homecoming*" by William Baker and Stephen Ely Tabachnick, in their *Harold Pinter,* 1973; "Pinter As a Radio Dramatist" by Mary Jane Miller, in *Modern Drama,* XVII(4), December 1974, pp. 403–12; "A Pattern of Need" by Steven H. Gale, in his *Butter's Going Up: A Critical Analysis of Harold Pinter's Work,* 1977; "Harold Pinter: A Retrospect" by Peter Thomson, in *Critical Quarterly,* 20(4), Winter 1978, pp. 21–28; *Pinter the Playwright* by Martin Esslin, 1984; *The Pinter Ethic: The Erotic Aesthetic* by Penelope Prentice, 1994; *Harold Pinter: A Question of Timing* by Martin S. Regal, 1995; *Understanding Harold Pinter* by Ronald Knowles, 1995..

Theatrical Activities: Actor: Plays—several of his own plays.

*   *   *

At the end of the twentieth century Harold Pinter was generally acknowledged as Britain's finest living playwright. He was born on 11 October 1930 in the East End of London, the son of a Jewish tailor. Following World War II he experienced a rise in anti-Semitic activity in London and politically classified himself as a conscientious objector opposed to performing military service for his country. At the age of 19 he dropped out of college and began a career as an actor in a touring Shakespearean company in Ireland.

Pinter's playwriting career began with a one-act play, *The Room* (1957), in which he explored some of the themes and styles that would become associated with his later work. It is a mysterious play about a middle-aged woman, Rose, who anxiously dwells in a room with her brutal, racist younger husband and who is commanded by a blind black stranger to remember the past. In this play and in others Pinter uses a circuitous structure that shies from specific explanation, preferring to make its points through implication. An early critic and biographer, Martin Esslin, described Pinter's plays as comedies of menace, in which protagonists are filled with anxiety, awaiting some brutal downfall. Many of his plays and film scripts also explore marriages and friendships as states of persecution, as competitions over memory, and as contests for language. Control or power becomes the central motivating force in human interchanges; whoever controls the language controls memory and controls both the present and the future.

These themes have been consistently present from *The Birthday Party* (1958) and *The Dumb Waiter* (1959) through *The Caretaker* (1960), *The Homecoming* (1965), *Old Times* (1971), and *No Man's Land* (1975). Pinter earlier eschewed precise political readings of his plays, preferring ambiguity to statement, even though his plays were peppered with clues. In the 1980s, however, he began openly expressing his political views in such works as *One for the Road* (1984), *Mountain Language* (1988), *The New World Order* (1993), and *Ashes to Ashes* (1996). Again, Pinter has shied away from specifically identifying his plays, especially as Holocaust or post-Holocaust theater. While the subject of *Mountain Language*—an ethnic group is denied not only all political rights but also its own language—was inspired by the actions of Turkey against its Kurd population, the play's unstated locale also allows the reader or viewer to infer the condition of Jews under the Third Reich in the 1930s and 1940s. Likewise, *Ashes to Ashes* utilizes images from the Jewish experience of being selected at railway stations, separations of families, and large groups being led to their deaths while carrying their personal belongings.

In only one script, his screen adaptation of Fred Uhlman's novel *Reunion* (1989), has Pinter directly confronted the Holocaust. In the script an elderly Jewish-American businessman named Henry Strauss returns to the Germany of his youth, where he lived before he was sent away by his parents to escape the escalating anti-Semitic violence of the 1930s. While he is in his hotel room, he watches a film clip of Laurence Olivier as Henry V giving the Saint Crispin's day speech to his troops. Henry's issue is the necessity for those who were present at the event to remember the past, a remembrance challenged by a television intellectual contesting the king's sincerity. Yet Strauss's visit to his childhood home is predicated on his need to confront his own conflicting memories and to discover what has happened to a former childhood friend who had abandoned him for the Nazis.

Pinter's place within Holocaust literature may be found in his exploration of the modes of persecution and in his analysis of the uses of language and its ability to control the past by refashioning memory. Although he did not personally experience the loss of the Holocaust, he has continued, with considerable power and imagination, to open discussion on these issues to a post-Holocaust generation.

—Steven Dedalus Burch

See the essay on *Ashes to Ashes*.

POTOK, Chaim

Nationality: American. **Born:** Herman Harold Potok, New York City, 17 February 1929. **Education:** Yeshiva University, New York, 1946–50, B.A. (summa cum laude) in English 1950; Jewish Theological Seminary, New York, 1950–54, M.H.L. and rabbinic ordination, 1954; University of Pennsylvania, 1959–65, Ph.D. in philosophy 1965. **Family:** Married Adena Sarah Mosevitzky in 1958; two daughters and one son. **Military Service:** United States Army chaplain in Korea, 1956–57. **Career:** National director of Leaders training fellowship, Jewish Theological Seminary, 1954–55; director,

Camp Ramah, Ojai, California, 1957–59; instructor, University of Judaism, Los Angeles, 1957–59; scholar-in-residence, Har Zion Temple, Philadelphia, 1959–63; member of faculty, Teachers' Institute, Jewish Theological Seminary, 1963–64; managing editor, *Conservative Judaism,* New York, 1964–65. Editor-in-chief, 1965–74, and since 1974 special projects editor, Jewish Publication Society, Philadelphia. Visiting professor, University of Pennsylvania, 1983, 1992–98, Bryn Mawr College, 1985, and Johns Hopkins University, 1995–98. **Awards:** Edward Lewis Wallant award, 1968, and National Book Award nomination, both for *The Chosen;* Athenaem award, 1969, for *The Promise;* Jewish National book award, 1997, for *The Gift of Asher Lev;* National Foundation for Jewish Culture achievement award. **Address:** c/o Alfred Knopf Inc., 201 E. 50th Street, New York, New York 10022, U.S.A.

PUBLICATIONS

Novels

The Chosen. 1967.
The Promise (sequel to *The Chosen*). 1969.
My Name Is Asher Lev. 1972.
In the Beginning. 1975.
The Book of Lights. 1981.
Davita's Harp. 1985.
The Gift of Asher Lev (sequel to *My Name Is Asher Lev*). 1990.
I Am the Clay. 1992.

Other

Jewish Ethics (pamphlet series; 14 vols.). 1964–69.
The Jew Confronts Himself in American Literature. 1975.
Wanderings: Chaim Potok's History of the Jews. 1978.
Ethical Living for a Modern World. 1985.
Theo Tobiasse: Artist in Exile. 1986.
The Tree of Here (for children). 1993.
The Sky of Now (for children). 1995.
The Gates of November: Chronicles of the Slepak Family. 1996.
Zebra and Other Stories. 1998.
My First Seventy-Nine Years, with Isaac Stern Knopf. 1999.
Conversations with Chaim Potok, edited by Daniel Walden. 2001.

*

Film Adaptation: *The Chosen,* 1982.

Bibliography: ''Chaim Potok: A Bibliographic Essay'' by Cynthia Fagerheim, in *Studies in American Jewish Literature,* 4, 1985, p. 107–20.

Critical Studies: ''The Phenomenon of the Really Jewish Best Seller: Potok's *The Chosen*'' by Sheldon Grebstein, in

Studies in American Jewish Literature, 1(1), 1975, pp. 23–31; "*My Name Is Asher Lev:* Chaim Potok's Portrait of the Young Hasid As Artist" by Ellen Serlen Uffen, in *Studies in American Jewish Literature,* 2, 1982, pp. 174–80; *The World of Chaim Potok,* edited by Daniel Walden, 1985; Chaim Potok issue of *Studies in American Jewish Literature,* 4, 1985; *Chaim Potok* by Edward A. Abramson, 1986; "Freedom, Faith, and Fanaticism: Cultural Conflict in the Novels of Chaim Potok" by Sanford E. Marovitz, in *Studies in American Jewish Literature,* 5, 1986, pp. 129–40; "An Interview with Chaim Potok, in *Contemporary Literature,* 27(3), Fall 1986, pp. 291–317; "Chaim Potok's *Book of Lights* and the Jewish-American Novel" by Edward Margolies, in *Yiddish,* 6(4), 1987, pp. 93–98; "Eternal Light: The Holocaust and the Revival of Judaism and Jewish Civilization in the Fiction of Chaim Potok" by S. Lillian Kremer, in *Witness through Imagination: Jewish American Holocaust Literature,* 1989; "Chaim Potok's Plea for Jewish 'Gentleness' As an Answer to Hatred" by Paola Loreto, in *Reclaiming Memory: American Representations of the Holocaust,* edited by Pirjo Ahokas and Martine Chard-Hutchinson, 1997; *Chaim Potok: A Critical Companion* by Sanford Sternlicht, 2000.

* * *

Chaim Potok, born in 1929 to Hasidic Jewish parents who had emigrated to the United States from Poland, began writing fiction when he was 16 years old. His early novels are of the bildungsroman tradition, with the stories exploring the development of a person from childhood to maturity and with particular emphasis on the character becoming conscious of his or her role in the world. Potok's conception of himself as a writer at the age of 16 evokes the very core of a bildungsroman novel. In a 1995 interview Potok told the author Laura Chavkin that his father had wanted him to teach Talmud and was not happy about his decision to become a writer. Potok did, however, follow this path, and he lists his most significant literary influences as James Joyce, Evelyn Waugh, and Thomas Mann, authors he describes as taking him to worlds he never knew existed, authors making him conscious of language and its potential beauty in telling stories.

Potok earned a B.A. in English literature and went on to earn a Ph.D. in philosophy from the University of Pennsylvania. In 1954 he was ordained as a rabbi and the following year served as a chaplain for the U.S. Army in Korea. Potok has described his service in Korea as a pivotal life experience: "Crucial, fundamental, pivotal. It was a transforming experience. I was not the same person coming out of the army and Korea as I was going in." He went on to say that the experience reshaped his model of himself and of his place in the world.

This reshaping of the self after confrontation with another culture is a central theme in Potok's fiction. For example, in Potok's best-known work, *The Chosen,* both the narrator, Reuven Malter, and his enemy-then-friend, Danny Saunders, are confronted with cultural elements (although both are from Jewish homes) that cause them to question and be transformed. While the transformation is not without pain, it gives meaning to their lives. In *My Name Is Asher Lev* the main character is confronted with his artistic gift and must learn to paint the truth by using motifs from his own as well as other religions, regardless of the pain this may bring to those he loves. It is this search for personal meaning within a tradition that gives the novels their richness and lasting significance. Potok has acknowledged the religious tradition in his novels: "There is in my work a very strong religious foreground and background."

History provides a background in Potok's fiction as well. World War II and the Holocaust are ever present in *The Chosen,* with the war, the ultimate defeat of Hitler, the realization of the murder of six million Jews, and the establishment of a Jewish state providing a larger context for the lives of the boys. Jewish history and the Holocaust also provide a subtle background for the suffering in *My Name Is Asher Lev.* The world remaining silent in the face of such slaughter is a concept the young Asher internalizes and eventually works through as he comes to realize that he cannot remain silent about suffering and be true to his art or his humanity.

Potok's fiction explores the importance of family, of Jewish tradition, of cultures coming together, of discovering truth and transforming the self as a consequence of experience. His bildungsroman novels present questions of humanity as the young protagonists mature in post-World War II America.

—Jan M. Osborn

See the essays on *The Chosen* and *My Name Is Asher Lev.*

PRESSER, (Gerrit) Jacques

Pseudonym: J. van Wageningen. **Nationality:** Dutch. **Born:** Jacob Presser, Amsterdam, 24 February 1899. **Education:** University of Amsterdam, Ph.D. in history 1926. **Family:** Married 1) Debora Suzanna Appel in 1936 (killed by the Nazis in Poland during World War II); 2) Bertha Hartog in 1954. **Career:** Teacher, Vossiusgymnasium, Amsterdam, 1926–40, and Jewish Lyceum, Amsterdam, 1941. Went into hiding during World War II. Professor of modern history, University of Amsterdam, 1947–69. **Awards:** Wynaends Francken award for *Napoleon: Historie en legende*; Van der Hoogt award for *De Nacht der Girondijnen*; Jan Campert award and Remembrance award, World Federation of Bergan-Belsen Associations, for *Ondergang: De Vervolging en Verdelging van het Nederlandse jodendom.* **Member:** Historisch Genootschap; Maatschappij der Nederlandse Letterkunde; Royal Dutch Academy of Science. **Died:** 30 April 1970.

PUBLICATIONS

Novel

De Nacht der Girondijnen. 1957; as *Breaking Point,* 1958; as *Night of the Girondists,* 1992.

Poetry

Orpheus en Ashasverus (as J. van Wageningen). 1945.

Other

Das buch "De tribus impostoribus" (Von den drei Detrügern) (dissertation). 1926.
De Tachtigjarige Oorlog [Netherland's Wars of Independence]. 1941.
Napoleon: Historie en legende. 1946.
Amerika: Van kolonie tot wereldmacht (American history). 1949.
Historia hodierna (inaugural speech). 1950.
Gewiekte wielen: Richard Arkwright (biography). 1951.
Schrijfsels en schrifturen (essays). 1961.
Europe in een boek. 1963.
Ondergang: De vervolging en verdelging van het Nederlandse jodendom, 1940–1945 (2 vols.). 1965; as *Ashes in the Wind: The Destruction of Dutch Jewry,* 1968.
Meit hek werk van Dr. Jacques Presser (essays, addresses, and lectures). 1969.

Editor, *Antwoord aan het kwaad: Getuigenissen 1939–1945* [World War II Prisoners and Poetry]. 1961.

* * *

Jacques Presser was born on 24 February 1899 into a secular Jewish family in the old Jewish ghetto of Amsterdam. He was the oldest child and only son among three daughters. Presser's father was a diamond worker, and when he found work in Antwerp the family followed him there. While they were in Belgium, Jacob's name was changed to the more assimilated-sounding Jacques. In 1907 the family moved back to Amsterdam, where Presser received his primary and secondary education. At the University of Amsterdam he studied history, art history, and Dutch; in 1926 he earned his doctorate in history. He then began to teach at the Vossius Gymnasium, a prestigious Amsterdam high school.

Presser's relationship to Judaism was complex but probably no more so than any European Jew who wrestled with the problems of assimilation: he never denied his Jewishness, but he never turned to Zionism either. He considered himself both a "ghetto Jew" from humble beginnings and a socialist.

In 1936, at the age of 37, Presser married Deborah Suzanna Appel, or Dé, also the name of a character in Presser's novel *Night of the Girondists,* a former student of his. Four years

later, on 10 May 1940, the Germans invaded Holland. On the morning of 14 May, the day of the Dutch capitulation, Presser and his wife fled to Ijmuiden, where thousands sought to escape Holland by sea. Unsuccessful, the Pressers returned to Amsterdam, and together they attempted suicide. While already bleeding, however, Presser telephoned the doctor. Both Presser and his wife soon recovered from their self-inflicted stab wounds.

In November 1940 all civil servants who had identified themselves as Jewish in the "Aryan Declaration" of the previous month were removed from their positions. Presser, as a high school teacher, was considered a civil servant and was forced to leave the Vossius Gymnasium. The following year, he began teaching at the new German-mandated Jewish Lyceum in Amsterdam. In the course of 1942 he and his wife were twice arrested in large roundups in Amsterdam's southern districts; twice they were released. Their luck ran out in March 1943, however. Without her Star of David and in possession of crudely forged identification papers, Deborah was arrested on the train while en route to visit her mother, who was hiding in the east of Holland. She was arrested and sent to the penal barracks at the Westerbork transit camp. After only five days in Westerbork, she was sent to Sobibor in a transport of approximately 1,200 Jews and gassed upon arrival. Upon learning of his wife's arrest—but not, at this point, her ultimate fate—Jacques Presser went into hiding, spending time in various "safe addresses" around the country until the end of the occupation in May 1945.

After liberation Presser lectured at the University of Amsterdam and soon became a professor there. In 1950 the newly created Netherlands State Institute for War Documentation commissioned him to write the history of the Dutch Jews under German occupation. This monumental work was published 15 years later under the title *Ondergang. De vervolging en verdelging van het Nederlandse jodendom 1940–1945.* Its English translation, *Ashes in the Wind: The Destruction of Dutch Jewry,* appeared in 1968.

While working on *Ondergang,* Presser also wrote a number of shorter pieces, including the novel *De Nacht der Girondjinen* (*Night of the Girondists*), which he anonymously submitted as the winning entry for a local literary contest. *De Nacht der Girondjinen* also won the Dutch Society for Literatures' Van Hoogt Prize for Creative Literature. It was published in The Netherlands in 1957, and within the next few years saw publication in English, Swedish, German, Danish, Spanish, and Czech translations.

Until his death at the age of 71, Presser remained involved in academe, writing about a wide array of historical subjects. He also wrote poetry and a number of detective novels. *Ondergang,* however, remains his most important work, as it widened and forever altered the discussion of the occupation period in Holland. *Ondergang* is, essentially, the history of the Jewish victims in The Netherlands, as experienced and written by one of these selfsame victims.

Jacques Presser died suddenly on 30 April 1970, only days before he was to address the queen and the nation at the televised National Liberation ceremony on 5 May.

—Jennifer L. Foray

See the essay on *Night of the Girondists,* or *Breaking Point.*

R

RADNÓTI, Miklós

Nationality: Hungarian. **Born:** Budapest, 5 May 1909. **Education:** University of Szeged, 1930s. **Family:** Married Fanni Gyarmati in 1935. **Career:** Editor, translator, and author. Prisoner, forced labor and concentration camps in Yugoslavia, World War II. Co-editor, *Kortars* and *1928* magazines, late 1920s. **Awards:** Baumgarten prize for *Járkálj, csak, halálraítélt!* **Died:** Executed by firing squad, Abda, Yugoslavia, 8 November 1944.

PUBLICATIONS

Collection

Miklós Radnóti: The Complete Poetry. 1980.

Poetry

Pogány köszöntö [Pagan Salute]. 1930.
Újmódi pásztorok éneke [Song of the New Shepherds]. 1931.
Enek a négerröl aki a városba ment. 1934.
Ujhold. 1935.
Járkálj csak, halálraítélt! [Walk On, Condemned!]. 1936.
Meredek út [Steep Road]. 1938.
Ikrek hava: napló a gverekkorról. 1940; in *Under Gemini, A Prose Memoir and Selected Poetry* (selections in English), 1985.
Válogatott versek, 1930–1940. 1940.
Orpheus nyomában: Muforditások kétezer év költoibol [In the Footsteps of Orpheus]. 1943.
Karunga a holtak ura; néger musék. 1944.
Bori notesz [Camp Notebook]. 1944; as *Last Poems of Miklós Radnóti,* 1994.
Tatjékos ég. 1946; as *Clouded Sky,* 1972.
Radnóti Miklós versei. 1948.
Tanulmányok, cikkek. 1956.
Összes versei és müfordításai. 1959.
Ikrek hava; napló a gyerekkoról. 1959.
Eclogák. 1961.
Legszebb versei [Selected Poems]. 1972.
The Witness: Selected Poems (selections in English). 1977.
Forced March: Selected Poems (selections in English). 1979.
Költeményei. 1982.
Foamy Sky: The Major Poems of Miklós Radnóti (selections in English). 1992.
Miklós Radnóti 33 Poems (selections in English). 1992.

*

Critical Studies: *Miklós Radnóti: A Biography of His Poetry* by Marianna D. Birnbaum, 1983; *The Poetry of Miklós Radnóti: A Comparative Study* by Emery Edward George, 1986; "Edward Hirsch on Miklos Radnoti" by Edward Hirsch, in *Wilson Quarterly,* 20(4), 1996; *The Life and Poetry of Miklós Radnóti: Essays* by George Gömöri and Clive Wilmer, 1999; *In the Footsteps of Orpheus: The Life and Times of Miklós Radnóti* by Zsuzsanna Osváth, 2000.

* * *

When the body of Miklós Radnóti was conclusively identified after being exhumed in the summer of 1946, nearly two years after the poet had been murdered by retreating Hungarian fascist militia and buried in a shallow mass grave, a notebook with his last 10 poems and a plea to send them to his best friend after his death was the final vestige of a short and brilliant career overshadowed by tragedy from the onset.

Born to Jewish middle-class parents in Budapest in 1909, Radnóti was haunted by feelings of guilt and remorse for the death of his mother and his stillborn twin brother, expressed frequently in his early poems and in his Proustian prose memoir, *Under Gemini (Ikrek hava: napló a gverekkorról,* 1940). Raised after his father's death by his uncle, he studied Hungarian and French literature at the University of Szeged—his uncle had intended him for a career in the textile industry—encouraged by the publication of his first collection of poems, *Pagan Salute (Pogány köszöntö),* in 1930. At the university he first came into conflict with the increasingly powerful fascist regime of Miklós Horthy, which charged him with subversion and offending public taste after the publication of his second volume of poetry, *Song of the New Shepherds (Újmódi pásztorok éneke,* 1931). Most of these early poems are on the whole affirmative and socially engaged or celebrate his love for Fanni Gyarmati, whom he married in 1935; after 1937 his poetry becomes dark and foreboding. Beginning with the poems in his volumes *Walk On, Condemned! (Járkálj csak, halálraítélt!,* 1936) and *Steep Road (Meredek út,* 1938), written in the shadow of the Spanish Civil War, Radnóti's poetry turns into a prophetic vision of the impending cataclysm and of his intensifying certainty that he was not destined to survive the Holocaust. This doomsday prophecy is particularly obvious in his poems dedicated to Federico García Lorca, whose death at the hands of the Franco fascists he foresees as his own. During these years he also devotes considerable energy to literary translation and the editing of other Hungarian authors, almost as if he were attempting to save some of these authors' works from the approaching purges. Never a devout Jew, Radnóti converted to Catholicism in 1943.

Radnóti's predictions were unfortunately all too accurate. From September to December 1940 he served in a forced labor camp in the Carpathian Mountains, mainly dismantling mines. After the publication of his collection *In the Footsteps of Orpheus* in 1943, he was pressed into service in a sugar factory, and in May 1944 he was taken to Lager Heidenau near the town of Bor, in German-occupied Yugoslavia, together with 6,000 other conscripts, mainly to build a railroad line in support of the local copper mines. Radnóti was largely spared the inhumane treatment meted out to the inmates of neighboring camps, but when the area was threatened by advancing Russian army units, the inmates were force-marched first to Bor and then sent in two groups of 3,000 men each on a grueling 14-day march to western Hungary. Radnóti, who had managed to be included in the first group to leave, survived the first massacre of 500 Jews near the town of Cervenka and that of another 500 in Sivac, among them the violinist Miklós Lorsi, an event described in Radnóti's last poem. On 8 November 1944, however, his premonitions of sharing Lorsi's fate came true: sick and unable to walk, Radnóti and 21 equally weakened comrades were loaded onto ox carts, presumably to be taken to a nearby hospital at Györ. According to local witnesses, the men were driven to a dam on the Rabca River, near the village of Abda, ordered off their carts, told to dig a ditch, and then shot and pushed into the shallow grave; the last survivor, who had been ordered to cover the bodies, was killed with shovels. Ironically, nearly all the 3,000 men in the second group to leave Bor survived.

While Radnóti had established his reputation as a poet before his time in the labor camps, the circumstances of his death and the sensational discovery of his last poems vaulted him into international prominence; he is certainly one of the most translated twentieth-century Hungarian poets. Radnóti is particularly admired for his stoicism in the face of his certainty about his and Europe's impending doom and his conviction, similar to T.S. Eliot's, that brutality and mechanized indifference must be met with humanistic faith and with reference to those fragments from classical literature and art that "we must shore against our ruins." A posthumous selection of his poetry after 1937, *Tatjékos ég,* appeared in 1946 and was translated into English in 1972 as *Clouded Sky. Miklós Radnóti: The Complete Poetry,* translated by Emery George, was published in 1980.

—Franz Blaha

See the essay on *Clouded Sky.*

RAWICZ, Piotr

Nationality: French (originally Polish: immigrated to Paris after World War II). **Born:** Lvov, 1919. **Career:** Prisoner, Auschwitz, World War II. **Died:** Suicide, 1982.

PUBLICATIONS

Novels

Le Sang du ciel. 1961; as *Blood from the Sky,* 1964.
Bloc-notes d'un contre-révolutionnaire ou la Gueule de bois. 1969.

*

Critical Studies: "Art and Testimony: The Representation of Historical Horror in Literary Works by Piotr Rawicz and Charlotte Delbo" by Lea Fridman Hamaoui, in *Cardozo Studies in Law and Literature,* 3(2), Fall 1991, pp. 243–59; *Engraved in Flesh: Piotr Rawicz and His Novel Blood from the Sky* by Anthony Rudolf, 1996.

* * *

Like many other Holocaust survivor-authors, including **Jean Améry**, **Bruno Bettelheim**, **Tadeusz Borowski**, **Paul Celan**, **Primo Levi**, and Benno Werzberger, Piotr Rawicz committed suicide. **Elie Wiesel**, in his book *And the Sea Is Never Full* (1999), admitted to being haunted by these suicides: "Was it because as guardians of memory they felt misunderstood, unloved, exiles in the present, guilty of having failed in their task? Were they afraid of having spoken too much—or not enough? In the light of the tragedies that continue to tear apart society, did they admit defeat?" Rawicz, who was a close friend of Wiesel, shot himself a few weeks after the death of his wife, Anna, from cancer. Both Rawicz and Levi specifically affirmed the sanctity of human life in their Holocaust writings, but that was not enough to prolong their own hold on life.

Rawicz was deported to Auschwitz in 1942 under the pretense of being a non-Jewish Ukrainian. He possessed a medical certificate explaining away his Jewish ritual circumcision. He became known for his fortitude under interrogation and torture, and his novel *Blood from the Sky* was highly autobiographical. Wiesel was impressed with the work, which he regarded as a masterpiece and which he described in the following terms: "It is only with sobbing and blaspheming that one can write about the death of a Jewish community betrayed by heaven and earth. Piotr Rawicz has made his choice. His book is an outcry, not an echo; a challenge, not an act of submission. Facing a grave filled with corpses, he does not recite Kaddish, he sheds no tears . . ."

Wiesel lamented that a human being who had contributed so much to making society better, as did Rawicz, could succumb to suicide. In remembering Rawicz and Levi, Wiesel discussed the Holocaust writer's attitude toward memory: "Like Kafka's unfortunate messenger, he realizes that his message has neither been received nor transmitted. Or worse, it has been, and nothing has changed. It has produced no effect on society or human nature. Everything goes on as though the messenger had forgotten the dead whose message he had carried, as though he had misplaced their last testament.'' Although Wiesel maintained that he understood Rawicz, he could not leave the subject without a word of reproach to his compatriot: ''What message did he leave us when he opened his lips to welcome death?''

—Peter R. Erspamer

See the essay on *Blood from the Sky.*

REMARQUE, Erich Maria

Nationality: American (originally German: immigrated to Switzerland, 1931; immigrated to the United States, 1939, naturalized citizen, 1947). **Born:** Osnabrück, 22 June 1898. **Education:** University of Münster. **Military Service:** German Army during World War I: wounded. **Family:** Married 1) Jutta Zambona in 1925 (divorced 1932); 2) Ilsa Intta Zambota in 1938 (divorced); 3) Paulette Goddard in 1958. **Career:** Substitute teacher, Osnabrück, c. 1919. Worked as a stonecutter, drama critic, salesman for a tombstone company, test driver for a Berlin tire company, organist in an insane asylum, and advertising copywriter for an automobile company. Lived in the United States, 1939–49; moved to Switzerland, 1949. Editor, *Sport im Bild* magazine, Berlin, 1925. **Award:** German Grand Cross of Merit, 1967. **Member:** German Academy of Speech and Poetry. **Died:** 25 September 1970.

PUBLICATIONS

Novels

Die Traumbude: Ein Künstlerroman [The Dream Room]. 1920.
Im Westen nichts Neues. 1928; as *All Quiet on the Western Front,* 1929.
Der Weg zurück. 1931; as *The Road Back,* 1931.
Drei Kameraden. 1937; as *Three Comrades,* 1937.
Liebe deinen Nächsten. 1941; as *Flotsam,* 1941.
Arch of Triumph. 1945; as *Arc de Triomphe,* 1946.
Der Funke Leben. 1952; as *Spark of Life,* 1952.
Zeit zu Leben und Zeit zu Sterben. 1954; as *A Time to Live and a Time to Die,* 1954.
Der schwarze Obelisk: Geschichte einer verspaeteten Ju gend. 1956; as *The Black Obelisk,* 1957.
Der Himmel kennt keine Günstlinge. 1961; as *Heaven Has No Favorites,* 1961; as *Bobby Deerfield,* 1961.
Die Nacht von Lissabon. 1961; as *The Night in Lisbon,* 1964.
Schatten im Paradies. 1971; as *Shadows in Paradise,* 1972.

Play

Die lezte Station [The Last Station] (produced 1956). As *Full Circle,* 1974.

Screenplays: *Der letzte Akt* [The Last Act] (*Ten Days to Die*), adaptation of *Ten Days to Die* by Michael A. Musmanno, 1955; *A Time to Love and a Time to Die,* 1957.

Other

Das unbekannte Werk: Fruhe Prosa, Werke aus dem Nachlass, Briefe und Tagebucher. 1998.

*

Film Adaptations: *All Quiet on the Western Front,* 1930, 1979; *Arc de Triomphe,* 1947; *A Time to Love and a Time to Die,* 1957.

Critical Studies: ''Autobiographical Elements in the Novels of Erich Maria Remarque,'' in *West Virginia University Philological Papers,* 17, 1970, pp. 84–93, and ''Humor in the Novels of Erich Maria Remarque, in *West Virginia University Philological Papers,* 29, 1983, pp. 38–45, both by Harley U. Taylor; *E. M. Remarque* by Franz Baumer, 1976; *Erich Maria Remarque* by Chrstine R. Barker and R. W. Last, 1979; *Erich Maria Remarque: A Critical Bio-Bibliography* by C. R. Owen, 1984; *Erich Maria Remarque: A Thematic Analysis of His Novels,* 1988, and *All Quiet on the Western Front: Literary Analysis and Cultural Context,* 1993, both by Richard Arthur Firda; *Erich Maria Remarque: A Literary and Film Biography* by Harley U. Taylor, Jr., 1989; *Understanding Erich Maria Remarque,* edited by Hans Wagener and James Hardin, 1991; *Opposite Attraction: The Lifes of Erich Maria Remarque and Paulette Goddard* by Julie Goldsmith Gilbert, 1995; *Erich Maria Remarque's All Quiet on the Western Front,* edited by Harold Bloom, 2001.

Theatrical Activities: Actor: Film—*A Time to Love and a Time to Die,* 1957.

*   *   *

Erich Maria Remarque once confessed that nothing worse can happen to a writer than to launch his career with a worldwide success. He was referring, of course, to his novel *Im Westen nichts Neues* (*All Quiet on the Western Front*), which appeared in 1929 and which overnight rose to the top of the best-seller list and appeared prominently on the Nazis' index as so much pacifist agitprop and as an outrage against the German infantryman. Remarque, in fact, disavowed any political agenda in writing what has been called the most widely read German novel of the twentieth century. (Elsewhere the primacy has been claimed for **Lion Feuchtwanger**'s *Jud Süss*). Remarque's purpose in writing *All Quiet* was simply to show how young people were herded to death just as they were embarking on adult life. Twenty years later **Heinrich Böll** was to take up precisely the same subject in some of his greatest stories, such as ''Wanderer, When You Come to Spa—'' and ''Reunion with Drüng,'' in which the figures are taken directly from school to the front and in which the stretcher takes on an almost iconic function.

On 29 January 1933, a day before Hitler's power seizure, Remarque fled in his Lancia to his villa on Lago Maggiore, which he had purchased the year before and which, with long intermittences, was to remain his home until his death in 1970. The next few years found him shuttling between Paris and Asconia. In 1939, on the eve of World War II, he left the Ticino for the United States, installed himself for the time being in Hollywood, and then, in 1942, settled in New York City. Our own vigilantes, who assumed every refugee writer and intellectual to be a carrier of the Red scare, barely took notice of Remarque, who shunned refugee circles in California and New York, hardly gave interviews, and (in this antagonizing his fellow exiles) remained essentially apolitical. Besides, his lifestyle markedly differed from theirs. Although almost pathologically publicity shy, he could scarcely escape the gossip dredged up about people who divided their passion between fast cars and Marlene Dietrich, frequented the Stork Club and Twenty-One, collected Monets and oriental rugs, and sold six novels to Hollywood studios, F. Scott Fitzgerald tinkering with the script of *Three Comrades*. Despite bouts of alcoholism and depression and a strenuous three-year affair with Dietrich, Remarque managed to see two of his novels through the press during the 10 years he spent in the United States: *Liebe deinen Nächsten* (1941; published in English under the title *Flotsam*) and the immensely successful *Arch of Triumph* (1945; the original appeared as *Arc de Triomphe* a year later). In 1949 he returned to his home in southern Switzerland, where he spent his last 20 years and produced half of the novels in the Remarque canon, including *Der Funke Leben* (1952; *Spark of Life*), *Zeit zu Leben und Zeit zu Sterben* (1954; *A Time to Live and a Time to Die*), and *Die Nacht von Lissabon* (1961; *The Night in Lisbon*).

Leaving aside the question of merit—but leaving the question of popularity very much in the equation—Remarque arguably contributed more to Americans' awareness of the miseries of exile and the horrors of Nazi Germany than did his detractors, whose names are legion. Remarque knew all about the conditions of flight, of statelessness, of commuting between gendarmeries and consulates at a time when a person was fairly lost without a passport, a visa or transit visa, an affidavit, and all of the instruments of survival on paper. Evidently, too, Remarque had no firsthand knowledge of the camps. What needs to be remembered is that Holocaust fiction did not really come into its own until about 1960 and that *Spark of Life*, published in 1952, presented virtually the first full-length fictional treatment of a death camp. It is perhaps no surprise that in 1952 a book about the Shoah could hardly be sold to the Germans, nor is it a surprise that at the time of Remarque's death *Spark of Life* was the least read of his novels

in Germany, whereas *The Night in Lisbon,* in which the concentration camp surfaces peripherally but which zeroes in on the adventures of a refugee couple, placed second after *All Quiet on the Western Front*.

Remarque died rich and, though hardly forgotten—certainly not by the judges of the Book-of-the-Month Club—was dismissed as a second-rater, read by people who enjoyed the productions of James Hilton, Nevil Shute, and Daphne du Maurier. Beyond having a street in Osnabrück named for him, after much wrangling among the city fathers, he died without public tributes or marble monuments. At the time he published *All Quiet on the Western Front,* he was thought a candidate for the Nobel Prize—for Peace. But a few years after her death the authorities paid Dietrich the ultimate homage of circulating her face on a postage stamp, in the same Famous German Women series in which they featured Hannah Arendt. Exile and second thoughts among Germans produce strange bedfellows.

—Edgar Rosenberg

See the essays on *The Night in Lisbon* and *Spark of Life*.

REZNIKOFF, Charles

Nationality: American. **Born:** Brooklyn, New York, 31 August 1894. **Education:** Boys High School, Brooklyn, graduated 1909; University of Missouri, School of Journalism, 1911–12; New York University Law School, 1912–15, LL. B. 1915; Law School of Columbia University postgraduate courses, 1915–18. **Military Service:** Joined Reserve Officers Training Corps, 1918: war ended before he served. **Family:** Married Marie Syrkin in 1930. **Career:** Worked as a salesman in his parents' hat-manufacturing business, 1912; admitted to the Bar of the State of New York, 1916; member of editorial staff, American Law Book Co., Brooklyn, early 1930s; associated with Louis Zukofsky, George Oppen, and Carl Rakosi, known as the Objectivist group of poets and founders of the Objectivist Press, 1930s; worked as a screenwriter in Hollywood, late 1930s; freelance writer beginning 1940s; member of editorial staff, *Jewish Frontier,* New York, beginning 1955. **Awards:** Jewish Book Council of America Kovner prize, 1963; National Institute of Arts and Letters Morton Dauwen Zabel award for poetry, 1971. **Died:** 22 January 1976.

Pᴜʙʟɪᴄᴀᴛɪᴏɴꜱ

Poetry

Rhythms. 1918.
Rhythms II. 1919.
Poems. 1920.

Uriel Acosta: A Play and a Fourth Group of Verse. 1921.
Five Groups of Verse. 1927.
Jerusalem the Golden. 1934.
Separate Way. 1936.
Going To and Fro and Walking Up and Down. 1941.
Inscriptions: 1944–1956. 1959.
By the Waters of Manhattan: Selected Verse. 1962.
By the Well of Living and Seeing: New & Selected Poems, 1918–1973. 1974.
Holocaust. 1975.
The Complete Poems of Charles Reznikoff, edited by Seamus Cooney (2 vols.): *Poems, 1918–1936.* 1976. *Poems, 1937–1975.* 1977.

Novels

By the Waters of Manhattan. 1930.
The Lionhearted: A Story about the Jews in Medieval England. 1944.
The Manner Music. 1977.

Plays

Chatterton, the Black Death, and Meriwether Lewis: Three Plays (playlets). 1922.
Coral, and Captive Israel: Two Plays (playlets). 1923.
Nine Plays (playlets). 1927.

Other

Testimony, In Memoriam: 1933. 1934.
Early History of a Sewing Machine Operator, with Nathan Reznikoff. 1936.
The Jews of Charleston: A History of an American Jewish Community, with Uriah Z. Engelman. 1950.
Family Chronicle, with Nathan and Sarah Reznikoff. 1963.
Testimony: The United States 1885–1890: Recitative. 1965.
Testimony: The Unites States 1891–1900: Recitative. 1968.
By the Well of Living and Seeing, and The Fifth Book of the Maccabees. 1969.
Selected Letters of Charles Reznikoff, 1917–1976, edited by Milton Hindus. 1997.

*

Bibliography: ''An Annotated Bibliography of Works about Charles Reznikoff: 1920–1983'' by Linda Simon, in *Charles Reznikoff: Man and Poet,* edited by Milton Hindus, 1984.

Critical Studies: *Charles Reznikoff: A Critical Essay* by Milton Hindus, 1977; *Charles Reznikoff: Man and Poet,* edited by Milton Hindus, 1984; '''Detailing the Facts': Charles Reznikoff's Response to the Holocaust'' by Robert Franciosi, in *Contemporary Literature,* 29(2), Summer 1988, pp. 241–64; Charles Reznikoff issue of *Sagetrieb,* 13(1–2), Spring/Fall 1994; '''And Breathe upon These Slain, That They Shall Live': Charles Reznikoff's Holocaust,'' in *Reclaiming Memory: American Representations of the Holocaust,* edited by Pirjo Ahokas and Martine Chard-Hutchinson, 1997, and ''Charles Reznikoff: New World Poetics,'' in *Strategies of Difference: Case Studies in Poetic Composition,* edited by Pierre Lagayette, 1998, both by Genevieve Cohen-Cheminet; ''Tradition and Modernity, Judaism and Objectivism: The Poetry of Charles Reznikoff'' by Norman Finkelstein, in *The Objectivist Nexus: Essays in Cultural Poetics,* edited by Rachel Blau DuPlessis and Peter Quartermain, 1999; '''Palestine Was a Halting Place, One of Many': Diasporism in the Poetry of Charles Reznikoff'' by Ranen Omer, in *MELUS,* 25(1), Spring 2000, pp. 147–80; *A Menorah for Athena: Charles Reznikoff and the Jewish Dilemmas of Objectivist Poetry* by Stephen Fredman, 2001.

*   *   *

Charles Reznikoff, born in 1894 in the Jewish Brownsville section of Brooklyn, New York, produced a large body of work, including poetry, fiction, drama, history, and memoir. While much of this material was concerned with American and Jewish American identity, Reznikoff wrote only one work that focused directly on the Holocaust—an extended poem, or, as he described it, a recitative, titled *Holocaust* (1975). As Reznikoff's last book of poems, *Holocaust* bears the hallmarks of the poetic style distinguishing his earlier writings, most notably his affinity with objectivist poets writing in the United States in the 1930s, the influence of his professional training on his aesthetics, and his commitment to witnessing history through poetry.

Objectivist poetry (a literary movement founded by Reznikoff's fellow Jewish poet Louis Zukofsky) can generally be understood as writing characterized by concise language; attention to detail; sparse, if any, use of symbol and metaphor; and an emphasis on the image itself as the most worthy object of poetic focus. Reznikoff explained his own understanding of the term in a 1969 interview: ''By the term objectivist I suppose a writer may be meant who does not write directly about his feelings but about what he sees and hears; who is restricted almost to the testimony of a witness in a court of law; and who expresses his feelings indirectly by the selection of subject matter and, if he writes in verse, by its music.''

This aesthetic philosophy was accentuated by Reznikoff's training as an attorney, his aspirations toward a career as a historian, and his job as an editor of court records. In the latter position he condensed and summarized court cases for publication in legal reference texts, a practice that clearly influenced his poetic writings. *Holocaust,* for example, which was based directly on archival records from the Nuremberg and Eichmann war trials, appears at first glance simply to consist of brief recapitulations of wartime atrocities. Under the section titled ''Research,'' for example, Reznikoff writes:

A number of Jews had to drink sea water only

to find out how long they could stand it.
In their torment
they threw themselves on the mops and rags
used by the hospital attendants
and sucked the dirty water out of them
to quench the thirst
driving them mad.

But the poem is far more than a mere summary of the historical record. On the contrary, *Holocaust* is stylistically pioneering in its portrayal of the abominations that took place in starkly detached detail. Paraphrasing an eleventh-century Chinese poet whom he admired, Reznikoff described the function of poetry to be the "present[ation] of the thing in order to convey the feeling. It should be precise about the thing and reticent about the feeling." Reznikoff artfully culls, arranges, and juxtaposes the documentary material to present the horror of "the thing" while resisting the urge to prescribe "the feeling." In so doing he creates a poem seemingly devoid of emotion but that has profound emotional impact on his readers. In fact his very refusal to comment upon the abuses portrayed in *Holocaust* makes the poem all the more disturbing in that the absence of interpretation in the poem demands that the gap be closed by the reader. As poet Michael Heller claimed upon Reznikoff's death, the "sheer factualness" of Reznikoff's poetry "commands" but does not "dictate" our response.

For Reznikoff, who was ultimately neither a trained historian nor a practicing lawyer with the potential to avenge past wrongs in a court of law, writing poetry provided a means of witnessing the inhumanity of the Holocaust. He saw the poem itself as a form of testimony: "Now suppose in a court of law you are testifying in a negligence case," he explains. "You cannot get up on the stand and say, 'That man was negligent.' That's a conclusion of fact. What you'd be compelled to say is how the man acted. Did he stop before he crossed the street? Did he look? The judges of whether he is negligent or not are the jury in the case and the judges of what you say as a poet are the readers. That is, there is an analogy between testimony in courts and the testimony of a poet." In writing *Holocaust* Reznikoff produced one of the most powerful testimonials in literature to witness, confirm, and condemn the event.

—Heather Hathaway

See the essay on *Holocaust.*

RICH, Adrienne (Cecile)

Nationality: American. **Born:** Baltimore, Maryland, 16 May 1929. **Education:** Radcliffe College, A.B. (cum laude) 1951. **Family:** Married Alfred Haskell Conrad in 1953 (died 1970);

three sons. **Career:** Poet and writer. Workshop conductor, YM-YWHA Poetry Center, New York, 1966–67; visiting lecturer, Swarthmore College, Swarthmore, Pennsylvania, 1967–69; adjunct professor in writing division, Columbia University, Graduate School of the Arts, New York, 1967–69; lecturer, SEEK English program, 1968–70, instructor, creative writing program, 1970–71, assistant professor of English, 1971–72, 1974–75, City College of the City University of New York; Fannie Hurst Visiting Professor of Creative Literature, Brandeis University, Waltham, Massachusetts, 1972–73; Lucy Martin Donnelly fellow, Bryn Mawr College, 1975; professor of English, Douglass College, Rutgers University, New Brunswick, New Jersey, 1976–78; A. D. White Professor-at-Large, Cornell University, Ithaca, New York, 1982–85; Clark Lecturer and distinguished visiting professor, Scripps College, Claremont, California, 1983, 1984; visiting professor, San Jose State University, California, 1984–96; Burgess Lecturer, Pacific Oaks College, Pasadena, California, 1986; professor of English and feminist studies, Stanford University, California, 1986–92; Marjorie Kovler visiting fellow, University of Chicago, 1989. Since 1992 national director, National Writers' Voice Project. Columnist, *American Poetry Review,* 1972–73; coeditor, *Sinister Wisdom,* 1981–84; contributing editor, *Chrysalis: A Magazine of Women's Culture;* founding editor, *Bridges: A Journal of Jewish Feminists and Other Friends,* 1989–92. **Awards:** Yale Younger Poets award, 1951, for *A Change of World;* Guggenheim fellowships, 1952 and 1961; Ridgely Torrence memorial award, Poetry Society of America, 1955; Grace Thayer Bradley award, Friends of Literature (Chicago), 1956, for *The Diamond Cutters and Other Poems;* Phi Beta Kappa Poet, College of William and Mary, 1960, Swarthmore College, 1965, and Harvard University, 1966; National Institute of Arts and Letters award for poetry, 1961; Amy Lowell traveling fellowship, 1962; Bollingen Foundation translation grant, 1962; Bess Hokin prize, *Poetry* magazine, 1963; National Translation Center grant, 1968; Eunice Tietjens memorial prize, *Poetry* magazine, 1968; National Endowment for the Arts grant, 1970, for poems in *American Literary Anthology: 3;* Shelley memorial award, Poetry Society of America, 1971; Ingram Merrill Foundation grant, 1973–74; National book award, 1974, for *Diving into the Wreck: Poems, 1971–1972;* National Medal of the Arts (declined), 1977; National Book Critics Circle award in poetry nomination, 1978, for *The Dream of a Common Language: Poems, 1974–1977;* Fund for Human Dignity award, National Gay Task Force, 1981; *Los Angeles Times* book prize nomination, 1982, for *A Wild Patience Has Taken Me This Far: Poems, 1978–1981;* Ruth Lilly Poetry prize, Modern Poetry Association and American Council for the Arts, 1986; Brandeis University Creative Arts medal in poetry, 1987; National Poetry Association award, 1989, for distinguished service to the art of poetry; Elmer Holmes Bobst award in arts and letters, New York University Library, 1989; Bay Area Book Reviewers award in poetry, 1990, 1996; The Commonwealth award in literature, 1991;

Robert Frost silver medal for lifetime achievement in poetry, Poetry Society of America, 1992; William Whitehead award, Gay and Lesbian Publishing Triangle for Lifetime Achievement in Letters, 1992; Lambda book award in lesbian poetry, 1992, for *An Atlas of the Difficult World: Poems, 1988–1991,* and 1996, for *Dark Fields of the Republic, 1991–1995;* Lenore Marshall/*Nation* poetry prize and Los Angeles Times book award, 1992, and Poets' prize, 1993, all for *An Atlas of the Difficult World: Poems, 1988–1991,* MacArthur Foundation fellowship, 1994; Tanning prize, Academy of American Poets, 1996; Lifetime Achievement award, Lannan Foundation. Litt.D.: Wheaton College, 1967; Smith College, 1979; College of Wooster, Ohio, 1988; Harvard University, 1990; Swarthmore College, 1992. **Member:** Modern Language Association (honorary fellow beginning in 1985); Poetry Society of America; American Academy of Arts and Letters; American Academy of Arts and Sciences; Phi Beta Kappa. **Agent:** W. W. Norton Co., 500 Fifth Avenue, New York, New York 10110, U.S.A.

PUBLICATIONS

Poetry

A Change of World. 1951.
Poems. 1952.
The Diamond Cutters and Other Poems. 1955.
Snapshots of a Daughter-in-Law: Poems, 1954–1962. 1963; revised edition, 1967.
Necessities of Life. 1966.
Selected Poems. 1967.
Leaflets: Poems, 1965–1968. 1969.
The Will to Change: Poems, 1968–1970. 1971.
Diving into the Wreck: Poems, 1971–1972. 1973.
Poems: Selected and New, 1950–1974. 1974.
Twenty-one Love Poems. 1977.
The Dream of a Common Language: Poems, 1974–1977. 1978.
A Wild Patience Has Taken Me This Far: Poems, 1978–1981. 1981.
Sources. 1983.
The Fact of a Doorframe: Poems Selected and New, 1950–1984. 1984.
Your Native Land, Your Life. 1986.
Time's Power: Poems, 1985–1988. 1988.
An Atlas of the Difficult World: Poems, 1988–1991. 1991.
Collected Early Poems, 1950–1970. 1993.
Dark Fields of the Republic, 1991–1995. 1995.
Selected Poems, 1950–1995. 1996.
Midnight Salvage: Poems, 1995–1998. 1999.

Plays

Ariadne: A Play in Three Acts and Poems. 1939.
Not I, but Death, A Play in One Act. 1941.

Other

Of Woman Born: Motherhood As Experience and Institution. 1976.
Women and Honor: Some Notes on Lying (pamphlet). 1977.
On Lies, Secrets and Silence: Selected Prose, 1966–1978. 1979.
Compulsory Heterosexuality and Lesbian Existence (pamphlet). 1980.
Blood, Bread and Poetry: Selected Prose, 1979–1986. 1986.
Birth of the Age of Women, with Susan Morland. 1991.
What Is Found There: Notebooks on Poetry and Politics. 1993.

Coeditor and translator, *Poems by Ghalib.* 1969.
Editor, *Best American Poetry of 1996.* 1996.
Translator, *Reflections* by Mark Insingel. 1973.

*

Manuscript Collection: Schlesinger Library, Radcliffe College, Cambridge, Massachusetts.

Critical Studies: "The Mirrored Vision of Adrienne Rich" by Susan R. Van Dyne, in *Modern Poetry Studies,* 8(2), Autumn 1977, pp. 140–73; *Adrienne Rich: The Poet and Her Critics* by Craig Hansen Werner, 1988; "Philoctetes Radicalized: Twenty-one Love Poems and the Lyric Career of Adrienne Rich" by Kevin McGuirk, in *Contemporary Literature,* 34(1), Spring 1993, pp. 61–87; "The Dream of a Common Language: Vietnam Poetry As Reformation of Language and Feeling in the Poems of Adrienne Rich" by Elissa Greenwald, in *Journal of American Culture,* 16(3), Fall 1993, pp. 97–102; "Contradictions: Tracking Adrienne Rich's Poetry," in *Tulsa Studies in Women's Literature,* 12(2), Fall 1993, pp. 333–40, and *The Dream and the Dialogue: Adrienne Rich's Feminist Poetics,* 1994, both by Alice Templeton; "Wrestling with the Mother and Father: 'His' and 'Her' in Adrienne Rich" by Betty S. Flowers, in *Private Voices, Public Lives: Women Speak on the Literary Life,* edited by Nancy Owen Nelson, 1995; *Stein, Bishop & Rich: Lyrics of Love, War & Place* by Margaret Dickie, 1997; *Fashioning the Female Subject: The Intertextual Networking of Dickinson, Moore, and Rich* by Sabine Sielke, 1997.

* * *

Adrienne Rich was born in Baltimore, Maryland, in 1929 and graduated from Radcliffe College in 1951. That same year, W. H. Auden selected her book *A Change of World* as the winner of the prestigious Yale Younger Poets first book award. Her writing has evolved significantly since then, and she has become, unquestionably, one of the major American poets of the last century and a shaping force of the poetic conscience of the twenty-first century.

In the course of a distinguished writing life, Rich has published more than 20 books of poetry, prose, and plays, and her work has been anthologized extensively. She has received many awards and most of the major honors that can be bestowed upon a poet. Among these are the Ruth Lilly Poetry Prize, the Commonwealth Award in Literature, a MacArthur Foundation Fellowship, the National Book Award, the Tanning Prize for mastery in the art of poetry, and the Frost Medal for distinguished lifetime achievement as well as a Lifetime Achievement Award from the Lannan Foundation. Among other significant contributions, her life and her work have served to open doors for the oppressed; she has both invited them in and insisted that they be heard in the important conversations about justice, power, and the meaning of citizenship.

Rich has become an American icon of artistic and moral integrity. It is difficult to read her work and not admire how unflinchingly she confronts all kinds of injustice, insisting that we examine those things we do not want to know but must know. She both questions and challenges privilege to make her readers increasingly aware of its consequences for others. The ethics of her work are rooted in her belief in poetry's "incalculable power to help us go on." In naming the names of things as they are, we begin the processes of awareness and change.

Given her politics, her unwavering integrity, and her belief in speaking on behalf of those without voice, Rich is not always a comfortable poet to read, yet her voice, often bristling, is of major importance to our intellectual, political, ethical, and communal lives. Her straightforward gaze and her keen sensitivity to the consequences of privilege and power are at the core of both her person and her poetry. This may well be founded in formative events obliquely referred to in "Eastern War Time," when her parents—and especially her Protestant mother—fearing for Adrienne's well-being, urged her not to let others know that she was the child of a Jewish father.

Rich is a hero to the feminist movement in part for her book *Of Woman Born: Motherhood As Experience and Institution* and increasingly because of her straightforward engagement of such issues as sexism, lesbian identity, and homophobia. Her essays and poems go well past specific political concerns to focus, as they almost always do, on the broader challenge of struggling to live in this complex world with integrity, compassion, and unblinking awareness.

—Michael S. Glaser

See the essay on "Eastern War Time."

RICHLER, Mordecai

Nationality: Canadian. **Born:** Montreal, Quebec, 27 January 1931. **Education:** Sir George Williams University, 1949–51. **Family:** Married Florence Wood in 1960; three sons and two daughters. **Career:** Freelance writer, Paris, 1952–53, London,

1954–72, and Montreal, 1972–2001. Writer-in-residence, Sir George Williams University, 1968–69; visiting professor of English, Carleton University, 1972–74. Member of editorial board, Book-of-the-Month Club, 1972–2001. **Awards:** President's medal for nonfiction, University of Western Ontario, 1959; junior art fellowships, 1959 and 1960, and senior arts fellowship, 1967, Canadian Council; Guggenheim Foundation creative writing fellowship, 1961; *Paris Review* humor prize, 1967, for section from *Cocksure* and *Hunting Tigers under Glass;* Governor-General's literary award, Canada Council, 1968, for *Cocksure* and *Hunting Tigers under Glass,* and 1971, for *St. Urbain's Horseman; London Jewish Chronicle* literature awards, 1972, for *St. Urbain's Horseman;* Berlin Film Festival Golden Bear, Academy Award nomination, and Screenwriters Guild of America award, all 1974, for the screenplay *The Apprenticeship of Duddy Kravitz;* ACTRA award for best television writer—drama, Academy of Canadian Cinema and Television, 1975; Book of the Year for Children award, Canadian Library Association, and Ruth Schwartz Children's book award, Ontario Arts Council, both 1976, for *Jacob Two-Two Meets the Hooded Fang; London Jewish Chronicle* H. H. Wingate award for fiction, 1981, for *Joshua Then and Now;* named a Literary Lion, New York Public Library, 1989; Commonwealth Writers prize, Book Trust, 1990, for *Solomon Gursky Was Here.* **Died:** 3 July 2001.

PUBLICATIONS

Novels

The Acrobats. 1954; as *Wicked We Love,* 1955.
Son of a Smaller Hero. 1955.
A Choice of Enemies. 1957.
The Apprenticeship of Duddy Kravitz. 1959.
The Incompatible Atuk. As *Stick Your Neck Out,* 1963.
Cocksure. 1968.
St. Urbain's Horseman. 1971.
Joshua Then and Now. 1980.
Solomon Gursky Was Here. 1989.
Barney's Version. 1997.

Novels (for children)

Jacob Two-Two Meets the Hooded Fang. 1975.
Jacob Two-Two and the Dinosaur. 1987.
Jacob Two-Two's First Spy Case. 1997.

Short Stories

The Street: Stories. 1969.

Plays

Duddy, adaptation of his *The Apprenticeship of Duddy Kravitz* (produced Edmonton, Alberta, 1984).

Screenplays: *No Love for Johnnie,* with Nicholas Phipps, 1962; *Tiara Tahiti,* with Geoffrey Cotterell and Ivan Foxwell, 1962; *The Wild and the Willing,* with Phipps (*Young and Willing,* 1965), 1962; *Life at the Top,* 1965; *The Apprenticeship of Duddy Kravitz,* 1974; *Fun with Dick and Jane,* with David Giler and Jerry Belson, 1977; *Joshua Then and Now,* 1985.

Television Plays: *The Acrobats,* 1957; *Friend of the People,* 1957; *Paid in Full,* 1958; *The Trouble with Benny,* 1959; *The Apprenticeship of Duddy Kravitz,* 1960; *The Fall of Mendel Krick,* 1963.

Radio Plays: *The Acrobats,* 1956; *Benny, the War in Europe, and Myerson's Daughter Bella,* 1958; *The Spare Room,* 1961; *Q for Quest,* 1963; *It's Harder to Be Anybody,* 1965; *Such Was St. Urbain Street,* 1966; *The Wordsmith,* 1979.

Other

Hunting Tigers under Glass: Essays and Reports. 1969.
Shoveling Trouble (essays). 1973.
Notes on an Endangered Species and Others (essays). 1974.
Images of Spain. 1977.
The Great Comic Book Heroes and Other Essays. 1978.
Home Sweet Home: My Canadian Album (essays). 1984; as *Home Sweet Home,* 1985.
Broadsides: Reviews and Opinions. 1990.
Oh Canada! Oh Quebec! Requiem for a Divided Country. 1992.
The Language of Signs. 1992.
This Year in Jerusalem: An Israeli Journal. 1994.
Belling the Cat: Essays, Reports, and Opinions. 1998.
On Snooker. 2001.

Editor, *Canadian Writing Today.* 1970.
Editor, *The Best of Modern Humor.* 1984.
Editor, *Writers on World War II: An Anthology.* 1991.

*

Film Adaptations: *The Acrobats,* 1957; *The Apprenticeship of Duddy Kravitz,* 1960, 1974; *Jacob Two-Two Meets the Hooded Fang,* 1977; *Joshua Then and Now,* 1985.

Manuscript Collection: University of Calgary, Alberta.

Critical Studies: *Mordecai Richler* by George Woodcock, 1970; *Mordecai Richler,* edited by G. David Sheps, 1971; "Mordecai Richler and the Jewish-Canadian Novel" by F. M. Birbalsingh, in *Journal of Commonwealth Literature,* June 1972, pp. 76–82; "Revaluing Mordecai Richler" by Kerry McSweeney, in *Studies in Canadian Literature,* 4(2), Summer 1979, pp. 120–31; *Mordecai Richler* by Victor J. Ramraj, 1983; "A. M. Klein and Mordecai Richler: Canadian Responses to the Holocaust" by Rachel Feldhay Brenner, in *Journal of Canadian Studies,* 24(2), Summer 1989, pp. 65–77; "Canada Wry" by Pearl K. Bell, in *New Republic,* 202(19), 7

May 1990, pp. 42–44; "Mordecai Richler Was Here" by Kenneth McNaught, in *Journal of Canadian Studies,* 26(4), Winter 1991–92, pp. 141–43.

*   *   *

Mordecai Richler was one of North America's most prolific, talented, and controversial Jewish authors, whose works explore themes ranging from Jewish identity and self-image and Holocaust-related guilt to the dilemma of how to live in a secular Canadian society where humanistic values have largely failed. Richler grew up in the Jewish community of Montreal, Quebec Province, Canada, in the 1930s and 1940s, a period during which his secondhand knowledge of the atrocities of the Holocaust overseas combined with his immediate experience of anti-Semitism and Quebec's own Fascist movement. A stay in Europe in the early 1950s put him into direct contact with expatriate existentialist ideas (in the style of Ernest Hemingway) and the disillusionment of the Beat generation. These two major historical and literary trends have found unique expression throughout Richler's fiction.

Although Richler's first novel-length work of fiction, *The Acrobats* (1954), focused primarily on the angst of an expatriate Canadian painter-rebel without a cause rather than on Jewish issues, Richler found his voice and expressed his greatest comic and literary talent in exploring Jewish topics closer to home. Much as William Faulkner's fictional Yoknapatawpha County and its inhabitants became the basis for exploring twentieth-century themes in a microcosm, Jewish Montreal and particularly the area around St. Urbain Street became Richler's laboratory of character development for his protagonists. *Son of a Smaller Hero* (1955) concerns young Noah Adler's efforts to break free of a rigid and strict Orthodox Jewish family at the same time that he deals with the anti-Semitic attitudes of the Canadian Gentiles in the world outside his family. Several years later Richler expanded his use of irony and satire to denounce hypocrisy and cruelty in all layers of Canadian society in *The Apprenticeship of Duddy Kravitz* (1959). This novel indirectly reflects the Holocaust experience in its portrayal of social hierarchies, victims, and exploiters. Although the Jews and Gentiles in this novel are removed from the immediate atrocities of the Holocaust concentration camps, the precarious position of Jews in Montreal society impels Jews such as young Duddy Kravitz, Mr. Cohen, and Jerry Dingleman to become ruthless hustlers and exploiters in business so that they can avoid becoming victims themselves. At the same time, people such as Simcha Kravitz, Duddy's grandfather, are helpless and ineffective in their efforts to uphold traditional Jewish values against the onslaught of exploiters.

Two other novels by Richler that confront the shadow of the Holocaust through the eyes of Jews from St. Urbain Street are *St. Urbain's Horseman* (1971) and *Joshua Then and Now* (1980). In *St. Urbain's Horseman,* Jacob Hersh is a famous and successful writer with a fair amount of financial security, but he cannot escape the fears of anti-Semitic persecution that dominated his childhood in Montreal. Jacob Hersh finds personal meaning and identification with the victims of the Holocaust. He travels to continental Europe and Israel in search of his cousin Joey, who was supposedly an avenger of the Holocaust and a type of mythical messiah for him, but his search proves fruitless. Joshua Shapiro, the protagonist of *Joshua Then and Now,* also has to deal with issues of guilt and moral crises. His father, Reuben, was an exploitative and ruthless businessman like Duddy Kravitz, and Joshua, a prominent sportswriter, feels guilty for his own success and his marriage to a Gentile woman, as well as for his family's history. During a trip to Spain he tries to find truth and morality in identifying with the International Brigades of the Spanish Civil War. He recognizes, however, that the history of even his most beloved Spain is rife with anti-Semitism, and he is humiliated by an ex-Nazi whom he meets. In short neither Jacob Hersh nor Joshua Shapiro can find the equality, brotherhood, or moral resolution that he seeks inside or outside his own community.

Some works of Richler's journalism and nonfiction, such as *This Year in Jerusalem: An Israeli Journal* (1994) and the essay ''The Holocaust and After,'' also demonstrate Richler's complex attitude toward the Jewish state and his view of Jews in the role of victim or oppressor. Richler continued to assert his claim that the writer is an advocate of the oppressed. And while he stood for a Jewish state in the aftermath of the Holocaust, he also sympathized with the sufferings of the Palestinians. Richler's most important contributions to the literature of the Holocaust, however, are his works of fiction that portray North American Jews' responses to the anti-Semitism around them and to the Holocaust. The modern crises of Jews' identities in multicultural societies and in the face of a long and difficult history crystallize with incisive humor and satire in Richler's fiction, which illustrates the persistent barriers and prejudices that both Jews and non-Jews still must understand and overcome.

—Alisa Gayle Mayor

See the essay on *The Apprenticeship of Duddy Kravitz.*

RINGELBLUM, Emmanuel

Nationality: Austro-Hungarian. **Born:** Nowy Soncsz, 1900. **Education:** University of Warsaw, 1919–27, Ph.D. 1927. **Family:** Married; one son. **Career:** Teacher, gymnasium in Warsaw, 1927–39; worked for the Joint Distribution Committee (JDC), established working and personal relationship with Yitzhak Gitterman; leader, Oneg Shabbat, a secret group of writers and underground activists that chronicled life under Nazi occupation, beginning 1939; worked in the political underground and for the institute for social self-aid among Warsaw Jews. Participant, Warsaw Ghetto Uprising, 1943; prisoner, labor camp, Poniatow, 1943; escaped but recaptured, 1944. **Died:** Murdered, victim of the Holocaust, 1944.

PUBLICATION

Diary

Notitsn fun Varshever geto. 1952; as *Notes from the Warsaw Ghetto: The Journal of Emmanuel Ringelblum,* edited by Jacob Sloan, 1958.

*

Critical Study: *Emmanuel Ringelblum: Historian of the Warsaw Ghetto* by Mark Beyer, 2001.

* * *

When World War II broke out, Emmanuel Ringelblum was a young scholar and teacher of social history, but within the next five years he himself became a significant part of history. On 1 September 1939, the day the Germans marched into his native Poland, he was attending the World Zionist Congress in Geneva. While some of the Polish delegates went to Palestine and others fled to Paris or London, Ringelblum decided to return to Warsaw. There were two main reasons for his decision to return: his relief work for the Joint Distribution Committee and his position as one of three leaders in the Zionist Labor Party. Realizing the significance of the events unfolding around him, in October 1939 Ringelblum took the first steps toward establishing a group of people devoted to recording everything that transpired during the Nazis' assault upon the Jews. Later known as the Oneg Shabbat circle, the group produced many diaries and documents that became crucial to understanding the scope and nature of the Nazis' actions. Among the most important documents is Ringelblum's own diary, which was published in Yiddish in 1952 under the title *Notitsn fun Vareshever geto* (*Notes from the Warsaw Ghetto,* 1958).

Born in 1900 in the Polish town of Nowy Soncsz, Ringelblum worked his way through gymnasium and enrolled at the University of Warsaw in 1919. Throughout his years at the university he was involved in reform movements and social action organizations for Jews. After completing his doctoral degree in 1927, he taught at a gymnasium in Warsaw until 1939. By May 1940 he had gathered together the leading figures in the Oneg Shabbat group. Rabbi Shimon Huberband, of Piotrków was his chief deputy; Hirsch Wasser, a refugee from Lodz, was his secretary; and Menachem Kon was his chief financial supporter. Once the Warsaw Ghetto was established in November 1940, the organization had dozens of volunteers working with them. Ringelblum, however, would not allow journalists or anyone associated with the Jewish Council into the Oneg Shabbat circle.

The Oneg Shabbat members lived in fear for their lives, and many were arrested and deported by the Jewish police. They were not deterred by the danger, however. Indeed, Ringelblum began recording his own diary on the Nazis' slaughter of the Jews before the end of 1939. Nor did he refrain from more active modes of resistance. A participant in the Warsaw Ghetto Uprising that broke out at Passover 1943, Ringelblum was captured by the Germans in May 1943 and sent to the slave labor camp at Poniatow. He escaped from Poniatow two days before an uprising broke out in the camp and found a hiding place in Warsaw for himself, his wife, and their son. There he continued his work on a volume that was later published under the title *Polish-Jewish Relations during the Second World War* (1992). In March 1944 Ringelblum and his family were discovered by the Gestapo. On 7 March the three of them— Emmanuel, his wife, and their 12-year-old son Uri—were executed, along with 35 other Jews, in the midst of the ruins of the Warsaw Ghetto. What later became his *Notes from the Warsaw Ghetto* was retrieved from the ruins in two parts; the first was discovered in September 1946, the second in December 1950.

—David Patterson

See the essay on *Notes from the Warsaw Ghetto: The Journal of Emmanuel Ringelblum.*

ROTH, Philip (Milton)

Nationality: American. **Born:** Newark, New Jersey, 19 March 1933. **Education:** Newark College, Rutgers University, New Brunswick, New Jersey, 1950–51; Bucknell University, Lewisburg, Pennsylvania, 1951–54, B.A. 1954 (Phi Beta Kappa); University of Chicago, 1954–55, M.A. 1955. **Military Service:** United States Army, 1955–56. **Family:** Married 1) Margaret Martinson in 1959 (separated 1962; died 1968); 2) Claire Bloom in 1990 (divorced 1994). **Career:** English instructor, University of Chicago, 1956–58; visiting writer, University of Iowa, 1960–62; writer-in-residence, Princeton University, New Jersey, 1962–64; visiting writer, State University of New York, Stony Brook, 1966, 1967, and University of Pennsylvania, Philadelphia, 1967–80; general editor, Writers from the Other Europe series, Penguin Publishers, London, 1975–89; distinguished professor, Hunter College, New York, 1988–92. **Awards:** Houghton Mifflin literary fellowship and Guggenheim fellowship, both in 1959; National Book Award, 1960, 1995; Daroff award, 1960; American Academy grant, 1960, 1995; O. Henry award, 1960; Ford Foundation grant for

drama, 1965; Rockefeller fellowship, 1966; National Book Critics Circle award, 1988, 1991; National Jewish Book award, 1988; PEN/Faulkner award, 1993; Pulitzer prize for fiction, 1998, for *American Pastoral.* Honorary degrees: Bucknell University, 1979; Bard College, Annandale-on-Hudson, New York, 1985; Rutgers University, 1987; Columbia University, New York, 1987; Brandeis University, Massachusetts, 1991; Dartmouth College, New Hampshire, 1992. **Member:** American Academy, 1970.

PUBLICATIONS

Novels

Letting Go. 1962.
When She Was Good. 1967.
Portnoy's Complaint. 1969.
Our Gang (Starring Tricky and His Friends). 1971.
The Breast. 1972; revised edition, in *A Roth Reader,* 1980.
The Great American Novel. 1973.
Life As a Man. 1974.
The Professor of Desire. 1977.
The Ghost Writer (novella). 1979; in *Zuckerman Bound: A Trilogy and Epilogue,* 1985.
Zuckerman Unbound. 1981; in *Zuckerman Bound: A Trilogy and Epilogue,* 1985.
The Anatomy Lesson. 1983; in *Zuckerman Bound: A Trilogy and Epilogue,* 1985.
Zuckerman Bound: A Trilogy and Epilogue (includes *The Ghost Writer; Zuckerman Unbound; The Anatomy Lesson; The Prague Orgy).* 1985.
The Counterlife. 1987.
Deception. 1990.
Operation Shylock: A Confession. 1993.
Sabbath's Theater. 1995.
American Pastoral. 1997.
I Married a Communist. 1998.
The Human Stain. 2000.
The Dying Animal. 2001.

Short Stories

Goodbye, Columbus, and Five Short Stories. 1959.
Novotny's Pain. 1980.

Play

Television Play: *The Ghost Writer,* with Tristram Powell, from his novella, 1983.

Other

Reading Myself and Others. 1975; revised edition, 1985.
A Roth Reader. 1980.

The Facts: A Novelist's Autobiography. 1988.
Patrimony: A True Story. 1991.
Conversations with Roth, edited by George J. Searles. 1992.
Shop Talk: A Writer and His Colleagues and Their Work.
   2001.

*

Bibliography: *Roth: A Bibliography* by Bernard F. Rodgers
Jr., 1974; revised edition, 1984.

Critical Studies: *Bernard Malamud and Philip Roth: A Criti-
cal Essay* by Glenn Meeter, 1968; *The Fiction of Philip Roth*
by John N. McDaniel, 1974; *The Comedy That ''Hoits'': An
Essay on the Fiction of Philip Roth* by Sanford Pinsker, 1975;
Philip Roth by Bernard F. Rodgers Jr., 1978; introduction by
Martin Green to *A Roth Reader,* 1980; *Philip Roth* by Judith
Paterson Jones and Guinevera A. Nance, 1981; *Critical Essays
on Philip Roth,* edited by Sanford Pinsker, 1982; *Philip Roth*
by Hermione Lee, 1982; *The Fiction of Philip Roth and John
Updike* by George J. Searles, 1985; *Reading Philip Roth,*
edited by Asher Z. Milbauer and Donald G. Watson, 1988;
Understanding Philip Roth by Murray Baumgarten and Bar-
bara Gottfried, 1990; *Beyond Despair: Three Lectures and a
Conversation with Philip Roth* by Aron Appelfeld, 1994; *The
Imagination in Transit: The Fiction of Philip Roth* by Stephen
Wade, 1996; *Philip Roth and the Jews* by Alan Cooper, 1996;
Silko, Morrison, and Roth: Studies in Survival by Naomi R.
Rand, 1999; *Philip Roth Considered: The Concentrationary
Universe of the American Writer* by Steven Milowitz, 2000.

*   *   *

Philip Roth has been writing for more than four decades,
mostly about Jewish Americans finding their place in a country
washed over by countless waves of immigrants searching for
their version of the American dream. His name, therefore, does
not immediately come to mind when thinking about Holocaust
literature because Roth is a writer who usually fictionalizes
people and events with which he is familiar. For example, all
the stories in his first successful book, *Goodbye, Columbus*
(1959), are astute observations of Jewish life often in the area
of New Jersey where he grew up. Only one of his early stories
in that book, ''Eli, the Fanatic,'' even mentions the Holocaust.
While illuminating the plight of a Holocaust survivor, it subtly
suggests the insensitivity of upwardly mobile suburban Jews
who are fearful that the sight of a desperately poor Hasid
dressed in tattered black clothes might excite dormant anti-
Semitism in their Gentile neighbors. They are more concerned
about preserving their new prosperity than helping a fellow
Jew who, during the Holocaust, had been robbed of everything
except his life. Whether Roth intended to or not, ''Eli, the
Fanatic,'' comes closer than any of his other Holocaust-related
stories to making a moral statement about the attitude of
American Jews during that time.

Ironically the reception to the other stories in *Goodbye,
Columbus* that did not deal directly with the Holocaust proved
to be heavily influenced by the catastrophe in ways unanticipated
by Roth himself. As a young writer in his 20s, he was aware
how deeply Jews in this country, feeling comparatively safe on
American shores, feared that the clouds of anti-Semitism could
potentially darken life here. When he wrote about certain
human frailties he observed among his fellow Jews, some
people worried that his writing would be just the catalyst to
awaken latent anti-Semitism, a fear Roth considered unfounded.

In *The Ghost Writer* (1979) Roth fictionalizes the real-life
debate that ensued between himself and his critics. The novella
also looks at what it means to be a writer, comparing Nathan
Zuckerman, Roth's literary alter ego, to Anne Frank. Zuckerman
suggests that his stories of Jewish life are not judged by the
same criteria as a Holocaust story like *The Diary of Anne
Frank.* This quiet criticism implying the exaggerated literary
merits of Holocaust stories is softened in *Epilogue: The
Prague Orgy* (1985), the last story in *Zuckerman Bound*
(1985). Zuckerman finds that he, too, is attracted to stories of
life during the Holocaust because they represent resistance on
the part of their authors toward repressive politics. Totalitarian
regimes like the Nazis' attempt to quash freethinking and limit
the expression of art. The freedom of the artist to develop his
ideas has been one of Roth's lifelong interests. Although Roth
briefly mentions Holocaust survivors and their stories in two
other books, *The Professor of Desire* (1977) and *Patrimony*
(1991), he focuses most intently on the Holocaust in *Operation
Shylock* (1993), where stories about the Holocaust serve as a
way to talk about writing, in general, and, more specifically,
about the value of fiction to illuminate truth. To accomplish
that, Roth incorporates some real-life elements into his novel:
the trial of John Demjanjuk, an alleged Nazi war criminal, and
a discussion with the Israeli novelist and Holocaust survivor
Aharon Appelfeld. This intermingling suggests that for Roth
the Holocaust is a perfect example of his belief that there is
much truth in fiction and much fiction in what we believe to be
the truth.

—Ellen Gerstle and Daniel Walden

See the essays on ''Eli, the Fanatic,'' *The Ghost Writer,*
   Operation Shylock: A Confession, and *Zuckerman Bound:
   A Trilogy and Epilogue.*

ROUBÍČKOVÁ, Eva Mändlová

Nationality: Czechoslovakian. **Born:** Eva Mändlová, Žatec,
16 July 1921. **Family:** Married Richard Roubicek in 1945
(died 1992); one daughter and one son. **Career:** Prisoner,
Theresienstadt ghetto, 1941–45. Administrative assistant,

KOOSPOL, Prague, 1957–75. Since 1980 private teacher of German.

PUBLICATION

Diary

We're Alive and Life Goes On: Theresienstadt Diary. 1998.

* * *

Eva Mändlová Roubíčková was born in 1921 in northern Bohemia (known as the Sudetenland; now the Czech Republic). She led a privileged life in the town of Žatec, where her father was a professor of the classics. Her life as such came to an end in 1938 when her entire family was forced to move to Prague. Her family attempted in vain to obtain visas to emigrate out of Czechoslovakia, and Roubíčková was forbidden to attend school by 1939. In 1941 she and her family were forced into the Theresienstadt (Terezín) ghetto. There Roubíčková spent several years before she was smuggled out of the ghetto during a typhus epidemic by a Czech train engineer with whom she had become friendly. The rest of her family perished in Auschwitz.

Roubíčková's only published work, *We're Alive and Life Goes On: A Theresienstadt Diary,* reflects her experiences as an inhabitant of the Theresienstadt ghetto. Although she is not a well-known Holocaust writer, her contribution to Holocaust literature should not be overlooked. Indeed, this work is informative about her life as a young girl in the ghetto and shows the dreadful conditions under which she was forced to live and ultimately survive. Her experiences are comparable to those of **Arnošt Lustig** and **Anne Frank,** though Roubíčková's writing is not nearly as detailed or in-depth as Frank's. In 1996 Roubíčková had her memoirs video recorded by Chanan Adar, who then donated this video to the Theresienstadt Memorial Museum. In these memoirs Roubíčková tells of the hatred her family was up against in their town of Žatec, and she relates in detail her job as a farm worker and shepherdess in Theresienstadt. The sheep that were under her care had been brought to Theresienstadt from the Czech town of Lidice, which was completely destroyed by the Nazis in 1942 in retaliation for the assassination by Czech underground fighters of Reinhard Heydrich, the Nazi ''Protector of Bohemia and Moravia,'' known as ''Hangman Heydrich'' and ''The Butcher of Prague'' by those who despised him.

After a six-year separation from her fiancé, Richard Roubíček, the two married shortly after their reunion.

—Cynthia A. Klíma

See the essay on *We're Alive and Life Goes On: A Theresienstadt Diary.*

ROUSSET, (Elisee) David

Nationality: French. **Born:** Roannc, 18 January 1912. **Education:** University of Paris, licencie es lettres 1932. **Military Service:** Joined the Resistance movement, 1939–43: arrested by the Gestapo and deported to Nazi concentration camps, 1943–44. **Family:** Married Susie Elliott in 1939; three sons. **Career:** Joined Socialist Students, 1931; leader, Trotskyist movement, 1935–43; member, Central Committee of the Workers' International Party, 1936; political and economic correspondent, *Life* and *Fortune* magazines, 1939–40; writer, *Revue Internationale, Temps Modernes Franc-Tireur, Combat, Figaro, Confluences,* and *The Nation,* 1947, *Preuves,* 1950–64, *Le Monde,* 1950–69, *Nouvel Observateur,* 1952, *Esope, Demain,* 1956, *Problems of Communism,* 1959, *Arguments,* 1961, *Atlas,* 1962, *Candide* and *Le Nouveau Candide,* 1963–67, and *The New Leader,* 1963; grand reporter, *Figaro,* 1963–66, *Notre Republique,* 1966, *L'Express,* 1973, *Match* and *La Nation,* 1968, *Nouvel Observateur,* 1984. Also worked as a radio and television commentator. Cofounder, Rassemblement Democratique Revolutionnaire, 1948; founder and vice president, International Commission against Concentration Camp Practices, 1949–58; organizer of enquiries on forced labor camps and political prisons in the U.S.S.R., Spain, Greece, Tunisia, People's Republic of China, and Algeria, 1951–58; deputy, fifth constituency of Isere, French Assemblee National, 1968–73. Founder and editor, *Saturne,* 1955–59, and of English edition, 1957. **Awards:** Prix Theophraste Renaudot, 1946, for *L'Univers concentrationnaire.* Inducted as officer of French Legion of Honor; named to Order of Orange-Nassau, ordre de L'Etoile brillante, and Greek Legion of Honor. **Died:** 1997.

PUBLICATIONS

Memoir

L'Univers concentrationnaire. 1945; as *A World Apart,* 1951.

Other

Les Jours de notre mort [The Days of Our Death]. 1947.
Le Pitre de Rit Pas. 1948.
Les Entretiens sur la politique, with Gerard Rosenthal and Jean-Paul Sartre. 1949.
Pour la verite sur les camps concentrationnaires, with Theo Bernard and Rosenthal. 1951; as *Police State Methods in the Soviet Union,* 1953.
Le Sens de notre combat. 1957.
La Societe eclatee de la premiere la seconde revolution mondiale. 1973; first volume translated as *The Legacy of the Bolshevik Revolution,* 1982.
Sur la guerre: Sommes-Nous en danger de guerre nucleaire? 1987.

*

Critical Study: *The Boundaries of Holocaust Literature: The Emergence of a Canon* (dissertation) by Naomi Diamant, Columbia University, 1992.

*   *   *

Born in 1912, David Rousset was a member of the resistance and a militant Trotskyite (he was a key member of the International Workers Party). He was arrested in 1943 and tortured and deported to Buchenwald in 1944. Later he was sent to various camps, including Neuengamme.

His account of the camps, *L'Univers concentrationnaire,* was published in 1945 and won the Prix Theophraste Renaudot in 1946. It was translated into English as *A World Apart* in 1951. Although he may have had surrealist sympathies—especially in relation to the black humor of the absurd—his account of the camps *L'Univers concentrationnaire* is not at all surreal in form (despite the incredible events it describes), as is sometimes claimed. It is a realist report on the ''depths of the camps.'' It covers not only a litany of atrocities and murder but also the range of different nationalities in the camps.

The fact that this book was one of the earliest accounts has had both good and bad consequences. As a report of the events, it was clearly very influential. In many ways it set the agenda for the early reception of the Holocaust, introducing the idea that the camps, a polyglot and evil kingdom of their own, were cut off from the world. On the other hand, the immensity of the Nazi genocide of the Jews is not immediately apparent (although Rousset does describe the gas chambers, it is not from firsthand evidence). More than this, he offers an interpretation of the Holocaust along conventional Marxist lines, suggesting that, although the camps came from Germany, they ''sprang from the economic and social foundations of capitalism and imperialism'' and so they may reappear anywhere. It ''would be easy to prove that the most characteristic traits of SS mentality and of social substructure may both be found in many other sectors of world society, although they may not be as pronounced.'' One effect of this is that he finds positive things quite easily in his experience: human solidarity, individual bravery, and resources to both confirm Marxist doctrine and combat Fascists and capitalists.

The experience had a profound effect on Rousset. As his career as a journalist and political figure flourished, he continued to support leftist causes. In the 1950s he was one of the first to denounce Soviet gulags and Stalinism—a brave action for somebody from the left. He was opposed to French colonial actions in Algeria, Morocco, and Indochina. He was connected with Sartre, Camus, and Breton and later became a deputy (a ''Gaullist of the Left'') in the French parliament.

Other Holocaust texts by David Rousset include *Les Jours de notre mort* (1947; *The Days of Our Death*), a ''novel'' based on the acts of witnessing to the camps and death camps, and sections of his *Fragments d'autobiographie.* Neither of these has the same power, however, as *L'Univers concentrationnaire,* not least because it was written so soon after the events.

—Robert Eaglestone

See the essay on *A World Apart.*

RÓŻEWICZ, Tadeusz

Nationality: Polish. **Born:** Radomsk, 9 October 1921. **Education:** Studied art history, Jagiellonian University, Kraków, 1945–49. **Military Service:** Served in the Polish Underground. **Career:** Poet, playwright, fiction writer, essayist, and screenwriter. Worked as a factory laborer and tutor during World War II. **Awards:** State prize for poetry, 1955, 1962, and 1966; Krakow City literary prize, 1959; prize from minister of culture and art, 1962; Jurzykowski Foundation prize (United States), 1966; prize from minister of foreign affairs, 1974 and 1987; Austrian National prize for European literature, 1982; Golden Wreath, Struga Poetry Festival, Yugoslavia, 1987. Commander, Cross of Order, Polonia Restitua, 1970; Order of Banner of Labor, 2nd class, 1977. **Member:** Bavarian Academy of Fine Arts; Academy of Arts.

PUBLICATIONS

Collection

Poezja, dramat, proza [Poetry, Drama, Prose]. 1973.

Poetry

Wlyzce wody. 1946.
Niepokój [Faces of Anxiety]. 1947.
Czerwona rekawiczka [The Red Glove]. 1948.
Piec poematow [Five Longer Poems]. 1950.
Czas ktory idzie [The Time to Come]. 1951.
Wiersze i obrazy [Poems and Images]. 1952.
Wybor wierszy. 1953.
Rownina [The Plain]. 1954.
Usmiechy [Smiles]. 1955.
Srebrny klos [Silver Ear of Grain]. 1955.
Poemat otwarty [The Open Poem]. 1956.
Poeszje zebrane. 1957; as *Collected Poems,* 1976.
Formy [Forms]. 1958.
Rozmowa z ksieciem. 1960.
Glos anonima [Voice of an Anonymous Man]. 1961.
Niepokoj; Wybor wierszy, 1945–1961. 1963.
Twarz [Face]. 1964.

Wiersze i poematy. 1967.
Poezje wybrane [Selected Poems]. 1967.
Twarz trzecia [The Third Face]. 1968.
Regio. 1969.
Wiersze [Poems]. 1969.
Wybor poezji. 1969.
Faces of Anxiety (English translation). 1969.
Wiersze. 1974.
"The Survivor" and Other Poems (selections in English). 1976.
Duszyczka [Little Spirit]. 1977.
Unease (English translation). 1980.
Green Rose (English translation). 1982.
Conversation with a Prince and Other Poems (selections in English). 1982; revised edition, as *They Came to See a Poet,* 1991.
Na powierzchni poematu i w srodku. 1983.
Poezje wybrane. 1984.
Poezje. 1987.
Poezja (2 vols.). 1988.
Plaskorzezba [Bas-Relief]. 1991.
Forms in Relief: And Other Works (Polish and English). 1994.
Poezja wybrane/Selected Poems. 1994.
Zawsze Fragment; Recycling (English translation). 1996.

Novel

Smierc w starych dekoraocjach [Death amidst Old Stage Props]. 1970.

Short Stories

Opadly liscie z drzew [The Leaves Have Fallen from the Trees]. 1955.
Przerwany egzamin [The Interrupted Exam]. 1960.
Wycieczka do muzeum [Excursion to a Museum]. 1966.
Opowiadania wybrane [Selected Stories]. 1968.

Plays

Beda sie bili. First serialized in *Echo Tygodnia,* 1949–50.
Grupa Laokoona [The Laocoon Group]. 1961.
Spaghetti i miecz [Spaghetti and the Sword]. 1966.
Utwory dramatyczne. 1966.
Przyrost naturalny. In *Dialog,* 1968; as *Birth Rate: The Biography of a Play for the Theatre in Twentieth-Century Polish Avant-Garde Drama,* 1977.
Kartoteka (produced Warsaw, 1960). As *The Card Index,* in *"The Card Index" and Other Plays,* 1969.
Wyszedl Kartoteka (produced Warsaw, 1960; as *Wyszedl,* Warsaw, 1960; as *Wyszedl z domu,* 1964). As *Gone Out,* in *"The Card Index" and Other Plays,* 1969.
Akt przerwany (produced 1964). As *The Interrupted Act,* in *"The Card Index" and Other Plays,* 1969.

"The Card Index" and Other Plays (English translations; includes *The Card Index; Gone Out; The Interrupted Act*). 1969.
Teatr niekonsekwencji (includes *Smieszny staruszek; Stara kobieta wysiaduje*). 1970.
Świadkowie, albo nasza mala stabilizacja (produced 1962). As *The Witnesses,* in *"The Witnesses" and Other Plays,* 1970.
Smieszny staruszek (produced 1964). As *The Funny Old Man,* in *"The Witnesses" and Other Plays,* 1970.
Stara kobieta wysiaduje (produced 1968). As *The Old Woman Broods,* in *"The Witnesses" and Other Plays,* 1970.
"The Witnesses" and Other Plays (English translations; includes *The Witnesses; The Funny Old Man; The Old Woman Broods*). 1970.
Sztuki teatralne [Pieces for the Theatre]. 1972.
Biale malzenstwo (translated as *White Marriage* and produced New Haven, Connecticut, 1977). In *Biale mtilzenstwo i inne utwory sceniczne,* 1975.
Biale mtilzenstwo i inne utwory sceniczne (includes *Biale malzenstwo; Dzidzibobo czyli milosc romantyczna czeka juz pod drzwiami; Sobowtor; Dramat rozbiezny; Czego pyrzbywa czego ubywa*). 1975.
Pułapka. 1982; as *The Trap,* 1997.
"Marriage Blanc" and "The Hunger Artist Departs" (English translations). 1983.
Teatr (2 vols.). 1988.
Reading the Apocalypse in Bed: Selected Plays and Short Pieces (selections in English). 1998.

Other

Zielona roza [The Green Rose] (poetry), with *Kartoteka* [The Card Index] (play). 1961.
Nic w plaszczu Prospera [Nothing in Propsero's Cloak] (poetry and plays). 1963.
Kartki z Wegier. 1953.
Przygotowanie do wieczoru autorskiego [Preparation for an Author's Evening]. 1971.
Proza [Prose]. 1972.
Proba rekonstrukcji. 1979.
Echa lesne. 1985.
Proza (2 vols.). 1990.

Editor, *Kto jest ten dziwny nieznajomy* [Who Is This Odd Stranger] by Leopold Staff. 1964.

*

Media Adaptation: *My Little Daughter,* from the novella *Moja coreczka,* 1966.

Critical Studies: *Różewicz* by Henryk Vogler, 1972; "Tadeusz Rózewicz and the Poetics of Pessimism" by Robert Hauptman, in *North Dakota Quarterly,* 50(3), Summer 1982, pp. 77–82; "Theatrical Reality in the Plays of Tadeusz Rózewicz," in

Slavic and East European Journal, 26(4), Winter 1982, pp. 447–59, and *A Laboratory of Impure Forms: The Plays of Tadeusz Rozewicz,* 1991, both by Halina Filipowicz; "On Różewicz" by András Fodor, in *Acta Litteraria,* 30(1–2), 1988, pp. 152–60; "Gardens of Stone: The Poetry of Zbigniew Herbert and Tadeusz Rozewicz" by Paul Coates, in *The Mature Laurel: Essays on Modern Polish Poetry,* edited by Adam Czerniawki, 1991; "Without Boundaries" by Jonathan Aaron, in *Parnassus,* 9(1), Spring/Summer 1991, pp. 110–28; "Rózewicz at Seventy: Rebirth of a Survivor," in *Polish Review,* XXXIX(2), 1994, pp. 195–211, and "Sources of Tadeusz Różewicz's Correspondence: Julian Przybos, 1945–1962," in *Polish Review,* XLI(1), 1996, pp. 3–36, both by Richard Sokoloski.

* * *

Tadeusz Różewicz belongs to the Kolumbowie Generation, also called the Generation of the Fulfilled Apocalypse. The main experience of the group's members, who were taking final exams in high school in 1939, was World War II and the fight with the Nazi invaders. Young and talented poets from Warsaw such as K.K. Baczyński, T. Gajcy, and A. Trzebinski died at the time. Różewicz fought in Armia Krajowa clandestine guerrilla troops in the country. Such experiences left a deep mark both in Różewicz's writing and in the writing of the most outstanding writer of that generation, **Tadeusz Borowski**. The tragic experience of wartime in Różewicz's life was intensified by the fact that his mother was of Jewish origin, and in November 1944 his elder brother was murdered by the Gestapo. His brother was for him the embodiment of patriotism as well as his spiritual and artistic confidant.

The war motif—moral degradation of the human race and the Holocaust crime—has been present in Różewicz's works since his debut until present times. He has specified it in his poetry, prose, and drama. It is best seen in two volumes of poems, *Niepokój* (*Faces of Anxiety*) and *Czerwona rekawiczka* ("The Red Glove").

At once Różewicz became a revelation for readers as an outstanding poet and a moral radical who had lost his faith in beautiful lies of art and in the effectiveness of ethical standards that were deeply downtrodden by those responsible for the Holocaust, though he did not share the dilemma of the antifascist Theodore Adorno, who questioned the purpose of creating poetry after Auschwitz. It is significant that Adorno was answered by two poets who survived the Holocaust in Poland. In the poem "Widziałem cudowne monstrum" ("I Saw the Miraculous Monster"), Różewicz writes, "a task is waiting for me / at home: / To create poetry after Auschwitz." **Henryk Grynberg**, in his poem "Popioły i Diamenty" ("The Ashes and the Diamonds"), firmly emphasizes, "let me add one more thing / it is possible / to write poems after Auschwitz."

What do these ironically heroic declarations of two poets who survived the Holocaust have in common? First of all is autobiographical compulsion, the necessity of personal trauma.

There is also the crucial need to reveal the truth about "the times of contempt" as well as the need to save the memory of those millions of Jews from Europe who died of hunger in ghettos or were cremated at Auschwitz. Each poet was also aware of the fact that goals can be reached only when language adequate for expressing these extremely depressing events is found—the debate focused on the truth and the bare facts recording, which are so scary and hard to imagine.

Tadeusz Różewicz invented a kind of poetic debate that rejected ornamental style. It was called Różewicz's type, or a peculiar variety of the type IV free verse system. Soon after, a school of poets imitating the author's formal innovations of *Faces of Anxiety* emerged in Poland and in some other countries.

Różewicz's merits for modernization of the drama form in Poland are also of great importance. In his famous book *The Theatre of the Absurd,* Martin Esslin juxtaposes the drama revelations of the author of *Kartoteka* and of European playwrights such as Sławomir Mrożek and Václav Havel. In spite of the fact that the problem of the Holocaust does not constitute the main theme in Różewicz's plays, some Holocaust motifs can be found in the following dramas: *Świadkowie* (*The Witnesses*), *Grupa Laokoona* ("The Laokoon Group"), *Odejśie Głodomora* (*The Hunger Artist Departs*), and *Pułapka* (*The Trap*), especially in those related to Franz Kafka.

Różewicz's poetics have gone through some changes. As a playwright he has used categories of tragedy, ridicule, absurd, and sublime. He has mixed genres and styles. He has made use of fantasy and contrasted it with aesthetic norms of realism in one piece. As a searching and pessimistic diagnostician of twentieth-century mass culture, he has perceived ideas and themes of modern art on "the scrap heap of life" just as Samuel Beckett did in *Endgame.* This Polish pessimist and innovator of poetry and drama is known for his original works. Like Friedrich Hölderlin, Różewicz believes that "what persists does so thanks to poets" despite crises in our civilization and the madness of a human race capable of committing horrible crimes such as the Holocaust or some other ethnic purge, which nowadays can be observed on racial, national, or religious grounds.

—Stanisław Gawliński

See the essay on *Collected Poems.*

RUDASHEVSKI, Yitskhok

Nationality: Russian. **Born:** Vilna, Lithuania, 10 December 1927. **Career:** Member, Pioneers youth organization, division of the Komsomol (All-Union Leninist Communist League of Youth). Forced into the Vilna ghetto, 1941–43. **Died:** Murdered, Ponary Forest, October 1943.

PUBLICATION

Diary

Yomano shel na'ar mi-Vilnah: Yuni 1941–April 1943. 1968; as *The Diary of the Vilna Ghetto, June 1941–April 1943,* 1973.

* * *

Born in Vilna on 10 December 1927, Yitskhok Rudashevski was the only child of Rose and Elihu Rudashevski. He was known to his family members as Itsele. His father was from a small town and had gone to Vilna to work as a typesetter for the publisher of the well-known Yiddish newspaper *Vilner Tog.* His mother, a native of Kishinev, was a seamstress, a job she continued to hold in the Vilna ghetto. Yitskhok enjoyed a comfortable childhood and a loving extended family. Growing up in Vilna, he was in the middle of a world center for Jewish and eastern European culture, and he took every educational advantage of it. He completed a year of study, for example, at the Realgymnasium, a Vilna secondary school noted for its academic excellence, where he was a good student and excelled in literature and history. He was not religious, however. In fact, he belonged to the Pioneers, a youth organization that was a subdivision of the Komsomol (the All-Union Leninist Communist League of Youth).

When the Germans invaded Lithuania on 22 June 1941, Yitskhok was just 13 years old. With ample cooperation from the Lithuanians, the Germans immediately set about the task of persecuting the Jews of Vilna. Within a month of their arrival they had taken 35,000 men, women, and children some six miles into the Ponary forest and murdered them. Soon Ponary had become one of the most notorious killing sites in eastern Europe. Sensing the gravity of the historical moment, Yitskhok began keeping a diary when the Germans were advancing toward his native city. The first entry of the diary is dated 21 June 1941, with the last entry dated 7 April 1943.

When Yitskhok's family was forced into the Vilna ghetto on 6 September 1941, the boy was traumatized by being separated from his maternal grandmother, to whom he had always been close. She was soon murdered by the Nazis. The Rudashevski family remained in the ghetto until it was liquidated on 23 September 1943. Throughout his time Yitskhok secretly continued to attend school, and he participated in various clubs and literary societies. Among his most important activities was the gathering of tales, testimonies, and other materials documenting the history of the Vilna ghetto.

When the ghetto was liquidated and the last of its Jews were sent to be murdered at Ponary, Yitskhok and his parents went into hiding with his Uncle Voloshin, who had a residence on Disne Street where five other people were also hiding. On either 5 or 7 October the Rudashevskis were discovered and sent to the killing field at Ponary. Among those whom the Nazis discovered in the hiding place was Yitskhok's cousin, a

young woman named Sore Voloshin. She was the one member of the group who managed to escape into the woods. She joined a partisan unit, and when she returned to Vilna with the partisans in July 1944, she found a city bereft of Jews. But she also discovered Yitskhok's diary in the house on Disne Street, where they had hidden together. She entrusted the diary to the care of the partisan poet Abraham Sutskever, who saw to it that the diary reached the archives at Yad Vashem.

—David Patterson

See the essay on *The Diary of the Vilna Ghetto, June 1941–April 1943.*

RUDNICKI, Adolf

Nationality: Polish. **Born:** 19 February 1912. **Military Service:** Fought in the campaign to defend Poland, 1939. **Career:** Writer. Imprisoned during World War II; lived in Lwów, Poland, 1942, before returning to Warsaw; participant, Warsaw Ghetto Uprising, 1944. **Died:** 1990.

PUBLICATIONS

Collections

Blic; Drobiazgi zolnierskie; Zolnierze; Po latach. 1967.
Opowiadania, edited by Marianna Sokolowska. 1996.

Novels

Szczury [Rats]. 1932.
Żołnierze [Soldiers]. 1933.
Lato. 1938.
Profile i drobiazgi zolnierskie. 1946.
Wniebowstąpienie (novella). 1948; as *Ascent to Heaven,* 1951.
Krowa. 1959.
Kupiec lódzki: Niebieskie kartki. 1963.
Teksty male i mniejsze. 1971.
Noc bedzie chlodna, niebo w purpurze. 1977.
Rogaty Warszawiak. 1981.
Sto jeden [One Hundred and One]. 1984.
Dzoker Pana Boga. 1989.

Short Stories

Niekochana [Unloved]. 1937.
Szekspir [Shakespeare]. 1948.
Ucieczka z Jasnej Polany [Escape from Jasna Polana]. 1949.
Wybór opowiadan. 1950.
Paleczka: Czyli kazdemu to, na czym mu mniej zalezy. 1950.
Narzeczony beaty: Niebieskie kartki [Beata's Fiancé]. 1961.

Złote okna i 9 innych opowiadań [Golden Windows and Nine
    Other Stories]. 1964.
50 opowiadan. 1966.
Daniela naga. 1977.

Memoirs

Wrzesien. 1946.
Żywe i martwe morze. 1952; as *The Dead and the Living Sea,
    and Other Stories,* 1957.

Other

Zolnierski dzien powszedni. 1936.
Major Hubert z armii Andersa. 1946.
Czysty nurt. 1946.
Kon. 1946.
Wielkanoc. 1947.
Manfred: Dramat w czterech aktach. 1954.
Mlode cierpienia. 1954.
Niebieskie kartki: Slepe lustro tych lat (essays) 1956.
Kartki sportowe. 1956.
Niebieskie kartki: Przeswity. 1957.
Obraz z kotem i psem. 1962.
Pyl milosny: Niebieskie kartki. 1964.
Weiss wpada do morza: Niebieskie kartki. 1965.
Wspólne zdjęcie: Niebieskie kartki [Collective Photo] (es-
    says). 1967.
Zabawa ludowa: Niebieskie kartki. 1979.
Krakowskie Przedmieście pełne deserów [Krakowskie
    Przedmieście: A Street Full of Desserts]. 1986.
Teatr zawsze grany. 1987.
Sercem dnia jest wieczór, with Janusz Majcherek. 1988.
Sto lat temu umarl Dostojewski (literary criticism). 1989.

Editor, *Wieczna pamiec.* 1955; as *Lest We Forget,* 1955.

*

Critical Study: "Assimilation into Exile: The Jew As a Polish
Writer" by Zygmunt Bauman, in *Poetics Today,* 17, Winter
1996, pp. 569–97.

*   *   *

Born in Warsaw into a Jewish family and often called the
"Jeremiah of the Warsaw Ghetto," Adolf Rudnicki started his
literary career in 1932 by publishing his first novel, *Szczury*
("Rats"), which manifested the author's specific anti-aesthetic program. His next work, *Żołnierze* (1933; "Soldiers"),
confirmed that his writing is documentary or, more precisely,
combines the elements of real life with his own imaginary
invention. He uses the elements of reportage but frequently
modifies them and thus has created this genre's new forms. His
prose contains features of a document, fiction, and a psychological account at the same time. Present in all his writings, this

"internal contradiction," as stated by Czesław Miłosz, suggests perhaps where the essence of his artistry is located. The
long short story *Niekochana* (1937; "Unloved") is full of this
contradiction and is widely regarded as Rudnicki's best prewar
achievement. It is also classified as a psychological study of an
unwanted love.

Although Rudnicki was prolific in the early years of his
career, his creativity peaked during and after the Second World
War. The impact of the war's tragedies and especially of the
fate of the Polish Jews on Rudnicki's writings is most powerful. From then on he embarked upon a major project to leave a
testimony to the tragedy of the Jews in Nazi-occupied Poland.
He was well predisposed to carry out his project, as his war
experiences testify: he took part in the failed September 1939
campaign to defend Poland and was taken prisoner by the
Germans but managed to escape; until 1942 he lived in the
Polish city of Lwów, then occupied by the Soviets; when Hitler
invaded the Soviet Union, he moved back to Nazi-occupied
Warsaw, where he managed to survive outside the ghetto while
being active in clandestine cultural organizations; and in 1944
he participated in the Warsaw Uprising.

Rudnicki's project aimed at depicting, in various narrative
forms, the whole array of the Nazis' victims and their experiences. Faithful to his prewar anti-aesthetic program, his narrative forms continued to consist of short stories (he did not
consider the novel a genre suitable for his project) that again
mixed fiction and reality through the use of the elements of
literature and reportage, the personal diary, and the feuilleton.
Shuffling factual data and rewriting the personal lives of real
persons in diverse narrative forms are the most typical features
in Rudnicki's postwar works, including *Szekspir* (1948; "Shakespeare") and *Ucieczka z Jasnej Polany* (1949; "Escape from
Jasna Polana"). The short stories from these two collections
later constituted a short-story cycle known as "Epoka pieców"
("The Epoch of Ovens") and are regarded as both Rudnicki's
best literary achievement and one of the most poignant testimonies of the Holocaust. A revised and extended version of the
cycle was published later under the title *Żywe i martwe morze*
(1952; *The Dead and the Living Sea, and Other Stories,* 1957).
It contains a strong moral message that expressed faith in the
dignity of man. It also signifies the author's ever-present
concern that his work is never perfect or even complete and
that it needs constant revision.

The aims and possibilities of literary art faced with the
imperative task of giving an account of the Jews' plight
constitute a major problem in Rudnicki's work. He chooses to
describe the moral aspect of the tragedy of the Jews rather
than their martyrdom. His heroic characters in, for example, *Wniebowstąpienie* (1948; *Ascent to Heaven,* 1951),
"Narzeczony Beaty" (1961; "Beata's Fiancé"), and "Wspólne
zdjęcie" (1967; "Collective Photo") defend their dignity,
find strength, and remain faithful to themselves through solidarity with their dying nation. They oppose its tragic plight not
only by fighting for their survival but also by preserving the

highest human values of love, compassion, and dignity. In his presentation of these values, Rudnicki combines a lyrical, even sentimental, commentary full of pathos with dry reporting filled with irony and sarcasm. Standing alongside other notable Polish authors who gave convincing literary accounts of the war's genocide, such as **Tadeusz Borowski** and Kornel Filipowicz, Rudnicki unquestionably remains one of Poland's leading chroniclers of the Holocaust. Numerous collections of his old and new short stories, feuilletons, essays, and memoirs (notably *Złote okna i 9 innych opowiadań* [1964; "Golden Windows and Nine Other Stories"], *Sto jeden* [1984–88; "One Hundred and One"], and *Krakowskie Przedmieście pełne deserów* [1986; "Krakowskie Przedmieście: A Street Full of Desserts"]) were published between 1960 and 1990.

—Andrzej Karcz

See the essay on *Ascent to Heaven.*

RYBAKOV, Anatolii (Naumovich)

Nationality: Russian. **Born:** Chernigov, 14 January 1911. **Education:** Moscow Institute of Railway Engineers, 1934. **Military Service:** Red Army, 1941–45: major-engineer. **Family:** Maried Tatiana in 1928; two sons from other marriages. **Career:** Exiled to Siberia for alleged involvement in counterrevolutionary activity, 1933–36. Engineer for motor vehicle transport companies, Ufa, Kalinin, and Ryazan, 1930s. Also worked as a truck driver and ballroom dance instructor. Contributor of fiction to periodicals, including *Novy Mir, Oktyabr,* and *Druzhba narodov.* President, Russian Soviet PEN center, 1989–91. **Awards:** Stalin prize, 1951, for *Voditeli;* Vasil'ev Brothers prize, Russian Soviet Federative Socialist Republic, 1973, for *Neizvestny soldat.* **Died:** 24 December 1998.

PUBLICATIONS

Collection

Sobranie sochineniy [Collected Works] 1981–82.

Novels

Voditeli [The Drivers]. 1950, in *Oktiabr'.*
Ekaterina Voronina [Catherine Voronin]. 1955; revised editions, 1958, 1960, 1970.
Leto v Sosniakakh [Summer in Sosniaki]. 1964.
Tiazhelyi pesok. 1978; as *Heavy Sand,* 1981.
Deti Arbata (first novel in tetralogy). 1987; as *Children of the Arbat,* 1988.
Tridcat'pjatyi i drugie gody [1935 and Other Years] (second novel in tetrology). 1989.

Strah [Terror] (third novel in tetralogy). 1990.
Dust and Ashes. 1994.
Remembrance. 1997.

Novels (for children)

Kortik (novella). 1948; as *The Dirk,* 1954.
Bronzovaya ptitsa (novella; sequel to *Kortik*). 1956; as *The Bronze Bird,* 1958.
Prikliucheniia Krosha [Krosh's Adventures] (novella). 1960.
Kanikuly Krosha [Krosh's Holiday] (novella). 1966.
Neizvestnyi soldat [The Unknown Soldier]. 1970.
Vystrel [The Shot]. 1975.

Plays

Screenplays: *Kortik,* 1954; *Ekaterina Voronina,* 1956; *Priklyucheniya Krosha,* 1962; *Eti neviuuije zabavy* [These Innocent Games], adaptation of his *Kanikuly Krosha,* 1968; *Minuta molchania* [A Minute of Silence], adaptation of his *Neizvestny soldat,* 1971; *Neizvestny soldat,* 1971; *Bronzovaya ptitsa,* 1975; *Poslednee leto detstra* [The Last Summer of Childhood], 1975; *Kanikuly Krosha,* 1980; *Voskzesenie, polorina sedmogo* [Sunday, Half Past Six], 1989.

Other

Roman-vospominanie (autobiography), 1997.

*

Film Adaptations: *Kortik,* 1954; *Ekaterina Voronina,* 1956; *Priklyucheniya Krosha,* 1962; *Minuta molchania,* 1971; *Poslednee leto detstra,* 1975; *Bronzovaya ptitsa,* 1975; *Kanikuly Krosha,* 1980; *Neizvestny soldat,* 1985.

Critical Studies: In *Commentary,* June 1979, pp. 85–88; in *Time,* 27 April 1987, pp. 45–46; in *Atlantic Monthly,* June 1988, pp. 102–05; in *New Yorker,* 12 September 1988, pp. 108–14.

* * *

Ever since the publication of Anatolii Rybakov's first book, *Kortik* (1948; *The Dirk,* 1954), an adventure story for teenagers in commemoration of the 30th anniversary of the Young Communist League (Komsomol), and his second book, *Voditeli* (1950; "The Drivers"), a socialist-realist production novel that earned its author a 1951 Stalin Prize for literature, the story of his success in the censorship-stricken Soviet Union has been interpreted by some of his critics (for example, Aleksandr Gladkov) as that of a gifted opportunist. Even the appearance of *Tiazhelyi pesok* (1978; *Heavy Sand,* 1981), Rybakov's only book on the Holocaust, which had been a taboo subject in Soviet Russia for decades, could justifiably be credited to his uncanny ability to make the most of a current political climate, whatever it was. As the 1975 signing of the Helsinki Agreement on Security and Cooperation in Europe, with its emphasis on human rights, forced the Soviet Union to soften its emigration policy, the mass exodus of Soviet Jews, leaving for either the United States or Israel, started gaining momentum (and reached its peak in 1979). With the concomitant partial liberalization of the restrictions on the discussion of the ''Jewish question,'' Rybakov must have felt that this was his chance to tell as much truth as possible about the fate of the Soviet Jewry during World War II. (In his 1997 autobiography, *Roman-vospominanie,* he claimed that even the estimated number of Holocaust victims, 6 million, was first revealed to the Soviet reader in no other source than *Heavy Sand.*)

In an unrelated chain of events, the year 1974 saw the appointment of the writer Anatolii Anan'ev as editor in chief of an influential Moscow literary magazine, *Oktiabr'* (''October''), notorious for being a bastion of communist conservatism. Anan'ev was anxious to turn the magazine around and gladly accepted the challenge of helping Rybakov's controversial manuscript to see the light of day after it had been turned down by the reputedly more liberal journals *Novyi mir* (''The New World'') and *Druzhba narodov* (''The Friendship of Nations'').

This was not an easy task. The editorial board of *Oktiabr'* demanded a large number of changes as a prerequisite for the novel's serialization. (It was eventually published in 1978, in numbers 7–9.) Thus the anti-Semitic leaflets with quotations from Dostoevsky, distributed during the war as part of the Nazi propaganda, were to be replaced by a reference to Knut Hamsun. Zürich, the birthplace of a main character in the novel, Yakov Ivanovsky, was to be changed to Basel because of the fear of possible associations with Aleksandr Solzhenitsyn's anticommunist book *Lenin v Tsiurikhe* (1975; *Lenin in Zürich,* 1976). In Soviet Russia, in those days, Solzhenitsyn's name was unmentionable. The topic of the late 1930s show trials, because of which Yakov's son Lyova perishes, was also deemed highly undesirable, and Lyova had to die by accident, under a train instead. (It was not by chance that the critic E. Starikova, in her review of *Heavy Sand,* appearing in *Druzhba narodov* in 1979, found this accidental death ''artistically unconvincing.'') Rybakov's treatment of World War II had to be readjusted to highlight the fact that not only Jews but also representatives of other Soviet nations suffered at the hands of the Germans. Even the original title of the novel, *Rakhil'* (''Rachel''), was apparently considered to be patently Jewish and could not stay unaltered.

These demands were largely in tune with the general line of *Oktiabr'.* (Almost 30 years previously, prior to the serialization of *Voditeli* in 1950, the then editorial board requested to replace the allegedly Jewish surname of a character called Verbitsky with the more Russian-sounding Vertilin.) They arguably could not inflict serious damage, however, on *Heavy Sand.* Regardless of how consistently editors (including the

chief ideologist of the Communist Party of the Soviet Union, Mikhail Suslov) sought to impose a multinational agenda on the novel by eradicating the word ''Jew'' from it, it remained, in essence, a novel about Jews and about the Holocaust. (Rybakov restored most of the censored episodes and the original story line when republishing *Heavy Sand* in *Sobranie sochineny.*

Neither Rybakov himself nor members of his immediate family had firsthand experience of the Holocaust. Rybakov's Jewish roots, however, contributed to his taking the issue personally. For obvious reasons his printed sources were limited mostly to the officially published protocols of the Nuremberg war trials (with some additional information drawn from the Moscow Samizdat journal *Evrei v SSSR* [''Jews in the USSR''], the access to which Rybakov gained courtesy of the dissident Sarra Babenysheva). Rybakov's visit to the Ponary forest near Vilnius (the burial site of some 70,000 Lithuanian Jews) and especially his extensive inquiries in the Ukrainian town of Shchors (formerly Snovsk), where his mother's family resided for a while, helped him to re-create the atmosphere of a typical ghetto, which was recognized as authentic by many Holocaust survivors. Almost the entire Jewish population of Shchors was exterminated in the early 1940s. Rybakov's main informer on the plight of the Shchors ghetto, a local hairdresser, is portrayed in *Heavy Sand* under the name of Bernard Semyonovich. The memorial gravestone at the Shchors Jewish cemetery, with the Hebrew inscription from Joel 3:21, is depicted in the final scene of the novel (contrary to Gary Rosenshield's statement that such ''a monument could not have existed in 1972'').

Heavy Sand has been branded by some as a piece of propaganda, but its critics seem to disagree on what ideas precisely it was supposed to spread. One reading of the novel suggested that Rybakov ''was aesopically advising his Soviet Jewish readers against trying to emigrate to Israel,'' whereas another, referring to the fact that Basel, mentioned in *Heavy Sand,* had been a popular location for Zionist Congresses, suspected the book of sending a cryptic Zionist message to the public. Perhaps the most balanced assessment of *Heavy Sand* belongs to Peter Lewis, who maintained that it ''may leave itself open to political criticism . . . , but at heart it is a profoundly humanistic novel in the great tradition of Russian literature.''

—Andrei Rogachevskii

See the essay on *Heavy Sand.*

RYMKIEWICZ, Jaroslaw (Marek)

Nationality: Polish. **Born:** Warsaw, 1935. **Education:** Studied Polish philology at the University of Lodz; holds a Ph.D.

Career: Worked at the Literary Research Institute of the Polish Academy of Sciences and Letters, Warsaw.

PUBLICATIONS

Poetry

Konwencje [Conventions]. 1957.
Czlowiek z glowa jastrzebia. 1960.
Metafizyka. 1963.
Animula. 1964.
Anatomia. 1970.
Co to jest drozd. 1973.
Thema regium. 1978.
Moje dzielo posmiertne [My Posthumous Works]. 1993.

Novels

Umschlagplatz. 1988; translated as *The Final Station: Umschlagplatz,* 1994.

Plays

Kochankowie piekla [The Lovers of Hell]. 1975.
Krol Miesopust; Porwanie Europy [The King of Meat; The Abduction of Europe]. 1977.
Dwie komedie (includes *Dwor nad Narwia* and *Ulani*). 1980.

Other

Kwiaty nowy, starych romanc, czyli, Imitacje i przeklady hiszpanskich romances. 1966.
Czym jest klasycyzm: Manifesty poetyckie [What Is Classicism? Poetical Manifestos]. 1967.
Mysli rozne o ogrodach [Various Thoughts about Gardens]. 1968.
Wybór wierszy. 1976.
Aleksander Fredro jest w zlym humorze [Aleksander Fredro Is in a Bad Mood] (biography). 1977.
Juliusz Slowacki pyta o gozine [Juliusz Slowacki Inquires about the Time] (biography). 1982.
Wielki ksiaze z dodaniem rozwazan o istocie i prymiotach ducha poskiego (Polish history). 1983.
Rozmowy polskie latem [Conversations in a Polish Summer]. 1984.
Zmut (biography). 1987.
Baket (biography). 1989.
Ulica Mandelsztama i inne wiersze z lat 1979–1985. 1992.
Kilka szczegolow [A Few Particulars]. 1994.
Mickiewicz, czyli, Wszystko: z Jaroslawem Markiem Rymkiewiczem rozmawia Adam Poprawa. 1994.
Do Snowia i dalej [To Snow and Beyond]. 1996.
Znak niejasny, basn pólzywa. 1999.

Translator, *Zycie jest snem,* by Pedro Calderón de la Barca. 1971.

*

Critical Study: "A New Generation of Voices in Polish Holocaust Literature" by Monika Adamczyk-Garbowska, in *Prooftexts,* 9(3), September 1989, pp. 273–87.

* * *

Born in Warsaw in 1935, Jaroslaw Marek Rymkiewicz is a literary critic and historian of literature, an essayist, a poet, a translator, and a playwright. He studied Polish philology at the University of Lodz, and his first volume of poems was published in 1957. He has translated poetry into Polish from English (Eliot and Stevens) and Spanish (Lorca and Calderón). Rymkiewicz's only novel was originally published in Polish under the title *Umschlagplatz* in Paris in 1988. According to Monika Adamczyk-Garbowska, what made the novel unacceptable to the Polish censorship authorities was not so much that it was critical of Polish attitudes toward Jews as that it presented a critical image of Communist rule. The novel was published in French under the title *La Dernière Gare (Umschlagplatz)* in 1989 and in German under its original title of *Umschlagplatz* in 1993. Nina Taylor's English translation was published in the United States under the title *The Final Station: Umschlagplatz* in 1994.

Parts of Rymkiewicz's research for the novel are represented within the text. The narrator's aim is to describe the Umschlagplatz, which was the area of the Warsaw Ghetto where Jews were gathered for deportation by train to Treblinka. As he knows neither Hebrew nor Yiddish, the narrator consults only works written in, or translated into, Polish, of which he has read "several dozen." Many of these works are cited and discussed in the novel. The same applies to his research on the deportation of Jews to Treblinka from a resort near Warsaw called Otwock; conflicting testimony is considered and evaluated.

Adamczyk-Garbowska describes *Umschlagplatz* as "the first full-length novel written by a Polish gentile writer that deals exclusively with the Holocaust." It was published soon after Jan Blonski's controversial 1987 article "The Poor Poles Look at the Ghetto." Blonski argued that the Poles should "stop haggling, trying to defend ourselves" and accept responsibility for insufficient resistance to the murder of Polish Jews: "We should acknowledge our own guilt, and ask for forgiveness." Rymkiewicz has a similar agenda in *Umschlagplatz.*

Umschlagplatz was well received. Michael André Bernstein has praised Rymkiewicz for successfully making the Holocaust the center of his work without relying on historical back shadowing or caricature and for making a confrontation with the moral dilemmas of writing about the Holocaust a central part of his text. Bernstein describes the dramatization in *Umschlagplatz* of Rymkiewicz's quandary about his right as a Pole to speak about the Holocaust at all as the author's most significant breakthrough, which "owes as much to [Rymkiewicz's] willingness to take artistic risks as it does to the seriousness of his moral imagination and historical scrupulousness."

—Alan Polak

See the essay on *The Final Station: Umschlagplatz.*

S

SACHS, Nelly

Nationality: Swedish (originally German: immigrated to Sweden, 1940, granted Swedish citizenship, 1952). **Born:** Leonie Nelly Sachs, Berlin, 10 December 1891. **Education:** Hoch Töchterschule; educated privately. **Career:** Writer and translator. Fled to Sweden, 1940. **Awards:** Prize of the Poets' Association (Sweden); Jahrespring Literature prize, 1959; Kulturpreis der deutschen Industrie, 1959; Annette Droste prize for poetry, 1960; won the first Nelly Sachs prize for literature (created in her honor by the town of Dortmund, Germany), 1961; Peace prize, West German Booksellers, 1965; Nobel prize for literature, 1966. **Member:** Bayrische Akademie fuer schoene Kuenste (Munich), Freie Akademie der Stadt Hamburg, Darmstaedter Akademie fuer Sprache und Dichtung. **Died:** 12 May 1970.

PUBLICATIONS

Poetry

Legenden und Erzaehlungen. 1921.
In den Wohnungen des Todes [In the Habitations of Death]. 1947.
Sternverdunkelung [Eclipse of the Stars]. 1949.
Und niemand weiss weiter [And No One Knows How to Go On]. 1957.
Flucht und Verwandlung [Flight and Metamorphosis]. 1959.
Noch feiert Tod das Leben [Death Still Celebrates Life]. 1960.
Fahrt ins Staublose: Die Gedichte der Nelly Sachs [Journey into a Dustless Realm: Poems of Nelly Sachs]. 1961.
Die Gedichte der Nelly Sachs (2 vols.). 1961–71.
Ausgewaehlte Gedichte [Selected Poems]. 1963.
Glühende Rätsel [Glowing Enigmas]. 1964.
Spaete Gedichte [Later Poems]. 1965.
Die Suchende [The Seeker]. 1966.
Wie leicht wird Erde sein: Ausgewaehlte Gedichte. 1966.
O the Chimneys: Selected Poems, Including the Verse Play, Eli (selections in English). 1967; as *Selected Poems: Including the Verse Play 'Eli,'* 1968.
The Seeker and Other Poems (selections in English). 1970.
Teile dich Nacht: Die letzten Gedichte. [Open Yourself, Night: The Last Poems]. 1971.
Suche nach Lebenden: Die Gedichte der Nelly Sachs. 1971.
Gedichte. 1977.

Plays

Eli: Ein Mysterienspiel vom Leiden Israels [Eli: A Mystery Play of the Sufferings of Israel] (radio broadcast 1951; produced 1962). 1951. In *Das Leiden Israels,* 1962; in *O the Chimneys: Selected Poems, Including the Verse Play, Eli,* 1967; in *Selected Poems: Including the Verse Play 'Eli,'* 1968.
Zeichen im Sand: Die szenischen Dichtungen der Nelly Sachs [Traces in the Sand: Collected Plays of Nelly Sachs]. 1962.
Das Leiden Israels (includes *Eli; In den Wohnungen des Todes; Sternverdunkelung*). 1962.
Simson fällt durch die Jahrtausende und andere szenische Dichtungen [Samson Falls through the Ages]. 1967.
Verzauberungen: Späte szenische Dichtungen [Magic Plays: Late Scenic Poems]. 1970.

Other

Das Buch der Nelly Sachs. 1968.
Briefe. 1984.
Paul Celan, Nelly Sachs: Correspondence. 1995.

Editor and translator, *Aber auch diese Sonne ist heimatlos: Schwedische Lyric der Gegenwart* [Once Again the Sun Is Homeless: Swedish Poetry of Today]. 1957.
Editor and translator, *Weil unser einziges Nest unsere Flugel sind* by Erik Lindegren. 1963.
Editor and translator, *Schwedische Gedichte* [Swedish Poetry]. 1965.

Translator, *Von Wolle und Granit: Querschnitt durch die schwedische Lyric des 20. Jahrhunderts* [From Wool and Granite: A Cross Section of Swedish Poetry of the Twentieth Century]. 1947.
Translator, *Poesie* by Gunnar Ekelof. 1962.
Translator, *Gedichte* by Erik Lindegren. 1962.
Translator, *Poesie* by Karl Vennberg. 1965.

*

Critical Studies: ''Journey into Dustlessness: The Lyrics of Nelly Sachs'' by Paul Konrad Kurz, in his *On Modern German Literature,* 1967; ''A Theosophy of the Creative Word: The Zohar-Cycle of Nelly Sachs'' by W. V. Blomster, in *Germanic Review,* XLIV, 1969, pp. 221–27; ''The Process of Renewal in Nelly Sachs' *Eli*'' by Dinah Dodds, in *German Quarterly,* XLIX(1), January 1976, pp. 50–58; ''Toward the Point of Constriction: Nelly Sachs's 'Landschaft aus Schreien' and Paul Celan's 'Engführung,''' by Hamida Bosmajiam, in his *Metaphors of Evil: Contemporary German Literature and the*

Shadow of Nazism, 1979; ''The Imaging of Transformation in Nelly Sachs's Holocaust Poems'' by William H. McClain, in *Hebrew University Studies in Literature,* 8(2), Autumn 1980, pp. 281–300; *The Phenomenon of Speechlessness in the Poetry of Marie Luise Kaschnitz, Gunter Eich, Nelly Sachs, and Paul Celan* by Robert Foot, 1982; *Jewish Writers, German Literature: The Uneasy Examples of Nelly Sachs and Walter Benjamin* by Timothy Bahti and Marilyn Sibley Fries, 1995; *Post-Shoa Religious Metaphors: The Image of God in the Poetry of Nelly Sachs* by Ursula Rudnick, 1995.

* * *

(Leonie) Nelly Sachs was born on 10 December 1891 in Berlin. Her father was a well-to-do businessman who dabbled in the arts. The family was Jewish but was assimilated to such a degree that it did not observe the high holidays. Sachs was first educated at a public school, from 1897 to 1900, but she then went to a private school in Berlin. She lived the typical life of a young woman of her class and was interested in literature, music, and dance. Most of her time was devoted to literature, and she began writing poetry, puppet plays, and legends in the style of the Swedish writer Selma Lagerlöf. In 1921 Sachs published a book of Christian legends and short stories and sent a copy to Lagerlöf, who responded positively to her young admirer. The first major change in her protected life took place when her father died in 1930. Sachs and her mother had to move from their villa to an apartment house, but her father had left them enough money to live a comfortable life. The next change was the Nazi takeover in 1933, which affected their lives with the endless chicaneries of the racist regulations against German Jews and finally, in 1940, with the threat of deportation to a concentration camp. Sachs was able to obtain a visa for Sweden. Lagerlöf intervened with the Swedish royal family and the Swedish government on behalf of Sachs and her mother, and on 16 May 1940 they escaped from Nazi persecution on one of the last planes of the regular service between Berlin and Stockholm.

Sachs spent the rest of her life in Sweden and, except for a few short visits after World War II to accept literary prizes in recognition of her Holocaust poetry, did not return to Germany. In 1952 she obtained Swedish citizenship. In the beginning Sachs and her mother were supported by Jewish welfare organizations in Stockholm and by a number of Swedish publishers. They lived in a small one-room apartment in the house of a Jewish welfare organization in the harbor district. Later Sachs earned a living by translating. She became a highly recognized translator of contemporary Swedish poetry into German. In the end she also received restitution payments from the West German government.

Sachs dismissed her poetry before 1945 and did not allow it to be published or even listed in bibliographies. During her first years in Sweden she continued writing some poetry in the style of her Berlin poems. It was the news of the German

extermination camps that caused the breakthrough of her Holocaust poetry. Her first book of poems was published in 1947 under the title *In den Wohnungen des Todes* (''In the Habitations of Death''), and another volume, under the title *Sternverdunkelung* (''Eclipse of the Stars''), followed in 1949. In 1951 her mystery play *Eli* was published for subscription in Sweden. The Swedish composer Moses Pergament set the play to music, and it was produced as an opera by Radio Sweden in 1959. A collection of her ''scenic poetry,'' as Sachs called her plays, was published under the title *Zeichen im Sand* (''Traces in the Sand'') in 1962. Two additional titles followed: *Simson fällt durch die Jahrtausende und andere szenische Dichtungen* (''Samson Falls through the Ages'') in 1967, and *Verzauberungen: Späte szenische Dichtungen* (''Magic Plays: Late Scenic Poems'') in 1970. Only a few of her plays were ever produced, and those mostly by small experimental theaters or by radio stations in Germany.

In 1950 Sachs's mother, on whom she had emotionally been very dependent because of their common exile, died after a long illness. Between 1957 and 1961 Sachs published a number of collections of poetry devoted to mourning death and bearing witness to the Holocaust. They appeared under the titles *Und niemand weiss weiter* (''And No One Knows How to Go On'') in 1957, *Flucht und Verwandlung* (''Flight and Metamorphosis'') in 1959, *Noch feiert Tod das Leben* (''Death Still Celebrates Life'') in 1960, and *Fahrt ins Staublose* (''Journey into a Dustless Realm'') in 1961. While her poetry and plays of the 1940s were based on Sachs's familiarity with Jewish legends and Martin Buber's books on Jewish mysticism, she was influenced by the mysticism of the cabala during the 1950s. She read excerpts from the *Zohar,* the ''Book of Splendor,'' in German translation and Gershom Scholem's monograph *Major Trends in Jewish Mysticism.*

Glühende Rätsel (''Glowing Enigmas'') began a cycle on which she worked between 1962 and 1966. Sachs transcended the Holocaust theme without leaving it behind. The cycle shows her concentrating on riddles as a new short-form genre. Her long poem *Die Suchende* (''The Seeker'') of 1966 was based on the Siberian exile of Marja Wolonskaja, a historical saint figure from Russian history. After 1966 Sachs did not publish. Her posthumous poems appeared under the title *Teile dich Nacht: Die letzten Gedichte* (''Open Yourself, Night: The Last Poems'') in 1971 and were never translated.

In 1960 Sachs met **Paul Celan** in Zurich, and she later visited him in Paris. He was the other well-known German-language poet who had focused his work on the Nazi genocide against the Jews. Celan, who suffered from depression because of anti-Semitism in West Germany, confided his fears to Sachs. When she returned to Stockholm, she had a nervous breakdown caused by persecution anxiety. She required medical treatment and was committed to a sanatorium for a long time. Celan visited her in Stockholm to support her, but she did not want him to see her in her state of severe mental illness. She was able to return to writing poetry but needed hospitalization again and again.

In 1965 Sachs was awarded the Peace Prize of the German Book Trade in Frankfurt, and in 1966 she shared the Nobel Prize for Literature with **S.Y. Agnon**. She was praised ''for her outstanding lyrical and dramatic writings that interpret Israel's destiny with touching strength.'' In 1967 she planned to visit Israel but had to cancel her visit for reasons of health. Although she declined to speak on behalf of Israel, she considered it her spiritual homeland. Sachs died on 12 May 1970, on the same day Celan, who had committed suicide, was buried in Paris.

Next to Celan, Sachs is the best-known German-language poet and playwright dealing with the Holocaust. She was celebrated as ''the voice of the suffering of the Jewish people'' when she received the Nobel Prize, but her voice has largely been forgotten since. This may be because of her exalted language and her mysticism. She wrote mystic poetry and drama in an age that was averse to mysticism. Her poetry invites either celebration or rejection rather than critical reading. Because of their experimental staging requirements, her plays are rarely performed. Although Sachs used Samuel Beckett's dramas as models, she never achieved a similar success as a playwright. Her plays never found a home on the German or the international stage. Nonetheless, hers is an authentic voice of Holocaust literature, and her achievements cannot be denied.

—Ehrhard Bahr

See the essays on *Eli: A Mystery Play of the Sufferings of Israel,* ''Landscape of Screams,'' and ''O the Chimneys.''

SARTRE, Jean-Paul (-Charles-Aymard)

Nationality: French. **Born:** Paris, 21 June 1905. **Education:** Lycée Montaigne and Lycée Henri-IV, Paris; École Normale Supérieure, Paris, agrégation in philosophy 1929. **Military Service:** Meteorological Corps, 1929–31; French Army, 1939–40: prisoner of war in Germany, 1940–41; resistance movement, 1941–44. **Family:** Began lifelong relationship with the writer Simone de Beauvoir in 1929; one adopted daughter. **Career:** Professor, Lycée du Havre, 1931–32, and 1934–36, Lycée de Laon, 1936–37, Lycée Pasteur, Paris, 1937–39, and Lycée Condorcet, Paris, 1941–44; traveled and lectured extensively during the 1950s and 1960s; member of Bertrand Russell's International War Crimes Tribunal, 1966. Founding editor, with de Beauvoir, *Les Temps Modernes,* beginning 1945; editor, *La Cause du Peuple,* beginning 1970, *Tout,* 1970–74, *Révolution,* 1971–74, and *Libération,* 1973–74; founder, with Maurice Clavel, Liberation news service, 1971.

Awards: French Institute Research grant, 1933; Roman populiste prize, 1940, for *Le Mur;* New York Drama Critics Circle award, 1947, for *No Exit;* Grand Novel prize, 1950, for *La Nausée;* Omegna prize (Italy), 1960; Nobel prize for literature, 1964 (refused). Honorary doctorate: Hebrew University, Jerusalem, 1976. French Legion d'honneur, 1945 (refused). **Member:** American Academy of Arts and Sciences (foreign member). **Died:** 15 April 1980.

PUBLICATIONS

Collection

Oeuvres romanesques, edited by Michel Contat and Michel Rybalka. 1981.

Novels

La Nausée. 1938; as *The Diary of Antoine Roquentin,* 1949; as *Nausea,* 1949.
Les Chemins de la liberté [Paths of Freedom]: *L'Âge de raison.* 1945; as *The Age of Reason,* 1947.
Le Sursis. 1945; as *The Reprieve,* 1947.
La Mort dans l'âme. 1949; as *Iron in the Soul,* 1950; as *Troubled Sleep,* 1951.

Short Stories

Le Mur. 1939; as *The Wall and Other Stories,* 1949; as *Intimacy and Other Stories,* 1949.

Plays

Bariona; ou, Le Fils du tonnerre (produced 1940). 1962; as *Bariona; or, The Son of Thunder,* in *The Writings 2,* 1974.
Les Mouches (produced Paris, 1943). 1943; translated as *The Flies* and published with *In Camera,* 1946.
Huis clos (produced Paris, 1944). 1945; translated as *In Camera* and published with *The Flies,* 1946; as *No Exit,* with *The Flies,* 1947.
Morts sans sépulture (produced Paris, 1946). 1946; as *Men without Shadows,* in *Three Plays* (UK), 1949; as *The Victors,* in *Three Plays* (US), 1949.
La Putain respectueuse (produced Paris, 1946). 1946; as *The Respectable Prostitute,* in *Three Plays* (UK), 1949; as *The Respectful Prostitute,* in *Three Plays* (US), 1949.
Les Jeux sont faits (screenplay). 1947; as *The Chips Are Down,* 1948.
Les Mains sales (produced Paris, 1948). 1948; as *Crime Passionnel,* in *Three Plays* (UK), 1949; as *Dirty Hands,* in *Three Plays* (US), 1949.
L'Engrenage (screenplay). 1948; as *In the Mesh,* 1954.

Three Plays (UK; includes *Men without Shadows; The Respectable Prostitute; Crime Passionnel*). 1949.

Three Plays (US; includes *The Victors; The Respectful Prostitute; Dirty Hands*). 1949.

Le Diable et le bon Dieu (produced Paris, 1951). 1951; as *Lucifer and the Lord,* 1953; as *The Devil and the Good Lord,* in *The Devil and the Good Lord and Two Other Plays,* 1960.

Kean, adaptation of the play by Dumas (produced Paris, 1953). 1954; translated as *Kean,* 1954; as *Kean, or Disorder and Genius,* 1990.

Nekrassov (produced Paris, 1955). 1956; translated as *Nekrassov,* 1956.

Les Séquestrés d'Altona (produced Paris, 1959). 1960; as *Loser Wins,* 1960; as *The Condemned of Altona,* 1960.

Les Troyennes, adaptation of a play by Euripides (produced Paris, 1965). 1965; as *The Trojan Women,* 1967.

Le Scénario Freud (screenplay). 1984; as *The Freud Scenario,* 1985.

Screenplays: *Les Jeux sont faits,* 1947; *L'Engrenage,* 1948; *Les Sorcières de Salem* [Witches of Salem], 1957.

Other

L'Imagination. 1936; as *Imagination: A Psychological Critique,* 1962.

Esquisse d'une théorie des émotions. 1939; as *The Emotions: Outline of a Theory,* 1948; as *Sketch for a Theory of the Emotions,* 1962.

L'Imaginaire: Psychologie phénoménologique de l'imagination. 1940; as *Psychology of the Imagination,* 1949.

L'Être et le néant: Essai d'ontologie phénoménologique. 1943; as *Being and Nothingness,* 1956.

L'Existentialisme est un humanisme. 1946; as *Existentialism,* 1947; as *Existentialism and Humanism,* 1948.

Explication de ''L'Étranger.'' 1946.

Réflexions sur la question juive. 1947; as *Anti-Semite and Jew,* 1948; as *Portrait of an Anti-Semite,* 1948.

Baudelaire. 1947; translated as *Baudelaire,* 1949.

Situations 1–10 (10 vols.). 1947–76; selections translated as *What Is Literature?,* 1949; *Literary and Philosophical Essays,* 1955; *Situations,* 1965; *The Communists and Peace,* 1965; *The Ghost of Stalin,* 1968 (as *The Spectre of Stalin,* 1969); *Between Existentialism and Marxism,* 1974; *Life/Situations,* 1977; *Sartre in the Seventies,* 1978.

Saint Genet, comédien et martyr. 1952; as *Saint Genet, Actor and Martyr,* 1963.

The Transcendence of the Ego: An Existentialist Theory of Consciousness. 1957.

Critique de la raison dialectique: Théorie des ensembles pratiques. 1960; as *Critique of Dialectical Reason: Theory of Practical Ensembles,* 1976.

On Cuba. 1961.

Les Mots (autobiography). 1963; as *Words,* 1964; as *The Words,* 1964.

Essays in Aesthetics, edited by Wade Baskin. 1963.

The Philosophy of Sartre, edited by Robert Denoon Cumming. 1966.

Of Human Freedom, edited by Baskin. 1967.

Essays in Existentialism, edited by Baskin. 1967.

On Genocide. 1968.

Les Commununistes ont peur de la révolution. 1969.

L'Idiot de la famille: Gustave Flaubert de 1821 à 1857 (3 vols.). 1971–72; as *The Family Idiot: Gustave Flaubert 1821–1857,* 1981–82.

Un Théâtre de situations, edited by Michel Contat and Michel Rybalka. 1973; as *Sartre on Theatre,* 1976.

Politics and Literature. 1973.

The Writings 2: Selected Prose, edited by Contat and Rybalka. 1974.

Cahiers pour un morale. 1983.

Les Carnets de la drôle de guerre: Novembre 1939–Mars 1940. 1983; as *War Diaries: Notebooks from a Phony War: November 1939–March 1940,* 1984; as *The War Diaries of Jean-Paul Sartre: November 1939–March 1940,* 1985.

Lettres au Castor et à quelques autres, edited by Simone de Beauvoir. 1983.

Mallarmé; or, The Poet of Nothingness. 1987.

Thoughtful Passions: Intimate Letters to Simone de Beauvoir. 1987.

Witness to My Life: The Letters of Sartre to Simone de Beauvoir 1926–1939, edited by de Beauvoir, 1993.

Quiet Moments in a War: The Letters of Jean-Paul Sartre to Simone de Beauvoir, 1940–1963. 1993.

*

Bibliography: *The Writings 1: A Bibliographical Life* by Michel Contat and Michel Rybalka, 1974; *Sartre: A Bibliography of International Criticism* by Robert Wilcocks, 1975; *Sartre and His Critics: An International Bibliography 1938–1980* by François and Claire Lapointe, 1981.

Critical Studies: *Sartre, Romantic Rationalist* by Iris Murdoch, 1953; *Sartre: A Literary and Political Study,* 1960, *Sartre: A Biographical Introduction,* 1971, and *Sartre,* 1992, all by Philip Thody; *The Marxism of Jean-Paul Sartre* by Wilfrid Desan, 1965; *Jean-Paul Sartre* by Henri Peyre, 1968; *Jean-Paul Sartre* by Arthur Coleman Danto, 1975; *Critical Fictions: The Literary Criticism of Sartre* by Joseph Halpern, 1976; *Jean-Paul Sartre, Philosophy in the World* by Ronald Aronson, 1980; *The Existential Sociology of Jean-Paul Sartre* by Gila J. Hayim, 1980; *Jean-Paul Sartre: Contemporary Approaches to His Philosophy,* edited by Hugh J. Silverman and Frederick A. Elliston, 1980; *The Philosophy of Sartre,* edited by Paul Arthur Schilpp, 1981; *Jean-Paul Sartre* by Catharine Savage Brosman, 1983; *Sartre and His Predecessors: The Self and the Other* by William Ralph Schroeder, 1984; *Sartre and Marxist Existentialism: The Test Case of Collective Responsibility* by Thomas

R. Flynn, 1984; *Sartre, Literature and Theory* by Rhiannon Goldthorpe, 1984; *Sartre, Life and Works* by Kenneth and Margaret Thompson, 1984; *Freedom As a Value: A Critique of the Ethical Theory of Jean-Paul Sartre* by David Detmer, 1986; *Sartre: An Investigation of Some Major Themes,* edited by Simon Glynn, 1986; *Critical Essays on Sartre,* edited by Robert Wilcocks, 1988; *In the Shadow of Sartre* by Liliane Siegel, 1990; *Vulgarity and Authenticity: Dimensions of Otherness in the World of Jean-Paul Sartre* by Stuart Charmé, 1991; *Jean-Paul Sartre, the Evolution of His Thought and Art* by Harold W. Wardman, 1992; *Understanding Sartre* by Philip R. Wood, 1992; *Jean-Paul Sartre and the Politics of Reason: A Theory of History* by Andrew Dobson, 1993; *Jean-Paul Sartre and Crime Passionnel* by Clive Emsley, 1994; *Sartre's Existentialism and Early Buddhism: A Comparative Study of Selflessness Theories* by Phra Methithammaphon, 1995; *Sartre and Evil: Guidelines for a Struggle* by Hayim Gordon, 1995; *Sartre for Beginners* by Donald Palmer, 1995; *The Bodily Nature of Consciousness: Sartre and Contemporary Philosophy of Mind* by Kathleen Wider, 1997; *Jean-Paul Sartre: Politics and Culture in Postwar France* by Michael Scriven, 1999; *Feminist Interpretations of Jean-Paul Sartre,* edited by Julien S. Murphy, 1999; *Jean-Paul Sartre,* edited by Harold Bloom, 2001.

* * *

Known as the father of French existentialism, Jean-Paul Sartre is not generally considered a writer of Holocaust literature. Indeed, only one of his numerous stories, novels, plays, essays, and treatises—*The Condemned of Altona*—deals explicitly with the cataclysm. But the legacy of World War II, the Nazi Occupation of France, and the Holocaust itself had dramatic impacts on Sartre's thought and led to a refocusing of his artistic ambitions.

Prior to World War II Sartre viewed writing as an apolitical discipline. As he explained in his literary autobiography *The Words,* he was initially focused only on the aesthetics of his works. While the insights that subsequently coalesced into his philosophical system were apparent in early works such as the novella *La Nausée* (1938) and the short story collection *Le Mur* (1939), Sartre did not connect these themes to a call for political action—as he did in almost all his postwar writings. The events of World War II and the Holocaust marked a crucial turning point.

Sartre was called up for military service in 1939 and was captured by the German forces in 1940. He spent nine months as a prisoner of war in a German stalag, an experience that marked both his character and his subsequent writing by confronting him with his own historicity. As Sartre told his lifelong companion Simone de Beauvoir in 1944, he no longer saw his writing as separate from the social and political circumstances in which he existed. This realization led to a shift in his artistic goals; no longer content with crafting simply an aesthetic tour de force, Sartre henceforth strove to change the way his readers thought, felt, saw the world, and acted in it.

It was also during the Nazi Occupation of France that Sartre wrote his great philosophical treatise *Being and Nothingness.* Dense and technical, the work presented Sartre's ''phenomenological ontology''—an exploration of the nature of being. Sartre believed that freedom was the primary characteristic of an individual's consciousness. Living in a world devoid of extrinsic verities, each individual is ultimately responsible for her own choices and actions. Sartre viewed this freedom as a curse as much as a blessing: in his famous phrase, ''man [wa]s condemned to be free.'' Yet rather than simply bemoan the inherent absurdity of life, Sartre argued, each individual had a duty to engage in social and political action. Sartre further developed this existentialist vision in his plays and novels of the early postwar period, many of which were set against the backdrop of World War II. In *The Flies,* for example, Sartre reworked the Greek myth of Orestes and Electra and denounced Nazism through Orestes's slaying of the tyrant Clytemnestra. Sartre's well-known play *No Exit* explored the adverse consequences that occur when one lives only for and through others, abjuring one's own obligation to act freely. Another work of this period, *The Victors,* focused on French resistance soldiers captured by the Vichy militia. Although the soldiers were facing death, Sartre believed that they were still free—free to choose the moment they ''broke'' under the torture—and remained morally responsible for those choices.

Sartre's belief in the absolute freedom of human consciousness was tempered somewhat during the 1950s, as he nuanced his views to consider the possibility that a person's social and cultural conditioning could limit the universe of possible choices before her. This shift informs Sartre's only work directly addressing the Holocaust, *The Condemned of Altona,* and is also explored more fully in his second major work of philosophy, *Critique of Dialectical Reason,* in which Sartre sought to harmonize existentialism with Marxism. *The Condemned of Altona* centers on a German family living in the aftermath of the Nazis' defeat. The play thematically treads familiar ground for Sartre, dealing with questions of freedom, responsibility, and choice. The family's youngest son, Frantz, is a Nazi war criminal, the notorious ''Butcher of Smolensk.'' Abetted by his family, Frantz descends into madness to escape the reality of his past actions and of his country's defeat. *The Condemned of Altona* problematizes Frantz's ability to be free by exploring the role that his familial and cultural upbringing played in leading to his barbaric actions. Ultimately, however, Sartre concludes that Frantz did indeed choose to participate wholeheartedly in the slaughter of the Holocaust and bears responsibility for that choice.

Like most of Sartre's other postwar work, *The Condemned of Altona* uses political events as a lens through which to examine the core components of individual consciousness. By the time he completed *The Condemned of Altona,* however, Sartre was beginning to lose faith in his art's ability to be an instrument of change for his readers. Nevertheless, Sartre continued to espouse the view that one's choices are freely made and that each individual is accountable for the decisions—and indecisions—that she makes.

—Rebecca Stanfel

See the essay on *The Condemned of Altona.*

SCHINDEL, Robert

Nationality: Austrian. **Born:** Robert Soel, Bad Hall bei Linz, 4 April 1944. **Education:** Studied philosophy and pedagogy in Vienna, 1968–72. **Career:** Magazine correspondent; teacher, Viennese School for Poetry. Since the mid-1980s freelance writer. Publisher, *Hundsblume,* 1970–71. **Awards:** Hans Erich Nossack prize, 1989; City of Vienna Elias Canetti scholarship, 1991; Federal Ministry for Instruction and Art prize, 1992; Erich Fried prize, 1993; City of Fellbach Mörike prize, 1999; Eduard Mörike prize, 2000.

PUBLICATIONS

Poetry

Ohneland [Without Country]. 1986.
Geier sind pünktliche Tiere. 1987.
Im Herzen die Krätze. 1988.
Ein Feuerchen im Hintennach. 1992.
Immernie. 2000.

Novels

Der Mai ist vorbei. 1982.
Gebürtig. 1992; as *Born-Where,* 1995.

Short Stories

Die Nacht der Harlekine. 1994.

Other

Gott schütz uns vor den guten Menschen: Jüdisches Gedächtnis, Auskunftsbüro der Angst. 1995.

Editor, *Klagenfurter Texte: Ingeborg-Bachmann-Wettbewerb 1999.* 1999.

*

Critical Studies: "Jewish Identity and the Holocaust in Robert Schindel's *Gebürtig*" by Thomas Freeman, in *Modern Austrian Literature,* 30(1), 1997, pp. 117–26; "1992 Robert Schindel's Novel *Gebürtig* Continues the Development of

Jewish Writing in Austria after the Shoah" by Ingrid Spork, in *Yale Companion to Jewish Writing and Thought in German Culture, 1096–1996,* edited by Sander L. Gilman and Jack Zipes, 1997; "The Politics of Recognition in Contemporary Austrian Jewish Literature" by Matthias Konzett, in *Monatshefte fur Deutschen Unterricht, Deutsche Sprache und Literatur,* 90(1), Spring 1998, pp. 71–88.

*   *   *

Robert Schindel, born in 1944 in Bad Hall bei Linz, is the oldest of the three most prominent contemporary Jewish writers of fiction in Austria. (The others are **Robert Menasse,** born in 1954, and Doron Rabinovici, born in 1961.) From early on he was an accomplished poet on a wide number of topics that ranged from mythology to the modern city, and a number of his early poems, such as "Errinerungen an Prometheus" (1964) and "Wolken I" (1988), deal with the murder of the Jews during World War II. It was not until the publication of his popular novel *Gebürtig* (1992), however, that Schindel became known as a major contributor to postwar Austrian fiction dealing with the Holocaust.

In a public reading at the Literaturhaus in Vienna on 14 June 2001, Schindel accounted for the delay in giving an in-depth exploration of the Holocaust by citing his negative identification with Judaism as he was growing up in Austria. Born to assimilated Jewish parents deeply involved in the resistance movement as members of the Communist Party, Schindel spent the first years of his life hidden in a Viennese orphanage while his parents were active in France against Hitler. Both his mother and his father were eventually discovered and sent to concentration camps, and only his mother survived and returned. Growing up in an Austrian society largely silent about the participation of its citizens in the Holocaust, Schindel was also personally confronted with anti-Semitism a number of times.

Although not religious, Schindel maintains that the identity of all Jewish Austrians, regardless of their level of observance, is rooted in the existence of the concentration camps. Before 1980 he was not an official member of the Jewish community of Vienna. His avoidance of official identification as a Jew, along with his earlier membership in the Communist Party and his engagement in the student uprisings of the 1960s, indicates a search for identity that reaches far beyond Judaism. The fact, however, that Schindel never fully denied his Jewish background is clear from much of his work, for a number of early poems deal with the issues of both the Holocaust and Jewish identity. Poems such as "Errinerungen an Prometheus" ("Memories of Prometheus") and "Klagenfurter Frühlingsballade" (1986; "Spring Ballad of Klagenfurt") contain autobiographical elements and details about his parents' experiences during World War II and also deal directly with his identity as a Jewish Austrian.

The popularity of the novel *Gebürtig* turned Schindel into an internationally recognized author for its critical examination of the relationships between Austrian Jews and non-Jews in the contemporary era. The novel covers a wide range of topics on the subject, including the silence of Austrian society regarding the Holocaust and the difficulties of the second generation of Jewish victims and of Austrian perpetrators and bystanders. Containing both autobiographical elements and general commentaries on anti-Semitism in Austria, as well as a critical look at how Jews themselves confront the past, Schindel's work illuminates the complex situation of being both Jewish and Austrian 40 years after the end of the Holocaust. In more recent years Schindel has returned to the publication of poetry, and he has continued to deal with the Holocaust in some of his works, as in the poem "Dreiundzwanzig Jahre (Eine Chronik nach R. Hilberg)" ("Twenty-Three Years: A Chronicle according to R. Hilberg"), from the collection *Immernie* (2000).

—Lisa Silverman

See the essays on "Errinerungen an Prometheus" and *Gebürtig.*

SCHLINK, Bernhard

Nationality: German. **Born:** Bielefeld, 1944. **Education:** Studied law at the University of Berlin; University of Heidelberg, J.D. 1975; Freiberg University, qualified to lecture at universities 1981. **Career:** Professor, University of Bonn, 1982–91, and University of Frankfurt am Main, 1991–92. Since 1988 justice, Constitutional Law Court, Bonn, and since 1992 professor, Humboldt University, Berlin. **Awards:** Glauser prize, 1990, for *Die Gordische Schleife;* German Krimi-Preis, 1993, for *Selbs Betrug;* Hans Fallada prize, 1995, for *Der Vorleser.*

PUBLICATIONS

Novels

Selbs Justiz, with Walter Popp. 1987.
Die Gordische Schleife. 1988.
Selbs Betrug. 1992.
Der Vorleser. 1995; as *The Reader,* 1997.
Selbs Mord. 2001.

Short Stories

Liebesfluchten: Geschichten. 2000; as *Flights of Love: Stories,* 2001.

Other (studies on law and society)

Abwägung im Verfassungsrecht. 1976.
Die Amtshilfe: Ein Beitrag zu einer Lehre von der Gewaltenteilung in der Verwaltung. 1981.
Grundrechte, Staatsrecht II, with Bodo Pieroth. 1985.

Streik und Aussperrung als Verfassungsproblem: Untersuchung anhand der neueren Rechtsprechung von Bundesarbeitsgericht und Bundesverfassungsgericht, with Walter Pauly. 1988.
Heimat als Utopie. 2000.
Der Verfassungskompromiß zum Religionsunterricht: Art. 7 Abs. 3 und Art. 141 GG im Kampf des Parlamentarischen Rates um die "Lebensordnungen." 2000.

Editor, with Arthur J. Jacobson, *Weimar: A Jurisprudence of Crisis.* 2000.

*

Critical Studies: "Bernhard Schlink: *The Reader* and Grete Weil: *Last Trolley from Beethovenstraat* by T. Lewis, in *The New Criterion,* 16(4), 1997, p. 74; "The Language of the Past: Recent Prose Works by Bernhard Schlink, Marcel Beyer, and Friedrich Christian Delius" by Stuart Parkes, in *'Whose Story?':Continuities in Contemporary German-Language Literature,* edited by Parkes, Arthur Williams, and Julian Preece, 1998; "The Uses of Illiteracy: *The Reader* by Bernhard Schlink, Translated by Carol Brown Janeway" by Eva Hoffman, in *The New Republic,* 23 March 1998, p. 33–34; "The Caesura of the Holocaust in Martin Amis's *Time's Arrow* and Bernhard Schlink's *The Reader*" by Ann Parry, in *Journal of European Studies,* 29(3), 115, September 1999, pp. 249–67; "Compassion and Moral Condemnation: An Analysis of *The Reader*" by Jeremiah P. Conway, in *Philosophy and Literature,* 23(2), October 1999, pp. 284–301; "Doubts about *The Reader*" by Ian Sansom, in *Salmagundi,* 124–125, Fall 1999/Winter 2000, pp. 3–16; "Bernhard Schlink's *Der Vorleser* and Binjamin Wilkomirski's *Bruchstucke:* Best-Selling Responses to the Holocaust" by J.J. Long, in *German-Language Literature Today: International and Popular,* edited by Arthur Williams, Stuart Parkes, and Julian Preece, 2000; "The Return of the Past: Post-Unification Representations of National Socialism: Bernhard Schlink's *Der Vorleser* and Ulla Berkewicz's *Engel sind schwarz und weiss*" by Helmut Schmitz, in *Cultural Perspectives on Division and Unity in East and West,* edited by Clare Flanagan and Stuart Taberner, 2000.

* * *

Bernhard Schlink, born in 1944 outside Bielefeld, Germany, published *Der Vorleser (The Reader)* in 1995. This novel has been translated into at least 27 languages and has sold more than 2.5 million copies. First published as a novelist in 1987, Schlink has consistently displayed an interest in investigating the repercussions of the Nazi era on contemporary German society and elucidating the moral questions surrounding guilt, punishment, and responsibility.

A law professor at Humboldt University in Berlin, Schlink began his career as a novelist with a series of detective novels, which, except for *Die Gordische Schleife* (1988), far exceeded the typical conventions of the genre. *Selbs Justiz* (1987) and *Selbs Betrug* (1992) manage to introduce into the plot of a whodunit the element of a private detective protagonist whose past is less than salutary: Gerhard Selb, age 68, was a public prosecutor in the Nazi era. This twist on the questions of crime and punishment typical of the genre allows Schlink to examine larger historical questions, such as the culpability of individuals under the Nazis and the fallout of guilt that permeates postwar German society.

Schlink's oeuvre takes a turn toward a more complex and involved examination of the effects of the Holocaust on German society with *The Reader*. The novel can be interpreted in a variety of contexts: *éducation sentimentale;* love story; analysis of guilt, both personal and societal; representation of the indelible influence of Nazism on German society after the war; the commensurability of abstract, objective legal principles with a subjective awareness of justice; and critical evaluation of what Germans call *Vergangenheitsbewältigung* (coming to terms/overcoming the past).

Critically acclaimed, *The Reader* was also a tremendous commercial success across the world: It was the first German novel to occupy the top of the *New York Times* best-seller list and also became a choice for Oprah Winfrey's book club. This success primarily stems from Schlink's courage to address taboos and break silences. Significantly, his novel appeared nearly contemporaneously with Daniel Jonah Goldhagen's *Hitler's Willing Executioners* (1996), after whose publication Germany intensified an internal dialogue, still ongoing, about ordinary Germans and the Nazi past. Similarly, the novel's success in the United States is in part indicative of a cultural moment in which the Holocaust has become the paradigmatic example of genocide.

The Reader is also successful because it manages to encapsulate morally complex questions in pellucid and accessible prose. The following passage may serve to illustrate this point: "What should our second generation have done, what should it do with the knowledge of the horrors of the extermination of the Jews? We should not believe we can comprehend the incomprehensible, we may not compare the incomparable, we may not inquire because to inquire is to make the horrors an object of discussion, even if the horrors themselves are not questioned, instead of accepting them as something in the face of which we can only fall silent in revulsion, shame, and guilt. Should we only fall silent in revulsion, shame, and guilt? To what purpose? . . . That some few would be convicted and punished while we of the second generation were silenced by revulsion, shame, and guilt—was that all there was to it now?"

Evident in this passage as well is Schlink's strategy of posing more questions than providing answers. One critic has termed *The Reader* "[a] counterpointing of two stories, or a story and a history, of victim and victimizer, culpability and disavowal, indictment and extenuation"; thus the novel unfolds moral complexities without providing ready-made answers for the reader.

Liebesfluchten (2000; *Flights of Love*, 2001) is a collection of seven short stories, some of which continue Schlink's interest in the second and third post-Nazi generation of Germans and in the relationship between Germans and Jews. One story focuses on a German living in New York City who, tired of what he perceives as being defined by the Nazi past, submits to a circumcision to please his Jewish girlfriend, who ironically had no plans to ask him to submit to the procedure. In a sense this ritual fails in its intent to create a space of putative commonality between the two lovers and can be seen as a plea, on the part of the author, for tolerating and engaging cultural and religious difference. Another story from this collection, "Girl with Lizard," published in the United States in the *New Yorker,* addresses once more the response of the generation following the Nazi perpetrators to their parents' past. The mystique surrounding the painting identified in the title (the protagonist's father, a Nazi judge, stole it from its painter, a Jew) dominates the boy's life and functions as a metaphor for the secrets kept by the perpetrators that influence following generations to this day.

Schlink's work concerns itself centrally with puncturing the silence that has surrounded the Nazi years in Germany. It asks questions about the culpability of the perpetrators and about how collective memory is to be transmitted responsibly; in that sense it is a perfect reflection of questions that have come to the fore in Germany in recent years.

—Stefan Gunther

See the essay on *The Reader*.

SCHWARZ-BART, André

Nationality: French. **Born:** Metz, Lorraine, 1928. **Education:** Sorbonne, University of Paris. **Military Service:** French Resistance during World War II. **Family:** Married Simone in 1961. **Career:** Prisoner in German concentration camp during World War II. Has worked as a mechanic, salesman, miner, librarian, and foundry laborer. Since 1959 writer. **Awards:** Prix Goncourt, 1959, for *Le Dernier des justes*; Jerusalem prize, 1967, for *Un Plat de porc aux bananes vertes*.

PUBLICATIONS

Novels

Le Dernier des justes. 1959; as *The Last of the Just,* 1960.
Un Plat de porc aux bananes vertes [A Plate of Pork with Green Bananas], with Simone Schwarz-Bart. 1967.
La Mulatresse Solitude, with Simone Schwarz-Bart. 1972; as *A Woman Named Solitude,* 1973.

Other

Hommage à la femme noire (6 vols.), with Simone Schwarz-Bart. 1989; as *In Praise of Black Women,* 2001.

*

Critical Studies: "History and Martyrological Tragedy: The Jewish Experience in Sholem Asch and André Schwarz-Bart" by Stanley Brodwin, in *Twentieth Century Literature,* 40(1), Spring 1994, p. 72.

*   *   *

André Schwarz-Bart, born in Metz in 1928 to Polish immigrants, was 11 years old when World War II broke out. Over the next five years he joined the Maquis, was captured by the Nazis, escaped, and finally fought with the Free French Army until the liberation of Europe. By the time the war was over, however, his own survival was overshadowed by the murder of the rest of his family in Nazi extermination camps. It was undoubtedly this tragedy that supplied the influence for his first foray into literature, his celebrated novel *Le Dernier des justes* (1959; *The Last of the Just,* 1960).

Because the onset of war had severely disrupted his education, Schwarz-Bart was largely ignorant of critical events and motifs in Jewish literature and culture. Perhaps due to these gaps the traditional legend of the *Lamed-Waf* was transformed— some say distorted—in his novel. Whereas in most versions of the legend the Righteous Men appear as isolated individuals, unknown both to one another and indeed to all other people until a time of anti-Semitic crisis, in Schwarz-Bart's story the *Lamed-Waf* belong to the one clan, the Levy family, with the mantle of righteousness passing as an inheritance from one generation to the next.

As a consequence the legend is changed in his version into a story of preordained self-sacrifice. Thus, in a curious paradox, although the novel stands as a particularly bitter indictment of European Christendom's anti-Semitic history, there remains a semi-Christian flavor to the text that for some readers jars oddly with the legend's intrinsic Jewishness.

It is possible, however, that this transformation of the legend is not in fact the result of cultural ignorance on Schwarz-Bart's part. Rather it is perhaps better understood as the author's best interpretation of Jewish survival in the midst, and in spite, of centuries of persecution. In other words, in the dark shadow of the Holocaust, and with the horror of Nazi genocide having struck him a deeply personal blow, Schwarz-Bart's natural question concerned the possibility of survival in such circumstances. How, after all that European Jewry had undergone, could there still be a remnant left? In this context the trajectory of his novel becomes less a matter of self-sacrifice and more a matter of cautious hope. If Auschwitz was the great "No!" to the Jewish people, Schwarz-Bart's novel attempts to circumscribe that "No!" with a "Nevertheless!"

If this is the case then Schwarz-Bart's place in the pantheon of Holocaust writers possibly lies more with **Elie Wiesel** than Richard Rubenstein. The latter felt compelled by the Holocaust to reject the traditional Jewish perception of God and return in desperation to Camusian philosophy, nature worship and, later, mysticism. In contrast Wiesel employed his despair to offer up questions to God, to accept with humility the fatuousness of certainty, and to circumscribe his doubts with the ever present "And yet . . . "

Both Wiesel and Schwarz-Bart have raised the most serious questions about God and his dealings with the Jewish people. Neither have been able adequately to answer their own queries. For both, the Holocaust casts a shadow over the comfort of covenantal relationship. But both prefer to leave their questions open rather than closing them with the finality of unbelief. The necessity of their respective "Howevers" or "And yets" speaks of their despair in the wake of the Shoah but also of their reluctance to admit final defeat. It is for this reason that, in spite of its title, Schwarz-Bart's novel *The Last of the Just* does not resonate with ultimate gloom. The Holocaust does not have the last word. A presence remains, righteousness is alive—somewhere.

—Mark R. Lindsay

See the essay on *The Last of the Just.*

SEBALD, W(infried) G(eorg)

Nationality: British (originally German: immigrated to England, 1966). **Born:** Wertach-im-Allgäu, 1944. **Education:** University of Fribourg, Switzerland; University of Manchester, England; University of East Anglia, Norwich, England. **Career:** Since 1970 professor of European literature, University of East Anglia, Norwich. Director, British Center for Literary Translation, University of East Anglia, 1989–94. **Awards:** Berlin literature prize, Johannes Bobrowski medal, Literature Nord prize, and *Jewish Quarterly* literary prize for fiction, all in 1997, for *The Emigrants;* Henrich Böll prize (Cologne); *Los Angeles Times* book award for fiction, 1998, for *The Rings of Saturn: An English Pilgrimage.* **Address:** Office: University of East Anglia, Norwich, Norfolk NR4 7TJ, England. **Agent:** c/o New Directions Publications, 80 Eighth Avenue, New York, New York 10011, U.S.A. **Died:** 14 December 2001.

PUBLICATIONS

Novels

Nach der Natur: Ein Elementardgedicht. 1988.
Schwindel, Gefühle. 1990; as *Vertigo,* 1999.

Die Ausgewanderten. 1993; as *The Emigrants,* 1996.
Die Ringe des Saturn: Eine Englische Wallfahrt. 1995; as *The Rings of Saturn: An English Pilgrimage,* 1998.
Austerlitz. 2001; translated as *Austerlitz,* 2001.

Other

Carl Sternheim: Kritiker und Opfer der Wilhelminschen Ära. 1969.
Der Mythus der Zerstörung im Werk Döblins. 1980.
Die Beschreibung des Unglücks: Zur Österreichischen Literatur von Stifter bis Handke. 1985.
Unheimliche Heimat: Essays zur Österreichischen Literatur. 1991.
Logis in Einem Landhaus: Uber. 1998.
Luftkrieg und Literatur: Mit Einem Essay zu Alfred Andersch (lectures). 1999.

Editor, *A Radical Stage: Theatre in Germany in the 1970s and 1980s.* 1988.

*

Critical Studies: "An Interview with W.G. Sebald," in *Brick,* 59, Spring 1998, pp. 23–29, and "W.G. Sebald's Uncertainty," in *The Broken Estate,* 1999, both by James Wood; "W.G. Sebald: A Profile" by James Atlas, in *Paris Review,* 41(151), Summer 1999, pp. 278–95; "W.G. Sebald: A Holistic Approach to Borders, Texts and Perspectives" by Arthur Williams, in *German-Language Literature Today: International and Popular,* edited by Williams, Stuart Parkes, and Julian Preece, 2000; "Writing in the Shadows" by Margo Jefferson, in *New York Times Book Review,* 18 March 2001, p. 27; "Only Connect: In His Novel *Austerlitz,* W.G. Sebald Captures Germany's Tense Relationship with the Debris of the Past" by A.S. Byatt, in *New Statesman* (England), 15 October 2001, p. 52–3.

* * *

W.G. Sebald, born in 1944 in the Allgäu area of Bavaria, Germany, emerged by the end of the twentieth century as one of the preeminent German-language writers. After studies at the universities of Fribourg (Switzerland), Manchester, and East Anglia (Norwich), he became a professor at the School of English and American Studies at East Anglia.

One of Sebald's primary topics is the exploration of the nature and transmission of memory as it intersects with notions of time and identity (personal and collective). His first fictional text, *Nach der Natur: Ein Elementargedicht* (1988), already makes use of the intertextual technique of allowing a mutual permeation of fiction and nonfiction and of using documentary and biographical information and their simultaneous fictionalization. The resulting generic instability, a hallmark of Sebald's style, emerges even more forcefully in his next novel, *Schwindel, Gefühle* (1990; *Vertigo,* 1999). Published in the United States after the success of *The Emigrants* and *Rings of Saturn, Vertigo* is part travelogue, part scholarship, part biography—a text, as one critic has written, that "kneads history, fiction, reportage, fantasy, pictures, travel notes and autobiography into a dense impasto of fatefulness."

The relationship between memory and the perception of the world are a constant theme in *Vertigo:* "On this occasion in the midst of the holiday season, the night train from Vienna to Venice, on which in the late October of 1980 I had seen nobody except a pale-faced schoolmistress from New Zealand, was so overcrowded that I had to stand in the corridor all the way or crouch uncomfortably among suitcases and rucksacks, so that instead of drifting into sleep I slid into my memories. Or rather, the memories (at least so it seemed to me) rose higher and higher in some space outside of myself, until, having reached a certain level, they overflowed from that space into me, like water over the top of a weir." Facts in this universe are by definition overdetermined, and the piling up of memories and secondary memories leads to an epistemological instability that is, on a textual level, also enacted by the insertion of photographs that may or may not verify or destabilize whatever the narrative tells us.

Die Ausgewanderten (1993; *The Emigrants,* 1996) further intensifies this technique (the novel includes 86 photos and illustrations) in the exploration of the lives of four Jewish protagonists who were forced to emigrate, in some cases during the Nazi era. *The Emigrants* marks the first time Sebald explicitly combines the exploration of memory's mechanics with the loss of homeland for German Jewry and the Holocaust. While never mentioned explicitly, the Holocaust forms the still point of the worlds depicted in *The Emigrants,* an event that can barely sustain direct mention but informs the present, indelibly and without the potential solace of sublimation or Freudian working through. To have demonstrated the circumstances of a present that is always pregnant with the past is one of *The Emigrants'* merits.

Die Ringe des Saturn (1995; *Rings of Saturn,* 1998), on its surface a travelogue about a hike undertaken in Suffolk by the narrator, is a text whose rhetorical tangents and scholarly examinations are barely contained within the structure of its putative genre. As so often is the case with Sebald, all individuals and events discussed seem to share a submerged correspondence of sorts, and the narrator constantly attempts to extract what is hidden from what is visible. One critic has described this plethora of details as a sort of rhetorical "curiosity cabinet, a *vanitas* still life, where every artifact has an allegoric meaning."

Luftkrieg und Literatur (1999), a collection of slightly expanded critical lectures Sebald gave in Zurich, returns to the traces the Nazi terror has permanently left in the collective memory—this time the memory of Germans. Sebald argues that the absence of detailed representations of the Allied bombing campaign toward the end of World War II indicates a

German inability to face the pain caused by their nation, as well as a tendency to allow this trauma sway over the collective psyche. Sebald further intimates that this inability to acknowledge psychological disturbances and to revert to "business as usual" as quickly as possible has also characterized Germans' approach to the Holocaust and has prevented them up to this point from addressing it with complete honesty.

Sebald's novel *Austerlitz* (2001) further refines the author's poetics of memory. As a four-year-old, Jacques Austerlitz, a Jew from Prague, loses his parents in the Holocaust and is brought to England on a *Kindertransport* in 1939. Thus the book chronicles how Austerlitz, after losing his name and mother tongue, spends a lifetime attempting to reclaim his identity—initially without being aware of either the specifics of his loss or how those specifics condition his unwitting activities at reclaiming his past.

Tellingly Austerlitz is at work on a project that reveals architectural progress as a displacement of history and the past. He realizes that these intellectual activities are an expression of a profound search and represent, in their avoidance of his own history, a flight from the truth. Austerlitz buries all his documents in his garden, meets his erstwhile nurse Vera in Prague, and finds out that his parents, Agáta Austerlitz and Maximilian Aychenwald, were murdered in the Holocaust. As in his other novels, Sebald weaves a dense tapestry of déjà vu moments, correspondences, and echoes of the past—in short, a tapestry of memory that demonstrates that the past never passes.

—Stefan Gunther

See the essays on *Austerlitz* and *The Emigrants.*

SEBASTIAN, Mihail

Pseudonym for Iosif Hechter. **Nationality:** Romanian. **Born:** Braila, 1907. **Education:** Studied law and philosophy at a Bucharest university. **Career:** Journalist. Worked for the Romanian Ministry of State. **Died:** 29 May 1945.

PUBLICATIONS

Collection

Opere, edited by Cornelia Stefanescu. 1994.

Diary

Jurnal: 1935–1944. 1996; translated as *Journal: 1935–1944: The Fascist Years,* 2000.

Novels

Orasul cu salcîmi. 1935.
De doua mii de ai [For Two Thousand Years]. 1936.
Accidentul [The Accident]. 1968.
Femei [Women]. 1992.

Plays

Teatru (includes *Jocul de-a vacanta*; *Steaua fara nume*; *Ultima ora*). 1946.
Derniere heure, comedie en trois actes. 1954; as *Stop News, a Comedy in Three Acts,* 1954.

Other

Opere alese, edited by Vicu Mîndra. 1956.
Proza publicistica, edited by Vicu Mîndra (vol. 2 of *Opere alese*). 1962.
Intîlniri cu teatrul. 1969.
Eseuri, cronici, memorial. 1972.

*

Critical Studies: "Excerpts from a Trouble Book: An Episode in Romanian Literature" by Irina Livezeanu, in *Cross Currents,* 3, 1984, pp. 297–302; "Romania's 1930s Revisited" by Matei Calinescu, in *Salmagundi,* 97, Winter 1993, pp. 133–51; "The Incompatibilities: *Journal, 1935–1944* by the Romanian-Jewish Writer M. Sebastian" by Norman Manea, translated by Patrick Camiller, in *New Republic,* 218(16), 20 April 1998, pp. 32–37.

*   *   *

Born Iosif Hechter in Braila on the Danube in 1907, Mihail Sebastian, a writer and an author of successful plays, was well known in the literary and political circles of Bucharest. Besides his novels and plays, Sebastian left behind a diary that covers the years 1935–44.

Sebastian was a sensitive storyteller who always sided with democracy against dictatorship and aggression, as well as a Romanian Jewish intellectual who struggled to write in a meaningful way and to find an existential sense to his life. He socialized with rich and famous liberal aristocrats, with genuine democrats or reptilian opportunists, with Zionist or Communist Jews, and with actors, novelists, and literary critics. He wrote his novels and plays in Bucharest but also in the not-so-distant Bucegi mountains. He took vacations on the Black Sea and sometimes traveled abroad, especially to France. An assimilated Jew, Sebastian was brutally rejected by the society that he loved. He had a strange destiny: He belonged to a group of gifted young people close to the newspaper *Cuvintul.* The mentor of these young people was Nae Ionescu, who was described by his contemporaries as inconsistent, without scruples, opportunistic, and cynical. He became the main ideologist of the Iron Guard; *Cuvintul* ended up as the official newspaper of the same organization and many of Sebastian's friends drifted toward Romanian fascism. Even before becoming a fascist, Ionescu published a viciously anti-Semitic forward to one of Sebastian's books. There is no clear explanation for the acceptance by Sebastian of this forward.

The tragedy of the Romanian intelligentsia in the interwar period was that rather than trying to improve an imperfect political system they chose to throw it overboard, instead linking themselves with totalitarian personalities and political regimes. During the interwar period some of Sebastian's friends, such as Cezar Petrescu, changed their opinions according to last-minute interests, being only crass opportunists. Others, such as Emil Cioran, sincerely embraced xenophobia and anti-Semitism, responding to the "attractive" nationalistic "qualities" of the Iron Guard regime. Very few of Sebastian's friends and acquaintances refused to compromise with the dominant fascist ideology of the war years.

Sebastian understood quickly the planned essence of the anti-Semitism of the Romanian state, which he called a huge anti-Semitic factory. He was exasperated by the fascist fanaticism of the society in which he lived, and he tried often to give a rational explanation that sometimes came close to an excuse for the fascist political engagement of his friends. Nevertheless, it remains puzzling that he continued to socialize with his anti-Semitic fascist friends. This weakness allowed him to remain an intimate witness of the barbarization of the Romanian intelligentsia. After liberation he condemned what he called the "indoctrinated stupidity" of the new emerging Communist regime, but he also agreed to work for its ministry of foreign affairs before being killed in the spring of 1945 in a road accident.

—Radu Ioanid

See the essay on *Journal: 1935–1944: The Fascist Years.*

SEMPRUN, Jorge

Pseudonyms: Gerard Sorel; Federico Sanchez. **Nationality:** Spanish. **Born:** Madrid, 1923. **Military Service:** Fought for anti-Franco forces during Spanish Civil War; French Resistance during World War II. **Career:** Exiled to France, 1939; prisoner, Buchenwald concentration camp, 1943–45; member of Politburo of outlawed Spanish Communist Party, 1952–62; secretary, French Communist Party; expelled from Communist Party, 1964; Minister of Culture, Spain, 1988–91. **Awards:** Planeta award for fiction (Spain), for *Autobiografia de Federico Sanchez;* Formentor prize for *Le Grand Voyage;* Jerusalem prize, 1997. Honorary doctorate: University of Turin, 1990.

Member: Academie Goncourt. **Agent:** Editions Gallimard, 5 rue Sebastien-Botton, 75341 Paris, Cedex 07, France.

PUBLICATIONS

Memoirs

Le Grand Voyage. 1963; as *The Long Voyage,* 1964; as *The Cattle Truck,* 1993.
Autobiografia de Federico Sanchez. 1977; as *The Autobiography of Federico Sanchez and the Communist Underground in Spain,* 1979; as *Communism in Spain in the Franco Era: The Autobiography of Federico Sanchez,* 1980.
Quel beau dimanche. 1980; as *What a Beautiful Sunday!,* 1982.
Federico Sanchez se despide de ustedes. 1983.
L'Ecriture ou la vie. 1994; as *Literature or Life,* 1997.

Novels

L'Evanouissement. 1967.
La Deuxieme mort de Ramon Mercader. 1968; as *The Second Death of Ramon Mercader,* 1973.
L'Algarabie. 1981.
La Montagne Blanche. 1986.
Netchaiev est de retour. 1987.

Plays

Stavisky (screenplay). 1974; translated edition, 1975.

Screenplays: *La Guerre est finie,* 1967; *Z,* with Costas-Gavras, 1968; *The Confession (L'Aveu),* 1969; *State of Siege,* 1973; *Stavisky,* 1974; *Special Section,* 1975; *Les Routes du Sud,* 1978.

Other

Montand, la vie continue. 1983.

*

Critical Studies: "Three Holocaust Writers: Speaking the Unspeakable" by Patricia A. Gartland, in *Critique,* 25(1), Autumn 1983, pp. 45–56; *The Dialogical Traveler: Discursive Practice and Homelessness in Three Modern Travel Narratives* (dissertation) by Sally Margaret Silk, University of Michigan, 1989; "'Cuanto mas escribo, mas me queda por decir': Memory, Trauma, and Writing in the Work of Jorge Semprun" by Ofelia Ferran, in *MLN,* 116(2), 2001.

* * *

Jorge Semprun was a Spanish Communist and later a member of the French resistance. Captured in 1943, he was deported to Buchenwald in 1944. After the war he was involved in the Spanish Communist Party, attaining a high rank. He became disillusioned with the hypocrisy of the Communists, however, and left the party. He became an award-winning author and screenwriter and later Spain's minister for culture. He is perhaps the most self-consciously literary of all the major Holocaust memoirists, and his style is comparable to the fragmentary modernist style of Charlotte Delbo. His books are dazzling intellectual and stylistic performances, defying genre and conventions to develop ways of writing about—or around—the camps.

Semprun recounted a meeting with Carlos Fuentes, who joked, "And so . . . you will have realized every writer's dream: to spend your life writing a single book, endlessly renewed." For Fuentes this is a lighthearted remark. For Semprun—with the black humor of the inmate that **Primo Levi** discussed—it is both a commentary and a reaffirmation of his Holocaust work. Semprun tells and retells the stories of his imprisonment. His work is as much about the nature of writing and narrative and its intersection with memory as about the events remembered.

There are three of Semprun's accounts readily available in English, each from a different decade: *The Long Voyage* (1964), *What a Beautiful Sunday!* (1982), and *Literature or Life* (1997). Each of these works in a similar way: Taking a set period of time—the journey to Buchenwald, a Sunday during his time there, the days immediately after liberation—as a narrative frame, they weave an account of this with accounts of events before, during, and after the war. Memories of one moment inevitably invoke other memories, and it is only through the whole contextual mesh of memories that make up a person that the events can be approached. Moreover, the nature of writing and narrating, too, effect what can be told. The style of the books aims to reflect this movement of memory and the problems of writing; they are shifting, uncertain. The narrator addresses readers personally, warns them of his fallibility, of his fabrications. There are slips in the chronology—conversations in 1944 slide into conversations in the 1950s, for example—that serve to disrupt the conventions of literary realism. Yet the texts—because of the subject matter, because of the power of the narrator, because, at base, of their ethical intentions—never slide into surrealism or trivial playfulness for its own sake.

Semprun's position in the Communist Party before, during, and after the war, and his eventual expulsion from it, as well as his range and depth of philosophical and political awareness and formal innovation make his accounts particularly interesting. While his texts cover the range of events that make up the core history of Europe in the twentieth century (from the Spanish Civil War to the collapse of the USSR and beyond) and his intellectual span draws in the range of major thinkers (Ludwig Wittgenstein, Martin Heidegger, Emmanuel Levinas) and writers (**Paul Celan, Bertolt Brecht,** Marcel Proust, Maurice Blanchot, for example), the Holocaust is at the center

of these works. They are works that testify not only to the disaster but also to the writing of the disaster.

—Robert Eaglestone

See the essays on *Literature or Life, The Long Voyage,* and *What a Beautiful Sunday!*

SENESH, Hannah

Nationality: Israeli (originally Hungarian: immigrated to Israel, 1939). **Born:** Budapest, 17 July 1921. **Education:** Nahalal Agricultural School, Palestine (now Israel). **Career:** Farm worker, Sdot-Yam kibbutz, Caesarea, Palestine (now Horbat Qesari, Israel), beginning in 1939. Anti-Nazi activist and member of Jewish resistance forces; member, British parachute team, c. 1944. **Died:** Executed by Nazi firing squad, 7 November 1944.

PUBLICATIONS

Diary

Hanah Senesh: Yomanim, Shirim, Eduyot (diary and poems). 1966; as *Hannah Senesh: Her Life and Diary,* 1971.

*

Media Adaptations: *A Time to Blossom* (musical composition), adaptation of poems by Hannah Senesh, 1995; *String Quartet No. 5, with Soprano* (musical composition), adaptation of translated poems by Hannah Senesh.

Critical Studies: *Palestine Parachutist: The Story of Hannah Senesh* by Chava Scheltzer, 1946; *Hannah Senesh, Halutza and Fighter for Freedom,* 1950; *The Summer That Bled: The Biography of Hannah Senesh* by Anthony Masters, 1972; *Three Battles, Three Heroines* by Faith Rogow, 1978; *Hannah Senesh: Tribute to a Woman of Valor* by Lydia C. Triantopoulos, 1982; *In Kindling Flame: The Story of Hannah Senesh, 1921–1944* by Linda Atkinson, 1985; *Ordinary Heroes: Chana Szenes and the Dream of Zion* by Peter Hay, 1986; *The Testing of Hanna Senesh* by Ruth Whitman and Livia Rothkirchen, 1986.

* * *

Hannah Senesh, who has become one of Israel's national heroines, was born in Budapest on 17 July 1921. Her father, Béla Senesh, was a well-known Hungarian playwright. He died in 1927 at the age of 33, leaving behind the six-year-old

Hannah, her seven-year-old brother, George, and their mother, Catherine. Because her father's creed was humanism, Hannah did not have a religious upbringing. She attended a Protestant school known for its high academic standards and was an excellent student. She was active in the school's literary circles and early on became known for her poetry. In fact, she began keeping a diary when she was 13.

In 1937, at the age of 16, Hannah became painfully aware of the difficulties of being Jewish in a Protestant school. After having been an active member of the school's literary society, she was informed that she was not allowed to hold office in the society because she was a Jew. When in November 1938 Hungary announced its allegiance to Germany in the event of war, it became clear to Hannah that a Jewish homeland was the only haven Jews could hope for. By the time she was 17, then, she had immersed herself in Zionism; she started learning Hebrew and making plans to immigrate to Palestine. Convinced that the new Jewish homeland needed farmers more than it needed poets, she abandoned her dream of becoming a college-educated writer and applied for admission to the Agricultural School at Nahalal in Israel.

In the spring of 1939 Hannah went to visit her brother in France, where he was attending school. The two of them decided that Hannah would immigrate to Israel within the next few months and that George would follow after he had finished his studies in France. In September 1939, as the High Holy Days were approaching, Hannah set out to make her home in Eretz Israel. She worked the land while attending the Nahalal Agricultural School. Two years after her arrival in Israel she joined the Sedot Yam kibbutz in Caesarea, where she wrote some of her best known poetry. By the end of 1942, however, Hannah was growing more and more concerned over the plight of the Jews of Europe and her mother's situation in Budapest. In early 1943 she volunteered to join an elite corps of Jewish paratroopers that the British and the Haganah had formed for the purpose of rescuing Allied prisoners of war and organizing Jewish resistance. In January 1944 she and 31 other fighters were sent to train under the British in Cairo.

Senesh was part of a unit that parachuted behind enemy lines in Yugoslavia in March 1944. There, while working with Tito's partisans, she wrote her best known poem, "Ashrei ha-Gafrur" ("Blessed Is the Match"). The deportation of the country's Jewry was at its peak when she crossed into Hungary on 7 June 1944 and was arrested by Hungarian police. She underwent months of severe torture but revealed nothing to her captors. On 7 November 1944 she was executed by a firing squad in the courtyard of a Budapest prison. Because her brother managed to get to Palestine in January 1944, he survived the war, as did their mother.

In 1950 Senesh's remains were taken to Israel to be buried on Mount Herzl with Israel's other military and political leaders. She became a national symbol of devotion and self-sacrifice, and her diary was first published in Hebrew in 1966. Titled *Hanah Senesh: Yomanim, Shirim, Eduyot*, it came out in English in 1971 under the title *Hannah Senesh: Her Life and Diary*.

—David Patterson

See the essay on *Hannah Senesh: Her Life and Diary*.

SEXTON, Anne

Nationality: American. **Born:** Anne Gray Harvey, Newton, Massachusetts, 9 November 1928. **Education:** Garland Junior College, 1947–48. **Family:** Married Alfred M. Sexton II in 1948 (divorced 1973); two daughters. **Career:** Fashion model, Boston, 1950–51; teacher, Wayland High School, Massachusetts, 1967–68; lecturer in creative writing, 1970–71, and professor of creative writing, 1972–74, Boston University. Scholar, Radcliffe Institute for Independent Study, 1961–63; Cranshaw Professor of Literature, Colgate University, 1972. Contributor to periodicals, including *Harper's, New Yorker, Partisan Review,* and *Nation.* **Awards:** Audience Poetry prize, 1958–59; Robert Frost fellowship, Bread Loaf Writers Conference, 1959; Levinson prize, *Poetry,* 1962; American Academy of Arts and Letters traveling fellowship, 1963–64; Ford Foundation grant for year's residence with professional theater, 1964–65; first literary magazine travel grant, Congress for Cultural Freedom, 1965–66; Shelley memorial award, 1967; Pulitzer prize, 1967, for *Live or Die;* Guggenheim fellowship, 1969. Litt.D.: Tufts University, 1970, Regis College, 1971, and Fairfield University, 1971. **Member:** Royal Society of Literature (fellow); Poetry Society of America; New England Poetry Club; Phi Beta Kappa (honorary member). **Died:** Suicide, 4 October 1974.

PUBLICATIONS

Poetry

To Bedlam and Part Way Back. 1960.
All My Pretty Ones. 1962.
Selected Poems. 1964.
Live or Die. 1966.
Poems, with Thomas Kinsella and Douglas Livingstone. 1968.
Love Poems. 1969.
Transformations. 1971.
The Book of Folly. 1972.
O Ye Tongues. 1973.
The Death Notebooks. 1974.
The Awful Rowing toward God. 1975.
The Heart of Anne Sexton's Poetry (3 vols.; includes *All My Pretty Ones, Live or Die, Love Poems*). 1977.
Words for Dr. Y: Uncollected Poems with Three Stories. 1978.
Complete Poems, 1981. 1981.
Selected Poems of Anne Sexton. 1988.

Love Poems of Anne Sexton. 1989.

Play

43 Mercy Street (produced New York, 1969). 1976.

Other

Anne Sexton: A Self Portrait in Letters (correspondence). 1977.
No Evil Star: Selected Essays, Interviews, and Prose. 1985.

Other (for children)

Eggs of Things, with Maxine W. Kumin. 1963.
More Eggs of Things, with Kumin. 1964.
Joey and the Birthday Present, with Kumin. 1971.
The Wizard's Tears, with Kumin. 1975.

*

Media Adaptation: . . . *about Anne* (stage production), 1986, from a compilation of Sexton's poems.

Critical Studies: *Sylvia Plath and Anne Sexton: A Reference Guide* by Cameron Northouse and Thomas P. Walsh, 1974; *Anne Sexton: The Artist and Her Critics,* edited by J. D. McClatchy, 1978; "Seeking the Exit or the Home: Poetry and Salvation in the Career of Anne Sexton" by Suzanne Juhasz, in *Shakespeare's Sisters: Feminist Essays on Women Poets,* edited by Sandra M. Gilbert and Susan Gubar, 1979; "The Hungry Beast Rowing toward God: Anne Sexton's Later Religious Poetry" by Kathleen L. Nichols, in *NMAL,* 3, 1979; "Housewife into Poet: The Apprenticeship of Anne Sexton," in *New England Quarterly,* 56(4), December 1983, pp. 483–503, and *Anne Sexton: A Biography,* 1991, both by Diane Wood Middlebrook; "Anne Sexton's Suicide Poems," in *Journal of Popular Culture,* 18(2), Fall 1984, pp. 17–31, "How We Danced: Anne Sexton on Fathers and Daughters," in *Women's Studies,* 12(2), 1986, pp. 179–202, and *Oedipus Anne: The Poetry of Anne Sexton,* 1987, all by Diana Hume George; "Anne Sexton Remembered" by Maryel F. Locke, in *Rossetti to Sexton: Six Women Poets at Texas,* edited by Dave Oliphant, 1992; *Searching for Mercy Street: My Journey Back to My Mother, Anne Sexton* by Linda Gray Sexton, 1994; *Anne Sexton* by S. L. Berry, 1997.

* * *

Anne Sexton is known as a "confessional poet," a term coined in the 1960s to describe a half dozen American poets (mostly male) who seemed to put more of their private lives into their poems than was customary at the time. Her work is also, as Alicia Ostriker noted in *Stealing the Language: The Emergence of Women's Poetry in America,* an important part of a body of poetry by women that emerged in the early 1960s, poetry that "illuminates the condition of women and therefore of humanity in an unprecedented way." Sexton wrote of her body ("In Celebration of My Uterus," "Menstruation at Forty") and of intimate female experience (abortion, masturbation) and situations ("Housewife," "For My Lover, Returning to His Wife"). She explored motherhood (often subversively), female sexuality, anger, and submission and, above all, breakdown, madness (*To Bedlam and Part Way Back* was her first collection, and the theme continued), the longing for death, and, especially in her last work, a longing for God the Father and his divine Son. Why, then, would Sexton, a New England WASP to boot, be included in a reference guide to literature on the Holocaust?

The answer lies in the poet's intense experience of evil and in the way she represented it in her poems. Evil was first felt as inner. One need not know that Sexton killed herself at the age of 46 to see that she sporadically, but increasingly, felt herself to be unworthy, crazy, bad. In Sexton, as in other women poets of the time, anger against the traditional condition of women, supposedly happy as procreators not creators, was often turned back against the self. Sometimes in earlier work, like the famous "Her Kind," she defiantly affirmed her status as "not a woman, quite"—"a possessed witch." Later, in "Loving the Killer," she saw herself as needing and loving the man who killed her; it is significant that she called him "my Nazi, / with your S.S. sky-blue eye." (Seven years earlier, in "The House," World War II in her family merely meant "rationed gas for all three cars.") In her last books self-destructive desire is accompanied by a proliferation of images suggesting inner evil ("the rat inside of me," "a bellyful of dirt," a "dead heart") and by multiple allusions to the Holocaust, signifying the evil both outside and within, public and private. In the posthumously published "Uses" she imagined and identified with the Jewish speaker, whose father was gassed, whose "Mama died in the medical experiments / they had stuffed a pig into her womb." (Note how the killing and violation of Jews is here associated with male violation of women.)

At the same time Sexton's poetry came to focus more and more on a difficult religious quest. In "Hurry Up Please It's Time" (*The Death Notebooks*), where Ms. Dog (clearly Sexton but also perhaps "God" spelled backwards) struggles with God, her mother "sent away my kitty / to be fried in the camps." In "For Mr. Death Who Stands with His Door Open" (*The Death Notebooks*), time itself is a "Nazi Mama with her beer and sauerkraut." In *The Awful Rowing toward God,* a collection written in two and a half weeks, whose religious passion "swept [her] up" and whose galleys she proofread the very day she committed suicide, Sexton produced what is arguably the most moving Holocaust poem in the English language: "After Auschwitz."

If the themes of Sexton's poetry are desperately serious, the poems are written in familiar American English ("Ms. Dog" and "Mr. Death" are typical), often close to ordinary speech. They are full of the objects of material culture (toilet seats, coffee mugs, Coke, frozen haddock) and names from popular culture (Joe DiMaggio, Skeezix, Long John Nebel), and they are often quite funny—sometimes savagely ironic, sometimes darkly funny, and sometimes just funny. Paradoxically, while her early verse may be the most "confessional," it often uses regular meters, rhymes, and is closer to the American academic poetry fashionable in the 1950s than to, say, the poetic experiments of **Paul Celan**. Yet as her poetry became more grounded in general myth, beginning with *Transformations* (the 1971 collection in which she retold Grimm's fairy tales), it became looser in form. The 10 wonderful "Psalms" in *The Death Notebooks* use the long free lines of the King James Bible and of the mad eighteenth-century poet Christopher Smart, whom she imagined as a kind of twin. *The Awful Rowing toward God* is in free verse. Sexton increasingly appears as a highly original religious poet, very American, who found a way to write like a woman and who found in the Holocaust objective signs of her own sense of evil.

—David Ball

See the essay on *The Awful Rowing toward God.*

SHERMAN, Martin

Nationality: American. **Born:** Philadelphia, 22 December 1938. **Education:** Boston University, 1956–60, B.F.A. 1960. **Career:** Playwright-in-residence, Mills College, Oakland, California, early 1960s, and Playwrights Horizons, New York, 1976–77; founder, Act Up. Moved to London, 1980. **Awards:** Wurlitzer Foundation of New Mexico grant, 1973; Dramatists Guild Hull-Warriner award, 1980, for *Bent;* National Endowment for the Arts fellowship, 1980; Rockefeller Foundation fellowship, 1985. **Agents:** Johnnie Planko, William Morris Agency, 1350 Avenue of the Americas, New York, New York 10019, U.S.A.; Margaret Ramsay Ltd., 14A Goodwins Court, London C.W.2, England.

PUBLICATIONS

Plays

A Solitary Thing, music by Stanley Silverman (produced Oakland, California, 1963).
Fat Tuesday (produced New York, 1966).
Next Year in Jerusalem (produced New York, 1967).
Change (opera libretto), music by Drey Shepperd (produced New York, 1969).
The Night before Paris (produced New York, 1969).
Things Went Badly in Westphalia (produced Storrs, Connecticut 1971). In *The Best Short Plays 1970,* edited by Stanley Richards, 1970.
Passing By (produced New York, 1974; London, 1975). In *Gay Plays,* edited by Michael Wilcox, 1984.

Soaps (produced New York, 1975).
Cracks (produced Waterford, Connecticut, 1975). In *Gay Plays, Volume II,* edited by Michael Wilcox, 1985.
Rio Grande (produced New York, 1976).
Blackout (produced New York, 1978).
Bent (produced Waterford, Connecticut, 1978; London and New York, 1979). 1979.
Messiah (produced London, 1982). 1982.
When She Danced (produced Guildford, Surrey, 1985; London, 1988; New York, 1990). 1988.
A Madhouse in Goa (produced London, 1989). 1989.
Some Sunny Day (produced London, 1996). 1996.
Rose (produced London, 1999; New York, 2000). 1999.

Screenplays: *Alive and Kicking/Indian Summer,* 1996; *Bent,* 1997; *See Under: Love,* adaptation of the novel by David Grossman, 1997; *The Dybbuk,* 1997; *Callas Forever,* with Franco Zeffirelli, anticipated 2002.

Television Play: *The Summer House,* adaptation of *The Clothes in the Wardrobe,* by Alice Thomas Ellis, 1992.

*

Film Adaptations: *The Summer House,* 1993; *Alive and Kicking/Indian Summer,* 1996; *Bent,* 1997.

Critical Studies: "Images of the Gay Male in Contemporary Drama" by James W. Carlsen, in *Gayspeak: Gay Male and Lesbian Communication,* edited by James W. Chesebro, 1981; *Acting Gay: Male Homosexuality in Modern Drama* by John M. Clum, 1992; "Martin Sherman" by Matthew S. Wolf, in *New York,* 30, 17 November 1997, p. 60–61; "Inventing History: Toward a Gay Holocaust Literature" by Kai Hammermeister, in *German Quarterly,* 70(1), Winter 1997, pp. 18–26; "Opening the Forbidden Closet" by Edward R. Isser, in his *Stages of Annihilation,* 1997; "Martin Sherman" by Sander Hicks, in *BOMB,* 62, Winter 1998, pp. 74–80.

Theatrical Activities: Actor: Films—*Radio Days,* 1987; *Alive and Kicking/Indian Summer,* 1996.

* * *

Few plays about the Holocaust have appeared on Broadway. Of the handful produced there, Martin Sherman has written two, plus two film scripts and other Holocaust plays.

Although known as a gay playwright, Sherman says his Judaism imbues his work more than does his sexual orientation. His heritage figures in his early plays, especially *Next Year in Jerusalem* (1967), his more recent *Rose* (1999), and most of those in between. This son of immigrants from the Polish-Ukrainian border shtetl of Yultishka writes about the "other"—that is, those not able-bodied, straight, white, Christian men. Repeatedly he chooses Jewish characters, and three times these characters originate in Yultishka. The seventeenth-century Rachel, a female Job, lives there long before the Holocaust, but the twentieth-century Chonnon and Rose have survived that horror. Over and over Sherman intertwines his twin themes: outsider status and survival. They coexist in his Holocaust scripts, even in one that takes as its central character the ultimate alien, a creature from outer space.

The playful yet chilling *Some Sunny Day* (1996) takes place in Cairo during July 1942 as five foreigners—Sherman outsiders—prepare for the city's expected fall to Rommel. A British propagandist and his wife, a British soldier and his lover—an impostor posing as a Maori journalist but really far more alien—and a disguised Jewish refugee trying to flee Egypt all react to their fears by exhibiting narcissism or altruism. Sherman plants suspicions about Nazi spies among them as he examines not just their identities but the nature of being, that is, ontology. Deceit permeates the play, as the alien proves selfless by blackmailing the diplomat for a pass so the Jew can escape to Palestine.

In 1997 Sherman wrote three screenplays. *See Under: Love,* which he based on **David Grossman**'s magic-realist novel of the same name, dramatizes a child's experiences in postwar Israel trying to learn about the Holocaust. Sherman juxtaposes these to flashbacks to the boy's great-uncle—a writer imprisoned by the Nazis—and scenes of heroic children, which the same writer created in the 1920s. Dramatizing the power of literature to transform hearts and alter destinies, this film revisits the Holocaust, which Sherman had treated years earlier in his most famous play, *Bent* (1979).

In *Bent* the dramatist characterizes his protagonist Max as a casual anti-Semite, then provides this gay man with a different perspective when he claims he's Jewish and encounters his once ridiculed landlord at Dachau. During Max's evolution toward humanity, compassion, and courage, he comes to accept himself, assert his true identity, defy the Nazis, love another, and die heroically.

See Under: Love's plot arcs differently. Sherman has changed the order of events in Grossman's tale, highlighted images of the SS officer as a child, and eliminated contemporary segments set after the Israeli boy has grown up, thereby throwing concentration camp scenes into greater prominence. In these scenes the prisoner, a Jewish Scheherazade, by means of his artistry both survives and transforms the camp's commandant.

The third 1997 screenplay, *The Dybbuk,* Sherman set only a few years after the Holocaust, in 1953 Atlantic City, where Chonnon, who has just arrived from Poland, begins working as a busboy at the Majestic Hotel. There he falls in love with his boss's daughter, uses cabala to win her, and dies after she plans to wed another. To prevent this, his spirit merges with hers. Possessed by his dybbuk, the young woman shares his memories, most compellingly those of how the Nazis came to Yultishka, herded everyone but him into the schoolhouse, locked the doors, and burned it. Chonnon escaped by crawling through his chimney to the roof, where he watched the fire, heard the screams. Sherman based this chilling account on

historical fact. While attempts occur to exorcise the dybbuk, we learn the possessed woman's father also came from Yultishka but left before the Nazis slaughtered his friends and relatives. Sherman dramatizes the importance of knowing what happened and remembering the Holocaust—an important theme in all these works.

When plans to film this screenplay evaporated, Sherman took some of its details and created his millennium piece, *Rose*. Both in London in 1999 and on Broadway in 2000, Olympia Dukakis memorably played this role of a Holocaust survivor who also knows she must remember, even as she tries to forget. Sitting shiva, the 80-year-old recalls her childhood in Yultishka, her marriage in Warsaw and suffering in its ghetto (where her child dies), her survival in the sewers, her internment as a displaced person, her journey on the exodus to Palestine and back, her years in Atlantic City, her retirement in Miami. Now she laments extremists in Israel behaving, she believes, no better than Nazis when one massacres Arabs in the Hebron mosque and another, her grandson, kills the Palestinian child for whom she sits shiva. Rose says Kaddish for the Yiddish language and culture, killed by the Nazis and by subsequent responses to hatred with hatred.

—Tish Dace

See the essay on *Bent.*

SIEDLECKI, Janusz Nel

Nationality: British (originally Polish: immigrated to England after World War II). **Born:** 1916. **Education:** Studied engineering in London after World War II. **Military Service:** Liaison between Polish Emigration Government in France and Polish underground movement, World War II. **Career:** Political prisoner in Auschwitz and Dachau during World War II. Worked as an engineer, London. **Died:** 2000.

PUBLICATIONS

Memoirs

Byliśmy w Oświęcimiu, with Tadeusz Borowski and Krystyn Olszewski. 1946; as *We Were in Auschwitz,* 2000.
Beyond Lost Dreams. 1994.

*

Critical Studies: ''When the Earth Is No Longer a Dream and Cannot be Dreamed through to the End'' by Jan Walc, in *Polish Review,* 32(2), 1987, pp. 181–94; ''Beyond Self:

A Lesson from the Concentration Camps'' by Piotr Kuhiwczak, in *Canadian Review of Comparative Literature/Revue Canadienne de Litterature Comparee,* 19(3), September 1992, pp. 395–405; *Suffering Witness: The Quandary of Responsibility after the Irreparable* by James Hatley, 2000.

* * *

Janusz Nel Siedlecki became an Auschwitz prisoner in November 1940. He got there while engaged in carrying out a confidential military mission. He was a liaison between the Polish Emigration Government in France and the underground movement in Poland. Imprisoned by the Gestapo, he was sent to Auschwitz, where he was given number 6643. Of the three coauthors of *We Were in Auschwitz* (2000; originally published in 1946 as *Byliśmy w Oświęcimiu*), he stayed the longest in concentration camps. He was also several years older than **Tadeusz Borowski** and **Krystyn Olszewski**, which in wartime was quite significant.

Nel Siedlecki was born in 1916. He went to school in Warsaw. He was a graduate of the famous high school named after King Stephen Batory. After the liberation he became friends with Borowski, Olszewski, and Anatol Girs, the future publisher of their common Munich book.

Nel Siedlecki was a man of high humanistic culture. The history of the book *We Were in Auschwitz* begins with his literary attempts. He was the first one to start jotting down his memories. Knowing that, Girs suggested that he should publish a book together with Borowski and Olszewski.

According to Borowski's testimony, which was written down by Professor Tadeusz Mikulski, Nel Siedlecki is the author of three stories: ''Between the Sola and the Vistula Rivers,'' ''You'd Better Not Get Ill,'' and ''The Story of a Certain Table.'' On the other hand, the stories ''With a Baedecker between the Wires,'' ''Homo Sapiens and the Beast,'' and ''Iodine and Phenol'' were written in cooperation with Borowski. Nel Siedlecki is also the author of the anecdote on the basis of which Borowski wrote ''The Fire Congeals.''

As Tadeusz Drewnowski and Andrzej Werner wrote, the longtime imprisonment of Nel Siedlecki was important for the overall shape of the book. Its authors used and transformed his knowledge and perspective, which were those of an ''old number.'' It was his knowledge of survival strategies that helped Borowski create his narrator, Tadek, who was such a shock for the literary audience.

In his letter to Maria Rundo, Borowski wrote of Nel Siedlecki: ''The other one is also from Auschwitz, he is not a publisher though, but a store-keeper from the Gypsy camp. He has a very old number, but he is a man of technical education and very knowledgeable.''

After the war Nel Siedlecki did not return to Poland. He went to live in London, where he studied engineering. Until

1994, when he published his memoirs, *Beyond Lost Dreams,* he was not concerned with literature. He died in 2000.

—Kazimierz Adamczyk

See the essay on *We Were in Auschwitz.*

SIERAKOWIAK, Dawid

Nationality: Polish. **Born:** Lodz, 25 July 1924. **Died:** Victim of the Holocaust, 1943.

PUBLICATION

Diary

Dziennik. 1960; as *The Diary of Dawid Sierakowiak: Five Notebooks from the Lodz Ghetto,* edited by Alan Adelson, 1996.

* * *

Dawid Sierakowiak was born on 25 July 1924 in Lodz, Poland. He and his younger sister, Nadzia, lived with their parents in Lodz and appear to have had a close immediate family, despite tensions between Dawid and his father. When Dawid returned to Lodz from several weeks away from home at summer camp in July 1939, he wrote, ''On the way I meet Mom. God, what joy! At home the same with Father and sister.'' The next day he remarked, ''I feel terrific being at home.''

Though diaries always reveal only fragments and glimpses of the true inner and outer life of the writer, the length and scope of Dawid's diary—written over almost four years under the most trying of circumstances—offer much to consider about the young writer. He emerges first and foremost as a young intellectual gifted at languages, reading and writing in English, German, Hebrew, Yiddish, and French. He was deeply committed to books and writing, not only reading philosophy and literature but experimenting in prose and poetry and the art of translation.

In this context it is not surprising that Dawid kept a diary. Though some volumes are lost, and gaps in the narrative thus exist, nowhere in the surviving notebooks did Dawid explicitly state his reasons for writing or his intentions for his text. At the same time, the very fact that he wrote virtually every single day, and his tenacity and determination in continuing to write even as he wasted away from hunger, illness, exhaustion, and despair, leaves little doubt that he viewed his diary as a deliberate testimony of his life. His attachment to the diary comes through in a few lines written on 27 May 1942. After considering the possibility of volunteering for deportation (the true nature of those departures still unknown to the ghetto inhabitants), Dawid gave up on the idea, citing among his reasons, "I would miss my books and 'letters', notes and copybooks. Especially this diary." As was the case for many young writers of the period, the diary was not only his record of the demise of his community and his family but also a confidant and a friend in an increasingly isolating world.

The struggle to maintain an intellectual life in the context of starvation and illness is a prevailing theme in the diary. Many young writers of this period shared the impulse to continue studying, reading, writing, and learning as if in defiance of the stagnation imposed upon them in the ghetto. But few expressed as vividly as Dawid the dwindling of intellectual and mental energy that made the struggle to continue to learn such a herculean one. Dawid's despair mounted through the diary as he found himself increasingly unable to concentrate, unable to read, and unable to learn. On 29 April 1942 he wrote, "Again I don't have any will, or rather any strength, for studying. I want to do something, but everything is exceptionally difficult for me, so I just stick to reading most of the time. Time is passing, my youth is passing, my school years, my power and enthusiasm are all passing. Only the Devil knows what I will manage to save from this pogrom."

Despite his determination to write, and to continue writing even as he recorded his rapid decline toward death, Dawid ceased his entries on 15 April 1943 with the ominous words, "There is really no way out of this for us." By the time he ceased writing, he had endured the deportation of his mother and the death of his father. His sister Nadzia is presumed to have been deported to Auschwitz in the final liquidation of the ghetto in August 1944 and murdered there.

According to the published edition of Dawid's diary, Waclaw Szkudlarek, a non-Jewish inhabitant of Lodz, returned to his apartment after the war and there found Dawid's notebooks piled on the stove. In his testimony regarding the discovery of the Sierakowiak diary, Mr. Szkudlarek speculated that the gaps in the sequence of the diary may be attributable to the fact that some notebooks were burned for fuel during the winter of 1945. Two of the original notebooks are now housed in the archives of the Jewish Historical Institute in Warsaw; the remaining three are in the Collections of the United States Holocaust Memorial Museum.

The five notebooks of Dawid's diary were published in English under the title *The Diary of Dawid Sierakowiak: Five Notebooks from the Lodz Ghetto* (1996). They were translated from the original Polish by Kamil Turowski and introduced by the editor of the volume, Alan Adelson.

—Alexandra Zapruder

See the essay on *The Diary of Dawid Sierakowiak: Five Notebooks from the Lodz Ghetto.*

SINGER, Isaac Bashevis

Pseudonym: Isaac Warshofsky. **Nationality:** American (originally Polish: immigrated to the United States, 1935, granted U.S. citizenship, 1943). **Born:** Icek-Hersz Zynger, Leoncin, 14 July 1904. **Education:** Tachkemoni Rabbinical Seminary, Warsaw, 1921–23. **Family:** Married Alma Haimann in 1940; one son from a previous marriage. **Career:** Proofreader and translator, *Literarishe Bletter,* Warsaw, 1923–33; associate editor, *Globus,* Warsaw, 1933–35. Journalist, *Jewish Daily Forward,* New York, 1935–91. Founder, *Svivah.* **Awards:** Louis Lamed prize, 1950, for *The Family Moskat,* and 1956, for *Satan in Goray;* National Institute of Arts and Letters and American Academy award in literature, 1959; Jewish Book Council of America Harry and Ethel Daroff Memorial fiction award, 1963, for *The Slave;* Foreign book prize (France), 1965; National Council on the Arts grant and *New York Times* best illustrated book citation, both in 1966, Newbery Honor book award, 1967, for *Zlateh the Goat and Other Stories;* National Endowment for the Arts grant and *Playboy* magazine award for best fiction, both in 1967; Newbery Honor book award, 1968, for *The Fearsome Inn;* Bancarella prize, 1968, for Italian translation of *The Family Moskat;* Newbery Honor book award, 1969, for *When Schlemiel Went to Warsaw and Other Stories;* Brandeis University creative arts medal for poetry-fiction, 1970; National Book Award for children's literature, 1970, for *A Day of Pleasure;* Association of Jewish Libraries Sydney Taylor award, 1971; Children's Book Council children's book Showcase award, 1972, for *Alone in the Wild Forest;* National Book Award for fiction, 1974, for *A Crown of Feathers and Other Stories;* Agnon gold medal, 1975; Nobel prize for literature, 1978; *Present Tense* magazine Kenneth B. Smilen literary award, 1980, for *The Power of Light;* Parents' Choice Foundation award, 1983, for *The Golem;* Handel Medallion, 1986; American Academy and Institute of Arts and Letters gold medal for fiction, 1989. D.H.L.: Hebrew Union College, 1963. D.Litt.: Texas Christian University, 1972; Colgate University, 1972; Bard College, 1974; Long Island University, 1979. Honorary doctorate: Hebrew University, Jerusalem, 1973. **Member:** American Academy, 1965; American Academy of Arts and Sciences, 1969; Jewish Academy of Arts and Sciences; Polish Institute of Arts and Sciences. **Died:** 24 July 1991.

PUBLICATIONS

Novels

Der Sotn in Gorey. 1935; as *Shoten an Goray un anderer Dertailungen,* 1943; translated as *Satan in Goray,* 1955.
Di Familie Mushkat, as Isaac Bashevis (2 vols.). 1950; as *The Family Moskat,* 1950.
The Magician of Lublin (translation of original Yiddish manuscript). 1960.

The Slave (translation). 1962.
The Manor (translation). 1967.
The Estate (translation). 1969.
Sonim, di Geshichte fun a Liebe. 1966; as *Enemies: A Love Story,* 1972.
Shosha (translation). 1978.
Reaches of Heaven: A Story of the Baal Shem Tov (translation). 1980.
The Penitent (translation). 1983.
The King of the Fields (translation). 1988.
Scum (translation). 1991.
The Certificate (translation). 1992.
Meshugah (translation). 1994.
Shadows on the Hudson (translation). 1998.

Short Stories

Gimpel the Fool and Other Stories (translation of original Yiddish manuscript). 1957.
The Spinoza of Market Street and Other Stories (translation). 1961.
Short Friday and Other Stories (translation). 1964.
Selected Short Stories, edited by Irving Howe. 1966.
The Séance and Other Stories (translation). 1968.
A Friend of Kafka and Other Stories (translation). 1970.
A Crown of Feathers and Other Stories (translation). 1973.
Passions and Other Stories (translation). 1975.
Old Love (translation). 1979.
The Collected Stories of Isaac Bashevis Singer. 1982.
The Image and Other Stories (translation). 1985.
Gifts (English and Yiddish). 1985.
The Death of Methuselah and Other Stories (translation). 1988.
The Safe Deposit and Other Stories about Grandparents, Old Lovers, and Crazy Old Men, edited by Kerry M. Orlitzky. 1989.

Plays

The Mirror (produced 1973).
Shlemiel the First (produced 1974).
Yentl, adaptation, with Leah Napolin, of his own short story ''Yentl, the Yeshiva Boy'' (produced 1974). 1977.
Teibele and Her Demon by Eve Friedman (produced Minneapolis, 1978; New York, 1979). 1984.
A Play for the Devil, adaptation of his own short story ''The Unseen'' (produced New York, 1984).

Other (for children)

Zlateh the Goat and Other Stories (translation of original Yiddish manuscript). 1966.
Mazel and Shlimazel; or, The Milk of a Lioness (translation). 1967.
The Fearsome Inn (translation). 1967.

When Schlemiel Went to Warsaw and Other Stories (translation). 1968.
A Day of Pleasure: Stories of a Boy Growing Up in Warsaw (translation; autobiographical). 1969.
Elijah the Slave: A Hebrew Legend Retold (translation). 1970.
Joseph and Koza; or, The Sacrifice to the Vistula (translation). 1970.
Alone in the Wild Forest (translation). 1971.
The Topsy-Turvy Emperor of China (translation). 1971.
The Wicked City (translation). 1972.
The Fools of Chelm and Their History (translation). 1973.
Why Noah Chose the Dove (translation). 1974.
A Tale of Three Wishes (translation). 1976.
Naftali the Storyteller and His Horse, Sus, and Other Stories (translation). 1976.
The Power of Light: Eight Stories for Hanukkah (translation). 1980.
The Golem (translation). 1982.
Stories for Children (selections). 1984.

Other

Mayn tatn's bes-din shtub (autobiography). 1956; as *In My Father's Court,* 1966.
An Isaac Bashevis Singer Reader. 1971.
Love and Exile: A Memoir (autobiographical trilogy). 1984.
  A Little Boy in Search of God: Mysticism in a Personal Light. 1976.
  A Young Man in Search of Love. 1978.
  Lost in America. 1981.
Nobel Lecture (in English and Yiddish). 1979.
Isaac Bashevis Singer on Literature and Life: An Interview, with Paul Rosenblatt and Gene Koppel. 1979.
Conversations with Isaac Bashevis Singer, with Richard Burgin. 1985.
Isaac Bashevis Singer: Conversations, edited by Grace Farrell. 1992.

Editor, with Elaine Gottlieb, *Prism 2.* 1965.

Translator, *Pan,* by Knut Hamsun. 1928.
Translator, *Di Vogler* [The Vagabonds], by Knut Hamsun. 1928.
Translator, *In Opgrunt fun Tayve* [In Passions's Abyss], by Gabriele D'Annunzio. 1929.
Translator, *Mete Trap* [Mette Trap], by Karin Michäelis. 1929.
Translator, *Roman Rolan* [Romain Rolland], by Stefan Zwcig. 1929.
Translator, *Viktorya* [Victoria], by Knut Hamsun. 1929.
Translator, *Oyfn Mayrev-Front keyn nayes* [All Quiet on the Western Front], by Erich Maria Remarque. 1930.
Translator, *Der Tsoyberbarg* [The Magic Mountain], by Thomas Mann (4 vols.). 1930.
Translator, *Der Veg oyf Tsurik* [The Road Back], by Erich Maria Remarque. 1931.

Translator, *Araber: Folkstimlekhe Geshikhtn* [Arabs: Stories of the People], by Moshe Smilansky. 1932.

Translator, *Fun Moskve biz Yerusholayim* [From Moscow to Jerusalem], by Leon S. Glaser. 1938.

*

Film Adaptations: *The Magician of Lublin*, 1978; *Yentl*, 1983; *Enemies: A Love Story*, 1989.

Bibliography: By Bonnie Jean M. Christensen, in *Bulletin of Bibliography*, 26, January/March, 1969; *A Bibliography of Isaac Bashevis Singer 1924–1949* by David Neal Miller, 1983.

Manuscript Collection: Butler Library, Columbia University, New York.

Critical Studies: *The Achievement of Isaac Bashevis Singer*, edited by Marcia Allentuck, 1967; *Isaac Bashevis Singer and the Eternal Past* by Irving H. Buchen, 1968; *Isaac Bashevis Singer* by Ben Siegel, 1969; *Critical Views of Isaac Bashevis Singer*, edited by Irving Malin, 1969, and *Isaac Bashevis Singer* by Malin, 1972; *Isaac Bashevis Singer and His Art* by Askel Schiotz, 1970; *Isaac Bashevis Singer: The Magician of West 86th Street* by Paul Kresh, 1979; *Isaac Bashevis Singer* by Edward Alexander, 1980; *Fear of Fiction: Narrative Strategies in the Works of Isaac Bashevis Singer* by David Neal Miller, 1985, and *Recovering the Canon: Essays on Isaac Bashevis Singer*, edited by Miller, 1986; *From Exile to Redemption: The Fiction of Isaac Bashevis Singer* by Grace Farrell, 1987, and *Critical Essays on Isaac Bashevis Singer*, edited by Farrell, 1996; *Understanding Isaac Bashevis Singer* by Lawrence S. Friedman, 1988; *Transgression and Self-Punishment in Isaac Bashevis Singer's Searches* by Frances Vargas Gibbons, 1995; *Isaac Bashevis Singer: A Life* by Janet Hadda, 1997; *Lost Landscapes: In Search of Isaac Bashevis Singer and the Jews of Poland* by Agata Tuszyanska, translated by Madeline G. Levine, 1998.

*   *   *

Arguably the greatest Yiddish writer, Isaac Bashevis Singer was born in Leoncin, Poland, on 14 July 1904. When Singer was four years old, his family moved to 10 Krochmalna Street, Warsaw, which serves as the setting for much of Singer's novel *Shosha* (1978), some of his finest stories, and his childhood reminiscences. To escape the hunger and disease caused by World War I, Singer and his mother fled (in 1917) to Bilgoray, where the youth spent the next four years observing the rural Jewish life that he would re-create in his fiction. Singer claimed that without this experience he never could have written his first novel, *Satan in Goray* (1935).

In the year that work appeared, Singer immigrated to the United States. Hence, as he wrote in the preface to *Enemies: A Love Story* (1972), he ''did not have the privilege of going through the Hitler holocaust.'' That event did, however, deeply influence his writing. In the August 1943 *Di tsukunft* Singer

published ''Arum der yidisher proze in polyn'' (''Concerning Yiddish Literature in Poland,'' 1995). After surveying the state of Yiddish letters from the coming of the Enlightenment to Poland in the early 1900s to the Nazi invasion, Singer concluded that this world had now vanished. ''For the Yiddish writer who comes from there, the very ground from which he derived literary sustenance has been destroyed along with Jewish Poland. His characters are dead. Their language has been silenced. All that he has to draw from are memories.''

Singer would evoke these memories in much of his subsequent fiction and in his autobiographical works. His ''Short Friday'' and ''Gimpel Tam'' (both 1945) are set in the old-world shtetls of Lapschitz and Frampol, respectively. The first story re-creates the loving relationship of Shmul-Leibele and Shoshe, who suffocate together one Sabbath because their oven's flue is closed. Their deaths represent the fate of millions of their coreligionists who perished in Hitler's ovens. The Frampol of ''Gimpel Tam'' is less endearing than Lapschitz; its inhabitants repeatedly deceive the title character. Yet ultimately Gimpel discovers that ''there were really no lies,'' that ''the world is entirely an imaginary world.'' Singer repeatedly emphasizes that through memory and imagination the vanished world of pre–World War II European Jewry could be preserved.

Singer's family chronicles, patterned after those of his older brother, Israel Joshua Singer, present a panoramic view of Jewish life in Poland. Taken together, *The Family Moskat* (1950), *The Manor* (1967), and *The Estate* (1969) portray life in Polish villages and in Warsaw from 1863 to the coming of the Nazis. As in ''Gimpel Tam,'' Singer does not sentimentalize the past, nor does he offer easy answers to explain the hard life Jews endured. When the Jews in *The Family Moskat* are expelled from Tereshpol Minor, the local rabbi wonders, ''Where are your worldly remedies?'' At the same time, the secular Jekuthiel asks, ''Where is your Lord of the Universe now?''

The Slave (1962) is set in seventeenth-century Poland in the aftermath of the Chmielnicki massacres, a series of pogroms that must recall the Holocaust to Singer's readers. Despite the devastation wrought by the Cossacks here and by the Nazis in *Enemies: A Love Story*, Singer offers hope for the future. Both novels show the rebuilding of the Jewish community through conversion and birth. *Shosha*, set in pre–World War II Poland, is more ambivalent. It shows that Holocaust survivors have rebuilt their lives, but the book ends with Aaron Greidinger and Haiml Chentshiner sitting in a dark room waiting for an explanation of the deaths and suffering they have witnessed, an explanation that will not be offered.

For Singer modernism is a false messiah: one cannot escape one's past. Asa Heshel Bennet in *The Family Moskat* leaves his village for Warsaw and abandons his Hasidic dress for a new wardrobe that makes him look like a Gentile. But when he orders lunch at a restaurant, the owner instantly recognizes him as a Jew and insults him. The nonbelievers Masha in *Enemies* and Betty Slonim in *Shosha* kill themselves. Without a past they also have no future. To deny God's existence is to destroy oneself. As "Gimpel Tam" illustrates, the greatest credulity is the belief in nothing. Singer does not, however, endorse unthinking orthodoxy. Yasha Mazur in *The Magician of Lublin* (1960) and Joseph Shapiro in *The Penitent* (1983) adhere so rigidly to the law that they isolate themselves from their family and community.

In his Nobel Prize address Singer joked that he wrote in Yiddish because a dead language was ideal for one who wrote about ghosts. More seriously, he described Yiddish as "the wise and humble language of us all, the idiom of frightened and hopeful humanity." That is the humanity that fills his fiction, that searches for answers in a silent world where anything is possible, even salvation.

—Joseph Rosenblum

See the essays on *Enemies: A Love Story*, "The Lecture," and "The Letter Writer."

SOBOL, Joshua

Nationality: Israeli. **Born:** Yehoshua Sobol, Tel Mond, Palestine, 1939. **Education:** Studied philosophy at the Sorbonne University of Paris. **Career:** Playwright-in-residence and artistic director, Haifa Municipal Theatre, Israel, 1984–88; has taught drama and playwriting workshops at Tel-Aviv University, Seminar Hakibbutzim, Beit Tzvi Drama School, and the Ben-Gurion University of Beersheva; playwright-in-residence, Wesleyan University, Connecticut, Fall 2000. **Awards:** Davidis Harp award for best play of the year (Israel), 1984, *Evening Standard* (London) best play of the year, and London's Critics' Circle best play of the year, 1989, all for *Ghetto;* has received the Davidis Harp award for four other plays. **Address:** c/o Or-Am Publishing House, P.O. Box 22096, Tel-Aviv 61220, Israel.

PUBLICATIONS

Plays (all originally produced in Hebrew)

The Days to Come (produced Haifa, Israel, 1971).
Status Quo Vadis (produced Haifa, 1973).
Sylvester 1972 (also known as *New Year's Eve 1972;* produced Haifa, 1974).
The Joke (produced Haifa, 1975).
Nerves (produced Haifa, 1976).
Leyl ha'esrim (produced Haifa, 1976). 1976; as *The Night of the Twentieth* (produced London, 1978).
Gog and Magog Show (produced Haifa, 1977).
Repentance (produced Haifa, 1977).
The Tenants (produced Haifa, 1978).

Beyt Kaplan [The House of Kaplan] (produced Israel,1978–79; trilogy).
The Wars of the Jews (produced 1981).
Nefesh yehudi (produced Haifa, 1982). Published as *Halaylah ha'acharon shel Oto Vaininger* [The Last Night of Otto Weininger], 1982; as *The Soul of a Jew* (produced London, 1983), published as *Jewish Soul,* in *Modern Israeli Drama in Translation,* edited by Michael Taub, 1993.
Geto (produced Haifa, 1983). 1983; translated as *Ghetto* (produced London and New York, 1989), in *Art from the Ashes: A Holocaust Anthology,* edited by Lawrence L. Langer, 1995.
Hapalestina'it [The Palestinian Woman] (produced Haifa, 1985). 1985.
Sindrom Yerushalayim [Jerusalem Syndrome] (produced Haifa, 1987). 1987.
Shooting Magda (produced 1987).
Adam (produced Tel-Aviv, 1989). 1989; translated as *Adam,* in *Israeli Holocaust Drama,* edited by Michael Taub, 1996.
Bamartef [In the Cellar]. 1990.
Underground (produced 1991).
Solo (produced Tel-Aviv, 1991). 1991.
Girls of Toledo (produced Jerusalem, Israel, 1992).
Kefar: Mahazeh bi-shete ma'arakhot [Village]. 1996.

Other

Almah: Mahazeh [Alma]. 1999.
Shetikah: Roman [Silence]. 2000.

Translator, *Draifus,* by Jean-Claude Grumnerg. 1980.
Translator, *Milhemet Troyah lo tihyeh,* by Jean Giraudoux. 1984.

*

Critical Studies: "Zionism: Neurosis or Cure? The 'Historical' Drama of Yehoshua Sobol" by Yael S. Feldman, in *Prooftexts,* 7(2), May 1987, pp. 145–62; "In Search of Sobol" by Rachel Shteir, in *Theater,* 21(3), Summer/Fall 1990, pp. 39–42; "When Choosing Good Is Not an Option: An Interview with Joshua Sobol" by Douglas Langworthy, in *Theater,* 22(3), Summer/Fall 1991, pp. 10–17; Joshua Sobol/Larry Kramer section of *Text and Performance Quarterly,* 12(4), October 1992; "Memory and History: *The Soul of a Jew* by Jehoshua Sobol" by Freddie Rokem, in *Jews & Gender: Responses to Otto Weininger,* edited by Nancy A. Harrowitz and Barbara Hyams, 1995; "Meeting Joshua Sobol" by Marion Baraitser, in *The Jewish Quarterly,* 46(1), Spring 1999, p. 68.

* * *

Playwright Joshua Sobol is the author of three of the best dramas concerning the Holocaust: *Geto* (1983), *Adam* (1989), and *Underground* (1991). Sobol, one of Israel's finest playwrights, is with good reason considered one of the finest dramatists—if not the greatest—regarding the Holocaust. Of his three plays concerning the Shoah, *Ghetto* is unquestionably the most popular. All three plays are testaments to the vitality of life in the ghetto. The characters are always busy and acting as if this day might be their last. Sobol claims that when he directs *Ghetto,* he instructs his actors and actresses to comport themselves as if the action in which they are currently engaged might be their last, that at any moment the Nazis might come and liquidate the ghetto. Similarly in *Adam* a life-or-death crisis presents itself, and the ghetto inhabitants must decide if they will follow Jacob Gens's orders to find and turn over Yitzhak Wittenberg to the Nazis or side with the United Partisan Organization; they have only a few hours to find Wittenberg or the ghetto might be liquidated on the orders of Kittel. In *Underground* the doctors must contain the typhus outbreak and hide it from the Nazis, which becomes a serious problem when Kittel and SS Doctor Jaegger come to visit the hospital. Again a life-or-death situation occurs, because the news of a typhus outbreak would result in the liquidation of the ghetto.

Unlike earlier dramatists, who sometimes created plays regarding the Holocaust in which the Jews were always innocent victims or survivors who continued to suffer psychologically years after the Shoah, Sobol wrote more complex and controversial plays. His Jewish characters are more three-dimensional and are capable of being selfish and sinful. In *Ghetto* Sobol portrays the tailor Weiskopf as an accomplice, a Jew willing to sacrifice other Jewish lives for the Nazi cause—and for his personal benefit. In *Adam* Sobol dramatizes Wittenberg Day—16 July 1943—the day that Vilna ghetto Judenrat leader Jacob Gens turned over to the Nazis Yitzhak Wittenberg, the leader of the partisan group that intended to lead an armed rebellion against the Germans and to save the lives of the Jews, including that of Gens himself. In *Underground* the dramatist portrays Doctor Lishafsky, a Jewish doctor who, despite the suffering that he witnesses in the hospital, sells medical drugs, intended for patients, for personal profit. Sobol, furthermore, dramatizes Jewish brutality onstage, such as the murder of the Hasid by Jewish smugglers in *Ghetto* as well as the brutality of the Jewish ghetto police in the same play. In his introduction to *Israeli Holocaust Drama,* Michael Taub attributes the shift in drama of the Shoah, embodied by Sobol's triptych, to the wars fought in the Middle East (the Six-Day War in 1967, Yom Kippur War in 1973, and Lebanon War in 1982), as well as the Jewish occupation of the West Bank and Gaza. Taub argues that during these situations Jews came to be in control of another group of people: "Consciously or not, this unique situation has, to some extent, led to a reexamination of the Shoah where the victims were, of course, Jews." Freddie Rokem concurs, making a connection between drama of the Shoah and the fighting in the Middle East in his book *Performing History: Theatrical Representations of the Past in Contemporary Theatre.* Rokem claims that in *Ghetto* Sobol implies that to some extent Israeli society has assimilated the violence that Jews experienced at the hands of the Nazis and has employed it to victimize the Palestinians. Such a theory is, of course, controversial. Nonetheless people who disapprove of this implication still acknowledge Sobol's great talent as a playwright.

Joshua Sobol concedes that his plays are controversial, but he insists that he is passing on a legacy. Sobol has always been fascinated by documents and thus conducted much research and interviews in preparation for writing his plays. He realized one day that there was a theater in the Vilna ghetto and managed to locate and interview the director of the Ghetto Theatre, Israel Segal, which led him to further research, in particular the diary of ghetto librarian Herman Kruk, which the playwright read in Yiddish. In an interview Sobol claims that "during the events of the Holocaust, people used to write to express themselves, to look for any form of expression that was available to put their experience into form, which is art. If they did it, we probably should not play the nice souls who are shying away from doing it . . . They are trying to pass a legacy, and if we deny ourselves the freedom to make the legacy ours, we are in a way interrupting that legacy." In the Ghetto Theatre in Vilna, actors, actresses, and playwrights attempted to preserve their culture, which they saw being annihilated by the Nazis; they consequently performed plays for the ghetto inhabitants. Decades later, when Sobol's play opened in Tel Aviv, Israeli actors performed the drama, indicating that the legacy has continued.

—Eric Sterling

See the essays on *Adam, Ghetto,* and *Underground.*

SPERBER, Manès

Nationality: Russian. **Born:** Zablotow, Austria-Hungary, 12 December 1905. **Education:** Studied psychology, Vienna, Austria, 1920s. **Military Service:** Volunteer with the French Army during World War II. **Family:** Married twice; two sons (one from each marriage). **Career:** Immigrated to France, 1934. Teacher and lecturer in Austria and Germany; professor of psychology, University of Berlin, 1927–33; literary director, Calmann-Lévy publishers, Paris, 1936–80. Also contributor to periodicals, including *New York Times Book Review, Encounter,* and *Merkur.* Editor, psychological journal *Zeitschrift für individualpsychologische Pädagogik und Psychohygiene,* until 1933. Member, Communist Party, 1927–37. **Awards:** Remembrance award, World Federation of Bergen-Belsen Associations, 1967, for *. . . Like a Tear in the Sea;* Literature prize, Bavarian Academy of Fine Arts, 1971; Goethe prize, city of Frankfurt am Main, Germany, 1973; Georg Buechner prize, German Academy of Language and Poetry, 1975; Austrian State prize for European literature, 1977; Peace prize, German Booksellers Association, 1983. **Died:** 5 February 1984.

PUBLICATIONS

Collections

Qu'une larme dans l'ocean, translated to French by Sperber and Gidon (novels). 1951; original German edition published as *Win eine Träne im Ozean: Romantrilogie,* 1961; as *Like a Tear in the Ocean,* 1988.
All das Vergangene . . . (biographies). c. 1983.

Novels

Et le buisson devint cendre, translated to French by Sperber and Blanche Gidon. 1949; original German edition published as *Der verbrannte Dornbusch,* 1950; translated as *The Burned Bramble,* 1951; in England as *The Wind and the Flame,* 1951.
Plus profondque l'abime, translated to French by Sperber and Gidon. 1950; as *The Abyss,* 1952; in England as *To Dusty Death,* 1952; original German edition published as *Tiefer als der Abgrund,* 1961.
La Baie perdue (Victi vincendi), translated to French by Sperber and Gidon. 1952; as *Journey without End,* 1954; original German edition published as *Die verlorene Bucht,* 1955; translated in England as *The Lost Bay,* 1956.
Wolyna. 1984.
Der schwarze Zaun [The Black Fence]. 1986.

Other

Alfred Adler: Der Mensch und sein Lehre [Alfred Adler: The Man and His Teaching]. 1926.
Zur Analyse der Tyrannis; Das Unglueck, begabt zu sein: Zwei sozialpsychologische Essays. 1938.
Le Talon d'Achille: Essais (essays). 1957; as *The Achilles Heel,* 1959.
Zur taeglichen Weltgeschichte (essays and lectures). 1967; as *Essays zur taeglichen Weltgeschichte,* c. 1981.
Man and His Deeds (essay selections in English). 1970.
Alfred Adler; oder, Das Elend der Psychologie. 1970; as *Masks of Loneliness: Alfred Adler in Perspective,* 1974.
Wir und Dostojewskij: Eine Debatte mit Heinrich Boell, Siegfried Lenz, Andre Malraux, Hans Erich Nossack, gefuehrt von Manes Sperber. 1972.
Leben in dieser Zeit: Sieben Fragen zur Gewalt. 1972.
Die Wassertraeger Gottes: All das Vergangene . . . (biographies). 1974; as *God's Water Carriers,* 1987.
Die vergebliche Warnung: All das Vergangene . . . (biographies). 1975; as *The Unheeded Warning,* 1991.
Bis man mir Scherben auf die Augen legt: All das Vergangene . . . (biographies). c. 1977; as *Until My Eyes Are Closed with Shards,* 1994.
Geist und Ungeist in Wien, with others (essays and lectures). 1978.

Individuum und Gemeinschaft: Versuch einer sozialen Charakterologie. 1978.
Churban; oder, Die unfassbare Gewissheit: Essays. 1979.
Nur eine Bruecke zwischen Gestern und Morgen. 1980.
Die Wirklichkeit in der Literatur des 20 Jahrhunderts; Der Freiheitsgedanke in der europaeischen Literatur: Zwei Vortraege (essays and lectures). c. 1983.
Ansprachen aus Anlass der Verleihung des Friedenspreises des Deutschen Buchhandels. 1983.
Ein politisches Leben: Gespraeche mit Leonhard Reinisch (conversations originally recorded for radio). c. 1984.
Geteilte Einsamkeit: Der Autor und sein Leser. 1985.
Sein letztes Jahr. 1985.

*

Critical Studies: *Pan und Apoll: Alfred Adler's Individualpsychologie, erste Uberwindung Sigmund Freuds; Franz Kreuzer im Gespraech mit Alexandra Adler, Manes Sperber, und Walter Toman* by Franz Kreuzer, 1984; *Manes Sperber zur Einführung* by Alfred Paffenholz, 1984.

* * *

Manès Sperber was an Austrian psychologist, author, essayist, translator, and political activist. His major work of fiction is the trilogy *Like a Tear in the Ocean* (1988). Originally published in his own French translation in 1951, it addresses the manner in which the spread of Fascism intersected with the exposure of the dark underbelly of Soviet Communism to sabotage and betray the hopes and philosophical beliefs of a whole generation of committed and humanitarian leftist intellectuals.

Sperber was born in 1905 in Zablotow, a Jewish shtetl in the eastern reaches of Austrian-occupied Poland. It was permeated by Hasidic mysticism, but like many similar communities, it was on that crossroads of East European cultures that also gave rise to the likes of Marc Chagal, Sholem Aleichem, and Bruno Szulc. During World War I Sperber's family sought refuge in Vienna. He felt uprooted and disenfranchised; he had become involved with a Zionist group but by 1920 formally broke with both Zionism and his faith. He was searching for something that held the promise of overcoming the poverty, suffering, and destitution he had seen while growing up and now again in Vienna. Despite giving up the formal aspects of his background, he retained its messianic thrust throughout his life.

In 1921 he was, as he put it, "discovered" by the leading psychologist Alfred Adler, under whom he then studied and whose theories of individual psychology he actively disseminated as his leading associate. He believed that Adler's theories, carried into practice, could lead to a significant improvement in the conditions of individuals and communities.

Sperber had earlier become a highly placed member of the Communist Party in Germany. His radical political ideas led to his eventual break with Adler although he never entirely abandoned his principles. In 1934 he was arrested by the Nazis and tortured, but friends and family were able to arrange his release. He quickly immigrated to France via Yugoslavia. In Yugoslavia he had worked with the Communist resistance, while in France he lectured and worked as a psychologist and as an organizer for the Communist Party. He became frustrated, however, with its rigidity and increasingly sinister tendencies, and he left it for good in 1937. The final though not the sole impetus for his decision came from the infamous purges and show trials of that year. He never again joined any political organization, and his frustrations with all such organizations plays a large role in the trilogy.

Before the outbreak of the war Sperber was active in anti-Fascist activities, primarily writing and lecturing, and working for a French publisher. After serving in the disastrous campaign of 1939, he relocated to the south of France, where he began work on the first volume of the trilogy. After a period of exile in Switzerland, he returned to France, and from 1946, with the assistance of André Malraux, he found work with a major publishing house, becoming head of its foreign language division. This allowed him time to work on his own writing and facilitated the publication of his work. He only published one other strictly literary work, *Der schwarze Zaun* ["The Black Fence"], which came out posthumously in 1986 and was not very successful. His other writings include three volumes of autobiography, which are closely connected with the thematic material of his fiction, as well as collections of essays on political and social questions. He was awarded a number of important literary and other prizes, including, shortly before his death, the prestigious Peace Prize of the German Book Trade Association.

Although the trilogy follows the spread of Fascism chronologically, and the shadow of the Holocaust falls on virtually every page, its specific events and details are not the raw material that make up most Holocaust literature. They are there, but for the most part he does not dwell on them. What is unique in Sperber's writing, as in his life, is how he interrogates the question of how, faced with unimaginable but very real evil, one can justify resistance. He rejects pacifism and nonresistance, no matter how enlightened, and essentially all competing ideologies, especially Communism. In the end he offers only a fragile belief in the inherent value of humanity and the genuine possibility of goodness.

His literary achievements have been assessed unevenly, and in general he is not viewed as a great writer. On the other hand, his work was highly valued by many of the outstanding intellectuals who were his contemporaries. He has often been compared with Arthur Koestler, although some feel he falls short of that comparison. On the other hand, Koestler spoke highly of his work, and the second volume of the trilogy is

dedicated to him. Among those who were most enthusiastic about Sperber's work are Upton Sinclair and André Malraux.

—Allan Reid

See the essay on *Like a Tear in the Ocean.*

SPIEGELMAN, Art

Pseudonyms: Joe Cutrate; Skeeter Grant; Al Flooglebuckle. **Nationality:** American (originally Swedish: immigrated to the United States, 1951). **Born:** Stockholm, 15 February 1948. **Education:** New York High School of Art and Design; studied art and philosophy, Harpur College (State University of New York at Binghamton), 1965–68. **Family:** Married Françoise Mouly in 1977; one daughter and one son. **Career:** Creative consultant, artist, designer, editor, and writer for novelty packaging and bubble gum cards and stickers, Topps Chewing Gum, Inc., 1966–88; editor, *Douglas Comix,* 1972; instructor in studio class on comics, San Francisco Academy of Art, 1974–75; editor, with Bill Griffith, and contributor, *Arcade, The Comics Revue,* 1975–76; instructor in history and aesthetics of comics, New York School of Visual Arts, 1979–87. Since 1980 founding editor, with Françoise Mouly, *Raw* (graphic magazine), and since 1991 contributing artist and editor, *New Yorker.* **Awards:** Playboy editorial award for best comic strip and Yellow Kid award for best comic strip author (Italy), both in 1982; Print magazine regional design award, 1983, 1984, 1985; Joel M. Cavior award for Jewish writing, 1986, for *Maus—A Survivor's Tale: My Father Bleeds History;* San Diego Comics Convention Inkpot award and Stripschappening award for best foreign comics album (Netherlands), both in 1987; Before Columbus Foundation award, Los Angeles Times book prize, National Book Critics Circle award, and Pulitzer prize, all in 1992, for *Maus II—A Survivor's Tale: And Here My Troubles Began;* Alpha Art award (Angoulerne, France), 1993; Guggenheim fellowship; Jewish Culture award, 1996. D.H.L.: State University of New York, Binghamton, 1995. **Address:** Office: Raw Books & Graphics, 27 Greene Street, New York, New York 10013–2537, U.S.A. **Agents:** Wylie, Aitken & Stone, 250 West 57th Street, Ste. 2106, New York, New York 10107, U.S.A.; Deborah Karl, 52 West Clinton Avenue, Irvington, New York 10533, U.S.A.

PUBLICATIONS

Comics

The Complete Mr. Infinity. 1970.
The Viper Vicar of Vice, Villainy, and Vickedness. 1972.
Zip-a-Tune and More Melodies. 1972.
Ace Hole, Midge Detective. 1974.
Language of Comics. 1974.

Breakdowns; From Maus to Now: An Anthology of Strips.
  1977.
Every Day Has Its Dog. 1979.
Work and Turn. 1979.
Two-Fisted Painters Action Adventure. 1980.
Maus—A Survivor's Tale. 1986; as *Maus I—A Survivor's
  Tale: My Father Bleeds History,* 1991; with *Maus II—A
  Survivor's Tale: And Here My Troubles Began,* in *Maus—
  A Survivor's Tale,* 1997.
Maus II—A Survivor's Tale: And Here My Troubles Began.
  1991; with *Maus I—A Survivor's Tale: My Father Bleeds
  History,* in *Maus—A Survivor's Tale,* 1997.
*Comix, Essays, Graphics and Scraps: From Maus to Now to
  Maus to Now* (exhibition catalog). 1999.
Jack Cole and Plastic Man: Forms Stretched to Their Limits,
  with Chip Kidd. 2001.

Other

Open Me, I'm a Dog (for children). 1997.

Editor, with Bob Schneider, *Whole Grains: A Book of Quota-
  tions.* 1972.
Editor, *Raw: The Graphic Aspirin for War Fever,* by Françoise
  Mouly. 1986.
Editor, with Françoise Mouly, *X,* by Sue Coe. 1986.
Editor, with Mouly, *Read Yourself Raw: Comix Anthology for
  Damned Intellectuals* (selections from the first three issues
  of the magazine). 1987.
Editor, with Mouly, *Agony,* by Mark Beyer. 1987.
Editor, with Mouly, *Jimbo: Adventures in Paradise,* by Gary
  Panter. 1988.
Editor, with Mouly, *Raw: Open Wounds from the Cutting
  Edge of Commix, V. 2, No. 1.* 1989.
Editor, with Mouly, *Raw: Required Reading for the Post-
  Literate, V. 2, No. 2.* 1990.
Editor, with R. Sikoryak and Mouly, *Warts and All,* by Drew
  Friedman and Josh Alan Friedman. 1990.
Editor, with Mouly, *Raw: High Culture for Low Brows, V. 2,
  No. 3.* 1991.
Editor, with R. Sikoryak, *Skin Deep: Tales of Doomed Romance,*
  by Charles Burns. 1992.
Editor, with R. Sikoryak, *The Narrative Corpse: A Chain-
  Story by 69 Artists.* 1995.
Editor, with Mouly, *Little Lit: Folklore & Fairytale Funnies*
  (for children). 2000.
Editor, with Mouly, *Little Lit: Strange Stories for Strange Kids*
  (for children). 2001.

*

CD-ROM Adaptation: *The Complete Maus,* 1994, from
Maus I and *II.*

Critical Studies: *Comic Books As History: The Narrative Art
of Jack Jackson, Art Spiegelman, and Harvey Pekar* by Joseph

Witek, 1989; "'We Were Talking Jewish': Art Spiegelman's
Maus As 'Holocaust' Production" by Michael Rothberg, in
Contemporary Literature, 35(4), Winter 1994, pp. 661–87;
"The Shoah Goes On and On: Remembrance and Representa-
tion in Art Spiegelman's *Maus*" by Michael E. Staub, in
MELUS, 20, Fall 1995, pp. 33–46; "The Language of Sur-
vival: English As Metaphor in Spiegelman's *Maus*" by Alan
Rosen, in *Prooftexts,* 15(3), September 1995, pp. 249–62;
"Art Spiegelman's *Maus:* Graphic Art and the Holocaust" by
Thomas Doherty, in *American Literature,* 68(1), March 1996,
pp. 69–84; "The Holocaust As Vicarious Past: Art Spiegelman's
Maus and the Afterimages of History" by James E. Young, in
Critical Inquiry, 24(3), Spring 1998, pp. 666–99; "The
Orphaned Voice in Art Spiegelman's Maus I & II" by Hamida
Bosmajian, in *Literature and Psychology,* 44(1–2), 1998, pp.
1–22; *Holocaust Literature: Schulz, Levi, Spiegelman and the
Memory of the Offence* by Gillian Banner, 2000; "*Maus,*
Holocaust, and History: Redrawing the Frame" by Barry
Laga, in *Arizona Quarterly,* 57(1), Spring 2001, pp. 61–90.

* * *

Art Spiegelman, best known as the author of *Maus* and a
regular contributor of cover images to the *New Yorker,* has
been involved in drawing serious comics since the late 1960s.
He has described his own artistic development as follows:
"*Maus* . . . I was doing with the understanding that it would be
seen in one way or another. But nevertheless it was something
born out of trying to meet two needs at once. One, tell a story. It
finally dawned on me after being a cartoonist for a good twenty
years or more that what people wanted out of comics was a
story, so I had to find a story worth telling, because the kind of
comics I'd been working on up to the moment I started *Maus*
were involved in kind of taking narratives apart and messing
with them, rather than telling them. So it was fulfilling that
need. On the other hand, it also filled the more central need for
me of trying to make sense of my own personal past and of
history as I intersected with it."

Spiegelman's rise from an obscure comics artist drawing
for underground publications to a Pulitzer Prize-winning author parallels the increasing seriousness with which comics as
a genre have been approached critically. While he had been
drawing comics from an early age and had even printed and
distributed them in high school, Spiegelman's oeuvre did not
find a wider readership until he, together with his wife,
Françoise Mouly, began publishing *Raw* in 1980. *Raw,* published annually, provided a forum for comics artists to publish
serious material that was intended for an adult audience; that it
also maintained an ironic edge, however, is evident from the
third issue's title, *High Culture for Low-Brows.*

It was in *Raw* that Spiegelman's greatest success to that
point, *Maus,* was published serially. In 1986 Pantheon published *Maus—A Survivor's Tale* in book format; it was later
followed by a second part, *Maus II—A Survivor's Tale: And
Here My Troubles Began* (1991). Reflecting the uncertainty

concerning the genre under which to classify a comics novel about the Holocaust, the *New York Times* initially assigned it to its fiction best-seller list, only to reassign it to nonfiction once Spiegelman wrote a letter of protest. Despite these initial confusions, *Maus* has been routinely hailed as one of the most brilliant contributions to Holocaust literature and has become a staple of college courses on the Holocaust.

Maus, implicitly or explicitly, addresses issues such as the proper form (if any) of fictional (or semifictional) responses to the Holocaust; the relationship between testimonial literature and fictional text; the role of survivors' children in transmitting knowledge about the horrors of the Holocaust; the production of meaning about a historical event at a generation's remove; the meaning of the commercial success of a book describing and depicting the Holocaust; the possibility of combining personal narrative with historiography; and the question of how to interpret the Shoah after the survivors' generation will have passed away.

In *Maus,* Spiegelman has written a text that is as much about the quandaries and difficulties associated with producing meaning about the Holocaust as it is about the Holocaust itself. *Maus* stands as a metonymic reminder of the desire to tell a story and the simultaneous inability to do so due to the problems associated with representing the Holocaust adequately.

Spiegelman (together with Mouly) has begun what appears to be a *Little Lit* series: *Little Lit: Folklore & Fairytale Funnies* (2000) combines contributions from a number of renowned comics artists and continues Spiegelman's interest in bringing a serious edge to comics, this time to an audience that too often is patronized by children's books. *Little Lit: Strange Stories for Strange Kids* (2001) promises more of the trademark Spiegelman strategy of blurring generic boundaries and producing work that elevates comics into the status of work of art.

—Stefan Gunther

See the essay on *Maus—A Survivor's Tale.*

STEINER, George A(lbert)

Nationality: American (originally French: immigrated to the United States, 1940, granted U.S. citizenship, 1944). **Born:** Paris, 23 April 1929. **Education:** University of Chicago, B.A. 1948; Harvard University, Cambridge, Massachusetts, M.A. 1950; Balliol College, Oxford (Rhodes scholar), Ph.D. in English literature 1955. **Family:** Married Zara Alice Shakow in 1955; one son and one daughter. **Career:** Member of editorial staff, *Economist,* London, 1952–56; fellow, Institute for Advanced Study, Princeton University, 1956–58; Gauss Lecturer, Cambridge University, England, 1959–60; founding fellow, 1961–69, and since 1969 extraordinary fellow, Churchill College, Cambridge University; professor of English and comparative literature, University of Geneva, Switzerland, 1974–1994. Visiting professor, New York University, 1966–67, and University of California, 1973–74; Maurice lecturer, University of London, 1984; Leslie Stephen lecturer, Cambridge University, 1985; W.P. Ker lecturer, University of Glasgow, 1986; visiting professor, College of France, 1992; First Lord Weidenfeld professor of comparative literature, Oxford University, 1994–95; Charles Eliot Norton Professor of Poetry, Harvard University, 2001–02. **Awards:** Bell prize (Harvard), 1950; Fulbright professorship, 1958–59; O. Henry short story prize, 1959; National Institute of Arts and Letters Morton Dauwen Zabel award (United States), 1970; Guggenheim fellowship, 1971–72; Cortina Ulisse prize, 1972; Remembrance award, 1974, for *Language and Silence;* Macmillan Silver Pen award, 1992, for *Proofs and Three Parables;* PEN Macmillan fiction prize, 1993; Truman Capote Lifetime Achievement award, 1998. Honorary doctorates: University of East Anglia, 1976; Lovain, 1980; Mount Holyoke, 1983; Bristol, 1989; Glasgow, 1990; Liege, 1990; Ulster, 1993; Durham, 1995. Fellow: Royal Society of Literature; British Academy. King Albert Medal, Royal Belgian Academy; Chevalier, Legion d'Honneur (France), 1984; Commander, Order of Arts and Letters (France), 2001. **Member:** American Academy of Arts and Sciences (honorary).

PUBLICATIONS

Novel

The Portage to San Cristóbal of A.H. 1981. In *Kenyon Review,* 1979.

Short Stories

Anno Domini: Three Stories. 1964.
Proofs and Three Parables. 1992.
The Deeps of the Sea (includes *The Portage to San Cristóbal of A.H.*). 1996.

Play

The Portage to San Cristóbal of A.H., adaptation of his own novel (produced 1982).

Other

Tolstoy or Dostoevsky: An Essay in the Old Criticism. 1958.
The Death of Tragedy. 1960.
Language and Silence: Essays on Language, Literature, and the Inhuman. 1967.
Extraterritorial: Papers on Literature and the Language Revolution. 1971.
In Bluebeard's Castle: Some Notes toward the Redefinition of Culture. 1971.

Fields of Force: Fischer and Spassky in Reykjavik. 1973; as
    The Sporting Scene: White Knights in Reykjavik, 1973.
Nostalgia for the Absolute. 1974.
After Babel: Aspects of Language and Translation. 1975.
The Uncommon Reader. 1978.
On Difficulty and Other Essays. 1978.
Martin Heidegger. 1978.
George Steiner: A Reader (selections). 1984.
*Antigones: How the Antigone Legend Has Endured in Western
    Literature, Art, and Thought.* 1984.
Real Presences: Is There Anything in What We Say? 1989.
*What Is Comparative Literature?: An Inaugural Lecture Deliv-
    ered before the University of Oxford on 11 October 1994.*
    1995.
No Passion Spent: Essays 1978–1995. 1996.
Barbarie de l ignorance: Juste l ombre d un certain ennui, with
    Antoine Spire. 1998.
Errata: An Examined Life (autobiography). 1998.
Ce qui me hante, with Antoine Spire. 1999.
Grammars of Creation. 2001.

Editor, with Robert Fagles, *Homer: A Collection of Critical
    Essays.* 1962.
Editor, *The Penguin Book of Modern Verse Translation.* 1966;
    as *Poem into Poem: World Poetry in Modern Verse Trans-
    lation,* 1970.
Editor, with Aminadav Dykman, *Homer in English.* 1996.

*

Film Adaptation: *The Tongues of Man* (television documentary), 1977, from *After Babel.*

Critical Studies: ''Steiner's Holocaust: Politics and Theology'' by Robert Boyers, in *Salmagundi,* 66, Winter/Spring
1985, pp. 26–49; ''George Steiner: On Culture and on Hitler''
by Bernard Bergonzi, in his *The Myth of Modernism and
Twentieth Century Literature,* 1986; ''George Steiner's *Por-
tage:* Holocaust Novel or Thriller?'' by Michael Popkin, in
Apocalyptic Visions Past and Present, edited by JoAnn James
and William J. Cloonan, 1988; ''Interrogation at the Borders:
George Steiner and the Trope of Translation'' by Ronald A.
Sharp, in *New Literary History,* 21(1), Autumn 1989, pp.
133–62; ''Judaism and the Rhetoric of Authority: George
Steiner's Textual Homeland'' by Norman Finkelstein, in his
The Ritual of New Creation, 1992; ''The Mind of a Critical
Moralist: Steiner as Jew'' by Edith Wyschogrod, in *New
England Review,* 15, Spring 1993, pp. 168–88; *Reading George
Steiner,* edited by Nathan A. Scott and Ronald A. Sharp, 1994;
''The Struggle between Text and Land in Contemporary
Jewry: Reflections on George Steiner's Our Homeland, the
Text'' by Dow Marmur, in *History of European Ideas,* 20(4–6),
February, 1995, pp. 807–13; ''The Holocaust, George Steiner,
and Tragic Discourse'' by Joan Peterson, in *Rendezvous,*
34(1), Fall 1999, pp. 93–105; ''Between Repulsion and Attrac-
tion: George Steiner's Post-Holocaust Fiction'' by Bryan

Cheyette, in *Jewish Social Studies,* 5(3), Spring/Summer 1999,
pp. 67–81.

* * *

Born in 1929, George Steiner grew up in Paris and New
York City. His father was a Czech Jew who emerged from
humble circumstances to achieve considerable success as an
investment banker, and his mother was Viennese. Steiner's
education in languages began early. As he himself put it in his
autobiography, *Errata,* ''My mother, so Viennese, habitually
began a sentence in one language and ended it in another. She
seemed unaware of the dazzling modulations and shifts in
intent this produced.'' His formal schooling began at a French
lycée in New York, took him briefly to the University of
Chicago, and concluded at Oxford University, where he received a Ph.D. in English literature. For many years Steiner has
taught literature at both Cambridge University and the University of Geneva.

While still in his mid thirties, Steiner became one of the
West's most formidable literary critics. There are a number of
reasons for his swift rise. Steiner's learning is vast, but his
sentences are short. Even when he takes on the most recondite
themes, for example, the motif of Antigone in world literature,
theories of translation from antiquity to the present, or the
differences between Tolstoy and Dostoyevsky, he writes with
compelling lucidity. Since the 1950s he has been a major
presence in popular intellectual forums, such as the *Times
Literary Supplement.* In fact, several of Steiner's most widely
read books consist of essays he wrote for nonacademic publications. Furthermore, he has produced works of fiction. Like
the German romantics, Steiner regards performance as the
deepest form of criticism.

But Steiner is more closely allied with a more immediate
intellectual tradition, what he calls ''central European humanism,'' an amalgam of classical humanism and German dialectics. Steiner has suggested—albeit obliquely—that he inherited it from his father, whose passion was letters even if his
profession was finance. And when he describes central European humanism, Steiner clearly could be sketching the main
features in a self-portrait. He has written, ''It has its markers: a
sound knowledge of Goethe, and the realization that Goethe is
one of the few genuine examples of a human being for whom
civilization was a homeland. An uneasy, yet profound admiration of Wagner. Intimacy with Heine and Stendhal, with
Lessing, Voltaire, and Ibsen. Men of that background tend to
use Greek poetry, and particularly Homer, as a tuning-fork of
the ideal. They regard Shakespeare as, in some essential way, a
European, nearly a continental possession. They read Karl
Kraus.'' The connection with Kraus, turn-of-the-century Vienna's most prominent cultural critic, is significant. Steiner
shares Kraus's moral urgency. He also often adverts to Kraus's
fascination with language, to which he feels ''indebted.'' The
same passion animates Steiner's own criticism.

Of course, Steiner belongs to a later generation, to a generation that came of age shortly after World War II. He is relentlessly candid about how history weighs on his belief in the creative miracle of language. Directly after claiming that his breakthrough work, *Language and Silence* (1967), is about the "life of language," Steiner poses the harrowing question "What are the relations of language to the murderous falsehoods it has been made to articulate in certain totalitarian regimes?" Elsewhere in the same preface he formulates his challenge even more poignantly: "We come after. We know now that a man can read Goethe or Rilke in the evening, that he can play Bach and Schubert, and go to his day's work at Auschwitz in the morning. To say that he has read them without understanding or that his ear is gross, is cant. In what way does this knowledge bear on literature and society, on the hope, that has grown almost axiomatic from the time of Plato to that of Matthew Arnold, that culture is a humanizing force, that the energies of the spirit are transferable to those of conduct?" Above all, Steiner's cultural importance derives from the fact that he has brought his enormous erudition and rare perspicacity and articulateness to bear on this problem, while addressing it more insistently than anyone else. Not only is it the subject of *Language and Silence,* his most successful book of criticism, but the shadow cast on language by the Holocaust is one of the main themes in Steiner's most influential foray into the writing of fiction, *The Portage to San Cristóbal of A.H.*

—Paul Reitter

See the essay on *The Portage to San Cristóbal of A.H.*

STEINER, Jean-François

Nationality: French. **Born:** 1938.

PUBLICATION

Novel

Treblinka. 1966; translated as *Treblinka,* 1967.

*

Critical Study: "Jean-Francois Steiner's *Treblinka:* Reading Fiction and Fact" by David J. Bond, in *Papers on Language and Literature,* 26(3), Summer 1990, pp. 370–78.

*   *   *

Jean-François Steiner was born in 1938 of a Jewish father who was killed at Treblinka and a Catholic mother. According to **George Steiner,** it was a trip to Israel and the malaise felt by younger Jews throughout the Adolf Eichmann trial about the passivity of Holocaust victims that prompted Jean-François Steiner to interview the handful of survivors of Treblinka and to write an account of the revolt in the extermination camp. His book *Treblinka* was first published in France in 1966, and Helen Weaver's English translation was published the following year.

Treblinka proved to be a controversial best-seller. Praised in a preface by Simone de Beauvoir as a vindication of Jewish courage, it was bitterly attacked by others, including **David Rousset** and Léon Poliakov, for its alleged inaccuracies, racism, and general thesis of Jewish passivity. **Richard Glazar**, a survivor of Treblinka, wrote an open letter to Steiner in which he expressed the "profound dismay felt by all the survivors at the politically or personally motivated misrepresentations of real events and real people, most of them now dead and unable to defend themselves." The survivors were particularly incensed by what was said to be Steiner's false claim that a *kapo* named Kurland personally administered fatal injections to those of the elderly and infirm who were incapable of walking to the gas chambers.

Neal Ascherson has criticized Steiner's view of the SS, referred to throughout *Treblinka* as "the Technicians." Ascherson has disputed the image of SS members as intellectual and coolheaded characters and has objected to what he describes as Steiner's "easy equation of their disgusting ingenuities with the 'de-humanizing efficiency' of modern factory practice." Terrence Des Pres, while acknowledging the technical expertise of the German higher officials who designed and ran the death camps but who were not directly involved in their day-to-day operations, believes that we now know there to have been a great deal of sloppiness, trial and error, and heavy drinking among the SS personnel, which suggests that they were not as fully in command as they were thought to be.

Ascherson has praised Steiner for his description of the state of mind of the Jews within the camp and for the way he traced their recovery from total enslavement toward the will to resist and save themselves. Sidra DeKoven Ezrahi, on the contrary, sees Steiner's depiction of the regeneration of the Jewish slave prisoners as an ideological bias that led him to distort the history of the camp: "In *Treblinka,* [Steiner] tailors the evidence of a revolt in a death camp to a rigid procrustean concept of Jewish history." Steiner's ideological commitment, she asserts, "directs the organization of his material; he attempts to trace a progressive emergence out of slavery to a point where the Jews are seen as masters of their own fate."

Steiner and his book continue to be controversial and are the target of a number of revisionist websites.

—Alan Polak

See the essay on *Treblinka.*

STIFFEL, Frank

Nationality: American (originally Polish: immigrated to the United States, 1950, granted U.S. citizenship, 1955). **Born:** Franz Josef Stifel, Boryslaw, 23 November 1916. **Education:** Studied medicine, University of Naples, Italy, 1936–37, University of Lieges, Belgium, 1937, University of Brussels, Belgium, 1938, and University of Nancy, France, 1939; studied French philology, University of Ivan Franko, Lwów, 1939–41; City College of New York, 1953–58, B.A. in romance languages 1958 (Phi Beta Kappa); advanced studies in French philology, Columbia University, New York, 1959–60; New York University, 1970–73, M.A. in occupational counseling 1973. **Family:** Married Ione Sani in 1946; one daughter. **Career:** Prisoner, Treblinka and Auschwitz, during World War II. Worked for Velpost Import/Export, Rome, Italy, 1946–47; agriculture secretary, American ORT, Rome, 1947–50; laborer and shipping manager, Salton Manufacturing, Inc., New York, 1950–55; import manager, J.H. Frankenberg, New York, 1955–58; president, Wallpaper Originals, New York, 1958–68; counselor, New York State Department of Labor, 1968–83. **Award:** Editors book award, 1983, for *The Tale of the Ring: A Kaddish.*

PUBLICATIONS

Memoirs

The Tale of the Ring: A Kaddish. 1984.
The Oxymoron Factor: Franek: Stranger in My Land. 2001.
*The Oxymoron Factor: The Tale of the Ring: A Kaddish for
  Civilization.* 2001.

*

Critical Study: *Passages of Annihilation: Holocaust Survivors' Autobiographies As Midrash* (dissertation) by Deborah Lee Ames, Oklahoma State University, 1999.

* * *

Frank Stiffel was born in 1916 in Boryslaw, then a city in the Austro-Hungarian Empire's sub-Carpathian region. In 1918, by an edict of the Versailles Treaty, the new Poland was established, and Boryslaw, Drohobycz, and other significant oil centers of the previous Galacia became a part of Malopolska, a southeastern province of Poland. When he was four, Stiffel moved with his parents and three brothers to Lwów (now Lvov, Ukraine), the capital city of Malopolska. There he attended school, studying humanities, history, Latin, and Ancient Greek. He passed his Matura examination in May 1935 and tried to attend the medical school in Lwów but was rejected

because of a quota on the acceptance of Jews. He subsequently enrolled in universities in Belgium, France, and Italy. He was studying to be a physician in Naples when the Italian fascist government issued anti-Semitic decrees. Stiffel decided to return to Poland rather than have his passport stamped "Ebreo," for Hebrew. At the end of June 1939, he returned to Poland, hoping to become a soldier in his country's fight against the Nazi invaders.

Three weeks after the German invasion of Poland in September 1939, Germany occupied the western part of the country, and the Soviet Union occupied the eastern part. During the year and half of German rule, Stiffel studied French philology at the University of Lwów. In June 1941 Germany attacked the Soviet Union. Anti-Jewish laws were introduced, and in March 1942 Stiffel, his parents, his eldest brother, and his sister-in-law sought refuge in the Warsaw Ghetto. On 4 September 1942, he and his family were deported to the death camp Treblinka, where one day after their arrival Stiffel's parents and sister-in-law were murdered in a gas chamber. Stiffel and his brother were put on a work detail, sorting the clothes of those who perished in the gas chambers. Seven days after their arrival at the camp, Stiffel and his brother escaped Treblinka by hiding in the bundles of clothes they sorted and riding out on a railway car. It was in Warsaw, after Treblinka, that Stiffel started keeping a notebook of wartime recollections, keeping the book secret by stowing it under the beams of a roof where he was hiding.

In Warsaw Stiffel and his brother aided Jews in illegal immigration to Palestine. Stiffel was arrested in January 1943. He was denounced by the Gestapo, arrested, and sentenced to death, a verdict that was later changed to imprisonment in the concentration camp Auschwitz. In his memoir, *The Tale of the Ring: A Kaddish,* Stiffel compares the organization of Auschwitz to a small corrupt city. He was assigned to a lumber camp outside of Auschwitz where killings were a daily occurrence. Because he had a degree as a doctor, he was later assigned to a medical unit at the camp.

Stiffel lived to see the collapse of Hitler's empire. The first thing he did after being liberated in 1945 was to begin writing his book. He left Poland for Italy, married, had a child, and, in May 1950, moved to New York City. While working to build a new life in America, Stiffel attended the City College of New York and graduated in 1958. He completed his M.A. from New York University in 1973. He eventually worked as a counselor for the New York State Department of Labor. He continued to work on his Holocaust remembrances, translating them from Polish to English, throughout his working years. In 1983 his Holocaust memoir won the Editors Book award and was published in subsequent years by numerous presses.

—Martha Sutro

See the essay on *The Tale of the Ring: A Kaddish.*

STOLLMAN, Aryeh Lev

Nationality: American. **Born:** Windsor, Ontario, Canada, 1954. **Education:** Studied at a rabbinical college in Cleveland, Ohio; studied the Talmud and medicine at Yeshiva University, New York; Albert Einstein Medical School, New York; fellowship in neuroradiology, New York University. **Career:** Neuroradiologist, Mount Sinai Medical Center, New York. **Awards:** Lambda literary award for gay men's fiction, 1998, and Wilbur award, both for *The Far Euphrates.*

PUBLICATIONS

Novels

The Far Euphrates. 1997.
The Illuminated Soul. 2002.

*

Critical Study: "The Great Miracle" by Laura Furman, in *Saturday Night,* 112(7), September 1997, p. 119–20.

* * *

Aryeh Lev Stollman, who was born in 1954 in Canada, typifies the new wave of religiously informed and Israel-inflected Jewish American/Jewish Canadian writers. Unlike Jewish writers of previous generations, from Henry Roth through **Philip Roth**, whose major subject was the immigrant experience and who, with a few exceptions, wrote outside any particular knowledge of or commitment to ritual observance and with at best only a fleeting interest in Zionism or the state of Israel, Stollman's novel, *The Far Euphrates,* and his short stories reverberate with a profoundly educated, cabalistically oriented modern-day Jewish consciousness. This Jewish consciousness is unabashed and takes the form of allusions as unselfconscious as those to science and classical culture, which also permeate his texts. Thus, his short story "Mr. Mitochondria," which, like other of his stories, makes extensive use of Stollman's expertise as a neuroradiologist at the Mount Sinai Medical Center in New York City, takes place in Beersheba, while "The Dialogues of Time and Entropy," in which biology and physics constitute nothing less than the philosophical weave of the story itself, is set in part in an Israeli settlement town. The story "The Adornment of Days," on the other hand, which is set in Jerusalem, has as much to do with the history of music as with Jewish mysticism, less well known Jewish holidays such as Tishah-b'Ab, the false messiah Shabbetai Tzevi, and the Shechinah. Punctuated by German, Yiddish, and Hebrew words, fragments of prayers and biblical texts, and figures from an esoteric past, the stories feel no obligation to clarify or translate every one of their obscure allusions, as if the work of understanding the Jewish past might be as legitimate an undertaking for a reader of contemporary writing as any other aspect of literary interpretation.

Indeed, Stollman's fiction may be understood as something of an act of recovery, restoring the Jewish past that has been snatched not only from Jewish but also from world culture. Although the short stories deal little if at all with the Holocaust—this is the province of the novel *The Far Euphrates,* winner of the Wilbur Award and Lambda Literary Award and chosen as a notable book by the American Library Association and recommended as a book of the year by the *Los Angeles Times*—many of them reverberate with the devastation of European Jewry and its world. Although the fiction is highly intellectual, it is also powerfully affective, haunted by death and loss that often take up residence in the story as a ghostly presence neither to be dismissed nor comprehended. Thus, in "Mr. Mitochondria" the child protagonist, through whose consciousness the story gets its focus, is actually a double consciousness, representing both himself and his deceased brother, who speaks through the living brother's mouth in much the way the Holocaust survivor Hannalore in *The Far Euphrates* speaks through the voice of the young narrator-protagonist of that work. The parents' migration from Stollman's own birthplace, Canada, to Israel, where, like another character in *The Far Euphrates*, they plant the shrubs and trees that are their "special babies," becomes then a journey both personal and collective. The family, the people, attempts to transplant itself in the modern ancient homeland only to be once again threatened, and overcome, by devastation and loss and in which the promise of the future cannot but speak in the voice of past torments and horrors.

Yet in that speaking the voice of the past enables the present to happen. "To keep our world alive," says the female protagonist in "The Dialogues of Time and Entropy," "we need, we absolutely must, reduce the entropy within history." The alternative to entropy is time, with all of its unpredictable, even heartrending, transformations. Set against Ahuva's mysticism and belief in miracles in the land of Israel (the name Ahuva means "love" in Hebrew) is the scientific rationalism of the story's narrator, the husband-scientist who, trying to discover a cure for an epidemic of deadly dizziness, in the end succumbs to the disease himself. But the mystical Ahuva survives, "borne up [in her husband's dying vision] at last by waves of miracles and hope," and even if she is temporarily defeated by the political world (her settlement is being dismantled by the government), she continues to "hover" like the Shechinah itself in "The Adornment of Days" and *The Far Euphrates* or like the "green line" in "The Creation of Anat," which represents the same life force of birth and growth as do the plants in "Mr. Mitochondria" and *The Far Euphrates.*

The alternative to such dizziness is the autism of the daughter in "The Dialogues of Time and Entropy." And dizziness itself, from which the protagonist in *The Far Euphrates* also suffers, can represent either death or ascendency. Apparently only faith can separate the one from the other. Stollman's is in that sense a faithful fiction, faithful to the poignancy of the human experience and to the specifically Jewish context of that experience, which is his own particular legacy.

—Emily Budick

See the essay on *The Far Euphrates.*

STYRON, William

Nationality: American. **Born:** Newport News, Virginia, 11 June 1925. **Education:** Davidson College, Davidson, North Carolina, 1942–43; Duke University, Durham, North Carolina, 1943–44, 1945–47, B.A. 1947. **Military Service:** United States Marine Corps, 1943–45, 1951. **Family:** Married Rose Burgunder; three daughters and one son. **Career:** Associate editor, McGraw-Hill, 1947; moved to Paris and helped establish the *Paris Review,* 1952; writer-in-residence, American Academy, Rome, 1952–53. **Awards:** American Academy of Arts and Letters Prix de Rome, 1952, for *Lie Down in Darkness;* Pulitzer prize, 1968, and American Academy of Arts and Letters William Dean Howells medal, 1970, both for *The Confessions of Nat Turner;* American Book Award, 1980, for *Sophie's Choice;* Connecticut Arts award, 1984; Prix Mondial del Duca, 1985; Edward MacDowell medal and Duke University Distinguished Alumni award, both in 1988; Bobst award, 1989; National Magazine award, 1990, for *Darkness Visible;* National Medal of Arts, 1993; National Arts Club medal of honor and Common Wealth award, both in 1995. D.Litt.: Duke University, 1968; Davidson College, 1986. Commandeur, Ordre des Arts et des Lettres (France), 1987; Commandeur Legion d'Honneur (France). Fellow, Silliman College, Yale University, 1964. **Member:** American Academy of Arts and Sciences; American Academy of Arts and Letters.

PUBLICATIONS

Novels

Lie Down in Darkness. 1951.
The Long March. 1952.
Set This House on Fire. 1960.
The Confessions of Nat Turner. 1967.
Sophie's Choice. 1979.
A Tidewater Morning: Three Tales from Youth. 1993.

Other

This Quiet Dust and Other Writings (essays). 1982.
Darkness Visible: A Memoir of Madness. 1990.

*

Film Adaptations: *Sophie's Choice,* 1982.

Bibliography: *William Styron: A Descriptive Bibliography* by James L.W. West III, 1977; *William Styron: An Annotated Bibliography of Criticism* by Philip W. Leon, 1978.

Critical Studies: *William Styron: A Critical Essay* by Robert H. Fossum, 1967; *William Styron* by Cooper R. Mackin, 1969; *Guilt and Redemption in the Novels of William Styron* by Peter Nicholas Corodimas, 1971; *William Styron* by Marc L. Ratner, 1972; *William Styron* by Melvin J. Friedman, 1974; *The Achievement of William Styron,* edited by Robert K. Morris and Irving Malin, 1975; *William Styron: A Reference Guide* by Jackson R. Bryer and Mary Beth Hatem, 1978; *William Styron: An "Unfamous" Great Writer Brings Out a New Novel, Sophie's Choice* by Andrew Fielding, 1979; *Critical Essays on William Styron* by Arthur D. Casciato and James L.W. West III, 1982; *William Styron, or, The Pangs of Mediocrity* by James J. Thompson, 1982; *William Styron* by Judith Ruderman, 1987; *Violence and Compassion in the Novels of William Styron: A Study in Tragic Humanism* by Murthy S. Laxmana, 1988; *William Styron Revisited* by Samuel Coale, 1991; *The Critical Response to William Styron* by Daniel William Ross, 1995; *The Novels of William Styron: From Harmony to History* by Gavin Cologne-Brookes, 1995; *Gynicide: Women in the Novels of William Styron,* by David Hadallar, 1996; *William Styron, A Life* by James L.W. West III, 1998.

*   *   *

William Styron, elder statesman of American letters, has earned a reputation for tackling big events and themes in provocative ways. His first novel, *Lie Down in Darkness,* which came out in 1951 when the author was only 26, introduced the fascination with mental illness, addiction, victimization, guilt, and doom that would characterize Styron's entire canon—the heaviness leavened not only by a sense of humor but also by an affirmation of the redemptive power of love.

Lie Down in Darkness is closely connected to *Sophie's Choice* (1979), Styron's one Holocaust novel. After graduating from Duke University in the late 1940s and setting off for New York City to find his calling as a writer of fiction, Styron worked on a novel about a disturbed and suicidal young woman from Tidewater, Virginia, married to a New York Jew who tries in vain to save her from destruction. Styron put his struggles with that novel to use in the autobiographical *Sophie's Choice,* published 30 years later. In that book the narrator recounts how as a young man he had met a Polish Catholic survivor of Auschwitz in his Brooklyn boarding house and, through their friendship, had gained the recognition of darkness and the power of love that enabled him to go on to write important works of literature—beginning with *Lie Down in Darkness* itself (called, in *Sophie's Choice, Inheritance of Night,* its real-life early title).

In actuality Styron's postwar encounter with this Holocaust survivor was brief and superficial; the story behind her tattooed numbers remained elusive to him until one morning in 1974 when, awakening from a dream about this woman, Styron decided to create an imaginative portrayal of her ordeal. The novel was also stimulated by a memoir of Auschwitz entitled *Five Chimneys,* by survivor **Olga Lengyel,** which he had read at Duke in 1947. Lengyel's story of how she had inadvertently sent her mother and son to the gas chambers provided for Styron a lasting impression of a horrific action that he could adapt for his own literary purposes.

The inspiration that Styron found in large historical events and grand themes had already led to what may be Styron's most famous, some would say infamous, novel *The Confessions of Nat Turner* (1967). Taking on the subject of slavery, Styron crafted a "meditation on history" (as he characterized it in his foreword) about the 1831 slave rebellion fomented by Nat Turner near the Styron home place in Virginia. Although the work won a Pulitzer Prize, Styron not unexpectedly was also lambasted: for writing in the first person as Nat, for inventing situations, and for attributing Nat's actions in large part to sexual frustration. Similarly intrigued by the inhumanity evidenced in the slave societies of the concentration camps, Styron refused to be intimidated by the notion that a Gentile could not, indeed should not, write on the Holocaust, especially if he had no firsthand experience of it and certainly not if his protagonist was not Jewish. Criticism of this novel came from several sources, among them Holocaust survivors and Poles, but it has been tame compared to the furor that arose at the publication of *The Confessions of Nat Turner* at the height of racial tensions in the United States.

Perhaps the criticism has been tempered by the thorough research on the Holocaust that the narrative structure permits *Sophie's Choice* to foreground; among the many formative works that Styron read to prepare him for this novel are **George Steiner**'s *Language and Silence,* Richard Rubenstein's *The Cunning of History,* and the memoirs of Rudolph Höss. He also traveled to Kraków, the childhood home of his Sophie, and to Auschwitz itself; an essay on Auschwitz is included in Styron's 1982 collection of nonfiction prose, *This Quiet Dust.*

By the time he wrote *Sophie's Choice,* Styron—whose childhood in Newport News, Virginia, was largely spent in the company of fellow Protestants—had married a Jew (the poet Rose Burgunder) and formed solid friendships with Jews. Jews play pivotal roles in each of his novels and his play, as outsiders, rebels, and/or moral touchstones. Although Styron's Holocaust novel gives voice to the millions of non-Jews who perished under the Nazi regime, it simultaneously and on several levels underscores the anti-Semitism that led to Hitler's attempts at extermination of the Jewish people. Honored with the American Book Award for Fiction and the subject of

an Academy Award-winning film starring Meryl Streep, *Sophie's Choice,* like all of Styron's works, makes "darkness visible"—to use the title of Styron's 1990 account of his clinical depression—in order that, by confronting the darkest reaches of the human soul and psyche, we might see the imperative for, and the possibilities of, redemption.

—Judith Ruderman

See the essay on *Sophie's Choice.*

SUTZKEVER, Abraham

Nationality: Israeli (originally Russian: immigrated to Palestine, 1947). **Born:** Smorgon, Belorussia, 1913. **Family:** Married; one daughter. **Career:** Lived in Vilna, 1920–43. Member, literary and artistic group Young Vilna, 1930s; member, United Partisans Organization in the Vilna ghetto, early 1940s. Editor, *Di Goldene Keyt* (The Golden Chain), 1949–96. **Awards:** First prize, Vilna Ghetto Writers Union literary contest, 1942; B'nai B'rith literary award, 1979; Israel prize in literature.

PUBLICATIONS

Collections

Burnt Pearls: Ghetto Poems of Abraham Sutzkever. 1981.
A. Sutzkever: Selected Poetry and Prose. 1991.
Laughter beneath the Forest: Poems from Old and Recent Manuscripts. 1996.

Poetry

Lider [Poems]. 1937.
Valdiks [Woodlore]. 1940.
Di Festung [The Fortress]. 1945.
Lider fun geto [Poems of the Ghetto]. 1946.
Geheymshtot [Secret City]. 1948.
Yidishe gas. 1948.
In fayer-vogn. 1952.
Sibir. 1953; as *Siberia: A Poem,* 1961.
Fun drai weltn (De tres mundos). 1953.
Ode tsu der toyb. 1955.
In midber Sinai. 1957; as *In the Sinai Desert,* 1987.
Oazis. 1960.
Gaystike erd [Spiritual Soil]. 1961.
Five Yiddish Poets, with Naftoli Gross, Eliezer Greenberg, Riesel Zhichlinsky, and Jacob Glantz. 1962.
Poetishe verk [Poetic Works]. 1963.
Lider fun yam-hamaves [Poems from the Sea of Death]. 1968.
Firkantike oysyes un mofsim. 1968.
Tsaytike penemer. 1970.

Griner akvarium. 1972; translated by Ruth Wisse as *Green Aquarium,* in *Prooftexts,* 2(1), January 1982.
Di fidlroyz. 1974; as *The Fiddle Rose,* 1990.
Lider fun togbukh. 1977.
Dortn vu es nekhtikn di shtern. 1979.
Di ershte Nakht in Geto [The First Night in the Ghetto]. 1979.
Fun alte un yunge ksav-yadn. 1982.
Tsviling-bruder. 1986.
Der yoyresh fun regn. 1992.
Tsevaklte (and stories). 1996.

Short Stories

Di nevue fun shvartsaplen [Prophesy of the Inner Eye]. 1989.
Baym leyenen penimer [Face Reading]. 1993.

Memoir

Vilner geto: 1941–44 [Vilna Ghetto]. 1945.

Other

Fun Vilner geto. 1946.
Editor, with Chone Shmeruk, Benjamin Harshav, and Mendel Piekarz, *A shpigl oyf a shteyn: Antologye: Poezye un proze fun tsvelf farshnitene yidishe shraybers in Ratn-Farband.* 1964.

*

Bibliography: *Avrom Sutskever-bibliografye* by Avrom Nowersztern, 1976.

Critical Studies: *Abraham Sutzkever: Partisan Poet* by Joseph Leftwich, 1971; "The Last Great Yiddish Poet?" by Ruth R. Wisse, in *Commentary,* 76, November 1983, pp. 41–48; *Avrom Sutzkever: Tsum vern a ben-shivim* by Avrom Nowersztern, 1983; *Against the Apocalypse: Responses to Catastrophe in Modern Jewish Culture* by David G. Roskies, 1984; "Abraham Sutzkever's Vilna Poems" by David H. Hirsch, in *Modern Language Studies,* 16(1), Winter 1986, pp. 37–50; "Mirrors of Memory: The Poetry of Abraham Sutzkever," in *Tikkun,* 6(3), May 1991, p. 67, and "Sutzkever: Life and Poetry," in *A. Sutzkever: Selected Poetry and Prose,* translated by Benjamin and Barbara Harshav, 1991, both by Benjamin Harshav.

*   *   *

It has been said of the poet Abraham Sutzkever that "he is not a man, he is a legend." More than the work of any other Yiddish writer of his generation, Sutzkever's poetic biography was seen to reflect the anxieties, tragedy, and drama of the eastern European Jewish experience. As a member of the prewar literary and artistic group Young Vilna, he resisted the dominant literary trend of social realism in favor of an aesthetic standard that mined the nuances of Yiddish language and

poetic form while exploring an intimate sense of his relationship with nature. Even before the Holocaust, Sutzkever aligned himself metaphysically with the natural universe of recurring cycles rather than the human domain of finite history. By "living poetically"—that is, by focusing his energies on the creation of refined poetic objects that were beyond the corrosive forces of worldly evil—Sutzkever felt that he could preserve not only his own moral compass but also the vivid memory of all his personal dead in an uncorrupted, dignified textual universe.

The myth of Sutzkever as partisan poet developed out of his commitment to the highest standards for his art and his activism in both the cultural and physical resistance in the ghetto. At the same time that he crafted emotionally controlled, stylistically innovative, and classically measured verse in the most extreme of conditions, he also organized public literary and theatrical events, joined the underground United Partisans Organization, and participated in a secret project to rescue irreplaceable cultural treasures from the Yiddish Scientific Institute (Yivo). As a member of the Paper Brigade, Sutzkever risked his life to smuggle documents relating to the history and culture of eastern European Jewry into the ghetto, where they were buried for posterity. In "Grains of Wheat" (1943) Sutzkever's first-person speaker gives voice to the sense of national mission that motivated members of the Paper Brigade.

Sutzkever's writing during the ghetto years ranged from the elegiac to the metapoetic, from self-accusatory lyrics to moving national epics. He invented new archetypes of Jewish spiritual and physical resistance that were based on actual personalities and events in the ghetto ("Teacher Mira," "Itsik Vitenberg," "To the Yiddish Theater," "The Grave-Child," "Kol Nidre," "The Prophet"). Elsewhere, he confessed his private grief about lost family and friends ("My Mother," "To the Child," "Under Your White Stars," "I Lie in a Coffin," "A Wagon of Shoes") or raged at the humiliation and degradation of a people that could not defend itself ("The Circus," "This Is How to Answer an Orphan," "Poem to the Last," "How?"). In *Poems from the Sea of Death* (1968)—Sutzkever's official canon of his wartime poetry—he edited out the angriest of works so as not to add further shame to the memory of the murdered.

Sutzkever quickly came to appreciate the special role of the poet-witness in the context of national catastrophe. In "The Prophet" he included the image of a bird pecking the eye out of a morally refined ghetto Jew and placing it in the eye socket of the poet. Elsewhere, he signaled more directly that he was prepared to assume the burden of collective memory.

In 1943 Sutzkever escaped to the Lithuanian forests to join Jewish partisan units. When one of his ghetto poems was smuggled into the U.S.S.R. and published, a rescue plane was sent into the war zone to bring him to the Soviet Union as a symbol of Jewish resistance to fascism. Once he was out of immediate danger Sutzkever thought it crucial to write a detailed history of the ghetto years (*Vilna Ghetto 1941–1944*). Not only does this chronicle testify to Sutzkever's recognition that it was essential to preserve a reliable record of what was perpetrated against the Jews and their varied reactions to it but it also accentuates just how much his artistic oeuvre both borrowed from and stylized these experiences.

In 1948 Sutzkever completed the first of several epic poems through which he would craft a new myth of national survival and rebirth. *Geheymshtot* (''Secret City'') communicates Sutzkever's notion that memorialization would not be complete until all the dead were brought to participate in the redemption of the people in their new homeland. (This might explain why Sutzkever later felt it important that his Yiddish master the Israeli landscape as sensitively as it had the Polish one in the 1930s.) Sutzkever arrived in Israel in time to experience the moment of its rebirth as an independent nation. His decision to establish *Di Goldene Keyt* (The Golden Chain)— a publication that emerged as the most prestigious Yiddish journal in the world—was designed to express the moral imperative of bringing Yiddish and the highest level of Yiddish scholarship to the new Hebrew-speaking homeland. In *Gaystike erd* (1961; ''Spiritual Soil'') Sutzkever recounted the story of his illegal sea journey to Palestine. At a time in Israeli cultural history when the Holocaust was often treated as a subject of national shame, Sutzkever's poem staked a claim for his generation of survivor-immigrants as heroes of the spirit who chose to rebuild themselves by helping to build a new nation. Sutzkever's poetic account of the Sinai campaign, ''In the Sinai Desert'' (1956), similarly reverberates with a mood of restored dignity as he forges a link between the new generation of brave, fighting Israelis and his comrades who took up arms in the ghettos of Europe.

Perhaps the most developed statement of Sutzkever's poetic philosophy occurs in his series of prose poems *Green Aquarium,* in which words (and the act of writing itself) are imagined to have ultimate power over life and death. This idea conveys a larger truth about Sutzkever's sense of the relationship between the Holocaust and culture. If, to other writers, the Holocaust came to rest at the center of Jewish culture, to Sutzkever culture—that is, the most elevated examples of national creativity—must occupy this privileged position.

—Justin D. Cammy

See the essays on *Di ershte Nakht in Geto, Di Festung,* and *Green Aquarium.*

SYLVANUS, Erwin

Nationality: German. **Born:** 1917. **Awards:** Leo Baeck Preis, 1959; Jochen-Klepper-Medaille, 1960; Joseph-Winkler-Stiftung prize, 1961. **Died:** 1985.

PUBLICATIONS

Collection

Drei Stücke (includes *Korczak und die Kinder; Jan Palach; Sanssouci*). 1973.

Plays

Korczak und die Kinder. 1957; as *Dr. Korczak and the Children,* 1968.
Emil Schumacher. 1959.
Jan Palach. In *Fünf moderne Theaterstücke: Volker Braun; Marieluise Fleisser; Ödön von Horváth; Erwin Sylvanus; Peter Weiss,* 1972.
Sanssouci. In *Drei Stücke,* 1973.
Victor Jara. In *Spectaculum: 26 Acht moderne Theaterstücke,* 1977.
Exil—Reise in die Heimat [Exile—Travel in the Homeland] (produced 1981). Published as *Ein Purim-Spiel oder Badische Heimatkunde* [A Purim Play or the Local History of Baden].
Leo Baeck: A Radio Play Based on Authentic Texts, edited by David Dowdey and Robert Wolfgang. 1996.

Radio Play: *Leo Baeck,* 1988.

Novel

Der Paradiesfahrer. 1942.

Poetry

Der Dichterkreis. 1943.
Die Muschel. 1947.

Other

Familie in der Krise, with Robert Bosshard. 1974.

*

Critical Studies: ''Erwin Sylvanus and the Theatre of the Holocaust'' by Anat Feinberg, in *Amsterdamer Beitrage zur Neueren Germanistik* (Netherlands), 16, 1983, pp. 163–75; ''Toleranz? Noch spur ich sie nicht': Erwin Sylvanus' Modern Sequel to Lessing's *Die Juden*'' by Alison Scott-Prelorentzos, in *Seminar* (Canada), 21(1), February 1985, pp. 31–47; ''Sylvanus'' by Walter Olma, in *Literatur-Lexikon,* edited by Walther Killy, 1991; ''German Theatrical Responses'' by Edward R. Isser, in *Stages of Annihilation,* 1997.

* * *

Erwin Sylvanus wrote three plays explicitly about the Holocaust, though he also wrote other plays dealing more generally with the subjects of anti-Semitism, racism, and other prejudices. In each of his three Holocaust plays he uses documentary evidence as his starting point. He did not, however, choose to create documentary theater; on the contrary, he often chose nonrealistic theatrical conventions, such as those popularized by **Bertolt Brecht** and Luigi Pirandello, to forge a unique theatrical experience for his audiences.

His first play, *Dr. Korczak and the Children* (1957), was one of the first plays produced in Germany to deal with the Holocaust. Sylvanus wrote the play not so much in response to the atrocities committed during the Third Reich. Rather his play was a protest against the rapidity with which the German public seemed to have forgotten or covered up the past during the 1950s, the years of the "economic miracle." The play, based on the true story of Dr. Janusz Korczak, utilizes a presentational style of playing. The narrator speaks directly to the audience and casts the actors in various roles. The actors are not pleased to be playing SS officers or Jews, but they must confront their own fears and prejudices and question their own complicity in the events of the past as they take on various parts. This play, Sylvanus's most famous, has often been labeled Pirandellian because of its philosophical questioning of moral issues and its use of a play-within-a-play format. The actors stepping out of their roles and questioning what they are doing is also characteristic of Brecht's epic theater.

Sylvanus's next play about the Holocaust was presented in 1981, having been commissioned by a German theater that annually presents plays about regional history. The play is based on Paul J. Schrag's book *Heimatkunde: Die Geschichte einer deutsch-judischen Familie,* the history of a local Jewish family during the Holocaust, whom the author traced through eyewitness accounts, both written and oral. Sylvanus's version has two titles: the official published version, called *Ein Purim-Spiel oder Badische Heimatkunde* ("A Purim Play or the Local History of Baden"), and the performance text, entitled *Exil—Reise in die Heimat* ("Exile—Travel in the Homeland"). Sylvanus once again uses documentary evidence as his starting point but takes some poetic license in his own version. For example, the book involves the Jewish businessman Fritz Kusel, whose family was murdered in the Holocaust. One of his best friends, Wolfgang Imhoff, was arrested for homosexuality and imprisoned in a concentration camp where he was later killed. In Sylvanus's version, however, Imhoff commits suicide after the war because of his realization that society is still just as intolerant as it had been during the Third Reich. The play, like *Dr. Korczak and the Children,* shifts back and forth between the present and the past, presenting not only the events of the Holocaust but also drawing parallels between contemporary prejudices and the atrocities of the past. The play also utilizes theatrical conventions such as presenting a play within a play and having an angry youth come out of the audience and ask questions about the performance, a technique often used by Brecht to increase audience involvement in the issues. Sylvanus also uses the format of the Jewish festival of Purim to structure the events of the play.

In his third play about the Holocaust, *Leo Baeck: A Radio Play Based on Authentic Texts,* Sylvanus traces the life story of Rabbi Leo Baeck, the chief rabbi of Berlin who later became a prisoner in the concentration camp Theresienstadt. Rabbi Baeck survived the Holocaust and provided succor for many others who did not through his teaching and humane example. Adolf Eichmann himself ordered Rabbi Baeck's death and was en route to Theresienstadt to carry it out personally, but the Russian Army arrived first. The English version of this play was adapted in 1988 to commemorate the 50th anniversary of *Kristallnacht* (Crystal Night). This play is presented more realistically than the other two and is, as the title suggests, based on documentation, including eyewitness accounts, of the rabbi's life.

Sylvanus, who spent his youth writing poems in support of Nazism, was seriously wounded in World War II and spent the remainder of his life writing plays, television scripts, and radio plays, many of which pointed out the wrongs of prejudice, hatred, and brutality. His first and most famous play, *Dr. Korczak and the Children,* was the earliest Holocaust play to struggle with the creation of a new stage language to deal with the unfathomable realities of the Holocaust and its aftermath.

—Susan Russell

See the essay on *Dr. Korczak and the Children.*

SZLENGEL, Wladyslaw

Nationality: Polish. **Career:** Poet and songwriter; wrote and read for Sztuka Café, a social club in the Warsaw Ghetto; contributor to various periodicals, including *Szpilki, Przegląd Polski,* and *Żywy Dziennik.* **Died:** Killed in the Warsaw Ghetto Uprising, April 1943.

PUBLICATION

Collection

Co czytalem umarlym [What I Read to the Dead]. 1977.

*   *   *

Wladyslaw Szlengel spoke in two kinds of verse—in satire and in lyrical poetry. He commenced his literary career by creating occasional texts to serve the needs of various stage shows as well as verse and satirical prose that was published in the periodical *Szpilki* (Pins). During the same period, before the outbreak of World War II, some of his pieces were also published in *Przegląd Polski* (Polish Review). In works such as "Nie kupujcie nowych kalendarzy" ("Don't Buy New Calendars") and "Przerazone pokolenie" ("The Fearful Generation") the poet focused on the approaching catastrophe and attempted to examine the threats looming over the Jewish community in Poland. Szlengel was a singer as well as a poet, and he appeared in the shows of the Sztuka Café and published the texts from these performances in *Żywy Dziennik* (Living Daily). Jokes and satire served as a form of collective therapy in the Warsaw Ghetto, for they integrated the community and allowed it to be prepared for the hour of doom. A series of humorous poems dedicated to the fictitious character Majer Mlinczyk enjoyed great popularity. The majority of Szlengel's satirical works, however, did not survive the war. Szlengel shared the fate of other Jewish writers who were murdered in the Warsaw Ghetto, including Franciszka Arnsztajnowa, Gustawa Jarocka, Henryka Lazowertówna, and **Janusz Korczak**. Szlengel was killed in the April uprising of 1943. His testimony of the resistance of the ghetto has the unique quality of a literary document.

Some of Szlengel's literary output was collected in the volume entitled *Co czytalem umarlym* ("What I Read to the Dead"), published in 1977. His lyrical writing in this volume is closely connected to his autobiography. The poet becomes a spokesman for the Jewish community condemned to death and a witness to the extermination of Jews. This experience opens up new ways of expression and contributes to the shaping of the poet as a witness. The deep force of Szlengel's poems is based on their authentic quality. The poet does not refrain from describing the most extreme details; it is as if the truth of the inconceivable suffering of the people trapped in the ghetto must be conveyed in its entirety. Szlengel avoids the lofty and the pathetic, resorting instead to colloquial Polish, with obvious references to local speech. The unmasking of the system of evil, which comprises both the world of the torturers and the world of the victims, the crisis of human values, the descriptions of the daily doomsday reality, the antiheroic attitude, and the rejection of moralistic comments have led many to compare Szlengel's poetry to the prose of **Tadeusz Borowski**. The events presented in the works included in *Co czytalem umarlym*, whose heroes are common people, form a synthesis of the tragic history of the ghetto.

The poet purposefully introduces a prosaic quality into his texts, exploiting meaningful concealment through short, broken sentences that imitate the speech of a hunted-down, chased man. The factuality of the documentary is overcome, however, through the use of parables and literary and cultural allusions that refer to Jewish and Polish traditions as well as through metaphoric images that represent the degradation of the human being in the world of routine, everyday crime.

—Wojciech Ligęza

See the essay on *Co czytalem umarlym*.

SZPILMAN, Wladyslaw

Nationality: Polish. **Born:** Sosnoviec, 5 December 1911. **Education:** Studied piano and composition, Chopin School of Music, Warsaw; Berlin Academy of Music, 1931–33. **Family:** Married Halina Grzecznarowski; two sons. **Career:** Pianist and composer, Polish Radio, Warsaw, 1935–39 and 1945–63; cofounder, with Bronislaw Gimpel, and performer, Warsaw Piano Quintet, 1962–86. **Awards:** Poland's Gold Cross of Merit, 1950; Polish radio industry award for children's songs, 1953; Polonia Restituta Cavalier's Cross, 1954; Polish People's Republic Tenth Anniversary medal and Polish Composers Union award, both in 1955; Officer's Cross, 1959; Merited Cultural Leader award, 1978. **Died:** 6 July 2000.

PUBLICATION

Memoir

Smierc miasta [Death of a City]. 1946; as *The Pianist: The Extraordinary Story of One Man's Survival in Warsaw, 1939–45,* 1999.

* * *

Wladyslaw Szpilman—a world-famous virtuoso and composer, graduate of the Berlin Academy of Music, and author of popular hits—preserved his war experience in a book. The unusual memoir describes the outbreak of the war, the defense of Warsaw, the first days of the Nazis' presence in the town, his life in the ghetto, and the years spent hiding in the capital occupied by the Germans. His memoir was called by critics a record of the human will to survive, which perseveres even in time of mass destruction.

Not accidentally this wartime biography is entitled *The Pianist*. For the narrator and protagonist of the book music is not a job but a way to live and to survive. Music became a refuge for the author in the critical days of the September campaign of 1939 when, despite the escalation of bombings, he prepared musical broadcasts together with other employees of Polish Radio until the last moment. Also, at the beginning of the occupation, playing music at home became a way of escaping from the more and more sinister reality imprinted with the escalating repressive measures aimed at the inhabitants of Warsaw, especially at the Jews. Music helped Szpilman survive the ghetto experience. Concerts in the restaurants of the Jewish district, to some degree at least, preserved Szpilman himself as well as his family from the hunger present in the ghetto. Music saved Szpilman's life on 16 August 1942 when he and his family landed at the Umschlagplatz. He was recognized as a musician and composer and dragged away from the shipment, which was heading for gas chambers, and pushed outside the police cordon by a Jewish policeman who supervised the loading.

With the help of his friends—Polish artists—Szpilman managed to escape from the ghetto and find a hideout outside the Jewish precincts. At the outbreak of the Warsaw Ghetto Uprising Szpilman lost the help of his murdered or exiled friends. He was hiding alone in the ruins, imprisoned in the district of Warsaw that was occupied by the Germans. He watched the agony of the town, the evacuation or executions of civilians. Even in this critical moment repeating his own compositions in his mind was his rescue from resignation, fear, and even madness.

In the last chapter of *The Pianist* Szpilman, found in the ruins by a German officer, plays Chopin's Nocturne in C-sharp minor at the officer's request. Thus one of the last scenes involves the meeting of two people who outwardly have nothing in common but are united by their love of music and their faith in the value of human life. This German officer is Captain Wilhelm Hosenfeld, whose wartime memoirs have been attached to the latest edition of *The Pianist*. Hosenfeld, a practicing Christian living by the rules, opposed Nazism to the best of his ability by helping the Jews. The German officer recorded shocking images of murders committed by the German army both on the Poles and the Jews.

—Joanna Hobot

See the essay on *The Pianist: The Extraordinary Story of One Man's Survival in Warsaw, 1939–45.*

SZYMBORSKA, Wisława

Pseudonym: Stancy Kowna. **Nationality:** Polish. **Born:** Prowent-Bnin, 2 July 1923. **Education:** Jagellonian University, Kraków, 1945–48. **Family:** Married 1) Adam Wlodek (divorced); 2) Kornel Flipowicz (died). **Career:** Poetry editor and columnist, *Zycie Literackie* (literary weekly magazine), 1953–81. **Awards:** Kraków literary prize, 1954; Gold Cross of Merit, 1955; Ministry of Culture prize, 1963; Goethe prize, 1991; Herder prize, 1995; Polish PEN Club prize and Nobel prize for literature, both in 1996; poet laureate of Poland, 1997. Knight's Cross, Order of Polonia Resituta, 1974. **Address:** Office: Zwigzel Literalow Polskich, ul Krolewska 82m 18, 30–079, Kraków, Poland.

PUBLICATIONS

Collections

Wiersze wybrane. 1964.
Wybor wierszy. 1973.

Poetry

Dlatego zyjemy [What We Live For]. 1952.
Pytania zadawane sobie [Questions Put to Myself]. 1954.
Wołanie do Yeti [Calling Out to Yeti]. 1957.
Sol [Salt]. 1962.
Sto pociech [A Hundred Joys]. 1967.
Poezje wybrane: Wybór i wstep autorki. 1967.
Poezje [Poems] (selections). 1970.
Wszelki wypadek [There but for the Grace]. 1972.
Wielka liczba [A Great Number]. 1976.
Tarsjusz I inne wiersze [Tarsius and Other Poems]. 1976.
Sounds, Feelings, Thoughts: Seventy Poems (selections in English). 1981.
Poezje wybrane (II) [Selected Poems II]. 1983.
Ludzie na moscie. 1986; as *People on a Bridge: Poems* (selections in English and Polish), 1990.
Poems (selections in English and Polish). 1989.
Wieczor autorski: Wiersze [Authors' Evening: Poems]. 1992.
Koniec I poczatek [The End and the Beginning]. 1993.
With a Grain of Sand: Selected Poems. 1995.
Zycie na poczekaniu: Lekcja literatury z Jerzym Kwiatowskim I Marianem Stala (with criticism). 1996.
Widok z ziarnkiem piasku: 102 Wiersze. 1996.
Nothing Twice: Selected Poems (in English and Polish). 1997.
Poems, New and Collected, 1957–1997 (selections in English). 1998.
Nothing's a Gift (in English, Polish, Yiddish, German, and Hebrew). 1999.
Miracle Fair: Selected Poems of Wislawa Szymborska. 2001.

Other

Lektury nadobowiazkowe [Non-Compulsory Reading] (collection of book reviews). 1973.
Wislawa Szymborska Nobel lecture 1996: The Poet and the World. 1996.

*

Critical Studies: ''Mozartian Joy: The Poetry of Wislawa Szymborska'' by Krzysztof Karasek, in *The Mature Laurel: Essays on Modern Polish Poetry,* edited by Adam Czerniawski, 1991; ''Eastern Europe: The Szymborska Phenomenon'' by Stanislaw Baranczak, in *Salmagundi,* 103, Summer 1994, pp. 252–65; ''Wislawa Szymborska and the Importance of the Unimportant'' by Bogdana Carpenter, in *World Literature Today,* 71(1), Winter 1997, pp. 8–12; ''Wislawa Szymborska: Naturalist and Humanist'' by Edyta M. Bojanska, in *Slavic and East European Journal,* 41(2), Summer 1997, pp. 199–223; ''Poetry and Ideology: The Example of Wislawa Szymborska'' by Clare Cavanagh, in *Literary Imagination,* 1(2), Fall 1999, pp. 174–90; ''Parting with a View: Wislawa Szymborska and the Work of Mourning'' by Charity Scribner, in *Polish Review,* 44(3), 1999, pp. 311–28; ''Sky, the Sky, a Sky, the Heavens, a Heaven, Heavens: Reading Szymborska Whole'' by Stephen

Tapscott and Mariusz Przybytek, in *American Poetry Review*, 29(4), July/August 2000, pp. 41–47; ''Szymborska's Two Monkeys: The Stammering Poet and the Chain of Signs'' by John Blazina, in *Modern Language Review* (United Kingdom), 96(1), January 2001, pp. 130–39.

* * *

Wisława Szymborska is one of the leading poets of postwar Poland. She was awarded the Nobel Prize for Literature in 1996 and named poet laureate of Poland in 1997. Born in western Poland in 1923, she moved to Kraków when she was eight years old. She studied Polish literature and sociology from 1945 to 1948, and her poetic debut dates to 1945, when she published her first poem. She had a volume of poems ready for publication as early as 1948, but it did not pass the test of political acceptability. She revised her work to make it conform to the exigencies of socialist realism, and a collection entitled *Dlatego zyjemy* (''What We Live For'') was published in 1952, when Stalinist tendencies in literature had reached their peak in Poland. This volume, and to a lesser extent her next one, have dogged her reputation ever since, because in them she has responded to the muse of political expediency as well as that of poetry. Despite her repudiation of this early work, she has been accused by many of a lack of integrity in connection with it, although there has been little attempt to determine her real political inclinations at the time. Comparisons with poetic hacks and careerists are hardly defensible, however, since even the second collection overcame many of the deficiencies of the first. It is noteworthy that her poetry and career since the mid-1950s have been largely unmarked by political events. This is not to say she has not taken principled stands at critical moments in Polish history, but she has done so quietly and largely outside of her poetry.

Since 1957, when she published her third collection, *Wołanie do Yeti* (''Calling Out to Yeti''), the number of volumes she published rose to about 20 by the end of the twentieth century. From 1953 to 1981 she worked for the important weekly *Zycie Literackie* (Literary Life), where she was poetry editor and wrote a book review column, the only other literary form she has practiced. These reviews have been collected and published in four separate volumes. She has also translated French poetry, mainly of the seventeenth and eighteenth centuries, into Polish.

Szymborska has been as reticent to discuss her biography as to discuss theoretical aspects of her poetry. In one poem she asks what poetry is and replies firmly, ''I don't know and I don't know and I hold on to that / like to a life raft.'' Her work is characterized by humility, a wry and frequently ironic sense of humor, and a profound sense of the joy and tragedy inherent in individual human existence and in the collective history of the species. Commentators generally agree with her that there is no need to know anything of her life to appreciate or understand her poetry. This is one of the few theoretical questions on which her position is unambiguously known, and while it may not apply equally well to all poets, it does seem to hold true for her work. Each of her poems successfully creates its own world, and there is little to connect them beyond some stylistic and methodological consistency. This makes it difficult to locate her views of the Holocaust within her opus, although some patterns do emerge. Three poems that bear directly on the Holocaust are ''Hunger Camp near Jaslo,'' ''Still'' (''Jeszcze''), and ''Hitler's First Photograph.'' Each of them manifests key elements of her poetic technique and fixes the reader's attention on the subject matter with a sense of urgency and newness, despite the familiarity of the thematic material. In ''Hunger Camp near Jaslo,'' besides identifying the important role to be played by poets in addressing such atrocities, she tries to remove the numbing effect of large numbers by forcing our attention onto the importance of each individual and the tactile and personal elements of their existence. She has written a number of poems about numbers, including ''Pi'' and ''A Large Number,'' where she says, ''Four billion people on this earth, / but my imagination is still the same. / It's bad with large numbers. / It's still taken by particularity.''

In ''Still'' she employs an extended metonymy, another frequently encountered technique in her work. She describes prisoners in a train headed for a concentration camp as if they were names only. The obvious Jewishness of these names marks them and sets them apart from their Slavic neighbors, making it easier for bystanders to ignore their situation. She describes with remarkable force the ''crash of silence on silence.'' This poem, from the mid-1950s, carries a strong charge of shared complicity disguised as passivity: ''and will they ever get out, / don't ask, I won't say, I don't know.'' ''Hitler's First Photograph'' is one of the most chilling poetic inspections of the psychopathological phenomena associated with its namesake and Nazism ever written. By describing Hitler in his first year of life from the perspective of his parents (any parents), she jolts us out of our complacency around the question of how this could have happened: ''And who's this little fellow in his itty-bitty robe? / That's tiny baby Adolf, the Hitlers' little boy!'' She prods us to question whether the signs were there and, if they were not, to ask what gives rise to such abominations and to recognize the need to be vigilant.

In these poems Szymborska explores aspects of the Holocaust in the same way as she approaches the minutiae of daily life, probing common details with phenomenological thoroughness to force us to reintegrate our experience of them with greatly increased and intensified awareness of their complexity, richness, and power.

—Allan Reid

See the essays on *Poems, New and Collected, 1957–1997*.

T

TABORI, George

Nationality: British (originally Hungarian: immigrated to England, 1936, granted British citizenship, 1945; moved to the United States, 1947; moved to Germany, 1971; moved to Austria, 1986). **Born:** Budapest, 24 May 1914. **Education:** Studied with L. Strasberg. **Career:** Worked in a hotel in Berlin, 1932–34; journalist and translator in Budapest, 1935; correspondent in Bulgaria and Turkey, 1939–41; Middle East correspondent, British Army intelligence service, 1941–43; correspondent, British Broadcasting Corporation (BBC), 1943–47; lived in New York writing film scripts and plays, 1953–71; started The Strolling Players (theatre group), 1966; worked as a director in various German cities, 1971–81; founder and manager, Der Kreis (theatre group), Vienna, 1987–90; director, Burgtheater and Akademietheater, Vienna. **Awards:** German Academic Exchange Service scholarship for study in Berlin, 1971; Federation of German critics prize for literature, 1976; Prix Italia, 1978; city of Mannheim film prize and city of Berlin art prize, both in 1981; city of Mülheim dramatist prize, 1983; city of Munich Ernst-Hoferichter prize, 1987; J. Kainz medal, 1988; Peter Weiss prize for theatre, 1990; Georg Bücher prize, 1992; distinguished service cross, 1994; city of Vienna gold medal of honor, 1995.

PUBLICATIONS

Collection

Theaterstücke (includes *Die Kannibalen*; *Pinkville*; *Die Demonstration*; *Clowns*; *Die 25 Stunde*; *Mutters Courage*; *Der Voyeur*; *Jubiläum*; *Peepshow*; *Mein Kampf*; *Weisman und Rotgesicht*; *Der Babylon Blues*; *Goldberg-Variationen*; *Requiem für einen Spion*). 1994.

Plays

Flight into Egypt (produced New York, 1952). 1953.
I Confess, with William Archibald, adaptation of a play by Paul Anthelme (screenplay). 1952.
The Emperor's Clothes (produced New York, 1953). 1953.
The Young Lovers (screenplay). 1954.
The Journey (screenplay). 1958.
Brou Ha Ha (produced London, 1958).
Brecht on Brecht (produced New York, 1960). 1967.
The Cannibals (produced New York, 1968). 1974.
Niggerlovers (produced New York, 1969).
Secret Ceremony, adaptation of a story by Marco Denevi (screenplay). 1968.

Pinkville (produced New York, 1970). In *Theaterstücke*, 1994.
The Resistible Rise of Arturo Ui; A Gangster Spectacle, adaptation of a play by Bertolt Brecht. 1972.
Clowns (produced Tübingen, Germany, 1972). In *Theaterstücke*, 1994.
Die Demonstration (produced Berlin, 1972). In *Theaterstücke*, 1994.
Sigmunds Freude, based on *Gestalt Therapy* by Frederick S. Perls (produced Bremen, Germany, 1975).
Talk Show (produced Bremen, 1976).
Die 25. Stunde (produced 1977). 1994.
Die Hungerkünstler, adaptation of the novel by Franz Kafka (produced Bremen, 1977).
Verwandlungen, adaptation of the novel by Franz Kafka (produced Munich, 1977).
Ich wollte, meine Tochter läge tot zu meinen Füßen und hätte die Juwelen in den O. based on *Shylock, the Merchant of Venice* by William Shakespeare (*Shylock Improvisations*) (produced Munich, 1978). 1979.
Mutters Courage [My Mother's Courage] (produced Munich, 1979). In *Theaterstücke*, 1994.
Der Voyeur (produced Berlin, 1982). In *Theaterstücke*, 1994.
Jubiläum [Jubilee] (produced Bochum, Germany, 1983). In *Spectaculum: 38, Sechs moderne Theaterstücke*, 1984.
Peepshow (produced Bochum, 1984). In *Theaterstücke*, 1994.
M, based on *Medea* by Euripedes (produced Munich, 1985).
Stammheim (produced Hamburg, 1986).
Mein Kampf (produced Vienna, 1987). 1988.
Masada, adaptation of *De bello Judaico* by Flavius Josephus (produced Graz, 1988).
Weisman und Rotgesicht: ein jüdischer Western (produced Vienna, 1990). 1990.
Nathans Tod, adaptation of *Nathan der Weise* by Gotthold Ephraim Lessing (*Nathan's Death*) (produced Wolfenbüttel, Germany, 1991).
Goldberg-Variationen (produced Vienna, 1991). 1992.
Der Babylon Blues oder wie man glücklich wird, ohne sich zu verausgaben (produced Vienna, 1991).
Der Großinquisitor, adaptation of *The Brothers Karamazov* by Fyodor Dostoyevsky (produced Seville, Spain, 1992).
Unruhige Träume (produced Vienna, 1992). 1992.
Requiem für einen Spion (produced Vienna, 1993).
Die Massenmörderin und ihre Freunde (produced Vienna, 1995).
Die Ballade vom Wiener Schnitzel (produced Vienna, 1996). 1996.
Die letzte Nacht im September (produced Vienna, 1997). 1997.
Purgatorium (produced Vienna, 1999).

Screenplays: *I Confess,* 1952; *Young Lovers,* 1954; *The Journey,* 1958; *The Holiday,* 1961; *No Exit,* 1962; *Secret Ceremony,* 1968; *Insomnia,* 1974; *Mutters Courage,* 1995.

Novels

Beneath the Stone. 1944; as *Beneath the Stone the Scorpion,* 1945.
Companions of the Left Hand. 1946.
Original Sin. 1947.
The Caravan Passes. 1951.
The Good One. 1960.
Tod in Port Aarif. 1995.

Other

Betrachtungen über das Feigenblatt: Ein Handbuch für Verliebte und Verrückte (essay). 1991.

*

Film Adaptations: *Secret Story,* 1968; *I Confess,* 1952; *The Journey,* 1959, *Mutters Courage,* 1995.

Critical Studies: *Embodied Memory: The Theatre of George Tabori* by Anat Feinberg, 1999; ''George Tabori's Jubilaum: Jokes and Their Relation to the Representation of the Holocaust'' by Timothy B. Malchow, in *German Quarterly,* 72(2), 1999, pp. 167–84; ''Speaking of American Theater: George Tabori and the Jewish Question'' by Jack Zipes, in *Theater,* 29(2), 1999, pp. 98–108.

Theatrical Activities: Director: **Plays**—Several of his own plays; *Das Buch mit sieben Siegeln,* Salzburg, Austria, 1987; *Schuldig geboren,* Vienna, Austria, 1987. **Film**—*Frohes Fest,* 1981. Actor: **Film**—*Bye, Bye America,* 1993.

* * *

George Tabori began writing about the Holocaust as a way to cope with his father's murder at Auschwitz. Tabori has occupied a unique position as a Jewish playwright working in Germany and Austria persistently confronting his audience with the memory of the Holocaust. Tabori's distinctive style has included black comedy and techniques of Theater of the Absurd in his depiction of German history.

Tabori, who was born in Budapest, fled to England and became a war correspondent in the Middle East. During World War II he began writing novels, but in the late 1940s he met the German playwright **Bertolt Brecht,** who hooked him on the theater. Tabori's playwriting was also affected by his work in the experimental theater of the 1960s in New York City. His style has been described by various critics as chutzpah, cynicism, black humor, and tasteless. Tabori claimed that for him, ''humor and horror always dance together.'' He admitted that

he has never been concerned with ''good taste or pious 'coping with the past.''' In his plays, as in Brecht's, the tragedy of the Holocaust does not preclude the use of comic irony to shock his audiences.

The Holocaust occupies a different role in each of his plays. *The Cannibals,* his earliest Holocaust play, is set in Auschwitz itself where sons of survivors have gathered to reenact their fathers' stories. Tabori utilized some of the ideas of Brecht's epic theater—e.g., actors play many different roles. His dark humor and indebtedness to absurdism is apparent in the insertion of numerous jokes and musical numbers throughout the play. The hero of the play, Cornelius, is modeled after Tabori's own father. The play revolves around whether or not the inmates will stoop to cannibalism. Cornelius and most of the others refuse and are gassed to death.

His second Holocaust play, *Mutters Courage* (''My Mother's Courage'') is a step removed from Auschwitz. It is also based on his family's experience: his mother was arrested and placed on a train to Auschwitz. Along the way a German officer decides to let her escape. Although her story has a ''happy ending,'' the tragic fate of other Jews is the darker subtext of the play. As in *The Cannibals,* the telling of the story—and the impossibility of knowing the truth—is foregrounded. In *Mutters Courage* the mother's memories sometimes clash with the narrator/son's desire to whitewash the past. The play, like *The Cannibals,* highlights the next generation's (and all future generations') puzzled sorrow about the events of the past.

Tabori's third play, *Jubiläum* (''Jubilee'') is set in 1983 in a Jewish cemetery where the dead return to demand justice. The play grapples not only with the past but also with the rise of neo-Nazism and xenophobia in contemporary Germany. *Jubiläum*'s setting (a graveyard where the characters pop up out of graves) is reminiscent of Samuel Beckett's mise-en-scène. Once again Tabori borrowed from epic theater by having actors portray many different parts. Like Tabori's other plays, *Jubiläum* not only involves a shocking confrontation with the past but it also suggests hope for the future.

The play that led to international fame for Tabori was his black comedy *Mein Kampf,* a prequel to the Holocaust involving a Jew, Schlomo Herzl, and his roommate, the aspiring art student Adolf Hitler, in a shabby flophouse in 1907. Here, even more so than in his other plays, Tabori borrowed from Beckett, Charlie Chaplin, the Marx Brothers, *Faust,* and Theater of the Absurd. This play premiered in Vienna at a time when Austria was embroiled in the controversy over the presidential election of Kurt Waldheim, a former Nazi official. As with *The Cannibals,* Tabori was accused with *Mein Kampf* of intentionally shocking people and tastelessly breaking taboos. As in his other Holocaust plays, the metaphor of eating plays a prominent role in *Mein Kampf.* At the end of the play Hitler burns Schlomo's beloved chicken, Mitzi, and Schlomo is forced to eat her in order to build his strength against the evil to come. Hitler waltzes off with his new companion, Frau

Death, who has come to help him fulfill his destiny as an "exterminating angel."

Several of Tabori's other plays deal with the Holocaust more tangentially. For example, he has adapted two classic works, Shakespeare's *The Merchant of Venice* and Gotthold Ephraim Lessing's *Nathan the Wise,* in light of the Holocaust. In the former, called *Shylock Improvisations,* Tabori investigated the history of anti-Semitic representations on the stage. In *Nathan's Death* he tied together the history of oppression of Jews with the twentieth century version: the Holocaust. Over many years as playwright and director, Tabori has continued to shake up his audiences by deliberately offending them, making them wonder whether or not to laugh, and causing them to question their own complacency through his unique mixture of what he calls "the celestial and the excremental."

—Susan Russell

See the essays on *The Cannibals, Jubiläum,* and *Mutters Courage.*

TEC, Nechama

Nationality: American (originally Polish: immigrated to the United States, 1952, naturalized citizen, 1960). **Born:** Nechama Bawnik, Lublin, 15 May 1931. **Education:** Columbia University, New York, B.A. 1954, M.A. 1955, Ph.D. 1963. **Family:** Married Leon Tec in 1950; one daughter and one son. **Career:** Research sociologist in biometrics, New York State Department of Mental Hygiene, 1956–57; research director, Mid-Fairfield Child Guidance Center, Norwalk, Connecticut, 1968–79. Since 1974 professor of sociology, University of Connecticut, Stamford. Also taught at Columbia University, Rutgers University, and Trinity College. Scholar-in-residence, Yad Vashem, 1995; senior research fellow, U.S. Holocaust Memorial Museum, 1997. **Awards:** Anti-Defamation League of B'nai B'rith merit of distinction award, for *When Light Pierced the Darkness* and for *Dry Tears*; Christopher award, 1991, for *In the Lion's Den;* International Anne Frank Special Recognition prize, 1994, and World Federation of Fighters, Partisans, and Concentration Camp Survivors prize for Holocaust literature, 1995, both for *Defiance;* American Society for Yad Vashem achievement award, 2001.

PUBLICATIONS

Memoirs

Dry Tears: The Story of a Lost Childhood. 1984.
When Light Pierced the Darkness: Christian Rescue of Jews in Nazi-Occupied Poland. 1986.

Other

Gambling in Sweden: A Sociological Study. 1962.
Family and Differential Involvement with Marihuana: A Study of Suburban Teenagers. 1970.
Grass Is Green in Suburbia: A Sociological Study of Adolescent Usage of Illicit Drugs. 1974.
In the Lion's Den: The Life of Oswald Rufeison (history). 1990.
Defiance: The Bielski Partisans (history). 1993.
Jewish Resistance: Facts, Omissions, and Distortions (history). 1997.

*

Critical Studies: "When Light Pierced the Darkness: Christian Rescue of Jews in Nazi Occupied Poland, Nechama Tec" by Vera Laska, in *International Journal on World Peace,* VII(4), December 1990, p. 92; "In the Lion's Den: The Life of Oswald Rufeisen" by Neal Pease, in *Catholic Historical Review,* LXXVII(2), April 1991, p. 323.

*   *   *

Nechama (Bawnik) Tec's formal education and early career were in the fields of sociology and mental health, and she wrote about these subjects in *Grass Is Green in Suburbia: A Sociological Study of Adolescent Usage of Illicit Drugs* (1974). Beginning in 1977, however, she focused her research on issues relating to the Shoah, including altruism, resistance to evil, the rescue of Jews during World War II, and gender and the destruction of European Jewry. She spent 1995 as a scholar-in-residence at Yad Vashem, Israel's national museum and archive of Holocaust commemoration, and 1997 as a senior research fellow at the U.S. Holocaust Memorial Museum, where she researched Jewish resistance. Among her published works are *Dry Tears: The Story of a Lost Childhood* (1984), her personal story of survival in Nazi-occupied Poland; *When Light Pierced the Darkness: Christian Rescue of Jews in Nazi-Occupied Poland* (1986), in which the rescuers exhibit a universalistic sense of caring, an independence of moral judgment, and a refusal to be persuaded by Nazi propaganda in defining the identity of the Slavic self as servile, base people and of the Jewish other as nonhuman; *In the Lion's Den: The Life of Oswald Rufeison* (1990), a sympathetic biography of Brother Daniel, a Jewish-born Shoah survivor and convert to Catholicism, who passed as half-German and half-Polish and saved hundreds of Jews and Christians, yet whose appeal in 1962 for Israeli citizenship under the Law of Return was denied by the Israeli Supreme Court based on national-historical not religious grounds, becoming a cause célèbre in the ongoing and widespread debate over the question of who is a Jew; and *Defiance: The Bielski Partisans* (1993), the virtually forgotten story of Tuvia Bielski, who, from his base of operations in the Nalibocka Forest (primarily) in western Belorussia, helped organize and led the largest armed Jewish self-help *otriad* in the rescue of Jews in World War II.

Tec is among the handful of female Holocaust researchers and survivors who have been making the "invisible female voice" of the event heard. She has written not only about Christian and Jewish acts of altruism but also about the emotional and conceptual longing that occurred before, during, and after the act of rescue. Her protracted investigation makes clear and distinct the voices of ordinary men and women, Christian and Jew, who are not neutral to the victim's cry "Do not forget." Her works reflect a slice of Shoah history in behavioral terms. For example, in *When Light Pierced the Darkness* she focused on the question of what constitutes Christian concern for Jews; in *Defiance* she sought to understand the Jew as victim and rescuer. And old-new questions continue to surface. Consider the ethical paradox posed by Bielski's credible conviction, "It is more important to save one Jew than to kill twenty Germans," and the passionate scream of a 75-year-old Jewish partisan when he killed a captured SS man, "God, my grandfather was not a murderer, my father was not a murderer, but I will be a murderer." Tec offers no judgment.

—Zev Garber

See the essay on *Dry Tears: The Story of a Lost Childhood.*

TEDESCHI, Giuliana (Brunelli)

Nationality: Italian. **Born:** Milan, 1914. **Education:** Studied linguistics, University of Milan, 1932–36. **Family:** Married Giorgio Tedeschi in 1939 (died); two daughters. **Career:** Prisoner, Auschwitz-Birkenau, 1944–45. Teacher in Turin, Liceo Cavour, 1945–47, Liceo Alfieri, 1947–48; Magistrale Regina Margherita, 1948–55, Magistrale Berti, 1955–56, and Liceo V. Gioberti, 1956–72.

PUBLICATIONS

Memoir

Questo povero corpo [This Poor Body]. 1946; revised and expanded edition, as *C'è un punto della terra: Una donna nel Lager di Birkenau,* 1988; translated as *There Is a Place on Earth: A Woman in Birkenau.* 1992.

Other

Lingua, grammatica, stile. 1971.
Spazio umano: Problemi in prospettiva: Le dimensioni del raccontare: Per il biennio delle Scuole Medie Superiori, with Fausto M. Bongioanni. 1972.
Come comunichiamo: Grammatica italiana ed educazione linguistica (grammar textbook). 1979.

France et étranger dans la "Revue de littérature comparée," 1921–1980, with Pier Antonio Borgheggiani (bibliography). 1983.
Uomo e ambiente nei continenti extraeuropei: Testo/atlante, with Andreina Post (geography aid). 1993.
Memoria di donne e bambini nei Lager nazisti. 1995.

* * *

Guiliana Tedeschi was born in Milan in 1914 and educated in the middle-class milieu of Turin. She completed an honors degree in linguistics as a student of the noted linguist Benvenuto Terracini and worked as a teacher. Married with two small children, she was arrested on 5 April 1944 and deported together with her architect husband and mother-in-law to Auschwitz-Birkenau. Her two girls, one a baby, survived in hiding cared for by her Roman Catholic housekeeper. The Jewish population of Italy had remained relatively safe until late in the war and relatively few (8,369 out of 44,500) were deported; of those who were sent to the camps, little more than 10 percent survived; of Tedeschi's family, both her husband and mother-in-law were killed.

On Tedeschi's return she resumed teaching and was the author of school texts for the study of Latin and Greek, a manual of Italian grammar and usage, and other texts in ancient history and geography. She wrote one of the first memoirs of camp experience, published in 1946. Involved in the survivor community and its organization, the National Association of Ex-Deportees, she reworked her 1946 text in the context of burgeoning 1980s interest in the Holocaust, published in 1988 as *C'é un punto della terra* and translated into English as *There Is a Place on Earth* in 1992.

Although providing a narrative of experiences in Auschwitz-Birkenau, the main focus of her writing is on the experience of the deportee. Her work is unusual in having almost no reference to life before deportation (or subsequent to liberation) and its attempt, primarily in its first stage, to depict feeling rather than a precise description of place and detail of events. Carole Angier has written that "more than Primo Levi, she makes us see, feel and smell the bodies, the disgust of dirt, disease and diarrhoea, of rags and sores and rough blankets." It has been said that her book is one of the few works of testimony with literary value, in parts poetically written.

In common with many women's accounts, Tedeschi is concerned with the nature of relationships and less concerned to analyze and explain a system whose reason is constituted by unreason, "the systematic organisation of disorganisation," the impossibility of logical deductions. Her interactions with—and descriptions of—the women whose fate she shares are heavily influenced by stereotypes of national character and social class, seen by one commentator as a reflection of Tedeschi's relatively privileged background. She generalizes from her own experience to supposed characteristics of all Italians: their "open southern nature, so alien to brutality and hardship, so tenderly unprepared for camp life." She is drawn to the cultured French, disdains the Greeks and Hungarians, and is revolted by the Poles.

The account of relationships is focused on nurturing cooperation and bonds of unity, not the fierce competition for survival. The system seeks to strip women of their femininity but does not invariably succeed; memories return, maternal feelings remain, there are fleeting, unexpected reminders of home. This situation is, however, radically transformed during the brutal struggle for life that marks the last stages of the war, when friends who acted as "anchors to each other" had "moments when they were overcome by bestiality."

—Andrew Markus

See the essay on *There Is a Place on Earth: A Woman in Birkenau.*

THOMAS, D(onald) M(ichael)

Nationality: British. **Born:** Redruth, Cornwall, 27 January 1935. **Education:** New College, Oxford University, B.A. (honors) in English 1958, M.A. 1961. **Military Service:** British Army (national service), 1953–54. **Family:** Married twice; two sons and one daughter. **Career:** Teacher, Teignmouth Grammar School, Devon, 1959–63; senior lecturer in English, Hereford College of Education, 1964–78. Visiting lecturer in English, Hamline University, St. Paul, Minnesota, 1967; lecturer in creative writing, American University, Washington, D.C., 1982. **Awards:** Richard Hillary memorial prize, 1960; British Arts Council award, for translation, 1975, for novel, 1980; Cholmondeley award, for poetry, 1978; *Guardian-Gollancz* Fantasy Novel prize, 1979; *Los Angeles Times* prize, for fiction, 1981; Cheltenham prize, for novel, 1981; Silver Pen award, 1982.

PUBLICATIONS

Collection

Selected Poems. 1983.

Novels

The Flute Player. 1979.
Birthstone. 1980.
The White Hotel. 1981.
Russian Nights (tetralogy):
  Ararat. 1983.
  Swallow. 1984.
  Sphinx. 1986.
  Summit. 1987.
Lying Together. 1990.

Flying into Love. 1992.
Pictures at an Exhibition. 1993.
Eating Pavlova. 1994.
Lady with a Laptop. 1996.

Poetry

Personal and Possessive. 1964.
Two Voices. 1968.
Logan Stone. 1971.
The Shaft. 1973.
Symphony in Moscow. 1974.
Poem of the Midway and Other Poems. 1974.
Love and Other Deaths. 1975.
The Honeymoon Voyage. 1978.
Dreaming in Bronze. 1981.
Protest. 1982.
News from the Front, with Sylvia Kantaris. 1983.
The Puberty Tree: New and Selected Poems. 1992.

Plays

The White Hotel, adaptation of his own novel (produced Edinburgh, 1984).

Radio Plays: *You Will Hear Thunder,* 1981; *Boris Godunov,* adaptation of the play by Alexander Pushkin, 1984.

Memoir

Memories and Hallucinations. 1988.

Other

The Devil and the Floral Dance, with John Astrop (for children). 1978.
Alexander Solzhenitsyn. A Century in His Life. 1998.
Charlotte Brontë Revelations: The Final Journey of Jane Eyre. 2000.

Editor, *The Granite Kingdom: Poems of Cornwall: An Anthology.* 1970.
Editor, *Poetry in Crosslight.* 1975.
Editor, *Songs from the Earth: Selected Poems of John Harris, Cornish Miner, 1820–84.* 1977.

Translator, *Requiem, and Poem without a Hero,* by Anna Akhmatova. 1976.
Translator, *Way of All the Earth,* by Anna Akhmatova. 1979.
Translator, *Invisible Threads,* by Yevgeny Yevtushenko. 1981.
Translator, *The Bronze Horseman and Other Poems,* by Alexander Pushkin. 1982.
Translator, *A Dove in Santiago,* by Yevgeny Yevtushenko. 1982.
Translator, *Boris Godunov,* by Alexander Pushkin. 1985.

Translator, *You Will Hear Thunder: Poems,* by Anna Akhmatova. 1985.

Translator, *Vozvrashchenie pushkinskoi Rusalki/The Return of Pushkin's Rusalka,* by Alexander Pushkin and Vladimir Retsepter. 1998.

*

Manuscript Collection: Department of Special Collections Memorial Library, University of Wisconsin, Madison.

Critical Studies: "D.M. Thomas" by David Brooks, in *Helix* (Australia), 21(22), Spring 1985, pp. 33–41; "Oracle and Womb: Delphic Myth in D.M. Thomas' *The White Hotel*" by Chris Ellery, in *Notes on Contemporary Literature,* 19(3), May 1989, p. 3–4; "Art and the Unseen Pattern in the Universe: An Interview with D.M. Thomas" by Rosa Gonzalez, in *BELLS,* 3, 1989, pp. 63–70; "D.M. Thomas' *The White Hotel:* Mirrors, Triangles, and Sublime Repression" by Robert D. Newman, in *MFS,* 35(2), Summer 1989, pp.193–209; "The Phalaris Syndrome: Alain Robbe-Grillet vs. D.M. Thomas" by K.J. Phillips, in *Women and Violence in Literature: An Essay Collection,* edited by Katherine Anne Ackley, 1990; "The Soul Is a Far Country: D.M. Thomas and *The White Hotel*" by Richard K. Cross, in *Journal of Modern Literature,* 18(1), Winter 1992, pp. 19–47; "Translation and Plagiarism: Puskin and D.M. Thomas" by Lauren G. Leighton, in *Slavic and East European Journal,* 38(1), Spring 1994, pp. 69–83; "Solomon's Fair Shulamite in D.M. Thomas' *The White Hotel*" by David Leon Higdon, in *Journal of Modern Literature,* 19(2), Fall 1995, pp. 328–33; *D.M. Thomas* by Rachel Wetzsteon, 1997.

* * *

The British novelist, poet, translator, and biographer D.M. Thomas is an extremely controversial figure. His connection to Holocaust literature lies principally in his 1981 novel *The White Hotel,* about which there is a small critical industry, and to a lesser extent through his later novels *Pictures at an Exhibition* (1993) and *Eating Pavlova* (1994).

Thomas began publishing poetry in the 1960s and novels in the 1970s. Critics usually single out his interests in sex and death, often mediated by psychoanalysis. They comment less often, however, on the fact that, unusually and unfashionably for an English novelist of his generation, his range of reference and erudition is deeply European. He has a special interest in Russian literature and ideas and wrote a four-volume sequence called *Russian Nights.* He has translated Anna Akhmatova, **Yevgeny Yevtushenko,** and Alexander Pushkin's *Boris Godunov* and has written a well-received biography of Alexander Solzhenitsyn. The crucial scenes of *The White Hotel* are set in the Ukraine.

His most celebrated Holocaust novel, *The White Hotel* was controversial for a number of reasons. Its climatic scene drew

heavily on **Anatoli Kuznetsov**'s "true novel" *Babi Yar,* which Thomas read on tour in the United States in 1980. A year after *The White Hotel* was published, this "plagiarism" was revealed in a letter to the *Times Literary Supplement,* and a controversy ensued in which Thomas was accused of appropriating both Kuznetsov's work and the life story of the survivor, Dina Pronicheva. (Kuznetsov also uses Pronicheva's account, in a way similar to that of Thomas, to guarantee authenticity but makes it clear that it is her account and does not interweave it into his narrative). In his defense Thomas stated that he "wanted the events to be authentic. It would have seemed immoral had I, a comfortable Briton, fictionalised the Holocaust."

A number of critics, notably Susanne Kappeler in *The Pornography of Representation,* also suggested that the novel was pornographic. Like much of Thomas's work, it certainly does not shy away from graphic representation. Nonetheless, it is both less graphic and more comprehensible, in its psychoanalytic context, than the lurid and exploitative scenes in, for example, **Jerzy Kosinski**'s *The Painted Bird.* Sue Vice, in her *Holocaust Fiction,* gives a good account of both these controversies.

The novel certainly is experimental, mixing intertextually historical accounts and fictional characters and combining different styles and genres. In this it is very different from realistic novels such as *Sophie's Choice* or from so-called true novels in the realistic style such as *Schindler's List.* It could be argued that *The White Hotel,* for all its failings, laid the literary groundwork for other more experimental Holocaust novels, such as **David Grossman**'s *See Under: Love,* Martin Amis's *Time's Arrow,* and Anne Michaels's *Fugative Pieces,* and should perhaps be read in this context. Unlike many British literary responses to the Holocaust, which approach the events much more obliquely if at all, Thomas does engage with the issues of Holocaust representation straight on.

Thomas's later works that involved the Holocaust were not so well received and seemed to be less complex and ambiguous. Brian Cheyette has argued that *Pictures at an Exhibition* was "a cold and calculated piece of writing, extremely self-conscious about its intentions and designed to make its author a great deal of money." These books, unlike *The White Hotel,* were not literary or commercial successes.

Jago Morrison has written that at "the extremes of his career Thomas has been hailed a genius, praised as a scholar, and dismissed as an unreadable degenerate. It remains to be seen in which combination his reputation will finally be fixed." Although the Holocaust is not the center of his work, because of *The White Hotel* and the issues the book raised, his role in the development of Holocaust fiction is an important one.

—Robert Eaglestone

See the essay on *The White Hotel.*

TILLION, Germaine (Marie Rosine)

Nationality: French. **Born:** Allegre, 30 May 1907. **Education:** University of Paris, M.A.; diplomas from Practical School of Advanced Studies, National School of Living Oriental Languages, and School of the Louvre. **Career:** Conducted ethnographic missions in the Aures (Algeria), 1934–40; member, Musée de l'Homme (French resistance network), 1940–42; prisoner, Paris, 1942–43; prisoner of war, Ravensbrück, Germany, 1943–45; investigated German war crimes and Soviet concentration camps, 1945–54; conducted inquires into injustices in Algeria, 1954–62. Director and chair in ethnography of the Maghreb, Ecole Pratique des Hautes Etudes, Paris, beginning 1957. Participated in National Science Research Center missions among the Tauregs and Moors, 1964–65 and 1966. **Awards:** Officer, French Legion of Honor, 1975; Croix de Guerre; Rosette of Resistance.

PUBLICATIONS

Memoir

Ravensbrück. 1946; revised and expanded edition, 1973; translated as *Ravensbrück,* 1975; revised edition, 1988.

Other

L'Algérie en 1957. 1957; as *Algeria: The Realities,* 1958.
Les Ennemis-complémentaires. 1960; as *France and Algeria: Complementary Enemies,* 1961.
L'Afrique bascule vers l'avenir; L'Algerie en 1957 et autres textes. 1960.
Le Harem et les cousins. 1966; as *The Republic of Cousins: Women's Oppression in Mediterranean Society,* 1983.
La Traversée du mal: Entretien avec Jean Lacouture, with Jean Lacouture. 1997.
Il était une fois l'ethnographie. 2000.

*

Critical Studies: ''Reflections on Three Ravensbrucks'' by Pierre Vidal-Naquet, translated by David Ames Curtis, in *South Atlantic Quarterly,* 96(4), Fall 1997, pp. 881–94; *Le Témoignage est un combat: Une biographie de Germaine Tillion* by Jean Lacouture, 2000.

* * *

When she joined one of the first cells of the French resistance in Paris in 1940, Germaine Tillion was a rising star in the field of ethnography and cultural anthropology and had spent several years researching the Berber population in North Africa. One of her mentors was Marcel Mauss, the famous Jewish anthropologist, who helped open her eyes to the seriousness and scope of Nazi crimes. Tillion was arrested in 1942 and spent the next 14 months in French prisons, where she was allowed to continue her scholarly activities. In 1943 she was deported along with other female prisoners to the Ravensbrück labor camp for women, where she remained until the end of the war. Tillion used her tenacity and scientific skills to gather information both during and after the period of her captivity. After the war she devoted much of her life to documenting and analyzing the Holocaust, using her personal experience as a guide but not limiting herself to it. Her three books on Ravensbrück, published in 1946, 1973, and 1988, respectively, are therefore valuable not only as eyewitness accounts but also as examples of rigorous, comprehensive scientific inquiry into the Nazi practices of deportation, slave labor, and mass murder. Though she has been criticized at times for allowing her personal experience to be overshadowed by a wall of academic research, such as in the review by Nancy R. Chiswick in *Contemporary Sociology* (1977), the combination of testimonial and scientific method help place *Ravensbrück* among the most important French works on the Holocaust.

Tillion's scientific career is not easily dissociable from her political activities both before and after the war or from her wartime captivity. Her early research on the Berbers centered on the role of ethnicity in a social and political context, which in turn led her to examine developments in Germany, especially the policies affecting Jews, with more insight and objectivity than many of her contemporaries. She started her North African research over again in the 1950s (all her earlier notes and manuscripts had been lost or destroyed at the time of her transfer to Ravensbrück), just in time to witness the rise of the Algerian independence movement. When the Algerian war broke out, Tillion became an outspoken critic of French colonialism and military policy. Her growing scientific reputation, along with her own wartime experiences, contributed to her credibility. In the 1950s and '60s she published numerous articles and several books on France's relationship with Algeria, on family structures and women in North African society, and on postcolonialism.

Tillion achieved scientific fame as an Africanist but never strayed very far from her commitment to the growing field of Holocaust studies. Much of her insight into the Algerian conflict stems from connections she perceived with World War II, including some historical and, at times, ironic continuities between the two conflicts: in the 1973 edition of *Ravensbrück,* for example, she includes a testimonial by an Algerian woman who, after being tortured by French soldiers, was treated by a German doctor of the French Foreign Legion who had been a member of the SS.

It was not only Tillion's ongoing research on Nazi camps that compelled her to publish the revised and expanded versions of *Ravensbrück* but also the growing phenomenon of Holocaust denial, including some that emanated from the academic establishment. She specifically mentions Olga Wormser-Migot's doctoral thesis, *The Nazi Concentrationary System* published by Presses Universitaires de France in 1968, in which the existence of gas chambers at Buchenwald, Dachau, and Mauthausen is questioned. Sensing that the attacks on the Holocaust would only grow more frequent, Tillion promoted the work of other Holocaust historians and went into the archives to find corroboration of her own memories and those of her fellow survivors. Her contribution to the history of the Holocaust consists primarily of her skill in gathering and recording information while a prisoner and her subsequent lifelong quest to recover and synthesize data as a means of correcting and supporting the growing number of eyewitness accounts, including her own. In addition, she consistently displays in her work an ability to discuss the broad historical context of the Holocaust, as well as an attempt to explain its causes and effects from a philosophical, rather than strictly historical or sociological, perspective.

—M. Martin Guiney

See the essay on *Ravensbrück*.

TORY, Avraham

Nationality: Israeli (originally Russian: immigrated to Palestine, 1947). **Born:** Avraham Golub, 10 December 1909, Lazdijai, Lithuania. **Education:** Lithuanian University Kovno, Faculty of Law 1933; also studied at the University of Pittsburgh. **Military Service:** Military attorney (reserve), 1954–63. **Family:** Married Pnina Ushpiz in 1944; three daughters. **Career:** Gymnast, Lithuanian Maccabi sports team, early 1930s; central committee member, General Zionist Union, ca. 1930s; secretary, Kovno Jewish Ghetto Committee, 1941–44; cofounder and leader, Matzok, underground Zionist organization, early 1940s. Lawyer in Tel-Aviv, 1952–96. Secretary general, International Association of Jewish Lawyers and Jurists, and Maccabi World Union. Editor, *Al Hoopin* (Italy), 1945–47. **Awards:** Maccabiah World Games award, 1966; Union of Jewish Academicians certificate, 1977, 1983; Maccabi World Union "Yakir World Maccabi" award, 1985. **Died:** 24 February 2002.

PUBLICATIONS

Diary

Geto yom-yom: Yoman u-mismakhim mi-Geto Kovnah, edited by Dina Porat. 1988; as *Surviving the Holocaust: The Kovno Ghetto Diary,* edited by Martin Gilbert, 1990.

Other

Editor, *Ha-Makabiyah ha-Revi'it: Yisra'el Sukot 714.* 1953.
Editor, *Mariyampol: 'Al gedot ha-nahar Sheshupeh (Lita)* [Marijampole on the River Shewshupe (Lithuania)]. 1986.

Editor, *Terumat Yehudim mi-Lita le-vinyan ha-arets u-Medinat Yisra'el* [Lithuanian Jews in the Upbuilding of the Land and the State of Israel]. 1988.

*   *   *

Avraham Tory (originally Avraham Golub) was born in the Lithuanian village of Lazdijai in 1909, the youngest of six children. He was educated at a cheder, then elementary school and at the Hebrew Gymnasium in Marijampolé, the district town. At the age of 19 he began the study of law in Kovno, then spent some time in the United States at the University of Pittsburgh before returning to complete his degree in Kovno in 1933. After graduation he was denied an opportunity to practice and held several assistantships, one to a judge, another to a university professor.

In his youth he became an active Zionist, at one stage heading a Zionist student fraternity and serving on the central committee of the Maccabi Sports Association. In 1932 he led the Lithuanian Maccabi sports team at the first Maccabiah Games held in Tel Aviv, where he participated as a gymnast. After the games he represented Lithuanian Jewish students at a world convention held at the Hebrew University of Jerusalem. He served as a central committee member of the right-wing General Zionist Union and in March 1939 was sent as delegate to a convention of Eastern European Zionists in Warsaw; five months later he was in Switzerland at the 21st Zionist Congress. Although war broke out during the congress, he chose to return to Lithuania. For a time he worked for the Soviet administration but came under increasing scrutiny because of his Zionist connections and went into hiding in the last weeks of Soviet rule.

Following the establishment of German control, marked by massacres in the streets of Kovno, a Council of Elders was ordered to be established. Tory served as a member and subsequently as head of its secretariat. He was also one of the founders and leaders of Matzok, the Zionist underground group in the ghetto. He began to keep a diary, its first entry dated 22 July 1941. He also collected documents issued by the German authorities and the council and encouraged artists and photographers to maintain a visual record.

The diary was written at all hours, whenever opportunity presented. At meetings he sometimes made jottings to help him compile an accurate record. Some entries were dictated to Pnina Sheinzon, his future wife. The chairman of the council, Dr. Elchanan Elkes, knew about the diary, as did his deputy Leib Garfunkel, and at times checked the accuracy of Tory's account. One other member of the council knew of the diary, as did several who assisted with the collection of material and its safekeeping. The records were carefully wrapped and packed in five small wooden crates lined with tar paper and buried beneath a cellar. In the summer of 1943, with fear of mass deportations increasing, Tory visited a priest, V. Vaickus, and gave him details of the hiding place lest he and his confidants not survive.

Tory's purpose, as recorded in his last will and testament written in December 1942, was to provide evidence for the prosecution of Nazi criminals and their collaborators after the war. Written in simple, readily accessible, unvarnished language, the diary aims to provide a precise and detailed description of daily events and record of interaction with those Germans and Lithuanians placed in positions of authority. Author Louise Erdrich has commented that "the power of this book lies precisely in its lack of poetry, in its refusal to generalize."

Tory was driven by the fear that no member of the Jewish community would survive to bear testimony; he saw it as his duty to "put into writing what my eyes had seen and my ears had heard, and what I had experienced personally." Survivors were adjured to punish the perpetrators. He ended his will with the demands: "Revenge! Never Forget! Never Forgive!." Tory left the ghetto on 23 March 1944 and evaded capture. During the week after his escape more than 1,000 of the remaining residents were killed; three months later, between 8 and 11 July, the surviving 8,000 were deported to Germany and the buildings set on fire.

Kovno was liberated on 1 August 1944. Tory returned several days later and, at considerable risk, recovered three of the five crates. The Germans had earlier learned of the existence of records but, despite the use of torture, had been unable to locate where they were hidden. Tory subsequently left most of the contents for safekeeping and transport with a member of Brichah, the organization helping Jews reach Palestine. He arrived in Palestine in 1947 and subsequently regained most but not all of the material. He practiced as a lawyer in Tel Aviv and became secretary general of the International Association of Jewish Lawyers and Jurists and secretary general of the Maccabi World Union. His diary was authenticated and used in trials and other legal proceedings against Nazi officials and their collaborators. It was published in a Hebrew edition in Israel in 1988 and in English in 1990 together with a short biographical sketch by the book's editor, Sir Martin Gilbert.

—Andrew Markus

See the essay on *Surviving the Holocaust: The Kovno Ghetto Diary.*

U

URIS, Leon (Marcus)

Nationality: American. **Born:** Baltimore, Maryland, 3 August 1924. **Education:** Baltimore public schools. **Military Service:** United States Marine Corps, 1942–45: served in the Pacific at Guadalcanal and Tarawa. **Family:** Married 1) Betty Katherine Beck in 1945 (divorced 1968), one daughter and two sons; 2) Margery Edwards in 1968 (died 1969); 3) Jill Peabody in 1970, one daughter; one other child. **Career:** Circulation district manager, *San Francisco Call-Bulletin.* **Awards:** Daroff Memorial award and National Institute of Arts and Letters grant, both in 1959; California Literature Silver Medal award, 1962, for *Mila 18,* and Gold Medal award, 1965, for *Armageddon;* Irish/American Society of New York John F. Kennedy medal, 1977; Eire Society of Boston gold medal, 1978; State of Israel Jobotinsky medal, 1980; Concord Academy Hall fellowship (with wife, Jill Uris), 1980; Hebrew University of Jerusalem Scopus award, 1981. Honorary doctorates: University of Colorado, 1976; Santa Clara University, 1977; Wittenberg University, 1980; Lincoln College, 1985. **Address:** c/o Doubleday & Co. Inc., 666 5th Avenue, New York, New York 10103, U.S.A.

PUBLICATIONS

Novels

Battle Cry. 1953.
The Angry Hills. 1955.
Exodus. 1958.
Mila 18. 1961.
Armageddon: A Novel of Berlin. 1964.
Topaz. 1967.
QB VII. 1970.
Trinity. 1976.
The Haj. 1984.
Mitla Pass. 1988.
Redemption (sequel to *Trinity*). 1995.
A God in Ruins: A Novel. 1999.

Plays

Ari, adaptation of his *Exodus,* music by Walt Smith (produced New York, 1971).

Screenplays: *Battle Cry,* 1954; *Gunfight at the O.K. Corral,* 1957.

Other

Exodus Revisited, with Dimitrios Harissiadis (photo essay). 1959; as *In the Steps of Exodus,* 1962.
The Third Temple (essay). Published with William Stevenson's *Strike Zion,* 1967.
Ireland: A Terrible Beauty: The Story of Ireland Today, with Jill Uris (photo essay). 1975.
Jerusalem, Song of Songs, with Jill Uris (photo essay). 1981.

*

Film Adaptations: *Battle Cry,* 1954; *Gunfight at the O.K. Corral,* 1957; *The Angry Hills,* 1959; *Exodus,* 1960; *Topaz,* 1969; *QB VII* (television), 1974.

Critical Studies: *Exodus, A Distortion of Truth* by Aziz S. Sahwell, 1960; ''*Trinity:* The Formulas of History'' by Wayne Hall, in *Eire-Ireland,* 13(4), 1978, pp. 137–44; ''Semi-Aesthetic Detachment: The Fusing of Fictional and External Worlds in the Situational Literature of Leon Uris'' by Sharon D. Downey and Richard A. Kallan, in *Communication Monographs,* 49(3), September 1982, pp. 192–204; ''Voicing the Arab: Multivocality and Ideology in Leon Uris' *The Haj*'' by Elise Salem Manganaro, in *MELUS,* 15(4), Winter 1988, pp. 3–13; *Leon Uris: A Critical Companion* by Kathleen Shine Cain, 1998; '''Rambowitz' Versus the 'Schlemiel' in Leon Uris' *Exodus*'' by Henry Gonshak, in *Journal of American Culture,* 22(1), Spring 1999, pp. 9–16.

* * *

The Holocaust and World War II are central concerns of most of the works of Leon Uris. His first novel, *Battle* Cry (1953), was based largely on his own experiences in the U.S. Marine Corps in the Pacific. His second novel, *The Angry Hills* (1955), was largely based on the experiences of his uncle, who fought in the Greek resistance against the Nazis. Working on *The Angry Hills* seems to have led to his interest in the European theater during the war and consequently to his best known work, *Exodus* (1958). For Uris the persecution of the Jews in Europe, and especially the Holocaust, led directly to the founding of Israel. As part of his story of the beginning of the Jewish state, he tells about the survival of several of his central characters in Nazi-occupied Europe and consequently depicts some of the more horrible aspects of the Holocaust. He also treats the work of some of his other central characters, in particular his protagonist, Ari Ben Canaan, in fighting for the

British against the Nazis. He describes the aftermath of the Holocaust, with Jews wandering throughout Europe, unwanted by any country but kept out of Israel by the British so that they had to be smuggled into the Middle East by the very people who had fought for the British during the war. And he describes the fighting, both diplomatic and actual, that led to the establishment of the State of Israel.

Another work in which the Holocaust is central is *Mila 18* (1961), about the uprising in the Warsaw Ghetto, an event Uris treats briefly in *Exodus*. In addition, *QB VII* (1970) focuses on the American author Abe Cady, a fictitious character based in part on Uris himself, who writes a book called *The Holocaust* about a Polish Roman Catholic surgeon, Adam Kelno, who was a prisoner in the fictitious Jadwiga Concentration Camp, where many of Cady's relatives were murdered. Cady accuses Kelno of collaborating with the Nazis by performing unnecessary experimental surgery on Jews in the camp. The surgeon sues Cady for libel in the Court of Queen's Bench in London. The novel deals with both the Holocaust and its aftermath, including continuing anti-Semitism in Poland and the possibility that "we are wrecking our world beyond our ability to save ourselves." As the trial ends, the Six-Day War is being fought. The last section of the novel includes an Associated Press dispatch from Tel Aviv dated June 6, 1967, reporting on the "light" casualties the Israeli Defense Ministry announced for that day, including the death of "Sergen (Captain) Ben Cady, son of the well-known author."

Uris's works tend to be based on fact. He researches carefully the backgrounds of the historic episodes he treats. In fact, he tends to be so accurate on historic facts that some reviewers have labeled certain of his works nonfiction novels.

Central to many of Uris's works lies the Jewish superman, a genuine larger-than-life hero whose physical size, strength, and extreme intelligence enable him to win victories that others could not. Ari Ben Canaan of *Exodus* and Andrei Androfski of *Mila 18* are examples of this kind of hero. So is Abe Cady of *QB VII,* a former college and semiprofessional baseball player, flyer in World War II, novelist, and journalist. After the war he travels throughout Europe, visiting, among other places, the Jadwiga Concentration Camp. Out of that visit his book on the Holocaust grows. When a Jewish university in the United States contacts Cady to participate in a fundraiser to support the school's academic work, he responds that he will participate only if the money he raises can be used to create a football team composed of "big buck Jews" who could severely beat Notre Dame and other non-Jewish schools. In this Jew, who combines both physical and intellectual superiority, Uris sees the hope of never experiencing another Holocaust. Still, his portraits of Jews are not as unbalanced as they at first might seem. In *Mila 18,* for example, he also treats Jewish smugglers, collaborators, members of the Judenrat, or Jewish Council, and Jewish police. His ultimate goal seems to be to depict Jews as human beings subject to the same drives, weaknesses, and strengths as other human beings.

—Richard Tuerk

See the essay on *Mila 18.*

V

VARGA, Susan

Nationality: Australian (originally Hungarian: immigrated to Australia, 1948). **Born:** Hungary, 1943. **Education:** Sydney University, M.A.; University of New South Wales, law degree. **Family:** Married (divorced). **Career:** Lawyer and journalist; also worked in film and video. Since 1990 full-time writer. Lives in New South Wales. **Award:** Fellowship of Australian Writers Christina Stead award for biography, 1994, for *Heddy and Me*. **Agent:** c/o Sceptre Hodder Headline Australia, Level 22, 201 Kent St., Sydney, New South Wales 2000, Australia.

PUBLICATIONS

Memoir

Heddy and Me. 1994.

Novel

Happy Families. 1999.

Other

Broometime, with Anne Coombs. 2001.

* * *

Susan Varga is one of the most accomplished of Australia's second-generation, post-Holocaust autobiographers. She is a survivor's daughter and a child survivor, and her writing is deeply shaped by the Holocaust, but she also addresses issues of gender, sexual orientation, race, and Australian cultural identity. Varga was born in Hungary in 1943. Her father died in a labor camp during the war. She spent much of the war in hiding with her mother, Heddy, and her sister. After the war her mother married a survivor who had lost his wife and two sons at Auschwitz. The family emigrated to Australia in 1948.

Like many first-person narratives by postwar eastern European Australian Jews, Varga's autobiography, *Heddy and Me* (1994), gives a compelling account of the migrant experience, especially of the way migrant children learned to move "between our two worlds," the European and the Australian. *Heddy and Me* won the 1994 Fellowship of Australian Writers Christina Stead Award for biography/autobiography and was short-listed for three other major awards. It has been translated into German and Hungarian. The book is also one of several Hungarian-Australian Jewish autobiographies (others include Andrew Riemer's *Inside/Outside* and *The Habsburg Café* and

Paul Kraus's *A New Australian, A New Australia*) that record a return journey, undertaken when the author is an adult, to the scenes of ancestral catastrophe. After the family had settled in Australia, Varga's stepfather and his brother established a clothing business in Sydney. Other successful business ventures followed, and with them came increasing material security. Varga earned an M.A. in English from Sydney University and later a law degree from the University of New South Wales. After pursuing various careers, including work in film, video, and the law, she settled into full-time writing in 1990. Married and divorced, she has lived in the southern highlands of New South Wales with fellow writer Anne Coombs since 1991.

Varga's first novel, *Happy Families* (1999), gives a broad sociological overview of contemporary Australian life and the often contrasting elements that comprise it: city and country, "old" Europe and "new" Australia, black and white Australians, male and female values. Coauthored with Coombs, *Broometime* (2001) is the sometimes controversial record of a nine-month period the couple spent in Broome, a large town on the northern coast of Western Australia. Varga has also written poetry. She has been active in movements to promote reconciliation with indigenous Australians and to create more enlightened policies for the treatment of refugees to Australia.

Varga's writing about the Holocaust is distinctively relational in its orientation. *Heddy and Me* combines an account of the Holocaust and its aftermath with a history of the daughter's relationship with her mother. The two narrative strands are intimately entwined. The Holocaust has powerfully shaped the often difficult relationship between the two, but researching the Holocaust has helped Varga better to understand Heddy and to arrive at a less fraught relationship with her. The book's last lines are "I chat often with Heddy on the phone. We rarely talk about anything important, but it is comfortable chat. We like each other. We have things in common, Heddy and I." The shift from the "me" of the title to the concluding "I" signals a new existential security and a new sanguinity in the outlook of this hitherto troubled post-Holocaust Jew.

—Richard Freadman

See the essay on *Heddy and Me*.

VERSTANDIG, Mark

Nationality: Australian (originally Polish: immigrated to Australia after World War II). **Born:** 1912. **Education:** Studied law, Jagellonian University, Kraków, graduated 1936. **Family:** Married Frieda Reich in 1940. **Career:** Involved with the Revisionist Student Organization, ca. 1920. Lived in Germany following World War II; moved to Paris, 1949, then to Australia. Textile manufacturer, Melbourne, until 1973. Also worked as a Yiddish broadcaster, public speaker, and journalist. Contributor, *Ibergang* and *Unzer Welt* newspapers, Germany.

PUBLICATION

Memoir

I Rest My Case. 1995.

* * *

Mark Verstandig was born in 1912, the youngest son in a Hassidic family of seven children. His father owned a substantial country estate, Sadkowa Gora, with a second home in the shtetl of Mielec in western Galicia, near Kraków, Poland. While his father had substantial assets in land, his cash income was limited.

Verstandig received his first years of education in the local cheder and Talmud Torah, then attended gymnasium, where he excelled. At the age of 17 he became a Betar activist. He attended the Jagellonian University in Kraków to study law but for much of his time was involved in the politics of the Revisionist Student Organization. One of his responsibilities was to provide for the needs of revisionist notables on visits to Kraków. He frequently skipped classes and crammed to pass exams, although he showed outstanding ability, winning essay prizes and receiving a commission from one of his professors to prepare a comparative analysis of Hebrew and Roman law. He continued this task after graduation in 1936 and would have earned a doctorate but for the outbreak of war.

After graduation he returned to Mielec to practice law, establishing good contacts with non-Jewish practitioners. In the first years of the German occupation he continued to work clandestinely with the approval of local practitioners and judges. He married Frieda Reich in December 1940. Following the deportation of the town's 10,000 Jews and the shooting of thousands, including his father, he spent more than two years in hiding, for some time in Warsaw separated from his wife, then hidden by peasants in the neighborhood of his home. The substantial wealth of the two families, reliable contacts, sound judgment of risk, and good luck enabled Verstandig and Frieda to survive. With the exception of his brother, who escaped to Russia with his wife and children, all the close relatives of both families were murdered.

After liberation Verstandig worked for a period for the Soviet authorities in a legal capacity; following the Kielce pogrom he escaped to Germany with his wife and became prominent in the politics of the Sheyris Hapleyta, his name recognized across the world. After moving to Paris in 1949, he visited Israel but, recognizing the difficulties of establishing himself in the new nation, he opted to immigrate to Australia, attracted by what he perceived as its nonpolitical culture and opportunities to forget the nightmares of the past. After leaving Poland he gave up the prospect of continuing law, and he and Frieda retrained themselves for work in the textile trade. Settling in Melbourne, he quickly built up a flourishing business, within a year of his arrival employing some 100 workers and reputed to be producing the best leather jackets in the country. He continued to diversify and prosper but did not find the work of accumulating wealth satisfying and retired at the age of 61, having provided for his old age. As a matter of principle he never applied for compensation from the German state.

An accomplished writer, Verstandig had long experience in journalism, beginning in his university days. In postwar Germany he joined the editorial board of *Ibergang*, published by the Federation of Polish Jewry in the American zone, and contributed to that paper and to the revisionist *Unzer Welt*, at one stage journalism providing his major source of income. In Australia he was a prominent representative of the revisionist interest, regularly the main speaker at the Vladimir Jabotinsky Yahrzeit celebrations and writer for the Yiddish press. After retirement he lessened his involvement in sectional politics, shifting his attention to cultural and welfare pursuits.

His autobiography was written late in life, in part as a legacy for his grandchildren. He states that he was initially reluctant to write because he had not been in a concentration camp or ghetto, but this reluctance was overcome by his daughter. The text is clearly aimed at a general readership and seeks to add to the record of a world laid waste, to present his understanding of issues that he views as inadequately covered in the existing literature.

On display is the persona of a man of principle, committed to a lifelong quest for justice, blessed with superior intelligence and education, self-assured, of independent means and outlook, who invariably succeeded in what he set out to do. The book brings a lawyer's discipline to the detailed description of events and analysis of the factors motivating human action and the impact of major religious institutions, political movements, and governments. He draws not only on his own direct experience and those told to him by his broad network of friends and acquaintances but also has made a limited study of historical work and documents deposited in the Yad Vashem archives and other institutions. While the writing of history based on documentary sources intrudes rarely in the book, it indicates the author's effort to be fully informed.

I Rest My Case stands at the forefront of memoirs dealing with the structure of Jewish life in pre-Holocaust Poland and survival in hiding. It has been described as "cool, precise, densely detailed," "enlivened by a sharp sense of humour," and, in the words of the leading Australian commentator Sam

Lipski, as "a major work of sociological and historical significance . . . [that] transcends the academic to become memorable journalism and literature."

—Andrew Markus

See the essay on *I Rest My Case.*

VRBA, Rudolf

Nationality: British and Canadian (originally Czechoslovakian: British citizenship, 1966; Canadian citizenship, 1972.) **Born:** Walter Rosenberg, Topolcany, 11 September 1924. **Education:** Czech Technical University, Prague, 1945–49, Ing. Chem. 1949; Dr. Techn. Sc. 1951; Czechoslovak Academy of Science, Prague, C.Sc. 1956. **Military Service:** Czechoslovak Partisan Units 1944–45: Chechoslovak Medal for Bravery, Medal of Meritorious Fighter, and Order of Slovak National Insurrection. **Career:** Escaped from Auschwitz, 1944. Researcher, Institute of Industrial Hygiene and Occupational Diseases, Ministry of Health, Prague, 1953–58; biochemist, Veterinary Research Institute, Ministry of Agriculture, Beth Dagan, Israel, 1958–60; scientific staff member, British MRC, Neuropsychiatric Research Unit, Carshalton, Surrey, England, 1960–67; associate, Medical Research Council of Canada, 1967–73; visiting lecturer, Harvard Medical School, and research fellow, Massachusetts General Hospital, Boston, 1973–75. Since 1976 associate professor, Faculty of Medicine, University of British Columbia, Vancouver, Canada. Helped produce several films on the Holocaust, 1972–85. **Awards:** Laufberger Medal for Physiology, Czech Academy of Science and Medical Society J.E. Purkinje, Prague, 1993. Ph.D.: Honoris Causa, University of Haifa, 1998.

PUBLICATIONS

Memoir

I Cannot Forgive, with Alan Bestic. 1963; as *44070: The Conspiracy of the Twentieth Century,* 1989.

Other

The Auschwitz Report of April 1944, with Alfred Wetzler. 1981; annotated edition, as *London Has Been Informed,* edited by Henryk Swiebocki, 1997.

* * *

Rudolf Vrba was one of the few who escaped from the Nazis during World War II, doing so from Auschwitz on 7 April 1944. With Alfred Wetzler, with whom he escaped, he wrote the Vrba-Wetzler report, which played no small role in alerting the world to the Holocaust.

The book has a swift and enthralling narrative with an adventure-like feel to it. This is because of the events it discusses (escapes, evasions of capture) and because, unlike most of the victims, the men and women discussed in this memoir were not the most wretched of the camps. It is also, however, because of the time and place it was published, and the audience for which it was written, more used to John Buchan than **Primo Levi.**

The book's genesis sheds some light on the way it tells its horror-filled story. In 1958 Vrba, who had been studying and living in Prague, left to take up a place with the British Medical Research Council in London. At the time of the Adolf Eichmann trial, Vrba was encouraged to go to a major British paper, the *Daily Herald,* to tell them his story. Falling in with an Irish journalist, Alan Bestic, he wrote five pieces for the paper, which were a great success. One morning, however, Vrba was buttonholed by the man who delivered his milk, a war veteran. "I thoroughly disliked your articles . . . To be frank with you, I think that you came to this country from Czechoslovakia with the aim of disturbing our good post-war relations with Germany," he said. "What you are saying now is just malicious and incredible." Like many ordinary people, the story of the camps was too much for this milkman: while the concentration camp at Belsen was well known, the death camps of the east were less familiar to Britain at that time. Vrba realized that, although he had described what had happened, he had not explained well enough how it had come to be, how "this was all arranged by the perfidious German administration of the time." A year later the prosecutor at Frankfurt wrote to Vrba too: "I have got here eighty books of evidence about Auschwitz, and I still do not know anything about Auschwitz." Vrba says that he would have to write 81 books to make sure no detail was missed but has to settle for "choosing from my recollection those pieces which in their totality would enable even my honest old milkman to understand the principles used by the Germans to make the unthinkable and unspeakable machinery of Auschwitz a reality." Along with **Kitty Hart**'s memoir *I Am Alive!* the book was one of the first in Britain addressed to the general public. There were few Holocaust memoirs in Britain (or in the anglophone world) in the early 1960s, despite the influence of Anne Frank's diary.

Vrba was a witness in many trials and made a deposition for the Eichmann trial. He is also one of the narrators in **Claude Lanzmann**'s film *Shoah.*

The book—accessible, clear, and narrative driven—made a big impact and remains a major Holocaust text, not least for the extraordinary story of the escape from Auschwitz and the creation of the Vrba-Wetzler report.

—Robert Eaglestone

See the essay on *I Cannot Forgive.*

WALLANT, Edward Lewis

Nationality: American. **Born:** New Haven, Connecticut, 19 October 1926. **Education:** Pratt Institute, 1947–50; New School for Social Research, 1954–55. **Military Service:** United States Navy, 1944–46. **Family:** Married Joyce Fromkin in 1948; one son and two daughters. **Career:** Graphic artist for various advertising agencies, 1950–61. **Awards:** Bread Loaf Writers' Conference fellow, 1960; Jewish Book Council of America Harry and Ethel Daroff Memorial fiction award, 1961, for *The Human Season;* Guggenheim fellow, 1962; National Book Award nomination, 1962, for *The Pawnbroker.* **Died:** 5 December 1962.

PUBLICATIONS

Novels

The Human Season. 1958.
The Pawnbroker. 1961.
The Tenants of Moonbloom. 1963.
The Children at the Gate. 1964.

*

Film Adaptation: *The Pawnbroker,* 1964.

Critical Studies: ''The Secular Heart: The Achievement of Edward Lewis Wallant'' by Nicholas Ayo, in *Critique,* 12(2), 1970, pp. 86–94; ''The Sudden Hunger: An Essay on the Novels of Edward Lewis Wallant'' by Charles A. Hoyt, in *Minor American Novelists,* edited by Hoyt and Harry T. Moore, 1971; ''The Renewal of Dialogical Immediacy in Edward Lewis Wallant'' by William V. Davis, and ''The Hung-up Heroes of Edward Lewis Wallant'' by Robert W. Lewis, both in *Renascence: Essays on Value in Literature,* 24, 1972, pp. 59–84; *Edward Lewis Wallant* by David Galloway, 1979; ''From Buchenwald to Harlem: The Holocaust Universe of The Pawnbroker'' by Lillian S. Kremer, in *Literature, the Arts, and the Holocaust,* edited by Sanford Pinsker and Jack Fischel, 1987; ''The Mistral of Sol Nazerman: Nature Imagery in Wallant's *The Pawnbroker*'' by Arnold L. Goldsmith, in his *The Modern American Urban Novel,* 1991; ''Hollywood and the Holocaust: Remembering *The Pawnbroker*'' by Leonard J. Leff, in *American Jewish History,* 84(4), December 1996, pp. 353–76.

* * *

Known primarily as the author of *The Pawnbroker,* his only work to directly address the Holocaust, Edward Lewis Wallant wrote four novels before his untimely death at age 36 in 1962. David Galloway, in *Edward Lewis Wallant,* claims Wallant may have been inspired to address the trauma of the Holocaust after meeting a Jewish refugee who had survived the death camps when both were students and adds that visits to a relative's pawnshop in Harlem informed the novel's setting. Wallant's writing concerns Jewish American protagonists who struggle with mourning, guilt, ethics, and ethnic identity. Jewishness becomes juxtaposed to other American ethnicities, offering a sociological inscription of attitudes and problems found in urban and suburban New York City at the end of the 1950s and the beginning of the 1960s. His narratives particularize the tensions between Jews, Blacks, Hispanics, and WASP inhabitants of microcosmic enclaves ruled more often by relationships of commerce, exchange, and daily circumstance than they are by intimacy. Distance and disaffection rule even familial interactions, and the past shadows the present, giving the novels a psychoanalytic dimension, most often without the aid of therapeutic listeners. If Wallant's racial and ethnic portrayals may be accused of reproducing stereotypes and his symbolism of being too obvious, his novels tellingly evoke their historical moment.

Beginning with *The Human Season* (1958), Wallant uses a flashback structure to link a postwar U.S. environment to that of European Jewry before immigration. Each of the 18 chapters begins with incidents in the1950s linked to dreams of events in the past, giving the novel a frame that bears witness to Wallant's concern with form. His approach to temporal segmentation may be seen from the outset as strikingly cinematic, a comparison that the film adaptation of *The Pawnbroker* will later confirm. The dreams in *The Human Season* recall incidents focusing on the protagonist's relationship to his father and contrast the epochal changes across a single generation, as displacement undercuts rituals seen as anchoring previous generations to a sustaining heritage.

With the publication and acclaim of *The Pawnbroker* (1961) Wallant, who had graduated in commercial art from Pratt Institute to become an advertising art director, was able to devote himself entirely to writing, sustained by a relationship with publisher Harcourt, Brace & World and a Guggenheim grant. After Wallant's fatal stroke in December of 1962, his last two novels were published posthumously.

Wallant's *The Tenants of Moonbloom* (1963) examines the daily life of a rental agent, Norman Moonbloom, who, in effect, is the front man for his brother, a lower Manhattan slumlord. As in *The Pawnbroker,* the history of urban migration serves as the novel's backdrop, as an anachronistic ritual of face-to-face rent collection forces the protagonist to visit tenants who complain about the many malfunctioning and decrepit aspects of their dwellings. They either try to con the collector out of their debt or enlist his attention to display their sex fantasies, their anger at the world, or their diseases. Dark comedy changes to a poignant vision of the economically oppressed. His final novel, *The Children at the Gate* (1964), juxtaposes a Jewish hospital orderly, Sammy, betrayed by an acquaintance, Angelo DeMarco, who comes later to regret his accusations. Throughout Wallant's work the reader listens to conversations and hears of invasive, troubling dreams, placed in the position of an analyst helpless to intervene. The novels each end with a coupling of sacrificial and redemptive actions, though the transformation willed as symbolic closure lingers less in memory than the dystopian vision of the body of these works.

—Maureen Turim

See the essay on *The Pawnbroker*.

WEIL, Jiří

Nationality: Czech. **Born:** Praskolesy, Bohemia, 1900. **Education:** Prague University. **Family:** Married Olga Frenclova in 1942 (marriage forcibly annulled). **Career:** Journalist, Moscow, 1933–35; editor, Prague, 1946–49; worked in the Prague Jewish Museum, 1950–58. **Died:** 1959.

PUBLICATIONS

Novels

Moskva-hranice [From Moscow to the Border]. 1937.
Zivot s hvězdou. 1949; as *Life with a Star*, 1989.
Na streše je Mendelssohn. 1960; as *Mendelssohn Is on the Roof*, 1991.
Drevená lzíce (sequel to *Moskva-hranice*). 1980.

Short Stories

Vezen chillonský [Prisoner of Chillon]. 1957.

Other

Makanna otec divu. 1945.
Vzpominky na Julia Fucika. 1947.
Zalozpev za 77,297 obetí [Elegy for the 77,297 Victims]. 1958.
Harfeník. 1958.

Hodina pravdy, hodina zkoušky. 1966.

*

Critical Studies: "Introduction: Jiri Weil, Two Stories about Nazis and Jews" by Philip Roth, in *American Poetry Review*, September/October 1974, p. 22; by Josef Skvorecky, in *New Republic*, 4 September 1989, 201(10), pp. 31–35.

* * *

Jiří Weil was actively engaged in the tumultuous cultural and political life of Europe in the 1920s, '30s, and postwar period up to his death in 1959. As a journalist he was abreast with the developments not only in his native, newly proclaimed Czechoslovakia but also in a Europe that was largely under the sway of fascist dictatorships. As a communist he observed the events in the rapidly changing Soviet Union—not always with approval—and he followed the changing trends in Soviet art and literature closely. In 1932 he edited a collection of Soviet revolutionary poetry, and, as Hitler was consolidating power in Germany, he left Czechoslovakia to spend two years in the Soviet Union (1933–35). His interest in Soviet matters led not only to journalistic articles and reportage but also to accomplished translations of Vladimir Mayakovsky, Boris Pasternak, and Maksim Gorky.

Weil was also a member of the Czech cultural avant-garde, including the Devetsil group. Having observed and experienced not only Czech anti-Semitism during the prewar years but more particularly the alarming escalation of the German anti-Jewish measures in the Protectorate of Bohemia and Moravia, Weil, a Jew, went underground in 1942 until the war ended in 1945. After the war he continued his journalistic work as an editor (1946–49) and then worked in the Prague Jewish Museum (1950–58). In the forefront of European literary trends, Weil exemplifies in his postwar writings the "absurd" and demonstrates as well an affinity with his still as yet largely unrecognized compatriot Franz Kafka.

His novel *Zivot s hvězdou* (1949; *Life with a Star*), written shortly after the liberation, tells the story of a Jewish bank clerk, Josef Roubiček, who progressively loses all his possessions, his lover, his cat, and even his identity. He is finally able to resist total effacement and, with the aid of socialist resisters, survives. The story is, however, less a description of the Jewish tragedy in 1940s Czechoslovakia than a story of alienation, of a simple human being caught, like Kafka's heroes, in an absurd world that works inexorably and machine-like against the individual. The novel *Na streše je Mendelssohn* (1960; *Mendelssohn Is on the Roof*) deals with the order to remove the statue of Felix Mendelssohn, a Jew, from the roof of the Prague concert hall. There is confusion as to which statue, precisely, is Mendelssohn's, and the statue itself exerts an uncanny influence against those who are trying to remove it. Again, the absurdity of the world of totalitarian rule is a major theme.

Weil's writings are suffused with European existentialism, as exemplified in the works of Kafka and Albert Camus. They combine, in simple language, both the real and the surreal. No matter what he had chosen for his subject matter, Weil would have been a leading writer of his time. Experiencing and observing the German occupiers as they oppressed and finally exterminated some 78,000 of the estimated 92,000 Jews living in Bohemia and Moravia in the war years, Weil took the Holocaust as material for his novels. His real theme, however, is the alienation of the individual and the destruction of human identity in an absurd world.

—David Scrase

See the essay on *Life with a Star.*

WEISS, Peter

Nationality: Swedish (originally German: immigrated to Sweden, 1939, granted Swedish citizenship, 1949). **Born:** Nowawes, 8 November 1916; spent most of childhood in Bremen; fled Germany with family to England, Switzerland, Czechoslovakia, and finally Sweden, 1934–39. **Education:** Polytechnic School of Photography, London; Prague Art Academy, 1937–38; Stockholm Art Academy. **Family:** Married 1) Helga Henschen in 1943 (divorced), one daughter; 2) Carlota Dethorey in 1949 (divorced), one son; 3) Gunilla Palmstierna in 1962, one daughter. **Career:** Correspondent, *Tidningen,* Stockholm; worked as a commercial artist; joined the Swedish Experimental Film Studio, 1952; painting teacher, People's University, Stockholm, 1950s. **Awards:** Prague Art Academy award, 1938, for his painting *Gartenkonzert;* Charles-Veillon prize, 1963; Lessing prize (Hamburg), 1965; Heinrich Mann prize, 1966; Carl Albert Anderson prize, 1967; Thomas Dehler prize, 1978; Cologne literature prize, 1981; Georg Büchner prize, Bremen literature prize, De Nios prize, and Swedish Theatre Critics prize, all in 1982. **Died:** 10 May 1982.

PUBLICATIONS

Collections

Dramen. 1968.
  Dramen. 1 (includes *Der Turm; Die Versicherung; Nacht mit Gästen; Mockinpott; Marat-Sade*). 1968.
  Dramen. 2 (inlcudes *Die Ermittlung; Lusitanischer Popanz; Viet Nam Diskurs*). 1968.
Gesang vom Lusitanischen Popanz und andere Stücke (includes *Gesang vom Lusitanischen Popanz; Nacht mit Gästen; Die Versicherung*). 1969.

Peter Weiss Werke in sechs Bänden, edited by Gunilla Palmstierna-Weiss. 1991.
  1. Band, Prosa 1 (includes *Von Insel zu Insel; Die Besiegten; Der Fremde; Das Duell*). 1991.
  2. Band, Prosa 2 (includes *Der Schatten des Körpers des Kutschers; Abschied von den Eltern; Fluchtpunkt; Das Gespräch der drei Gehenden; Rekonvaleszenz*). 1991.
  3. Band, Prosa 3 (includes *Die Ästhetik des Widerstands*). 1991.
  4. Band, Dramen 1 (includes *Der Turm; Die Versicherung; Nacht mit Gästen; Mockinpott; Marat/Sade*). 1991.
  5. Band, Dramen 2 (includes *Die Ermittlung; Lusitanischer Popanz; Viet Nam Diskurs*). 1991.
  6. Band, Dramen 3 (includes *Trotzki im Exil; Hölderlin; Der Prozess; Der Neue Prozess*). 1991.
Marat/Sade; The Investigation; and The Shadow of the Coachman's Body, edited by Robert Cohen. 1998.

Plays

Der Turm (produced 1949). In *Dramen. 1,* 1968; as *The Tower,* 1968.
Die Versicherung (produced Germany, 1952). In *Dramen. 1,* 1968.
Nacht mit Gästen (produced Berlin, 1963). 1966; as *Night with Guests* (produced 1968).
Die Verfolgung und Ermordung Jean Paul Marats dargestellt durch die Schauspielergruppe des Hospizes zu Charenton unter Anleitung des Herrn de Sade (Marat/Sade) (produced Berlin, 1964). 1964; as *The Persecution and Assassination of Jean-Paul Marat As Performed by the Inmates of the Asylum of Charenton under the Direction of the Marquis de Sade* (produced New York, 1965), 1965.
Wie dem Herrn Mockinpott das Leiden ausgetrieben wird (produced 1963). 1968; as *How Mr. Mockinpott Was Cured of His Sufferings* (produced 1972).
Die Ermittlung (produced Germany, 1965). 1965; as *The Investigation,* 1966.
Gesang vom lusitanischen Popanz (produced 1967). In *Gesang vom Lusitanischen Popanz und andere Stücke,* 1969; translated as *Song of the Lusitanien Bogey* and published with *Discourse on the Progress of the Prolonged War of Liberation in Viet Nam,* 1970.
Diskurs über die Vorgeschichte und den Verlauf des lang andauernden Befreiungskrieges in Viet Nam als Beispiel für die Notwendigkeit des bewaffneten Kampfes der Unterdrückten gegen ihre Unterdrücker sowie über die Versuche der Vereinigten Staaten von Amerika die Grundlagen der Revolution zu vernichten (Viet Nam Diskurs) (produced Frankfurt am Main, 1968). 1967; translated as *Discourse on the Progress of the Prolonged War of Liberation in Viet Nam* and published with *Song of the Lusitanian Bogey,* 1970.
Trotzki im Exil (produced Düsseldorf, 1970). 1969; as *Trotsky in Exile,* 1971.

Hölderlin (produced Stuttgart, 1971). 1971.
Der Prozeß, adaptation of the novel by Franz Kafka (produced 1974). 1979.
Der neue Prozeß (produced Stockholm, 1982). 1982; as *The New Trial* (produced Duke University, 1998), 2001.

Novels

Från ö till ö. 1947.
De Besegrade. 1948.
Der Vogelfreie. 1948.
Dokument I. 1949.
Duellen. 1951.
Der Schatten des Körpers des Kutschers. 1960; as *The Shadow of the Coachman's Body,* in *Bodies and Shadows: Two Short Novels,* 1969.
Abschied von den Eltern. 1961; as *Leavetaking,* 1968.
Fluchtpunkt. 1962; translated as *Vanishing Point* and published with *Leavetaking,* 1968.
Das Gespräch der drei Gehenden. 1962; as *The Conversation of the Three Wayfarers,* in *Bodies and Shadows: Two Short Novels,* 1969.
Die Ästhetik des Widerstands. 1975; as *The Aesthetics of Resistance,* 1996.
   Volume I. 1975.
   Volume II. 1978.
   Volume III. 1981.
Die Situation. 2000.

Other

Avantgarde Film, edited by Beat Mazenauer. 1956.
Rapporte. 1968.
Meine Ortschaft. 1968; as *My Place,* 1978.
Rekonvaleszenz. 1970.
Rapporte 2. 1971.
Notizbücher 1971–1980. 1981.
Notizbücher 1960–1971. 1982.
Briefe, edited by Beat Mazenauer (correspondence). 1992.

*

Film Adaptations: *Marat/Sade,* 1966.

Critical Studies: *Peter Weiss: A Search for Affinities* by Ian Hilton, 1970; *Peter Weiss* by Otto F. Best, 1976; *Metaphors of Evil: Contemporary German Literature and the Shadow of Nazism* by Hamida Bosmajian, 1979; *The Theme of Alienation in the Prose of Peter Weiss* by Kathleen A. Vance, 1981; *Patterns of Ritual and Symbols in the Plays of Jean Genet, Peter Weiss, and Edward Bond* (dissertation) by Miriam Yahil-Wax, Stanford University, 1983; "Aesthetics and the Revolutionary Struggle: Peter Weiss's Novel *The Aesthetics of Resistance*" by Peter Horn, in *Critical Arts,* 3(4), 1985, pp.

7–54; "Auschwitz and Its Function in Peter Weiss' Search for Identity" by Jurgen E. Schlunk, in *German Studies Review,* 10(1), February 1987, pp. 11–30; *Peter Weiss in Exile: A Critical Study of His Works* by Roger Ellis, 1987; *The Mother in the Work and Life of Peter Weiss* by Åsa Eldh, 1990; *Understanding Peter Weiss,* 1993, and "The Political Aesthetics of Holocaust Literature: Peter Weiss's *The Investigation* and Its Critics," in *History & Memory: Studies in Representations of the Past,* 10(2), 1998, pp. 43–67, both by Robert Cohen; "I Have Arrived Twenty Years Too Late' The Intertext of Peter Weiss' Investigation into Auschwitz" by Gunther Pakendorf, in *Acta Germanica: Jahrbuch des Germanistenverbandes im Sudlichen Afrika,* 23, 1995, pp. 69–78; *Not of This Time, Not of This Place: Diasporic Imagination in Peter Weiss, Nelly Sachs, and Paul Celan* (dissertation) by Katja Garloff, University of Chicago, 1998; *Rethinking Peter Weiss,* edited by Jost Hermand and Marc Silberman, 2000.

*   *   *

The impossibility of representing Auschwitz on the stage led German philosopher Theodor W. Adorno in his radio lecture *Engagement oder künstlerische Autonomie* (published in *Noten zur Literatur III,* 1965) to launch a massive attack against images of a reality. He claimed that the very process of the depiction of these images by means of the artistic shaping of naked corporeal pain softened the impact of this reality and contained the potential "to yield pleasure." Nevertheless, in his *Negative Dialektik* Adorno justified the survival of art after Auschwitz, claiming that "perennial suffering" has the right to be expressed. This right means that oblivion or forgetfulness cannot be accepted. The "drastic guilt of him who was spared death"—who experiences his escape as guilt at evading the death sentences of the SS—causes Adorno to doubt whether life is worth living after Auschwitz. For him every form of bearing witness is made possible only through the distance of time that separates the survivors from the victims of the death camps.

Painter, film director, novelist, and playwright Peter Weiss—born near Berlin in 1916—was also tormented by guilt for, as he said, "not having been one of those who had had the number of devaluation branded on their flesh." He was spared death thanks to the foresight of his mother, an actress who worked with Austrian theater director Max Reinhardt, and his Jewish father. The family members, Czech citizens, fled Germany in 1934, emigrating via England and Czechoslovakia to find refuge in Sweden in 1939. Weiss studied at the Polytechnic School of Photography in London and at the academy of arts in Prague as well as at the Art Academy in Stockholm before he started his career as a painter and writer. In 1949 he received Swedish state citizenship. His attempt to be integrated into Swedish society proved difficult although he received benevolent reviews and public orders for his paintings and exhibitions. In his first book, *Från ö till ö,* written in

1944 in Swedish and published in 1947, he draws up the utopia of the art in the picture of the island, which is threatened by a decayed outside world.

Weiss went back to Germany as a correspondent of a Swedish daily in 1947. In one of his *Sechs Reportagen aus Deutschland* ("Six Reports from Germany"), he describes his dismay upon reading **Eugen Kogon**'s book *Der SS-Staat* ("The SS State"). Kogon's publication revealed to him the first really clear picture of the extremely complicated organized inferno, in which sadism was transformed to science and the hangmen became the truest representatives of the time. Weiss interpreted his visit to Germany as the beginning of his own politicization. Traces of this politicization, however, cannot be found in his publications *De Besegrade* (1948) and *Der Vogelfreie* (1948) nor in the play *Der Turm* (1949; *The Tower*).

Weiss failed in his attempt to get the Suhrkamp publishing house to publish his novel *Der Vogelfreie*. Swedish publishing houses also refused the publication of his texts, so he decided to publish them in his own publishing house. The year 1952 proved to be a crisis year for him due to missing artistic recognition. He therefore devoted himself to shooting films and recorded successes with some of his movies, which are both surreal experiments and socially inspired documentary movies. The death of his parents at the end of the 1950s caused Weiss to write a self-critical autobiographical novel, *Abschied von den Eltern* (1961; *Leavetaking*, 1968). His following publication, *Fluchtpunkt* (1962; "Vanishing Point"), is also decisively influenced by experiences of his own life. In this novel the narrator, who is identical with Weiss, discusses the question of guilt in his youth: He unsuccessfully tried to rescue his girlfriend Lucie Weisberger out of the concentration camp in 1941 by marrying her. Weiss's serious self-accusation for having failed to rescue Weisberger led to an increasing politicization in his literary activity. With his play *Marat/Sade* (1964)—a play within a play, which combines historical facts of the French Revolution with dramatic fantasy—the engaged intellectual Weiss succeeded in his worldwide breakthrough. After this success Weiss dealt with the further-reaching repression of fascism. He went to the place of the destruction, Auschwitz, and he attended the Frankfurt am Main Auschwitz trial to be able to write his short prose text *Meine Ortschaft* (1968; *My Place,* 1978) and the play *Die Ermittlung* (1965; *The Investigation,* 1966). Weiss's work on the Auschwitz material intensified his interest in Marxism. Instead of realizing his plan to write a canto about colonialism, racism, conquest, robbery, and murder, he thematized with his play *Viet Nam Diskurs* (1968) the Vietnamese struggle for liberation, in which Weiss—in the meantime declaring his belief for socialism—saw a new quality of human engagement. In his *10 Arbeitspunkte eines Autoren in der geteilten Welt* (September 1965), he announced that the guidelines of socialism contained the intellectual truth for him. Some months before, in March, he had announced that the acceptance of truth consists of

doubts and contradictions. The failure of the Prague Spring—Warsaw Pact forces invaded Czechoslovakia over the night of 20–21 August 1968—caused him to have sharp criticism of the politics of the socialist states. Weiss increasingly dissociated himself from socialism during the 1970s while writing his magnum opus, the one thousand-page novel *Die Ästhetik des Widerstands* (1975; *The Aesthetics of Resistance,* 1996).

Weiss, who died in 1982, discusses his moral political problem of guilt in multiple ways in his oeuvre, in which the victims of national socialism and also of the postwar period have got the right to express their "perennial suffering."

—Olav Schröer

See the essay on *The Investigation*.

WIECHERT, Ernst (Emil)

Pseudonym: Ernst Barany Bjell. **Nationality:** German. **Born:** Forsthaus Kleinort, Prussia, 18 May 1887. **Education:** University of Königsberg, teaching diploma, 1911. **Military Service:** German Army during World War I: lieutenant. **Family:** Married 1) Meta Mittelstädt in 1912 (separated late 1920s; died 1931); 2) Paula Marie Junker in 1931. **Career:** Private tutor near Königsberg, ca. 1906; teaching assistant, Königsberg, 1911–14; teacher, beginning 1914; lived and wrote in Bavaria, beginning 1933, and in Switzerland, beginning 1946. **Died:** 24 August 1950.

PUBLICATIONS

Collection

Sämtliche Werke (10 vols.). 1945.

Novels

Die Flucht [The Flight] (as Ernst Barany Bjell). 1916.
Der Wald [The Woods]. 1920.
Der Totenwolf [The Death Wolf]. 1924.
Die blauen Schwingen [The Blue Wings]. 1925.
Der Knecht Gottes, Andreas Nyland [God's Servant, Andreas Nyland]. 1926.
Die kleine Passion [The Little Passion]. 1929.
Jedermann: Geschichte eines Namenlosen [Everyman: Story of Anonymous]. 1931.
Die Magd des Jürgen Doskocil. 1932; as *The Girl and the Ferryman,* 1947.
Die Majorin: Eine Erzählung. 1934; as *The Baroness,* 1936.

Hirtennovelle. 1935.
Das einfache Leben. 1939; as *The Simple Life,* 1954.
Der Totenwald: Ein Bericht. 1945; as *The Forest of the Dead,* 1947.
Die Jerominkinder: Roman (2 vols.). 1946; as *The Earth Is Our Heritage,* 1950.
Missa sine nomine. 1950; translated as *Missa sine nomine,* 1953; as *Tidings,* 1959.
Der Exote. 1951.

Short Stories

Der silberne Wagen: Novellen [The Big Dipper]. 1928.
Die Flöte des Pan: Novellen [The Pipe of Pan]. 1930.
Der Todeskandidat; La Ferme morte; Der Vater: Drei Erzählungen. 1934.
Atli der Bestmann; Tobias: Zwei Erzählungen. 1938.
Demetrius und andere Erzählungen. 1945.
Erzählungen. 1947.
Die Gebärde; Der Fremde. 1947.
Der Richter. 1948.
Die Mutter: Eine Erzählung. 1949.
Fahrt um die Liebe: Erzählung. 1957.
Regina Amstettin; Veronika; Der einfache Tod; Die Magd: 4 Novellen. 1969.

Plays

Das Spiel vom deutschen Bettelmann [The Play of the German Beggar]. 1933.
Der verlorene Sohn [The Prodigal Son]. 1935.
Okay; oder, Die Unsterblichen: Eine ernsthafte Komödie in drei Aufzügen. 1946.

Other

Die Legende vom letzten Wald. 1925.
Der Kinderkreuzzug [The Children's Crusade]. 1935.
Von den treuen Begleitern [On the Loyal Companions] (essay). 1936.
Der Dichter und die Jugend. 1936.
Wälder und Menschen [Forests and People] (autobiography). 1936.
Eine Mauer um uns baue. 1937.
In der Heimat. 1938.
Vom Trost der Welt. 1938.
Der ewige Stern: Eine Adventsgeschichte. 1940.
Totenmesse. 1945.
Rede an die deutsche Jugend 1945. 1945; as "Address to the Youth of Germany," in *The Poet and His Time: Three Addresses,* 1948.
Der Dichter und seine Zeit: Rede, gehalten am 16. April 1935 im Auditorium Maximum der Universität München (lecture). 1945; as "The Poet and His Time," in *The Poet and His Time: Three Addresses,* 1948.

Der weisse Büffel; oder, Von der grossen Gerechtigkeit. 1946; as *The White Buffalo, or, Concerning Great Justice,* 1986.
Der brennende Dornbusch. 1946.
An die deutsche Jugend: Drei Reden und ein Aufsatz. 1946.
Über Kunst und Künstler: Aus einer ungesprochenen Rede. 1946.
Märchen (2 vols.). 1946.
Rede an die Schweizer Freunde. 1947; as "Address to My Swiss Friends," in *The Poet and His Time: Three Addresses,* 1948.
The Poet and His Time: Three Addresses (includes "Address to the Youth of Germany," 1945; "The Poet and His Time," 1935; "Address to My Swiss Friends," 1947). 1948.
Der grosse Wald. 1947.
Das zerstörte Menschengesicht: Rede an der Goethe-Feier in Stäfa (Zurich) am 22. IX. 1947. 1948.
Jahre und Zeiten: Erinnerungen [Years and Times] (autobiography). 1949.
Das Antlitz der Mutter: Eine Bilderfolge. 1949.
Ernst Wiechert: Lebensworte aus seinem Schrifttum, edited by Adolf Wendel. 1950.
Es geht ein Pflüger übers Land: Betrachtungen und Erzählungen, edited by Lilje Wiechert. 1951.
Vom bleibenden Gewinn: Ein Buch der Betrachtung. 1951.
Meine Gedichte [My Poems]. 1952.
Gesegnetes Leben: Das Schönste aus den Werken des Dichters, edited by Gerhard Kamin. 1953.
Am Himmel strahlt der Stern: Ein Weihnachtsbuch. 1957.
Briefe an einen Werdenden, and Ein deutsches Weihnachtsspiel, edited by Sumner Kirshner. 1966.
Häftling Nr. 7188; Tagebuchnotizen und Briefe, edited by Gerhard Kamin. 1966.
Der Vogel Niemalsmehr: 12 Märchen. 1973.

*

Bibliography: "A Bibliography of Critical Writing about Ernst Wiechert" by Sumner Kirshner, in *Librarium* (Switzerland), 7, 1964.

Critical Studies: *The Island Motif in the Prose Works of Ernst Wiechert* by Marianne R. Jetter, 1957; "Lithuanian Folksong As a Philosophical Leitmotif in German Literature: Ernst Wiechert" by Anatole Matulis, in *Lituanus,* 12(4), 1966, pp. 49–55; "'Even if They Were Guilty': An Unpublished Letter by Ernst Wiechert about the Jews" by Sumner Kirshner, in *German Life and Letters* (England), 23, 1970, pp. 138–43; "The Symbolic Role of Fire in the Works of Ernst Wiechert," in *New German Studies* (England), 10(1), Spring 1982, pp. 33–42, and *Ernst Wiechert: The Prose Works in Relation to His Life and Times,* 1987, both by Hugh Alexander Boag; "Ernst Wiechert's Dissident Novella, *Der weisse Buffel oder von der grossen Gerechtigkeit*" by Ford B. Parkes-Perret, in *Neophilologus* (Netherlands), 73(4), October 1989, pp. 560–73;

"Ernst Wiechert and His Role between 1933 and 1945" by Bill Niven, in *New German Studies,* 16(1), 1990/1991, pp. 1–20.

* * *

In July 1933 and April 1935 the East Prussian novelist Ernst Wiechert delivered two speeches to the students at the University of Munich in which he attacked the regime with understated astringency, taking aim at the mindless cult of youth, the deadening effort to institutionalize literature, and the reversion to anarchy in the curricula. The speeches, couched in elaborately courteous, ironically flattering language and the soft-spoken tones Wiechert cultivated, not only displayed great spunk but were the more surprising in a writer whose right-wing views were well known. Nor did the Nazis lift a finger against him. Wiechert himself disparaged any claims to courage: he confessed that he spoke on the chance that his very popularity might keep the Nazis at bay. But he also knew that a reprieve is by definition contingent, and in 1938 he virtually committed himself to Buchenwald. It pays to look at the conclusion of his two speeches: in 1933 he told his listeners, "I don't know what the poet who will stand in this place after me will talk about"; in 1935, "I don't know whether I shall be allowed to speak to you again two years hence." And he was honest enough to add: "Nor do I know what I shall have to say to you then."

Wiechert, in fact, remains one of the more difficult "cases" to place ideologically. His father was a forest ranger, and this, as well as the landscape in which the young Wiechert grew up, determined his lifelong theme: the splendor of life in the woods, the intimacy between man and nature, the character of the self-reliant recluse. In many ways Wiechert's novels bore all the characteristics of the party-approved blood-and-soil literature—the literature whose greatest exponent remains Knut Hamsun, one of the Nazis' eminent showpieces. (The hero of Wiechert's first serious novel, *Der Wald* [1920], burns down his forest before he leaves home to keep it from being polluted by alien hands.) Wiechert shared the doctrinal anticosmopolitanism: until his death he looked on the city as the source of a soul-destroying "civilization." In the same year in which he delivered his second Munich Philippic, in the childhood memoir *Wälder und Menschen,* all urban life, "in its greed, its obsession with rank, the paltry homage it pays to spiritual distinction," is indiscriminately written down as "wholly contemptible." If his novels were rooted in nature, Wiechert disclaimed any belief in the sanctity of the race (that is, the "blood" component of the formula), but book after book reveals that "blood is man's only immortal element," more binding than any divine prophecy, that blood is "destiny." And though he palmed himself off as a basically nonpolitical animal, Wiechert remained solidly *deutschnational:* he loathed the postwar revolutions, despised the Weimar Republic, and stipulated that no Jewish publications were to print his work. At the same time, he expressed his equivocation

in a telling gesture; he rejected a book cover prominently featuring the swastika: "The swastika absolutely has to go, even though I am closely enough kinned to it—or perhaps for that very reason."

Though it is idle to date such conversions, very likely by 1929 or 1930 the Nazis had begun to get under Wiechert's skin. (The novel *Jedermann,* published in 1931, contains his first appealing portrayal of a Jew.) An intensely private person, Wiechert found the Nazis' rowdy mass movement increasingly repellent. In his Munich speeches he drew a thick line between the eternal verities (which are the proper domain of the poet) and the ephemera churned out by Hitler's young lions and old hangers-on (what a splendid thing that Goethe refrained from writing battle hymns in 1813; what a pity that Gerhart Hauptmann wrote them a century later); and in Wiechert this distinction always suggests the distinction between silence and noise: the silence of the stars and the noise of the brown rabble.

In the end Wiechert's place in the ideological spectrum remains disturbingly fuzzy. No doubt he capitalized on his martyrdom, which he may have inflated. Even after his release from Buchenwald, he collected handsome royalties and read to standing audiences. His autobiography *Jahre und Zeiten* (1949), like lesser species of *Selbstrechtfertigungsliteratur*, naturally suppresses these unpleasant minutiae. He promoted himself as an almost messianic figure, someone who was forever being handed a halo and forever rejecting it, who hoarded praise only to repudiate it—the repudiation itself confirming the praise. The peasant in him found the splitting of the psyche and of the atom the cardinal sins of the century. And to the end he remained true to his creed, a creed by which such books as *The Magic Mountain* remained hopelessly cosmopolitan, tendentious, a plaything of time, measured against the eternal truths of the magic East Prussian woods.

—Edgar Rosenberg

See the essay on *The Forest of the Dead.*

WIESEL, Elie(zer)

Nationality: American (originally Romanian: immigrated to the United States, 1956, granted U.S. citizenship, 1963). **Born:** Sighet, Transylvania, 30 September 1928. **Education:** Sorbonne University of Paris, 1948–51. **Family:** Married Marion Erster Rose in 1969; one son and one stepdaughter. **Career:** Worked at various times as foreign correspondent for *Yedioth Ahronoth,* Tel-Aviv, *L'Arche,* Paris, and *Jewish Daily Forward,* New York, 1949–68. Distinguished Professor of Judaic Studies, City College of the City University of New York, 1972–76. Since 1976 Andrew W. Mellon Professor in the Humanities, and since 1988 university professor, Boston University. Distinguished visiting professor of literature and philosophy, Florida International University, Miami, 1982; Henry Luce Visiting Scholar in Humanities and Social Thought, Whitney Humanities Center, Yale University, 1982–83. Chair, United States President's Commission on the Holocaust, 1979–80, U.S. Holocaust Memorial Council, 1980–86. **Awards:** Remembrance award, 1965; Jewish Heritage award for excellence in literature, 1966; Prix Medicis, 1969; French Academy Prix Bordin and Eleanor Roosevelt Memorial award, both in 1972; Jewish Book Council Frank and Ethel S. Cohen award, 1973; Prix Livre-International and state of Israel Jabotinsky medal, both in 1980; Prix des Bibliothecaires, 1981; United States Congressional Gold medal, 1984; International League for Human Rights humanitarian award, 1985; Nobel Peace prize, 1986; B'nai B'rith Profiles in Courage award, 1987; International Human Rights Law Group award, 1988; Human Rights Campaign Fund humanitarian award, 1989; Soka University award of highest honor, 1991; Ellis Island medal of honor and Council of Jewish Organizations Humanitarian of the Century, both in 1992; Golden Slipper humanitarian award and Interfaith Council on the Holocaust humanitarian award, both in 1994; National Civil Rights Museum, Memphis, Tennessee, freedom award and Socio Honorario de la Sociedad Hebraica Argentina, both in 1995; American Academy of Achievement golden plate award, 1996; Clark University Fiat Lux award and Rennert Center for Jerusalem Studies, Bar-Ilan University, Guardian of Zion prize, both in 1997. Approximately 95 honorary doctorates. Commander, Legion d'Honneur, 1984, elevated to Grand Officer, 1990. **Agent:** Georges Borchardt, 136 East 57th Street, New York, New York 10022, U.S.A. **Address:** University Professors, Boston University, 745 Commonwealth Avenue, Boston, Massachusetts 02215, U.S.A.

PUBLICATIONS

Novels

La Nuit, L'Aube, Le Jour. 1969; as Night, Dawn, The Accident: Three Tales, 1972; as The Night Trilogy: Night, Dawn, The Accident, 1987.
   L'Aube. 1960; as Dawn, 1961.
   Le Jour. 1961; as The Accident, 1961.
La Ville de la chance. 1962; as The Town beyond the Wall, 1964.
Les Portes de la foret. 1964; as The Gates of the Forest, 1966.
Le Chant des morts. 1966; as Legends of Our Time, 1968.
Le Mendiant de Jerusalem. 1968; as A Beggar in Jerusalem, 1970.
Le Serment de Kolvillag. 1973; as The Oath, 1973.
Le Testament d'un poete juif assassine. 1980; as The Testament, 1981.
The Golem: The Story of a Legend As Told by Elie Wiesel. 1983.

Le Cinquieme fils. 1983; as The Fifth Son, 1985.
L'Oublie. 1989; as The Forgotten, 1992.
Les Juges. 1999.

Plays

Zalmen; ou, la Folie de Dieu. 1966; as Zalmen; or, The Madness of God, 1968.
Ani Maamin: A Song Lost and Found Again, music by Darius Milhaud. 1974.
Le Proces de Shamgorod tel qu'il se deroula le 25 fevrier 1649: Piece en trois actes. 1979; as The Trial of God (As It Was Held on February 25, 1649, in Shamgorod): A Play in Three Acts, 1979.
The Haggadah, music by Elizabeth Swados. 1982.

Memoirs

Un di velt hot geshvign [And the World Has Remained Silent]. 1956; as La Nuit, 1958; as Night, 1958.
Tous les fleuves vont a la mer: Memoires. 1994; as All Rivers Run to the Sea: Memoirs, 1995.
Et la mer n'est pas remplie: Memoires, 2. 1996; as And the Sea Is Never Full: Memoirs, 1969–, 1999.

Other

Entre deux soleils. 1965; as One Generation After, 1965.
The Jews of Silence: A Personal Report on Soviet Jewry (originally published in Hebrew as a series of articles for newspaper Yedioth Ahronoth). 1966.
Celebration Hassidique: Portraits et legendes. 1972; as Souls on Fire: Portraits and Legends of Hasidic Masters, 1972.
Celebration Biblique: Portraits et legendes. 1975; as Messengers of God: Biblical Portraits and Legends, 1976.
Un Juif aujourd'hui: Recits, essais, dialogues. 1977; as A Jew Today, 1978.
Four Hasidic Masters and Their Struggle against Melancholy. 1978.
Images from the Bible, illustrated with paintings by Shalom of Safed. 1980.
Five Biblical Portraits. 1981.
Somewhere a Master. 1982; as Somewhere a Master: Further Tales of the Hasidic Masters, 1984.
Paroles d'etranger. 1982.
Against Silence: The Voice and Vision of Elie Wiesel, edited by Irving Abrahamson (selections; 3 vols.). 1985.
Signes d'exode: Essais, histoires, dialogues. 1985.
Job ou Dieu dans la tempete. 1986.
Le Crepuscule au loin. 1987; as Twilight, 1988.
The Six Days of Destruction, with Albert H. Friedlander. 1989.
Mal et l'exil. 1988; as Evil and Exile, with Philippe-Michael de Saint-Cheron. 1990.

From the Kingdom of Memory: Reminiscences. 1990.
A Passover Haggadah, illustrated by Mark Podwal. 1993.
Monsieur Chouchani: L'Enigme d'un Maitre du XX Siecle: Entretiens avec Elie Wiesel, suivis d'une enquete, with Salomon Malka. 1994.
Memoire a deux voix, with Francois Mitterrand. 1995; as *Memoir in Two Voices,* 1996.
Ethics and Memory. 1997.
Celebration prophetique: Portraits et legendes. 1998.
King Solomon and His Magic Ring (for children). 1999.

*

Bibliography: *Elie Wiesel: A Bibliography* by Molly Abramowitz, 1974.

Critical Studies: *Elie Wiesel: A Small Measure of Victory* by Gene Koppel and Henry Kaufmann, 1974; *Conversations with Elie Wiesel,* 1976, and *Responses to Elie Wiesel,* 1978, both by Harry J. Cargas; *Confronting the Holocaust: The Impact of Elie Wiesel,* edited by Alvin Rosenfeld and Irving Greenberg, 1978; *A Consuming Fire: Encounters with Elie Wiesel and the Holocaust* by John Roth, 1979; *Elie Wiesel* by Ted L. Estess, 1980; *Legacy of Night: The Literary Universe of Elie Wiesel* by Ellen Fine, 1982; *Elie Wiesel: Messenger to All Humanity* by Robert McAfee Brown, 1983; *Elie Wiesel: A Challenge to Theology* by Graham B. Walker, 1988; *Elie Wiesel: Between Memory and Hope,* edited by Carol Rittner, 1990; *Elie Wiesel: God, the Holocaust, and the Children of Israel* by Michael Berenbaum, 1994; *Elie Wiesel's Secretive Texts* by Colin Davis, 1994; *Elie Wiesel: Bearing Witness* by Michael Pariser, 1994; *Silence in the Novels of Elie Wiesel* by Simon P. Sibleman, 1995; *Celebrating Elie Wiesel: Stories, Essays, Reflections,* edited by Alan Rosen, 1998; *Elie Wiesel and the Politics of Moral Leadership* by Mark Chmiel, 2001; *The Worlds of Elie Wiesel: An Overview of His Career and His Major Themes* by Jack Kolbert, 2001; *Elie Wiesel's Night,* edited by Harold Bloom, 2001.

*   *   *

After World War II, because many publishers were reluctant to publish Holocaust memoirs, it was difficult for Holocaust survivors to confront the world as witnesses to their suffering. New York trade publishers and their counterparts throughout the world felt that the subject was too depressing to be commercially viable. Even such luminous authors as Elie Wiesel and **Primo Levi** had difficulty finding publishers. By becoming best-selling authors, however, they won the right to be internationally recognized Holocaust witnesses, both for themselves and for other Holocaust authors who followed them.

Wiesel's citation for the Nobel Prize for Peace reads, "Wiesel is a messenger to mankind. His message is one of peace and atonement and human dignity. The message is in the form of a testimony, repeated and deepened through the works

of a great author." In his book *All Rivers Run to the Sea* (1995), Wiesel openly admits that, when he was at Auschwitz and Buchenwald, he never expected his Holocaust experience to turn him into such a messenger:

> Was it the will to testify—and therefore the need to survive—that helped pull me through? Did I survive in order to combat forgetting? I must confess that at the time such questions did not occur to me. I did not feel invested with any mission. On the contrary, I was convinced that my time would come and that my memories would die with me. When I heard fellow inmates making plans for "afterward," I thought it was no concern of mine. I repeat: It is not that I wanted to die, just that I knew I would not survive, first of all because I was convinced the Germans would keep their promise and kill us all, down to the last Jew, if necessary in the final hour before their defeat. And also because I knew that beyond a certain point I would be incapable of bearing the hunger and the pain.

Ruth Klüger similarly mentions in her memoir *Still Alive: A Holocaust Girlhood Remembered* (1992) that survival in the concentration camps was as improbable as winning the lottery. Bearing witness, therefore, was not likely to be the first thing on the inmates' minds.

Nonetheless, Wiesel forcefully describes the need to bear witness for those internees who survived the concentration camps. As a witness and a messenger, Wiesel laments the defensive amnesia that prevented many Jews from taking flight from the Nazis prior to their internments in concentration camps and seeks to prevent new forms of amnesia from taking root. Wiesel recalls how his non-Jewish housekeeper wanted to save the entire Wiesel family:

> Maria—our old housekeeper, wonderful Maria who had worked for us since I was born—begged us to follow her to her home. She offered us her cabin in a remote hamlet. There would be room for all six of us and Grandma Nissel as well. Seven in one cabin? Yes, she swore it, as Christ was her witness. She would take care of us, she would handle everything. We said no politely but firmly. We did so because we still didn't know what was in store for us.

Wiesel celebrates Maria's unselfish offer but grieves that there were not more Christians like her:

> Dear Maria. If other Christians had acted like her, the trains rolling toward the unknown would have been less crowded. If priests and pastors had raised their voices, if the Vatican had broken its silence, the enemy's hands would not have been so free. But most

of our compatriots thought only of themselves. Barely was a Jewish house emptied of its inhabitants, than they descended like vultures on the abandoned possessions, breaking into closets and drawers, stealing bedsheets and clothing, smashing things, looting. For them it was a party, a treasure hunt. They were not like our Maria.

He thereby gives credence to the need for the survivor to act as a witness-messenger by mentioning that even small numbers of opponents can lessen the monstrosity of a crisis like the Holocaust.

In his essay ''Why I Write'' Wiesel states, ''Why I write? To wrench these victims from oblivion. To help the dead vanquish death.'' This is similar to the Russian author Aleksandr Solzhenitsyn's statement ''A writer must tell society what he has seen.'' Wiesel's intellectual roots are not only in Hasidism and Jewish mysticism but also in the European existentialism of such authors as Camus and Dostoyevsky. His angry exhortations against God in *Night* are particularly reminiscent of Dostoyevsky, who unleashes angry laments and accusations upon God but who also acknowledges that he cannot live without him. Wiesel explains his religious feelings by saying, ''I had seen too much suffering to break with the past and reject the heritage of those who had suffered.''

In his works Wiesel emphasizes the meaning the telling of the story has had for him after liberation. Survivors attempting to chronicle the Holocaust experience a conflict between the internal pressure to express themselves and the psychological barriers of reliving traumatic experiences. The courageous act of memoir and novel writing is examined by Andrea Reiter in her study of Holocaust literature, *Auf dass sie entsteigen der Dunkelheit: Die literarische Bewältigung von KZ Erfahrung* (1995). According to Reiter, the unique thing about these texts is the attempt to portray a life-threatening personal experience and to attribute meaning to this traumatic experience in such a way that the requisites for a satisfactory continuation of life can be guaranteed.

Wiesel's memoirs and novels of dehumanization and subsequent rehumanization under impossible circumstances also can have a beneficial impact upon their readership. His works have the potential of instilling in their readers the power of reflection, of self-determination, and of noncooperation with evil, which is the only true antidote to the principle of Auschwitz. Wiesel has revealed how anti-Semitic persecution threatens the very fabric of civilization, and in so doing he and a number of other Holocaust authors have redrawn the map of civilization itself to make it more just and more humane.

—Peter R. Erspamer

See the essays on *The Accident, Dawn, The Forgotten, The Gates of the Forest, Night, One Generation After,* and *The Town beyond the Wall.*

WIESENTHAL, Simon

Nationality: Austrian (originally Austro-Hungarian). **Born:** Buczacz, Galicia, 31 December 1908. **Education:** Technical University, Prague, Czechoslovakia, 1929–32, architectural engineering degree 1932. **Family:** Married Cyla Muller in 1936; one daughter. **Career:** Practicing architect in Lvov, Poland, 1936–39; mechanic, bedspring factory, Lvov, 1939–41; arrested and imprisoned in Nazi forced labor and concentration camps, 1941–45; worked for War Crimes Commission, U.S. Office of Strategic Services, and Counter-Intelligence Corps, 1945–47; founder and director, Jewish Historical Documentation Center, Linz, Austria, 1947–54; director, Jewish welfare agencies, Linz, 1954–61; founder, Jewish Documentation Center, Vienna, 1961. **Awards:** International Resistance Diploma of Honor; Austrian Resistance Movement Needle of Honor; League of the United Nations Diploma of Honor; the Netherlands and Luxembourg freedom medals; Congressional Medal of Honor; Jerusalem Medal. Honorary doctorates: Hebrew Union College; Hebrew Theological College; Colby College; John Jay College of Criminal Justice of the City University of New York. Commandeur of Oranje-Nassau; Commendatore de la Republica Italiana; Commandeur de ordre pour la merite. **Agent:** Robert Halpern, 225 Broadway, New York, New York 10007, U.S.A. **Address:** Office: Jewish Historical Documentation Center, Salztorgasse 6/IV/5, 1010 Vienna, Austria.

PUBLICATIONS

Memoirs

KZ Mauthausen [Concentration Camp Mauthausen]. 1946.
The Murderers among Us: The Wiesenthal Memoirs. 1967.
Die Sonnenblume: Von Schuld und Vergebung. 1970; as *The Sunflower,* 1970; revised edition, as *The Sunflower: On the Possibilities and Limits of Forgiveness,* 1998.

Novels

Max und Helen: Ein Tatsachenroman. 1981; as *Max and Helen: A Remarkable True Love Story,* 1982.
Flucht vor dem Schicksal: Roman. 1988.

Other

Grossmufti-Grossagent der Achse [Head-Mufti, Head-Agent of the Axis]. 1947.
Ich jagte Eichmann [I Hunted Eichmann]. 1961.
Anti-Jewish Agitation in Poland: A Documentary Report. 1968.
Segel der Hoffnung: Die geheime Mission des Christoph Columbus. 1972; as *Sails of Hope: The Secret Mission of Christopher Columbus,* 1973.

Krystyna: Die Tragödie des polnischen Widerstands. 1986; as
  Krystyna: The Tragedy of the Polish Resistance, 1991.
Le Livre de la mémoire juive: Calendrier d'un martyrologue.
  1986; as *Every Day Remembrance Day: A Chronicle of
  Jewish Martyrdom,* 1987.
Recht, nicht Rache: Erinnerungen. 1988; as *Justice Not Venge-
  ance,* 1989.
*Denn sie wussten, was sie tun: Zeichnungen und Aufzeichnungen
  aus dem KZ Mauthausen.* 1995.

Editor, *Verjährung? 200 Persönlichkeiten des öffentlichen
  Lebens sagen nein; Eine Dokumentation.* 1965.
Editor, *Projekt Judenplatz Wien: Zur Konstruktion von
  Erinnerung.* 2000.

*

Film Adaptations: *Murderers among Us* (television), 1988;
Max and Helen (television), 1990.

Critical Studies: *Nazi Hunter: Simon Wiesenthal* by Iris
Noble, 1979; *Simon Wiesenthal: The Man and His Legacy* by
Lydia Triantopoulos, edited by Rhonda Barad, 1984; *The
Wiesenthal File* by Alan Levy, 1993; *Simon Wiesenthal: A Life
in Search of Justice* by Hella Pick, 1996.

* * *

Simon Wiesenthal was born in 1908 in Buczacz, Galicia, at
that time a part of the Austro-Hungarian Empire. He studied
architecture at the Technical University of Prague, from which
he was awarded a degree in architectural engineering in 1932.
He lived and worked as a practicing architect in Lvov, Poland.
At the start of World War II, a nonaggression pact between
Germany and the USSR divided Poland, and Lvov became
part of the Soviet Ukraine. During the Soviet occupation
Wiesenthal's stepfather was arrested by the Soviet secret
police and died in prison, and Wiesenthal himself lost his
employment as a successful architect. At the outbreak of the
German-Soviet war, the Germans displaced the Russians from
Lvov and proceeded to enact anti-Jewish restrictions, which
contributed to the near-total liquidation of the Jews in Lvov
and the environs by June 1943. They were assisted by the local
Ukrainian population. Wiesenthal, however, was arrested by
the Ukrainian police in 1941 and spent most of the war years in
more than a dozen forced-labor and concentration camps. His
5-feet 11-inch frame was down to 95 pounds at the time of his
liberation from Mauthausen on 5 May 1945 by the United
States Army.

From *The Murderers among Us* (1967) we learn that
Wiesenthal's career as a Nazi-hunter began shortly after the
war, when he was employed by the War Crimes section of the
United States Army in Austria to track down SS murderers. At
the time there were more than 100,000 survivors living in 200
displaced-persons centers in Germany and Austria. With the
help of friends, he established a network of correspondents in

the centers who interviewed former prisoners and documented
their accounts of brutal SS activities and crimes. After his
service to the Americans, Wiesenthal established in 1947 the
Jewish Historical Documentation Center in Linz, Austria,
where these affidavits were filed and augmented. They represented living testimony to a historical carnage that "we must
not forget" and helped in the prosecution of a number of Nazi
war criminals. A combination of factors, among them the Cold
War between the Soviet Union and the United States and the
waning of public interest in bringing Nazi war criminals to
trial, however, influenced Wiesenthal to close the first-ever
documentation center in 1954. While he continued to direct a
number of Jewish welfare agencies in Linz, he never abated in
his efforts to bring Adolph Otto Eichmann, the chief architect
of the Final Solution, to justice. Thus, encouraged by the
worldwide interest in the capture and trial of Eichmann, he
reopened the Documentation Center in Vienna in 1961, devoted exclusively to documenting "Nazi (or SS) crimes." His
important work of gathering and analyzing Shoah-related
material has continued.

On Holocaust issues Wiesenthal has written articles, re-
ports, and books. Among his nonfiction are *Ich jagte Eichmann*
(1961; "I Hunted Eichmann"), his own account as *der
Eichmann-Jäger* ("the Eichmann hunter"), who discovered
Eichmann's hiding place; *The Murderers among Us* (1967)
and *Justice Not Vengeance* (1989; from the German *Reht nicht
Rache*), selected vignettes depicting his modus operandi; *The
Sunflower* (1970; from the German *Die Sonneblume*), a narrative that asks a serious ethical and moral question; *Max and
Helen: A Remarkable True Love Story* (1982; from the German
Max und Helen), an anguished story of two Holocaust survi-
vors bearing an unbearable secret who refuse to bring their
tormentor to justice; and *Every Day Remembrance Day: A
Chronicle of Jewish Martyrdom* (1986), a chronicle of every-
day anti-Semitic events highlighted with the anniversary dates
of the deportation and destruction of European Jewry during
World War II.

—Zev Garber

See the essay on *The Sunflower.*

WILKOMIRSKI, Binjamin

Pseudonym for Bruno Dössekker. **Nationality:** Swiss (originally Latvian: immigrated to Switzerland after World War II).
Born: Riga, ca.1939; grew up in Majdanek and Auschwitz
concentration camps, an orphanage in Kraków, Poland, and
foster care in Switzerland. **Career:** Classical musician. **Awards:**
National Jewish book award and Prix Memoire de la Shoah,
both for *Fragments.* **Agent:** c/o Schocken Books, 201 East
50th Street, New York, New York 10020, U.S.A.

Memoir

Bruchstücke: Aus einer Kindheit 1939–1948. 1995; as *Fragments: Memories of a Wartime Childhood,* 1996.

*

Critical Studies: "The Man with Two Heads" by Elena Lappin, in *Granta,* 66, Summer 1999, pp. 7–65; "Ethos, Witness, and Holocaust 'Testimony': The Rhetoric of Fragments" by Michael Bernard-Donals, in *JAC,* 20(3), Summer 2000, pp. 565–82; "Memorizing Memory" by Amy Hungerford, in *Yale Journal of Criticism,* 14(1), Spring 2001, pp. 67–92; *The Wilkomirski Affair: A Study in Biographical Truth* by Stefan Mächler, translated by John E. Woods, 2001; *A Life in Pieces: The Making and Unmaking of Binjamin Wilkomirski* by Blake Eskin, 2001.

*   *   *

Binjamin Wilkomirski is the pseudonym of the Swiss classical musician Bruno Dössekker. *Fragments: Memories of a Wartime Childhood* was published in English translation in 1996, having appeared in German the year before, as the testimony of Wilkomirski, a child survivor of the Holocaust. The text itself is written from a child's viewpoint and so lacks specific dates and locations, but in interviews Wilkomirski established the background to his text. He claimed to have been born in Latvia in 1939. He saw his father killed in the Riga ghetto and spent six years in Majdanek and Auschwitz. After the war the orphaned Binjamin was taken to Switzerland, where he was adopted by a couple, the Dössekkers, who urged him to forget his past. In the early 1990s, after entering into therapy, Wilkomirski wrote *Fragments,* initially as a private document that friends then urged him to publish. The book was a critical and commercial success, and Wilkomirski toured the United States to deliver lectures sponsored by the United States Holocaust Memorial Museum on being a child survivor.

In August 1998 the article "Die geliehene Holocaust-Biographie" ("The Borrowed Holocaust Biography"), by the Swiss journalist Daniel Ganzfried, appeared in the Zurich newspaper *Die Weltwoche.* It argued that Binjamin Wilkomirski had been born in Switzerland, not Latvia, in 1941, that he was not Jewish, and that, except as a tourist, he had spent no time in Majdanek or Auschwitz. On the contrary, the article said, he was the illegitimate son of a woman named Yvonne Grosjean (now dead) and had been placed in various orphanages and foster homes before being adopted by the Dössekker family. After protracted investigations the German publisher of *Fragments*—Jüdischer Verlag, the Jewish-interest wing of Suhrkamp Verlag—withdrew the book from sale. An exhaustive report of the investigation, Stefan Maechler's *The Wilkomirski Affair: A Study in Biographical Truth,* which was published in 2001 and which includes the text of *Fragments* as an appendix, provided

conclusive evidence that *Fragments* was fiction and that Wilkomirski was really Bruno Dössekker, who had never left his native Switzerland during the war years.

It appears that Dössekker was not so much a confidence trickster as a troubled individual who had transposed the details of a genuinely traumatic childhood onto the historical catastrophe of the Holocaust and who had come to believe in this story of his own past. In his overidentification with the Holocaust, Dössekker may appear to resemble Sylvia Plath, whose confessional poems "Lady Lazarus" and "Daddy" use Holocaust imagery and who has been accused of "larceny" for appropriating historical events in order to convey an individual angst. In Plath's case, however, the larceny was a poetic matter and not the personal one it was for Dössekker. His case is more similar to that of writers who have fraudulently published as autobiography what turned out to be fiction—for instance, Martin Gray's *For Those I Loved* (with Max Gallo), which purported to be a memoir by a survivor of the Warsaw Ghetto and Treblinka but is at least partly invented, and Helen Darville's novel *The Hand That Signed the Paper,* originally published under the name Helen Demidenko as autobiographical fiction about being a second-generation perpetrator.

—Sue Vice

See the essay on *Fragments: Memories of a Wartime Childhood.*

WOJDOWSKI, Bogdan

Nationality: Polish. **Born:** 1930. **Career:** Spent two years in the Warsaw Ghetto. Worked as a writer. **Award:** Second prize, Polish government literary contest, 1971, for *Chleb rzucony umarlym.* **Died:** Suicide, 1994.

Novels

Konotop. 1966.
Chleb rzucony umarlym. 1971; as *Bread for the Departed,* 1997.
Tamta strona. 1997.

Short Stories

Wakacje Hioba [Job's Summer]. 1962.
Maly czlowieczek, nieme ptasze, klatka i swiat. 1975.
Manius Bany. 1980.
Wybór opowiadan. 1981.
Krzywe drogi. 1987.

Other

Proba bez kostiumu [Rehearsal without Costumes] (theatrical sketches). 1966.
Mit Szigalewa [The Myth of Shigalev] (literary sketches). 1982.

*

Critical Study: ''Bogdan Wojdowski, My Brother'' by Henryk Grynberg, in *New England Review,* 18, Fall 1997, pp. 8–10.

* * *

The Holocaust dominated Bogdan Wojdowski's life and writing. His most essential literary works concern, both thematically and problematically, the physical and psychical outcomes of the Nazi extermination of the Jews in Poland under German occupation. They owe their powerful artistic expression and authenticity equally to Wojdowski's talent and his tragic biography. Wojdowski spent two nightmarish years in the Warsaw Ghetto. When he finally managed to get out of there, his mother's friends and the Council for Help to Jews (Żegota) supported his subsistence. Those caring Poles were addressed in his preface to *Bread for the Departed* when he said, ''I spent the last years of the war 'on this side' among those who remained my close friends. I was told, 'these were absolutely infallible papers.' I didn't see any such papers. But what I saw was infallible people who put their own life at risk to save another man's life.'' Then the saved boy stayed among food and weapons smugglers, tended peasants' cows near Wyszków, and in the winter of 1943 hid with a partisans' group. He lived to see the liberation, and he returned to a totally demolished Warsaw with workers displaced from the capital city. That homelessness is quite reminiscent of **Henryk Grynberg**'s fortunes depicted in his *The Jewish War* (1965).

Both Wojdowski and Grynberg share the same traumatic experience of childhood. They made a similar type of debut in prose. Wojdowski published a collection of dismal short stories, *Job's Summer* (*Wakacje Hioba*), in 1962, and Grynberg, who is six years his junior, made his debut with *The ''Antigone'' Crew* in 1963. The transition from minor narratives about immense misfortune to an epic synthesis of the truth about the nation's extermination, which was unprecedented in history and therefore hardly possible to relate, is distinctive of the two writers. Relating the Holocaust becomes still more difficult for a Jewish writer whose good fortunes helped him avoid being killed and who can never forget what he has been through and give up the memory of those who perished. Writing about the Holocaust stands for him as a categorical imperative. Therefore, a writer who has embarked on such a literary mission must neither experiment upon the structure of the novel nor fathom egotistically the mysteries of his soul. Wojdowski's knowledge of this fact was absolute when he directed ''An open letter to the writers of the Shoah generation,'' where he stated, ''Shoah is not just a theme to write about. It is a living pain, care and memory of the hurtful experience, a universal tragedy of disgraced humanity, a problematic question of man's existence on earth.''

Twenty years after *Bread for the Departed,* this discourse perfectly justifies the origin of Wojdowski's outstanding novel and the whole literature as a testimony to the holocaust and an appeal to the readers' morally sensitive conscience. The same intentions underlined *Samson* (1948) by Kazimierz Brandys and a few narrative masterpieces by **Adolf Rudnicki**—*Shakespeare* (1948), *An Escape from the Bright Meadow* (1948), and *The Live and Dead Sea* (1952). Wojdowski benefited from his predecessor-writers' literary experience. The critics noted that the author of *Job's Summer* owed a lot for his poetics to other Polish writers such as **Tadeusz Borowski** and Jarosław Iwaszkiewicz.

Since *Bread for the Departed* came out in print, Wojdowski has been publicly considered as one of the most original and distinguished Holocaust writers. This opinion was further confirmed by his next collections of stories, which gave his principal theme its final shape that is suggestive of a special kind of hermeneutics or recurrent fictional motifs making a circling movement. David's going to the Umschlagplatz in the final scene of *Bread for the Departed* and the old tailor's coming back to the ghetto (as in the story ''Passover'' included in the collection *Winding Roads* [*Krzywe drogi*]) mark costly obsessive returns both in literature and real life. And the more so for a Jewish survivor, who existed in a society with the warring party factions of communist Poland encouraging anti-Jewish campaigns in times of political crisis. Wojdowski calculated the cost of cultivating the memory of the Holocaust and the price he had to pay for being Jewish in the eschatological text *Judaism—The Fate*: ''I have no longer a society to belong to, a society whose traditions make me recognise it, nor can a society recognise me. I am by myself. The bonds are broken. My loyalties towards the purpose and the values of living have been invalidated and no appearances can save me, for the limits of being have been violated.''

As a writer, Wojdowski reached to the limits of human existence. As a man, he continued to search through the Holocaust for its existential, ethical, and artistic implications. He was passionate doing it. And like the other ex-Auschwitz prisoners—Borowski and **Primo Levi**—he wholeheartedly drifted toward his own self-destruction.

—Stanisław Gawliński

See the essay on *Bread for the Departed.*

Y

YEHOSHUA, A(braham) B.

Nationality: Israeli. **Born:** Jerusalem, 9 December 1936.
Education: Jerusalem Hebrew Gymnasium; Hebrew University, Jerusalem, B.A. 1961; Teacher's College, graduated
1962. **Military Service:** Israeli Army, 1954–57. **Family:**
Married Rivka Kirsninski in 1960; one daughter and two sons.
Career: Teacher, Hebrew University High School, Jerusalem,
1961–63; director, Israeli School, Paris, 1963–64; secretary-general, World Union of Jewish Students, Paris, 1963–67;
member, board of art, *Keshet* literary magazine, 1967–74.
Dean of students, 1967–72, and since 1972 professor of
comparative literature, Haifa University. Visiting fellow, St.
Cross College, Oxford University, 1975–76; guest professor,
Harvard University, 1977, University of Chicago, 1988, 1996,
and Stanford University, 1990; visiting professor, Princeton
University, 1992. Editorial consultant, *Siman Kria, Tel-Aviv
Review,* and *Mifgash.* **Awards:** Akum prize, 1961; Municipality of Ramat-Gan prize, 1968; University of Iowa fellowship,
1969; Prime Minister's prize, 1972; Brenner prize, 1983;
Alterman prize, 1986; Bialik prize, 1989; National Jewish
book award (U.S.), 1990; Israeli Booker prize and Israel prize,
both in 1992; Koret prize AP, 2000. Honorary degrees: Hebrew
Union College, Cincinnati, 1990; Tel-Aviv University, 1998.
Address: Office, Haifa University, Department of Literature,
Mount Carmel, 31999, Haifa, Israel.

PUBLICATIONS

Novels

Bithilat kayits 1970 (novella). 1972; as *Early in the Summer of
1970,* 1977.
Hame'ahev. 1977; as *The Lover,* 1977.
Gerushim me'ucharim. 1982; as *A Late Divorce,* 1984.
Molcho. 1987; as *Five Seasons,* 1989.
Mar Maniy. 1990; as *Mr. Mani,* 1992.
Ha-shiva me-hodu [Return from India]. 1994; as *Open Heart,*
1996.
Masa el tom haelef. 1997; as *Voyage to the End of the
Millennium,* 1999.

Short Stories

Mot hazaken [Death of the Old Man] (novella). 1962.
Mul haye'arot [Facing the Forests]. 1968; translated in *Three
Days and a Child,* 1970.
Three Days and a Child (selections). 1970.
Tishah sipurim [Nine Stories]. 1970.

Ad horef 1974: Mivhar (selections). 1975.
The Continuing Silence of a Poet. 1988.
Kol ha-sipurim. 1993.

Plays

Laylah beMai (produced Tel-Aviv, 1969). As *A Night in May,*
in *Two Plays,* 1974.
Tipolim acharonim (produced Haifa, 1973). As *Last Treatment,* in *Two Plays,* 1974.
Two Plays: A Night in May and Last Treatment. 1974.
Hafetsim (produced Haifa, 1986). Translated as *Possessions,*
in *Modern Israeli Drama in Translation,* 1993.
Tinokot laylah [Babies of the Night] (produced 1992).

Screenplays: *Sheloshah yamim veyeled* [Three Days and a
Child], 1967; *Hame'ahev* [The Lover], 1986; *The Continuing Silence of a Poet* (Germany), 1987.

Other

Bizechut hanormaliyut. 1980; as *Between Right and Right,*
1981.
Israel, with Frederic Brenner. 1988.
Hakir vehahar: metsi'uto halosifrutit shel hasofer beYi'sra'el
[The Wall and the Mountain: The Literary Reality of the
Writer in Israel]. 1989.
*Kohah ha-nora shel ashmah ketanah: Ha-heksher ha-musari
shel ha- tekst ha-sifruti.* 1998; as *The Terrible Power of a
Minor Guilt: Literary Essays,* 2000.

*

Critical Studies: "An Appraisal of the Stories of Yehoshua"
by Baruch Kurzweil, in *Literature East and West,* 14(1), 1970;
"Yehoshua As Playwright" by Anat Feinberg, in *Modern
Hebrew Literature,* 1, 1975; "A Touch of Madness in the
Plays of Yehoshua" by Eli Pfefferkorn, in *World Literature
Today,* 51, 1977; "Distress and Constriction" by Haim Shoham,
in *Ariel,* 41, 1976; "Multiple Focus and Mystery" by Leon I.
Yudkin, in *Modern Hebrew Literature,* 3, 1977; "A Great
Madness Hides behind All This" by Gershon Shaked, in
Modern Hebrew Literature, 8(1–2), 1982–83; "Casualties of
Patriarchal Double Standards: Old Women in Yehoshua's
Fiction," in *South Central Bulletin,* 43(4), 1984, and "The
Sleepy Wife: A Feminist Consideration of Yehoshua's Fiction," in *Hebrew Annual Review,* 8, 1984, both by Esther
Fuchs; Possessions As a Death Wish" by Gideon Ofrat, in
Modern Hebrew Literature, 12(1–2), 1986; "Yehoshua:
Dismantler" by Chaim Chertok, in his *We Are All Close:*

Conversations with Israeli Writers, 1989; ''Yehoshua,'' in *The Arab in Israeli Literature,* 1989, and ''Yehoshua and the Sephardic Experience,'' in *World Literature Today,* 65(1), 1991, both by Gila Ramras-Rauch; ''Yehoshua's 'Sound and Fury': A Late Divorce and Its Faulknerian Model'' by Nehama Aschkenasy, in *Modern Language Studies,* 21(2), 1991; *Facing the Fires: Conversations with A.B. Yehoshua* by Bernard Horn, 1997.

* * *

Like **Amos Oz** and **Yehudah Amichai**, A.B. Yehoshua belongs to what was dubbed the new wave of Israeli writers born in the 1930s and '40s who came to prominence in the 1960s. While ruptures in the diaspora and the advent of Israeli statehood defined their historical moment and shaped them sociopolitically, such writers (largely inspired by the poet Natan Zach) reached back a generation to figures like **S.Y. Agnon**, Y.H. Brenner, and David Vogel for models of a renegotiated literary tradition. Their social milieu also contrasted dramatically with that of their counterparts in the immediately preceding generation, molded as they were by the kibbutz or the War of Independence. Thus, Yehoshua's formative development at Hebrew University rather than a youth organization or military unit was representative and to a certain extent explains the academic and aestheticizing thrust of the *gal hadash* (new wave) in literary prose that sought to exchange an earlier social-realist program for subtler and more formally complex modes. Agnon, Kafka, and Faulkner are the primary influences Yehoshua acknowledges in the body of his fiction and also in critical studies he has penned.

In order of composition, Yehoshua has published three collections of short stories (1963–72), two books of essays, *Between Right and Right* (1981) and *The Wall and the Mountain* (1989), and six novels, *The Lover* (1977), *A Late Divorce* (1984), *The Five Seasons* (1989), *Mr. Mani* (1992), *Open Heart* (1996), and *Voyage to the End of the Millennium* (1999). While *Open Heart* was his greatest popular success, *Mr. Mani,* appropriately enough, precipitated a unique cultural conversation—two collections of reviews and essays within five years of the novel's release—as befits a book that revoices a debate about Israel's present outside the limiting discursive confines of nationalism and fundamentalism. Additionally many of Yehoshua's works have been dramatized, filmed, or, in the case *Mr. Mani,* given public readings; he has been awarded the Brenner, Alterman, Bialik, Israeli Booker, and Israel prizes, the last being the most eminent literary honor his country bestows.

The poetics of Yehoshua's writing—narrative technique, symbolist structures, literary influences—deserve the closest kind of scrutiny, yet, to borrow from the English title to one of his novels, it is their ''open heart,'' particularly in *Mr. Mani,* that might best situate the author in the present context. Before ideology, history, and myth, Yehoshua has said, that novel tells

a story of patrimony. And in Yehoshua's case, paternity and sonship (while also paralleling, albeit critically, a determinative masculinist bias in modern Hebrew literature up through the State generation) possess a special resonance inasmuch as his family is Sephardic with roots in Jerusalem going back to the early nineteenth century. By contrast both Oz and Amichai are the sons of fathers whose surnames and national origins reflect the legacy of Ashkenazic (European) Jewry. Moreover the novel's proliferation of identities says as much about the author's own various personal allegiances—to forebears both familial and literary, to Sephardic, secular, and Zionist cultures, to a presentist ethic informed by a novelist's sense of history—as it does about its characters'.

In the last regard Yehoshua has been an outspoken critic of the government's treatment of Palestinians within and without the green lines that separate territory annexed in 1967 from the rest of Israel. His peer Amos Oz and younger contemporary **David Grossman** are most often associated with him as writers and Jews who perforce speak as citizens co-responsible for the decisions of state. More revealing, however (once again, apropos of the obliquity at the core of *Mr. Mani*), has been an ongoing adversarial dialogue, along with reciprocal admiration, with the Arab-Israeli author Anton Shammas, whose novel *Arabesques* portrays a Yehoshua-like figure satirized for his paternalism. Perhaps the most important of the extraliterary supplements to the conversations in *Mr. Mani,* that exchange—with an equally adept writer who is also an Israeli citizen though not a Jew—merely participates in and extends the logic of Yehoshua's own literary intuitions: beyond where he can go ideologically perhaps but in the same spirit of bending axis toward margin, of subtending polarities with what the novelist Robert Musil called ''the third possibility.''

—Adam Zachary Newton

See the essay on *Mr. Mani.*

YEVTUSHENKO, Yevgeny (Alexandrovich)

Nationality: Russian. **Born:** Stanzia Zima, Siberia, 18 July 1933. **Education:** Gorky Literary Institute, 1951–54. **Family:** Married 1) Bella Akhmadulina in 1954 (divorced); 2) Galina Semyonovna in 1962 (divorced); 3) Jan Butler in 1978 (divorced); 4) Maria Novikove in 1986; five children. **Career:** Since 1996 faculty member, Queens College, New York. **Awards:** U.S.S.R. Commission for the Defense of Peace award, 1965; U.S.S.R. state prize, 1984; Order of Red Banner of Labor; finalist, Ritz Paris Hemingway award for best 1984 novel published in English, 1985, for *Wild Berries.*

PUBLICATIONS

Poetry

Razvedchiki gryaduschego [The Prospectors of the Future].
1952.
Tretii sneg: Kniga liriki [Third Snow]. 1955.
Shosse entusiastov [Highway of the Enthusiasts]. 1956.
Stantsiya Zima. 1956; as *Winter Station*, 1964.
Obeschanie [Promise]. 1957.
Luk i lira: Stikhi o gruzii [The Bow and the Lyre]. 1959.
Stikhi raznykh let [Poems of Several Years]. 1959.
Yabloko [The Apple]. 1960.
Nezhnost: Novyii stikhi [Tenderness: New Poems]. 1962.
Posie Stalina [After Stalin]. 1962.
Selected Poems (selections in English). 1962.
Vzmakh ruki [A Wave of the Hand]. 1962.
Zamlung. 1962.
The Poetry of Yevgeny Yevtushenko, 1953–1965 (selections in
English and Russian). 1965; revised and enlarged edition,
1967.
Bratskaia GES. 1965; translated as *Selections from the Bratsk
Hydroelectric Station and Other Poems*, 1965; as *Bratsk
Station and Other New Poems*, 1967.
Yevtushenko Poems (selections in English and Russian). 1966.
Poems Chosen by the Author, Yevgeny Yevtushenko (selec-
tions in English and Russian). 1966.
Kater sviazi [Torpedo Boat Signaling]. 1966.
Babii Yar and Other Poems (in English and Russian). 1966.
The City of Yes and the City of No, & Other Poems. 1966.
Flowers and Bullets, & Freedom to Kill (translation of *Tsvety i
puli*). 1970.
Stolen Apples (in English and Russian). 1971.
Kazanskii universitet. 1971; as *Kazan University and Other
New Poems*, 1973.
From Desire to Desire. 1976.
The Face behind the Face. 1979.
Ivan the Terrible and Ivan the Fool (translation of *Ivanovskie
sittsy*). 1979.
Invisible Threads (selections in English). 1981.
A Dove in Santiago: A Novella in Verse (translation of *Golub'
v Sant'iago*). 1982.
Early Poems (selections in English). 1989.
Belorusskaia krovinka: Otryvok iz poemy, stikhi. 1990.
The Collected Poems 1952–1990 (selections in English). 1991.
Net let: Liubovnaia lirika. 1993.
Moe samoe-samoe. 1995.

Novels

Yagodnyye mesta. 1981; as *Wild Berries*, 1984.
Ardabiola: A Fantasy. 1984.
Ne umira prezhde smerti. 1993; as *Don't Die before Your
Death: An Almost Documentary Novel*, 1994; as *Don't Die
before You're Dead*, 1995.

Plays

Poiushchaia damba: Stikhi i noema (Pod kozhei statui Cvobody)
[Under the Skin of the Statue of Liberty] (produced 1972).
1972.

Screenplays: *I Am Cuba*, with Enrique Pineda Barnet, 1963;
Kindergarten, 1983; *Pokhorony Stalina*, 1990.

Other

A Precocious Autobiography. 1963.
Almost at the End (selected prose and poetry in English). 1987.
Divided Twins: Alaska and Siberia (essays; translation of
Razdelënnye bliznetsy). 1988.
*Fatal Half Measures: The Culture of Democracy in the Soviet
Union* (speeches and essays). 1991.
Pervoe sobranie sochineniaei v vosmi tomakh. 1997.
Medlennaeiia leiiubov. 1997.
Volchiaei pasport. 1998.
Izbrannaia proza. 1998.

Editor, with Albert C. Todd and Max Hayward, *Twentieth
Century Russian Poetry: Silver and Steel: An Anthology*.
1993.

*

Film Adaptations: *I Am Cuba*, 1964 (as *Soy Cuba*, 1964, *Ia
Kuba*, 1964); *Kindergarten*, 1983; *Pokhorony Stalina*, 1990.

Critical Studies: ''The Politics of Poetry: The Sad Case of
Yevgeny Yevtushenko'' by Robert Conquest, in *New York
Times Magazine*, 30 September 1973; ''The Poetry of Yevgeny
Yevtushenko in the 1970s'' by Irma Mercedes Kaszuba, in
Language Quarterly, 25(1–2), Fall/Winter 1986, pp. 31–34;
''Yevtushenko Feels a Fresh Wind Blowing'' by Katrina
Vanden Heuvel, in *Progressive*, 24 April 1987, pp. 24–31;
''Russian Roué'' by Anthony Wilson-Smith, in *Maclean's*
(Canada), 108, 12 June 1995, p. 60.

Theatrical Activities: Director: **Film**—*Kindergarten*, 1984.
Actor: **Film**—*Pokhorony Stalina*, 1990.

*   *   *

Yevgeny Yevtushenko, born in 1933 in the village of Zima
Junction in Siberia, is a profoundly Russian, profoundly Siberian writer. He is also, like most Russian writers, acutely aware
of history. His hundreds of works are steeped in the geography,
history, and daily life of Russia. Even his poems about other
countries, while perceptive and accurate portrayals, remain
nonetheless ''Russian'' poems, their subjects seen through the
eyes of a Russian observer. The same holds true for his
treatment of historical events. The roots of his morality are to
be found in his love of Russia, his belief in the brotherhood of
all people, and his belief in the ideals of the revolution.

Yevtushenko's career took off with the "thaw" following Joseph Stalin's death in 1953. He became a popular poet whose readings filled football stadiums and who was given unprecedented freedom to travel abroad. This prominence made it possible for him to take strong critical positions and to tackle such taboo subjects as anti-Semitism. In his political poems Yevtushenko praises Salvador Allende and Che Guevara and condemns nuclear weapons at the same time that he warns against militarists, dishonest bureaucrats, and toadies of all kinds at home.

Even the semi-offical poet was not immune from censorship, however. A number of poems written during the 1960s, such as "Russian Tanks in Prague" (written in 1968; published in 1990) could not be published until years later. Even "Babii Yar," his best-known poem, about a Nazi massacre of Jews and others near Kiev during World War II, was to reap both tumultuous public praise and official disapproval.

Yevtushenko's poems dealing with World War II are illustrative of his socialist vision and his civil courage as well as his conviction that a poet has an ethical duty to perform. Most of them fall into two categories: personal, patriotic poems about his experiences as a child in Siberia, and those focusing on Jewish themes. In "The Companion" (1954) the narrator and another child strive to act bravely after the train in which they are riding is bombed. In "Party Card" (1957) a little boy brings strawberries to a Russian officer in the forest, then takes the dying officer's Communist Party card and carries it next to his own heart. In "Grandma" (1956) Yevtushenko recalls listening to his grandmother's revolutionary tales while his mother was at the front. "Army" (1959) portrays a children's chorus singing to wounded soldiers in a hospital in Siberia, while in "Weddings" (1955) he describes the desperate gaiety of wartime weddings, as young men married only to go off to the front the next day. Uniting all these poems is a sense of the resolve and human solidarity of ordinary Russians in the face of the fascist menace.

The second category contains the few poems Yevtushenko wrote about the Holocaust. All are interwoven with the poet's thoughts on his own identity and contemporary political concerns. "Russians and Jews" (1978) celebrates the unity of the peoples who fought together for "moral justice" and "died for their common land." In the opening lines of the antiwar poem "On the Question of Freedom" (1967) the lines "Dachau's ashes burn my feet / The asphalt smokes under me" link the Holocaust to later crimes such as the Vietnam War and the assassination of John F. Kennedy.

"The Apple Trees of Drobitskii" (1989) recalls the mass murder of Jews and Ukrainians by Nazis at Drobitskii Yar near Kharkov. In a powerful evocation of the common humanity of the victims Yevtushenko portrays a group of apple trees growing from the killing ground, each rooted in a child that whispers through the trees—Sarah in Yiddish, Khristia in Ukrainian, Manechka in Russian, Dzhan in Armenian. "All the skeletons embrace one another in the ground." But like Yevtushenko's more famous poem "Babii Yar" it is also an indictment of contemporary Russian anti-Semitism. He asks "Ruvin Ruvinovich," who survived the massacre, if he had escaped only so "some day / they could charge your gray hairs / with Jewish Freemasonry?" But, the poet insists, "we are working our way out . . . from under the ruins."

In 1961 Yevtushenko wrote the poem that made his a familiar name in the West, "Babii Yar," about the Nazi massacre of tens of thousands at a ravine outside Kiev. In it he makes his strongest statement of solidarity with the Jews, as victims both of the Holocaust and of ongoing anti-Semitism. Yevtushenko appeals to the goodness of his fellow Russians who are, he insists, "international to the core." The poem ends with the now-famous words "I am as hateful as a Jew / to all antisemites / In their callous rage. / For that reason I am a true Russian!"

—Patricia Pollock Brodsky

See the essay on "Babii Yar."

Z

ZABLE, Arnold

Nationality: Australian. **Born:** Wellington, New Zealand, 1947; grew up in a suburb of Melbourne, Australia. **Education:** Melbourne University; Columbia University, New York. **Career:** Lecturer in the Arts faculty, Melbourne University. Worked as an English and creative writing teacher and as a freelance journalist. Coeditor, *The Melbourne Chronicle;* columnist, *The Age,* Melbourne. **Awards:** National Council Lysbeth Cohen award and NSW Ethnic Affairs Commission award, both in 1991, and Braille Book of the Year award and Talking Book of the Year award, both in 1992, all for *Jewels and Ashes.*

PUBLICATIONS

Novel

Cafe Scheherazade. 2001.

Memoir

Jewels and Ashes. 1991.

Other

Clown Boy (for children). 1982.
The River Man (for children). 1982.
Wanderers and Dreamers: Tales of the David Herman Theatre. 1998.

Editor, *The Industrial Yarra: Possibilities for Change.* 1976.

* * *

Arnold Zable, the son of prewar Polish Jewish migrants, was born in New Zealand in 1947 and grew up in Carlton, an inner-city suburb of Melbourne that then had a substantial Jewish population. He was an academic and migrant educator before becoming a full-time writer and journalist. Zable is one of the best known and most respected Australian Jewish writers of his generation. The writings, like the man, bring two potentially conflictual tendencies into close accord: on the one hand, a joyous cosmopolitanism that revels in cultural difference and passionately endorses Australian multiculturalism; on the other, a fierce loyalty to Jewish cultural traditions (though he is not an observant Jew)—in particular, to traditions of Jewish storytelling.

In addition to many shorter pieces, Zable has published three books: the award-winning *Jewels and Ashes* (1991), an autobiographical account focused on his travels in eastern Europe in 1986; *Wanderers and Dreamers* (1998), a history of Yiddish theater in Australia; and *Café Scheherazade* (2001), a novel in which Holocaust survivors, all patrons of the Café Scheherazade (a real-life eatery in St. Kilda, one of the centers of Melbourne Jewish life), recount their tales of survival. Each of these books evinces a powerful reconstructive impulse.

Jewels and Ashes seeks to reconstruct aspects of family and wider Polish Jewish history that were decimated by the Holocaust. It is an awesome quest: ''Perhaps this is how it has always been for descendants of lost families: we search within a tangle of aborted memories, while stumbling towards a mythical home which seems to elude us as it recedes into false turns and dead ends.'' Yet the journey proves more availing than this might suggest. The second generation Australian's return journey reveals not just the ''ashes'' that the horror left behind but also the ''jewels''—the people, the memories, the locales, the stories—that survived. The narrative's meld of lament and celebration is typical of Zable's writings; but in his work, unlike that of some other well-known Australian Jewish writers like Morris Lurie and Serge Liberman, the main emphasis falls on celebration. Perhaps in the final analysis Zable is a chronicler of enchantment.

This chronicling of enchantment is evident in *Wanderers and Dreamers,* with its celebration of the quixotic, chancy, inspired, unlikely but also passionately willed history of Yiddish theater in Australia. ''Yiddish theatre,'' he writes, ''is a tale of miraculous journeys.'' Since organized Yiddish theater in Australia began in the first decade of the twentieth century, many of the journeys in question occur prior to the Holocaust; but many also unfold in its shadow, as in the case of Mila and Moshe Potashinski, Auschwitz survivors who are reunited after the war and exercise the ''power'' of their ''ancient craft'' with special passion and poignancy in Europe and later Australia.

Miraculous journeys are also the essence of *Café Scheherazade.* Martin Davis, a journalist who is the principal narrator of the story, is ''engaged in reconstructing other times, other worlds,'' as he listens to the stories of three Holocaust survivors, Yossel Bartnowski, Laizer Bialer, and Zalman Grintraum, and to those of Avram and Marsha Zeleznikow, the proprietors of the café. These narratives contain many terrible things; yet the book is also rich in romance, as in the story of how the café got its legendary name, and in moments of transcendence that pierce the darkness. As Zalman, the speaker most attuned to transcendence, says: ''In every darkness there is a spark.'' He discerns ''crevices of peace'' in a nightmare world, and says: ''This is what all my wanderings have taught me: that the moment itself is the haven, the true sanctuary.''

But some places offer more secure sanctuary than others, and, like most Australian Jewish writers, Zable is in little doubt that for Jews, at least in relative terms, Australia is a *gan eiden*—a ''golden land.'' In Zable's work storytelling is a matter of urgency as well as enchantment. Martin is acutely aware that ''a generation is moving on. And with each passing life I feel it more keenly: there are tales aching to be told, craving to be heard, before they disappear into the grave.'' In the author's note with which the book concludes, Zable explains: ''This is not a book about history. Rather, it is a homage to the power of story-telling, a meditation on displacement, and on the way in which the after-effects of war linger on in the minds of survivors.'' Here, as always, his vision, while rooted in Jewish history, is deeply attuned to that larger history of which the Jewish past, harrowing yet sublime, is but a part.

—Richard Freadman

See the essay on *Jewels and Ashes.*

ZEITLIN, Aaron

Nationality: American (originally Russian: immigrated to the United States from Warsaw, Poland, 1939). **Born:** Gomel, Ukraine, 1898; son of the writer Hillel Zeitlin. **Career:** Moved to Warsaw with family, 1907; lived in Jaffa, Jerusalem, and Zichron Yaakov, 1920–21. Professor of Hebrew literature, Jewish Theological Seminary of America, New York, beginning in 1939. Also worked as a journalist. Literary editor, *Unzer Ekspres* newspaper, 1926; editor, *Globus* journal, 1932–34. **Died:** 1974.

Publications

Poetry

Metatron: Apokoliptishe poeme. 1922.
Shotns oyfn shney [Shadows on Snow]. 1922.
Gezamlte lider [Collected Poems]. 1947.
Shirim u-fo'emot. 1949.
Lieder fun churban 'on lieder fun gloybin [Poems of the Holocaust and Poems of Faith]. 1967.
Ruah mi-metsulah: Shirim u-fo'emot. 1975.
Darko ha-aharonah shel Yanush Korts'ak: Po'emah bi-ferozah [Last Journey of Janusz Korczak]. 1989.

Plays

Brenner. 1929.
Yakob Frank: Drame in Zeks Bilder. 1929.

Esterke [Esther]. 1939.
Ben ha-esh veha-yesha': Po'emah dramatit. 1957.
Min ha-adam va-ma'lah: Shete po'emot dramatit. 1964.
Gezamlte drames [Collected Dramas]. 1974.
Drames. 1980.
Brener, Esterke, Vaitsman ha-sheni: Sheloshah mahazot. 1993.

Novel

Brenendike erd [Burning Earth]. 1979.

Other

In keynems land [In No Man's Land]. 1938.
In kamf far a Idisher melukheh. 1943.
Medinah va-hazon medinah. 1965.
'Al yahase ha-gomlin ben ha-medinah la-golah: (Hartsa'at oreah ba-hug li-fe'ile ha-tefutsot). 1966.
Ha-Metsi'ut ha-aheret: Ha-parapsikhologyah ... 'uvdot ve-eru'im mi-tehum ha-mufla ... 1967.
Ben emunah le-'omanut: Kerekh rishon Mi-dor le-dor: Kerekh sheni Be-'ohole sifrut ... (each of the three titles also published separately in 1980). 1980.
Literarishe un filosofishe eseyen [Literary and Philosophical Essays]. 1980.
Bi-reshut ha-rabim uvi-reshut ha-yahid: Aharon Tseytlin ve-sifrut Yidish: Pirke mavo ve-igrot mu'arot be-livui te'udot le-toldot tarbut Yidish be-Polin ben shete milhamot ha-'olam (correspondence). 2000.

Translator, *Shirav ha-idiyim,* by Hayim Nahman Byalik. 1956.

*

Critical Studies: ''Singer on Aaron Zeitlin'' by Isaac Bashevis Singer (translated by Joseph C. Landis), in *Yiddish,* 6(2–3), Summer/Fall 1985, pp. 117–19; ''The Holocaust Poetry of Aaron Zeitlin in Yiddish and Hebrew'' by Emanuel S. Goldsmith, in *Reflections of the Holocaust in Art and Literature,* edited by Randolph L. Braham, 1990.

* * *

Aaron Zeitlin, son of the noted Yiddish writer and thinker Hillel Zeitlin, was born in Gomel, Ukraine, in 1898 and raised in Vilna and Warsaw, where his family moved in 1907. Together with his brother, Elchanan, he sojourned for nine months in 1920–21 in Jaffa, Jerusalem, and Zichron Yaakov. The experiences of this period are reflected in Zeitlin's literary works in Hebrew and Yiddish, including the drama *Brenner* (1929), about the gifted Hebrew writer of the ''uprooted'' generation who was murdered on 2 May 1921 in Jaffa during the Arab riots; the novel *Brenendike erd* (1979; ''Burning Earth''), on the World War I Jewish espionage network Nili and the nature of a future Jewish state; and poetry. In 1939 he was invited to New York by director Maurice Schwartz for the production of his play *Esterke* (''Esther''). The start of World

War II on 1 September 1939 prevented his return to his family, all of whom were murdered in the Shoah. He settled in New York City where he worked as a journalist and a professor of Hebrew literature at the Jewish Theological Seminary of America. Zeitlin died in New York in 1974.

Zeitlin's literary writings include bilingual (Hebrew and Yiddish) poems, narratives, dramas, essays, and criticism. Noteworthy is his contribution from the Warsaw period. In the 1920s and '30s he was totally immersed in the Yiddish cultural life of Warsaw. He was a moving force in the inclusion of Yiddish literature and Yiddish writers as members of the World PEN Organization (late 1920s), whose branch in Warsaw he chaired in the 1930s. In 1926 he became literary editor of the Warsaw Yiddish daily *Unzer Ekspres,* and he founded and edited the Yiddish literary monthly journal *Globus* (1932–1934). His extant collections of interwar Yiddish poetry and drama include *Shotns oyfn shney* (1922; "Shadows on Snow"), *Metatron* (1922), *Yakob Frank* (1929), and *In keynems land* (1938; "In No Man's Land"), a premeditation of the German horrors on the horizon. Tragically, German militarism destroyed a number of his unpublished manuscripts and works in progress, including five volumes of poetry ready for publication; unpublished plays; a novel co-written with **Isaac Bashevis Singer** on the Austrian Jewish psychologist and philosopher Otto Weininger (1880–1923), whose brand of Jewish self-hate influenced Nazi ideology; and personal correspondence.

Zeitlin's works represent a reflective reservoir that is fed by a wide range of sources, classic and contemporary. Feeding the depths are tributaries of sacred and secular semantics as well as old new currents, such as mysticism, philosophy, Shoah, and Zionism. What unites his writings is his cosmopolitan traditional way of thinking. This talent, which he honed as a literary critic and editor and perfected in his journalistic work and polemics, sustained the "kultural-kampf" between traditional and antitraditional *yiddishists* in pre-war Poland and beyond. He was a devoted loyalist who left an indelible mark on the development and advancement of Yiddish culture and literature. Singer, at his Nobel lecture, said of his friend Aaron Zeitlin, "He left a spiritual inheritance of high quality." Few critics would disagree.

—Zev Garber

See the essay on *Lieder fun churban 'on lieder fun gloybin.*

ZUCKERMAN, Yitzhak "Antek"

Nationality: Israeli (originally Polish: immigrated to Israel after World War II). **Born:** 13 December 1915. **Family:** Married Zivia Lubetkin. **Career:** Active throughout the Nazi occupation of Poland in underground resistence activities

including the Jewish Fighting Organization and Warsaw Ghetto Uprising. Editor, *The Fighting Ghetto* newsletter. Cofounder, Kibbutz Lohamei Haghetaot and Beit Lohamei Haghetaot (Ghetto Fighters' Kibbutz and Memorial). **Died:** 17 June 1981.

PUBLICATIONS

Memoirs

Ba-geto uva-mered. 1985.
Sheva' ha-shanim ha-hen: 1939–1946. 1990; as *A Surplus of Memory: Chronicle of the Warsaw Ghetto Uprising,* 1993.

Other

Sefer Milhamot ha-geta'ot: Ben ha-homot, ba-mahanot, ba-ye'arot, with Mosheh Basok. 1954.
Ketavim aharonim: 700–704, with Shelomo Even-Shoshan and Itzhak Katzenelson. 1956.
Kapitlen fun izovn, with Shmuel Barantchok and Re'uven Yatsiv. 1981.

*

Critical Studies: "The Road Leads Far Away: *A Surplus of Memory: Chronicle of the Warsaw Ghetto Uprising* by Yitzhak Zuckerman" by Irving Howe, in *New Republic,* 208(18), 3 May 1993, p. 29; "Ghetto Fighter: Yitzhak Zuckerman and the Jewish Underground in Warsaw" by Michael R. Marrus, in *American Scholar,* 54(2), Spring 1995, p. 277.

*   *   *

Although Yitzhak Zuckerman was not a prolific writer on the Holocaust, his contribution to Holocaust remembrance is not to be overlooked. Zuckerman was an organizer of and a commander in the *Żidowska Organizacja Bojowa* (ŻOB; Jewish Fighting Organization), and his work offers Holocaust scholars invaluable insider information into an operation that was superbly organized but doomed to fail. This failure was not due to the fact that these fighters were young, middle-class, and inexperienced in battle; they were outnumbered in manpower and in weaponry. The spirit of the ghetto fighters, however, surpassed all comprehension that the Germans had of Jews. They had not suspected that a "non-resistant, weak people" would be capable of going up against a clearly more powerful Nazi army. Indeed, in spirit these ghetto fighters were the true victors, and their bravery is a tribute to the extraordinary potential that more often than not lies dormant in most people.

When studying the Warsaw Ghetto Uprising, one must also keep in mind that at this time the fighters had an extremely difficult time recruiting others in the ghetto to join their cause. Many knew it would be a fruitless effort; many others had already resigned themselves to the fact that the ghetto was the place they were supposed to be. Understanding the meaning of "ghetto mentality" is imperative in gaining an even stronger understanding of just what these young fighters were up against—not only the Nazis and the Judenrat, with its fair share of informants, but a resistance of the inhabitants to fight against what they perceived to be the fate that had been dealt to them.

Zuckerman's mainstay in his life was his wife, Zivia Lubetkin, who, even though a shy, middle-class woman from a small village, became a central figure in the organization of the Warsaw Ghetto Uprising. Her work *In the Days of Destruction and Death* provides an overview to many others' contributions to the organization of the uprising and can be read in addition to Zuckerman's *Surplus of Memory: Chronicle of the Warsaw Ghetto Uprising*. The Warsaw Ghetto Uprising is only a small section of the entire Holocaust experience, and it is many times passed over in favor of the "larger picture" of the Holocaust. But the significance of this resistance cannot be denied. As stated in the foreword of *Surplus of Memory,* simply entitled "Antek," Barbara Harshav states, "... in that Hell they [the fighters] lived in, they've maintained a human image. Because they stared down the reality of their situation directly in the face and took control of their own lives, holding onto their definition of who they were and what they valued—difficult enough in the best of circumstances; well-nigh impossible under Nazi occupation." Not many of the leaders of the uprising survived that nearly month-long period from 19 April to 16 May 1943, and among those killed was the leader of the ŻOB, Mordecai Anielewicz. Many of the fighters committed suicide rather than face what punishment the Nazis had in store for them. Zuckerman led many to safety out of the Warsaw Ghetto through the underground sewer system. He continued rescuing Jews during and after the war. In 1946, when massacres of great numbers of Jews in the town of Kielce commenced, Zuckerman and Lubetkin were there to lead survivors to safety.

Zuckerman was also the editor of a newsletter called *The Fighting Ghetto.* He and Zivia established the *Kibbutz Lohamei Haghetaot* (The Ghetto Fighters' Kibbutz), whose members are all Holocaust survivors. He continued paying tribute to the uprising by establishing a museum, *Beit Katznelson,* at his kibbutz. The 12 archives and more than 60,000 volumes and documents in the museum made its collection larger than that of the U.S. Holocaust Museum.

To the end of his life Zuckerman continued his tribute to the resistance of the Warsaw Ghetto fighters. He fervently worked in his kibbutz and maintained the *Beit Katznelson* for many years. The entire ordeal of his youthful days, however, had indeed taken a toll on his health. He died of a heart attack in Galilee on 17 June 1981.

—Cynthia A. Klima

See the essay on *A Surplus of Memory: Chronicle of the Warsaw Ghetto Uprising.*

ZWEIG, Stefan

Nationality: British (originally Austrian: immigrated to England, 1934, granted British citizenship, 1940). **Born:** Vienna, 28 November 1881. **Education:** Studied German and Romance literatures, University of Vienna, Ph.D. 1904; also studied at University of Berlin and the Sorbonne, Paris. **Family:** Married 1) Friderike Maria Burger von Winternitz in 1919 (divorced); 2) Elisabeth Charlotte Altmann in 1939. **Military Service:** Worked in the Austrian War Archives during World War I. **Career:** Traveled to China, India, Africa, and North America in the years prior to World War I; moved to Salzburg, 1919; lived in England, 1934–40; traveled to the United States and South America, 1940–42. **Award:** Bauernfeld prize for lyric poetry, 1906. **Died:** Suicide, 22 February 1942.

PUBLICATIONS

Collection

Gesammelte Werke in Einzelbände (10 vols.). 1981.

Novels

Brennendes Geheimnis: Eine Erzahlung (novella). 1911; as *The Burning Secret,* 1919.
Angst (novella). 1920.
Der Zwang (novella). 1920.
Die Augen des Ewigen Bruders (novella). 1922.
Der begrabene Leuchter (novella). 1936; as *The Buried Candelabrum,* 1937.
Ungeduld des Herzens. 1939; as *Beware of Pity,* 1939.
Schachnovelle (novella). 1942; as *The Royal Game,* 1944.

Memoir

Welt von gestern. 1941; as *The World of Yesterday: An Autobiography,* 1943.

Short Stories

Die Liebe der Erika Ewald (novellas). 1904.
Erstes Erlebnis. 1911.
Amok (novellas). 1922; translated as *Amok,* 1931.
Passion and Pain (selections in English). 1924.
Verwirrung der Gefühle (novellas). 1927; as *Conflicts,* 1927.
Kaleidoscope (translation of *Kaleidoskop*). 1934.
The Old Book Peddlar, and Other Tales for Bibliophiles (selections in English). 1937.
Legenden. 1945; as *Jewish Legends,* 1987.
Ausgewählte Novellen. 1946.
Stories and Legends (selections in English). 1955.

Plays

Tersites: Ein Traurspiel (produced Dresden and Kassel, 1908). 1907.

Der verwandelte Komödiant: Ein Spiel aus dem deutschen Rokoko. 1912.

Das Haus am Meer (produced Vienna, 1912). 1912.

Der verwandelte Komodant. 1913.

Jeremias (produced Switzerland, 1917). 1917; translated as *Jeremiah,* 1922.

Legende eines Lebens. 1919.

Volpone, adaptation of a play by Ben Jonson. 1926; translated as *Ben Jonson's Volpone: A Loveless Comedy in Three Acts,* 1926.

Die Flucht zu Gott. 1927.

Das Lamm des Armen. 1929.

Die schweigsame Frau, adaptation of a play by Ben Jonson (opera libretto), music by Richard Strauss. 1935.

Poetry

Silbern Saiten [Silver Strings]. 1901.
Die frühen Kränze. 1906.
Die gesammelten Gedichte. 1924.

Other

Verlaine (biography). 1905; translated as *Paul Verlaine,* 1913.

Emile Verhaeren (biography). 1910; translated as *Emile Verhaeren,* 1914.

Das Herz Europas: Ein Besuch im Genfer Roten Kreuz. 1918.

Fahrten: Landschaften und Städte. 1919.

Drei Meister: Balzac, Dickens, Dostojewski (biography). 1920; translated as *Three Masters: Balzac, Dickens, Dostoeffsky,* 1930.

Marceline Desbordes-Valmore: Das Lebensbild einer Dichterin (biography). 1920.

Romain Rolland (biography). 1921; translated as *Romain Rolland,* 1921.

Sainte-Beuve. 1923.

Der Kampf mit dem Damon: Holerin, Kleist, Nietzsche (biography). 1925; as *The Struggle with the Demon,* 1929.

Abschied von Rilke (essay). 1927; as *Farewell to Rilke,* 1975.

Sternstunden der Menschheit: Fünf historische Miniaturen. 1927; as *The Tide of Fortune: Twelve Historical Miniatures,* 1940.

Drei Dichter ihres Lebens: Casanova, Stendhal, Tolstoi (biography). 1928; as *Adepts in Self-Portraiture: Casanova, Stendhal, Tolstoy,* 1928.

Joseph Fouche (biography). 1929; translated as *Joseph Fouche,* 1930.

Die Heilung durch den Geist: Franz Anton Mesmer, Mary Baker Eddy, Sigmund Freud (biography). 1931; as *Mental Healers,* 1932.

Marie Antoinette (biography). 1932; translated as *Marie Antoinette,* 1933.

Triumph und Tragik des Erasmus von Rotterdam (biography). 1934; as *Triumph and Tragedy of Erasmus of Rotterdam,* 1934.

Maria Stuart (biography). 1935; as *Mary, the Queen of Scotland and the Isles,* 1935.

Castellio gegen Calvin; oder, Ein Gewissen gegen die Gewalt (biography). 1936; as *The Right to Heresy: Castellio against Calvin,* 1936.

Begegnungen mit Menschen, Buchern, Stadten (essays and criticism). 1937.

Magellan (biography). 1938; as *Conqueror of the Seas,* 1938.

Brazilien: Ein Land der Zukunft (travel). 1941; as *Brazil, Land of the Future,* 1941.

Amerigo: A Comedy of Errors in History (biography; translation of *Amerigo; die geschichte eines historischen Irrtums*). 1942.

Zeit und Welt: Gesammelte Aufsätze und Vorträge, 1904–1940, edited by Richard Friedenthal. 1943.

Balzac, edited by Richard Friedenthal (biography). 1946; translated as *Balzac,* 1946.

Briefwechsel: Stefan Zweig-Friderike Maria Zweig, 1912–42 (correspondence). 1951; as *Stefan Zweig and Friderike Maria Zweig: Their Correspondence,* 1954.

Briefwechsel zwischen Richard Strauss und Stefan Zweig, edited by Willi Schuh. 1957; as *A Confidential Matter: The Letters of Richard Strauss and Stefan Zweig, 1931–35,* 1977.

Fragment einer Novelle, edited by Erich Fitzbauer. 1961.

Durch Zeiten und Welten, edited by Erich Fitzbauer. 1961.

Im Schnee, edited by Erich Fitzbauer. 1963.

Der Turm zu Babel, edited by Erich Fitzbauer. 1964.

Unbekannte Briefe aus der Emigration an eine Freundin, edited by Gisella Selden-Goth (correspondence). 1964.

Frühlingsfahrt durch die Provence: Ein Essay, edited by Erich Fitzbauer. 1965.

Die Monotonisierung der Welt: Aufsätze und Vorträge, edited by Volker Michels. 1976.

Brief an Freunde (correspondence). 1978.

Die Hochzeit von Lyon, edited by Erich Fitzbauer. 1980.

Das Stefan Zweig Buch, edited by Knut Beck (selections). 1981.

Das Geheimnis des künstlerischen Schaffens, edited by Knut Beck. 1981.

The Correspondence of Stefan Zweig with Raoul Auernheimer and with Richard Beer-Hofmann, edited by Donald G. Daviau, Jorun B. Johns, and Jeffrey B. Berlin. 1983.

Stefan Zweig/Paul Zech: Briefe 1910–1942, edited by Donald G. Daviau (correspondence). 1984.

Briefweschsel mit Hermann Bahr, Sigmund Freud, Ranier Maria Rilke und Arthur Schnitzler, edited by Jeffrey B. Berlin, Hans-Ulrich Lindken, and Donald A. Prater (correspondence). 1987.

Rainer Maria Rilke und Stefan Zweig in Briefen und Dokumenten, edited by Donald A. Prater (correspondence). 1987.

Editor, *Eine Anthologie der besten Übersetzungen,* by Paul Verlaine. 1902.
Editor, *Gesammelte Werke,* by Paul Verlaine (2 vols.). 1922.
Edtior, *Literarische Portraits aus dem Frankreich des XVII.–XIX. Jahrhunderts,* by Charles Augustin Sainte-Beuve (2 vols.). 1923.
Editor, *Romantische Erzählungen,* by Francois René Auguste and Vicomte de Chateaubriand. 1924.
Editor, *Goethes Gedichte: Eine Auswahl,* by Johann Wolfgang von Goethe. 1927.

Translator, *Ausgewählte Gedichte,* by Emile Verhaeren. 1904.
Translator, *Die visionäre Kunstphilosophie des William Blake,* by Archibald B.H. Russell. 1906.
Translator, *Drei Dramen: Helenas Heimkehr; Phillipp II; Das Kloster,* by Emile Verhaeren. 1910.
Translator, *Hymnen an das Leben,* by Emile Verhaeren. 1911.
Translator, *Rembrandt,* by Emile Verhaeren. 1912.
Translator, *Rubens,* by Emile Verhaeren. 1913.
Translator, *Den hingerichteten Völkern,* by Romain Rolland. 1918.
Translator, *Die Zeit wird kommen,* by Romain Rolland. 1919.
Translator, *Weib: Roman,* by Madeline Marx. 1920.
Translator, with Erwin Rieger, *Cressida,* by André Suarès. 1920.
Translator, *Clérambault: Geschichte eines freien Gewissens im Kriege,* by Romain Rolland. 1922.
Translator, *Man weiss nicht wie,* by Luigi Pirandello. 1935.
Translator, with Richard Friedenthal, *Ein Schimmerlicht im Dunkel,* by Irwin Edman. 1940.

*

Film Adaptations: *Beware of Pity,* 1946; *Letter from an Unknown Woman,* 1948, from the novella; *Fear,* 1954, from the novella *Angst; Brainwashed,* 1960, from the novella *The Royal Game.*

Bibliography: *Stefan Zweig: A Bibliography,* 1965, *Stefan Zweig: An International Bibliography,* 1991, and *Stefan Zweig: An International Bibliography, Addendum I,* 1999, all by Randolph J. Klawiter.

Manuscript Collection: Daniel Reed Library, State University of New York College, Fredonia.

Critical Studies: *Stefan Zweig, Great European* by Jules Romains, translated by James Whitall, 1941; *Stefan Zweig* by Friderike Maria Burger Winternitz Zweig, translated by Erna McArthur, 1946; *Stefan Zweig; A Tribute to His Life and Work* by Hanns Arens, translated by Christobel Fowler, 1951; "Jewish Themes in Stefan Zweig" by Harry Zohn, in *Journal of the International Arthur Schnitzler Research Association,* 6(2), 1967, pp. 32–38; *European of Yesterday: A Biography of*

Stefan Zweig by Donald A. Prater, 1972; *Stefan Zweig: A Critical Biography* by Elizabeth Allday, 1972; Stefan Zweig issue of *Modern Austrian Literature,* 14(3–4), 1981; *Stefan Zweig: The World of Yesterday's Humanist Today: Proceedings of the Stefan Zweig Symposium,* edited by Marion Sonnenfeld, 1983; *Moral Values and the Human Zoo: The Novellen of Stefan Zweig* by David Turner, 1988; "Stefan Zweig and Franz Werfel: Humanism and Mysticism as Responses to Antisemitism and the Holocaust" by Lionel B. Steiman, in *Holocaust Studies Annual,* edited by Sanford Pinsker and Jack Fischel, 1990.

* * *

Arthur Schnitzler, a contemporary of Stefan Zweig, once remarked that many people have to hear a shot in order to realize that a murder has been committed. This observation may be applied to Stefan Zweig, who escaped the Nazis, was not overtly deprived of his freedom, and was not killed in a concentration camp but who, nevertheless, can be considered a victim of the Holocaust. He was driven from Austria and especially from Vienna, a city that supplied him the psychological energy to write. Without cultural roots, he became more and more melancholic and depressed. He could not envision an end to the barbarism of the Nazis, and he, together with his wife, took his own life.

Zweig, the author of *The Royal Game* and *The World of Yesterday,* was born in Vienna, Austria, to the son of a well-to-do Jewish industrialist on 28 November 1881. Although an Austrian by birth, he can be considered a truly European writer since he transcends national borders. His essays, novels, short stories, and biographies are characterized by elements of psychological realism, testifying to Zweig's interest in psychology, especially in Sigmund Freud. His publications, including his translations (he was fluent in French), embrace the life and era of many well-known figures in various walks of life, artists as well as diplomats. A lifelong friendship connected him with the pacifist Romain Rolland and the Belgian Émile Verhaeren. Having studied at the University of Vienna, the University of Berlin, and the Sorbonne, Zweig settled in Salzburg in 1919. Since political events endangered his personal safety (his books were openly burned by the fascists in Berlin on 10 May 1933, and his home in Salzburg was searched by the Austrian police for weapons in 1934), he left for England in 1934. His first marriage to Friderike, with whom he continued to stay in contact until the end of his life, ended in divorce; in 1939 he moved to Bath and married for the second time, to German immigrant Elisabeth Charlotte Altmann. After becoming a British citizen in 1940, he left with his wife for South America in the same year by way of New York. On 22 February 1942 he and his wife committed suicide in Petrópolis, near Rio de Janeiro.

Zweig set down his humanistic credo and also the personal justification for his political noninvolvement in his *Triumph and Tragedy of Erasmus of Rotterdam* (1934). In Erasmus, a figure with whom he strongly identified and whose aims he shared, Zweig showed the strength and weakness of liberal-humanistic thinking, the strength being that humanism is not tied to national boundaries but is a force of the spirit and mind uniting all Western nations. This kind of humanism can ''never be revolutionary,'' he stated in *Erasmus*; ''[a] man of intellect had, such was Erasmus's conviction, nothing other to do in this world than to determine and elucidate truths; his was not to march forth and fight for these truths.'' Erasmus did not attempt to translate his theories into action, in his case against the ''fanatic'' Martin Luther, just as Zweig, and other Austrian intellectuals, did not take the dangers of the rising Nazi movement seriously. Erasmus, as well as Zweig, neglected to include the masses in his elitist humanistic circle, and in this exclusion lay also the tragedy of the humanistic movement. The masses, the moving force of social change, were excluded from realizing this noble goal: ''[Erasmus] considered the masses . . . unworthy the attention of a refined and educated man, and it would be beneath his dignity to woo the favours of 'barbarians.''' Zweig considered this attitude to be the tragic flaw of this optimistic utopian worldview; the ''armchair philosophies'' created an ideology that did not take into account the irrational elements of the people as well as human weaknesses and national wars; this humanistic world order proved ineffective when confronted with actual reality. Zweig

pointed to the dichotomy between the introverted humanistic thinker and the extroverted man of action also in his biographical novel *The Right to Heresy: Castellio against Calvin* when he remarked that humanists are not activists and vice versa. Zweig was on the side of Erasmus, the cosmopolitan thinker; an intellectual ''cannot afford to take sides, his realm is the realm of equable justice; he must stand above the heat and fury of the contest.''

Zweig's belief in the victory of the spirit over war and aggression was shattered during and after World War I. For him the world of the Austro-Hungarian Empire, in which he felt at home, became a world of yesterday. Disillusioned, he left his native land, but in exile Zweig did not have the psychological security and cultural environment that he needed for his productivity, and he ended his life. If there was a shortcoming in his life, then it can be seen in his decision to be apolitical in a time when political involvement was necessary for physical and cultural survival. This political passivity, however, also characterized some other intellectuals living in the waning days of the Austrian fin de siècle of the 1900s.

—Gerd K. Schneider

See the essays on *The Royal Game* and *The World of Yesterday: An Autobiography.*

WORKS

A

THE ACCIDENT (Le Jour)
Novel by Elie Wiesel, 1961

Elie Wiesel's *The Accident* (1961) is a possibly autobiographical account of being hit by a car. The narrator slips into stream of consciousness as he vacillates between death and life, providing the accident victim with bizarre, surrealistic impressions as he remembers his grandmother and his father, who perished in the Holocaust. The trauma of the Holocaust haunts him: "Shame tortures not the executioners but their victims."

Against this backdrop, the narrator remembers the humanity of his physician, Paul Russel: "Each prey torn away from death made him happy as if he had won a universal victory." The physician admonishes the narrator: "During the operation. You never helped me. Not once. You abandoned me. I had to wage the fight alone, all alone. Worse. You were on the other side, against me, on the side of the enemy." The Holocaust experience has sapped the narrator of his ability to fight near-death experiences. The fact that he endured the Holocaust has made his outlook on life bleak.

He ruminates on his experiences in the Holocaust as he sits in his hospital bed in New York City:

> They were about ten in the bunker. Night after night they could hear the German police dogs looking through the ruins for Jews hiding in their underground shelters. Schmuel and the others were living on practically no water or bread, on hardly any air. They were holding out. They knew that there, down below in their narrow jail, they were free; above, death was waiting for them. One night a disaster nearly occurred. It was Golda's fault. She had taken her child with her. A baby, a few months old. He began to cry, thus endangering the lives of all. Golda was trying to quiet him, to make him sleep. To no avail. That's when the others, including Golda herself, turned to Shmuel and told him: "Make him shut up. Take care of him, you whose job it is to slaughter chickens. You will be able to do it without making him suffer too much."

This passage explains how experiencing the grim situational ethics of the Holocaust lessened the ability to fight for his life when he is injured in an automobile accident.

As he continues to convalesce in the hospital, he ruminates about the prostitute Sarah, whom he met in Paris: "Maybe I had only lived for this meeting, I thought. For this meeting with a prostitute who preserved within her a trace of innocence, like madmen who in the midst of their madness hold on to a trace of their lucidity." The Holocaust survivor relates to this prostitute who had been impressed into service in a military brothel at the age of 12 because she, too, had suffered physical abuse and emotional trauma.

—Peter R. Erspamer

ADAM
Play by Joshua Sobol, 1989

Adam (1989), the second of three plays in a Holocaust triptych by Israeli playwright Joshua Sobol, dramatizes the historical struggle for power in the Vilna ghetto between Judenrat leader Jacob Gens and United Partisan Organization (UPO) leader Yitzhak Wittenberg, whom Sobol calls Adam Rolenick in the play. Unlike in Sobol's most popular and widely known drama about the Holocaust, *Ghetto*, Gens in *Adam* is not portrayed favorably but rather as an accomplice of the Nazi ghetto liquidator Kittel. In this play Gens and the members of the UPO disagree strongly on the most suitable course of action to take against the Nazis. Gens, believing that the Russian army will rescue them in a few months (they are approaching from the east), demands that the Jews be patient and act peacefully in order to avoid the attention and the wrath of the Nazis. The UPO believes, contrariwise, that the Jews in the ghetto must arm themselves with weapons and fight against the Nazis because the liquidation of the ghetto is inevitable; they must take their fate into their own hands and, if successful in their attempt to fight their way out of the ghetto, join the partisans in the forest. The clash in the methodology pits the two sides on a collision course because Kittel is under orders, as a consequence of the Warsaw Ghetto uprising, to liquidate any ghetto that shows evidence of armed underground activity. Therefore, the actions of the UPO could potentially save the lives of the Jews in the ghetto or at least allow them to die with dignity, but, conversely, their actions could incite the Nazis to destroy everyone in the ghetto. Both Gens and the members of the UPO have a plausible argument, but Sobol chooses to tell the story primarily from the perspective of Rolenick (Wittenberg) and his lover, Nadya, who survives the ghetto and whose purpose in the play is to serve as a narrator of the action and an eyewitness.

After a Lithuanian partisan named Kaslaskas is captured by the Nazis and, under torture, provides them with Rolenick's name, Kittel decides to capture Rolenick so that he can torture him, thus finding out all the information he can regarding the armed underground resistance in Vilna. Because of his desire to prevent the liquidation of the ghetto, which would occur if armed resistance and contact with partisans were discovered, Gens works against the UPO, arranging to turn their leader, Rolenick, over to Kittel. When Gens sets up a meeting at night with Rolenick, Kittel is there with some Nazi soldiers to arrest the UPO leader. To Kittel's surprise there are UPO members conducting surveillance of the arrest; they attack the Nazis and free Rolenick, thus allowing him to hide in the ghetto. The UPO attack on Kittel's Nazi officers is simultaneously a success and a failure, for the underground rescues their leader but at the same time exposes their military operations and insults the Nazis, jeopardizing the lives of the 15,000 Jews who inhabit the Vilna ghetto. Gens is then faced with an ultimatum from Kittel: turn Rolenick over to him within a few hours or the ghetto will be liquidated and all of the Jews will die. Once again Gens comes into conflict with the UPO. Kittel successfully turns the Jews against themselves: Gens sends a frantic message to his constituents, claiming that all of them will die unless they find Rolenick within a few hours and turn him over to Kittel. The inhabitants of the Vilna ghetto proceed with a desperate search for Rolenick; the members of the UPO decide initially to fight in order to protect Rolenick, yet they back down because that involves fighting against and injuring their fellow Jews. Ultimately the UPO agrees reluctantly to surrender their leader, much to his dismay. Rolenick asserts prophetically that any organization willing to surrender its leader will never succeed.

Adam Rolenick turns himself over to Gens, who, surprisingly, is rather disappointed. Gens has expected—and even desired—an armed revolt against the Nazis. Gens, therefore, is a very complex character: He works against the armed resistance because of his role as ghetto leader, but he, conversely, sympathizes with the movement and would have enthusiastically joined it if the revolt had occurred. Because Rolenick turns himself in, however, the UPO becomes fragmented and never attempts the military battle that they had planned. As Rolenick correctly predicts, the ghetto is ultimately liquidated with no resistance, as the Jewish inhabitants, who turned against the underground movement, go meekly to their deaths. As for the members of the UPO, some of them escape to the forest, where they join the partisans.

In *Adam* Sobol dramatizes one instance, based on historical documents and eyewitness accounts, of how the Nazis successfully turned the Jews against themselves. The Jewish inhabitants of the ghetto wanted so desperately to live that they, ironically, helped to destroy the only organization that could have saved them.

—Eric Sterling

ADAM RESURRECTED (Adam ben kelev)
Novel by Yoram Kaniuk, 1969

Adam Resurrected by Yoram Kaniuk, published in Hebrew in 1969 under the title *Adam ben kelev* ("Son of Dog") and in English translation in 1971, centers on an insane asylum populated by Holocaust survivors. The asylum, the Institute for Rehabilitation and Therapy, was founded with the donation from an American tourist convinced by the Schwester twin that a refuge for all the insane members of society in the desert—God's castle—must be established. One of these people, rejected by society, could after all be the messiah. The Israeli medical staff members fail in their aim to cure the patients until Adam (Herbert) Stein, a Holocaust survivor who is also a clown, magician, and supposed clairvoyant, appears in the institution. In the concentration camp Stein would entertain the internees, alleviating some of the terror. He amused his wife and daughter in their last moments. He also acted as a second pet dog for the head of the camp, Klein. This grotesque behavior, walking on all fours, barking, and eating out of the dog's bowl, earned him his life.

Stein identifies so strongly with his identity as a dog that he cannot accept his new life as a member of Israeli society. He not only mocks Israel and holds onto his past life as a dog, however horrific it may have been, but he also maintains a friendly relationship with Klein after the war. The institute, a high-tech hospice for various asocials, emerges as a nightmarish reflection of life in Israel. Stein discovers a dog in one of the rooms of the institute and develops an intimate relationship with it, a confidant. The dog is in fact a child who has assumed the identity of a dog and through his relationship with Stein, reverts back to his human self. Stein is the messiah for which the Schwester twin searches. He is a modern Christ who finds salvation only after rescuing the child from his own trauma; only after giving life to another may Stein recover his own life as a human. His recovery, however, does not mark the beginning of a new life. Rather, he lives a sedate and calm life as an old man. The story ends on an optimistic note tinged with hints of sadness that arise out of accepting reality, however grim it may be. As Stein states after his recovery, sanity is sad, nothing happens. He says, "I live in a beautiful, good valley, the peaks are forever gone."

Adam Resurrected deals with the Holocaust of humankind. Kaniuk purports that the Holocaust must not be viewed as an aberration or as an extraordinary event in human history but as an event that gave full expression to human existence. In discovering the inhuman aspect of all humans, the real essence of humanity may be revealed. Stein's real sickness is in his failure to recognize the advantages of being a human as opposed to a dog. He can only recover once he recognizes these benefits. It is important to note, however, that the novel ends inconclusively because humanity is not drawn as categorically superior to animality.

One may read allegorical meaning into many of the elements in *Adam Resurrected*—the insane asylum as the Zionist project: a large segment of the Jewish population has perished, the only people remaining are the crazy individuals who came to build the country. Walking to the desert is a return to one's roots: the attempt to rebuild the Jewish state out of its historical and biblical origins. The rich American who donates the funds for the building of the asylum mirrors American financial support of the Zionist project. These allegorical elements, however, overlook the important role that fantasy plays in the novel. Fantasy forms the main thematic element in this Holocaust novel. Often compared with Gabriel García Márquez's *One Hundred Years of Solitude*, Kaniuk's novel contains an inner logic that validates the madness that propels its plot.

Kaniuk's sentiment toward the Holocaust is summed up in *Adam Resurrected*. Kaniuk writes about the survivors and witnesses of the Holocaust, articulating that "the knowledge, the wisdom in knowing that they were the raw materials in the most advanced factory in Europe, under a sky in which God sits in exile, like a stranger . . . this knowledge makes us go insane, and so the whole country has become the biggest insane asylum on earth."

—Ziva Shavitsky

ALL BUT MY LIFE
Memoir by Gerda Weissmann Klein, 1957

Gerda Weissmann Klein's memoir *All but My Life* is a mesmerizing account of one Polish teenager's three-year struggle to survive not only in body but also in spirit. Like **Anne Frank**'s *Diary*, the book is a classic of Holocaust literature. Divided into three parts, it begins with the German invasion of Poland in September 1939 and continues through the days following Gerda's liberation in Volary, Czechoslovakia, in May 1945. It is an unforgettable story of courage. For Gerda, memory sustains hope, and hope provides the strength to continue in spite of losing everything but her life.

In the first days of Nazi rule, the Weissmanns must move from the comfort of their home in Bielsko, Poland, to their damp basement, where there is no electricity and little food. Gerda can no longer visit her beloved garden, only a few feet away. Gerda and her mother unravel old clothes, dye them, and knit new sweaters to earn money for food. With little coal to heat their two rooms, the Weissmanns are warmed by their love for one another and their memories of happier days. They share the hope that Gerda's brother Artur will return from a forced labor camp and they will be reunited as a family. Soon even that hope is taken from them.

A heartbreaking letter from a school friend telling of the murder of her family foreshadows the excruciating loss that Gerda will soon experience. The question "How does one bury a heart?" echoes throughout the book. Yet no matter how great her suffering, Gerda never chooses to bury her heart.

The family's downward spiral continues when they must leave their home for the ghetto. Even there, their love sustains them. For her birthday, Gerda's mother sells a valuable ring to present her daughter with the priceless gift of an orange. Gerda's friend Abek gives her roses, a reminder of the beauty outside the ghetto. Soon the family is torn apart. Gerda paints a luminous portrait of their last hours together, as her parents talk long into the night of their love for one another and their children. Even when Gerda is separated from her parents, their love continues to protect her. Although it is June when the deportation order comes, her father orders her to wear her ski boots. Three years later, they save her life during a brutal winter death march. Her mother's last words, "Be strong," sustain her through loneliness and near despair.

Gerda demonstrates an extraordinary ability to recall and describe scenes that offer the reader a strikingly vivid portrait of the small, often forgotten, threads of the Holocaust. One sees her father's hands upon her brother Artur's head as he blesses and bids him farewell for the last time; one tastes the bittersweet cocoa, saved for months, that her mother gives her as a special treat the last morning they are together.

Part II of the memoir recounts Gerda's trials as she is moved from one slave labor camp to another. Friendships sustain her through illness, deprivation, and brutality, as do occasional scribbled sentences from her brother Artur. Her nineteenth birthday comes, bringing precious presents from her friends: margarine scraped from bread, bobby pins made from wire—testimonies to love and loyalty.

In January 1945, as liberation seems imminent, Gerda's worst days begin. She and her friends are sent on a brutal death march. Out of a column of 2,000 girls and women, fewer than 120 survive. Ilse, her best friend, dies in her arms. Unwilling to allow any of their prisoners to survive, the guards drive them into a factory building and plant a bomb. It does not detonate, therefore Gerda's life is spared once more.

Part III of the book opens with Gerda's liberation on 7 May 1945, one day before her twenty-first birthday. For Gerda this moment begins a new chapter in her life. She sees the young American lieutenant who liberates her as a gallant hero. He is, in fact, much more. A fellow Jew, he left Germany for the U.S. in 1937; however, State Department bureaucracy thwarted his efforts to rescue his parents. He, too, has known suffering and loss. In her, Kurt Klein sees a woman of extraordinary nobility.

Gerda's struggle back to health is a long one. In the end all she has left are the precious photos of her family, hidden for three years in her ski boot, and her life. With Kurt Klein's love and support (the two were married in 1946), she creates from that life a remarkable testimony to the power of love and the magnificence of the human spirit.

—Marilyn J. Harran

AND THE SUN KEPT SHINING (Un di zun hot geshaynt)
Memoir by Bertha Ferderber-Salz, 1965

And the Sun Kept Shining, originally published in Yiddish in 1965 and in English translation in 1980, is Bertha Ferderber-Salz's first-person account of her horrific experiences as a Jewish woman in Nazi-occupied Poland and her survival of the death camps Auschwitz and Bergen-Belsen. Ferderber-Salz tells of her futile attempts to escape the Nazi terror, first fleeing Kraków, then hiding in a small village. She describes the hardship of life in the Kraków ghetto and finally the dehumanizing existence in the camps, first at Plaszow, where her husband falls ill and is condemned to die, then at Auschwitz, and finally at Bergen-Belsen. In addition to the deadly diseases of the camps caused by the deliberate starvation, the insurmountable work and the inhuman treatment at the hands of the Nazis and their collaborators, and the ever present danger of being sentenced to death, Ferderber-Salz must constantly fear for the lives and well-being of her two daughters whom she had left in the care of a Polish woman in Kraków. Ferderber-Salz's ordeal does not end with her liberation from Bergen-Belsen by the British troops. She must fight for the right to her children and her two nephews, who together with two older children are the only survivors of her once large family. After a devastating journey though Western Galicia in a futile attempt to find surviving members of her family, Ferderber-Salz and her children leave Poland for the United States.

Ferderber-Salz tells her story in a straightforward manner with little regard for aesthetic concerns. Like other Holocaust survivors' personal narratives, Ferderber-Salz's memoir is intended as a testimony to the victims of the Holocaust and their sufferings as well as a warning to future generations. For her, writing her story, reliving the past, and keeping the memory alive is the price she has to pay for surviving. The biblical precept ''And you shall tell it to your children'' provides the answer to the question ''Why did I survive'' asked by so many of the survivors. In order to establish narrative authority, Ferderber-Salz emphasizes the immediacy of her memories: She recorded them shortly after her liberation from Bergen-Belsen. Moreover, she diminishes her authorship in them: ''But it is almost as if the pages were written by themselves . . . or perhaps the sighs of those who were burned and slaughtered dictated to me what I should write.''

Although the narrative centers on Ferderber-Salz's own experiences, they are imbedded in the larger sufferings and faith of the Polish Jewish population. Her own desperate attempts to keep her family safe and alive and her loyalty, kindness, and selfless concern for those around her are mirrored in the actions of the other Jewish victims. They help each other to find employment so the Nazis would not think them dispensable, they take on part of the work of those who could

not keep up with the ordered quota, and they sacrifice themselves for the children and others. The inmates of the concentration camps suffer starvation, torturous working conditions, and sadistic abuse and degradation by prison guards without compromising their dignity or spiritual belief. In their refusal to abandon their ethical standards, Ferderber-Salz's Jewish victims triumph over the Nazis and their conspirators who have long relinquished their humanity.

Ferderber-Salz relates the unspeakable acts of terror and brutality committed by the Nazis in a factual, nondramatic manner. With equal restrain she tells stories of repeated betrayals of Polish Jews by their compatriots who ruthlessly profit from their desperate situation. Bitterness over the world's indifference to the suffering of the Jews, however, is evident in the title of her memoir, the meaning of which she explains at the end: ''Our tormented people suffered a thousand tortures, was massacred and burned. AND THE SUN KEPT SHINING.''

—Helga Schreckenberger

AND WHERE WERE YOU, ADAM? (Wo warst du, Adam?)
Novel by Heinrich Böll, 1951

And Where Were You, Adam?, first published in English translation as *Adam, Where Art Thou?* in 1955 and later as *And Where Were You, Adam?* in 1973, is part of Heinrich Böll's literary output from 1947 to 1952, which draws extensively from autobiographical events during his time as a soldier in World War II. It was originally published in German as *Wo warst du, Adam?* in 1951. In nine loosely connected chapters, the novel discusses the fate of the protagonist Feinhals and of his fellow soldiers on the eastern front in the closing months of the war. What characterizes all of Böll's war literature is the fact that there are no heroes; his protagonists are ordinary, downtrodden soldiers who lack control over their lives and whose deaths are usually presented as being completely pointless, often painful, and always ugly. In keeping with his condemnation of war, Böll's style is realistic; he saw the war not as an exciting adventure but as an illness ''like typhoid.''

Böll prefaces *And Where Were You, Adam?* with two quotations: one from Antoine de Saint-Exupery which likens war to typhoid; the other from Theodor Haecker which provides the title of the work and suggests that the basic problem of German contemporary society is that it uses the war as an alibi—'' 'And where were you, Adam?' 'I was in the World War.''' For Böll, Adam's excuse is typical of society's refusal to accept responsibility for its actions; this is also true for such seemingly sympathetic characters as Feinhals and his fellow soldiers who are conscripted into serving a cause that they regard as senseless. Unfortunately, their passivity—or inability to take action—allows the truly destructive elements in society to rise, in this case, Nazism, which leads inexorably to the Holocaust.

Böll depicts the horror of the Holocaust in an encounter between SS Captain Filskeit, leader of an extermination camp, and the baptized Jewish girl, Ilona. Böll cynically portrays Filskeit as an unattractive pyknic type with latent homosexual tendencies who is a fanatic believer in the Nazi doctrine of the superiority of the racial purity, beauty, and superiority of the Aryan race. His detailed characterization of Filskeit is an extended satire of Nazi characteristics in general: an exaggerated respect for order, slavish following of superiors' commands, and a shallow love of art. Filskeit loves choral music and creates a choir in every camp he is sent to during the war. When Ilona arrives, Filskeit orders her to sing while he recruits members for his shrinking choir from the Jews sent to him. As she sings the "All Saints Litany," Filskeit recognizes the fallacy of the Nazi ideology of the racial superiority of the Aryan race that had been central to his life. In Ilona he finds what he had in vain sought in himself: "beauty and nobility and racial perfection, combined with something that completely paralyzed him: faith." His reaction is true to his distorted human nature: he shoots the young woman and orders the extermination of the rest of the Jews.

This episode (developed in chapters five and seven of the novel) is the most explicit example of Böll's attitude to the Holocaust. If at times Böll seems to accuse all Germans of responsibility for its occurrence, he qualifies this charge in his portrayal of ordinary Germans who preserve their humanity in the face of widespread brutality. When the soldier Feinhals meets Ilona, their love for each other transcends questions of race or nationality. His senseless death at the novel's end echoes Ilona's and underlines the inhumanity of the Nazi regime as represented by the Holocaust.

—Renate Benson

ANDORRA: A PLAY IN TWELVE SCENES
(Andorra: Stück in zwölf Bildern)
Play by Max Frisch, 1962

Andorra—set in a fictitious town, not in the European region of the same name—was completed in 1961 and premiered in November of the same year at Zurich's Schauspielhaus. In January 1962 it was performed on various German stages. The idea for the play came much earlier; in his *Sketchbook 1946–1949* (translated by Geoffrey Skelton) Max Frisch recorded an entry under the heading "The Andorran Jew":

In Andorra there lived a young man who was believed to be a Jew. It will be necessary to describe his presumed background, his daily contacts with the Andorrans, who saw the Jewishness in him: the fixed image that meets him everywhere. Their distrust, for instance, of his depth of feeling—something that, as even an Andorran knows, no Jew can possibly have. A Jew has to rely on the sharpness of his wits, which get all the sharper because of it. Or his attitude toward money, an important matter in Andorra as elsewhere. . . He could not become like all the others, and so, having tried in vain not to make himself conspicuous. he began to wear his otherness with a certain air of defiance, of pride. . .

Andorra is a play about political and personal issues, specifically about racial and national prejudice, stereotypes, identity, and collective guilt. Andri, a young man considered a Jew by the Andorrans, has been "adopted" by a teacher who, as he finds out later on, is his real father, although he does not admit to his paternity because he is ashamed of having a child out of wedlock. Andri tries to assimilate with the Andorrans and to their way of life, but they reject him because of his seeming "otherness." The Andorrans see in Andri what they consider "Jewish" traits—cowardice, greed, sexual urges, and ambition—traits they themselves have and project onto him. Andri is confused about his identity, and he finally adopts the image society has made of him. At the end the invaders who occupy Andorra take him away on the pretext that the Andorrans have murdered Andri's real mother. Andri is slaughtered, while his father hangs himself and his sister goes insane.

In *Andorra* Frisch uses devices reminiscent of **Bertolt Brecht**'s Epic Theater, although he does not share Brecht's optimism that society can be enlightened through the theater. Between the scenes the perpetrators, except members of Andri's immediate family, step up to a ramp where they rationalize their behavior to the audience and take refuge in their collective guilt, denying personal responsibility. This whitewashing technique, which Frisch introduces at the beginning of the play when Andri's sister is whitewashing the facades of the house, is very effective inasmuch as it makes the audience aware of the dangers inherent in image-making. In order to prevent a recurrence of this personal tragedy, which ultimately could lead to a Holocaust, Frisch admonishes the viewer in the section of "The Andorran Jew": "Thou shalt not, it is said, make unto thee any graven image of God. The same commandment should apply when God is taken to mean the living part of every human being, the part that cannot be grasped. It is a sin that, however much it is committed against us, we almost continually commit ourselves—except when we love." Frisch points out that each individual carries the responsibility of preventing a future Holocaust by accepting and affirming every person's unique being.

—Gerd K. Schneider

THE APPRENTICESHIP OF DUDDY KRAVITZ
Novel by Mordecai Richler, 1959

Mordecai Richler's *The Apprenticeship of Duddy Kravitz* (1959) strongly reflects the impact of the Holocaust on the Jewish communities in North America. This work, set in the poor Jewish district of St. Urbain Street in Montreal, depicts the ethnic and class contradictions and difficulties of a tricultural Canadian society: wealthy white Anglo-Saxon Protestant managers and executives, largely poor French Canadian workers, and the Jewish community caught between both groups. The novel shows the world primarily through the eyes of young Duddy Kravitz, the second son of a poor and uneducated Jewish taxi driver. Throughout the novel Duddy is struggling to find a clear identity, respectability, and prosperity in both his own family and the world around him. Upon completing high school, Duddy decides he must make a name for himself in business and achieve the dream of acquiring some land of his own, for his revered *zayde* (grandfather), Simcha Kravitz, has impressed upon him the idea that a man without land is nothing. Duddy's adventures in business take him through nearly all layers of Montreal society, both Jewish and Gentile. Through Duddy's interactions with different people, Richler uses his satiric wit to demonstrate the moral corruption and distortion that take place in a society founded on hypocrisy, prejudice, and injustice. By the end of the novel Duddy acquires his prize of a "promised land" at the price of his honor and nearly all his most important relationships.

Although this novel is not set directly in the lands of the Holocaust, some of the situations depicted by Richler shockingly parallel the hierarchies and class structures of the countries that had the concentration camps and other atrocities. In many ways Duddy is a type of survivor and hustler in that he constantly seeks ways around the rules of Canadian society to achieve his ends. He understands that he cannot trust most of the people around him, and he feels compelled to use every situation to achieve some advantage over others or to escape a bleak fate as a taxi driver or waiter for the rest of his life. As some European Jews were compelled to escape the fate of most Holocaust victims through false identity papers or secret deals, Duddy persuades his French Canadian girlfriend, Yvette, to use his money for purchasing land in areas where the owners will not sell land to Jews and to sign her name for it. Duddy also makes secret deals with the wealthy Gentile businessman Mr. Calder so that Mr. Calder will not have Duddy's older brother, Lennie Kravitz, expelled from medical school for illegally performing an abortion on Mr. Calder's daughter. Duddy's worst act is to buy some land with a check he had forged in the name of Virgil Roseboro, an epileptic man who became crippled when he had a seizure while driving a delivery truck for Duddy's business. Other hustler-survivors who have made their fortunes through less than ideal means include Mr. Cohen, a wealthy scrap metal dealer who does not mind endangering his French Canadian workers if it helps his business, and Jerry Dingleman, a Jewish gangster and drug dealer whom Duddy's father idealizes as a type of local messiah.

Even when Jews are isolated from the rest of society, their interactions are a microcosm of the inequities of the larger society. At Rubin's scenic summer resort camp for Jews in Quebec Province, where Duddy works as a waiter in the early part of the novel, wealthy Jews take advantage of their poorer brothers and of poor French Canadians by making them hustle for scarce money. Duddy's brother, Lennie, and wealthy Jewish college students such as Irwin Shubert seek to hide their Jewishness and imitate Gentile society. They point at Duddy as an example of a stereotypically pushy Jewish businessman, but in essence they all are acting in response to both outer and inner pressures. In satirizing the state of Canadian society, Richler views no social group as innocent or immune. All three groups in the society are intertwined and are responsible for the state of affairs. Unfortunately Richler sees no clear way to improve the situation for any of the three different communities.

Richler's novel can be deftly compared with works of other North Americans who have handled issues of Holocaust-related Jewish alienation, distorted Jewish self-images, and survivor guilt. **Arthur Miller**'s play *Broken Glass* (1994) and Barry Levinson's film *Liberty Heights* (1999) also deal with the ways that Jews' moral quandaries about fitting into Gentile society without betraying themselves paralyze their relations with Gentiles and within their own community. As Richler, Miller, and Levinson indicate, Jews in North America may have escaped the most drastic effects of the Holocaust, but they must not forget the parallels between their lives and those of their indirect kin in Europe.

—Alisa Gayle Mayor

ASCENT TO HEAVEN (Wniebowstąpienie)
Novella by Adolf Rudnicki, 1948

Ascent to Heaven (1951; *Wniebowstąpienie,* 1948) by Adolf Rudnicki remains one of his most representative works on the subject of the Holocaust. In the manner typical of this Polish writer, the novella combines the elements of fiction and reality and uses such diverse narrative forms as the short story, reportage, and historical document. It is a tragic tale of a young Jewish couple who strives and does not succeed to survive the darkest days of the Nazi occupation of Poland. The main characters, Raisa and Sebastian, get married shortly after the Nazi army attacks the Soviet Union in June 1941. The Polish city of Lwów, where the couple lives, was occupied by the Soviets until the German invasion. The city's inhabitants flee eastward to the Soviet Union, but Raisa and Sebastian decide to stay. The terror that immediately follows the Nazis' entrance to Lwów, however, makes the couple escape to Warsaw. While they find help and shelter with the Poles, the couple's life continues to be full of anxiety and fear. To survive they constantly have to move from one apartment to another. Their tormented life becomes even more difficult after Sebastian, who "does not acknowledge the presence of the Germans" and attempts to live a normal life, shows signs of a serious mental illness caused by constant fear. His unpredictable behavior endangers the life of Raisa and their cohabitants. She does everything to protect her husband, but her heroic efforts are in vain, as one day he leaves the house and gets arrested. After two months in a Nazi prison, he is taken out to work, and one night, apparently during an escape attempt, is shot dead. Raisa also gets killed, but a little later: she is buried under the rubble of a bombed house during the Warsaw Uprising in September 1944.

Alongside the story of Raisa and Sebastian, Rudnicki also tells a more general tale of the realities of life in Nazi-occupied Poland. He presents, even if sketchily, other characters and their efforts to survive the war, and lists, rather dryly, many facts about the Second World War and the lives of the Polish Jews during the German occupation of Poland. Many facts are contained within both the conversations between the characters and the descriptions of their actions. Yet it is not only the novella's unforgettable dramatic content but also the distinct voice of the narrator and diverse narrative forms that make *Ascent to Heaven* a highly valuable testimony to the Holocaust. The distinct narrator, found in all Rudnicki's short stories, is able to be emotional, sometimes even sentimental, and also show presumably little or no passion. His emotionality is voiced almost throughout the entire presentation of the main characters' love. But Raisa's obsessive love for her mentally ill husband ("ascent to heaven" is a metaphor for her love) is depicted against the stark images of the tragedy of the Jews. This contrast provides the narrator with enough motives for his almost uncontrolled emotionality combined paradoxically with his dry and dispassionate voice. In it one can even hear irony or sarcasm, as in his comment on Raisa's honeymoon (one that should be wished to no one) or in his observation that the radiant moments of a person's life do not always harmonize with history. The fictitious tale of Raisa and Sebastian intertwined with such comments and observations, along with the dry reporting of the war's historical events, make *Ascent to Heaven* a work of diverse narrative forms, expressing effectively a strong moral message about the highest of human values.

—Andrzej Karcz

ASHES TO ASHES
Play by Harold Pinter, 1996

Ashes to Ashes, Harold Pinter's extended one-act play of 1996, opens with a man and a woman, Rebecca and Devlin, in the comfortable living room of a country house. She is seated,

and he stands. At first she appears to be talking about a past lover and her sadomasochistic relationship with him. Her first words indicate that she is answering an unheard question from Devlin, giving an example of how she was sexually tormented or toyed with by her lover. Devlin's gently interrogative responses condition us to think that he may be a psychiatrist, although later we think that he may be her husband.

Devlin attempts to get Rebecca to define, to explain, to put a stable meaning to her words and descriptions. They have an exchange over the term "darling." Devlin uses the term with her. Did her lover? Devlin insists not. Rebecca's recollections begin with her lover's threat of physical abuse and its attendant eroticism and then continue with her accompanying him to his factory, a damp and inhumane place where the workers doff their hats to him out of either respect or fear. Rebecca also describes seeing her lover at a railway station and watching him tear babies from their screaming mothers' arms. Later she tells Devlin about watching a group of people being led, fully clothed, to their deaths by drowning in the sea.

In his interrogation of her Devlin describes himself as a dichotomy; he is a man who both does not care and who possesses a rigid sense of duty. He attempts to restore order, to claim control, and to force Rebecca to kiss his fist, the action she originally described her lover as forcing on her. By the end of the play Rebecca has related a story, which is repeated in an echo during the telling, of being forced to give up her own baby in a place where babies were being taken away. Pinter describes the physical setting of the drama as becoming progressively dimmer, in spite of the fact that the light from the table lamp intensifies throughout the play, although it must do so without further illumination.

Ashes to Ashes can be seen as a post-Holocaust play, even though Pinter usually disavows any such specific meaning. Nevertheless, many of Pinter's earlier plays present a profound sense of the anxiety of the outsider and focus on persecution and torture—psychological, emotional, physical—as nightmarish conditions that require no logical source. After two decades of explicitly and implicitly denying the existence of any political themes in his work, Pinter began incorporating specific political speech and addressing the conditions of torture and persecution against groups of people in a series of short one-act plays in the 1980s, for example, *One for the Road* (1984), *Mountain Language* (1988), *The New World Order* (1993), and *Party Time* (1993). Born in London in 1930, Pinter grew up in the East End, the son of a Jewish tailor. His coming-of-age coincided with World War II and the Holocaust, as well as with the rise of British fascism in the years immediately following the war. In *Ashes to Ashes* the descriptions of railway stations, of the forcible removal of babies from their mothers, and of large groups of people being led to their deaths are shared images from the Holocaust that have become commonplace in our cultural vernacular.

Pinter's explorations, although they have become more openly politically engaged, still resonate with mysteriousness.

There is no logical explanation for hate, for the targeting of any specific group, or for the bestial and eroticized power games of the persecutors. Words cut as deeply as conventional weapons, and the control of language and memory is presented as the strongest of the torturer's implements. Rebecca, although initially prodded by Devlin, remembers witnessing others' brutalization and murder. Her final memory, of the loss of her own child, occurs as an act of defiance, however. Devlin demands that she kiss his fist and then ask him to put his hands around her throat. She does neither and remains silent, and he loosens his grip. She then speaks of her own loss, repeated by an echo in the room. He takes his hand away, and Rebecca and the echo continue the story of how she had her baby taken from her and how she was forced to deny the baby's existence. This becomes the play's final image, not that of Rebecca's personal story, painful as it is, but of her silent defiance and then reiterated memory. Although Pinter continues to work in his patented ambiguities—just where all of this is taking place and who these people are he refuses to indulge—nevertheless, the final image of defiance and remembering may be seen as the central thesis of the play and of Holocaust literature in general, suggesting perhaps that strength, for an individual or a group, comes from a willingness to retain the past, to insist on experience.

—Steven Dedalus Burch

AT THE MIND'S LIMITS: CONTEMPLATIONS BY A SURVIVOR ON AUSCHWITZ AND ITS REALITIES (Jenseits von Schuld und Sühne: Bewältigungsversuche eines Überwältigten) Autobiographical essays by Jean Améry, 1966

The collection of essays *At the Mind's Limits,* published in English in 1980, is probably Jean Améry's best-known book. The first of three autobiographical works (followed by *Über das Altern* and *Unmeisterliche Wanderjahre*), it was explicitly written for a German radio audience and broadcast before publication. Améry reflects in five essays on his experiences as an intellectual and cultural German Jew during the Nazi period and examines the consequences of the Holocaust for his self-understanding after the war.

In its German original, the title reads *Jenseits von Schuld und Sühne: Bewältigungsversuche eines Überwältigten* and suggests that Améry did not believe in the possibility of reconciliation. The subtitle is an ironic word play on the German term for "coming to terms with the Nazi time," *Vergangenheitsbewältigung.* The essays are compiled in the order in which they were written, rather than according to the chronology of the events they describe. The reader is thereby able to follow Améry's own development of thought and journey in memory and reflection. Beginning with "At the

Mind's Limits" which deals with the (nonreligious) intellectual in Auschwitz, Améry moves on to describe his experience of being tortured by the Gestapo and the consequence of having lost trust in the world. He reflects on the notion of *Heimat* (Home), particularly to a German-Jewish refugee and Auschwitz survivor. In "Ressentiments" Améry deals with his disillusionment with the developments in West Germany's political left. The collection closes with an essay on his Jewishness.

All essays are characterized by sharp observations and a disarming sense of honesty and irony about his own life. In particular, when addressing the consequences of the Holocaust on his relationship to German culture, Améry's observations about his alienation from both contexts and his struggle to identify are clearly reflected in his style. He defines *Heimat* as "security," a context that can be taken for granted. Living in a different cultural context, especially when that was not chosen freely but had been enforced, means the loss of one's entire cultural system of reference. In particular, German-Jewish survivors of the Holocaust were thrown into an existential crisis different from the crisis of other survivors, since they had no other cultural context to fall back on and in which to feel at home. The alienation from one's origins was particularly poignant in relation to the German language. Overnight German had become the language of the enemy. The violence done to the German language by its misuse during the period of National Socialism was felt particularly in the camps, where the German-Jewish prisoner was identified by fellow inmates as part of the enemy culture while being tortured by representatives of that same culture.

Améry contends that the number tattooed on his arm tells more about his Jewishness than any religious text or tradition could. The tattoo stamped a forced identity on him, and merely looking at it makes him realize the loss of *Heimat* all over again, regularly shattering his trust in the world. His Jewishness was forced on him rather than being naturally part of his self-understanding, and it is bound up with fear of renewed persecution and loneliness. Because Améry grew up assimilated with no positive awareness of his Jewish roots, he could not invent a positive relationship to this part of his heritage once the Nuremberg Laws expelled him from German culture. He subsequently identified with Jean-Paul Sartre's (negative) definition of Jewishness, which relied on being identified as Jewish by others. This was not necessary for Jews who, with or without assimilation, had a strong sense of belonging to the Jewish community. Yet Améry, once identified as a Jew, did not resign himself to this fate. He accepted this identification and rebelled against it, struggling to find his own identification in the one that was forced on him by distinguishing between "being Jewish" and "Judaism."

The autobiographical essays in the collection are more than memories of a contemporary witness. They remain relevant, reflecting on the human consequences of atrocity. The theme uniting the essays is Améry's concern for a "radical humanism," which communicates the consequences of inhumane behavior in order to prevent its reoccurrence.

—K. Hannah Holtschneider

ATROCITY (Karu lo Piepel)
Novel by Ka-Tzetnik 135633, 1961

In his book *The Seventh Million* Tom Segev writes, "I was a boy when I first read *Piepel* [the Hebrew title of *Atrocity*]. I have never read anything about the Holocaust that so disturbed me." More striking was Haim Shorer's 1961 plea to Gideon Hausner, the state prosecutor in the trial of Adolf Eichmann:

> Leave aside your concluding speech and take Ka-Tzetnik's latest book *Piepel* and read it out loud to the court and its listeners and don't stop . . . Read in a loud voice and we will listen and cry for two-three days and nights. All of us, all of Israel, we will cry and wail without end; perhaps we could wipe away with the sea of tears the great horror, whose depth we yet do not know. We will cry until we faint with our dear Ka-Tzetnik, with his pure and holy book.

A layered mosaic of unimaginable, inconceivably traumatic vignettes, this novel by Ka-Tzetnik 135633 (published in 1961 in Hebrew as *Karu lo Piepel* and in English as *Piepel* before its publication in 1963 as *Atrocity*) has as its main subject the sexual exploitation of children in the concentration camps. The nub of the narrative follows Moni, a seven-year-old boy who is forced to become a child prostitute, a *Piepel,* to serve the homosexual needs of the older guards and section orderlies. First appearing in *House of Dolls,* the naïf, tender, and refined child, modeled after the author's own brother, arrives at Auschwitz and is immediately noticed by the block ruler Franzel because of his gentle, tempting eyes. Traversing familiar territory, Ka-Tzetnik manages to brilliantly transcribe, from the perspective of a youthful hero, the horrifying crimes committed against children in the Holocaust and to embed the story's fabric with illuminating insights about the torture and destruction of innocent lives.

At its epicenter the book is a rite-of-passage tale unfolding in an insane universe where cruelty and subjugation go hand in hand. The story is also about the struggle of children to grasp the intolerable reality they are thrust into and to behave heroically in a corrupt, abnormal world. In many respects *Atrocity*'s keynote theme is Moni's attempt to preserve his sanity and integrity even as he is ceaselessly preyed upon by the vicious, evil men of the block.

Looming large among the pages of *Atrocity* are consuming images of the sadistic debasement of human life that chillingly flash throughout. In one disturbing passage Fruchtenbaum, a Jew and scion of a Zionist family who was once a *Piepel* himself but who now runs one of the blocks, hacks to death a fellow Jew for recognizing him and reminding him of his suppressed heritage. Ka-Tzetnik repeatedly hammers home the idea that perversity and murder were polymorphous in the Nazi phenomenon. In a terrifying catalog of scenes a Nazi officer chokes a young boy to death after his rape, an old *Piepel* is seesawed from side to side with a cane laid across his neck, a cell block master smothers one his captives by pushing his head into the latrine hole, and an adolescent is punished with death for stealing jam for the rabbi who yearns for the sweet taste.

In common with Ka-Tzetnik's other texts, the *Mussulmen* (living skeletons) once again comprise a central part of the symbology of depravity and expunction of life. At one point Moni, escaping the unprecedented savagery of Robert, seeks shelter among the *Mussulmen* and is hardly noticed by them, for they have had any trace of life snuffed out by the debauchery of their enslavers. Notably, the *Mussulmen* are entrusted with safeguarding the food rations, for it is known that their desire to eat has dissipated and that they no longer possess any consciousness of their surroundings. Above all, the blank, hollowed-out, spiritually emaciated corpses, slowly crawling toward their liberating death, personify the surreal and subhuman depths a person can be reduced to.

As is to be expected, Moni's odyssey into the netherworld is graphically charted, emphasizing his inability to shake off the "fetters" of his Judaic past. Doubtless, Moni is acutely aware of the fate that awaits him if he allows those values to surface, as they are in direct opposition to the demands of Robert, the block chief. For instance, Moni refuses to eat, though he has access to all of the food he craves and though he knows that this act will surely lead to death, since his tormentors like their sexual objects to be of supple and round flesh. Inevitably, the sensitive young protagonist, who longs for his parents, grows too thin to continue his function as a *Piepel* and is replaced by Lolek. Still, he cannot hate his substitute, because he believes that Lolek, just like him, yearns to see his mother, who is interned at the women's camp. Indeed, despite the relentless suffering and pervasive anguish around him, Moni never loses his humanity. We reflect, for instance, that he embraces the Talmudic teachings of the rabbi of Shilev, who through his Yom Kippur prayer and mere presence in the camp is able to infuse Moni's wretched existence with a modicum of meaning and hope.

In the end, after stealing a turnip and receiving a ruthless beating for his "sin," Moni finds release when he valiantly attempts to escape by lunging at the barbed wire. Significantly, his brave, life-affirming act elicits unexpected praise from Robert and Vatzek, a German *kapo,* who recognize his courageous refusal to succumb to the impending death from starvation that awaits the others: "'Bravo, old whore' he cried out as though to cheer him on." Perhaps the deepest message of the book is that it is only in the world of Auschwitz, where all values had been so overtly inverted, where all moral prescriptions were eclipsed by ritualized monstrosity, where the usual distinctions between right and wrong had vanished, that the death of a little boy is preferable to life.

—Dvir Abramovich

AUSCHWITZ AND AFTER (Auschwitz et après)
Memoir by Charlotte Delbo, 1970

Charlotte Delbo wrote *Auschwitz and After* (published in French in 1970 and in English translation in 1995) in the style of the new factuality, a type of realism where the cold precision of language shows that a profound sadness has replaced the admiring attitude of the former and older styles of realism. The structure of the text is superficially confusing, consisting of factual accounts and poems, but her method is effective. She brings out the beauty of the horrible, and many of the accounts of the extreme cruelty and hardship that she and her companions had to endure are written in incandescent language. A clue to her ability to write in this way can be seen by her occasional reference to her thinking of herself as already dead, someone who died and yet is still alive, in a sense, and who has set herself the task of describing what took place. The book is the opposite of dramatic: it is so concerned not to highlight or emphasize anything that happened that everything is viewed as extraordinary. But there are references to drama itself, to the author's previous experience of drama before she was sent to the camps, and she sometimes analyses what happened in terms of the highly artificial strategies of the stage and explains in this way how particular participants made themselves noticed. The occasional reference to artifice brings out the artificiality of the whole system of the camps, as does the stray reference to her life in France before her arrest, a time of normalcy that seems from the perspective of the camps to be surreal rather than normal.

The interspersing of poems between the chapters of prose sounds rather complicated, but it represents a way of varying the presentation of what is constantly grim descriptive material. The poems are a pause in the unremitting recitation of the horrors of the camps and the impression that she gives that the camps are real and everything else is illusory. This point is repeated when the author reflects that she really is dead, although legally she is alive. The sections of the book that relate her life after the rescue from the camps are similarly so concentrated and descriptive that they are evocative of the extraordinary nature of the ordinary given the backdrop of the experience of the camps and the fact that survivors often felt that they had to pay particular attention to what was happening to them to keep a grip on the reality of the situation and stop slipping back into the thinking of the camps. In short, they

needed to remind themselves constantly that they were really alive and not dead, something that runs right through the content of the book.

—Oliver Leaman

AUSCHWITZ: A DOCTOR'S EYEWITNESS ACCOUNT (Dr. Mengele boncolóorvosa voltam az auschwitzi krematóriumban)
Memoir by Miklos Nyiszli, 1947

Miklos Nyiszli wrote only one book about the Holocaust, but that book, based on his experiences in Auschwitz, opens a door into the nethermost regions of the Auschwitz death camp. Few people survived to tell of life in the *Sonderkommando* at Auschwitz-Birkenau, the special group assigned to transport the bodies from the gas chambers to the crematoriums, stoke the fires, and turn the bodies into ash. To save his life, Nyiszli became the chief physician of the Auschwitz crematoria and the personal research pathologist of Dr. Josef Mengele, the "Angel of Death."

Auschwitz: A Doctor's Eyewitness Account, published in English translation in 1960, is composed of 38 brief chapters and an epilogue. The chapters, organized chronologically, begin in May 1944, following the Nazi invasion of Hungary.

Nyiszli's descent into the abyss begins with a four-day journey, accompanied by his wife and daughter, in a sealed cattle car from their Hungarian home to the concentration and death camp of Auschwitz, in Poland. Immediately upon arrival, on 29 May 1944, he is separated from his family and thrust into a life and death decision. He obeys the command for all physicians to step forward. He then must decide if he will respond to Mengele's call for specialists trained in German universities and skilled in forensic medicine. Nyiszli chooses to do so, hoping that his decision will save his life and perhaps protect his wife and daughter.

His expertise is tested immediately in a macabre examination. Mengele and other senior SS officers sit in attendance while Nyiszli performs two autopsies. He passes the test and becomes Mengele's personal research pathologist, with additional duties as the physician to the 860 members of the *Sonderkommando* who routinely at four-month intervals are sent to their deaths.

Nyiszli tells his story in straightforward, objective language. At times his tone is eerily dispassionate. In a foreword to the 1960 edition of the book, **Bruno Bettelheim** criticizes Nyiszli for deluding himself into thinking that he was still functioning as a physician. There are instances that lend support to Bettelheim's judgment. Nyiszli reports that on one occasion he held forth with Mengele as if he were a colleague at a medical conference, engaging him so totally that Mengele offered him a cigarette. It is a measure of Nazi evil that Nyiszli could speak of such an offer with seeming pride.

Along with **Filip Müller**'s book, *Eyewitness Auschwitz: Three Years in the Gas Chambers,* Nyiszli's memoir tells of life in the innermost circle of hell. He recounts moments of almost unbelievable inhumanity, as in the story of a 16-year-old girl who survives the gas chamber and is nursed back to life by the *Sonderkommando,* only to be shot by the SS. Toward the end of his Auschwitz imprisonment, he sees the horribly scarred bodies of the 13th *Sonderkommando,* burned to death by flamethrowers.

With adequate food and housing, even alcohol and drugs, the men of the *Sonderkommando* earn a privileged life with their gruesome labor, but they work with a death sentence hanging over them. Only the men of the 12th *Sonderkommando* choose to rebel against this sentence. Nyiszli offers a firsthand account of their revolt, in which nearly all die, but not without first killing 70 SS members, destroying one crematorium, and damaging another. Nyiszli and a few of his coworkers are spared a sentence of death only because they are still useful to Mengele.

Nyiszli was confronted daily by cruel ethical dilemmas, set in a world in which canisters of Zyklon-B gas are delivered in Red Cross vans. Soon after his arrival, Nyiszli saves an inmate from dying from an overdose of sleeping pills. Later he questions whether his decision was humane. He refuses to give poison to *Sonderkommando* members but regrets that decision when he learns they died a horrible death. Whenever possible, he steals medicine, vitamins, and bandages to give to inmates. His privileged position enables him to help his wife and daughter, supplying them with food and medicine and even arranging for them to be assigned to a labor camp in Germany, although they are ultimately sent to Bergen-Belsen.

Nyiszli's book leaves one with much to ponder. It offers a glimpse into another part of the universe of Nazi evil, disguised as the pursuit of science. It is a world in which to save his life a doctor cooperates in the worst abuses of medicine.

—Marilyn J. Harran

AUSCHWITZ: TRUE TALES FROM A GROTESQUE LAND
Memoir by Sara Nomberg-Przytyk, 1985

Translated from an unpublished Polish manuscript written in 1966, Sara Nomberg-Przytyk's memoir *Auschwitz: True Tales from a Grotesque Land,* which appeared in 1985, marked the emergence of a penetrating expression of women's ordeals in the universe of the concentration camp. Exploring various individuals and incidents from that realm in a series of brief vignettes, Nomberg-Przytyk captures the horrific essence of the death factory. A skilled storyteller, she conveys the unbearable nature of her experience in a manner accessible to her reader, bringing out the depths of a will to live even within the confines of the kingdom of death.

One especially powerful motif that runs through the tales in Nomberg-Przytyk's memoir is the assault on the mother as the origin of life and of love in the world. She recalls, for instance, songs about the loss of the mother that were sung in the camp at Stutthof and in Auschwitz. She often refers to the phenomenon of the "camp mother" or "camp daughter," in which one woman took another under her protection. And she presents a beautiful, tragic portrayal of a mother and daughter in the tale of Marie and Odette. Perhaps the most devastating example of the assault on the mother is found in the story "Esther's First Born." It is the tale of a young woman who gave birth to a beautiful child in the camp only to be told by her fellow inmates that newborns in the camp must be killed in order to spare the mothers. Esther refuses to allow them to take her infant and goes to her death with her baby in her arms.

As harrowing as the tale of Esther is, the story in "A Living Torch" is even more so. Here the women in the camp are inundated with the sound of children crying out, "Mama!" as if "a single scream had been torn out of hundreds of mouths." As the children are sent to be burned alive in pits of flames, a scream breaks out from the women in the block. Nomberg-Przytyk ends the tale with a question that continues to haunt the world: "Is there any punishment adequate to repay to criminals who perpetrated these crimes?"

Not all of Nomberg-Przytyk's portraits of women in the camp are about bonding and nurturing. Images of something monstrous can be found in her memory of women like Orli Reichert and the infamous Cyla, who was in charge of Block 25, the block where women were sent to await their turn for the gas chambers. Cyla was one of Josef Mengele's favorites in the camp, and Nomberg-Przytyk's memoir contains several accounts of Mengele's words and deeds, including his explanation of why he sent mothers to their deaths with their children. "It would not be humanitarian," said Mengele, "to send a child to the ovens without permitting the mother to be there to witness the child's death." Such was the Nazi notion of kindness.

A question that recurs in Nomberg-Przytyk's memoir is whether or not new arrivals should be informed of the fate that awaits them. While the matter of giving people a short time to prepare themselves for their deaths is left unresolved, Nomberg-Przytyk presents a heroic example of such a preparation in her tale "The Dance of the Rabbis." Here the Nazis order a transport of Hasidic rabbis to dance and sing before they are murdered, but the rabbis—even as they are going to their deaths—transform the Nazi order into their own affirmation of the holiness that imparts meaning to life. This they accomplish by refusing to allow the Nazis to determine the meaning of the words that come from their lips.

Indeed, Nomberg-Przytyk is especially attuned to the Nazis' assault on words and their meaning and how the assault most profoundly defined the Holocaust. Realizing that the violence done to the word parallels the violence launched against the meaning of the human being, she writes, ''The new set of meanings [imposed on words] provided the best evidence of the devastation that Auschwitz created in the psyche of every human being.'' Skillfully making use of words to remember this assault on words, Nomberg-Przytyk returns meaning to words in a way that not only attests to the kingdom of death but also bears witness to the dearness of life.

—David Patterson

AUSTERLITZ
Novel by W.G. Sebald, 2001

W.G. Sebald's final novel, *Austerlitz,* published in German and in English translation in 2001, tells the story of a Jewish child who escapes the Holocaust by being part of a children's transport to Britain. He thus gains his life by circumventing the Nazi occupation, but he loses his identity when his foster parents withhold his real name and origin. As an adult, in his quest for self-knowledge, Austerlitz recounts his stark childhood in Wales, his adolescence in boarding schools and college, his work as an architectural historian, and finally his wrenching search for his identity in Europe.

In 1939 four-and-a-half-year-old Jacquot Austerlitz is put aboard a children's transport by his mother, Agáta Austerlitzová. She acts out of fear and love, desperate to save him from the Nazis. Leaving behind his mother and his mother's best friend, Vera Ryšanová, who has been his loving nanny, Austerlitz travels by train with the other children. They pass through the German Reich and The Netherlands to Holland, where they board the ferry *Prague.* In England his journey continues, by train again, to London where, surrounded by strangers whose words he does not understand, young Austerlitz loses his past among the omnipresent shadows of a strange land. His foster parents, Emyr Elias, a Calvinist preacher, and his timid wife take Austerlitz to their home in Bala, Wales, a cold setting that is physically and emotionally isolated. Austerlitz begins life over as their child, with a new name, Dafydd Elias, and a new language. During his 12th year, when his foster mother dies, Austerlitz enters a boarding school, where the activity and opportunities to learn stimulate his physical and intellectual life. Eventually he makes a close friend, Gerald, whose mother and uncle provide a sense of family during Austerlitz's remaining years of adolescence. It is also at this time that Austerlitz learns his true name.

As Austerlitz goes through adulthood, he shuns efforts to trace his origins. Apart from friendships with Gerald and a teacher who encourages him in his studies, Austerlitz never forms close relationships. He avoids thinking deeply about his identity and cannot express his emotions to the one woman in his life, Marie de Verneuil. When Gerald dies, Austerlitz's emotional health begins to decline until, in 1992, he suffers a total breakdown and finds himself hospitalized. Finally he hears a broadcast about children's transports prior to the war, and they arouse fleeting memories. In particular the narrative of a woman from Prague inspires him to embark on a journey of self-discovery. In Prague he finds his aged caregiver, Vera, whose tales reconstruct the story of Austerlitz's mother, Agáta, and the secret of his own origin. Austerlitz discovers that Agáta was sent from Prague to the Theresienstadt ghetto in 1941 and then to her death in 1944. He also learns that his father, Maximilian Aychenwald, had gone to Paris before its occupation but that Agáta had never heard from him again. Austerlitz then travels to decrepit Terezín, where his mother spent her final years as a prisoner in the Nazi-constructed ghetto. Using books and a Nazi propaganda film about Terezín, Austerlitz investigates the circumstances of his mother's fate. As the novel ends, he plans to learn more about his father and to find Marie, the woman whose love Austerlitz could not accept earlier in his life.

Austerlitz's life resembles the lives of characters from Sebald's *The Emigrants* (1996). As in that work and others by Sebald, characters who physically avoid the Holocaust do not manage to escape it emotionally. There are further similarities between this and other works by Sebald in style. Similar to Proust's *Remembrance of Things Past,* Sebald's novels make use of details from the present to develop the characters' past lives. The minutiae of observations trigger feelings of uncertainty and hazy recollections in Austerlitz throughout his life until his odyssey brings him back to the city of his birth. The haphazard odyssey, comprised of several journeys, provides a narrative structure for the novel, which utilizes the characteristics of memoir and travel book.

All of these events in Austerlitz's life are recounted by a nameless narrator whose meetings with Austerlitz, some random and some planned, take place 20 years apart. Similar to the intent listener on the ship in **Elie Wiesel**'s *The Accident,* the narrator provides catharsis for the estranged Holocaust victim. But unlike the unwilling repository of painful memories in Wiesel's work, Sebald's listener relishes every word that Austerlitz speaks and desires to hear more. The meetings occur internationally, in keeping with the travel motif established as part of Austerlitz's life, whose work as an architectural historian takes him to cities throughout Europe. Many times on his journeys Austerlitz has a sense of déjà vu without realizing that, on his childhood journey from Prague to London, he had actually seen the sights that stir his memory. Austerlitz describes each of these locations in explicit detail to his acquaintance who, in turn, writes about their conversations in memoir fashion. The stories of Austerlitz's youth weave in and out of the descriptions of the places he has been and the intriguing accounts of books he has read, museums he has visited, natural phenomenon he has studied, and existential thoughts he has had about the passing of time.

As a further distinguishing trait, the book includes photography that illustrates places and people Austerlitz has described. These photos have been included, ostensibly, because as Austerlitz embarks on the last segment of his quest he hands the narrator the key to his London home and offers him access to the photos he has acquired of all the places he has been. The narrator then uses these photos to document Austerlitz's life and to support recollections of the conversations. Their effect is to add such validity to the work that a reader could believe he is reading a nonfiction memoir or a travel book. They also engage the reader so that, by the end, Sebald has succeeded in extending to the reader the narrator's fondness and hope for Austerlitz.

—Sharon Brown

THE AWFUL ROWING TOWARD GOD
Poems by Anne Sexton, 1975

The Death Notebooks was the last book of poems published while Anne Sexton was alive; she checked the proofs of *The Awful Rowing toward God* on the day she committed suicide. The first line of the earlier volume, like the title of the latter, suggests the main theme ("Mrs. Sexton went out looking for the gods") of both volumes and sets the tone: an ironic, often funny, yet terribly serious quest for a God she can believe in despite the evil world he (presumably) made and who would love her despite the evil she feels inside herself. Allusions to the Holocaust sometimes represent both evils. Her own death impulse ("the death baby") fuses with the destruction of the Jews: "I went out popping pills and crying adieu / in my own death camp with my own little Jew" ("For Mr. Death Who Stands with His Door Open" from *The Death Notebooks*). In *The Awful Rowing toward God* a syllogism equating lack of belief and absolute evil uses Hitler as a code for the latter: "The priest came, / he said God was even in Hitler. / I did not believe him / for if God were in Hitler / then God would be in me" ("The Sickness unto Death"). Sexton has a ferocious need to believe, "each day, / typing out the God / [her] typewriter believes in. / . . . like a wolf at a live heart" ("Frenzy").

The quest is further complicated by gender. Sexton's imagined God is no abstract being. He is daddy supreme, precisely the kind of dominating male figure she has been struggling with throughout her poetic life. No wonder the "rowing" toward such a God (Sexton uses the ancient metaphor of the sea journey) is "awful." As William Shurr has indicated, she also explores and modernizes the mystical concept of Logos, the embodied word of God. But the final encounter with that

body ("The Rowing Endeth") is ambiguous; having cheated her at cards, "He starts to laugh, / . . . such laughter that He doubles right over me." The words echo Sexton's evocation of incestuous rape in earlier work.

On Sexton's journey hope and sometimes terrifying joy ("Riding the Elevator into the Sky") alternate with disgust and despair. The latter dominate in "After Auschwitz," the one Holocaust poem of *The Awful Rowing toward God*. A number of Sexton's themes intersect in these 33 short lines. "After Auschwitz" is also one of many questionings of God and humanity in Holocaust literature.

Typically, Sexton's opening simile is not logical but catches the feeling of anger: "Anger, / as black as a hook, / overtakes me." The savage hyperbole and homey vocabulary that follow are also typical: "Every day, / each Nazi / took, at 8:00 A.M., a baby / and sautéed him for breakfast / in his frying pan." Next a two-line stanza encapsulates the indifference of the world, expands its significance into the metaphysical plane, and begins the "dirt" motif, Sexton's signifier for evil: "And death looks on with a casual eye / and picks at the dirt under his fingernail." This provokes the poet's despair over human nature, dramatized by the fact that she is stirred to actually speak it (as we are ritually reminded) and intensified by the short, choppy verses:

> Man is evil,
> I say aloud.
> Man is a flower
> that should be burnt,
> I say aloud.
> Man
> is a bird full of mud,
> I say aloud.

The image of evil within ("bird full of mud"), a theme of Sexton's poetry, intensifies the feeling, and "should be burnt" suggests the curse that will follow the horrible two-line refrain "And death looks on with a casual eye / and scratches his anus." (We recall that Auschwitz was called "the anus of the universe.") First, however, the poet evokes what is typically, wonderfully human, only to reveal its disgusting evil:

> Man with his small pink toes,
> with his miraculous fingers
> is not a temple
> but an outhouse,
> I say aloud.
> Let man never again raise his teacup.
> Let man never again write a book.
> Let man never again put on his shoe.
> Let man never again raise his eyes,
> on a soft July night.
> Never. Never. Never. Never. Never.
> I say these things aloud.

This curse on all human activity—an emotionally comprehensible reaction to Auschwitz (if this is what man can do, then let him cease to function)—culminates with King Lear's famous lament. The expanded ''saying'' refrain, slightly more distanced now (the poet, aware of her reaction, seems to reflect on her own speaking), sets up the final, whispered line, detached from the others: ''I beg the Lord not to hear.''

Why? Because he might be tempted to retaliate against the woman cursing his creation? At any rate, if he can hear, then he exists. But is this really sufficient consolation ''after Auschwitz''?

—David Ball

B

BABI YAR: A DOCUMENTARY NOVEL (Babii Iar: Roman-dokument)
Novel by Anatoli Kuznetsov, 1966

Anatoli Kuznetsov's *Babi Yar* (1966, republished in an expanded version in 1970), which the author described as a documentary in the form of a novel, offers significant insight into the experience of the Holocaust and World War II in the lands of the Soviet Union. Furthermore, the extraliterary context of this work's editing, censorship, and subsequent republication in an expanded edition outside the Soviet Union reveals much about further atrocities of the period that Soviet censorship had suppressed.

Babi Yar details life during World War II and the Holocaust period primarily through the point of view of a non-Jewish preadolescent boy, Tolia Semerik, who is based on the author's life and experiences. The novel depicts general living conditions and the catastrophic events that took place in Kiev, Ukraine, during the Nazi occupation from fall 1941 to fall 1943. Tolia's own experiences of famine, repeated escapes from possible capture by the Nazis, and confusion about nationality and patriotism are mixed with his impressions of the September 1941 massacre and mass burial of nearly the entire Jewish population at Babi Yar, a ravine not far from his family's home. Tolia reports hearing the gunfire of the massacre and of the continuing executions that resulted in the deaths of more than 100,000 local residents at the hands of the Nazis. In the novel's structure Tolia's reports are complemented by eyewitness accounts of the massacre at Babi Yar and of conditions in a concentration camp, which Kuznetsov had recorded from Jews who had miraculously escaped from both places. Throughout the novel Kuznetsov intersperses Tolia's impressions and the eyewitness accounts with relevant excerpts from Nazi and Soviet propaganda statements released during the German occupation period of Ukraine, as well as descriptions of what happened differently from the material contained in the propaganda. Furthermore, particularly in the uncensored version of his novel (1970), Kuznetsov rounds out the perspectives in the novel with the extensive commentary, warnings, exhortations, and reflections of Tolia as an adult years after the war. In this way Kuznetsov achieves a syncretic or mixed work that makes its points by combining features of several different genres: the novel, the memoir, and the general wartime documentary.

Even in its censored form, Kuznetsov's novel played an important role in spreading awareness about the atrocities at Babi Yar, which the Soviet government had previously downplayed. His work expands on **Yevgeny Yevtushenko's** poem "Babii Yar" (1961), which also focuses on the overpowering image of devastation and death at the ravine and the importance of this place for all Soviet citizens. Like Yevtushenko's poem, Kuznetsov's novel repeatedly returns to the image of the ravine as the symbol of the Holocaust and World War II for the Soviet people and the world as a whole. The thematics and fate of Kuznetsov's work are also particularly comparable to those of **Vasily Grossman**, whose novels *In a Good Cause* (1952) and *Life and Fate* (written in 1960, published first outside the Soviet Union in 1980) also treat the Soviet experience of World War II, including anti-Semitism and the Holocaust. The publication of Grossman's *Life and Fate* was suppressed at least partly because this work depicted a Nazi concentration camp and a Soviet gulag in equal measure. Similar sections in Kuznetsov's novel that detail and criticize Soviet atrocities toward Jews and prisoners of war were completely excised by censors. Kuznetsov's work is also comparable to Aleksandr Solzhenitsyn's *One Day in the Life of Ivan Denisovich,* which treats conditions in a gulag for an ordinary worker who has been sent there for forced labor. Kuznetsov's novel, like Solzhenitsyn's, makes use of some conventions of socialist realism, which was the generally accepted set of literary norms for Soviet writers. Kuznetsov deals with conditions and details of everyday life for average citizens and workers to demonstrate the crushing and divisive impact of the war and the Holocaust. Kuznetsov, however, openly breaks with socialist realism in that rather than wholeheartedly extolling the glories and progress of his Soviet homeland and the virtues of the Soviet citizen and proletarian, he depicts in full the presence of anti-Semitism and other atrocities in his country and presents people as atomized individuals who must struggle for mere existence, sometimes against each other.

Kuznetsov's novel is valuable to the literature of the Holocaust for several important reasons: for its candor in revealing crucial facts about the Babi Yar massacre, for its continuation of a previously suppressed dialogue about the Holocaust and World War II in the Soviet Union, and for its own history of composition as evidence of the impact of censorship on knowledge and awareness.

—Alisa Gayle Mayor

BABII YAR
Poem by Yevgeny Yevtushenko, 1961

Babii Yar is a ravine on the outskirts of the Ukrainian city of Kiev, where in 1941 the SS murdered more than 100,000 people—Jews and non-Jewish Ukrainians, Russians, and others—and buried them in a mass grave. In 1961, when Yevgeny Yevtushenko visited the site with fellow writer **Anatoli Kuznetsov,** the site was still unmarked, the event mostly buried in the memories of those who had witnessed or—rarely—survived it.

Yevtushenko responded with a poem of eleven rhymed iambic stanzas that was to galvanize audiences in Russia and abroad, call down a rebuke from nervous Soviet censors, and serve as an inspiration for other Russian artists including Dmitrii Shostakovich and Kuznetsov himself in his 1966 novel *Babii Yar*. Yevtushenko, who was not Jewish, took a radical and courageous stand when he wrote and performed this poem, which identifies with the Jews and condemns native anti-Semitism.

Yevtushenko was outraged that ''Above Babii Yar there are no monuments,'' as he wrote in the first line. He was acutely aware of the need to address the past and perceived the neglect of this Nazi atrocity as an insult both to the victims and to the honor of his own people, who had led the long fight against fascism. Yevtushenko sees everything through the filter of conscience and of his own Russianness. His love for the Russian people and his commitment to warning them of manipulation by anti-Semites are central to this poem that focuses on Jewish victims.

Yevtushenko's reaction is deeply personal. The sight of the ravine evokes the response, ''I am afraid . . . / . . . taking off my cap, / I feel how I slowly turn grey / . . . and I myself am like a massive, soundless scream / above the thousand thousand buried here.'' In the central device of the poem the poet ceases to be an observer and through his empathy becomes the victims. His persona fades as he takes on those of a series of Jews across the centuries. Beginning ''Today I'm as old / as the whole Jewish race,'' he goes on, ''Here I am wandering through ancient Egypt.'' He then assumes, one after another, the identities of a Jew crucified in Palestine; Dreyfus, reviled and imprisoned; a child begging for mercy during a pogrom in Bielostok; and Anne Frank, in love and ''transparent as a twig in April.'' Returning to Babii Yar, he becomes, finally, ''every old man shot dead here, / every child shot dead . . .''

The Soviet worldview officially condemned the Russian tradition of anti-Semitism. In this spirit Yevtushenko makes it clear that he speaks not only as a Russian but as a Soviet citizen: ''The 'Internationale,' let it thunder / when the last antisemite on earth / is buried forever.'' The poem ends with the defiant paradox that though ''there is no Jewish blood in my blood,'' because he has taken the side of the Jews, anti-Semites will now hate him as if he were one himself, and he is ''for that reason—a real Russian.''

These moving declarations alone caused consternation among right-wing nationalist critics. But there is an ambiguity in the poem that caused Soviet officials more serious concern about

its possible destructive effects: nowhere in the poem does he mention Germans or Nazis. In 1961, at the height of the Cold War, anything that Western audiences could construe as anti-Soviet was welcomed there, and many gleefully read ''Babii Yar'' as a condemnation of Soviet anti-Semitism alone. Given the lack of general knowledge of the atrocity in the USSR at the time, it was even possible to read the poem as an accusation of Ukrainian complicity in the murders. In addition there was fear that Yevtushenko's poem would foster divisive identity politics (a term nonexistent then) by focusing on one group of victims to the exclusion of the others. Thus Soviet officials were understandably worried about the popularity of this work, and despite Yevtushenko's insistence that his poem had been misinterpreted, after its initial publication in *Literaturnaia gazeta* it was not published again until 1983, and then with the addition of a footnote stating that Jews had not been the only victims.

The poem continued to reach audiences in another form, however. Dmitri Shostakovich, like Yevtushenko both a critical voice and a Soviet patriot, used five Yevtushenko poems, including ''Babii Yar,'' as the basis for his Thirteenth Symphony, which debuted in 1962 to enthusiastic crowds. For the next performance censors required that a few lines be changed to emphasize the Soviet victory over fascism. This was the only change ever required in the text, but hostile critics spun persistent rumors, either accusing Yevtushenko of anti-Soviet writing or conversely accusing the Soviet state of suppression of a great poet. Despite the poem's continuing ambiguity, Yevtushenko created that monument to Babii Yar whose absence he decries in its opening lines.

—Patricia Pollock Brodsky

BADENHEIM 1939 (Badenheim, 'ir nofesh)
Novel by Aharon Appelfeld, 1975

Published in Hebrew as *Badenheim, 'ir nofesh* in 1975 and in English five years later, *Badenheim 1939* established Aharon Appelfeld as an important, serious writer. This ''small masterpiece,'' as critic Irving Howe described it, introduced readers to Appelfeld's minimalist, controlled, restrained style, reminiscent of Franz Kafka not only in technique but also by the presence of a ubiquitous, oppressive, remote bureaucratic authority. Badenheim is an Austrian resort, high in the mountains, the summer home of middle-class assimilated Jews who had, in previous seasons, enjoyed its music festival. The summer population of Jews includes the spectrum of intellectuals, artists, entrepreneurs, merchants, and professionals that

Appelfeld recalled from his boyhood summers in similar spas: ''shockingly petit-bourgeois and idiotic in their formalities. Even as a child I saw how ridiculous they were.''

Local shopkeepers and hotel staff round out the panoply of Badenheim's residents, all of whom balk slightly at the arbitrary, incremental measures imposed on them by the Sanitation Department. These intrusions parallel the process that led to the Final Solution—first, identification through registration, then the isolation made visible by the barbed wire that transforms the resort into a ghetto and by the cessation of both telephone service and the distribution of food and medicine, and eventually deportation to the east. Stripped of all contact with the rest of the world, the Jews are left alone, paralyzed by circumstances that deceive and disable them. They create a semblance of their cultural life of previous summers and entertain one another unenthusiastically with concerts, poetry readings, endless intellectual and banal talk, and finally petty accusations and arguments about their Jewish identities. They try to interpret the severe edicts by concocting plausible reasons. Unable to relinquish their trust in rational thought and logic, they delude themselves and find excuses for optimism. They await the inevitable train to Poland, which some anticipate as a homecoming and others accept with resignation. Placing the novel in its historical reality, readers are well aware of the doom that awaits the Badenheimers, but Appelfeld allows his characters no such foreknowledge. This is, after all, 1939, a difficult time for all Jews but less so, some of the characters reason, for those who consciously and optimistically have molded themselves into the general, sophisticated non-Jewish culture of central Europe. By 1939, as Appelfeld so artistically portrays, there was no way out except surrender to the authorities or suicide, which both history and the novel demonstrate.

Appelfeld's Badenheim is dreamlike, with few but unmistakable concrete images that evoke the absurd: the prodigious supply of medicines of the pharmacist's wife that do not heal, the new fish in the aquarium that massacre other fish, dogs too weak to jump fences, pink ice cream and pastries that lull the summer visitors into self-deception. Irony pervades the novel, although there are no explicit or unambiguous references to the Nazis or the Holocaust. In an interview with **Philip Roth** in March 1988, Appelfeld explained his ahistoricity as an expression of his childlike, innocent memory of ''contact with . . . a kind of dark subconscious the meaning of which we did not know, nor do we know to this day . . . This world appears to be rational . . . but in fact these were journeys of the imagination, lies and ruses, which only deep, irrational drives could have invented. I didn't understand, nor do I yet understand the motives of the murderers.''

—Myrna Goldenberg

BENT
Play by Martin Sherman, 1979

Martin Sherman's *Bent,* first produced in Waterford, Connecticut, in 1978, dramatizes the Third Reich's incarceration and extermination of gay men. Set in its later scenes in Dachau, the play initially depicts a hilarious domestic farce that could occur in 1979 London or New York. Only when the SS burst in and murder the boyfriend of an SA leader do we recognize the date as the Night of the Long Knives (28 June 1934) and the place as Berlin.

The gay slaughter that occurred from 28 June to 3 July rid the Nazi leadership of homosexuals and put Heinrich Himmler, the virulent homophobe who ran the SS, into the top position under Hitler. Himmler's obsession with eradicating gay men underlies *Bent*'s action, which occurs between mid-1934 and late 1936, when the Nazis systematically persecuted, arrested, imprisoned, and killed them.

Following the arrival of the SS in their apartment, Max and Rudy run, but Max refuses to leave the country alone. Because of his loyalty, he's apprehended with Rudy. Frightened while on the train to Dachau into betraying Rudy in order to survive, Max denies knowing him, even hits him, contributing to Rudy's death. At Dachau Max meets Horst, who advises him on how to stay alive. Max reacts to what he learns by obtaining a yellow star rather than a pink triangle on his prison clothing because in 1936—still early in the Holocaust—his odds of survival in a concentration camp were slightly higher posing as a Jew.

At Dachau Max works one of his deals to get Horst assigned to move rocks with him. When they first carry out their repetitive, pointless task together, they argue. Then they joke. Then, in a section of the play written in a minimalist style reminiscent of Beckett, they begin to fall in love and learn to have sex merely by talking to each other, since they cannot touch. Sherman daringly employs sex as rebellion against fascism and assertion of simple human dignity; this coup de théâtre challenges bigots who watch it to embrace the human right to ''pursue life, liberty and the pursuit of happiness.''

Horst acknowledges his love for Max, saying it gives him a reason to live. Max, consumed by guilt and self-contempt, tells Horst not to love him because he can't return Horst's love and ''Queers aren't meant to love.'' Indeed, he insists Horst should hate him. But slowly Max begins to learn tenderness and selflessness, and he suggests he and Horst can one day have a life together in Berlin. Shortly after that birth of hope, the SS captain orders Horst to electrocute himself on the fence. Horst signals that he loves Max, then chooses to attack the captain and be shot. Rather than die passively, he resists.

When ordered to dispose of the corpse, Max holds Horst for the first time and also for the first time tells Horst he loves him. Few dramatic scenes pack such power, as Max continues to carry rocks, counts to 10 (as he did in the parallel scene in the first act), then jumps into the pit of bodies and comes out of the closet by removing Horst's jacket and donning it. Now, finally wearing a pink triangle, Max defies his captors by choosing to run onto the fence and die. Not a despairing suicide but an act of embracing his identity and asserting his courage, it shows his denials and deals put too high a price on survival. Max has grown enormously.

Bent dramatizes themes of cowardice and courage, betrayal and loyalty, deception and truth-telling, self-contempt and self-respect, love and hatred. Above all it indicts bigotry that demonizes outsiders, and it depicts the struggle by the persecuted to survive or to defy those who dehumanize others. The play proves universally moving and speaks to contemporary atrocities against the "other"—whether it be slaughter in Kosovo or the devastation wrought by extremists pursuing an Islamic jihad against the United States.

Theaters in such world capitals as Tokyo, Paris, Athens, and London have repeatedly presented Sherman's Holocaust masterpiece. Productions have occurred in some 40 countries around the globe; everywhere it has sent spectators home crying. London's Royal National Theatre named it an NT 2000 play—that is, one of the most important dramas of the twentieth century. The 1997 film version, financed largely by Japanese investors, had its world premiere in Tokyo after winning the coveted Prix de Jeunesse at Cannes. Sir Ian McKellan, who starred as Max in London in 1979 and 1990, recalls Jewish Holocaust survivors stopping him to display numbers burned onto their arms, share their memories, and praise this harrowing play. Sherman's iconic work brought to public consciousness the Nazis' oppression and murder of gay men and made the pink triangle a universal gay symbol.

—Tish Dace

BIEDERMANN AND THE FIRE RAISERS: A MORALITY WITHOUT A MORAL (Biedermann und die Brandstifter: Eine Lehrstück ohne Lehre, mit einem Nachspiel)
Play by Max Frisch, 1958

The play *The Firebugs* was written in several stages, first appearing in Max Frisch's *Sketchbook 1946–1949*. In the entry under the title *Burleske*, he recorded the first version, beginning with: "One morning a man comes to your house, a stranger, and you cannot help yourself, you give him a plate of soup and some bread. For the injustice he has suffered according to his own account, cannot be denied, and you don't wish him to take it out on you. And there is no doubt, the man says, that he will one day have his revenge . . ." In the first completed prose version, a radio play completed in 1952 and published in 1955, Biedermann is portrayed more as a capitalist exploiter than in the final stage version, *Biedermann and the*

Firebugs: A Learning Play without a Lesson (U.K. title, *Biedermann and the Fire Raisers: A Morality without a Moral*, published in 1962), which premiered on 29 March 1958, at the Zurich Schauspielhaus.

The protagonist in the play is the hair-lotion manufacturer Gottlieb Biedermann, a middle-class, small capitalist, who wants to be considered by the world as a kind man although he has driven his employee, who has provided him with the successful formula for his business, into suicide. Biedermann lets two vagrants, actually arsonists, into his house. He feeds them and lets them sleep in the attic, where they store gasoline canisters. Although the two terrorists actually tell Biedermann the truth about themselves, he does not believe them, and when they become overly demanding, he is too much of a coward to throw them out of his house. When asked, he even gives them matches with which they ignite the canisters and burn down not only Biedermann's house but the whole town, setting in motion an armageddon.

Biedermann does not want to see the truth, although it is literally driven home to him, and in that he is reminiscent of the German attitude toward Adolf Hitler, who clearly laid out his intentions to wipe out the Jews in *Mein Kampf* and in his speeches. Hitler's contemporaries did not take him and his threats against the Jews seriously; their naive disregard ultimately led to the Holocaust, which even the intellectuals did not foresee. This last point is indicated in the words of the doctor who was intent on improving the world, but who misjudged the murderous activity of the terrorists.

The impossibility of preventing or reversing the tragedy is evident in the lines of the chorus, which informs the audience of the morality of the play without a moral and also that the happenings are not inevitable fate but brought on by the people themselves: "For arson, once kindled, / Kills many. / Leaves few, / And accomplishes nothing. . . Fate—so they call it!"

—Gerd K. Schneider

BITTER HERBS: A LITTLE CHRONICLE (Het bittere Kruid: Een kleine Kroniek)
Novel by Marga Minco, 1957

In most of her writings Marga Minco returns, to a greater or lesser extent, to the period of the German occupation of her native Holland (1940–45). Her experiences of this time are central to her first novel, *Bitter Herbs* (1960; *Het bittere Kruid*, 1957), which consists of 21 chapters and an epilogue. Each chapter is devoted to one event or one aspect of life under the Germans. The epilogue is set in the postwar period and poignantly states the difficulty many survivors had in coming to terms with the loss of family.

The first-person narrator, who is never named and whose age is never given, begins with the return of her Jewish family who, along with everyone else in their community, had fled when the Germans invaded in May of 1940. Back in their hometown, they meet other returnees and briefly discuss the situation. Offhand comments reveal differing reactions: some have left The Netherlands for France, as yet not under German control; some feel that the German presence will be brief; and others are more pessimistic. The narrator's father shows no great concern. Life, he feels, will go on more or less as before, so why worry?

Other chapters describe the relatively benign anti-Semitism that Jews in The Netherlands experienced in their communities, along with the anti-Jewish measures introduced by the Germans almost on a daily basis. The narrator misses much of what happened in the early period of the occupation because of a sickness and lengthy hospital stay. With her return to the community, she is shocked by the changes that have occurred. Her family, however, shows little concern. Even when Jews are forced to wear the Star of David, they accept the measure with, for the most part, no great apprehension. The father buys more than are needed, and the mother sees that they are sewn on neatly. Only the narrator's brother seems a little worried—he would like to remain "normal."

Minco describes the reactions to each new measure, each fresh development. Dave, the brother, resorts to the contents of a mysterious bottle to render him temporarily unfit for labor when he is obliged to report for a medical examination. Fearing separation, they, along with many other Jews, have family portraits taken as a reminder of times when they were together. Gradually families disappear, either through deportation or because they go underground. The narrator's sister is caught in a *razzia* (raid), and the rest of the family begins to pack and acquire useful objects for their own impending deportation. Suitcases and certain rooms in their apartment are sealed, but still the father remains optimistic. The ghetto will be like a large parish, he believes. Jews will be together as one united community. Dave and the narrator have medical certificates and remain in their pajamas throughout the day to appear ill should they unexpectedly receive official visitors. Non-Jewish "friends" turn up and ask whether they might have this possession or that, because, after all, Jews are not going to be able to keep such objects. The parents, over the age of 50, are forced to move to the ghetto in Amsterdam. One day the narrator decides to cast off her pajamas, remove her yellow star, and visit them. In the ghetto she is forced to hide as a roundup takes place. Meanwhile the Sabbath is celebrated and some semblance of normal Jewish life continues, even as the family's fear begins to grow, and they are accosted in the street by sinister men seeking out individuals for arrest and transportation. Finally, they are sought out by the authorities. The narrator escapes and at last goes underground, staying in a series of safe houses arranged by the resistance. After liberation she discovers that her parents, brother, and sister have perished. The narrator encounters an uncle who waits at a tram stop on a daily basis, convinced that his brother is about to return. He does so in vain but continues his vigil until, grief stricken, he dies.

Minco's style throughout is sober and understated. Sentences are short, description is minimal, and many details are omitted—the reader is expected to fill them in. Chapters often revolve around a central image: a child's toy top figures prominently in one chapter. It is crushed by a German truck and, at the end of the chapter, a little girl cries over her broken toy. Minco does not graphically describe how her family disappears. Often there is simply a report by a third person or an allusion with no mention of name. The growing fear of the narrator's parents is also not stated but is patent by virtue of their actions and responses. *Bitter Herbs*—the title alludes to the ceremony in which the youngest in a family asks why they eat unleavened bread and bitter herbs and is then told the story of the Exodus from Egypt—is, as the subtitle states, "a little chronicle." It is also a very effective, understated account of how a Jew survived in the occupied Netherlands.

—David Scrase

BLOOD FROM THE SKY (Le Sang du ciel)
Novel by Piotr Rawicz, 1961

In Piotr Rawicz's novel *Le Sang du ciel* (1961), published in English translation as *Blood from the Sky* in 1964, the precariousness of survival for a Jew in Europe during World War II is presented in a series of stream-of-consciousness vignettes that take place in the Ukraine and in Paris. Rawicz reveals the difficulties and challenges of his hero, Boris, trying to pass as a Gentile in Paris: "A jumble of distinctive gestures handed down from our forefathers and resuscitated by our life in the walled-up town seemed the greatest threat to our survival: relics of sign language, fugitive expressions of the people around us . . ." Boris finds on the ground a birth certificate of a Ukrainian named Yuri Goletz and decides to pass as a Ukrainian nationalist:

"I had thus swapped races, bartering one that for thirty centuries had regarded itself as Chosen for another that had been harboring a similar belief for only some thirty years. Both had been molded, sculpted, chiseled out of sufferings vaster and richer than those endured by the races around them. In different degrees, I was indifferent to the destiny of neither. But the second, with its Cossack past, its traditions of life in the steppes, its sad songs and incomparable landscapes, was joining in the task undertaken by the invader of exterminating my own people. The masquerade that we were enacting had a particular flavor to it: from a slave doomed to immediate cremation I was turning into a slave who assisted and vindicated the fine attendant in his task.''

After his arrest Boris's circumcised penis reveals him to be a Jew: ''The ripped trouser-fly reveals the bluish penis. On it, the sign of the Covenant is inscribed in indelible lettering, all too easy for these bustling men to read.'' Nonetheless, Boris does not abandon his uncompromising effort to cling to life: ''Since he persisted in denying his origins, he was transferred to another cell—this one inhabited by people who were not doomed to immediate extermination.''

An examination by a Nazi Ukrainian intellectual, Professor Humeniek, leads to the conclusion that Boris is not a Jew: ''As I said politically I wouldn't trust him an inch. A pernicious character, on quite the wrong side of the fence. But he isn't a Jew. No question of that. He speaks our language too well, he knows too much about our history, our literature, our way of life . . .'' Boris then explains away his Jewish ritual circumcision by claiming that it was an operation to cure a penile infection.

Central to Boris's survival are his strength and fortitude in resisting torture during interrogation. In an effort to break down his will, electrical current is run through a steel ring around his penis:

> ''Whoever is interrogating you sits down at his desk and runs his finger over a button. Obviously, however much you are affecting indifference, you can't help looking at him. For his part, he doesn't look at you: only at the button. The moment he moves his finger toward it, you screw up all your strength: I must resist, I will resist! You clothe yourself in anticipation, in your thickest armor. You bid agony come, and set it nought. He can pluck the living heart from me and I won't cry out, I won't confess to anything. I'll pull through. You have summoned all your resources: huge they are, haughty as a mountain.''

The book is permeated with the will to resist death at all costs, even when the Nazis are knocking at the door. Rawicz shows how even the slightest coincidence can prolong a tenuous hold on life under the most hostile of circumstances. His description of the effort to hold on to life even in the face of death reveals his belief in the sanctity of human life.

—Peter R. Erspamer

THE BOOK OF QUESTIONS (Le Livre des questions)
Miscellany by Edmond Jabès, 1963–73

The Book of Questions is the masterpiece of Edmond Jabès. Written from 1963 to 1973, this magnum opus encompasses the Jewish experience in its essence. It is a text that is extremely difficult to read, especially in translation, offering the reader discontinued and disparate sets of short stories, quotations, monologues, dialogues, poems, aphorisms, dedications, some graphisms, and isolated sentences. There is no evident plot or development, simply the presence of recurring voices and addressees. The addressees bear such symbolic names as Yukel, Yaël, Elya, and Aely, all variations on the name of God, or El, the heading of the last book: (*El, or The last book*). This heading is explained by a quotation from the cabala: ''God, El, to reveal Himself, manifested Himself by a period.''

A poet of exile and the desert, Jabès tries to create a space of meditation rather than a continuous telling. The only place where man can find solace is in ''The Book,'' the one each of us is invited to write in our own silence. Jabès's text is, by definition, an open book where all can find their own space. The search for silence as a source of knowledge and the power of silence to create a space of creativity for the reader is at the heart of this writing. As music is the silence between notes, so the blank space between the words is the true story. Like the Jew, defined by his millennia of wandering with no rest or peace, reading here is defined as a long search for meaning that can only be guessed at rather than secured as a certainty. Always fluctuating, the word cannot be trusted to transfer meaning adequately, and to stop at its graphism is to limit oneself to a superficial reading of the world. Words are simply indexes of something else, and only by dismantling our reading habits can we be made aware of their fragility. We are thus invited to create another, more personal version of the world.

The question is by far the most prevalent means by which Jabès confronts the world and the word. While a question may be expressed in words, the answer does not necessarily require expression; the essential answers concerning the human condition and our relation to the world do need to be expressed in words but can be felt intimately in the soul. Indeed, the attempt to express them is only restrictive. The question is important, but the silence of the answer is more revealing and, ultimately, a path to the discovery of the self. Jabès asks the questions; we, the readers, answer, each in our own way. The text is only a starting point, the very beginning of a long process of self-improvement.

While the word ''El'' is present throughout the text, it refers ultimately to silence and is used as a focal point for meditation that is, in many ways, deeply atheistic: God is present in His negation. Man's search must progress through questions; as such, the exegetic study of the Torah, a deep hermeneutic process without definite answers, provides the best example and guide. Transcendence can exist only in the word; the questioning of God is the essential questioning of the Word: thus the Book is the World.

Just as the most elaborate rabbinical commentaries barely skim the meaning of the Torah, so our understanding of the word/world is barely a shadowing of "The Letter." Yet like the rabbis who remain totally devoted to the Book, we must spend our existence in a feeble and limited attempt to grasp, in an intuitive way, the way of existence. *The Book of Questions* uses the traditional enthymemic system of Jewish heritage: the mind is invited to wander among the words and allow imagination to flower so long as it preserves a connection with the primal text. That link can be very loose and may not obey rational logic. This approach allows for the free association of images and concepts and encourages us to think across time and space and unite what seems to be distant. In that movement we can join the elders of the tradition and, ultimately, the prophets and patriarchs. From this perspective Jabès's books become an anthology of Jewish thinking and mysticism and a guide for fruitful meditation.

—Alain Goldschlager

BREAD FOR THE DEPARTED (Chleb rzucony umarlym)
Novel by Bogdan Wojdowski, 1971

Bogdan Wojdowski's extensive novel *Bread for the Departed,* published in English translation in 1997, covers a strictly limited period of time. The book starts with the formal establishment of the Warsaw Ghetto and ends with the Nazi deportation of the Jewish inhabitants numbering 300,000 in September 1942. The novel is considered important in the world of literature for its comprehensive and reliable account of the specific historical events and its elaborate artistic composition. The principal character of the book, David Fremde, a son to an upholsterer, Jakow, is of the same age as Wojdowski was in his days in the ghetto. Wojdowski's father, Szymon Jakub Wojdowski, ran a carpentry shop on the corner of Srebrna and Towarowa streets, and David was the author's real name. Those autobiographical allusions reinforce the general expression of the novel. The arrangement of the book offers a panorama of the ghetto community divided along economic, professional, and social lines—from the Jewish elite to poor craftsmen to thieves and wretched prostitutes.

The wide perspective of the novel determines its composition. There is no uniform plot over a few hundred pages. The book is episodic with snapshot presentations of various groups of people living in the minor ghetto. The jargon they speak is far from grammatical by Polish, German, and Yiddish standards. Wojdowski aims at rendering the ghetto reality as exactly as he remembers it from his childhood. Therefore, innumerable instances of human degradation caused by brutal repression, the increasingly intensive hunger, and the decimating diseases abound in the book, so naturalistic and drastic in detail. The writer neither endorses nor condemns the human acts dismissed abhorrently by the Nazi propaganda as "Juden, Lause, Fleckfieber" ("Jews, lice, typhus"). And by no means does he approve of reducing a humiliated Jew to animal instincts and a merciless fight for bread to stay alive at any price. That is evident due to the unrealistic features of Wojdowski's poetics applied in the narrative, which makes the book a special kind of prose focused on a narrow group of people, a historically biographical documentary and a poetic requiem for the victims of the Warsaw Ghetto.

Bread for the Departed places spiritual values in two planes—in the principal character's psychic, in his dreams and fantastic associations, and in feverish David's somnambular lyricism. David's personal data is clearly symbolic. His surname Fremde stands for a foreigner, an alien. And the origin of his forename can be traced to another source of religious beliefs—to the Bible. That was also where the Jewish faith, and not only it, originated from. Wojdowski took the opening sentence for his ghetto epic from the Bible. This introductory utterance brings to David's memory the reminiscence of his father's prayers and of the happy days they had lived before their captivity in the ghetto. Then the Holocaust began. The patriarch of the family, the most pious one of all, has the child taken away from his parents and sent to the Aryan side of the wall. He also instructs David, "Forget you are Jewish. You must forget to stay alive . . . Live a wild dog's life. Skirt away people but go on living . . . Forget who you are. Forget who your father and mother are. Forget who your grandparents were . . . You must have a heart of stone." The grandson finds that desperate advice as a curse of an old man dying of starvation. And this is not the only curse to be found in the novel. David's father is even more blasphemous arguing with God, "Jakow, Jakow. Where are you? . . . I am here. I am dying therefore I am."

With Wojdowski neither the Bible nor René Descartes's rationalistic philosophy can account for the cause and the scale of innocent Jews' suffering. The logic of faith is hopeless when faced with the reality of Shoah. Wojdowski, who is making repeated references to the Holy Books and Judaic history, is quite aware that drawing any analogy between Gomorrah and the ghetto is groundless. Also interpreting the present Jewish tragedy in terms of religious guilt and punishment is futile. Nevertheless both the writer and the victims of the Nazi extermination are haunted by the same nagging question, "Why should they have been killed, forsaken by the indifferent world?" The same passionate determination to find the answer is revealed in *The World of Stone* (1948), a collection of stories by **Tadeusz Borowski,** and in *And the World Remained Silent* (1956), a literary interpretation of the Auschwitz experience by **Elie Wiesel.**

The title of Wojdowski's novel can be understood both realistically and symbolically. On the real side there is an authentic event when German soldiers shoot dead a Polish tram driver who secretly delivered bread to starving Jews in the ghetto. The symbolic aspect needs a confrontation with *What I Read to the Dead,* a narrative by **Wladyslaw Szlengel,** who was killed in 1943. In this sense "the dead" describes figuratively the condition of the captives living in the Warsaw Ghetto. And the book itself becomes a voice from beyond the grave calling out to the readers.

Wojdowski goes another way. He himself was saved from extermination, and after years he preserves the memory of those exterminated. His novel symbolically keeps them alive just as bread kept alive the ghetto inhabitants. The two books differ fundamentally for the stands their authors assume. Szlengel wrote his *What I Read to the Dead* in the ghetto, and that made him assume a victim's perspective. Wojdowski enjoyed liberty writing *Bread for the Departed,* and therefore his perspective was that of a witness to the Holocaust. That determined his literary strategy. Naturally it became a Jewish survivor's obligation to testify to the Holocaust and reproach the world for the suffering of millions of the victims of Hitler's Nazi ideology.

Wojdowski's autobiographical story breaks in autumn 1942, before the heroic uprising of the Jewish insurgents on 13 April 1943 followed by the final liquidation of the ghetto. The Jewish uprising became a literary theme for *The Holy Week* (1945) by Jerzy Andrzejewski and *Easter* (1947) by **Adolf Rudnicki.** *Bread for the Departed* is closely related in subject matter to *A Man with a Cart* (1961) by Stanisław Wygodzki and *A Merchant of Lodz* (1963) by Rudnicki. These two novels give a realistic and expressive relation of how life looked in the ghettos of Będzin and Lodz. Wojdowski, Rudnicki, and Wygodzki's stylistics are poles apart with that of *The Liberal's Death* (1947) by Artur Sandauer, an ironic-grotesque story of a Jewish intellectual in a ghetto in the former Polish eastern borderlands.

Wojdowski's novel seems the most closely related to *The Empty Water* (1964), an autobiographical book by Krystyna Żywulska, who survived the ghetto and Auschwitz pretending to be Aryan. Żywulska's novel, less elaborate in its composition, deals with similar episodes of the ghetto anguish and the same torturers.

Wojdowski made use of his predecessors' literary achievements, but he retained his individual character no matter what he exploited—the aesthetic standards of realism, lyrical pathos, or the style of elegy and prayer. His continuous inclination toward pursuing the Holocaust experience was further confirmed in his later collections of stories. *A Little Man, a Dumb Bird, a Cage and the World* (1975; *Mały człowieczek, niemę ptaszę, klatka i świat*) is a lyrical counterpart of his remarkable novel. His later narratives of the 1970s and '80s touch the same questions of the Jewish tragedy and reveal

Wojdowski's predilection for the parabolic composition. This is a general tendency of Holocaust literature with an individual experience being translated into a universal one and becoming archetypal.

—Stanisław Gawliński

A BRIGHT ROOM CALLED DAY
Play by Tony Kushner, 1991

Written and first produced Off-Off-Broadway in 1985, *A Bright Room Called Day* was Tony Kushner's New York debut. In 1991 it received a major production in New York City at the Joseph Papp Public Theatre, where it was critically lambasted. Though the critics more favorably received other productions in San Francisco and Chicago, the play has been frequently dismissed because of an Adolf Hitler-Ronald Reagan equation that has continued to discomfort many critics.

The play, in two parts, focuses on a group of friends in Berlin from 1 January 1932 to 12 November 1933, during which the Nazi Party secured its power in Germany. The friends, made up of leftists, artists, and refugees, congregate in Agnes's apartment, seeking safety and security. Agnes, Paulinka, and Husz all work in the film industry while Annabella makes her living as a graphic designer and Baz, openly homosexual, works at the Berlin Institute for Human Sexuality. Over the course of the play, they see their hopes for a socialist Germany collapse and their friendships tattered by their fears and denials over what is happening in their country. By the end of the play, Agnes, alone among her friends, refuses to flee the country, preferring to remain ensconced in her room, afraid of what is taking place in the outside world.

Throughout the play there are eight "Interruptions," so called because the play's chronological narrative is broken into by Zillah, a contemporary Jewish American woman. Her interruptions attempt to draw the focus on this group of powerless individuals in 1930s Germany into a parallel with the play's current audience. In the mid-1980s to early 1990s, Kushner angrily perceived the moral abandonment and surrender by the American leftist intelligentsia to the rightward lurch of American politics in the Ronald Reagan/George Bush years. Writing the play, Kushner watched as the American Left and the media withdrew from protesting as the Reagan/Bush administrations oversaw an illegal war against a popularly elected government in Nicaragua, attempted to dismantle many governmental social services that assist the poor and the disenfranchised, traded arms for hostages with America's enemies, ignored the growing epidemic of AIDS, and fractured the country's economy with irresponsible tax cuts and overspending on the military. This moral abandonment Kushner has likened to the failure of the German Left to rise up against the Nazis, even as he took pains within the text as well as in his published afterword to acknowledge that it was not an exact parallel. In Zillah he has created a dramatic Jeremiah for the times, accosting each audience and demanding that they see themselves mirrored in what Kushner described as the ineffectual decency of Agnes and her friends.

Kushner's postmodern dramaturgy utilized an array of styles, most notably realism and a form of expressionism mixed with a medieval morality argument. This latter style occurred with the uses of two other characters in the play. The first character is Die Alte, an elderly woman of indeterminate age who appears suddenly in Agnes's apartment at odd and alarming moments, claiming that she once lived there, but who appears to be currently homeless. Each time she appears through the window, indicating that she lives on the fire escape, and each time she demands rolls to eat.

The second character, seen once only in the final scene of Part One, is Satan, introduced as Herr Swetts, an exporter from Hamburg. Husz, a Hungarian cinematographer who has lost an eye during the communist revolt in 1919, suddenly admits to his friends that he can conjure the Devil and does. Herr Swetts appears sickly, almost asthmatic, until he delivers an extraordinarily powerful monologue cataloging his years in the European wilderness, culminating in a resurgence of strength and confidence as his position is restored in the world. As he exits, Agnes, who has been unable to utter a word during this display, finally finds her voice, but all she can utter is a polite and friendly welcome to Germany.

Rather than confront the Holocaust in the more familiar terms of earlier writers, Kushner focused his study on the fears, the excuses, the petty tyrannies and jealousies, and the denials that the German Left offered as its excuse for inaction and political fragmentation. Kushner was less concerned with remembering the events as history and more committed to a historical narrative that would connect to a contemporary American audience and force them to examine their own complicity in the general and wholesale overturning of the American progressive social agenda in place since the Depression. Some critics have faulted Kushner for manipulating the facts and the emotions of the Holocaust to express his outrage over the U.S. government's handling of the AIDS epidemic. But Kushner's spirited defense of his using the Holocaust as the established parameter of evil in categorizing society's current ills can be persuasive, and his questions regarding the German Left are both legitimate and insightful.

—Steven Dedalus Burch

BRONSTEIN'S CHILDREN (Bronsteins Kinder)
Novel by Jurek Becker, 1986

In his 1976 novel *Der Boxer* (''The Boxer''), Jurek Becker introduces a father and son, both Holocaust survivors, who are reunited in East Berlin. The novel portrays their struggles to rebuild their lives together and depicts the ultimate failure of their relationship due to factors—including the Holocaust—that neither of them understands.

In 1986 Becker published another novel about a father and his children. Some of the characters in these two novels and many of their difficulties are similar, but the latter novel, *Bronsteins Kinder* (translated in 1988 as *Bronstein's Children),* is set in the 1970s and focuses more on the still lingering effects of the Holocaust. Indeed, while the text does refer to contemporary events in East Berlin (where it is set), the context which shapes the text and the members of the Bronstein family is the Holocaust. Even though the story takes place almost 30 years after the war, the characters cannot overcome the grip of their past, and the ways in which they deal with this past form the thematic core of the text.

The father, Arno Bronstein, and his daughter, Elle, are Holocaust survivors. The son, Hans, was born after the war. Arno and Hans live together, while Elle is confined to an institution. Hans Bronstein, who is just about to begin his university studies, is the first-person narrator of *Bronstein's Children.* For much of Hans' childhood, his family's past and their Jewishness has played only a marginal role. When he arrives at his family's forest cottage to set the scene for an illicit rendezvous with his girlfriend, Martha, however, he discovers his father and two of his father's friends in the house along with a fourth man whom they are holding captive. He learns that the three captors, all elderly concentration camp survivors, have tracked down a former camp guard and are holding and interrogating him.

The text alternates between two strands. One relates the discovery of the guard's captivity and Hans's attempts to decide how to react to this discovery. The other follows Hans in the subsequent year as he continues to work through the experience and the events stemming from it. After encountering the tortured and bruised body of the guard, Hans begins to gain new insight into the deep, yet easily-hidden scars the Holocaust has left on his father. With the additional information he gains through discussions and arguments with his father, Elle, Martha, and others, Hans is forced for the first time to take an active role in tracing his own identity as a Jew and a German.

While Jewish characters in Becker's earlier novels, such as *Jakob the Liar* and *Der Boxer* were all direct victims of Nazi persecution during the Holocaust, with Hans we meet a character who is Jewish but is not a Holocaust survivor. While survivors in those earlier texts could be grouped together based on their common suffering and the common historical bond, *Bronstein's Children* asks whether succeeding generations can also be included in such a group, since they were not directly involved in the Holocaust. Ever since the publication of *Jakob the Liar,* when Becker was forced to comment on his own Jewishness, Becker had been opposed to such categorization. And, of course, the notion of categorization was of great importance in Germany after World War II not only for Jews but also for non-Jews in Germany who were confronted with questions of collective guilt for the Holocaust.

In *Bronstein's Children*, various characters in Hans's life attempt to categorize him, often presenting him with only two options: you are either with us or you are against us. Hans rejects such simple, objective, and often polarized options, and chooses instead to search for more flexible, subjective possibilities marked by multiplicity.

Around the time that the novel was published, prominent historian Jürgen Habermas wrote a series of essays that included criticism of those who would limit the possibilities for historical interpretation. Hans's resistance to the prescribed roles he is offered echoes Habermas's criticism. In his own awkward way, Hans seeks to position himself critically within the ambivalences of the historical traditions and discourses in which he is situated. His story begins a process in which he may work toward the kind of nuanced and pluralistic notion of identity that Habermas advocates—a sense of identity based not on symbols or denial but instead on a critical confrontation with and examination of the past. Becker's novel is, then, a call for a more nuanced examination of the way both Jewish and non-Jewish Germans deal with and live with their history, and especially with the Holocaust.

—Gregory Baer

BRUDER EICHMANN
Play by Heinar Kipphardt, 1983

During Adolf Eichmann's imprisonment a young police officer who had been charged to look after his emotional well-being lent Eichmann a copy of *Lolita,* which had been translated into German a few years before. Greatly offended, Eichmann handed the book back to his young warden two days later: "Das ist aber ein sehr unerfreuliches Buch!" (This is a thoroughly unpleasant book!). Hannah Arendt, who cites the episode, quotes it to support the notion expressed by the prison psychiatrists that Eichmann's inability to talk in anything but bureaucratic clichés showed him to be a perfectly normal specimen and that his utter dependence on officialese should be interpreted as a "positive" side of his character. Of course, it also demonstrates what has itself become a commonplace: that mass murderers can be very prudish family men.

It is a pity that Heinar Kipphardt omits this anecdote from his last docudrama, *Bruder Eichmann* ("Brother Eichmann"). But Eichmann's vis-à-vis, the pretrial interrogator Avner Less, would have acted totally out of character—and the thrust of the whole play would have been blunted—had he allowed himself to get personal with his cliché expert. We have Less's word

that Eichmann's presence filled him with loathing during his 260 hours in the man's company, but Less's revulsion is wholly irrelevant to the drama. Kipphardt's Less neither loathes nor likes the man in the glass booth. Before his trial got under way, Eichmann had expressed the desire to tell his story; Less listened and asked questions. The entire action, as somebody once groused, revolves around two chain-smokers facing each other across a wooden table and talking into a tape recorder. At one point Less breaks through the sound barrier and mentions parenthetically that his family had been gassed; Eichmann professes to be honestly horrified. Beyond this Less treats the entire proceedings as strictly professional, at most offering his client a smoke once he observes that cigarettes sharpen his powers of concentration and boost his already highly developed volubility.

But after weeks of this, Kipphardt's Less finds it increasingly difficult to maintain his distance. He flatters Eichmann by telling him that among the guards Eichmann's fortress has come to be known as "Eichmannigrad" (Eichmann: "Eichmannigrad, Donnerwetter!"); Less begins to scream at him, "Cain! Cain! Cain! Monster! Jew Killer!"; in a brief scene cast in the form of a soliloquy, Less concludes that "the monster, it seems, is the ordinary functional man, who oils every machine and is out to improve himself," and that if Eichmann is the model bureaucrat so is he. In what is perhaps the most quoted line in the play, he bursts out, "In these months we are getting horrifyingly close." This, not only for Less but also for most intelligent readers, is the point at which the drama (however docu) parts radically from the biographical actuality—and from narrative logic. Less himself found Kipphardt's thesis so offensive that he entered a sharply worded objection entitled "So war es nicht!" ("That's Not How It Was!"), and after the first performances he was fitted out with a different name. Less would have taken special exception to a production in Weimar, in which each of nine actors who portrayed Eichmann in nine different scenes assumed the role of Less in the scene that followed, as if Less and Eichmann were interchangeable items of mortality. I add that the two solitary chain-smokers remain at it only in the first part of the play. In the second part the cell fills up with a (fictitious) woman psychiatrist (who, however, has already sounded out Eichmann in the first part), the prison commander Ofer, and a Canadian clergyman and his wife. These people serve to convey something of Eichmann's emotional and religious vita, even, or especially, when he lies, and he lies almost uninterruptedly.

By the time Kipphardt's play appeared, Eichmann, thanks largely to his seedy looks in court, had long ceased to be demonized. **Simon Wiesenthal** thought that "he looked like a bookkeeper who is afraid to ask for a raise," and Robert Servatius, Eichmann's lawyer, used still more derogatory language. Kipphardt goes a step further: given certain conditions, we all have it in us to assume "the Eichmann position," the position, that is, of functional man, a frighteningly average specimen whom time and routine have taught to surrender his conscience to the head boss and to do simply what he is told. (This, of course, was Eichmann's own *plaidoyer,* and in his preface to transcripts of the interrogation Less convicts himself out of his own mouth—and assumes the Eichmann position—by admitting that he took on his distasteful job only "because somebody had to do it.") To make his point, Kipphardt peppers the play with what have been its most embattled parts, "analogical scenes" in which the Eichmann position and its consequences keep surfacing elsewhere in the recent past. These include film sequences of atomic explosions followed by the testimony of a Nagasaki survivor, a toddler reciting an anti-Semitic parody of Goethe's "Wanderers Nachtlied" from the pages of Julius Streicher's *Der Stürmer,* Ariel Sharon reporting on the prospect of a military solution to the PLO, plus the testimony by a Palestinian woman, a survivor of Sabra and Shatila. The analogies do not bear much scrutiny, if only because both functionary and situation differ, sometimes radically, from Eichmann and his hobbyhorse. As all of these atrocities were hatched by the Western powers, it is no wonder that *Bruder Eichmann* fared singularly well in East Germany.

Most objectionable is the comment by the attending clergyman in his curtain speech that the ovenlike structure in which Eichmann's corpse has been placed and the rails leading to it remind him of nothing so much as the photos of crematoria in the death camps. The final lines of the play—"Standing at the railing, we watched as Ofer solemnly opened the container and from the stern of the boat slowly poured the ashes into the swirling waters"—suggest that Eichmann literally embodied the Holocaust, the sacrificial burnt offering that purifies. Kipphardt's play is powerful enough to sustain these macabre identifications, but perhaps the ultimate answer to the heresy that we are all Eichmanns-*in-posse* ("evil lurks in the heart of man") has been most succinctly expressed by **Primo Levi**: "I do not know, and it does not much interest me to know, whether in my depths there lurks a murderer, but I do know that I was a guiltless victim and I was not a murderer."

—Edgar Rosenberg

BURNED CHILD SEEKS THE FIRE: MEMOIR
(Bränt barn söker sig till elden)
Memoir by Cordelia Edvardson, 1984

Cordelia Edvardson's *Memoir,* as it is subtitled, is more than what is normally meant by that word. It originally appeared in Swedish in 1984, in German two years later, and in English in 1997. It is, to be sure, an account of the noteworthy experiences of its author, but it is also a deep and penetrating self-appraisal by the author of her character and psyche within the framework of the Holocaust and its aftermath.

Although Edvardson does so in a sober and almost understated way, she reveals in an economical but eloquent fashion all that is pertinent to her own particular experience and her own problematic development. She spells out the essential elements of her memoir in the short first chapter: an outsider—different, singled out, with a deep guilt complex—is clearly of Christian heritage but has a Jewish father; her mother is a writer whose works are suffused with myth. The myth of Proserpina, or Persephone, who was abducted by Pluto, taken to the underworld, and able to return to the world only periodically—thus giving rise to the seasons—is alluded to throughout the memoir. The relevance of this myth to the fate of Cordelia Edvardson is obvious.

Edvardson's situation is, however, even more complicated than it seems at the outset of the book. Her biography, reflected to be sure in her memoir, is essential for an understanding of the work. Her mother was Elisabeth Langgässer (1899–1950), a prominent poet and novelist loosely connected with the German school of magic realism. Langgässer, the illegitimate child of a Rhenish, Roman Catholic mother and a married Jewish father, grew up as a practicing Roman Catholic. When she was 29 years old, Langgässer in turn gave birth to an illegitimate child, Cordelia. The father was likewise Jewish, and Cordelia was likewise raised as a Catholic. Like many others, Cordelia was soon forced to come to terms with her status first as a "mixed breed" then later as a *Volljüdin* ("full Jew"), as the Gestapo decreed. Her experiences as a child in Berlin, in the German school she was soon forced to leave, in the Jewish school she then attended, in forced labor, and in the camps (including Theresienstadt and Auschwitz) are all described in this book. They are, however, not described in lurid detail, but soberly, and always with an explanation of the effects on the child's human growth, on her scorched psyche. Although, in essence, not truly Jewish, Edvardson was obliged through her ordeal to become Jewish; hence, the title transforms the German proverb, "a burned child avoids the fire" into the "burned child *seeks* the fire." Given the ovens of the Holocaust, the title is, of course, all too apt.

Edvardson was a precocious child, and her mother fed her a rich diet of serious literature, including her own novels and poems, together with fairy tales and myths. Her use of language, and of literary and mythic references, reflects this upbringing. Like **Jiri Weil** and **Marga Minco**, Edvardson became a journalist. It was, in part, her journalist experiences that helped to establish a new, truly Jewish identity that became complete and permanent at the time of the Six-Day War, which she covered for a Swedish newspaper. Her writings were all in Swedish, not her native German. One might readily understand that coming to terms with her native land is at least as fraught with difficulty as was her acceptance of her Jewish identity. The book's dedication is eloquent in its brevity: "To my mothers / Elisabeth Langgässer, Berlin / Stefi Pedersen, Stockholm / Sylvia Krown, Jerusalem." She has, in short, had to come to terms with three identities: German and

Catholic, an adopted Swedish persona, and an Israeli Jewish self. *Burned Child Seeks the Fire* ranks very high as a Holocaust memoir, along with such works as **Ruth Klüger's** *Weiter leben* (*Still Alive*).

—David Scrase

C

THE CANNIBALS
Play by George Tabori, 1974

The inception of George Tabori's first Holocaust play, *The Cannibals* (1974), lay in his desire to cope with his father's murder at Auschwitz 25 years earlier. Tabori subverted certain conventions of traditional narrative form through Brechtian techniques, while at the same time he created a traditional hero based on his father, Cornelius.

The Cannibals is a reunion of sorts. Two survivors of Block 6, Auschwitz, along with ten men who are the sons of the other inmates who did not survive, are gathered together to reenact the events that preceded and precipitated the murder of their fathers. The two survivors are successful businessmen now. They inform the audience they are the only two survivors. The others enter, remove their everyday clothes, and put on camp uniforms. The actors are gradually revealed to be the sons playing their fathers. At various times during the play the sons stop the action to question the survivors about details of their fathers' appearance and behavior. Or they refer to their fathers in the third person. For example, when Uncle (Tabori's father) realizes that the others have killed Puffi, he chastises them: "See what you've done? You animals! (*to audience*) He was shaking with indignation." The use of direct address to the audience and the deliberate "distancing" or interruption of audience identification with the character are techniques championed by the German playwright **Bertolt Brecht,** who had a profound effect on Tabori.

When one of the inmates is accidentally killed in a scuffle over a bread crust, someone suggests serving him up in a stew. Uncle considers this act to be against God's laws and convinces them to forego such an abomination, no matter how hungry they are. Later a Nazi guard arrives and forces them to either eat the stew or be sent to death immediately. Tabori took the literal fact that often prisoners could only survive at the expense of others and incorporated it into a stage metaphor that allows the audience to witness how the characters arrive at their choices. The death camp slogan "One man's death is another man's bread" becomes literally and horribly true onstage.

The play's plot involves the argument "to eat or not to eat." Uncle is the moral leader whose gesture of resistance, of not eating, is portrayed in a positive light. Along the way we learn that he also hid a knife that was to be used to resist during their deportation to Auschwitz. Some critics have argued that Uncle's passivity is critiqued in the play, but overall Uncle embodies a traditional hero. This portrayal is in sharp contrast to Tabori's *My Mother's Courage,* in which he dramatized his mother's escape from Auschwitz and deliberately deconstructed traditional notions of heroism.

Although the play's premise is serious, Tabori sometimes has been criticized because of his style, which includes black humor, song, and dance, along with hints of Samuel Beckett and Franz Kafka and other absurdist elements. The play is a staging of remembrance—the sons are trying to understand their fathers' pasts by embodying them. But Tabori insisted on "mixing the celestial and the excremental," as he put it. For example, at one point, while lamenting their starvation and trying to justify eating their comrade, the inmates burst into "Yes, We Have No Bananas."

Jewish and Christian symbolism also inform Tabori's Holocaust plays. In *The Cannibals* the ritual meal is referred to as a "black mass," with 12 diners, reminiscent of the 12 apostles at the Last Supper and the Twelve Tribes of Israel. In the end only two eat, along with the Nazi guard, who turns out to be not him, but his son, who also questions his father's behavior during the war.

The play premiered during the late 1960s, a time in Germany when the next generation was coming of age, filled with questions about the past their parents wanted to forget. The trial of Nazi official Adolf Eichmann in 1961, the Auschwitz trials in Frankfurt (1963–65), the premieres of **Rolf Hochhuth**'s *The Deputy* (1963) and **Peter Weiss**'s *The Investigation* (1965), and the student revolts of 1968 all led to a breakdown of the silence surrounding the Nazi era. Thus, the time was ripe for this play, whose impetus was the struggle of the grown child (Tabori) to deal with the past. The character of the Nazi guard played by his son also articulated the frustrated accusations of the postwar generation in direct conflict with the often desperate defensiveness of those who survived. When Tabori came from New York to Berlin to produce what he called his "horror farce," he wrote in the program notes that sentimentality is an insult to the dead because "the event is beyond all tears." In Tabori's Holocaust plays the tragedy of the Holocaust did not preclude his use of comic irony to shock and confront his audience.

—Susan Russell

A CANOPY IN THE DESERT (Hupah ba-midbar)
Poem by Abba Kovner, 1970

A Canopy in the Desert (1973; *Hupah ba-midbar,* 1970) by Abba Kovner is a lengthy narrative poem that describes a journey through the Negev and Sinai Desert in Israel. Divided into several sections, the poem merges biblical motifs with the memory of the Holocaust and with life in modern Israel. The poem has been compared to H.N. Bialik's "The Dead of the Wilderness" for its form, structure, and theme. It is divided into 12 "gates," or chapters, and contains approximately 100 shorter poems.

The journey into the desert is a journey into the past, both near and distant. At the end of the travels a wedding is to take place, but it does not. The desert is a charged location: here Moses led the Hebrews out of Egypt, here Moses made his Covenant with God, here the state of Israel fought three wars. It is a location of struggle with both man and God. These different phases in Jewish history are collapsed into a vast wasteland in which one can see no trace of the past, as the sand forever blows over the footsteps of those who have gone before. But the narrator of the poem, the wandering poet, carries the voices of all those who died—in the Holocaust, in the Vilna forests where Kovner fought as a partisan, and in the wars of Israel.

The Covenant received at Mount Sinai ordained "Thou shalt not murder." The location looms as a constant battlefield. The traveler wishes to renew the Covenant by becoming one with the little sister, reminiscent of Kovner's *My Little Sister*, to whom he wishes to be betrothed at the end of the journey. The wedding, however, does not take place, and the Covenant is forever broken. Kovner depicts many forms of death in this location—from soldiers and local Arab and Jewish inhabitants to dead dreams and hopes, which cumulatively negate any possibility of change. There are many allusions to the bible; for example, the whale that throws the poet narrator up on the shore is a reference to Jonah's whale, and in rabbinic tradition it alludes to coming out of exile. Many words in Kovner's poems carry references to biblical or Midrashic themes.

The poem alludes to the Holocaust indirectly, by calling on and recalling characters from more specifically Holocaust-oriented poems, namely the little sister, but also in its overriding agenda. In *A Canopy in the Desert* Kovner asks whether the order of things cannot be broken, whether it is possible to bring order into the chaos of humanity, whether another beginning is possible. This question of humanity in an inhuman world clearly relates to the poet's own experience and other artistic treatments of the Holocaust.

—Ziva Shavitsky

A CAT IN THE GHETTO: FOUR NOVELETTES
(Kiddush Hashem)
Novelettes by Rachmil Bryks, 1952

Rachmil Bryks's *A Cat in the Ghetto: Four Novelettes,* published in its original Yiddish in 1952, was translated into

English by S. Morris Engel in 1959. Preceding the introduction is a letter from Eleanor Roosevelt, who states: "This work was difficult for me to read." Indeed, the situations are very graphically portrayed by Bryks; unique to his writing, however, is that the foundation of faith and rays of hope constantly shine through. Whereas many Holocaust writers portray those who take for themselves and who are extraordinarily cruel in their own struggle for survival, Bryks introduces the reader to those whose humanity is never lost under the most extreme circumstances. The songs of *A Cat in the Ghetto* have also been immortalized at the back of the collection, and the score has been added by Bryks. This is certainly an unusual tactic by an author, but it provides the reader with the actual sounds of the ghetto. Included in the song collection are the sarcastic "Rumkowski Chayim" and "Our President Chayim," which "honor" the head of the Judenrat of the Łodź ghetto; the hopeful "I am Going Home"; and the saccharin-hawker's melody "Saccharin."

The first novelette, *A Cat in the Ghetto*, centers around Schloime Zabludovitch, who has a cat in his possession. It is said in the ghetto that whoever turns in a cat will receive bread in return. Bryks's humor in this novelette is somewhat surprising considering that the ghetto is a sea of emaciated beings who dream of only simple staple items to keep them alive, if only just to the next day. Zabludovitch realizes, however, that what he has heard about bread for cats is just a rumor. In the end, truth triumphs over falsehood, and the pureness of the human heart conquers suspicion and distrust.

A Cupboard in the Ghetto reflects the truly inventive nature of man when faced with horrific circumstances. Ersatz food and imaginatively created sugar treats mark the desperation of those determined to lead lives of dignity in a world of despair. "It's true, we are dying out because of hunger, but we have not become wild beasts . . . On the outside we look like corpses, but inside we have preserved the image of God," Mr. Bluestein states in this novelette. The small triumphs in life are what carry the Jews forward and instill in them the determination to succeed in surviving past the expectations of those who continuously place roadblocks in their paths.

Sanctification of God's Name is the longest novelette in the collection. Again, the steadfastness of faith in the approaching Russian army and the belief that good will come to the Jews permeate this work. Despite the disappointment in their fellow man, the Jews remain believing that they will be liberated shortly and must only endure a short time of torture at Auschwitz. But the reader soon realizes that liberation is sometimes only possible by marching willingly to one's own death. It is this willingness to march that marks the victory of the inmates over their keepers.

Berele in the Ghetto is a fine representation of how quickly small children must enter an adult world in the ghetto in order to survive. Berele, a nine-year-old boy who has lost his entire family, begins life as an adult as soon as the last member of his family disappears. His admirable determination to survive and his ability to organize unionist strikes by the other children carry him way beyond his years. As Sol Liptzin stated in the introduction to the collection: "It is such children, of whom alas only a pitiful remnant survived, that are today helping to rebuild the Jewish people as a significant moral force on the world scene."

—Cynthia A. Klíma

CHILD OF THE HOLOCAUST
Memoir by Jack Kuper, 1967

Jack Kuper's *Child of the Holocaust* relates the story of Jankele Kuperblum, a young Jewish boy whose impoverished family arranges for him to be taken on as a farmhand by a local Polish woman in the summer of 1942. While suffering the fear and pain of being separated from his family and being thrust into an alien and menacing reality, this food and shelter for work arrangement saves Jankele's life. While he is working on the farm, the Germans liquidate the Jews of his hometown.

Child of the Holocaust belongs to that domain of Holocaust literature concerning children hidden during the Holocaust years. As such, this leads to a natural comparison between this work and what may be arguably the two most well-known works concerning children and the Holocaust: *Anne Frank: The Diary of a Young Girl* and **Jerzy Kosinski**'s *The Painted Bird*. Like those works, in this work there are none of the more harsh elements of the Holocaust experience such as transports, concentration camps, and death marches. There exist significant differences in style, tone, and content, however, between Kuper's childhood memoir and the aforementioned works.

Criticism has pointed to the fact that those involved in the original publication of the diary of Anne Frank and its subsequent inclusion in the school curriculum sought to normalize both Anne and the Holocaust. Despite the fact that later editions of the diary include material initially viewed as inappropriate, the original sanitized diary (and subsequent stage and film productions) established a somewhat otherworldly Anne, perhaps best remembered for one specific entry where she reaffirms her basic belief in the goodness of humanity.

If the story of Anne Frank has served to deliver a rather benign view of the Holocaust experience and its meaning, Kosinski's *The Painted Bird* does quite the opposite. The pseudo-memoir of a young boy who roams the Polish countryside during the Holocaust years presents a reality so nightmarish and fantastic that the reader is all but compelled to ultimately view the events described as not being of this world.

As opposed to the above, *Child of the Holocaust* presents in a direct and uncompromising fashion the story of a child who meets tremendous goodness, indifference, and evil as he seeks to save himself from the Germans and starvation. The events, people, and behaviors described are very much of this world: friendship and bigotry, love and blind hatred, faith and doubt.

Through the eyes of the child that he was, Kuper shows how Jankele confronts his reality. While Kuper believes that his young age saved him from realizing the full impact of the events around him, it also was a factor in the slow disintegration of Jankele's self—identity—and his emotional health—described in the book. While in face of the hatred he eventually comes to deny and hate himself and his identity, Kuper shows the power of the individual and leaves the reader with hope for the regeneration of the self.

The book opens with nine-year-old Jankele on his way to visit his family for the first time since he left home months before: "A heavy layer of mist covered the village of Kulik, disclosing a few chimneys and thatch roofs as if they were suspended in the air ... Mrs. Paizak sat in the front [of the wagon] holding the reins, her back toward me. "Vio!" she called out to the horse whenever he slowed down, and hit him across the back. The horse too could barely be seen, and it seemed as if we were sitting on a cloud being pulled by some magic force. Perhaps all this is a dream I thought. When I awake I'll find Mrs. Paizak and Genia gone." Not only does the dream not end but it quickly turns into a nightmare when Jankele learns that the Jewish residents of the ghetto have been sent to a concentration camp. Jankele subsequently must attempt to make sense of the events swirling around him like the mist covering the village of Kulik. Deprived of the advice and instruction of family and friends, young Jankele begins to struggle with debates that develop among voices that appear in his head. Dream and reality interchange as he struggles against both known and unknown dangers.

Hiding his Jewish identity as he wanders the Polish countryside, Jankele transforms himself into Kubush the shepherd boy, Franek the farmhand, and Zigmund. He eventually reinvents himself so often that he finds it increasingly more difficult to remember the young boy who he once was. Indeed, after years of pretending to be a Christian, Jankele begins to look, act, and feel like the peasants among whom he has lived. Regretting being born a Jew, he identifies in Jews (including himself) the very traits about which he heard from the peasants. Reaching a Jewish orphanage at the end of the war, Jankele discovers that neither he himself nor the other boys see him as a real Jew. The disintegration of his previous self is so complete that by the end of the war he cannot even understand or speak his native tongue of Yiddish.

At the edge of the ultimate self-negation, standing near a church in Lublin and considering conversion to Christianity, Jankele encounters a man garbed in a turban and white sheet: "His arms outstretched toward passerbyers, he kept repeating the same phrase in a strange language ... 'Who is he?' I asked ... 'An Indian,' answered a boy. 'What is he saying?' I asked. 'No one knows,' answered the same boy. 'He's been walking around like this for weeks. He's lost and nobody understands what he's saying.'" The image of the man lost without his people returns Jankele to himself and to his people. He makes a mad race to the center for missing persons. Panting, he reaches a room where people smile at him "as if expecting" him. Regaining his faith in both his past and his future, he lists his name among those looking for the living and makes it known to the world that "Jankele Kuperblum is alive."

Out of the depths of despair, reaching out for a hand to take his, Jankele (Kuper) concludes his memoir with a reaffirmation of life. Offering comfort for himself (and the reader), he concludes: "It's possible, I told myself. Everything is possible."

—Avi Kay

CHILD OF THE SHADOWS (Zydowska wojna)
Novel by Henryk Grynberg, 1965

Henryk Grynberg published *Child of the Shadows* in 1965 in Poland under the title *Zydowska wojna* ("The Jewish War") corresponding to the work by Joseph Flavius from the first century. That original title is important because the author intended to argue with a certain anti-Semitic stereotype emphasizing the passive attitude of the Jews in the face of the Holocaust. The English title links Grynberg's book too obviously to the literature concerned with the experiences of the children of the Holocaust, and thus it veils its thematic richness. The writer points out that the heroic, though passive, struggle for each hour and day of life was for the Jews the only possible form of fighting.

The audience learns that the author's younger brother, sent into hiding with a peasant family, was recognized as a Jewish child and killed. He fell into the hands of his murderers because of the circumcision—a symbol of the covenant between Abraham and God. Clear autobiographical denotations are apparent in Grynberg's introduction to this book, which is a eulogy for the author's mother.

Child of the Shadows, published in English translation in 1969, is divided into two parts. The first describes the situation of the author's family in the first months of the German occupation of Poland, beginning with the eviction and ending with the escape on the night preceding the deportation of the Jewish community to Treblinka and with the protagonist's separation from his father, who bought Aryan documents for his wife and son and then, because of his Semitic features, hid in forests but did not survive the war. The second part deals with the life with the "Aryan papers," first in Warsaw and later in the country. The novel concludes with the coming of the Red Army in the summer of 1944.

In this tiny book by Grynberg the reader will easily identify a number of typical situations determining the fate of the Jews during the Shoah such as evictions, deprivation of property,

forced labor, spontaneous murders, organized murders, loneliness, fear of denunciation, blackmail, paying for survival, the life with the Aryan papers, and rejection of Jewish identity—but also the rescue thanks to the help of some Poles. Such a fate of a Polish Jew, trapped between the hunt for victims and the help offered by a fellow man, is expressed in a brief and ingenious way in the most cruel sentence in the novel: "Praised be the Lord, Mr. Sliwa, we are coming to you to look for Jews." Here, uttering a Christian greeting, a Polish peasant alarms another one—the one who keeps the protagonist and his family in hiding.

In *Child of the Shadows* the characteristics of Grynberg's writing and his conception of literature became crystallized. It is also the first of the series of four books with the same protagonist, all of which constitute a chronicle of life during the Holocaust and under Communism. Their author is concerned with the various forms of Nazi, Polish, communist, and religious anti-Semitism. He also strongly emphasizes another great issue: the problem of identity.

The life with the Aryan papers requires constant alertness, a talent for mimicry, and the lack of physical likeness to a Jew. It means a constant fear of being recognized by the Poles. The narrator and protagonist of the novel is brought up as a Catholic child, and his mother teaches Polish and religion to anti-Semites. In church her son learns that the Jews killed Jesus Christ, and he asks his mother an anti-Semitic question: Why? "I don't know, sonny," she replies, "but I think that if he had not been born among the Jews, the Gentiles would have killed him." This answer invalidates religious anti-Semitism.

Grynberg's power of the artistic description of his family history stems not only from the authenticity of personal experience but also from the form of its presentation. The language of the narrative is very sparse, limited to a matter-of-fact, reporting style. It avoids revealing emotions and imitates the awkward language of a child with a poor command of vocabulary. The narrator is a survivor who lives in the post-Shoah world. The tension between the discourse of a child and the perspective of the author who possesses a post-war knowledge about the catastrophe is the source of the rhetoric of paradox. The world of the novel is in fact a counterworld described in a neutral and sometimes naive language.

—Kazimierz Adamczyk

THE CHOCOLATE DEAL ('Iskat ha-shokolad)
Novella by Haim Gouri, 1964

The dramatic backbone of Haim Gouri's poetically written and viscerally expressionistic novella *The Chocolate Deal* (1968; *'Iskat ha-shokolad*, 1964) focuses on the rived souls of two Holocaust survivors wandering aimlessly through postapocalyptic Europe and their attempt to come to terms with their experiences and in the process establish normality. It is about the scarred psyche of the victims as they grapple with the sudden descent upon them of normality and the attendant battle to rebuild their identity and find a way, as **Aharon Appelfeld** once put it, beyond despair. Instead of foregrounding the Nazi horrors, Gouri deliberately sidesteps entering the concentrationary experience, preferring instead to pin the nucleus narrative to the period immediately following the Shoah and show the immutable terror within the floating clove of emptiness gnawing inside every survivor. As if holding a sieve, Gouri picks through the ruins and ruptures of the past that have been bequeathed to him as someone who was not in Europe during the atrocities, trying to transform this cracked marquetry into an architectural unified story that ropes the reader into empathic identification with the wounded. Drenched in symbolic allusiveness and repeatedly blurring the line between realities, leaping from character to character and from time to time, these oscillations leave the reader blinking and groping in desperate attempts to follow. For instance, at the start of the book it is unclear who the two protagonists are or who at times is the narrator, and revelatory details are proffered in shards and driblets. Since Gouri's aim is in presenting emblematic personas that represent contrasting types and not veritable, fully fleshed characters, as well as adumbrating the lingering aftermath of the survivor universe, the plot's drama is conveyed not through a penetrating strobe light but through a hazy obscure lens that stultifies any clear decoding of the personage of the story.

Set in an unidentified postwar German city, the story is told through the eyes of the two central characters, Mordi (Mordechai) Neuberg and Rubi (Reuben) Krauss, whose interior monologues serve as the piston engine of the narrative. In many ways this aesthetic device underscores the unstaunched psychological nature and structure of the tale and the author's penchant in working along the lower levels of consciousness in depicting his heroes' torrent of agony. In essence, the two childhood friends who had survived the inferno and who meet unexpectedly in a train station are the recto and verso of the survival experience. To be sure, their characters function as an all-purpose metaphor for the disparate ways one can deal with the past and live in an amoral world. In other words the two men parabolically embody some dimension of survival larger than just the personal.

One critic shrewdly observed that at the outset the main protagonists live as if in a spiritual wasteland, sapped of vigor and riddled with psychic lesions. Denuded of family, they spend copious hours futilely looking through the missing persons section of the newspapers for remaining relatives. And although the reader is not told how Rubi managed to stay alive during the Holocaust, we discover that Mordi, a talented journalist in France who, prior to the war, was conducting research on troubadour poetry for a doctoral dissertation, was

housed in a monastery by his university teacher. Hiding in the cellar and cared for by a righteous monk, he is savaged with guilt after learning that his mentor was tortured and interrogated for his act of kindness.

The conniving Rubi, whose dreams of prosperity are smashed when he discovers that his wealthy relatives have perished in the hands of the Nazi beast, is hell-bent on reconstructing his shattered existence and becoming rich, figuring that the only way to arise from the ashes is through fraudulence and revenge on the perpetrators. To that end he confects a black market scheme that exploits the excess leftover of military chocolate unloaded on the local market by the stationed American forces. In his pursuit he plans on manipulating a Dr. Hoffman into medically confirming the rumors that the consumption of chocolate affects male sexual potency and then selling the surplus for a high price after the rumors are debunked. Rubi, the mathematical wunderkind, demands the doctor's cooperation since he knows about his lack of moral rectitude during the German barbarity. Rubi's moral indifference is further illustrated when he takes up with a German woman, unmoved that she once was a Gestapo devotee and now moonlights as a prostitute.

In contradistinction Mordi is introspective and passive, constantly enrobed and swathed by the past from which he cannot escape. The conscience-stricken young man is obsessed with the knowledge that he alone survived and finds it increasingly difficult to live in this vicious and cruel world, while at the same time dealing with the existential alienation that like a ring gradually stretches out and envelops his fragile existence. During the course of the book the pensive and morbid Mordi comes to represent the survivor who is unable to forget the unspeakable tragedies, wholly burdened by the painful memories that are slowly eating away at his energy and willingness to live. Tellingly, the hypersensitive hero mysteriously dies when Rubi momentarily abandons him for Gerti, his German mistress, underscoring the symbiotic relationship of dependence and need that has flowered between the two boyhood friends. On a deeper level one could argue that Rubi's proposed swindle to trade on German shame and guiltiness is the author tipping his self-reflexive hat, subtly hinting at the divisive issue of German reparation. Gouri is remarkably able to limn this terrain without moralizing or judging his principals' actions, sagaciously understanding that in the aftermath of the Shoah the response of the survivors was multiplex and variegated rather than monolithic. What Gouri seems to suggest is that there are twin roads that the survivors can travail. The first is to maintain and preserve one's ethical integrity in continuously brooding over the terrible loss—a path that ultimately results in the destruction of the soul. The other is to forge ahead, to discard the mental anguish of the past that perennially overhangs the victims and embrace the present, pathetic and ravaged as it may be.

—Dvir Abramovich

THE CHOSEN
Novel by Chaim Potok, 1967

Chaim Potok's novel *The Chosen* takes place in New York City, with World War II and the Holocaust a constant presence as two boys from different Jewish traditions meet and are transformed by one another. The novel is organized into three books. The first book establishes the war as a background and presents the central theme as Reuven Malter's father asks him to choose Danny Saunders as his friend, a choice that is to have consequences for both boys. The second book focuses on the boys' growing friendship, the end of the war, a realization that six million Jews have been murdered, and the first calls for a Jewish homeland. The third book immerses the boys in the aftermath of the war, both the internal war between Jewish sects—Reuven's father is a Zionist, and Danny's father, the tzaddik for his Hasidic community, is totally opposed to a homeland—and Reuven's own battle with hatred for the choice Reb Saunders made in using silence to raise his son Danny.

War is clearly a central theme in *The Chosen*. As the two boys from different Jewish traditions meet in a hate-filled battle on the baseball diamond, the world, too, is at war. David Malter asks Reuven to be aware of a world that is larger than his anger at Danny: "It is expected Rome will fall any day now. And there are rumors the invasion of Europe will be very soon. You should not forget there is a world outside." The war and Hitler provide a backdrop for the boys' lives in the Bronx: "The millions of soldiers fighting Hitler are part of the world," and as Danny tells Reuven of wanting to read Freud in German, he must defend his decision: "Just because Hitler speaks German doesn't mean that the language is corrupt." As the war escalates, it takes on a greater presence in the novel: "And then the news of the war in Europe suddenly reached a peak of feverish excitement." Reuven notes that even Danny's father mentions the war: "It is the end of Hitler, may his name and memory be erased." And finally news of the Holocaust reaches the boys: "there came the news, at first somewhat guarded, then, a few days later, clear and outspoken, of the German concentration camps." Reuven struggles with this reality: "I just couldn't grasp it. The numbers of Jews slaughtered had gone from one million to three million to four million, and almost every article we read said that the last count was still incomplete, the final number would probably reach six. I couldn't begin to imagine six million of my people murdered. I lay in my bed and asked myself what sense it made. It didn't make any sense at all."

The question of the "sense" of the world is a central theme in *The Chosen*. It is introduced early by Mr. Savo, a character in the eye ward at Brooklyn Memorial, and Potok turns again and again to the phrase "Crazy world. Cockeyed." When Danny contemplates how he and Reuven are so different, he echoes Mr. Savo: "'It's funny,' he said. 'It's really funny. I have to be a rabbi and don't want to be one. You don't have to

be a rabbi and do want to be one. It's a crazy world.'" Reuven's father is also deeply affected by the insanity of the world as he considers the Holocaust: "Did we know, he asked us, that on December 17, 1942, Mr. Eden got up in the House of Commons and gave the complete details of the Nazi plan . . . and not a thing was done . . . No one had cared enough. The world closed its doors, and six million Jews were slaughtered. What a world! What an insane world!"

In the midst of this insanity choices are all-important. Reuven is asked to "choose" Danny as his friend: "Reuven, if you can, make Danny Saunders your friend." He is asked to understand his father's passion for Zionism, the importance of giving loss meaning: "Six million of our people have been slaughtered . . . It will have meaning only if we give it meaning . . . We have a terrible responsibility . . . If we do not rebuild Jewry in America, we will die as a people." Reuven is asked to understand his father's drive, to accept his father's mortality. "A span of life is nothing," David Malter tells his son, "But the man who lives that span, *he* is something . . . A man must fill his life with meaning, meaning is not automatically given to life. It is hard work to fill one's life with meaning . . . A life filled with meaning is worthy of rest. I want to be worthy of rest when I am no longer here." And ultimately Reuven must come to understand Reb Saunders's choice to use silence in the raising of his son Danny, a painful choice but one made to save him: "A *heart* I need for a son, a *soul* I need for a son, *compassion* I want from my son, righteousness, mercy, strength to suffer, and carry pain, *that* I want from my son, not a mind without a soul! . . . I had to make certain his soul would be the soul of a tzaddik no matter what he did with his life." Reuven's understanding of this choice, his acceptance of a culture other than his own, is at the heart of the novel.

This story of two Jewish boys growing to adulthood in the shadow of the Holocaust is ultimately a story of choosing to love, of choosing to serve others with love. Potok tells the story in a way that gives meaning to the suffering; he tells a story in which understanding provides hope for the future.

—Jan M. Osborn

CITY OF GOD
Novel by E. L. Doctorow, 2000

E. L. Doctorow's experimental, unconventional novel *City of God* displays a vast jumble of diversified materials that fill the mind of a movie scriptwriter, Everett, and are recorded in his workbook. Its contents include excursions into theology, psychology, and cosmology; fictional fragments; factual elements; direct quotations from important writers; other direct borrowings from outside sources; tributes to the City (New York); commentary on the writing of movie scripts and on old standard songs; and imaginary plots for movies. The tragedy of the Holocaust, described in personal terms, plays a major role in the book.

City of God has a discontinuous story line about a mysterious event in a small, progressive Jewish synagogue in Manhattan's Upper West Side and its consequences for the rabbinical couple who lead the congregation and the Episcopal clergyman, from a church in lower Manhattan, who becomes involved with them. The narrative elements are introduced randomly, often without proper identification. Moreover, Doctorow's scriptwriter changes names and locations of his three major characters and two houses of worship. It remains unclear as to whether Doctorow intended a meaningful story line or a set of notes for a movie-script plot.

The mystery concerns the astounding theft of the huge brass cross hanging behind the altar of Rev. Thomas Pemberton's Episcopal church and its incredible reappearance on the roof of the building that houses the progressive Synagogue for Evolutionary Judaism, led by Rabbi Joshua Gruen and his wife, Rabbi Sarah Blumenthal. The heist and its possible implications draw Pemberton to the couple, socially and emotionally. As they vainly continue to seek answers, Pemberton, whose commitment to his church's doctrines has been steadily eroding, begins to direct his commitment to Sarah and her brand of Judaism. As a very young victim-survivor of the Final Solution, Sarah's father kept a diary of the tribulations of the Jews in the Kovno ghetto, Lithuania. (He also discussed his experiences there with Sarah.) To trace this archival record to its source, Sarah's husband travels to Lithuania, where he believes the diary has been preserved. Before he can find and recover the valuable book, however, he is brutally murdered.

Pemberton takes the heist of the large cross from his church and its removal to the roof of the Evolutionary Judaism synagogue as a cryptic sign of something portentous. Having lost his church (which is now deconsecrated), he reassigns himself to hospice work on Roosevelt Island. He then goes to Moscow in search of the problematical ghetto diary, which apparently is no longer in Kovno. Finally, he gives up his own religious faith entirely, takes on Sarah's form of Judaism, marries her, and together they continue the mission of her synagogue.

As for the book's overall philosophical view, the drift of the contents of Everett's "teeming mind" is an evolutionary one. A good deal of his rumination is devoted to the big-bang theory and the expanding, ever-evolving universe. Also, the story line itself, through its major characters, points to the need for both Christianity and traditional Judaism to evolve into more progressive forms of religion; Pemberton—the real conscience of the book— seems to "hope that a revelation [is] evolving," and Sarah herself believes that even God is evolving. But the Holocaust material, which is not limited to Everett's transcription of what Sarah's father experienced and witnessed in the Kovno ghetto, remains "an ever-fixèd mark" (a phrase from Shakespeare's Sonnet 116), the most valuable portion of this grab bag of a book.

As memorable in its own way as Doctorow's extensive borrowing from **Avraham Tory**'s diary with its death-camp horrors, offered as selections from the personal record of Sarah's father, is Pemberton's sermon to his congregation, which leads to his leaving the church. He desires his congregation's opinions on Holocaust matters. What had the Holocaust done to their religion and to the "story of Christ Jesus"? Given the weak Christian response, was it only the Jewish theologians' problem? What behavioral change would have been a suitable Christian reaction to the Holocaust, drastic enough to assure them "of the holy truth" of their religion's story? Finally, utilizing the City in general as a high concept (though New York is dearest to him as its embodiment), Doctorow reveals a far-reaching philosophy about the City's breakdown tendencies (crime, disease, overgrowth, decay, and corruption) and barely hints at its possibilities for purification and renewal. His model apparently was St. Augustine's *City of God* from the early fifth century, which dichotomizes the earthly, worldly city and the divine eternal city of the worshipers of the true God. But Doctorow concludes only with an introduction to his hero and heroine—Sarah and Pemberton, the post-Holocaust, "vitally religious couple"—running the progressive synagogue that is already familiar to the reader.

—Samuel I. Bellman

CLOUDED SKY (Tatjékos ég)
Poems by Miklós Radnóti, 1946

The discovery of Miklós Radnóti's body in a mass grave near the western Hungarian town of Györ in 1946 catapulted the martyred poet to worldwide fame. Critical interest focused naturally on the works written during his last years, from his conscription into forced labor camps in 1940 to his brutal execution in the fall of 1944 at the age of 35. In particular his last 10 poems, found in a notebook when his decomposing body was exhumed, attracted international attention. It is therefore understandable that his posthumous collection *Clouded Sky*, published in English translation in 1972, includes only poems from the second half of his career—from August 1937 to October 1944—and omits the generally more upbeat poems of his early life.

The first two selections, "Spain, Spain" and "Federico García Lorca," both from 1937, set the tone for *Clouded Sky*: the dark clouds of the Spanish Civil War are gathering ominously over an autumnal wasteland, and the death of the Spanish antifascist poet foretells Radnóti's own fate. Friends and acquaintances who were killed or committed suicide populate the poems of the following years; in the poem from which the title of the collection is taken, the poet not only expresses his amazement that he is still alive but also his conviction that "I am the one they'll kill, finally, because I myself never killed.'' Against this impending catastrophe Radnóti puts up sonnets and other tightly organized poetic forms, as if to attempt to reign in the chaos and dissolution he foresees. In particular his ''Eclogues'' (the collection contains six of the eight extant ones) shows this approach: the traditional bucolic poems, usually in the form of dialogues or soliloquies, idealize the simple, idyllic life of shepherds and country people. By describing the horrors of the war and of the Holocaust in this classical form, Radnóti points an accusing finger at the horrors of his age. All that is left for him to hope for is to keep his sanity and to be allowed, as he states in ''Maybe'' (1940), ''to die, without fear, a clean lovely death, like Empedocles, who smiled as he fell into the crater.''

Radnóti's last creative phase begins in May 1944, when he was conscripted for the last time at the Lager Heidenau, near the Yugoslav town of Bor. These so-called ''Lager Poems'' are preceded by the terrible accusation against his age in ''Fragment'' (19 May 1944):

> I lived on this earth in an age
> when man fell so low
> he killed willingly, for pleasure, without orders.
> . . .
> I lived on this earth in an age
> . . .
> when women were happy if they miscarried,
> a glass of thick poison foamed on the table,
> and the living envied the rotten silence of
> the dead.

In between there are glimpses of hope that he will see his wife again: ''I'll use magic but I'll get back'' (''A Letter to My Wife,'' August/September 1944), but already he sees himself no longer as a flower but as a root, with ''heavy black earth above me'' (''Root,'' 8 August 1944). His last poem written at Heidenau, ''The Eighth Eclogue,'' is an angry doomsday jeremiad, in which the poet envisions himself and his wife standing next to the prophet Nahum at the fiery destruction of Nineveh. Then follow the broken lines of ''Forced March,'' written after having been force-marched from Heidenau to Bor: ''You're crazy. You fall down,_____stand up and walk again, / your ankles and your knees move_____pain that wanders around, / but you start again_____as if you had wings,'' with the spaces indicating the tortured, stumbling trek of the prisoners.

There finally are the last four poems, the *Razglednicák* (''picture postcards'') from the march to his place of execution. Radnóti chose the title carefully to remind the reader of the completely different, carefree *cartes postales* he wrote 10 years earlier from a trip to Paris. Here they become frightening vignettes of an air and artillery bombardment during his last march, as in ''Postcard 1.'' In the second the unmentioned massacre of 500 Jewish marchers near Cervenka is made doubly terrible by the seeming unconcern of nature and some bystanders. Three weeks further into the death march, ''Postcard 3'' shows the fatally fatigued and sick men waiting like oxen to the slaughter, and in his final poem, written 10 days before his own execution, he describes the execution of the violinist Miklós Lorsi near Sivac on 31 October 1944, predicting the circumstances of his own death:

> I fell next to him. His body rolled over.
> It was tight as a string before it snaps.
> Shot in the back of the head—''this is how
> you'll end.'' ''Just lie quietly,'' I said
>   to myself.
> Patience flowers into death now.
> ''Der springt noch auf,'' I heard shout
>   above me.
> Dark filthy blood was drying on my ear.

The death of the violinist as compared to a broken string and the sarcastic German words of the executioner (''He'll jump back to his feet again'') are a shocking conclusion to one of the most moving poetic testimonies of the terrors of the Holocaust.

—Franz G. Blaha

CO CZYTALEM UMARLYM
Poems by Wladyslaw Szlengel, 1977

The poet Wladyslaw Szlengel was killed in April 1943 in the Warsaw Ghetto Uprising. Not all of his works were saved from the wartime conflagration. Although he had plans to publish several volumes, his entire heritage is contained in the collection *Co czytalem umarlym* (''What I Read to the Dead''), published in 1977. In the prose piece that gives the volume its title Szlengel explains the most important principle of his writing. The poems are addressed to his murdered friends as well as to the nameless masses of the Nazi victims of crime. The poet thus speaks on behalf of the absent. The poet creates a ghetto chronicle that covers the period of time in 1943 between the liquidation and the uprising. The poetic evidence of the experience of this extreme evil, as the author himself suggests however, may not be fully understood by someone who had not been through the hell of the ghetto. In sequences of short, dynamic sentences, the ''chronicler of the dying'' wrote down his psychical reactions to enclosure and encirclement. He reconstructed the aura of fear and uncertainty and described the methods of killing and of depriving people of the remainer of their humanity. Szlengel uses statistics to reveal the scale of the tragedy, and he shows how soon the anonymous martyrs are forgotten. The exceptionally dramatic scenes focus on the motifs of bailing oneself out from death and of survival bought for money. In this inhuman world there is no room for heroic gestures. The low value of contemporary history on human lives is judged severely.

The poetic recording of the "dying / of the largest Jewish Community in Europe" in "Wołanie w nocy" ("Calling at Night") is carried out from an individual perspective. The poems "Okno na tamta strone" ("A Window with the View of the Other Side") and "Telefon" ("The Phone") constitute shrill studies of solitude, the bonds with the inhabitants of Warsaw on the other side of the wall having been irrevocably broken. For the poet Warsaw from before the war becomes a kind of the paradise lost. Authenticity plays a special role in the poems; it intensifies the credibility of the poet's reports and strengthens the ties of the speaking lyrical "I" with the sufferings of the common people. In the epitaph for Jewish mothers the small scale of life is provocatively contrasted with threnodies commemorating heroes, as in "Pomnik" ("A Monument"). In "Rzeczy" ("The Things") a story of objects becomes a suggestive epitome of the collective historic disaster. "Dzwonki" ("The Bells") traces life from before the catastrophe to reveal the dominating emptiness the murdered nation leaves behind. Heroic sacrifices belong to the everyday order of things. In "Kartka z dziennika 'akcji'" ("A Page from the 'Action' Diary") Szlengel compares the act of **Janusz Korczak**, who chooses death, to the defense of the Westerplatte outpost.

By unmasking the frail bases of hatred, as in "Dwaj panowie na sniegu" ("Two Men on the Snow"), the poet proves how ludicrous the divisions are to the races of the victims and the victors. In "Dwie śmierći" ("The Two Deaths") the extermination of the Jews is contrasted with death on the battlefield, where significance comes from patriotic values. In his accusation against the Holocaust crimes the poet resorts to sarcasm, irony, and a grotesque and macabre sense of humor, as, for example, in "Mala stacja Treblinki" ("The Little Station of Treblinka"), "Cylinder," ("A Top Hat"), and "Resume" ("A Resume"). The overwhelming degradation imposed on the victims affects both the spheres of feelings and of behavior, as is shown in "Romans współczesny" ("A Contemporary Romance") and in "Piękna niedziela" ("A Beautiful Sunday"). In Szlengel's accusing poetry the images borrowed from Jewish culture undergo a change from their original sense in the ghetto reality. Thus, in its new version as revised by history, the Festival of Tabernacles (Sukkoth) becomes a festival of shelters, while the story of the golem of Prague shows the loss of human features among the inhabitants of the ghetto condemned to death.

—Wojciech Ligęza

COLLECTED POEMS
Poems by A. M. Klein, 1974

Montreal poet A. M. Klein began writing and publishing poems in his late teens while an undergraduate at McGill University. In his mid-40s Klein contracted a disabling illness that effectively ended his career as a poet. In the course of that career he had published four books of poetry and a large number of occasional poems, scattered in various Canadian and American poetry magazines.

After Klein's death in 1972 a Canadian scholar, Miriam Waddington, gathered together all of his published poetry in a single volume, which appeared in 1974 as *Collected Poems*. The great value of this compilation is that it presents, as nearly as possible in their order of composition, all of the poems Klein chose to publish in his lifetime, thus affording the reader a privileged insight into his development and evolution as a creative artist.

What strikes the reader first, upon opening *Collected Poems,* is that so many of the earliest poems are concerned with death. Sometimes the tone is droll or ironic, as in "Epitaph Forensic," a lawyer's amusing recital of what he wants on his tombstone, or "Threnody," a mock lament for the demise of Klein's student literary magazine, *The McGilliad.* Other times the tone is ominously foreboding, as in the sequence of seven short stanzas herded together under the title "Obituary Notices" or the group of five sonnets entitled "Five Weapons against Death."

Why this early preoccupation with death is not known, but in many of Klein's later poems he returns obsessively to the same theme, often in connection with historic mass murders of Jews, such as the slaughters committed by the Crusaders or the pogroms that occurred in Slavic countries. References to the pogroms are especially frequent, probably because in his youth Klein had heard firsthand accounts of pogroms from his parents and other relatives. It is also possible that his memory was permanently haunted by his personal experience of trauma in his infancy, namely the death of his twin brother when he was one year old. That trauma, Klein knew, was what precipitated his parents' decision to flee the pogrom-prone Ukrainian village of Ratno and settle in Montreal. Whatever the origin, we do know that the theme of death is a persistent leitmotiv in Klein's poetry, and it is not without significance that when Klein turned his attention to the Holocaust, in the late 1940s, he tended to speak of it as "the great death."

Klein's recurrent invocation of the themes of death and destruction, though fundamental to him, are by no means the whole man. A man of many parts, Klein had an engaging sense of humor, even on the subject of death, as in his poem "Invocation to Death," in which young lovers ponder the grotesqueries of old age that await them and conclude, "O let us die before we will be old." He had an evident delight in language and its infinite possibilities for creative expression. Ingenious wordplay is the hallmark of all his many comic and satiric poems, even the angry polemic *The Hitleriad* (1944), in which he rings joyful changes on Hitler's family name, Schicklgruber, observing that "no poet's nor mob's tongue / Could shake from shekel-shackle-gruber-song!"

Klein seems quite simply to have fallen in love with English, especially the rich expressiveness and elegant diction of the Elizabethan-era writers like Shakespeare, and he made it his own medium, believing that the dignity of poetry required nothing less. The most striking feature of Klein's poetry is that he never wrote a line, regardless of subject matter, that did not meet the requirements of elevation of tone and refinement of language proper to poetic diction. Even on so coarse-grained a subject as his caustic poem ''Public Utility,'' about pimps and prostitutes, he is careful to preserve the propriety of poetic diction throughout.

Finally one may note that Klein was a masterful prosodist, both knowledgeable and skillful in the use of meter and rhyme. A superb example of his mastery is the much admired ''Design for Medieval Tapestry,'' in *Hath Not a Jew* (1940), in which he expertly adapts Dante's terza rima to his depiction of the inferno-like relationship between medieval Jewry and medieval Christianity.

To peruse *Collected Poems* is to journey through the mind and spirit of a richly gifted poet, steeped in the traditions to which he was born, imbued with the English and French traditions among which he lived, and determined to develop his expressive powers to their maximum, in order to preserve and honor all the traditions that gave meaning to his own life.

—Murray Sachs

COLLECTED POEMS (Poezje zebrane)
Poems by Tadeusz Różewicz, 1957

Among the many ways in which Tadeusz Różewicz's various works can be interpreted, critics are fond of talking of ''being paralyzed by death.'' This is true of the characters of his works as well as of the personal fears and existential experiences of the author himself.

Różewicz was born and lived in Radomsk, a provincial Polish town with a Jewish population of nearly 13,000, more than 50 percent of the town's total. The outbreak of World War II changed this radically. After the defeat of the Polish army, German repression affected all Poles, but the Polish Jews were particularly hurt during their isolation in the ghetto, after which, in 1943, they were transported to the concentration camp in Treblinka. Różewicz did not remain indifferent to the tragic fate of the Jews, with whom he had close ties.

During 1947–56 the poet published seven poems directly related to the problem of the Holocaust. These poems are found in *Poezje zebrane* (1957; *Collected Poems*, 1976). ''The Living Were Dying'' describes Jewish families dying of hunger in the ghetto, while ''Chaskiel'' deals with a young boy killed by the Germans during the liquidation of the ghetto. One can make an analogy with the fate of the child in the poem

''Ballads and Romances'' by Władysław Broniewski, in which members of the SS murder a 13-year-old girl, Ryfka. Broniewski has Jesus accompany the girl as both are executed because they are Jews. Różewicz elevates the death of Chaskiel with a reference to Exodus in these closing lines: ''A red sea / hid him.'' He thus sanctifies the death of an innocent Jewish child. ''The Slaughter of Boys'' equates the Nazi murders with the biblical acts of Herod. The despair produced by the sudden, irreversible destruction of the innocent lives of children is expressed by the poet in the metaphor ''a tree from dark smoke / vertical / a dead tree / without a star in the tree-top.''

Another dimension of the hideous efficiency of the Nazi murders is revealed in ''A Little Tress.'' Before the women in the concentration camps were sent to the gas chambers, their heads were shaved. (Those who visit the Auschwitz Museum can see in glass cases what remains of the tresses of the victims, hair the Germans did not had enough time to convert into mattresses.) The tress of the title of Różewicz's poem refers to the hundreds of thousands of Jewish women who were first deprived of their hair and then of their lives. By describing the tress, the author pays homage to the victims.

''Stony Imagination'' deals with the bestial methods of killing Jews. The merchant ''Rozenberg will never see / the islands of the Great ocean / the Ukrainians caught up with him in the latrine / he died suffocating in excrement / you cannot imagine / Rosenberg's death in a town / near Piotrków in Poland.'' Różewicz is offering here his own definition of the poet as an insignificant, anonymous human being who is possessed of a ''little, stony, implacable'' imagination. What the poet needs after Auschwitz is, not the sham of old beauty, but remembrance petrified by pain and murder and yet relentlessly disavowing all sham and falsity. **Czesław Miłosz**, in solidarity with the dying Jews of the Warsaw Ghetto, evaluated memory in an identical way. In ''A Poor Christian Looks at the Ghetto'' Miłosz became the first of the Polish poets to identify with the victims as a ''Jew of the New Testament,'' and he condemned the unfeeling mob in ''Campo dei Fiori.''

Różewicz emphasizes the similarities of the Polish and the Jewish tragedies in his poems ''From My Home'' and ''Polish Thermopylae.'' In the former he shows the destruction of a house and its inhabitants, and in the latter he contrasts the pathos of ancient heroism with the modern hideousness of slaughtering people with a spade, a bullet, a bayonet, poison, or the gallows. While the former illustrates the traditions of the lyricism of the threnody, the latter is an example of the more innovative poetry of Różewicz, a realist who does not avoid the ugliness of human words and acts. Różewicz puts logic and hard facts, without a romantic veil or classical conventions, above emotion. He does not shock the reader with words, but he paints brutal scenes, showing heads split with a spade, walls spattered with brains, a Polish underground fighter with spilling guts, and a hanged Jew with ''a six-pointed star in his eyes.'' He condemns murder with tremendous power, and he shares the responsibility. Różewicz the poet has survived not

REFERENCE GUIDE TO HOLOCAUST LITERATURE   COME SPRING

to enjoy life but to expose a civilization that has sunk into degradation and to identify every human evil.

This uncompromising search for the truth about the attitude to recent history has also affected Różewicz's prose. For example, the theme of the story "A Visit to the Museum" is close to that of the poems "A Little Tress" and "The Slaughter of Boys." Here Różewicz offers his reflections after a visit to the Auschwitz Museum. The textual background of "A Visit" is a story by **Tadeusz Borowski**, "People Who Were Walking," which describes the last walk people condemned to gas chambers had to take from the railway loading ramp. Writing a dozen or so years later, Różewicz was hardly less critical. He pointed out that after the end of World War II those who had become free did not become any less hypocritical. They forgot all too easily about the past because they wanted to enjoy themselves without any qualms of conscience. The author reveals his moral aversion indirectly, however. He gives different participants in the visit their own voices so that, without his interference, they themselves reveal their infantile awareness and trivial needs against the background of this terrifying graveyard, where they should remain silent in order that their hearts might speak.

In the poem "Der Tod ist ein Meister aus Deutschland," published in *Płaskorzeÿba* ("Bas-Relief") and dedicated to **Paul Celan**, Różewicz states with desperate courage, "During the time that came to be after a worthless time / after gods had left / the poets are leaving / I know I will die complete." In this way the poet came full circle to the themes, questions, and obsessions with which he began his creative journey. The old poet attempts to confront them through a diversification of the forms, genres, and styles of his strongly intertextualized artistic output, which is imbued with the thoughts of the great creators of a universal culture. This is particularly true of Franz Kafka, who with a brilliant intuition predicted in *In the Penal Colony* the hell of the totalitarian systems and of the genocide.

—Stanisław Gawliński

COME SPRING: AN AUTOBIOGRAPHICAL NOVEL
Novel by Maria Lewitt, 1980

Maria Lewitt, a volunteer guide at the Jewish Holocaust Museum in Melbourne, Australia, has been troubled by the fluidity of narratives that are constantly retold, reshaped, and polished. She was a 15-year-old schoolgirl in Lodz, Poland, when World War II started. Her wartime diaries did not survive, but when she embarked on her autobiographical novel, *Come Spring,* she made a conscious effort to preserve its authenticity as testimony. *Come Spring* relives the vicissitudes and perils of the German occupation from the viewpoint of a touchy, vulnerable adolescent. This first novel won a major Australian literary award prior to publication in 1980. At a

time when knowledge of the Holocaust was limited, it attracted great publicity and interest. Publication by the Australian/New Zealand edition of the *Reader's Digest* gave it a readership of more than 180,000.

The raw material of most Holocaust memoirs is an individual's struggle for survival against the odds. The historical event that destroyed most of European Jewry is mediated by an individual story in which the reader is exposed to the conventional dynamics of fiction and the cathartic effects of suspense, awe, and pity. *Come Spring* also conforms to this pattern as Lewitt records how people reacted to extreme conditions. But in addition it is a novel about thresholds of awareness and development. At the beginning of the occupation, Lewitt's father was beaten to death in his own home by a member of the SS. Shortly afterward her mother fled with her daughters to Warsaw. Lewitt and her mother symbolized the traumatic rupture with the past, the sudden loss of a prosperous home and family, by burning treasured letters and photos. Lewitt also cut off her schoolgirl plaits. From this point one follows the girl's unconscious struggle to fulfill the developmental norms of ordinary adolescence in extraordinary circumstances. The tensions of adolescent separation and independence from family are complicated by a hostile environment in which family is the only resource for survival.

As in Anne Frank's diary the reader is drawn into an ordinary teenager's inner life. Self-pity over her perceived victimization by her mother is as intense as awareness of external danger. Sexual and romantic impulses contrive fulfillment in the most confined, awkward settings. Though there are many touching similarities, the canvas is broader than Frank's diary. In 1940–41 Lewitt lived in relative security and comfort in the Warsaw Ghetto, while children died on the street of disease and starvation. She witnessed summary executions and other arbitrary brutality. Often hungry and frightened herself, she also had to contend with survivor guilt, which intensified after leaving friends behind in the ghetto.

Apart from their own danger, inability to help or protect others was often unbearable, and her mother experienced an acute episode of depression. The strains of clandestine existence outside the ghetto never eased. A visit by thugs (*szmalcowniki*) whose racket was blackmail and denunciation of hidden Jews forced the family to move to the secluded village home of Lewitt's aunt, who was married to an impoverished Polish nobleman.

Lewitt also began to grapple with the implications of her parents' mixed marriage. Her mother Lydia's "good look" (that is, blond and Slavic) was the family's passport to survival. Unlike documents, the "good look" was an internalized category that could not be forged or bought. The emotional fault lines within the family were deepened by this ethnic divide.

A convert to Judaism, Lewitt's mother remained Russian to the core. She saved her children and their extended family and was generous to a fault to others. But those she protected often questioned her judgment. They resented her risk-taking and feared their security was compromised by her irrepressibly extroverted temperament.

Lydia and her sister Olga are depicted through the eyes of a dependent yet increasingly critical teenager. The ironic obliqueness of this portrayal is one of the novel's artistic highlights. Outside the square the reader sees how the risky, ambiguous allegiances that Maria and her Jewish relatives so distrusted were their salvation. Lydia and Olga liked, and were liked by, all kinds of men. Equally at ease with professed anti-Semites and Jews, they bridged a divide that had become a fatal chasm in wartime. Olga had married an outspokenly anti-Semitic Polish aristocrat of the old school who sheltered his in-laws and their extended family in their hour of need. The sisters' indiscreet relationship with the local leader of the Polish underground also produced unexpected dividends at a time of crisis. Their undisciplined Russian ways represented a small victory for humanity over murderous ideology. By the time it was Lewitt's turn to love, the teenager had learned from her mother not to let anything, least of all fear or caution, get in the way of her happiness.

Lewitt spent five extraordinary years under German occupation. When the war ended she was a young adult of 20, about to marry and have a child. The effect of the suffering she witnessed and experienced is probably still immeasurable, even to her. By nature Holocaust testimonies are skewed to the resilience of survivors. This late twentieth-century coming-of-age novel faithfully records the interplay of light and shadow.

—Felicity Bloch

THE CONDEMNED OF ALTONA (Les Séquestrés d'Altona)
Play by Jean Paul Sartre, 1960

Jean-Paul Sartre's *The Condemned of Altona* is the author's only work that directly addresses the Holocaust. First produced in Paris in 1959, the play is a tense family psychodrama that explores issues of German guilt and responsibility for wartime and Holocaust atrocities. At the center of *The Condemned of Altona* is Frantz Gerlach, a German World War II veteran who has locked himself in his bedroom for more than a decade and deluded himself into believing that Germany is the ultimate victim of the war. The play slowly reveals the source of Frantz's psychological torment in ever-deepening layers of darkness. Although it is not immediately clear from the surface of the work, Sartre—who wrote *The Condemned of Altona* as France brutally strove to maintain its colonial rule over Algeria in the late 1950s—intended the play to be a comment on French involvement in Algeria as well as on Holocaust-era Germany.

The Condemned of Altona has two narrative threads. One follows the Gerlach family, which has survived World War II intact and whose members live comfortably in their home in the German town of Altona. The Gerlach father is busy rebuilding the family's shipping business. Under the general amnesty granted by the Allies, and buoyed by Germany's postwar economic recovery, the Gerlachs are regaining their fortune, though the patriarch is dying of throat cancer. Aware that he will soon be dead, Gerlach *père* wants his son Werner to return home to live and run the business. On the surface the Gerlachs are a staid, respectable bunch. "We may lose our principles, but we keep our habits," a daughter comments.

But beneath this placid, bourgeois surface run the raving monologues of the family's insane son Frantz, who returned from the Russian front 13 years before the action of the play begins. Frantz has barricaded himself in a windowless upstairs room of the Gerlach family home. He paces, eats oysters, and rants constantly into a tape recorder, making a tape for "the thirtieth century." He refuses to speak to anyone but his sister Leni, with whom he is having an incestuous affair. With Leni supporting his delusions, Frantz has convinced himself that Germany is suffering at the hands of the Allies, that German children starve in orphanages, and that its cities lie in ruins. Above all, Frantz refuses to accept the fact of Germany's renewed prosperity.

These two plots collide when Werner's wife Johanna decides to confront Frantz in an effort to free the entire family from his domination. In peeling back the layers of Frantz's insanity like onion skins, the play moves forward and backward in time, slowly revealing the horrible secret that has condemned Frantz to Altona. These flashbacks also serve to heighten the dramatic tension of the play, as the reader is only slowly shown the full truth. It initially seems that Frantz is in hiding because of trouble with an American soldier who tried to rape his sister. But the truth is far more complicated. As the play progresses, we learn that Frantz saw his father sell off family land for use as a concentration camp. Further, during the war years Frantz tried to save a rabbi, but his father intervened to ensure that the Jew was sent to his death. Then his father forced Frantz to enlist in the German army. In the army Frantz allowed captured enemy soldiers to be shot. For some time Sartre leaves the reader with the impression that this is the real reason Frantz went into hiding. In the final act, however, the stinging final layer is exposed. Frantz not only allowed the murder of men placed in his custody but he was also a full-fledged torturer, the "Butcher of Smolensk." If his father had not bribed some German soldiers, Frantz would have been tried as a war criminal. In the family's attic Frantz has been hiding both from his guilt and because of it.

Responsibility is the key issue that underlies *The Condemned of Altona*. Like much of Sartre's other work, the play explores human freedom—in this case by asking whether Frantz committed his barbarous acts freely. In *The Condemned of Altona* Sartre limns the question of whether Frantz was inexorably drawn down that path by the conditioning influences of his family and society or whether he made a conscious—and therefore morally culpable—choice. Frantz's final words provide Sartre's answer to the question of who was responsible: ''I have been,'' he cries. Frantz's madness, Sartre judges, was his own choice as well, one freely made. His delusions were merely his attempt to justify his actions.

—Rebecca Stanfel

THE CONVERSATIONS WITH AN EXECUTIONER
(Rozmowy z katem)
Memoir by Kazimierz Moczarski, 1977

The Conversations with an Executioner by Kazimierz Moczarski were first published in the years 1972–74 in a literary monthly, ''Odra.'' The publication in a book form took place in Warsaw in 1977. Both versions were red-penciled. The first Polish completed edition appeared in 1992, after the downfall of Communism. The work has been translated into many languages, and it is frequently republished. The first English translation was published in 1981.

Besides the sociopsychological study of a Nazi criminal and the reflections on the phenomenon of the Nazi system, the Holocaust is the most important aspect of the book. Its special status results from the uniqueness of the author's fate. Moczarski is a Polish patriot, a Home Army soldier, who for 225 days in 1949 shared a death cell with Nazi war criminal General Jürgen Stroop, the liquidator of the Warsaw Ghetto, and Gustaw Schielke, a German police officer in the General Gubernya.

Moczarski published his recollections 27 years after his detention by the Communists and 16 years after his release from prison and rehabilitation. In his memoirs he recalls his death-cell experience and shares with the reader his impressions of the meeting with the executioner of the Warsaw Ghetto.

Beginning the Grossaktion Warshau, the Germans entered the ghetto on 19 April 1943 at 6 A.M. The action was officially finished on 16 May at 8:15 P.M. after blowing up the Great Synagogue in Tlomackie Street. Single fighting and hunts for the hiding Jews took several more months. The SS troops under Stroop's command murdered 70,000 Jews and turned the ghetto into a burned desert.

The prison portrait of the executioner reveals an average man, rather limited intellectually, who is a product of Nazi training and literature. Stroop is a party dogmatist, believing in the superiority of the German race and treating the Jews and Gypsies as an inferior species. This is a man of party morality for whom sources of satisfaction are discipline, party promotions,

and well-obeyed orders. Stroop told Moczarski of many details concerning the liquidation of the ghetto, of the surprise with the resistance, and of the extension of the action that took much longer than the originally planned three days. He mentioned the fighting tactics and the fact that putting the city on fire was the only effective method of exterminating the rebels. He also talked about the role of the canal communication, night fighting, the armament of his troops, and the numbers of the ghetto defenders killed and caught daily as well as the plans of building a German representative housing estate on the site of the former ghetto. Pressed by his interlocutor, Stroop many times expresses his admiration and appreciation for the architecture of the bunkers and for the determination of the fighting Jews.

It is difficult to classify this book as a genre. The author tries to reconstruct faithfully the prison dialogues of 1949. It begins with diary notes, only to change into memoirs enriched with elements of essaylike discourse or academic study. The report also has some literary values. Stroop's confession composed in retrospect, many years later, is arranged in thematic sequences. The chapters have interpretative headings, which at the same time have the value of a generalizing metaphor. This is also a drama of three actors. A considerable role is played here by Schielke, who from the point of view of a realistically minded, lower-rank subordinate compromises Stroop's frequent propagandist and ideological slogans. Moczarski is particularly predestined to conversations with Stroop, since being an officer of the Home Army Information and Propaganda Bureau he was well informed about the situation in the Warsaw Ghetto and in the underground movement. He often completes and corrects the report of the SS general, reveals his lies, and forces him to tell the truth. Thus, in spite of the declared emotional detachedness resulting from the common fate in prison and from the attitude of an explorer, Moczarski confronts Stroop several times. Such moments, as well as the ever present, though not always manifested, clashes of two separate attitudes determine the dramaturgy of the book.

—Kazimierz Adamczyk

COUNTING MY STEPS: AN AUTOBIOGRAPHY
Memoir by Jakov Lind, 1969

Counting My Steps, published in 1969, recounts Jakov Lind's traumatic experiences during the Holocaust when he was forced as an 11-year-old to leave his parents and home in Vienna, Austria, for The Netherlands, where he lived with various foster families. After the country's occupation by the Nazis, Lind was moved into the Amsterdam ghetto. He avoided deportation, and after having obtained false identification papers, Lind went into hiding. He spent the last stages of the war in Nazi Germany dodging discovery by the Nazis and Allied air raids.

Lind's work is not merely a story of miraculous survival but a deeply personal account of the author's inner crisis resulting from his experiences. The author poignantly reveals loss of identity, cultural alienation, and guilt feelings about having lived as being the price of survival. Nevertheless, his exploration of the horror that he escaped is accompanied by the assertion of an overwhelming lust for life, which undoubtedly helped him survive the ever-present danger.

The text is composed of three parts: ''School for Metaphysics,'' ''School for Politics,'' and ''School for Alchemy.'' These titles clearly place the emphasis on the author's inner developments instead of on outer events. In the first part Lind reflects on his childhood in Vienna. He describes the influences that shaped his early identity and, consequently, his outlook on life. This includes descriptions of his family and his fascination with German and Russian literature and socialist and Zionist ideas, as well as his experiences with the covert anti-Semitism in Vienna, which became rampant with the Anschluss of 1938. In the second part Lind describes his desperate struggle for survival. He escapes deportation by the Nazis by refusing to show up at the collection place. Instead he assumes the identity of the fictitious young Dutchman Jan Overbeek, later volunteering as a foreign laborer for Nazi Germany. He works on a large barge plying the German rivers and, after Allied bombs destroy his ship, he moves on to work for the director of a research unit in the German Air Ministry. The constant danger, the rough milieu in which he moves, and the continual need to change his identity take an emotional toll: ''I thought I had fallen out of all spheres and beyond and underneath all levels. I was not part of humanity . . . I am not speaking of loneliness and isolation. I am speaking of nonexistence . . . Not because my initials had changed and I listened to another name; my consciousness had ceased to function altogether.'' The alienation from self extends beyond the end of the war. In the last part the reader learns of Lind's aimless drifting in Palestine. His peregrinations come to an end after he writes and publishes the diaries of a young man who escaped the death camps of Europe only to be killed in battle shortly after his arrival in Palestine. Writing this story helps Lind come to terms with his own experiences and rid himself of his crippling emotions. The memoirs end with Lind's return to Europe in search of a new personal and cultural identity.

Counting My Steps marks Lind's shift from writing in German to English. In the introduction to the German edition of the work, which Lind helped translate, Lind explains that he couldn't have written his autobiography in German as he needed distance from his subject matter. Seemingly the linguistic distancing made it possible for him to analyze his experiences and actions objectively and to reveal honestly the emotional turmoil that led him to reject his Jewishness. In addition this distance made it possible for him to situate his own story within the larger context of the Nazi terror. He describes German occupation of neighboring countries; persecution, ghettoization, and deportation of the Jewish population; forced labor practices; and finally the misery of the displaced-persons camps after the war. The work successfully reveals the connections between an individual life and the historic events of the Holocaust without privileging one over the other. With its lucid style and its perfect balance of reflection and dramatic narration, Lind's autobiography is a most successful example of this genre.

—Helga Schreckenberger

A CUP OF TEARS: A DIARY OF THE WARSAW GHETTO
Diary by Abraham Lewin, 1988

Abraham Lewin kept a diary in the Warsaw Ghetto in connection with his activities as a member of the Oneg Shabbes group, an archival project under the direction of **Emmanuel Ringelblum**. The two hidden archives recovered after the war each included one part of Lewin's diary: ''From the Notebooks,'' written in Yiddish and covering the period from 26 March to 12 June 1942; and ''Diary of the Great Deportation,'' written in Hebrew and covering the period from 22 July 1942 to 16 January 1943. The extant text may be incomplete. The final entry date suggests that Lewin broke off because he was himself deported to his death in the major *Aktion* that commenced two days later. The diary was interrupted before Lewin could give an account of the resistance of the Jewish Fighting Organization at that time and thereafter in the Warsaw Ghetto Uprising that began on 19 April 1943.

The diaries are carefully circumscribed by the designs of an archivist rather than by the desire to articulate personal experience. Typically, Lewin limits his own presence in his narrative while concentrating attention on the stories of his informants. In this approach Lewin fulfills Ringelblum's prescription for '''good' work.'' ''The method,'' writes Ringelblum in his own diary (*Notes from the Warsaw Ghetto,* 1958) on 23 May 1942, ''[is to] sit down with the informant over a glass of tea, and write up the information afterward.'' Only the tea appears to be missing. Ringelblum, in turn, has words of praise for Lewin's text: ''The clean and compressed style of the diary, its accuracy and precision in relating facts, and its grave contents qualify it as an important literary document.'' Lewin himself makes the same point about style when he asserts in the midst of the massive deportations of the summer of 1942, ''Future generations will not believe it. But this is the unembellished truth, plain and simple.'' His generally understated tone allows the facts to speak for themselves, thus casting the breaks in his rhetorical restraint into high relief. When Levin allows himself to exclaim, ''It is horrific, quite horrific,'' the pathos of a dignified observer pushed to the edge of his sensibilities is patent. That tone of utter despair is most often evoked when he receives testimony of the killing of children. And when he permits himself to speak in such terms as "annihilation machine" (for example, with respect to Treblinka) or "the war against them" (that is, against the Jews), one recognizes that this, too, is not embellishment but rather the language of accuracy and precision.

The ideal of the unembellished truth guides Lewin's reportage. He is attentive to the difference between rumor and "a very reliable source"; he compiles conflicting viewpoints; and he provides follow-up accounts of incidents. Lewin is especially zealous in seeking out the numbers and names of victims, thereby giving voice to two impulses fundamental to the diary. The numbers speak to the inhuman magnitude of the crime committed against the Jews; the names nevertheless humanize each tragedy. Lewin's dedication to the truth also demands of him an unsentimental view of the Jews themselves. He records moments of mutual aid, but he is also unrelenting in setting down Jewish crimes: the complicity of the Jewish police, above all, as well as the looting in the wake of deportations. In a related note of personal poignancy, having already expressed a hope that no Jews would volunteer to join the labor battalion organized by the Nazis for the removal of the possessions of the deported, Lewin is pained to note that his own daughter Ora was now thus employed.

Lewin's view of Ora's labor points beyond the personal realm to a leitmotif that runs through the diaries and the ghetto. On the one hand, the well-informed and astute Lewin is determined to hold no illusions, to pierce the ruses of the Nazis. But he cannot defend himself entirely from hope—not so much the hope of surviving, which he relinquished almost entirely, especially after the deportation of his beloved wife, Luba (née Hotner), but more the hope that reason itself might be salvaged. As late as 28 December 1942 Lewin can still find it noteworthy that "the Germans killed five men, without carrying out any kind of investigation." He is still hoping that rational inquiry remains an operant principle under the Nazis. If he does not see his hopes fulfilled, he does succeed in making a powerful record of the killings.

—Andrew Bush

D

THE DANCE OF GENGHIS COHN (La Danse de Genghis Cohn)
Novel by Romain Gary, 1967

The Dance of Genghis Cohn, published in French as *La Danse de Genghis Cohn* in 1967 and in English translation in 1968, is at once a detective novel and an extended essay on the challenges Romain Gary believed the Holocaust posed for European civilization. A satirical treatment of the reluctance of postwar Germany to remember or draw lessons from the Holocaust, *Genghis Cohn* uses a police investigation as the occasion for a "psychological examination" of German culture. In a small German town an inquiry into serial murder leads the local police into "the Forest of *Geist*" (Spirit) in pursuit of the beautiful Baroness Lily Von Pritwitz and her accomplice, symbols of "Germany's" murderous past. Gary's grandiose and highly speculative psychological analysis of "German" brutality was a well-established device for writers who sought after 1945 to uphold the virtues they attached to German culture while insisting that the ills that had made Germany genocidal were still deeply embedded in the culture. At its blackest Gary's biting satire does not aim to be humorous, but the book is nevertheless a conscious effort to show that mass murderers and the societies that try to ignore them are a fit subject for humor and ridicule.

The most perceptive attempts at laying bare the flawed representatives of humanity in *The Dance of Genghis Cohn* lie in the relationship between the ghost of a Jewish comedian, Genghis Cohn, and the detective charged with the investigation, the former SS officer who killed him, Lieutenant Schatz. (His name means "treasure," a common term for a lover in Germany.) Schatz struggles in vain to free himself of his Jewish ghost but instead is forced to learn to speak Yiddish and to observe Jewish customs. Nevertheless, he continues to make remarks that indicate he has forgotten the murders he committed, and Cohn chooses such moments to appear to Schatz. As Cohn tells the reader, appearing any more frequently might give Schatz cause to seek psychological treatment, and the last thing a ghost wants is to be exorcized. The Jewish ghost exists only because he continues to haunt his erstwhile assassin.

The parallels between his bitter commentary and the sense of alienation felt by many Jews in Europe in the 1960s make Cohn a fascinating character. Like the Jewish philosopher André Neher, Gary wrote with evident anxiety at the attempts of other Europeans to rehabilitate the "new" Germany, apparently oblivious to the signs of continuity with the Nazi past that continued to appear in news reports across the West. *The Dance of Genghis Cohn* presents a subtle commentary on the interdependence of antagonistic European Jewish and German memories of the Holocaust 20 years after the events, with both groups increasingly affected by their responses to the different premises on which they relate to the past. On the basis of their shared experiences and bound by a history of mutual antagonism, Schatz and Cohn also develop an intimacy and solidarity that neither has chosen. By interweaving this complicated fictional relationship with descriptions of real events in postwar German history, Gary created one of the most sophisticated commentaries on Jewish-German relationships that has ever been published.

It is significant that Genghis Cohn (the name suggestive of his own part Jewish, part Asian identity) is a Yiddish speaker from Warsaw, where Gary had spent part of his childhood and which he visited again on the publication of the book. Clearly familiar with the life of eastern European Yiddish-speaking communities, Gary took the opportunity to describe some of the features of the religious and cultural life of a traditional Jew exposed to the modern world. Indeed, the book is as much an exploration of contemporary Jewish identity as it is an essay on the Holocaust. We learn only of the occasion of the killing of the Jews shot with Cohn before the book passes on to a more general discussion of German-Jewish relations in the 1960s. In Cohn's commentary on current events the development of a new generation in Germany with no knowledge of the Holocaust is as dangerous as the persistent survival of former Nazis, who at least were haunted by the ghosts of the past, in leading positions in German society. In Cohn's perspective Jewish and German identities were bound for one brief generation, and for the younger generation the Jews of Europe have already become entirely invisible.

That the Holocaust happened is not Gary's primary target. Rather, it is the apparent fact that the civilized postwar world could respond to the persistence of Nazi influences on the new Germany as if the Holocaust had not happened. The ghost in *The Dance of Genghis Cohn* embodies a pessimism about both Jewish and non-Jewish memory of the Holocaust that fittingly marked an end to Gary's literary preoccupation with the subject. His subsequent novels on Jewish themes abandoned reference to the Holocaust altogether.

—George R. Wilkes

DARK SOLILOQUY: THE SELECTED POEMS OF GERTRUD KOLMAR (Das lyrische Werk)
Collection of Poems by Gertrud Kolmar, 1955

Dark Soliloquy provides in side-by-side German original and English translation a panoramic selection from Gertrud

Kolmar's lyrical work from roughly 1928 to 1937. It contains material from the poem cycles "Image of Woman," "Animal Dreams," "Rose Sonnets," "Prussian Coats of Arms," and "Worlds." With the exception of "Worlds," in which Kolmar abandoned her otherwise consistent adherence to strict forms, Kolmar's poems show a conservative approach to form (strictly maintained common meters, end rhyme, and consistent verse and stanza length). What is striking and innovative about Kolmar's formally traditional poetry are her exceedingly rich and sensual language, her daring portrayals of female sexuality, and her ability to identify with and give voice to the mute or marginalized through a vast array of lyrical personae, including social outcasts (primarily women), children, animals, and plants. None of the poems collected in *Dark Soliloquy* address explicitly the Holocaust or the persecution of Jews and other groups in Germany under National Socialism. Many of these poems, however, were clearly influenced by Kolmar's experiences during this time as a member of multiple marginalized and persecuted groups (as a Jew, a woman, and an artist). The collection was originally published as *Das lyrische Werk* in 1955, and the English translation appeared in 1975

The lyrical "I" of "The Troglodyte" is a cave-dwelling, animal-like woman, at once sexual predator and mother. The troglodyte, in heat, lies in wait for a lost wanderer, whom she rapes (the translator misleadingly renders this clearly sexual passage as a hunt for food). After the attack she returns to her cave where both child and bat hang on her "swollen udders." Through her association with bats, as well as with other despised animals (vipers, snails, and toads), she resembles a she-vampire, a common stereotype of female Jewish sexuality (Kolmar employs similar imagery in "Metamorphoses"). Kolmar's portrayal, however, is not without compassion for the troglodyte, who herself fears the dark forest and its creatures and is not only the hunter but also the hunted (*gehetzt*).

In "The Toad" the lyrical "I" assumes the persona of a toad, a lowly despised animal, a Jew among animals. The toad is depicted as a soulful creature who loves the sunset, stars, and "whispering of the night." Cognizant of man's disdain for her, the toad nonetheless confidently asserts her self-worth, "Come and kill me! Though to you I'm but a [disgusting] pest: I am the toad, and wear a precious jewel." Unlike many contemporaneous poets (Rainer Maria Rilke, for example), Kolmar does not simply use animals as metaphors but is interested in the animals themselves. In "Judgement Day, Held by Animals Tortured to Death" (not included in *Dark Soliloquy*), Kolmar condemns humans' use of animals for food, clothing, and luxury goods, as well as the capture of zoo animals and animal testing. Dagmar Lorenz suggests in her book *Transforming the Center, Eroding the Margins* that Kolmar, like other Jewish authors, such as Elias Canetti, sought to reevaluate the hierarchical categories of man versus animal, recognizing that the degradation of animals was the first step in the degradation of human beings, "open[ing] the door to the extermination of lives 'unworthy of living.'"

In a 1 October 1939 letter to her sister, Kolmar reports that the "events of the world" no longer "moved" her as before. The poem "Asia" is reflective of Kolmar's withdrawal from the harsh realities of everyday life into an inner world where she is transported to "exotic" locales far from Europe. The idealization of Asia in particular can be attributed to her sympathy for Zionism. In a 13 May 1939 letter to her sister, Kolmar describes herself as a "hindered Asian." Although she never seriously considered emigration, in another letter (24 November 1940) she rejects America as a potential destination, explaining, "My face looks Eastward, Southeast." The poem "Asia" positions Asia as homeland: "Mother, Mine before my own had held me, I am going home." Corresponding to the German designations of Europe as "Eveningland" and Asia as "Morningland," Europe appears in the poem as a jealous old maid, "She mimics you . . . this gray maid, and mocks your movements and your words." The same Zionist yearning is expressed in "The Jewish Woman." The lyrical "I" expresses feelings of alienation in her present surroundings, "I am a stranger," and the wish to "mount an expedition into my [own] ancient land." The journey is clearly not aliyah but travel inward. From within the locked towers that gird her, she explores her people's distant past, returning to sites of Jewish history and reuniting with the Jewish matriarchs.

In "We Jews" the lyrical "I" embraces the suffering of her people, celebrating martyrdom as the hallmark of Jewish identity, "The gallows and torture wheel made us what we are" (translation by Elizabeth Loentz). She welcomes her destiny, "When the bitter hour strikes I want to rise up, like all of you did, and be a triumphal arch through which suffering will march" (translation by Loentz). The willingness to accept fate is echoed in the poem "The Sacrifice" and in Kolmar's 24 January 1943 letter to her sister, where she reports that she has learned *amor fati*. This seeming passivity does not preclude the poet's wish to be a voice for her people. Although her "lips are sealed in glowing wax," the poet "I" longs to "be the voice that echoes down the shaft of all eternity" and "raise [her] voice to be a blazing torch . . . and thunder: Justice! Justice! Justice."

—Elizabeth Loentz

DARKNESS CASTS NO SHADOW
Novel by Arnošt Lustig, 1976

Darkness Casts No Shadow by Arnošt Lustig is his most autobiographical work. The film adaptation appeared in 1964 under the direction of Jan Němec and is a milestone of Czech New Wave cinema. It is the story of two boys, Manny and

Danny, who escape a train that has been bombed on its way to a German death camp. As seen in the novel *Diamonds of the Night,* the action is interspersed with memories of the past, ranging from family activities to the horrors of concentration camp life. The characters' thoughts are clearly defined for the reader, but still it is not known what course of action any character will take. Will the boys kill in order to survive? Is killing right when one could be killed? Is it worth the risk not to kill? Moral dilemma permeates the work, and the boys learn that what a person says is not always the action he or she will take. One example of this is the boys' friend, Frank Bondy, who talks boldly of escape. But when the train is bombed, he stays behind with his mortally wounded Polish girlfriend, thus leaving Manny and Danny to deal with escape into the forest on their own. He states: "Just remember, boys, every person in the world always lives at least two lives. In one, he plays with an open hand of cards so that everybody can see, and in the other, he's the only one who knows what he's got. I hope you know what I mean." In another example, a rabbi, who has taken Danny under his wing like a son, preaches of God's trickery upon and testing of people. He then proceeds to steal Danny's bread ration: "'That's how it goes here,' a Hungarian rabbi had said once. 'You don't have to accept the idea that everyone lives and dies alone,' he said. It was like a huge sinking ship, where no one cries out any longer, but each hears the same old refrain, 'Every man for himself.' That was before his bread ration was stolen. But even that is not fatal."

Lustig's work portrays people not as individuals but rather as madmen who are all members of a larger group of madmen. They cease to be what they were and become instead creatures who can only depend upon themselves for survival. The rabbi is a prime example of this fact for Danny.

After the train wrecks, the forest into which the boys have run will either swallow them up or lead them to freedom, though what sort of freedom it is remains to be seen at the end of the novel. The specter of death is well represented by crows, birds that will eat anything. The boys are surprised that they are still picky about what they eat, a reference to the fact that they are alive and, therefore, still consider themselves to be human. They have not yet joined that circle of madmen. Danny is crippled by a nail in his shoe and the wound begins to fester, hindering the boys' escape. One cannot help but to surmise, however, that Danny has purposely left the nail exposed in order to hasten his own death, leaving him to become food for the crows.

The work is indeed dark and suspenseful. The imagery of the forest, the blackness of the crows, and the apprehension at nightfall serve to feed the reader's mind with the horror of the boys' fate. The novel ends with the boys' death, and there ceases the similarity with Lustig's own life.

—Cynthia A. Klíma

DAWN (L'Aube)
Novel by Elie Wiesel, 1960

In Elie Wiesel's *Night* he writes about Jews reacting to persecution and threats to their existence with a kind of defensive amnesia—a refusal to believe the horrors confronting them combined with a passive inaction. One example of this is when Wiesel's cousin urges Elie's father, Chlomo Wiesel, to try to escape from the ghetto on the eve of deportation to Auschwitz and he refuses to do so. Another example of this defensive amnesia is when Moché the Beadle survives a mass killing at the hands of the Nazis and the Jews of Sighet refuse to believe him when he comes to warn them.

Wiesel wrote *Dawn* (1961; *L'Aube,* 1960) to signal that Jews were no longer willing to accept threats to their security with an impassive defensive amnesia but had, in fact, become very militant in defense of their vital interests. The novel takes place in 1945, when Jewish settlers were fighting the British in order to erect a Jewish homeland in Israel/Palestine (which happened in 1948.)

The protagonist Elisha is an 18-year-old survivor of Buchenwald who, after living in Paris, agrees to go to Israel as a member of a militant organization fighting the British. The British have decided to hang one of the organization's leading members, David ben Moshe, and Elisha is assigned to kill an English hostage, Captain John Dawson, in retaliation.

Elisha's killing of John Dawson is done without anger or hatred or any vendetta whatsoever against the British officer but with deep sorrow that Elisha tries to reinterpret as hatred. Indeed, his decision to go through with the killing causes him inner turmoil: "I didn't hate him at all, but I wanted to hate him. That would have made it all very easy. Hate—like faith or love or war—justifies everything."

Elisha's thoughts as he is contemplating the execution of John Dawson signify a transition from the defensive amnesia of the Jews who were sent to the concentration camps to the militant Jews of Palestine: "Without hate, everything that my comrades and I were doing would be in vain. Without hate we could not hope to obtain victory. Why do I try to hate you, John Dawson? Because my people have never known how to hate. Their tragedy, throughout the ages, has stemmed from their inability to hate those who have humiliated and from time to time exterminated them." With this reflection, Wiesel signifies that pacifism is not a part of the Jewish future, particularly not the Jewish future in Israel, because of what Jews suffered during the Holocaust. The Jews of Israel continue to be haunted by the grim situational ethics of the Holocaust as they struggle to make the Jewish homeland a viable place to live.

—Peter R. Erspamer

DEATH FUGUE (Todesfuge)
Poem by Paul Celan, 1948

Paul Celan's "Death Fugue" was originally written in Romanian in 1944, put in its final form in 1945, then translated into German in 1948, the date of its first publication. It has appeared in several English translations. In its German version the poem has become widely known and is frequently invoked as a principal instance of Holocaust poetry. It juxtaposes and provocatively links the two German achievements of masterful artistry and unprecedented mass murder. Celan patterns his poem—about a blue-eyed German master who rules over a death camp where Jews shovel their graves—after the cyclical theme-and-repetition model of a baroque fugue. The poem's central image depicts Jewish prisoners forced to dig their graves and play music while being told that they will rise like smoke in the air. In the poem's most trenchant formulation, which has served as title for innumerable anthologies and documentaries, Celan declares that "death is a master from Germany." Celan based "Death Fugue" on accounts by survivors of concentration camps returning to Romania in late 1944. He describes no particular camp but invokes an unspecified murderous setting outside of Germany where individual agency and perspective all but vanish in the numbing monotony of forced laborers toiling on the brink between life and death.

The poem's incantatory rhythm is propelled by a haunting refrain of "Black milk of daybreak we drink it at nightfall." The recurring line introduces a series of stark and quasi-surrealist images recounted in the present tense by an unidentified "we" which presumably encompasses all Jewish victims of the Holocaust. Each of the poem's six varied-length stanzas includes disturbingly concrete descriptions of "a man" alternately writing to his sweetheart in Germany, playing with snakes, whistling his dogs, swinging an iron bat, ordering "his Jews" to dig and to sing, and shooting them "with perfect aim." In this decidedly modernist poem, sentence fragments are spliced and recombined to create the impression of a scene of suffering, fear, and death that is at once chaotic and random, yet entirely self-contained.

In response to critics' suggestions that the artistic achievement of "Death Fugue" transcends all suffering, Celan insisted in a letter in the 1960s that the "grave in the air" in "*this* poem, God knows, is neither a borrowed reference nor a metaphor." At the time "Death Fugue" had become a touchstone in debates about the possibility of writing "poetry after Auschwitz," which German philosopher Theodor W. Adorno had famously declared to be "barbaric." Since Celan feared that his poem might be misunderstood as whitewashing German crimes or overcoming the Holocaust by means of art, he stressed the literalness of his images.

The poem contains both explicit and oblique references to German and Jewish literary sources. Its rhythmic structure is a decidedly modernist adaptation of a long tradition of dances of death in works as diverse as medieval verse, the poetry of Heinrich Heine, and the lyric modernism of Georg Trakl. Although "Death Fugue" is a severe indictment of the notion of German-Jewish coexistence, it refuses to forsake the artistic achievements often associated with the German tradition, or to uncouple these achievements from Jewish influence. Celan places the German camp commander's "golden-haired Margarete" from Goethe's *Faust* tragedy next to and ultimately contrasts her with an "ashen-haired Shulamith" from the "Song of Songs." Celan even employs the Nazis' cynicism ("we are digging a grave in the air there we won't lie too cramped") to assert his right to speak on behalf of Jewish survivors, and to condemn the German crimes all the more severely by relying on artistic means associated with German culture. The deceptively straightforward poem becomes a powerful dirge for the Jewish victims of German violence through Celan's technique of layering several contradictory meanings into a single compacted image.

In the 1960s Celan's poem became a standard literary representation of the camp experience. Partly in response to overly formalist readings of "Death Fugue" where the poem's theme was downplayed in favor of metrical analyses or buried with praise of its literary achievement, Celan refused reprinting it in anthologies. He was also dismayed at seeing his poem included in collections with poets of erstwhile ultra-conservative or fascist political leanings or with writers who had previously been associated with the surrealist poet Yvan Goll's widow, who waged an unfounded campaign charging Celan with plagiarism. It is possible to find occasional veiled references to images from "Death Fugue" in Celan's later work. In light of the poet's suggestion that every poem is as much "wounded by reality" as it is in "search of reality," "Death Fugue" remains one of the most powerful directives in efforts to map the terrain of the Holocaust in literature.

—Ulrich Baer

THE DEATH TRAIN: A PERSONAL ACCOUNT OF A HOLOCAUST SURVIVOR
Memoir by Luba Krugman Gurdus, 1978

The Death Train: A Personal Account of a Holocaust Survivor is comprised of a double testimony, a written memoir and accompanying illustrations, both by Luba Krugman Gurdus. The text and pictures follow her along a varied and brutal path of survival, such that Gurdus's personal experiences constitute an unusually comprehensive account of the Holocaust. They include life in Warsaw at the outset of the Nazi occupation; clandestine crossings in and out of Russian territory to support her fugitive husband and brothers; displacement to the countryside and labor under Polish and Nazi authorities; flight, hiding, and passing; and internment in Majdanek, while still passing among the Polish prisoners. The precaution of maintaining multiple false identities in the camp, along with a knowledge of German, was crucial in securing release from Majdanek, after which Gurdus traveled back to Warsaw, surviving on the "Aryan side" along with her sister and the aid of helpful Poles. In a brief epilogue Gurdus relates that her husband, Jacob Gurdus, who had escaped to Palestine and joined the British army, returned to Warsaw at the close of the war and arranged for both his wife and her sister, Mira, to leave Poland.

In the wide array of personal experiences to which Gurdus attests, the death train of her title seems absent. The apparent discrepancy, however, points to the very heart of the double memoir, for Gurdus enunciates the title through her son, whose testimony is also incorporated into the book. *Death Train* is the title Gurdus ascribes to a drawing Robert Michael "Bobus" Gurdus had produced on his fourth birthday, on 24 August 1942. The child had seen the countless trains passing near the family's room in a house on the outskirts of the town of Zwierzyniec and was aware of their purpose. One of his little Polish playmates had helped to dispel any doubts: "'You will soon be in a train like that.'" His mother reassures him, "'No, no, it's not true my darling . . . Janusz is small and stupid; we will not go, I promise you.'" It is a promise Bobus reminds her of when the family is included in a later roundup of Jews, from which they obtain a last-minute reprieve. "[Bobus] often argued with his playmates that he would never be forced to mount the monster train because I would find a way to protect him," Gurdus recounts. "But the fear, looming in his subconscious, suddenly appeared with unmistakable clarity in his drawing of the death train." She reproduces the drawing facing a full-page portrait of Bobus, and in addition to the "force and conviction" she finds in her son's artwork, one also notes the manner in which his testimony is encased. It appears, coffinlike, within the frame of her own drawing, which is crowned by her own motif of the death train that she uses in other illustrations and that echoes the architecture of the Warsaw Ghetto. It is as though Gurdus were bearing her son's final resting place within herself. The particular edge of this melancholic incorporation derives from the irony that undermines the fulfillment of her promise. For, indeed, she does keep her word. Bobus never rides the death train of his drawing. Instead, he dies of diphtheria in Zwierzyniec before the roundup in which Gurdus's parents are murdered and from which she and her sister escape.

The manner in which Gurdus narrates Bobus's death is exemplary of her laconic style. "I summoned the only Polish physician in Zwierzyniec, who came in spite of German restrictions forbidding him any contact with Jews," she writes. "His prognosis was grim, and the lack of medicine sealed my son's fate." Without further elaboration, she immediately opens a new paragraph: "Our entire life now revolved around the factory." Much as in this climactic moment, her stark narrative seldom pauses for expressions of horror, outrage, or

lament. The passage is also characteristic in that, while Gurdus remarks on Polish complicity with the Nazis, she often includes brief notice, as here, of instances in which she received assistance from Poles as well. Her streamlined approach goes beyond style to touch upon the general narrative structure of the memoir. Gurdus develops neither a background of prewar tranquility nor a postwar romantic denouement, frequent features of memoir literature, as a contrast to her experience of the Holocaust. Instead, she keeps a steady focus upon the rigors of survival and chief among them the burden of loss.

—Andrew Bush

DIE DENUNZIATION
Novella by Gert Hofmann, 1979

Gert Hofmann's first major work of fiction was *Die Denunziation* ("The Denunciation"), published in German in 1979. Along with **Rolf Hochhuth**'s 1978 novel *Eine Liebe in Deutschland,* it constituted one of the few serious case studies in postwar German literature of denunciation under the Nazi regime. Unlike other authors who used references to denunciations in order to characterize in a somewhat clichéd way the poisonous moral climate during the Nazi regime, Hofmann delved deeply into the manifold impact of denunciations as they affected individual victims during the course of their entire lives.

In the novella an anonymous report of the harmless activities of the half-Jewish tailor L. Silberstein sets off a chain of events that destroy two families in the last year of the war. Silberstein, who is said to have given free lessons in tailoring, "had for such a long time and in such a miraculous manner eluded the attention of the bureaucrats or had been tolerated by them." One day in early May 1944, however, he is betrayed and "removed from the city for the purposes of liquidation." Shortly thereafter, his wife commits suicide by drowning. The German family Hecht is also affected by the denunciation of the tailor. Mr. Hecht, presumably because he has commented on the deportation of Silberstein and because of denunciation, is sent to a penal battalion on the Eastern Front and is killed within a month. Although the text is not explicit about the point, it suggests that his wife, who had taken lessons with Silberstein, is also reported to the authorities by an anonymous denouncer. She drowns herself as well. The Hechts' 14-year-old twins, Karl and Wilhelm, are separated and never see each other again.

These events are reconstructed 31 years later by one of the twin sons, Karl Hecht, now a successful lawyer in West Germany, living and working in the same small town where he grew up. Upon hearing "news of the sudden passing" of his brother, Wilhelm, who has died in a mental hospital in New

York, Karl spends the night awake, reminiscing about the events leading to their separation, browsing through his brother's notes, and at the same time preparing for the next day's trial, which deals with a case of denunciation. The narrative line seems to be held together by Karl's perspective, but it is at the same time disjointed, elliptic, and full of uncompleted sentences and fragmented thoughts. Karl's feelings and observations are recorded in the form of a letter to a mysterious colleague named Flohta, whose voice is also interjected into the narrative in the form of comments on the letter, thus bringing an additional sense of disorientation.

Hofmann called *Die Denunziation* a *Novelle,* and his work owes a great part of its effect and success to the ways in which it both conforms with and transgresses the conventions of the genre. The initial denunciation seems to be that "unheard-of event," a key element of the traditional novella, that occurs abruptly and disrupts the normal flow of life. The act of betrayal is presented as a source of irreparable ruptures as well as a poisonous web that envelopes the personal tragedies and moral failures of both brothers. Yet in Hofmann's work, unlike the traditional novella, there seem to be far more denunciations—both in the Nazi past and in the narrative present of the 1970s—each of them triggering a new set of ruptures and thus conveying a sense of the endless repetition of history and of the impossibility of an exit and a closure. Not only is Silberstein betrayed, but Hecht's father and mother are as well for their presumed sympathy with Silberstein. In addition, the original denunciation of Silberstein is mirrored in the lawsuit that Karl Hecht is participating in 30 years later. In this case a teacher, Wilhelm Treterle, is charged with assaulting a citizen whom Treterle has accused of denouncing him. Treterle, as with the Hecht brothers, finds it impossible to prove the exact terms and perpetrators of the denunciation against him and becomes a victim of the establishment.

As he compares and contrasts the lives of each of the brothers after their separation, Hofmann pronounces his moral verdict both on the shameful Nazi past and on the various ways in which postwar generations have come to terms with it. Wilhelm Hecht left Germany when he was very young and traveled around the world in a restless effort to find the "truth" about the denunciation. That has been his way of dealing with the original trauma. Failing to locate the "guilty persons," Wilhelm has not succeeded in healing the ruptures in his own life either and dies after a mental breakdown. Karl Hecht, however, has remained in the same town, become a prominent lawyer, and participated in the economic miracle in West Germany. In other words, he has sought to recover from the shock of his initial childhood trauma by relentlessly trying to forget the events of 1944.

Both models of coping with the tragic past—repression or self-absorbed explorations—are doomed to end in fiasco. The death of both brothers—the one of insanity in a New York hospital and the other of heart failure at his home after a long

night of reminiscing over repressed experiences—underscore Hofmann's pessimistic view of his generation's attitude toward the Holocaust. As long as German society continues to condone anonymous denunciations and to tolerate the persecution of people who are perceived as racially or socially different, the hope of a meaningful closure of the past does not exist.

—Mila Ganeva

THE DEPUTY (Der Stellvertreter: Ein christliches Trauerspiel)
Play by Rolf Hochhuth, 1963

From its first performance in 1963, Hochhuth's *Der Stellvertreter: Ein christliches Trauerspiel* (*The Deputy,* translated as *The Representative* in Britain) quickly became the focus of heated debate across the West over papal policy during the Holocaust. While Hochhuth's polemic against Pope Pius XII is unmistakable, *The Deputy* remains one of the most useful treatments of the context of the pope's decision not to break his Concordat with the Nazis. Dismissed by many critics for its leftist and anti-Catholic polemic, *The Deputy* has nevertheless won plaudits for its sustained liberal focus on the ability of bystanders and perpetrators to choose their response to the development of the Nazis' Final Solution. Hochhuth's documentary approach to the history of the Holocaust sits uneasily with his more philosophical objectives: *The Deputy* is also a rewriting of the Christian drama in the light of the challenges to faith presented by the Holocaust. All characters are abstracted into stereotypes to fit this dramatic schema, and not even the victims escape the distorted lens through which Hochhuth's philosophical insights unfold.

The Deputy is structured so as to contrast the Vatican's measured criticisms of Nazi policy toward the Jews with the heroism of individual Christian opponents of the Nazis. The two heroes of the play, *SS-Oberstumbannführer* Gerstein and Riccardo Fontana, find that, like Christ, they have no option if they wish to remain truly Christian but to break with their churches and to sacrifice their lives for and with the Jews, the first stage in this Christian tragedy. Their passion begins with a recognition that the Catholic hierarchy is unwilling to take even small risks to save Jews, a caution which Hochhuth suggests was partly motivated by an overriding concern to combat Soviet influence at all costs. Time and again, according to his understanding of the historical record, church protests succeeded in modifying Nazi policies. When Germany made clear it needed the Vatican in order to sue for peace, the Vatican chose to use its influence to encourage a peace settlement instead of intervening more vigorously in favour of the Jews, for Hochhuth a deeply un-Christian choice.

The action begins and ends not in Rome but in Germany. From the outset it is clear that Hochhuth saw his subject as Germany as much as Christianity. The perpetrators who appear in the cast—led by the evil Auschwitz Doctor—are faceless archetypes of bigotry and brutality, "civilised" men who made a Faustian pact with the Nazi regime at the expense of Jewish lives. In Germany Hochhuth's play was a landmark in the debate over the connections between Germany's recent past and contemporary politics, shaking the assumption that there was a fundamental breach between the perpetrators of the Holocaust and the rest of the German political elite. Hochhuth's sharpest critiques, set in Berlin and in Auschwitz, center on the cultural norms that he felt relieved Germans of any sense of responsibility for their action or inaction. Though inspired by the archetypal figures of medieval mystery plays, Hochhuth's bystanders and perpetrators nevertheless only differ from his heroes because of their decision to scorn the humane values of Christianity. The inability of any of the churches to challenge the marginalization and inversion of Christianity by its erstwhile supporters is the second key to Hochhuth's view that the Holocaust represented a Christian tragedy.

The marginal role played by Jews in *The Deputy* reflects Hochhuth's dismay at the passivity of Jews as they were led to their deaths (a view he owed to Hannah Arendt). The play opens with instructions that the cast is to play perpetrators and victims as if they are interchangeable. Sensitive to the victims' suffering, Hochhuth nevertheless had little understanding or sympathy for the way Jewish victims saw themselves. Thus, he cast all of his Jewish characters as Christian or nonreligious Western Europeans (a minority of the actual victims) and even introduced one with a brief commentary on his "Old Testament harshness." In Auschwitz the limits to Hochhuth's much-vaunted emphasis on free will are most evident. Only in order to add final insult to injury did the Doctor create the semblance of choice, tricking mothers into sending their children to a speedier and more certain death. With devilish cunning the Doctor shows Riccardo the total inability of Christians to affect the bureaucratic killing machine and the impossibility of seeking, through martyrdom, to suffer the same choiceless fate as the Jews. This presents the third level on which the Holocaust merits the description of a Christian tragedy. In the anonymous machine of Auschwitz, according to Hochhuth, God was dead, and Christianity too.

—George R. Wilkes

DEUTSCHES REQUIEM
Short Story by Jorge Luis Borges, 1949

Although well known for his erudite short stories in which he blended fantasy and realism to address complex philosophical problems, Jorge Luis Borges has played a significant role in

bringing his readership closer to topics that relate both directly and indirectly to Nazi Germany and the Holocaust. In his story "Deutsches Requiem" (published in *El Aleph*, 1949) he shows the perversity of Adolf Hitler's Germany from the perspective of an unrepentant torturer and murderer who rejoices in his horrendous deeds and does not show any remorse. After being found guilty and having been sentenced to death for crimes against humanity, Otto Dietrich zur Linde writes his confession in order to show that man can transcend all compassion and "ancient acts of tenderness."

An avid reader of Arthur Schopenhauer, Friedrich Nietzsche, and Oswald Spengler, zur Linde believes himself to be innocent in spite of his crimes (which he does not attempt to cover up) because he believes he has been part of a larger scheme, and his fulfillment of his duties as a high-ranking German officer and concentration camp director were both necessary and desirable: "The world was dying of Judaism, and of that disease of Judaism that is belief in Christ; we proffered it violence and faith in the sword . . . There are many things that must be destroyed in order to build a new order; now we know that Germany was one of them . . . What does it matter that England is the hammer and we the anvil? What matters is that violence, not servile Christian acts of timidity, now rules . . . My flesh may feel fear; I *myself* do not."

The last lines written by the protagonist of the story radiate a certain kind of nostalgia for the past rather than remorse. As a faithful believer in the larger cause of Nazism in both theory and practice, zur Linde rejects any and all acts of mercy. This becomes apparent from the outset when he writes about a Polish man imprisoned in his camp, David Jerusalem, a Whitmanesque poet from Breslau, who is seen by zur Linde as a persecuted and destitute member of a depraved and hated race. Although zur Linde reads many of his works and is moved by the poet's profound sensibility, in the end he destroys him: "I let neither compassion nor his fame make me soft. I had realized many years before I met David Jerusalem that everything in the world can be the seed of a possible hell." He kills the poet (one is never told how, although one is led to believe he commits suicide) not out of bigotry or racial hatred but out of fear and loathing of his own feelings kept deep inside him. Yet the true reason for ending the life of Jerusalem is pure destructiveness and cruelty for its own sake. Zur Linde is an intellectual who has not only read extensively but also has written on a variety of topics. He is neither a natural born killer nor a person who is mentally insane; he is rather a servant of Nazi ideology and a dutiful follower of its principles.

Though it has been hinted at by some critics that Borges's attempt to deal with the Holocaust puts the reader at too great a distance from the physical and moral horror of the events, one must take into account the fact that the story was published in 1949 (and was written even earlier), shortly after the Nuremberg trials of 1945–46 and long before the Holocaust became a topic for writers of fiction, especially in Argentina and the rest of

Latin America. Borges's stories were not concerned solely with the real events of the horror that took place in the Shoah but rather with the destruction of German culture as a whole by the Nazis. In his epilogue to *The Aleph* Borges explained how "Deutsches Requiem" was an attempt to try to come to terms with the Nazi horror and his sorrow for the tragic destiny of German culture.

—Alejandro Meter

DIAMONDS OF THE NIGHT (Demanty noci)
Short stories by Arnošt Lustig, 1958

Diamonds of the Night, published in 1958 and in English translation in 1986, is a collection of nine short stories. The stories progress to the end of World War II, and, therefore, some of Lustig's most optimistic and humanistic stories appear in this work. The cruelty and savagery of the Nazis, however, is ever present. Several stories are intertwined with memories of the past that are in stark contrast to the occurrences of the present. Unpleasant situations are used not as an excuse for revenge but rather as learning devices. The Germans, as well as the Jews, have suffered losses in the war. Characters are interdependent, and comradeship becomes a necessity of survival. As an old man in "The White Rabbit" relates, "We only live for ourselves, but to do even that, we need others." This indeed rings true in this collection. It is this statement that binds together these works and conveys the stories toward the conclusion of the war.

The stories can be grouped into five different themes: hopelessness/despair, reliance, the old and forgotten, glimpses of humanism, and the end of the war. In "Lemon" hopelessness and despair are represented by a lemon that a young boy named Erwin must procure for his ailing sister. Without it he feels his sister will surely die. The despair felt by Erwin is his realization that he is now the man of the family, his mother relies on him, and his sister is near death, yet he is powerless to change the circumstances. "The Lemon" ranks as one of the most heart-breaking stories in this anthology.

"The Old Ones and Death" and "Last Day of the Fire" relate the fate of the elderly—too weak to work and too much of a burden for the young. In "The Old Ones and Death" even the delousing agent has forgotten about Aaron Shapiro and his dying wife, Markéta. Memories of their past are integrated into the moment of her death. "What is death?" is the question that is pervasive throughout this work. In "Last Day of the Fire" a grandfather must wait for his grandson Chick to return each day. Although the two have never been close, Chick shows his love for the old man in an ironic fashion, by rigging a method of suicide for his grandfather should the fire bombing or the

Nazis get too close. Discussion of death is a normal pattern of conversation among the old, but what method they succumb to always keeps the reader on edge in Lustig's stories.

Reliance is the theme tying "The Second Round" and "The White Rabbit" together. Children learn to depend upon one another for survival in these works. "The White Rabbit" is especially symbolic. Young Thomas believes he can give one last glimmer of hope to Flea, a girl who has been institutionalized with brain damage at their camp. He borrows a white rabbit from the camp commandant's hutches. The rabbit represents hope for the girl, but its dark fate is inevitable. It is caged like the camp inhabitants, and like their own, its life will end in an oven.

Humanism makes its breakthrough in "Beginning and End," where young Jiří reveals his belief that the German lieutenant in charge of his group may be a decent sort of fellow. His intuition parallel's that of Lustig, who relied on his own perception of human behavior to determine the goodness or evil of a person in order to survive. Jiří realizes he will never know this lieutenant when he discovers his body in a pile of rubble. Michael's predicament in "Michael and the Other Boy with the Dagger" also takes a humanistic approach. He saves a Hitler Youth's life when he falls. In turn the boy does not blow the whistle on Michael; instead, he turns away, only to fall to his death down a broken ladder. The realization that they both might have been friends had circumstances been different comes too late, but the bridge has at least been crossed.

The war has ended with the last two stories of the anthology: "Black Lion" and "Early in the Morning." Both stories raise the question, "How do we make the Germans suffer as we have?" The answer in "Black Lion" is to let them run or leave them to wonder about their own fate. Not knowing is the worst torture with which the survivors can leave them, and, besides, none of the characters in these stories really want to become Nazis toward the Nazis. "They aren't jumping anymore," relates the old man to the young concentration survivors in "Early in the Morning." As for the Germans, he concludes, "They're not interesting anymore. They lost all their mystery, their secrets."

—Cynthia A. Klíma

DIARY OF A YOUNG GIRL (Het achterhuis)
Diary by Anne Frank, 1947

Diary of a Young Girl tells Anne Frank's story of her life in hiding in the secret annex in Amsterdam from July 1942–August 1944. She paints a vivid picture of the eight people who spent more than two years cooped up in the annex, with little food, little space, and virtually no privacy. Published in Dutch in 1947 and in English translation in 1952, the book has been translated into more than 50 languages.

Anne Frank describes with great admiration her intelligent and loving father, writes of her sometimes rocky relationship with her mother, and discusses her accomplished and talented sister, Margot. She writes with great disdain of the Van Daans, in particular of their constant bickering and their selfishness. Mr. Van Daan spends much of his money on cigarettes, even selling his wife's beloved fur coat in order to purchase more; furthermore, he steals some of the food that the inhabitants are rationing. Mrs. Van Daan is self-absorbed, flirting alternately with Mr. Frank and Mr. Dussel; in addition, she is prone to bursts of hysteria, insisting that the Nazis will win the war and that the group in the annex will be captured. The couple fights not only with each other but also with Anne and her mother. Anne characterizes Dussel as temperamental and finicky, difficult to get along with. She writes in great detail of her relationship with Peter, of their strong feelings for each other and of developments in their relationship. She does express some concerns about Peter, such as his immaturity and lack of interest in religion. And perhaps most importantly, Anne Frank writes about herself.

Part of the greatness of the diary derives from the profound introspection within it—quite rare for someone as young as Anne. The reader learns a great deal about Anne as she discovers more about herself. She confides in the diary, which she calls "Kitty." She writes introspectively about her relationship with Peter and about her behavior and personality in general. Some of these moments occur immediately after arguments with other inhabitants of the annex, such as when she writes a letter to her father (5 May 1944), complaining about life in the annex and claiming that she, at the age of fourteen, is now capable of being independent. In the letter (written in response to being told not to spend so much time alone with Peter), Anne tells her father that she has cried much since she moved into the annex in July 1942 and that if he knew "how desperate and unhappy I was, how lonely I felt, then you would understand that I want to go upstairs! I have now reached the stage that I can live entirely on my own, without Mummy's support or anyone else's for that matter." She discusses how life in the annex has rendered her an atypical fourteen-year-old girl. In a 3 May 1942 entry, Anne maturely discusses politics, society, and war. She considers it foolish that large airplanes and bombs are built in order to destroy houses, which then have to be rebuilt, and that large amounts of money are spent on weapons while the poor go hungry. She claims that there exists within human beings an urge to destroy others. It is fascinating that a fourteen-year-old girl, hiding to save her life in cramped quarters with little food, concerned herself with the plight of others. It demonstrates great precociousness and altruism.

The passages covering an attempted burglary are suspenseful and descriptive; the fear that the burglars, the police, or the Nazis will find them renders the annex inhabitants white with fear. It is noteworthy that the teenagers Anne and Peter are the most calm: Anne comforts Mrs. Van Daan and tells her to be strong and brave, and Peter brings the burglary to the attention of Otto Frank while attempting to avoid making the other inhabitants nervous. These passages show that the Jews hiding in the annex had to be on their guard at all times, and that the slightest mistake (such as when Mr. Van Daan shouted, "Police!" to scare away the burglars) could cost them their lives. (Anne remarks that in a time of such terrible socioeconomic times, burglaries are prevalent.)

Toward the end of the diary, Anne and the others become more optimistic, believing that the Allies will save the inhabitants of the annex; this is especially true after the D-Day invasion. Anne even mentions that she hopes to return to school by the end of 1944—after the Nazis have lost the war and life has returned to normal. These sections of the diary are quite poignant, given the fact that the readers know Anne's tragic end.

—Eric Sterling

THE DIARY OF ANNE FRANK
Play by Frances Goodrich and Albert Hackett, 1956

The Diary of Anne Frank, the dramatic adaptation by Frances Goodrich and Albert Hackett, was first produced in 1955 and published in 1956. Goodrich and Hackett's play tells the story of the intelligent and lively **Anne Frank**, a teenage girl who is perhaps the most famous victim of the Holocaust. The playwrights begin the drama after Otto Frank, Anne's father, returns home in November 1945 and receives his daughter's diary from Miep, a friend of the family who has helped to hide the Franks from the Nazis. Otto Frank then reads the diary of his daughter for the first time, and the words in the diary serve as the action of the play.

The audience observes as Anne and her family arrive at the secret annex and encounter the family with whom they will spend the next two years and one month: the Van Daans. (This is the name that Anne gives them to protect their identity; the real name of the family is Van Pels.) The playwrights deviate from historical truth by having the Van Daans waiting in the annex for the Franks to arrive. Historically the Van Pels family arrived in the annex one week after the Franks went into hiding. Goodrich and Hackett alter the order in which the two families arrive, perhaps because the playwrights want to demonstrate Mrs. Van Daan's hysteria (she becomes hysterical as she awaits the arrival of the Franks, thinking that they have been captured by the Green Police—and that they might mention that the Van Daans are hiding in the annex). Also Mrs. Van Daan specifically thanks Mr. Frank for allowing her family to stay there but neglects to thank Mrs. Frank, which foreshadows her attraction to Otto Frank and her concomitant disdain for his wife. And the early arrival of the Van Daans might make it more comprehensible why they subsequently become territorial (in terms of space and food) toward the people they initially consider to be their friends and benefactors.

Goodrich and Hackett immediately foreshadow the problems that the Van Daans will cause by focusing on the cat (Mouschi), Mrs. Van Daan's fur coat and her previously mentioned hysteria, and the squabbling between the married couple. The Van Daans bring their cat even though they realize that food will be scarce and that there is supposed to be no noise for hours every day; Goodrich and Hackett demonstrate the poor decision of the Van Daans when Anne remarks to Peter that her parents refused to allow her to bring her cat. Mrs. Van Daan demonstrates her willingness to jeopardize all of the inhabitants of the annex by wearing her fur coat to the annex. Although all of them realize that it is crucial that they do not attract the attention of the Green Police on their way to the annex, Petronella Van Daan insists on wearing her fur coat rather than leaving it behind—even though she wears it to the annex on 13 July 1942, the middle of summer. In order to save one of her possessions, she thus takes a big risk by obviously calling attention to herself. The discussion of the fur coat leads to bickering between the Van Daans, making manifest to the audience the cantankerous nature of the husband and wife and foreshadowing the many arguments that will arise in the annex. The bickering increases when the petulant dentist, Mr. Dussel (real name, Fritz Pfeffer), joins the other Jews in the annex.

Dussel's arrival complicates the logistics of the annex because the limited food, space, and W.C. time are further reduced; this problem, together with the inevitable frustrations that ensue when people are confined in a small area and are not allowed to make noise, leads to short tempers. Goodrich and Hackett adroitly delineate the characters of Mr. Frank and Mr. Van Daan by juxtaposing them in the scene in which Mr. Kraler, who along with Miep is hiding the Jews, brings Dussel to the annex. Otto Frank immediately agrees to take in Mr. Dussel while Mr. Van Daan sulks and complains about the already low supply of food. Goodrich and Hackett's stage direction shows Peter turning away in shame of his father's selfishness and hypocrisy—it is, after all, only four months since the Franks brought the Van Daans into the annex, possibly saving their lives. The scene also manifests the benevolence of Mr. Frank.

The inhabitants of the annex survive for more than two years until they are betrayed by a thief and subsequently arrested. Pages of Anne's diary are scattered on the floor as the Jews are taken prisoner. Miep informs Otto Frank that she has kept the diary, waiting to return it after the war is over. Frank reads through his daughter's diary with pride; after reading her

famous line "I still believe that people are really good at heart," he concludes with admiration, "She puts me to shame."

—Eric Sterling

THE DIARY OF DAWID SIERAKOWIAK: FIVE NOTEBOOKS FROM THE LODZ GHETTO (Dziennik)
Diary by Dawid Sierakowiak, 1960

The five notebooks of Dawid Sierakowiak's diary span a period of almost four years in Lodz, Poland, making it one of the longest and most sustained individual accounts of daily life during the Holocaust. He began his diary at age 14 in June 1939, enjoying a hearty outdoor life at a Jewish youth camp in southern Poland. He ended it in April 1943 in the Lodz ghetto, crippled by starvation, illness, and loss. His diary provides a brutal account of his terrible passage from youthful vitality to exhaustion, despair, and imminent death. Originally published in Polish in 1960, the diary appeared in English translation in 1996.

Dawid grew up in Lodz with his parents and younger sister, Nadzia. His first notebook captures a few moments of calm before the war and the explosion of violence that marked its beginning on 1 September 1939. Well informed of world events and curious about history and politics, Dawid reported on the rising tensions in Europe, the nonaggression pact between the Soviet Union and Germany, and the frantic mobilization in Poland as the German attack became imminent. Once war began he vividly described the air raid bombings, the disruption throughout Lodz, and the desperation of the city's inhabitants who struggled to decide whether to flee or to remain in the city.

On Friday, 29 September, Dawid wrote, "The pact has been signed in Moscow. The division of Poland between Germany and Russia has been settled . . . Well, well, what an insult!" With this Dawid's diary shifts in tone and content from the tension-filled entries written just prior to and during the brief fight between Germany and Poland to the resigned and eerie calm of life under German occupation. Like many diarists of this period, Dawid noted in sharp and careful detail virtually every restriction that he and his community endured. Reports of confiscations, seizures for forced labor, imposition of the Star of David, restricted movement, expulsions, and countless other repressive measures fill the pages of Dawid's notebook, offering glimpses of the ever-shrinking world of Jews under Nazism. Dawid ended his first notebook on 31 December 1939.

Dawid's next notebook does not begin until 6 April 1941, the long gap most likely attributable to volumes lost during or after the war. The beginning of the second surviving notebook finds Dawid and his family in the Lodz ghetto, where they had already been imprisoned for almost a year. The diarist wrote this and the other three remaining notebooks while in the ghetto itself, and despite their gaps, his account offers an astonishingly thorough picture of his life. Dawid not only reported on his own family's suffering—describing the relentless struggle against hunger, starvation, illness, family tensions, lethargy, and despair—but also turned his gaze to the wider misery shared by the collective community in the Lodz ghetto. To cite only two examples of many, Dawid bitterly denounced the corruption and privilege that divided the ghetto inhabitants and at the same time evoked the shared waiting and hoping for liberation that joined them together.

In his diary Dawid returned often to the subject of his desperate fight against his own physical and mental decline. It is a theme often echoed among other young writers' diaries of this period. Dawid's diary reveals his efforts to overcome the lethargy and stagnation caused by exhaustion and hunger and his own painful acknowledgment of the effect of his ill health on his ability to study, read, and learn. But perhaps most striking of all is the image Dawid recorded of the slow decimation of his own family. His mother was deported and murdered in September 1942; his father died of illness in March 1943. Dawid himself succumbed in August 1943, at the age of 19, four months after he wrote his last entry. His sister Nadzia surely perished, though the details of her fate are unknown. The diary he left behind testifies to the daily life of this writer and to the collective story of the doomed community of Lodz.

—Alexandra Zapruder

THE DIARY OF EVA HEYMAN: CHILD OF THE HOLOCAUST (Yomanah shel Evah Hayman)
Diary by Eva Heyman, 1964

Eva Heyman began her diary in the city of Nagyvárad in northern Transylvania (the modern Oradea, Romania) on 13 February 1944. Her notes cover a period of just under three months, during which time she witnessed and experienced all aspects of the German occupation of the city and the repression of the Jews there. One of a very few diaries written by young people in this region of Europe during the war, Eva's diary offers a close-up contemporaneous view of the decimation of a fragment of Hungary's Jewish community. It was originally published in Hungarian in 1947, as *Yomanah shel Evah Hayman* in 1964, and in English translation first as *The Diary of Eva Heyman* in 1974 then as *The Diary of Eva Heyman: Child of the Holocaust* in 1988.

The only child of divorced parents, and surrounded by highly educated, liberal adults, Eva reported on many historical events that might have normally passed over the head of such a young girl. Though she confessed that she often "didn't understand" the exact implications of the events she mentioned, she nevertheless touched on major historical currents as they affected her immediate family and friends. In particular, she remembered when her hometown of Nagyvárad (part of Romania since 1919) was given to Hungary in 1940, and its humiliating consequences for her grandfather, whose pharmacy was expropriated. She also described her stepfather Bela Zsolt's entry into the Hungarian Labor Service, which was comprised of Jews who were forcibly drafted and sent to aid the Hungarian army on the Eastern Front. And, she returned again and again to the memory of her friend Marta Munzer, whose family was among 16,000 people deported by the Hungarians from Nagyvárad to Kamanetz-Podolsk, where they were turned over to the SS and brutally slaughtered.

Above all, however, Eva's diary captures the German onslaught and the daily events that culminated in ghettoization and deportation. In this part of the diary, Eva was not remembering the past and filling in its details, but reporting on events as they unfolded. Unlike diaries written in many other parts of Europe, in which the escalation of repression against the Jews unfolded over a period of years, Eva's diary vividly reflects the sudden and swift attack on the Jews of Hungary. From the moment she announced that the Germans had taken power in Hungary, Eva's diary is filled with the whirlwind of laws, decrees, and events that affected the Jews of Nagyvárad. She witnessed the eviction of Jews from their homes, and poured out her own experiences of oppression, including the imposition of the Star of David, the rapid confiscation of personal property, the departure of the family's Christian cook and friend Mariska Szabo, and the arrest of her father.

In May 1944 the family was crowded with the Jews of their community into the Nagyvárad ghetto. Eva wrote at length about the humiliating and traumatic move from home and its affect on her family. Once in the ghetto, Eva aptly captured the dramatic change in their circumstances. She wrote, "Everything is forbidden, but the most awful thing of all is that punishment for everything is death. . . . No standing in the corner, no spankings, no taking away food, no writing down the declension of irregular verbs one hundred times . . . Not at all: the lightest and heaviest punishment—death."

The family remained in the ghetto for one month. Eva continued to write during this period, confiding in her diary her growing terror that she would share the fate of her murdered friend Marta. When the ghetto was liquidated at the end of May, Eva and her family (except her mother and stepfather) were deported from the ghetto to Auschwitz and murdered. Her notes stand not only as a record of the life of one little girl but as a powerful and moving account of the German attack and annihilation that engulfed the vast majority of Hungarian Jewry.

—Alexandra Zapruder

THE DIARY OF THE VILNA GHETTO: JUNE 1941–April 1943 (Yomano shel na'ar mi-Vilnah: Yuni 1941–April 1943)
Diary by Yitskhok Rudashevski, 1968

Portions of the diary that Yitskhok Rudashevski kept in the Vilna ghetto were first published in 1953 in their original Yiddish in volume 15 of the Yiddish journal *Di Goldene Keyt* (The Golden Chain). A Hebrew translation of the diary was published in 1968, and the complete English edition appeared in 1973 under the title *The Diary of the Vilna Ghetto: June 1941–April 1943*.

Before the war Vilna had been a major center of Jewish learning. Even after the Nazi invasion, the Vilna ghetto continued to be a place where Jews engaged in the study of letters as long as they were alive. Despite his young age—he was 13 at the time of the Nazi onslaught—Yitskhok was heavily involved in learning. He belonged to a circle of Yiddish writers, for example, and declared that "ghetto folklore which is amazingly cultivated in blood, and which is scattered over the little streets, must be collected and cherished as a treasure for the future." He recorded the establishment of a Jewish historical society in the ghetto on 10 November 1942, and he was careful to note the literary celebration on 13 December 1942 that was held in honor of the circulation of the 100,000th book from the ghetto library, adding, "The book unites us with the future, the book unites us with the world."

As he wrote his own book, then, Yitskhok exhibited a deep understanding of the significance of the book for history and for humanity. To be sure, he saw a definitive connection between the status of the book and the status of the human being. "Into what kind of helpless, broken creature can man be transformed?" he asks. Of course, in Vilna the Jews were not just broken, they were murdered—primarily at Ponary—and Yitskhok's diary bears witness to the meaning of Ponary from beginning to end. In the fall of 1941 he wrote, "Ponar[y]—the word with a wound written in blood . . . Ponar[y] is the same as a nightmare, a nightmare which accompanies the gray strand of our ghetto-days." And in one of the diary's last entries, dated 5 April 1943, he noted, "Around 5,000 persons were not taken to Kovno as promised but transported by train to Ponar[y] where they were shot."

Like many Holocaust diaries, Yitskhok's also chronicles the assault on the holy within the human as that assault is carried out on the holy days. On Yom Kippur 1941, for example, he recorded the uprooting of several thousand people

from the ghetto and added, "These people never came back." The Yom Kippur roundup was followed by one of many pogroms, whereupon he wrote, "The old synagogue courtyard is pogromized. Phylacteries, religious books, rags are scattered under one's feet." And on Yom Kippur 1942 he affirmed that, even though he was not religious, "This holiday drenched in blood and sorrow which is solemnized in the ghetto, now penetrates my heart." The holiday penetrated his heart because the holiness of the holiday manifested itself through the human beings who embraced it, and those human beings had been murdered.

Yitskhok's youth found eloquent expression in his longing for a place in the world; indeed, that is one reason books were so dear to him. The more intense the destruction of the world, the more intense the longing. Seeing how ruined lives paralleled ruined families, homes, and buildings, he cried out, "How much tragedy and anguish is mirrored in every shattered brick, in every dark crack, in every bit of plaster with a piece of wallpaper." As a natural longing for a sense of place, his longing is also a yearning for nature. He joined a nature group and declared, "We are not cut off from nature in spirit." And in the spring of 1943, the year of his death, he wrote, "I revel in the spring breeze, catch the spring rays and my heart is full of strange yearning." Those who have been young know that yearning. Reading Yitskhok's diary, one realizes that even such yearning was subject to annihilation.

Hauntingly prescient, Yitskhok's diary ends with the words, "We may be fated for the worst." The question confronting the reader who comes to the end of this testimony is, "What will be the fate of his diary?"

—David Patterson

DR. KORCZAK AND THE CHILDREN (Korczak und die Kinder)
Play by Erwin Sylvanus, 1957

Erwin Sylvanus's play *Dr. Korczak and the Children* (1968; *Korczak und die Kinder,* 1957) was written not in direct reaction to the atrocities of World War II but in response to a phenomenon that Sylvanus, along with other playwrights like **Rolf Hochhuth**, **Peter Weiss**, and **George Tabori**, felt was perhaps even more horrifying: the "amnesia" that overtook many Germans during the period of the "economic miracle" of the 1950s. His play, based on the true story of Dr. Janusz Korczak, confronts German audiences with their complicity during the war and their rapid postwar forgetfulness. The central motif of the play is the one lie Korczak told—it is a stark contrast to the many lies and the denials practiced by the Germans after the war.

The real Dr. Korczak ran a Jewish orphanage where he advanced his progressive theories of education. He was also an

412

author and beloved national star of a children's radio program in Poland. When the orphanage was moved to the Jewish ghetto established in Warsaw in November 1940, Dr. Korczak went too, despite many offers to save him. In August 1942 he and nearly 200 children were rounded up for deportation to Treblinka, where they were all murdered. Eyewitnesses described the children laughing and singing as Dr. Korczak led them, refusing to let them be frightened by their captors. Several other more recent plays and films, including Michael Brady's *Korczak's Children* (1983) and the Polish film *Korczak* (1990), directed by Andrzej Wajda, realistically depict the experiences of Dr. Korczak and his orphans. Sylvanus, however, chose nonrealistic theatrical conventions to portray the Holocaust.

Chief among these are conventions made famous by **Bertolt Brecht** and Luigi Pirandello. In what he called his epic theater, Brecht advocated a presentational style of playing. Thus, he often had his actors speak directly to the audience. In this way he hoped to force the audience to take a position, not just sit back passively. For example, at the beginning of *Dr. Korczak and the Children*, the narrator tells the audience that the play will deal with World War II: "Ah, you're startled, are you? There's still time to get up and leave, you know. You're not involved yet in what we're going to show you here." The play also calls for actors who play actors, taking on various characters. As the actors are forced to take on certain roles that are uncomfortable for them (for example, the one who plays the SS officer who insists he was "only doing his duty"), the audience also begins perhaps to feel a similar discomfort.

The other playwright who influenced Sylvanus is Pirandello, whose plays, especially his most famous, *Six Characters in Search of an Author,* often emphasize the tensions between illusion and reality and between the identities of the actors and the characters they play. During the course of *Dr. Korczak and the Children,* as in *Six Characters in Search of an Author,* the actors/characters discuss the play itself as they are performing. They, the contemporary German actors, complain about the casting and discuss the issues in the play. Thus, the audience is also encouraged to view the play skeptically, particularly the Nazi perspectives. Korczak is presented as a tragic hero who tried to live the truth but was ultimately forced to lie to comfort his children. The play takes up the question of lying versus truth telling. Korczak is presented as a man who never lied— except once. When his children are going to be taken away to die, he decides to lie to them about their destination. He tells them that they're going to the Promised Land, so the children feel happy and unafraid.

In the final scene the narrator takes on the role of a rabbi who describes the landscape that Korczak and his children inhabit, borrowing the words from the prophet Ezekiel. Ezekiel has a vision of a valley of dry bones. It seems to be a world of death and hopelessness. But the Lord tells Ezekiel to prophesy to the bones and the bones will rise up; breath will enter them, flesh will come upon them, and they will live. And as Ezekiel speaks the bones do indeed rise up and become human beings. And the Lord promises to bring the people of Israel, who had been dead, hopeless heaps of bones, into the Promised Land, as Korczak promised his children. Thus, the play ends on a note of hope and as a tribute to Korczak's dream for his orphans. The ending also emphasizes Korczak's dream of a future Israeli state.

—Susan Russell

DREAMS OF ANNE FRANK: A PLAY FOR YOUNG PEOPLE
Play by Bernard Kops, 1993

Dreams of Anne Frank is a play that is intended for younger audiences. Bernard Kops believed that a theater should be a place of education. In his essay "The Young Writer and Theater," Kops pleads his case for a change in traditional theater, stating, "We [writers] write about the problems of the world today because we live in the world of today. We write about the young, because we are young. We write about Council Flats and the H-bomb and racial discrimination because these things concern us and concern the young people of our country, so that if and when they come to theatre, they will see that it is not divorced from reality, that it is for them and they will feel at home." Kops's play *Dreams of Anne Frank,* first produced in England in 1992, is written in a light style, with musical continuity and sudden action, all of which serves to keep the attention of a younger audience. Anne's imagination is stressed, and she uses it to transport herself and others in the Annex to magical, as well as to frightening, places. "In captivity you can be free inside your head ... use your imagination and it's all yours!" she exclaims. The reality of life always returns with a blow, and it is always a reality with which children can relate, such as their own powerless in an adult world, a world that not only takes away a child's property but also a child's life. The personality of Anne has also been reinvented in this play, as opposed to the version of Anne's personality portrayed in films about her. In the 1959 film version starring Millie Perkins as Anne, Anne is much older looking and barely utters a harsh word. Kops's Anne is much more childish and talks back quite readily. Even in her diary, she does not come across as such an upstart. This is a facet of Anne's personality to which children can relate much more easily. The character of Mrs. Van Daan has also been given a much beefier and more cantankerous role. Kops sarcastically portrays her describing herself in a prideful manner, using adjectives such as polite and courteous. Of all the adjectives she uses to her benefit, not one fits her.

In this play Anne is much more the optimist and the one to whom others turn for answers. Her writing while in hiding lends her a more contemplative character, making her seem to be the one who knows more than any of the other Annex inhabitants and the interpreter of what they are all hearing on the radio. Her diary is her world of truth, hope, and humanity, attributes that Mrs. Van Daan is not only in short supply of but also abstract connotations for which she lacks any comprehension. Anne's imagination wreaks havoc with the adults; she often believes that what her imagination is telling her is the truth. Helpful on stage are the visuals that are used to portray Anne's dreams and nightmares, from the wedding to Peter that she will never have a chance to experience to a gingerbread house in the Black Forest, guarded by Mrs. Van Daan, the evil witch. Anne's nightmares are the result of a childhood that she has had to prematurely give up. She dreams of loss of life, of death, and of tragedy. In the gingerbread house there is a large oven, an efficient one built by the Germans. "There's lots of Jews waiting to be admitted. Gingerbread and hard work makes free," says the evil witch (Mrs. Van Daan).

One character that is intentionally absent from the play is Miep Gies, who, along with her husband, provided news and food to the Franks and the others. Her role is symbolized by the helping hand that often appears through a hatch on stage. In this way Kops has simplified the actual diary by allowing only a minimal number of characters on the sparsely set stage. The entire focus of the play is thus on Anne and her dreams, a young person with yearnings and fears like any other child, but a child who is living under conditions that are far different from those of the play's audience.

The play ends not with Nazi violence but with a simple disappearance of the diary from Anne's hands, symbolizing the fact that the inhabitants have been betrayed. There is no violence on the stage, but it is evident to the young audience members that Anne will now go away. Her nightmare is about to begin, as all the Annex inhabitants remove their clothing to reveal prison camp stripes underneath. Anne addresses her audience in a touching monologue at the end, and the stage darkens. There is only a light shining upon her diary.

"All the books ever written cannot be weighed against the value of one child's life. I would gladly swap it, throw it away, or have it unwritten if only I could have Anne again, living." It is with these words that Otto Frank closes the diary and the curtain falls.

—Cynthia A. Klíma

THE DROWNED AND THE SAVED (I sommersi e i salvati)
Memoir by Primo Levi, 1986

I sommersi e i salvati (1986; *The Drowned and the Saved*, 1988), Primo Levi's last great work of witness, was published less than a year before his death in 1987. It incorporates within the context of new material some pieces that had been published over the previous nine years.

In this book Levi reverses the balance characteristic of his earlier works of witness, such as *Survival in Auschwitz* and *The Reawakening*. There he had employed narrative, with himself as "author-protagonist," and had interwoven into those carefully crafted narratives considerable analysis and commentary. In *The Drowned and the Saved* the emphasis is on analysis and commentary; narrative is used episodically, for purposes of illustration or support of a point. An especially powerful example of this practice is the section on Chaim Rumkowski in the chapter "The Gray Zone."

The book, which is composed of eight chapters plus a substantial preface and a conclusion, seems, in its title, to allude to Dante, who refers (*Inferno* 20.3) to those in hell as *i sommersi* (the submerged, or the drowned). It is Levi's phrase for those who perished in camp. Levi uses as an epigraph to this work lines from Coleridge's "Rime of the Ancient Mariner" that refer to a huge urgency to tell a terrible tale: "And till my ghastly tale is told / This heart within me burns." Levi is greatly concerned in this work not to fall prey to those distorting effects on memory that he observed and commented on with somber brilliance in the chapter "Vanadium" in *The Periodic Table* as well as in the preface and first chapter, "The Memory of the Offense," of the present book. He reports in his preface, in fact, that he checked his memory in rigorous ways and found that it remained powerful and reliable, undistorted in the passage of years by forgetfulness or by shifting deep motivations.

Levi had from his first writings crafted striking phrases for certain realities associated with the operation of the camps and the moral issues involved. His first chapter deals not only with memory but also with offense. That latter word is for him a technical term and points not only at the evil of the camps but also at the fact that in order to break the humanity of those imprisoned there practices were developed that specifically outraged their sense of what was most sacred in their identity. The tattooing of the prisoner's number on his or her arm is itself an example of this. A law in Torah forbids Israelites to be tattooed. Similarly, prayer shawls were taken away on entry into Auschwitz and made into underwear, which the prisoners were then forced to wear and befoul.

His chapter "The Gray Zone" represents a profound plea that one not generalize and suppose that all, tormentor and tormented alike, were in some sense equally victims. There are, according to Levi, those who obviously are pure victimizer or are pure victim. And even for those whom we might think to inhabit a sort of gray zone between the two poles, Levi insists that we not give over the act of judging, of making distinctions, of determining the balance of exoneration and opprobrium. Only in one case does he ask that we suspend judgment—that is for the case of those in the Special Commando, prisoners themselves who, before they knew the nature of the work they would be asked to do, were offered privileges for special labor. Only after they agreed did they find that their work was at the crematoria, putting bodies in and taking the ashes out. To refuse then would have meant immediate death. For them Levi asks that we continue to consider their case but suspend judgment. For all others he asks that we continue the act of judgment—assessing culpability according to the degree of their consent to and participation in the operation of the Final Solution.

Chapters follow on "Shame" (survivor shame), the topic also of one of his most powerful poems, "The Survivor" ("Il superstite"); on "Communication"; on "Useless Violence"; on "The Intellectual at Auschwitz"; and on "Stereotypes"; and there is one in which he refers to a number of letters he had received from Germans and in which he analyzes the response to the Holocaust indicated or implied there. These chapters are followed by a conclusion as intense, though controlled, as it is brief.

The chapter on "Communication," perhaps the central concern of Levi's great and very substantial oeuvre, argues vigorously against the contemporary tendency in literary studies to assert that all meaning is individual and subjective and that we cannot effectively communicate with one another what it is most important to know about our condition. Levi believes this idea to be an "aesthetic vice," asserting that we can know adequately the mental intent of another's utterance and suggesting that if we wish to know what real incommunicability is, we examine the case of Auschwitz. There language was used with the intent not to communicate significantly in any mode save that of unquestionable command. But, as Levi observes, not only did language in Auschwitz involve great problems of communication but also language about Auschwitz is extremely difficult, because common discourse, which derives from the world of general human experience, has no vocabulary for dealing with its singularities. Common language therefore characteristically betrays and palliates.

Seen in retrospect from the fact of his death, the frequency of mention of suicide in this book is worth attention, beginning in the early pages with the notice of the suicide of **Jean Améry**. So, too, in an astonishingly composed and restrained work of luminous analysis about the horror of the Holocaust and its aftermath is the outrage and disdain that brings the conclusion of the work to its close. There he notes the responsibility borne by the great majority of Germans, "who accepted from the beginning, through mental laziness, through myopic calculation, through stupidity, through national pride, the 'beautiful words' of Corporal Hitler, who followed him so long as fortune and the lack of scruples favored them, who were overthrown by his ruin, lashed with sorrows, misery, and remorse, and rehabilitated a few years later through a disingenuous political game." Obtuse self-interest and a willingness to come to terms with power Levi saw as the defining fault

of the Germans in the Holocaust—and not only of the Germans and not only in the case of the Holocaust.

—Ralph G. Williams

DROWNING: GROWING UP IN THE THIRD REICH
(Drenkeling kinderjaren in het derde rijk)
Memoir by Gerhard Durlacher, 1987

Five-year-old Gerhard Durlacher was growing up in the German town of Baden-Baden when the Nazis came to power. He describes hearing the news of their takeover of the city. A room in his home falls silent while an excited voice on the radio reports that the new chancellor of the German Reich is Adolf Hitler. *Stripes in the Sky* was Durlacher's first memoir, in which he described his experiences in Auschwitz-Birkenau from 1942 to the end of the war. *Drowning* is the prequel, a small collection of penetrating remembrances from the years 1933 to 1936. *Drowning* was published in English translation in 1993.

In one scene Durlacher describes an experience at a Christmas pantomime when he is called to the stage to sit on Santa's knee. The young boy immediately recognizes his Uncle Herbert behind the beard and says so loudly. While the boy returns to his seat a man sitting nearby, with perfectly Aryan daughters, whispers menacingly to him, "Smart-aleck little Jewboy." Other scenes in the book capture the eerie sense of the unreal initial years of Nazi rule. Increasingly the sense of menace that alters his world begins to cave in on him: the windows of the hotel of friends of his family are smashed; his parents' non-Jewish cleaning lady stops coming to his house; his father gradually loses his business clients. The younger Durlacher sees the Brownshirts as "devils stamping their hooves" and led by a man on horseback who resembles "the cruel knight" in his book of fairy stories.

Despite the experience at Birkenau that enshrouded Durlacher's teenage years, he is able to retrieve from the past not only his memories but his sense of childish innocence and wonder. According to Durlacher his memories came back after reading two books in the early 1980s: Martin Gilbert's *Auschwitz and the Allies* and Walter Laqueur's *The Terrible Secret*. Both books attempt to investigate why the Allied forces ignored pleas for help after the true purpose of the concentration camps became known. Laqueur's conclusion, which Durlacher also espouses, focuses on the nature of belief. The horror of some atrocities is so harrowing that they are impossible to accept. Durlacher illustrates how even people new to Auschwitz, people on the brink of their own destruction, could still not believe that the smoking chimneys did not belong to factories and interpreted the stories from other prisoners as a kind of cruel initiation rite.

Although the tone of *Stripes in the Sky* is one of anger and vengeance, the tone of *Drowning* is that of acceptance mixed with sorrow. The title story refers to one illuminating incident. While on a holiday in Riva young Gerhard watches two boys playing with toy boats at the edge of the jetty. Adults nearby are intent on listening to Italian and German radio announcements coming from loudspeakers when first one boy, then the other, falls in. Gerhard screams for help, but the parents listen with undivided attention to the radio: the Nazis have assassinated the Austrian leader Dolfuss in a failed coup attempt. It was the first palpable demonstration of Hitler's real menace. The boys are rescued only at the last minute.

This story becomes Durlacher's metaphor for the Jewish experience in Nazi Germany. A kind of desperate optimism comprises the paralysis that takes over Durlacher's family, even as full realization of their plight begins to dawn on them. By the time they flee to an uncertain safety in Holland it is already too late; they are deported to Auschwitz-Birkenau in 1942. Durlacher ultimately puts the blame for the destruction of Jewish families like his own on "those countless Germans, indifferent or paralyzed by fear, [who] watched us drown before their eyes."

—Martha Sutro

DRY TEARS: THE STORY OF A LOST CHILDHOOD
Memoir by Nechama Tec, 1984

There is a caste system in the Holocaust survivor's community. At the top is the concentration-camp survivor who is obsessed with the experience and feels compelled to tell his story, and on the bottom is the hidden child who lived his childhood as a non-Jew, neither deported nor incarcerated, and who keeps the *milhomeh yahren* (war years) to himself. Though both groups acknowledge that to honor the memory of the brutally murdered is to never forget—and, thus, to reveal what was concealed, denied, minimized, and destroyed—there are distinct variables between them. A common thread among camp survivors is forever living the guilt and pain of surviving, and that for the hidden children is forever remembering the idiosyncrasy of surviving by any means necessary. Such is the grist of Nechama Tec's memoir.

In the whole of Jewish history there has been no more murderous an age, no period more villainous for the Jew, than the Shoah. With so much that is painful to remember—dislocation, despair, death—Tec's memoir is that rare story of one Jewish family's ability to survive intact. Tec (née Bawnik) was eight years old when World War II began with Nazi Germany's invasion of Poland on 1 September 1939. As a child she did not understand her mother's cry, "We are lost, we are lost," which foretold her family's destiny in the coming

years. Despite her ignorance and confusion about the situation at hand, she learned enough to remain alive and to be quiet about it. Survival and secrecy became the matrix around which she attempted to recapture her childhood in order to comprehend the character of her being.

Tec's coming-of-age story details the perils involved in Jews passing as Christians among anti-Semitic people who sheltered them, loved them, lived off them, and despised them. Typical is the family Homar, of Kielce, who sheltered the Bawniks during the war. Tec wrote: "All the Homars made me feel welcome. They were so warm and friendly that I was hurt when I discovered that they were anti-Semitic, and totally uninhibited about being so. Unabashed by my presence, they would talk disparagingly about Jews, and even scold me half jokingly: 'Don't be a nosy Jew,' 'Don't be clumsy like a Jew.' I said nothing, but my face must have registered some surprise or opposition or both, because they would then add, 'You know that you are not a real Jew. You are not *really* Jewish.'" Ironically, the truth behind their mean-spirited remarks is vouched for by Tec herself: "Early in life I became aware of my 'non-Jewish' appearance. Blond and blue-eyed, I had what was considered to be a 'typically Polish' look." This look enabled Tec to pass as a Gentile and sell rolls on the black market to help sustain her family in hiding.

Collectively, events remembered in this book may well resemble those found in other memoirs in form but not necessarily in content. What is unusual is the dilemma of a young girl who became a Pole and a Catholic on the outside, thereby separating herself from her real self and from her family, religion, and ethnicity. Seemingly, by giving up her Jewish identity—born Helen Bawnik, she became Pelagia Pawlowska and later Christina Bloch—and embracing silence, she found solace "inside a church [where] I felt neither a Christian nor a Jew, but only a human being, who had a terrible need to confide in someone. In the stillness I could whisper my secrets without fear, and whether it was a Christian God or a Jewish God who listened to me did not matter. What mattered was that I had someone to confide in, and that he was listening." Though Tec emerged from the war with a personal vow to "never again pretend to be someone else," her conflicted identity continued to prevail. Her need to heal is the raison d'être of *Dry Tears*. For the most part she succeeded in overcoming her bifurcate identity.

—Zev Garber

DURING THE EICHMANN TRIAL
Poem by Denise Levertov, 1961

In "During the Eichmann Trial," a poem about the Holocaust that was included in *The Jacob's Ladder* (1961), Denise Levertov provides her thoughts about the trial of the Nazi henchman Adolf Eichmann in Jerusalem. The poem is divided into three sections: ''When We Look Up,'' ''The Peachtree,'' and ''Crystal Night.''

The poet begins with an epigraph from fellow poet and friend Robert Duncan: ''When we look up / each from his being.'' Duncan's epigraph concerns introspection, looking at oneself objectively, from without. The epigraph is correlated with the first section of Levertov's poem, which is about Eichmann's cruelty. Levertov suggests that Eichmann's evil derives at least in part from his refusal to look at Jews as he does himself, his inability to consider them as human beings. Instead, because ''he had not looked,'' he considers Jews to be ''the other.'' Levertov adds that people ''must pity if they look / into their own face.'' The word ''if'' suggests that people in general are not introspective, that people cannot look at themselves from without in order to be objective. Instead, people are self-centered and egoistic, which helps to explain how countless bystanders neglected to help Jews during the Holocaust. They did not see themselves and the Jewish victims as part of the same whole but rather as separate.

Eichmann subsequently issues his excuse for his part in the atrocities: he was a mere cog in the machine, merely following orders. Eichmann remarks, ''I was used from the nursery / to obedience / All my life . . . Corpselike / obedience.'' The defendant claims that he is not an evil man but merely a loyal and an obedient one, a passive man who carried out the orders of others. The phrase ''from the nursery'' suggests his position that such passivity is now part of his being and cannot be altered; in fact, it makes him lifeless, corpselike. But the term ''corpselike'' also suggests that he was part of an emotionless bureaucracy and thus acted not out of malice but without thinking. Eichmann stresses legal positivism and social law but chooses purposefully to ignore moral law, ideas such as ''Thou shalt not kill.'' Eichmann's claims of innocence conflict with what other prominent Nazi officials had declared in their testimony during the Nuremberg trials when they blamed him for the atrocities they themselves were accused of. Levertov implies that Eichmann's defense that he simply followed orders is merely a sham, a feeble excuse.

Levertov makes her position clear in the second segment of the poem, ''The Peachtree.'' This section is based on a incident, brought up during the trial, in which Eichmann was charged with murdering a young Jewish boy in his garden. The charge was unique because in the other accusations against Eichmann, counts such as crimes against humanity, he was not said to have taken part in the killings personally. According to Levertov's account, a Jewish boy working near Eichmann's villa climbed a wall into his garden and, out of desperation and hunger, stole a yellow peach. Angry because he had planned to eat the peach with sour cream and brandy, Eichmann murdered the boy. The crime was malicious and senseless, in part because Eichmann committed it over a mere peach. Furthermore, the poet wants her audience to juxtapose Eichmann's decadent dessert with the starving boy's desire to eat in order to survive. Yellow represents the peach as well as the boy, who wears a yellow star, and both are destroyed by Eichmann.

As it turns out, Levertov had the details wrong. The boy did not actually scale the wall into Eichmann's garden but was working there, and he stole cherries, not a peach. Even though Levertov later realized that she had made these mistakes, she kept them in the poem. She was writing the poem during the trial and did not want to change the details later, when she might not have been feeling the same intensity. In addition, by changing the object of theft from peaches to cherries, she would have lost the yellow imagery that pervades ''The Peachtree.''

The last section, entitled ''Crystal Night,'' refers to *Kristallnacht,* the terror that ensued on 9–10 November 1938. Synagogues were destroyed, and businesses owned by Jews were ruined, littering the streets of Germany with broken glass. The black-and-white imagery of this section contrasts with the color imagery of the preceding segment and provides the poem with a documentary, newsreel impression. One tie with the rest of the poem is that the father of Herschel Grynszpan, the man who incited *Kristallnacht* by killing a Nazi functionary, testified at the trial of Eichmann. Levertov uses words such as ''brick,'' ''stone,'' ''glass,'' ''ice,'' and ''knives'' to convey the cold and heartless horror that prevailed during the wave of terror. The broken glass suggests the dangerous situation that the Jews remaining in Germany—and the countries that Germany would occupy—faced and is also juxtaposed with the strong glass that protected Eichmann during his trial.

—Eric Sterling

E

EASTERN WAR TIME
Poem by Adrienne Rich, 1989–90

The difficulty of comprehending something that is impossible to understand and yet must be understood is at the heart of Adrienne Rich's poem ''Eastern War Time.'' Through the fog of memory's ''smoky mirror,'' the poem juxtaposes the innocence of a young Jewish schoolgirl in America in 1943, her parents' desire to protect her from the terror that is happening in Europe, and the blaring wires and telegrams that are reporting the destruction of millions of human beings:

> how do you teach a child what you won't
>   believe?
> how do you say *unfold, my flower,*
>   *shine, my star*
> and *we are hated, being what we are?*

How does an American child, studying Latin and *Jude the Obscure* in 1943, understand the Holocaust? How does one understand it today—the camps? the six million? the incalculable individual acts that created, allowed, and acted out that great horror we call the Holocaust? Like the cryptic telegrams and messages sent or smuggled out of Europe, how does one even begin to name the horror?

> PARENTS DEPORTED UNKNOWN DESTI-
>   NATION EAST
> SITUATION DIFFICULT ether of messages
> in capital letters   silence

What can one do but bear witness, even if that is only to one's experience, and then, as Stanley Kunitz puts it, ''report out.'' This poem is an example of that kind of reporting out: of re-creating and thus sharing the experience of a young Jewish schoolgirl in America, studying the history of the ancient world and, with ''permed friz of hair / her glasses for school and movies / . . . trying to grasp the world / through books.'' What child could ever be prepared to understand the telegrams? Or say, Rich suggests in the sixth section of the poem, you are not in America but in Poland, in Vilna, and you are young and walking with your boyfriend into the woods to support the resistance. Even then, knowing what you know, how could you possibly understand what is soon to happen to your village, your family, your neighbors, your friends, you?

Memory, with its imperfect voice and vision, calls on us. It reaches into the past to the known and the unknown, to the avoided and the ignored. It is a ''roll of film,'' a ''mirror,'' an intrusive ''bitter flashing.'' ''Unkillable though killed,'' it confronts us with questions: What now? What is right? What does one do?

The theme, central to Rich's poetry, points over and over to our dangerous obsession with the self—with our forgetting how to say ''we,'' with thinking, even, that there is a separation between the ''I'' and the ''we.'' Whether we think we are trying to save ourselves and our family during a war or are simply ''trying to live a personal life,'' we soon find ourselves losing the meaning of ''we''—a concept explored more fully in Rich's poem ''In Those Years.''

The tenth and final section of ''Eastern War Time'' is a long recollection of memory that speaks in the inclusive first person:

> I'm a canal in Europe where bodies are floating
> I'm a mass grave . . .
> . . . .
> I'm a woman bargaining for a chicken
> . . . .
> I have dreamed of Zion . . .
> . . . .
> I am a woman standing in line for gasmasks
> . . . .
> I am standing here in your poem . . .

Here the ''I'' becomes the ''we,'' inviting others to become selves included in the community. We need to see ourselves, the poem argues, as interconnected, as brothers and sisters living in community because memory, offering us its own eyes from which we might see and learn, is ''standing here in your poem unsatisfied / lifting [its] smoky mirror.''

With every word Rich reminds us what it means to be fully awake and aware. Her poetry is an engagement with the question of how one lives faithfully and honestly with the hard questions and realities with which the Holocaust—and, indeed, any injustice—confronts us. Her poetry bears witness to the horror and consequences that come from not knowing how to say ''we.''

—Michael S. Glaser

ELI, THE FANATIC
Short Story by Philip Roth, 1959

Like all the other stories in *Goodbye, Columbus,* ''Eli, the Fanatic'' is distinctly Jewish in its subject and tone, and yet it is assuredly American, too. Indeed, all the stories reflect the Jewish experience of America as a testing ground for equality, liberty, and the infinite opportunities denied to their immigrant forebears who fled Russia and Europe. The stories resonate with an underlying conflict of identity that continues to engage Roth's interest: Can a person identify himself as an American and still hold on to those ethnic traits that distinguish him as different? This conflict seems to have grown out of the more basic, archetypal query: Who am I?

The answers to these questions are made all the more poignant in "Eli, the Fanatic," the only story in *Goodbye, Columbus* to deal with the Holocaust. Roth weaves a kind of rabbinic parable that describes the ways in which the more modern concerns with the self have superseded for many Jews the traditional biblical dictum to be their brother's keepers. Thus the story relates how the peril for a group of Hasidic Jews, a Holocaust victim in particular, ironically comes from other Jews, not Gentiles.

Roth is sensitive to the fact that while American Jews were galvanized by the Holocaust and united against anti-Semitism, many also felt an underlying imperative to discard what had outwardly marked them as Jews. They wanted to avail themselves of the chance to shed their image as outsiders despite the fact that assimilation had not protected Jews in Hitler's world. Roth fictionalizes what happened to American Jews who, with newly acquired financial means and increased social mobility, feel their achievements threatened.

Having ventured beyond their self-imposed ghettos of urban America into Gentile suburbia, the secular Jews of Woodenton are anxious to evict some Hasidic Jews who have taken up residence on the outskirts of their newly found paradise. They are especially disturbed by the presence of one embarrassing interloper who, with his black frock coat, black pants, and black hat, is a nagging reminder of their Jewish ancestry whenever he parades past the manicured lawns and upscale shops.

Roth singles out the Hasid's black suit as a highly visible sign of being a Jew and makes it a dual symbol of what assimilating Jews have tried to forget and, ironically, what they need to remember: their link to Judaism and their tie to victims of anti-Semitism. This message is encoded in the story of Eli Peck, the lawyer persuaded by his fellow secular Jews to use the law, if need be, to evict the Hasidim from encroaching on their territory. Since eviction seems a drastic step, Eli insists that Mr. Tsuref, the head of the Yeshiva, at least tell the young Hasid to change from the black outfit that his clients find so objectionable. Such attire, Eli heartlessly suggests, probably made victimization of the Jews much easier. Eli's obtuseness about the condition of Holocaust survivors forces Tsuref to starkly inform the lawyer: "The suit the gentleman wears is all he's got." This unalterable fact prompts Eli to donate his own Brooks Brothers tweed suit to the survivor, who in return gives Eli his black one. After Eli impulsively dons the black garb, a transformation ensues. Slowly Eli becomes aware, perhaps for the first time, of what it has meant to be a Jew—the ostracism,

the persecution, the stigma of being different, and also the fierce commitment to a moral code that involves compassion, charity, and a sense of justice.

Eli's wife and the doctors at the hospital where she has just given birth to a son judge his epiphany to be a sign of a nervous breakdown. Their assessment of Eli's madness reaffirms symbolically the position of America's secular Jews who kept not only a geographic but also an emotional and philosophical distance from their more religious, less fortunate, fellow Jews. Reading this story as a quasi sermon also suggests that Eli is the sole wise man, destined perhaps to be misunderstood. In terms of the Holocaust, Roth's story reflects the inability or the refusal of American Jews to know about and to have sufficient compassion for the indescribable suffering of their own people.

—Ellen Gerstle and Daniel Walden

ELI: A MYSTERY PLAY OF THE SUFFERINGS OF ISRAEL (Eli: Ein Mysterienspiel vom Leiden Israels) Play by Nelly Sachs, 1951

Among the plays of Leonie (Nelly) Sachs, *Eli,* first produced and published in the early 1950s as *Eli: Ein Mysterienspiel vom Leiden Israels* and published in English translation in the collection *O the Chimneys* in 1967, is the one that deals most directly with the Holocaust. The play concerns the murder of Eli, an eight-year-old boy, a God child, as indicated by his name in Hebrew. The action takes place in a small town in Poland where Jewish mysticism was prevalent. The time of the play is defined symbolically rather than historically as the period after martyrdom. Eli was killed by a soldier when his parents were led through the streets of their town to be deported to an extermination camp. Trying to follow them, Eli blew his shepherd's pipe as a call to God for help. In a postscript to the play Sachs interprets the shepherd's pipe with which the boy, in his despair, called to God as an "attempted outbreak of the human in the face of horror." At that moment, as Eli called to God, one of the soldiers turned around and, assuming the pipe to be a secret signal, killed the boy with his rifle butt. The soldier's fear of a secret signal is explained by the playwright as a symbol of unbelief.

After the war a new city is being built outside the gates of the old town. But the townspeople continue to grieve over the murder of their loved ones, especially over Eli, the God child. Michael, a shoemaker who has the eyes of the Baal Shem, the saint-mystic of eastern European Jewish mysticism (Hasidism), cannot find peace. Shoemaking traditionally is a mystic trade. Sachs was aware that Jakob Böhme, for instance, the German mystic of the early seventeenth century who was strongly influenced by Jewish cabalism, was a shoemaker. It was

Böhme who became a source of inspiration for Sachs, in whose works the parallel strands of Jewish and German mysticism are united. Michael is also one of the Thirty-Six Pious, or Just, Men for whose sake, according to Jewish legend, the world was saved. As one of these men, Michael takes his people's grief into his own heart so that they are relieved of the burden of their sorrow and thus able to build the new town without grief.

Taking with him Eli's pipe, the instrument for invoking God, Michael leaves the town and goes into the world in search of Eli's murderer. Wherever he meets people, he takes their sorrows unto himself so that they can live or die in peace. Finally Michael finds work in a village in the west, where Eli's murderer lives. Again the locale is indicated symbolically rather than geographically or politically. Michael works at his shoemaker's trade, but he cannot mend the murderer's shoes. It is impossible for Michael to connect the ''lower'' sole to the ''upper'' leather, because the murderer has split the ''lower world'' into two pieces. When the murderer's child comes to Michael's shop with his father, he wants to play Eli's pipe, but the father will not permit it. Denied the pipe, the child is overcome by a strange, powerful yearning for the instrument the father tries to ridicule. In his harshness the murderer prevents his child from establishing a relationship with God through the instrument that gives voice to religious longing. Instead, he promises the child the flute of the Pied Piper, expressing world domination and demagoguery. He does not allow his child to play the shepherd's pipe whose sound reaches God. The child dies, not because of the sins of his father, but because of the denial of his religious yearning. The former soldier thus repeats his murderous act of the past. In his innocence his own child dies as did Eli, both victims of the same evil.

Confronting the murderer, Michael now becomes the guardian angel of Israel. A primordial light shines from a symbolic embryo in the sky, representing the original God child. The murderer crumbles into dust before the divine light, a picture of remorse, as Sachs explains the scene in her postscript. The murderer is destroyed by his sense of guilt, not by the revenge of the survivors. With the primordial light now shining from his brow, Michael is taken to God. His mission as one of the Thirty-Six Pious Men is fulfilled, and as the anguish and fear of the past are lifted, the town can be rebuilt.

The Jewish New Year's liturgy that forms the central part of the play, promising the Lord's return, is fulfilled in the last scene. Jewish religion and Hasidic mysticism merge to provide Sachs with objective correlatives to present the mystery of religious promise and redemption. Employing the figure of the mystic shoemaker, Sachs believed that she was able to ''raise the unutterable to a transcendental level, so as to make it bearable,'' as she says in the postscript.

Sachs's other plays, or ''scenic poetry'' as she preferred to call them, deal with similar topics of persecution and collaboration and of guilt and redemption on a symbolic level, using mysticism and religious ritual as means to express the ineffable. They have nothing in common either with lyrical drama, contemporary social drama, or the epic theater of **Bertolt Brecht**. Yet they are characterized by bold experimentation with music, dance, and even film projections. It is not surprising that several of her plays have been produced as radio dramas, while others, including *Eli*, have been set to music. It provided the libretto for two operas, one by Moses Pergament (1959) and the other by Walter Steffens (1967).

—Ehrhard Bahr

ELLI: COMING OF AGE IN THE HOLOCAUST
Memoir by Livia E. Bitton-Jackson, 1980

Elli: Coming of Age in the Holocaust is the graphic memoir of Livia E. Bitton-Jackson, born Elli L. Friedman in Somorja at the foot of the Carpathian Mountains in what had been Czechoslovakia but was at the time occupied by Hungarian forces. She describes her journey from the bucolic village to the horrors of the concentration camps. In the spring of 1944 the 13-year-old budding poet, her mother and father, and her 16-year-old brother, Bubi, suffered the Nazi invasion and were deported to several ghettos, first to Nagymagyar. As the second ghetto at Dunaszerdahely was liquidated, the able men, including her father, were summoned for transport to labor camps. Elli, her brother, mother, and Aunt Szeren were then sent on a hellish three-day train ride to Auschwitz.

Separated from both Bubi and her aunt, Elli and her mother, because of their *goldene Haar,* were sent not to the gas chambers but to labor in Auschwitz and then to Plaszow to shovel dirt and move stones. But seven weeks later they were returned to Auschwitz, where they met Bubi, who had fared well as an interpreter for the Germans. In Auschwitz, however, the mother was paralyzed when a bunk collapsed on her. Aided by Elli and other inmates, she survived, and she and Elli were then shipped to yet another labor camp, at Augsburg, where the officers could not believe that they are women because of their ''porcupine'' hair and stick bodies. Their brief confinement in Augsburg working at an airplane factory revived them since the food and conditions there were relatively good. But they were soon shipped to Mühldorf, once again encountering Bubi, by this time a skeleton covered with dreadfully numerous lice. He was alive, however, despite the many dead around him.

Even when liberation was near, the deaths continued. The Nazis shot inmates in cornfields and in cattle cars, and even the Americans strafed the train the Friedmans were riding in, killing yet more of the pitiful number of survivors. On 28 April 1945, Elli, her mother, and her brother were liberated. Elli was then 14, fatherless, a displaced person, emaciated, mistaken for a 60-year-old. She and her remaining family returned to their home but still felt like refugees. In 1951 Elli and her family emigrated to the United States.

As in many coming-of-age texts, the protagonist in *Elli* experiences painful and, surprisingly, joyful lessons as she matures. This first-person account, written in 1980 at the prodding of her husband, is remarkable not only for its shocking descriptions of human depravity and brutality but also for its amazing descriptions of the kindnesses Elli experienced even in the hell of the camps. Her determination to support her mother and brother in their efforts to stay alive is especially noteworthy. Her recounting of these years, culminating in her triumphant survival as well as the survival of her mother and brother, is inspiring for all ages.

Elli, published in 1980, won the Christopher Award, the Eleanor Roosevelt Humanitarian Award, and the Jewish Heritage Award. In1997 Bitton-Jackson adapted *Elli* for a teenage audience, retitling the memoir *I Have Lived a Thousand Years: Growing Up in the Holocaust.*

—Maryann McLoughlin

THE EMIGRANTS (Die Ausgewanderten)
Novel by W.G. Sebald, 1993

The Emigrants, an eloquent rumination on the nature of memory and loss, is the first of W.G. Sebald's novels to garner critical and popular acclaim in English translation. Published as *Die Ausgewanderten* (1993) in the German original and translated into English in 1996, it presents four thematically interrelated life stories of emigrants who were forced to leave their home countries, in some cases due to their Jewish origin.

The Emigrants is characterized throughout by the use of fictional techniques that locate the novel in the interstices of generic convention. Sebald combines elements of biography, autobiography, travelogue, and photographic representation to arrive at a narrative form all his own. The combination of historiography with fictional elements results in a style that points beyond the portraiture of individuals toward allegory.

The book's first section, ''Dr. Henry Selwyn,'' relates how Hersch Seweryn emigrated from Grodno, Lithuania, when he was seven years old. He settles in England where his secrecy about his Jewish origin, as well as his increasing sense of his deracination and consequent hollowness of identity, result in his suicide. ''Paul Bereyter,'' the second section, introduces the narrator's grade school teacher, who is prevented from teaching by the Nazis because of his being a so-called *Dreiviertelarier* (one of his grandparents was Jewish), subsequently emigrates and returns to Germany, but can never assimilate into a postwar culture bent on forgetting about the

Third Reich. He kills himself by lying down on the train tracks, an uncanny echo of the role the railways played in the deportation of the Jews.

The third section, ''Ambros Adelwarth,'' depicts a great-uncle of the narrator who emigrates to the United States between the wars and serves as a personal servant and travel companion to Cosmo Solomon. By depicting the relationship between a German émigré and a Jew in the United States, Sebald evokes the very different relationship between Jews and Germans in Germany and thus mourns the absence of Jewish life from Germany. The book's lengthiest section, ''Max Ferber,'' depicts a German Jew who fled to Manchester and lives in the shadow of smokestacks—literally, due to Manchester's industrial heritage, and figuratively, because his parents were killed in the Holocaust.

Ferber is a painter, and his artistic technique could be seen as emblematic of Sebald's understanding of memory's processes:

> Since [Ferber] applied the paint thickly, and then repeatedly scratched it off the canvas as his work proceeded, the floor was covered with a largely hardened and encrusted deposit of droppings, mixed with coal dust, several centimetres thick at the centre and thinning out towards the edges, in places resembling the flow of lava . . . It had always been of the greatest importance to him, Ferber once remarked casually, that nothing should change at his place of work, that everything should remain as it was, as he had arranged it, and that nothing further should be added but the debris generated by painting and the dust that continuously fell and which, as he was coming to realize, he loved more than anything else in the world. He felt closer to dust, he said, than to light, air or water . . . And indeed, when I watched Ferber working on one of his portrait studies over a number of weeks, I often thought that his prime concern was to increase the dust. He drew with vigorous abandon, frequently going through half a dozen of his willow-wood charcoal sticks in the shortest of time; and that process of drawing and shading on the thick, leathery paper, as well as the concomitant business of constantly erasing what he had drawn with a woollen rag already heavy with charcoal, really amounted to nothing but a steady production of dust, which never ceased except at night.

Despite their conversations, the narrator does not find out anything about Ferber's biographical background until he returns to Manchester from a sojourn in Switzerland and reads about the painter in a newspaper's Sunday supplement. Ferber left Germany in 1939, and his parents were exterminated in the Holocaust in 1941. When the narrator visits him once more in Manchester, Ferber tells him in great detail his life history and says that ''time . . . is an unreliable way of gauging these things, indeed it is nothing but a disquiet of the soul. There is neither a past nor a future.'' Upon departure, Ferber hands the narrator a package containing his mother's memoirs of her youth and upbringing, written between 1939 and 1941—a document where ''remembering, writing and reading'' intersect.

In *The Emigrants* the prism through which the present is viewed is a gray one, one that refracts the light against the backdrop of emptied cities, the color of ashes, and the all-pervasiveness of dust, all of which are recurrent images of the ''Max Ferber'' section. The pastness of history does not guarantee an escape from its maw. The narrator experiences this bond at Bad Kissingen's Jewish cemetery: ''A shock of recognition shot through me at the grave of Maier Stern, who died on the 18th of May, my own birthday; and I was touched, in a way I knew I could never quite fathom, by the symbol of the writer's quill on the stone of Friederike Halbleib, who departed this life on the 28th of March 1912.'' This realization extends beyond the narrator imagining the universality of human experience—such a sentiment appears limited by virtue of attempting to extract metaphysical meaning from biographic coincidence. Seen against the backdrop of Jewish life in Germany contained in the memoir of Max Ferber's mother and the cemetery's ''wilderness of graves, neglected for years,'' it also bespeaks a loss that transcends the individual—a loss of a culture and a world whose only present traces are those of the past, where presence is indicated only by markers of absence. The phenomenal reality the photographs and, by extension, *The Emigrants* depict is one that captures more than the present-day object: They capture an aura of the past and are as accurate a depiction of ghosts as is possible to a device that depends on expressing memory through linguistic means.

—Stefan Gunther

ENEMIES: A LOVE STORY (Sonim, di Geshichte fun a Liebe)
Novel by Isaac Bashevis Singer, 1966

Enemies: A Love Story, originally published in Yiddish (1966) and later in English (1972), recognizes the enduring dark legacy of the Holocaust even as it indicts modern Judaism. Before World War II Herman Broder, the novel's protagonist, married and separated from Tamara Luria. Trapped in Poland during the Holocaust, Herman was saved by Yadwiga, the Broder family maid, who hid him in a hayloft. Believing that his wife is dead, Herman marries Yadwiga after the war, and the couple move to Brooklyn. Wherever he goes in New York, Herman seeks places to hide from imaginary Nazis. Yet Broder is a victim not only of the Nazis but also of his own personality. He works as a ghostwriter, a fitting occupation for someone who has rejected life, who wants no children. He also

has rejected religion, and he is unfaithful to Yadwiga, carrying on an affair with Masha Tortshiner, another Holocaust survivor.

Like Herman, Masha is bitter and self-centered, caring only for her own pleasures. She cannot believe in a God who would permit the Holocaust, but without belief her life lacks meaning. Although she thinks that she is pregnant, she is suffering from nerves: she cannot bring forth new life. At the end of the novel she kills herself. Her materialism is shared by Yadwiga's Jewish neighbors. When Yadwiga talks to them to learn about Judaism, to which she is going to convert, she gets the impression from their conversations that ''the insurance policy and the dishwasher were both necessary aspects of Jewish observances.''

Contrasting with these tormented figures are those who are saved by belief and tradition. When Herman puts on his skullcap and returns to the sacred books, he feels peace, but he cannot remain faithful to God any more than he can to Yadwiga. At the end of *Enemies* he vanishes from the world of the book. Shifra Puah Bloch, Masha's mother, yet another Holocaust survivor, remains a believer, and her religion gives meaning to her life. Tamara, who in fact survived the war, has been chastened by her experiences and has learned compassion. And Yadwiga, who risked her life to save Herman's, brings forth new life as the book ends. Her daughter, Masha, represents a renewal that can occur only by accepting tradition. The new Masha, safe from the Nazis and surrounded by love, offers hope.

Though *Enemies* was Singer's fourth novel to be translated into English, it was the first with a contemporary American setting. His New York is bleak, wintry, gray—a fitting valley of ashes for the hollow men and women who inhabit it. Yet the novel is essentially comic in the sense that it ends with the promise of renewal. In a kind of fertility ritual, the old Masha and her bitterness die, and in the late spring, the season of rebirth, a new Masha is born.

In presenting Singer with the Nobel Prize for Literature in 1978, the Swedish Academy praised ''his impassioned narrative art which, with roots in a Polish-Jewish cultural tradition, brings universal human conditions to life.'' This novel's paradoxical title exemplifies Singer's concern with the eternal struggle of good and evil, the search for self, the desire for and fear of love.

—Joseph Rosenblum

THE ENGLISH GARDEN
Short story by Walter Abish, 1977

''The English Garden'' is the first of seven short stories (referred to by the author as ''fictions'') that Walter Abish published in *In the Future Perfect* (1977), his second collection. However, to label these pieces "short stories," or their presence in the same volume a "collection," would be to underestimate the fact that they resist subsumption under one generic heading and cannot be easily summarized or explicated. In the most general sense, they can be seen as "metafiction"—fiction about fiction, less concerned with the traditional categories of plot and character than with the representational qualities of language itself.

"The English Garden" undoubtedly is a precursor to Abish's later novel *How German Is It* (1980). The novel's examination of the strategies of displacement undertaken by the Germans in the wake of the Holocaust and World War II is clearly foreshadowed in the story. The epigraph of "Garden" is a quotation from John Ashbery's "The New Spirit" (in *Three Poems*) that programmatically announces the story's epistemological approach: "Remnants of the old atrocity subsist, but they are converted into ingenious shifts in scenery, a sort of 'English Garden' effect, to give the required air of naturalness, pathos and hope."

Abish sums up the text's narrative thrust and thematic concerns as follows: "The story describes an American who has come to Germany to interview a German writer. On his arrival the American buys a coloring book, really a children's coloring book, at the airport. During his brief stay he keeps questioning the signs in the coloring book and comparing them to other signs in Germany. That immediately reduces the landscape, everything I describe, to a set of signs and images and also introduces, not the interpretation itself, but the need for interpretation as well as the level on which the speculation is to be conducted." The narrator, a writer, visits Brumholdstein, a town named after Germany's preeminent living philosopher (clearly modeled after Martin Heidegger) and built on the ruins of Durst, a concentration camp. Throughout the narrative, the device of the coloring book serves as a foil to contemporary German life, and its images of normalcy and quotidian activity are juxtaposed with the sense of the past constantly breaking through the veneer of the guiltless present Germans attempt to construct.

This sense emanates from the following passage from the story: "After a careful search that afternoon I found the old railroad tracks. They run parallel to the main highway. There was very little traffic at that hour. I parked my car on the side of the highway and followed the tracks on foot for a mile or so. No one saw me. I encountered no one. In the distance I could make out the taller buildings of Brumholdstein. On a siding I passed an old railroad freight car. Its sliding doors wide open. It was a German freight car. For no reason in particular I scratched a long row of numbers on its side."

This passage anticipates a similar one in *How German Is It*. In both cases Abish makes the point that in a postwar dispensation, an innocent or even prewar look at a "railroad freight car" in and of itself, or even as a distinct object functioning

within an economy designed to move goods expeditiously, has simply become impossible. Any viewer of this specific image would by necessity see the railroad freight car as automatically implicated in the Nazi economy of moving humans, Jews, as expeditiously as possible to the locus of the *Endlösung* (Final Solution). Objects that are presented as innocent in postwar Germany cannot be seen innocently any longer. They always refer back to their implication in the unspeakable and carry a referential, if not always immediately visible, remainder/reminder of that past.

—Stefan Gunther

ERIKA: POEMS OF THE HOLOCAUST
Poems by William Heyen, 1984

William Heyen's procession into the Holocaust inferno is threefold. The first is nurturing and upbringing by German immigrant parents in a German-speaking environment and the security of a pastoral childhood on Long Island. The second is a gradual loss of that world in an adulthood quest of personal history that merges with the history of the Shoah. The third is a visit to the landscape of camps and crematoriums in order to make sense of shattered innocence and uncertain destiny. For Heyen the quest to understand began early, when swastika signs appeared on his boyhood home, "how the heart beats with it, / how the eyes remember." His *Swastika Poems* (1977) included in *Erika: Poems of the Holocaust* (1984; reissued in 1991) represents one of the earliest Gentile efforts to directly confront issues of the Shoah.

Erika is divided into four sections. The second section, entitled "Erika," is a prose memoir of a one-day visit to Bergen-Belsen. At the camp museum Heyen encounters the statistics and face of death; outside he walks among the markers of death, whose mass graves are covered with Erika, "Erika, bell-heather, *heide,* a heath plant, wild and strong." The beauty of the Erika plant growing over the graves and the objects the caretaker at Belsen finds when he tills the soil in spring—a piece of human bone, a frame of someone's glasses, a heel of a shoe, a wedding band—are memories that spring eternal and christen an anguished and sensitive soul of an American poet of German heritage to seek how and why.

The epilogue juxtaposes counsel from Susan Sontag and a dream-poem from Heinrich Heine, and together they set the intent of this work. From the former, to remember the murder of the six million European Jews is right, proper, and moral though it runs the risk of not being practical or good. And from Germany's outstanding Jewish poet and essayist,

I dreamed I had a lovely fatherland

The sturdy oak
Grew tall there, and the violets gently swayed.
Then I awoke.
I dreamed a German kiss was on my brow,
And someone spoke
The German words: ''I love you!'' (How
    they rang!)
Then I awoke.

Heyen's pledge at the end of ''Erika,''—''I will always remember''—is a testimony of attachment to his cultural heritage and how far he must exorcise the demons from within and without.

The first section of poems painfully describes Jewish life in Nazi-occupied Europe in life and death hues. Childhood memory of crooked crosses etched on ''our doors [which] father cursed and painted over'' and joyful *Volksfesten* and boundless *Deutsche Geistigkeit,* which destroyed the Jew in the street, ghetto, community, and camps. Streams of consciousness connect these entries. But what happens years after the Event, when forgetfulness reigns? The penultimate poem, ''Darkness''—a descent into ''Treblinka green, / Nordhausen red, / Auschwitz blue, / Mauthausen orange, / Belsen white''—answers surrealistically that there are fragments of killer and victim although the distinction is blurred. The section ends in ''The Legacy'' and the terrible revelation said thrice-over by the author: ''I am dead. They are dead.''

The third section, called ''The Numinous,'' confronts in stanza and verse the brutality of the Shoah on its own ground. In the title poem Heyen and his wife are walking on a Hannover street when suddenly their trancelike disposition is disrupted by an ''explosion'' of pigeons, which ''we will always remember.'' ''The hundred hearts [of blue-gray pigeons] / beating in the air'' suggest the transcending moments of Jewish children murdered in blue flame and rising to a blue sky, to the Lord of blue. In ''Blue'' and ''Simple Truths,'' feelings about God's presence or nonpresence are expressed. ''The Children'' is an anguished personal testimony that ''within my dream / . . . I do not think that we can save them'' but there is solace in the speaking voice that affirms ''they are safe in my body.'' Other poems are fragments of dreams (''Listener, all words are a dream / You have wandered into mine''), which talk of nature (the Erika over the graves, the wind and the dawn sun mixed with the smoke of Belzec, ''The Tree,'' in Lidice, Czechoslovakia, destroyed with the village in reprisal for the killing of Gestapo chief Reinhardt Heydrich by Czech partisans) and the nature of the Nazi program of ''willed chaos'' (''Poem Touching the Gestapo'').

The third section begins with ''The Baron's Tour'' of the führer's castle on the Rhine where ''we have always lived'' and ends in ''This Night'' by querying Who am I? Who are you?—necessary questions about the human predicament that come out of the inferno. To wit Heyen advises in ''The Tree,''

''Read the book made from the leaves of that tree from Lidice and see the faces of what was and the face of what must be.''

—Zev Garber

ERRINERUNGEN AN PROMETHEUS
Poem by Robert Schindel, 1964

Included in Robert Schindel's collection of verse entitled *Im Herzen die Krätze* (1988), the lengthy autobiographical poem ''Errinerungen an Prometheus'' (''Memories of Prometheus''), written in 1964, deals with the poet's birth and upbringing during the years of Hitler's reign over Austria. As such, it includes details regarding his parents' incarceration in concentration camps and the death of his father, as well as the murder of millions of Jews as a result of the Holocaust. The poem thus intertwines the general tragedy of the Holocaust with the poet's own personal history.

The main body of the poem is divided into three stanzas, labeled a, b, and c, and it is preceded by modified short excerpts from each of the sections, which are also labeled a, b, and c. Each of the three introductory sections begins with a question, playing on the three meanings of the word *bestehen:* ''What are our origins?'' ''Of what are we composed?'' and ''What do we demand?'' Each of the answers contains a range of vivid imagery from the longer sections, such as ''Knochengerüst,'' ''Monde,'' and ''Himmel.''

The first and longest stanza begins with a reference to Schindel's birth, which he describes as a matter of fate, of his being ''thrown'' into the town of Bad Hall, located in the middle of the Ostmark, the name for the Austrian territory annexed by the Nazis. He also refers to his being the offspring of ''racially low-quality'' parents who participated in the resistance against Hitler as foreign workers in Alsace. The bitter, ironic tone used here, as well as the description of each event and person through the perspective and language of the Nazis, lends the poem a sense of resentment that he happened to be born a Jew in the middle of annexed Austria during the Holocaust. The tone also conveys a sense of distance, from which the author chooses to write about the first years of his life, normally a most intimate subject. That Schindel wrote a poem dealing with the subject at all is surprising, however, for at the time there was little public discussion of the events of the Holocaust in Austria, whether by Jews or non-Jews.

The first stanza also interweaves the events of his earliest birthdays, when he was not yet fully aware of the world around him, with the fate of his parents under the Nazis. He ''hears'' that there existed a good relationship between the parents and their child in the year before the identities of the parents were discovered and they were transported to concentration camps, and he "hears" that the conditions in the cattle car in which his mother was transported were terribly crowded. He also "hears" that his father, who died in Dachau, loved music and gymnastics. Of course, he can have heard this information only from his mother, the lone witness to the events, as she, but not his father, returned from the camps. His refusal to quote directly the source of his information, however, and his distanced language and tone support his reference to his own childhood as "myth," as if he is uncertain of its occurrence. He writes that it is possible, but not probable, that the "brat" of those years and the current writer of the poem are the same person. Almost 30 years later Schindel returned to the theme of doubling to describe his identity as the child of Nazi victims in the novel *Gebürtig* (1992), in which Demant, the main character, who is also the son of Jewish parents who resisted Hitler, has a twin brother who is writing the story.

Although the poem is autobiographical in content, each section maintains its distance from the direct identification of experience. The second and third stanzas refer to the perpetrators of the Holocaust alongside imagery of the landscape in which the murders took place, the efforts of most people to forget the gruesome events, and finally the myth of Prometheus, which links the stanzas together.

—Lisa Silverman

DI ERSHTE NAKHT IN GETO
Poems by Abraham Sutzkever, 1979

Written between 1941 and 1943, the poems in *Di ershte Nakht in Geto* ("The First Night in the Ghetto") represent Abraham Sutzkever's response to the setting up of the Vilna (Vilnius) ghetto and the rapid destruction of the Jewish population. A feature of the poems, and indeed a feature of the poet's life, is that they are defiant and muscular, full of hope even when all hope seems to be futile. Sutzkever was fairly noncommittal about Judaism as a faith and the passivity of the Jews as a community, and yet he gave evidence of his feelings of guilt that he survived while his family had been murdered. In some ways his ability to resist is seen as bought at the expense of his family, and thus many of the poems convey a good deal of despair and raging against the futility of the position in which he was put. They represent the uneasiness Sutzkever felt about being concerned about his own fate while the fate of so many of his own people had already been sealed.

There is evidence that the absence of a positive note led the poet to edit the poems severely before publication, removing those that were negative and critical of the contemporary Jewish community. Some of the poems are very lyrical, particularly the title poem, as if to demonstrate the phenomenon Sutzkever described in which the unbearable becomes part

of everyday life and prepares the victims for yet greater horrors in the future. His descriptions of aspects of Jewish life and practice in an environment in which only death seems to rule are effective in linking him with Judaism while eschewing any reliance on an individual God. Survival becomes the supreme value, and yet in a universe in which such cruelty reigns survival appears to be both impossible and irrelevant.

What Sutzkever often referred to as crucial is the role of the witness. The witness sees and experiences, and it is his duty to transmit that information to the future. But Sutzkever also expressed the idea that the audience for the reports of the witness is being destroyed at the same time as the community is being destroyed. The destruction is so total that the witnessing eye ultimately survives by blending with nature, and although the report survives there is a suggestion that it is irrelevant, since what is meant by survival is ironic. At the end of the poem that gives this collection its title, Sutzkever referred to "the familiar, the living stars of my town [Vilna] . . . . the after-Sabbath stars . . . . a happy new week." Then he explained that he is resuscitated and must live, "for my mother's good star is alive," the mother who wished him a good week at the end of the Sabbath. Yet it is clear that both his life and his mother's afterlife were far from what would normally be called life, and that Sutzkever's theme is one which is familiar in Holocaust literature, the blurring of the distinction between the living and the dead.

—Oliver Leaman

EVA: A NOVEL OF THE HOLOCAUST
Novel by Meyer Levin, 1959

When Meyer Levin turned to write *Eva* (1959), he was coming off the tremendous critical and popular success of *Compulsion* (1956), a documentary fiction on the famous Leopold-Loeb murder case that anticipated works by American authors such as Truman Capote, Norman Mailer, and the cluster of writers known as the New Journalists. Levin worked best from source materials, and the relative success of *Eva* as a piece of Holocaust fiction seems owing to its documentary lineage. Borrowing his story line from the personal history of a survivor named Ida Lev, Levin had originally intended to preserve as much of Ida Lev's real life history as possible, but the novel soon evolved into a curious hybrid form. In it the fictionalized heroine Eva Korngold remembers her life more than a decade after the end of the war and approximates, through Levin's narrative style, the rhythms, cadences, and even some of the rhetorical markers of testimonial speech. If for this reason only, *Eva* is a fascinating work that troubles generic distinctions, especially the line, much insisted on, that is drawn between the novel and Auschwitz, or fiction and authentic witness.

Eva is a young Jewish girl from Hrebenko, a village in Poland occupied mostly by Ukrainians who have hated being governed by the Poles. In the fall of 1941, with the Germans at the height of their power and actions against the Jews becoming more severe, Eva's family decides that she must cease to be Eva and enter the Gentile world as a Ukrainian Polish girl named Katya (Katarina Leszczyszyn). For almost its first two thirds the novel functions as a passing story. As a Jew under Christian cover, the novel's heroine recalls an odd detail from Levin's career—the period during which he was forced to adopt a Christian pseudonym for his *Esquire* bylines because of racial sensitivities among the magazine's readership. Though often resentful about the restrictions placed upon the Jewish perspective in his writings, Levin consistently advocated both a Jewish particularism he thought compatible with America's language of ethnic inclusiveness and a democratic universalism he thought the best face of the Judeo-Christian cultural heritage. This led to a rhetorical habit in which, as both journalist and fiction writer, Levin expressed a solidarity with Christian language and culture because it had provided, along with Judaism, the very idioms of justice and freedom by which a liberal society could continue to be measured. This posture of politic passing comes out in Eva's Holocaust tale of passing. So when Eva dons a crucifix as part of her disguise, she consoles herself with the thought that Jesus himself had been a Jew, and when she later worries about losing her true self to her Christian identity, she first identifies her common ground with the Christian faith—admiring it "when it helped people and they were true to it"—before she ponders its hegemonic tendencies and dissents in her self-remembrance from Christian culture's attempt to erase the other as Jew.

With most of the novel taking place in the world outside of the camps, Levin makes the historical threat of extermination run parallel with another dimension of genocide, which had been part of the 1948 Geneva Convention's definition of genocide, namely the canceling of cultural identity. In carrying out his legal fight with Otto Frank over the Broadway *Diary* production and the cultural interpretation of Anne Frank's story, Levin frequently referred to this other aspect of genocide, as he argued that the distortion of Anne's real words and the censorship of his truer account amounted, in effect, to a killing of Jewish identity consistent with the politics of Nazi Fascism. Thus the greatest fictional imperative of Levin's *Eva* derives through a cultural filter: Eva's struggle to maintain her Jewishness in a world in which it would be easier not to remember her true identity is a version of the attempt of Anne Frank, as someone coming from an especially assimilated family, to reckon with her Jewishness and, by implication, Levin's own attempt to keep this aspect of Anne's identity alive. It is not hard to imagine that for Levin, having so long immersed himself in Anne Frank's perspective, Eva would have seemed a slightly older version of Anne and a vehicle for him to give expression to the imaginative energy he had already exerted toward telling the Holocaust through the eyes of a young woman. Whether or not Levin is entirely effective in achieving the androgynous voice one of his reviewers sympathetically attributed to him, it is nevertheless admirable that he offered a Holocaust story sensitive to the intersection between gender issues and the Nazi repression of Jewish identity. Part of the appeal of treating a woman's story of passing was that Eva's identity could remain, if only for reasons of anatomy and the dictates of Jewish law, a matter of personal choice.

Much of the early portion of the novel employs an associative narrative structure according to which a scene from the narrative present of Eva's story falls back into the past and her life in the small town of Hrebenko. Only some of these recollections are directly attributable to Eva's memory, and Levin's point seems to be that one's identity is greater than the patterns of conscious remembrance. Once Eva crosses the threshold and enters "that other world, the world without Jews," she finds work in Vienna, where she lives with the possibility that she will be discovered at any moment by the Germans. If the external threat of exposure remains a real concern throughout the story, closer to its center there is the risk of losing oneself to the requirements of a self-preservation that is at the same time potentially self-destructive. Much of the drama of the second half of the novel develops from Eva's persistent need to be known as herself. Comparing her own story to tales she has heard about criminals who fled their homes, changed their lives, and married under new names and yet 20 years later revealed their true identities, Eva fantasizes about surrendering her virginity only with her great secret and, as she confesses her true identity in the moment of passion, perhaps finding out that her lover is also secretly Jewish. This fantasy to reveal her true self competes at times with her survival, and Levin's novel runs into difficulty, as Steven J. Rubin has suggested, when he allows the connotations of surviving to make the Nazi genocide seem the occasion for testing and affirming Eva's identity. Eventually Eva does reveal her secret to a Czech man with whom she is in love and again to a Polish woman who has befriended her and turns out to be, in fact, another Jew in cultural disguise. When Eva is finally apprehended by the Gestapo, she is caught because she tells more of her own story than was strictly necessary, almost as though her secret has weighed too heavily upon her and become, at least in her own mind, criminal in connotation.

In the end Eva's ability to preserve her identity is indistinguishable from her ability to survive, since in either case she is marked by what she thinks of as her "special fortune." Even as Eva enters the world of Auschwitz, she tells herself that she has "been caught by a mistake of [her] own rather than by some act of bad fortune," and she fully expects her luck to see her through Auschwitz, as it indeed does. Levin may well intend to draw our attention to the survivor's tendency to rationalize her own fate as if it had been marked all along by a necessity proportionate to character, yet he can do little to separate himself from such a claim. So firmly has the novel been located inside the truth of Eva's testimonial voice that Levin fails to dissent from the way such a perception might distort the luckless world of Auschwitz.

—R. Clifton Spargo

EXILE IN THE FATHERLAND: MARTIN NIEMÖLLER'S LETTERS FROM MOABIT PRISON
(Martin Niemöller: Briefe aus der Gefangenschaft Moabit)
Memoir by Martin Niemöller, 1975

In his forward to *Exile in the Fatherland: Martin Neimöller's Letters from Moabit Prison* (1986), the English edition of *Martin Niemöller: Briefe aus der Gefangenschaft Moabit*, Franklin H. Littell, the doyen of American Protestant scholars on the Shoah, recognizes Karl Barth and Martin Niemöller as the leading architects of the Confessing Church's resistance to National Socialism and the German Christians' Faith Movement (Reich Church). Niemöller's public activity and sermons support this claim. Reflecting Niemöller's strategic leadership in the church's struggle are these sentiments from his last church sermon in the Third Reich, "We have no more thought of using our own powers to escape the arm of authorities than had the Apostles of old. No more are we ready to keep silent at man's behest when God commands us to speak. For it is, and must remain, the case that we must obey God rather than man" (1937).

Niemöller never saw himself as a theologian nor did he view the church in terms of ecclesiastical structures. Influenced by his father's stern Christian commitment, he saw the Church as a way of life imbued with a Christian philosophy and system of morals circumscribed by the question, *Was würde Jesus sagen?* ("What would Jesus say?"). The young Niemöller showed hints of anti-Judaism when he declared that the Jews bear the curse of "Positive Christianity," that is to say, "a pure-blooded, race-conscious nation" who rejected and resisted "Negative Christianity," meaning repentance to and faith in Jesus as the savior of all sinners. But he broke from his anti-Jewish feelings, which he never denied and attributed to his home environment and seminary training, beginning in 1933, when he rejected everything that the Nazis stood for, including the persecution of the Jews. This is expressed adroitly and succinctly in his famous "Confession of Guilt," which originated orally in his postwar American travels and became the concluding words of his many addresses to American audiences. "First, they came for the socialists, but I did not speak out because I was not a socialist. Then they came for the trade unionists, and I did not speak out because I as not a trade unionist. Then they came for the Jews, and I did not speak out because I was not a Jew. Then they came for me and there was no one left to speak for me."

On 1 July 1937 Pastor Niemöller was arrested by the Gestapo and confined to Moabit prison in Berlin without the due process of a court trial. His letters from prison during his eight months of confinement bear the testimony of an engaged Christian soul on fire who was sustained by his peace with his Lord. His numerous letters to his wife Else (she died in 1961) reflect the strain and adjustment to the prison stay coupled with concern, devotion, and love for her and his family. He anguished over the insinuation that he was "an enemy of the people" and found comfort in "Give thanks to the Lord, call on His name; make known His deeds among the nations; proclaim that His name is exalted" (Isaiah 12:4). He complained not of his cell of 10 meters by 10 meters—"The Lord is on my side, I have no fear; what can any man do to me?" (Psalm 118:6)—but of his fear that the people on the outside do not keep the faith firmly. By this he meant those members of the German Evangelical Church who bent their knee to Ba'al/Caesar and thus impeded the "spread of confessionalism." Between 10 November 1937 and 4 December 1947, nearly a thousand Confessing Church pastors were arrested or brought in for interrogation by the Gestapo. Nonetheless, Niemöller's letters from prison charged the brethren not to lose hope or direction and to fight the good fight for the church of our Lord Jesus Christ. His popularity and steadfastness irked Adolf Hitler, whose personal order imprisoned and later transferred him to Dachau and parenthetically, "in (to) all the textbooks of church history," according to Bishop Dibelius.

But Niemöller was not one to rest on his laurels readily. He perceived his calling as a servant of the people appointed by a higher power to resist the propaganda of unbelief even when persecution comes. In 1936 he succored Christians who opposed the word of the Führer, "Rejoice and be glad, because great is your reward in heaven, for in the same way they (Jews) persecuted the prophets who were before you. You are the salt of the earth. You are the light of the world" (Matthew 5:12–13a–14a). Admittedly, suggesting that Jews persecuted Christians contributed to the teachings of the Reich Church, but he publicly confessed and begged forgiveness for his part in spreading this teaching of contempt. After his liberation from Dachau, he said, "I knew my alibi was good between 1937 to 1945 [where he spent eight months in Moabit, three years in Sachsenhausen, and four years in Dachau], but here God was asking me: where were you between 1933–1937? And I had no answer. I felt a cold chill creep up my spine and knew that this was God's warrant against the Pastor Niemöller." And later before students at Göttingen, he berated the ineptness of traditional Christian theological anti-Judaism: "Those six millions are a heavy burden on Christendom and on the church and cannot be blamed on the Nazi party, the SS, and the one mass murderer. Yes, the church bears the heaviest burden because it knew what it did when it did nothing. Antisemitism is the one acute threat to the church as a church. An antisemitic church being a contradiction in itself.'' So spoke Niemöller, a genuine hero of the church struggle, who lived each day as it came to fight evil (Matthew 6:31).

—Zev Garber

EYEWITNESS AUSCHWITZ: THREE YEARS IN THE GAS CHAMBERS (Sonderbehandlung: Drei Jahre in den Krematorien und Gaskammern von Auschwitz)
Memoir by Filip Müller, 1979

Filip Müller's testimony *Eyewitness Auschwitz: Three Years in the Gas Chambers* (1979; in some editions *Auschwitz Inferno: The Testimony of a Sonderkommando*) is one of the bleakest and sparest of all Holocaust memoirs. Müller worked in the *Sonderkommando,* the special units that were most closely involved with the extermination of the victims of the Holocaust. He was one of the few survivors of these units, as they were systematically murdered by the Nazis in an attempt to avoid the secret of the camps getting out.

Unlike many testimonies, this text begins in the camps and ends, literally, at the moment of liberation. On being told that he is free, he struggled from his hiding place, ''stretched out on a woodland ground and fell asleep.'' This concentration on the ''three years in the Gas chamber''—we find out little of Müller before or after this period—makes the book all the bleaker and focuses the reader's attention less on Müller and his story and more on the horrors of the camp.

One of the recurring themes in this memoir is the role of the *kapos* and the SS men and commanders. Even more than in the camps as a whole, the *kapos* in the *Sonderkommando,* because of their tasks and the proximity of the SS, were brutalized and brutal. Müller discusses those who were just and those who were unjust. One, for example, Fischl, manages to get the favor of a commanding SS man by ''pretending to be brute.'' In fact, ''he never once jeopardised our health or well-being, let alone our lives.'' The role of the *kapos* and the SS, their rivalries, and the prices of these rivalries, however, take up no small part of this book. Many famous Auschwitz stories are here too: for example, the beautiful woman who fascinates the SS guards seductively and then shoots SS man Schillinger. In addition to the day to day defiance through survival, there are some accounts of resistance in the book, described in the same reporting style with little extra elaboration.

Most harrowing are the accounts of those who are going to die. Müller gives a number of detailed and unstinting accounts of the whole murderous process, from disembarkation through to the chambers to, finally, the crematoriums. Müller often tells of how the SS tried (and usually succeeded) in tricking their victims. One consignment from Czechoslovakia began to sing, first the Czechoslovak national anthem and then the Hebrew song ''Hatikvah'': ''And all this time the SS men never stopped their brutal beatings.'' Müller writes that ''I proudly identified'' with the Czechoslovak victims. This incident brings on a deep despair, and he tries to join them in the gas chamber. ''I managed to mingle with the pushing and shoving crowd.'' A young woman, however, speaks to him: ''We must die, but you still have a chance to save your life. You have to return to the camp and tell everyone about out last hours . . . perhaps you'll survive this terrible tragedy and then you must tell everybody what has happened to you.'' He leaves the chamber and is then beaten by an SS man, Kurschuss, who says, ''We decide how long you stay alive and when you die, and not you.''

Müller begins to accumulate information and to help with attempts to tell the world about Auschwitz. He steals a label from a Zyklon-B cylinder and two days ''before his escape I handed the label to Alfred Wetzler to enable him to produce it as another piece of evidence of the systematic extermination of Jews.'' (The story of Wetzler's escape is told in *I Cannot Forgive* by **Rudolf Vrba** and Walter Rosenberg, who escaped with him.) Müller is also involved in the doomed revolt of the *Sonderkommando:* however, as the SS regained control, he managed to hide and survive. Later he is involved in death marches and frantic movement around the collapsing Reich.

—Robert Eaglestone

F

THE FALL (La Chute)
Novel by Albert Camus, 1956

Albert Camus's novel *The Fall* is a satirical tour de force that mocks the Christian doctrine of the fall of man, because of Adam's original sin, as pious hypocrisy by the device of setting the novel in the old Jewish quarter of Amsterdam's harbor area after World War II. The novel's lone protagonist, a Frenchman who pointedly calls himself Jean-Baptiste Clamence (that is, the biblical figure John the Baptist, known as the voice crying in the wilderness), proudly declares in the novel's opening chapter that he has chosen to live in the Jewish quarter, where there is now a lot of room because "our Hitlerian brothers," with methodical efficiency, wiped out the entire Jewish community during the war. Clamence consequently adds, "I am living on the scene of one of the greatest crimes in history." Clamence also notes that the concentric canals of Amsterdam remind him of the circles of hell described by Dante and that the harbor and the old Jewish quarter are thus in the last or innermost circle, the ninth in Dante's hell, which is the circle of the traitors, those who have betrayed the highest values of their society: family, friends, country, or religion. Combining the symbolism of a Holocaust-like devastated Jewish quarter and a Dantesque ninth circle of treachery-ridden hell, Camus, alias Clamence, has thereby defined the novel's main theme from the outset as a grimly comic demonstration that man's fall from grace, in the twentieth-century Christian world, has been far more precipitous and far more universal than anything the biblical world could have imagined and that much of the fall had occurred in the name of religion.

The novel emerged from a troubled and unproductive period in Camus's career and therefore reflected his deepened pessimism about human nature. The entire content of *The Fall* is a transcription of a rapidly delivered speech—actually one side of an oddly unbalanced dialogue—by Clamence, whose facile comic verve is artfully contrived to obscure his meaning and thus keep both his interlocutor and the reader constantly off balance. Nevertheless, Clamence never loses their attention, because his steady stream of chatter is an irresistibly brilliant virtuoso performance, as spellbinding as that of Samuel Taylor Coleridge's "The Rime of the Ancient Mariner," both to the person he is addressing and to the reader who, by an ingenious twist, turn out at the end to be the same person.

As the novel opens, Clamence is in mid-conversation with a total stranger, with whom he has just become acquainted, in a sleazy bar of the harbor district in Amsterdam. This conversation will go on for five full days, represented by the book's five chapters. Clamence brazenly makes pronouncements on all sorts of matters, most of which are plainly not true, including

his name. To compound the confusion he later remarks that, before coming to Amsterdam, he had been a lawyer but that now his occupation is "judge-penitent," a calling of his own invention that will not be fully explained until the last day.

Clamence purports to be telling the stranger his life story, but it is actually a carefully calculated fiction in which he manages to "confess," contritely, to having committed all the commonest sins of man in his past when he was a prosperous Paris lawyer, admired for his defense of widows and orphans. He confesses further that in those days he took great satisfaction in being able to consider himself a person of superior virtue until one day, as he looked smugly at himself in the mirror, he thought he heard a woman's mocking laugh. The laugh compelled him to recall an occasion when he was crossing a bridge over the Seine late at night and saw a young woman preparing to throw herself into the river, then heard the splash. But instead of attempting to rescue her or get help, he walked quickly away without looking back. He now realizes that the mocking laugh was really his conscience telling him that the man of superior virtue he considered himself to be was in fact a pious fraud and a sinner, like everyone else.

It was that revelation that prompted him to give up his practice, do penance in the seediest district of Amsterdam, and take up the profession of judge-penitent. His new profession, Clamence explains, requires him to be of whatever assistance he can to all tourists who come to that sin-laden quarter of Amsterdam. His assistance consists of offering to listen sympathetically to their confessions of sin. He can only do this, however, by first accusing himself of all seven deadly sins. That is what gives him the right to judge them and allows him the pleasure of once again basking in the warmth of his own superiority. As a judge-penitent, he points out, he can once more confer upon himself the right to be called virtuous, as he was wont to do as a Parisian lawyer.

The novel naturally concludes with the disclosure that, as Clamence had guessed from the start, his interlocutor is in fact a Paris lawyer. Clamence had shrewdly shaped his own invented life story on that premise so that his offer to listen sympathetically to his interlocutor's confession would be more readily accepted and he would have one more opportunity to experience the pleasurable sensation of his own moral superiority, necessary to his personal comfort and self-esteem. That ending compels the reader to recognize the calculated sophistry of Clamence's purely self-seeking performance. Disguised as high-minded moral philosophy, it is merely a device for exerting a kind of moral blackmail on others to feed his own emotional needs.

The thoughtful reader might well discern a broader meaning in the novel as well, intended by Camus—namely, the danger of the Christian doctrines of original sin and the fall of man. Those doctrines, which proclaim that all humans are sinners, subtly sanction the actions of authoritarian minds, allowing them to feel justified in creating such oppressive regimes as Fascism or in perpetrating such genocide as the Holocaust because their victims are certifiably sinful and deserve harsh punishment.

—Murray Sachs

THE FANATIC
Novel by Meyer Levin, 1964

Despite Meyer Levin's disclaimer in his preface that *The Fanatic* was "a story, and not a report or portrayal of events in which I was involved, or of people involved in those events," it is hard to read this 1964 novel except as a roman à clef concentrated on the author's decade-long feud with Otto Frank over the adaptation of Anne Frank's famous *Diary*. Contemporary reviews agreed that the book was narrowly topical, a too close account of the politics of the publishing trade and the Broadway coterie whose commercial and ideological motives thwart the ambitions of the book's protagonist, Maury Finkelstein. In a plot parallel to Levin's own involvement with the *Diary,* Maury discovers a book written in Auschwitz by a young Jewish man (Leo Kahn) who died there, whereupon Maury dedicates himself to getting the book published, launches it with a successful review, and then lobbies and earns the drafting rights to a dramatic adaptation, only to be rewarded for all his efforts by having his draft inexplicably rejected by the producer. Replaced by a pair of Hollywood writers, Maury soon perceives a commercially motivated plot to oust him as a lesser-known author and, launching a public campaign for his repressed play, claims to be the victim of an ideological conspiracy to de-Judaize Leo's story and offer a vaguely anti-Fascist tale to the American public.

So overt are the transpositions of history in *The Fanatic* that when Frank's lawyers received a prepublication announcement concerning the book, they sued to have it suppressed, protesting that Levin was in breach of an October 1959 agreement in which he promised not to raise any further controversy over the *Diary*. Though the cover of fiction protected Levin from direct legal repercussions, it did little to prevent the mounting public perception of Levin as an author obsessed by a wrong done to him who insisted on airing his grievances time and again in public. All of this intersects problematically with any attempt Levin might be making in *The Fanatic* to render the world of Auschwitz and force us to wrestle more seriously with the historical and philosophical implications of the Holocaust. As Lawrence Graver succinctly put it, one has the impression reading this novel that Levin cared more about the damage done to his career than the

atrocities committed against Jews or the misrepresentation of Anne's *Diary* before the American public. Told from the perspective of the Holocaust victim Leo Kahn, who watches over the actions Maury performs on his behalf, *The Fanatic* evokes the traditional Jewish lore of the dybbuk, almost as if Leo were living through the imaginative enterprises of the man who has married his former lover. The rhetorical point of the device is to ratify the blamelessness and dignity of Maury (as a stand-in for Levin), since Leo Kahn (as the stand-in for Anne Frank) insists that if he could choose someone among the living to represent him, he would choose "such a one" as Maury. Having imagined himself the faithful interpreter of the *Diary* and the true representative of Anne Frank's spirit, Levin several times during his drawn-out contention with Otto Frank made appeals to Anne's authority, almost as if she could have defended the author who had taken up her cause among the living. Thus when Leo narrates the story unable to imagine a more appropriate substitute for his own life and vision than Maury, he posthumously grants permission to Maury to use his aesthetic talents in service of a more literal historical truth—"to write the play," as Leo himself puts it, "as I myself would have written it." Referenced here is the very boundary line Levin had a hard time discerning, namely, the line between his own interpretive adaptation and the *Diary*'s original vision. In his 1973 memoir *The Obsession* Levin himself recalls how Frank's lawyers charged him with having the hallucinatory impression "that he actually wrote the *Diary*."

It has to be said that Levin does not appropriate his own personal history and the larger set of issues about the proper cultural memory of the Holocaust for which it stood without some degree of self-consciousness. He chooses the somewhat surprising—and one might add, refreshing—strategy of portraying himself as a rabbi author of minor liturgical dramas, a strangely humble self-representation that may have been offered as a gentle caricature of his opponents' views. Over the course of the novel Maury struggles with the question of whether he has been right to pursue his cause, even at such great costs to his family life. The novel resolves all questions of conscience by ending in the courtroom, where a $100,000 verdict (far in excess of Levin's $15,000 no-fault settlement with Frank) finally vindicates Maury and his fight to tell the truth about the Holocaust. Though *The Fanatic* often makes for tedious reading, since Maury is so earnest, wronged, and renewedly hopeful that we have a hard time imagining how his evil opponents can live with themselves, it is also significant in the history of American fiction on the Holocaust because Levin's novel suggests that the American cultural memory of the Holocaust of the 1950s—with the Broadway and Hollywood versions of the *Diary* at the very center—lacked any serious engagement with the Jewish background of the Nazi's central victims and thus perhaps the central cultural meaning of the Nazi genocidal ideology.

—R. Clifton Spargo

THE FAR EUPHRATES
Novel by Aryeh Lev Stollman, 1997

Like most American and Canadian Holocaust fiction, Aryeh Lev Stollman's *The Far Euphrates* is less concerned with depicting the events of the Holocaust than in tracing the consequences for its survivors. Indeed, and also like the majority of texts written in the last two decades of the twentieth century, it is even more concerned with the effects of European Jewish history on the next generation of Jews, both on the children of survivors and on others of the post-Holocaust generation.

Alexander, the narrator-protagonist of Stollman's novel, is the single offspring of two Jewish Canadian families, both of whom have been singed by the Holocaust. Alexander's father, a rabbi, is the son of refugees who fled before the war. His parents' best friend and neighbor is a cantor who survived not only the concentration camps but also Josef Mengele's infamous experiments on twins. As the lone, haunted child in these two families, Alexander is a figure not only of the distortion and wounding by the past of the Jewish present but also of the real possibility of a literal end to Jewish continuity. Not only can the two families bring to term only a single child (Alexander's mother suffers miscarriage after miscarriage, and the cantor has been rendered sterile), but Alexander's budding homosexual preference takes him further outside the possibility of biologically determined reproductive futurity. It is Hannalore, the cantor's twin, however, who provides the novel's most shocking and painful image of the disfigurement of the Jewish people and of the generations who, biologically speaking, will never be. Though to its credit the text does not descend into graphic detail, Hannalore, born "Elchanan son of David," has chosen to live what is left of his life after the devastation of the concentration camps as a woman and, just as significantly, as a Christian.

Yet "whatever weird creature" Hannalore is—male/female, Jewish/Christian, German/Canadian—she and Alexander, who, by his mother's account, is no less weird, are the rich human resource out of which the future is to be constructed. For Stollman, Hannalore in particular brings together both the everlasting wound, which is not accidentally represented as a perversion of the mark of the covenant (circumcision), and the heroism of Jewish survival, which she bequeaths to her spiritual offspring, Alexander. Hannalore is, as the text puts it, the "ghost" that haunts the post-Holocaust present, but she is also one more of Alexander's many mothers. In the context of her own conversion to Christianity, she is a sort of virgin mother who gives birth not to a savior but to a writer, to one who writes not in the Christian tradition of texts but in the Jewish tradition. Thus, she is less the Holy Ghost of Christianity than the Jewish Shechinah, on which the Holy Ghost is based, and she offers not redemption but hope. "The Shekinah followed Adam and Eve out of Eden," Alexander reports, "and the Shekhinah follows all of us in our time of Exile to provide us with a home . . . It is Her love we must seek." On this side of the far Euphrates, which is to say on this side of Eden (which is where the Euphrates is supposed to take its origins), all we have is this exilic home that we share with others and in which the voices we speak are not always or only our own. For what the novel is also about is how, in imitation of God, we create the world anew in language that speaks the past in and as the present.

In the most dramatic moment of the text Hannalore, at the unveiling of her tombstone, which is also the revelation of the awful truth of her sexual identity, speaks through Alexander. He "look[s] underneath the English lettering to the small Hebrew inscription that contained the same honeyed letters that God used to create His universe in several days: *Ud matzal m'aish.* 'An ember saved from the fire.' Then I read Hannalore's Hebrew name: 'Elchanan ben David.' Elchanan son of David."

Elchanan son of David will never literally engender a next generation. She will not bodily keep alive the Davidic, the messianic, line. Yet insofar as the present generation permits itself to become the willing medium of the voice of the past, she will continue to speak and live. Like other writers of Holocaust fiction, Stollman universalizes, even Christianizes, the Holocaust. At the same time, densely learned and deeply steeped in Jewish history, ritual, and even language, *The Far Euphrates* in no way compromises the specifically Jewish character of the Holocaust. Indeed, it recovers the origins of Christianity within Judaism and the origins of Western culture in Jewish tradition and writing. Like Alexander speaking Hannalore's words, *The Far Euphrates* speaks the Jewish past in the voice of a very live, very contemporary Jewish present.

—Emily Budick

FATELESS (Sorstalanság)
Novel by Imre Kertész, 1975

Imre Kertész insists that in *Sorstalanság* (1975; *Fateless*, 1992) he did not intend to write a Holocaust novel, or indeed a novel in the conventional sense. "The greatest danger for me lay in the temptation of giving way to anecdotal digressions, intriguing, colorful but inessential details, singularly interesting little stories," he said in a 1999 interview. "The action had to follow a clearly devised structure, it had to be reduced to essentials. The story of Auschwitz has become part of the repository of European knowing and European memory. I had to fashion my story as a collective myth." Indeed, each scene, each episode and character in the novel is at once concrete and emblematic; each detail used is crucial and representative.

Nevertheless, on the surface *Fateless* reads like a typical concentration camp narrative about a 14-year-old Hungarian boy's journey to Auschwitz and back. In light of what we know about the world he enters, nothing out of the ordinary happens to him. And because the story is told from the perspective of an "innocent" narrator, this ordinariness is further highlighted, with the result that the boy's responses to what he sees and experiences strike the reader as odd, inappropriate. When he first sees men in prison stripes in Auschwitz, he is "curious to discover what their crimes were." Later, in Buchenwald, he reflects on the difference between prison and a concentration camp. One can eventually get used to prison life, but in the camps "they didn't give you enough time to try." When he becomes very sick and is removed from his barracks, he waits apathetically for the end; but when he realizes he is in the hospital, he says yearningly, "I would so much like to live a little longer in this beautiful concentration camp."

Throughout his ordeal Kertész's young hero assumes nothing; he doesn't anticipate, judge, or rebel. At first his compliance and passivity appear to be shocking evidence of a victim's self-denigration, his identification with the aggressor's view of him. But as we read on we realize that his readiness to accept and understand actually enables him to retain his sanity and even a modicum of dignity. What he discovers for himself in the camps is the "banality of evil," and his "normal" reaction to the process of dehumanization is at once a confirmation of this banality and an unconscious rejection of it.

When the boy returns to Budapest, weighed down and enriched by his experiences, people want him to act like a victim and say things a survivor might say. But he can't—and won't. "We can never start a new life," he tells a journalist who expects appropriate—that is, stock—answers to his questions. "We can only continue the old one. I took my own steps. No one else did. And I remained honest to the end to my given fate . . . Do you want all this horror and all my previous steps to lose their meaning entirely? . . . Why can't you just see that if there is such a thing as fate, then there is no freedom? If, on the other hand . . . there is freedom, then there is no fate."

Fateless may be seen as a universally valid meditation on evil in the twentieth century or an existentialist novel in which an absurd universe appears in the guise of a totalitarian system that strips one of his or her real self and imposes a role, a fate. Yet there is nothing abstract about the novel—for Kertész, lived reality is too important. He is a survivor who bears witness, but he is also a writer. Implicit in *Fateless* (as well as in Kertész's other works) is the belief that there is—there must be—art after Auschwitz.

—Ivan Sanders

FEAR AND MISERY OF THE THIRD REICH (Furcht und Elend des Dritten Reiches)
Play by Bertolt Brecht, 1941

Bertolt Brecht began writing *Fear and Misery of the Third Reich* in 1933, when he fled Germany for Denmark. Outraged by the rise of the Nazi dictatorship in his homeland and all too aware of the character of Hitler's regime, he set out to create a work that portrayed the fear, repression, and violence of life in Nazi Germany. Consisting of 27 dramatic sketches (which Brecht believed could be performed individually or together), the work documents the lives of everyday men and women and the misery they experienced under the Third Reich. Brecht completed *Fear and Misery* in 1938, well before he and the rest of the world learned the full scope of Nazi atrocities. Therefore, although the work deals pointedly with Nazi Germany's omnipresent anti-Semitism, it does not address the Holocaust in a direct manner. But this only serves to make the work richer, as it is underpinned by the reader's knowledge of what comes after. It was first published, as *Deutschland: Ein Greuelmärchen,* in 1941.

When Brecht began writing the sketches—or playlets, as they are sometimes called—he was not planning to synthesize them into a single dramatic work. Instead, he sought to provide material for amateur theater groups of German exiles. It was only in 1938 that he combined the 27 terse sketches, using an introductory poem, connecting poems, and a scenic device to link the disparate scenes. This method proved effective because the playlets fit naturally together. They range in length from ten lines to coherent one-act plays, but each one examines the impact of the Nazi regime on everyday German men, women, and children. The sketches are set between 30 January 1933, when Hitler became chancellor, and 13 March 1938, when Hitler marched into Austria. Instead of using historical figures or the likenesses of prominent people, Brecht portrays a cross section of "average" German citizens—soldiers, workers, farmers, butchers, housekeepers, teachers, doctors, and judges—and the impact of their government on them. Although *Fear and Misery* is a political work, it is in no way a propaganda piece. Brecht eschewed melodrama in favor of a quiet, semi-documentary style that is ultimately more resonant for its restraint.

One of the best-known sketches, "The Jewish Wife," typifies Brecht's detached style. The scene depicts a Jewish woman, Judith Keith, deciding to leave her non-Jewish husband and move to Amsterdam. He is a prominent physician, and she does not want to risk either his safety or career, both of which are threatened by the fact that he has a Jewish wife. Brecht distilled the dilemma into three powerful portraits, which together take only about 20 minutes to deliver: Judith makes farewell phone calls to acquaintances, she practices a speech she plans to deliver to her husband, and the couple meets in a final confrontation. The scene where she packs is typically spare, yet powerful. As she places items in her suitcase, she rehearses what she will say to him, becoming, in the process, increasingly upset that she is forced to leave. Men are "not even allowed to choose their own wives anymore," she says to herself. She predicts that her husband will not fully accept her decision, that he will be ostrich-like and will discount her leaving as only a short-term hiatus. Her fears are borne out, and the vignette ends on this note of betrayal.

Brecht explores the consequences of Nazism on everyday lives in the other playlets as well. "Chalk Crosses" touches on a theme that runs through the collection. In this play Brecht examines how conscious choices made by ordinary individuals helped cement Hitler's hold on power. This vignette is centered on paramilitary storm troopers in 1933. It depicts their chilling transformation. At first they play their brutal roles out of self-preservation, but over time they begin to live these roles fully. "The Informer" presents a domestic scene rife with the paranoia Nazism bred: a high school teacher and his wife fear that their own son will denounce them to the authorities.

—Rebecca Stanfel

DI FESTUNG
Poems by Abraham Sutzkever, 1945

Di Festung ("The Fortress")—a collection of 39 lyric and epic poems published after the war but composed during Abraham Sutzkever's entrapment in the Vilna (Vilnius) ghetto and his time as a partisan fighter in the forests of Lithuania— was among the earliest volumes of Yiddish poetry to explore the experience of the destruction of Jewish eastern Europe. Inspired by actual events and personalities, the volume's contents range from poetic confessionals to elegiac verses written for murdered family and friends, from poems of frustration, anger, and resistance to one of the earliest attempts to interpret the extent of human destruction symbolically through disembodied, everyday objects. During the war Sutzkever, whose mastery of the introspective nature lyric had first put him on the Yiddish literary map in the 1930s, continued to rely upon precisely constructed lyrics and the imaginative use of the Yiddish language as a means to assert control over the external chaos. While some critics have suggested that Sutzkever's life in the ghetto transformed him from a socially disengaged aesthete into a self-consciously national poet, the contents of *Di Festung* show a writer who managed to maintain his poetic poise by privileging the authority of the internalized experiences of the poet-witness. By combining this perspective with motifs from the library of Jewish catastrophe through the ages, he transformed the Vilna of his personal memory into a new prooftext for Jewish suffering, heroism, and survival.

Among the most famous poems from this volume are those in which Sutzkever attempted to construct new archetypes of physical and spiritual resistance. In "Teacher Mira" he took the example of real-life ghetto teacher Mira Bernshteyn and transformed her into a model of cultural endurance. In "The Lead Plates of the Rom Press" Sutzkever offered up a legend about local partisans melting the plates that had once been used to print a famous edition of the Babylonian Talmud to manufacture bullets; the ghetto fighters are shown to exist in a continuum of national heroes stretching back to the Maccabees. Despite the fact that the events described by the poem never occurred, its myth contributed to a literary revolution in Jewish self-respect.

Sutzkever was also among the first writers to rely upon a collection of objects to communicate both the magnitude of national destruction and his private grief. When the speaker of "A Wagon of Shoes" notices a cartload of shoes still twitching with the memory of their owners, the reader recognizes that they are now the only tangible symbols of lost children, brides, friends, and ultimately even the speaker's mother (whose Sabbath shoes he recognizes in the pile). Elsewhere, as in "On My Thirtieth Birthday," Sutzkever ruminated on the function of the artist in the ghetto. For the poet, the act of retelling that which he has witnessed serves as a regenerative gesture that will defy the abyss of history.

In *Di Festung* Sutzkever also experimented for the first time with longer works of epic ambition. In "The Grave-Child" he staged a scene of national rebirth set amid the graves of Vilna's Jewish cemetery. The haunting but moving sound of a violin in the distance punctuates the end of the work, suggesting that the creative process itself (whether physical or artistic) is a mark of Jewish endurance. Such a motif was powerful to Sutzkever not only for its dramatic effect but also because his own baby had been killed under German orders only hours after its birth in the ghetto hospital. In recognition of its achievement, the poem was awarded first prize in the initial literary contest of the Union of Writers and Artists in the Vilna Ghetto in 1942.

The epic monologue "Kol Nidre" starkly conveys both the terror of the German extermination squads and the struggle of the faithful to hold God accountable for his inaction. Unlike the majority of Sutzkever's writing in *Di Festung*, which is composed from the perspective of the secular Yiddish writer, the speaker of "Kol Nidre" is an observant survivor in a roundup of Jews on Yom Kippur eve 1941. The work's climax occurs when he discovers that his only remaining family, a son who had left home 20 years earlier, has also been captured and faces imminent torture. When the speaker enacts the biblical Akeidah (the sacrifice of Isaac) to keep his son beyond the grasp of the Nazi guards, he both undermines and redefines categories of holy and profane. The poem's intertextual reliance on such familiar themes as Job's suffering, Ezekiel's vision of the Valley of Dry Bones, and portions of the High Holiday liturgy inserted the material of contemporary history into the continuum of Jewish responses to catastrophe. In a concluding gesture that reflected Sutzkever's own sense of poetic mission, the speaker relates this story to the ghetto poet in the hope that the Jewish writer will now assume the burden of collective memory. Such a self-image was realized when the poem was smuggled out of the ghetto and published, in Russian translation, by critic Ilya Ehrenberg in Moscow. It became the earliest work to reach the U.S.S.R. to testify to the brutality and extent of Jewish destruction, leading to Sutzkever's eventual rescue from the partisan forests and his testimony on behalf of Soviet Jewry at the Nuremburg trials.

—Justin D. Cammy

THE FIFTIETH GATE: A JOURNEY THROUGH MEMORY
Memoir by Mark Raphael Baker, 1997

Ostensibly the story of a son's attempt to access and narrate his parents' fragmented Holocaust biographies, Mark Raphael Baker's *The Fiftieth Gate* also subverts the convention of second-generation memoir writing. A composite of detective story, love story, tales of hiding, and vignettes of discovery, *The Fiftieth Gate* has themes that are synonymous with the difficulties of the narrative construction of the Holocaust as an event "at the limits": the search for appropriate interpretive vessels sensitive to the expression of often unspeakable memories of first-generation survivors, the traumas of intergenerational transmission, and the child's adoption of a vicarious Holocaust identity as one of many complex responses. Baker's relentless subjection of his parents' memories to forensic historical analysis based on empirical evidence also revisits the vocabulary of speaking the unspeakable commonly associated with the long-standing debate about the Holocaust and its preferred modes of representation.

The motivation for the story emanates from Baker's quest to find the thread that might weave the fragmented narrative of his parents' largely unspoken pasts in which his childhood and adolescent Jewish identity were clothed. The environments that propelled Baker to this quest festered in an urban social context of dislocation: the absurdity of his parents' Holocaust pain muted in the suburban isolation and material complacency of his home in Melbourne: "And there was the pain of displaced identification. I invented a biography for myself and elements of my parents' lives, characters more valorous than any protagonist found in fiction. As a child, I even gave myself a number, imagining myself as a ghetto fighter . . . What was I doing? I now ask myself. Was it Australia I wished to escape, its suburban dross and culture of leisure? In the absence of a Holocaust, I was compelled to create my own."

The most invigorating and frustrating moments of Baker's path to his parents' memories are found in his attempt to validate their pasts with the evidentiary apparatus of the historian—the archive. Documents in regional archives in Radom and Jerusalem are scoured with a feverish intensity in order to verify the droplets of memory that are revived upon touring the scarred European landscapes to which the family returned in 1995. Genia Krochmal, Baker's mother, was born

in Bolszowce, in Galician Poland, in 1934 and was the only child to survive the deportation of 1,380 Jews to Belzec in October 1942. She did so as a young girl, for two years, hiding in blackness in a bunker in a nearby village. But history does not validate her memory. Baker's search for archival signs of her former existence in Bolszowce prove redundant and force him to dispense with the historians' truth and rely on his mother's memory as the evidence and hence justification for her pain: "[I]t was not the facts that were held under suspicion, but her credibility as a survivor. Unlike my father, she could never show her children the scars on her arm; hers were invisible, numbered in the days and years of her stolen childhood."

Baker's father, Yossl Bekiermaszyn, was from Wierzbnik, southeast of Warsaw. The Nazis' murder of his two younger sisters, Martale and Yentale, and the missing history of his father, Lieb Bekiermaszyn, unequivocally freight his story. Baker returns with his father to one address from his past: Buchenwald. There he is able to depend on history, since he can quote his father's incarceration and validate his experiences: "My father is on pages forty-two and 109 of a Register of Jewish Survivors published by the Jewish Agency of Palestine in 1945 . . . He is listed as Josek Bekiermaszyn, officially arrested by SS on 28 October 1942, after which he was imprisoned in Starachowice, Auschwitz and Buchenwald."

The narrative style of *The Fiftieth Gate* reshapes the genre of conventional memoir writing. The book is divided into as many chapters, each symbolizing a gate on the path to a religious revelation, the triumph of good over evil. Vignettes of memory are juxtaposed in the context of the present-tense journey of Baker's investigation of archives, the acquisition of historical details, and a self-reflexive analysis of the right to occupy his parents' pasts as a historian and son. While spirited by the historical weight and empiricism of archival evidence, Baker surrenders to his mother's memories of unspeakable darkness in particular, to her story of a young girl denied the right to be one, to her dual roles as Holocaust survivor and mother, permitting her to speak without qualification, and is almost ashamed for having required the initial documentation of history. The details of the physical return to Poland—as the source of both wound and revelation—recalls the methods of writing the detective genre: the burial of evidence and its rediscovery, the travel from archive to archive, with documents in hand, desperate to corroborate his parent's memories forged in the addresses of Birkenau, Bolszowce, and Buchenwald.

In *Remnants of Auschwitz: The Witness and the Archive,* an examination of survivor testimony, Giorgio Agamben remarked that the vocation of the survivor is to remember. *The Fiftieth Gate* is a vivid incarnation of that particularly Jewish vocation of the storyteller and the commandment of Zakhor, as we watch Baker inhabit the roles of the vicarious witness—the teenage son, historian, writer, heir and embodiment of this vocation. The narrative content of Baker's reconstruction of the everyday journey of the intimate, physical, and empirical topography of Genia's and Yossl's persecution, incarceration, survival, and postwar refuge reveals not simply a son in search of knowing his parents but also his own Australian-Jewish identity that is anchored to an incomplete present. The responsibility to write the story of that identity, the text of his memory of their shared history, is reflected in Baker's monumental gift to his parents, which is, finally, to enter into the fiftieth gate, in which memory has survived the attempt to destroy it and where blackness is overwhelmed by light.

—Simone Gigliotti

THE FINAL STATION: UMSCHLAGPLATZ
(Umschlagplatz)
Novel by Jaroslaw Marek Rymkiewicz, 1988

The Final Station: Umschlagplatz, by Jaroslaw Marek Rymkiewicz, was published in Polish in 1988 and in English in 1994 in a translation by Nina Taylor. Like many literary works about the Holocaust, *Umschlagplatz* mixes a number of different genres. Madeline G. Levine describes it as a "hybrid blend of novel, confessional journal, meditative essay, and record of investigative research." It is classified by the Library of Congress system as both personal narrative and fiction. Levine places *Umschlagplatz* alongside other recent Polish literature, by authors such as Tadeusz Konwicki and Kazimierz Brandys, that also employs the "genre of the hybrid not-quite-autobiographical narrative that mixes deliberate fictions with apparently confessional autobiography." *Umschlagplatz* is not simply the creation of literary imagination, for the numerous sources of Warsaw Ghetto testimony cited and discussed in the text are not invented.

The narrator of *Umschlagplatz* is given the author's name and like the author is a Gentile Pole born in 1938. This multileveled book includes the author's research into the description of the Umschlagplatz, from where the Jews of the Warsaw Ghetto were herded onto the trains that would take them to their deaths in Treblinka. It also depicts a group of Jewish intellectuals and artists, invented by the narrator, who are on holiday in 1937 at the summer resort of Otwock, not far from Warsaw. In addition, there are switches to the present, where the narrator discusses with Hania, his assimilated Jewish wife, the historical reality of the book he is writing. Hania acts as a foil to the narrator, questioning the morality of his fictionalizing the lives of Jewish characters and giving him the opportunity to try to justify what he is doing. In reality the author's wife is not Jewish. The dividing line between fiction and reality in *Umschlagplatz* is deliberately blurred. Not only is the status of the "autobiographical" passages left open ("Maybe I invented it all . . . [but] even if I've invented it all,

including you [Hania] . . . it is no less true for all that"), but they are not always clearly separated from those passages that are acknowledged as fictional within the text.

The importance of *Umschlagplatz* is not as an essay about the physical layout of the Umschlagplatz or about the details of the deportation of the Jews from Otwock but, rather, as an inquiry into what the murder of Polish Jews on Polish soil signified or should signify for Poles now: "I am chiefly interested in the future. What does Umschlagplatz signify in Polish life and Polish spirituality, and what does it portend for posterity? We live within the orbit of their death." Although the narrator stresses that "'it is only as a Christian that I can address the problem. And a Christian testimony, to my mind, is what we need,'" his lack of "practical experience of Polish-Jewish life . . . prevents [him from] writing an unfictionalized testimony," although his ideal remains for the book to tell "the common history of Poles and Jews as it really was, with no imaginary additives."

Umschlagplatz then is partly an attempt to persuade Poles to confront their true history, despite their lack of any desire to do so: "Perhaps we genuinely don't want to remember—I don't mean what happened to our Jews, but what happened to us as onlookers. Perhaps it is ourselves we would rather forget about." The book is also noteworthy, however, for its discussion of the limits of fictional representation in Holocaust literature within the text, when it has become almost a characteristic of the genre (**Thomas Keneally**, Martin Amis, Helen Darville) to confine this to an author's note placed outside the text.

The book is centered on an emotional assertion of the narrator's right to testify as a witness despite the fact that he was a child at the time and remembers nothing but "broken scraps and fragments": "I think I am a suitable witness, and I feel that I not only can but should testify. Even if I cannot testify to their lives, it will be my own personal act of remembrance . . . So you [Hania are] wrong to accuse me of wholesale fiction-mongering. You surely can't mean that my great dirge for the Polish Jews is imagined . . . And surely, my testimony is not imagined either. My dirge is a lament for myself. When I mourn for the Polish Jews it is an act of self-mourning, the lament of a Pole forever forsaken by Polish Jews."

—Alan Polak

FIVE CHIMNEYS (Souvenirs de l'au-delà)
Memoir by Olga Lengyel, 1946

Olga Lengyel's memoir *Five Chimneys* tells the story of her survival in Auschwitz and on the frantic death march after the camp was abandoned. Written just after the war and published in English in 1947, this account spares nothing. It is on a par with the best Holocaust narratives.

Lengyel's harrowing narrative begins with her charge against herself that she was "in part responsible for the destruction of my own parents and of my two sons." She was a surgical assistant (to her husband) in Cluj in Transylvania (Klausenburg in German, also known as Kolozsvar). In 1944 she and her family were deported to Auschwitz. A trained medical assistant, she was ordered to work in the infirmary. There she is contacted by the underground and volunteers to act spreading news as a "post office," passing on messages and parcels and observing events: her contact says to her, "We must observe everything that goes on here. When the war is over the world must know about this. It must know the truth." Her role in the underground gives her fresh reason to live, and she makes detailed observations about the camp.

As with many accounts of Auschwitz, after the initial arrival the strict chronology breaks down and the account describes key incidents that highlight life in Auschwitz. These are discussed in other accounts: for example, the liquidation of the Czech camp and their failed rebellion (discussed in **Rudolf Vrba**'s memoir), the escape and recapture of Maya the translator, and the rebellion by the *Sonderkommando*. Aspects of camp life—organization and the multitude of languages, for example—are discussed. The book also describes, at some length, Irma Griese, the Angel of Auschwitz (who "inspired in me the most violent hatred I ever experienced") and Dr. Josef Mengele (she writes that one "could have called him handsome were it not for the expression of cruelty in his features").

Lengyel also discusses more intimate parts of camp life, inaccessible to some other inmates. For example, she has a chapter that explains how the infirmary staff would kill newborn babies. The Germans would send newborn and their mothers to the gas chambers, so, in order to save the mothers, the staff—after long debate—would kill the babies and say that they were stillborn. "Without our intervention they would have endured worse sufferings, for they would have been thrown into the crematory ovens while still alive. Yet I try in vain to make my conscience acquit me. I still see the infants issuing from their mothers. I can still feel their warm little bodies as I held them. I marvel to what depths these Germans made us descend!" She also discusses sex: the lesbian activity in the camp, the odd, broken love affairs, the bestialities of the SS, the inmates who preyed on the starving women who sold their bodies for food. Like **Primo Levi,** however, she is aware of the "gray zone": it "would be heartless to condemn the women who had to sink so low for half a crust of bread. The responsibility for the degradation of the internees rested with the camp administration."

The book is bleak and unsparing ("At Birkenau rats were feeding on the children of Europe"), full of detail and information, told in a clear, unaffected style. Lengyel declares finally that those who were not degraded morally by the Nazis means

that "there is hope indeed. It is that hope which keeps me alive."

—Robert Eaglestone

THE FOREST OF THE DEAD (Der Totenwald: Ein Bericht)
Novel by Ernst Wiechert, 1945

In the spring of 1938, in protest against the re-arrest of **Martin Niemöller**, the head of the Confessional Church and an outspoken critic of the regime, Ernst Wiechert, one of the leading German novelists, informed the branch office of the Nazi Party that hereafter his contributions to the party's welfare agencies would be diverted to help Niemöller's family. This was not, in fact, Wiechert's only offense. In the February plebiscite preceding the *Anschluss,* Wiechert, as the party very well knew, had failed to vote (the explicit naysayers were half-beaten to death within half an hour after the polls had closed).

Wiechert was arrested on 6 May. For the first two months he was detained in "protective custody" in the Wittelsbach Palace in Munich—"all revolutions," he wrote, "have a hankering after palaces"—and here the first half of the book takes place. In early July he was deported to Buchenwald, which gives his report its title. (In the original the title reads *Der Totenwald,* the name given to the camp by its inmates in a spirit of near-literal gallows humor). Written in 1939 (and concealed at night beneath a red currant bush in Wiechert's garden), the book owes its importance not least to being nearly the earliest insider's account of the concentration camp—strictly speaking, the first, the actor-director Wolfgang Langhoff's Dachau-based *Die Moorsoldaten,* appeared as early as 1935.

The Forest of the Dead, published in 1945 and in English translation in 1947, has sometimes been unfairly dismissed as tame stuff compared with the *littérature concentrationaire* that has been prevalent since the 1960s. Readers who are steeped in the more recent texts tend to disparage the brevity of Wiechert's sentence and the relatively light tasks he performed. What needs to be remembered is that while Wiechert himself escaped physical torture, he witnessed degrees of sadism that nearly matched those of the death camps. By 1938 a crematorium had been installed; prisoners were hanged as examples to rookies, always on Mondays and Thursdays, or flogged to death; the camp physician seized the day by tossing stones at his patients; the personnel observed Christmas by hanging a prisoner from a Christmas tree. A sympathetic commentator, writing in 1945, noted (without the least political animus, years before David Irving was heard from) that if these scenes had appeared in a work of fiction, nobody would have believed them. In the first half of the book Wiechert is initiated into these horrors by his cellmates—one, an alleged criminal, the other, a homosexual; in the second half he delivers an eyewitness account of the "high horrible screams . . . that dwindled to the voiceless rattle of an animal whose life-blood evaporates" and the fun and games of the guards who, on a hunting spree, enlivened the game by picking on human targets. Since World War II plenty of documentaries have "acclimated" viewers to the sight of "skeletons with phantom arms and legs, covered with sores and stained with clotted blood"; but Wiechert, when he wrote those words, had not been treated to so much as the clips shown at the Nuremberg trials.

Nor was Wiechert exempt from hard labor. For some 13 hours a day he carried limestone blocks in 95°F heat, forbidden to straighten up or, under penalty of flogging, to drink a drop of water (on the pretext that the water was cholera-suspect). Wiechert, then nearly 50 years old, already suffered from severe cardiac complications and contracted edema and dysentery during his days in camp—though the days were to run their course by the end of August. Perhaps Goebbels, who summoned Wiechert after his release to tell him that one more publication by him would lead to a terminal vacation in camp, couldn't afford to have anybody of Wiechert's prominence die of heart failure just then. Toward the end of his stay, in an incident he himself called "grotesquely funny," Wiechert received permission to order all his books for the camp library—in duplicate. (One of the guards asked him if he had really written them "all by himself.") Perhaps Sidrah Ezrahi, who cites this incident, cannot be blamed for calling Wiechert's account "an autobiographical novel." Nor, after **Charlotte Delbo** and **Primo Levi**, is it easy to listen to Wiechert's jeremiads about his sloppy looks at the Wittelsbach Palace or really appreciate his complacency in "tak[ing] care of his body by buying lard and chocolate." But we should look for the deeper truths on which the book ends: that "No leave-taking is harder than the leave-taking from a concentration camp," and the comment about him by an inmate: "A queer man. When he first came, his face was just like stone. Now that he goes, it looks the same."

—Edgar Rosenberg

THE FORGOTTEN (L'Oublie)
Novel by Elie Wiesel, 1989

The theme of Elie Wiesel's novel *The Forgotten* (1992; *L'Oublie,* 1989) is the sanctity of human life among the infirm and the handicapped. In the person of Elhanen Rosenbaum, Wiesel describes a dignified man with a heroic past struggling with the onset of Alzheimer's disease. The Jewish psychiatrist had spent World War II as a partisan in the Transylvanian

forest fighting against the Nazis. His son Malkiel makes a trip to Hungary to try to understand more of his father's past before it slips away from Elhanen's memory altogether.

While in Hungary, Malkiel meets Herschel the Gravedigger who was also a partisan. Herschel tells the story of a great reunion. Having survived a roundup of Jews in the ghetto, Herschel went to a Jewish cemetery to contemplate the next phase of his survival strategy. The throes of crisis drive him into a psychotic breakdown. He believes himself to be communing with the deceased rabbis of the Jewish community, who urge him to escape to the forests and join the partisans. The contents of his hallucinations during the breakdown show him to be a man of great intelligence, well versed in Hasidic Judaism. Wiesel experiments with the notion that the mentally ill may have unusual prophetic powers. In the case of Herschel, mental illness does indeed seem to have some life-saving properties. His psychotic voices give him a suggestion that is a reasonable alternative to waiting for the Nazis to round him up.

The mentally ill gravedigger establishes a reputation for himself by telling people stories of the war era. Nonetheless, he appears to be a man who is shunned and disregarded by most of the locals, due to prejudice against him.

As Malkiel makes preparations to return to the United States and contemplate further care for his father, he is as perplexed as ever:

> I know: even the most eminent doctors are some-times wrong. I sometimes wonder if the diagnosis is correct. I wonder if my father is suffering from amnesia or some other disease. He may know everything that's happening to him, everything said in his presence, everything going on around him and within him, and he may want to react, to respond, but he may be incapable of it. Or he may not want to. He may be disappointed in mankind. And in its language. He may reject our worn and devalued words. He may need others, he may be choosing to feign forgetfulness so that he can remain speechless.

Malkiel speculates that Elhanen's case of Alzheimer's disease may be a feigned madness like that of Hamlet, brought about so that Elhanen can deal with survivor's guilt.

—Peter R. Erspamer

FRAGMENTS OF ISABELLA: A MEMOIR OF AUSCHWITZ
Memoir by Isabella Leitner, 1978

Isabella Leitner's memoir *Fragments of Isabella* (1978) is striking for its brief but powerful images of people and moments from the unreality of Auschwitz. Keeping her sentences simple and her chapters short, she poetically captures the depth and the horror of the Holocaust a sentence, a page, and a paragraph at a time.

One dimension of the Holocaust her memoir drives home most powerfully is the Nazis' assault on the mother as it unfolded on various levels. Leitner makes it clear that the Nazis set out to murder not only mothers but also the very idea of a mother. Early in the memoir, for example, she recalls the almost supernatural force of her mother's love as her mother gazed upon her with an eerie smile during the deportation of the Jews from the Kisvárda ghetto. "She knows that for her there is nothing beyond this," wrote Leitner. "And she keeps smiling at me, and I can't stand it . . . I gaze at her tenderly and smile back." Upon their arrival in the camp, she remembered, Josef Mengele selected her mother for death before they could exchange a last look of good-bye. And once in the camp the prisoners were engulfed by the murder of the mother: "The smoke was thick. The sun couldn't break through. The scent was the smell of burning flesh. The burning flesh was your mother."

In a one-page chapter titled "The Baby" Leitner brings out the Nazis' most profound assault on the mother: deeming the existence of the Jew to be criminal, these murderers of the human image made becoming a Jewish mother a capital crime. Therefore, the women in the camp were placed in the position of having to kill newborns in order to save the mothers. "Most of us are born to live," she addresses one such infant. "You, dear darling, are being born only to die . . . Your mother has no rights. She brought forth fodder for the gas chamber. She is not a mother." In keeping with her concern for the assault on the mother, Leitner ultimately understands her liberation—to the extent that liberation is possible—in terms of becoming a mother. Crying out to her mother upon the birth of Peter, her first child, she declares, "Peter has started the birth of the new six million." Jews were liberated, she suggests, not just by emerging from the camps but by becoming mothers and fathers.

Parallel to Leitner's expression of her relation to the mother is an issue of identity. It begins when her mother is taken away to the gas chambers, and it continues as she struggles to cling to her surviving sisters. Upon their initiation into the antiworld of Auschwitz, they are rendered unrecognizable to one another. "Within seconds," she writes, "Chicha is somebody else. Some naked-headed monster is standing next to me. Some naked-headed monster is standing next to her." This crisis persists throughout her struggle to survive and even beyond. For when she finally leaves Auschwitz to be transferred to Birnbaumel, she cries out, "Bye, Auschwitz. I will never see you again. I will always see you." At the end of her memory of the universe of the concentration camp, her despair assumes the form of this image eternally before her eyes, an image that assumes a voice of its own. Trying to rid herself of her despair as liberation draws nigh, she affirms what she feared from this new shadow self: "She tells me what I was afraid she'd say: '*I*

will live as long as you do.'" Thus Leitner reveals the extent of the Nazis' violence against the soul of the Jew: Auschwitz extends beyond the barbed wire to the very end of the survivor's life. Auschwitz is a specter that darkens every joy and lurks in every happiness.

And yet Leitner ends her memoir with a cry of joy and a return to the mother. She ends by becoming a mother, telling her own mother about the beautiful child she has had. His name is Peter, the rock: "You were the rock, Mama. You laid the foundation. Peter has started the birth of the new six million."

—David Patterson

FRAGMENTS: MEMORIES OF A WARTIME CHILDHOOD (Bruchstücke: Aus einer Kindheit 1939–1948)
Memoir by Binjamin Wilkomirski, 1995

Binjamin Wilkomirski's *Fragments: Memories of a Wartime Childhood,* translated by Carol Brown Janeway and published in 1996, was presented as a memoir but has since been revealed to be fiction. Before it was known to be fictional, *Fragments* was compared to works by **Anne Frank** and **Primo Levi**, and it won a string of international prizes. Although the prizes were awarded on the basis of the authenticity of *Fragments,* they also testify to its power as a literary work. Its most striking features are the construction of a view of organized genocide through a child's eyes and the resulting defamiliarization of facts that we have come to accept as comprehensible. These features are both of literary value even though *Fragments* no longer has value as a historical document.

The construction of the child's-eye view may in the future come to distinguish *Fragments* as a text that tried stylistically to evade Holocaust "image-fatigue," as does, for instance, Martin Amis's novel *Time's Arrow,* which is about the life of a Nazi doctor written backwards. In *Fragments* the boy Binjamin has no historical or other understanding of what is going on around him; events occur at random for no apparent reason. The reader has to supply the missing background. This is clear when Binjamin first arrives at Majdanek and asks a soldier what his weapon is; instead of replying, the soldier hits the child in the face with a whip. This episode painfully juxtaposes a child's innocence with adult knowledge. We, as adult readers, know what the whip is right from the start, yet we are made to see the weapon and the act of violence as if for the first time.

A second striking feature of this scene is its lack of any historical context; there is little to suggest that we are reading about incidents in a wartime death camp. Throughout *Fragments* historical details are far and few between, and the word "Jew" is used only rarely, with at least one of these instances in reported speech. We could take the dehistoricized nature of many scenes in *Fragments* as an insight into the text's composition. Emotions that may have been familiar to the author from childhood experience—the betrayal of good faith, unwarranted punishment, even physical cruelty—reappear in a specific historical setting in an apparent effort to make sense of personal suffering. This would explain why *Fragments* bears some resemblance not only to Holocaust novels but also to authentic testimony by child survivors: they have in common a way of remembering. It also explains the strikingly split structure of the text. It is divided, in alternating sections, between the past of the camps and the present of postwar orphanages and also, we can speculate, divided between invented and remembered detail.

When *Fragments* was shown to be fiction, many readers pointed to the loss of authenticity in particular incidents in the text, which had often been singled out as the most memorable in reviews of the book as a memoir. These events include the death of Binjamin's father, the child's visit to his dying mother, women's corpses being eaten by rats, and starving babies chewing their own fingers. It is revealing that these episodes are identified as the text's most striking. Of course they are harrowing to read, but they are also not difficult to understand, because they have a universal meaning. In other words *Fragments* does not demand special knowledge of the Holocaust or of Jewish history in order to understand the suffering depicted in the book. We might speculate that the necessarily dehistoricized and fragmentary child's-eye view of the Holocaust was relatively easy for a nonsurvivor to re-create; hence also the text's reliance on cruel individual incidents.

Precisely because it is such an extreme case, the scandal surrounding *Fragments* has been instructive. For instance, the case has highlighted the fact that it is impossible to decide what is authentic testimony and what is fiction from internal textual evidence alone and that there is a place in the canon of Holocaust literature for fiction written by nonsurvivors.

—Sue Vice

FROM THE ASHES OF SOBIBOR: A STORY OF SURVIVAL
Memoir by Thomas Blatt, 1997

Fewer than 60 prisoners survived the Holocaust to tell the world of the death camp Sobibor. Now, over half a century later, fewer than a dozen remain. Thomas Blatt is one of these few. His memoir *From the Ashes of Sobibor: A Story of Survival* tells of a boy thrust into an extermination camp in which at least 250,000 Jews perished.

In the preface, Blatt states that his book has no "dominant message except the struggle of a teenager to survive." Yet, the book does have a dominant message—one of courage, perseverance, and remembrance. It is the story of a boy who at the

age of sixteen witnessed his entire family (father, mother, and younger brother) sent to the ovens to be turned into ashes and who vowed to live to tell the world the horror he had seen.

Blatt's style is factual and straightforward. Emotion seems only to exist between the lines. But Blatt's accounts are often strikingly memorable. He recalls the words of his schoolmate who betrayed him to the Nazis, saying "I'll see you on a shelf of soap in a store someday." Similarly, Blatt's reproach to his mother for refusing him an extra glass of their carefully rationed milk are the unremarkable words of a teenager—except they were the last words he ever spoke to her. He had no chance to follow these harsh words with ones of love. Fifty-five years later Blatt is still haunted by his thoughtless remark.

Born in Izbica, Poland, Blatt and his family experienced occupation by the Germans followed by a brief respite under the Soviets and then renewed German occupation. Seeing their town transformed into a transit center, Blatt's parents hoped to save their elder son by securing false papers for him and sending him to Hungary. Unfortunately, that decision proved disastrous. Blatt was captured, jailed, and then hospitalized, nearly dying of typhus before finally returning home. Yet, whatever his situation, Blatt demonstrated an uncanny ability to plot the course that would mean his survival.

His book underscores a theme of nearly all survivor accounts, that luck was crucial to survival. Upon arrival at Sobibor, Blatt wills the Nazi officer to select him to live. He is one of only a few men who are chosen to work. The rest are sent immediately to the gas chambers. Hunger, brutal labor, and the sadistic violence of the SS turn each day into a gauntlet of unpredictable danger. One day a *kapo* could be a fearsome oppressor and the next day a savior, as he pitches in to help Blatt meet an almost impossible work quota. A few days later the same *kapo* is beaten and poisoned to death by his fellow *kapo*s.

The stark, objective tone of Blatt's book expresses well the trials of a boy who must reject all feelings to survive, whose life depends on working for the hated Nazis; he must destroy the documents of the thousands of prisoners who walk off the train and into the gas chambers.

Blatt's book is immensely valuable for the insight it gives into the Sobibor revolt and the planning that preceded it. Here again, Blatt's luck continues. He survives the revolt only because a collapsing fence temporarily pins him down, preventing him from being among the first to cross the minefield. Later, the farmer who hides Blatt and his two friends decides the situation has become too dangerous and shoots them. The farmer thinks Blatt is dead, and Blatt escapes death only because his would-be executioner decides to wait until morning to bury him.

Such moments of utter heartlessness alternate with stories of selfless generosity: the peasant woman who gives Blatt and his companions food even though they have no money to pay; the farmer Petla who allows Blatt to tend the cows and invites him to share the family's simple meal, a gesture that gives Blatt hope that there might be a better world.

For Blatt, liberation does not mean safety. He has no loved ones to greet him, no home to which he can return. In Izbica, he is seen as an intruder by his neighbors who fear that he may reclaim his family's property. In the end, Blatt must flee his home for good.

From the Ashes of Sobibor is the story of a courageous boy who vowed that he would live to witness for those who died, for those whose lives had been reduced to the ashes of Sobibor. It is an invaluable memoir of the Holocaust.

—Marilyn J. Harran

FROM THE DIARY OF A SNAIL (Aus dem Tagebuch einer Schnecke)
Novel by Günter Grass, 1972

Günter Grass's novel *From the Diary of a Snail,* published in English translation in 1973, appeared in German as *Aus dem Tagebuch einer Schnecke* in 1972. A significant part of the novel deals with the German election campaign of 1969, but one portion describes what happened to the Jews from Danzig (now Gdansk) while that city was under Nazi occupation. On the political level the novel is aimed at two targets. The first is Kurt Georg Kiesinger, of the Christian Democratic Union (CDU) on the right of the political spectrum, a former Nazi and at the time the chancellor of West Germany. The second is the so-called extraparliamentary opposition, composed of various left-liberal activists opposed to the establishment and to the policies of the federal parliament.

During the 1960s Grass was constantly involved in political activities. He supported the Social Democratic Party (SPD) as no other writer before him had done. The SPD's top candidate, Willy Brandt, became one of his best friends, and Brandt's writings have influenced Grass's works ever since. Yet political activism has to be learned by doing, and *From the Diary of a Snail* can be regarded as the final document of that phase of Grass's experience.

When asked by his son to define his profession, Grass replies that he sees himself as writing against the current of time. It is a seemingly futile occupation, but he keeps trying nevertheless. This attitude, in turn, allows his references to Albrecht Dürer's engraving *Melencolia I* (1514) to become defiant and anti-idealistic: "Only those who know and respect stasis in progress, who have once and more than once given up, who have sat on an empty snail shell and experienced the dark side of utopia, can evaluate progress."

In the novel Grass tells his children about the campaign. He concludes that democracy in action moves very slowly, which leads to the metaphor of the snail: "'What do you mean by the snail?' 'The snail is progress.' 'What's progress?' 'Being a little quicker than the snail' . . . and yet never getting there, children.'' The children hear another story that retraces the horrible plight of the Jews from Danzig. Before describing the actual circumstances, the author reflects on the difficulties involved in writing for or talking to his children about the Holocaust: "I hear Franz or Raoul asking about the Jews: 'What about them? What's the story?' You notice that I falter whenever I abbreviate. I can't find the needle's eye, and I start babbling. Because this, but first that, and meanwhile the other, but only after . . .''

Grass also notes the impersonal, technical nature of quantitative or scientific information regarding the Holocaust: "'Exactly how many were they?' 'How did they count them?' It was a mistake to give you the total, the multidigitate number. It was a mistake to give the mechanism a numerical value, because perfect killing arouses hunger for technical details and suggests questions about breakdowns. 'Did it always work?' 'What kind of gas was it?''

Grass begins the story by stressing its universality: "Now I'll tell you . . . how it happened where I come from—slowly, deliberately, and in broad daylight. Preparations for the universal crime were made in many places at the same time though at unequal speeds." Throughout the novel Grass weaves in historical facts. He mentions the 7,479 Jews left in Danzig in early 1938 and the "barely 4,000 Jews left'' at the end of November 1938, and he includes accounts of persecution, hate speeches, acts of violence, the boycott of Jewish stores, *Kristallnacht* (Crystal Night, 9–10 November 1938), expulsions from professional life, segregation, isolation from other communities, the ghetto, the emigration to the United States and Palestine, the fate of Jews who died in the German concentration camp at Theresienstadt, and the many others who were murdered in mass shootings or in the gas chambers of Auschwitz and Treblinka. He describes the last Jewish emigrants leaving Danzig "on August 26, 1940 (a Monday)'' and the drownings and diseases that killed most of them. Grass leaves his readers with a warning: "This ability to get used to genocide has its parallel in a premature readiness to shrug off the crimes of the National Socialists as momentary insanity, as an irrational aberration, as something incomprehensible and therefore forgivable."

As a political novel *From the Diary of a Snail* also generates a historical dimension. As a historical novel it includes both historical details and reflections on the writing of history, especially the obstacles one faces in trying to describe events that were part of the Holocaust.

—Mark Gruettner

G

THE GARDEN OF THE FINZI-CONTINI (Il giardino dei Finzi-Contini)
Novel by Giorgio Bassani, 1962

The Garden of the Finzi-Contini, published in Italian in 1962 and in English translation in 1965, is Giorgio Bassani's best-known book. The setting, as usual, is his hometown of Ferrara, a walled city in the Po Valley between Bologna and Venice. It is above all a love story. The obstacles to true love are not only wealth and aristocracy but also the Fascist racial laws heralding the Holocaust.

The Finzi-Contini family is a wealthy Jewish family that owns a house and park dating back to the renaissance rulers of Ferrara. The period covered begins in 1929 and ends in the all-important year of 1943, when 183 Jews were deported to Germany. Among them was the Finzi-Contini family, except the eldest son, Alberto, who died the year before. Bassani announces this stark fact in the prologue so that it is lodged in our imagination from the start. The event provides an unusual end-stop for a novel. The story is set against Bassani's main theme of anti-Semitism, fueled since 1937 by the Fascist press. (There was no other.)

The narrator is the sensitive Jewish boy who appears in Bassani's other fiction and bears some resemblance to him. He meets Micol, the daughter, in 1929 in a childish escapade played out under the high wall of the garden. She is something of a tomboy and, recognizing him on his bike, invites him to climb up the wall, showing him the footholds. On the garden side there is ladder. He misses his chance while hiding his bike, and Micol is called home. She is thirteen at this time, the age of Anne Frank when she got her diary for her birthday in 1942. That diary was first published in 1947. Micol is by far the most electrifying and memorable of Bassani's characters.

When the racial laws have been promulgated in 1938 and Jews are not allowed to play tennis on public courts, among other more serious discriminations, the Finzi-Contini family throws open its tennis court to the young people. The narrator and Micol are now both students, she at Venice working on a thesis on Emily Dickinson, he at Bologna reading Italian. An industrial chemist, Giampiero Malnate, Alberto's friend from Milan, is also invited. Micol is the name of King David's wife, who had mocked him for dancing before the Ark of the Covenant and therefore bore no children. Showing him around the garden Micol tells the narrator that she had fallen for him on that first meeting and had called him Celestino because of his pale blue eyes. He replies with a reference to Celestine V, who was condemned by Dante for abdicating the papacy. By their names we can tell their relationship has little future. The sense of nostalgia and death emanating from the Finzi-Contini garden is illustrated by Micol's complaint half way through the book that the family is obsessed with refurbishing rather than letting things decay with elegance and humility.

Their relationship unravels during the second half of the novel, partly through Celestino's diffidence. Micol leaves for Venice and asks him to keep her brother company. There is tea and conversation with Alberto and Malnate, who turns out to be a communist, critical of too many possessions and of the number of Jews who had joined the Fascist Party in its first years. Bassani is dealing with the plight of the Jews but he has not forgotten his antifascism, for which he was imprisoned in 1943. Celestino describes how he was asked to leave the town library because of the racial laws and is given the run of the Finzi-Contini family's library to finish his thesis. When Micol comes back for Passover in 1939 it is celebrated with a dinner party reminiscent of James Joyce's *The Dead.* The addition of a Ouija board pronouncing grotesque and garbled prophecies adds a cruel touch. Celestino manages to visit her in her bedroom when she has flu but gives a disastrous impression of immaturity. The relationship resembles Petrarch's failed courtship of Laura with the addition of the telephone and, of course, anti-Semitism and the knowledge of its appalling consequences. Micol rebuffs him and he turns to Malnate for friendship.

Celestino renounces Micol after his father, an insomniac since the racial laws, points out that there are class and financial differences between them. She is above him, and he is too sensitive; he has no job, though he may become a critic, a novelist, and a poet. He last visits the garden the next night, finally scaling the wall and finding Micol's ladder on the other side. He suspects Malnate is his rival and thinks of looking for them in the Hütte, the chalet by the tennis court. The clock reminds him that he is too late again. The opening and closing play on the ladder recalls the Romeo and Juliet story, from the Italian novella tradition. Shakespeare's Juliet was also thirteen at the beginning of the story. The epilogue confirms the expected closure. Celestino breaks with all the Finzi-Contini family. After Alberto's death the whole family is taken by Mussolini's Republican troops in September 1943 and deported to Germany in November. Malnate leaves for Milan, eventually to be posted to the Russian front without trace. Celestino is imprisoned in 1944. His mature verdict is that if he had been able to stop Micol's deceiving and desperate words with a "real" kiss things would have been different. As it is the words of the novel must reflect what his heart can remember.

Italian critics had difficulty fitting Bassani's fiction and its unparalleled theme into earlier literary traditions. They highlighted memory and melancholy, the themes of the decadents. The political situation was also ambiguous for some time after the civil war in the north. Perhaps Celestino's type of diffidence prevented him from taking the stance of witness against Fascism as Silone had for the peasants or **Primo Levi** would for the Jews. But his sensitive record of the evils of anti-Semitism from the position of the victims, particularly in this masterpiece, with one of the most striking heroines in recent Italian writing, leaves a lasting mark on any reader.

—Judy Rawson

THE GATES OF THE FOREST (Les Portes de la foret)
Novel by Elie Wiesel, 1964

The first section of *The Gates of the Forest* (1966; *Les Portes de la foret,* 1964), ''Spring,'' introduces us to Gregor, who is in many ways a latter-day Robinson Crusoe. A 17-year-old Jewish youth, he hides from the Nazis by living in a cave in the depths of the Transylvanian forest. In his sylvan hideaway, he feels himself in harmony with nature: ''Now that he was no longer a child, the forest gave Gregor a sense of security. When he stroked the bark of the pine trees he felt close to the earth; when he listened to the rustling leaves he understood that man's secret outlives man.'' This pantheistic concept of man in harmony with nature is borrowed from eighteenth-century writers like Daniel Defoe and Friedrich Hölderlin.

Gregor lives in complete seclusion until another Jewish refugee stumbles on his hiding place. Then the days of living in harmony with nature are over. Gregor's new companion is a madman who refuses to admit he has a name, so Gregor gives him his own Jewish name, Gavriel. Gavriel compromises the safety of the hideaway by begging for food in a nearby village, and the lives of both men are threatened by a manhunt. Gavriel gives himself up to the villagers to save Gregor from further manhunts. But once the forest has become an object of Nazi suspicion, there can be no more living in harmony with nature.

The second part of the book, ''Summer,'' finds Gregor living in a Hungarian village with an elderly woman, Maria. He pretends to be deaf, mute, and feeble-minded in order to pass as a Gentile and prevent the villagers from suspecting him. The section is in the tradition of Shakespeare's *Hamlet,* where Hamlet feigns madness in order to be free of intrigues from his father's court: ''Though this be madness, there be method in it.''

This silent period is an important period in Gregor's life: ''Even today Gregor thinks nostalgically of the peaceful, dream-like weeks under Maria's protection when liberty was not law but the absence of law. They allowed him to glimpse a universe which had nothing in common with words. He has kept scraps of this universe and ever since he lost it he has lived for the purpose of putting it together again. Sometimes he fancies he is succeeding; then the sounds of the faraway night become voices and he shuts his eyes in order to hear them.''

Gregor lives in a bizarre sort of inner emigration in which he observes other people but does not directly communicate with them. His survival depends upon his being unable to communicate the truths of his being to his new neighbors.

Gregor's inner emigration and the safety it allows come to an end when the villagers impress him into playing Judas in an Easter passion play. The village peasants are so convinced by Gregor in that role that they pelt him with rocks in a scene resembling Shirley Jackson's 1949 story *The Lottery.* Gregor shocks them by giving a speech in which he admits to being a Jew. A sympathetic spectator helps him escape once more to the forest where he joins a group of Jewish partisans. Leaving his world of silence behind cancels his right to live within civilization so he must once again retreat into the forest.

His relationship with the partisans becomes tenuous when he involves them in an ill-conceived scheme to rescue Gavriel that backfires when their leader, Loeb the Lion, is captured. Nonetheless, the book ends with an inexplicable feeling of safety: World War II comes to an end and Gregor celebrates with other Jews in a Hasidic village. He agrees to marry a female partisan, and he reconnects with Gavriel, who has also survived the war.

—Peter R. Erspamer

GEBÜRTIG
Novel by Robert Schindel, 1992

Set in Vienna in the early 1980s, Robert Schindel's *Gebürtig,* his second and most highly acclaimed novel, examines the effect of the Holocaust on contemporary relationships between Jewish and non-Jewish Austrians. Through smoothly written dialogue, with verses and a number of letters interspersed, he shows how the repercussions of the Holocaust continue to permeate virtually every corner of the daily life of all Austrians, be they survivors, bystanders, perpetrators, or their children. The novel consists of seven chapters, preceded and followed by a prologue and an epilogue. The prologue, entitled ''Doppellamm'' (double lamb), contains an opening scene in a Vienna coffeehouse that sets the tone for the rest of the novel. The non-Jewish Austrian Erich Stieglitz deliberately baits the Jewish Mascha Singer, a child of survivors, by praising Mauthausen, his hometown, for its beauty. While the reference to the idyllic town, best known for its concentration camp, is upsetting for Singer, the scene is more important for its illustration of how Stieglitz, despite his provocation, considers himself a victim of the Jews and of the past. Indignant because he is no longer allowed to admire the beauty of his hometown and peeved because he is considered a fascist for doing so, Stieglitz storms out of the coffeehouse. The scene parallels

Austria's postwar proclamation of itself as the first victim of Hitler's aggression, contrary to the warm reception Hitler received during the Anschluss.

The following chapters pursue more in-depth examinations of the relationships between Jewish and non-Jewish Austrians. The main character is Danny Demant, a lecturer who is the son of exiled Jewish Austrian communists and who pursues a stormy relationship with Christiane Kalteisen, some of whose relatives were Nazis and whose non-Jewish identity and lack of concern with the past form the basis of their difficulties. Demant's twin brother, Alexander, nicknamed Sascha Graffito, narrates the novel. This doubling underscores the fact that most of the Jewish characters in the novel appear to have two identities: a Jewish persona, which the characters either hide or emphasize, depending on the situation, and a neutral, Austrian, persona. In addition, the theme of doubling is reflected in the title of the prologue and in short verses interspersed among the text. "Das doppelköpfige Unschuldslamm" (the double-headed lamb of innocence) mentioned in one verse refers to the Jewish and non-Jewish Austrians whose present identities may seem so different but whose pasts are intricately and indelibly linked. Thus, the Jewish and non-Jewish characters in the novel, like Danny and Christiane, are constantly attracted to and form relationships with one another. These relationships, however, inevitably break down because of the past.

Schindel's writing also demonstrates the importance of language and names to each character's identity. The name of a Jewish woman who died in the war, Sonja Okun, comes to Demant's mind many times. When Konrad Sachs, the child of the Nazi official in charge of occupied Poland, tries in good faith to come to terms with his own identity, he stumbles over the name Demant so often that Demant finally lashes out at him for it. In addition, the book contains a glossary in which Yiddish and Hebrew words are listed along with Viennese terms; thus, Josefstadt, a section of Vienna, follows Yom Kippur, the holiest of the Jewish holidays. The city of Vienna also plays an important role in Schindel's examination of the past, particularly in the story of the trial of an Austrian Nazi guard from the camp at Ebensee. The story is told by way of a text within the text, through the manuscript of Emmanuel Katz, who has given it to Demant to read. In the story the only witness, a former Austrian Jew appropriately named Hermann Gebirtig (playing on the title of the book, which has been translated as "born where"), must return to Vienna to testify that he knew the guard while he was imprisoned in Ebensee. While he is in Vienna, the narrative follows him through the streets of his childhood to the justice ministry, where the guard is finally pronounced innocent, thus implicating the city itself in Austria's refusal to recognize its complicity in the events of the Holocaust. Gebirtig must return home to the United States, since for him Vienna remains forever tainted in its refusal to acknowledge its role in the persecution of the Jews.

The epilogue, entitled "Verzweifelt" (hopeless), follows Demant and 40 Jewish survivors as they travel to Theresienstadt on an eerie trip for the filming of a television series on the Holocaust. Demant, the child of Nazi victims, plays the role of a camp inmate, while an actual survivor plays an SS guard. Thus, the prologue's theme of the shifting identities of victims and perpetrators continues even to the end, indicating that the identities of "victim" and "perpetrator" shift increasingly with the passage of time.

—Lisa Silverman

THE GERMAN REFUGEE
Short Story by Bernard Malamud, 1963

"The German Refugee" concludes Bernard Malamud's second collection of short stories, *Idiots First* (1963). The setting is New York City in the summer of 1939, just before the outbreak of World War II. The principal character, Oskar Gassner, a Jew, has immigrated to the United States from Germany. He saw what was happening to Jews, especially after *Kristallnacht,* and knew that he had to get out of that "accursed country." On a trip to the United States a year earlier he had tried to find a job, which would enable him to immigrate more easily. He was promised one, not as a journalist, which was his profession, but as a lecturer, and that decided him finally.

Leaving his Gentile wife, the daughter of a virulent anti-Semitic mother, behind in Stettin, Oskar comes to New York and tries to perfect his English so that he can deliver his lectures to an American audience. He hires a young student, Martin Goldberg, to tutor him. The story is Martin's first-person account of trying to help Oskar and of the friendship that grows between them as Oskar struggles with his pronunciation and the vagaries of American English.

It is not an easy time for Oskar or for the others like him whom Martin also tutors, thus eking out a small living during his senior year in college. The men he tutors live in uptown Broadway, the area where many refugees settled at the time. Three other German refugees are among Martin's clients, one a former film star, another a brilliant economist, and the third a man who had taught medieval history at Heidelberg—all accomplished persons, all driven out of Hitler's Germany. But it is Martin's relationship with Oskar that is the main focus of the story.

The summer is hot, and Oskar's disordered, shabby hotel room is stifling. But the two persevere, despite Oskar's recurrent bouts of despair and depression. He has frequent nightmares of Nazis inflicting tortures on him, sometimes forcing him to look upon corpses of people they have slain. At one point he dreams of visiting his wife in Germany, where he is directed to a cemetery. On her tombstone he reads another person's name, although her blood seeps out of the shallow grave.

Oskar does not talk much about his wife or Germans, whom he has come to despise as pigs masquerading as peacocks who have destroyed his career and uprooted his life after half a century. He also believes that in her heart his wife is a Jew hater. But on one occasion Martin glimpses a note from Mrs. Gassner that says in part, "Ich bin dir siebenundzwanzig Jahre true gewesen" (I have been true to you for 27 years). On another occasion, after they have been friends for a while, Oskar admits to Martin that he had attempted suicide a week after he arrived in New York, but he claims that it was a mistake.

Despite his efforts to help Oskar master English so that he can write and deliver a lecture on Walt Whitman in Germany, Martin begins to feel that it is hopeless. In a last, desperate attempt to assist him, Martin gives Oskar some notes he has taken on *Leaves of Grass,* and this proves to be the breakthrough Oskar needs. He overcomes his writer's block, or paralysis of the will as he calls it, and completes the lecture, which he delivers in September with good success. Its theme, ironically, is the feeling for *Brudermensch,* his humanity, that Germans found in Whitman, although Oskar admits that such feeling does not grow long on German soil and is soon destroyed.

By this time the Germans have invaded Poland, and World War II has begun. But Oskar has changed, has come back to life—only to lose everything. Two days after hearing the lecture, Martin climbs up to Oskar's hotel room and finds a crowd there. Oskar lies dead, having gassed himself. A week later, going through Oskar's belongings as his sole heir, Martin finds the explanation for the suicide in a letter from his anti-Semitic mother-in-law. His wife had converted to Judaism and had been seized by the Brownshirts along with other Jews in their apartment building, taken to a Polish border town, and shot in the head. She was then toppled into an open ditch with naked Jewish men and their wives and children, some Poles, and a few Gypsies and thus buried.

Malamud's story is a powerful account of the effects of the Holocaust even upon those who managed to escape the direct onslaught of the Nazis. Not only is Oskar affected fatally, but Martin, his friend and tutor, is also terribly influenced by the events. Malamud, however, wisely refrains from a full description of these effects and lets the story end with the account of how both Gassners perished and with the effect of their deaths upon the reader.

—Jay L. Halio

GHETTO (Geto)
Play by Joshua Sobol, 1983

Israeli playwright Joshua Sobol's award-winning drama *Ghetto,* first produced in Haifa in 1983 then in English translation in New York and London in 1989, is the first of

three installments in his triptych concerning the Holocaust. Sobol's play dramatizes life in the Vilna ghetto in Lithuania shortly after approximately 33,500 Jews were murdered and buried in the Ponar forest during the summer of 1941. Sobol portrays several historical characters, such as Judenrat leader Jacob Gens, tailor and ghetto entrepreneur Weiskopf, ghetto librarian Herman Kruk, and Nazi ghetto liquidator Kittel. The play is a documentary drama in which Sobol employs historical information and eyewitness accounts from people such as Kruk (from his diary) to portray the vibrant life that existed in the Vilna ghetto.

After the mass murders at Ponar, the remaining Jews were herded into the ghetto (although Sobol's play mentions only one ghetto, historically there were two that were later consolidated into one). Gens attempts to use any means to keep the Jews alive; one such method is to start an acting company, for the actors are considered skilled workers and thus are entitled to food rations and soap. Although Kruk is vehemently against the creation of the acting company because he claims that it is sacrilegious to perform theater in a graveyard (a reference to those who died at Ponar), Gens believes that the theater will add vitality to the ghetto and allow the Jews to maintain their culture, spirit, and dignity—as well as serving as a diversion from the pain and suffering that they have experienced. Historically, as in Sobol's play, the theater was a huge success and even attracted Nazi soldiers such as Kittel. Sobol obtained his research about the theater from several sources, primarily from the ghetto theater director, Israel Segal, whom he interviewed in Tel Aviv shortly before writing the play. Segal serves as the model for the puppeteer Srulik in the play.

Jacob Gens, as ghetto leader, is in a precarious position for he attempts to save as many Jewish lives as possible while trying to maintain a working relationship with the Nazis, under whose control his power rests. He wants to help his people but must appease Kittel; thus his power is actually rather limited. Gens reluctantly agrees to selections but attempts to save as many Jews as possible. His path converges with the tailor Weiskopf, who creates a uniform-mending factory within the ghetto: Nazi uniforms are repaired in the ghetto, thus saving the Nazis much time and money because the uniforms do not have to be sent all the way back to Germany. Weiskopf achieves great fortune in the ghetto while many other Jews starve and are impoverished. A struggle ensues between Gens and Weiskopf because the ghetto leader wants to put as many Jews to work as possible in order to save their lives, yet the tailor wants to limit the number of his workers in order to make more money and save the Nazis some money as well—even at the expense of Jewish lives. Weiskopf becomes, to a large extent, a collaborator with the Nazis and even seems to want to become one. He becomes excited when he is led to believe that he will get to meet Hermann Göring, as if he considers the Nazi a hero. Shocked that Weiskopf is starting to comport himself as a Nazi, Kittel arranges for the destruction of the tailor. Weiskopf is a selfish person who becomes an opportunist in the ghetto.

When Kittel asks him the difference between partial and total liquidation of the ghetto, Weiskopf responds that partial liquidation occurs when 50,000 Jews are slain but he is spared, and total liquidation occurs when he is killed. Although the comment seems to be a joke, Weiskopf's actions suggest that he means the quip sincerely. Sobol thus manifests the selfishness and egoism that some Jews exhibited when faced with such a desperate situation. Although Sobol was accused by some critics for portraying collaboration during the Holocaust, the playwright counters that such behavior is historically true and based on documented evidence. As a playwright, Sobol dramatizes the actions of the characters onstage, yet he refrains from judging them.

In many interviews Joshua Sobol states that in *Ghetto* he attempts to portray the vibrancy of the people and the culture in Vilna under Nazi occupation. He wants his characters to act with a sense of desperation and vitality, as if they know that their lives can be taken away from them at any time. The theater manifests this vitality and also represents a form of Jewish resistance against the Nazis. Sobol concentrates on complex issues, such as collaboration, the ghetto police, selections, and the question regarding theater in an area where tens of thousands of Jews have been murdered. The clothes onstage are a constant reminder of those unfortunate Jews who lost their lives at Ponar; these clothes are then worn by the characters who have survived. **Elie Wiesel** has criticized *Ghetto* because of the portrayal of complicity as well as other unscrupulous behavior by Jews in the play. Sobol, however, fervently defends his play from Wiesel's criticism, indicating that the characters and content of the play derive from historical documents and eyewitness accounts.

—Eric Sterling

GHETTO DIARY (Pamietnik z getta)
Diary by Janusz Korczak, 1978

Janusz Korczak's *Ghetto Diary* is remarkable both for its eloquence and for its insight. In the diary, which was published in English translation in 1978, Korczak's devotion to the orphans of the Warsaw Ghetto reveals itself in a number of ways. What was most disturbing to him was that the sight of dead children had become part of the ghetto landscape. He recalled, for instance, a group of youngsters playing in the ghetto streets, while nearby the body of a dead boy was lying in the gutter. "At one point," he wrote, "they note the body, move a few steps to the side, go on playing." The dead boy lying in the street added to Korczak's vision of dead children, until his nights were haunted by a nightmare: "Bodies of dead children. One dead child in a bucket. Another skinned, lying on the boards in the mortuary, clearly still breathing." When dead

children became commonplace, children were no longer children. Korczak underscores this overturning of existence when he comments that his orphanage has turned into a home for the elderly. Thus, Korczak realizes a definitive dimension of the Nazis' extermination project: they set out to annihilate not only children but also the very image and essence of the child.

Devoted as he was to the children, Korczak incorporated texts from their diaries into his own. In keeping with his lifelong commitment to make the children heard, Korczak demonstrated the profundity of the children's outcry by including lines from their notebooks such as this one: "A widow sits at home and weeps. Perhaps her older son will bring something from smuggling. She does not know that a gendarme has shot her son dead." Here is another example: "That siddur [prayer book] which I want to have bound is a souvenir since it belonged to my brother, who died, and it was sent to him for the day of his bar mitzvah by his brother in Palestine." In these passages Korczak shows that during the Holocaust the tearing of the essence from the child was a tearing of the child from mothers and brothers, from prayers and memory. Restoring the outcry of the child by adding it to his own outcry, Korczak attempts to restore at least the testimony to that tearing.

As he indicated in the entry for July 15, 1942, Korczak also shared his diary with the children: "The children moon about. Only the outer appearances are normal. Underneath lurks weariness, discouragement, anger, mutiny, mistrust, resentment, longing. The seriousness of their diaries hurts. In response to their confidence, I share mine with them as an equal." Sharing his diary with the children, Korczak shared both the responsibility and the helplessness in the face of the death that surrounded them. In an entry from July 1942, for example, he wrote, "There are problems that lie, like bloodstained rags, right across the sidewalk. People cross to the other side of the street or turn their eyes away in order not to see. I do the same." As Korczak's diary assumes a confessional tone, his humanity and his humility unfold to the extent that his sense of shame deepens. His greatest shame was that he remained alive in the face of so much death, as he saw the finest human beings among the first to fall. Indeed, he knew that when children died before their elders, the world had been turned on end. Perhaps this was where the Nazis attained their most devastating victory: deeming the very life of the Jew to be criminal, they led the Jew to feel guilty for being alive.

And yet this assault on life's substance made Korczak's daily testimony to life's dearness a matter of even greater urgency. Hearing shots fired, for example, as he wrote on the night of 21 July 1942, he wondered whether his windows were sufficiently blacked out to hide his "crime" of writing. "But I do not stop writing," he asserts. "On the contrary: it [the shooting] sharpens (a single thought) the thought." Lamenting what the Nazis had made of life, Korczak remained committed to the dearness of life. In the world created by the Nazis, however, the person who persisted in being a witness to life was often condemned to death for his persistence. So it happened with Korczak. Although in one of his last entries he struggled in vain to bless the world, he did not act in vain when he joined the children in the sealed train to Treblinka. The man who was a spokesman for the children of the ghetto lived by his words and died by them.

—David Patterson

GHETTO FACTORY 76: CHEMICAL WASTE CONVERSION (Geto fabrik 76)
Poem by Rachmil Bryks, 1967

Rachmil Bryks' poem *Ghetto Factory 76: Chemical Waste Conversion* was written in Yiddish in 1943 in Łódź and was published in English translation in 1967. The significance of this poem lies in the fact that Bryks recited it at a banquet in the Łódź ghetto in 1943, and this recitation nearly cost him his life. He was placed on a list for deportation to Auschwitz but quick-thinking, clever friends hid him and thus rescued Bryks from the sure fate of death. In the forward to this work, Isaac Bashevis Singer wrote: "It is a duty to read this work; it will be remembered for generations." The original manuscript was discovered in the ghetto and is now housed in the Jewish Historical Institute in Warsaw, Poland.

In this poem, Bryks speaks of Ghetto Factory 76, as each factory in the Łódź ghetto was numbered. Here the "sweepings" of flour, sand, dust, and ashes swept from the mill and bakery floors are collected and used in the manufacture of liquor and alcohol for ghetto commissars. Ghetto inhabitants could instead use the sweepings to create gelatin, goulash, and pastry for their own consumption. Potato skins, left over from the creation of thin soup for ghetto inhabitants, become an overwhelming temptation for the starving workers within the factory. They dare not partake of these scraps, for discovery of this "theft" could mean jailing, cleaning latrines with one's bare hands, or even death. The theme of hunger is the thread that binds the entire poem together. To see food, no matter how mixed with other matter it may be, and to have it shoveled into bags before the eyes of starving souls is the ultimate cruelty. Bryks refers to these souls as "famished animals" and portrays their vicious behavior toward one another in the soup lines. Hope continues to thrive in typical Bryks fashion, however, and this work becomes reminiscent of his novelette *A Cat in the Ghetto*. The inhabitants dream of Adolf Hitler's demise and speak of Winston Churchill's threats toward Nazi Germany. As Bryks writes: "Eyes glower with envy and hatred and hearts thirst for revenge." Many are sure that the Nazi machine will quickly be destroyed, bringing forth the liberation of the ghetto.

The poem continues to describe the factory's goal of producing alcohol that will provide a pleasant drink for those in charge of the ghetto, while those who must toil at its production are left with nothing but empty stomachs and yearning hearts. Bryks scolds the administrators of the ghetto with the following lines:

> Seeing directors and commissars
> In brightly-lit halls,
> At linen-covered tables,
> Amid sounds of music
> Swallowing liquor,
> Gulping down alcohol,
> Fancy dishes—gorging themselves
> And carrying on harlotry.

With these accusatory lines, it is not difficult to see why Bryks's life was endangered by the recitation of this poem in public.

Selected lines from *Ghetto Factory 76* were also set to music by William Gunther and are included at the end of the piece. Gunther also set Bryks's poems *Nisht vartzwaifeln (Don't Despair)*, *Tzwaigen (Twigs)*, and *Du a Nenufar Wasserlilie (You are a Water Lily)* to music. They are included with the poem *Ghetto Factory 76*. This work should be read in conjunction with Bryks's novelette *A Cat in the Ghetto* to gain full understanding of Bryks's style and his message regarding life in the Łódź ghetto.

—Cynthia A. Klíma

THE GHETTO FIGHTS (Getto walczy: Udział Bundu w obronie getta warszawskiego)
Memoir by Marek Edelman, 1945

A small book (sixty-seven pages) by Marek Edelman, published in 1945 in Warsaw and in 1946 in English translation, is not just a report on the events in the ghetto but rather a shocking, though lacking in pathos, testimony of a witness and participant. *The Ghetto Fights* is dedicated not only to the armed activity of the Jewish underground organizations but also to their merits in raising the spirit of resistance among the Jewish population that was intimidated, oppressed, and disoriented by German propaganda. The chronological report encompasses the period from the moment the German invaders entered Warsaw (September 1939) until the downfall of the Warsaw Ghetto Uprising. The author carefully analyzes the causes of the inaction of the Jewish community, seeing them in light of the fact that the process of extermination was a culmination of long-lasting and methodical persecutions. The order to wear the Star of David and the bans on traveling, possessing gold, baking bread, treatment of Aryan patients, and working in state-owned institutions are just some of the repressive means mentioned by Edelman, all of which preceded the total isolation of Jews in the form of the Warsaw

Ghetto created by Germans in November 1940. Most attention, however, is paid to the activity of the Jewish youth, who dealt first with charitable activities and then with political and military activities within the confines of such organizations as the bund. Young activists, including Edelman himself, did not give in even when Jews, public opinion, and Western politicians did not believe their information on the gassing of Jews or the true purpose of supposed evictions. As Edelman emphasizes, the ghetto did not believe that the world was unwilling to believe the disillusioning reports of witnesses. Members of the resistance took up the fight in defiance of those who wanted to survive at all costs, including the cost of the human quota delivered to the Umschlag, the ''deportation'' site. The armed clashes with the police—who followed the orders of the oppressor and the obedient Jewish Council—that began in July 1942 was the first sign of opposition, visible to the ghetto and the whole city of Warsaw. The fighters deemed putting up resistance as a moral duty of any Jew. Therefore, they criticized the behavior of Adam Czerniakow (an engineer), the president of the Jewish Council, who in July 1942 on the second day of the deportation action committed suicide to avoid the responsibility for the death of hundreds of thousands in gas chambers. In *The Ghetto Fights* Edelman contrasts Czerniakow's attitude with the determination of Edelman's comrades—activists of the Jewish opposition, who in 1942 decided to coordinate their efforts by creating *Zidowska Organizacja Bojowa* (ZOB; Jewish Fighting Organization). He describes the armed actions undertaken by ZOB from December 1942, such as freeing prisoners held by the police or executing death sentences on the Jewish Gestapo informers.

The author avoids any mention of his own function in the organization, his personal achievement, or his participation in individual operations. The narration is done in the first person plural. The tension between the matter-of-fact report and the emotional commitment of the writer can be seen especially in the part devoted to the uprising, the outbreak of which was the response to the liquidation of the ghetto attempted by the Germans in April 1943. In short, interrupted sentences Edelman writes about the desperate defense of every shelter, about the fights within the walls of the ghetto set on fire by the Germans, about the evacuation of survivors through sewers beyond the walls of the Jewish district.

The part of the guardian of memories is assumed by the author, especially in the ending of the book, remembering those who have fulfilled their task to the very end, ''to the last drop of blood which soaked into the pavement of the Warsaw ghetto.'' The author talks with admiration and engagement about Abrasha Blum, the spiritual leader of the ghetto resistance; about David Hochenberg, who blocked the passage in one of the bunkers with his own body; about Tobcia Dawidowicz, a wounded liaison woman who remained in the ghetto not wanting to delay others in their escape.

By focusing on the facts Edelman avoids pathos but without giving up his emotional commitment. Therefore we call his

book—quoting Zofia Nalkowska, a Polish writer and a member of *Komisja Badania Zbrodni Niemieckich* (Committee for the Investigation of German Crimes)—''a record of a common martyrdom.''

—Joanna Hobot

THE GHOST WRITER
Novella by Philip Roth, 1979

When Philip Roth wrote *Goodbye, Columbus* (1959) and *Portnoy's Complaint* (1969), he could not have predicted the hostile response by some American Jews who feared Roth's unflattering portraits of Jewish life might foment latent anti-Semitism in the wake of the Holocaust. His detractors insisted that his identity as a Jew and his identity as a writer were irrefutably connected; he had a responsibility to portray Jews in ways that would not nourish the souls of anti-Semites. He argued then and has repeatedly stated since that a writer, indeed any artist, must be free to express his ideas. In ''Writing about Jews,'' an essay reprinted in *Reading Myself and Others* (1975), Roth rejects the claims of those who ''argue or imply that the sufferings of the Jews throughout history, culminating in the murder of six million by the Nazis, have made certain criticisms of Jewish life insulting and trivial.''

A few years later his novella *The Ghost Writer* (1979) enlarged the discussion about a writer's freedom to express his ideas, and, to a degree, offered Roth a fictional forum in which he could continue to debate his views. At the same time, Roth put forth an idea that he has revisited in a number of other books: Jews tend to sanctify stories about the Holocaust and to elevate the storytellers by virtue of their victimization without subjecting either to any literary scrutiny.

In the novella Roth's alter ego, the young writer Nathan Zuckerman, goes to visit his literary idol, E.I. Lonoff, describing him as someone ''who, some ten years after Hitler, seemed to say something new and wrenching to Gentiles and Jews, and to Jews themselves, and to readers and writers of that recuperative decade . . .'' There he encounters another Lonoff admirer, Amy Bellett, who alleges to be the deceased Anne Frank, the juvenile author of the famous Holocaust diary. She claims to have assumed an alias rather than reveal her identity in order to preserve the hallowed position maintained by her celebrated work. The circumstances allow Roth to pursue a defense of his writing, with Holocaust literature serving as a point of reference in his discussion of Jewish writers, their subjects, and the reception of their work by Jewish audiences.

As part of his argument Zuckerman sets up a counterpoint between himself and Anne Frank. He made a conscious choice to be a writer; ''as for developing into a writer—she owed that not to any decision to sit down each day and try to be one but to their stifling life.'' He elected to write about Jews, to make them his subject; she wrote about them by default. Yet Jews find fault with his presentation of Jewish life and praise *The Diary of Anne Frank*. For Zuckerman, and one may assume for Roth, the adoration of the diary was based less on artistic merit than on the tragic circumstances of its subject. The diary invited sympathy for Jews; Zuckerman's work did not.

Zuckerman, like Roth, had felt the long arm of Hitler's endless persecution since fear of anti-Semitism had created its own unique brand of censorship. For example, Zuckerman's father, although claiming to be proud of his son's literary success, worries about the harmful potential of one story, ''Higher Education.'' He admonishes him: ''I wonder if you fully understand just how very little love there is in this world for Jewish people. I don't mean in Germany, either, under the Nazis. I mean in run-of-the-mill Americans.'' And his father's friend Judge Wapter, apparently a stand-in for numerous critics of Roth, concocts ''Ten Questions for Nathan Zuckerman'' on the subject of the responsibility of Jewish writers. The first question reads: ''If you had been living in Nazi Germany in the thirties, would you have written such a story?'' and the last question circles back to the same issue: ''Can you honestly say there is anything in your short story that would not warm the heart of a Julius Streicher or a Joseph Goebbels?'' Roth is, of course, satirizing the concerns of his critics and, through Zuckerman, restating his argument that fiction has no power to propagandize—that the artist must be free to express his thoughts.

—Ellen Gerstle and Daniel Walden

GREEN AQUARIUM (Griner akvarium)
Poems by Abraham Sutzkever, 1972

These prose poems, written by Abraham Sutzkever in Israel between 1953 and 1954 and published originally as *Griner akvarium* in 1972, deal with the poet's experience of life in the Vilna (Vilnius) ghetto. The English translation appeared in 1982. The text deals with the very last days of the ghetto, when the few survivors were being rounded up and murdered. Evocative in style, each poem is quite brief and self-contained, with an emphasis firmly on the personal rather than the historical. If there is a theme it is that of the value of life in the midst of death and the importance of regarding each moment of life as significant. The Germans appear by proxy as the agents of death and capture; they are never personalized, and

thus they are made to seem omnipotent. God is completely absent from the text in one sense, yet in another sense the whole world—including animals and inanimate objects—is imbued with transcendental meaning. Poetry itself is seen to embody the forces of salvation because it serves as a witness to the strength of those few human actions during the violence that represent the ability of life to reassert itself and to deny the overwhelming influence of death and destruction.

The title poem's image of a green aquarium as the environment in which the participants of the Holocaust were living is interesting. Green has two meanings here: it represents not only the stagnant atmosphere of ghetto life but also the possibility of rebirth and growth. It is an image that Sutzkever also used in *The First Night in the Ghetto* (1971), where the *gliverdike gufim* (stiff bodies), the corpses lying on the ground, are described as *grine* (green) twice, contrasting with the black poison, the forces of death. It is important to emphasize the secular character of Sutzkever's verse, which suggests that the power of survival and redemption has to lie, if anywhere, in nature itself, in the ability of the natural and the human world to resist and ultimately triumph against the apparently omnipotent forces of death.

Nature itself becomes a source of poetry in this collection and plays an important role in putting the horrors of the destruction of the Vilna Jewish community into a context where they can be discussed by the Angel of Poetry, who appears throughout the collection as the antagonist of the Angel of Death. Sutzkever seemed to yearn to use classical forms of poetic expression, but the pressure of real-life events intervened and made those forms no longer appropriate. Since Sutzkever was determined not to return to the images and beliefs of religion, except as a historical source of ideas, the only other place that he could look to for poetic stimulation and artistic allusion was nature; and it is the ability of nature to regenerate itself, to have a spring come after winter, that provided the only hope he could find in the events of the Holocaust. Nevertheless, the poems also suggest that nature is a weak repository for memories. Although the world will continue, it does not continue in a way that can give the survivors or the dead any serious consolation. Once the world of Vilna Jewry is smashed and destroyed, it is as impossible to reconstitute as a smashed aquarium. On the other hand, what pours out of the aquarium may continue as part of nature, albeit in a radically changed form. The tightness of Sutzkever's style neatly replicates what he sees as the fragility of what has been destroyed.

—Oliver Leaman

H

HANNAH SENESH (Hanah Senesh)
Play by Aharon Megged, 1958

The play *Hannah Senesh* (produced in Tel-Aviv in 1952; published in Hebrew in 1958 as *Hanah Senesh*) by Aharon Megged describes the events of a woman who became a hero in Israel. Hannah Senesh escaped from Hungary to Palestine and then returned as part of the Jewish brigade formed by the British to help organize the resistance to the Nazis and work on behalf of what remained of the Jewish community. In the play she is captured and offered a lesser sentence in return for her cooperation, but she nobly refuses to compromise, despite torture and imprisonment, and implicitly criticizes those of her Hungarian peers who went to their deaths without resistance or principle. This represents a common view held by Israelis in the 1950s about Jews in the Holocaust: that they did not do anything to avert their murder, while Israelis had vigorously resisted their enemies. Even though Senesh is under the control of the Nazis, she remains able to resist to a certain extent and loses no opportunity to do so. She takes on a mythic role in the play, being said to be stronger than her captors; on one occasion while torturing her, they collapse before she does. She never exhibits any doubt about what she has done and is a constant source of strength to all around her.

In a later work (*Shulkhan ha-Ketivah,* 1989; ''The Writing Desk'') Megged reflects the fact that Israelis came to better appreciate the impossible situation in which most European Jews found themselves during the Holocaust. He outlines two kinds of heroism, the kind exhibited by Senesh, in which one demands one's rights and does not bow one's head in submission (*ve-lo lakhof et roshekha*), and another kind of heroism, hitherto unappreciated. The latter is where one has the courage and spiritual strength to survive a long, drawn-out persecution that continues for months and even years, where each moment is a struggle. Senesh is able to resist the Hungarian collaborators for a long time. Even when they bring in her mother and threaten to harm her if Hannah does not give them information, there is no indication of any wavering on her part, there is no real mental turmoil or hesitation in her mind about her conduct.

Although Senesh is originally from Hungary and has spent only a few years in Palestine before returning for her assignment, Megged represents her as very much the new Israeli, determined not to be seen as impotent in front of her enemies even when they overwhelm her. The Holocaust is the backdrop to her resistance, and by contrast with the other Jews in Europe who are just victims, she is determined to take charge of her life and so indicate the appropriate role for Jews if they are to survive. She transcends the Holocaust and is a powerful literary treatment of one way of overcoming.

—Oliver Leaman

HANNAH SENESH: HER LIFE AND DIARY (Hanah Senesh: Yomanim, Shirim, Eduyot)
Diary by Hannah Senesh, 1966

One of the most courageous tales to come out of the Holocaust was first published in Hebrew in 1966. It was *Hanah Senesh: Yomanim, Shirim, Eduyot*, which appeared in English in 1971 under the title *Hannah Senesh: Her Life and Diary*. The volume contains not only the diary of a girl from the time she was 13 almost until her death at 23 but also letters she wrote to her family from Palestine, many of her poems, and testimonies of people who knew her, including her mother. The diary shows that, for Hannah Senesh, growing into adulthood meant realizing her role in life as a Jew. Revealing a sense of responsibility for people and a devotion to family, the diary is characterized by a profound sense of destiny. ''In my life's chain of events,'' Senesh wrote in one of her last entries, ''nothing was accidental. Everything happened according to an inner need.'' These words become especially powerful in the light of the fate that befell their author. After parachuting behind enemy lines in a special unit of British-trained Israelis, she was captured and murdered by the Hungarians.

Reading the diary of Senesh, one is struck by the parallels between the historical developments of the period and the development of a remarkable young woman. In an entry dated 15 May 1937, she considered whether anti-Semitism had not made the Jews stronger, since it forced them to take on the strength to overcome even more obstacles. With the passage of more and more anti-Semitic legislation in Hungary in 1938, however, she believed that whatever strength the Jews might have acquired should be devoted to the Zionist movement rather than to trying to live in an anti-Semitic Christian Europe. On 17 October 1938, for example, she wrote, ''One needs to feel that one's life has meaning, that one is needed in this world. Zionism fulfills all this for me.'' Once she moved to Israel in 1939, her sense of mission grew even deeper; indeed, in Israel she came to believe that ''almost every life is the fulfillment of a mission.''

Like many teens growing into adulthood, Hannah endured an identity crisis and experienced doubts about herself while she was in the very process of cultivating a deeper sense of meaning in her life. In an entry dated 12 April 1941, for example, she wrote, "I'm filled with discontent, hesitancy, insecurity, anxiety, lack of confidence. Sometimes I feel I am an emissary who has been entrusted with a mission." As her sense of mission grew, so did her sense of responsibility for the lives of others. In the entry dated 9 July 1941—just as the Nazi killing units were advancing on the Eastern Front—she asserted that she must do something "exerting, demanding, to justify" her existence. Therefore, she rejected the temptation "to seek personal happiness" and chose to find ways to join "the difficult and devastating war" for what was good for humanity.

Indeed, Senesh believed that "the world was created for good," but she understood this to mean not that people were good but that they must do good. This realization shifted her attention to her home in Hungary, where the situation of the Jews was growing more and more precarious. "I feel I must be there," she noted on 8 January 1943, "to help organize youth emigration, and also to get my mother out." Within a month of recording the entry she was training to join a military mission to the Balkans. "I see the hand of destiny in this," she said of her military assignment, "just as I did at the time of my Aliyah." Because she died in an effort to save the lives of Jews at a time when the world had generally turned its back on them, her destiny was to die as a Jew.

Just before she went into Nazi territory in Hungary, Senesh said farewell to her friend Reuven Dafne and gave him a slip of paper. "If I do not come back," she told him, "give this to our people." It was her best-known poem, "Blessed Is the Match," written on 2 May 1944, just after she and her comrades had landed in Yugoslavia. The poem ends with a line that best describes the life of Hannah Senesh: "Blessed is the match consumed in kindling flame."

—David Patterson

HASIDIC TALES OF THE HOLOCAUST
Oral History by Yaffa Eliach, 1982

Yaffa Eliach's work *Hasidic Tales of the Holocaust* presents an interesting and well-documented collection of tales that, had it not been for the assistance and enthusiasm of Eliach's students in Brooklyn, might have not come to fruition. Eliach's tenacity in following up on each tale collected is admirable, and the work is the result of a project that lasted six years. Interviews were conducted in nine languages and several dialects, all translated by Eliach. Eliach's work demonstrates the typical wit and anecdotal style that is associated with Hasidic storytelling. "The very nature of the Hasidic tale made it a most appropriate literary form through which to come to terms with the Holocaust and its aftermath," she wrote. The role that women play in these tales is very evident— their bravery, religious conviction, and love for family show

the strong and important position of women in Hasidic life. The stories provide a means of coming to terms with having to face unspeakable reality.

The foreword of the work provides a good explanation on the origins of Hasidism. This is a must-read section for those unfamiliar with Hasidic tradition, a tradition filled with a strong belief in humanity and God. The glossary and notes at the end of the work give the reader excellent explanations for uncommon terminology. The collection is divided into four sections, three representing stages of life in the concentration camps and one depicting life for survivors after World War II. The first section, "Ancestors and Faith," reflects stories about the power of one's departed family members. These stories depict the first stage of concentration camp life, the belief that God will always protect and the spirits of loved ones will carry camp inmates to safety. In "Hovering Above the Pit," Rabbi Israel Spira believes that he has been carried aloft by his ancestors over a large, open grave. The stories powerfully relate the strength of unrelenting faith. Religious services are carried out, despite the penalty of death, and traditions survive the worst of conditions, as seen in "The Zanzer Kiddush Goblet."

In the second part of the collection, entitled "Friendship," relationships in camps begin to develop. Loneliness and loss have provided a means for many to accept others as "sisters" or "brothers." In "What I Learned at My Father's Home," a woman named Bronia gives away her last white bread to a rabbi dying. By doing so, she saves his life. Simple words, as heard in "The World Needs You," save a rabbi's life, and quick thinking saves a cousin in "Stars." In "The Mosaic Artist's Apprentice," an elderly Polish Jew saves the life of a 13-year-old boy by lying for him. Adoption of others was not an uncommon practice, and placing one's own life in danger for another became regular practice, such as in the tale, "A Girl Called Esterke."

"The Spirit Alone," the third part of the work, contains representations of those barely clinging to life—human skeletons whose spirit could not be trampled by the Nazi regime. Senseless murders and other evil actions committed by the SS and the Gestapo are overcome by deep, unflinching faith. The Nazis especially liked to use Jewish holidays for particularly disturbing methods of inflicting fear and taking lives, such as represented in "Even the Transgressors in Israel." Wisdom, spirit, and faith never disappear, even when one is in deep pain, as evidenced by the Zaddik of Belz in "Death of a Beloved Son" when he states, "How can one mourn the death of an individual, even a beloved son, when one is overwhelmed by the collective pain of a nation mourning its six million dead!"

The fourth section, "At the Gates of Freedom," contains stories of survivors who are left to suffer alone as they return to empty or destroyed houses, decimated villages, and the taunts of hateful townspeople who have taken over Jewish property. Many camp survivors leave for America, as in "The Plague of Blood." Some deny their own Jewish heritage. In "Puff . . ."

one of the most pious Hasidic men turns to the former enemy whom he now considers to be "the future." Still others refuse to let go of their religious upbringing or those who have left it return, as in "The Grip of the Holy Letters."

Hasidic Tales of the Holocaust is a collection of stories that exemplify the power of the human spirit, the will to survive, and the immense capacity of man to overcome seemingly impossible odds. They serve as a connection between the past to overcome the reality of the present and to carry the faithful into the future.

—Cynthia A. Klíma

HEAVY SAND (Tiazhelyi pesok)
Novel by Anatolii Rybakov, 1978

Heavy Sand (1981), originally published in Russian as *Tiazhelyi pesok* (1978), is a family chronicle that combines elements of a parable, a thriller, and a soap opera. It is loosely based on the true story of the life and death of the parents of Rybakov's friend Robert Kupchik. Rybakov and Kupchik first met before World War II in the central Russian city of Riazan', where Rybakov worked in a motor-transport depot and Kupchik was an economist in an industrial cooperative. Robert's grandfather, a Jew from the city of Simferopol' (in southern Russia), went to Switzerland to study for a degree in medicine, became a successful doctor in Zürich, married a German woman there, and in 1909 came back to Russia with his younger son, who was about to become a student, to visit relatives. When in Simferopol', the son fell in love with the beautiful daughter of a local shoemaker and married her. At first the newlyweds left for Zürich, but the shoemaker's daughter quickly understood that she would not adapt there and chose to return to Simferopol', together with her husband (Robert's father, who served as a prototype for Yakov Ivanovsky in Rybakov's novel). Because of his all-consuming love for his wife, he threw away his career as a student and began working as a cobbler for his father-in-law. In the 1930s, during Stalin's purges, he was imprisoned on account of his suspicious foreign origins but released in 1940 as a half-German in the wake of the Molotov-Ribbentrop pact. In 1942, however, both Robert's mother and father, together with other Simferopol' Jews, were killed by the Nazis and buried in a mass grave near the Crimean town of Sudak.

When at the preparatory stage Rybakov made a research trip to Simferopol', he discovered that the city failed to stimulate his imagination, as it could not resonate with his own childhood memories of Jewish life in the Russian South. For this reason he not only transferred the action to the Ukrainian town of Snovsk (in 1935 renamed Shchors, after a local Russian Civil War hero), where he spent some time as a little boy, but he also populated the Kupchiks' story with real-life members of his own family on his mother's side. Thus,

Rybakov's maternal grandfather became the prototype for *Heavy Sand*'s patriarchal boot maker Abraham Rakhlenko, his great-uncle served as an inspiration for the character of the retired noncommissioned officer Khaim Yagudin, and certain features of both his mother and sister provided the basis for the image of the heroine, Rachel Rakhlenko-Ivanovsky. Even the narrator's voice with its distinctly Jewish intonation is modeled on Rybakov's aunt Ania (who recorded eight audiocassettes of her own reminiscences to help Rybakov with his book), although in *Heavy Sand* it actually belongs to a man, Rachel's son, Boris Ivanovsky.

Rybakov successfully used the first-person narration on behalf of a fictional character before, in his trilogy about Sergei Krasheninnikov (*Prikliucheniia Krosha* ["Krosh's Adventures"], *Kanikuly Krosha* ["Krosh's Holiday"], *Neizvestnyi soldat* ["The Unknown Soldier"], 1960–70), who is endowed with the authentic speech patterns of a 1960s Russian youth. Throughout the trilogy Krasheninnikov is growing up, as does Misha Poliakov, the hero of yet another Rybakov trilogy (*Kortik* [*The Dirk*], *Bronzovaia ptitsa* [*The Bronze Bird*], *Vystrel* ["The Shot"], 1948–75), with their views and attitudes changing accordingly. Rybakov's technique of showing characters in their development was skillfully applied in *Heavy Sand*, which follows the fortunes of a Jewish family over the time span of some 50 years. Both trilogies were either filmed or televised, often in several episodes per part, with Rybakov's working on the screen versions of his own books. This taught him the basic principles of broadcast drama, which he competently employed in *Heavy Sand*. The novel could be divided into rather self-sufficient units, with the reader's attention being focused on each family member in turn. Engaging domestic themes, such as complicated relations with neighbors and love affairs, are interspersed with work-related issues, which could easily become tedious but in fact never are. Thus, in the story of Yakov's arrest and trial for the alleged embezzlement at the shoe factory, the abundance of technical details even adds to the interest provided by the unexpected twists of the case. In such episodes Rybakov's expertise in the genre of production novel (see his *Voditeli* [1950; "The Drivers"], *Ekaterina Voronina* [1955], and *Leto v Sosniakakh* [1964; "Summer in Sosniaki"]) manifested itself to the full.

Chronologically *Heavy Sand* consists of three parts, consecutively describing Jewish life in pre-revolutionary Russia, in post-revolutionary Russia, and under the German invaders. This allows Rybakov to gradually build up the reader's empathy with the main characters to a degree when their execution, one by one, at the end of the book produces a truly devastating effect. *Heavy Sand* has been criticized for its linear structure and traditional plot—that is, too harmonious a form to reflect the genuine experience of the Holocaust. Such a criticism underestimates the fragmented nature of the narration, which now interrupts itself to make a digression or now runs ahead and prematurely discloses important components of the plot, instead of keeping the reader in suspense. This "homey" style, says M. Eidelman, "ultimately creates a disintegrative effect." On the other hand, *Heavy Sand* needed a fairly popular, widely accessible literary frame to get the message about the Holocaust across to as many people as possible. From this point of view even the novel's Soviet-style internationalism played a positive role by enabling those Russians, Belorussians, and Ukrainians whose relatives died because of the war to identify, at least partly, with the Nazi victims of Jewish origins. (It appears that Rybakov's choice of the fictional family name Ivanovsky, reminiscent of one of the most common Russian surnames, Ivanov, serves the same purpose.)

A close examination of *Heavy Sand* reveals that it is less Sovietized than people usually assume. Its imagery is based on three quotations from the Bible, strategically placed at the very beginning and at the very end of the novel. (Citing from the Bible in itself was a daring act in a country ruled by militant atheists.) The first explains the symbolism of heavy sand and hints that the author cannot speak freely (my grief and calamity "would be heavier than the sand of the sea: therefore my words are swallowed up," Job 6:3). The second (Genesis 29:20) reminds the reader of the biblical story of Rachel and Jakob, which has obvious parallels with *Heavy Sand*'s Rachel and Yakov. The slightly modified third (Joel 3.21) expresses Rybakov's attitude toward the Holocaust ("those who have spilled innocent blood shall never be forgiven") and toward the "Jewish question" as a whole (he meaningfully omitted the second half of the verse, "for the Lord dwelleth in Zion"). The novel's parabolic features become further reinforced when Rachel suddenly dissolves into thin air on her way to the partisans' camp, where she is leading the ghetto survivors after their rebellion. It is quite characteristic that the communist commander of the partisan detachment, who is not supposed to give credence to supernatural phenomena, seems to believe in Rachel's mysterious disappearance, although he prefers not to admit this openly. This scene graphically demonstrates that, contrary to what the communist ideology claims, certain things are simply beyond the communists' grasp. This is also confirmed by the final episode, when the same partisan commander asks the narrator whether the Hebrew inscription on the bilingual memorial gravestone to the ghetto victims is a correct translation of the neighboring Russian sentence. Although the Hebrew phrase has nothing to do with the Russian original, the narrator gives the commander the affirmative answer. This can be interpreted as a symbolic representation of Rybakov's discreet and successful attempt to fill the socialist-realist frame of *Heavy Sand* with powerful Jewish subtext.

The novel was translated into 39 languages and came out in 26 countries. The *Heavy Sand* files, including thousands of readers' letters, were donated by Rybakov to the University of Tel Aviv, which conferred on him an honorary Ph.D. degree.

—Andrei Rogachevskii

HEDDY AND ME
Memoir by Susan Varga, 1994

Heddy and Me (1994) is a collaborative autobiography that literally grew out of a narrative contract between a mother and daughter. Susan Varga had been reluctant to probe their European past, but in early 1990 she found to her surprise that, in fact, her mother, Heddy, wanted to talk about it, indeed had been "waiting for Susan" to help her do so. She wanted to talk not only about her life in hiding with the children during the Holocaust but also about being raped by Russian soldiers and much else. As the conversation proceeded, it became clear that for the daughter the issue of the Holocaust was inseparable from the issue of her relationship with her mother. The Holocaust had heavily shaped that relationship, and the process of exploring the catastrophe together—of seeing it from a relational vantage point—enabled the mother-daughter bond to mature. It allowed them to shed some of the tensions and misunderstandings that had impeded their relationship.

Varga began recording her mother's recollections in March 1990. At that point she was 47, and Heddy was 73. The sessions lasted for six months, after which they met with Gyuszi, Varga's stepfather, and her partner, Anne Coombs, in Hungary. The narrative interleaves four principal time perspectives. First is the period from Heddy's birth in 1916 to 1960, the point at which the narrative ends, bringing Heddy to age 44 and her daughter to age 17. Second is the present of the interview, the account of which includes commentary about the two women's experience of the narrating situation and about the way it impinges on their already complex relationship. Third is the post-interview return to Hungary, with its many probes into the memory of life before, during, and just after the war. Fourth is the writing present, which renders the interview phase and the return to Hungary as parts of the past the women share and provides a perspective from which the various pasts, together with the evolution of the torn but fond mother-daughter relationship, can be accorded a kind of provisional summation.

As Varga's early warning to her mother makes clear, this is not a simple story of the life of a mother-as-survivor: "I've told her it won't be her life story, not properly. It will be filtered through my reactions and thoughts, my second generation eyes." These "second generation eyes" belong to one for whom being a daughter involves a kind of existential doubleness: she is a daughter who seems to ascribe enormous causal power to the mother-daughter bond, but she is also a particular kind of daughter—the daughter of a Holocaust survivor. The book's epilogue provides a final and decisive twist. Varga tells of attending a conference called "Child Survivors of the Holocaust" and of its transformative impact on her. She writes of going to the conference: "I went as a member of the second generation. I came home a member of the first. I was there." She was not just the child of a survivor but a survivor herself, a child survivor. This put her in a dramatically revised relation to herself and to Heddy. Of the baby she was during the war, she says, ''I know who she is now. She is a child who survived the War, at the outer edges of the Holocaust. I can trace her through who I am now. She is my fears, my sense of displacement, my omnipresent sense of threat. She is also my resilience and accommodation, my will to find meaning and to make things work.'' After the trip to Hungary, Varga writes, ''Only recently have I started to think of Heddy and myself as part of something bigger.'' That something, of course, is the Holocaust. Toward the end of the return trip she senses ''a new ease, born of something shared, between Mother and me.'' The book's title is *Heddy and Me,* but the newfound sense of internal coherence and the commonality that has emerged through narrative collaboration occasion a change in Varga's use of the first-person pronoun. The last line of the book is ''We have things in common, Heddy and I.''

Heddy and Me is a distinguished, intense, somber, and carefully researched and structured work of personal and historical inquiry. Its concern with the Holocaust extends to such issues as the Jewish migrant experience in Australia, gender relations, and the nature of memory.

—Richard Freadman

HELDENPLATZ
Play by Thomas Bernhard, 1988

Thomas Bernhard's play *Heldenplatz* is the story of a Jewish professor who emigrated to Oxford in 1938 when Hitler invaded Austria. When he returns to Vienna 50 years later, he finds the country still rife with anti-Semitism. His wife thinks she hears the cheers from the Nazi rally that was held on Heldenplatz many years ago. Heldenplatz, or Heroes' Square, is a big, open plaza in the center of Vienna, near the former imperial palace. There, in March 1938, Adolf Hitler announced ''the completion of the most important act of my life, the entry of my homeland into the Great German Reich'' and was hailed by an enthusiastic crowd of some 300,000 Austrians. Unable to deal with his situation and his wife's madness, Professor Schuster commits suicide by jumping out of his apartment window onto Heldenplatz. The play deals with his family's response to his suicide and their fears for the future.

Heldenplatz, which premiered in November 1988, was written for the 100th anniversary of Vienna's most prestigious theatre, the Burgtheater. That year also marked the 50th anniversary of Hitler's triumphant arrival in Vienna. Several editorials called for the play to be banned because of its critique of Austria. The president of Austria at the time, Kurt Waldheim, himself a former Nazi official, also denounced the play, and neo-Nazis attempted to blockade the theater by dumping a heap of manure at the entrance. Bernhard, who died several months after the premiere, continued his vilification of

his native Austria in his will, where he strictly forbade the performance of any of his works in Austria for 70 years, except for the plays that were currently running at the Burgtheater. Those plays would then also be prohibited once their contracted run was over.

In this play, as in many of his others, Bernhard decries the idyllic, fairytale reputation of Austria as a quaint land of high culture and music. Instead, his characters rant about its prejudiced provincialism, calling it ''a brutal and stupid nation . . . a mindless, cultureless sewer which spreads its penetrating stench all over Europe.'' The deceased professor's brother, Robert, asserts that ''If they were honest, they would admit what they would most like to do to us today is exactly what they did fifty years ago—gas us . . . I don't delude myself. If they could, they would again today—without a great fuss—murder us.'' Ironically, however, the deceased professor, whom his relatives and housekeeper constantly quote, seems himself rather fascist in his treatment of his housekeeper, wife, and children, and in his outlook on humanity.

Bernhard, like several other contemporary Austrian writers (Peter Handke, **Paul Celan**) was influenced by the theories of the philosopher Ludwig Wittgenstein, who emphasized the unreliability of language as a means for communication. Bernhard's work also resembles Antonin Artaud's Theatre of Cruelty, which sought to shock audiences out of their everyday conformity and comfort zones. Bernhard's plays resemble those of Samuel Beckett's and other works of the Theatre of the Absurd in their stark settings, grotesque situations, and repetitious, exaggerated language. His plays also contain long monologues—similar to those in expressionist plays—that reveal the characters' inner obsessions. These rants are usually expressed to a silent listener who may occasionally comment on the speaker's torrent of words. Thus, the emphasis in the play is not so much on plot as on character development and the overall atmosphere and ideas of the play. For example, in the first scene, one hears the perspective of Mrs. Zittel, the housekeeper. She parrots the professor's rants, which reveal his tyrannical personality and pessimistic, even paranoid, obsessions. As she describes the professor's tyranny, she also behaves abusively towards another servant who is her subordinate. In the second scene, which takes place after Professor Schuster's burial, Robert raves about Austria's horrifying synthesis of Nazism and Catholicism. Occasionally, the professor's daughter Anna chimes in. In the final scene, the widow Schuster and her relatives sit down for a meal. Robert continues his harangue against the government, the church, society, the theater, and all high culture. The widow Schuster begins to hear the cheers of the mob on Heldenplatz again. The sound becomes more and more unbearable until she falls over onto the dinner table, presumably dead.

Significant themes in this and other plays by Bernhard include the moral decay of Austria, which comes to symbolize despair about Western civilization and the entire human condition; Nazism; death, especially by suicide; mental illness;

destructive family relations; and existential fear. Many critics see Bernhard as an uncompromising pessimist; others maintain that his dark view of humanity stems from a deeply rooted idealism that was disappointed by World War II and its aftermath. Waldheim's election to the Austrian presidency in 1986 seemed to confirm Bernhard's contention that Austrians have yet to thoroughly confront their Nazi past.

—Susan Russell

HEROD'S CHILDREN (Die größere Hoffnung)
Novel by Ilse Aichinger, 1948

Ilse Aichinger's first work, the novel *Herod's Children* (1963; *Die größere Hoffnung*, 1948), established her as a major figure in postwar German literature. Although the book deals with the atrocities of the war and the Holocaust, its symbolism (often surreal in character), its imagery (often drawn from dreams), and its use of parable set it apart from works by such contemporary writers as Wolfgang Borchert (*Draussen vor der Tür*, 1947; *The Man Outside*) and **Heinrich Boll** (*Wo warst du Adam?*, 1951; *Adam, Where Art Thou?*), who approached these topics more directly.

Aichinger's protagonists in *Herod's Children* are a group of Jewish children living in Vienna during World War II. Ellen, who plays a leading role in the novel, is half Jewish and shares a number of autobiographical similarities with Aichinger. When she is denied a visa to the United States, she joins the other children and shares in their games, hopes, and fears. Except for the painful death by suicide of Ellen's grandmother and the beating of the child Bibi by a Nazi police guard, Aichinger does not overtly point at the horrors of the Holocaust. Indeed, the chapter "Das grosse Spiel" ("The Great Play") is a parable not only about the persecution of the Jewish people, forever in search of a homeland, but also about Christians (the play depicts the Nativity story) who are persecuted because of their stand against evil. Aspects of the Holocaust are presented in many details that chillingly depict the brutal Nazi ideology that turns children without the "right grandparents"—they are Jews—into victims destined to die in concentration camps. Aichinger is impressive in her depiction of the children's naïveté. They still hope for a better future—dreaming about life as a dancer, soccer player, artistic director, and a housewife with seven children—and they fantasize that if they save a child from drowning they will again be permitted "to sit on benches" with non-Jews. Ironically, Ellen does rescue a child from drowning but nothing changes for the children. Inexorably they are confronted with the bleak reality threatening them: Ellen's grandmother forces her to help her commit suicide so that she will not fall into the hands of the Nazis; when Ellen proudly displays the Star of David, which she believes to be a symbol of life, not death, she is scorned by

the non-Jewish; furthermore, she is rejected by her Gentile Nazi father. Not knowing where to hide or escape since the borders are closed to them, the children make the cemetery their playground; it is a grim symbol of their future. Despite their fear and despair, the children continue to nurture their dreams and act them out in their plays, but at the novel's end Ellen is killed by a grenade and most of the other children are deported to a concentration camp.

The last chapter of *Herod's Children*, "Die groessere Hoffnung" ("The Greater Hope"), is also the German title of the book. It contrasts with the first chapter "Die grosse Hoffnung" ("The Great Hope"), which is mainly concerned with Ellen's hope for a visa allowing her to emigrate to the United States. In the last chapter the symbol of the building of a new bridge to reach across to other people and the symbols of light—especially of the morning star—seemingly reinforce Aichinger's message that while the body dies the soul survives. Despite the Christian aspect of the ending, however, *Herod's Children* is in fact a deeply sad and pessimistic novel about the Holocaust and the human condition. Not only are Jewish people killed, but Jan, a young foreign soldier and a friend of Ellen, is mortally wounded in one of the last battles of the war that takes on aspects of Armageddon. Furthermore, the novel's pessimism is deepened by the fact that Ellen and the other children die in the last days of the war when the Nazis are losing power. In *Herod's Children* Aichinger may be seen as trying to find a reason to explain the Holocaust, but the senselessness and brutality of the children's death echoes the novel's ultimate failure to find any satisfactory explanation.

—Renate Benson

HISTORY: A NOVEL (La storia: Romanzo)
Novel by Elsa Morante, 1974

The success of Elsa Morante's best-selling novel *La storia: Romanzo* (1974; *History: A Novel*, 1977) is perhaps best understood within the context of its thematic appeal and its publisher's marketing strategy, accentuated by the political tensions between the Italian right and left in the mid-1970s. It narrates the experiences of Ida Ramundo, her children, and their acquaintances in Rome from January 1941 through the summer of 1947. Other than the first and the last chapters, which are dated 19**, the seven remaining ones correspond to single years. They each open with a brief chronological commentary highlighting historical events, followed by a lyrical passage that negotiates the space between historical and fictional narration. Morante has referred to *History: A Novel* as a "work of poetry" and "an act of accusation against all the fascisms of the world." *History: A Novel* represents Morante's most articulate meditation on the Holocaust and its effects on Rome's Jewish community.

Inspired by her readings of Simone Weil, Morante first conceived of the novel toward the end of 1970 and the beginning of 1971. She completed the manuscript in 1973, and Einaudi published the book in 1974. As with her other works, *History* is an anti-conformist novel that resists facile categorization. The novel's polemical title alludes to the text's narratological and ideological concerns with the relationship between history and fiction. The private histories of those excluded from public history provide a compelling and necessary account for understanding History—always capitalized throughout the text—because the one without the other is incomplete. This dialectical identification is articulated through the formal juxtaposition of textbook history as fiction and fiction as history. Public history's representation as successive acts of violence perpetrated against the private unvoiced histories is reiterated in the novel's subtitle, which refers to History as "a scandal that has endured ten thousand years."

Morante bases many of the fictional episodes in the narrative on her personal experiences. A German soldier rapes Ida Ramundo, a widowed, half-Jewish schoolteacher, and nine months later she gives birth to Giuseppe [Useppe]. He is a magical and strange child who is representative of a poetic celebration of innocence. Ida also has an older son, Nino, from her marriage. He does not share Useppe's sensitivity to his environment, but instead seeks to change it. Just as her mother Nora had done, Ida lives in constant fear of racial persecution. She has always denied her Jewish identity—even going so far as to conceal from Nino his Semitic origins. As a result she is not arrested with the Roman Jews during the infamous deportation of 16 October 1943. Later she wanders through the deserted ghetto listening to the voices of the dead. When her home is destroyed by bombings she moves the family to a shelter in Pietralata. In this refuge they meet a Jewish anarchist named Davide Segre. He uses drugs to escape the present because, as he explains, "History, of course, is all an obscenity from the beginning, but years as obscene as these have never existed before." Davide is an authorial alter ego who articulates the horrors of the Holocaust. He understands History's scandal but ultimately succumbs to it by dying of an overdose. Nino joins the partisans and then, after the war, works in the black market. He is killed in an accident while being pursued by the police. History has bequeathed Useppe an early death from an epileptic seizure at the age of five. His passing reaffirms the impossibility of either poetry or innocence surviving in a violent world sustained by History's scandal. When Ida learns of Useppe's death she goes mad and is institutionalized. She dies nine years later.

Morante's lyrical prose emphasizes communication in the realist tradition. Despite employing a refined vocabulary the syntax is linear and accessible. The third-person female narrator's intrusive comments and questionable reliability challenge both the tenets of realist discourse and the conventions of the historical novel. Although the narrator resists omniscience by voicing the limitations of her knowledge, these affirmations reinforce her textual authority by subtly disporting the reader's textual dependence on her. Nevertheless, the narrator's subjectivity calls into question her reliability and mediates the textual opposition between History and fiction.

History: A Novel concludes with a brief bibliography in which Morante acknowledges those authors to whom she is indebted for providing documentation that inspired episodes in her narrative. She cites Giacomo Debenedetti's *16 ottobre 1943* (1959), Robert Katz's *Black Sabbath* (1969), Pino Levi Cavaglione's *Guerriglia nei Castelli Romani* (1945), Bruno Piazza's *Perché gli altri dimenticano* (1956), and two works by Nuto Revelli, *La strada del Davai* (1966) and *L'ultimo fronte* (1971). By framing her text within this academic discourse, Morante subverts generic categorizations and inserts *History* into History's bibliography.

—Piero Garofalo

HOLOCAUST
Poem by Charles Reznikoff, 1975

Holocaust (1975), an extended poem, or a recitative, by Charles Reznikoff, is the author's only work that focuses on the Holocaust. But, as Reznikoff expert and critic Martin Hindus argues in *Charles Reznikoff: A Critical Essay* (1977), "from one point of view, the whole of Reznikoff's long artistic life may be regarded as a preparation to cope with the challenge of such a subject." Reznikoff was considered one of the objectivist poets writing in the United States in the 1930s; as such, his poetry was characterized by concise language, attention to detail, sparse use of symbol and metaphor, and an emphasis on the uninterpreted image as the sole object of poetic focus. *Holocaust,* which was Reznikoff's last book of poems, bears all of these hallmarks.

Based wholly on archival records from the Nuremberg and Eichmann war trials, *Holocaust* offers a detached, nonjudgmental, and stark presentation of atrocities that took place during the war. The volume is divided into 12 sections: "Deportation," "Invasion," "Research," "Ghettos," "Massacres," "Gas Chambers and Gas Trucks," "Work Camps," "Children," "Entertainment," "Mass Graves," "Marches," and "Escapes." Each section consists of short numbered poems that describe specific events collected and culled from the historical records of the two trials.

Throughout *Holocaust* Reznikoff offers no commentary on the events he depicts. Rather he allows his lean and seemingly rudimentary recapitulations to speak for themselves. In so doing, he masterfully demands equal and full engagement from his reader. Consider, for example, the following excerpts from the section of the book titled "Children":

Once, among the transports, was one with
    children—two freight
cars full.
The young men sorting out the belongings of
    those taken to the
gas chambers
had to undress the children—they
    were orphans—
and then take them to the "lazarette."
There the S.S. men shot them.

. . . .

Women guards at the women's section of the
    concentration camp
were putting little children into trucks
to be taken away to the gas chambers
and the children were screaming and crying,
    "Mamma, Mamma,"
even though the guards were trying to give
    them pieces of candy to
quiet them.

By withholding judgment and offering only the image itself, Reznikoff forces the reader to interpret its significance on his or her own. Indeed, this quality of restraint makes the poem stylistically pathbreaking and tests the sensitivity, even the humanity, of its readers.

Reznikoff developed his objectivist technique when writing an earlier recitative titled *Testimony,* which testifies to injustices experienced by common, ordinary men and women in the United States between 1885 and 1915. *Testimony* was also based on trial records, and it again presented in concentrated verse glimpses of oppression. But the two texts differ in important ways, most notably in their use and omission of proper names. Whereas *Testimony* tells the stories of individual people occasionally even identified by proper name, *Holocaust* depicts only nameless groups of Jews suffering all forms of abuse. The effect of this is not simply to witness the denial of humanity and individuality that marks genocide, but as importantly to remind all readers of the possibility of similar acts occurring to anyone, at any time, in any place. As Reznikoff himself explained, "I believe in writing about the object itself, and I let the reader, or listener, draw his own conclusions."

Charles Reznikoff waited 30 years after the Holocaust before he was able to write about it, before he felt able to tackle a topic of such enormity. During those three decades the subject had been covered and even capitalized upon by writers, filmmakers, and journalists so often that to render it sincerely and objectively—without sentimentality, without exploitation, without melodrama—presented a formidable challenge. But Reznikoff was able to do so and, as a result, provided some of the most powerful poetic testimony to the Holocaust in American literary history.

—Heather Hathaway

THE HOLOCAUST KINGDOM
Memoir by Alexander Donat, 1965

Written with the insight of a skilled journalist, Alexander Donat's memoir *The Holocaust Kingdom* (1965) describes several incidents that have become well known in Holocaust studies. Commenting, for example, on the transport of children from the orphanage of **Janusz Korczak** in the Warsaw Ghetto, he recalls Korczak leading the little ones in an orderly procession to the trains and then joining them for their journey to Treblinka. Perhaps because Donat was himself a father, he was especially sensitive to the plight of the children. He saw his two-year-old boy go from a playful toddler to a child paralyzed with fear. Whenever Donat left the room, he relates, his son would "tighten his grip on me, uttering only the single word: 'Daddy.'" Here the memoir reveals a definitive dimension of the assault that characterized the Holocaust, an assault on the father as a father by rendering him powerless to respond to his little one's cry of "Daddy."

Donat recalls another commonly related incident, included, for example, in **Emmanuel Ringelblum**'s *Notes from the Warsaw Ghetto.* According to the story, a German who came into the ghetto was about to take away a mother's child when he turned and answered her pleas by saying, "If you can guess which of my eyes is a glass eye, I shall spare your child." When she correctly identified the artificial eye, he asked her how she could tell it was the one. She answered, "It looks more human than the other one." Here and elsewhere in his memoir, Donat shows that in their assault on the human image the Nazis lost their humanity.

Much of Donat's memoir is a remembrance of the unraveling of his world and of his identity. He writes, "The very bases of our faith had crumbled: the Polish fatherland whose children we had always considered ourselves; two thousand years of Christianity, silent in the face of Nazism; our own lie-ridden civilization. We were despairingly alone, stripped of all we had held sacred." What he laments is a situation in which, in order to remain a human being, one could not live as a human being but was forced to die as a human being. One of the few to survive the Warsaw Ghetto Uprising, Donat points out that, unlike any other uprising, this one was not carried out with the aim of victory. Rather, he says, "it was undertaken solely for death with dignity." Pursuing further the question of what it means to be a human being, Donat recalls the moment when he was inducted into Majdanek: "I looked at my number: 7,115. From that moment I ceased to be a man." Hence the advice he received from another inmate to "forget who and what you were." That forgetting, however, is precisely what Donat seeks to overcome in the writing of his memoir.

Donat overcomes the loss of his humanity by remembering how other people dealt with the assault. He recalls, for example, the importance of washing one's face, even with snow or dirty water, just to affirm the value of the face and therefore of the person. "Those who failed to wash every day," he observes, "soon died." He also recalls the profoundly lifesaving significance of the smallest act of kindness in that realm where kindness was all but unknown. Recalling a family he met in Radom, for instance, he writes, "What brought me back to life, pulled me up out of the depths of despair was warmth, compassion, kind words the Melcers gave me." Thus, Donat's human identity was awakened by the humanity of others.

And yet for Donat, as for many other survivors, the return to the world of humanity at the end of the war posed immense difficulties. "I was afraid of my new freedom," he explains. "I was afraid of returning to normal life and its activities because they seemed like desecration of the memory of those who had perished . . . But most of all I feared going home." Why did he fear home? He did so because the foundations of the home—the idea of the home—had been reduced to ashes, along with the mothers, fathers, and children who constituted the home. With this memory Donat reveals a difficulty confronted not only by him but by all humanity. Both emerged from the Holocaust in a state of exile.

—David Patterson

HOPE IS THE LAST TO DIE: A COMING OF AGE UNDER NAZI TERROR (Nadzieja umiera ostatnia)
Memoir by Halina Birenbaum, 1967

Hope Is the Last To Die, published in English translation in 1996, is the autobiographical account of Polish-Jewish writer Halina Birenbaum's adolescent journey through the horrors of the Holocaust. Beginning with the occupation of Warsaw, she recounts the constant fear and dangers of the ghetto and later the camps: Majdanek, Auschwitz, Ravensbrück, and Neustadt-Glewe. In outline it is a familiar story, but in her telling it is fresh, startling, and powerful. First published in Polish in 1967, *Hope Is the Last To Die* has been through three editions in that language and translated into several more, including multiple editions in English and German.

Like any successful travel narrative, it has a primary level that is spatial and geographical. It also, however, describes a journey on psychological, emotional, and spiritual levels. Set against external events—imposed and controlled by the alien forces of the Nazi occupiers—are the narrator's personal and internal experiences, which punctuate her accelerated growth as an individual. These experiences are primarily built around a series of personal relationships, first with family members, the most important of which is with her remarkable mother. When all the members of her immediate family have been exterminated or have disappeared, there are periods of isolation and alienation. Each time, however, she overcomes the inclination to despair and resignation and reaffirms her belief in and attachment to humanity through the establishment of new relationships, all of which reflect the need of the adolescent narrator to recreate her essential familial linkages.

Although it was written more than 20 years after the events, Birenbaum attempts to maintain the naïve perspective of a young adolescent. This difficult stylistic challenge has eluded many highly accomplished writers, but Birenbaum manages it with considerable success, primarily because her natural narrative voice has the directness, humility, and unpretentious sincerity of a child. Meanwhile, the pacing—combined with naturalistic detail of description, psychologically astute analysis, and emotional sincerity—carry the reader eagerly along.

The tone of the work is one of a profound belief in the enduring value of humanity and in the ability of the human spirit to overcome the most overwhelmingly evil obstacles. The writing is not artistically sophisticated—it occasionally lacks structure, is frequently uneven in its delivery of descriptive passages, and its characters are not equally well drawn. At the same time, there are characters and scenes that are unforgettable and powerfully drawn. In particular, the psychological description of the author's mother and of the mother-daughter relationship stands out as a noteworthy achievement. There are also scenes from the ghetto, transport trains, and camps that are simply unforgettable for their emotional power and sharpness of detail. For example, in a delicately understated passage reminiscent of Russian writer Varlam Shalamov's bleakest accounts of Soviet labor camps, Birenbaum describes hiding for hours on narrow shelves in a closet to avoid detection by the Nazis. Bringing together a remarkable mix of poignancy, tension, and absurd horror, she recounts how the younger children on the shelves above are unable to refrain from urinating on her, and she, a girl of 12, is unable to move or even to sigh. Like so many people of her generation, she was robbed of her youth, and one of the key sources of dramatic motivation in the story is the constant image of her forced to pretend to be 17 years old when she is actually only 13; the success of the stratagem will determine whether she lives or dies.

Obviously the writing of such a personal account is both painful and redemptive. Much of the success of the work lies in the balance Birenbaum strikes between the two processes. She does not refrain from describing evil acts and their perpetrators and effects in plain language. She also does not shield the reader from the fact that not all the evil was carried out by Nazis and describes the despicable things done by Jews and Poles as well. But, her true motivation is suggested in the title of her account and in the descriptions of acts of courage, selflessness, and compassion on the part of Jews, Poles, and others. She even tries to locate humane virtue in some of her oppressors and successfully puts a human face on both perpetrators and victims; her characters are human first and ethnically or racially grouped only secondarily. In a recent untitled poem she questions whether it is possible, through love and tears, to burn the old forms of evil and from their ashes to resurrect something better and of higher value. Birenbaum concludes that since she does cry and does love, it must indeed be possible.

—Allan Reid

HOUSE OF DOLLS (Beit ha-bubot)
Novel by Ka-Tzetnik 135633, 1953

Gershon Shofman, one of Israel's preeminent authors, once wrote that *House of Dolls* (1955) by Ka-Tzetnik 135633 is "a holy book." Certainly the most famous and widely read of his novels, *House of Dolls,* originally published in Hebrew as *Beit ha-bubot* in 1953, centers on a young Jewish girl, Daniella Preleshnik, in reality the writer's own sister. Three days before the outbreak of the war, the 14-year-old is captured in Poland while on a trip at the end of the school year and transferred to a Nazi women's camp, the ironically named Camp Labor Via Joy, where she is forced to become a prostitute for German soldiers. Formally, the plot is based on the notebook kept by Daniella.

The story is told in flashback, and the narrator is Daniella's brother Harry, who is assigned to the sick bay, although he had never graduated from medical school and although there are no medicines, no beds, no instruments, and, most importantly, no patients. Instead, he is charged with overseeing the burial of the piles of Jewish bodies, all the while struggling not to surrender to the impending debasement of life that turns those interned into *Mussulmen,* or "living skeletons." These are the deformed, crippled, near dead men who are the embodiment of human misery and lost hope. Over the course of the novel Harry loses all of those who are close to him, including his friend Tedek, once a member of the ghetto resistance who is now enamored with Daniella.

As the girls enter the camp and are directed to their division, they are first sterilized and then inducted into the abhorrent master-slave relationship of the so-called House of Dolls, for which they are simply not prepared. The extreme sexual abuse and their treatment as mere objects in this brothel clearly illustrate the familiar trope of Ka-Tzetnik's series of novels: the Holocaust as a unique event and as the most horrifying and obscene of modern situations. We learn, for instance, that the "dolls" must be in perfect physical condition for the visiting soldiers, those en route to the Russian front or those coming from the transit terminus, who stop by to prey upon the weak and vulnerable Jewesses. In addition, the discovery of a venereal infection means immediate doom, for any damage results in transportation to the ovens. Worse, if the concentration camp guards or other "German warriors" leave unsatisfied with their entertainment, they need only convey their displeasure and report the number tattooed on the girl's breast. In the event that three such complaints are recorded, death is instant.

In a similar vein, we read that every girl must smile to show her appreciation of the pervasive cruelty meted out day and night, knowing that her life depends on seeming happy and content for the "guests." One could venture the observation that, in portraying such events and situations, there exists the risk of trivialization and objectionable eroticism, of seducing the reader to participate voyeuristically in the sexual victimization presented rather than to focus on the horror perpetrated. Still, it is equally clear that on a different reading the text gravitates to the other central theme hovering over the novel, the facility of the women-victims to survive spiritually the gory dehumanization of the Nazis in spite of the beatings and rape. In fact, among the pages of the book can be found various instances of the will to live and to preserve one's sanity and dignity. One is the tale of Tzevia, an orthodox girl from the seminary of Beit Ya'acov who purposefully and stubbornly refuses to acquiesce to her tormentors' advances, although she knows the result of such repudiation. Inevitably, Tzevia is bludgeoned to her death, standing naked in the execution arena, defiant and strong, admirably victorious in keeping her chasteness and virtue whole, "as a tough shell." Another striking case is Daniella, who keeps her head up and who against the odds upholds her moral integrity. As the novel draws to a close, the heroine seeks to escape her dreaded existence by sauntering toward the barbed wire fence. Not surprisingly, she is shot by an SS sentry who knows that he will be rewarded with three days of leave for ending her bid for freedom. Following the murder, he bursts out singing, intoxicated with euphoria, for "Tomorrow he's going to his family. Maybe—to mother, waiting at home. Maybe—to sister, or—to little only—daughter who he so pines for as he stands here on the bridge."

Doubtless, the dark, violent barbarism of the German officers knows no bounds, and there is a panoply of monstrosities. Elsewhere, the same sentry clobbers Tzevia's sister Hanna to death in a methodical, gut-wrenching display. To the pious woman's shouts of "God all mighty, save me," he responds with well-directed and vicious blows to her head, legs, arms, and ankles, watching calmly as she writhes in pain, plunging her teeth into the ground, and tearing out her hair. Afterward he coolly rests to devour his sandwich. And there are the medical experiments conducted by the German professor on the girls, including artificial inseminations, tests on twins, and coerced abortions and castrations, or the raw cruelty of Elsa, the brothel overseer.

While the narrative limns in graphic detail Daniella's, Harry's, and the other inmates' ordeals and sexual exploitation, Ka-Tzetnik ensures that the teenager's memories of family love and tradition engraved deeply in her psyche are not erased. To wit, as a counterpoint the author undercuts his sequences of sheer Dantean hell with the quotidian innocence and loyalty that guyed Daniella and her brother Moni's life before the war in the town of Kongressia. Among other things, this serves to further underscore the nauseating degradation they are subjected to and to emphasize the two realities, each stridently polar from the other.

Through the succession of vignettes padded with interior monologues, Ka-Tzetnik pulls the reader into Daniella's world, dramatizing and compounding the sadism to which the protagonist must adapt but ultimately cannot. It is interesting that the scenes of battery and psychical defilements are inscribed in a nonjudgmental, neutral manner, perhaps as a tacit acknowledgment that what is being chronicled is at the peak of the objective mode since the satanic acts speak volumes and do not require a braiding of the subjective.

—Dvir Abramovich

HOW GERMAN IS IT
Novel by Walter Abish, 1980

How German Is It could be termed a postmodern novel about historical amnesia—more precisely, the amnesia post-World War II Germany chose to affect about its Nazi years and their political and psychological implications. While not overtly a book about the Holocaust, Walter Abish's novel nonetheless unfolds against the backdrop of the Holocaust: the newly constructed town of Brumholdstein rises from the location that used to house the concentration camp of Durst and a mass grave is discovered in the center of town. Tellingly, the epigraph of *How German Is It* is taken from Jean-Luc Godard and reads, "What is really at stake is one's image of oneself," perfectly characterizing the Germans' intent to develop a new communal and cultural identity for a new, postwar Germany. While criticizing these German attempts at self-reinvention, however, the novel can also be read as a critique on the dynamics of identity formation, both personal and societal.

In *How German Is It* Abish creates a German reality characterized by copies that seemingly repeat themselves in endless succession, while the originals have been destroyed:

> Next. Essentially a pleasant aimless stroll, looking—as if for the first time—at Würtenburg's buildings, at the war memorial, the churches, the objects in the shopwindows: lamp shades, silverware, carpets, radio, furniture, food, all attractively displayed—although not with the French flair to which he had, after only a six-month absence from Germany, grown so attached. It was something that his fellow countrymen, despite all their theories on aesthetics, their determined search for perfection, seemed to lack. In any event, it was difficult to believe that life could ever have been different here. And that these buildings were all recently constructed.

Evident in the casually laconic, truncated last sentence of this paragraph is a societal tendency to attempt normalization, to persuade the casual observer that the solaces inherent in pleasing displays reflect harmlessness and quotidian ordinariness. In the case of postwar Germany, this rhetoric of promulgating an innocuous self-image, of course, involves erasing 12 years of Nazi terror and, in the case of the buildings mentioned in the paragraph above, replacing all the structures that were destroyed with virtual replicas.

Thus, *How German Is It* constructs a kind of Germany less dependent on empirical truth that would be verifiable or falsifiable than on clichés about Germany that reveal as much—if not more—about the "real" Germany as any putatively objective documentary would. In this methodological approach, answering questions is less important than consecutively asking the right ones. Abish addresses this asymptotic relationship of the text to the events it depicts: "I sense that what I invent will become 'real'. . . that writing can and frequently does construct what is imminently about to take place. The question is, how free are we to invent? To embrace the 'real' events is to remain innocent. For it is to embrace the answers. That is, essentially, what the institutions in Western society churn out. A great many answers that authenticate the 'real' and 'familiar' world." Abish does not choose Germany (the nation or geographic entity) for mimetic reasons (for example, in order to write a novel "about" Germany) but for the paradigmatic quality this linguistic referent encloses with reference to the weight of historical embeddedness and transmission that is being born by signs. "Germany" is an example, says Abish: "For the most part, novels about Germany, or those simply located in Germany, without having to raise the question of 'How German is it?' resolve the unspoken question by explaining Germany. . . . They explain Germany away and thereby provide satisfaction." Not providing satisfaction is one way of foregrounding the impossibility of escaping history, especially when underwritten by a focus on the German desire to escape the specters of the past through the projected blessings of the future.

In its accumulation of detail and its simultaneous refusal to interpret for the reader (while, however, insinuating that meaning does accrue from these details), the novel does not display what could traditionally be called a unified narrative or a protagonist. Its main character—besides the ever-questioning and unreliable narrator—is Ulrich Hargenau, a writer and former student of Brumhold (modeled on the German philosopher Martin Heidegger, whose writings became entangled with Nazi ideology). Ulrich's father is executed by the Nazis due to his opposition to Adolf Hitler, and Ulrich lives in Paris after the war (as opposed to his brother Helmuth, who has become a nationally known architect). Ulrich's former wife, Paula, features as a member of the left-wing Einzieh group (possibly modeled after the Red Army Faction of the 1970s and '80s), which is engaged in a bombing campaign (that, incidentally, also affects one of Helmuth's buildings). It is this force field of German Nazi past, postwar reactions of the Germans to their history (different as they may be for Ulrich and the other Germans depicted), and the political fallout of both of these features (the novel insinuates that there is a causal link between the emergence of the Einzieh group and Germany's relationship to its past) that characterizes the novel's narrative situation.

—Stefan Gunther

HUMAN BEHAVIOUR IN THE CONCENTRATION CAMP: A MEDICAL AND PSYCHOLOGICAL STUDY (Het Duitse concentratiekamp: Een Medische en Psychologische studie)
Memoir and Study by Elie Aron Cohen, 1952

Human Behaviour in the Concentration Camp: A Medical and Psychological Study was originally written by Elie Aron Cohen as his doctoral thesis in 1952, seven years after his liberation from Ebensee. Although the scientific-sounding title might lead the reader to believe that it is merely a behavioral analysis based upon psychological research per se, it must be emphasized that the study is a result of the author's personal experiences as a prisoner in the concentration camps. As he states in the preface, "When I wrote my doctor's thesis in 1952 . . . everything I had suffered from in the concentration camps was still vivid in my mind."

Written in Dutch and published in 1954, it was then issued in an English translation in 1988 with a foreword by the British psychoanalyst Dinora Pines as well as a newly written preface by the author. Although Cohen had been a prisoner in various camps, including transport and death camps, as well as on a death march, he states that is his intent to write as objectively as possible, and he succeeds in doing so. The book is meticulously researched and very detailed. It is divided into four major sections: (1) general aspects of the camps; (2) medical aspects, including diseases of the prisoners as well as experiments conducted by Nazi physicians; (3) psychological aspects of the prisoners; and (4) psychological aspects of the SS.

In the first section, in order to acquaint the reader with life in a concentration camp, Cohen discusses general aspects of the camps. He begins by analyzing the differences between three categories of individuals: those who were never in a camp of any sort, those who were in other types of camps, such as prisoner-of-war or labor camps, and those who were in concentration camps themselves. Other topics he covers in this section include a discussion of the hierarchies of prisoners as well as SS personnel and the organization and layout of the camps, much of which is based upon the findings of **Eugene Kogon** in his book *Der SS Staat*. Cohen also discusses aspects of extermination, which is amplified by the use of statistics enumerating dates and the numbers of prisoners moved to

other camps as well as those who escaped or were released or executed. In this section, which is based upon his own experiences as well as on research from such sources as Ella Lingens-Reiner (*Prisoners of Fear*), G.M.Gilbert (*Nuremberg Diary*), and **Viktor E. Frankl** (*Ein Psycholog erlebt das K.Z*), Cohen concludes that there remains an emotional gulf between survivors of the concentration camps and those who never experienced imprisonment within them.

The second section is about medical aspects of life in the camps. Cohen focuses on diseases suffered by the prisoners as well as on medical experiments conducted by Nazi physicians. Because he administered care as a physician in the camps, he is able to speak with authority. He describes in detail several of the diseases the prisoners suffered, again providing statistics regarding the numbers of diseases in the camps and the mortality rates. In one part of this section he goes into great detail on the food given to the prisoners, both in the camps and in the ghettos, including data on calories and on the physical effects of chronic malnutrition. He compares malnutrition in the camps to the effects of starvation suffered by American soldiers in Japanese internment camps. One of his findings is that, secondary to malnutrition and starvation, some medical conditions, such as asthma and high blood pressure, seem to go into a stage of remission. In another part of this section Cohen gives details regarding medical experiments. In this he relies upon **Miklos Nyiszli** (*SS Obersturmführer Docteur Mengele*) and others, including Lingens-Reiner and **Olga Lengyel**, who in the book *Five Chimneys* wrote about her experiences as a physician in Auschwitz. He also relies to a great extent on testimony given before the International Military Tribunal in Nuremberg in 1945–46.

The third section deals with psychological aspects of the prisoners, and the fourth section deals with psychological aspects of the SS. Cohen's methodology in examining behavior in the camps is based upon Freudian analysis as set forth in works such as *Totem and Taboo, Civilization and Its Discontents, The Ego and the Id, Group Psychology and the Analysis of the Ego,* and *Mourning and Melancholia*. As regards the prisoners, Cohen finds that there were three psychological stages of adaptation to life in the camps. If the prisoner successfully passed through these stages, barring selection for the gas chambers or other circumstances beyond his control, there was at least some hope for survival.

Cohen analyzes the mental status of both the prisoners and the SS in depth. According to his findings, they were complete opposites. For example, the prisoners had no strong leader with whom they could identify and were in a situation in which their sense of identity gave way to a primal need for sustenance. Thus, they experienced a strengthening of the ego, or sense of their own needs, which resulted in a weakening of the superego. The SS, on the other hand, were following a strong leader and had a strong sense of identity. Their egos, therefore, gave way to their superegos, albeit criminal superegos. As a result, again largely based upon his reading of Freud, Cohen concludes that there was a crowd rather than a group mentality among the prisoners, while the SS, strongly united in its adherence to the state and its policies, had an unwavering group mentality.

Cohen obviously could not cover all aspects of the causes of the Holocaust. He does not mention the influence of socioeconomic factors or of Teutonic mythology on the Nazi mentality. Nevertheless, he fulfills his aim of giving a clear, objective, and well-researched analysis of aspects of and reasons for the human behavior that took place in the concentration camps.

—Diane Plotkin

THE HUMAN SPECIES (L'Espèce humaine)
Memoir by Robert Antelme, 1947

In *The Human Species* (1992; *L'Espèce humaine,* 1947) Robert Antelme traces his life as a *kommando* at Gandersheim, a particularly brutal subcamp of Buchenwald, then on a death march, and finally at Dachau's liberation. As he writes, the "horror in it is not gigantic. At Gandersheim there was no gas chamber, no crematorium. The horror there was darkness, absolute lack of any kind of landmark, solitude, unending oppression, slow annihilation. The motivation underlying our struggle could only have been a furious desire, itself almost always experienced in solitude; a furious desire to remain me, down to the very end." And this is the theme of the book: the nature of being human and its "indivisible oneness."

Throughout *The Human Species* this refrain is repeated. Toward the end Antelme writes that, even though he and his fellow inmates look like animals, they are human and "the distance separating us from another species is still intact." The Holocaust tests "the variety of relationship between men" and "at the point where we approach our limits" appears, for Antelme, the realization that "there are not several human races, there is one human race" and it is "because we're men like them that the SS will finally prove powerless before us." Even death reaffirms this since "the worst of victims cannot do otherwise than establish that, in its worst exercise, the executioner's power cannot be other than one of the powers men have, the power of murder. He can kill a man, but he can't change him into something else." This is similar to **David Rousset**'s leftist understanding of the Holocaust as a resource to stimulate a fight against capitalism and fascism and to other readings that attempt to redeem or, in Lawrence Langer's phrase, "pre-empt the Holocaust." The book is full of human actions, and Antelme finds proof of his thesis and the basis of resistance in the most human of functions—eating, defecating, and urinating.

This theme is heightened throughout the text by the constant discussion of power. The *kapo*s in the main were not political prisoners, with some sense of solidarity, but rather criminals, "murders, thieves, swindlers, sadists and black marketeers" who reveled in their (relative) power and privilege. He describes the process of becoming a *kapo* and the actions of bad and corrupt *kapo*s. Yet their humanity (not in the sense of "being humanitarian" but in the sense of "being a human being") comes through.

National identity also is a ground for Antelme's resistance. A rail car from the SNCF (the French national railway) raises the spirits of his colleagues: "the wind which wafts the west into our faces doublecrosses the SS, so do the four letter SNCF which he didn't even notice." And at liberation, when the prisoners are commanded in German, they shout, "You sons of bitches, we're free! Talk to us in French!" Part of being human seems to be, for Antelme, the sense of national belonging. In the final pages, this is both affirmed and transcended as a Russian survivor passes him a cigarette and they talk in their common language, German. "Ja" is the last word of the text, an affirmation, in German, of the unity of the human race, and yet, at the same time, a reminder of the attempt to destroy this unity.

Despite his argument, Antelme is also aware that the camps are a world away. He beings his account by suggesting that "no sooner would we begin to tell our story than we would be choking over it. And then, even to us, what we had to tell would start to seem unimaginable." These "stifling words," however, remain a call for human unity.

—Robert Eaglestone

I

I AM ALIVE!
Memoir by Kitty Hart, 1961

I Am Alive! is Kitty Hart's first account of her and her mother's survival during World War II—hiding in Germany and Poland, then in Auschwitz and an array of camps and journeys in the collapsing Reich.

Hart came from a Jewish family in Bielsko, Poland. She was very active, a swimming champion who enjoyed and excelled at all sorts of sports. After the invasion of Poland, her family fled to Lublin in eastern Poland and tried to escape to the Soviet Union. Their attempt, however, failed, and they returned to Bielsko, eventually hiding with a local count. A Catholic priest provided Hart and her mother with false papers, and they "hid" as foreign workers in Germany. Soon, however, they were discovered—possibly betrayed—and she and her mother were interrogated and sent to Auschwitz. On her first day there, Hart met a gypsy who told her that "you will be one of the very few to see freedom again. Remember, you must never lose your will to live." And, indeed, Hart did not. Her time in hiding had taught her to be very alert and self-sufficient, and in Auschwitz she also showed a great deal of courage and initiative: she smuggled in potatoes and dodged forced labor by hiding during the day with a resting night shift. Finally, she got a job in Kananda, which provided her and her mother with food to smuggle back into the main camp. Hart was also lucky: her mother worked as a nurse in the camp hospital and was able to care for and protect her when she fell ill with typhus. It is her work in Kanada that kept Hart and her mother alive, and she is very aware of the bleak irony of this.

Hart's memoir relates some Auschwitz stories that are familiar from other accounts: Alma Rose's concerts, the woman who killed Rapporfurher Schillinger, and the escape, recapture, and execution of Mala. She also describes a gassing in some detail, one of the earliest accounts to do so. As the Eastern front moved closer, she and others were taken from the camp. As she leaves she reflects that, although the Nazis stole her school years (a constant theme of the book), the camp had "been a good schooling. Only here one could get to know the true character of a person, not like in civilisation where people tend to hid behind masks."

Toward the end of the war, Hart and her mother were among the prisoners taken from Auschwitz in trucks. Then began a longer and bewildering period of movements and camps and work, all under the shadow of increasingly frightened guards and with almost no food. Hart, her mother, and the other Auschwitz girls band together and get more vocal as they are moved throughout the collapsing Reich. They refuse, for example, to enter a bomb shelter they suspect is a gas chamber;

at one point, starving, they beg to be allowed into a camp at whose gates they have been halted. Finally, they are liberated. They head off into the local town to find food but also to seek revenge. Hart, who has acquired a dagger, and others break into a house, and they find the family hiding in the cellar: "'Come on kill them, what are you waiting for?' ... I don't know why, but suddenly I simply could not do it." They do, however, smash up house after house: "It was certainly hard work and I ached all over. But how satisfying destruction can be!" Her home and the rest of her family—except an uncle in England—were destroyed, so she sets her face to the future, "to get on with the almost impossible task of wiping out the past and coming to terms with the future." The story of this is taken up, to some extent, in her book *Return to Auschwitz*.

I Am Alive! is one of the clearest of the camp memoirs. Hart is uncompromising in her account of the terrors she and her mother had to face and how she endured them.

—Robert Eaglestone

I CANNOT FORGIVE
Memoir by Rudolf Vrba (with Alan Bestic), 1963

Like many memoirs that have been written by the survivor with a ghostwriter, Rudolf Vrba's *I Cannot Forgive* begins in medias res with an account of Heinrich Himmler's visit to Auschwitz on 17 July 1942. This visit leads to the death of an inmate called Yankel Meisel because three buttons were missing from his tunic.

Vrba's actual story begins in Slovakia and with his attempts to escape the country before it is too late. After a number of close shaves, however, he is eventually captured and sent to Maidanek. He manages to get a job in the kitchens, but, when offered the chance to do farm work, he volunteers: "'Anywhere's better than this dump' I told him 'Auschwitz couldn't be worse.'"

After three months in Auschwitz, he was assigned to the Kanada, processing the stolen goods and food. It is there that his suspicions and the rumors are confirmed: "I was in a death factory." From August 1942 to June 1943 he worked on the ramps at which the transports arrived. He became a scribe and had his own room, chair, and table. This also put him in a position to have some knowledge about events in the camp among both captors and victims. Particularly harrowing is his account of his actions when he heard that the Czech Jews from Theresienstadt were to be killed. He attempts to persuade Freddy Hirsch to lead a revolt. Hirsch asks for an hour to think, and when Vrba returns, Hirsch has taken poison. The Jews are all killed.

His accounts of Auschwitz are detailed. A hardy man, full of initiative, tenacious and angry, Vrba manages to survive. He eats anything, "even if the bread contained sawdust and the tea looked like sewer water." He smuggles food and other tokens between men and women in the camp: "It brought me small rewards from the kapos and to a certain extent I was sheltered from unnecessary punishment." Although one such attempt leads to a vicious beating, he does not reveal the couples' name and survives. He even has a doomed love affair himself. Indeed, one of the interesting things about his testimony is the vision that it offers of those prisoners in the camp who had some positions of minimal authority. It is also concerned with the ways in which people are brutalized into becoming *kapos* and other figures of authority. He also tried to maintain some sort of count of how many were murdered by the Germans.

Vrba, however, is one of the few who escaped. He explains the details of his escape in great detail. He and Fred Wetzler hid in a ditch in the timber yard, covered by timber for three days and nights. Then they escape by walking to Slovakia. Vrba wrote a report that he gave to the Jewish communities in Slovakia and Hungary and then to the Papal Nuncio. After this he joined the partisans in Slovakia. The final pages of his account describe an attack on a building where 700 SS men were based: he writes that during the attack, "tears of happiness were coursing down my cheeks. I was running forwards not backwards."

Vrba went on to be a professor of pharmacology in Britain and Canada. His style is already scientific—detailed and objective, even about his own feelings. More than this, as a good scientist his text is full of details and references to other witnesses (**Filip Müller,** for example) and to external events. Moreover, he is never afraid to name the perpetrators when he can. The 1963 edition has an epilogue concerning postwar trials and two appendixes: one is his deposition for the Adolf Eichmann trial and the other is an account of Kurt Gerstein's report on Belzec. All these serve to support and corroborate Vrba's account. But perhaps most importantly the book is the story behind the Vrba-Wetzler report, which helped "in the mobilisation of the worlds conscience" and is "one of the key documents of the Holocaust."

—Robert Eaglestone

I KEEP RECALLING: THE HOLOCAUST POEMS OF JACOB GLATSTEIN
Poems by Jacob Glatstein, 1993

In 1934 Jacob Glatstein traveled to Lublin, Poland, to visit his ailing mother. His reminiscence about his voyage is contained in two volumes of elegant prose, *Ven Yash iz Geforen*

(1938; "When Yash Went Forth"; an earlier version was serialized in the Yiddish magazine *In Zikh*) and *Ven Yash iz Gekumen* (1940; "When Yash Arrived"), in which he narrates his personal dilemma of being a universal Jew in an anti-Semitic world. Through a series of interior monologues and dialogues in which strangers tell their stories to a seemingly silent protagonist, Glatstein bares a shocking discovery, namely the Jew, who in his historical wanderings embodies the ideal of international siblinghood, is in the end what he was in the beginning, a *yidele,* "a little Jew." The paradox becomes more compelling when in-your-face Jew hatred causes the narrator to hide his ethnicity from Nazi youths on a train ride to Poland, though his inner self wants to assert *Ich bin a Yid.* The writer's confessional struggle—that is, his Jewish selfhood was parsed and defined by an outside world—alludes to the fate of East European Jewry on the eve of World War II. And on the twisted journey to Auschwitz, the world was silent and, worse, indifferent.

Glatstein's Holocaust poems are meant to confront, shock, understand, give solace, and mend a shattered Jewish world. His poetry is informed by an authenticity that is anguished by memory and reflection. His striking imagery, ear for folk idiom, and ability to divest and invest words, sounds, and structure enhance his verse. His "Good Night World" is a shattering rejection of European culture, state and church included, in whose bosom the Shoah was thought, prepared, and executed. He exclaims,

> Good night, wide world
> Big stinking world!
> Not you but I slam shut the door.
> With my long gabardine,
> My fiery, yellow patch,
> With head erect,
> And at my sole command,
> I go back into the ghetto
> . . . .
> Swinish German, hostile Polack,
> Thievish Amalekite—land of swill and guzzle,
> Slobbering democracy,
> With your cold compress of sympathy,
> Good night, brash world with your elec-
>   tric glare.
> . . . .
> Good night, I give you in good measure
> All my redeemers;
> Take your Jesus Marxes; choke on their daring.
> Burst with each drop of our baptized blood.

What he laments is the Jews' enticement and entrapment in a Gentile world, and he exhorts,

> I need no comforting.
> I walk again my straight and narrow way:
> From Wagner's heathen blare to Hebrew chant

And the hummed melody.
I kiss you, cankered Jewish life,
The joy of homecoming weeps in me.

Glatstein's bellwether poem (written in 1938), which speaks to the downtrodden Jew not to exchange *Yiddishkeit* (Jewishness) for all the emancipation in the world, echoes the lessons of Ahad Ha'am and Chaim Nahman Bialik on enlightenment and pogroms.

Glatstein anticipated the horror of the *Khurbn*. His reflection on the dawn of the Shoah are expressed with a tear-laced quill on burning parchment. His portrayal of the life and anguish of the Jew in the ghetto and in the camps is a vivid reminder that the shtetl, the thousands of small-town Jewish communities of Eastern Europe, is no longer. Some of his poems are anguished testimony to the difficult privilege of Jewishness and the moral crisis of faith. In "Wagons" (1938) he relates that the *wegener*—sign of a once robust shtetl life—return at night with no one there to greet them. A fearful plea is offered to heaven: "Let me not remain the only one, / Do not pass over me with my thin bones." Yet the Voice of Compassion and Justice does not reply and the heavens do not cry.

In "Smoke" the poet explains and wonders,

Through the chimney of the crematorium,
A Jew wafts upward to eternity.
And as soon as his smoke disappears,
His wife and child curl upward too.
And up above, in the heavenly pale,
Holy ghosts keen and wail.
O God, up where Your glories resound
Not even there can we be found.

What emerges is that the everyday becomes unbearable and the Eternal is uncovered as mystifying and baffling. Reacting to the destruction of the Six Million, Glatstein's elegiac challenge to God, seeded in the rabbinic genre of *klapei shemayya'* (against heaven), is not without merit.

Who will dream You?
Remember You?
Deny You?
Yearn after You?
Who will flee You?,
only to return
over a bridge of longing?
No end to night
for an extinguished people.
Heaven and earth wiped out.
Your tent void of light.
Flicker of the Jews' last hour.
Soon, Jewish God,
Your eclipse.

The suggestion that the Shoah twins Jewish history and the Jewish conception of God is decisive and stark.

For Glatstein, to honor the memory of the brutally murdered is to never forget nor forgive ("I Keep Recalling"). True, his elegies cannot restore the autonomy of the victims, but they reconstruct flesh to bones, personality to numbers, and novelty to *novum*—a written memorial to honor those who suffered and hoped in the eye of the storm.

—Zev Garber

I REST MY CASE
Memoir by Mark Verstandig, 1995

Mark Verstandig's *I Rest My Case* is a whole life autobiography: 90 pages deal with the prewar years in southern Poland; 100 pages with the period of German occupation; and 100 pages with life in Soviet-controlled Poland, refuge in Germany, and experiences in France and Australia. The work is distinguished by its precision: its clarity and economy of words, sharpness and depth of detail, richness of character sketches, and acuteness of observation. Written late in life in Yiddish and translated into impeccable English by Verstandig's daughter, Felicity Bloch, it was first issued by a small commercial publisher in 1995 and republished by Melbourne University Press in 1997.

The first section of the book covers life in prewar Poland. Born into a prosperous family, Verstandig presents a detailed account of his education from yeshiva to university. In 1936 he graduates in law and in his subsequent small town legal career experiences little discrimination; after German occupation he manages for two years to make a living preparing briefs and representing clients through the connivance of the local legal profession in flouting Nazi dictates. The discussion extends from family history and personal experience to an attempt to explain the political forces shaping Poland's development. There is also discussion of the workings of the Jewish community, presented from the vantage point of one with a lifelong commitment to Vladimir Jabotinsky's revisionist movement.

The year 1942 witnesses a radical change of fortunes for the Jews of Mielec, grown in number to 10,000—deportation (in March) and immediate murder of thousands. Following rumors sweeping the town, Verstandig escapes to Polaniec and later reconstructs events from the accounts of survivors. He learns of the order to gather in the marketplace; the separation of the young men and the forced march of the remaining men, women, and children to a military airfield seven kilometers distant; the shooting on arrival of 1,500 elderly women and men, including his father; the housing of those temporarily spared in an aircraft hangar; the continued murders, over seven days, in full view from the hangar; and the transportation of survivors to Lublin and other locations.

Throughout this and subsequent accounts there is great attention to detail, including character sketches depicting the gamut of reactions to the murderous fury, from the Gestapo collaborator who dispatched his wife and two children to their deaths in a vain effort to save his life, to the president of the Judenrat of Sandomierz, who, when ordered to provide a list of Jews for ''deportation,'' handed over a sealed envelope containing only one name, that of his own. His reward was a bullet in the back of the neck, delivered on the staircase outside his office. Quoting **Primo Levi,** Verstandig observes that ''there are few men who know how to go to their deaths with dignity.''

Verstandig subsequently details his experiences in hiding on the Aryan side of Warsaw and in remote rural locations. A major interest is the motive of those who assisted Jews in hiding; he writes that there were honorable people, such as a doctor who answered a call to treat his wife after she was shot, but they were few in number. The great majority who provided aid did so because they were well paid and judged that there was little risk to themselves. He notes that the Blue Police, when they caught Jews, rarely handed to the Gestapo those who had been providing shelter. He documents the denunciations and murders committed by civilians, including the betrayal and execution of two of his sisters.

He is also concerned to describe the murderous impact in Poland of the Roman Catholic church's anti-Semitism and to place on record his experience of the Armia Krajowa: the rejection of his request to join the underground, the murder of his companions in hiding by a detachment of partisans, and the heightened intensity of attacks in the last stage of the war, which he understands as a policy orchestrated by the Polish government-in-exile to complete Hitler's work, important for the reestablishment of the Polish nation.

—Andrew Markus

I WAS A DOCTOR IN AUSCHWITZ
Memoir by Gisella Perl, 1948

Before the Nazi invasion of Hungary, Gisella Perl led a rewarding and successful life as physician, wife, and mother. Trained as an obstetrician and gynecologist, she worked alongside her surgeon husband, operating a hospital in Sighet. The Nazi invasion of Hungary ended her days of normalcy.

Her memoir, *I Was a Doctor in Auschwitz,* is brief but unforgettable. Each of the short chapters conveys striking portraits of Nazi oppressors and those they persecuted. The book was first published in 1948.

The opening chapter, ''Dr. Kapezius,'' sets the stage for all that follows. Perl's life is transformed into a labyrinth of suffering, defined by unpredictable and cruel twists and turns,

where nothing is what it seems. In December 1943, as the German army was suffering heavy losses on the Eastern Front, Perl is visited in her office by an erudite and charming German physician, Dr. Kapezius. Overcoming her suspicions, Perl invites him to spend an evening at her home. Kapezius seems a reassuring reminder of German culture and humanity. His eyes fill with tears when Perl recites the poetry of Heine and Lessing, and he is lavish in his praise following a violin performance by the Perls' gifted son. Kapezius reminds the family that not all Germans are Nazis and urges them to keep up their courage, for one day soon the war will end.

Five months later, in Auschwitz-Birkenau, Perl, torn from her family and stripped of everything she owns, encounters Dr. Kapezius again. The veneer of civility is stripped away, and he is unmasked as the monster he is. A colleague of Josef Mengele, Kapezius compels Perl to become the camp gynecologist. It is a cruel assignment, for Perl receives neither medicine nor instruments. Yet she saves lives, with compassion and conversation as her only tools.

This opening vignette presents one of the themes of the memoir: in a world gone mad, things are not what they appear. Normal values are turned upside down. Perl, who had treasured the moments when she could bring new life into the world, becomes a secret abortionist, killing babies to save their mothers' lives. A bag of diamonds has value only when it can purchase three uncooked potatoes; women entering the hell of Auschwitz receive flimsy party dresses that barely cover their bodies. A piece of string to tie one's shoes becomes the difference between life and death, and Perl must decide how high a price she will pay for that piece of string.

Perl's memoir recounts acts of kindness as unforgettable as the episodes of cruelty. Conversation functions as a healing balm; margarine is rumored to be a miracle drug. A smile brings a desperate prisoner through another day. Auschwitz through Perl's eyes is a land of extremes, oppressive heat and bitter cold, unfathomable cruelty and extraordinary compassion.

While the book centers on the author's experiences in Auschwitz-Birkenau, it also recounts her struggle to survive when she is torn from her friends there and sent first to Berlin, then to a labor camp near Hamburg, and finally to Bergen-Belsen. The theme of cruel contradiction continues. Had Mengele permitted her to remain with her patients in Birkenau, she would have been liberated months earlier. When she arrives at the train station in Berlin, dressed in rags and with her number upon her coat, people turn away from her as if she is a murderer, but, as Perl knows, these seemingly normal people are the true criminals.

Even liberation is not what it should be, an experience of unmitigated joy. For with freedom Perl receives the devastating news of the death of her husband and son. Overwhelmed by grief and bereft of hope, Perl, who has survived so much, now chooses suicide. She is rescued and brought back to the land of the living through the kindness of a young Catholic priest who ministers to her as she has ministered to so many others. Kindness once again becomes the antidote to poison.

Perl's memoir contains few dates to guide the reader. Yet that seems appropriate. When Perl enters Auschwitz her striking wristwatch, which Kapezius had admired at her home, becomes his possession. For Perl time loses all meaning; only the struggle to survive another day matters.

—Marilyn J. Harran

I WILL BEAR WITNESS: A DIARY OF THE NAZI YEARS (Ich will Zeugnis ablegen bis zum letzten: Tagebücher 1933–1941)
Diary by Victor Klemperer, 1995

The title is Victor Klemperer's own formulation. On 27 May 1942 he wrote in his diary, "I will bear witness, precise witness." That is what he had been doing since 1933 and what he proceeded to do during the last years of the Third Reich, at great personal risk. Indeed, Klemperer's secret diaries represent one of the most evocative accounts we have of the Nazi years in Germany.

There are a number of reasons for their effectiveness. Klemperer's training in textual analysis figures prominently among them. From 1920 until 1935, when he fell victim to the Nazi policy of coordinating German culture (Gleichschaltung), Klemperer worked as professor of Romance languages at the Technical University in Dresden. And the diaries abound with trenchant readings of Nazi propaganda and its impact on the speech and thought of everyday Germans. Many of the readings, in fact, appear in Klemperer's highly regarded monograph about Nazi discourse, LTI: Lingua tertii Imperii (1947). Because in his diaries Klemperer scrutinizes communist as well Nazi ideology, they did not find a publisher in East Germany, his home after the war until his death in 1960. Not until 1995 were they published, in abridged form, in the original German (Ich will Zeugnis ablegen bis zum letzten). In 1998 they were published in English translation.

Klemperer's status as an academic shaped his diaries in other ways as well. In their first parts he discusses at length the reactions of both students and fellow professors to Nazism. He has much more sympathy for the former group, whose attitudes he depicts as often ambivalent and conflicted. For example, in 1936 Klemperer wrote about his colleagues, "If one day the situation were reversed and the fate of the vanquished lay in my hands, then I would let all the ordinary folk go, and even some of the leaders, who might perhaps after all have had honorable intentions and not known what they were doing. But I would have all the intellectuals strung up and the professors three feet higher than all the rest; they would be left hanging from the lampposts for as long as was compatible with hygiene."

This sense of betrayal pervades the diaries. Like many assimilated German Jews, Klemperer greatly valued the humanistic tradition in German culture. It was the center of German identity, according to him. And for all Klemperer's insight he maintained a kind of willful blindness during the first years of the Nazi regime, insisting that the Nazis were fundamentally un-German and that they would be supplanted by recrudescence of true Germanness. Eventually he came to realize, with great acrimony, that many quondam purveyors of humanistic values had definitively abandoned their cause. But Klemperer's quixotic ideas about German identity, and his perception of himself as a German, lingered, fatefully keeping him in Germany until it was too late to get out. Money and lack of connections played a role here too, as did the fragile health of his non-Jewish wife. (Klemperer's marriage enabled him to avoid deportation.) Yet above all Klemperer stayed because he believed that no other culture could sustain him and his intellectual passions. As this culture quite literally collapsed around him, and with neither an academic position nor publishing prospects, he continued to write about French and Italian literature, noting his progress and frustrations in his diaries. From Klemperer's wry and also moving comments on having to give up his car and his typewriter to his vivid portrait of the Dresden bombings, I Will Bear Witness contains a wealth of information about quotidian experiences in the Third Reich and their psychological toll. The life it records is, however, that of a scholar.

Klemperer does not only inveigh against the treachery of fellow intellectuals. In some of the diaries' most disquieting passages he condemns the reemergence of a ghetto mentality among assimilated Jews whose response to Hitler differed from his. For Klemperer giving up on the German cultural mission of Dichten und Denken engendered parochialism or, again, a ghetto mentality. This is how he sees Zionism, for example. And Klemperer attaches the same term to the mindset of Jews who tried to survive financially by propitiating the Nazi regime. Jewish behavior in the Third Reich, he goes so far as to suggest, is enough to make one into an anti-Semite.

Such thoughts testify to more than the complexity of German-Jewish attitudes in the mid-1930s. Klemperer knows that his feelings are ugly. That he expresses them nonetheless is an indication of his candor, of the compelling authenticity of the diaries. Furthermore, Klemperer dissects his own response to Nazism and the difficulties it brought with the same ruthlessness he brings to bear on everything else he addresses. The paradoxical effect is that the diaries have their greatest force where Klemperer dwells on his own weaknesses. Here we have the impression of utter self-honesty under the most difficult circumstances, circumstances that must have made the refuge of delusion very attractive.

—Paul Reitter

ICE FIRE WATER: A LEIB GOLDKORN COCKTAIL
Novel by Leslie Epstein, 1999

The irrepressible Leib Goldkorn, the protagonist of *Ice Fire Water,* made his first appearance in ''The Steinway Quartet,'' a l976 novella that centered on a group of Eastern European musicians working at the Steinway restaurant on Rivington Street in New York City. The work introduced Leslie Epstein's characteristic ploy of intertwining screwball comedy with moral seriousness. What should not have worked in fact did— partly because his longhaired protagonist has a sprightly narrative voice and partly because he stands for Old World values in a debased, often violent, New World setting.

There are at least a hundred ways of getting Goldkorn's accent wrong, but Epstein, as sportscasters like to say, ''nails it.'' The convoluted, thickly textured paragraphs are as much a part of the Goldkorn leitmotiv as are his Admiral television set, Bulova watch, ersatz alligator briefcase, and much-lamented flute. Goldkorn's years at the Steinway are a study in fortune spiraling ever downward: he ends up working inside the restaurant as a shoe shine boy and outside it as a street musician, waving his highly trained musician's hands over water glasses. What remains in *Ice Fire Water,* despite Goldkorn's now sickly wife, Clara (diabetic, incontinent, altogether a burden), is a voice, seasoned by sorrow, that turns quotidian woe into bursts of language and dashes of poetry: ''Waking? I had not once through the long night of anticipation closed my eyes. I heard, from my corner of the Posturpedic, the snores of my wife. In a glass, formerly containing seedless jelly, her dentures lay like a mollusk under inches of water.''

Fire Ice Water alternates between memory and desire. Its italicized portions take the reader back to the era of Adolf Hitler and Goldkorn's seriocomic effort to produce what he regards as his masterpiece: *Esther, A Jewish Girl at the Persian Court.* The opera, Golkorn insists, might yet ''change history's course. Surely the subtle French, so wise in the ways of the world, would understand the association of Haman with Hitler. Both begin with the letter H. *Formez vos bastaillons.''* That Goldkorn, a graduate of Vienna's Akademie fur Musik, Philosophie, und darstellende Kunst, is destined to endure comic disappointments and oversized misadventures should not be surprising. The three novellas collected in *Goldkorn Tales* (an expanded version of ''The Steinway Quintet''; ''Music of the Spheres,'' about an over-the-top production of *Othello*; and ''The Magic Flute,'' about an assassination plot hatched against a suspected Nazi now serving as the restaurant's new owner) provide the template from which *Ice Fire Water* was struck. The difference, however, is that the Goldkorn the reader has come to love is now surrounded by a richer, more mature texture. Historical personages intermingle with a bulging cast of fictional extras. The result is playfulness of a high and delightful order, but the high jinks sometimes make for a complicated, unwieldy read. In each case, Hitler or his

Nazi agents make cameo appearances as Sonja Henie finds herself at the mercy of Hollywood's Daryl Zanuck or Esther Williams gazes at the bubbling cauldron a group of cannibals have prepared for her death and their dinner.

Epstein, in short, gives Hollywood melodrama the comic send-up it deserves, and in the process turns the altogether predictable into art. This is so because Epstein renders his characters with just the tight-lipped, ironic treatment they deserve and also because he hides tragedy under the guise of an ever-darkening comedy. Only Goldkorn is immune because he holds fast to his belief that music constitutes mankind's slim hope for redemption. For Epstein the question, possibly the only one that matters, is how to limn the twentieth century and the oceans of blood it has occasioned.

Epstein chooses outrageous comedy as his preferred way of confronting the outrageousness that turned a generation of Eastern European Jews into ash. He seems never to have met a pratfall, pun, or misplaced preposition that he did not love. These entities attach themselves to the hapless Goldkorn like bananas to unsuspecting shoes. In this sense, Epstein's protagonist seems less a variation of **Saul Bellow**'s aging, increasingly disgruntled Artur Sammler than an avatar of James Joyce's bumbling Leopold Bloom. Like Bloom, Goldkorn's stream of consciousness is awash in misinformation. In one memorable scene, he convinces himself that the *New York Times* book reviewer Michiko Kakutani is, of all things, a Finn and thus misses a luncheon date. In another equally outrageous scene, a famished Goldkorn devours the artificial fruit that tops Carmen Miranda's trademark headdress.

Ice Fire Water is a ''Goldkorn cocktail'' that successfully mixes ''real'' characters with imagined ones, the beautiful with the ugly, and aspects of goodness with unspeakable evil. Granted, Goldkorn's beverage of choice is schnapps rather than a cocktail, but no matter. Epstein knows where understatement and misdirection can take the reader, just as he knows that the Holocaust remains the twentieth century's most enigmatic mystery. In old age Goldkorn retains his essential trademarks, but his insights are both wiser and decidedly earned.

—Sanford Pinsker

IF NOT NOW, WHEN? (Se non ora, quando?)
Novel by Primo Levi, 1982

Among Primo Levi's works of witness to the Holocaust, *Se non ora, quando?* (1982; *If Not Now, When?,* 1985) stands out, at first consideration, as a striking but unlikely project. Levi had set his remarkable powers of observation, his almost flawless memory, and his taut narrative style unyieldingly against the Nazi will to obliterate all record of the Holocaust and to denigrate as fiction whatever accounts did survive. In this work, which he was beginning to conceive already in 1966—though it did not appear in print until April 1982—Levi dares to write a *romanzo,* a ''novel of adventure,'' concerning a group of Jewish resisters in Eastern Europe who made their way from Russia to Italy en route to Palestine.

His will to do so is best understood in terms of three reference points. One was the experience, which he recounts in *The Reawakening,* of meeting in his journey home a band of young Zionists on their way to Palestine. A second was an account of such a band that passed through Milan told him in detail by a friend, Vita Finzi; Levi drew heavily on the notes he made of this narrative and added to it the results of a year's study in historical sources, chiefly on resistance in Eastern Europe. A third impulse was added by the charge, already leveled by the Nazis and revived in one form or another in the years after the war's end, that the Jews were cravenly docile and compliant in the face of the slaughter they endured. Levi wrote this book in part because no one else seemed to be writing a work of witness that would refute this libel and because he had, in this story, the means to counter the charge. Elsewhere, in answers to questions in the schools he visited in the decades after the Holocaust, he elaborated on the reasons why such resistance was virtually unthinkable, psychologically and physically, either on the way to Auschwitz or when in camp. Levi makes abundantly clear, then, that this is a work of historical fiction and refuses to be constrained from telling an important truth even though it must at times be told through fiction.

It is in this context that the title of the work should be understood: Levi takes it from the famous phrases of Hillel recorded in the *Pirke Avot* (''The Sayings of the Fathers''), ''If I am not for myself, who will be for me? And when I think only of myself, what am I? If not now, when?'' Mighty and urgent phrases these; they echo in a poem that Levi composed and for which he creates a fictional author, Martin Fontasch, a Jew captured and killed by a German who nonetheless allowed Fontasch one last wish—which was to compose this poem. In the book the poem reaches a character by the name of Gedale, and it became known, then, as ''Gedale's Song.'' Containing some of Hillel's lines quoted above, it also bears the marks of Levi's reading of **Paul Celan**'s shatteringly evocative poem ''Totesfuge'' (''Death Fugue''). At the end of this entry I give the poem in its entirety as a concise presentation of the huge impact of this novel and as an example more generally of the complexity and power of Levi's verse.

Perhaps the best summary of the work, which involves the acts of resistance and the project of survival and freedom undertaken by a group of Jews who band together and join with other, non-Jewish resisters, is that given by a character named Pavel to a relief worker, as the group arrives in Italy: ''Gruppo, lovely signora. Group. Sempre together. Russia, Polandia. March. Forest, river, snow. Dead Germans. Many. We partizani,

all of us, porca miseria. No DP. We, war, partizanka. All soldiers, madosha. Women, too.''

The story follows the huge strains the group experienced, partly rejected because they are Jews, partly accepted by other resisters. In presenting the community thus formed, Levi creates a number of striking individuals, both men and (to a degree outstanding in his work) women, including one man, Mendel, who, of the figures in this work, is most like Levi himself. The work, as is characteristic of Levi, never sentimentalizes, showing not only the rancorous prejudice the Jewish resisters encountered but also their own internal conflicts and tensions, sexual and otherwise, their limitations of energy and patience, and their huge tenacity. The extent of their courage and calculation in damaging German rail lines and disrupting German retaliation is told without easy heroization but without diminution either.

''Gedale's Song'' both quotes from Hillel's lines and is a midrash on them for the world after the Holocaust. It conveys much of the spirit of this work and many of the key terms and elements of Levi's work as a whole. Like much of his verse, of which this poem is here presented as an example, it is less reticent than is characteristic of the prose of his works of witness and, while highly allusive, is more direct in its evocation of anger and pain.

> Do you recognize us? We are the flock of
>   the ghetto,
> Fleeced for a thousand years, resigned to the
>   offence.
> We are the tailors, the scribes, and the cantors
> Withered in the shadow of the Cross.
> Now we have learned the paths of the forests,
> We have learned to shoot, and we hit
>   straight on.
> If I am not for myself, who will be for me?
> If not thus, how? And if not now, when?
> Our brothers have risen to heaven
> Through the ovens of Sobibor and of Treblinka,
> They have dug themselves a grave in the air.
> Only we few have survived
> For the honor of our submerged people,
> For vengeance, and for witness.
> If I am not for myself, who will be for me?
> If not thus, how? And if not now, when?
> We are the sons of David and the stubborn
>   ones of Massada.
> Each of us bears in his pocket the stone
> Which smashed the forehead of Goliath.
> Brothers, away from the Europe of tombs:
> Let us climb together toward the land
> Where we will be men among other men.
> If I am not for myself, who will be for me?
> And if not thus, how? And if not now, when?
> —Ralph G. Williams

THE IMMORTAL BARTFUSS (Bartfus ben ha-almavet)
Novel by Aharon Appelfeld, 1988

Another "small masterpiece" (the epithet frequently evoked by reviewers and critics about Aharon Appelfeld's novels), *The Immortal Bartfuss,* published in Hebrew and in English translation in 1988, focuses on a survivor living in Israel and haunted by his Holocaust experiences. He devotes 15 minutes a day to earning a living in underground dealings, spends endless days and nights in a Jaffa café or wandering about the beach or the city, and takes uneasy satisfaction in the knowledge that he has hidden three bars of gold, gold watches, two necklaces, some cash, and old photographs of his parents and sister. He is estranged from his wife and retarded daughter, distrustful of them and almost everyone else, and always deep in his private thoughts. With sparse details and tight, spare narrative, Appelfeld sets a dreamlike tone, a gauzelike backdrop for inaccessible characters. Bartfuss, like Appelfeld himself, is, in the words of Leonard Michaels, "a figure of awesome interiority."

Elaborating on his obsession with survivors whose lives are marked by the absence of both language and mutual personal relationships, Appelfeld explained to Philip Roth that the "Holocaust belongs to the type of enormous experience which reduces one to silence." Bartfuss is the essence of the survivor who remains alienated by choice as well as by circumstance. He trusts no one, not even himself. He blames his wife, Rosa, beyond forgiveness for surviving by sleeping with a peasant and his sons and repeatedly accuses her of selling herself: "There's a limit to disgrace. Life is valuable, but not at any price." He lives and sleeps alone in a sparse room in the same apartment as his wife and daughter. Contemptuous of them, he provides for them, but he does not share a life with them. He has not seen his older daughter, Paula, since the day of her wedding more than two years earlier, yet he clumsily tries to form a relationship with Bridget, his retarded daughter, whose smile warms him.

In coffeehouses and cafés Bartfuss sees other survivors, with whom he does business and who regard him as a hero; he has, after all, 50 bullets in his body and a reputation for selfless bravery, which may be an explanation for the adjective "immortal." Although he has many acquaintances among the survivors, some of whom he knew in prewar Europe or in Italy just after the war, he is not friends with them. They are merely numb players on the same stage. Like them, he protects himself by protecting his loneliness. "No one," he thinks while recovering in the hospital from an ulcer attack, "knew what to do with the lives that had been saved." At times he resolves to dedicate himself to the "general welfare . . . inspire faith in people overcome by many disasters." After all, "a man is not an insect," he thinks, echoing a sentiment that resonates in other Appelfeld novels. Preoccupied with finding purpose

after experiencing the Holocaust, Bartfuss asks another survivor, "What have we Holocaust survivors done? Has our great experience changed us at all?" He answers his own question ironically, "I expect greatness of soul from people who underwent the Holocaust." We see glimpses of an emerging generosity as he begins to show less contempt for Rosa and Paula. We see a generous Bartfuss helping another survivor he knew in his days of smuggling and illegal immigration in Italy, a woman whose poverty renders her dependent upon favors.

Is Bartfuss transforming himself, closing the "gap between his actions and his verbal declarations," in the words of Gila Ramras-Rauch, and moving "forward in the painful process of coming to terms with oneself"? Appelfeld's Bartfuss finds no consolation in Zionism or religion. He is alive, however, and that, says the author, "isn't a great deal, but it's something."

—Myrna Goldenberg

IN FULL VIEW
Essays by Lily Brett, 1997

Lily Brett's literary productions reflect a dominant and singular fact: her obsession with an event that she did not experience directly but which, irrespective of that fact, shaped her life in ways she has still been trying to work out. Brett's writing has had its source, one could say, in her belated determination to face, and somehow come to terms with, the appalling reality of her parents' experiences during the Holocaust. Her writing has also been (perhaps above all) tied to her need to deal with the devastating effects she believes the event had on her mother in particular and on the ways these effects then came to be registered, both physically and psychically, in her as her daughter. Whether Brett is writing explicitly about herself and her parents or other members of her family, as in her poetry and in the collection of autobiographical essays *In Full View,* or whether she disguises herself as one of the protagonists in her collections of short stories and novels, what her works persistently thematize is the complex, conflicted, and ambivalent relationship she had with her mother, the traumatic effect this has had on Brett (and on her body in particular), and how all this is connected to the history of her mother's Holocaust experiences. What is also strongly thematized has been Brett's pervasive desire, of which the writing is itself a significant expression, to re-create the broken connections between herself and her mother. As her writing shows, Brett has attempted to do this through identifying with her mother's experiences both before and during the Holocaust.

The associative and conversational style that is the hallmark of Brett's writing suggestively links her literary productions to her long stints of psychoanalysis. In a similar way to what happens through the technique of free association in an analysis, her writings are able to convey to the reader the traumatic nature of the message that her mother must have transferred to her about her experiences during the Holocaust, a message that marked Brett and that has continued to live on, especially in her body. Something traumatic in the mother's history, both before and during the Holocaust, seemed always to have been at stake in the difficult relations between mother and daughter, and it is the legacy of that traumatic history that is the source of so many of the stories Brett has told in poetry, fiction, and autobiography of her experiences growing up as the child of Holocaust survivors. It would seem that what was apparently most indigestible about the Holocaust for her mother got itself written on Brett's body; thus, the body that Brett's writing puts on display for us in her writing functions as an unhappy memorial to that trauma. As Brett has said about her body: "I created this havoc within myself because of a complicated confluence of history and family. Death camps, starvation, greed, a beautiful mother who'd lost everything except her looks. It was a heady brew. I took my regular, symmetrical, attractive features, and I huffed and I puffed until I distorted myself and resembled somebody else."

Brett's writing testifies to how her body not only attempted to avoid resembling a mother whom she could not help but resemble physically but was also her unconscious defense against the anxiety she always experienced in face of a suffering that threatened to devour her whole. As she says in "I Wear Your Face," one of *The Auschwitz Poems*: "I wear the glare / you froze me with / . . ./ I wear your fear / with practised ease / pleasing you / I wear your face / and mother / the green witch howls behind it." And yet, her writing also testifies to a contrary desire. Against this desire to flee from the voracity of a mother's suffering, Brett's very writing becomes an attempt to perform the impossible: to undo miraculously with the use of words the losses suffered by her parents, to use her writing to stitch herself seamlessly to their histories, above all to the time and place of her mother's pre-Holocaust past when life, not death, seemed possible. This latter desire, and the fantasy it stages, to reconnect the link between daughters and mothers that Hitler severed, is constantly dramatized in Brett's works. "If / with / my white biro / I could string / some strong words / into a thread / I would spin / myself a cocoon / a second womb / and / gently / tuck us in together."

This fantasy of loving union in which Brett is connected to a past she did not live unfortunately also has something potentially deathly about it. The question such an impossible fantasy poses (so poignantly evoked in these lines: "When I am pickling and preserving, I am joined to the past. Joined to another time, another life; a life I was destined to live before Hitler intervened. I am in Lodz. I am joined to my mother. I am not just her Australian child. I am joined to a city and a time that was never mine") is how it can support a usable present and future, not only for Brett but also for others of the second generation that her literature speaks of and to.

—Esther Faye

IN THE DAYS OF SIMON STERN
Novel by Arthur A. Cohen, 1973

In the Days of Simon Stern is a richly textured, fantastical narrative describing the coming of the Messiah in the aftermath of the Holocaust. Combining serious theological reflection with elements of farce, Cohen's novel represents a statement of faith in the ongoing possibility of redemption. At the same time it qualifies this faith by underscoring the dangers inherent in premature efforts to "force the end." In an illuminating analogy Cohen has described his novel as an attempt to "transcribe for full orchestra what the *aggadah* had scored for the small voice." Like the *aggadah*—the homiletical stories told by the rabbis of the Talmud—Cohen's work is a fiction that participates in Jewish tradition by offering a commentary on fundamental theological questions.

The story is narrated by a blind scribe named Nathan Gaza who describes himself as a "proclaimer of visions" and an "impresario" for the world's redeemer. His story recounts the life and adventures of Simon Stern, who comes of age in New York City during the years of the Great Depression. Before Simon's birth in an East European shtetl his parents bring him to America, where he becomes a brilliant student of Jewish Law—and an even more brilliant entrepreneur. Working his way up from a janitor in the real estate company of Baumgarten & Fitzsimmons, Simon takes over the operation and becomes, by the outset of World War II, a real estate tycoon worth $60 million. Simon's biography suggests a burlesque version of the rags-to-riches Horatio Alger story. Rather than embracing a life of opulence, however, he decides to marshal his resources toward the salvation of a remnant of European Jewry.

Simon's transformation is prompted by a visit from a mysterious personage who recounts an extended parable entitled "The Legend of the Last Jew on Earth." It describes a mass conversion of the Jews during a modern version of the Spanish Inquisition. Only one Jew, Don Rafael, has the tenacity to withstand the pressures to convert, and when he is murdered by the Inquisition the memory of his deeds inspires a mass return to Judaism. The parable underlines the possibility for spiritual rebirth, even under extreme duress, and it prepares Simon for his own errand to the Jews. Simon attends a rally in Madison Square Garden where he hears Chaim Weizmann describe the mass murder of European Jews. Immediately thereafter Simon decides that it is time "to begin the work of redemption." Amassing an eccentric group of assistants Simon drafts (while sitting in Ratner's restaurant on Delancy Street) the "Ratner's Declaration of Conscience," in which he describes his plan to build a sanctuary for a selected group of survivors from the Nazi death camps.

Modeled upon King Solomon's Temple, the sanctuary will provide "an enclave in which to cultivate the resources of stubbornness." Simon travels to Europe to collect a remnant of European Jewry. Together with a thousand survivors Simon and his assistants return to New York and take up residence in the "Temple," which covers an entire block on the Lower East Side. (The facade retains the appearance of a conventional tenement building.) Not long after their arrival, Janos Baltar, the one evil character they have allowed to join the group, smuggles into the compound $2 million worth of ammunition and attempts to stimulate an insurrection. The ammunition sets off a gigantic explosion, destroying the Temple and killing Baltar. The survivors flee "to the city beyond," Simon moves uptown, and Nathan writes the narrative.

The account of these events is filled with allusions to Talmudic and Biblical texts, Greek mythology, European literature, and Jewish history. For example, the name Simon Stern recalls that of Shimon Bar Kokhba, who in 132 C.E. led a doomed rebellion against the Roman emperor Hadrian ("Bar Kokhba" means in Hebrew "son of the star"; "stern" means star in both German and Yiddish). Many of Bar Kokhba's contemporaries, including Rabbi Akiva, saw in him the coming of the Messiah. Another key allusion links the scribe, Nathan Gaza, to the historical Nathan of Gaza, who in 1665 proclaimed the messiahship of Sabbatai Zevi, setting off the most notorious episode of messianic fervor in Jewish history. Yet while these historical references associate the character Simon Stern with false messianism, the novel's narrator insists otherwise. At the end of his tale, he writes "I have told you the story of a fulfilled moment." The implication is that Simon Stern's action on behalf of the survivors of the Holocaust reflects a step toward redemption, even if ultimate redemption remains deferred. This conclusion is anticipated by Nathan's running discussion throughout the novel of the difference between Greek tragedy and Jewish literature. Whereas the former reflects the doctrine of implacable human fate, the latter reflects a faith in the human ability to turn toward the divine and alter the terms of fate.

—Julian Levinson

INCIDENT AT VICHY
Play by Arthur Miller, 1964

In the German-occupied but still free French town of Vichy in 1942, there has been a general roundup of ten men, suspected of being Jews, for deportation to the concentration camps. At first the men are shocked and bewildered by their treatment, and several are in denial over the meaning of these events. Gradually the truth of their situation is revealed to them. Not only are their identity papers being checked but their penises are also examined for circumcision. Two of the ten are not Jews: a Gypsy (also among the racially condemned) and Von Berg, a Viennese aristocrat who was mistakenly arrested in the roundup. This is the central event of this long one-act play. Over its course the men will argue with each other, will

struggle to comprehend the enormity of the evil they are experiencing, and will, all but one, go off to their certain deaths.

Miller returns to his great thematic preoccupations: the relationship of men to their society around them, the responsibility of the community, and what we as individuals owe to a corrupted society. A secondary thematic question to Miller's work, that of self-knowledge (after knowledge of the outside world), is articulated for the first time in his plays as Who is a Jew? For the first time in his plays, however, Miller's questions are now met with the profound silence of the Holocaust. Unlike the characters and their struggles in his other plays, these men, even if they understand and face the overwhelming destruction that awaits them, have no agency with which to thwart or diminish that destruction. Their individual strengths and weaknesses as human beings have no bearing on their fate. They are Jews and their world has determined to be rid of them. Basing his story on an actual occurrence during the war, Miller has the one Gentile among the prisoners, the Austrian prince Von Berg, take a specific and individual action against the Nazis. By handing his pass to Leduc, one of the Jews, Von Berg buys Leduc a few moments in which to flee the detention center. He and he alone still retains any agency, and it is from his sense of shame and from his guilt that he acts.

One of Holocaust drama's formal problems for all writers is the fact of its victims' lack of agency, a condition that can create a motivational passivity in a play's protagonist. Drama, unlike the novel, does not take to such passivity, demanding that its central character, whether Hamlet or Oedipus or Willy Loman, take an active role in pursuit of their objective. But the Holocaust stripped its victims either from taking any action or effecting any change from their action, and any dramatization of this monumental event must remain true to this. The characters in *Incident at Vichy* are active primarily in their denial or in their pursuit of an explanation yet remain sadly inert to even the fantasy of escape. Though the psychiatrist Leduc is given the longest and most anguished speeches, the central character in the play is Von Berg. Miller links these two men through an articulation of Von Berg's own passivity in recognizing that his cousin had assisted in the removal of all the Jewish students at Leduc's school. Thus Von Berg's slight yet profound rejection of his own silent complicity in not vocally opposing the actions of his cousin when he pushes his safe conduct pass into Leduc's hands at the play's ending resounds dramatically and remains truthful to the realities of the Holocaust.

Miller refuses to spare any of his characters from his conclusion that victims and perpetrators have acted in concert. While those victims clearly are not held responsible for their own destruction, their systematic denials and various individual levels of selfishness nevertheless have contributed to the handing over of all power to their enemies. The Waiter, for instance, only sees the German Major as a pleasant customer, while Monceau, the actor, refuses to believe that his cultured theater audiences in Germany would ever stoop to such barbarism. Each man has his excuses as to why he has been picked up, and each dismisses the reports of mass executions. Likewise the humane German Major is troubled by what he is abetting but realizes that he has no means of protest and retreats into drunkenly bullying Leduc in an attempt to reduce cynically Leduc's ethical questions into selfish pleading.

Written and produced at the start of the United States' heavy military involvement in Vietnam and shortly after Adolf Eichmann's historic trial and execution in Israel, *Incident at Vichy* attempts to set out the multilayered questions as to how genocide flourished. Miller's examination of the chain of command among the perpetrators as well as the incapacitating denial of the victims creates a dramatically vivid contemporary morality play that continues to resonate as nations and individuals continue to allow the genocidal impulse among groups to play out.

—Steven Dedalus Burch

THE INFORMED HEART: AUTONOMY IN A MASS AGE
Memoir and Study by Bruno Bettelheim, 1960

In *The Informed Heart* Bruno Bettelheim examines the interplay between two fundamental issues using his experiences during the Holocaust to highlight this interplay. First he explores changes in personality development and personality integration as a result of life during the machine age. Bettelheim then discusses the nature-versus-nurture debate, emphasizing the inborn internal mechanisms (organismic) from a psychoanalytic perspective as well as the impact of the environment on personality change and development. Bettelheim's experiences in Dachau and Buchenwald form the foundation for much of this argument. Organizationally *The Informed Heart* is structured such that Bettelheim's theoretical beliefs and ideas form the beginning and ending chapters, with the narrative of his time in the camps comprising the middle sections of the text.

It is difficult to describe Bettelheim's account of his experiences in Dachau and Buchenwald as typical memoir. Rather it reads as an extended research study based on personal descriptions and memories of camp life with accompanying analyses. Bettelheim describes his initiation into the concentration camp experience, including his original transport to Dachau. Faced with overwhelming brutality and personal disorientation, Bettelheim argues that each prisoner had to find ways to survive. Bettelheim states that he drew upon his psychoanalytic training and expertise to reframe his camp experiences as research and to maintain personality integration and provide a rationale for survival.

In 1943 Bettelheim published ''Individual and Mass Behavior in Extreme Situations,'' an article intended for a professional audience. The narrative chapters of *The Informed Heart* essentially represent a revision of this earlier work. Thus, psychoanalytic terminology and theoretical constructs are interspersed throughout. Individuals not familiar with these constructs may find parts of the narrative difficult to understand.

Bettelheim, in his analysis of concentration camp life, first discusses the impact of coercion. He focuses principally on the stages of adjustment to the daily life and difficulties in the camp, including an analysis of the social stratification of the camp, differentiation between old and new prisoners, and the Musselmen, or walking corpses. His essential premise is that life in the camps over time reduces the prisoners to the psychological equivalent of children. Behavior changes to infantile dependence on the aggressor or leads to a state of death in life. A chapter examining the psychological defenses to the camp experience follows this discussion. Bettelheim reexamines the role of social stratification in the camps, discusses the process of psychological identification of the prisoner with the SS and Gestapo, and addresses a variety of other defenses such as anonymity and work. Essentially he argues that the prisoner must be informed and aware of the choices being made or the prisoner risks personality disintegration.

As noted previously, Bettelheim claims to have based his analysis on professional expertise and research. It was later learned, however, that Bettelheim had no formal psychological or psychoanalytic training prior to his internment in the camps. Additionally it is highly improbable, considering the condition of concentration camp life, that Bettelheim could have conducted the type of interviews or questioned the number of prisoners at Buchenwald or Dachau that he claimed. Bettelheim may have also misinterpreted situations within the camp to provide evidence supportive of his own hypotheses. For example Bettelheim argues that prisoners begin to identify with and want to become like their captors. He uses as a main source of evidence the desire by prisoners to have old police uniforms. According to Bettelheim the desire to dress in police uniforms demonstrates that the prisoners wish to be like the SS. Survivors, however, reported that the desire to have these uniforms was based on the fact that the old police uniforms were warmer and more resistant to water than the striped prisoner uniform. Thus the acquisition of an old police uniform was motivated by survival needs and not identification with the SS. The motivations behind Bettelheim's exaggerations and misrepresentations are unclear, but they call into question the validity of much of what he has written.

Bettelheim has received much criticism for his argument that Jews went like sheep to the slaughter in the concentration and death camps. Bettelheim emphasizes that few resisted and that little organized active resistance by Jews took place during the Holocaust, both inside and outside of the camps. Unfortunately Bettelheim fails to acknowledge the resistance that took place, the military, political, economic, and physical problems associated with active resistance, the historical precedents of anti-Semitism affecting Jewish response, the limitations of some due to age or infirmity, and the role of passive resistance. His description and blame of the Frank family clearly demonstrates a lack of understanding of the conditions associated with resistance and rescue in the Netherlands under Nazi occupation. In an apparent contradiction Bettelheim provides numerous arguments and rationales for lack of German resistance to Nazism.

—Linda M. Woolf

AN INTERRUPTED LIFE: THE DIARIES OF ETTY HILLESUM, 1941–43 (Het vestoorde leven: Dagboek van Etty Hillesum, 1941–1943)
Diaries of Etty Hillesum, 1981

Etty Hillesum's diaries under the title *An Interrupted Life* (1983; *Het vestoorde leven: Dagboek van Etty Hillesum, 1941–1943*, 1981) are one of the treasures of world literature. They were written by Hillesum from age 27 to 29. She wrote them from the very beginning with publication in mind, which accounts for the elegant style of her rhetoric. Prior to her internment in Westerbork and her subsequent deportation to Auschwitz, she gave the diaries to a friend in the hope that they would be published even if she did not survive.

The diaries have a dialectical construction: Hillesum's fear for eventual death in the concentration camps is played against her irrepressible, exuberant zest for life, fueled by her joyous sexuality with the psychotherapist-palm reader Julius Spier and with a man identified as Father Han, as well as her ever-deepening spiritual relationship with God, which she defines in terms of a personal relationship with the deity. Another aspect of her indefatigable joie de vivre is her study of great authors such as Rainer Maria Rilke, Carl Gustav Jung, Fyodor Dostoyevsky, Leo Tolstoy, and Saint Augustine.

The dichotomy between Hillesum's joy for life and fear of eventual annihilation at the hands of the Nazis is expressed in this passage: "Because I am still so young and utterly resolved not to go under, and also because I feel that I am strong enough to pull myself together, I tend to forget how deprived we young people have become and how lonely. Or have I simply been anaesthetised? Bonger is dead, Ter Braak, Du Perron, Marsman, all are dead. Pos, and Van den Bergh and many others are in concentration camps." Hillesum describes the desire to hold on to a feeling of inner peace while her outer world lapses into catastrophe. She explicates both the difficulty and the necessity of holding on to this inner peace in the face of increasing terrorization: "More arrests, more terror, concentration camps, the arbitrary dragging off of fathers, sisters, brothers. We seek the meaning of life, wondering whether any can be left. But that is something each of us must settle with himself and with God. And perhaps life has its own meaning, even if it takes a

lifetime to find it. I for one have ceased to cling to life and to things, I have the feeling that everything is accidental, that one must break one's inner bonds with people and stand aside for all else. Everything seems so menacing and ominous, always that feeling of total impotence."

Hillesum's religious outlook appears to have been influenced by Buddhism and other forms of Eastern spirituality with the teaching that everything is temporary and that one cannot cling too closely to worldly things and people. Too close a bond to the worldly leads to sorrow because nothing lasts forever.

In another passage she describes the importance of literature in her search for self-realization: "Slowly but surely I have been soaking Rilke up these last few months: the man, his work and his life. And that is probably the only right way with literature, with study, with people or with anything else: to let it all soak in, to let it mature inside you until it has become part of yourself. That, too, is a growing process. Everything is a growing process. And in between, emotions and sensations that strike you like lightning. But still the most important thing is the organic process of growing." This exposition reveals how the study of literature is a major component of Hillesum's inner strength. Another major component of her inner strength is her unabashed enjoyment of her sexuality: "I only know that I love him, a bit more every day, and that I ripen beside him into a genuine and adult human being." Literature and sexuality help Hillesum to keep some semblance of inner tranquillity in the awareness and expectation of impending disaster.

Hillesum discusses religion as an important internal bulwark against Nazi terror: "The threat grows ever greater, and terror increases from day to day. I draw prayer round me like a dark protective wall, withdraw inside it, as one might into a convent cell and then step outside again, calmer and stronger and more collected again. I can imagine times to come when I shall stay on my knees for days on end waiting until the protective walls are strong enough to prevent my going to pieces altogether, my being lost and utterly devastated."

Generations of postwar readers have drawn inspiration and wisdom from Etty Hillesum's undefeatable spirituality when she herself was in the midst of a grave spiritual crisis. *An Interrupted Life* is therefore among the greatest books of the twentieth century.

—Peter R. Erspamer

THE INVESTIGATION (Die Ermittlung)
Play by Peter Weiss, 1965

In his work Peter Weiss was confronted with the fundamental problems of an artistic reckoning with the Holocaust as well as the representability of the Holocaust. He was himself an eyewitness of the Nazi regime, though not a witness to the destruction of the European Jewry in the death camps. He could not remember the actual events but only make use of the personal testimonies mediated to him as a spectator of the Frankfurt am Main Auschwitz trial by survivors and perpetrators, as well as the photographs, radio reports, and newspaper articles published by Bernd Naumann during the trial and later edited as a book. The Auschwitz trial against the murderers of the death camp Auschwitz and their odd-job men took place from December 1963 until August 1965. Twenty defendants and more than four hundred witnesses took part in the trial, in which the activities of all persons involved in the extermination camp Auschwitz were investigated.

Naumann's and Herrmann Langbein's respective documentations of the Auschwitz trial were used as raw material for Weiss's documentary drama *The Investigation* (1966; *Die Ermittlung,* 1965). Weiss wished to write a world drama on the course of history of the twentieth century, following the pattern of Dante's *Divina commedia,* which he found both fascinating and irritating. In his triptych, Inferno represents the world in respect to perennial suffering and Purgatory the present time of action, of searching, doubt, hope, and the fight against the evils of the world. Although Weiss later abandoned his plans for a world triptych project, he found an aesthetic form for a play on the Auschwitz trial, adopting Dante's aesthetic structural principle of numerology in order to treat his abundance of material, reducing it to a compelling indictment of what happened at Auschwitz. *The Investigation* consists of eleven cantos, each subdivided into three segments, in which the account of imaginary spokespersons stride through the site of destruction, Auschwitz, in nine stations. The play begins with "The Platform" where the trains arrived, proceeds to "The Camp," and ends with two cantos, "Zyklon B" and "The Fire Ovens." Although the situation of examining witnesses and defendants may appear to guarantee unity of time and place, neither directions of time nor place are actually given by Weiss.

Weiss managed not to mention the words "Jew," "German," or "Auschwitz" in his play. He did not draw attention to the national or ethnic background of the victims. The nine witnesses of the extermination camp—in which, according to the German philosopher Theodor W. Adorno, specimens, not individuals, died—are not differentiable dramatic characters but anonymous figures one to nine without discernible individuality. They appear in the play as nameless mouthpieces, their statements speaking for the many. The representatives of the jurisprudence appear as not individualized function carrier: "Judge," "Representative of the charges," and "Representative of the defense." Only the 18 defendants, listed at the beginning as anonymous numbers, are identified during the course of the play by the witnesses and the three legal representatives.

The two cantos in the center of the play, cantos 5 and 6, are different from the other nine songs: In these two cantos the individual destiny of two persons of the same age—a victim, Lilly Tofler, who died in Auschwitz, and a perpetrator, the 19-year-old Nazi, SS Corporal Stark—are described. Individuality is admitted only to this victim and this perpetrator in Weiss's play.

The artistic, artless, toneless, laconic, monotonous, and unemphatic language of the various mouthpieces, which is characterized by the parataxial sentence construction, the renunciation of metaphors, and punctuation and language, gives the wrong impression, as if Weiss has only quoted and assembled the trial's testimonies. A comparison of the Auschwitz trial documentation with the text of *The Investigation* shows how Weiss simplifies and reduces the language material to create a distance between the spectator and the event in order to anesthetize the feelings of the spectators/readers who have to work through this text. This play removes Auschwitz from the pure realm of religious, metaphysical, or mythological discourse. One of the key witnesses in *The Investigation* demands: "We must drop the lofty view that the camp world is incomprehensible to us." The theatrical but nondramatic documentation of Auschwitz offers no catharsis or resolution of any sort; it renounces use of naturalistic dialogues, a traditional dramatic structure, and individually drawn characters, who make audience identification possible.

The atrocities of Auschwitz are not scenically represented in *The Investigation*—according to Weiss any mimetic representation of Auschwitz or scenic reconstruction of the trial must be renounced—but naked testimonies are described in gruesome detail to the court negotiation by the witnesses and defendants. According to Lawrence Langer, a noted scholar specializing in the field of Holocaust literature and testimony, "Peter Weiss lowers the barriers of the unimaginable." His theatrical testimony of physical suffering "gradually narrows the space separating the imagination from the camp."

—Olav Schröer

THE ISLAND ON BIRD STREET (Ha-I bi-rehov ha-tsiporim)
Children's Novel by Uri Orlev, 1981

In the introduction to his novel for children *The Island on Bird Street* (1984; *Ha-I bi-rehov ha-tsiporim,* 1981), Orlev asks his readers to imagine a city occupied by a foreign army and divided by walls that separate neighborhoods in which people have been imprisoned and separated from each other based upon some arbitrary characteristic such as the color of their skin or of their eyes. In this imaginary city the rich can still buy what they want, but the poor die of hunger. This city resembles Warsaw, where Jerzy Henryk Orlowski, known as Uri Orlev, was born in 1931. The hero of *The Island on Bird*

Street, Alex, also strongly resembles the boy Orlev once was, though Alex is a fictional character.

Orlev uses literary models and a mixture of keen observation of reality and his main character's imaginative inner life to convey the experience of surviving alone in the ghetto during German occupation after his father is deported. His primary literary model, which becomes a metaphor for Alex's isolation, is Robinson Crusoe's sojourn on a distant island. Alex scavenges to survive, as Crusoe did, and he feels as distant from the rest of the world as his literary role model did. Alex also is aided in his struggle to survive by his pet mouse, Snow, who takes on almost human characteristics in Alex's imagination. But most of all, he endures because he has hope: he is waiting for his father to return. He has to deal with neighbors with whom his father established a hidden cache of food, but who, now that his father is gone, refuse to share the food with him. Instead of casting his lot with these untrustworthy neighbors, he decides to attempt to survive on his own. He observes the life in the neighboring Polish street from his hidden lookout and eventually even dares to venture out into the Polish sector, in search of companionship with other children.

The novel is not only a vivid depiction of the fear and pain of living under the threat of death, it is also a philosophical exploration of the ambiguities of good and evil, fate, and human nature, from the perspective of a thoughtful and imaginative 11-year-old. For instance, thinking about the process of ''selection,'' Alex reflects on what it would be like to be someone on whom others' lives depended. ''I'd think, for instance, that if it were up to me, I'd decide to save anyone who had a big space between his front teeth, because I had one myself. But father and Boruch didn't have spaces. It would

have to be something else, then, like blue eyes.'' But he quickly realizes the absurdity of using any criteria to select some people for survival and allow others to be destroyed.

Alex also confronts the question of violence and its justification in self-defense. His father teaches him to shoot, and says, ''What counts most is the element of surprise. They'll never guess that you're armed. Take your time. You'll be more accurate from close up. If one is behind the other, you can thread them both with one shot.'' Alex laughs at the idea of ''threading'' people he shoots ''as if they were a bunch of beads,'' but he is also keenly aware that his mother would not laugh at this. She hates the war books and stories Alex loves. ''If you relate to people with trust and human kindness, they will always help you,'' is his mother's teaching. These conflicting messages are difficult for Alex to reconcile. His father says, ''Be kind but trust only yourself.''

Alex has to act on his father's advice when he encounters a German soldier pursuing two fleeing men during the Uprising. Alex shoots the soldier but goes into shock later. With great ingenuity and courage, he aids the two underground fighters, crossing over into the Polish sector to find a doctor to operate on the one who is injured. Despite hunger, danger, and long stretches of loneliness, Alex endures for five months until his father, against all the odds, returns. Alex is both child and man, seeing the surreal world of the ghetto and its surroundings with convincing clarity and retaining his sanity in an insane universe. Oddly, yet believably, Alex's ordeal is not bleak, though it is terrifying at times. It is a heroic story about a boy who is forced to become a man but who does not lose his childlikeness or his humanity.

—J.D. Stahl

J

JACOB THE LIAR (Jakob der Lügner)
Novel by Jurek Becker, 1969

The concept for *Jakob der Lügner* first appeared in a film script Jurek Becker wrote around 1962. When sensitivity to Soviet reception of the film lead to the East German government halting its production, Becker transformed the script into a novel (1969). The novel was published in English in 1975 and in a new translation in 1996. The title character is an unwilling hero who captures the attention of his fellow Jews in a Nazi-run ghetto by supplying them with news of the Soviet army's imminent liberation of the ghetto—news garnered from an overheard radio broadcast. Many readers will be captivated by the novel's poetic language and by the humor with which people in this most horrifying place confront life and death. This novel, which can be an entertaining and funny read, also has much to say, however, about the mechanisms of power and the truths that support it.

The "lie" of the title refers to Jakob's lies about having a radio. Jakob's first report of the advancing Soviets is real, but when ghetto residents begin asking for follow-up stories, Jakob refuses their requests, until he realizes that his story has brought the rarest of commodities to the ghetto: hope. In order to maintain that hope, he must manufacture news. The notion that lies can produce positive and desired results—results that are accepted as truth—points to one of the novel's major themes: the role of narrative in the production of truth.

The world of Becker's novel is untruthful on several levels. As an historic depiction of a Nazi-run ghetto, it lacks accuracy. On an even broader level, truth and lies have become entirely inverted in the ghetto. Horrendous acts, such as murder, starvation, deportation, and humiliation, have become commonplace truths, while things common outside the ghetto, such as watches, trees, and hope have become criminal or untruthful.

Becker's characters react to this bizarre world—this new "truth" imposed by the Nazis—in different ways. Though he is the only one in the ghetto to have an actual radio, the actor Frankfuter destroys it without ever listening in to a single broadcast. He tacitly accepts the Nazis' lies, hoping to survive them. In contrast, Dr. Kirschbaum, a renowned cardiologist, grasps an opportunity to free himself from the twisted values of the Nazis, in the process committing the only overt act of resistance in the novel. In Lina, the young orphan, we see a lack of experience outside the ghetto that would have provided the critical capacity to distinguish between truth and lies. Rosa, on the other hand, represents more critical approaches to truth and lies. The painful reality of losing her parents places her in opposition to the hopeful optimism of Jakob's fictional news.

Through these characters, Becker invites readers to consider the ways we react to truth and lies.

With Jakob's character, Becker takes the additional step of examining the production of truth. In his various attempts to find real news to incorporate into his fictional "broadcasts," Jakob learns that transforming truth into lies is difficult. Clearly, he learns, the lines between truth and lies are sometimes blurred. At the same time, Jakob realizes that those with the ability to produce truth gain control and power. This realization is vital to an understanding of the Holocaust and the mechanisms by which dictatorships take control.

Becker's examination of the mechanisms of truth production is underscored by the structure of *Jakob the Liar*. A modern-day narrator establishes a narrative frame around the linear main narrative of Jakob's story. The narrator's attempts to get the facts of Jakob's story, and to warn us when he cannot, establish narration as the dominant theme of the novel.

The most dramatic example of narrative possibilities and of the role of narration in establishing truth comes at the conclusion of the novel, when the narrator provides two possible endings. The contrast between the two—one true, the other a lie—highlights the tension between truth and lies that pervades the novel. This tension encourages readers to examine the truth content of the text in order to discern who is defining truth and how the process of definition affects the story and its interpretation.

The theme of truth and lies and the two endings also offer a critique of socialist realism, a literary doctrine that insisted on positive heroes and constructive, forward-looking themes. At the same time, the novel subverts traditional antifascist interpretations of the Holocaust still sanctioned at that time in East Germany. By questioning these doctrines, and by showing the disastrous consequences of insisting on adherence to specific truths, *Jakob the Liar* questions the use of power inherent in the production of truth and furthers understanding of the misuses of power during the Holocaust and since.

—Gregory Baer

JAKOB LITTNERS AUFZEICHNUNGEN AUS EINEM ERDLOCH: ROMAN
Novel by Wolfgang Koeppen, 1948

In the preface to the 1993 edition of his novel *Jakob Littners Aufzeichnungen aus einem Erdloch,* Wolfgang Koeppen states that in 1946–47 his friend the publisher Herbert Kluger told him about the fate of Jakob Littner. Based on his friend's narration, Koeppen reconstructed Littner's story: "I had dreamed of it." Littner was born in 1883 in Oświęcim (Auschwitz) and died in 1950 in New York City. A Polish citizen, he had escaped from Munich to Prague and then to Kraków, remaining there until the German army marched on the city and he was forced to go further east. He lived in the ghetto in the Polish-Ukranian city of Zbaraz until it was demolished on 8 June 1943. Littner and his longtime companion, Janina, were able to hide in a hole in the cellar of an impoverished Polish noble only by paying him immense sums of money. His narration is one of the few authentic documents of the German policies against the Jews before they were killed.

Returning to his hometown—which, as Koeppen writes in his preface, "was destroyed by the bombs of his saviors"— Littner believed that he had "seen murderers. He wanted to scream, but he only choked. He wanted to speak and look in the faces that had tolerated everything." He emigrated to the United States and, after his arrival, began sending CARE packages to Koeppen as payment for writing the book. Koeppen says, "I ate food from American cans and wrote down the woeful story of a German Jew. This is how it became my story." The book was issued by Kluger's publishing house in 1948 and was reissued in 1985. In 1993 the book was issued again by Jüdischer Verlag, a branch of the publishing house Suhrkamp, and a paperback edition followed in 1994, this time without the subtitle "Novel." Meanwhile, a public debate had begun over the authorship of Koeppen, with some critics attacking him on the issue of copyright. Littner's heirs had found a manuscript, of 183 pages, entitled *Mein Weg durch die Nacht* ("My Way through the Night"), which apparently had served as Koeppen's model.

Littner's introduction is dated 9 November 1945. He says that with this document he wanted to provide evidence, to "find out facts in the interest of truth," and to offer an example "for the innumerable and nameless who have shown their noble ethos." To this end Littner tried to depict his experiences as accurately as possible, and his work is striking in its attention to detail. At the same time Littner repeatedly emphasizes his faith in God's leadership. Even as a child he was filled with the fear of God and with faith in God: "Due to the disastrous events I was only confirmed in my faith of God." In his book he sets his faith against the dominant "spirit of unbelief and materialism."

While Koeppen copied a number of passages from Littner's manuscript, he also generalized and mythologized Littner's factual account and turned it into literature. As the critic Roland Ulrich has said, "an inner diary" was created "reminiscent of Hiob, Kierkegaard and Dostoyevsky." In his version of Littner's story Koeppen focuses on symbols of death, and Littner's life becomes a parable for modern existence in a dark world, the metaphors for which are the prison and the ghetto. Littner appears as a new Ahasver, the victim of a kafkaesque bureaucracy of evil. Only gradually does he find

his way from doubt to faith in God. But Koeppen also stresses the role of the so-called good Germans: "They have withstood the slogan of inhumanity." In the end Koeppen's Littner emphasizes that he does not hate those who were guilty. He will not forgive them, however, because what has happened cannot be judged by man but only by God. The interpretation of Littner's manuscript as a poetic work and the identification with the victim are actually Koeppen's reflections on his own guilt: he was in opposition but without the courage to stand up to the Nazis for his beliefs. In this way Littner becomes an image projected by Koeppen, a reinterpretation that has been widely criticized.

—Walter Schmitz

JEWELS AND ASHES
Memoir by Arnold Zable, 1991

Arnold Zable's *Jewels and Ashes* is one of several Australian Jewish narratives in which second generation post-Holocaust Australian Jews travel to central or eastern Europe to visit ancestral places destroyed in the Holocaust. Other well-known examples include **Mark Baker**'s *The Fiftieth Gate,* **Lily Brett**'s novel *Too Many Men,* Andrew Riemer's *Inside Outside* and *The Habsburg Café,* and **Susan Varga**'s *Heddy and Me.* Riemer and Varga are child survivors whose early childhoods were spent in hiding with parents. In some instances—Baker, Brett, and Varga—parent survivors accompany their children on their journeys to the scenes of wartime catastrophe.

Zable's parents left Bialystok before the war. The families that remained were decimated. *Jewels and Ashes* recounts what amounts to a spiritual return to Poland, a journey Zable undertakes on his own, but with an imagination fired by parental and other stories. For Zable the world—not least the gone world of eastern European Jewry—is alive with stories, some enchanted, some catastrophic. The book's title alludes to the "elders" who "left a legacy of fragments, a jumble of jewels and ashes, and forests of severed family trees which their children now explore and try somehow to restore."

For the project of restoration Zable employs a nuanced narrative structure comprised of the physical journey, intermittent flashbacks to his childhood, Polish history up to the Holocaust and beyond, personal and metaphysical rumination, and a circular framing configuration whereby the narrative begins and ends with images of his parents. Amid these many currents there is a predominant movement from darkness, confusion, and pain toward intimations of acceptance, harmony, and even peace. The book's final scene recalls a picnic during which the young Arnold finds a dented Ping-Pong ball.

His mother delights him by dropping it in boiling water until its spherical shape is restored. But the sense of resolution is always necessarily partial, and it is hard-won: ''Perhaps this is how it has always been for descendants of lost families: we search within a tangle of aborted memories, while stumbling towards a mythical home which seems to elude us as it recedes into false turns and dead ends.''

Upon arrival at Bialystok he senses the profound doubleness of the place and of the world more generally: ''Romance and terror, light and shadow, replicas and originals, hover side by side, seeking reconciliation . . . yet, somehow, never have I felt so much at peace.'' Zable is not only a skilled narrator of place but also of those who inhabit places and who invest them with the magic and indestructibility of story. One of several memorable figures in the book is Buklinski, ''one of the very last Bialystoker Jews,'' a survivor, a man of frenetic intensity who ''weaves tall stories in a frenzy'' before he subsides into tearful recollection of his two years in Auschwitz. Aside from Arnold, the most powerful single human presence in the book is his father, Meier, also a man of great intensity, whose memory ''unravels like the scrolls that were paraded on Simchas Torah.'' It is in large part from his father that the son learns his love of words, of stories; from him, too, he gleans a life trajectory that begins in tumult, loss, and darkness and ''moves towards inner balance, an integrity.'' For Zable, as for so many Jewish writers and thinkers, words bear the power of transcendence; they can summon the inexpressible. His own understatedly poetic style can do this beautifully, as when visiting Auschwitz he notes that:

> In recent months I have come to know many levels of silence. It is a language with an extensive vocabulary. There are silences which echo ancestral presences; silences in which it is possible to observe the slightest movement of dust, an insect in hiding, a pod floating from a dandelion with the faintest promise of rebirth; and the awesome silence of forest clearings where mass executions took place against mute backdrops of stunning beauty. Yet here, in the headquarters if the Reich terror network, the vocabulary of silence reaches beyond its own limits. It overwhelms with the sheer force of numbers: and the fact that here, lived and worked a company of technicians and bureaucrats who went about the task of efficiently and quickly annihilating over a million human beings.

There are also stories that can reveal the silence of ''perfection and a hint that somewhere, very close, there hovers another realm in which can be found an understanding and acceptance of things that go far beyond mere words.'' This is a statement of faith, but not of specifically Jewish faith.

Jewels and Ashes's yearning for restoration reflects a double acknowledgment: an acknowledgment not only that the Holocaust and other catastrophes have happened but also that

human potentiality is so much greater than this. Zable's sometimes harrowing memoir is finally an act of affirmation.

—Richard Freadman

JOEL BRAND: DIE GESCHICHTE EINES GESCHÄFTS
Play by Heinar Kipphardt, 1965

In *Joel Brand: Die Geschichte eines Geschäfts* (1965; ''Joel Brand: The Story of a Business Transaction''), Heinar Kipphardt takes up one of the murkiest episodes of the Holocaust: Adolf Eichmann's proposal to trade 10,000 trucks for one million Jews during his ''cleansing operations'' in Hungary. The deportations in the summer of 1944 were to be Eichmann's last hurrah, and they were opposed by rival agencies, who, in the face of Hitler's collapse, preferred to dissolve the camps and enter into secret negotiations with the Allies. Eichmann's chief rival within the Nazi Party, Kurt Becher, a member of the Waffen-SS and a notorious war profiteer who took his orders from Heinrich Himmler and Oswald Pohl, the head of the Economic Office, was bent on pursuing the deal. Eichmann, who took his orders from his old buddy from Linz, Ernst Kaltenbrunner, Reinhard Heydrich's successor as head of the Reich Security Main Office, was bent on ridding Europe of all remaining Jews and thought the proposed exchange a farce. A maliciously chummy banter between Eichmann and Becher opens the play.

Eichmann arrived in Budapest in March 1944, and on April 15th (Brand's 38th birthday) he summoned Brand, one of the leaders of the quasi-legal Jewish Relief and Rescue Committee, to pass on Himmler's offer. What follows are a series of disastrous stalling devices, alibis, bogus claims that Brand's demands exceed the claimant's jurisdiction, and feuds among the perpetrators, bystanders, and victims. Brand approaches the Zionist agency in Istanbul and the myopic and rattled Swiss branch of the Joint Distribution Committee for the needful moneys. The members of the Istanbul-based Sochnuth refuse all aid without official sanction from the people in Jerusalem, and the Swiss representative, Saly Mayer, ''a national disaster'' and ''a man who lives on the moon,'' proposes to offer Eichmann funds from his blocked Swiss account. In all of these (futile) transactions Brand asks (vainly) for (spurious) written assurances that sufficient funds will be transmitted to stay all deportations, while his volatile colleague, Reszö Kasztner, remains in Budapest and tries to practice the same stalling tactics on Eichmann with apparent astuteness and common sense. En route to Syria, where he expects to negotiate with the head of the Jewish Agency in Palestine, Brand is kidnapped by British agents and taken, not to Jerusalem, but to Cairo. By now the Allies regard him as a nuisance whose traffic (in all senses) impedes their effort to get on with the war. A captain in intelligence assures him that the impending invasion of Europe, when the Germans will need all of their trucks as troop transports, is bound to forestall further deportations, an assurance Brand will not buy. Ultimately the commissioner for the Middle East, Lord Moyne—as outraged as the Swiss naïf by Eichmann's demand to trade human beings for merchandise—asks Brand what he expects him to do with the shipment of a million Jews to Palestine, apart from provoking an explosion among the Arabs. ''If there's no room on the planet for us,'' Brand tells him, ''there's nothing for us but to go into the gas.''

Despite its ho-hum reception, *Joel Brand* remains a grim reminder that if (*pace* Marx) ''reification reifies the reifier'' it may equally reify the victims. And if he stresses the exploitative nature of Eichmann's transactions, Kipphardt is fair enough to allow his two most mischievous (non-Nazi) characters—Mayer and Moyne (who remains offstage throughout the play)—to express the inhumanity of such deals. Brand himself meets the evasions of his bogus apologists (the people whom Lillian Hellman calls ''the civilized men who are sorry'') head-on. ''But my dear Mr. Brand,'' the British agent tells him, ''you must see the entire picture.'' Brand simply replies, ''I see my children [going into the gas].''

The action is so fast paced that Kipphardt has been taxed with writing a conventionally suspense-ridden play at the expense of all of the regulation props of ducodrama. (A television version of *Joel Brand,* which was aired a year before its stage debut, conformed much more nearly to the genre in using photomontage—Eichmann in a sailor suit, at a picnic, as a bridegroom; lastly, the shoes of his victims—and a speaker who introduced the actors, perhaps as a sop to the people who did not know who was who.) The filmic fluidity of the play suggests that Kipphardt might have done well to follow the procedure of supplying—on a screen or by use of a speaker—the conventional forward flashes: Eichmann tried by an Israeli court and executed on 1 June 1961; with Kasztner's help, Becher acquitted at the Nuremberg trials and set up as a wealthy Bremen businessman; Lord Moyne shot by Jewish terrorists in Cairo two months after the Brand conversations; Kasztner accused by Israeli Zionists in January 1954 of alleged complicity with Eichmann in suppressing evidence of the Auschwitz atrocities from Hungarian Jews, found guilty in June 1955, murdered in Tel Aviv in March 1957, and posthumously exonerated by the Israeli Supreme Court in January 1958. Brand survived to appear as one of the chief witnesses at the Eichmann trial and so, along with the villain himself, provides a nice link to Kipphardt's final play, *Bruder Eichmann.*

—Edgar Rosenberg

JOURNAL 1935–1944: THE FASCIST YEARS (Jurnal: 1935–1944)
Diary by Mihail Sebastian, 1996

Sebastian's diary covers the not-so-glorious period of three anti-Semitic dictatorships in the Romanian national history: the dictatorship of Carol II (1938–40), which followed the short-lived, rabidly anti-Semitic government of Goga-Cuza (December 1937–February 1938); the dictatorship of Ion Antonescu in alliance with the Iron Guard (September 1940–January 1941); and the dictatorship of Antonescu without the Iron Guard (1941–44).

Of course Sebastian's diary was not the first literary description of the nazification of a European society seen through the eyes of a Jewish intellectual. Perhaps the closest example of a similar diary is **Victor Klemperer**'s *I Will Bear Witness: A Diary of the Nazi Years, 1933–1941*. Like Sebastian, Klemperer was in a brutal and merciless way rejected by this society only because he was Jewish. Like Sebastian, Klemperer registered the systematic shrinking of the physical and intellectual space around him. The comparison cannot go too far. If Klemperer lived in an ultimate Nazi society Sebastian survived in a world of opportunistic fascism. Like about half of the Romanian Jewry Sebastian remained alive because of the change of tactics of the Romanian authorities in terms of the solving of the ''Jewish problem.'' When he saw that Romania might not win the war in alliance with Nazi Germany, Antonescu and his clique tried to win the war changing sides. From a population targeted for extermination the Romanian Jews became a bargaining chip, a possible way through which the Romanian authorities were hoping to buy the goodwill of the Allies.

The diary refers often to Sebastian's friends, but it represents more than that: It is the political chronicle of the free falling of the Romanian intelligentsia toward fascism. As the diary enters the war period the physical space around Sebastian gets narrower; many of his friends are deserting him, and the heavy anti-Semitic legislation makes him a pariah. Already in 1937 Sebastian did not have too many illusions about his friends who became Iron Guards. He continued to socialize with them, acknowledging that this represents for him something almost unbearable.

One of the closest friends of Sebastian who became rabidly anti-Semitic under the influence of the Iron Guard was Mircea Eliade, whose fanatical involvement with the Iron Guard Sebastian records in a subtle and sad way. A well-known journalist and novelist in interwar Romania, Eliade had after World War II an outstanding scholarly career at the University of Chicago as a historian of religions. Unlike other famous representatives of his generation Eliade never truly acknowledged his past as an Iron Guard ideologist and never regretted his involvement with this criminal organization.

Another close friend of Sebastian was the well-known novelist Camil Petrescu, who was a casual anti-Semite. He was not an Iron Guard, but he reflected perhaps better than anybody else the nazification and the opportunism of a great part of the Romanian intelligentsia during World War II. Sebastian was very fond of him and considered him one of the finest minds in Romania. During the war Petrescu bought heavily into official anti-Semitic propaganda clichés of the Antonescu regime that accused the Jews of being responsible for all the military misfortunes of Romania and therefore responsible for their own tragic fate. Accordingly Petrescu thought that the Jews from Bessarabia and Transnistria deserved to be massacred or deported because they allegedly fired against the Romanian troops and because the Russians committed the same atrocities when they built the Volga Canal. According to Petrescu the Jews, especially the American ones, were also guilty for the continuation of the war because they were making any compromise impossible.

Of course not all of Sebastian's friends were insensitive or sensitive anti-Semites. Several friends—such as the diplomat and politician Constantin Visoianu, one of the leaders of the Romanian post-World War II emigration in the United States; Prince Antoine Bibescu, his benefactor; and professor Alexandru Rosetti—supported him morally and materially at the height of the fascist terror.

Sebastian described with a fascinating accuracy the Romanian Holocaust. Like most of the Jews from Regat (Romania in its pre-World War I borders) Sebastian was not deported to concentration camps. Unlike the Jews from Bessarabia, Bukovina, and Transnistria who were deported and massacred en masse Sebastian was taken out to do forced labor, his radio and bicycle were confiscated, he was denied almost all income, he was heavily fined, and he was given tiny discriminatory rations of food, but was not ghettoized. He continued therefore to witness what was happening to the less-fortunate fellow Jews from Romania's periphery. Sebastian saw and described the beginning of forced labor in Romania. During January 1941 Sebastian accurately described the "bestial ferocity" of the pogrom of Bucharest, a sort of Romanian *Kristallnacht* during which 121 Jews were killed, some of them hanged on butchery hooks at the abattoir with "kosher meat" inscriptions on their bodies. During the spring of 1941 Sebastian witnessed the first roundups of Jews and the harsh conditions under which the forced labor of Jews took place. He recorded promptly in his diary the pogrom of Iasi from June 1941, which is described as "a dark, sombre, insane nightmare," and its death trains in which 2,683 Jews died because of lack of air and water. Sebastian also recorded—with rich details later confirmed by archival documents—the conditions under which the deportations of Jews from Bessarabia and Bukovina to Transnistria took place during the summer and the fall of 1941. Quoting eyewitnesses Sebastian describes in his diary the deportees as "a long wretched line of women in tatters, with small children equally ragged."

Sebastian's diary was published for the first time in extenso in 1996 in Romania (*Jurnal 1935–1944*). French (*Journal, 1935–1944*, 1988) and U.S. editions (*Journal 1935–1944: The Fascist Years,* 2000) followed. The publication of the diary had the effect of a time bomb. Its explosion generated an ample debate in Romania and abroad about Romanian anti-Semitism and the Holocaust in Romania.

—Radu Ioanid

THE JOURNEY (Podróż)
Novel by Ida Fink, 1990

Ida Fink's novel *Podróż* first appeared in Polish in 1990. It was published in English translation as *The Journey* in 1992. Like her earlier collected stories, *A Scrap of Time,* it is set against the Holocaust and is so deeply rooted in her own personal experiences that it might just as easily be viewed as a memoir. It deals centrally with her escape, along with her sister, from the Nazi death machine. It is her physician father who realizes in 1942 that the only way to save his two grown daughters from the Germans' increasingly frequent and brutal roundups is to obtain false identity cards and working papers for them so that they can leave Poland and travel into Germany as volunteer laborers.

Pretending to be two young peasant girls, they dress up in "old winter coats . . . cinched with rawhide belts to make them look more peasant like," topped off with the most telling accessory, beautiful kerchiefs for their hair decorated in a popular pattern of "roses blooming among green leaves." Noting with satisfaction that she is a blond (her sister's "Jewish" dark hair is a constant source of anxiety), she is nonetheless concerned about her own appearance. Repeating to herself her brother's observation that "the craziest plans have the greatest chance of succeeding," she sets out with her sister on their journey, a "harrowing odyssey, as the *New Yorker* reviewer described it, which "has the quality of a fox hunt seen through the eyes of the fox."

The narrator's real name is never given, although we learn three different names that each sister assumes during their flight. From the outset, she realizes that only through "cleverness and luck" will they be able to survive—to deal with informers and blackmailers along the way who either recognize them from their hometown or who suspect they are Jewish and threaten to turn them in to the Gestapo. Wherever they go, they are aware, chillingly, that they are in enemy territory. At a stopover in Lvov, for example, a cabdriver calls their attention to a column of emaciated figures inching their way along a rainy street; they are probably prisoners, the narrator guesses, from a nearby detention or concentration camp. Pointing toward them, the cabdriver, a callous bystander, tells the sisters, "Look, the Yids are marching."

Once they arrive at the Ruhr Valley munitions factory to which they have been assigned, the sisters settle into a routine in the ironworks shop. They live in an adjoining camp barracks with a hundred other Polish-German girls who are also labor volunteers. Working under the German commandant of the camp, Johan Schmidt, the sisters must be ever vigilant to maintain their disguise as Christian peasant girls, fresh from the countryside, passive, a bit slow-witted. Even though they are ever on guard, they fall under suspicion, along with five other Jewish girls who are also in hiding. Betrayal is likely, if not for the reward, then simply for the satisfaction of their fellow workers. Even the youngest member of the volunteers, thirteen-year-old Anya, sighs with relief when the narrator denies the rumor that she is Jewish. "It would be such a pity," says Anya. "I don't like Jews." Recognizing that "only a fraction of a second separated us from the word 'Jew,'" and that at any moment they might be denounced, the narrator considers whether to try to bribe Schmidt or try to escape.

As it turns out, Schmidt has a spark of decency. After agreeing to help out a girl he has been sleeping with, he agrees to help the others as well by pretending he doesn't see them escaping. He even reminds them that their train will depart at seven: "You can still make it." It is a rare and unexpected act of kindness which leaves them "speechless with amazement," especially after he adds "You're a brave bunch . . . a brave bunch . . ."

On the final lap of their journey the sisters, still disguised as Aryan "country girls," are able to settle into farm labor for five months. Again they escape in order to travel south to Cologne, Bonn, Frankfurt, and Heidelberg—always in short segments since longer trips would require them to show identification. When the war is finally over, the sisters return to the city where their father, who has somehow survived on his own, is still living. Marvelously and miraculously, they return together "just as they had left together."

We travel with them through landscapes depicted in such rich and compelling detail that they become an integral part of the story. The natural world is always a presence hovering in the background—benignly indifferent to their suffering, as they sadly observe, but nonetheless comforting in its beauty and constancy. Indeed, at the end the narrator tells us that it is only the natural landscapes that she recalls: "the darkness of the autumn night, the gusting wind, the rustle of trees in the alley . . . the wide plain opening up before us." This is a tense and powerful novel, a tale of terror—as any work about the Holocaust must be—that is mitigated only by the tenderness of the telling and the humanity and rare artistry of the teller.

—Jacqueline Berke

JUBILÄUM
Play by George Tabori, 1984

George Tabori premiered his play *Jubiläum* ("Jubilee") in Germany on 30 January 1983, the fiftieth anniversary of Hitler's takeover. In the Bible the year of jubilee (the fiftieth year) is a holy year and is considered a time of reckoning, when justice is restored. Tabori, a Hungarian Jew, set his story in a Jewish cemetery in Germany where the dead are beginning to rise up, in the year in which, Tabori insinuated, justice might finally prevail. Utilizing the episodic form used by playwright **Bertolt Brecht,** Tabori based his play on contemporary newspaper articles, court records, and personal experiences. As in his earlier Holocaust plays, Tabori used dark humor to present a disconcerting case study of contemporary German society.

Originally conceived as a continuation of Brecht's anti-Nazi play *Fear and Misery in the Third Reich, Jubiläum* is a series of 12 episodes involving seven characters whose lives are intertwined. They include a Jewish couple, Lotte and her husband Arnold, whose father was killed at Auschwitz; a homosexual couple, Otto and his partner Helmut, whose concern over his neo-Nazi nephew Jürgen causes him to undergo circumcision out of guilt over the Holocaust; Jürgen, the young, brutal neo-Nazi; Mitzi, Arnold's crippled niece who is driven to suicide by Jürgen's taunts; and Wumpf, the gravedigger clown whose scenes echo his prototype's in *Hamlet.*

The play begins as Jürgen races up and spray paints "JEW DOG DIE" all over the Jewish graves. Arnold, one of the inhabitants of the graveyard, shakes his head ruefully and corrects the young man, "'JEW-DOG' with a hyphen, young man." Otto chimes in, "The cross [swastika] is wrong too— you missed a line on the left side." These ironic comments, which frighten Jürgen away, draw the audience into an unusual world of walking corpses who act out various roles in their conversations with one another: psychiatrist and patient, defendants and prosecutors, victims and perpetrators.

The scenes begin and end with no clear resolution; past, present, and future merge to form a collage that hints at Tabori's fears of the resurgence of the Nazi mind-set, personified by Jürgen, the young neo-Nazi who claims that "a little N-A-Z-I" is present in all of them. Some characters reveal their memories of abuse during the Holocaust; others relate contemporary incidents of anti-Semitism and xenophobia, asking questions, like the sons in Tabori's *The Cannibals,* about their parents' behaviors in the past.

The history of Jürgen's development is revealed in order to clarify the link between the Nazi period and the present. When Jürgen was a child, his father, an SS man, delighted him with glorious stories of his adventures during the war. In adolescence Jürgen joined a gang whose major interests included smoking, tormenting foreigners, and drinking. He was thrown out of school and into jail several times, but his uncle, "a judge of the old school," always managed to get him off. Later, in a scene between Jürgen and Helmut (where Jürgen forces Helmut to play his father), the audience learns how his father's crimes become transformed into acceptable behavior in the boy's eyes, confirmed by society's failure to prosecute many Nazis. Unlike Schreckinger's son in *The Cannibals*, Jürgen takes perverse pride in emulating his father.

While Jürgen serves to incarnate Tabori's fears, Arnold serves as a voice of hope and desire for reconciliation. He describes a recurring scenario of his childhood. His parents often fought, throwing things at each other, yelling and crying, while the child Arnold stood at the door, "waiting for them to get along again." Arnold pities Jürgen, just as he once pitied Hitler, who always seemed lonely to him. In the end Arnold's father, who was killed at Auschwitz, appears to Arnold, offering him bread, which Arnold shares with everyone, including Jürgen. As in *The Cannibals,* Tabori utilized the idea of Holy Communion or the sharing of bread in the Jewish Sabbath, but with a twist: the bread "tastes funny." Thus, it becomes a symbol both of reconciliation and of retribution. He also stressed the theme of the questioning son who survives his father, as in several of his other plays. Tabori's own father, Cornelius, was murdered at Auschwitz.

Brecht's influence on Tabori is evident in this play. Tabori borrowed liberally from the most famous episode of *Fear and Misery,* "The Jewish Wife." Lotte's predicament when she is trapped in a phone booth is clearly patterned after "The Jewish Wife." Also, Helmut wears a dress and reads "The Jewish Wife" as he recovers from his circumcision. Allusions to *Hamlet* and *The Merchant of Venice* also appear throughout the text. By referring to these other texts, Tabori added more layers to the horror he illustrated. Through the play's setting, form, and content, Tabori sounded an urgent warning to his German audiences, articulating his hopes and fears for the future.

—Susan Russell

K

KADDISH FOR A CHILD NOT BORN (Kaddis a meg nem született gyermekért)
Novel by Imre Kertész, 1990

In a sense Imre Kertész's *Kaddis a meg nem született gyermekért* (1990; *Kaddish for a Child Not Born,* 1997) is a sequel to his first novel. Here the narrator of *Fateless,* the 14-year-old Holocaust survivor who coolly recounts his experiences in the camps, has turned into a frantic middle-aged man, a writer taking stock of his botched life: his failed marriage, his unyielding obsession with Auschwitz, and his own Jewishness. At first he reminds us of one of Dostoevsky's desperate chatterboxes as he forever corrects and qualifies his words, acutely aware, both as a writer and an Auschwitz survivor, that often "words lose their form, their context, their signification; they simply turn to naught." He also realizes during the fevered, spellbinding monologue that constitutes the novel that "my urge to speak is nothing but noisy silence, articulated silence . . ."

The novel is an elegy—*kaddish* is a painfully ironic word from a man alienated from Judaism—not just for an unborn child but for the life of a mid-twentieth century, Middle European assimilated Jew who had been saddled with a fate he could neither evade nor accept. Not only does he mourn his fate but also he rails against it with an outraged sense of humanity that he regards, willy-nilly, as Jewish. His wife, born after Auschwitz, who had tried to save his benighted soul, his "sick and poisoned consciousness," had to give up—she chose life, another man, and children. What our tormented narrator tries to explain to his now ex-wife is that the reason he couldn't see himself bringing a child into this world had to do not only with his refusal to transmit the awful baggage of Auschwitz to another generation but also with the simple and terrible recognition that "I was incapable of assimilating myself to the existing, the real, to *life.*"

There was yet another reason this middle-aged Holocaust survivor living in communist Hungary didn't want to become a father. Recalling his own father, and the director of the boarding school where he was sent as a child after his parents' divorce, he sees them as stern and tyrannical authority figures. Indeed, he sees the tyrannies of the modern world, authoritarian rules that led to Auschwitz, in terms of forbidding fathers: "[T]he two terms, Auschwitz and father, resonate the same echoes in me, I told my wife. And if the observation is that God is an exalted father, then God, too, is revealed to me in the image of Auschwitz, I told my wife." Earlier in the narrative he puts his own gloss on a Thomas Bernhard quote: "Rule by terror invariably means rule by the father."

The narrator refers repeatedly to another childhood memory. He visited observant relatives in the country. One morning he accidentally opened the bedroom door and saw not his *sheitel*-wearing aunt but "a bald woman in a red gown in front of a mirror." He was shocked, appalled, and the image stayed with him—in the narrative it becomes a potent, many-layered symbol of Jewish vulnerability and shame. The narrator's life after the war becomes a temporary condition—he remains an inveterate renter rather than owner of things, a transient, a wanderer, and in the new political order he feels even more alienated. The ugliness of the housing project where he lives—the concrete slab of a building protrudes from an old Budapest neighborhood like an "oversized false limb"—not only is emblematic of the ugliness of "existing socialism" but also stands for the bleakness and hopelessness of his existence.

Kaddish is one long howl of negation, but as in Kertész's other novels of despair something strange, almost incomprehensible, happens that negates the negation. The narrator remembers a fellow inmate in Auschwitz, a "skeleton" everybody called Professor, who one day, upon seeing how very weak the narrator was, gave him his ration, though by doing this he lessened his own chance of survival. Under the circumstances, the narrator says, this act made no sense whatsoever. At the end of his recitation, the man without hope wants to be swept away by the "filthy flow of memories," he wants to drown in their "black warmth"—yet he lives on.

—Ivan Sanders

KING OF THE JEWS: A NOVEL OF THE HOLOCAUST
Novel by Leslie Epstein, 1979

Leslie Epstein's *King of the Jews* (1979) focuses on the morally ambiguous politics of a *Judenrat* (Jewish council) in the Lodz ghetto and on its flamboyant leader, Isaiah Chaim Trumpelman, a figure clearly modeled on the real-life Mordecai Chaim Rumkowski, a man who ruled his Polish ghetto with a combination of regal theatrics (stamps and script bore his image, and he often rode through the disease-ridden streets on a magnificent white horse) and political savvy. Heading the *Judenrat* was a game fraught with peril because it meant that a great number of Jews would have to be sacrificed so that a much larger number might survive. But it also meant, of course, that one was cooperating with the Nazis. History has not been kind to those who accepted the Nazis' offer.

Epstein's novel attempts to turn the facts of the Lodz ghetto into a grim moral fable. To this end, words such as "Nazi" or even "German" never appear. Instead, the murderers are called "the occupying power," storm troopers become "Warriors," and the SS is transmogrified into "Death-Headers." Writing in the pages of the *New York Times Sunday Book Review,* Robert Alter, who generally admired the novel, wonders about the effect that "this manipulation of names contributes to the peculiar generalizing effect of the novel as a whole." Others were more explicit about their objections. In his influential study, *A Double Dying: Reflections on Holocaust Literature* (1980), Alvin Rosenfeld worries that readers will be "drawn uncomfortably close to a cartoon version of life and death in the ghettos." The problem is not that the complicated, morally ambiguous story of a man such as Rumkowski lacks the stuff from which serious fiction can be made. Rather, Rosenfeld argues that what Epstein lacks "is imagination enough to set his players within and solid and memorable context and have them appear as something more than stick-figure, or caricatures of the 'types' they are meant to represent." Writing in the *Chicago Tribune,* Irving Abrahamson made no bones about how offensive he thought the novel was: "*King of the Jews* is a one-dimensional piece, failing utterly to explore the complex historical, philosophical, theological implications of the greatest crime in history."

Other critic-reviewers, however, found much to praise in Epstein's novel, including its penchant for dark, slapstick humor. How else to tell a story in which the material itself seems to resist even the best efforts of the imagination, and how to approach a character such as Rumkowski from the perspective of a third-generation American Jew who grew up in southern California? Satire, part of a long Jewish tradition, turned out, in Epstein's case at least, to be the answer.

So it is that Trumpelman comes to relish his role as the Lodz ghetto's larger-than-life representative, and so it is that he also wrestles with the rationalizations and uncertainties that vex him when he finally realizes the grisly destination of the trains that leave the small territory he ostensibly "rules." Still, to save 100 Jews by sending 10 away may, just may, be the stuff of sainthood. Thus, he thinks of himself as a "savior," the king of the Jews.

King of the Jews is also filled with the mordantly playful. As Rosenfeld points out, "cows fall suddenly into graves, guns fire or misfire at the wrong moments, feet stumble and buttons pop, the mad go strolling the crooked streets, starving mothers become the butt of mistaken jokes about cannibalism, the apparent dead return to life in whimsical and improbable fashion, even the sun and moon perform their rotations in odd and attention-grabbing ways." Rosenfeld, however, is not amused, insisting that these instances of glib humor have no place in a novel that aspires to seriousness and certainly not in a novel about the tragic circumstances surrounding the Lodz ghetto.

Others, however, would argue that Epstein's thickly textured portrait never completely abandons its sense that the Holocaust requires a distanced, even understated perspective if its painful story is to be told. Thus, at one point early in the novel, the reader encounters the following sentence: "On a bright afternoon in September 1939, a small dot, a speck, appeared high in the sky." To say more would diminish the power that Epstein's novel packs and the ways that it brings the reader slowly, even slyly, to its story of how I.C. Trumpelman deals with fantastic personal opportunities and the fearful consequences of shadow—and night—that eventually fell over every Jew in the Lodz ghetto.

Can a Jewish-American writer successfully imagine the horrors of what happened an ocean away? Some would say "No!" and say it in thunder. Others would be less rigid, especially when the novel in question is as skillfully rendered as that by Epstein. Much has happened since the pros and cons of *King of the Jews* were widely debated, and in large measure the voices of those who would automatically consign novels about the Holocaust to the ash heap have been silenced. For this Epstein's ambitious, daring novel rightly deserves a large share of the credit.

—Sanford Pinsker

KOL HA-SHIRIM: "ABA" (PIRKE PROZAH)
Poetry by Dan Pagis, 1991

Robert Alter notes displacement and playfulness as being singular features of Dan Pagis. This is particularly striking in Pagis's Holocaust poems, where both playfulness and displacement are means of restoring to the event the horror of initial confrontation or the impossibility of comprehending. Sometimes, as in the poem "Footprints," Pagis's playfulness falls into the category of black humor. Thus the poet, remembering his journey in a cattle car, combines it with associations from a banal prewar world. The incongruity is shattering, and once the point is made the thought breaks off in midsentence:

> Maybe there's a window here—if you
>   don't mind
> look near that body, maybe you can open up
> a bit. That reminds me
> (pardon me) of the joke about the two Jews
> in the train, they were traveling to

In the poem "Autobiography" the playfulness is once again expressed as a deliberate incongruity in tone. The biblical Abel narrates the poem, talking about his own death—and then, explicitly, about Holocaust death—in a deliberately offhand way. Jarred by the understatement (" . . . at first the details horrify / though finally they're a bore''), the reader is made to confront the event anew.

Displacement in these poems is sometimes a simple matter of presenting the self as separate from the event, as in "Roll Call": " . . . only I / am not there / am not there, am a mistake." In other poems separation is understood the opposite way, as the state of being of the survivor who cannot resume ordinary life. The poem "Instructions for Crossing the Border" tells a survivor in an ordinary railway car that he "is a man" and instructs him to "sit comfortably," but the man invoked in the opening line is "imaginary"—he cannot rejoin ordinary life. A different kind of displacement results from imagining the event itself from a distance or in a way that at first seems very far removed. Such is the case of the poem "In the Laboratory," about scorpions in a glass beaker. Someone blows poison gas into the beaker, and the poisonous insects turn into victims who feel loneliness, futility, and pain.

God is ambiguously involved in the events, sometimes as complicit, sometimes as distant and surprised, sometimes as provider of peace in an escape that is death. The experiment with scorpions from "In the Laboratory" is observed by "angels of punishment" who are startled. Who then ordered the punishment and why was its outcome surprising? The poem fails to answer. A different ambiguity is at the heart of the poem "Testimony," which begins with the statement that the murderers were created "in the image." The poet, by contrast, imagines himself of another origin: "A different creator made me." It is to this creator, who gives him a life that is like death (or a death that is like life), that the poet flees, describing this escape as "smoke to omnipotent smoke / that has no face or image." Like the initial metaphor ("in the image") that links God and murderer, this final metaphor, linking God and victim, comes from the Jewish tradition. Is it then the same God? Once again the poem gives no clear answer.

Pagis's poems often turn to the problem of understanding. In "Brain," which is not explicitly a Holocaust poem, Brain seeks insight but ultimately achieves peace—in death—when he can give up his quest. "Written in Pencil in the Sealed Railway-Car," Pagis's most anthologized poem, suggests either that there is nothing to say or that nothing can be said. The six-line poem is entirely circular:

> here in this carload
> i am eve
> with abel my son
> if you see my other son
> cain son of man
> tell him that i

The circularity (and its sense of entrapment) is more obvious in the Hebrew, which permits a seamless transition from the last word back to the first.

Related to the problem of understanding is the problem of memory. Among the instructions for crossing the border (in the poem of that name) is the paradoxical pair "You are not allowed to remember" (second line) and "You are not allowed to forget" (final line). The first is a condition for resuming life; the second is the survivor's inescapable burden. The need to forget is uppermost even for Brain, who has no connection with the Holocaust. The poem does not tell us what Brain needs to forget—as far as we can see, he has strictly lived the life of the mind. Pagis has perhaps lent him his own memory, or presents, in this poem, the need to forget as an overwhelming fact of existence.

Like "Brain" many Pagis poems that are not really about the Holocaust are not removed from it either. The narrator of "Spaceship" is "receiving a different light," a man apart. Like the hero of "Instructions for Crossing the Border," he cannot fathom the way ordinary surroundings are put together. "A Lesson in Observation" also begins far away from the subject—indeed, at the creation of the earth. Continuing the lesson, the class (whoever they are, they are plural) is shown a blue earth, and then children, and eventually screams and the abstract concept "memory." The final lines contain a question and an answer that is uncompromisingly bleak: "The little dot on the side? It seems to be / the only moon of that world. / It blew itself out even before this."

—Alice Nakhimovsky

L

THE LADY OF THE LAKE
Short Story by Bernard Malamud, 1958

Henry Levin, the protagonist of "The Lady of the Lake," from the collection *The Magic Barrel* (1958), is one of Bernard Malamud's New York Jews who seeks love and adventure by traveling abroad. When he comes into an inheritance, he quits his job and goes to Europe, ending up in Italy in a *pensione* in Stresa on Lake Maggiore. It is after World War II, and Italy is still a very poor country. Changing his name to Henry R. Freeman, symbolic of his attempt to change his life as well as his identity, Levin wanders around the area. The various islands in the lake fill him with a sense of expectancy, each an undiscovered world worth exploring, and he decides to visit them on a tour.

When his tours of two islands prove unsatisfying, his landlady suggests Isola del Dongo as an exceptionally beautiful place with exquisite gardens. One evening at sunset he rents a rowboat and goes out to the island alone. By this time the reader suspects that Freeman is something of a schlemiel, and his ineptness at rowing emphasizes the point. Nevertheless, he manages to get to the island, which is as lovely as his *padrona* has said. The island rises in terraces, the gardens filled with statuary, a palazzo at the top. Bathed in evening mists, it fills Freeman with "a sad memory of unlived life, his own, of all that had slipped through his fingers." At that moment he sees the figure of a young woman who is looking out at the water. Though tempted to speak to her, he notices how dark the night is getting. He returns to his rowboat and with difficulty makes it back to shore.

This is the start of Freeman's quest. When he finally meets the woman on the island, she identifies herself as Isabella del Dongo. Curiously, one of the first things Isabella asks him, after discovering that he is an American, is whether he is Jewish. Freeman is Jewish, but thinking that an admission would put off this obviously aristocratic Italian, he denies it.

Isabella is so beautiful that it does not take long for Freeman to fall in love. She allows him to visit, and on one occasion she disrobes and goes for a swim, inviting Freeman to follow. Finally summoning up his courage, he does, but by the time the awkward swimmer gets to the raft where she has lain down, she has returned to the island, and he has to swim back alone, where she awaits him with a towel.

Guiding Freeman on his visits to Isola del Dongo are Ernesto and his son, Giacobbe. The swimming episode occurs when Isabella tells Freeman that her family is away. Although Freeman is disappointed not to meet the del Dongos, he lets her show him through the palazzo, which is famous because Napolean supposedly once slept there. Isabella, however,

disabuses Freeman of the myth and admits that the Titians and other paintings are all copies. The incident is important in developing the theme of illusion. Freeman admits that he has a lot to learn since he cannot tell the fakes from the real.

Indeed, Freeman does have a lot to learn, as he later discovers when his passion for Isabella grows and he determines, after overcoming "a swarm of doubts concerning his plans and possibilities," to propose to her. When they finally meet again, this time in Stresa, Freeman learns the truth. Isabella is not a del Dongo after all but rather the daughter of Ernesto, the caretaker of the estate, and Giacobbe is her brother.

Despite Isabella's confession, Freeman does not admit who or what he is. Isabella says that she wanted to get to know him better, and Freeman again asserts that on his part he is not hiding anything. This is precisely what she is afraid of, she says, and she returns with her brother to the island, leaving Freeman in turmoil. Although hurt by her misrepresentations, and not thinking of his own, he still loves her and follows her to the island. When he finds her, Isabella again asks him if he is Jewish, and he again denies it. She uncovers her breast and shows him the tattooed number on it. An inmate at Buchenwald, she had hoped that he was Jewish so that she could marry him.

It is too late now for Freeman to come clean. Isabella disappears among the statues and the mists, and Freeman is left embracing only a moonlit stone. The Holocaust has taken a different toll here—robbed both Freeman and Isabella of a chance for possible happiness together. Her past is meaningful to her in a way that his apparently is meaningless to him. This is why he denies the truth of his origin, and this is why she cannot accept him.

—Jay L. Halio

LANDSCAPE IN CONCRETE (Landschaft in Beton)
Novel by Jakov Lind, 1963

Jakov Lind's literary work *Landscape in Concrete* (1966; *Landschaft in Beton,* 1963) clearly shows the imprint of his personal history, which has been shaped by his experience of the Holocaust and World War II. In 1938, 11-year-old Lind left his native Austria for the perceived safety of The Netherlands. Following the Nazi occupation in 1942 Lind escaped deportation, and after assuming the identity of the fictitious young Dutchman Jan Overbeek he lived out the war in Nazi Germany. Not surprisingly his experiences during the war emerged as his primary topic. In his autobiographical text *Crossing: The*

Discovery of Two Islands, published in 1991, Lind asserts, ''my theme was the war, my war, what it meant to me and what had happened. This was the theme with many variations I must write about.'' Lind's literary works are not only unified by their subject matter but also by the author's consistent choice of the grotesque, the absurd, and the fantastic as a literary means to re-create the atmosphere of terror inherent in his experience of National Socialism and war.

Originally published in German, *Landscape in Concrete* is Lind's first full-length novel. It tells the story of Gauthier Bachmann, a German soldier who wanders through Nazi-occupied Europe in search of a new regiment after his own perishes in a mud slide in Russia. Fearing discharge for a mental disorder and eager to prove himself worthy as a soldier, he is duped into carrying out atrocious acts of revenge for two other men. After he murders a Norwegian family at the command of a Nazi collaborator, Bachmann seems to regain some understanding of his situation and seeks medical treatment, only to be told that he is fit to serve. Losing his last grip on reality, Bachmann gruesomely murders the young woman he loves and embarks again on his search for his regiment.

Gauthier Bachmann embodies the average German soldier whose lack of identity and low self-esteem make him a perfect tool for the Nazis. He is not a Nazi himself—he is just eager to serve his country. In addition, being a soldier has provided him with an identity and a place within a collective that he desperately seeks to reclaim: ''I'd like to feel human again, that's what I'm really after, I'm sick of being an outcast, see what I mean?'' The need to prove himself worthy of both his country and the collective makes him the perfect tool to carry out the brutalities of war or rather the atrocities of the Nazis as is indicated by Bachmann's memory of his killing all prisoners taken at a Russian village. Bachmann's willingness to kill does not remain limited to the battlefield. He easily falls for the Norwegian Nazi collaborator's promises that the murder of the Norwegian family will gain him renewed respect. Finally killing becomes an almost unconscious response to his environment. Bachmann has, in Lind's words in *Crossing,* turned into the ''military Golem, which we created out of fear and must now live in fear of.''

As in his first published work, ''Soul of Wood'' (1962), Lind employs the stylistic means of grotesque alienation to re-create the horrors of war. It is a world of violence in which the lines between victim and perpetrator become increasingly indistinguishable, as is demonstrated in the character of Bachmann. Already mentally destabilized by the horrors of the war, Bachmann's longing for a secure identity as a soldier makes him a willing victim of the manipulations of others, but a victim nevertheless. He commits his last murder in a hallucinatory daze following a bombing attack. The circular structure of the novel indicates that Bachmann is irretrievably caught in the insane world of war and anticipates his future acts of violence. The title, *Landscape in Concrete,* refers not only to

the natural landscape covered with the concrete remains of buildings destroyed by bombs but to Bachmann's humanity, which was also buried in the atrocities of war.

—Helga Schreckenberger

LANDSCAPE OF SCREAMS (Landschaft aus Schreien)
Poem by Nelly Sachs, 1957

In ''Landscape of Screams,'' first published in *Und niemand weiss weiter* (1957), Nelly Sachs depicts a world overrun by violence. The landscape of the poem is immense in terms of time and space; it spans history, from the Biblical era to the twentieth century, and encompasses the entire globe, from Hiroshima to the concentration camp at Maidanek. The violence of the scream is not a noise but something that is seen, a horrific vision. While the scream still represents the most primal human response to terror in the poem, it has been silenced, dispossessed of its power of expression. With this negation—of the human voice's ability to make sound, of its ability to describe—any attempt to find sense in atrocities like the Holocaust becomes impossible. What remains is a barren tableau, a terrain devoid of meaning.

The ''landscape of screams'' is dominated by the language of color and gesture rather than sound. The first stanza introduces us to the screams in the act of tearing open ''the black bandage'' of the night. Attempts to speak, even breathe, are continually choked, like ''the gulping train of breath of the very old, / slashed into seared azure with burning tails.'' Blood flows throughout the poem: ''wildly rearing manes of sacrificial blood,'' arrows ''released / from bloody quivers,'' ''trees of sleep rear blood-licking from the ground.'' The effect of such graphic imagery is to render the screams speechless. Sight overpowers the voice.

Sachs strips the scream of its power to articulate in stanza three:

> O hieroglyph of screams
> engraved at the entrance gate to death.

Here the scream has effectively become a written language, something to be deciphered rather than heard. Sachs dislocates the scream from its meaning; it is not only silent but unintelligible.

This sense of dislocation is further aggravated by the absence of any clearly defined connection between scream and source. While Sachs populates her landscape with people—Abraham, Job, prisoners, and saints—she has rendered their voices impotent. ''Abraham's scream'' for his son Isaac is left ''preserved''—and, presumably, unheard—''at the great ear of the Bible''; ''Job's scream'' is swallowed up by the ''four winds.'' Their screams have become disembodied, forced to act on their own. And yet their ability to make noise is continually stifled. They are ''shut tight with the shredded mandibles of fish'' or else ''concealed in Mount Olive/like a crystal-bound insect overwhelmed by impotence.'' Throughout the poem the effort of the scream is met by extreme violence, a violence inflicted repeatedly on the human throat. The reader encounters ''shattered throat flutes,'' throats slashed by the ''knife of evening red.'' Rendered useless, the throat becomes a mere image, a ''nightmare pattern'' on a tapestry.

This disembodiment is taken to its logical extreme when the scream is ripped away from the throat completely and reinvented as a function of the sense of sight, ''the visionary eye tortured blind'':

> O you bleeding eye
> in the tattered eclipse of the sun
> hung up to be dried by God
> in the cosmos—

The image of the wounded eye suggests that soon vision, too, will be lost. Here Sachs has withdrawn the poem from the landscape of screams and thrust it into the void. The words seek vainly for resolution, just as the word ''cosmos'' seeks its end point. We are left with a calm and silent God—implicated, somehow, in these crimes, yet indifferent to the consequences.

—Stephen Meyer

THE LAST JEW
Play by Yaffa Eliach, 1977

The Last Jew is a four-act play written by Yaffa Eliach and Uri Assaf. It was first produced and broadcast live by Israel's National Broadcasting Company on 7 April 1975 in the Zavta Theater, Tel-Aviv, to commemorate the Day of Heroes and Martyrs. This work compares the worlds of two very different generations that are dealing with the Holocaust in dissimilar fashions. The first generation consists of two madmen who cannot distinguish present from past, Nachumadman and Maftir-Yonah; the Last Jew of the Eisysky shtetl, Avraham Schneiderman; and Vasily Levangorski, who was responsible for following German orders by massacring all of the Eisysky Jews in September 1941. Schneiderman is the only Eisysky Jew who remained alive, living for the past 30 years in the Eisysky shtetl. The younger generation represents the present Israeli reality in 1971. Dr. Bluma Maoz Lev is the daughter of Avraham Schneiderman; her husband, Dr. Vladimir Maoz

Lev, is the son of Vasily Levangorski. Vladimir is also in charge of the asylum where Nachumadman and Maftir-Yonah are interned. He is a converted Jew who has gone to the Holy Land to start a new life while internally combating the guilt and turmoil that the Holocaust left behind. Yigal Sinai, an Israeli security officer, represents the New Israel, but he wishes to see Israel not just move forward but to make sure that a Holocaust never occurs again. These characters set the backdrop for a play that wrestles with the tremendous guilt enveloping not only those who were left behind to survive but also those whose generation is guilty of unspeakable crimes. The play raises many questions: How does the younger generation deal with the Holocaust and with being the offspring of survivors or perpetrators of a gruesome past? What problems must they overcome or at least attempt to resolve? The new generation of Jews wants to start over, but the old generation of survivors docs not allow it, nor docs Vladimir, whose guilt runs so deep for what his father committed that he constantly lives in the past. Flashbacks in the play also provide the audience with a connection to the past and a view to the dilemma that both generations are trying to surmount.

Symbolic in this play are the effigies that have been set up on the stage, nine figures that represent the missing minyan. This symbolizes the demise of the Eisysky shtetl. In the first act a carriage enters the scene carrying four images that represent Hitler, Stalin, Churchill, and Roosevelt. These images, as well as the flashbacks, are constant reminders of the past. Nachumadman's and Maftir-Yonah's antics concerning the past and the Holocaust also serve to remind the audience of Vladimir's own past and reinforce the guilt he carries on his shoulders. The younger generation knows of the past via the stories from its parents, but the main difference lies in the fact that the young Jewish generation, represented by Bluma and Yigal, wishes to go forth and build a strong Israel, while the children of perpetrators, embodied by Vladimir, wish to suffer for the deeds of their parents. Vladimir is so burdened by guilt he wears a necklace of barbed wire. This provides a constant struggle between people of the same age who have suffered the outcome of the war in very different ways. For both Bluma and Vladimir the Holocaust is kept alive by Avraham Schneiderman and Vasily Levangorski, who also struggle with being victims and perpetrators. Schneiderman's own background is questionable as well, for one must wonder how he managed to be the only survivor of the shtetl. Did he reveal Jewish hiding places in order to protect his collection of gold? Although he has come to Israel to visit his daughter Bluma, is he actually acting as an agent of the Soviet authorities (namely Levangorksi) by bringing Vladimir back to his father? Is this yet another attempt to save himself at the expense of another? The main question that comes forth throughout the play is, ''Can he who sank deeply in a black, filthy mire in order to save his body be clean without stain or blemish?''

The play is an excellent representation of the dilemmas that have faced survivors, persecutors, and their children. There is no easy answer for either generation and the cold, dark reality is that the atrocities of the Holocaust can never be forgotten by Vladimir or Schneiderman, nor escaped by Bluma, who struggles to lead a normal life in Israel as the daughter of the Last Jew.

—Cynthia A. Klíma

THE LAST MOHICAN
Short Story by Bernard Malamud, 1958

An American named Fidelman, the subject of a number of stories Bernard Malamud later collected for *Pictures of Fidelman* (1969), first appears in "The Last Mohican" in the collection *The Magic Barrel* (1958). He has arrived in post-World War II Italy to study the art of Giotto, the subject of a monograph he is writing. He carries with him a new briefcase and a draft of his opening chapter, on which he plans to work before moving from Rome to Florence to continue his studies. But his education in Rome turns out to be far different from the study of Giotto's art that he had planned and far more important.

At the train station in Rome Fidelman immediately meets Shimon Susskind, a refugee, formerly from Israel but evidently a person displaced after the war and a likely Holocaust survivor. Poor, gaunt, "oddly dressed in brown knickers and black, knee-length woollen socks," conversant in Yiddish as well as other languages—Susskind appears as a relic of the formerly flourishing Hasidic communities of central Europe. Recognizing Fidelman as Jewish, he greets him with "Shalom," to which the student hesitantly replies, using the word for probably the first time in his life.

This is how the relationship between the two men begins. Susskind explains how he came to leave Israel and live in Italy, which he finds more congenial to his health and general well-being, though he is without a passport (stolen, he claims) and without any means of earning a livelihood except peddling and—to raise the capital for his investment—schnorring. Soon he starts asking Fidelman to give him a suit, which he says he badly needs, what with winter coming on. But Fidelman has only two suits to his name; therefore, he tries to palm him off with a dollar instead. Not satisfied, Susskind asks for more, until finally Fidelman shakes him off and goes to his hotel.

Susskind follows him and continues to harangue him for his suit. Fidelman continues to resist, asking why he should be responsible for this stranger, when Susskind responds that if he, a human being and a Jew like himself, is not, who is? Exasperated, Fidelman again tries to fob Susskind off with some of his meager funds and gives him five dollars. Hoping to be rid of him for good, he changes his residence. Nevertheless, Susskind finds him again and resumes his harangue, this time trying to get Fidelman to go into business with him selling women's stockings and again asking him for a suit.

Susskind finally leaves Fidelman alone, and the latter returns to his hotel, only to find his new briefcase and the important, and so far only, chapter of his book on Giotto missing. Nothing else is missing—only that. He suspects Susskind as the thief but cannot understand why he would take those items and nothing else. He sets out next day to find Susskind, but his hunt turns up nothing. Weeks turn into months as Fidelman searches in the ghetto, in synagogues, and among peddlers but finds no trace of the refugee. He is desperate, because without the initial chapter he feels that he cannot continue his work. Told that Susskind sometimes works in a cemetery, Fidelman looks for him there, but he sees only a grave whose inscription starkly recalls the Holocaust: "My beloved father / Betrayed by the damned Fascists / Murdered at Auschwitz by the barbarous Nazis / O Crime Orribile."

A month later Fidelman discovers Susskind peddling holy beads near the Vatican and surreptitiously follows him home into the ghetto. His home is a poor, barren hole in the wall, but before Fidelman returns the next day to look for his manuscript, he dreams of "Virgilio Susskind," a ghost that leads him into a synagogue, where he sees Giotto's painting of Saint Francis handing an old knight his cloak.

Enlightened by his dream, Fidelman stuffs his gabardine suit into a bag and runs to Susskind's hovel. He sees the refugee lighting a candle, apparently with a page of a typewritten manuscript, but he gives him the suit anyway. As Fidelman leaves, Susskind goes after him and returns the briefcase, empty of the missing chapter, which he has burned, claiming that he has done Fidelman a favor. Furious at him and threatening to slit his throat, Fidelman chases after Susskind until, catching his breath, he remembers what he has learned and shouts, "Susskind, come back. The suit is yours. All is forgiven." But Susskind keeps running and disappears into the ghetto.

Responsibility for one's fellow human beings, not only for one's fellow Jews (but perhaps especially for them), is the theme of Malamud's story. While not a dominant or explicit motif, the Holocaust and its significance nonetheless play their essential part. The failure of responsibility, of human compassion, such as Saint Francis had for the poor knight and Fidelman finally has for poor Susskind, permitted the Holocaust to occur, Malamud seems to be implying.

—Jay L. Halio

THE LAST OF THE JUST (Le Dernier des justes)
Novel by André Schwarz-Bart, 1959

The French Jewish author André Schwarz-Bart's first novel, *Le Dernier des justes* (1959; *The Last of the Just,* 1960), stands as a most somber, and at the same time poetic, depiction of the historical path of suffering trodden by the Jewish people. Framed by a period of 760 years, the narrative follows the ancient legend of the Just Men—the *Lamed-Waf*—through the Levy dynasty. Beginning with the martyrdom of York's Jews under the leadership of Rabbi Yom Tov Levy in 1185, the story winds its way through the European geography of anti-Semitism until it ends in the gas chambers at Auschwitz. By the book's end the reader has been exposed not only to the passions of the Just Men of the Levy clan but, through them, to the sufferings of the entire Jewish people. Indeed, this note of vicariousness, as the foundation of the Just Man tradition, rings consistently throughout the novel. Auschwitz, Majdanek, Buchenwald, Sobibor, and Belzec (the names of Nazi infamy are listed, almost liturgically, on the final page) become, therefore, entrenched within the boundaries of historical context as the not altogether unforeseeable (but not, for that reason, any the less horrific) climax to the centuries-long stain of European Christendom's anti-Semitism. Inevitably, therefore, the book stands as both a testament to the paradoxical triumph of the Just Men in the face of such terror and an accusation against the culture that, in Christian piety, took the cross of Christ by its other end and made a sword out of it.

Schwarz-Bart orders his narrative strictly chronologically. He begins with the story of Rabbi Yom Tov Levy, who, in defiance of Bishop William of Nordhouse's inflammatory sermon and the devout Christian mob that sought to put his words into bloody action, martyred himself and his coreligionists and thus segued his deed of pious resistance into the tradition of the *Lamed-Waf*. From here Schwarz-Bart traces the Levy dynasty in rapid succession for 12 generations, before jumping finally to the figure of Mordecai Levy, grandfather of the eventual hero Ernie, with whom he commences a fuller history.

The novel makes no sense, however, if it is read merely as a genealogy of Jewish suffering. Nor does it resonate if it is taken as a historical fiction designed to illustrate the inevitability of the Holocaust. Rather it is only within the paradigm of the *Lamed-Waf* legend that the novel acquires its poetic and pedagogical significance.

According to that ancient Talmudist tradition, "the world reposes upon thirty-six Just Men, the Lamed-Vov [*sic*], indistinguishable from simple mortals . . . But if just one of them were lacking, the sufferings of mankind would poison even the souls of the newborn, and humanity would suffocate with a single cry. For the Lamed-Vov are the hearts of the world multiplied, and into them, as into one receptacle, pour all our griefs." It is this tradition that provides the interpretive paradigm for the novel and in which the main characters, from the venerable Rabbi Yom Tov Levy to his distant descendant Ernie, are positioned. Throughout it all the Just Men are shown to be fallible, at times unlikable, often unsure of their status and usually trying to escape from it—but nevertheless indispensable.

Intoning consistently throughout the narrative is this question: How can one possibly be a Jew? As Mother Judith puts it,

"When will God stop *miracling* us that way?" The paradox of Jewish election thus becomes a defining motif throughout the text: How is it that a people can be so precious to God and yet at the same time so cruelly forsaken to persecution? The answer at which Schwarz-Bart arrives, of course, is that the *Lamed-Waf* bear in themselves the suffering of the Jews in the same way that the Jews bear in themselves the suffering of the rest of humanity. There is, in other words, a twin dialectic of vicariousness at work throughout the novel. It is in the necessity of this dialectic that the answer to Judith's question lies.

The dialectic is also, however, paradoxical. As Schwarz-Bart says at the close of the novel, Ernie Levy, as the cipher of all the Just Men, remains yet alive, even though dead six million times. There remains a presence—of Ernie? of indestructible Jewish spirit? of vicarious burden?—that testifies to the essence of the *Lamed-Waf* that continues to bear the soul and history of humanity, even in the wake of the Holocaust. And for that reason the novel ends on a note of cautious optimism. "Yes . . . sorrow. *But . . . preferably,*" concludes the author. There is cause, however muffled, for hope. Sorrow is circumscribed by the remembrance of this "But . . . preferably." And it is in this that the Just Men find their reason and vindication.

—Mark R. Lindsay

THE LECTURE
Short Story by Isaac Bashevis Singer, 1967

In midwinter the narrator, N., is traveling from New York City to Montreal to deliver a lecture that he describes as an "optimistic report on the future of the Yiddish language." The journey begins auspiciously, but near the Canadian border the train becomes snowbound, and in his imagination N. is transported to the Poland of his youth. Because of this delay N. arrives at his destination in the middle of the night, to be greeted only by two Holocaust survivors, an old woman and her daughter, Binele. The old woman's appearance and accent again recall Poland, as do the street and the very apartment to which they take N. "No stage director," he remarks, "could have done a better job of reproducing such a scene of old-country misery." The mother cannot stop talking about her experiences in Auschwitz and the loss of her family members under the Nazis.

While the apartment and its inhabitants recall pre-World War II Poland, N.'s room reproduces life in a concentration camp. The cot is as narrow and rickety as a plank, the air freezing. He hears scratching so loud it seems to come from some monster trying to raze the building. N. lies in agony thinking, "Well, let me imagine that I had remained under Hitler in wartime. Let me get some taste of that, too." He imagines himself in Treblinka or Maidanek. "Tomorrow there would be a 'selection,' and since I was no longer well, I would be sent to the ovens . . . I won't come out of here alive.'' He does live to tell the tale, but during the night the mother dies, and the optimistic lecture mysteriously vanishes.

This series of disasters reveals the lingering effects of a dark past. Binele objects to her mother's morbid stories and tries to live in the present, but her wrist bears the tattooed reminder of her inability to escape history. Though the narrator lives safely in America, he, too, thinks that the present has been rendered ''totally remote and insubstantial'' amidst these mementos of a former existence. N. calls the disappearance of his manuscript Freudian in the sense that even before leaving New York he had felt it presented too glowing a vision. After the harrowing night in Montreal he could not give this lecture; the mother's death reflects the disappearance of N.'s (that is, Singer's) Yiddish-speaking audience.

Set in a midwinter night, ''The Lecture'' is a dark story, but it contains elements of humor and hope. The scene of the mother's death becomes farcical when N. and Binele repeatedly collide with each other as they chase about the apartment trying to get help. The story, which first appeared in the January 1968 *Playboy,* even offers a bit of the erotic. Binele runs about only half-dressed, and N. inadvertently touches her breast. The story ends with the coming of day. Singer writes in the penultimate paragraph, ''Life had returned. The long nightmare was over.'' N. embraces Binele and promises to care for her. The old world and old life still exert their dire influence, but a new life is possible for those who have survived. In the curious way that life imitates art, Singer in 1978 would deliver that lost optimistic lecture not in Montreal but in Stockholm in accepting the Nobel Prize for Literature.

—Joseph Rosenblum

THE LETTER WRITER
Short Story by Isaac Bashevis Singer, 1968

Isaac Bashevis Singer's fiction does not directly describe the Holocaust, yet that cataclysm underlies much of his writing, including this story. Herman Gombiner lives in New York, but he grew up in Poland, where his family perished when the Nazis destroyed their village of Kalomin. Alone, Gombiner has only one companion, a mouse he names Huldah (Hebrew for mole). He does, however, maintain an extensive correspondence with distant women whose names he finds in magazines devoted to mysticism and the occult.

Gombiner's belief in the supernatural is vindicated when one of his correspondents, Rose Beecham, appears at his door after he contracts pneumonia. Rose tells him that her dead grandmother sent her to Gombiner, thus saving his life. One night when Gombiner awakes, he sees Rose's lips moving in

her sleep, and he understands that she is conversing with her dead relative.

In his own dreams Gombiner also communes with the dead. In one dream he is back in Kalomin walking with a girl. In another his mother and sisters argue over a comb. Before his illness, in daydreams he would return to heder, to yeshiva, to the Kalomin cemetery. To Gombiner these experiences prove that there is no oblivion. He recognizes that ''six million souls must exist somewhere,'' and he imagines the spirits of the dead Jews fighting with the spirits of the dead Nazis. ''The Letter Writer'' thus offers consolation for the horrors of World War II. Though physically gone, the old Jewish world exists on a metaphysical plane as long as memory remains faithful to it, as long as writers like Singer continue to invoke it.

Singer offers a second consolation as well. Gombiner in this story recapitulates the experience of the Holocaust. He loses his job with the closing of the Hebrew publishing house for which he works. He then confines himself to his apartment, a form of ghetto. The furnace explodes, leaving him without heat, and he becomes so ill that he nearly dies. Huldah also suffers, since Gombiner is too ill to feed her. Singer explicitly links Huldah to European Jewry when he thinks, ''In relation to [animals], all people are Nazis; for the animals it is an eternal Treblinka.'' Yet both survive. They are thinner, weaker, after their ordeal, but alive. The story ends with a cascade of images of renewal. A pigeon flies through the snowfall, recalling the dove that brought hope to Noah. Children awaken. The sun casts a rosy glow on Gombiner's windowpanes, symbolizing the end of the storm and the dawning of a new day. Even the old bindings in the bookcase shine, indicating a revival of Jewish literature. Synecdoches of Judaism and the Jewish nation, Gombiner and Huldah have come close to extinction but have miraculously been recalled to life.

—Joseph Rosenblum

LETTERS FROM WESTERBORK (Het denkende hart van de barak: Brieven van Etty Hillesum)
Correspondence of Etty Hillesum, 1982

Because of her contacts as a special assistant to the Jewish Council, Etty Hillesum received several offers to go into hiding before she herself became an inmate at Westerbork and Auschwitz, but she refused those offers. She did not want to be saved when thousands of Dutch Jews just like herself were being sent to the concentration camps. In the summer of 1942 she accompanied the first transport of Jews to Westerbork not as an inmate but as an employee of the Jewish Council and was permitted to come and go at will. She did everything she could to alleviate the suffering around her, and she developed from being an introspective intellectual to being a heroic and altruistic activist on behalf of her Jewish coreligionists.

Later in 1942 she briefly returned to Amsterdam while her boyfriend Julius Spier was dying. In November 1942 she returned to Westerbork. The book *Letters from Westerbork*, published in 1982 and in English translation in 1986, contains correspondence and some diaries from this time frame that document her impressions of Westerbork. She comments on the death of Spier: ''My friend has died; I heard the news a few hours ago. Ever since I saw him last week, I have prayed that he might be released from his suffering while I was still here on leave. And now that it has really happened, I am grateful. And on the whole, gratitude that he was part of my life will always be greater than my grief at his no longer being here, physically here.'' The letter demonstrates Hillesum's deep reserves of inner strength during a time of immense personal sorrow and grieving and points to those characteristics that led her to heroically assume august communal responsibilities as a social worker for the Jewish Council in Westerbork during a time of grave societal pandemic.

Hillesum bears witness to the bleak social circumstances with which she is confronted in the concentration camp: ''The whole of Europe is gradually being turned into one great prison camp. The whole of Europe will undergo this same bitter experience. To simply record the bare facts of families torn apart, of possessions plundered and liberties forfeited, would soon become monotonous. Nor is it possible to pen picturesque accounts of barbed wire and vegetable swill to show outsiders what it's like. Besides, I wonder how many outsiders will be left if history continues along the paths it has taken.'' The passage reveals both Hillesum's determination to be a witness for the suffering caused by the Holocaust and personal frustrations with this role as she encountered indescribable depravity and barbarism. There is considerable food for thought in her statement that society outside the concentration camps of European countries under the totalitarian heel of Nazi Germany was beginning to resemble society inside the concentration camps.

She reflects on the barbed wire that is an important synecdoche of concentration camp life: ''If the barbed wire just encircled the camp, then at least you would know where you were. But these twentieth-century wires meander about inside the camp too, around the barracks and in between, in a labyrinthine and unfathomable network. Now and then you come across people with scratches on their faces and hands. There are watchtowers at the four corners of our wooden village, each a windswept platform on four tall posts. A man with a helmet and a gun stands outlined against the changing skies. In the evening one sometimes hears a shot echo across the heath, as it did once when the blind man stumbled too close to the barbed wire.''

Hillesum does not shy away from documenting the random terror of the concentration camps as characterized by the arbitrary shooting of inmates by the guards. These frequent occurrences have also been critiqued in our popular culture, particularly in Steven Spielberg's majestic film *Schindler's List*.

She also describes the fear and agony experienced by the inmates who were being transported from Westerbork to concentration camps in Eastern Europe: ''Anyway, it is terribly crowded in Westerbork, as when too many drowning people cling to the last bit of flotsam after a ship has sunk. People would rather spend the winter behind barbed wire in Holland's poorest province than be dragged off to unknown parts and unknown destinies deep within Europe, from where only a few indistinct sounds have come back to the rest of us. But the quota must be filled; so must the train, which comes to fetch its load with mathematical regularity. You cannot keep everyone back as being indispensable to the camp, or too sick for transport, although you try it with a great many. You sometimes think it would be simpler to put yourself on transport than have to witness the fear and despair of the thousands of men, women, children, infants, invalids, the feebleminded, the sick, and the aged, who pass through our helping hands in an almost uninterrupted flow.''

Hillesum's poignant and evocative words convey the excruciating sorrow she felt as a benefactor to the Jewish community and as an eyewitness to the malefaction of the Nazis when she saw how people were horrified by the unbearable conditions of their transport to the East. She reflects on the inmates and their dehumanization through the wretched circumstances in which they found themselves: ''These figures wrenched from their context still carry with them the restless atmosphere of a society more complicated than the one we have here. They walk along the thin barbed-wire fence. Their silhouettes move, life-sized and exposed, across the great stretch of sky. You cannot imagine it . . . Their armor of position, esteem, and property has collapsed, and now they stand in the last stretch of their humanity. They exist in an empty space, bounded by earth and sky, which they must fill with whatever they can find within them—there is nothing else.''

Hillesum also reflects on the fact that deep reserves of inner strength can to some extent counteract the dehumanization caused by extreme situations like the Nazi concentration camps and the horror they evoked.

—Peter R. Erspamer

LIEDER FUN CHURBAN 'ON LIEDER FUN GLOYBIN
Poems by Aaron Zeitlin, 1967

Aaron Zeitlin's standing in the field of Yiddish belles lettres is nurtured by two seemingly opposing sources—namely, postimpressionistic ideas and techniques and a strong commitment to Jewish traditional sources. These aspects are imbued in the style and content of Zeitlin's work, and they stem from his Orthodox upbringing and education and his evolvement as an independent Jewish thinker. His drama on the pseudo-Messiah *Yakob Frank* (1929) and his Zionist novel, *Brenendike erd,* portraying the heroic deeds of Nili, which is an acronym for the title *Netsah Yisrael Lo' Yeshaker* ("The Glory of Israel Will Not Lie" [1 Sam. 15:29]), both highlighting counter-culture traditional themes, illustrate this.

In a similar fashion, Zeitlin's muse inspires his poetry of Holocaust and faith in *Lieder fun churban 'on lieder fun gloybin* ("Poems of the Holocaust and Poems of Faith"). His topics include identity, faith, destruction, and remembrance and are interwoven with threads of piety, mysticism, and folklore in addition to strong pronouncements against entrapment by non-Jewish cultures. He acknowledges that he, like his enlightened Warsaw friends of letters, followed Goethe's path to the seemingly heavenly palace only to discover in Hitler's belligerent night "how short is the distance between Faust and fist, from Goethe's *übermensch* to the *untermensch* and to the Hitlerites." In the Nazi "Night and Fog" Zeitlin sees a dastardly link between Europe's wordsmiths and murderers. His faith in building bridges between the husks of the abyss (exile) to the *tikkun* (redemption) is shattered with "another sleepless night (of) a thousand curses." In his poem "A khalom fun noch Majdanek" (1946; "A Dream Still from Majdanek") he counts into the endless night names of Jewish children whose whereabouts is nameless: "Gone and not here anymore the Heshelekn, Heshelekn, Peshelekn, Hindelekn. Sounds, only sounds, only poetic sounds—Names of Jewish children. Where is your little foot, Zisele? Zipele, where is your little braid? You are smoke, Yentele's little hand! You are ashes, Kopele's little head!" In addition to the terrible physical loss to the Jewish people, the smoldering embers of Jewish children recall for Zeitlin the cultural and spiritual price paid for leaving the way of *Yiddishkeit* for European civilization. From the depths of evil amidst a vanished Jewish world, who will recall the life that was the Jewish community of Eastern Europe?

The *Khurban* ("catastrophic destruction," the preferred term in Yiddish for Holocaust) poetry of Zeitlin is confused, infused, and suffused with fate and faith. He wonders, "Where is God?" and wanders into Kabbalah. What is to be now that "A knife flashes through all the *sefirot . . . Malkhut* is away from *Yesod* and fallen before *Keter.*" The ripping of the communion of Israel away from its foundation daringly teaches that non-sense has replaced sense and that nothingness has eclipsed Nothingness. If the *'Oybershter* (the Most High) is silent then "*even* an outcry is now a lie, *even* tears are mere literature, *even* prayers are false." And he meditates in "'Ani ma'amin" (1948; "I Believe"): "Why so volcanic as my God? If He is Sinai to me, He is Majdanek as well." Zeitlin's conflict and struggle give way to protest, and he professes: "No matter how much I rebel, no matter how much I grow weary, I must be Jew. We cannot let go of each other, not He of me, nor I of Him. You say 'Israel,' when you say 'Elokim.'" In

retrospect this reflects Zeitlin's anti-secularist/modernist reminder to his generation, "Zayn a Yid" (1936; "To Be a Jew"): "Being a Jew means running forever to God *even* if you are His betrayer, means expecting to hear any day, *even* if you are a nay sayer, the blare of Messiah's horn; means, *even* if you wish to, you cannot escape His snares, you cannot cease to pray—*even* after all the prayers, even after all the 'evens.'" To rid a Jewish soul of *'afilus* ("evens") is to (re)discover *dos pintele Yid* (the essence of a Jew).

—Zev Garber

LIFE AND FATE (Zhizn' i sud'ba)
Novel by Vasily Grossman, 1980

Vasily Grossman was no mere passive observer of the horrific events that befell his country; at one and the same time he was both the witness and the victim of the Holocaust, of the atrocities of both the German and the Russian versions of totalitarianism, and of both Nazi and Soviet anti-Semitism. In his work *Life and Fate* (1985; *Zhizn' i sud'ba,* 1980) a novel that may be compared in scope to Leo Tolstoy's *War and Peace,* he sets out to examine, among other things, what has been aptly described as the "diabolical pact" between Adolf Hitler's Germany and Joseph Stalin's Russia. After his father's death in 1956, Grossman, virtually ignored at this time by the Soviet writing establishment, decided to dedicate all his remaining energies to the completion of a work in which he would attempt to portray the truth about both Stalingrad and Berdichev, truths that had already been clouded and obscured by the officially approved postwar Soviet versions.

Grossman employs the device of the omniscient narrator to tell his tale. The work presents both historical and imaginary characters, and it additionally invites comparisons between Napoleon's invasion of Russia and that of Hitler. In many of the digressions the various degrees of anti-Semitism are discussed, the conclusion being that there are three, the last one the most dangerous and one that can arise only in a totalitarian state. The action of *Life and Fate* begins in 1942, at the point when the Germans are pushing the Russians defending Stalingrad back toward the Volga. It is autumn. The novel ends in the spring of the following year, some months after the final surrender of the German 6th Army at Stalingrad in February. The novel, however, also contains various flash-forwards—to the Hungarian uprising of 1956, for example—and the various philosophical digressions by the narrator help to create a sense of timelessness for the work, thus underlining the important moral issues that lie at its deepest level. It is a work that deals with, among other things, the problems of individual freedom, of making moral choices, and it faces too the quest for life's meaning in the midst of chaos and horror (a theme that is also central to the much earlier work *Red Cavalry* by the Russian Jewish writer Isaac Babel).

It has been noted many times that the Russian victory at Stalingrad "prolonged the agony of the Russian people"; many of the characters in *Life and Fate* express their hopes for greater personal freedoms in postwar Russia while, on the other hand, Party officials prepare to curtail all such freedoms once the German danger has been routed. In *Life and Fate* Grossman, in his search for the truth about the Holocaust and Hitler's invasion, stirs up and challenges many of the myths that the Soviet government had used to conceal the reality of the indifference and incompetence of the leadership. Grossman shows, for example, how the ordinary Soviet soldier becomes the victim not only of the German enemy but also of Soviet Party officials. It still is possible that Grossman's novel might not have been "arrested" if its criticisms of Soviet society had gone no further. As noted above, however, the greatest "danger" contained in *Life and Fate* was to be found in the author's investigation of totalitarianism. From the official Soviet point of view, the Nazi state had nothing at all in common with the Soviet regime. Grossman in *Life and Fate* argues persuasively that they are but two sides of the same coin. Seen from this perspective it is not then surprising that the manuscript was seized and publication of the novel was denied in Grossman's lifetime. This is a work that appeared late on the Soviet literary scene and one that caused the same powerful impact as Mikhail Bulgakov's *Master and Margarita* had done some 20 years before. Like the latter, it is a work that testifies to the greatness of the human spirit, and it bears a message that is relevant to all readers.

—Margaret Tejerizo

LIFE WITH A STAR (Zivot z hvězdou)
Novel by Jiří Weil, 1949

Jiří Weil's novel *Life with a Star* (1949; *Zivot z hvězdou*) reflects the three major influences on his work: his experiences as a Jew in the Protectorate of Bohemia and Moravia, as Adolf Hitler designated that part of Czechoslovakia that the Germans occupied on 15 March 1939; his knowledge and experience of European totalitarianism in the 1920s, '30s, and '40s; and his espousal of the Kafkaesque qualities of human alienation in an incomprehensible world, a world devoid of meaning. In short, although the word was not yet current, he attempted to come to grips with what Albert Camus called *l'absurde*. It is no coincidence that Weil's hero, Josef Roubiček, shares the same first name as Kafka's Josef K.

Written in the first person, the novel relates how Roubiček, a lowly Jewish bank clerk, loses everything: his job, his

material possessions (which he in part destroys so that "they" won't get them), his lover Růžena, who is executed, and, finally, his identity and every shred of humanity. Throughout the tale Roubiček describes the various people he runs across as they react (or do not react) to the decrees and measures applied to the Jews: the identification of them as Jews, the expropriation and exploitation they suffer, the ever more frequent deportations, and the final extermination, which, however, is presumed rather than described. The oppressors are never identified but simply called "they." Neither are there, strictly speaking, any other true characters—the persons throughout appear more as figures that barely function in the world of the oppressors, figures tangential to Roubiček, who through them reveals the absurd nature of the world he exists in as it increases inexorably in its incomprehensibility. This world finally effaces all that live with a star. Roubiček's narration, with its frequent imagined conversations with his absent lover Růžena, its depiction of his encounters with his fellow sufferers, with its conversations conducted with the stray cat, Thomas, that he adopts and tries, unsuccessfully, to protect (it is, after all, illegal for him to possess a pet), succeeds brilliantly in depicting the alien machine that progressively crushes the human beings sought out and identified for destruction.

Very near to his own destruction—deportation is imminent— Roubiček, who has been surreptitiously visiting Materna, a socialist in the resistance, finally decides, with Materna's help, not to accede to the demands of the oppressors. He will drop out of sight, hide, and thereby survive. Perhaps his intention is, through this action, to thwart "them" in their attempt to destroy him.

Although "they" would clearly seem to be the Germans, and although *Life with a Star* would seem to be based on Weil's own experiences as a Jew in the Protectorate, the novel is really about modern alienation, about living a pseudolife imposed on one from the outside. Humans are caught in a machine-like and unfeeling system, constantly degraded and finally destroyed. Only at the brink of the abyss does Roubiček, who has always been fed with cake and tea by the socialists around Materna, finally break free and rejoin the true humanity that the socialist resistance represents.

Although the Czech experience of the Holocaust is essential to the novel, *Life with a Star* is primarily a novel of the absurd, in which estrangement unto death in a meaningless and inimical world is the real theme. Like the Dutch writer **Marga Minco,** he subscribes to the school of existentialism as it took hold in postwar Europe. Despite the secondary importance of the Holocaust in Weil's work, however, he remains the best portrayer of the Holocaust in Czechoslovakia. The book is always accessible, sober in its descriptions, clear in its structure and syntax, and effective in its depiction of the incomprehensible nature of the crushing Nazi oppression.

—David Scrase

LIKE A TEAR IN THE OCEAN (Qu'une larme dans l'ocean)
Novels by Manès Sperber, 1951

Like a Tear in the Ocean (1988; originally published in French in 1951), Manès Sperber's trilogy of novels about the major political and social processes of the period from 1931 to 1944, is set against the background of the spread of Fascism and the Holocaust. (Confusion frequently arises because the same title is often applied to the third volume of the trilogy, and it does serve as the title of one of the chapters of that volume. That chapter was also published as a separate volume in French under the same title, with a preface by André Malraux.) Although vigorously denied by the author, many consider the trilogy to be autobiographical or a roman à clef. His protestations notwithstanding, at the very least it reflects many aspects of Sperber's personal and complex journey through political and ideological commitment, betrayal, and discovery during those turbulent years. Sperber was one of that group of politically engaged intellectuals who supported revolutionary Communism but gradually came to see that the movement's humanitarian goals had been corrupted by its Soviet managers, and inevitably he arrived at the realization that its claims to ultimate truth were as vacuous as similar claims of any other movement or organization. Indeed, in Sperber's case he had already rejected religion and Zionism, and in 1937 he parted from the Communist Party and resigned from the high posts he held within it.

The central conflict of the trilogy involves the dilemma faced by individuals who, once committed to the humanitarian values of the left, have since rejected its manifest tyranny but now must come to terms with the pressing need to oppose Nazism, which, however, necessarily implies allying themselves with the agents of Stalin and the Soviet Union and the evil they in turn present. The choices are between two evils, neither of which, in the long view, is lesser. Faber, Rubin, and the others who arrive at the same crossroads, as Sperber liked to describe it, elect to struggle against the Nazis out of love for humanity, for a greater though undefined good, and against evil, but not for any ideology or political alignment. The uncertainty of such a goal requires a much more powerful and profound personal commitment than to a packaged ideology.

If this had been played out in abstract terms—that is, as a debate of ideas—it would have been a simple political treatise, as indeed some readers have referred to it. In fact Sperber avoids this by having his characters not only debate ideas but also be actively and passionately involved in the struggles with which they are intellectually engaged. They are passionate and fallible, and they change and grow. Moreover, they do not simply read or hear about the treachery of Soviet GPU agents and the evil and violent policies of the Nazis; these things arrive at their doors and claim as victims not only their conscience and innocence but frequently also their own lives, their families, friends, and collaborators.

The peripatetic protagonists cross back and forth across continental Europe, from East to West, and their moral and ideological struggles intersect in complex ways. Sperber's training and experience as an Adlerian psychologist is compellingly manifested in the drama and passion of his characters' inner struggles and social confrontations.

Perhaps the most dramatic and pointed section of the entire trilogy, and certainly one of its most artistically successful parts, is the penultimate chapter of the third volume, the one entitled "Like a Tear in the Ocean." It describes the fate of the inhabitants of the town of Wolynya, a Jewish enclave in eastern Poland in 1944. It is virtually the only remaining Jewish community in Poland, and its Jewish residents are faced with a hopeless situation. They are to be rounded up and either killed or sent to camps. Their perceived options can be reduced to two: martyrdom or resistance. Resistance is a complex option because not only will it likely not succeed, but for some it presents the morally unacceptable choice of violence, and it hinges on an alliance with local Poles, most of whom represent the same threat as the Nazis. The majority are wiped out by the Nazis, and only a small number choose resistance. Their fate is as predicted. The portrayal of Bynie, the memorable and enigmatic rabbinical leader of this last group, is imbued with the same tragic ambiguity as Isaac Babel's Last Rebbe from *Red Cavalry*.

The tragedy of Wolynya is consistent with the entire trilogy: Sperber provides no easy solutions, no simple answers, and no comfort. The intellectual resolution he suggests is that to search for wisdom and understanding for the sake of humanity is endless but unequivocally worthwhile; while the psychological resolution he indicates in the innocence and promise of children is entirely Camusian.

—Allan Reid

LITERATURE OR LIFE (L'Ecriture ou la vie)
Memoir by Jorge Semprun, 1994

Literature or Life (1997; *L'Ecriture ou la vie,* 1994) is perhaps the most dazzling of Semprun's Holocaust memoirs translated into English. It takes the literary techniques of *The Long Voyage* and *What a Beautiful Sunday!* a stage further. Its "studied disorder" shows the difficulty, or impossibility, of describing the experience and the power of memory that disrupts both the past and the present.

The first part uses a familiar Semprun technique. Taking the days immediately after liberation as the basic time frame, the book then weaves chronologically from his life before the war to his life afterward and all points in between, with each chronological leap illustrating or developing questions about the nature of memory and writing as well as the events of the days following the liberation of Buchenwald. These ''slips'' in the narrative happen frequently and without warning.

As the memoir is in part about writing (''literature or life?''), Semprun tells and retells stories, often with warnings. (''Watch out—I'm fabricating.'') For example he retells the story from an earlier novel of how, in the resistance, he shot a German soldier: ''But I was with Julien . . . and not with Hans . . . I'd invented Hans Freiberg in order to have a Jewish friend. I'd had Jewish pals at that time of my life, so I wanted to have one in the novel as well.'' But he finds himself, in his attempt ''to placate the god of a credible narration,'' unable to convey the ''hell of radical evil'' of the camps. This memoir is very philosophically informed: Semprun had been a philosophy student and had read, among others, Immanuel Kant, Karl Marx, Martin Heidegger, and Emmanuel Levinas before the war. Not only are his meditations on these thinkers fascinating in their own right, they also suggest to him that the ''essential thing is to go beyond the clear facts of this horror and get at the root of radical Evil, *das radikal Böse*,'' a Kantian term.

The second part of the book is more essayistic. Leaving the tight narrative time frame Semprun tells about his decisions to write or not to write. He begins to put down his experiences after the war but the ''memory was too dense, too pitiless for me to master immediately . . . Whenever I awoke at two in the morning, with the voice of the SS officer in my ear, blinded by the orange flame of the crematory, the subtle and sophisticated harmony of my project shattered in brutal dissonance. Only a cry from the depths of the soul, only a deathly silence could have expressed that suffering.'' This tension—the need to record, the need not to record—effects Semprun deeply.

The third and final part tells of his decisions to write. A moving chapter on Levi's suicide refers to the terribly final chapter of *The Truce* and suggests that one ''last time, with no help for it, anguish had quite simply overwhelmed him . . . Nothing was real outside the camp, that's all. The rest was only a brief pause, an illusion of the sense, an uncertain dream. And that's all there is to say.'' He returns to Weimar and Buchenwald, both actually and in memory. He is given a copy of his registration card (despite his protests at the time, he was recorded as a ''stucco worker,'' not a student, a clearly intentional slip that may well have saved his life). This return, a mediation on **Primo Levi, Paul Celan, Bertolt Brecht,** and others, and a memory of the night sky, beautiful like the tree in *What a Beautiful Sunday!,* allow Semprun to write.

Literature or Life is a demanding, literary, fascinating, and revealing book. Its form and style make it one of the clearest prose accounts of the labyrinths of memory and of writing memory.

—Robert Eaglestone

LITTLE EDEN: A CHILD AT WAR
Memoir by Eva Figes, 1978

The British writer Eva Figes emerged as a writer in the mid-1960s with the publication of the novel *Equinox* (1966). She has since published numerous novels, translations, and works of nonfiction. Her works, especially her early novels, have been well received, and she won the prestigious *Guardian* Fiction Prize in 1967 for the novel *Winter Journey*. Despite critical acclaim, her readership has remained small due to her experimental and aesthetically challenging style of writing. In her article ''The Long Passage to Little England,'' published in the *Observer* on 11 June 1978, Figes connects her discomfort with the prevalent aesthetic traditions in postwar England with her personal history as a German refugee from the Holocaust. This experience left her with a sense of permanent statelessness that precludes the notion of continuity, be it aesthetic or political. Although the Holocaust is evoked directly in only two of Figes's novels—*Konek Landing* (1969), a complex, highly experimental text exploring the relationship between victims and their executioners, and the autobiographic *Little Eden: A Child at War* (1978)—the recurring themes of alienation, angst, and paranoia point to its underlying impact on the author's entire work.

Born Eva Unger on 15 April 1932 into a culturally assimilated German Jewish family in Berlin, Figes, along with her younger brother, experienced a typical upper-middle-class childhood without any instruction in the Jewish faith. On 9 November 1938—the notorious *Kristallnacht*—her father was arrested and imprisoned in Dachau. After his release the family succeeded in obtaining an exit visa, and in March 1939 they emigrated to England. The political realities of Nazi Germany, their father's imprisonment, and their grandparents' later deportation were kept from the children. Only much later did Figes comprehend these events, which she then experienced as a loss of innocence.

These events and her early years in England are the subject of the autobiographical text *Little Eden: A Child at War* (1978). Writing from an adult perspective, Figes links her childhood experiences to her later artistic views and convictions. The majority of the book is devoted to the description of the small town of Cirencester, Gloucestershire, where the child is sent to attend a small, unconventional school in order to escape the daily bombings of London. In this ''Little Eden'' she discovers the world of literature and the beauty of language as an outlet for her imagination and sensitivity, and it is there she conceives the notion of becoming a writer. Nonetheless, a shadow is cast on this Eden when a classmate calls her a Jew. Once again she feels the sense of alienation and otherness that she had experienced so keenly in London. Only shortly before the end of the war, when her mother sends her to the local cinema ''to go and see for yourself,'' does she understand and relate to the term ''Jewish'': ''I sat alone in the dark cinema and watched the newsreel of Belsen: mounds of corpses, dazed survivors with huge haunted eyes staring out of skulls which had become too heavy for the frail emaciated bodies, mute evidence for the prosecution posing for the camera. At last I knew what it meant to be a Jew, the shameful secret which had been hinted at but kept from me for so many years . . .'' For Figes this new knowledge marked both a final expulsion from Eden and the beginning of a sense of guilt. For years she was haunted by the memory of her family's departure from Berlin: ''And a row of abandoned loved ones standing outside the airport building, waving wistfully at survivors whom they could no longer see.''

A tension created by the knowledge of the adult narrator (and the reader) and the political innocence of both the child and the place is tangible throughout the text. Figes's portrayal of Cirencester, consisting of her fragmented memories augmented by research into the history of the area, reveals a place that is touched little by the horrors of the war and the Holocaust. Seemingly unchanged, Circencester appears to have sustained the innocence, which the child has lost irretrievably. Figes's memoir reflects a longing not only for the innocence of childhood but also for the innocence of a pre-Holocaust world.

—Helga Schreckenberger

THE LONG VOYAGE (Grand voyage)
Memoir by Jorge Semprun, 1963

Published in 1963 in France and first translated and published in the USA in 1964 and again in 1994, *The Long Voyage* is the first of Jorge Semprun's Holocaust narratives. It won the Formentor Prize. Like all Semprun's works on this subject, it is carefully crafted and self-consciously literary. It is the story, roughly, of Semprun's journey in 1943 from France to Buchenwald. Originally a Spanish Communist who had fled Franco, he was captured as a member of the resistance in 1943 under the alias of Gérard and imprisoned first in France and then in Germany. The journey to Buchenwald in early 1944 takes five days and nights. The key relationship of the ''present'' time line, the long journey, is ''the guy from Semur'' who becomes his companion during the journey. Although they (probably) do not exchange names the ''guy from Semur'' dies in his arms on the last night of the journey. ''Don't leave me, pal,'' are his last words. The final section of the book, narrating his arrival at Buchenwald, is, unlike the rest, told in the third person, reflecting not only Semprun's series of aliases but also the change of self that the camps engender.

Like all of Semprun's work, however, the account is much more about the memory of these events and the other events of his life and also the writing and representation of these events. The book jumps about in its chronology, slipping from events

in the main time line (the journey to Buchenwald) back to his time in the resistance, forward to his time in the camp—its liberation and later. These jumps happen suddenly and often with very little or no textual sign of the jump. Different conversations from different times merge with each other—an interwoven tapestry of past and present. The book disrupts the idea of the present constructed by the generic assumptions of the realist novel and so begins to reflect what **Saul Friedländer** called ''extraordinary mechanism of memory.'' ''You're tossing the salad, voices are reverberating in the courtyard . . . you let your mind wander . . . and suddenly, like a scalpel slicing cleanly in to the soft tender flesh, the memory explodes . . . And if someone, seeing you there, petrified, asks 'What are you thinking?' you have to answer: 'Nothing,' of course.''

Semprun displays both understanding and a granite hardness. After liberation an elderly German woman in Weimar tells him that both her sons are dead. He replies: ''I hope so, I really hope they're dead . . . I haven't the strength to tell her that I understand her sorrow, but I'm happy both her sons are dead, I mean I'm happy the German Army is wiped out.'' Indeed, this is a theme in the book: the way in which people find themselves fighting and could choose not to but do, in fact, choose to fight, making conflict inevitable.

The book has some terrible moments. The worst, perhaps, is his initiation into the horror of the Holocaust: the murder of a group of Polish Jewish children by the SS and their dogs. Semprun builds up to this epiphanitic event. The awful story ''has never been told . . . [it has] lain buried in my memory like some mortal treasure preying on it with a sterile suffering.''

Finally, Semprun—who had been a very high-ranking Communist—is also a philosopher. This book, quietly, perhaps, takes issue with Robert Anteleme's much more celebrated account of the Holocaust, *The Human Species*. ''Actually, we didn't need the camps to understand that man is a being capable of the most noble as well as the basest acts. How banal can you get!'' Instead, here and in Semprun's later *Literature or Life,* the question is one not of inhumanity but of radical evil. The ''long voyage'' is not just a five-day journey in a cattle truck, it's a journey to the universe of the camps and back.

—Robert Eaglestone

THE LOST CHILDHOOD: A MEMOIR
Memoir by Yehuda Nir, 1989

In acknowledging his Holocaust memoir, *The Lost Childhood* (1989), Yehuda Nir pays tribute to the many people who were instrumental ''in enabling a remaining witness to give testimony to a story that must be set down.'' The intensity of his commitment, with all its urgency, more than the terrifying events he recounts, empowers the narrator voice of his Holocaust memoir. The prose is spare, authentic, and devoid of stylish devices but crammed with a breathless raciness of hairbreadth episodes and dangerous escapes that mirror wartime treacheries yet defy belief even within the genre of the Holocaust memoir.

Dedicated to his savior, Ludwig Selig, Nir's domain is clearly that of a Holocaust witness. With an understated yet retaliatory tone of irony, he sets down the experiences of his peaceful Polish Jewish childhood detonated by the 1939 German invasion. Nine-year-old Yehuda Nir's story begins in Lvov, Poland, when following the German invasion, the Red Army in a counterattack occupied his city. The family's initial deprivations under the Soviets include the appropriation of his father's factory, relocation, and reduced living quarters shared with a Russian officer and his wife. Two years later when the Germans invade the Soviet Union, the real horrors for Yehuda's family begin. The occupying Germans, assisted by Ukrainians, begin shooting Jewish men on the street and then begin arresting others. When his father is arrested Yehuda follows to the police station and describes the parting glance he has with the parent he will never see again. Many years later at the end of the war, he learns that his father was murdered the same day by the Germans. The three surviving family members—Yehuda, his mother, and his sister, Lala—merge into what he describes as ''an interdependent triangular symbiosis,'' adopting new roles to prevail in the endgame of survival.

Before long they are ordered into the ghetto, taking only a bed, a table, and a few chairs. When the German annihilation plan unfolds, they escape deportation through talents of Lala's boyfriend, Ludwig. With his extraordinary talent for forgery, Ludwig fashions baptismal certificates and gives Yehuda's mother a new identity. Ingeniously he procures baptismal papers by writing to his landlady's church in Lithuania requesting her replacement baptismal papers. These papers establish a new identity for Yehuda's mother, that of Halina Skrybaylo, Ludwig's landlady. Then by purchasing a blank baptismal form on the black market from an ''enterprising priest,'' Ludwig fills in the name Julian so it will closely match Yehuda's name Julius. The safe identity of Roman Catholics with Aryan papers forever alters his destiny. It enables the family's flight from Lvov to Warsaw, where unrecognized they live out three more years of their ordeal until Poland's surrender in October 1944. Ludwig's heroism takes on a tragic poignancy when Yehuda learns later that he has been denounced and murdered.

In anonymous Warsaw life remains precariously dangerous despite Aryan papers. Yehuda finds work as an assistant to a German dentist, an officer of the Wehrmacht. He is almost denounced when, posing as a Catholic Pole, he asks what day in December Christmas falls on. Quick thinking saves him when he threatens to reveal a suspected affair. Later when he becomes ill it is Lala's idea that he can conceal his circumcision by feigning modesty with the female doctor she summons

to treat him. He poses as a member of the Hitler Youth, an identity that will backfire from the anti-German fury of his Polish concierge. The ironies continue when after heroic acts of resistance, posing as a Pole in the failed Polish uprising, Yehuda and his family are sent to Germany as Polish slave laborers. Bribing a German camp guard with her wedding ring, Yehuda's mother asks him to call the German industrialist Rockschmidt, for whom she had previously worked as housekeeper in Poland. Once again the luck that has marked Yehuda's existence intervenes when Rockschmidt sends his uncle to bring them to his estate at Erzberg, where they live out the war.

Yehuda escapes several dangerously close calls only with sheer nerve and chameleon-like changes. He manages to escape the German death machine that is murdering European Jews in Poland's death factories. Living by his wits, he triumphs and trumps German efforts to murder him. He has lost his childhood but he will recast his future in the role of witness.

The Lost Childhood at times closely parallels the award-winning novel *Wartime Lies* by **Louis Begley**, whose survivor fiction recounts the exploits of Maciek, a six-year-old boy living on the run with an aunt in wartime Poland. The six-year-old protagonist of Begley's novel lives with forged Aryan papers and establishes a Catholic identity. The composite character Aunt Tania shares some of the characteristics of Begley's mother and is reminiscent of the resourcefully ingenious Lala, Nir's sister. Tania's daring boldness makes her the novel's heroine shepherding Maciek through duplicitous traumas such as concealing circumcision, escaping blackmailers, and posing as a pious Catholic. Adopting multiple identities scars his nascent identity, and young Maciek, unable to grasp a sense of who he is, never fully answers that question. His fractured identity, not unlike that of the small boy in **Jerzy Kosinski**'s *The Painted Bird*, provides Begley with the novel's leitmotiv. Recollections of a plundered childhood mute memory, and thus questions of identity and selfhood haunt adulthood. In *The Lost Childhood*, nine years old when his six-year trauma begins, Yehuda Nir also has to adopt multiple identities to survive. The voice in his memoir, however, reverberates with the intensity of a survivor invested with a mission to bear witness to German and Polish atrocities.

Begley purposely chose the fictive form of a novel, more to confront the enduring dilemma of unraveling a fractured identity rather than to recount the horrors of a childhood forfeited to Holocaust treachery. The legacy of fabricated lies so vital to survive an evil universe leaves Maciek, who was born in Poland the same year as the author, with an existential dread. Who is he and what has become of his past are questions Maciek reckons with in the closing passage of the novel: ''And where is Maciek now? He became an embarrassment and slowly died. A man who bears one of the names Maciek used has replaced him. Is there much of Maciek in that man? No: Maciek was a child and our man has no childhood that he can bear to remember; he has had to invent one.''

And while *The Lost Childhood* describes a relentless struggle with multiple identities Nir assumes in a universe determined to exterminate him, his memoir is less a search for self than a resounding call to heed the voice of a witness to the Holocaust crimes committed against his people.

—Grace Connolly Caporino

M

MALINA: A NOVEL
Novel by Ingeborg Bachmann, 1971

Ingeborg Bachmann's novel *Malina,* published in German in 1971 and in English translation in 1990, recounts one woman's "murder" at the hands of the three men closest to her: her Hungarian lover, who loves only his children (in the first chapter, "Happy with Ivan"); her abusive father and the fascist society he represents (in the second chapter, "The Third Man"); and, most pernicious of all, her other self, Malina, who shares her apartment and works at the arsenal in the Austrian Army Museum (in the third chapter, "Last Things").

The destruction of the nameless female, first-person narrator is so gradual as to be almost imperceptible, while on the novel's surface almost nothing appears to be happening: she smokes and waits for Ivan (chapter 1); she dreams and remembers her father's silencing of the past (chapter 2); she realizes her condition and disappears into a crack in the wall (chapter 3). Leading up to the final sentence, "It was murder"—which unequivocally attests to the criminal nature of her disappearance—each of the three chapters focuses on her relationship with a different "murderer."

In the novel's central chapter the narrator recounts "the dreams of last night." The first of these 36 nightmares opens with the image of a lake on which, she recalls, expressive men's choral societies had once stood when the water was frozen, a lake surrounded by many cemeteries, one of which is the "cemetery of the murdered daughters." This frightening landscape beneath a dark block of clouds leads to one of the most horrible scenes ever written, the dream of "the world's biggest gas chamber." A daughter has been locked in the chamber with her father, who then leaves her alone in the gas: "My father, I say to him, who is no longer there. I would not have betrayed you, I would not have told anyone. Here you do not resist."

This beginning of the dream chapter contains the prime scene of German literature after 1945. A child of the perpetrator generation asks about a way out of the world of the Holocaust and, in so doing, is abandoned by her father. Just as he pulls his hand back from her shoulder in the first dream when the old grave digger approaches them and tells her that this is the "cemetery of the murdered daughters," so does he leave her alone in the gas chamber in the second dream. With Bachmann it is no longer the son, but the daughter, who is separated from the world of the father, which in the German novel after 1945 is the world of the Holocaust.

The dreams document the many ways in which the daughter is silenced: her father writes no lines for her to sing in his grand opera; he takes paper and pencil away from her in prison and destroys her letters; he even tries to find the sentences she has hidden in her parched mouth and to take them into custody as she dies of thirst. At the same time the dreams also chronicle the daughter's repeated attempts at resistance, most of which, however, remain ineffectual. Words prove to be least effective of all, and she uses all of the words she has available: "I say: Ne! Ne! and in many languages: No! No! Non! Non! Nyet! Nyet! No! Ném! For in our language, too, I can only say no, I can't find any other word in any language." When she screams, her voice is without sound; she speaks, but no one hears her. Amid the daughter's repeated, futile attempts to be heard, the father offers a busy front to distract attention from the truth of his past.

The novel ends with the disappearance of the narrator into a crack in the wall, "a very old wall, a very strong wall . . . from which nothing can ever be heard again," as the novel's penultimate sentence announces. Unlike the novel's narrator, the writer Bachmann was not silenced by her father's world. Her work tells the story he struggled to keep her from writing.

—Karen R. Achberger

THE MAN FROM THE OTHER SIDE (Ha-Ish min ha-tsad ha-aher)
Children's Novel by Uri Orlev, 1988

In this story of 14-year-old Marek, told in the first person voice with great immediacy and persuasive power, we learn of the adventures of a boy who is torn between revulsion and admiration for his stepfather, Antony, who smuggles food through the sewers to the Warsaw ghetto. Marek's ambivalence about his stepfather becomes more intense as he becomes Antony's assistant and observes Antony's skill at smuggling both food and escaping Jews but also his ruthlessness in eliminating someone who threatens to reveal their illegal activity.

Marek has absorbed anti-Semitic attitudes from the Polish society he is part of, but he discovers that he cannot despise or exploit Jews without a sense of guilt. His mother has taught him tolerance. Because the plight of the Jews in wartime Warsaw is seen from the perspective of a Catholic boy who is initially neutral about what is happening in the ghetto, his growing sympathy for the Jews is particularly convincing. What is more, he discovers that his father was a Jewish

Communist who was tortured and killed by the Nazis. In a young Jew named Pan Jozek, Marek finds a surrogate image of his father, and Marek's efforts to hide and save Jozek culminate in his risking his life to fight at Jozek's side in the Uprising. And, after Jozek is killed, Marek honors his friend by seeing to his honorable burial, despite extreme danger.

Orlev introduces the story with a preface titled "A Word About My Friend Marek," in which Orlev tells of his friendship with a Polish newspaperman named Marek, who, after sharing memories of Nazi-occupied Poland and touring the north of Israel with the author, told him the story of his life in Warsaw as a boy. The reality of continuing anti-Semitism in Poland becomes clear when Orlev tells Marek that he wants to write the story of Marek's boyhood but Marek is alarmed because "nobody [in Poland] knows my background . . . that's still a very sensitive subject there." Orlev promises not to tell his story as long as Marek is alive. Soon after, Marek is killed in an airplane crash, and Orlev is free to tell Marek's story. This introduction, which might have worked better as an afterword, suggests that Orlev is fictionalizing based partly on autobiography but also on his convincing novelistic imagination.

Particularly striking in this novel is the completely persuasive presence of Marek himself, a boy whose family situation many contemporary readers can identify with. His widowed mother has remarried, and Marek dislikes his stepfather, who seems coarse and crude to him. Nevertheless, Marek needs a father figure, and ironically through his discovery of his dead Jewish father and through his friendship with Jozek, who resembles his lost father in some ways, Marek travels a distance toward acceptance and reconciliation with Antony. He comes to admire Antony's courage and, most importantly, learns that Antony loves and cares for him, which changes his attitude toward Antony. Antony is an interesting character because he is such a mixture of good and bad. At the same time, Marek learns complicated lessons about Jews and Christians, decides to fight for the Jews in the uprising, and wrestles with his own complicated identity, though the introduction makes clear that he never publicly acknowledges his Jewish roots.

The Man from the Other Side (1991; *Ha-Ish min ha-tsad ha-aher,* 1988) is a gripping psychological novel for older children and young adult readers that also conveys a great deal of realistic historical information about the Nazi occupation of Poland and the relations between Jews and Christians in Poland during World War II. Orlev honors the heroism of those who fought against the Nazis. He also conveys the complicated political situation in wartime Poland with a minimum of didacticism or editorial commentary. Orlev is well served in the American editions of the book by the excellent translation by Hillel Halkin.

—J.D. Stahl

MAN'S SEARCH FOR MEANING: AN INTRODUCTION TO LOGOTHERAPY (Ein Psycholog erlebt das Konzentrationslager) Memoir and Study by Viktor E. Frankl, 1946

Man's Search for Meaning (1963; *Ein Psycholog erlebt das Konzentrationslager,* 1946) introduces readers not only to Viktor E. Frankl's experiences as a prisoner within the Nazi concentration camp system but also to the fundamentals of logotherapy, a branch of existential analysis that he founded. Frankl begins with "Experiences in a Concentration Camp," a gentle description of daily life and death within the concentration camp. Frankl's theoretical analyses are interwoven into the context of this narrative, which is presented chronologically and in the first person. The latter two sections of the book are principally theoretical. "Logotherapy in a Nutshell" is divided on the bases of explication of terms and therapeutic processes. This is followed by "The Case for a Tragic Optimism," an update of his theory that includes the idea of an optimistic future built from a tragic past.

Many may elect to read about Frankl's experiences in the concentration camps but then not follow up by reading the latter two parts of the book. The essence of Frankl's analysis of life in the camps, however, can be better understood, internalized, and valued if one reads his more theoretical chapters. It is important to remember that the basic framework for Frankl's ideas were well established prior to his deportation and internment. His perceptions of logotherapy and the search by individuals for meaning provide a context for his Holocaust experiences. In fact many may find it useful to read the latter two sections of the book prior to reading about Frankl's experiences in the camps.

While most of his family perished during the Holocaust, Frankl survived imprisonment in four concentration camps: Theresienstadt, Auschwitz, and two satellite camps of Dachau. In *Man's Search for Meaning* he presents an intimate glimpse into his camp experiences. His narrative is laden with descriptions of his fears, frustrations, and thoughts as he and others survived the camps. While he doesn't focus on the gruesome, it is ever-present. Instead he focuses on the everyday experiences, such as the incessant thoughts of food, the various work details, and relations with other victims as well as those in positions of power, such as the *kapos* and SS. He also discusses why others, when meaning for life and survival was lost, often slipped into a path toward death.

Frankl's existential approach is not based on the idea of lack of meaning associated with life but rather the inherent need in humans to achieve a meaningful existence. Associated with this will toward meaning is the need to transcend oneself, to seek meaning through one's focus toward others and the world. He argues that meaning can be found in achievement (not success), through relations with others, and through suffering. It is the latter that is particularly relevant to an understanding of Frankl's interpretation of his camp experiences. Frankl's descriptions of his relationship with his wife through memory while in the camp and his attempt to reconstruct his lost writings illustrate how such a transcendent focus and will toward meaning worked to assist with his survival. It should be noted that Frankl does not portray a picture of survival based simply on whether one is successful at achieving such meaning. He clearly relates the arbitrariness of luck associated with life in the camps that factored heavily into whether one lived or died each day.

One major problem with *Man's Search for Meaning* is Frankl's dichotomous presentation of those who lived in the camps into two primary categories: devils and saints. While arguably Frankl clarifies that most individuals are not totally in either category, he fails to fully acknowledge the difficulties of morality in the camps. He focuses on the choices that individuals make at every moment of their lives, whether in extremity or in everyday life. At each moment individuals can make choices that are positive and bring meaning to their lives, or they can make choices that are negative and serve to waste their lives or harm others. He fails to acknowledge situations in extremity in which individuals may be faced with what has often been termed "choiceless choice." When an individual faces choices that have no possible positive outcome or times of extreme adversity outside the range of normal human experience, the issue of morality becomes much more clouded. Thus, one must use care in reading and interpreting the work of Frankl so as to not blame the victim.

Frankl also received criticism for his failure to examine or mention that the focus of the Holocaust was the destruction of European Jewry. The word "Jew" does not even appear in the text of *Man's Search for Meaning*. For those who define the Holocaust as a unique event perpetrated against Jews, this remains problematic.

—Linda M. Woolf

MAUS—A SURVIVOR'S TALE
Story by Art Spiegelman, 1986 and 1991

Maus—A Survivor's Tale, whose two volumes, *My Father Bleeds History* and *And Here My Troubles Began,* were published, respectively, in 1986 and 1991, is a graphic narrative (or comic book) in which Art Spiegelman tells the story of his father Vladek's life—life in pre–World War II Poland, survival in Auschwitz, postwar life in the United States—as well as his own efforts to come to terms with that past. The book is also an homage to his mother, Anja (Vladek's first wife), who too survived the camps but later committed suicide. In a representational twist that seems to heighten the reader's empathy, Spiegelman makes use of the conventions of the animal fable by drawing the Jews as mice, the Germans as cats, the Poles as dogs, and so on.

The Library of Congress's Cataloguing-in-Publication Data inform us that *Maus*'s call number is D810.J4 S643 1986—in other words, *Maus,* which attempts to analyze the Holocaust primarily through historiographical means, can be found on library shelves next to historical volumes. And indeed the book's title, *Maus—A Survivor's Tale,* would place the text squarely in the realm of testimonial literature—that is, among nonfictional texts. On the other hand, the very medium (the comic strip) that Spiegelman has chosen to represent his father's recollections and his own relationship to his father is one that displays markers of fictionality and does not normally concern itself with historical accuracy or the strictures inherent in writing history. This very hybridity is evident from the moment the reader faces the cover of the first volume, where decisions about design and promotional text indicate immediately that the text at hand cannot be located in either camp exclusively.

On the back cover Jules Feiffer notes that *Maus* is "at one and the same time a novel, a documentary, a memoir, and a comic book"; the *Washington Post*'s review opines that the book is "impossible to describe accurately"; and the *New York Times* (on the front flap) points to *Maus*'s "remarkable feat of [blending] documentary detail and novelistic vividness." Similarly the back cover combines a map of wartime Poland, which also includes the locations of the Nazis' death camps, with a comic strip panel depicting Vladek sitting in an armchair and telling his story to Art, who is lying on the floor. Quite literally this combination of images bespeaks *Maus*'s insistence on mapping a personal existence into and onto historical space, of fixing individual specificity within a larger context. In addition these two graphic elements elegantly draw together *Maus*'s main concerns: Vladek's survival at Auschwitz and Art's attempts to come to grips with his father and his father's story. In other words, *Maus* fruitfully exploits the putative disjunction between the work's narrative genre (autobiography-memoir-testimonial) and the chosen medium, the comic strip.

Possibly the best expression of the hybridity of *Maus*'s genre is the use Spiegelman makes of photographs within the text. Toward the end of the second volume, Spiegelman includes a picture of Vladek in a concentration camp uniform. The putative power of a photograph to bestow authenticity to its surroundings, however, is annihilated in the following panel, when Vladek explains the circumstances in which it was taken: "I passed once a photo place what [*sic*] had a camp uniform—a new and clean one—to make souvenir photos." This photograph stands in a synecdochic relationship to the text at large: it makes the point that a mimetically realistic authenticity is impossible while also stressing that a radically antimimetic and completely nonrepresentational depiction is not desirable either. In other words, then, this admission of the relative inauthenticity of any discourse about the Holocaust prepares the ground for the sublation of the binary opposition between representability and nonrepresentability. *Maus* attempts a balancing act between these two extremes. On one hand, the text seems to affirm the fact that the Holocaust cannot be represented: after all, it employs a quasi-Brechtian *Verfremdung* by way of the animal imagery and steers clear of any potential aestheticization through the use of a pictorial technique that is deliberately flat and monochromatic. On the other hand, *Maus* clearly believes in the possibility of rendering intelligible historical events by way of constructing a narrative and by grounding the validity of that narrative in the authenticity of a survivor's life story. Based on his interviews with Vladek, Art attempts to render history realistically and accurately in comic book panels whose chronological and narrative sequentiality is constantly interrupted by epistemological parentheses; reflections on the appropriateness of the medium to the historical events; and the consistent foregrounding (rather than the elision) of the ways in which obtaining, processing, and representing information are interlinked in rendering visible Vladek's life story.

Maus thus locates itself within the force field that, more than 50 years after the end of World War II, informs the dissemination of representations of the Holocaust: by necessity it faces chronological remove; transmission of its narrative by someone other than a survivor; awareness of the existence of a media industry from which texts cannot escape; and an increasing awareness of the impossibility of fixing the one putatively correct way of representing the Holocaust while being acutely aware of the desire for locating that one proper way.

Maus makes the point that any desire to finally and successfully "work through" the Holocaust is an illusion—no ultimate resolution is possible, and despite chronological finality the Holocaust will extend itself into the lives of successive generations. It is patently obvious that the lives of survivors will forever be influenced by the shadow of the Holocaust. *Maus* also demonstrates that even if the representatives of Art's generation chose deliberately not to make the Holocaust a subject of their discourse, the Holocaust would by necessity insert itself into their lives, by virtue of the role it played in their parents' lives. *Maus* indissolubly links the necessity to make the Holocaust a subject of discourse and the ultimate futility of speaking about the Holocaust. In fact, these two strands are linked into a Möbius strip of sorts of our century, in which, as Jean-François Lyotard has theorized, the Holocaust was an earthquake that destroyed the very instruments that were customarily used to measure the strengths of earthquakes and in which the belief in a linearly progressive conception of history has been severely undermined, not least due to the Holocaust.

—Stefan Gunther

THE MESSIAH OF STOCKHOLM
Novel by Cynthia Ozick, 1987

Cynthia Ozick's *The Messiah of Stockholm* (1987) is a compact and highly provocative narrative that may be read as a parable about Holocaust memory and postwar Jewish identity. Its playful, quasi-fantastical mode recalls the postmodernist techniques of **Jorge Luis Borges** and **Italo Calvino**. In both its style and content, the novel also presents an homage to the Polish Jewish writer Bruno Schulz, who was killed by the Nazis in 1942. The narrative centers on a few days in the life of Lars Andemening, an eccentric and reclusive book reviewer for a newspaper in Stockholm. His name, Swedish for "spirit" or "inward sense," points to his fantasy that he has been singled out for an elevated spiritual mission. As for his actual life, he sleeps during the day, rarely communicates with anybody, and spends his nights writing cryptic reviews of highbrow central European writers. His obsession is literature, which he imbues with the sanctity of a religion: "He had long ago thrown himself on the altar of literature." Alongside this quasi-religious devotion is Lars's deep-seated conviction that he is the son of Bruno Schulz, who was shot by the Nazis on the streets of Drogobych during the early stages of the Holocaust. Lars focuses all of his energies on this lost "father," studying Polish and devoting himself to learning as much about Schulz as possible.

Lars has one confidante, the bookseller Mrs. Elkund, who reluctantly assists him in tracking down Schulziana. She herself hardly believes Lars's story about himself and has little interest in examining personal histories: "You're a Swede like any Swede," she says. "Why be a fool and dredge all that up—nobody cares, old Nazi stories . . ." But Lars insists on tracking down any remains of Schulz's work, particularly the lost manuscript of his last work, entitled *The Messiah*.

Playing on this title, Ozick invites the reader to examine the relationship between a textual and a real messiah. Lars has kept alive a faith in Schulz's textual *Messiah,* but what about the divine Messiah? Does his investment in the one preclude a genuine faith in the other? This question comes to the fore in the second half of Ozick's text, which gradually shifts register from narrative to parable. Lars learns that a woman calling herself Schulz's daughter has arrived in Stockholm in possession of Schulz's original manuscript. Fearing that he is being fooled, Lars is nonetheless drawn to the manuscript as if to his salvation. When he gets the opportunity to inspect the manuscript for himself, Ozick describes his process of reading with metaphors of consumption, suggesting an idolatrous relation to the text: "The terrible speed of his hunger, chewing through hook and blade, tongue and voice, of the true *Messiah*! Rapacity, gluttony!"

The text that Lars reads contains an implicit message to him to abandon his obsession with the manuscript. It describes a sort of postapocalyptic future, when "no human beings remained in Drohobycz; only hundreds and hundreds of idols."

The idols begin to worship each other, and all over town there are sacrificial bonfires, the stronger idols seizing and burning the weaker ones. Into this scene of destruction the Messiah emerges from the cellar of the Drohobycz synagogue where an old man named Moses the Righteous One used to sleep on a huge bundle of hay. Lars seems to be on the verge of receiving from this text a warning against his own idolatrous reading practices. The Messiah in the text embodies the message to stop hungering after, and seeking to devour, substitute messiahs. Yet Lars cannot register such a message and determines instead that the manuscript must be a fake. He retreats in despair to the conclusion that the real *Messiah* "went into the camps with its keeper . . . *The Messiah* was burned up." Where he had previously insisted upon "dredging up" the past, now he accepts the view that the past is irretrievable. As if retroactively to impose on the manuscript in his hands the same fate, Lars sets fire to it.

In the novel's postscript to this apocalyptic ending, Lars returns to his ordinary life. Having abandoned his fantasy of being Schulz's son, he resigns himself to the life of a "normal" reviewer of mediocre books. But the questions raised by the novel remain unanswered: How can we honor the dead without using them for our own purposes? How can we use literature as a genuine form of commemoration? How can we remember the past if our memories are driven by our fantasies and personal needs? The novel suggests that where Lars ultimately fails, others may succeed in responsibly bearing witness to the memory of the Holocaust.

—Julian Levinson

MILA 18
Novel by Leon Uris, 1961

Leon Uris's novel *Mila 18* (1961) is a fact-based treatment of the heroic resistance of the Jews in the Warsaw Ghetto during their uprising against the Nazis in 1943. The Nazis had been systematically emptying the ghetto, promising the inhabitants that they were being shipped to labor camps but actually shipping them to Treblinka for extermination. After word reached the ghetto of the Jews' real fate, some of the ghetto dwellers decided to confront the Nazis. On 18 January a group led by the Jewish Combat Organization met a Nazi attempt to round up Jews with armed resistance. Not until 16 May did the Nazis manage to defeat the defenders of the ghetto, even though the Nazis had at their disposal almost limitless manpower and one of the best-trained and best-equipped armies in the history of the world, while the Jews had on their side a group of largely untrained volunteers, many of whom were children, with few arms, most of which were homemade. The Germans eventually used artillery fire and aerial bombing to level the ghetto, but still the defenders fought on. That they held out for as long as they did demonstrated to the world that the Nazis could be defeated and that the Jews could fight. Uris extensively researched this historic episode both in archives and by interviewing survivors.

Uris's novel begins before the Nazi conquest of Poland. His protagonist, Andrei Androfski, is an officer in the Polish army who leads his horse-mounted regiment against the Nazi panzer troops. He manages to achieve a short-lived victory but is eventually forced to flee back to Warsaw when his outmanned and outgunned troops are defeated. After the surrender of Warsaw he and the other Jews of the city and, eventually, of the surrounding area are put into a walled-off ghetto the Nazis have created. While Androfski argues for the Jews to arm themselves and tries to join the Free Polish Forces, other groups, especially the Zionists, preach patience, having no idea of the fate that lies in store for them. After it is too late, Androfski wins the argument, and the Jewish command sets up its headquarters at Mila 18, from which it directs attack after attack against the Nazis and their allies.

Uris shows that, although some non-Jews help the inhabitants of the ghetto, most turn their backs on them. The Free Polish Forces refuse to aid the ghetto dwellers, even stealing some of the money being directed from the United States and England to the ghetto. The Nazis feed on preexisting Polish anti-Semitism to make the populace feel that the problems of occupation are the fault not of the Nazis but of the Jews.

In the book Uris also depicts Jewish characters who collaborate with the Nazis either for the illusion of power or for wealth, which they quickly lose when they are deported. He also depicts some who collaborate in the misguided idea that they are helping the Jewish people survive. Believing that the Nazis are determined to exterminate the Jews, they feel that working with the Nazis will make things easier on the Jews. He also indicates that many inhabitants of the ghetto cannot grasp what is happening to them and do not believe the reports that they are being deported for mass extermination.

Nonetheless, Uris focuses on the heroic resistance fighters, involved in what they know is a losing battle but nonetheless willing to sacrifice their lives to show the world that defiance of the Nazis is possible. He treats the idea that immense pressure brings out the worst in some people but the best in others. He also deals with the importance many of the ghetto dwellers place on recording the story of what is happening to them and of getting their story to the rest of the world. His book is in part an attempt to tell that story.

Through no stretch of the imagination is *Mila 18* a great piece of literature. When it appeared, many reviewers attacked it for stereotypical characterization and superficiality. Others compared it unfavorably to **John Hersey**'s *The Wall* (1950), also about the uprising in the Warsaw Ghetto. Even those who attacked the work, however, tended to praise Uris's plotting and his passion. Like most of Uris's works, it was written for a popular audience, and it was a best-seller. It tells a gripping tale of both human perfidy and sacrifice, self-delusion and clear sight, and cowardice and heroism. And it attempts to illustrate the idea that individual actions can make a difference even in the face of modern destructive technology.

—Richard Tuerk

THE MISSION (Die Mission)
Novel by Hans Habe, 1965

Hans Habe's novel *The Mission,* published in German as *Die Mission* in 1965 and in English translation in 1966, was intended to be a reminder of the nearly forgotten Évian Conference of 1938. The purpose of the conference, which took place at the initiative of U.S. President Franklin D. Roosevelt, was to discuss the Jewish refugee problem, which had become even more urgent with the German annexation of Austria. Fascist Germany refused to participate but suggested unofficially that it was willing to sell the freedom of Jews. It was the mission of the Vienna medical practitioner Heinrich Neumann to get support for the proposal. The vast part of the international public never had knowledge of the German proposal, and the politicians gathered in Évian-les-Baines, France, opposed it.

As a League of Nations correspondent, Habe reported on the conference throughout July 1938, and his articles were published in the Budapest newspaper *Ujság.* Prior to the conference he had learned about the mission of Neumann, who had been a friend of the family, and the novel was meant to be a tribute to him. From an artistic standpoint Habe's intent was to give to this singular event a universal significance. At the time he was working on a cycle of novels that dealt with the cardinal virtues and the deadly sins, and he devoted *The Mission* to the "lethargy of the heart," the sin he believed to be the most significant. In the epilogue to the novel he wonders, "Does a man whose heart is too sluggish to stop the wheel of disaster become an accomplice of the disaster?" His answer is yes, for guilt, he concludes, is always individual. While there may not be collective guilt, there is, however, collective complicity: "The bad happens because it is quietly tolerated by the good."

The Mission is a historical novel, and Habe wants to tell a story that adheres closely to the facts, which is why he adds a documentary appendix. In the novel the private life of the physician is rendered as fiction, enabling Habe to express Neumann's "mission" in symbolic terms. His personal mission becomes the mission of an entire people and its history, especially significant since he, as an assimilated Jew, has forsaken his people. At first Neumann hesitates to accept the idea of being a "new Moses," and thus he initially fails to

perform his task. In this sense his mission confronts the question of the dignity of mankind and, in so doing, seeks to create an identity for Neumann that goes beyond his fame and success as a doctor: "He himself—what was that?" The physician is unable to heal the disaster of his times, just as he cannot overcome his own frailty. Returning from his mission, he dies of a heart attack; the physical failure of his own heart corresponds to the world's moral failure to respond to the crisis confronting the German Jews. His personal dignity is saved, however. He has not gained advantages for himself or his family, and he has avoided becoming an accomplice of the fascists. Instead, he has fulfilled his true mission by demanding some form of accountability: "Those who are Jews force the world to take sides—maybe this is the core of anti-Semitism."

In 1967 the novel served as the basis of a successful television production, "Die Mission," directed by Ludwig Cremer and with a screenplay by Jochen Huth.

—Walter Schmitz

MR. MANI (Mar Maniy)
Novel by A.B. Yehoshua, 1990

Obliquely yet still inescapably about the Shoah, A.B. Yehoshua's *Mr. Mani* (1992; *Mar Maniy,* 1990) ranks as perhaps the most important Israeli novel of the 1990s and one of the landmark fictions in any contemporary national literature. The novel is Yehoshua's fourth, and while continuous with the earlier three (together with short fiction of the 1960s and '70s) in its penchant for Faulknerian narrative technique and the grotesque, mythic underpinnings, and what Yehoshua has elsewhere called the "tuning" of identity both cultural and personal, *Mr. Mani* undertakes nothing less than an allegory of modern Jewish history, refracting five spatio-temporal crossroads—Athens, 1848; Kraków, 1899; Jerusalem, 1918; Crete, 1944; the Negev, 1982—through the thematic motif of the *akedah,* the binding of Isaac. Narrative fiction, as both the secularization of myth and the actualization of what remains merely latent or threatened within it, is thus made to draw a line inexorably connecting the site of Jewish national and religious origin—the Temple Mount in Jerusalem—to the site of modern Jewish catastrophe.

As the boldest sort of creative intervention into history, *Mr. Mani* could thus be said to pick up where Freud's essay in psychocultural analysis, *Moses and Monotheism*—a work Freud referred to as a "historical novel"—left off, having been completed in London exile following the Nazi occupation of Vienna in 1939. In the context of the *dor hamedinah,* the new wave of modern Hebrew fiction (the 1960s–80s), *Mr. Mani* represents Yehoshua's own most sophisticated revision of the Zionist narrative by proposing a *kivun negdi,* a counter-move or alternate possibility, in the physical past for each of five formative moments in modern Jewish history.

Beyond being "the anti-family anti-saga," in Gershon Shaked's useful designation for the novel, *Mr. Mani* is even more flagrantly anti-hegemonic in its narrative poetics. Moving backward at 20–50 year intervals, the plot trajectory—five generations in a Sephardic family whose scions nurture both a death wish and inchoate genealogical longing—is narrated through the device of half-dialogue, the interlocutor's half of each conversation being left out and to be inferred in the reading. The novel's diegesis is thus a mix of story and confessional self-accounting in what might be called polyphonic Hebrew—five different registers to simulate the modern Hebrew, German, English, Yiddish, and Ladino spoken in each linguistically specific conversation. But with the exception of Abraham Mani in the final conversation (the only Mani family member given narrating responsibilities), the other dialogic partners all recapitulate certain family dynamics of the Mani family (missing fathers, listeners that are their speakers' elders) without, however, actually belonging to it.

As plot-driven as any saga of Yoknapatawpha County (Yehoshua has never concealed his authorial debt to William Faulkner), *Mr. Mani* makes final sense of its closest-to-present events (the first conversation on the outbreak of Israel's incursion into Lebanon and on the eve of the *intifada*) only with reference to those most historically remote (the fifth conversation that relates incidents taking place in Jerusalem in 1848, "the Springtime of Nations"). But at the same time, the text configures itself on a vertical axis, so that reading becomes archaeology—an intricate process of sifting through carefully sedimented details, layered artifacts of individual, collective, and mythic identity. For example, the second conversation takes place on the island of Crete because (1) Crete is the geographically closest that the Nazi occupation came to approaching Palestine; (2) in Greek mythology it is the womb in which Europe was reared, its cultural source and root; (3) it is the reputed origin of the *p'lishtim* who journeyed to Israel at about the same time the Israelites made their crossing from Egypt; and (4) as Knossos, it exemplifies civilization without religion. Cutting athwart all these layers is the transverse line of the Mani family, always proximate to historical movement or event but bypassed nevertheless. Thus, it is precisely their Sephardic cosmopolitanism that, while insulating them from Zionist idées fixes and benighted allegiances to European culture, keeps them stranded and askew.

Contrary progression, negative narration through omission, and not least historical and ideological roads not taken—such multiple decenterings explain the overarching thrust of Yehoshua's novel, which lays bare national choices confronting Israel in the present by narrating in reverse the immediate historical past. Yehoshua is himself a fifth-generation Sephardic Jerusalemite, a personal connection that in his own admission justifies both the centrality of Jerusalem in *Mr. Mani* and the

formal device of its five-generation plot. Yet the need for the centripetal pull of Jerusalem as neither ruin nor endlessly deferred return but lived Jewish history and geography is structurally crucial to the novel, biography notwithstanding.

Similarly, in its consistently centrifugal shift to the historical margins, a subtly mongrelized Sephardi identity becomes a metaphor for an alternate or refocused national destiny (a Sephardi is thus held captive in Heraklion in 1944 rather than centrally positioned in 1948, the year of Israel's statehood). As Jews of the Ottoman Empire, the Manis are not world-historical figures. Rather in tangentially making contact with the British-mandated Palestine in 1918 and the rise of Arab and Jewish nationalism, or the Third Zionist Congress (1899), or the war in Lebanon, or the Nazi occupation of Crete, they are made inadvertently to interrogate what otherwise appears to be an inexorable historical process.

Yehoshua has spoken of the "cool clarity" vouchsafed him by his Sephardi identity; one might likewise understand the role played by the Manis in his text as a self-occlusion, like a fish-eye lens, through which we can more clearly apprehend what is at stake for a Jewish world leading up to and away from the Shoah and recrudescent national will. But perhaps, finally, Yehoshua's profoundest and most distinctly novelistic achievement in *Mr. Mani* is its ethics of form—dialogues that must be cocreated in the reading that thus suggest a way left permanently open, ballast of human voices over the determinative weight of plot.

—Adam Zachary Newton

MR. SAMMLER'S PLANET
Novel by Saul Bellow, 1970

Artur Sammler of Saul Bellow's *Mr. Sammler's Planet* (1970) is a Holocaust survivor living in New York City. Forced to strip naked, Mr. Sammler was shot along with his wife and many other Jews in a pit he and the others had dug in the woods in Poland. Wounded (he was blinded in one eye so that he can distinguish only light and dark with it), he dug himself out through the corpses on top of him and the loose soil piled over them. Symbolically reborn, he joined the Polish resistance, but toward the end of the war the resistance began shooting its Jewish members. Sammler escaped and hid in the Mezvinski family tomb, where he was cared for by Cieslakiewicz, a Gentile. Thus, this time he literally emerged from the tomb.

Found in a camp for displaced persons, Sammler and his daughter, Shula, were taken in 1947 to the United States by his nephew, Arnold (Elya) Gruner. The nephew supports Sammler and his daughter during the time of the novel and assures his uncle that he will have no financial worries after his death. A retired surgeon, Gruner is rumored to have made money by providing illegal abortions to the girlfriends of members of the Mafia. At the time of the novel he is in a hospital dying.

Shula had survived the Holocaust by hiding in a Polish convent for four years, an experience that helped drive her insane. She is torn between her identity as a Jew and as a Roman Catholic, sometimes using her Jewish name, Shula, and sometimes her Catholic name, Slawa, and consulting both rabbis and priests. Shula went to Israel and married Eisen, another mad survivor. After Eisen began beating Shula, Sammler rescued her, and they both returned to New York.

During the war, Sammler says, he lost his faith in God. The novel shows him wandering in an America that also seems to have lost faith in God, and Sammler finds himself wondering, "Is our species crazy?" Many readers initially see him as an observer who prefers not to participate in life. But by the end of the novel he participates in life once again, feels faith in God and humanity, and even prays for the soul of Gruner. Sammler becomes a kind of one-eyed man in the kingdom of the blind, seeing people as they really are.

Sammler's change can best be traced in connection with a pickpocket he spies while riding the bus from Columbus Circle. Fascinated by the man, Sammler watches what he does. He tries to report him to the police, but they are not interested. The man sees Sammler watching him, follows Sammler to the lobby of his apartment building, and exposes himself. Sammler tells friends about the pickpocket, and one, Lionel Feffer, uses a miniature camera to photograph the pickpocket at work. The pickpocket sees Feffer and starts to beat him, trying to get the camera. Sammler, who is trying to get to the hospital to visit the dying Gruner, sees what is happening and calls upon Feffer to give the pickpocket the camera, and he begs the people in the gathering crowd to help Feffer. No one responds except Eisen, who is in America trying to make a fortune selling iron medallions. Eisen starts mercilessly beating the pickpocket with a sack full of the medallions. Sammler stops Eisen before he kills the pickpocket. He is horrified at what has happened to the pickpocket and feels tremendous sympathy for him. Eisen, who smiles throughout the beating, cannot understand his father-in-law's horror and reminds Sammler of his own experiences during the war, when he too had to kill people. As a result, Sammler realizes that for him merely to observe is impossible; he has to take a stand.

At the same time Sammler recognizes similarities between New York City in the 1960s and Europe in the 1930s and 1940s. In both the thin veneer of civilization was being stripped aside, revealing the chaos beneath. As a result of his experiences Sammler learns that utopian schemes like those of H.G. Wells, whom he had known in London before the war, and Govinda Lal, whom he meets after Shula steals Lal's manuscript on colonizing the Moon, cannot be fulfilled. But he also learns to value human life, to forgive his fellow humans for their faults, and even to love them, just as he recognizes that Gruner, in spite of his faults, was basically a good human

being. Thus, although several of the central characters in the novel experience the horrors of the Holocaust, it ends with what critics find at the conclusion of most novels by Saul Bellow, an affirmation of life.

—Richard Tuerk

MR. THEODORE MUNDSTOCK (Pan Theodor Mundstock)
Novel by Ladislav Fuks, 1963

In a world that offers little hope but much fear, Ladislav Fuks blends comedy and tragedy in his novel *Mr. Theodore Mundstock,* published in Czech as *Pan Theodor Mundstock* in 1963 and in English translation in 1968. Mundstock is a man who, until he reads the letters of his friends and neighbors, has given very little thought to the fact that the transport of Jews is taking place. Like everyone else, he follows the orders he is given, and, being a man who is alone except for a pet pidgeon and his own shadow to talk to, he has never communicated any clear opinion on the transports. It is not until he visits his friends the Sterns and in a night vision observes the struggles of his friend Mr. Vorfahren while being transported that he comes up with an idea that is so unbelievable it just might work. From the Sterns, Mundstock learns that people are hiding property and giving valuables to friends for safekeeping. Hope has existed in the Stern family that the war may be over in the spring, but as the spring passes, their hopes begin to fizzle, and resignation to a terrible fate begins to drive them crazy. When Mr. Vorfahren is called to be transported, it is the last straw for Mundstock. He begins to formulate his "road to salvation," and he thus creates a master plan, a "ME-THOD" of survival. It is "the way out of the Jewish history of suffering. The secret of salvation. It was the happiest day of his life."

In his vision he sees the troubles Mr. Vorfahren has heaving a suitcase that is too unwieldy and from having to sleep on a bed that is much too hard. The road to salvation, Mundstock concludes, rests upon one's preparation for the hardships of life in a concentration camp. A person must prepare for his fate and get used to things that are very different from current existence. One must also harden oneself to the fact that mistreatment and starvation will be part of the process. But these situations can be overcome, he believes. It is at this moment that intense happiness envelops Mundstock, for the formulation of his plan has not only given him hope for survival, but it also keeps his mind on the preparation instead of the transport to the concentration camps.

Although one might think that there is nothing comical about preparation for transport, Fuks has developed a character who is gifted with incredible foresight and keen powers of observation as well as a creative imagination. Mundstock begins to practice carrying a heavy suitcase, even counting the number of steps he must take before he changes hands. He uses an ironing board as a plank bed to get used to concentration camp life. He even envisions getting beaten by a Nazi and losing his teeth so that the soldier will feel that the beating has produced a result and cease. Mundstock surmises that this situation must also be practiced, for he has had little experience with anger and violent behavior. While he is at a kindly butcher's shop, he antagonizes the butcher and calculates the precise time at which he must spit out his false teeth.

Several letters appear throughout the novel and propel the story forward. The reader learns of the misery and the fear within the minds of Mundstock's friend Ruth Kraus and his friends the Sterns. "We have been flung into a terrible Hell," Kraus writes. In addition, the reader is privy to Mundstock's thoughts and actions throughout the novel. "What was so bad about being born under the Star of David?" he wonders. This thought indeed drives him to perfect his plan. In fact, Mundstock's preparation, as comical as it appears to be, develops a real purpose, and the reader finds himself cheering Mundstock on when he concocts another ME-THOD of overcoming the fate the Nazis have in store for him. His efforts are certainly valiant. In her last letter Mrs. Stern announces that the entire family, except for Simon, the young son, will be transported. It is his love for this young boy that will drive Mundstock to his death, for when they are both summoned for transport, Mundstock spots Simon on the platform and calls his name. Although Mundstock has meticulously prepared himself and Simon for transport and for survival in the camps, he neglects to take care in the street and is struck dead by a military transport.

One cannot help but feel psychologically drained by the entire endeavor undertaken by Mundstock. His comically detailed preparation and his fervent hope for salvation are undermined by fate, not in the form of his prediction of the hardships of the concentration camps but in the very unpredictable nature of life itself.

—Cynthia A. Klíma

MUTTERS COURAGE
Play by George Tabori, 1994

In *Mutters Courage* ("My Mother's Courage," 1994), first produced in Munich in 1979, playwright George Tabori subverted traditional narrative form while deconstructing conventional notions of heroism. Tabori wrote, "Certainly this anecdote is an exception. But my mother's rescue by a German is just as true as it is true that my father was killed at Auschwitz." But the way in which Tabori relayed this "truth" is through the use of deliberately contradictory and constantly shifting perspectives: the story of his mother's deportation and escape, based on real life incidents, is relayed by a son/storyteller who beautifies the tale in an attempt both to validate his mother's unconventional courage and to illustrate the tension between a neat narrative and an unwieldy and horrible reality. In this way Tabori recognized the difficulty of articulating experiences of atrocity while validating a more nuanced notion of resistance.

The play, "a fairy tale in which no one was saved from baking in the oven except one," opens with the tape-recorded voice of the storyteller (Tabori himself): "A summer day in January '44, an outstanding harvest year for death, my mother put on her good black suit with the lace collar that she, as is appropriate for a lady, was accustomed to wearing to the weekly game of rummy at her sister Martha's." So begins the tale of one day in Elsa Tabori's life. She is arrested on the way to her sister's. When her bumbling captors accidentally lose track of her, she obediently turns herself in again. She is then placed on a train to Auschwitz; along the way she tells a German officer a mistake has been made, whereupon she is allowed to go back, arriving at her sister's late in the evening to play rummy, seemingly unscathed by her adventures. But the suggestion of the darker fate of many Jews remains despite Elsa's fortunate escape.

Throughout the son's narration the mother interrupts occasionally to correct him. Often Elsa praises him for his poetic descriptions of her experiences, though she reminds him that his version is not entirely accurate. But later she claims she has forgotten what happened. Thus, the playwright's emphasis is as much on the discrepancies between the son's story and his mother's memory as on the actual experience.

One way Tabori foregrounded the "produced" nature of representation was through his mockery of traditional narrative form, such as one finds in fairy tales. This "fairy tale" includes stock formulas such as a "love affair," a thrilling chase scene, and heroic struggles against obstacles, but always with an ironic twist. For example, the sequence the son entitles "the love story" involves an unseen male on the train to Auschwitz who begs Elsa to allow him to have anal intercourse with her because this would be his last time. Elsa grants the man's request and even experiences a certain pleasure from it, according to her son. Before the story can be fully told, however, the mother protests. She asks permission to leave the stage, too embarrassed to listen. Meanwhile the "past Elsa" (played by the same actress) remains onstage, pantomiming the son's version. Of course it is ironic and macabre to call this incident a "love story." The audience is also left wondering exactly what the real story is. These discrepancies between the son's tale and the mother's untold memory serve to distance the audience's identification with the characters, disrupting and at times even refuting the son's well-made narrative.

Tabori also deconstructed traditional notions of courage, as **Bertolt Brecht** did in his play *Mother Courage*. Elsa's conception of herself is a far cry from the traditional hero she is familiar with from her afternoons at the cinema. At one point

Elsa confesses she lacks the skills required for such adventures and would do better if she were ''her idol, Douglas Fairbanks, who could . . . swing from roof to roof and fence with a horde of crooks.'' Swept away from her ''woman's world'' of domestic cares, she behaves passively, and her destiny is constantly being determined by the men around her, just as her story is by her son's narration. The kind of courage she demonstrates seems small in comparison with the more dramatic and clear-cut moral stance exhibited by a traditional hero such as Uncle in Tabori's earlier play *The Cannibals*. But Tabori nonetheless validated his mother's courage by depicting her less dramatic but perhaps more realistic resistance.

By presenting narrators who are at times unreliable (as he also did in his plays *The Cannibals, Jubiläum,* and *Mein Kampf*), Tabori has dramatized the problematic stance of the Holocaust writer. He realized that no representation of the Holocaust could adequately portray the ''objective'' truth. In this play, as well as in his other Holocaust plays, Tabori therefore has attempted through black humor, irony, and theatricality to avoid sentimentality but still focus on the horrible realities of the Holocaust.

—Susan Russell

MY FATHER'S HOUSE
Novel by Meyer Levin, 1947

Based on Meyer Levin's screenplay for the movie of the same title and year, *My Father's House* (1947) employs any number of heavily symbolic, quasi-cinematic scenes in a vaguely propagandistic allegory in support of a Jewish state in Palestine. Part of Levin's technique—and it is hard to say just how much of this is indebted to the novel's cinematic origins—is to render the entire fictional world of this novel subject to the rules and logic of fable, assigning his characters singular and highly symbolic meanings. The impulse, it seems, comes from the mythic soil upon which the novel is set, quite as if Levin had been unable to imagine contemporary Palestine other than through the lens of the biblical imagination. Among the main characters it is especially the Zionist hero Avram who represents the novel's fabulous design. As the head of a Jewish settlement into which a number of survivors of the Holocaust have been smuggled illegally, Avram plots the incorporation of these living remnants of European history into the promise of the biblical, yet also modern and socialistic, homeland. Standing strong against the political adversities imposed by British rule and the varied ambivalences and hostilities of the indigenous Arabs, as also against the weighty sorrows and effete cultural heritage of the European Jewish past, Avram embodies the hope of the Jewish people. Thus he persistently foresees—at times seeing for others—a redemptive future into which all of the Jewish people, no matter how abject their personal histories, may be incorporated.

In later years Levin would note that his largely overlooked novel had anticipated the tremendous success of **Leon Uris**'s *Exodus* (1958), and indeed it might be said of Levin, as of Uris, that he employs the Holocaust in service of Zionist politics—at the expense of Holocaust history. Levin and Uris share the impulse to search for redemptive meanings in the midst of immense historical catastrophe, and each testifies to the endurance and dignity of the Jewish people by creating Zionist characters who seem less human material than the stuff of future legend. Yet even as Levin's novel works toward a redemptive future, it also resists the trajectory of its own plot. *My Father's House* delineates a conflict between Holocaust consciousness and the Zionist project, thus remembering a real tension within the emergent Israeli state. As Tom Segev and others have noted, the requirements of nationalist ideology meant that a cultural memory of the Holocaust was slow to take root in Israel, as was also the case, for different reasons, in America. In Levin's novel two survivors, Daavid and Miriam, have an especially hard time reconciling their Holocaust past with the promises of Palestine, and their struggle signifies Levin's apprehension of the chasm that lay between the Holocaust and the usable past of Jewish religion and culture. For Miriam, a young woman who we eventually learn has been a survivor of Nazi medical experiments and becomes sterile as a result, it is the memory of what has been done to her and to those Jews who perished at the hands of the Nazis that forbids any belief in the mythic language of rebirth advocated by the Jewish settlers. Conceiving a special attachment to Daavid, the maternal connotations of which are unmistakable to almost everyone in the novel except herself, Miriam is nevertheless adamant that Daavid not be allowed to persist in his delusionary belief that his father and family have survived the war and are waiting for him somewhere in Palestine. For his part, faithful to this delusion and to a father whom he was too young to remember, Daavid soon flees the settlement and comes for a while under the guardianship of a man who shares with Daavid the surname Halevi. Recognizing that this boy has come to him looking for family, the gentle-hearted man pretends to be Daavid's uncle, takes him into his home, and agrees to help Daavid continue his search for his father. Eventually Daavid discovers the man's well-intentioned lie and departs for Jerusalem looking for the Search Bureau, an agency responsible for listing the dead and locating survivors of the Holocaust.

As the boy finally confronts the full horror of history, Levin employs an extraordinary device to deliver him from the trauma of the past. Having learned that everyone in his family has been killed at the hands of the Nazis, Daavid walks into the middle of a group of children who are singing a Purim song and playing a game that reenacts Haman's persecution of the Jews. With this device Levin incorporates the Holocaust into a biblical story of oppression and suggests the historical continuity of anti-Semitism. Suddenly Daavid's search for his identity in the past of the Holocaust has been placed in a larger context of Jewish identity and suffering, and the novel's fabulous trajectory within the mythic resources of biblical lore. Still Levin recognizes that the Holocaust is on a far greater scale than any previous injustice suffered by the Jews. When Daavid collapses as the children sing gleefully of oppression, the contrast between this more immediate catastrophic history and the injustices of the mythic past could not be more starkly emphasized. Yet this will prove to be the device through which Levin delivers the child from his recusant Holocaust memory. Only through a mental breakdown brought on by extreme grief can Daavid find his way to a new identity. Attributing to Daavid what are more symbolically apt than clinically precise symptoms, Levin shows the boy regressing to a younger age— to a time, as it were, before the Holocaust—in order to be reborn a child of the emergent Jewish homeland. While the Zionist Avram foresees a future for Daavid and Miriam, and Levin ostensibly supports such a vision, what the novel fails to imagine is how the Holocaust can be included in the triumphalist and redemptive narrative of Zionism. Beginning anew from an earlier innocent age, Daavid is reborn absent the memory of the Holocaust, his memorylessness offered in the service of a cultural continuity of Jewish identity.

—R. Clifton Spargo

MY GERMAN QUESTION: GROWING UP IN NAZI BERLIN
Memoir by Peter Gay, 1998

In *My German Question* (1998) Peter Gay discusses the Holocaust from two viewpoints. From a historical perspective he explains why German Jews did not leave the country as soon as Adolf Hitler became chancellor on 30 January 1933 and why they meekly submitted to increasingly anti-Semitic decrees and violence. On a personal level Gay explores how growing up in Nazi Germany affected him.

In his examination of the behavior of German Jews, Gay rejects the claim made by Gershom Scholem that while the Jews loved the Germans, the Germans never loved the Jews. Gay was born in 1923 and recalls his first ten years as idyllic. Even after the Nazis came to power, he continued to spend summers with the Gentile parents of the family's maid; they were like a second set of parents to him. Another Gentile, Emil Busse, was a close family friend who took many risks to help the Gays escape Germany. The decency of some Germans served to lull Jews into a false sense of security, as did the Nazi regime's uncertainty about how it would deal with the Jews. In 1935, the year of the implementation of the Nuremberg Laws, which severely restricted Jewish civil rights, Gay's uncle Siegfried Kohnke received the Iron Cross for his service in

World War I. The award was made in Hitler's name. According to Gay, ambivalence rather than a determination to annihilate German Jewry marked the Nazi's attitude, allowing Jews to convince themselves that they would be able to remain and survive in the only home they had known. He also notes that even if Germany's Jews had wished to emigrate, they had no place to go. Gay directs his anger not only at the Germans who killed the Jews but also at the rest of the world that refused to provide a safe haven.

With his mother and father, Gay narrowly escaped the fate of his two aunts, who died in the Holocaust. Still, the years 1933–39 left their mark on the historian. To compensate for his low status in his native land, he became a fan of winning sports teams. For more than two decades he refused to return to Germany. When he finally did go back in 1961, the visit was ruined by his paranoia.

Over the years Gay has come to reject the view that the only good German is a dead German; he has adopted a more nuanced attitude towards Germany and its inhabitants. His Columbia University dissertation dealt with the German political philosopher Eduard Bernstein, and his two-volume study of the Enlightenment (1966–69) and his five-volume survey of the Victorian era (1984–97) discuss a variety of German intellectuals and artists. While Gay has thus reintegrated Germany into his intellectual world, *My German Question* demonstrates that the pain inflicted in the 1930s has not vanished. As of 1998 Gay had never watched the movie *Shoah*, had not visited the Holocaust Museum in Washington, D.C., and had not gone to Auschwitz. As Gay writes, "Some sixty years later, fragments of Nazi Berlin still sometimes haunt me and will haunt me to the day I die."

—Joseph Rosenblum

MY HATE SONG
Poem by Itzik Manger, 1961

Itzik Manger's writing occupies a central place in Jewish literary identity, spanning poetry, essays, cultural history, rabbinic writings, politics, and fiction. Characteristic of his work are a cosmopolitan sophistication combined with an equally strong sense of folk identity. Traditional stories, including biblical stories were material that could be revitalized and used in ways that brought them new life. Manger's career was profoundly shaped by the Holocaust. He chose to write in the ballad form in his aim to encourage a sense of the Yiddish folk epic.

In "My Hate Song" Manger's use of irony in the title characterizes his intensely emotional and bold sense of lyrical expression. His song of hatred is his attempt to break hatred of its constraints, those constraints that have defined it in the Nazi consciousness. The first stanza of the poem situates a lone remaining singer before his ultimate host. This direct confrontation is the only way for him to define his own vengeance. Manger's heightened rage, urgency, and sense of imminent peril are the driving emotions in the poem. His fate, which he both fears and desires, is to sing a song to a ''massacred host,'' the destroyed lodging of Israel. In the early stanzas of the poem, Manger emphasizes the ironies inherent to his song. What its rhythms have rendered before, the ''Spring blossoming,'' has come to pass over the Kaddish, the Jewish song of the dead, which he has ultimately come to sing. The ''shadow of gloom,'' evocative of the archetypal despair of children's stories, especially as he suggests it will be sung to children, becomes the sole remaining agency of his song.

In stanzas four and five the poet sings a hate song itself. The ultimate embodiment of hate will be the extermination of children; once he expresses this, it seems like a horror too emphatic to take. The poem turns to the abstract, to the realm of dreams and the subconscious: ''Divide me, God, a thousandwise, / Into evil dreams where I man devour / The flesh of the blond Cains.'' The violent, vaguely metaphysical initial image renders the speaker irrevocably ruptured before the poem evokes the son of Adam and Eve and murderer of his brother Abel: Cain. Yet this is an Aryan Cain, in multitude. In moving and dramatic images the final stanza of the poem sings in direct address to God: ''Send over that bloody land all your carrion crows'' is an image that rings with a dark beauty. As the rhythms and language proceed, the density of hatred gathers momentum and creates out of itself something vital and perseverant. Hate, Manger's hate, has been the thing that has ultimately divided and fallen into step with itself. The ending image, of dogs licking blood from German knives, depicts not only the violence of a gory predation but it also powerfully draws an illustration of a survivalist will, a will to take life from the instrument of one's demise. ''My Hate Song'' ultimately describes two impulses. It sings a song, and it does so in a traditional form that links it to life-sustaining, culture-sustaining utterances throughout history. Within that form it sets down an undeniable motivation for retribution for wrongs inflicted. This is a motivation so intense that it stems from and, to some extent, operates within the very vehicle of the Holocaust's tragedy—hate.

—Martha Sutro

MY LITTLE SISTER (Ahoti ketanah)
Poem by Abba Kovner, 1967

The poem *My Little Sister* (published as *Ahoti ketanah* in 1967 and appearing in English translation in *My Little Sister*

and Selected Poems, 1965–1985 in 1986), bearing much likeness to the Song of Solomon, is constructed as part of five series of 46 shorter poems and forms a eulogy for the people of Vilna who perished in the Holocaust. It tells the story of a young Jewish girl who crawls up over the corpses buried in a mass grave near Ponar, a labor camp near the Vilna ghetto, and returns to the ghetto to report the tragic fate of the thousands of victims. The poem gradually leads toward the suffering of the narrator's mother. The poem is Abba Kovner's most focused delivery of Holocaust poetry.

The poem is narrated by one of the girl's dead brothers speaking omnisciently from his grave. He mourns the fate of his sister, who emerges as somehow deader than he. The girl, finding refuge in a convent, lives in solitude, submerged in a surreal world of deadening silence and replete with Christian allusions. Kovner voices subtle protest against Christian acquiescence to the Holocaust, drawing links between the priest and nuns of the convent and the Holy Trinity of Christianity and the Jewish victims. His protest extends to the Jewish God, who simply stares at the morbid fate of the little girl in silent disapproval.

The suffering and chasteness of the nuns are contrasted with the unwilling martyrdom of the little girl. The nuns' love for Christ takes on an erotic quality, while the love Kovner and the narrator of the poem feel for the little girl emerges purer and superior to that experienced by the nuns for their God. Love in Kovner's poem does not take on masculine or satisfaction-oriented qualities but instead connotes yearning and loss.

In *My Little Sister* Kovner succeeds in creating a suitable fusion of poetic expression and symbolic representation of the victims of the Holocaust. He does so by diverting from normal grammatical guidelines and discarding personal and geographical demarcations—except for the monastery and the nuns. Thus, by abstracting the main character of the poem, the fate of the entire Jewish nation converges with that of the little girl.

One of the most prominent motifs in the poem is the image of a bride and groom—the sister and her beloved brother—and the coming together in a covenant of marriage. This motif, used in the Bible to represent the Covenant between God and his people, expands the theme of the poem from the love of the individuals animated in it and the national tragedy. The wretched misery of the sister and the fate of the Jewish nation are transmitted through a network of visual and lyrical allusions that relive the memories of the dishonoring of the Covenant.

Another way in which Kovner evokes the collective fate of European Jewry is by repeatedly changing the speaking voice—it may be that of the ancient sages, the brother, or the young girl—that alternates with the voice of Jesus. The fragmentation of speech is aided by grammatical and visual lack of flow in the poem.

—Ziva Shavitsky

MY MOTHER'S SABBATH DAYS (Der mames shabosim)
Memoir by Chaim Grade, 1958

The original Yiddish title page of Chaim Grade's *My Mother's Sabbath Days* (1986; *Der mames shabosim,* 1958) classifies the work as *dertseylungen*—a collection of stories. An English translation appearing in 1986, four years after the author's death, bears the words ''a memoir'' on its cover. In fact, the work operates somewhere in between these two genres. Grade draws upon his memories to craft a series of vignettes, rich in lyricism and detached character study, linked chronologically and by the recurrence of subjects and settings, flickering between the past and present tenses and poignantly evocative of the devastation visited upon him by the events of the Holocaust.

The book is divided into three sections, representing the before, during, and after periods of Grade's wartime experience. In the first of these, eponymous with the entire volume, he summons forth from death the lost Vilna of his youth—the lives and ways of life decimated by the Nazis. His mother, Vella, is the central figure, and as a spirit pouring out of Grade's pen she radiates a loving tenderness, long-suffering poverty, and simple piety that coalesce into the emotional core of the work. Around her, as she struggles through her circumstances toward the tenuous peace of her weekly Sabbath, whirl a host of characters and concerns: goose dealers carrying on illicit affairs with butchers' assistants beneath the watchful eyes of professional gossips, aged widows calculating the quickest path to an easeful death, young men and women yearning for the new lives shimmering in dream visions of Zionism and Soviet communism, and the generational conflicts that ensue as old religious structures crumble beneath the weight of modernity.

Though Grade writes in the first person, his own life in this era is predominately explored only in so far as it bears upon his mother's. His rejection of religious Judaism and burgeoning success as a modern Yiddish poet are reflected in Vella's anxious ruminations, the traditional mother lamenting, and even shamed by, her son's abandonment of his faith. At these moments the text shifts most obviously from memoir to storytelling, Grade the author exploring his mother's consciousness from a perspective he would not have been privy to as Grade the son. The major exception to this fixed focus on his mother is the introduction of his wife, the young nurse Frumme-Liebche, in lingering and reverent prose. With the emotional relevance of these two women firmly established, the stage is set for the agony to follow.

When the Germans invade Lithuania in 1941, following Hitler's double-crossing of Stalin, Grade flees with the retreating Soviets, leaving behind his consenting wife and mother, under the common misapprehension that the Nazis pose a mortal danger only to able-bodied men. The next four years of his life, his meager existence in the refugee limbo of the Asian Soviet republics, are covered in ''The Other End of the World.'' He survives the arduous flight, witnessing death, degradation, the severing of families, and the chaos of the early Russian war effort, sneaking through dark, patrolled forest, and riding amidst the squalor of open railway cars. Through depictions of his fellow travelers he highlights the preoccupations of the refugees. Misha Troiman, uncertain of his wife's fate, contemplates finding comfort in the arms of a willing stranger, while eking out a dangerous living on the black market, to support the family of his imprisoned brother. Ornstein devolves into a bitter sarcasm, disabused of his earlier idealism by his experience of the poverty and repression of the actual Soviet Union. Chaim Grade wanders in a haze of guilt and longing, visited by visions of his mother and wife, who, he is to learn, have gone to the slaughter in the forests of Ponary.

He returns to Vilna after the war, and ''The Seven Little Alleys'' finds him haunting the ruins of the ghetto, searching for remnants of his lost loved ones and fearing what he may find. He describes the psychological strategies of other survivors: the shoemaker who dulls his pain by obliterating the evidence of his former identity and the pediatrician who speaks openly of the past out of a belief that the dead can be revived in words. Grade allows no suggestion to coalesce into a solution. In the final pages he flees from the house of worship on Yom Kippur, as the last Jews of Vilna pray for reconciliation with God, and wanders among the wreckage of other synagogues, asking only for the strength to enter at last into his mother's old dwelling. There, in the violated sanctuary, in the company of a stray cat, he murmurs the only words of understanding he can muster: ''Mother has gone to the synagogue and cannot return . . . she will not return . . . will not return . . . ''

—Binyomin Weiner

MY NAME IS ASHER LEV
Novel by Chaim Potok, 1972

My Name Is Asher Lev, Chaim Potok's third novel, is a story of the search for truth and of a way to communicate that truth. It is a story of the search for meaning and balance in a world that contains suffering. In the novel Potok continued to work in the bildungsroman tradition, with the main character choosing his place in the world as he matures from childhood to adulthood. As in his earlier work *The Chosen,* Potok's main character must confront Jewish tradition and make meaning of it in his own life.

As a young boy with a gift for drawing, Asher Lev is driven to his art in the face of his father's disdain: ''He seemed awed and angry and confused and dejected, all at the same time.'' The boy struggles with his internal desire to draw what he sees, what he remembers, what he feels in the face of his community's fear that his gift is from the ''Other Side'' (that is, from the Gentiles) rather than from Ribbono Shel Olom (from Judaism). In Asher's journey to fulfill the promise of his gift, he connects to the journeys of his family. It is in this connection that he discovers that his art must speak the truth if it is to bring balance to a world with suffering.

Throughout his life Asher had heard stories of how his father's great-great-grandfather had transformed the estates of a Russian nobleman into a source of immense wealth. The nobleman, however, had persecuted his serfs and once burned down an entire village. Asher realizes that his ancestor's later travels had to do with atonement for an ability that led to suffering. His father's father, too, traveled, as does his own father. In coming to understand these journeys as methods of atonement, Asher finds his own meaning: ''Now the man who had once been the child asked it again and wondered if the giving and the goodness and the journeys of that mythic ancestor might have been acts born in the memories of screams and burning flesh. A balance had to be given the world; the demonic had to be reshaped into meaning . . . Traditions are born by the power of an initial thrust that hurls acts and ideas across centuries.'' And so Asher reshapes the anguish and torment of his people into art: ''No one says you have to paint ultimate anguish and torment. But if you are driven to paint it, you have no other way.'' Yet to paint this suffering, this torment, Asher must journey into another tradition to find the aesthetic mold necessary to convey the pain. This mold is the crucifix he has been studying for much of his life. The master of the universe whispers to him through the leaves of the trees: ''Now journey with me, my Asher. Paint the anguish of all the world. Let people see the pain. But create your own molds and your own play of forms for the pain. We must give a balance to the universe.''

The themes of balance and truth and journey in *My Name Is Asher Lev* are played out in the context of a post-Holocaust world. Although his mother wants him to paint pretty pictures, Asher cannot because he realizes that the world is not pretty; rather, it contains suffering, a suffering he must depict, a truth he must paint. When there is silence, where there is a fear of the truth, agony persists. Asher learns this from the Russian émigré Yudel Krinsky, who had been imprisoned in Siberia. The image of his cold, his suffering, is of interest to the young Asher. ''Did Stalin send many people to Siberia?'' Asher asks. When Yudel replies that he sent millions, Asher wants to know what the world did for this inhumanity. ''Absolutely nothing,'' Yudel responds. It is this nothing, this silence, that Asher cannot allow in his own life, in his art. Risking everything, he must paint the truth. He must bring balance to the world, for such suffering has no meaning if it is kept quiet, if it is not communicated, not set out for all to see.

Once again, in *My Name Is Asher Lev,* Potok explores issues of confronting the past, confronting cultures, and understanding the self and others. It is as if Potok were saying to the readers of his work, ''Journey with me.''

—Jan M. Osborn

MY QUARREL WITH HERSH RASSEYNER (''Mayn krig mit Hersh Rasseyner'')
Short story by Chaim Grade, 1982

In the early 1950s Chaim Grade, a leading Yiddish poet, began to write prose fiction, and ''My Quarrel with Hersh Rasseyner'' was among his first pieces. Drawing upon his own background in the Noveredok Yeshiva of the Mussar movement, the story anticipates the fuller portrayal and more sustained questioning of that milieu in his subsequent novel, *Tsemach Atlas.*

''My Quarrel with Hersh Rasseyner'' presents the lifelong debate between two classmates from the Noveredok yeshiva. Hersh Rasseyner remains committed to the stringent mussar movement, characterized by extreme piety, with an emphasis on ethics, and an ascetic tendency. His companion, known as Chaim Vilner, a stand-in for the author, abandons the mussar movement to pursue a life in secular letters. The tale begins with a brief conversation on a street in Bialystok in 1937 seven years after Chaim has left the yeshiva, followed by a second, chance encounter in Vilna in 1939. These moments serve to delineate the characters and to set the lines of their quarrel. The largest portion of the text is devoted to their meeting on the Paris metro in 1948, at which time the experience of the Holocaust drives them to a passionate elucidation of their respective positions: for Hersh, greater piety; for Chaim, deeper questions. In the course of that discussion the friends ask one another what change the Holocaust has wrought in their thinking, and they answer in turn. Yet Grade presents the post-Holocaust reflections as continuous with their pre-war quarrel. The Holocaust casts a stark, clarifying light on their differences and also raises the stakes, as it were, of the contest, but the debate remains a confrontation between Jewish tradition, as interpreted by the mussar movement, and modernity, as it has been embraced by secularizing Jews.

The first round in Bialystok goes to modernity. Hersh castigates his friend for abandoning piety for the vain pursuit of fame. But Chaim responds with a critique that takes traditional piety by its blind side. He points out that ''Women exhausted from work bring you something to eat.'' Hersh's spirituality denies a place for women and yet depends on them and on the labor of those whom Hersh himself maligns for lack of piety. A telling criticism will have an important post-Holocaust echo: ''You scold the hungry for being sinners.''

Will the pious similarly blame the victims of the camps for their victimization?

In round two the balance shifts. The two friends meet in a Vilna plagued by the Russian NKVD and in sight of Red Army tanks. Hersh asks the rhetorical question, ''Is this what you wanted?'' The implication has been developed in much post-Holocaust discussion, namely, that the totalitarian regimes of Stalin and Hitler are not aberrations but rather the logical extension of the premises of modernity. Chaim's retort is unconvincing and easily overturned. He asserts, like the biblical Cain, ''Hersh, I bear no more responsibility for all that than you do for me.'' The adherent of mussar need only accept his responsibility for his brother to suggest the parallel responsibility of the secularist for the modern totalitarian condition.

The experience of the Holocaust appears, at first, to have transformed the acerbic and judgmental Hersh into a milder man. But eventually he is led to speak aloud the challenge that he claims to have practiced in the camps. His argument is forceful, particularly as he presses the former themes, such as the basic irresponsibility of the credo of liberalism: ''Let me alone and I'll let you alone.'' Reason, the characteristic instrument of modernity, makes the freedom of the individual, critical intelligence the principal value. Reason, then, is not inevitably wed to ethics, and, moreover, the free individual is not wed to a community. Without community the Jew cannot be a Jew, Hersh argues, and without a basis in ethics modernity can and does lead to the Holocaust. At the limit Hersh declares that the Jew who leaves his community (for Hersh, but also for Chaim, Jews are gendered male) to emulate the gentiles will find himself, when Holocaust comes, wishing to become—that is, to exchange places with—his torturer in the camps. Hersh easily brushes away Chaim's objection that the gentile philosophers also understood and strove for the good, suggesting that upholding ethical values did not prevent the Holocaust. Hersh responds that good deeds, not a good ethical system, was called for, and only the Jewish law conceives of ethics in those terms, thus leading the Jew, and only the Jew, to true goodness.

Chaim counters with the example of the pious Christians and humanitarian atheists who saved Jewish lives: ''Now you come along and repudiate everything in the world that isn't piously Jewish.'' He goes on to contest Hersh's understanding of the chosen character of the Jewish people, which, he demonstrates decisively, excludes not only pious gentiles but also all Jews who do not share the mussar way of life. Many who suffered as Jews would be denied their Jewishness by Hersh's standard, and this, Chaim urges, would be a further crime against the living and the dead.

Grade gives the final word to Chaim. Freedom, Chaim argues, does make for individuals, but so too it breeds equality, whence comes fraternity. Community is not to be achieved by the ascetic who withdraws from human contact and by the pious traditionalist who excommunicates fellow Jews for their modernity. After Auschwitz, argues the modern Jew, let us have fellowship. Thus Chaim's closing refutation is to invite his adversary to enlarge the tragically diminished circle of Jewish life. After Auschwitz, and before the friends separate forever, Chaim proposes, ''let us embrace each other.''

Andrew Bush

N

NAKED AMONG WOLVES (Nackt unter Wölfen)
Novel by Bruno Apitz, 1958

Bruno Apitz was a socialist activist from adolescence on. As such, he experienced jail for the first time during World War I, then in the Weimar Republic, and again for most of the Third Reich. It was his experience in the Nazi prisons and camps in Colditz and Sachsenburg (1933), Waldheim (1934–37), and Buchenwald (1937–45) that provided the material for his most successful work, *Naked among Wolves* (1958; *Nackt unter Wölfen*).

When he came to write the book in the 1950s, Apitz was a socialist living in a restrictive socialist Germany. The German Democratic Republic subscribed to the doctrine of socialist realism in its narrowest Zhdanovian interpretation. The tenets of socialist realism entailed the promotion of revolutionary socialism, which was portrayed optimistically and was future oriented. In socialist realist literature, moreover, one avoided all experimentation (formalism) and psychological subtlety. Stylistically, socialist realism demanded, above all, clarity, accessibility, and readability. Apitz fulfilled all these criteria admirably.

Naked among Wolves is set in Buchenwald. Although it relies on its author's own experiences and is based on fact, Apitz freely invented and embellished his material—he wrote as a novelist, not as an historical chronicler. In the last weeks of the war a Jewish child is smuggled into the camp during the chaos as Jews and other prisoners were evacuated west from Polish camps by cattle cars and forced marches. The presence of such a child, hidden in the camp, endangers the resistance that is soon to be put into action by the ILK, or international camp committee. The leadership of the ILK is split between those who take the humane view and wish to save a life, a Jewish life, and those who see the child as an impediment— once the SS learns of the hidden Jew, they will turn the camp upside down and thus discover the arms that are to be used in the imminent uprising.

The German camp personnel is also split. Some hard-liners, prepared to fight to the end and implement Nazi doctrine rigorously, want to use the child to locate the resisters and murder them. Others, seeing the impending end and anticipating defeat, fear for their lives and wish to use what they see as an opportunity to appear more humane than they actually are. As it turns out, the child soon unites the camp's inmates—ILK members and non-members alike. Solidarity thus prevails, and, as the American liberators approach, the revolt takes place and the camp is liberated from within.

The plot is simple but full of tension. There are unexpected developments, mysteries that long remain unsolved, and graphic descriptions of camp life. The Nazi policy of appointing prisoners to organize the day-to-day routine of the camp (kitchen, infirmary, electrical installations, etc.) also serves to provide the prisoners with information and opportunities as they prepare their uprising. The novel is never dull, and the reader is rapidly drawn into the action, eagerly awaiting each new development.

The language and syntax are simple and clear. The persons, although types rather than fully rounded characters, are believable, if exaggerated. The socialist message is patent throughout but falls short of being irksome. The symbolism is largely limited to the child, who signifies life, hope, and the future and who is a strong unifying factor that inspires unity and self-effacement.

Naked among Wolves is an early German camp novel. The camp, however, is not an extermination camp for the Jews, who, apart from the child, are almost entirely absent. The assumed solidarity of socialist and Jewish victimhood, as it is portrayed, for example, by **Sara Nomberg-Przytyk** in her *Auschwitz: True Tales from a Grotesque Land*, is not part of the novel (and was certainly not a reality in Buchenwald). Furthermore, the resistance itself has little in common with Jewish resistance, which operated, whenever it did, under totally different conditions and constraints. As such, the novel's importance is less as an example of Holocaust literature and more as a novel of concentration camp life written by a socialist in a form appropriate for his communist homeland.

—David Scrase

THE NAZI AND THE BARBER (Der Nazi und der Friseur)
Novel by Edgar Hilsenrath, 1971

One can scarcely imagine a tale more twisted, more deeply sarcastic, and more humorous than the story of Max Schulz, the "illegitimate, yet pure-blooded Aryan" hero of Edgar Hilsenrath's *Der Nazi und der Friseur* (1977; *The Nazi and the Barber*, 1971). From his birth in 1907 in a small German town to his death in Israel more than 60 years later, Max Schulz takes part in some of the most important events of the twentieth century, including the rise of Nazism, the Holocaust, the defeat of Germany, and the founding of the Jewish state. Max's story is so unusual because in each of these historical periods he changes or re-forms himself in order to take advantage of the situation. He begins as a small-town barber's apprentice and becomes in turn a member of the Nazi Party, a concentration camp guard, and an executioner, and then, slipping into the identity of one of his victims, he becomes a black marketeer, a fighter for Israeli independence, and finally a respected citizen of Tel Aviv. Each of his identities is laden with stereotypes and clichés, demanding that the reader reexamine accepted notions of identity, guilt, and atonement.

A few examples of these stereotypes from just the opening pages of the novel are as follows: As a child Max Schulz, with his very German-sounding name, grows up in a lower-class home at the crossroads of Goethe and Schiller Streets, names that signify the height of classical German culture. His best friend is Itzig Finkelstein, whose name resembles something invented by an anti-Semitic propagandist. (In fact, Itzig during the Nazi period was a derogatory name for any Jewish man.) The Finkelsteins, while practicing Jews, are highly assimilated members of the local community. The list of groups to which Itzig's father belongs is a ridiculous overexaggeration of the stereotypical German tendency to join and organize: a bowling club, the animal protection society, the garden club, the barbers guild, the love-your-neighbor league. This stereotype of German Jewish assimilation and coexistence is, however, turned on its head by the descriptions of the two boys. Max is dark, has a hooked nose and flat feet, and generally fits the historical stereotype of Jews established by anti-Semitic tracts. Itzig, on the other hand, is blond, fair, and blue-eyed—the ideal of stereotypical Aryan masculinity. Later in the text, when Max needs to escape prosecution as a war criminal and takes the identity of his murdered friend, Itzig, his name and his dark complexion are so convincingly Jewish that his identity as a Jewish concentration camp survivor is never questioned.

The novel begins as a first-person narration and is told through the eyes of the perpetrator, Max Schulz, in stark contrast to Hilsenrath's novel *Nacht* (1964; *Night,* 1966), in which the victim's perspective is dominant. There are, however, some slight shifts in narrative voice. The second of the novel's six books has a third-person narrator, and the fourth book consists of a letter written by Max Schulz (now posing as Itzig Finkelstein) to his murdered friend Itzig. Despite these slight shifts on the narrative level, each part of the novel has a clear role in the story as a whole, and the text is held together by the presence of the main character, Max Schulz.

Critics have noted various influences on *The Nazi and the Barber.* Hilsenrath's use of short and often repetitive sentences as well as themes like transformation, characters like witches, and settings like forests are obvious references to the romantic German fairy tale tradition. More modern influences may include works by **Günter Grass** or Evelyn Waugh and comic films by Charlie Chaplin, Ernst Lubitsch, Billy Wilder, and the Marx Brothers. While some (including many German publishers who originally balked at publishing the novel) may take issue with viewing the Holocaust through a humorous lens, Hilsenrath, like the authors, directors, and performers just mentioned, is able to use comedy and exaggeration to raise

important issues and reveal the triviality of valued ideals without providing simple answers.

Throughout the text, with its storybook-like use of repetition, stereotypes are constantly recalled and turned on their heads as Hilsenrath unmasks the clichés associated both with the victims of the Holocaust and with its German perpetrators. In so doing he reveals psychological, cultural, and personal barriers that have prevented us from closely examining the dynamics by which one group victimizes another, both during the Holocaust and since.

—Gregory Baer

NIGHT (Nacht)
Novel by Edgar Hilsenrath, 1964

Like **Eli Wiesel**'s more famous novel of the same title, Edgar Hilsenrath's *Nacht* (1964; *Night,* 1966) is an attempt to probe the depths of horror in an inhuman landscape during the Holocaust. The text is set in Prokow, a fictional Jewish ghetto established by the Nazis in the Bukovina region of present-day Romania and Ukraine. The main character, Ranek, and most of the other characters in the novel struggle daily to survive in a bleak, bombed-out, disease-ridden city with little food or shelter. Each night bands of police roam the ghetto picking up anyone they find outside, thus making it imperative that ghetto residents wishing to avoid deportation and certain death in the camps fight each other to find shelter for the night. Reduced to stealing from the dead and dying in order to find valuables that might afford them another night or another piece of bread, the Jews in the ghetto are robbed of their humanity and reduced by their captors to virtual animals. Human values such as warmth, forgiveness, and mutual solidarity are nearly absent from this place.

A few characters, whose talents are sought out and paid for or who have been able to bring wealth with them into the ghetto, do enjoy a place of privilege among their fellow captives. The narrative privileges them as well—with names. Most of the characters that Ranek encounters, however, are known simply by their descriptions. In this landscape of hopelessness there is one voice of hope: Debora. She is married to Ranek's brother, Fred, who dies in the course of the novel, but she is in love with Ranek. This love, and her ability to laugh, which would seem insignificant in another context but rises to the level of resistance here, makes her an antidote to the ghetto's message of complete desolation and savagery. Her ability to hope and act on her hope is seen too in her decision to adopt a young child others have rejected.

While Debora does offer the narrative a glimmer of hope and goodness, the portrayal of Jewish characters willing to prey on their fellow captives, whether dead or not, broke a postwar German taboo. The image of people who have obviously come from polite and cultured society but who have been deindividualized and reduced to animals was upsetting to both critics and the public. Indeed, though written in German, only about 1,000 copies of the novel were printed in 1964 by its original German publisher, and the book was virtually ignored by the reading public in Germany. Hilsenrath blames this on the philo-Semitism prevalent in Germany at the time, which would not allow seemingly negative portrayals of Jews. Only after more than a decade had passed and after it had been translated into several languages and achieved great success abroad was *Nacht* republished in Germany, where it has since been accepted into the canon of important literary works on the Holocaust. Readers have also come to understand that Hilsenrath's depiction of the Jews in Prokow docs not reflect their inhumanity but the barbarity of those who forced them into the ghetto.

Scholars and reviewers have criticized the episodic and sometimes halting structure of the text and called Hilsenrath's language in the text repetitive or even awkward. This style and structure may be attributed to the immature skills of a young author, but they may also represent Hilsenrath's attempt to portray the ghetto as Ranek and the other residents might have perceived it. Ranek's story is told by an omniscient narrator, albeit one with a somewhat limited viewpoint: he presents only the perspective of the victims. The police and the Nazis remain shadowy figures rarely stepping into the action, though their power is revealed in the fear that they are able to create. Various scholars have discussed the novel's lack of narrative description or emotion and the fact that it presents the horror of Ranek's situation and the desolation around him without reflection. Yet the author manages to straddle the fine line between being distanced and engaged with his characters and his subject, and he does this in a way that keeps readers absorbed by the text. And indeed, if we accept the description of the work as a novel of existence rather than of becoming or developing, the form and the narrative style of *Nacht* would seem appropriate for a text set in a bleak landscape where existence is all one can hope for.

—Gregory Baer

NIGHT (La Nuit)
Memoir by Elie Wiesel, 1958

Elie Wiesel's *Night* (1958, *La Nuit*) was one of the earliest and most renowned of the Holocaust memoirs. It is characterized by a dramatic style and swiftness of action that has made it a popular book in high school as well as in college literature and history courses. Three themes dominate the book: a respect for the sanctity of life for everyone, including the impoverished and the mentally ill; a lament over the defensive amnesia of many Jews which led them to not believe the existence of Hitler's Final Solution until they themselves were deported to the concentration camps; and a Kaddish (Jewish prayer of memorial) for Wiesel's father, Chlomo Wiesel, who perished in the Holocaust.

In his childhood reminiscences in the first part of *Night,* Wiesel remembers Moché the Beadle very fondly. Although he was abjectly poor and mentally ill, Moché was a man of great piety and substantial intellectual reserve. His erudition was apparent as he tutored Wiesel in the ways of Jewish mysticism, the cabala and the *Zohar.*

Foreign Jews were expelled from Wiesel's hometown of Sighet, Hungary, and Moché the Beadle was among them. Sometime later when Moché the Beadle returned to Sighet with news of having survived a mass execution of Jews, the Jews of Sighet reacted with a kind of defensive amnesia: they did not wish to hear the stories they were hearing. Because they knew of Moché's bouts with mental illness, they refused to ascribe any credibility to him despite the fact that he had heroically risked his life to return to Sighet and warn his fellow Jews to escape from the Nazis before it was too late.

While being transported to Auschwitz on cattle cars, Wiesel notices that one of his neighbors, Madame Schächter, has gone mad. She keeps screaming about fires, possibly because she has had a paranormal vision of the fires in the crematorium of Auschwitz. She is mistreated by the other deportees who tie a gag in her mouth. When they arrived at Auschwitz, Wiesel recollects: ''I threw a last glance toward Madame Schächter. Her little boy was holding her hand. In front of us flames. In the air that smell of burning flesh.'' This respect for the intellectual and prophetic sagacity of the mentally ill also finds reflection in Wiesel's later writings and is an important cornerstone of his belief in the sanctity of human life. In this connection, it is important to mention that prior to the Final Solution, the Nazis had implemented several programs to euthanize the mentally ill.

The sanctity of life theme is also seen in Wiesel's relationship with his father. While Elie is taking care of his father shortly before Chlomo's death in Buchenwald, a camp doctor gives Elie a grim lesson in the situational ethics of the concentration camp: ''Listen to me, boy. Don't forget you're in a concentration camp. Here, every man has to fight for himself and not think of anyone else. Even of his father. Here, there are no fathers, no brothers, no friends. Everyone lives and dies for himself alone. I'll give you a sound piece of advice— don't give your ration of bread and soup to your old father. There's nothing you can do for him. And you're killing yourself. Instead, you ought to be having his ration.'' The doctor's admonition to a 15-year-old boy who deeply loved his father is testimony to the barbaric and animalistic tendencies that prevailed in the Nazi death camps.

Wiesel recalls his first reaction on learning of the death of his father:

> I awoke on January 29 at dawn. In my father's place was another invalid. They must have taken him away before dawn and taken him to the crematory. He may still have been breathing. There were no prayers at his grave. No candles were lit to his memory. His last word was my name. A summons, to which I did not respond. I did not weep, and it pained me to feel that I could not weep. But I had no more tears. And, in the depths of my being, in the recesses of my weakened conscience, could I have searched it, I might perhaps have found something like—free at last.

Nonetheless, his father's careful thinking had often kept Wiesel alive in Auschwitz and during a death march en route to Buchenwald. *Night* is therefore a more permanent Kaddish, a more permanent memorial, to Chlomo Wiesel than any graveside ceremony would have been.

—Peter R. Erspamer

NIGHT AND HOPE (Noc a nadeje)
Short stories by Arnošt Lustig, 1958

Night and Hope, published as *Noc a nadeje* in 1958 and in English translation in 1989, is a collection of seven short stories, all of which are emotionally charged and profoundly moving. Each story deals with feelings of guilt, trust, betrayal, or loss. The first story, "The Return," relates the story of Hynek Tausig, a middle-aged, unattached Jew who has taken the identity Alfred Janota in order to survive. Tausig is at a crossroads: does he accept the identity and constantly live in fear of being discovered by the Gestapo, or does he give himself up and join the others (mostly families) in the transports? The dilemma is similar to that of Raskolnikov in Fyodor Dostoyevsky's *Crime and Punishment*: to confess or not to confess. Much like Raskolnikov's case, paranoia sets in, and Tausig fears that everyone knows the truth behind his facade. While others suffer for being Jewish, he is free on the outside, and the enormity of his guilt is palpable. He begs to be let into the ghetto for transport: "Would you do me a favor and put me among the crowd there behind the fence? Or take me with you. But if you would be so kind, I'd prefer the first, behind the fence. It won't mean a thing to you, you can just say you found me here and that I belong in this transport and not in the one that has gone. For you it means only a few steps and for me—just now, it means everything that is called life."

He does not feel alive as Alfred Janota—only as who he is—Hynek Tausig. But he soon discovers life is mere existence on the other side of the fence. The reality of the ghetto is too much and he escapes. False identity thus becomes Tausig's reality.

In an interesting twist guilt is not only felt by the Jews but also by those who are in charge of them. In *Rose Street* an elderly Jew by the name of Elizabeth Feiner is beaten senseless in her shop by the Nazi officer Herz, whose only goal is to rise in the Nazi ranks. In an interesting contrast Lustig introduces Herz's status-conscious wife and unbearable mother-in-law, both of whom Feiner embodies for Herz and both of whom Herz cannot stand. Feiner's beating is therefore symbolic of Herz's own shortcomings as a husband, father, and son-in-law. Werner Binde, a driver for the Reich, witnesses this cruelty and is powerless to do anything, but his guilt forces him to return to Feiner's shop and leave her a can of sardines. Lustig brings forth optimism about the human spirit not often seen in Holocaust literature. Binde is a character who represents the goodness of those who were caught up in the madness of the Holocaust and whose sympathetic inner struggle against the cruelty of the Nazis could lead to his own demise.

Children are also important characters in "The Children," "Moral Education," and "Stephen and Anne." In the camps they must become adults and fend for themselves. Growing up well beyond one's actual years is key to survival. Memories of the past are tied in to the present, and these memories are what sustain the children. Pain and loss are also emotions with which these children must deal, as seen in "Stephen and Anne," a couple of teenagers who fall in love at first sight and whose love is dashed when Anne is called to the transports the next day.

Envy and betrayal confront Ignatz Marmulstaub in "Blue Flames." The newly appointed council chairman of the ghetto has distanced himself from his community and has been a "pet Jew" of the Nazi Herr von Holler. Marmulstaub believes that his status with von Holler will save him from being transported, and it is this arrogance that will eventually lead to his departure for the East. He even takes a mistress, Liselotte, a teenage girl who realizes that sex is tantamount to her own survival. She represents an adult wisdom that is seemingly lacking in Marmulstaub, for she knows that the end is near, whereas he tends to ignore the inevitable. In the end Marmulstaub is sent to the East with the transports, much to the glee of a ghetto community that has always known that friendship and trust mean nothing to the Nazis.

A glimmer of optimism appears at the end of the collection. In "Hope" an elderly married couple, Simon and Chana, are waiting for the Germans to come and take them. Simon, however, anticipates the arrival of the Allies, who are gaining the upper hand over the Nazis. Who will knock at their door? The final line of the story leaves the reader with a ray of hope: "'We shall wait, my dear,' he whispered. He could not sleep that night; he was waiting."

—Cynthia A. Klíma

THE NIGHT IN LISBON (Die Nacht von Lissabon)
Novel by Erich Maria Remarque, 1961

The Night in Lisbon (1964; published in German as *Die Nacht von Lissabon* in 1961) is the last of three of Remarque's novels, along with *Flotsam* (1941) and *Arch of Triumph* (1945), that deal with the plight of émigrés at a time when German anti-Nazis were treated as if they were Nazis by the countries to which they had fled. It was a time when the "host" governments did not want these wandering Jews but then again refused to let go of them and when a person was lucky to get an exit visa from France before his transit visa to Spain expired. The novel is framed by a refugee narrator who, sometime in 1942, has made it to Lisbon with his dying wife. The book begins when he runs into a landsman who offers him two passports to the United States on condition that the lucky beneficiary serve as his captive audience during the night it takes him to unravel his tale. The recitalist (and main figure) has himself inherited the passports from a dying emigrant, Schwarz, whose name he has taken. In 1934 Schwarz the narrator had been denounced by his SS brother-in-law and sent to a camp, from which he escaped to Paris. During the 1930s and 1940s Paris—and the French outposts—served as the inevitable destination, the locus classicus, of intrigue and nostalgia for the Schwarzes, Rick Blaines, and Victor Laszlos, who had their choice of being interned by the Gestapo or the gendarmerie. In 1939 Schwarz returns to Westphalia to look up his wife, from whom he has been parted for five years and who insists on returning to Paris with him illegally. (Twenty years earlier Remarque had used a similar plot in *Flotsam*.) The bulk of the novel charts the course of the two from Germany to Lisbon between 1939 and 1942. En route to the Pyrenees, both escape from internment camps in Marseille; Schwarz's wife dies of cancer the day before he hands the passports to his listener and joins the resistance.

The novel shares the stylistic and narrative flaws of all of Remarque's later books. The frame narrative itself merely provides Schwarz with a sounding board, and, to judge from the dialogue that takes up three-fourths of the novel, he seems to have total recall or else talks under hypnosis. (This framing device works beautifully in **W.G. Sebald**'s *Austerlitz*—surely one of the great Holocaust novels of the new century—if only because the *style indirect libre* the speaker uses in tracing his past is totally suited to the confessional genre.) Nor is it good form to tell one's wife that she "smell[s] of summer and freedom" and that "heartbreak kills as easily as dysentery." Besides, Schwarz keeps insisting that his story is riddled with miracles and coincidences, so that the reader is forever reminded that "the unbelievable happened" or that "I did the impossible." He walks out of the main gate of a prison in broad daylight and tells the sentries that he has been discharged (unbelievable), and later on he comes by two visas thanks to "the drunken whim of a chance acquaintance" (miraculous).

The open escape from prison can, in fact, be read in another way, one that redounds to Schwarz's credit. What refugee chutzpah! What refugee bluffing! Schwarz knows that if he crawled out of prison at night he would be shot. By now he has learned all of the tricks of survival. He knows, for instance, that in occupied Paris (or occupied anywhere) to be seen alone invites suspicion; to be seen with a woman disarms it. That to brandish a (fake) passport and yell at an irresolute border patrol will get a person across the border. That a foolish modesty is the hobgoblin of naive refugees. That it pays to confront the authorities with a clean-shaven face. By pretending to be an electrician hired to inspect the wiring, Schwarz bluffs his way into the camp in which his wife is being held. And for all its derring-do, *The Night in Lisbon* betrays Remarque's intimacy with his subject, if not his full control. The old Viennese (the original donor, the first Schwarz) has smuggled a couple of drawings by Ingres across the border by putting them into hideous frames and palming them off as sketches of his old parents. The fiction is as authentic as the Ingres are. So is the refugee from Frankfurt who makes his living by peddling rosaries and pictures of saints.

And for all its too frequent flippancy, the book contains genuine glimpses into the heart of darkness. A friend of Schwarz's, who has watched a Jew being arrested and beaten, tries to come to his help by knocking the SS monster unconscious and telling the Jew to run. Instead, the Jew curses his would-be liberator. Now, he tells the man, he is truly lost; the beating will simply fuel the Nazi's wrath. Sobbing, the Jew goes for water to revive the SS official, who can now lead him to his slaughter. Actions like these may grate on people who bristle at all the talk about the Jews' docility under pressure, but Remarque knew better. Had Chekhov been his contemporary, he would have bought the rights to the story.

—Edgar Rosenberg

NIGHT OF THE GIRONDISTS, or BREAKING POINT (De Nacht der Girondijnen)
Novel by Jacques Presser, 1957

Night of the Girondists is a work of fiction, although both the main character and the events portrayed in the novel bear striking resemblance to the person and experiences of the author, Jacques (or Jacob) Presser. First published in The Netherlands in 1957, *Night of the Girondists* appeared in English translation the following year. The English translation has also appeared under the title *Breaking Point*.

As the novel opens, it is mid-1943, and the narrator and main character, Jacques Suasso Henriques, is interned in the penal barracks of the Westerbork transit camp in the east of The Netherlands, where he is frantically attempting to record how he got there, or to make the "figures add up." He has tried to write it all down twice before but without success, and this is to be his final attempt.

In the beginning of his recounted story, it is obvious that Henriques, a secular Dutch Jew of distant Portuguese descent, feels himself more Dutch than Jewish. In fact although Henriques hates the Germans, he also hates the Jews attempting to flee them. He now belongs to the ranks of this accursed people, despite the fact that his mother was a convert to Protestantism (and even applied, unsuccessfully, to the Dutch Nazi Party) and his father had renounced his family's practice of the Jewish faith.

Henriques traces much of what has happened to him—and, more important, what he has become—to his experiences teaching at the Jewish Lyceum in Amsterdam, and in particular to a meeting with Georg Cohn, one of his students. Cohn is the son of the "uncrowned king of Westerbork," the head of the camp's Jewish administration. In early 1943 Georg confided to Henriques that he too hated the Jews but that he knew they were all doomed to a common fate. He then offered his teacher a position with his father at Westerbork: as Georg saw it, the naive and unsuspecting Henriques could shield himself from this fate only by accepting his offer.

Henriques returned to his teaching position in Amsterdam, although each day students went missing and never returned. Following an incident involving a student whose mother had been arrested the night before, Henriques quits his job in disgust and decides to work at Westerbork. He becomes the adjutant to Siegfried Israel Cohn, the "Blond Beast" of Westerbork. As such, he is a member of the Jewish SS (*Ordedienst*), the group of men that assists with the transports from Westerbork to Auschwitz and other eastward destinations. His primary responsibility, however, as stated by Cohn, is to "grow hard as iron, hard as concrete," or else board the train.

Henriques describes one disturbing encounter after another: the incredible terror brought about by the arrival of the trains, the constant administrative haggling over the deportation list, the language used to mask the horrible realities of the situation, the crazed behavior of those called for transport, and, most devastating, the roundup and deportation of his former students, including one that he was "completely crazy" about. Henriques must constantly reaffirm the current state of his existence: though someone reading his story may think him mad, he is not. If he were, then at least the awful things his eyes have seen could be attributed to delirium and the ravings of a lunatic.

In the course of his stay in Westerbork, Henriques had become close with one of his barrack-mates, a man by the name of Jeremiah Hirsch. Through his relationship with Hirsch, whom he calls "the Rabbi," Henriques becomes less of a Jew-hater, learning, for the first time in his life, Jewish prayers and readings. It is this relationship that leads him to confront both Cohn and everything he represents. In the final pages of the

novel, the reader learns that Henriques' bold act against Cohn and in defense of Hirsch and his religion has caused Henriques' internment in the penal barracks.

The reader last encounters the narrator the night before he is scheduled to leave on a transport. He has finished writing and is kept company by Dé, the wife of a former colleague at the Jewish Lyceum, who was sent to the Westerbork penal barracks after she was arrested during a check of identification papers on the train. She too is scheduled to leave on the next day's transport but not before she has smuggled Henriques' writings out of the camp. Dé, who reaffirms Henriques' identity as a Jew, also reveals the final destination of their transport and, thus, their ultimate fate as Jews under German occupation.

In exploring these events and themes as experienced through the eyes of a former outsider to the Jewish community, *Night of the Girondists* succinctly but forcefully examines the wartime situation of Dutch Jews. Henriques, Cohn, and Hirsch demonstrate the various behaviors and reactions that were possible, and their actions demonstrate how, in the face of increasing German persecution and Dutch complicity, ethical and religious concerns often collided with the sheer struggle for survival. The historical context selected by Presser for this struggle is particularly poignant: during the four-month period of early March to late July 1943, 19 trains carrying 34,000 people left Westerbork for Sobibor, where all but a few Dutch Jews were killed upon arrival.

—Jennifer L. Foray

NIGHT OF THE MIST
Memoir by Eugene Heimler, 1959

In many respects Eugene Heimler's account of the year in his life that he was forced to spend in the Nazi camps of Auschwitz, Buchenwald, Tröglitz, and Berga-Elster exhibits many of the classic features of the genre. It follows in chronological order what happened to a young Hungarian Jew, Jansci, from the day he and his bride, Eva, were dragged away from the ghetto to the liberation of the Berga-Elster camp in Saxony. Like other Holocaust memoirs, *Night of the Mist* (1959) is a kaleidoscopic collection of stories that not only forms a full picture of the narrator's personal ordeals and suffering but also reveals the pain and agony of numerous others he met in the camps. Heimler immortalizes in his writing a couple of unforgettable characters who will continue to be loved and respected despite their physical demise. The book raises also the expected questions about the meaning of this tragedy—for the Jews as well as for every individual victim—and about the role of faith and religion both in cases of survival and of cruel death.

What makes Heimler's book distinct among the group of comparable masterpieces (**Primo Levi**'s *Survival in Auschwitz* and **Elie Wiesel**'s *Night,* to name just a few) is the strong presence of the narrator himself. His story is permeated by an "immense yearning to live" and by a resilient will to overcome the horror and hardships. Heimler often uses the verb "to live" not only in the sense of mere physical survival but also as a synonym of "to learn" and "to comprehend." His journey through the stations of terror is presented as a dense lesson in spiritual maturing, in discovering and analyzing one's own self as well as the meaning of humanity in times of tremendous crisis. As a person Heimler realizes that his survival is due to pure luck more than to anything else, and as a poet he makes it his mission to bear witness and write about his experiences.

Night of the Mist is an extremely self-reflective book filled with detailed descriptions of dreams, daydreams, images, and phantoms that often appear while the narrator is feverish, delirious with pain, or battling the cold. Heimler's account is especially effective when it reveals how complex psychological states and puzzling mystical experiences bordering on hallucination and superstition have become part both of the arsenal of survival strategies and of the state of insanity that reigns in the camps. With remarkable sincerity and poignancy Heimler offers some rare glimpses into the maddening persistence of sexual desire, the paralyzing return of childhood fears, and the overwhelming wish to escape. Several times he believes to have been saved, quite inexplicably, by a forceful premonition that comes to him in the form of a voice whispering warnings into his ear ("Stay away from Block 17 . . .") or by his own intuitive powers or by a dream that helps him make a crucial decision. At the same time, he shows with stunning veracity how there was just one step from extreme superstition to "abysmal depression" and then to death.

Night of the Mist presents an interesting case study of how memory works and what its role is in surviving the Holocaust. One theme that runs through the book is the protagonist's persistent and even heightened ability to review the past "from this cold and forbidding world of the barracks." In line with his emphasis on the heuristic power of the experience, Heimler claims that many times he had felt as if the Nazis "had shocked into consciousness" forgotten scenes and feelings of the past. Before the eyes of the reader the narrator resurrects the complex world of his past populated by members of his family and by the images of Jews from various social classes. He recovers fragments of experiences dating back to his childhood and retells the stories of people that the camps now have deprived of all human features. It seems that in that very ability to delve into the past Heimler found a way to preserve his own humanity and not become a "man of Auschwitz."

Alongside numerous self-reflective passages, Heimler's memoir contains remarkably realistic descriptions of life in the camps. Two examples stand out within the large field of Holocaust literature. One is Heimler's description of the Gypsy camp in Auschwitz. Up until the second half of 1944, when they were suddenly rounded up and sent to the gas chambers, Gypsies deported from various places in Europe were entitled to a special lifestyle: men and women could live together and even have children in the camp; they did not have to work and could use the other prisoners as household help. Another example of an engaging realistic account in the book is the chapter devoted to Buchenwald. Heimler's analysis of the peculiar social order and power dynamics in that camp as well as of his encounters with various other prisoners—from British POWs to German communists, Danish policemen, and ordinary criminals—belongs to the most illuminating passages on Buchenwald in the literature of the Holocaust.

—Mila Ganeva

NIGHTFATHER (Tralievader)
Novel by Carl Friedman, 1991

The narrator of Carl Friedman's first novel, *Nightfather* (1994; *Tralievader*, 1991), is a young girl whose father is a survivor of the Holocaust. Her child's perspective shapes the novel, which is written in short chapters reminiscent of a child's primer, each focusing on a word or concept. Like a primer, the chapters elaborate on the use of the term, but this is no easy primer. The novel's deceptively simple form throws into stark relief the devastation of the Holocaust and its continued impact on post-Holocaust life.

Nightfather highlights the difficulty of using language to share an experience that is fundamentally beyond comprehension. As many Holocaust writers have noted, the camp had a language all its own, and its vocabulary cannot simply be imported into postwar life. Friedman expresses this impossibility in the very first line of her novel: "He never mentions it by name." The father never names the concentration camps in which he suffered but rather distills them into a single term, "the camp." The book goes on to explore the difficulty of naming experiences that lie, in a profound way, beyond words. Words such as "hunger" and "camp" bear a very different meaning in the context of the Holocaust. This gap between the words (and world) of the father and the words of his children is at the center of the daughter's second-generation experience.

The book begins with the daughter's understanding that what makes her father different from her and her brother is that he has "had camp." "Camp is not so much a place as a condition," the girl explains. "'I've had camp,' he says. That makes him different from us. We've had chicken pox and German measles. And after Simon fell out of a tree, he got a concussion and had to stay in bed for weeks. But we've never had camp." From there the book takes on words such as "heaven" and "stranger" to mark the distance between the father's world and the children's. *Nightfather* makes it clear that camp is incurable; those who have it will always be different from those who do not.

Nightfather is not primarily about language, however, but about the impact of the Holocaust on the emotional life of the family. The author uses the difficulty of sharing language to foreground the difficulty of the father to share his experiences with his children. The father of *Nightfather* has been forever changed by the Holocaust, in ways that have also changed his family. This is no avuncular elder, sharing wisdom about life while his children sit on his lap. The father's "wisdom" comes in difficult lessons, brought on by the everyday behavior of his children. His son saying "I'm hungry" brings a lesson about true hunger; his daughter's desire to join the Girl Scouts evokes a story about Hitler Youth. Everyday objects in the house are linked to the Holocaust, like the knife the father made in the camp, which lies in the drawer with the rest of the knives but which is never used. The daughter understands that what makes these objects different is that they have a story to tell.

The daughter understands that this is also what makes her father different from other fathers—he too has a story to tell. Indeed, his story has changed her as well. She may not be able to fully understand her father's words, yet nor can she relate to the sunny experiences of her peers. While the other children in school draw cheerful pictures of pixies, the girl draws a prisoner being hanged. She understands she is different from the other children but sees this as a limitation of their understanding, not her own. When her friend Nellie comments on what a funny father she has, the girl does not know what to say. Nellie "knows nothing about hunger or the SS . . . She speaks a different language."

That the daughter is not named in *Nightfather* suggests that there is something about her experience too that is difficult to express. It also emphasizes her role as witness, as someone who is both part of her father's story and outside of it. *Nightfather* speaks extensively about the father's experiences in the concentration camps, but the novel is equally the story of the daughter. She bears witness not only to her father's history but also to the ways in which the Holocaust has shaped the life of her family, the ways in which the Holocaust reverberates today.

—Rachel N. Baum

NOT OF THIS TIME, NOT OF THIS PLACE (Lo me-akhshav, lo mikan)
Novel by Yehuda Amichai, 1963

Yehuda Amichai's only novel was originally published in Hebrew as *Lo me-akhshav, lo mikan* in 1963 and in English translation as *Not of This Time, Not of This Place* in 1968. Unique to the novel is its preoccupation with the author's German roots and with the Holocaust, a fact that has led many to observe that these were ghosts exorcized and laid to rest in the work. It is not the novel of a survivor, nor does it focus on the Holocaust as a Jewish national trauma. The novel describes "the summer of Joel" (Yoel in Hebrew), a 40ish married man

and an archeologist who suffers from the disenchantment all too common among a generation of protagonists in Israeli literature of the 1950s and 1960s. But while the diagnosis is typical, the remedy is highly untraditional. The novel hinges upon a bold structural experiment. In an innocuous conversation in the first chapter Mina, a schizophrenic woman, proposes to Joel that he resolve his midlife crisis in one of two ways: he can have a love affair, or he can return to Germany to visit "Weinburg," the city he fled just prior to his bar mitzvah. Joel does both. In alternating chapters two discrete plots unfold detailing these two illicit encounters. One, narrated in the third person, describes Joel's adulterous love affair with Patricia/Patrice, a non-Jewish American doctor, in Jerusalem; the second, a first-person account, takes him back to Weinburg to search for the slowly vanishing traces of his childhood.

How one understands the significance of *Not of This Time, Not of This Place* as a Holocaust novel depends in part upon how one interprets the fact that the novel is also a love story. In an 1982 interview with Esther Fuchs, Amichai explained, "I loved the girl in Germany, during my childhood, and I loved the American girl I met in Jerusalem . . . I wanted to be in both places with both girls at the same time." Yet beyond the double love story there is much in the novel to validate Mina's schizophrenic logic, to wit, that the two dramatically different plots are at bottom one. Both are tales of flight, betrayal, and ultimately self-discovery; there are numerous crossovers in motif and character; and they complement and interpret each other in myriad ways. For example, in Jerusalem, Joel regresses and becomes diverted from his archeological career. Yet in Germany he digs around for all kinds of evidence. He discovers a wide cast of characters, Germans and Jews, survivors and expatriate Israelis, children and elderly relatives, and he describes in great detail the topography of the city and the often grotesque ways in which an economically booming Germany has attempted to overlay the past.

The central focus of the Germany plot, however, is intensely personal; it details Joel's quest to retrieve the traces of his beloved Ruth, "who burned." Although there is much talk of vengeance, Joel is no avenger. His sword is "made of wax," and Ruth's face is his "eternal light," lending comfort rather than inciting rage. Ruth, a teenage girl and amputee, is the novel's single tragic figure; she is innocence, courage, pure loss embodied. As Joel pieces together her story, the result is nothing short of an elegy. Details from her life and death accrue gradually: her bed was covered with broken glass during *Kristallnacht*; the two argued as young children; she wrote him impeccable letters once he had left. The path to Ruth is not straightforward, for the nun who tended her has taken a vow of silence and is mute. Only later on does the nun send Joel a snapshot of Ruth taken on the day of her deportation: "Her eyes looked straight forward, clear and proud and courageous. The woolen scarf around her neck was carefully and neatly arranged, as was her custom . . . On her chest was a small sign with her number and the number of her transport . . .

The small sign given to the deportees was already punched in two places. 'Each deportee must provide his own string,' the instructions read.'' Passages such as these form the novel's most poignant moments.

Yet even the quest for Ruth is not sacrosanct. Ruth is subject to Joel's innate forgetfulness, to his tendency to leave even important matters to chance. At one point Joel goes so far as to track down what he imagines to be, and what cannot be, Ruth's artificial leg. But he inadvertently misplaces the leg, then puts an ad in the newspaper to locate it. The finding and losing of Ruth's leg encapsulate the novel's irreverent mood. In a similar vein an aging survivor gives Joel a comb that belonged to the daughter who died in her arms, but Joel gives the comb to Patricia, whom, in the Germany novel, he encounters only once, in the Orly airport, just before he flies home. The transaction is not exactly an act of commemoration; he reports that ''there wasn't time to tell her its history.'' Earlier Joel discovers the box of Rabbi Mannheim's sermons at a construction site. (Rabbi Mannheim, his childhood rabbi and the father of Ruth, survived the war and figures in the Jerusalem plot.) Yet the box opens up, and the pages fly away. They are not exactly lost, however, for Joel later purchases a bag of cherries and notices that the paper, stained with cherry juice, ''bore one of Dr. Mannheim's sermons,'' and, in fact, ''it is [Joel's] Bar Mitzvah speech the Rabbi had prepared and never given.'' The sermon is retained, only to fly again out of Joel's briefcase.

—Abigail Gillman

NOTES FROM THE WARSAW GHETTO: THE JOURNAL OF EMMANUEL RINGELBLUM (Notitsn fun Vareshever geto)
Diary by Emmanuel Ringelblum, 1952

Because Emmanuel Ringelblum was himself a scholar and a historian, his *Notes from the Warsaw Ghetto* (1958; originally published in 1952 in Yiddish as *Notitsn fun Vareshever geto*) is among the most informative of the Holocaust diaries. To be sure, the fact that it found its way to the light of day is truly remarkable. Before the Warsaw Ghetto Uprising of April 1943, Ringelblum placed his notebooks in milk cans and buried them. What later became his *Notes from the Warsaw Ghetto* was retrieved in two parts, the first in September 1946 and the second in December 1950.

Taking up his pen, Ringelblum not only recorded a history of atrocity but also offered a testimony to the dearness of humanity. Children, for example, play a prominent role in his entries. In an entry for September 1940 he attested to the devotion of children to other children when he wrote, ''At the

funeral for the small children from the Wolska Street orphanage, the children from the home placed a wreath at the monument with the inscription: 'To the Children Who Have Died from Hunger—From the Children Who Are Hungry.''' On 26 April 1941 he pointed out that ''three-year-old children are out begging in the streets,'' and on 31 August 1941 he told of a six-year-old boy who lay on the street ''gasping all night, too weak to roll over to the piece of bread that had been thrown to him'' from a balcony. The reader soon realizes that this assault on the child was a defining feature of the ghetto. And Ringelblum was deeply aware of the implications. ''In the past,'' he wrote on 10 June 1942, ''whatever was done with the grownups, the children were always permitted to live—so that they might be converted to the Christian faith . . . But the Hitlerian beast is quite different. It would devour the dearest of us, those who arouse the greatest compassion—our innocent children.'' Ringelblum demonstrates that under the Nazis the thing most threatened was precisely the holiest thing.

Although he was not religious, Ringelblum was careful to take note of the explicit attack on the holy dimensions of Jewish being. He reported, for example, the desecration of Torah scrolls and observed that when the ghetto was established the Nazis tore the mezuzahs—the small containers of Scripture that remind a Jew of God's sovereignty—from the doorposts of Jewish apartments. As the High Holy Days of 1940 were approaching, he noted that ''in one city they assembled all the rabbis *and they were killed*.'' And early in 1942, he related, ''a group of Jews were locked up in the synagogue until they hacked the holy ark to bits.'' The sign of Jewish tradition and teaching—the sign of a Jewish presence in the world—is the sign of the presence of the Holy One in the world. And that is precisely what the Nazis tried to erase from the world.

Here one discovers another remarkable dimension of Ringelblum's diary: his insight into the importance of meaning in life and the threat of madness in the assault on meaning. Early in his notes he observes a ''noticeable increase in the number of madmen'' in the ghetto, and the remainder of the diary is punctuated with references to madness and madmen as well as to mad children: ''In a refugee center an eight-year-old child went mad. Screamed, 'I want to steal, I want to rob. I want to eat, I want to be a German.''' If madness threatens one's humanity, Ringelblum shows that, in the effort to dehumanize the Jew, the Nazi lost his own humanity: ''A police chief came to the apartment of a Jewish family, wanted to take some things away. The woman cried that she was a widow with a child. The chief said he'd take nothing if she could guess which of his eyes was the artificial one. She guessed the left eye. She was asked how she knew. 'Because that one,' she answered, 'has a human look.''' The other eye, the human eye, resembled a dead eye.

This is one of the most earthshaking revelations in Ringelblum's diary: in their aim to exterminate the Jews from the world, the Nazis overturned the world to create a total confusion between life and death, leaving no place for either. In the universe of the concentration camps, the living were as though dead, and the dead were as though they had never lived.

—David Patterson

NOTES OF THE AUTHOR ON THE PAINTED BIRD
Essay by Jerzy Kosinski, 1965

Jerzy Kosinski's first novel, *The Painted Bird,* aroused controversy even before it saw print. The publisher, Houghton Mifflin, was concerned about whether the book should be sold as an autobiography, with claims to factual accuracy, or as a work of fiction. If the first, there would be legal issues should any people portrayed in the book sue for slander. Kosinski was also concerned about his brutal portrayal of the peasantry of his (unspecified) native Poland. That he had been exiled from that country since 1957 and had become an American citizen through marriage only added to his sensitivity about *The Painted Bird*. The book was published as fiction, and even though not translated into Polish, it was reviewed by Polish writers who attacked Kosinski for his literary and personal shortcomings. "Notes of the Author on *The Painted Bird*" is Kosinski's thoughtful response to his critics, and, as such, it embodies a useful commentary on the book and his intentions in writing it.

The essay was written in the months following the spirited reception of *The Painted Bird* and published by Kosinski himself in late 1965. (The reader can find the essay in *Passing By: Selected Essays, 1962–1991*, a posthumous collection edited by Kosinski's widow.) It begins in a formal, allusive, and abstract manner, invoking within its first few pages Marcel Proust, Susanne K. Langer, and Paul Valéry, while speaking about the artist's necessary "alienation from the specific experience" about which he writes. Reluctant at first to call *The Painted Bird* fiction, Kosinski states that the "*remembered event becomes a fiction, a structure made to accommodate certain feelings*" and that "*there is no art which is reality ...*"(his italics). Kosinski then moves to a more explicit discussion of *The Painted Bird*'s fictionality by admitting that the book "could be the author's vision of himself as a child, a *vision,* not an examination, or a revisitation of childhood ... The locale and the setting are likewise metaphorical." Even the landscape belongs to no specific national group but rather lies on borders "continually torn by strife." The peasants in the area of *The Painted Bird* are torn by "suspicion and fear, watching plague and waiting death," paying "grudged devotion to an unforgiving God." To them the child represents a mythic figure who "comes into their isolated world at the same time as the Germans, a very real threat of annihilation, arrive." The peasants treat him and one another with a cruelty

that is "extremely defensive, elemental, sanctioned by traditions, by faith and superstition, by centuries of poverty, exploitation, disease, and by the ceaseless depredations of stronger neighbors." But they are survivors, and so is the boy.

Kosinski presents the boy as a mythic hero by invoking Jungian archetypes. *The Painted Bird*, he says, "can be considered as fairy tales *experienced* by the child, rather than *told* to him ..." It is "undoubtedly remarkable" that such a boy could survive the war alone, but in the context of fairy-tale conventions, the boy must be seen as a heroic representative of us all. Children, Kosinski claims, are better equipped to survive adversity than adults because of their comparative simplicity: "Events to the child are immediate: discoveries are one-dimensional. This kills, that maims, this one cuffs, that one caresses. But to the adult the vision of these memories is multidimensional." In the fairy-tale narrative the young hero is put through test after test, "yet he must survive."

Kosinski paradoxically suggests that we must see the boy as a negative hero because of the purity of his hatred for all that has happened in the world. This hatred is more self-motivated and generated because the hatred of the peasants is so deeply rooted in their history and their traditions. It is also important, Kosinski notes, that the peasants did not originate the mass extermination program. This was developed by the "civilized" peoples in "the centers of European culture" who had experienced the Enlightenment, Bach, and Goethe. To a great extent, then, the author presents the peasants as also being victims of the war.

Authors do not get to have the last word on their books, much as Kosinski might have wished, because they frequently justify what they think they have done as much as they explain it. Such criticism can certainly be leveled at "Notes of the Author on *The Painted Bird*," but once beyond the essay's labored opening, the reader has much to learn from Kosinski's remarks. Not only does he offer a sophisticated justification of his own work, but he also situates himself as a philosophical novelist in the tradition of Camus and Sartre as well as a self-conscious student of literary traditions.

—Michael Hoffman

NOW THEY SING AGAIN: ATTEMPT OF A REQUIEM (Nun singen sie wieder: Versuch eines Requiems)
Play by Max Frisch, 1972

The surrealistic play *Now They Sing Again* by Max Frisch was finished in January 1945 and premiered at the Schauspielhaus in Zurich in March of the same year. The play's title derives from the recurring leitmotiv of a song that is sung by 21 killed hostages whenever an injustice is committed. The first four parts of the requiem deal with the inhumanity of the war, in which there is no victor. The last three parts depict the attempt and inability of the dead to communicate their newly gained truth to the living, leaving the audience with a feeling of sadness that derives from the senselessness of killing.

The play reveals the futility of humanistic endeavors. Herbert, one of the protagonists, is a cynical German officer who orders the shooting of the hostages, not because he did not receive a humanistic education but because he only learned the classical form without internalizing the humanistic message. He does not believe in the world of Platonic ideals but in reality, which for him is a valueless abyss, the Nothing. As he faces his former professor, whom he ordered to be shot, he asserts that all humanistic values, as taught in school, are lies. Otherwise, why would his best pupil order his old teacher to be executed? The right to live and the dignity of the individual have no value for Herbert. Frisch addresses here a question that baffled many people after 1945: How was it possible that a cultured nation such as Germany could commit such atrocities? Although Frisch does not directly refer to the Holocaust in the requiem, he does point out the flaw in a humanistic education, which equates aesthetics and ethics.

Frisch also addresses the question of personal and collective guilt. The play indicates a few times that flight is taken into collective guilt; the responsibility for the committed atrocities does not rest with the individual but with the superiors who gave the orders. Obedience was an existential question because noncompliance with an order meant certain death. This is shown clearly in the fate of the soldier Karl, who defies the order to execute hostages. Karl asks his father the question haunting him: Who is guilty in the killing of innocent women and children? His father's reply is that this was not his fault because his superiors had ordered it. Karl, however, does not accept this "flight into obedience." His conscience tells him that responsibility cannot be passed on; it rests with the individual.

The question of guilt and individual responsibility is a recurring theme in the postwar *Trümmerliteratur*, literally "the literature of the rubbles," referring to material possessions as well as the spirit. This was first taken up by **Wolfgang Borchert** in his *Man Outside* (1947), then in the short stories by **Heinrich Böll.** Frisch, despite the nihilistic tone of his requiem, suggests that men and women have the freedom to refuse an order to murder innocent people, even if it means that one pays for this heroic deed with one's own life.

—Gerd K. Schneider

O

O THE CHIMNEYS!
Poem by Nelly Sachs, 1947

"O the Chimneys" was the first poem in Leonie (Nelly) Sachs's collection *In den Wohnungen des Todes* ("In the Habitations of Death"), which was published in 1947. It also served as the title of the first book of translations of Sachs's poetry into English, in 1967, which contained a large body of texts from later work between 1949 and 1966. The poem addresses the smokestacks of the crematoria ovens of the German extermination camps. Although chimneys are associated with home and family life, the second line of the poem identifies them as being attached to "habitations of death." They do not stand as metaphors but rather represent the reality of genocide.

The poem's structure is based on a combination of irreconcilable elements. Houses with chimneys are usually designed as homes for the living, but here they serve as institutions for destruction. There is a murderous deception involved in the design of the houses; they are "invitingly" decorated, not for the welcome and entertainment of guests, but for their treacherous murder. Death, who was once only a guest, has now become the permanent host. The "fingers" addressed in the third stanza refer to selection by SS guards. Once fingers were used to show guidance and direction, but now they decide the life and death of the victims at the selection ramps, "laying the threshold / Like a knife between life and death." The perversion of the familiar meanings of "habitation," "host," and "helpful guidance" uncovers the deception that is practiced here and serves to denounce the inhumanity of the design as well as the cunning malice of the perpetrators. This sequence of realistic images is contrasted with a sequence of interspersed religious images. Quotations from the Book of Job contain images that change, the chimneys metaphorically to become "freedomways for Jeremiah and Job's dust" and "the road for refugees of smoke." These "freedomways" present a counterdesign to the maliciously "devised habitations of death." But there is no false claim of redemption: "When Israel's body drifted as smoke / Through the air— / Was welcomed by a star . . . / [That] star turned black." The last lines of the poem address the images again to commemorate and lament the brutal facts of extermination: "O you chimneys / O you fingers / And Israel's body as smoke through the air!"

Other poems in the early 1947 collection speak of the "children branded for death" and of "their terrible nursemaids" who have taken the place of their mothers and who flex their muscles to murder them ("O the night of the weeping children") and of the old men who are not allowed to die in peace, their "genuine hours of death" and their "last breaths" stolen ("Even the old men's last breath"). There is an insane mother in search of her dead child who kisses the air filled with the smoke from the crematoria ("Already embraced by the arm of heavenly solace"). And there is a child led to death who speaks of the "knife of parting" that someone raised to cut her from her mother ("A dead child speaks"). The survivors in the "Chorus of the Rescued" express their constant fear of death and ask for patience and compassion from bystanders. The children in the "Chorus of the Orphans" lament to the world that their mothers and fathers have been taken from them; they are "like no one in this world any more."

—Ehrhard Bahr

OCALENIE
Poems by Czesław Miłosz, 1945

This collection of poems, written during the Nazi occupation in the shadow of the Warsaw Ghetto and published in Polish as *Ocalenie* (1945; "Salvation"), marks the transition of Nobel Prize-winner Czesław Miłosz from the "catastrophism" of the 1930s when he was a key member of the "second avant-garde" to a mature expression of his sense of history and humanity and a profound understanding of his role as poet and his place in the traditions of world and Polish literature. A small number of the poems contained in this collection directly address the matter of the Holocaust, most notably "Campo dei Fiori" and "A Poor Christian Looks at the Ghetto." Miłosz's project in this collection is strikingly expansive: he seeks to place and define himself, his art, and his time in the context of the natural world, the movement of history and the development of humanity, and of eternal philosophical and spiritual values. In "A Poor Christian Looks at the Ghetto" he does not describe the ghetto, as one might expect from the almost banal title of this short poem written in 1943. Instead, he focuses on images from the natural world that are grotesque and concrete by turns and intersperses references to products of human civilization. He builds up an image of destruction of human reality on a background of mindless biological decay in the natural order; the picture is chillingly horrifying and disturbing in its despair and bleakness. A leader is identified, and it is a mole who, though obviously blind, wears a small red lamp like a miner as it works its way indifferently through the clammy underground world of decomposing humanity. He refers to this creature as a "Patriarch," one who has read "the great book of the species," and implies that, like Dostoevsky's Grand Inquisitor, he is profoundly and frighteningly mistaken in his view of the ends of human existence. But most of all Miłosz is concerned with his own, and hence everyone's, connection with the destruction he sees everywhere. His lyrical subject refers to himself as "a Jew of the New Testament" and fears he will be counted "among the helpers of death." He does not condemn the point to which Western civilization has arrived, but he identifies a crisis in which its greatest values have, at least temporarily, lost ground or have been overcome by forces external and inimical to them.

In "Campo dei Fiori" Miłosz connects the execution of Giordano Bruno during the Inquisition with the extermination campaign being carried out in the Warsaw Ghetto. In particular he addresses the indifference of the bystanders and their failure to recognize and empathize with the suffering of the individuals, whether the solitary Bruno or the individuals making up the group singled out for destruction in the ghetto. His choice of Bruno as a point of departure is hardly facile, for Bruno had been persecuted not only by the nefarious Catholic Inquisition but by Calvinists as well. His teachings were not dangerous, but his independence of mind marginalized him and situated him outside the masses, which were subject to control by the dark forces of the misguided religious hierarchy. In Miłosz's poem he suffers the agony of the executioner's flames utterly alone, while the citizens of Florence go about their casual quotidian affairs. In Warsaw people are shown enjoying the pleasures of a carousel while thousands are being hounded and rounded up for extermination just on the other side of the wall.

In "The Poor Poet," written in 1944, we can see how these experiences reshaped Miłosz's poetic and philosophical sensibilities. He speaks of himself as transformed and plotting his revenge, as he reflects with valiant optimism about the future. Despite the horrors he has witnessed and his profound doubts about what may yet come, he sees an important role for the poet: "To me is given the hope of revenge on others and on myself, / For I was he who knew / and took from it no profit for myself."

Miłosz has occasionally been referred to as a "poet of the Holocaust." While the dearth of references to the Holocaust in his writing over the next five decades makes the suitability of that epithet rather unlikely, the poetry he wrote during and immediately after the war clearly demonstrates that his experience of the Holocaust was crucial in his transformation into the remarkable poet he became from that point on.

—Allan Reid

OCCUPATION TRILOGY: LA PLACE DE L'ÉTOILE, LA RONDE DE NUIT, LES BOULEVARDS DE CEINTURE
Novels by Patrick Modiano, 1968, 1969, and 1972

La Place de l'étoile is the first novel in Patrick Modiano's so-called Occupation Trilogy, which also includes *La Ronde*

de nuit (1969; as *Night Rounds,* 1971) and *Les Boulevards de ceinture* (1972; as *Ring Roads,* 1974).

La Place de l'etoile, a play on the word *étoile* ("star"), which means both the place of the yellow star and the famous Parisian square, inscribes the Holocaust at the center of the Jewish experience, and the narrator's name, Raphael Schlemilovitch, defines him as the archetypal Jew. His absurd, farcical, autobiographical saga takes us through time and space into all the clichés of anti-Semitism. In his comical efforts to find roots or assimilate, the narrator tries to adopt France's values: religion, army, land. In his many transformations, incursions into different times and milieus, he must either hide or claim his foreign origins. But assimilation is impossible: when Schlemilovitch is in danger of taking roots (in the arms of a Proustian duchess, for example), he is sent to Vienna after a hallucinatory scene where a character acts out some of the worst representations of "the Jew" anti-Semites have constructed.

Under the parody, death permeates the book. There are numerous evocations of the Holocaust. In a ghostly Vienna the narrator's "I" turns into "we" and becomes six million Jews, a figure yelled at him by a grotesque incarnation of Adolf Hitler. Vienna's Prater becomes Theresienstadt; the narrator is briefly the lover of an Auschwitz survivor who, haunted by her memories, commits suicide with his help. After Vienna Schlemilovitch hops to Trieste, Budapest, Salonika, now all Jewless, and back to occupied Paris where he joins a sinister gang of the French Gestapo; he leaves them for the victim's side. But Auschwitz is not for him: he was born too late. He goes to Israel instead, to a Nazi-like, "disciplinary kibbutz" camp, to be cured of the memory of the Jewish tragedy and become a modern, positive Jew. Then he is back to wartime Paris, where Israeli Jews join the same Gestapo gang of criminal revelers. They finally shoot him. But the nightmare is not over. Back to Vienna, where Dr. Sigmund Freud also wants to cure him, of his Yiddish paranoia this time: "We now live in a pacified world. Himmler is dead. How can you remember all this? You weren't born yet."

That is exactly Modiano's point. In this nervous, dislocated narrative, devoid of coherence or logic (the narrator dies three times), where discontinuity rules and tenses and times collide, there is a sense of rage: how is it possible to be French, Jewish, and a writer after the Holocaust? Modiano said in *Dora Bruder*: "What I wanted to do in my first book was to reply to all these people whose insults had wounded me through my father, and silence them once and for all on their own turf, French prose."

Modiano's second novel, *La Ronde de nuit,* is set during the occupation. The same gang of criminals working for the Nazis are now foregrounded: these sleazy racketeers, swindlers, blackmailers, pimps, and prostitutes hold parties at their headquarters while torturing on the floor below. Swing Troubadour, the narrator, works as their informer—and as an informer for a resistance group too. First in a long line of

Modiano characters, he suffers from a lack of identity. Unlike Schlemilovitch, clearly defined as the Jew, Swing's double agent status is symbolic of his ambiguity. Never sure of who he is (innocent? corrupt? traitor? hero?), dizzy, guilt-ridden, inhabited by fear and a sense of doom, he roams Paris in search of himself. Only death seems certain in this murky era. Abrupt shifts of temporality, incoherence (the protagonist is killed at the end, yet earlier he was tried after the war), and ambiguity are embedded in the narrative. Although there is a hint that the narrator is Jewish, the Holocaust seems absent from this novel.

Les Boulevards de ceinture is about the search for the father. Baron Deckecaire is clearly a character inspired by Modiano's own father and their relationship. After a painstaking investigation, the protagonist/narrator, Serge Alexandre, finds him in the midst of another loathsome gang, operating now in the intellectual/artistic circles of the collaboration. Schlemilovitch's clownish, conspicuously Jewish father is now an enigmatic, terrified, pathetic Jewish collaborator. A tool in the hands of these criminal anti-Semites, he will be killed when they no longer need him. The narrator's efforts to approach, understand, and forgive his father lead him to proclaim his affiliation, thus reclaiming his own Jewish identity. The father is arrested. The son/writer stays with him until the end (the end of his narrative too): presumably Auschwitz.

The evocation of the occupation (and behind that, the Holocaust) is remarkable in the second and third novels. Narrative transgressions are not as extreme in *Les Boulevards de ceinture,* but the ghostlike characters, now blurred now clear, float between past, present, and future, as do events. The narrative, blending history with fiction, acquires a haunting, dreamy, poetic quality that will become Modiano's trademark.

—Nicole Ball

ON BOTH SIDES OF THE WALL (Fun beyde zaytn geto-moyer)
Memoir by Vladka Meed, 1948

On Both Sides of the Wall, Vladka Meed's only book-length work, is a memoir of the Warsaw Ghetto that was published in Yiddish in 1948 and in English translation in 1971. Meed, a member of the Zydowska Organazcja Bojowa (Jewish Fighting Organization), which led the Warsaw Ghetto Uprising, was able to serve as a courier in the resistance thanks to her ''Aryan'' appearance and command of Polish. The narrative begins in July 1942, at the time of the first deportations from the Warsaw Ghetto to Treblinka, two years after the Jews of Warsaw had been forced into the ghetto. In December 1942 she was smuggled to the Aryan side of Warsaw to try to obtain weapons, deliver literature for the resistance, and find hiding places for Jews. The memoir proceeds chronologically through

July 1944, when the Polish underground organized a unsuccessful revolt against the Nazis, which lasted two months before the Poles surrendered. The last few pages detail the return of Meed and her husband, Benjamin, to Warsaw after the city had been liberated, and the English version of the book includes an epilogue describing their return to Poland some three decades later.

Meed writes little about her life before the days of the ghetto, and thus the memoir does not provide the reader insight into the fabric of her life before the Holocaust. Her inner life is minimized, with the specifics of the larger struggle of the resistance, particularly of the Jewish Fighting Organization, the focus. Meed was a labor activist before Germany's invasion of Poland, participating in the youth organizations of the Jewish Labor Bund, which promoted workers' rights and the perpetuation of Yiddish culture.

In addition to a detailed account of the struggle of the resistance, Meed's memoir is notable for her insightful and sensitive description of the way many Jews came to give up the struggle to survive, whether because of debilitating hunger or because they refused to work longer or to go into hiding if this involved abandoning elderly parents, children, or younger brothers and sisters. The book describes in rich detail the struggle of the Warsaw Ghetto Uprising and the efforts of the resistance fighters to offer aid to Jews in other cities and camps. Meed recounts the day-to-day struggles of what was required to carry out the resistance efforts, giving the reader an understanding of the bravery and resourcefulness needed. This included obtaining money from the outside to bribe guards and officials, to painstakingly collecting bottles for Molotov cocktails, to trying to convince sympathetic Poles to shelter those who had to remain in hiding because of their Jewish features. As she makes clear, people took such actions even when doing so was likely to result in their own deaths.

Meed does not sidestep controversial issues, such as the roles of the small number of Jews who comprised the Jewish Ghetto Police and of other collaborators, of the retributions of the Jewish Fighting Organization, or of the collaboration of the Poles and Ukrainians. She writes about the fate of many Jews who, after managing to escape from camps or hiding, sought refuge in the forests, only to fall into the hands of Polish and Ukrainian partisans who killed Jews on sight. She relates the anti-Semitism of the Armja Krajowa (Home Army), the Polish resistance, which not only refused to allow Jews into its ranks but also killed them upon discovery. Meed includes resistance efforts in the labor camps of Czestochowa and Radom and explains how difficult it was for inmates there, away from the greater possibilities of aid from sympathetic Gentiles and the greater availability of hiding places in Warsaw, to organize.

Meed's memoir provides valuable insights into the lives of those survivors who historically have been considered the ''lucky ones,'' those who could ''pass'' as Gentiles, and poignantly describes their particular struggles. They had to avoid detection by the notorious Polish blackmailers and were subject to constant searches by the Nazis. These people had to adopt a Roman Catholic cultural identity, which included memorizing prayers and attending church, and they had to adopt Polish customs and scrupulously avoid any trace of Jewishness in their speech or mannerisms. Meed describes how exhausting it was to maintain these identities, especially after people had lost their friends and families in the deportations or in the uprising.

This important addition to the Holocaust literature details the story of the Warsaw Ghetto as told through the lens of a young woman who was a committed socialist. Meed's work is in the genre of **Gerda Weissman Klein**'s *All but My Life* and **Fania Fenelon**'s *Playing for Time*.

—Margie Newman

ONE DESTINY: AN EPISTLE TO THE CHRISTIANS
Essay by Sholem Asch, 1945

An eloquent essay in favour of Jewish-Christian reconciliation, *One Destiny* (1945) nevertheless also expresses a critical approach to Christianity absent from most of Sholem Asch's novels. *One Destiny* begins with a statement of his faith in the interdependence of Jews and Christians and then seeks to confront Christians with the Holocaust's implications for Christianity. Critics have long suggested Asch's naïve, idiosyncratic faith had little to do with traditional Christianity or Judaism. The characterization of the Holocaust in *One Destiny* highlights the features of Asch's approach to contemporary and historical Jewish-Christian relations that, on the contrary, made his perspective both sensitive and realistic.

Asch's declaration of faith in *One Destiny* was designed to elicit a contrite attitude toward the suffering of the Jews from his Christian "brothers-in-faith," not to engage with the critics of his Jewish-Christian vision within the Jewish community. Written in English, not Yiddish, its language was carefully selected to affirm as much of Christian belief as possible by means of imaginative interpretations of Jewish teaching. Asch sidesteps the distinctive aspects of Christian theology, not because he denies them but rather in pursuit of a rapport with the Christian reader. Creating a single community of Jews and Christians did not follow from the argument in *One Destiny*, and Asch did not argue that Christianity was simply a form of Judaism. He did, however, reaffirm his often-stated belief that at the core of both traditions lay a common "messianic" belief, and Adolf Hitler's Holocaust was but the latest attempt by "Satan" and his "pagan" allies to obliterate both (a conclusion reiterated in later essays such as "The Guilty Ones").

According to *One Destiny*, the Holocaust reconfirmed the eternal and interdependent Jewish and Christian missions. Prompted by the anti-Semitic legacy of two millennia of false Christian teaching, Christendom had nevertheless stood by while the Nazis killed millions of their Jewish "brothers." Worse still, the persecutors of the Jews—Jesus's people—"called themselves Christian." For that, the German people would always bear "the mark of Cain," but Christianity as a whole had contributed to this situation by de-Judaizing their faith and in the process transferring the anti-Christian hatred of the pagan world onto the Jews. Throughout Christian history, the Church had persecuted the Jews, Asch argued. The memory of Jesus, by contrast, had always stood with his people. Although *One Destiny* is similar to other contemporary American works written to forestall the development of Christian anti-Semitism in the United States, Asch also drew on scholarly works on the Jewishness of Jesus and the common bonds between Jewish and Christian ethics that originated in Europe. Like Franz Rosenzweig (*The Star of Redemption*, 1921), for instance, Asch saw the messianic or prophetic ideal as the distinctive basis for Jewish and Christian faith, marking them off from Islam and other false religions.

The destruction of Polish Jewry lies at the core of Asch's perspective on the Holocaust in *One Destiny*. Evoking the efficient inhumanity of the perpetrators through a description of Heinrich Himmler's visit to the Warsaw Ghetto, he suggests that the underlying polarity revealed in the Holocaust was the conflict between pagan modernity and the faith expressed first by the Jews, and then by Christians. Asch, trying to express in Christian terms the faith of what he claimed were the vast majority of victims, the religious Jews of rural Poland, suggests that most would have "seen their messiah" as they were killed. Even the assimilated Jews of Western Europe, as much as they had wished to escape their Jewishness, were "taught" about their Judaism by Hitler. Whereas the Judaism of the Eastern European working masses was affirmed by the Holocaust, according to Asch, the rationalism of Western European Jewry was discredited by Hitler, not least because it lacked the "messianic" essence of Jewish faith.

Asch's hope was pinned on his American Christian readers, for "only they" recognized the Jewish gift to civilization. At a time when the British and the Arabs were jointly obstructing Jewish immigration into Palestine, only the United States, he concluded, provided an adequate haven for the remnant of the Jewish people. Published in the midst of the public furor over Asch's Christological works, *One Destiny* was widely classed as part of a syncretistic attempt to marry the two faiths together not simply in "one destiny" but as "one faith." This would be to misjudge it. *One Destiny* was a skillfully crafted appeal for a change in Christian attitudes to Jews and Judaism after the Holocaust. Asch made clear he believed the Holocaust confirmed the distinctive historical "roles" of the two faith communities. He did not need more specific theological polemics to serve his purpose.

—George R. Wilkes

ONE GENERATION AFTER (Entre deux soleils)
Collection by Elie Wiesel, 1965

Elie Wiesel's *One Generation After* (1965; *Entre deux soleils*) is a collection of vignettes, stories, essays, and dialogues that reflect on the Holocaust and other themes central to his writing. In the essay "Journey's Beginning," he remembers a madman named Moshe who nonetheless was distinguished through great piety. In this remembrance Wiesel betrays his reverence for the mentally ill: "they see things we do not see." He also remembers Moché the Beadle (discussed in Wiesel's first book, *Night*), who tried to warn the Jews of Sighet of heinous crimes that would befall them but whose heroic sacrifice fell on deaf ears because people took him for a madman.

In his essay "Readings" Wiesel reflects on the many exhortations to testify on behalf of the victims of the Holocaust that occurred in the concentration camps. Such exhortations came from the prominent octogenarian historian Simon Dubnov, who knew he would not survive the concentration camps and from the inmates hosting literary evenings in Buchenwald; exhortations occurred in plays, poems, and autobiographical accounts of the Holocaust that continue to terrify and fascinate.

In the essay "Snapshots" we experience Wiesel's description of photographs of Holocaust victims: "I know that every image robs me of another reason for hope. And still my fingers turn the pages, and the shriveled bodies, the gaping twisted mouths, their screams lost in space, continue to follow one another. Then the anguish clutching me, choking me, grows darker and darker; it crushes me: with all these corpses before my eyes, I am afraid to stumble over my own." Reliving the Holocaust unleashes a massive cultural anxiety in us that in no way escapes the survivors of this catastrophic experience; however, "there is a thirst for knowledge, a desire to understand."

Wiesel describes a photograph of a man who committed suicide in one of the concentration camps: "Seen in profile, the prisoner seems strangely serene. One might think him seated, were it not for the belt tightened around his neck, its other end fastened to a pipe screwed into the ceiling. The hanged man could not have chosen a more fitting or symbolic place: the latrines." Wiesel expresses his pity for and solidarity with those who succumbed to the horrific and depraved environment of the concentration camps which presented monstrosities ordinary human beings could not endure.

—Peter R. Erspamer

OPERATION SHYLOCK: A CONFESSION
Novel by Philip Roth, 1993

The difficulty of identifying a perpetrator from the Holocaust in order to achieve justice for victims of the Holocaust, the deceased as well as the survivors, is the paradigm for Philip Roth's examination of the perplexing nature of truth in the 1993 novel *Operation Shylock*. While this work does not fall into the category of historical fiction, Roth has combined his fictional tale with the actual war crimes trial of John Demjanjuk and his real-life interview with **Aharon Appelfeld**, a Holocaust survivor and fellow novelist. This deliberate mixture of fiction with historical fact gives a structural representation to Roth's idea that in life nothing is purely factual and fiction offers important truths.

For Roth, the questionable nature of truth is reflected everywhere, even in a subject as serious as the Holocaust. At issue in the case of Demjanjuk are the counterclaims of the defendant and a group of six survivors. Demjanjuk insists that he is not the infamous torturer from Treblinka but rather is merely a man unfortunate enough to have the same baptismal name, age, and physical appearance. The defense asks: How could Demjanjuk, a law-abiding American citizen, skilled autoworker, and father of three grown children be Ivan the Terrible? The Jewish survivors contend that the defendant is unquestionably their former nemesis, despite any evidence to the contrary. They swear he is the same anti-Semitic wolf, except that he is now dressed in the sheep's clothing of American respectability.

For Roth, Demjanjuk's plight offers a real-life model to point out the ambiguities of truth. The discrepancy between the description of Ivan and the appearance of Demjanjuk is great enough to lend credence to the defense's claims but not substantial enough to discredit the prosecution's allegations. Could John and Ivan be one and the same? Demjanjuk, after all, could have discarded his old identity just as many Nazi criminals did. The story subtly asks: Wouldn't it be a miscarriage of justice to convict him on the testimony of survivors with fading memories who had not set eyes on the real Ivan for more than 40 years?

In the case of John Demjanjuk, there lurks the underlying irony to which Roth is so attuned. If the court makes an error, the State of Israel, the Jewish nation, would be guilty of killing an innocent man because of the same kind of lifelong prejudices against the "other" that Germany displayed toward the Jews. Yet Demjanjuk's guilty verdict seems assured since a deep-rooted dread that a Holocaust crime would go unpunished takes precedence over any assumptions of innocence and negates the chance that the testimony of Holocaust survivors might be impugned.

Looking at the difficulty of defining truth from a literary perspective, Roth inserts into *Operation Shylock* a part of his interview with Appelfeld published elsewhere in Appelfeld's book *Beyond Despair: Three Lectures and a Conversation with Philip Roth* (1994). In response to Roth's curiosity about why a writer would fictionalize his Holocaust experience, Appelfeld explains: ''My real world was far beyond the power of imagination, and my task as an artist was not to develop my imagination but to restrain it . . .'' According to Appelfeld, any effort to reconstruct those places and times was interrupted by ''visions of the trains and the camps . . .'' For example, his tainted memories led him to fictionalize life at Badenheim, to see those summers not as they were day to day but as a symbol. To detail the grotesque realities of the Holocaust was so awful that remaining true to the facts ran the risk of not being believed. Therefore, Appelfeld asserts, ''All my works are indeed chapters from my most personal experience, but nevertheless they are not 'the story of my life.''' Appelfeld's explanations in many ways echo Roth's own ideas about maintaining the truth when translating life into art.

Roth, however, is well aware that most survivors are not like Appelfeld, capable of transforming history into art. Some survivors have been less successful in separating themselves from their camp experience. In *Operation Shylock* Roth gives these survivors a fictional voice in the character of Apter, a man whose life remains filled with tales of continued victimization. The veracity of Apter's stories in which people ''steal from him, spit at him, defraud and insult and humiliate him virtually every day'' are somewhat beside the point. Their authenticity is unimportant for Roth, who believes the stories are ''fiction that, like so much of fiction provides the storyteller with the lie through which to expose his unspeakable truth.'' In this novel Appelfeld's and Apter's stories of the Holocaust are teaching tools for Roth, allowing him to demonstrate that truth and fiction are not antithetical, that fiction can be an important source of the truth, even when the subject is as grave as the Holocaust.

—Ellen Gerstle and Daniel Walden

THE OPPERMANS (Die Geschwister Oppermann)
Novel by Lion Feuchtwanger, 1933

Lion Feuchtwanger's novel *The Oppermanns* (1933; *Die Geschwister Oppermann*) describes the fate of an upper middle-class Jewish family in Berlin from November 1932 to late summer 1933. The story focuses on the independent scholar Gustav Oppermann, who has signed a manifesto against the introduction of barbarism in public life. Consequently, after the Nazi seizure of power and the burning of the *Reichstag,* he is in danger and therefore goes to Switzerland. When he

returns to Germany under a false name in order to collect evidence of Nazi crimes, he is arrested and sent to a concentration camp. After his release he dies from the aftereffects of his treatment there. His brother Martin, who manages the family business, the furniture company Oppenheim, is forced to merge the firm with that of his competitor, the storm trooper Wels. He will immigrate to London. His brother Edgar, a world-famous laryngologist, is removed from his hospital and will go to Paris. His brother-in-law Jacques Lavendel, an Eastern Jew with American citizenship, liquidates his business in Germany and moves to Switzerland. Whereas Jacques Lavendel's son Heinrich is able to cope with anti-Semitism at school, Martin's son Berthold is driven to suicide by his anti-Semitic German teacher. Edgar's daughter Ruth, an ardent Zionist, goes to Palestine.

The novel thus deals with anti-Semitism in Germany shortly before and after the Nazi seizure of power. Although Feuchtwanger also tries to include the lower classes by introducing the furniture salesman Wolfsohn, his concentration on anti-Semitism prevents him from dealing with the entire spectrum of German society. Hitler appears as a rather ridiculous character. The success of National Socialism is described as the result of crude agitation, targeting the lower middle class. It is supported by capitalists and big landowners who want to protect their financial interests and to fight Communism.

In spite of the rise of barbarism, Feuchtwanger optimistically believes that even National Socialism, which appeals to man's basic instincts, constitutes only a short, temporary episode in history's development toward a society governed by reason. In the end reason will win out over stupidity and barbarism although maybe not in the characters' lifetime.

The characters are not described in black-and-white fashion but with all their personal weaknesses, the Jews as well as the Nazis, who, as Feuchtwanger believes, represent only a small part of the German people. Feuchtwanger's style is conventional, almost naturalistic. On the basis of eyewitness reports he paints a stark and clear picture of the Nazis' anti-Semitic actions at the time, showing the discrimination of Jews, the effects of anti-Semitic propaganda, and the corruption of the German legal system. He takes his readers inside the Gestapo prisons and concentration camps confronting them with the inhuman treatment of human beings. By doing so, the novel was of tremendous informational value for the exiles and other readers outside Germany at the time. Already in the summer of 1934 all international editions together had sold more than a quarter million copies.

—Hans Wagener

P

THE PAINTED BIRD
Novel by Jerzy Kosinski, 1965

The Painted Bird (1965) remains a powerful work of Holocaust fiction, even though it makes few direct references to the Shoah beyond the occasional appearance of Nazi soldiers or trains carrying Jews to the camps. Throughout the book, however, we feel the presence of a world made possible by the dehumanizing values of the Third Reich. This brutal, episodic, and matter-of-fact narrative begins with a nameless six-year-old boy who is placed by his parents in the fall of 1939 with a peasant foster mother. When the foster mother dies, the boy is left on his own. Not only is he nameless, but so is the European country where the story occurs, and the boy—taken by the peasants for a Gypsy or a Jew—is not given an ethnic identity.

Most readers have assumed the country to be Poland and the boy Kosinski. The author himself was cagy about his life, and his publisher was unsure whether to market the narrative as history or fiction. A number of the book's episodes are so clearly fantastic that it is now difficult to believe they were taken as factual, but readers closer in time to the Holocaust were more willing to accept the book as ''truthful.'' Houghton Mifflin had legal concerns about such issues as slander, and the publisher finally decided to market the book as a novel, although this did not stop readers from treating its story as factual. Polish critics, for instance, reading the book in English (it was not translated until much later), interpreted it as a slander on Poland. Kosinski, unlike the book's protagonist, had survived the war in relatively comfortable circumstances, helped by his family's name change (from Lewinkopf) and their denial of their Jewish identity. Reacting to his various critics, Kosinski wrote a long essay called ''Notes of the Author on *The Painted Bird*'' (1965) that he published himself as a booklet. In it he justified his novel as being a kind of heroic fairy tale in the tradition of folk fiction.

The title comes from a folk legend enacted in one of the sections. In it a peasant captures a bird that he paints with bright colors. When he sets the bird free, it flies up to its native flock, which then attacks it because of its altered coloration, pecking at it viciously until it falls bloodily to earth. We associate the boy with the painted bird, rejected by its fellows because it looks different. In almost every episode of *The Painted Bird,* the boy experiences alienation, rejection, or violence at the hands of the peasants to whom he goes for protection.

The book's episodic structure reminds one of the picaresque novel, and the abrupt juxtaposition of most episodes without transition puts it also in the tradition of modernist fiction. The boy narrator's detached tone is particularly effective as he describes without emotional embellishment one scene after another of physical and sexual violence. This forces the reader to interact with the text throughout. Some critics have complained about the story's excessive violence; others have said that no amount of narrative violence was adequate to reflect what really happened during the war years. The novel contains a lot of mesmerizing action that represents individuals behaving in primitive and unrestrained ways. In an early scene a simpleminded peasant woman is slain by a group of village women jealous of her sexuality. They beat her without mercy, finally jamming a bottle full of excrement into her vagina and kicking it until it explodes. The boy witnesses a scene in which a peasant who is jealous of attentions a farmhand has paid his wife gouges out the boy's eyeballs, one at a time, with a spoon. In another scene a girl receives sexual attention from both her father and brother, finally being asked to couple with a goat. In yet another episode the boy witnesses the invasion of a village by Kalmuck soldiers who proceed to ravish both women and children, sometimes on horseback, before the Kalmucks themselves are shot by Russian liberators.

Just past the middle of the book the boy has been accepted as a Christian and has begun his religious training. While working as an altar boy, he drops the missal during a service, for which he is chased, beaten, and thrown into a pit of human excrement. After he pulls himself out, the boy discovers that he has lost his voice. Again we are asked to see the larger implications of this silence, a condition that continues until the book's last page, when the boy recovers his voice while talking on the telephone.

The book's final episodes occur after Russian liberators have arrived and the boy, while still mute, is protected by a few of them. Although these chapters are not as effective as the earlier ones, they do allow the narrator to reflect on the lessons he has learned from his experiences—that revenge, silence, and brotherhood are all essential elements needed for survival. When, at the end, the boy returns to his parents, he is not happy to see them. What he has learned has made him feel like a painted bird, a condition that is, no doubt, shared by many survivors.

—Michael Hoffman

PAPER BRIDGES: SELECTED POEMS OF KADYA MOLODOWSKY
Poems by Kadya Molodowsky, 1999

The final two lines of ''Dzshike Street'' (from the volume bearing the same name) reveal a tension that looms large throughout Kadya Molodowsky's poetic volumes and the poems selected, translated, and edited by Kathryn Hellerstein for inclusion in *Paper Bridges*: "And although tears well up behind my eyes, / I am in love with life like a bitch." The "although" in the line indicates something of the challenge that Molodowsky puts out to her readers: despite, and perhaps because of, pain, suffering, grief, loss, and an increasingly terrifying sense of abandonment, to love life, to embrace the body, to continue to speak directly to God. At the same time that her poetry bears witness and gives voice to this pain, it also demonstrates a vehement affirmation of life. The contrasts and oppositions that generate the movement of these volumes are many: the landscape both urban and pastoral, Molodowsky's tone both compassionate and caustic, despairing and uplifting, her governing motifs both deeply traditional and playfully heretical.

The selections from *Kheshvndike nekht* (1927; "Nights of Heshvan") include the entire "Women-Poems" cycle. The voices in this cycle ache with contrition, self-judgment, and conflicted longing—longing for lost love and lost youth but, most of all, longing to give birth, to be fertile. The maternal voice of tradition comforts, but cannot ameliorate, the varieties of sadness that these women face. The highly personalized experience of loss is carried into the other selections from this volume; the threat of death hovers barely concealed, broken only periodically by moments of tremendous intimacy with nature, family, and community, and even the rebellious exclamation of "At Blue Dawn"

> I'll start to run
> And overturn the tombstone,
> Mock the mourners,
> Kick dirt into the grave and dance on it,
> Clap my hands
> And call up the young and the strong,
> I will come and, then won't the graveyard
>   have fun!

does not suppress an escalating uneasiness. Quiet is increasingly undercut by impending doom; time creeps up, taking its toll not only on the body but on memory as well. There is a cynicism in this volume, a resignation that moral corruption is pervasive, that we are, in some sense, fallen creatures. At the same time, Molodowsky displays a painful nostalgia for a life and time on the brink of destruction, and she claims a responsibility to speak for those in this diminishing world:

> Sometimes I turn my face, as to an East-
>   ern wall,
> Toward my tiny shtetl,
> Almost entirely devastated,
> And pray for every single person
> left behind.

Her prayers continue, but they are conducted to a deepening silence, a silence becoming ever more threatening.

Molodowsky's *Mayselekh* (1931; "Tales") are poems written for children. As such, they provide a telling contrast to those of the previous volume. The selections from this volume portray the magic of the everyday, the promise of wonder tugging at the stark reality of daily life. This magic itself restores, just a little bit, the lost world that Molodowsky laments in the previous volume. Thus, in "Tale of a Washtub," a well-meaning washtub, voluntarily washing the clothes of all the world, performs *tikkun olam,* serves a sanctifying purpose: "Friday the washtub became quite devout, / And did nothing else but wash itself out." The selections from *Afn barg* (1938; "On the Mountain"), "Marzipans," and "A Letter," also written for children, promote self-sufficiency and creativity. The selections from *Freydke* (1935), similar in tone to the poems of these previous volumes, provide a glimpse into the shtetl; but the menace here is more defined

> the last bit of blue in the sky fades and fades—
> I hid it somewhere
> From the stones of enemies,
> From the cold in the room,
> From the dark nights of pogroms.

Dzshike Gas (1933; "Dzshike Street") continues to pursue the possibility for hope—for belief—even in a world tinged by devastating poverty and persecution, so that, in the title poem, Molodowsky hesitantly claims, "almost, it almost / Seems that God is there." In this volume Molodowsky is more deliberate and self-conscious about the writing process, a tendency that becomes more pronounced in her final volume, *Likht fun dornboym* (1965; "Light of the Thornbush"). She begins here to bemoan the inadequacy of language, of poetic language in particular, to capture depth of feeling, and presents the danger that the writing process will cheapen feeling:

> You leave. I can't recall the streets, alas,
> And those I recognize are strange, inert.
> The first line can be rhymed with
>   Montparnasse,
> The second, with a shirt.

Though gently mocking, these lines contain a fundamental caveat that guides this volume and those to follow: language can exploit just as it can bear witness.

In land fun mayn gebeyn (1937; "In the Country of My Bones") reflects an intense ambivalence, and, as Molodowsky explains in her autobiography, the fragmentation of identity that is almost inevitable for the East European Jewish émigré in America. In New York she is at once at home in a community of Jewish émigrés, in a community of Yiddish writers, and profoundly displaced, uprooted, separated from the country she carries with her but will never again be able to experience as a living reality. The final selection from this volume, "Legacy," drips with an almost palpable regret, with a haunting self-doubt that swings perilously close to despair:

> Who knows if a poet, who knows if a fraud
> In borrowed shoes,
> In a meandering bed.
> No thing is a symbol—
> Nothing to reveal.
> Maybe life is all wrong, a raw deal.

Molodowsky's last two volumes, *Der melekh dovid aleyn iz geblibn* (1946; "Only Kind David Remained") and *Likht fun dornboym* (1965), directly confront the Holocaust; the unnamable threat of the early volumes had shown itself as a terrifying reality, and the poet, in exile, commits herself to bearing witness. On the far side of the Holocaust, Molodowsky attempts, tentatively, to find a suitable language to depict the near-complete annihilation of her world, a language driven at once by rage and the deepest sorrow. Central to these volumes is a return to the spirit of the "Prayer" of her first volume, to a deeply traditional frame as a means of both challenge and comfort. In "The Rivalry of Writers Increases Wisdom," for instance, she casts herself as Job, accusing and implicating God in the devastation. To her surprise the grandmothers, the matriarchs, answer her instead of God. And their answer— "believe us, we are able / To open Paradise"—in some ways announces the task of these final volumes: to give voice to horrific devastation at the same time that they hold out the hope for a kind of redemption. This hope, she insists, cannot be blind. In one of her final poems, "I Am an Echo," Molodowsky places the words that both Abraham and Moses speak, "Here I am" (*hineni*), into the mouth of a fiddler, who fades into a mere echo. The world of Tevye becomes Scripture, and this world, she warns us, is rapidly disappearing, even as memory. And yet, as this fiddler's voice becomes more and more faint, he speaks a fragile hope, projects a future:

> You don't need what is real.
> My voice will reach you.
> Here I am, here I am,
> Take along my echo to the walls of Jericho.
> Soon I will play
> By the walls of Jericho.

Reality is ousted by the wish for renewal.

—Beth Hawkins

THE PARNAS: A SCENE FROM THE HOLOCAUST
Novel by Silvano Arieti, 1979

In *The Parnas: A Scene from the Holocaust*, Silvano Arieti combined his "psychiatrist's insight and the storyteller's skill," as **Elie Wiesel** expressed it on the book jacket, to produce one of the most penetrating novels written in response to the Holocaust. Indeed, **Primo Levi**, again quoted on the book jacket, described it as "a book to read again and again with the same piety with which it has been written." Based on the life of Giuseppe Pardo Roques—the *parnas,* or chief elder, of the Jewish community in Arieti's native town of Pisa—the novel explores how the spiritual sickness of an age can manifest itself in the soul of one of its victims. Arieti wrote *The Parnas* not only as a tribute to the courage and spirituality of Roques but also as an exploration of the bestial evil that characterized the Holocaust. "I feel as if I had written this book not only with ink but also with blood," Arieti said in his introduction. One powerful point he makes in the novel is that mental illness "may hide and express the spirituality of man," both individually and collectively. Pardo, as Roques is known in the novel, suffers from a phobia of animals, particularly dogs. Like any phobia, his appears to be completely irrational until the end of the tale, when the Nazis come to rob and murder the *parnas.*

As the Germans try to torture the *parnas* into praising Hitler, Pardo persists in his adoration of God. And as they proceed to beat him to death, Pardo sees the Nazis transformed into creatures that bark and howl, "with a snout, fur, four claws, and a tail." In other words he sees them transformed into what they have already become. At that point he realizes what he had truly feared all his life. It was the fear that haunts all humanity in the wake of the Holocaust, not a fear of animals but a fear of the human being who has allowed himself to be transformed into an animal. Who is worse off than the Jew murdered at the hands of the Nazi? When a German soldier puts this question to Pardo, he answers, "You." The Nazi who sets out to dehumanize the Jew loses his own human image in the process.

In the process of coming to this conclusion in the novel— and in keeping with his theories on the relation between mental illness and spirituality—Arieti examines the most profound spiritual questions that arise from the Holocaust. Pardo's friend Ernesto, in fact, believes that the mental illness is part of the Shechinah, of God's indwelling presence, that has descended upon the *parnas.* "What is ill in you," says Ernesto, "is intertwined with what is strong and holy and springs from the same source." Pardo replies by affirming his conviction that his illness has meaning; it is a warning against the illness of Nazism.

Because he sees meaning in his illness, the *parnas* does not believe that God has abandoned the world or the Jews. He hears his friend Angelo cry out, "What about the silence of God? Why is He mute? Why does He permit these things to happen?" The *parnas* answers, "God is not mute! Each crime bespeaks His lament, 'How far you are from Me!' . . . But we must choose to hear Him." In *The Parnas*, Arieti uses his skills as a psychiatrist and storyteller to enable his reader to hear the lament of the One whom Pardo affirms with his dying breath:

"Shemah Israel, Adonai Elohenu, Adonai Ehad—Hear, O Israel, the Lord our God, the Lord is One." What echoes in these words is the cry "How far you are from Me!"

—David Patterson

THE PATH TO THE NEST OF SPIDERS
Novel by Italo Calvino, 1956

The Path to the Nest of Spiders has become one of the key post-war novels in Italian literature, despite the fact that it is an anomaly, both in the context of Italo Calvino's other output and in the context of the developing neo-realist movement. The novel is at once far more realistic than those that would later bring Calvino fame and tinged with a certain fairy-tale symbolism that distinguishes it from most neo-realist novels. Nevertheless, by providing one of the most lucid and intelligent firsthand accounts of the new movement, Calvino's 1964 preface to the novel established it as a key neo-realist text. *The Path to the Nest of Spiders* was published as *Il sentiero dei nidi di ragno* in 1947, when Calvino was 24—a talented writer still testing his craft and attempting to process the traumatic events of the war. There are a few hints of the crystalline structure and playful fantasy that would characterize his later work, but for the most part this novel represents an attempt by Calvino to transform his own experiences as a partisan in the Italian resistance into fiction and to enter into the contemporary polemic about the nature of the partisans and the growing Communist movement.

In the 1964 preface Calvino writes: "For the fact is that those who now think of 'Neo-realism' primarily as a contamination or coercion of literature by non-literary forces, are really shifting the terms of the question: in reality the non-literary elements were simply there, so solid and indisputable that they seemed to us to be completely natural; for us the problem appeared to be entirely one of poetics, of how to transform that world which for us was *the* world into a work of literature." Concerns such as the role of socialism in Italy, resistance to dogma, and the desire to be an accurate and illuminating witness to history were paramount for Calvino. Interested in the ambiguous nature of human character and discontent with programmatic fiction, Calvino recalls himself as having aimed "to launch an attack both against the detractors of the Resistance and against the high-priests of a hagiographic Resistance that was all sweetness and light . . . What do we care about someone who is already a hero, someone who already has class-consciousness? What we ought to be portraying is the process by which those two goals are reached!"

Although there are moments where a clear conflict between good and evil seems to exist, such as the scene in which the boy-narrator Pin is beaten by Nazis who are interrogating him, the narrative focuses far more often on the vast, muddied, and mixed-up area between these two absolutes. The band of partisans that Pin joins is often incompetent and uncommitted to its cause; in fact, more than one of them seem to have difficulty choosing on which side to fight. Throughout it all our narrator Pin wanders, an urchin with too much experience of sex and violence (his sister is a prostitute) to play with the other children but still too immature to be accepted fully by the adults. His child's viewpoint allows Calvino to show the treachery, deception, or heroism of the characters without moralizing. Using Pin as the narrative filter also allowed Calvino to displace his own feelings and experience as a young bookish upper middle class man who felt out of place among the tough and often working-class partisans onto another marginalized character who is also younger and less capable than his companions.

The Holocaust, like the ideologies of fascism and Communism, are incomprehensible to Pin; the reader has the benefit of understanding the motivations behind actions that go over Pin's head while at the same time seeing what he sees, a world of adults who sometimes commit good actions and sometimes very terrible ones. The distinction between the ethical and the unethical adults is a question of personal character, not party. Pin sees individuals, without dehumanizing them into abstract ideological conceptions. In Pin's view, adults constantly play games with each other but break the rules. Death is the penalty of their game. Confusion and guilt are the visible signs of a larger corruption and evil whose roots are unguessable to Pin but clearly implied for the reader. The Holocaust is the most extreme result of a tendency the adults on both sides are vulnerable to—a tendency to betray oneself or others by treating people as abstractions or by acting in corrupt self-interest. No one is innocent, not even the orphan Pin.

Calvino's book was a watershed for readers used to more dogmatic and uncritical novels about the resistance movement, such as those by Elio Vittorini or Marcello Venturi, with whom Calvino shared a literary prize for a post-war collection of stories in 1946. He had mixed feelings, however, about the book: "The uneasiness which this book caused me for so long has to a certain extent subsided, but to a certain extent still remains: it resides mainly in my relationship towards something so much bigger than myself, involving emotions which affected all my contemporaries." As a form of collective memory, the book also endangered his own personal memory of the war years, involving a sense of loss that implies history can never be fully understood at the time it is experienced: "A completed book will never compensate me for what I destroyed in writing it: namely, that experience which if preserved throughout the years of my life might have helped me to compose my last book, and which is in fact sufficient only to write the first."

—Christina Svendsen

THE PAWNBROKER
Novel by Edward Lewis Wallant, 1961

Edward Lewis Wallant's 1961 novel, *The Pawnbroker,* presents a series of dreams (set in italics) that reemerge to trouble the title character, Sol Nazerman. The dreams constitute his memories of victimization in the Holocaust. Once a professor at the University of Kraków, Nazerman is now a suburbanite who runs a pawnshop in East Harlem, and he is haunted by images of the losses and tortures of his concentration camp past.

The adaptation of Wallant's book as a film directed by Sidney Lumet and starring Rod Steiger in an Oscar-winning performance served to bring this narrative to a large audience. The strength of the flashback associative imagery allows the film to enlarge upon the novel's work on Holocaust trauma, as stated in the book *Flashbacks in Film: Memory and History.* The present calls the past to our attention through a process of associative memory; this effect is even more pronounced in the film whose abrupt associative editing graphically matched the images from New York's East Harlem in the present with those from Europe. Leonard Leff's ''Hollywood and the Holocaust: Remembering *The Pawnbroker,*'' published in *American Jewish History* (1996), provides great insight into the film's conditions of production. He emphasizes how Wallant's novel intrigued those in Hollywood looking for a script to address the Holocaust, even while they struggled with its commercial viability in a cultural context that had not yet witnessed widespread mainstream production of films about the horrors of the Holocaust. Taken together, the book and the film can be seen as playing a crucial role in a broader U.S. reception of Holocaust narratives.

Controversial in its setting up of a metaphoric parallel between the concentration camp and urban poverty, Wallant's novel stems from that moment in U.S. history in which many U.S. Jews saw their involvement in the civil rights movement as a way of responding to the concomitant evils of racial prejudice and apathy that sustained the Holocaust. For them the legacy of the Holocaust was a call to social action. Wallant made the link but never assumed that mere equivalence must be implied by the comparison; it is less an issue of weighing a major disaster of history against the crushing poverty and suffering of everyday life than one of becoming aware of both in their specificity and difference. Wallant initially presents Nazerman as a character who refuses to feel or to care about others. Trauma brings about the loss of empathy, as the self closes down. Nazerman becomes an emblem of how misrecognized or foreclosed traumas of the present might be obscured by not having worked through the traumas of the past, especially insofar as one might have to understand those traumas empathetically, as they affect others.

When Nazerman learns that his pawnshop is a money laundering front for a pimp, he must confront both his complicity in exploiting women for profit and his will to ignorance in refusing to piece together the clues he might have recognized buried in everyday procedures. Participation in prostitution crushes him, for his Holocaust memories include being forced to witness his wife service a Nazi soldier.

Besides the witnessing of his wife's sexual enslavement, other dreams recount horrific scenes of helplessness: his family's deportation in a boxcar so crammed with others that Nazerman cannot hold his young son up out of the filth below, an operation being performed on him by Nazi doctors and nurses who taunt him as they enjoy their experiment, and his shoveling a mound of dead bodies, fearing he will recognize his family members among the corpses. Wallant transformed documented accounts of Holocaust atrocities into personal memories; Nazerman's nightmares become a dream condensation of all the horrible scenes one imagines a survivor may have witnessed. Some of the dreams present a documentary, though highly subjective vantage point, while others take on a surreal dimension. In one he sees a child's body suspended from a hook as if a butchered carcass, the face first appearing to be his daughter, then other members of his family and of his acquaintance, victims from the past ceding their place to others of the present. Toward the end a dream of a peaceful family picnic scene before their arrest and deportation freezes: ''Their faces all came closer; he would have liked to gather them all into him, to drink them, to breathe them. And then they stopped, every blade of grass froze, each of them was arrested in motion . . . All was silence; it was like a movie which has suddenly stopped while its projecting illumination continued. And he was paralyzed, too, forever out of reach of the dear faces, frozen a few feet short of all he had loved. And then it all began dimming; each face receded, the sunny afternoon turned to eternal twilight, dusk, evening, darkness.''

The Pawnbroker captures this mournful dream of the traumatized Holocaust victim even as it constructs circumstances in the present to move Nazerman beyond the oppression of his dreams of the dead and his survivor's guilt. Wallant created a redemptive sacrificial gesture as Nazerman's assistant in the pawnshop, Jesus Ortiz, takes a bullet intended for Nazerman in a robbery Ortiz helped plan. The novel ends in tears of mourning and forgiveness: ''he realized he was crying for all his dead now, that all the dammed-up weeping had been released by the loss of one irreplaceable Negro who had been his assistant and who had tried to kill him but who had ended up saving him.''

—Maureen Turim

THE PERIODIC TABLE (Il sistema periodico)
Memoir by Primo Levi, 1975

Perhaps the most brilliantly inventive formally of all of Primo Levi's works, *Il sistema periodico* (*The Periodic Table,*

1984), originally published in 1975, is a sort of personal memoir—not an autobiography but ''in some fashion a history,'' as Levi himself puts it. It consists of 21 chapters, each of whose titles is one of the elements in the periodic table, the first being ''Argon,'' and the final one ''Carbon.'' Each chapter focuses on a major issue, event, or figure in his life, or some combination of these.

In the first chapter Levi constructs a sort of genealogy for himself as a man of words, an intellectual, and a Jew by reporting and reflecting on phrases associated with various of his ancestors from the time they migrated from Spain after the expulsion of 1492 up to the generation before his own. Each of the phrases he introduces connects with one phase or another of the experience of a Jew in a Christian world. The words and phrases show, in short, the pressure of social experience and are only intelligible given that context. The chapter is concerned as well with other marks of difference—dietary practices, for example. The tone is often wry and ironic but never unserious; in a way characteristic of Levi the account asks the reader to be ready to decipher fugitive and oblique clues to the experience of others, if we are ever to communicate with and to treat one another humanely.

The chapters that follow open sequentially on Levi's life from age 16 (in the second chapter, ''Hydrogen'') to past age 48 (where the reader finds him, in 1967, in the penultimate chapter, ''Vanadium''). He does not deal at length with his time in Auschwitz. The chapter ''Cerium'' refers to that period, but Levi refrains from large and direct engagement with it here, remarking simply, ''The fact that I, a chemist, have lived a different season has been narrated elsewhere'' (referring to *Survival in Auschwitz* and *The Reawakening*). But the whole book is pervaded by the approach to the experience of Auschwitz, its results in his life, and its traces in language and society more generally. Nowhere is this more evident than in the two chapters ''Lead'' and ''Mercury,'' which were written before his capture and are here inserted into a book of retrospect. These chapters—one on a mysterious disease that causes early death generation after generation in a proud family of traders, the second a story of marriage—show the huge pressures about death within a genetic line and about marriage that the young Levi was feeling as the racial laws in Italy were taking effect.

Mixings and separations, then, are the constant theme of this book, as are the effects of trace elements in chemical (and social) experience. The point is made repeatedly that to understand we must decipher traces, reconstitute the combination of elements in which they had their original context, and study the effect to which (sometimes in the long term) they contribute. To forget, to lose a grip on the facts, and, worse, to practice ''willed ignorance'' of, say, conditions in Auschwitz, is, in Levi's view, to invite disaster in social reactions, just as such ignorance can lead to deadly explosions in chemical reactions; ''Vanadium'' is perhaps the most effective chapter in making this point.

The final chapter, ''Carbon,'' is a small masterpiece on the importance of trace elements in the conditions of life. Levi is obviously thinking of the way in which Jews, and other minorities, relatively rare elements in the composition of society, nonetheless are indispensable as conditions of its possibility. That chapter takes up too a question that looms large in Levi's response to Auschwitz—the question of responsibility. What, is the question, is the relationship between materially determined chains of events and free choice, if it exists at all? Levi creates a mini-epic, an odyssey, that recounts the travels of an atom of carbon from its inert state ''hundreds of millions of years ago'' to the point where it powers mental synapses in himself as a writer, in a ''labyrinthine tangle of yeses and nos.'' In that process it also directs his hand as he writes *The Periodic Table,* whose last chapter he ends with a period, a dot of carbon ink, to which he calls our attention. His responsibility as a writer of witness and our responsibility as readers come together in our common attention to what is signified by the multiplied millions of traces of carbon that end here with that dot of ink.

—Ralph G. Williams

THE PIANIST: THE EXTRAORDINARY STORY OF ONE MAN'S SURVIVAL IN WARSAW, 1939–45 (Smierc miasta)
Memoir by Wladyslaw Szpilman, 1946

Wladyslaw Szpilman was a composer, a pianist, and an animator of cultural life. He studied in the Berlin Academy of Music. In 1933, after Hitler had gained power, Szpilman returned home to Warsaw. He worked as a pianist for Polish Radio, at the same time composing symphonic music and movie soundtracks. He also wrote about one thousand songs.

He described his war experience—the stay in the ghetto and the years spent in hiding in occupied Warsaw—in a book entitled *The Death of a City*, which had a censored edition in 1946. The unabridged edition of the book, published in Germany in 1998, is entitled *The Pianist*. One year later it was also published in England, Holland, Italy, Sweden, Japan, and the United States. It appeared on the best-seller lists of such newspapers as the *Times* (London), the *Los Angeles Times,* and the *Guardian* (London).

The Pianist is an attempt at coping with the nightmare of the years under German occupation. It belongs to the stream of post-World War II memoir literature in which fiction had to give way to facts. In Szpilman's memoir there is no feeling of hate or the need for revenge. The author writes only about his own experience, about what he had witnessed. He describes the first German repressions aimed at Jews, the creation and the closing of the ghetto, the everyday life in the Jewish quarter, the ever-present hunger and death, the deportations of people destined to be murdered in gas chambers, and a wide spectrum of human reaction in extreme situations. But *The Pianist* is not only a story about the effects of fanaticism and the Nazi ideology. Szpilman's book is also a homage to music, which gave the narrator the strength and motivation to survive.

In addition to being the record of the fate of an individual, *The Pianist* analyzes the mechanisms of behavior of the whole community living under the pressure of fear. Szpilman shows the martyrdom of his nation. At the same time, however, he shows his readers a world of restaurants visited by the ghetto youths and Jewish Gestapo agents and their mistresses. He describes the streets where people were dying of hunger and the atmosphere of cafés where the rich tried to drown their fear.

Szpilman's story is balanced, free of hate or the wish of revenge. This restraint makes it possible for the facts to speak. Thanks to the story, scenes—such as a fleeting meeting with Stefan Starzynski, the president of Warsaw; a lamentation of a mother who has strangled her own child for fear that the crying would give them away to the Germans; or a picture of a man lapping up the soup straight from the pavement—become important symbols.

The Pianist was named Book of the Year 1999 by the *Los Angeles Times*. Director Roman Polanski was shooting a movie about the Holocaust based on the book.

—Joanna Hobot

PILLAR OF SALT (Statue de sel)
Novel by Albert Memmi, 1953

The novel *Statue de sel* (*Pillar of Salt*) by Albert Memmi is a veiled autobiography. It was published in French in 1953, when the author was 33 years old, and published in English translation two years later. The novel describes the evolution, through education, of the poor son of a worker. Based on the life of the author, it details the torment that accompanies every step of his social and personal change. The text relates the emergence of a poor, disenfranchised Jewish boy from the secluded dead end of the Tunis ghetto, where the only joy is the Sabbath dinner. Each step the child takes outside this protective world is marked by a double experience in which every instance of social or intellectual improvement exacts a personal price. In particular the boy must confront the guilt he feels in abandoning his family, who cannot understand what he is doing. At the same time, however, the boy's classical education fails to provide him with an alternate "home" and serves only to clarify the abyss that separates him from the world. A Jew, he is separated from classical literature even if he understands it better than his classmates. His accent points

to his lower-class origins, and because of it he is rejected by Christians and Jews alike. His education makes him see his parents' religion as a set of superstitions, and he thus abandons it, widening the gulf between himself and his father.

The boy is constantly reminded of his marginality, which he lives as an unfair draw. Even when he receives an award, he must follow the wishes of the donor and not his own inclination. His poverty makes him a misfit, always looking to an upper-class friend who will open a door, only to find that, even inside, he remains an outsider. From his first emotional encounter with a girl to his first visit to a prostitute, his experiences are marked by his position as an outcast who, unfamiliar with the ways of society, has had to find his own way by trial and error.

A large proportion of the book is devoted to the boy's intellectual and social evolution in the classroom, a microcosm of the outside world. The narrator—whose name, Alexandre Mordekhai Benillouch, is now revealed—shares the Arab experience of the colonized, suffers the Christian rejection of the African, swallows the snubs he endures from the bourgeois Jews and Gentiles alike, and internalizes his rejection by his father and his family. He faces the world alone, dispossessed of everything but his mind and his will to succeed. The only help he receives comes from some of his teachers, themselves misfits who perceive the human richness of their student and guide him in his final choice of the West over Africa, of language over dialect.

But the world intrudes. The war begins, Pétain breaks the promise of the French Republic, and Alexandre chooses to join his coreligionists in a work camp, where his status as part of the elite now places a barrier between him and the underprivileged. In the camp he learns again the value of religion as consolation and his own incapacity to help. He thus decides to escape, and the advance of the Allies offers him the possibility when the slave laborers are moved from the front lines. Having reached Tunis, he hides until the Americans deliver the city. He tries to join the French army of Charles de Gaulle but is rejected because he is Jewish, and in turn he rejects the West after this second betrayal. He studies to become a philosophy professor and, after suffering a new rejection from the French education ministry, decides to continue his life in a new world: Argentina.

Written with great tenderness and acute attention to detail, the text re-creates an entire society and does so without any obvious animosity or regret. The book is an exploration of identity, not only of a Jew in an oriental and Christian world but also of an underprivileged and outcast individual. As the narrator says, he is "indigenous in a country of colonization, a Jew in a antisemite universe, an African in a world where Europe triumphs." Constantly attempting to enter worlds where, ultimately, he perceives his status as an outsider ever more cruelly, the narrator succeeds only in severing himself from his roots. The dramas of North African Jews, of decolonization, and of Arab anti-Semitism are all captured in this beautiful and rich book.

—Alain Goldschlager

THE PLAGUE (La Peste)
Novel by Albert Camus, 1947

The longest and most ambitious of his fictions, Albert Camus's novel *The Plague* is widely regarded as his master-piece. It is certainly an artistic tour de force: a vividly realistic account of a harrowing imaginary event. It tells the story of an outbreak of bubonic plague in the Algerian city of Oran and is set in the 1940s, which is also when it was written. Published as *La Peste* in 1947 (*The Plague,* 1948), when the recent end of World War II was still fresh in everyone's mind, *The Plague* made painful but compelling reading, so nightmarishly real were its descriptions of the terror and suffering inflicted by the imaginary plague. Inevitably—and no doubt intentionally—such a novel would invite an allegorical interpretation.

In 1947 it seemed obvious that the story was intended as an allegory of the brutal German occupation of France during the war and of the heroic French opposition to it by the resistance. That interpretation was natural enough, since Camus had been a resistance hero himself, with his polemical articles in the clandestine newspaper *Combat,* and had, moreover, declared publicly that the original inspiration for his novel had been the panic and frustration he experienced in 1943 when he was alone in central France and suddenly discovered that all communication with his family in Algeria had been cut off because of the war.

Subsequently, however, readers of the novel began to find other themes in it in addition to that specific wartime allegory. It was noticed, for example, that the novel emphasized the dire human consequences of isolating those infected by the plague and the even graver distress that followed the isolating of the whole city from contact with the rest of the world. Those observations seemed to point to the urgent human need for community and to human helplessness before the random violence of nature as significant themes of the novel and to a broader interpretation of the symbolism of the plague as a more universal evil that would include war in general, as well as imprisonment and political oppression of every kind.

From these concepts it was a short but logical step to seeing *The Plague* as a veiled allegorical depiction of the German concentration camps, detailed knowledge of whose horrors were beginning to emerge from eyewitnesses during the last days of the war, even as Camus was composing his novel. Oran under siege by the invisible menace of the plague, as described in Camus's novel, has striking similarities to the extermination camps of the Holocaust, with their piling up of dead bodies, their shattered families, their squalid living conditions, their

brutal mistreatment, and the ever present menace of death. The plague is, in fact, as uncomfortably apt a symbol for the horrors of the Holocaust as it is for the harsh realities of the German occupation of France.

The Plague has numerous passages describing the heroic efforts of ordinary citizens, against impossible odds, to ease the suffering and control the epidemic. The central figure, Dr. Bernard Rieux, who risks his life every day fighting the plague, is shown as exhilarated by the satisfaction he feels at finding himself equal to his heroic task. The plague has given his life meaning. Yet on balance, *The Plague* is a bleakly pessimistic novel. Human beings in adversity are rarely shown to be noble or courageous. Most are selfish, corrupt, or paralyzed by fear. Though friendships and alliances are formed to combat the infection, they prove ephemeral, and Camus is at pains to show that ultimately each human being is isolated and alone. When the plague appears over, Rieux is left with the empty feeling that his life no longer has any purpose. The novel's closing sentence is especially despairing, reminding readers that the plague is never over but lies dormant for years or even centuries until one day "it will awaken its rats, and send them to die in a happy city."

—Murray Sachs

A PLAQUE ON VIA MAZZINI (Una lapide in Via Mazzini)
Novel by Giorgio Bassini, 1952

A Plaque on Via Mazzini was first published in 1952 and appeared in *Five Stories of Ferrara* in 1956. All of the stories in the latter examine the relationship between the Jewish community and the rest of the people of Ferrara. Many refer to the impact of Mussolini's "racial laws" of 1938.

As in most short stories the attention is focused on one person—in this case the sole survivor of the 183 Jews carried off to Germany in autumn 1943. There is an unobtrusive first-person narrator who is worried about the reality of his tale, set as it is in an ordinary street like Via Mazzini, though the street runs along the top of the old ghetto. Geo Josz appears in August 1945 while a builder is putting up a plaque on the synagogue commemorating the deportations. Geo says his name should be removed now that he has returned. The gathering crowd can see he is so fat that he looks like a drowned man; showing clearly on his right wrist are tattooed numbers preceded by the letter "J."

Bassani often conveys important elements of his narrative by describing emblematic objects such as the tattoo of the concentration camp inmates. Geo's fur hat and jerkin are the uniform of the escapee, the calloused hands the sign of the forced labor in the salt mines. There is much play on the beards that the men sport—from the little goatee of the early fascists to the full beard of the returning partisans—that are eventually shaved off as normality returns. The story has the task of chronicling the political events from Mussolini's fall to the elections of May 1948, which decided the fate of the partisans, forging the political shape of Republican Italy for decades to come.

Geo claims back his father's house, bought in 1910 from an aristocratic family. It had been used as the headquarters of the Fascist Black Brigade and then passed to the partisans, who after the 1946 elections and the disappearance of the Action Party would move to three rooms in the old Fascist headquarters in the main street. A house can be a comment on political history.

Geo and his uncle take up residence in the Ghibelline tower of the old house. Ferrara's medieval legacy thus gives him a lookout where he can survey the partisans and monitor any vengeful excesses they might have contemplated in the old prisons below. These were times of civil war.

Once installed Geo declares his Jewishness by wearing an olive "gabardine," italicized in the Italian, and maybe reminiscent of Shylock in *The Merchant of Venice*. The people in his favorite cafe are eager to hear Geo's story and have a spirit of hope for the new democracy. But his uncle Daniele, another returner but from the ranks of the partisans, who lodges in the room below in the tower, hears his slippered tread at night and knows that his room is covered with photos of his lost loved ones. On the day of Geo's return they had visited another uncle, a lonely example of a Jew surviving in the city because he had espoused the Fascist cause from the start, as many had. He had paraded his black shirt until 1938 and still wore a goatee.

In May 1946 Geo meets yet another elderly survivor, Count Scocca. He represents the Fascist machine, a paid spy of the secret police, sporting a black dyed Hitler moustache. Geo goes up to him and slaps his face twice like a Fascist bully. The count replies by whistling "Lili Marlene," the German army song. People see the assault as unmotivated. Others assert that the count had asked Geo if he was Ruggero, poor Angiolino's son, and inquired about his father's death, mentioning how he had always asked after his father and his little brother.

So everything changes. Geo puts on his fur hat and jerkin and neglects his new gabardine. In the cafe he sits beside the torturers, telling stories of Germany and Buchenwald, his father's last words on the way to the salt mines, his mother's farewell wave, and his little brother's disappearance in the dark. But now it is too late. People are bored and unbelieving. In August 1946 he appears in rags at a new dance hall opened near where five members of the resistance were shot two years before. Because he had agreed with the partisan secretary over his father's house, people think he has turned Communist. In February 1947 he is excluded from the club restricted to top people, both Catholic and Jewish, and also from the brothel, whose owner exercises her democratic right to exclude people

from her own house. The outcome is that Geo disappears rather as he had come, and no one knows if he has gone away or killed himself. They are sincerely sorry for not having been more patient.

The epilogue explains that in the May twilight one wonders why one is playing someone else's game. The slaps were Geo's reply to the count's polite but patronizingly hypocritical questions. They were Geo's revenge. The crowd thinks he was mad. (Now this might be described as post-traumatic stress.) Ferrara returns to its closed and provincial ways. And Bassani has captured some conflicting moods of desperate and bitter times.

—Judy Rawson

PLAYING FOR TIME (Sursis pour l'orchestra)
Memoir by Fania Fénelon, 1976

Fania Fénelon's autobiography tells the story of her imprisonment in Birkenau from January–November 1944 and in Bergen-Belsen from November 1944–April 1945, as well as her subsequent rescue by English soldiers who liberated Bergen-Belsen on 15 April 1945. It originally appeared in French in 1976 as *Sursis pour l'orchestra* and was published in English translation the following year. Fénelon's story is unique among memoirs by Holocaust survivors because she stayed alive by working for the female orchestra in Birkenau, hence the title of her autobiography. She begins her memoir with a climactic moment: her rescue as she lay dying of typhus. Despite being ill and dehydrated, and weighing a mere 62 pounds, she sang songs such as "La Marseillaise," "God Save the King," and the "Internationale." Her songs moved the liberating soldiers to tears and were heard on BBC radio. In fact, her cousin, who was living in London, was listening to the radio and discovered simultaneously that she had been captured by the Nazis and liberated by the Allies. The first chapter is significant because it shows the love and respect that the other prisoners had for her; she was their inspiration, their friend, and their leader. Even Irma Grese, the sadistic Nazi officer at Birkenau, pleaded with her not to die; this fact suggests how special Fénelon was because Grese rarely exhibited any concern for Jews and enjoyed torturing them.

After this opening chapter, Fénelon goes back in time to her deportation and her initial meeting with Clara, a spoiled prisoner who initially befriends Fénelon but then becomes selfish and egocentric. Upon earning her place in the women's orchestra, Fénelon risks her life in order to save Clara's—demanding that the Nazis allow Clara, who had a lovely soprano singing voice, to join also. Members of the women's orchestra enjoyed valuable perks, such as taking showers and obtaining shoes, better clothes, bedsheets, and soap. She risks all of this to help Clara, but a month later, her friend turns against her. Clara becomes obsessed with food, sleeping with *kapo*s for a small container of jam or a little sugar. Clara, who had insisted previously that she and Fania share a box that they "organize" (the word they used for accumulating possessions), changes her mind and uses separate boxes after she starts to gather a stash of food. Because Clara is pretty, has large breasts, and is obese in a camp in which almost all of the women are quite thin from malnourishment, the *kapo*s find her very desirable. Subsequently, Clara becomes the girlfriend of a *kapo* and eventually, in Bergen-Belsen, a brutal *kapo* herself. Fénelon expresses that she felt betrayed by Clara's actions, and the text manifests her belief that the desperate situations imposed by the Nazis in the camps led weak people such as Clara to sacrifice their morals and values in order to survive.

Fénelon's moving and introspective autobiography dwells on the women's orchestra, which was unique; there were male orchestras in other camps, but not female orchestras. She describes in great detail the other members of the orchestra, including Alma Rosé, the daughter of the first violinist in the Berlin Opera orchestra and the niece of notable composer Gustav Mahler. Fénelon discusses her frequent attempts to break down the emotional barrier that Rosé created between herself and the other members of the orchestra. The author also discusses other members, such as Marta and her love for little Irene (homosexuality was prevalent in Birkenau), the friction between the Jewish and Polish women prisoners, and the struggle to perform well enough to please the Nazis, knowing full well that their lives literally depend on it. The orchestra plays for the inmates as they leave for work in the morning and when they return in the evening, as well as concerts for Nazi officials such as Heinrich Himmler and Josef Mengele.

Fénelon scrutinizes the comportment of the Nazis in Birkenau as well as the behavior of orchestra members. The chief of the camp, *Lagerführerin* Maria Mandel, is seemingly a harsh woman and a strong advocate of Nazi ideology. One day she encounters a sweet, beautiful baby and desires the boy for herself. She separates the baby from his grieving mother, who is gassed. For a week she takes the baby everywhere and falls in love with him. Deciding that keeping the baby violates her sense of Nazi purity, however, she personally brings the boy to the gas chamber and then mourns his death. Fénelon hypothesizes that Mandel's devotion to Nazi ideology supersedes her love of the boy and humanity.

—Eric Sterling

POEMS, NEW AND COLLECTED, 1957–1997
Poems by Wisława Szymborska, 1998

The poetry of Wisława Szymborska is remarkably rich in imagery, subject matter, and intellectual scope. She has written on topics ranging from the purely quotidian ("Cat in an Empty Apartment") to the arts, history ("Reality Demands"), love, existential angst ("Four in the Morning"), and much more. Her work is highly complex and constantly reveals new dimensions of meaning and expression. If there is one thing that characterizes her approach, it would be the concretization of our abstract and fragmented perceptions of the physical, psychological, and moral world. It is highly reminiscent of Hegel's prephenomenological position in his famous essay "Who Thinks Abstractly?" in which he describes people watching a hanging and shows each spectator focusing on just one aspect of the man on the gallows. Each of them thinks he or she is seeing the totality of the phenomenon, but in actuality each only sees a single aspect: criminal, son, youth, and so on. Szymborska examines familiar phenomena, and by reminding her reader of their details and multifaceted nature ("eagerness to see things from all six sides"), she brings to consciousness a refocused and renewed sense of what is there.

She has written numerous poems to address social and political themes, including the conflicts and atrocities of the twentieth century. The three poems from her oeuvre that most directly address the Holocaust are "Still" ("Jeszcze"), "Hunger Camp near Jaslo," and "Hitler's First Photograph," and each in its own way demonstrates her poetic method and contributes to an understanding, both of the phenomena they address and of her poetic imagination. The three poems appear in a 1998 collection of Szymborska's poetry, *Poems, New and Collected, 1957–1997*.

"Still" is an extended metonymic evocation of a sealed boxcar containing Jewish "names" traveling across the Polish countryside to a sinister destination. The focus on the names instead of the people to which they are attached is not an exploration of nominalism but an indictment of the crude objectification of the "other," which lies at the core of anti-Semitism and other forms of racism: "Let your son have a Slavic name, / for here they count hairs on the head, / for here they tell good from evil / by names and by eyelids' shape." It diminishes their value as individual persons, as personalities, and it seemingly legitimizes the artificial alienation it engenders. Interestingly the poet's target here is not Nazism and its adherents but her compatriot inhabitants of the countryside through which the train is traveling. True, the Nazis may have filled and sealed the boxcars, but it is local anti-Semitism she refers to specifically, and in doing so she raises the always disturbing and thorny question of the passive complicity of bystanders. The train is neither invisible nor silent as it moves like a ghost ship through the countryside. Indeed, she contrasts the clickety-clack of the train moving along holding its grotesque cargo with the "crashing silence" of those on the outside who know but refuse to act or even acknowledge what is happening.

In "Hunger Camp near Jaslo" Szymborska also refers to the silence around such events, but like Anna Akhmatova in "Requiem" she enjoins her poetic persona to "write it," to tell the world. She takes the reader away from conceiving the

Holocaust as a phenomenon of unimaginable—and therefore abstract—proportions to confronting the individuality of each victim: "History counts its skeletons in round numbers. / A thousand and one remains a thousand, / as though the one had never existed."

Similarly, in "Hitler's First Photograph"—a truly remarkable poem—Szymborska with disturbing irony presents a picture of Hitler as a lovable little baby ("Precious little angel, mommy's sunshine, honey bun.") who embodies all the hope and potentiality of any other infant. He represents and embodies his parents' joys and dreams, he might grow up to be just about anything, but there is no mention, no hint, of the diabolical monster he in fact became. He is identical with all of us and all of our children at that age—indistinguishable: "Looks just like his folks, like a kitten in a basket, / like the tots in every other family album." The reader is left with the realization that everyone is obliged to try to understand and to be engaged, unlike the history teacher at the end of the poem who cannot hear what is going on around him and simply "loosens his collar / and yawns over homework."

These poems, while not occupying a large space within Szymborska's work, are closely connected with other works that, in combination, develop an expansive and profound expression of the worth and importance of every human being and every human existence.

—Allan Reid

THE PORTAGE TO SAN CRISTÓBAL OF A.H.
Novel by George Steiner, 1979

In the title of George Steiner's novel *The Portage to San Cristóbal of A.H.* (1979), the "A.H." stands for Adolf Hitler. The premise of the novel is that a group of Nazi hunters manages to capture Hitler, now 90 years old, in the depths of the Amazon jungle and attempts to transport him to San Cristóbal, where their leader awaits them. This might sound like literary wish fulfillment, but Steiner, who has been one of Britain's most eminent literary critics since the 1960s, develops his idea in the opposite direction. Rather than offering its readers the pleasure of fictional vengeance, the novel confronts them with an intricate mosaic of nightmare scenarios and ethical challenges. It is, as Steiner himself once said, "a warning."

First published in 1979 in the *Kenyon Review, The Portage to San Cristóbal of A.H.* immediately ignited controversy. When the play based on it opened three years later, popular protest, as well as further critical debate, resulted. The novel's incendiary qualities are largely an effect of its construction. It contains no authoritative voice. Instead of mediating the utterances of the various characters through the buffer of a

rational perspective, Steiner forces his readers to decide for themselves which claims have merit. Because some of the statements are at once nihilistic and intelligent, the process is often unsettling. For example, some of Hitler's captors meditate on their ennui, on their indifference toward an undertaking that costs one of them his life. In a chapter that both evokes and inverts the main themes of *Doktor Faustus,* Thomas Mann's novel about the rise of Nazism, the reflections of a German legal theorist on music's ability to transcend time give way to his musings on the "fullness" of life in the Third Reich. Here Steiner addresses what perhaps has been his gravest concern: the relation of the sinister and the sublime elements in Western culture. How, he insistently asks in the essays collected in *Language and Silence* (1966), can we have faith in the humanizing mission of the arts when we know that Beethoven was played in the shadow of death factories?

For Steiner language, more than any other medium, generates culture. Hitler's eloquence is, therefore, a devastating fact. This implies that "a word might be at the end" as well as at the beginning. And Hitler almost gets the final word in Steiner's novel about him. In the final chapter Hitler sheds his senescence and defends himself with chilling rhetorical force. In fact, he develops sophisticated arguments about the connections between the Holocaust and ongoing genocidal events that resonate with some of Steiner's own utterances. Hitler points out that the Holocaust would have been impossible had the Allies behaved differently and that it cost many fewer people their lives than did Stalin's purges. Occasionally Hitler is more bombastic. He suggests that he culled his ideas about the racial struggle from Viennese Jews and that he, in turn, created Israel, which perpetuates his attitudes about race and territory in its treatment of Arabs. Hitler, however, has a counterweight in the novel: Emmanuel Lieber, the driving force behind the expedition to capture A.H. He continues to pursue Hitler when everyone else has given up. Admonishing the men he sent after Hitler to be careful, Lieber tells why. In a pathos-laden monologue, which Steiner places at the center of the novel, Lieber enumerates Nazi crimes in damning, harrowing detail.

Remembrance and the pain this causes are also major themes. Here, too, Steiner is provocative. Of Hitler's five captors four are Holocaust survivors. Not only does their past torment them, but their most sincere responses to it conform to literary and filmic representations of war and suffering, in some cases to bad ones. The men are cruelly aware of this. Indeed, their oppressive sense of the scriptedness of their deepest emotions and desires torments them still further.

Physical distress mirrors their psychic pain. Much of the novel consists of accounts of Hitler being carried through the rankest jungle by Lieber's men, afflicted with diseases and sores, buckling under their load and their exhaustion, finding no relief from the insects and the damp. These scenes set the tone of the novel. Some of the characters are cynical and ironic, but for most Hitler's resurfacing brings an abundance of agony and very little hope. There is no sense in the past that returns with him. Significantly, posed in very different contexts, the question ''Why?'' makes several characters feel the same: foolish. As Steiner himself emphasizes, the very last word in the novel belongs to a figure whose name is Teku, the Hebrew word for issues that are beyond human understanding.

—Paul Reitter

A PRAYER FOR KATERINA HOROVITZOVA
(Modlitba pro Katerinu Horovitzovou)
Novel by Arnošt Lustig, 1964

Arnošt Lustig reveals a penchant for creating exceptionally strong female characters, and Katerina Horovitzova in *A Prayer for Katerina Horovitzova* (1973; *Modlitba pro Katerinu Horovitzovou,* 1964) is no exception. In an interview with *Contemporary Authors,* he stated, ''I like stories about brave people, about how they survived under the worst circumstances. I like people who are fighting for their fate, and who are better in the end, richer, in a sense, than they were in the beginning. I think that each writer has a certain duty—to imagine himself in theory as perhaps the last human being alive under certain circumstances and that perhaps his testimony will be the last one. He is obliged to deliver that testimony.'' *A Prayer for Katerina Horovitzova* certainly represents this statement.

Bribery, trickery, and deceit mark the road to nowhere in this novel. Twenty European-born Jews, all of whom are American citizens, have been captured in Italy and turned over to German authorities. These men have two things in common—their wallets and their egos. They are all immensely wealthy, and it is their affluence and egoism that will be used against them in their attempt to buy their way out of German hands. Mr. Herman Cohen, with permission of Mr. Friedrich Brenske, commandant of the camp's secret division, has managed to rescue young Katerina Horovitzova from the loading dock. She will join the group in its attempts to free itself from the clutches of the Nazis. She will also be used by the Nazis as a pawn in an intense game of falsehoods and sadistic acts. Mr. Brenske sees the potential in her very presence for more

manipulation of the group's monetary status and brilliantly employs her beauty and youth to bleed the men of their last francs. From the very beginning of their plight, it is evident that Mr. Brenske's promises to the prisoners will never be fulfilled. His entire plan is to lead them full-circle, from their internment at the camp, to the train, to the ship that will supposedly carry them all to freedom, back on board the train, ending with a return to the camp. On each foot of the voyage Mr. Brenske creates a new excuse to have the men write checks, until their money supply is depleted. This is all in an effort to gain more money for the German Reichsbank, and there is no intention whatsoever of releasing these captives. Lustig's ingenious plot, however, keeps the reader's hopes high that this story might turn out differently, although it becomes clearer with the multiple requests for Swiss francs that these 21 people are doomed. The ultimate act of sadism is placing the prisoners within view of the rescue ship that will never sail.

Throughout the entire ordeal Katerina keeps silent and seems detached from the group. Although many of the men protest Mr. Brenske's appeals for more cash, she observes and quietly obeys. The buildup of tension within her is evident throughout the novel and climaxes when the men run out of money. It is not evident that Katerina could become the hero of the work; after all, she is the only female in this group. She is forced to strip in front of all the men in an attempt to further humiliate her, but she performs the ultimate act of revenge by snatching a pistol from Lieutenant Schillinger and shooting several Nazis. Her act of revenge is indeed a dignified one, something that her 20 captives are powerless to commit. She retains her femininity to the end, and her execution of these Nazis does nothing but show the real power in her personality. She is able to act, whereas her 20 cohorts could do no more than write checks. Human dignity indeed reaches much deeper than one's pockets. All the prisoners are singularly executed, starting with Mr. Adler, ''as though things must always be done alphabetically,'' an act that further reveals the obsessive compulsion of the Nazi regime.

Katerina's body is burned along with the others, as Rabbi Dajem sings a song in the hair-drying room commemorating her bravery.

—Cynthia A. Klíma

Q

THE QUALITY OF WITNESS: A ROMANIAN DIARY 1937–1944 (Jurnal din vremur de prigoanæa)
Diary by Emil Dorian, 1982

Emil Dorian's diary *Jurnal din vremur de prigoanæa* is an eloquent text written by one of Romania's major Jewish literary figures. It is the work of a mature man who had devoted his life to the cause of peace and tolerance but who lived to see the atrocities of the Holocaust. Because of the censorship policies of Romania's Communist government, the diary was first published in English translation in 1982, and it did not appear in Romanian until 1996. It was only because of the devotion of a close friend to whom he entrusted the diary notebooks that they were preserved. The English edition was prepared by his daughter Marguerite Dorian, who excerpted entries from the first seven notebooks that Dorian kept from 1937 until his death in 1956.

With its first entry dated 30 December 1937, *The Quality of Witness* presents the reader with rare insights into prewar Romania and the rise of anti-Semitic legislation, as well as with other measures taken against the Jews before the outbreak of hostilities. The published excerpts of the diary end on 24 August 1944 with Dorian's reflections on Romania's surrender to the Allies. More than most other Holocaust diarists, Dorian recognized from the very beginning the profound nature of the historical upheaval that was taking place. On 11 February 1938, for example, he wrote, "One could feel every human being shiver at the intimate contact with the essence of historical events." Further, the more intense his collision with history, the more radical his experience of the collapse of time. On 22 October 1943, for instance, he declared that he had lost all interest in the future. Three years later, to the very day, he had lost his sense of the present, wondering, "What does it matter that I jot down dates?" This obliteration of a present and a future came in the wake of a radical assault on memory and therefore on the past. Thus measuring time a day at a time, Dorian's diary contains a record of the assault on time.

This collapse of time had implications both for the individual and for his or her world. For the Jew, Dorian pointed out on 22 May 1944, the world became a place where death itself—that is, the natural death that befalls a normal humanity—no longer existed. On 5 February 1941 he noted how other nations reacted to such a condition, lamenting that Jews "have been expelled, tortured, massacred—while people, or rather countries, looked on with total indifference." At a time when a Jew's crime was being alive, the world's crime was being indifferent. What this meant to the individual Jew came out in the entry of 15 August 1941: "Getting worse: I'm plunged in silence." Revealing the tension between the need to speak and the oppressive silence, Dorian's diary brings out the serious mental, emotional, and spiritual dimensions of the annihilation of European Jewry.

Because Dorian was a writer, his diary contains numerous reflections on the literary craft and the spiritual dimensions of writing. "All is not lost," he declared on 12 July 1938, "while the hope of writing a poem is still alive." He even ascribed a certain redemptive significance to his diary. In an entry dated 2 June 1943, he commented on the difference between "writing literature" and keeping the diary. The former he regarded almost as indulging in a luxury, the latter as engaging in a testimony. What is remarkable about Dorian's diary, then, is that it opens up the nature of the Holocaust diary as such. It is not a tranquil reflection on the day's events or on one's personal life for the sake of oneself. Rather, it examines a world, a truth, a horror, and a meaning for the sake of a community.

Dorian demonstrates that the Holocaust diary rests on a fundamental accountability; its cry of "Why?" is not a "Why me?" but "Why my neighbor? Why the children and the old ones?" On 25 January 1942, for example, he wrote, "The thought of what is happening to these human beings [the Jews] poisons every moment of my life." While other diaries offer an account of a life at the end of a day, Dorian's diary reveals the daily struggle to recover a life that is destroyed every day.

—David Patterson

THE QUARRY (Der Verdacht)
Novel by Friedrich Dürrenmatt, 1953

Der Verdacht, a short detective novel by Friedrich Dürrenmatt, was published in 1953 after being serialized in *Der Schweizerische Beobachter* in 1952. It later appeared in English as *The Quarry* (1962). It is a sequel to his better-known mystery *Der Richter und sein Henker* (1952; *The Judge and His Hangman,* 1954). Each work features the Bern police superintendent Hans Bärlach as the protagonist-sleuth bent on solving a murder mystery. Although both works have Swiss settings, the content and tone of the latter novel is Holocaust-specific.

The novel's two equally long portions take place, respectively, in two different Swiss health-care facilities over a two-month period at the end of 1948 and the beginning of 1949. The first half is set in a Bern hospital where the protagonist has just been diagnosed with terminal cancer and given only one year to live. The second half is set in a private clinic near

Zürich where he has placed himself incognito to apprehend the novel's antagonist-murderer. As in many Holocaust-related works, there are three different types of main characters: a bystander, the engaged Bärlach; the victimizer, the notorious Nazi physician Dr. Emmenberger of the Stutthof concentration camp, who was known for performing operations on inmates without an anesthetic and who was able to take flight from prosecution after the war; and the victim, Gulliver, a Jewish survivor of Stutthof and other camps who has made it his self-imposed mission to track down and murder Nazi criminals. Their interaction and the ensuing ethical questions dealing with crime and retribution are Dürrenmatt's chief concerns.

The dilemma that Bärlach finds himself facing from the outset of the work is whether the notorious Nazi physician at Stutthof was a German from Berlin called Nehle or, in fact, a Swiss doctor named Emmenberger, posing as Nehle, who after the war became head of the aforementioned clinic.

The burning drive that keeps the superintendent on track in locating the death-dealing physician and bringing him to justice is the *Verdacht*—literally the "suspicion"—of the work's original German title. In a twist that combines clever plotting with profound moral examination, it is the "neutral" Swiss rather than the German who turns out to be the villain, relishing the opportunity to perform sadistic experiments in the camps. The Holocaust thus illustrates a human problem rather than a merely national problem. What motivates Bärlach in going it alone so close as he is to death is the need to find an arch criminal often neglected by traditional law enforcement agencies: "The big criminals are running free while the small ones are stuck in jails. And anyway, there are all kinds of crimes nobody pays any attention to, only because they are more aesthetic than some sensational murder which gets into the headlines. But actually they are both the same, provided you look at the facts and have imagination . . . The really big

beasts are under the protection of the state, like beasts in the zoo.''

Provoked by Bärlach's relentless questioning, Emmenberger reveals himself as the impersonator of Nehle, whom he had sent away to South America in the 1930s and eventually murdered in Hamburg. As Emmenberger prepares to kill Bärlach in the clinic, he propounds the unregenerate satanic creed that allows him to feed his spirit by murdering his helpless victims using violent pain: "Freedom is the courage to commit crime, for freedom itself is a crime . . . For when I kill another human being . . . I become free . . . And the screams and the pain which flood toward me from glassy eyes and open mouths, the convulsing, impotent white flesh under my knife, reflect my triumph and my freedom and nothing else.''

In a reversal of Holocaust roles, the victim, Gulliver, a giantlike figure of remarkable physical strength once tortured by Emmenberger, rescues Bärlach. A few minutes before Emmenberger is to begin his lethal operation, this Wandering Jew (he is repeatedly referred to as Ahasverus) forces Emmenberger to take poison.

Two other Holocaust-related characters in the novel are Emmenberger's wife and accomplice, Dr. Marlok, a Communist who feels that her human spirit was murdered both in the Soviet gulag and in the Nazi camps, and a nameless dwarf, spared by Emmenberger from Nazi extermination in order to act as his murderous tool.

Although this is Dürrenmatt's only imaginative work specifically engaging the Holocaust, the questions it raises about crime and retribution and the quest for justice are major themes throughout his oeuvre. In 1958 he wrote one other short detective novel, *Das Versprechen* (*The Pledge,* 1959), set in Switzerland but with a different protagonist.

—Steven R. Cerf

R

RADICAL HUMANISM: SELECTED ESSAYS
Essays by Jean Améry, 1984

Radical Humanism, a collection of essays compiled and translated for an American audience by Sidney Rosenfeld, reveals the breadth of Jean Améry's intellectual work, spanning his experiences in the Holocaust, his postwar political engagement, and his philosophical interests. The essays are united by the theme of "radical humanism," a concept that appropriately describes Améry's life. Radical humanism, in a nutshell, means prioritizing the welfare of human beings in all circumstances. He suggests a "radically humane demand for a 'revolt against reality, which is rational only as long as it is moral.'"

Not all essays in this collection are autobiographical. The final five focus on Améry's philosophical studies and discuss philosophers whose work had occupied him during his life: Friedrich Nietzsche, Ludwig Wittgenstein, Simone Weil, and Jean-Paul Sartre. The collection closes with an interpretation of the Enlightenment and its enduring humanitarian values, in opposition to structuralism, which Améry sees as antihuman and even fascist in its relativism. The remaining six essays follow the autobiographical style of Améry's writing but discuss events that he did not witness himself. He comments on these events from the perspective of his experiences, such as the Warsaw Ghetto Uprising, as well as from the perception of emigrants in their host country and historiographical representations of the Third Reich. Subjects Améry had previously discussed are taken up again, including his identity as a Jew; anti-Semitism in the political left, especially in Germany; German attempts at "coming to terms with the past"; and his own sense of mission as a writer. As a whole the collection is representative of Améry's work written between 1967 and 1978.

The essays united in this volume address human, social, and political consequences of the Holocaust in a variety of contexts. In most of the autobiographical essays, the focus remains on Améry's self-understanding as a Jew, his disappointment and anger at anti-Semitism in the guise of anti-Zionism, and the loss of *Heimat* (Home), which is intensified in an analysis of West German public discourse on the legacy of the Holocaust, particularly in the political left.

At the Mind's Limits, another collection of essays by Améry, is a book of hope and measured optimism despite the terrifying nature of much of its content. It warns against the human capability of inflicting evil on others, while expressing a belief in the possibility of human beings changing for the good. In contrast, *Radical Humanism* largely speaks of Améry's disappointment with the way his message has been received. The collection conveys the intense sense that he has not only begun his career as a writer with much delay but also that he has failed in making himself heard. In his own interpretation his insights about the human condition after the Holocaust have not been received; in particular, West Germany's left has not lived up to the high ethical-political hopes Améry placed on it.

Améry's own philosophical and political allegiances remain the same. His profound sense of alienation from German culture and his native Austria as well as his sense of being abandoned by the world as a Holocaust survivor and Jew are manifest in his struggle to invest his Jewishness with meaning that conveys identity rather than only forced identification. In particular, his unwavering support of Israel at a time when criticism and condemnation of Israeli politics was popular among the political left demonstrate his frustration with and sense of betrayal by the political movement he had placed his faith in. The Holocaust, while not explicitly the subject of most of the essays, is the background against which all his reflections need to be read. His own experience of being a refugee and victim of atrocity motivated him to support political and humanitarian activities and can be seen as the driving force for his writings.

—K. Hannah Holtschneider

RAVENSBRÜCK
Memoirs by Germaine Tillion, 1946, 1973, 1988

The title *Ravensbrück* refers to three distinct works. Each has as its starting point French ethnographer Germaine Tillion's internment in the Ravensbrück women's labor camp between 1943 and 1945. The first, published in 1946, relates her firsthand knowledge as directly as possible, at a time when the world was only beginning to read eyewitness accounts of the Holocaust. In spite of an attempt at objectivity in the form of a thorough discussion of the camp's historical context, it is an angry document, containing unscientific comments such as the different degrees of moral and physical strength exhibited by prisoners depending upon their nation of origin. The second, published in 1973, includes a corrected version of the 1946 edition in which she disavows her earlier generalizations based on race and ethnicity and is augmented by histories of the camp and the Nazi policies of slave labor and extermination as well as by a study of the fate of 959 French women who were part of a convoy sent to Ravensbrück from Compiègne in 1944. Tillion ends with discussions of the broader question of German guilt (once again abandoning her earlier belief in the inherent vices of certain nationalities) and of the problem of truth in testimonies. Studies by other authors of the gas chambers in Mauthausen, Dachau, and Buchenwald appear as appendixes for the purpose of repudiating recently published denials of their existence. The third version, published in 1988, reflects 40 years of research not only on Ravensbrück but also on the Holocaust in general, including archival material that had only been made available after the 1973 version was written. It is her most important work.

Despite vast differences among the three books, a few central concerns and characteristics remain consistent throughout. From the start Tillion intended to provide more than a factual account; she was always concerned with placing her experience in the larger historical context and analyzing philosophical issues such as the trustworthiness of testimonials or the attribution of responsibility for genocide. She pays careful attention to concentration camp terminology, such as *verfügbar* ("available"), applied to women who were not assigned to work in factories outside the camp, or *Nacht und Nebel* ("night and fog"), applied to women considered security risks, such as political prisoners from occupied lands, such as herself (as opposed to common criminals, prostitutes, ethnic minorities, and others). She uses whatever written document can be found, whether her own notes taken secretly while in captivity or Nazi archives that had escaped destruction during the abandonment of the camps. Despite such scholarly trappings, the 1946 edition is valuable primarily for its ability to convey emotion and a sense of closeness to the events being described.

The most significant addition in the 1973 edition is a systematic attempt to document the scale of murders in Ravensbrück based on a German list of 959 French female prisoners who were sent to the camp in early 1944. By carefully tracking the fate of each woman on the list, Tillion arrives at a coherent picture of the camp in general, especially the various means of murdering prisoners before the gas chambers were put into service toward the end of the war. The *Revier,* or infirmary, was one way the Nazis increased the death rate, as was the *Jugendlager,* or youth camp, which was in effect a death camp annexed to the larger labor camp. Tillion's purpose in researching this data was to arrive at a more precise figure for the numbers of deaths and explain how they logistically could have occurred.

The scientific approach that dominates the 1973 edition reaches its fulfillment in the 1988 edition. Passages from the earliest edition have all but disappeared. A revised analysis of the list of 959 prisoners is preserved, though it is dwarfed by the quantity of research and analysis of other aspects of the camp. Tillion introduces her study by describing the state of knowledge of Nazi war crimes in France during the war and follows with an overview of Nazi policies, with special attention to Heinrich Himmler's business interests. She continues with a more complete history and sociology of the Ravensbrück camp than in the earlier editions, owing more to archival research, depositions by German army personnel arrested after the war, testimonies from other survivors, and research by other scholars than to Tillion's own experience. The penultimate chapter consists of her thoughts on some of the dominant themes of Holocaust research. As if to respond to criticisms that her work on the Holocaust was insufficiently personal, she includes for the first time a full account of her mother's deportation and murder. Few people have Tillion's combination of scientific credentials and experience, a fact that places all three versions of *Ravensbrück* in a special category in the bibliography of Holocaust literature.

—M. Martin Guiney

DI RAYZE AHEYM/THE JOURNEY HOME
Poem by Irena Klepfisz, 1990

The most salient stylistic feature of Irena Klepfisz's poem "*Di rayze aheym*/The journey home" is its English/Yiddish bilingualism. During her work on the Jewish women's anthology *The Tribe of Dina* (1986), Klepfisz became increasingly aware of, as she wrote in *Dreams of an Insomniac,* "how the Holocaust had robbed [her] generation of the language and culture which should have been [their] natural legacy" and was "struck that as a poet . . . [she] had never thought about the discrepancy between . . . the Jewish experiences [she] was trying to write about, and the language [she] was using." Influenced by Chicana writer Gloria Anzaldúa, who mixed Spanish and English in her poetry, Klepfisz began experimenting with bilingual poetry. She characterized "*Di rayze aheym,*" one of her first bilingual poems, as an attempt "to duplicate in language and form the thematic conflict in the poem itself— the loss of language and voice, the efforts to regain them."

Polish, not Yiddish, was Klepfisz's first language. She recalled that she had no language in which she felt "completely rooted" until her late teens. After immigrating to America in 1949 her Polish atrophied, never progressing beyond a childlike state. Although she thought and dreamed in English, it "seemed alien and lacked both intellectual and emotional resonance." The Yiddish she learned at the Workmen's Circle School and which was the language of the secular Jewish community in which she was raised "had the emotional and cultural substance" but "simply didn't feel natural." Although she has conceded that the Yiddish of her poetry was neither the same *mame-loshn* she would have used had she "been born into a different Poland" nor the anglicized Yiddish of American Jews, she insisted that her Yiddish was authentic and that Yiddish was not a dead or dying language. The Yiddish of her poetry "was very much alive. Not unlike a . . . survivor of an overwhelming catastrophe, it seemed to be saying . . . 'I am not what I once was . . . But I did not die. I live.'"

Although clearly autobiographical, inspired by Klepfisz's return to Poland in 1983, ''*Di rayze aheym*'' is written predominantly in the third person. In ''*Der fenster*/The window,'' the first of nine cantos, the poem's ''she'' looks out the window, alienated and estranged from the American cityscape. In America ''All is present / The shadows of the past fall elsewhere.'' The shadows are the ''shadows of Jewish-Polish culture'' that Klepfisz encountered on her trip to Poland, an experience she describes in *Dreams* as ''like stepping into a negative rather than a photograph.'' For Holocaust survivors, whose present is permeated by the past, America's constant present is perceived as a threatening wilderness, and the wilderness has ''dried out our tongues and we have forgotten speech.'' The absence of Yiddish from this canto underscores the loss of language.

In the wilderness and isolation of the eternal present, ''she'' tries to hold on, ''clinging like a drowning person to a flimsy plank,'' to her memory, which holds ''the entire history of the people.'' In an attempt to rescue fleeting memory and restore lost speech, ''she'' flies ''like a bird'' to Poland, landing near the wall of a Jewish cemetery. The cemetery wall, however, does not separate the living from the dead, ''*Der moyer a beys-oylem oyf der zayt un oyf der zayt*,'' as there is no living Jewish present on the other side of the fence. In her travel diary ''*Oyf keyver oves*: Poland, 1983,'' Klepfisz concludes, ''the major Jewish activity in Warsaw occurs in the Jewish cemetery and consists of the unchecked sinking of gravestones into the ground. Deeper and deeper.'' Cantos 5–8 further explore the inadequacy of language in mediating between present and past, the living and the dead. ''Among strangers on this side'' and ''among ghosts on this side,'' she wonders ''with whom,'' ''how,'' and ''with which words'' she should speak and is ultimately driven to silence, ''*un zi shvaygt*.''

Canto 5 lists four questions (*kashes*) but leaves them unanswered, underscoring the impossibility of dialogue. In canto 8, ''*Di tsung*/The tongue,'' communication breaks down completely, ''She lacks the words and all that she can force is sound unformed sound.'' In this canto the gutter down the middle of the page, which throughout the poem serves as a visual reminder of the unbridgable gap between Yiddish and English, the past and present, widens. Silence dominates, embodied in the empty space between the vowel sounds, the Yiddish words they signify, and their English translations. In the final canto, ''*Di rayze aheym*/The journey home,'' ''she'' returns to America, concluding, ''Among strangers is her home. Here right here she must live. Her memories will become monuments.'' Together with her travel diary, in which Klepfisz states, ''Poland remains *undzer heym,* our home . . . *Amerike iz goles,* America is exile, a foreign land in which I speak a foreign tongue,'' ''*Di rayze aheym*'' denies the possibility of a definite distinction between home and exile for the Holocaust survivor. Klepfisz has revisited this dilemma in her poem ''*Bashert*,'' in which the narrative voice explains: ''I am almost equidistant from two continents. I look back towards

one, then forward towards the other. The moment is approaching when I will be equidistant from both and will have to choose. Maintaining equidistance is not a choice.''

—Elizabeth Loentz

THE READER (Der Vorleser)
Novel by Bernhard Schlink, 1995

The Reader (1997; *Der Vorleser,* 1995) expands on an ancillary aspect of Bernhard Schlink's earlier work in the genre of detective fiction. This aspect had emerged by 1995 as the proper theme of the narrative: Germany's relationship to its own past and the concomitant examination of questions of culpability and transmission of cultural memory.

As Ernestine Schlant, in *The Language of Silence* (1999), her seminal examination of contemporary German literature engaging the Holocaust, writes: ''[*The Reader*] shows a thorough acquaintance with all the issues addressed in the 'literature about fathers and mothers' and recapitulates and simultaneously criticizes them.'' Schlant is alluding to the novel's position in a larger cultural dialogue that, as a belated continuation and intensification of efforts first made in the later 1960s, focused on examining the role of ordinary Germans in the Holocaust; questions of individual and potential collective guilt; the silence maintained about the Nazi era in early post–World War II (West) Germany; and the attempts to discuss appropriate channels for the future transmission of Holocaust memory.

The novel begins in 1958 with the 15-year-old protagonist, Michael Berg, suffering from hepatitis and becoming sick in the street one day on his way home from school. He is rescued by a stranger, a woman about 20 years his senior, who helps him to wash up and walks him home. Prompted by his mother, Michael later visits the woman to thank her and is drawn into a love affair with her: ''She felt me looking at her. As she was reaching for the other stocking, she paused, turned towards the door, and looked straight at me. I can't describe what kind of look it was—surprised, skeptical, knowing, reproachful. I turned red. For a fraction of a second I stood there, face burning. Then I couldn't take it any more. I fled out of the apartment, down the stairs, and into the street.''

Soon a routine develops that consists of a ritual of reading aloud (Michael reads to Hanna, at her request), taking showers, and making love. After a moment that confronts Michael with his own ambivalence regarding his loyalty to Hanna, she disappears, and Michael is overcome with guilt and loss: ''But even worse than my physical desire [for Hanna] was my sense of guilt. Why hadn't I jumped up immediately when she stood there and run to her! This one moment summed up all my halfheartedness of the past months, which had produced my denial of her, and my betrayal.''

The novel's second part begins with Michael describing the emotional aftermath of his relationship with Hanna and his subsequent inability to commit to anyone or anything possibly important enough to lose. Later, Michael is studying law and his professor asks a seminar group to attend one of the belated Nazi war crime trials. Five former concentration camp guards are on trial, and to Michael's surprise, Hanna is amongst them. During the trial it becomes clear that Hanna has a secret that is, to her, more shameful than murder, something she could use in her self-defense to invalidate some of the charges but that she chooses not to divulge. Belatedly, Michael understands: "Hanna could neither read nor write. That was why she had had people [that is, selected camp inmates and, later, him] read to her . . . That was why she had admitted to writing the report [about the crime in question during the trial] in order to escape a confrontation with an expert.'' She is sentenced to life in prison.

The third part chronicles Michael's increasing emotional numbness, which ruins his marriage—he had not told his wife about Hanna, and his continued feelings for her imprison him. Now a professor of legal history, Michael researches the question of law in the Third Reich and comes to appreciate how the German present is pregnant with the past, "the legacy of the past which brands us and with which we must live." He also suffers from insomnia and begins to read his favorite books aloud into a tape recorder, starting with the *Odyssey,* in which "Odysseus does not return home to stay, but to set off again." He sends these tapes to Hanna in prison and thus resumes the old bond between the two of them. After Hanna is paroled and Michael attempts to help her reenter society, Hanna commits suicide. Michael visits her cell, where he notices numerous books about the Holocaust (Hanna has by now learned to read), and is given a note asking him to give Hanna's life savings to one of the two survivors of the killings examined in the trial. Michael visits the survivor who rejects the intended gesture of atonement.

The Reader is, in a sense, a novel of confession. Michael admits to an entanglement with an individual from the German past and plumbs his moral entanglement, as well as Hanna's culpability. The novel thus enacts the relationship of the postwar Germans to the reality of the Nazi era, which, under a thin veneer of quotidian normalcy, continues to exert its poisonous influence.

Like much of his generation, Michael, as a law student, insists on holding the generation of his parents responsible. When confronted with the reality of seeing his erstwhile lover in the dock, however, his theoretically based moral principles seem to waver. The novel seems to argue that the central mystery of the love affair—Michael reading to Hanna—and Hanna's guilt are rooted in the same cause: her illiteracy.

One of the text's central interpretive cruxes lies in the difference between explaining the root causes of an action and the potential use of this explanation for exculpatory purposes. In other words, is Hanna's handicap a sufficient explanation for her wartime cruelties and could it serve to vitiate the

importance of abstract moral principles when judging Hanna's behavior? Given that once Hanna has learned to read she delves into literature of the Holocaust, the novel implies a causal link between literacy and moral agency. This argument seems to detract from the otherwise deft exploration of the concepts of crime and punishment and the unflinching examination of the relationship later generations have with their history's legacy. Any serious discussion about the responsible transmission of communal memory is potentially compromised by a rhetoric that qualifies moral concepts such as individual responsibility by reference to particular human qualities whose existence is not sufficient to invalidate those moral categories.

—Stefan Gunther

A READING OF ASHES: POEMS (Odczytanie popiołów)
Poems by Jerzy Ficowski, 1981

A Reading of Ashes: Poems (Odczytanie popiołów), which was first published in London (1979) and then reprinted in Warsaw (1983), with an English translation published in 1981, is in its entirety devoted to the Holocaust experience. After many years Ficowski takes up the issue of the crime committed on the Jewish people, particularly emphasizing the need for compassion, the ethical precept of perpetuating the sufferings, the issues of faithful memories, and the protest against lies and against the deliberate concealment of the tragedy. In *A Reading of Ashes* the author tries to reconcile three different approaches to the problem: the authentic documents in the form of excerpts from books quoted in extenso, voices, and testimonies, the personal experience taking the form of lyrical tales, and the rich language of images, metaphors, and rhetoric figures. Very moving is the force of the facts that cannot be replaced with a poetic comment. The impression of veracity is achieved through the exposed connection between the childhood biography and the Holocaust history. On the other hand, the high quality art of poetry does not serve the purpose of presenting artistic proficiency. It precisely expresses the truth, reveals inhuman cruelty, diversifies the spectrum of psychical perceptions, and, through a number of literary and cultural references, gives universal significance to the described facts.

In Ficowski's collection the obligation of remembrance expresses a paradox, since the speaker wishes his testimony to "be on time even if late." History is a closed chapter. The Shoah cannot be reversed. The rescuing power of the word can also be doubted. And yet the moving study of emptiness, as well as of moping about the nonexistent cemeteries, has a deep moral sense. In *A Reading of Ashes* the motif of absence is symmetrical to the oblivion motif. The lack of traces of the murdered and the silence over their fate are combined into one through the images of a desert (''Co jest'' [''What Is There'']; ''List do Marc Chagalla'' [''A Letter to Marc Chagall'']), wind and air (''Do Jeruszalaim'' [''To Jerushalaim'']; ''Opłakiwanie'' [''Mourning'']; ''Diagnozy'' [''Diagnoses'']), and snow and ashes (''Wniebowzięcie Miriam z ulicy zima 1942'' [''Assumption of Miriam of the Street Winter 1942'']; ''5.VIII.1942''). Since people tend to forget too quickly, nature mourns the murdered nation: ''a stone says the Kaddish'' (''Zbiegowisko kamieni'' [''A Gathering of Stones'']). In the discussed volume empathy is particularly significant. It is the understanding of psychical experience—of pain, fear, and humiliation—but also the penetration into the nature of physical experience of the body. In a series of suggestive images Ficowski describes the history of the people who ''were allowed to be just a little'' (''A Letter to Marc Chagall''). The reduction of the bodily existence means not only a live death (''Epitafium żywcem zmarłego'' [''An Epitaph for the Dead Alive'']) but also an awakening to the new existence outside the horror of the ghetto (''Twoje matki obie'' [''Your Both Mothers'']). The poet is particularly sensitive to the sufferings of the Holocaust children. Their behavior and words build up an unquestioned testimony of the truth and the accusation of an innocent victim reveals the crime in its utmost form. (''5.VIII.1942''; ''Sześcioletnia z getta zebrząca na Smolnej 1942 roku'' [''A Six-Year-Old from the Ghetto Begging in Ul. Smolna in 1942'']; ''Siedem słów'' [''Seven Words'']). Parallel to the stories of people the drama of spiritual and material culture develops. There is no one to read the holy words of the Scriptures, and Jehovah will no longer speak from the books that are now dead and abandoned (''Pismo umarłego cmentarza'' [''The Writing of a Dead Cemetery'']; ''Księga'' [''A Book'']). In Ficowski's poetry the moral judgment of the desensitized conscience of the Poles and of their inglorious behaviors is extended beyond the time of the war.

In *A Reading of Ashes* there are a number of references to the lamentations of the Old Testament prophets as well as to religion and images of Jewish culture. In his wailing the poet resorts to the traditions of such genres as an epitaph, a threnody, and an elegy. Ficowski's subtle imagination draws inspiration from Chagall's painting, though seeing graves in the air reveals some affinities to **Henryk Grynberg**'s poetry. In ''Opłakiwanie'' (''Mourning'') he conducts a dialogue with **Czeslaw Milosz**'s ''Campo di Fiore.'' In the poem entitled ''Diagnoses'' he uses a cryptic quotation from Wislawa Szymborska's poem ''Jeszcze'' (''Still''). And although the author of *A Reading of Ashes* does not epitomize the poetic language of that Polish Nobel Prize winner, we can point to their common artistic property, which involves conceptualism, paradoxes, and the difficult-to-translate language games consisting in the transformation of set phrases.

—Wojciech Ligęza

THE REAWAKENING (La tregua)
Memoir by Primo Levi, 1963

First published in 1963 as *La tregua* (*The Truce*, 1965), *The Reawakening* is the second of Primo Levi's books. In it Levi continues the largely narrative mode, with analysis and comment interwoven, that he had established in his first work of witness, *Survival in Auschwitz*. The book treats the issues that arose out of his experiences from January 1945, when the Russians liberated the camp, to his arrival home in Torino on 19 October 1946. As in his earlier book, he is (to use his own phrase) ''author-protagonist.''

The title of the book was a shift on the eve of publication; he had initially proposed ''High Wind'' as the title. The present form has a threefold valence. The first of these indicates the special nature of this period in his life: a sort of lull, marked by the stirrings of new life, between the terrible pressures of the camp and the complex process of reintegration into the life of home and the everyday from which he had been absent so long. To that home context he returned altered, inhabited by memories of an experience that others often did not wish to hear and about which it was almost impossible to communicate in any case. The second valence is more general. The war and the camps constituted precisely open war. The ending of the armed conflict and the liberation of the camps marked the entry, as he saw it, not into permanent peace and the cessation of the sort of hatreds and prejudices that anti-Semitism represents but into a period of uneasy and difficult truce, with the danger of the resumption of open conflict at any time. That is, in part, the significance of the following lines from the poem he wrote as an epigraph to this book; *wstawac* (get up) was the command in Polish used in Auschwitz.

> Now we have found home again,
> Our stomach is full,
> We have stopped recounting the experience.
> It is time. Soon we will hear again
> The command in a foreign tongue:
> ''Wstawac.''

The third, and most general, valence, Levi himself commented, is the fact that death is already implicit in life: that all of us will hear the summons into death at some moment. Until then we live in a period of truce.

As with *Survival in Auschwitz* the book in its present form is divided into 17 chapters. Though they follow the chronology of the journey, they are given titles that indicate persons or events thematically significant, or even the direction of the journey, or the stage on the way home reached at any point. The narrative and its interwoven analysis and commentary are at times somber, while at other times lightened by Levi's characteristic wit and self-deprecating irony.

A single image can often focus a whole issue and remain fixed in the mind and sensibilities. For example, he reports that as he left Auschwitz, ill, taken out on a horse cart, he saw for the last time "the roll-call square where the gallows and the gigantic Christmas tree still towered side by side." In an especially moving instance, he sets the case of three children side by side. He intends his testimony, as with his mention of all figures from Auschwitz, to give evidence that they lived. But more, these three show with great force and precision the impact of Auschwitz on human communication. Hurbinek, a child of Auschwitz, dies at perhaps three years of age, without ever being taught language, without ever being able therefore "to enter the world of men." Peter Pavel, about five years old, trusting no adult, lives furtively, speaking only among other children languages that Levi reports he could not understand. The third, Kleine Kiepura, about 13 years old and kept as a sexual plaything by one of the *kapos,* speaks a stream of vituperation against Jews—and therefore against himself—having absorbed the prejudices of his protector. A Greek, whose vision of life, all life, is as a sort of war, is contrasted with Cesare, a Roman who can find game anywhere.

Levi introduces in this book a theme he will develop elsewhere, notably in *The Monkey's Wrench:* the humanizing function of significant work and of the marketplace. He reports that in fact he was first reconciled again to life by the bargaining he observed after liberation—and in which he participated—in a Polish marketplace. What is represented in that bargaining is for him free communication. Human transactions about value are determined through the agreement of both parties, with the communication itself having something of the nature of a game. The working of the market among the slaves in Auschwitz, and of the discourse of command there, Levi intends to be still in the readers' minds as, by contrast, the discourse of the world of the lords of death.

Reference to the way in which one image system works will illustrate something of the narratorial and analytic power evident in this work. In *Survival in Auschwitz* Levi reports on the shower and the shaving off of all hair forced on those who were to be enrolled in camp rather than being sent immediately to the gas. A second description of a bath—marked by reference to that first one—is given at the beginning of *The Reawakening,* a bath given by the Russian liberators of the camp. Finally, just as he is nearing Italy, he and the others with him are given a third bath—and delousing with DDT—by Americans. These accounts of the three baths in their concise detail constitute acute analysis of the national cultures of those administering them and help to tie together the large narrative of his experience.

Reference to one more image or episode from the work will illustrate Levi's profound probing of the challenges to communication, to sharing one another's experiences. As his train neared Italy, Levi observed outside the window a vehicle he had never before seen—a jeep. A black American was driving it; inside were other soldiers. One of them shouted in Neapolitan dialect, "You're going home, you bums." Levi's point is clear on reflection: The American soldiers, in their vehicle

strange to him but familiar to them, had no notion of what those on the train had suffered. But how much could those on the train hearing those words know too of the experience of those soldiers, who had made their way up from southern Italy (the Neapolitan dialect), on a continent whose languages, land, and ways were unknown to them? And what did they know of the life of an American black man, the descendant of slaves, and of his experience in the war? The experiences of those on the train and in the jeep are not equivalent, but they are not unrelated, and the challenge to mutual understanding one knows Levi is surely suggesting is vast.

—Ralph G. Williams

THE RESISTIBLE RISE OF ARTURO UI (Der aufhaltsame Aufstieg des Arturo Ui)
Play by Bertolt Brecht, 1957

In March 1941 Bertolt Brecht and his family were refugees in Helsinki, Finland, anxiously waiting to depart for the United States; the Nazi army, which had just invaded Denmark and Norway, seemed all but invincible. In this atmosphere of desperate suspense, Brecht drafted a new parable play, a "gangster-history," meant for the American stage as a warning against the dangers of fascism. In part, his decision to frame the rise of the upstart Adolf Hitler as the story of Al Capone in Prohibition-era Chicago was an attempt to provide a milieu familiar to American audiences. Brecht intended "to render ridiculous the great political criminals, alive or dead" and "to destroy the common and dangerous respect for the great killers." Aided by his son Stefan and his assistant Margaret Steffin, Brecht completed *Arturo Ui* in early April 1941; the play was published in 1957 and appeared in English translation in *Collected Plays 6, ii,* in 1976.

When the curtain rises, the city is reeling from an economic downturn. There is violence in the streets. Ui (Hitler), a cheap hoodlum, approaches the members of the Cauliflower Trust (Junkers and industrialists) and offers to boost sales because "shopkeepers would rather buy cauliflower than coffins." Instead, the trust decides to make use of the impeccable reputation of the ward leader Dogsborough (Paul von Hindenburg) and reinvigorate its enterprise with a municipal loan designated officially for the construction of harbor works. The trust entices Dogsborough to acquire the majority of stock in a shipping company and to accept a country estate as a "gift." Once Dogsborough has secured the loan, Ui smells an opportunity. Threatening to expose the venerable politician, he becomes the protector of the racket. Ui and his henchmen—the devilish florist Givola (Joseph Goebbels), the wily populist Giri (Hermann Göring), and the brutish Roma (Ernst Röhm)—thus join the ranks of the major players. In order to succeed in the public arena, Ui takes lessons in speech and demeanor from an actor. Under the pretext of restoring order, he imposes a reign of terror on the small vegetable merchants (petty bourgeoisie). A man who refuses to pay for protection finds his warehouse in flames. The ensuing trial reveals that judge and prosecutors have been bought. In spite of the efforts of a brilliant defender (Georgi Dimitrov), an unemployed drifter (Marinus van der Lubbe) is convicted. Once in power, the members of Ui's gang begin to quarrel. Roma wants to extend the terror to the large businesses, including the Cauliflower Trust, but Ui plans to consolidate his power in collusion with big business, not against it. He has set his sights on the city of Cicero (Austria), where the newspaperman Dullfleet (Engelbert Dollfuss) controls the vegetable trade and agitates against Ui. Ruthlessly, Ui pursues his goals, first by having Roma and his group murdered, then by wooing Dullfleet's wife, Betty, and by threatening Dullfleet. Even though Dullfleet agrees to collaborate, Ui has him assassinated and takes over Cicero. In the final scene, Ui declares, in front of a subdued crowd of vegetable merchants from both cities, that Dogsborough has named him heir in a rueful will. He secures his own election by having dissenters shot and zealously presents his designs for armament and expansion.

Arturo Ui is a brash montage that oscillates between the parabolic simplicity of unmasking historical events and a complex and ostentatious artificiality. The play's relation to historical reality is reductive and allusive rather than representative. In 17 short scenes Brecht traces Hitler's rise to prominence during the depression and the crumbling Weimar Republic (1929–1933); the finance scandal involving Reich Pres. Paul von Hindenburg, which Hitler helped suppress (1933); the Reichstag fire (February 1933); the arson trial (September to December 1933); the elimination of the rogue paramilitary organization SA (Sturm-Abteilung) and its leader Ernst Röhm (June 1934); the murder of the Austrian Chancellor Engelbert Dollfuss (July 1934); and the annexation of Austria (March 1938). Those who view the play as an allegory of Hitler's rise to power have noted that Brecht falsified the historical record by, for example, allowing Dullfleet to appear as an honorable anti-fascist and by casting Roma in the role of a martyr. The twofold plot of gangsters and Nazis has also come under attack as an inadequate analytical tool for grasping the phenomenon of National Socialism. Brecht's Marxist focus on the hidden alliance between politicians, industrialists, and gangsters prevents him from addressing other aspects of Nazism, such as its popularity or its anti-Semitic policies. The play may therefore be viewed as exemplary of a trend discernible in Brecht's oeuvre in general: an evasion of race as a crucial category in the legitimation and implementation of the Nazi genocide. On the other hand, Brecht employs a number of alienation techniques (parody, satire, quotations from popular culture and from scripture, use of formal elements of the classical tragedy) that foster an estranged view of fascism and make visible the discrepancies between aesthetic form and cheap content. The audience is led to contrast the historical

grandeur and the messianic posturing of Hitler with his corrupt and murderous acts.

—Cornelius Partsch

THE RETREAT (Ha 'pisgah)
Novel by Aharon Appelfeld, 1982

Aharon Appelfeld's novel *The Retreat,* which appeared in English in 1984, was originally published in Hebrew as *Ha'pisgah* ("The Summit") in 1982. The fourth Appelfeld novel to be published in English, it is an ironic parable about death, the death of the illusion that pre-Anschluss and pre-war Jews will remedy their defects, "two hundred defects—no small number in relation to one human being," by taking on Gentile values and habits. The retreat itself is an isolated mountain hotel used for this single purpose. It fails, of course, and the residents who have not died or left for home await their fate with passive resignation.

Located near Vienna, the retreat is nearly inaccessible, reminiscent of Franz Kafka's castle. Not all of the residents choose to live there; some are forced to do so by circumstances. The aging, penniless actress Lotte Schloss, for example, has no choice because she cannot live with her daughter, Julia, who is married to a Gentile Austrian farmer of no culture or sensitivity. As in other Appelfeld stories that portray Gentile men who marry Jewish girls from assimilated families, this boor beats Lotte's daughter, who passively endures her life. Painfully aware that she was fired from the acting company because she was Jewish and that her three grandsons will, like their father, despise her, Lotte unwillingly journeys to the retreat where Jews, though vulgar and commonplace, are at least generous. Others have been lured to the retreat by Balaban, its founder, who promised them a life of physical activity—running, calisthenics, swimming, horseback riding—lessons in shedding their Jewish accents, indigestible diet, and ugly mannerisms. He promised the hotel guests that he would, as a result of this non-Jewish regimen, "turn the sickly members of his race into a healthy breed." Indeed, Herbert Zuntz, a renowned journalist who was fired because he was Jewish, tells Lotte that he is now taller because his back is straighter and that his nerves are calmer; he has managed to rid himself of a major Jewish defect: weak nerves. Balaban's experiment does not last, however. The residents go back to their old ways and grow flabby; when one of them, Isadora, commits suicide, Lotte reads Rilke at the graveside. Balaban and others die, and the remaining residents appear to begin to die. They grow as bleak as the landscape, but as Appelfeld has said elsewhere, Jews are by nature optimists. Thus, the residents do not surrender their illusions that they will become cultured Viennese if they continue Balaban's process.

The Retreat belies its quiet sparseness. Thematically similar to *Badenheim 1939* but much darker, Appelfeld's controlled narrative is deceptively simple and apolitical. The characters are desperate, urbane Europeans who delude themselves into believing that they are at blame because, says Engel, one of the residents, "Anything is possible, All you need is the will, and that we have in full measure." They have enough will, they are convinced, to overcome their "decayed inheritance," the reason another resident offers for his conversion. Like many other works by Appelfeld, *The Retreat* is a profound confrontation with alienation from the self, the embarrassment of having been born Jewish, and the memory of one's roots. The Appelfeld critic Gila Ramras-Rauch has interpreted Balaban's project as one of physical and spiritual suicide. For example, the mountaintop hotel, originally a monastery, was organized as a vehicle to accomplish the suicide of Jewish memory and thereby the elimination of the "defective" Jew, or inevitably the physical suicide of a people. Yet at the end, when the hotel is impoverished and the men are assaulted when they venture into town to sell the residents' jewels, clothes, and other material items, the community draws closer, and "they helped one another. If a man fell or was beaten he was not abandoned."

—Myrna Goldenberg

RETURN TO AUSCHWITZ: THE REMARKABLE STORY OF A GIRL WHO SURVIVED THE HOLOCAUST
Memoir by Kitty Hart, 1981

Return to Auschwitz (1981) was written in association with the prize-winning television documentary "Return to Auschwitz" (1979; also known as "Kitty—Return to Auschwitz). Like many Holocaust victims, Kitty Hart has retold her story. Much of the narrative is the same—in outline—as her previous account *I Am Alive!* (1961). There are, however, three general changes.

The first difference is that this account also tells of Hart's arrival and settling in England. After meeting Hart and her mother at Dover, her uncle says, "Before we go off to Birmingham, there's one thing I must make quite clear. On no account are you to talk about any of the things that have happened to you. Not in my house, I don't want my girls to know. And I don't want to know." When asked about the odd marks on her arm ("a laundry mark? . . . a boyfriend's number?"), she sometimes answers that it is her concentration camp number, and the "reaction was an awkward silence, as if I had said something terribly ill mannered." These stories set the tone for her immediate postwar experiences. After all that she has endured and now "in the light at the end of the tunnel," she is nearly overcome by despair and loneliness. However,

with the help of a psychiatrist, who thought "there was nothing wrong with me, but a lot wrong with the other people concerned," and Dr. Brailsford, a radiographer who "adopted" and helped her, she begins training as a nurse and radiographer. In March 1949 Hart marries Ralph, who had escaped from Germany as a boy of 13 in 1939.

The second difference between the two accounts is the level of detail. *Return to Auschwitz* is more detailed and grimmer throughout than *I Am Alive!* From prewar Poland and its anti-Semitism to the horrors of the camps, this book covers the events more closely than the earlier, more straightforward narrative. If her first book was, to some extent, written for her sons as children, this is written for adults. It supplements her experiences with what has been learnt since 1945 and explores her memories in greater depth.

The third difference is that *Return to Auschwitz* is more reflective. For example, Hart discusses how she and her husband established their business, and how, while some firms were fair to deal with, others "profit from slave labour. The more prosperous they are, the more the demand from those who do the real creative work, and for a smaller fee. Just as the SS would demand so many gold rings from the ghetto inhabitants . . . so there are great organisation in the so-called free world demanding your souls and life-blood for the most meagre rations." She sees "the features and routines" of Auschwitz everywhere. "How do men get and hold the most coveted jobs in big firms? By starting as 'trusties' . . . from Unterkapo to Kapo to Oberkapo. . . to camp executive and even higher if you're ruthless enough. You may even be able to eat with the SS and use their washroom if you're truly dedicated to the cause." She is equally candid about herself as well. In *I Am Alive!* she describes how she didn't stab some Germans just after liberation: "If . . . I had met one of those SS men while the dagger was still in my hand, would I have used it? I'm pretty sure I would. And I'd have had no guilty conscience afterwards." Likewise, her candour covers more positive things: the bonds of friendship in Auschwitz were "strong . . . more direct and more honest." She writes that "somehow those friends are still with me in spirit. If I do anything worthwhile, it's with their support."

On the last page Hart writes, "It has been said that to understand all is to forgive all. Perhaps one reason why the Nazis can never be forgiven is that their obsessive evil can never be understood."

—Robert Eaglestone

ROSA
Short Story by Cynthia Ozick, 1983

Cynthia Ozick's "Rosa" (1983) picks up the narrative of "The Shawl" approximately 30 years later. Both stories have been published together under the title *The Shawl* (1989). Stylistically "Rosa" represents a marked divergence from the earlier text. Whereas "The Shawl" is a compact, largely impressionistic description of a single traumatic experience, "Rosa" is a straightforward narrative that gradually builds to its denouement. "Rosa" is also written in the comic mode that recalls much of Ozick's other fiction. This stylistic distinction reinforces the ontological distinction between the stories' environments: the first takes place in a concentration camp, the second in Miami. By choosing an indirect, figurative style for the first story and a more direct, narrative style for the second, Ozick implies that different representational modes are necessary to describe experiences during the Holocaust and after.

"Rosa" centers on the character of Rosa Lublin, a concentration camp survivor who was forced to observe the murder of her infant daughter. Rosa is now a "madwoman and a scavenger" living in a community of retired Jews in Miami, where she has recently moved after smashing up her antique store in New York. Contemptuous of the Yiddish-speaking old socialists and idealists that surround her, she spends her days as a recluse. Her one pastime involves writing letters in "the most excellent literary Polish" to an imaginary correspondent: her daughter Magda, who was killed as an infant by the Nazis. Rosa variously imagines Magda as a professor of Greek history at Columbia, as a successful doctor living in the suburbs, or as an unblemished girl at 16. She also eagerly awaits a package from her niece Stella containing Magda's shawl, a token from the past Rosa has come to worship (according to Stella) like a religious relic. But Rosa's world of fantasy, in which she seems willfully to have enclosed herself, is an insufficient bulwark against all intruders. During a visit to the laundromat, she is approached by Persky, a flirtatious older man who is determined to bring Rosa back to the world of the living.

Rosa and Persky represent radically divergent forms of Jewish identity. She epitomizes the European Jew who worships the symbols of Western high culture while reviling anything that smacks of old-world Jewishness. She proudly recalls that her father did not have "a particle of ghetto left in him, not a grain of rot." As for Persky, he reads a Yiddish newspaper and playfully jabs at Rosa like a Borscht Belt comic. Having imagined herself "a future Marie Curie," Rosa is humiliated to find herself in America where she is routinely associated with unspectacular Jewish immigrants like Persky. When Persky points out that they are both from Warsaw, Rosa is quick to correct him: "My Warsaw is not your Warsaw." Her lofty self-conception leaves no room for his *heymish,* or old-world Jewishness.

The story develops into a quest narrative. Rosa realizes that a pair of underwear is missing from her laundry bag and, convinced that she has been robbed (perhaps by Persky), she searches for them along Miami's beachfront. Her futile quest for a lost object represents her own existential situation. Accordingly the gates around private beaches appear to her as barbed wire. Stumbling upon gay lovers in the sand and wandering through a palatial hotel, Rosa imagines she is stuck in Sodom. The turning point in the story occurs when she discovers, the next day in her apartment, her missing underwear curled inside a towel. After this discovery her first act is to reconnect her telephone, a gesture that signals a triumph (at least for the time being) over her self-imposed exile from the world. It seems she has glimpsed the folly at the root of her paranoia. Even Magda's shawl, which arrives and prompts one last epistolary outburst, begins to dim in significance. "And Magda! Already she was turning away." When the phone rings announcing a visit from Persky, Rosa decides to welcome him in.

Thus, according to one reading, "Rosa" stages the return to human relations of a woman who has become trapped in her own mourning. But while Persky's generous sociability might seem the antidote to Rosa's despair and cultural elitism, the story resists simply casting Rosa as victim and Persky as savior. Persky, it turns out, has a wife in a mental hospital, which, as he callously relates, "don't cost me peanuts." He also tells Rosa about her own situation that "sometimes a little forgetting is necessary." In her fidelity to the past, Rosa represents a witness, a bearer of historical memory in a world of amnesiacs. Her imaginative re-creation of Magda is a triumph as well as a delusion, and the story's conclusion is tentative enough to imply that Rosa has not completely abandoned her commitment to Magda and the lost world she represents.

—Julian Levinson

THE ROYAL GAME (Schachnovelle)
Novella by Stefan Zweig, 1944

The psychological novella *The Royal Game* (1944; *Schachnovelle,* 1942) is of special importance within Stefan Zweig's oeuvre since it was his last work, written shortly before his suicide in 1942 and published posthumously in Buenos Aires in the same year. The action takes place on an ocean liner bound for South America. The author-narrator, who functions as listener, commentator, and onlooker, is informed by Dr. B. that Mirko Czentovic, the chess world champion, is also onboard. Dr. B. is persuaded to play against the world champion. He wins the first game but gives up the second one, being unnerved by the cold and brutal strategy of his opponent.

Zweig described in this novella the quite different biographies of these two chess "monomaniacs." Dr. B. is a highly intelligent cultured man, a humanist in love with literature and philosophy, with a strong imagination. He comes from a family that for generations represented the business of the Roman Curia and had a close and personal relationship with the Austrian emperor. He has acquired his expertise in chess while incarcerated by the Gestapo in an isolated hotel room, during which time he learned and memorized the moves of the chess masters from a chess book he had stolen from his guard's pocket. He plays against himself and develops a kind of "artificial schizophrenia." This mental activity, however, helped him to sustain the torture of the infrequent interviews and his isolation. He had never played with another person and is, therefore, after some reluctance, persuaded to enter into a match with the world champion.

The champion, on the other hand, is the opposite of Dr. B. He plays with technical perfection, but mechanically, without imagination. He is unable to play "blind" like his opponent. His main interest in playing is for money, which is not too surprising if one considers Czentovic's peasant background. He keeps apart from intellectuals in fear that they might see through him, since he has hardly mastered the art of reading and writing. The difference between these two men is revealed in their manner of playing chess: "For in the course of the game the intellectual contrast between the two opponents became more and more physically apparent in their manner. Czentovic, the man of routine, remained as immovably solid as a rock the whole time, his eyes fixed unwaveringly on the board. Thinking seemed almost to cause him actual physical effort, as though he had to engage all his senses with the utmost concentration. Dr. B., on the other hand, was completely relaxed and unconstrained . . . he was physically relaxed and chatted to us during the early pauses, explaining the moves." This changes during the second game when Czentovic uses psychological terror against his opponent, a terror that to Dr. B. is reminiscent of the terrors during his incarceration. He grows more and more nervous and impatient while the champion, noticing the irritation in Dr. B., slows the speed of his moves. Dr. B. finally breaks down and gives up.

This novella is, just like other masterworks, subject to a variety of interpretations. Donald Daviau and Harvey Dunkle come to the conclusion that "[a]lthough Dr. B. is ostensibly defeated on the field of battle, he is preserved for the world to keep the humanistic attitude alive." Another approach is to interpret the novella along political lines, with Dr. B. standing for the humanist and Czentovic being the representative of the dictatorial power in the Third Reich, or as Joseph Strelka has called him, a "Miniature-Hitler." Although Dr. B. cannot be identified with its author, there exist many similarities: both men were humanists and both were interested in chess; Zweig also purchased a chess book and played frequently. This last interpretation would point to the conclusion that Zweig gave up in his struggle for a revitalization of humanistic values admitting the ineffectiveness of thought when confronted with brutal reality.

—Gerd K. Schneider

RUE ORDENER, RUE LABAT
Memoir by Sarah Kofman, 1994

Sarah Kofman's memoir *Rue Ordener, Rue Labat,* originally published in French in 1994 and in English translation under the same title in 1996, is an account of the effect on her life of the deportation of her father, a Parisian rabbi ("maybe all my books have been detours required to bring me to write about 'that,'" she says at the start of the memoir), and on her subsequent experiences as a Jewish girl in hiding in Paris during the war, torn between loyalties to her Jewish mother and to the Gentile woman who hides them.

Kofman describes her family life and upbringing in their house on the Rue Ordener: rigorously observing kosher rules, her father's duties, and the family's religious activities. As with so many memoirs, she describes the gradually worsening situation during the occupation of France: anti-Semitism in schools, roundups, yellow stars. Her parents try to send the young Sarah away to the country, but she cries inconsolably when separated from her mother and refuses to eat nonkosher food. On 16 July 1942, despite her mother's attempts to prevent it, her father is taken away, sent to the transit camp and Drancy and finally to Auschwitz: "One day when he refused to work, a Jewish-butcher-turned-Kapo (on returning from the death camp he reopened his shop on the Rue des Rosiers) supposedly beat him to the ground with a pickaxe and buried him alive."

After her father's deportation Kofman and her mother hide at various addresses in Paris. Their apartment is searched by the Gestapo and sealed (and was not returned to them after the war). They end up with a "lady" on the Rue Labat. The mother hides in one room, and the woman, Mémé, begins to treat the young Sarah as her own daughter. This is the central dynamic of Kofman's short memoir: the tension between her Jewish self (summed up by the metaphor of the Rue Ordener) and a developing non-Jewish self (Rue Labat). Mémé changes Sarah's diet and hairstyle, makes her new clothes, and gives her books to read. On "Mother's Day" Sarah buys cards for both her mother and Mémé. Although Mémé saves the Kofmans, she is not without anti-Semitic prejudices, which she teaches to Sarah. Trapped by a bombing raid away from home, Mémé and Sarah stay in a hotel overnight: "My mother was waiting, sick with worry, certain we'd been arrested . . . I had completely forgotten her. I was quite simply happy."

After the liberation her mother tires to "recapture" Sarah by taking her far away from the Rue Labat. Sarah escapes and returns to the "woman I now loved more than my mother." Her mother takes her back and beats her. Mémé goes to the law, and a Free French tribunal awards her custody of the child. Sarah's mother, however, takes her child back with force. "Deep down," she writes, "I was relieved."

As Sarah grows up, she is able to visit Mémé occasionally, usually with a friend, and she reestablishes her links to Judaism. Two motifs surfacing at the end of the book reflect her experience of having "two mothers." The first is Leonardo da Vinci's *Madonna and Child with St. Anne.* Freud explains the oddities of the picture by showing how it reflects the experience of the young Leonardo, torn from his real mother at five and brought up by his stepmother. The second is Alfred Hitchcock's film *The Lady Vanishes,* in which the "good maternal face of the old lady" is replaced by "a horribly hard, shifty face" of the impostor.

Similar in a way to **Saul Friedländer**'s memoir *When Memory Comes,* Kofman's account describes the trauma not just of her father's deportation but also of the difficult process of coming to terms with a concealed identity and all this implies.

—Robert Eaglestone

S

SCHINDLER'S LIST
Novel by Thomas Keneally, 1982

As the author of numerous historical novels, Thomas Keneally has been at once daring in what he imagines of characters' motives and rhetoric and conservative in his respect for his sources. The provenance of his novel *Schindler's List* (first titled *Schindler's Ark,* 1982) was the chance testimony of one of the so-called *Schindlerjuden,* a group of Jewish prisoners of the Nazis who were saved from the Holocaust. Keneally heard the story at the Los Angeles luggage store of Leopold Pfefferberg. From his account Keneally would reimagine a short period in the life, if never fully attempt to comprehend the motives, of the womanizer, drinker, and dandy, the indulgent libertine Oskar Schindler. This businessman and factory owner would elect—at the risk of his own life—to save from destruction his Jewish employees at Zablocie, in Poland. As a result of his perilous exertions, more than 1,000 of them survived World War II.

Part of Schindler's fascination for Keneally was this uncompelled, reckless, unquestioning generosity of spirit. Nothing in Schindler's past had anticipated or could explain what would "obsess, imperil and exalt him." Nothing in what the novelist depicts of Schindler reveals, retrospectively, the forces that energized him. Here is a rare instance of good works in action, along with the challenge to art that this represents. (As Keneally wryly remarked, "Fatal human malice is the staple of narrative.") Although alert to danger, Schindler was equally indifferent to self-justification, publicity, or posterity. As for the Schindler survivors, in Keneally's interpretation "the sum of his motives" would remain imponderable, their rescue a blessing hardly possible to credit.

Inspired initially by the astonishing gift of the Pfefferberg story, Keneally would interview 50 of those whom Schindler had protected, in Argentina, Australia, Austria, Brazil, Israel, West Germany, and the United States. In company with Pfefferberg he traveled to the forced labor camp at Plaskow, which had been commanded by the homicidal SS officer Amon Goeth, to Oskar Schindler's enamel factory in Zablocie, and to Auschwitz. This was the footslogging research of a historian whose imagination would be stirred by actual sites of horror—and hope. Yet as Keneally wrote in the author's note to *Schindler's List,* while "I have attempted to avoid all fiction . . . since fiction would debase the record," nonetheless he had to relate this true story by means of fictional techniques, by practicing "the only craft to which I can lay claim." Herein, incidentally, was the nub of the controversy over the award of the prestigious Booker Prize for fiction to *Schindler's List.*

At key moments in the novel Keneally appears to renounce or at least to qualify his claims. Early on he states bluntly that this is "the story of the pragmatic triumph of good over evil, a triumph in eminently measurable, statistical, unsubtle terms." It is as if an inventory of the saved will of itself generate wonder. Nowhere near so evident, as argued above, is the driving force for Schindler. Indeed at times the author seems amazed at the events that Schindler set in train and on which so scrupulously he based his narrative. Later in the book, as Keneally leads readers down the "Kafkaesque corridors" of the SS complex in Kraków, we are given the names of the departments. Revulsion arises from this dutiful documentation rather than the flourishes of art: "the SS Main Office, the headquarters of the Order Police . . . Jewish Affairs . . . Peace and Resettlement . . . the Reichskommisariat for the Strengthening of Germandom." By means of an antistyle, the bureaucratic complement of an evil ideology is starkly displayed.

Many of Keneally's characters live in terrible jeopardy. In *Schindler's List* the Kraków Jewry are one of the most desperate groups of them. They cling, deludedly, "to the idea of the ghetto as a small but permanent realm." Those who survive its destruction and are taken into Schindler's factory live an oxymoron. Their life, Keneally writes, is one of "fragile permanence." Schindler's miracle, or conjuring act, is to sustain that condition long enough to enable these people to last until the end of the war. For those who survive, the list of the names of those whom Schindler would attempt to save "is an absolute good. The list is life. All around its cramped margins is the gulf." The abysmal terror, the paralyzing uncertainty of their plight, is never dissembled, nor does Oskar Schindler's near desperate charismatic appeals to the German authorities distract us from it.

For all that he is skeptical of legends and legend making, Keneally's novel (and the Spielberg film based on it) contributed significantly to "the Oskar legend." He cautions that, in the scale of the annihilation of Jews in the Holocaust, "Oskar was only a minor god of rescue." Yet in the telling of the story, Keneally has made us acquainted with numerous individuals whom Oskar saved, with more than "statistics, unsubtle terms." It is a further paradox of Schindler's life, in Keneally's reckoning, that "the peace would never exalt him as had the war." After the war Schindler failed in businesses, moved from country to country, and was supported by some of those whom he had protected. That war and the Holocaust "summoned forth his deeper talents" is a strange and fortunate irony of history. It was also an enduring source of gratitude for those survivors who mourned Oskar Schindler "in every continent" when he died in October 1974.

—Peter Pierce

A SCRAP OF TIME AND OTHER STORIES
(Skrawek czasu)
Short Stories by Ida Fink, 1983

First published in Polish in 1983 and in English in 1987 (revised, 1995), Ida Fink's *A Scrap of Time and Other Stories* is a remarkable and powerful collection of 22 very short stories. The world she conjures up unveils the pitiless, harrowing world of the Holocaust as it unfolded in Nazi-occupied Poland—day by horrifying day. Here some three-and-a-half million Jewish men, women, and children were slaughtered as part of the Third Reich's Final Solution.

Born in Poland in 1921, Fink is herself a survivor of both the ghetto and of years in hiding. Almost all her stories are autobiographical; they are based either on her own experiences or those of people she knew and talked to. The town in the stories, for example, "is always the same town, the garden is our garden." The dog, Ching, who would not betray the family's hiding place, belonged to Fink's real-life family; the three-year-old in "The Key Game," pathetically practicing how to postpone opening the door for the police until after his father was hidden, was in fact the son of Fink's husband. One should not—and perhaps as we may speculate, cannot—make up stories about what happened during the Holocaust. In important ways, it is all unimaginable, inconceivable. One ought to present the Holocaust "in a very authentic manner," she says. "It seems to me that on this theme fantasy is harmful."

This is not to say that she has not used fantasy to make a point, as in the stunningly surrealistic ending to "The Garden That Floated Away." One of the early stories in the collection, it focuses on the time before the mass deportations when Jews were still desperately seeking means of escape. A Jewish doctor "on a warm and peaceful afternoon" in summer, negotiates secretly within the confines of his home office for forged documents that might possibly protect his family. The young narrator sits on the porch steps overlooking two gardens—really the single garden her family has long shared with their non-Jewish friends and neighbors. There is no fence, for they had long ago companionably agreed it "would be an intrusion."

But now, as the narrator overhears their muffled conversation, she realizes that fence or no fence, they are divided: they are in different worlds. The trees on their "Jewish" side are all bare; the family has already eaten the fruit, even when it was green. The neighbors are saying that "we were right to do so, because who knows what would happen to us by winter." Recognizing that "what they were saying was absolutely true," the narrator notes that "the garden of our childhood friend suddenly shuddered, swayed, began to pitch and roll, and slowly, slowly it started to float away, like a huge green ocean liner." Fink uses the garden as an objective correlative, a device whereby an object, a person, event, or situation represents more than itself and thereby elicits an emotional response from the reader. It is Fink's repeated and brilliant use of this device that helps to account for the intensity, economy, and power of her stories. "The Garden That Floated Away" elicits readers' keen disappointment, if not righteous indignation, regarding the sorry role of so many bystanders during the Holocaust, their widespread and ultimate indifference and passivity.

Fink's stories are arranged chronologically within the time frame of the Holocaust years in Poland, beginning with early harassment of Jews to ultimate deportations, disappearances, and death. She never takes us into the world of the camps: we remain outside on the tormented fringes. Later we move into the post-Holocaust period when grief-stricken survivors are obsessively trying to locate their loved ones or at least find out what happened to them. Those who know the worst may nonetheless be driven obsessively to talk about them, even though there are those—like the young girl in "Splinter"—who literally fall asleep when her young boyfriend insists on repeating yet again an account of how his mother, arrested by the Nazis, managed to spirit him away to safety.

Essentially two themes—time and memory—run through this masterful collection; both are introduced in the title story "A Scrap of Time." "I want to talk about a certain time," the narrator-author announces, "not measured in months and years." It is a time she feared had been "crushed and destroyed by regular time." But she tells us, "as I was digging around in the ruins of memory I find it fresh and untouched by forgetfulness." It is the time when people did not talk about days or months but rather about "the first action, or the second, or right before the third." Thus, each of the stories that constitute the collection represents the author's excavation into "the ruins of memory" from which she emerges repeatedly with another incomparable literary resurrection—or restoration—of what has been referred to as "a world that was and is no more." In Fink's remarkable writing, "scraps" of that world are returned to us with such clarity, fidelity, and force as to be—without exception—unforgettable.

—Jacqueline Berke

SCROLL OF AGONY: THE WARSAW DIARY OF CHAIM A. KAPLAN
Diary by Chaim Aron Kaplan, 1965

Chaim Aron Kaplan's Warsaw diary was first published in English in 1965. In 1999 it was edited and translated by Abraham I. Katsh and published in English as *Scroll of Agony: The Warsaw Diary of Chaim A. Kaplan.* Originally written in Hebrew, it begins with the invasion of Poland on 1 September 1939 and concludes on 4 August 1942 during the "great action" that started on 22 July 1942, in the course of which more than 300,000 Jews were deported from the Warsaw

Ghetto, the great majority of them to Treblinka, where they were gassed on their arrival.

Kaplan's diary is one of many journals and diaries written in the Warsaw Ghetto that have survived. The most famous include the journal of the historian and archivist **Emmanuel Ringelblum** and the diaries of **Abraham Lewin** and of the chairman of the Judenrat, **Adam Czerniakow**. Even in this exalted company, Kaplan's diary has a special place. Alvin H. Rosenfeld has identified a threefold focus in Kaplan's writing: the cruelty of the Nazis, the helplessness and misery of the Jews, and the passivity and acquiescence of the majority of Poles. The most striking aspect to a modern reader, however, is not so much Kaplan's description of Nazi cruelty but his almost uncanny prescience as early as 1939 and 1940 of the fatal consequences of the German invasion of Poland for Polish Jewry and his identification of the central role played by Nazi ideology in sealing their fate. As early as 1 December 1939, Kaplan noted that, although everything the German forces did bore ''the imprint of confusion and illogic,'' nevertheless, ''the Nazis are consistent and systematic only with regard to the central concepts behind their actions—that is, the concept of authoritarianism and harshness; and in relation to the Jews—the concept of complete extermination and destruction.''

Many of Kaplan's ideas about the origins of Nazi anti-Semitism anticipated those adopted at a later date by Raul Hilberg and others: ''Nazism found the primeval matter of religious hatred all prepared as a heritage of the Middle Ages. It merely reinforced it with economic hatred, in which it mixed . . . bits of ideology . . . from Houston Stewart Chamberlain, and from other bigots and racists.''

Kaplan repeatedly emphasized the ideological basis of the Nazis' persecution of the Jews: ''Their barbarism in relation to the Jews is ideological; and here lies the source of the evil. Ideological filth is hard to vanquish.'' This distinguishes him from most other diarists and memoirists, who tend to highlight the cruel behavior of particular individuals rather than the ideology underlying their actions. It also disproves the argument that Holocaust victims were always too close to the events to be capable of understanding them. Kaplan could not, of course, know with any degree of certainty what was to happen over the next few years, but this did not prevent him from understanding very clearly the essentials of what was really happening to the Jews and also what, barring the miracle of a speedy military defeat of the Nazis, was most likely to happen to them in the near future. In March 1940 Kaplan set out an analysis of German anti-Semitism showing that for the masses it was a hatred of emotion: ''They have absorbed their masters' teaching in a concrete corporeal form.'' For the Nazi leaders, however, ''Judaism and Nazism are two world outlooks, neither of which is compatible with the other, and for this reason they cannot live together.'' Given his understanding of Nazi ideology, Kaplan had no illusions about the true purpose of ghettoization: ''[The concentration of Jews] will make it easier for the murderers to destroy them, not one by one but wholesale.''

Kaplan employed the literary device of an imaginary friend called Hirsch, who presents the hopeless but realistic aspect of the situation of the Jews in the ghetto. Hirsch pulls no punches. From his first appearance in May 1942, he rails against the illusions of false hope, and his message is simple but devastating: '''Idiots! . . . Your hope is vain; your trust a broken reed. All of you are already condemned to die, only the date of execution has yet to be set.''' There is no patience here with the notion that illusions are a symptom of the will to survive, sheltering people from total despair. Hirsch's prophesies of doom have a biblical flavor, and echoes of the Jeremiah of Lamentations can sometimes be heard in Kaplan's prose.

—Alan Polak

THE SEASON OF THE DEAD (Le Temps des morts)
Novella by Pierre Gascar, 1953

Pierre Gascar's novella *Le Temps des morts* (*The Season of the Dead*) was appended to a collection of short stories entitled *Les Bêtes* that appeared in French in 1953 and in English translation in 1956 as *Beasts and Men*. By adding a longer text to the collection of short stories, Gascar's publisher succeeded in having the work considered for the Prix Goncourt, France's most prestigious literary prize, normally awarded only to novels. The strategy was successful, and Gascar received the prize for that year. In 1998 a new, strictly autobiographical version of *The Season of the Dead,* subtitled *The Russian Dream,* was published posthumously. The title therefore refers to two separate works: one a piece of fiction, the other a memoir, written about 45 years apart.

The Season of the Dead of 1953 is a fictionalized account of Gascar's experience in a Nazi prisoner-of-war camp in the town of Rawa-Ruska in the province of Galicia, then a part of occupied Poland and now in Ukraine. The town is called Brodno in the novella. Because of a chronic shortage of water, the mortality rate among the prisoners was high. The camp commander assigned a group of prisoners the task of building and maintaining a cemetery outside the camp, where the dead prisoners were buried with military honors. Every evening the prisoners dug one fresh grave to be ready for the next casualty.

The relative independence enjoyed by the prisoners on cemetery detail, combined with the humanity and even friendliness of the German soldiers, allows the narrator, Pierre (based on Gascar himself), to enter into contact with the locals. He flirts from a distance with a peasant girl named Maria and befriends a Jew named Isaac Lebovitch, who toils in a nearby sawmill. From the time of their first arrival in town, the French prisoners notice the Jews wearing white armbands with a blue Star of David, many of whom were pressed into slave labor by the Germans. As time goes by and the extermination process intensifies, the prisoners hear from the rail yard the cries of victims in transit inside the cattle cars. Finally, the Germans round up the Jews of Brodno and send them to the death camps or murder them on the spot.

The French prisoners believe that they are only passive witnesses, until they discover that someone has been hiding at night in the grave they dig every evening before returning to camp. Pierre corresponds with the fugitive by leaving a note in the fresh grave and finding an answer in the morning. He learns that it is Isaac Lebovitch who hides in the grave at night and stays in the trees during the day. In his messages Isaac begs Pierre to help him escape, as if Pierre himself were not a prisoner. Finally the workmen arrive one morning to find that Isaac's hiding place has been discovered, and they never find his trace again.

Gascar decided years later, during a long correspondence with a Ukrainian woman who sent him pictures of contemporary Rawa-Ruska and of the graveyard he had helped build, to rewrite *The Season of the Dead* as nonfiction. He believed that the original suffered from being too poetic and remote from the facts. Many of the events and descriptions in the later version are similar, although there is no longer an Isaac Lebovitch character. On the other hand, Gascar places more emphasis in his memoir upon his discovery in the forest of an abandoned Jewish cemetery, which the commander wants the workers to raid in order to use the tombstones for their own graveyard. Gascar speculates that the German officer, by encouraging this desecration, was trying to get the prisoners to share some of the guilt for the persecution of the Jews. At one point, seeing that the commander makes the local Jews engage in an enormous amount of busy work during the peak period of deportation, Gascar wonders if he is not trying to protect them from the death camps by inventing things for them to do, such as building a monumental stone entrance for the prisoner-of-war cemetery. He realizes that such is not the case, however, when he discovers one day that all of the Jews in the town have disappeared.

In their own way both versions of Gascar's story are valuable documents. The latter, nonfictional version, without the dramatic element of the Jew hiding inside a grave to escape deportation, is a more literal, detailed, and reflective account of what Gascar witnessed. It is also less memorable and less tightly structured, containing the author's thoughts on the Soviet Union, reminiscences from the more distant past, and his experience of the liberation, all accompanied by his own extensive analysis. By purging his account of its poetic and narrative qualities, however, he makes up in historical accuracy what he loses in rhetorical power.

—M. Martin Guiney

THE SECOND SCROLL
Novel by A.M. Klein, 1951

The last publication of Montreal poet A.M. Klein, before his disabling illness struck, was an audaciously conceived book entitled *The Second Scroll* (1951). Klein himself identified the book as a novel, but it was so unlike any other novel that it still defies easy classification as a literary kind. Most critics have settled on the phrase ''poetic novel,'' but to understand fully what a daring departure this work really is, one must first understand its title.

The inspiration for the book was Klein's idea that the twentieth-century history of the Jews had been strikingly parallel to the historical and religious beginnings of the Jewish people as recorded in the first five books of the Old Testament. According to Jewish tradition the Pentateuch was given to Moses by God and is therefore sacred. Its Hebrew name, Torah, identifies the five books as the embodiment of the laws of Judaism, and for that reason a copy of the Torah, in its original form as a handwritten parchment scroll, is to be found in every Jewish house of worship. Klein's book is thus intended to be a modern Torah, a second scroll, telling the most recent story of Jewish persecutions, slaughters, and banishments into exile and the diaspora. The defining event, of near total destruction of the Jews, would of course be the Holocaust, and the ending, its Deuteronomy, would record the saving of the remnant by their return to the homeland under the banner of Zionism.

Klein's story is told in five chapters bearing the English names of the canonical five books: Genesis, Exodus, Leviticus, Numbers, and Deuteronomy. In accordance with Jewish tradition, the five chapters are followed by five commentaries, called Glosses, numbered in Hebrew: Aleph, Beth, Gimel, Dalid, Hai. The chapters named in English, and the commentaries numbered in Hebrew, clearly signal Klein's intention to make his novel a hybrid. That intention follows logically from his basic concept of creating an authentic modern Torah and, at the same time, a story of interest to Jews and non-Jews alike. For that reason *The Second Scroll* duplicates, in its structure, a universally familiar biblical narrative but employs a language that deliberately mingles poetic English and hybrid elements derived from Yiddish, Hebrew, Latin, French, or Italian. An example of this occurs in the book's opening sentence: ''For many years my father—may he dwell in a bright Eden!—refused to permit in his presence even the mention of that person's name.'' The phrase ''may he dwell in a bright Eden!'' is a literal translation of a common Yiddish expression. The effect of the literalness is to impress on readers who know no Yiddish that the expression is not standard English and belongs to a different culture. The device, in many variations, is used repeatedly throughout the narrative to underline the hybrid nature of the whole.

The Second Scroll is a first-person narrative, strongly focused on just two characters: the narrator, a member of an orthodox Jewish family in Montreal, and the narrator's uncle, Melech Davidson, who is the brother of the narrator's mother and still lives in the Ukrainian village of Ratno, where the narrator's mother was born. The narrator has never met his uncle but knows his reputation as "a prodigy of learning and a scholar in Israel" and hopes to follow in his footsteps. The novel's central figure is the uncle, whose odyssey and quest for a righteous life provide the narrative thread. The uncle's celebrated piety is shattered when he witnesses a pogrom in Ratno. He abandons his faith and embraces Marxism, hoping to find justice. Years later, having rejected Marxism, he is deeply shocked, during the war, when he comes upon firsthand evidence of the Holocaust in Kamenets, Poland. Horrified, he flees to Italy, where he helps Jews in a displaced-persons camp and, still searching, has a brief flirtation with Catholicism. He finally finds a comforting peace in Israel, where he dies. The matured narrator then undertakes his own quest, traveling to Europe to find his uncle, first in Italy, then, following his trail, in Israel. He arrives too late to attend his funeral but is comforted to witness the establishment of the new state and the miracle, as he calls it, of the survival of the Jewish people after near extinction.

The novel includes unsparingly vivid descriptions of the massacre of Jews in Kamenets and earnestly addresses the major issues of the time, namely the nature of evil and the problem of faith in an all-powerful deity who can countenance the unimaginable horrors of the Holocaust. To that extent *The Second Scroll* is a powerfully moving history of our times and deserves its reputation as Klein's finest work and as one of the most original works of fiction in Canadian literature of the twentieth century.

—Murray Sachs

THE SECRET MIRACLE ("El milagro secreto")
Short Story by Jorge Luis Borges, 1944

"The Secret Miracle" ("El milagro secreto") was written by Jorge Luis Borges at the height of the Second World War in 1943 and was published in 1944 when it appeared in his renowned collection of short stories *Ficciones*. Set in Nazi-occupied Prague, "The Secret Miracle" is the story of a Jewish playwright, Jaromir Hladík, who is arrested by the Germans and is quickly sentenced to death for his dissenting views of the Third Reich. As his date of execution approaches, he becomes increasingly concerned about his legacy as a writer and in particular with his unfinished play entitled *The Enemies*. As he struggles to formulate and develop the plot in his head, he realizes he needs more time in order to complete his masterpiece. In the solitude of his cell he asks God to grant him one more year to complete his project, and thus, on the eve of his execution, the protagonist has an unsettling oneiric

experience: he dreams that he searches for God among the thousands of volumes contained in the Clementine Library (an authentic building in Prague). As he awakens from his dream, he hears a rewarding voice that assures him, "The time for your labor has been granted." Precisely on schedule, at 8:44 a.m., the guards arrive in his cell and escort him to the patio where the firing squad awaits. At 9:00 a.m. the sergeant raises his arm and gives the order to fire, but at that instant Hladík sees the world around him freeze. Time is suddenly stopped. He wonders if he has gone to hell or if he might be dead or perhaps crazy. Soon, however, he realizes that God has granted his wish. He has witnessed a secret miracle and has been given a one-year respite to complete his play. He immediately sets out to work and begins the writing process, rewriting the play word by word, scene by scene, aided only by his memory. In a year's time he is finished. His task is suddenly complete, and time picks up where it had left off before: "He began a maddened cry, he shook his head, and the fourfold volley felled him." In the last line of the story the narrator lets the implicit reader know that Hladík died that same morning barely two minutes after nine o'clock.

"The Secret Miracle" has been subject to various readings and interpretations. While some scholars have attempted to read the story as a mere intellectual game that blurs the line between the real and the fantastic, between what can be interpreted as a real occurrence or as a vivid oneiric experience, others have suggested that it may be read as a play within a play though presented in narrative form, thus suggesting this could have been Borges's one and only attempt to experiment with drama, a genre that always eluded the author.

Yet, to suggest that Borges's stories deal ultimately with writing, in the sense of art for art's sake, seems rather reductive and undeserving of the author. In the case of "The Secret Miracle" one cannot fail to notice the fact that the story is set in the context of the Second World War and was written and published at a time when Argentina, though formally neutral, was still siding with the Axis powers. In "The Secret Miracle" Borges explores the limits of representation and poses different methods through which to examine the Holocaust.

—Alejandro Meter

SEE UNDER: LOVE ('Ayen 'erekh-ahavah)
Novel by David Grossman, 1986

Given its bent toward the intertextual, David Grossman's *'Ayen 'erekh-ahavah* (1986; *See Under: Love,* 1989) might well be introduced with reference to another hybrid text, **W.G. Sebald**'s *The Emigrants,* in which a protagonist likens the memoirs of his deported mother to "one of those evil German fairy tales in which, once you are under the spell, you have to carry on to the finish, till your heart breaks, with whatever work you have begun—in this case, the remembering, writing, and reading." It is a conceit that captures both the textual dynamics and aesthetic ideology at the root of *See Under: Love*. What Sebald's text circles around obliquely, however, Grossman's interrogates directly, marking a watershed in Israeli fiction and the fictional representation of the Shoah generally. Although it was not the first such novel to stake such claims (that distinction must go to **Yoram Kaniuk**'s *Adam Resurrected* from two decades earlier), by dint of sheer formal ingenuity and moral daring, *See Under: Love* secures their exigency, not to be gainsaid.

From the opening sentences in each of its sections, the novel throws down three gauntlets: (1) not only its aftereffects but the Shoah itself will now reside in the topical foreground (Sebald's "carry on to the finish"); (2) nonrealistic narrative strategies (akin to Sebald's "evil German fairy tales") will assume their rightful place in its representation; and (3) the very act of narrative transmission will be reflexively charged and thematized (Sebald's "remembering, writing, and reading" understood as ethical and exegetical labor—what the novel and its readers will undertake as their collaborative work).

It is in its formal design and discursive styles that Grossman's text most conspicuously announces a new, postmodern departure. Where Israeli Holocaust fiction by statehood generation writers like **Yehuda Amichai** (*Not of This Time, Not of This Place*) or **Aharon Appelfeld** (*The Searing Light*) might look back to literary modernism for its antimimetic effects, *See Under: Love* directly thematizes the dilemma of writing the novel in the first place, under the double shadow of national catastrophe and the pressure of antecedent authors and writings. Thus both Anshel Wasserman (a figure in the novel's diegesis) and Bruno Schultz (reimagined in the narrative as a literary character) offer parallel cases as Jewish writers of mythopoetic literary fictions whom the writer in the text, Shlomo Neuman, imitates but must also transcend in order to legitimate his own voice.

The story that we read thus represents a recuperation of both the undersound of the human tongue muted by horrors of the Shoah and the oversound of literary influence (Bruno Schulz, Sholem Aleichem, Mendele Mokher Seforim). *See Under: Love* is thus an astonishing parable and enactment of what Elias Canetti has called "the tongue set free"—both on the plane of the story's events and on the authorial plane subtending it. The latter, for Grossman, means imagining the Shoah without having personally undergone its depredations, within a literary establishment for which the conventions of testimony were both authoritative and culturally sacrosanct.

The novel divides in four distinct but overlapping parts. The first, "Momik," tells the story of Shlomo "Momik" Neuman as the nine-year-old Israeli-born child of survivors belatedly introduced to his grand-uncle Anshel Wasserman, who has just been released from a sanatorium and is unable to communicate

except for incoherent fragments (a "code" Momik seeks to decipher). Assembling his grand-uncle along with other similarly marginalized Yiddish-speaking survivors, and armed with the few details extracted from his parents and relatives and a scrap of the author Anshel Wasserman's "The Children of the Heart" (tales written for a children's magazine published in 1912), Momik gives febrile authorial form to "the Nazi Beast" he imagines hiding in the cellar of his house in order to vanquish it. This first section of *See Under: Love* ends with Momik's nervous breakdown, as the narrative burden of the Holocaust remains unintegrated and inchoately realized.

In the second part (discursively the most difficult) Shlomo, now an adult, seeks to remedy that unresolved childhood trauma, which stands in for unassimilated large-scale cultural trauma, together with his own uncertainties about a literary vocation by transferring onto the figure of Bruno Schulz, whom he reimagines as having escaped death by metamorphosing into a sea creature. It is, however, simultaneously a liberation and a regression. Thus in the section's culminating episode, Bruno invites Shlomo to witness the triumph of hermetic literary creation over quotidian life—Schulz's "Age of Genius"—through which the fictionalizing imagination seeks to displace reality and, consequently along with it, individual choice and collective responsibility.

A self-criticized retreat into idolatry becomes the text's second failed resolution of its narrative and mimetic burden. The third and fourth sections, "Wasserman" and "The Complete Encyclopedia of Kazik's Life," represent Shlomo Neuman's (and David Grossman's) successful, Jewishly reimagined version of an evil German fairy tale in which, once you are under the spell, you have to carry on to the finish with whatever work you have begun—in this case, the remembering, writing, and reading. Yet here too the novel signals its awareness of its own wager, since, as critic Efraim Sicher has noted, the plot device in this second half of the novel—victimized Jewish storyteller becomes indestructible Scheherazade—allegorizes the risk of abandoning historical record for fantasy in the first place, even if the fictive ultimately justifies the meaning behind the novel's title.

The product of that fantasy, a homunculus generated by Wasserman's storytelling, provides a seam where an escapist Jewish past, the Shoah itself, and its survivor aftermath all meet; literary fiction is thus allowed to become a temporary and tenuous bridge for ruptures in time as well as representation. More important, however, this Jewish prototype for "the new man" justifies the organizing framework for the novel's fourth section. Called an encyclopedia, really a lexicon, it attests to the moral force of language at the level of the individual word. And thus, though easily missed, the supplementary glossary of Yiddish terms that ends the novel is really its last section. While registering its own precedent in contemporary Hebrew fiction, it marks one final heteroglot demonstration of the novel's romance with the power of fusion:

between the real and the fictive, authoring selves and narrating others, literature and destruction.

—Adam Zachary Newton

SEPTEMBER SONG
Poem by Geoffrey Hill, 1968

Geoffrey Hill's "September Song," which appeared in his second volume of poetry, *King Log* (1968), is a brief elegy written for a concentration camp victim. The poem revisits the subject of earlier poems such as "Two Formal Elegies." Characteristic of Hill's method, it exhibits the compression of layers of meaning in deceivingly simple words, irony (including irony directed at his own aesthetic motives), and a complex switch in tone that results in ambivalence sufficient to elicit markedly different interpretations.

The first lines of the poem, "Undesirable you may have been, untouchable / you were not. Not forgotten / or passed over at the proper time," convey irony in the balance between "undesirable" and "untouchable" and the "not. Not . . .'' In the third line "passed over" alludes to the Passover, but in this case there is a bitterly ironic reversal. Implicit in the reversal is a recurring theme in Hill's work about the mystery of God's ways. God's plague on the Egyptians resulted in the slaughter of the innocent as well as the guilty. Three instances of mass slaughter converge in these lines: the Egyptian plagues, Herod's killing of the innocents, and the Holocaust.

As a martyrologist, Hill focuses on victims and victimizers throughout history. Many commentators on his work, beginning with Christopher Ricks, have remarked that Hill does not restrict his use of the word "holocaust" to Jews only. He recognizes the danger in treating the Nazi slaughter as an aberration that is beyond the reach of understanding, a one-of-a-kind atrocity that will never be repeated. Ever wary of sophistic reasoning and the evasion of hard truths, Hill understands that the Nazis' Final Solution was not beyond reason but was a form of reason taken to hideous extremes, an instrumental reason in which human beings can be annihilated and the natural world destroyed as a means to a scientifically, rationally planned end.

The next several lines of the poem contain numerous words and phrases that convey a measured, marching rhythm and that reflect the transformation of human beings into things in a dehumanized, mechanized process of extermination by a Nazi machine:

> As estimated, you died. Things marched,
> sufficient, to that end.
> Just so much Zyklon and leather, patented
> terror, so many routine cries.

Efficient, patented, routine—things marched. Estimated, sufficient, just so much—the mathematics of mass murder was practiced.

Suddenly Hill interrupts the poem with a self-conscious aside in parentheses: "(I have made / an elegy for myself it / is true)." Coming after the seven tightly controlled and dense lines delivered in an apostrophe to the concentration camp victim ("you"), these three parenthetical lines deliver a jolt. They are obviously confessional and are delivered in a short, halting fashion, causing the reader to stutter and dwell with the poet in a self-conscious moment as he examines his relationship to the victim. The epigraph tells us that the victim was "born 19.6.32"—one day after Hill's birthday. Some readers have asked what Hill is up to in terms of his identification with the camp deportee, especially considering the fact that he is a professed Anglican. One is reminded of Sylvia Plath's controversially ironic assumption of Jewishness as a figure for the suffering of her persona in such poems as "Daddy" and "Lady Lazarus." The difference lies, arguably, in the two poets' uses of irony, with Hill's being much more self-conscious. He is knowingly traversing dangerous poetic ground to demonstrate the risk of appropriating the tragedy of someone else as the stuff of counterfeit elegy. Such appropriation and trivializing, which he has called "atrocities of the tongue," produce a literature of cliché and bathos. Hill never forgets the risk in taking Zyklon gas and crematorium smoke and making lyrical poetry of them. Although readers hear a confession, "I have made / an elegy for myself it / is true," the final three words also suggest that the elegy—despite being written for himself—is true, as witness to the historical truth of the horror of the Holocaust. The poem makes clear that elegies are always meant for the living.

Many readers have commented on the ambivalence of the last line, "This is plenty. This is more than enough." The line follows logically from the parenthetical confession, however, for Hill evokes the recognition that an elegy is always and inevitably inadequate as a commemoration. It can never bring back the dead, can never release the victim, because the dead are gone, and we are caught up in the present fullness and plenty of a September day. Therein lies the limit of poetry as witness and as an antidote to historical forgetting.

—Molly Abel Travis

THE SHAWL
Short Story by Cynthia Ozick, 1980

Cynthia Ozick's "The Shawl" (1980) is a tiny masterpiece of Holocaust literature. In seven pages Ozick evokes the horror and brutality of the Holocaust and relates a powerful narrative of death and survival. Originally published as a separate story in the *New Yorker,* it was followed by a sequel, "Rosa," which takes up the story 30 years later. The two stories have been published together in book form under the title *The Shawl* (1989). Written in a dense and highly metaphoric style, "The Shawl" resembles a prose poem more than a straightforward narrative. It centers around three characters—a mother (Rosa), her infant daughter (Magda), and her 14-year-old niece (Stella)—who are trapped in "a place without pity," an unnamed concentration camp. During the opening passages the characters are marching along a road, presumably part of a march toward a death camp. Rosa is cradling her infant daughter in a shawl that will become the central symbol of the story. We learn that it is on account of this "magic" shawl that Magda has managed to survive this long: the Nazis would have taken the girl away had she not been concealed. Magda also sucks on the shawl for comfort, the only form of nourishment available now that Rosa's breasts no longer provide sufficient milk. Moreover, the shawl becomes an animate creature in Magda's eyes, making her laugh when it moves about in the wind. Stella, who has become so emaciated that her knees are described as "tumors on sticks," is jealous of her baby cousin and yearns to be rocked to sleep in the shawl herself. The shawl is thus depicted as a necessary, but inherently limited, resource for navigating the concentration camp universe.

The scene shifts seamlessly from the road to the camp. The baby girl, Magda, has strayed from the barracks into the roll-call arena where, suddenly exposed to the camp guards, she cries out for her mother. Rosa is faced with a critical dilemma: should she go out to grab Magda, who will continue to cry until the shawl is recovered, or should she find the shawl first and allow Magda to remain exposed in the meantime? Rosa decides to find the shawl first and quickly discovers it covering the sleeping Stella. In the story's only words of dialogue, spoken in an undefined "afterward," Stella callously accounts for her act of theft: "I was cold." Although Rosa recovers the shawl, it is too late to save the screaming Magda. As Rosa watches, Magda is lifted onto the shoulder of a Nazi guard and hurled against the electrified fence. In order to squelch her cries, Rosa stuffs the shawl into her own mouth and tastes "the cinnamon and almond depth of Magda's shawl." Once again the shawl acts as a source of comfort and protection, a reminder of the tenderness that has been stamped out.

Throughout the story Ozick's style works by indirection. Rather than identifying the barracks as part of a Nazi concentration camp, she describes the "ash-stippled wind" and the "stink mixed with a bitter fatty floating smoke." Rather than identifying the figure that hurls Magda against the fence as a Nazi guard, Ozick writes that Magda was "riding someone's shoulder" and that "above the shoulder a helmet glinted." As a result of this style, the reader is denied access to the omniscient perspective generally afforded by a third-person narrative. In place of such a perspective, the reader is situated amidst a series of experiences so horrifying that they resist the categories of conventional language. Ozick's extensive use of figurative language—Magda's eyes are called "blue tigers,"

her legs are called "scribbling pencils"—suggests the desperate operations of a mind (both Rosa's and that of the implied narrator) striving to make sense of a bleak world. When Magda lets out her first scream in the roll-call arena, Rosa responds with "fearful joy": fear because recrimination is imminent, joy because Magda's silenced voice has finally been released. In a similar way Ozick's story lets out a lyrical outpouring that bears witness to unmitigated suffering.

—Julian Levinson

A SHAYNA MAIDEL
Play by Barbara Lebow, 1988

Barbara Lebow's play *A Shayna Maidel,* first produced in 1985, dramatizes the saga of the Weiss family, Polish Jews whose lives are irrecoverably altered by the Holocaust. The play begins in a Polish shtetl in 1876, when the patriarch of the family, Mordechai Weiss, is born during what appears to be a pogrom. This scene is significant in Lebow's play, for he is a good baby who does not cry, thus foreshadowing his resilience and tough spirit. *A Shayna Maidel* is a memory play in that it is set in three times: when Mordechai is born in 1876, when his two daughters (Rose White and Lusia Weiss Pechenik) are reunited in New York City during the present (1946), and when Lusia has flashbacks of her life in Poland immediately before and after the Holocaust. Lusia has survived Auschwitz, and the Red Cross and the Hebrew Immigrant Aid Society have contacted her father to inform him that she is coming to New York. Mordechai insists that she come to live with her sister, Rose. This order from her father upsets Rose because she does not remember her sister and thus feels uncomfortable about sharing an apartment with her. In addition, Rose, having come to New York at the age of four, has become fully Americanized and has even changed her name from Rayzel Weiss to Rose White. Although she is not ashamed of being Jewish, she has distanced herself from her past in Poland and her Jewish heritage; she does not even keep kosher, which disturbs Mordechai. The main reason Rose feels uncomfortable about living with Lusia is her guilt: she has enjoyed a peaceful and uneventful life in New York while her sister suffered unspoken atrocities during the Holocaust. Mordechai, his wife, and his two daughters were supposed to leave Poland for New York, but before they could leave, Lusia contracted scarlet fever and had to remain in Poland with her mother. Therefore, Mordechai had taken Rose (Rayzel) with him to New York and had intended to have his wife and Lusia join them after the daughter recovered. But when the war breaks out, mother and daughter cannot leave the country. Lusia initially does not mind being left behind because she can remain with her best friend Hanna and because she has fallen in love with Duvid. Lusia marries Duvid, and they have a child (Sprinze) together, but eventually Lusia, her mother, husband, child, and best friend are taken to Auschwitz. Only Lusia and Duvid survive the ordeal, and Lusia, grieving for her mother, baby, and best friend, arrives in New York to live with the relatives who left Poland before the war and to attempt to track down Duvid, whom she believes is alive and looking for her.

Rose does not know how to talk to her sister because they are strangers to one another and because Rose cannot comprehend the suffering that Lusia has experienced. Lusia recognizes almost immediately her sister's reluctance to be with her, which adds to the strain in the relationship. Lusia is also distracted because she is preoccupied with her search for her missing husband. As the audience later discovers, Lusia is also angry at Mordechai because just before the war started he had turned down an opportunity to bring his wife and Lusia to New York: someone had offered to lend him the money to bring the two over to New York, but because of his pride and dignity, Mordechai refused to accept the money. Mordechai's refusal prevented his wife and daughter from leaving Poland; as it turns out, if Mordechai had accepted the offer, his family would have survived and his daughter never would have suffered her ordeal in Auschwitz.

Mordechai and Lusia have each maintained a list of their relatives and what happened to them during the Holocaust. The two family members read their lists in ritualistic fashion, revealing that almost all their relatives have died. Rose is fascinated by the reading of the lists and wants to know more about her past; Mordechai has previously shielded her from any knowledge about her relatives, even her own mother, because he felt that it would cause her too much pain. Mordechai now reveals to Rose that he has kept a letter from her—a final letter written to her from her mother. In the poignant letter Rose's mother tells her that she loves her and sends along her baby spoon, which she has kept as a tangible reminder of their bond.

The play concludes on a positive note, for Mordechai manages to help find Duvid and bring him to Rose's apartment, where Lusia is waiting. Lebow's touching play demonstrates the indomitable nature of the human spirit and the importance of strong family bonds. Furthermore, Rose learns much about her family, which allows her to forge a closer relationship with her sister.

—Eric Sterling

SHIBBOLETH (Schibboleth)
Poem by Paul Celan, 1955

Paul Celan's poetry represents an attempt to universalize the Holocaust. It seeks to invent a new language for a horror without precedent. For Celan it is not enough merely to bear witness, to recount the facts, because his experience is composed not only of real events, and real pain, but also of the

agonizing emotional transformation these events have caused. For both the poet and the reader, the struggle to make sense of this transformation through poetry is arduous, even painful; the more personal the experience, the more deeply it is felt, the more difficult it becomes to express. The profoundly personal nature of Celan's poems, their multilingual quality, and their free use of obscure historical references turn the act of reading into a type of decoding in which the reader is compelled to formulate a distinct point of entry for individual stanzas, if not individual words.

Published in *Von Schwelle zu Schwelle* (1955), the poem "Shibboleth" both struggles to master this coded world and acknowledges the hopelessness of such a struggle. The derivation of the word is significant. It was first used in biblical times as a password by the soldiers of Jephthah during the defeat of the Ephraimites. Because the language of the Ephraimites did not contain a "sh" sound, the word "shibboleth" was unpronounceable, making them easy to identify when they tried to escape. This form of identification, rooted in ethnicity, finds its ominous echo in the Holocaust, where Jewish identity was the mark, predetermined by the enemy, that resulted in death.

In Celan's poem, utterance of the shibboleth constitutes a search for "homeland." Home is where memory, identity, and one's native language all intersect. For Celan this home was irredeemably destroyed when the Nazis occupied Romania and murdered his parents. In his exile the poet is seeking that one word, that secret code, that will restore him to familiar territory. The poem abounds with potential shibboleths, such as "February" and "No pasaran." On one level the interpretation of these words seems clear. February refers to the date of many of the events alluded to in the poem; "No pasaran" was a Republican slogan during the Spanish Civil War. And yet the transformative power of these phrases has been gutted by defeat. Instead, we find ourselves looking back, through the eyes of a prisoner, on the ruins of war: "remember the dark/ twin redness/of Vienna and Madrid." The landscape is unfamiliar, foreign:

> they dragged me out into
> the middle of the market,
> that place
> where the flag unfurls to which
> I swore no kind of allegiance.

Amidst this destruction the poet struggles to find his "homeland," to reestablish his citizenship. But the only remaining territory is memory, ravaged by death:

> Set your flag at half-mast,
> memory.
> At half-mast
> today and forever.

Unable to become repatriated through the language of his surroundings, the poet turns to his heart and seeks from it the "shibboleth" that will reconcile him to this "alien homeland." But the heart can only repeat the old, vanquished phrases: "February. No pasaran."

In the last stanza Celan launches his search into the realm of myth. Having failed to elicit a response from his heart, he turns to a unicorn, insisting that it understands:

> you know about the stones,
> you know about the water,
> come,
> I shall lead you away
> to the voices
> of Estremadura.

Here the poet is momentarily transported. Estremadura is a region in Portugal near southern Spain. It is close to the scene of disaster, but it is on the other side of the border, in a place where different "voices" can be heard. The fluid, exotic quality of the name itself suggests an escape from the harsh sounds of war. In this way the poet imbues the unicorn—as an image, as a word—with a sense of liberation. The bestowing of this quality becomes the definitive poetic act. And yet ultimately this gesture represents a capitulation, a turning away from history toward the impossible. The last stanza suggests real beauty, but it is purely imaginative, as elusive as the unicorn itself.

—Stephen Meyer

SHIELDING THE FLAME: AN INTIMATE CONVERSATION WITH DR. MAREK EDELMAN, THE LAST SURVIVING LEADER OF THE WARSAW GHETTO UPRISING (Zdazyc przed Panem Bogiem)
Interview by Hanna Krall, 1977

Hanna Krall's *Shielding the Flame* (1986) was originally published as *Zdazyc przed Panem Bogiem* in 1977 in the **Wrocław literary** magazine *Odra*. In it the author, at the time a reporter for the Warsaw magazine *Polityka*, draws a portrait of **Marek Edelman**, the last surviving leader of the Warsaw Ghetto Uprising. Compared to the earlier report of the German SS leader Jürgen Stroop, Krall's work provides a view from the opposite side of this historic event. Krall had originally planned a report about Edelman and a surgical method he had invented in the 1970s. According to Krall, the idea to ask him about his role in the uprising occurred only during the interviews with him.

In the interviews Edelman reflected publicly on the events of the uprising for only the second time in his life. He initially opposed talking about the horrors of the ghetto, using self-irony and speaking "between clenched teeth." He emphasized the coincidental aspect of the events and insisted on talking about his friends and comrades instead of producing a hero's legend of himself. When, for example, he told about a red woolen jumper he had worn while breaking out of a hiding place, he said derisively, "Add two revolvers. When you look elegant you need a revolver and crossed belts." To him the revolt was a way of maintaining human dignity and securing freedom. Nevertheless, he felt woven into the culture of death: "People always believed that shooting is great heroism. That's why we had to shoot." Edelman disappoints the hope for a legend: "Thus he never meant to be a spokesperson, because he couldn't scream. And he never meant to be a hero, because he lacked pathos."

Edelman speaks at great length, while Krall's comments, specific questions, and reflections are added on the side. Other witnesses are included in the search for the past and to find an answer to the question "What sense is behind remembering?" Krall challenges the media, not only interviews but also films like those of Andrzej Wajda. In addition, she tests the culture of memorials, which are based on destroying the remembered: "There is a park on this site now; a hill, a stone, an inscription." The reactions and expectations of readers are included, as, for example, when they request that the memories be censored. One reader complains, "Such banal things should not be told about the commander." The text, however, ends up subverting the anticipation of a "common" story. Even though the readers pay close attention to "the historical facts and the course of events," the "historical course is, as it is shown, nothing else but the course of dying."

A creative form is essential in the work in order both to emphasize and to break the routine of remembering; the past must not rest on a conventional image. Thus, the past forces itself into the present, and both merge in the conscience of a survivor. Several images stand beside one another: a 22-year-old rebel, a heart surgeon in a Warsaw hospital, the men and women who died in the ghetto, terminally ill patients, comrades from the past, doctors who fight diseases in the present. Edelman names the parallels. He believes that his task is to save "as many of his patients as possible," and at some stage he realizes "that it was the same task as back then in the Ghetto," when the victims for the next transport were pulled together. "Back then I stood at the gate" delegated by the Jewish committee and, disguised as a messenger of the ghetto hospital, tried to "free single people from the crowd of the condemned." In both cases it is a race with death: "God would like to blow out a candle, but I must be quicker in shielding the flame and use his temporary inattentiveness. It should burn a little longer than He wishes." It is not a story about the dignity of death but one about the dignity of life: "All it is about is shielding the flame of life."

—Walter Schmitz

SHOAH
Oral History by Claude Lanzmann, 1985

In its book form *Shoah* (Hebrew for "annihilation") is the complete text drawn from the nine-and-a-half-hour film *Shoah* (1985), widely considered the most profound film about the Holocaust. Though commonly regarded as a historical document or documentary, Claude Lanzmann called *Shoah* a "fiction of reality" that rejects any general representation of the Holocaust. The focus is on the processes of extermination as they emerged over the course of the Holocaust, engineered by the Nazis primarily in Poland. Rather than documenting the exterminations, *Shoah* aims specifically to "transmit the experience of the Holocaust," to "incarnate" the truth "in the present." In order to do so, the text relies entirely on present-day, eyewitness accounts and avoids any stock footage or photos as well as most original documents. Crucial to the aim to "relive" the Holocaust is Lanzmann's dictum "don't let the Holocaust be the past": in depicting the past only through the present, *Shoah* attempts, according to Lanzmann, "the abolition of all distances between past and present."

Shoah assays the incarnation of truth in the present via contemporary eyewitness testimony, in which the interlocutor (usually Lanzmann) plays an actively inquiring role. Comprised entirely of such oral histories, the text dispenses with a unifying voice-over, omniscient narrator, or background sound track. The only voice linking the various testimonies is Lanzmann's own, such that the unifying element in the work is a voice of inquiry.

The witnesses fall into approximately three categories: victim-survivors (mostly male Jews, often from the *Sonderkommando*), perpetrators (ex-Nazis, usually interviewed surreptitiously), and bystanders (usually Poles). The text juxtaposes fragments of their testimony into a collage that slowly gives shape to the machinery of annihilation. Lanzmann performs the interviews, often with translators whose presence is foregrounded. Most often Lanzmann interviews witnesses alone and as individuals, but occasionally also in groups, demonstrating the collective character of memory, understanding, and communication.

Some of the subjects are interviewed on location at the historical sites, usually in Poland, and some away from the original places. The film often cuts from the interviews to present-day images of the sites of the ghettos, deportations, and exterminations, creating a careful correspondence between voice-over and the contemporary topography of the Holocaust. The interviews themselves often focus on the details of the processes of killing: Lanzmann openly follows the advice of the historian Raul Hilberg—who is one of the only nonwitnesses in the text—that it is important to pose small, detail-oriented questions and slowly build to bigger answers. Among the topics covered in the interviews are Jewish life before the deportations, the roundups and deportations, the functioning of different kinds of camps, life and death in the camps, and resistance and uprising.

By juxtaposing a large number of interviews, *Shoah* offers a multiplicity of voices that underscores the radically differing perspectives on the Holocaust. This diversity of testimonies demonstrates the vagaries of memory as well as the difficulty of understanding what transpired. For ethical reasons Lanzmann rejected any meeting between victim-survivors and perpetrators, but in the collage of the text they are brought together to underscore the differences in how individuals see, understand, and remember the same events. The multivalence character of the text simultaneously corroborates the events while also elucidating radical differences in perspective and the ultimate gaps in understanding.

In addition to the spoken testimonies, the text is also careful to show how silence and forgetting emerge and create meaning. In one famous sequence one of only two Chelmo survivors, Simon Srebnik, listens silently as a present-day Polish villager voices persistent anti-Semitic sentiments (for example, "All this happened to the Jews because they were the richest"). In this sense the film explores the transmittance of the past into the present and shows how seeing, memory, and silence coincide to help create "today."

Despite much widespread acclaim, *Shoah* has been criticized on a number of fronts. Some have protested the depiction of Poles, which generally underplays any Polish attempts to help Jews. *Shoah* has also been criticized for staging elements of some of the interviews, including two of the most famous: one with a retired Polish train conductor who drives a rented locomotive along track to Treblinka reopened by Lanzmann for the interview; and one with a retired Jewish barber who cut the hair of Jews in Treblinka. For the barber Lanzmann rented a barbershop and asked him to cut a friend's hair while giving testimony. In the latter interview—one of the most famous of the film—another controversial technique of Lanzmann emerges: at the moment the interviewee breaks down in emotion and asks Lanzmann to cease the interview, Lanzmann continues to probe, asking even more precise questions. Many have criticized these techniques of staging interviews and ignoring the will of the interviewee, though many others—including some interviewees—have admitted that such dogged probing was necessary to resurrect the experience and incarnate the truth in the present.

—Jaimey Fisher

THE SHOVEL AND THE LOOM (Twee koffers vol)
Novel by Carl Friedman, 1993

The Shovel and the Loom (1996; *Twee koffers vol*, 1993) is Carl Friedman's second novel. Its protagonist, Chaya, is the 20-year-old daughter of Holocaust survivors, now living alone in Antwerp for the first time. A student of philosophy, she draws upon her reading to make sense of her world but finds the texts lacking. As the reader shares Chaya's philosophical quest, Friedman's point becomes clear: traditional philosophy is insufficient to make sense of the world after Auschwitz. Yet Friedman's novel does not provide an easy alternative; rather, the novel suggests that, like Chaya, each of us must wrestle with what it means to live after the Holocaust. That Chaya is Hebrew for "life" foregrounds further the difficulty of living after the Holocaust, trying to navigate between the demands of the past and the draw of the present.

Significantly the novel is told as a flashback, the older Chaya looking back on a photograph of herself at the age of 20. From the onset *The Shovel and the Loom* is concerned with history, with understanding how the past affects our identity. This broad concern with history and origins is foregrounded early in the novel through Chaya's intellectual questions: "Where do we come from?" she asks Mr. Apfelschnitt, a family friend and a Holocaust survivor. "Was a divine father or a slimy amoeba at our cradle? Why do we live? And if we truly aspire to good, how is it that we cause so much misery?"

The novel is not driven by Chaya's philosophical musings, however; to the contrary, Chaya's philosophical beliefs develop through the action of the novel, through the people she meets and the events she experiences. This too is central to Friedman's point that our beliefs cannot be developed in a closed room but must develop out of our experience in the world and our history.

Overlaying all is, of course, the Holocaust. Chaya's concerns with the past clearly stem from her experiences as the daughter of Holocaust survivors. The shovel and the loom of the novel's title reflect two different ways of dealing with the past. Chaya's father is obsessed with old maps of Antwerp as he searches for the suitcases he buried before the war. Chaya's mother, on the other hand, thinks her husband should let go of the past. A survivor of Auschwitz, she deals with her painful history by throwing herself into the present, specifically baking, weaving, and other crafts. As the child of these survivors, Chaya stands between these two responses to the Holocaust, trying to find her own way.

In need of a job to supplement her scholarship, Chaya finds employment as the nanny for the Kalmans, a Hasidic family with five children. The work is difficult, but she stays because of her love for the youngest son, Simcha. Simcha means "joy" in Hebrew, and for Chaya the boy represents the only spark of joy in the stern Kalman household.

Working for the Kalmans exposes Chaya to a depth of anti-Semitism she has not previously experienced. Every day she must contend with the anti-Semitic manager of the building where the Kalmans live; taking the boys to the park one day, she sees anti-Semitic epithets painted on the benches. Chaya does not know how to respond to such anti-Semitism. Again she is stuck between the shovel and the loom, between a return

to tradition and an embrace of modern life. Should Jews respond to anti-Semitism by becoming more religious, as Mr. Apfelschnitt argues? Or is her father right, that Hasidic Jews invite prejudice by holding on to the ways of the ghetto? Chaya is not sure and sees her own beliefs somewhere in the middle.

Chaya cannot identify with the Hasidic lifestyle of the Kalmans; she finds the way of life stifling, particularly to women. Yet neither can Chaya abandon her Judaism, which exhibits a pull on her that even she does not fully understand. Indeed, her love for Simcha draws Chaya to the sacred Jewish texts, in her desire to better understand his world. Here again we are in Friedman's realm, where actions are led not by ideology as much as by emotion, by the connections we forge with others.

The Shovel and the Loom presents a brief and intense exploration of the complexity of Jewish life after the Holocaust. Chaya struggles with the issues particularly, as the daughter of Holocaust survivors, but the novel's concerns bear on all post-Holocaust Jews struggling to create life out of the ashes.

—Rachel N. Baum

THE SIGN
Autobiographical Essay by Shmuel Yosef Agnon, 1972

Shmuel Yosef Agnon's "The Sign" is an autobiographical essay thinly disguised as a short story. It reaches far back into Agnon's past. Agnon's work as a writer in the Hebrew language goes back to the turn of the twentieth century (his work in Yiddish goes back even further). Modern Hebrew literature at the turn of the twentieth century was informed and influenced by a language and literature from a religious tradition that was its only antecedent, although Modern Hebrew literature strove for secular goals. Agnon's first successes as a writer came during the earliest efforts to revive Hebrew as an active language.

Agnon left Poland for Palestine in 1907, during the Second Aliyah (second wave of modern Jewish immigration to Palestine). During this time Hebrew literature labored to be a connecting link between the disintegrating Jewish life in the Diaspora and the new society being developed in Palestine. He left Palestine in 1913 and settled in Germany but returned to Jerusalem in 1924 when the Nazis were on the horizon.

Agnon's work vacillates between two loci of struggle: Jewish life in Buczacz, Poland, and Jewish life in Palestine/ Israel. He emphasizes the fragility of Jewish life in both locations but places great importance on the rituals of Judaism that give the Jewish community the strength to persevere.

"The Sign" begins with the Arab riots in Palestine in 1929, during which Agnon's home in Jerusalem is destroyed. At the same time he had heard that all the Jews in his hometown of Buczacz had been destroyed. He expresses a strong preference for the situation in Palestine: "With every sorrow I used to say how much better it was to live in the land of Israel than outside the land, for the Land of Israel has given us the strength to stand up for our lives, while outside the land we went to meet the enemy like sheep to the slaughter." Agnon laments that his European coreligionists reacted to the events of the Holocaust with a kind of defensive amnesia that disabled them from mounting any effective resistance to the monstrous persecution that engulfed them. Agnon prefers the more militant stance of Jews in Palestine and Israel in directly resisting their enemies.

Agnon recollects the holiday of Shavuot in terms of a dichotomy between bitter sorrow and needful celebration. He describes his new summer suit: it was a tradition to wear new clothes for the first time in the synagogue on a holiday. He discusses his amazement that he could celebrate a holiday while tens of thousands of his coreligionists were being killed in his hometown but maintains that religious celebration and ritual have given the Jews the strength to persevere through arduous hardships.

Agnon also reflects on the ritual candles in his contemporary House of Prayer that memorialize the victims of the genocide: "Six million Jews have been killed by the Gentiles, because of them a third of us are dead and two-thirds of us are orphans." He elucidates how his ties to Judaism are strengthened by reading the Jewish commandments every Shavuot as they were written down by Rabbi Solomon Ibn Gabriel. Agnon thereby links his religious ritual with his legendary penchant to be a bookworm.

—Peter R. Erspamer

SMOKE OVER BIRKENAU (Il fumo di Birkenau)
Short stories by Liana Millu, 1947

Smoke over Birkenau (1991; *Il fumo di Birkenau,* 1947) is a collection of six stories, each centered on a different woman. The women are prisoners at Birkenau, also known as Auschwitz II, a vast complex of barracks, gas chambers, and crematoriums about two miles from the older, smaller camp called Auschwitz I, near Kraków, Poland. Presumably each of the women underwent the selection process on the train ramp upon arrival and, because of her age, health, and strength, was chosen to enter the camp to perform forced labor until death. That selection process, involving forcible separation from most accompanying family members and the immediate gassing of those too young, old, or feeble to work, is not described here. Nor is the reader told when, how, and why the women, each from a different country, were arrested. Instead, author Liana Millu focuses entirely on the women's camp experiences and daily

routines. Their stories are universal—the chronicles of prisoners in circumstances of extreme brutality and deprivation.

At the same time, the stories are historically unique. It is late 1944 at Birkenau, where most of the prisoners are confined not because of political or criminal activities but because they were born Jewish. At Birkenau the forced labor is absurd, the intent is to exterminate, and the sick and the weak will be murdered rather than cared for. As **Primo Levi** relates in his introduction to the 1986 Italian edition of *Smoke over Birkenau,* there was "above all the haunting presence of the crematoria, located right in the middle of the women's camp, inescapable, undeniable, their ungodly smoke rising from the chimneys to contaminate every day and every night, every moment of respite or illusion, every dream and timorous hope." And yet, the women dare to hope. Allied planes fly over the camp. The guns on the Russian front are audible. The war, they think, may end any day. They struggle to stay alive until then.

The stories of the six characters are also unique by gender. They could only have happened to women, not to men. There is no suggestion that the experiences of male prisoners at Birkenau were not equally horrible. The focus here is simply on women. A single narrator, also a female prisoner and surely based on the author herself, introduces the women. The reader meets, for example, gentle "Lili Marlene" from Hungary, doomed because she dares to remain feminine and attracts the attentions of her female *kapo*'s lover. Maria's terrifying secret is that she was undetectably pregnant when she arrived at the camp and wants to have her baby. Bruna, from Milan, arrives at Birkenau with her 13-year-old son, who is confined in the men's section and whom she sees only when their labor battalions pass each other in the evening. Their wrenching love and anguish affect all the women. Zina, a Russian, struggles to see her husband, rumored also to be at Birkenau. Gustine, from The Netherlands, rejects her beloved sister Lotti, who has chosen prostitution as a means of survival. And Lise, desperately hoping to survive for her husband at home, must decide whether to encourage the attentions of a male prisoner who can keep her alive at a price. As they deal with their personal problems, the women perform tedious but grueling labor, eat little, and struggle against filth, disease, exhaustion, and human cruelty. Despite all odds they fight to survive and retain their humanity.

—Susan Zuccotti

THE SONG OF THE MURDERED JEWISH PEOPLE
(Dos Lid fun Oysgehargetn Yidishn Folk)
Epic Poem by Yitzhak Katzenelson, 1944

The epic poem *The Song of the Murdered Jewish People* (1980; *Dos Lid fun Oysgehargetn Yidishn Folk,* 1944) by

Yitzhak Katzenelson tells in 15 cantos the story of the destruction of Eastern European Jewry and their world, from the German invasion of Poland through the executions and deportations to the razing of the Warsaw Ghetto after the 1943 uprising. It begins, like Homer's *Odyssey,* with the exhortation to the poet to "Sing!" and ends, again like the classical heroic narrative, with a fight to the death between a small band of heroes and an overweening hostile force. Unlike Homer's epic, however, Katzenelson's ends in defeat: the heroes—the Warsaw Ghetto fighters whose death prefigures, in this poem, the fate of the Jewish people—dead, their possessions plundered, their lives and deaths unmourned, already half-forgotten. Katzenelson wrote his poem in the winter of 1943–44 while he was interned in Vittel. To increase the chances of his text's survival, he prepared six manuscript copies: two survive (one smuggled out of Vittel and taken to Palestine in the handle of a leather suitcase, the other buried on the camp terrain and exhumed after the war) and are preserved in the archive of the Beit Lohamei Haghetaot (Ghetto Fighters' House) in Israel. It was first published in Paris in 1945 in the original Yiddish in Hebrew script and has been translated into all the major European languages.

Encyclopedia Judaica has described Katzenelson's *Song* as "one of the greatest expressions of the tragedy of the Holocaust," and Hermann Adler has called it Eastern European Jewry's greatest poetic act of resistance. It is also an act of mourning, a lament for the dead: "Woe is me . . . There was a people once. All gone." The poet remembers them—the murdered millions who have been turned to fish food, to bone meal, and to soap—and bears witness on their behalf. This was the very job assigned the poet himself by his fellow partisans in the Warsaw Ghetto, who smuggled him out so that he could live to tell their story, the story of "the last Jews on Europe's earth." The poem thus begins with the poet's orders: "Sing! Take your harp in hand . . . and sing the last song of the last Jews who lived, who died, unburied, gone." And he accepts the charge: "I will sing . . . give me my harp that I can play."

Like all Katzenelson's work, this is an intensely oral text: its title, "*Song,*" can be taken literally. In this regard the poem bears the mark of the poet's previous work as a popular writer of lyric poetry, children's songs, and plays, designed for use within the life of the community. All the verses rhyme, the largely iambic meter is easily recitable, and large sections of the poem are written as dialogues. Indeed, the presentation constantly shifts from narration to dramatic action. In canto 8, for example, the brutal humiliation of two Jews—a rabbi and his shammes—by a German officer is staged as a terse three-person drama. By thus enacting the events, not just telling about them, the poet includes us, too, in the act of witnessing.

In stark contrast to the light and melodious tone that typified Katzenelson's pre-Holocaust lyrics, the language of this poem is violent, bitter, sarcastic, and often deliberately crude. The poet who once translated Heinrich Heine into elegant Hebrew has been replaced by a poet writing in the tradition of Chaim

Nachman Bialik's haunting Kishinev pogrom poems. Unlike Bialik, however, Katzenelson writes from within the disaster. His is a writing against time: the pace is breathless, the sentences fragmented, the repetitions frantic. At the same time, as if to stave off the end, the verses steadily increase in length; by the end of the poem they have literally doubled in length, and the prosodic frame is stretched to the breaking point. Chronology, too, no longer holds. Thus, the early days of the German occupation (canto 10) are remembered long after the deportations and the liquidation of the Warsaw Ghetto have begun to be described (cantos 4 and 5). What holds—and holds the poem together—is the rigorous discipline of textual form: fifteen cantos of fifteen four-versed stanzas each, each tightly framed by end-accented cross-rhymes. This form remains consistent from the first verse to the last.

Of all the unresolved questions in this poem, the one that most haunts it is the question of God. As the poet bitterly notes, God has disappeared as his people are being slaughtered: "No God, you heavens, lives in you!" The paradox is that, despite his absence, he is omnipresent in the text. For, according to the Hebrew tradition of *gematria,* the hermeneutic rule establishing the numerical equivalence of letters, 15 signifies God: יה. In the doubling of the number 15 (15 15-stanza cantos), God thus reappears as the poem's structuring principle. And so, in writing "as if there were a God," the poet reinscribes God as the wager on which creation is founded.

—Angelika Bammer

SOPHIE'S CHOICE
Novel by William Styron, 1979

Sophie's Choice is structured on the ungraspable principle puzzled over by George Steiner in his *Language and Silence* and referenced by the narrator of William Styron's novel: two orders of irreconcilable experience exist simultaneously, so that while some people are going about their daily and mundane business, others are suffering cataclysmic upheavals. It never fails to amaze Stingo that on that fateful April day in 1943, when Sophie was forced to make an evil choice between her children at the railroad station in Auschwitz, he was gorging on bananas in North Carolina in a last ditch effort to make weight for the Marines. The point is underscored not only by the repeated statements about this disparity of experience but, more dramatically, by the two very different stories that form the substance of the novel.

The first story is that of the randy 22-year-old would-be writer, recounted by his mature self at a distance of many years. This story focuses on two of the young Stingo's most feverish ambitions, to get laid and to write the Great American Novel; it frames the second story, that of Sophie Zawistowska, a Polish Catholic survivor of the concentration camps. Stingo provides the vehicle through which Sophie can gradually divulge her darkest secrets, since her Jewish lover, wrestling with his own demons, has proved himself to be a violently unpredictable recipient of her confidences. The full horror of her ''choice'' does not emerge until the final pages.

By being faithful to his youthful self's ambitions, and by distancing Sophie's story through the lens of those ambitions, the narrator tells a tale heavily centered on a callow young man. Not until well into the novel does the reader learn the details of Sophie's past, a rhetorical device that builds suspense and again reinforces the unsettling idea about disparate orders of experience. Sophie's frantic attempts to cope with her guilt, regain a semblance of normalcy and vitality, and start life anew exist in jarring juxtaposition to Stingo's equally frantic attempts to gain any experience at all. By having the stories intersect through Stingo's friendship with Sophie, Styron suggested that the two orders might well come, in fact must come, into some form of communication, imperfect though it might be.

Styron's controversial choice to concentrate so heavily in a Holocaust novel on Stingo's desire to lose his virginity serves several additional purposes. The novel is in great part a *Künstlerroman,* about the development of an artist, and therefore all aspects of the narrator's coming-of-age are relevant to his works as well as his life. The force of passion, sex, and love as life affirming drives plays a central role in the Styron canon as a whole, nowhere more importantly than in this novel, in which the urges toward destruction and self-destruction predominate. Stingo's sexual traumas also reflect the time in which the novel is set, when Freudian theories were on everyone's lips but sexual repressiveness reigned. Through Stingo's ridiculous encounters with Leslie Lapidus and Mary Alice Grimball, Styron provided comic relief from Sophie's sexual violations in the concentration camp and on the New York City subway; at the same time he pointed up the contrast between all those episodes and the liberating (and presumably instructional) sex that Stingo finally achieves with Sophie.

Other dual orders inform the novel. The home of the Auschwitz commandant is essentially cordoned off from the hellish activities taking place outside, with life proceeding for the Höss family on such a separate plane that it might as well be on a different planet. The style of the sections dealing with Stingo is hyperbolic, a mixture of pomposity, intensity, and insecurity befitting the subject, whereas Styron often reserved a matter-of-fact, understated vocabulary and tone for the scenes from Sophie's past, which set off the dreadfulness of those events. In these ways Styron melded style and content to greatest effect.

Styron's tactic of making the novel so heavily autobiographical, down to the thinly disguised listing of the Styron novels that Stingo will go on to publish, has appeared self-indulgent to some readers, but it does enhance the authority of the novel and implies that all people must acknowledge human degradation on a personal level if they are to be fully human

themselves. Through the revelations about Sophie's past and Stingo's as well, and through the connections Styron drew between European history and the American South's legacy of slavery, *Sophie's Choice* highlights the choices that all individuals make and the guilt that they bear in consequence. The novel is of a piece with Styron's other works in advocating rebellion against any bureaucratic system that would reduce its inhabitants to ciphers. *Sophie's Choice* ultimately teaches that, like Stingo, we must all shed our self-protective innocence without succumbing to despair.

—Judith Ruderman

SOUL OF WOOD (''Eine Seele aus Holz'')
Short Story by Jakov Lind, 1962

Born in 1927 to Jewish parents, Jakov Lind endured formative years shaped by the experience of overwhelming danger and fear. In 1938, shortly after Austria's Anschluss with Nazi Germany, the 11-year-old was forced to leave his parents and his home in Vienna to find safety with various foster families in The Netherlands. Following the Nazi occupation of The Netherlands, Lind together with the Dutch Jewish population was moved to the Amsterdam ghetto, where he escaped deportation by hiding in an attic. After being provided with false papers and a new identity, that of a young Dutchman named Jan Overbeek, Lind decided that he would be safer in enemy territory and went to work in Nazi Germany. There he worked as a sailor on a large barge, barely escaping the Allied bombings. During the final stages of the war, Lind worked for the director of a metallurgical institute in Marburg. He was 18 when the war ended.

Lind's early traumatic experiences had a profound impact on him, and they surface, in various ways, in his literary works, particularly in his early writings. These include the prose collections *Soul of Wood* (1964; first published as *Eine Seele aus Holz* in 1962) and *The Stove* (originally written in English but first published in German in 1973) as well as the novels *Landscape in Concrete* (1963) and *Ergo* (1966), which are set during the Nazi period, including the war years, and examine human behavior in the face of life-threatening danger. In these works Lind creates an absurd, nightmarish, and unpredictable world in which fear and guilt are the primary human experiences.

The initial, title story of Lind's first publication, *Soul of Wood,* a collection of short prose, includes the subject of opportunism as part of the author's exploration of central human experiences. In this story the grotesque atmosphere is created not only by the Nazi regime of terror but by the opportunistic compliance of its followers and bystanders. The main character is Wohlbrecht, a World War I veteran with a wooden leg who, although he does not subscribe to the Nazi ideology, nevertheless seeks to profit from it. After promising his Jewish employers he will hide their paraplegic son after their deportation in exchange for the deed to their apartment, Wohlbrecht transports the helpless Anton Barth to a mountain hut and leaves him there to die. When his plans to sell the apartment are thwarted by a Nazi, Wohlbrecht finds himself an inmate in an insane asylum. He survives by currying favor from the Nazi doctors who are administering fatal "special treatments" to the patients of the asylum. With the end of the war in sight and the Russians advancing on Vienna, Wohlbrecht and the doctors set off on a bizarre race to retrieve the remains of Anton Barth, whose body they hope will exonerate them by providing evidence that they had once attempted to save a Jew. Wohlbrecht, who does not want to share "his Jew," is shot and left on the mountainside.

While Wohlbrecht appears to personify the opportunistic bystander who adapts easily to whoever is in power and acts only in his own self-interest, Lind's text actually blurs the line between victim and perpetrator. Wohlbrecht has little or no control over his fate and repeatedly falls victim to men more unscrupulous than he. His victim status is indicated by his physical handicap, which connects him with the totally paralyzed Anton Barth, the true victim in the story. On the other hand, his wooden leg can be understood as the outer manifestation of his inner deformation, to which the title "Soul of Wood" refers.

Anton Barth's miraculous cure on the mountaintop after he is abandoned by Wohlbrecht and his existence as the mythical "Wild Man" on the mountain take Lind's text into the realm of the fantastic. As is the case with the grotesque elements in the story, the fantastic and bizarre inhibit reader identification, which detract from the central intention of the work: the exploration of the relationship between victims and perpetrators and the gray area where the difference between the two is blurred.

—Helga Schreckenberger

SPARK OF LIFE (Der Funke Leben)
Novel by Erich Maria Remarque, 1952

In one of **Tadeusz Borowski**'s greatest stories, "Silence," a dozen inmates of Dachau, which has just been liberated by the Americans, are trampling to death an SS guard. When an American officer enters the bunk for an absurdly polite pep talk, the campers shove their victim out of sight, and the moment the American has left, they finish the job. The story might serve as a commentary on Francis Bacon's essay on revenge: "Revenge is a kind of wild justice which the more man's nature runs to, the more ought law to weed it out." And he adds, "The most tolerable sort of revenge is for those

wrongs which there is no law to remedy; but then let a man take heed the revenge be such as there is no law to punish."

Erich Maria Remarque's *Spark of Life,* published in German as *Der Funke Leben,* points rather the same moral in what was one of the earliest novels about life in a death camp—Anna Seghers's *The Seventh Cross,* which appeared as early as 1942, takes the concentration camp as a point of departure, focusing on the landscape of flight from a camp. And it necessarily takes place years before *Spark of Life,* which minutely describes a camp in the last months of the war, at a time when the country was being scorched by Allied bombs and the Allied advance had begun to encourage at first resistance, then "wild justice," among the inmates. (The novel can be roughly dated by a reference to the Nazis' failure to blow up the Remagen Bridge on 11 March 1945 as having occurred "quite a while in the past.") The hero, an inmate since 1933, is simply identified as "509," and the disclosure of his name some two-thirds through the story rather transparently marks a turning point. (No one seems to have made anything of the name, Koller, which appears as a common noun dozens of times in *All Quiet on the Western Front* alone and can best be translated by its cognate "choler.") The refusal by 509 and a younger inmate, Berger, to submit to lethal experiments marks the first downright act of resistance, and 509 first experiences the sense of being a mensch again when he gets a revolver into his hand.

Remarque is no doubt at his best in extended descriptive passages. The minute details he lavishes on the operations at a crematorium are among the most horrifying scenes in concentrationary literature—and not merely by an "outsider." Then, too, he re-creates the bombing of the camp, the burning streets, and the panicked citizens with a wonderfully adroit combination of (never really vindictive) zest and lynx-eyed authority. Some of the scenes are eerily funny: Berger scaring off one of the *kapo*s by convincing him that in touching him the *kapo* has contracted cadaverine poisoning, or the commandant's panic when a new transport threatens to swamp the camp. The failure of the book ultimately lies in Remarque's stylistic gaffes and his feeble character definitions. Comments that are intended to shock too often sound so smart-alecky that they leave an acid aftertaste: "the camps in Germany had become rather humane . . . One only gassed, clubbed and shot, or simply worked people insensible and then left them to starve"; " . . . the commandant was particularly proud [that the camp] had no gas chambers. In Mellern, he liked to explain, one died a natural death." Sentences like these display an embarrassing insensitivity. Ditto Remarque's tone deafness in orchestrating his conceits: "The tension escaped from her like gas from a balloon"; "Impotence plunged over him like night."

In his foreword to the first edition Remarque tried to vouch for the authenticity of his people by citing his sources: anybody familiar with the material would recognize in the commandant's love for rabbits Heinrich Himmler's love for rabbits; in the electrically lit skull that lights up the bunk senior's room the human lamp shades in Buchenwald (and elsewhere). But surely creative fiction is not made of such mummery. In describing the camp personnel, Remarque notes, he tried to explore the ways in which they became the way they became. But except for a perfunctory comment that X grew up idolizing Y and that Z, who could not live on his wages as a postal clerk, "now [had] something," Remarque's attempts languish in the void. Here comparison with the figures in a novel like **Heinrich Böll**'s *Adam, Where Art Thou?* comes to mind. In a book one-fourth as long as Remarque's, Böll, by sketching their antecedents in a few pages, shows the reader why, given their past, Bressen shams his wound, Greck dies in his own excrement, and Ilona Kartök chooses to be baptized. The central female figure in *Adam,* Ilona is far more complex than the one female figure in *Spark of Life,* Berger's young woman. As the novel ends, these two take their solitary way from the inferno. But it is Berger who has the last word. The few surviving inmates are dispersing, and one of them sadly comments on their dispersion:

> " . . . we shouldn't lose sight of one another like this."
>
> "Oh, yes," said Berger. "We should."

—Edgar Rosenberg

STAR ETERNAL (Kokhav ha-efer)
Novel by Ka-Tzetnik 135633, 1966

In different ways *Star Eternal* (1971; *Kokhav ha-efer,* 1966) by Ka-Tzetnik 135633 is a remarkable, seminal achievement in the Holocaust canon. At once a disturbing and edifying work, it depicts in vivid, yet simple and direct detail the unspeakable horrors of concentration camp existence and functions as a *summum* of Ka-Tzetnik's thematic template. Above all, it describes the gruesome events of the Final Solution in a pared-down, staccato style and language that tangibly pierces the thick, impenetrable wall erected by readers that often prevents any cognitive or emotional engagement. Put simply, the novel arouses and extracts a deep chill of empathy and shock from the spectator and in the process opens a window for the younger generation so as to allow them to connect with the world being described.

Star Eternal possesses a mimetic surface clarity that is aided and abetted by the brevity of the basic Hebrew, pruned of metaphor and hyperbole. It is laconic, trimmed, and controlled, and the effect is so natural that the bewildered reader is increasingly unaware of how much detail is being described. Admittedly, the conflation of razor-sharp sentences with fragmented descriptions underscores the author's desire to reflect the crushed, disjointed reality that is outside any normative

framework and that does not fit into a logical, coherent mold. Likewise, it is not unreasonable to suggest that the message foisted upon the audience is that here is a perverted reality, stripped bare of the conventional constituents of time and space and that the monastic verbal representation is in consonance with the unthinkable reality.

The novel was originally published in 1960 in Hebrew under the title *Ha-shaon* ("The Clock"), and it is small wonder that the central operating motif informing the narrative is one of time, more specifically, the parallel time frames of normal Europe, where people live a typical, ordinary life, and "planet Auschwitz," where Jews suffer terror and inhumanity. In construction the book is made up of a series of jarring, loosely coupled episodes, which the author terms "stages." Each chapter is self-contained, encasing within its midst a separate title and story line, and pivots around disparate threads of camp living, leavened for the most part by a welter of jolts, gnomic words, and twists.

Bookended by a prologue and an epilogue, *Star Eternal* begins in the narrator's eerily quiet street, bathed in the searing heat of the sun and featuring a boulevard of display windows. The author adumbrates the tranquillity of the place, heightened by snippets of banality peppered throughout the opening pages, and then quickly dismantles it when the intensity of the date is revealed: 9 September 1939, the day on which Hitler's army marched into Poland, marking the start of World War II. Even more starkly, the city's electric clock is in synchronicity with the unfolding of events; its hands rest on 9 a.m. And thus we have an application of a direct and realistic portraiture devoted to the profound and sober chronicling of a specific place and time, setting down a visage of the "other planet," to borrow from Ka-Tzetnik once more, in precise detail and lineament.

After the hero, Ferber, is taken to Auschwitz, the narrative lens zeros in on this world with uncompromising eyes, capturing with perfectly modulated metrics the indigestible tableau, the images of annihilation, and the doing of evil that defies description. With a raw filmic gaze the author, possessing a strong grip on his material, leads the reader into the vortex of Auschwitz, into the black hole, condensing into a few passages the feeling of omnipresent death. Because the narrative is written in the second person, the reader is addressed openly and is thus positioned to see the inmate's world and is co-opted into participating in an experience from which, by reason of distance, he was explicitly excluded. In other words, the reader is positioned to adopt and comply with the mood, vulnerability, and torment the shaping of the plot seeks to present.

There are moments of uninhibited, infernal magnitude. In one episode we step into the "showers," surrounded by the bony, living dead, and stare into the sprinklers above our heads in anticipation of the stream of Zyklon B, which will spurt the blue gas into our lungs. If anything, the unflagging pace, the leaping from one visceral episode of agonizing torture to another, the repeated catalog of atrocities presented in explicit specificity are all chokingly disturbing. One need only consider a sequence in which a group throws itself at the ground to lick the remains of some spilled soup, one person's teeth biting into another, to understand the reduction of the human condition to its most basic level.

And still, in the midst of the machinery of death, a note of optimism for the future can be drawn from a striking theological conversation between Ferber and the rabbi of Shilev titled "The Last Debate." At one point Ferber ponders the question of the Jewish people's destiny, asking the rabbi why God has deserted his children and delivered them into the hands of the beast. In response the rabbi states that out of the ruins and ashes of the night the nation of Israel will arise in the promised land with its eternal star brightly shining. On the face of it, this is a false hope. Yet for the hero it is a nourishing vision: "Light of full understanding flashed within Ferber; his brothers there, in the land of Israel! Revelation bared itself to him. For a split second only. Round about him all was distillate, pure. No longer did he feel himself in his own skeleton. At that moment he was utterly oblivious to his body's existence. The Rabbi's eyes were like two open gates."

At the novel's conclusion, when the main protagonist returns from Auschwitz to his hometown of Metropoli, the clock has not stood still but is still running, but this time it is a changed world he encounters. A compendium of the devastating effects of the camp is supplied in the text's concluding lines. Here Ferber pleads that one hair of his sister's golden locks be returned, along with one of his father's shoes, one wheel of his brother's bicycle, and one speck from his mother's back.

—Dvir Abramovich

STEPS
Novel by Jerzy Kosinski, 1968

Jerzy Kosinski's eagerly awaited second novel, *Steps* (1968), received the National Book Award in 1969, perhaps in belated acknowledgment of *The Painted Bird* (1965). *Steps* shares several structural similarities with its disturbing predecessor. Although much shorter, it is also highly episodic, consisting of more than 50 separate sections narrated in the first person by a dispassionate voice that sounds like a grown-up version of the boy in *The Painted Bird*. Each section contains a complete story, really a vignette, and the whole is held together by the nameless narrator. None of the sections in roman type contains dialogue; all conversation is summarized by the narrative voice. Interspersed among these episodes are about a dozen sections printed in italics, totally in dialogue. Italicized speech is occasionally mixed into one of the other episodes. The taut narrative presents the brutal material in a matter-of-fact manner in both styles.

The narrative voice recalls a young Kosinski, with stories taking place in a postwar Poland as well as in a technologically advanced country like the United States, where Kosinski had migrated in 1957. In the countryside many gruesome episodes occur. In one a demented woman lives naked in a cage in a barn where village men use her sexually. The farmer who keeps her (it may be his daughter) profits from these visits. When the narrator reports the man to the police, they take away the woman. The narrator then accuses the village priest of knowing about the situation and protecting his congregants through the sanctity of the confessional.

In a few scenes Kosinski uses his own work experiences as a New York parking lot attendant to tie together episodes in which the narrator also does such work. Perhaps half the episodes are sexual, including some from the narrator's student days and some from his countryside experiences. In one, in which he gets lost on an archeological expedition, the narrator is saved from starvation by two enormously fat women who use him sexually in exchange for food. In most cases, however, the narrator victimizes women. For instance, he induces one of his lovers to sleep with another man to prove her devotion to him. In another he becomes that other man himself when a friend makes the same demand on his own lover. In yet another episode the narrator's girlfriend endures a gang rape when a group of men overpower him and attack her. This changes their relationship, so that by the end of the tale he has created a situation at a party in which—while he flees— she is about to be taken by another group of men.

The effect of the narrative is continually jarring. Violence and abuse occur so continuously that without a mitigating presentation we grow numb to what is going on. This is truly a post-Holocaust, Nietzschean world, in which "God is dead" and everything is permitted. Only a few sections toward the middle of the book refer specifically to the Holocaust. In one episode the extermination of rats is compared to the execution of prisoners in concentration camps. In another a professional boxer is brought to a camp to fight with a prisoner who is destined for the gas chambers. But the professional refuses to fight because of the prisoner's racial inferiority.

Readers of *The Painted Bird* will see other parallels between the two books. The emphasis on gaining revenge pervades both, and there are episodes in which the narrator perpetrates an almost gratuitous level of violent revenge. In addition, Kosinski once again makes an issue of silence. In some of the final episodes, for instance, the narrator of *Steps* pretends to be a deaf-mute, reminding us of how the boy in *The Painted Bird* was struck dumb. Students of Kosinski will notice how often suicide occurs, is contemplated, or is justified in *Steps*. The final vignette shows a woman stripping off her clothes before entering the ocean, much as Edna Pontellier does at the end of Kate Chopin's *The Awakening* and with the same ambiguous outcome. "A small rotten brown leaf brushed against her lips," Kosinski says, writing now in the third person. The woman's shadow crosses the ocean floor as she dives deep, and the "tiny leaf" appears above her. Does the fallen leaf represent death? Kosinski never tells us because this is where the narrative ends.

As he did with *The Painted Bird,* Kosinski wrote and published himself a long essay about *Steps* shortly after the book appeared. The title is "Art of the Self: Essays à Propos *Steps*" (1969), and readers can find it in *Passing By: Selected Essays, 1962–1991,* edited posthumously by Kosinski's widow. In the essay Kosinski identifies his primary narrative structure as montage, a key mode of both modernism and postmodernism, and he talks in particular about the active role the reader must play in relation to the work. The major themes Kosinski lays out in the essay are metamorphosis, domination, revenge, cruelty, and obsession. The list will work just as well with all of Kosinski's novels.

—Michael Hoffman

STIFLED WORDS (Paroles suffoquées)
Memoir by Sarah Kofman, 1987

Sarah Kofman's *Stifled Words,* published in French in 1987 as *Paroles suffoquées* and in English translation in 1998, takes its title from Robert Anteleme's account of his experience in the Holocaust death camps, *The Human Race.* It is not a memoir in the conventional sense—as is Kofman's *Rue Orderner, Rue Labat,* for example—but rather an extended meditation on the Holocaust and responses to it. There are three figures that lie behind and inspire the work.

The first figure is her father, Berek Kofman, a Parisian rabbi deported and murdered by the Nazis in Auschwitz. She gives the facts—"taken to Drancy on July 16th, 1942 . . . convoy no. 12, dated July 29, 1942"—in a "neutral" way, echoing the Serge Klarsfeld Memorial, which she incorporates into the text. This neutral voice, she writes, "leaves you without a voice, makes you doubt your common sense and all sense, makes you suffocate in silence." Yet the absence of her father is present throughout the text—and perhaps all of her writing—as a constant, haunting presence.

The second figure is Maurice Blanchot. Kofman writes that it "behoves me, as a Jewish woman intellectual who has survived the Holocaust, to pay homage to Blanchot." This is a very strong statement of support for the French writer, critic, and philosopher. Before the war, and despite his close friendship with the Jewish philosopher Emmanuel Levinas, Blanchot published articles in right-wing and anti-Semitic periodicals. During the war, however, he helped Jews hide from the Nazis in occupied Paris, and his reflections after 1945 on the Holocaust, principally in *The Writing of the Disaster* but also throughout his work, have been extremely influential on two generations of French thought. In this work his influence is most clearly seen in the understanding of otherness and in the idea of the community of those with nothing in common, an idea developed further by Jean-Luc Nancy in *The Inoperative Community.*

The third influence on Kofman is Robert Antelme. His book *The Human Race,* an account of his experiences in Auschwitz, was extremely influential in the French understanding of the Holocaust. Most of Kofman's book is a discussion of Antelme's memoir. She asks how it is possible to speak when the task—"to convey the experience just as it was, to explain everything to the other"—is impossible. To speak is to choke; words are stifled. Antelme's book and many other testimonies are examples of this "choking speech." For Kofman, Antelme's central argument is that the extreme situations in the death camps were simply a magnification of what happens in the "normal" world, that "we the detainees are not animals; and you the SS are not gods. We are nothing more or less than men and there is nothing inhuman or superhuman in man." She shows that, for Antelme, even the most basic vital functions show that a man is still a man. Antelme maintains that because the SS "sought to call the unity of the Human race into question . . . they will eventually be crushed."

In a four-page coda, influenced by Blanchot and Friedrich Nietzsche and implicitly by Martin Heidegger, Kofman reflects on Antelme's argument. She suggests that, because he does not posit an essence that the SS and the victims share, Antelme does not simply affirm an old-fashioned humanism. Yet they do share a community "without community . . . the relation without relation." It is a relationship based not on similarities of nationality, say, or of religion or of being reasonable but on an awareness of difference and of the unassimilable nature of human difference: "the abject dispossession of the deportees signifies the indestructibility of alterity, its absolute character." This sort of thinking—hard to summarize—has many affinities with the work of Levinas and the later Jacques Derrida, not least because of the shared influence of Blanchot. It seeks to ask about the conditions of the possibility of the idea of humanity and ethics after the Holocaust.

—Robert Eaglestone

STILL ALIVE: A HOLOCAUST GIRLHOOD REMEMBERED (weiter leben: Eine Jugend)
Memoir by Ruth Klüger, 1992

Originally published as *weiter leben* in Germany in 1992, the English translation and revised edition became available from Feminist Press as *Still Alive: A Holocaust Girlhood Remembered* in November 2001. In this award-winning book,

Ruth Klüger recalls her past and supplements these recollections with critical observations and reflections from the present, specifically addressing a German audience. Calling it a "German book," she has dedicated it to her friends from Göttingen, a city in northern Germany, where she has occasionally resided and taught at the local university. The text itself also addresses the readers directly (as "Dear friends," for instance) and repeatedly invites them to participate actively in the reading process. The specific episodes of her life are told from the perspective of an emancipated, self-confident Jewish woman who survived prejudice, persecution, the loss of her family, internment in three concentration camps, and displacement—a woman who is now an internationally respected scholar and writer. At the same time, the book has another dimension. Its critical candor extends to author and audience alike, and the narrative explicitly contemplates Klüger's own process of working through the past. The reader learns about personal issues ranging from the recurring preoccupation with her father and brother and the circumstances surrounding their deaths to her experience as an immigrant in the United States. Moreover, the text raises many controversial questions of interest, among them coming to terms with one's past (*Vergangenheitsbewältigung*), feelings of guilt, the culture of Holocaust memory (*Erinnerungskultur*), and the role of women within Judaism. The pertinence of her topics, the vivid and precise use of language with which she has traced the course of her life, her recognition of the problematic nature of memory, and her outspoken honesty constitute this autobiography's uniqueness. The reader not only learns about one survivor's life but also receives an education on questions central to the Holocaust.

Five large sections frame Klüger's account: "Vienna," "The Camps: Theresienstadt, Auschwitz, Christianstadt," "Germany-Bavaria," "New York," and "Epilogue: Göttingen." Each, she insists, is important to her identity. "Vienna" consists of childhood memories, particularly about her father, Viktor Klüger, and her brother George (Schorschi), both of whom died during the Holocaust. Her complicated relationship with her mother, who survived along with her daughter, also plays an important role throughout the book. "The Camps" begins in September 1942, when Klüger, not quite 11 years old, was deported with her mother to Theresienstadt. In this section she describes her living arrangements in what was called "The Children's Home," the friends she made, and the general experience of being in a camp. Fond of German literature, especially German poetry, she relates how she started to write what she later describes as "sehnsüchtige Gedichte über Heimat und Freiheit" ("poems of yearning about homeland and freedom"). In May 1944 mother and daughter are sent to Auschwitz, where they both are selected in June of the same year for work in Christianstadt, a satellite camp of Gross-Rosen in former Silesia. In addition to descriptions of everyday life in the camps (deportation, hunger and thirst, selection, slave labor), the reader also hears of the continued importance of poetry for her during this time.

Writing and reciting poetry give her comfort and support by providing a balanced, coherent, and well-structured language in times of utter chaos. She evokes how poetry helped to pass the time (during roll call, for instance, when she recited Friedrich Schiller's ballads) and exercised her mind, preserving her sanity. Memorization was necessary: since she often lacked pen and paper, she wrote poetry in her mind. The book quotes not only excerpts from the concentration camp poems but also those she wrote after the war about her traumatic experiences. Some recurring themes in her postwar work are the death of her father and brother and her preoccupation with the dead, the ghosts who intrude on the present. She analyzes each poem, assesses its aesthetic qualities, and tells the story behind its composition.

The third section, "Germany-Bavaria," recalls the immediate postwar period in Germany. After successfully escaping from Christianstadt with her mother and Ditha, her foster sister, whom her mother had adopted in Auschwitz, they join the flow of refugees from the East into Germany, obtain identity cards, and pass as Germans. Klüger tells of qualifying for the university and attending classes at the University of Regensburg before immigrating to the United States. Her acquaintance with the student she calls Christoph (actually the German writer Martin Walser) and their numerous conversations form a part of this section. "New York" portrays her difficulties as an unwelcome immigrant in the new country and the small group of female friends who sustained her. The chapter ends with her leaving her mother behind in New York after receiving a bachelor's degree from Hunter College in 1950. In the "Epilogue" Klüger describes the startling effects of a bicycle accident she suffered in Göttingen. This experience triggers the realization that the past is always present and inescapable. The ghosts of the dead require her to deal with her past and to work through it, prompting her to write her autobiography, which will surely stand as a lasting evocation of one person and an entire period.

—Sandra Alfers

STREETS OF THE RIVER: THE BOOK OF DIRGES AND POWER (Rehovot hanahar: Sefer ha'iliyot vehakoah)
Poems by Uri Zvi Greenberg, 1951

Uri Zvi Greenberg's collection of poems *Rehovot hanahar: Sefer ha'iliyot vehakoah* (*Streets of the River: The Book of Dirges and Power*), published in 1951 and awarded the Bialik prize, was the poet's anguished response to the Holocaust and is arguably the most magnificent model of lamentations in the pantheon of Holocaust poetry. Borrowed from a Sabbath prayer that rhapsodies the rivers of faith flowing with wisdom, the title represents the stream of bloodshed and tears shed by the victims as well as the constant wandering of the Jewish people that ultimately leads to the Holy Land.

The tempestuous bard's oeuvre is marked by an explosive rhetorical force, seething with exhortations and powerful declamations against the tormentors of his people. The speaker's individual persona that addresses the reader is on display, accentuating the subjective, potent voice and conflating the political with the personal. Not infrequently the "I" is employed to dramatize the horror of the European Jew and the nation, suffering destruction and clinging to their eternal longing for redemption. Skirting along the edge of egocentric obsessiveness and with an intense sense of thunderous fury, Greenberg assumes the role of a biblical prophet to bemoan the devastating terror of the Holocaust, willing to confront and denounce the God who instead of protecting his chosen people had surrendered them to the murderous gentiles. In one scathing verse he asks: "God, why hast thou made me a pillar among my people." And while the poet points an accusatory finger at the Nazis, he is intent on reminding us that the European genocide that engulfed his people is only but one link in a chain of a mythic narrative that has divided Christian from Jew. In this ahistorical version the modern catastrophe is situated within a broader story line in which the Jews, from time immemorial, have been subject to persecution by the same, archetypal enemy. On the whole the message hammered home to Israelis is that there exists a connective between those Jews who lost their lives in millennia of murderous sprees and those exterminated in the camps—both part of a holistic chain of catastrophes leading to the establishment of Israel.

At heart the poems lament both the gruesome fate that befell Greenberg's parents and sisters whom he could not save and the victims that perished in Auschwitz. In this respect, it is noteworthy that in Greenberg's literary universe there exists an acute bipolar dichotomy, an obtrusive duality that is the golden thread that runs through the 385 pages of vengeful utterances. The cycle of poems oscillates between passages, at times almost involuntary in mood, that explore the horrible calamity to imaginative modes of rebirth shot through with visions of regeneration. Indeed, Greenberg's *ars poetica,* while showcasing a tortured human soul that throbs beneath a cracked surface, abrim with feelings of mourning, guilt, and powerlessness, simultaneously betrays a shard of hope. As such, the poet renarrativizes the Holocaust experience, presenting it through the prism of the ancient covenant that God had made with Abraham and which encases within its midst ultimate salvation. Renewal and survival is based on the ancient doctrine that Jewish existence is immortal and cannot be brought to an end. Amid the scenes of massacres and mourning one discovers a note of faith—that out of the ruins, post Holocaust Jewry will triumphantly rise to once again establish sovereignty in the cherished homeland, restoring the Davidic destiny in fulfillment of manifest national destiny. Also looming large is the overarching topos of Greenberg's personal loss on which the poet tells a large part of his jeremiads. For the orphaned narrator the destruction of his childhood paradise extends far beyond the individual scale to include an entire people who stand at the edge of an abyss.

The theme of German barbarity looms large in "We Were Not Likened to Dogs Among the Gentiles," a disturbing poem that shines a light on the wicked and their treatment of the Jews. The artist gasps at the love and care bestowed upon the dog by his gentile owners, who grieve his passing as they would a family member, while denying the Jew any similar humane compassion afforded to the animal. According to Greenberg, the violation of the Jew is comparable to that meted out to a leprous sheep, "Before the slaughter they did not pull out the teeth of their sheep / They did not strip the wool from their bodies as they did to us / They did not push the sheep into the fire and make ash of the living." In a volcanic outburst the poem's coda contains the vehement warning that the desecration of Jewish life will forever be imbedded in the annals of western civilization, destined to become the axis of reference for all human atrocities to come: "He who compares will say: This analogy is of the Jewish kind." Elsewhere, Greenberg references the murder of his father by a Nazi soldier on a snowy hill, the invasion of the Jewish home by gentiles who engrave a cross onto the walls, and a yearning to be buried with his parents for he cannot live without them.

The intermingling of biblical motifs with the European genocide is further amplified in, "Lord! You Saved Me from Ur-Germany As I Fled." Employing the legend in which God saves Abram from the fire (Ur) after being tried and sentenced to death, the poet equates the furnaces of the ancient Chaldees with the crematoriums of Auschwitz. Further, the poet's survival (albeit with a scarred and rived psyche) and the shielding of Israel from Nazi attack is a redemptive affirmation of divine kindness and a sign that the holy covenant will be actualized with the return of the Jews to their homeland. Above all, Greenberg's central message is that the supreme form of retribution will be victory over his people's enemies and the effluence of Jewish pride in the land of their forefathers.

—Dvir Abramovich

STRIPES IN THE SKY: A WARTIME MEMOIR
(Strepen aus de hemel: Oorlogsherinneringen)
Memoir by Gerhard Durlacher, 1985

Gerhard Durlacher, who grew up in the German town of Baden-Baden, lived through the initial years of Nazi rule. He watched his community and his family disintegrate under the stresses of prejudice and institutionalized anti-Semitism. Ultimately they sought safety in Holland, but it was too late. They were shipped in 1942 to Auschwitz-Birkenau, where Gerhard and his parents were separated. His parents were sent to the gas chambers; he was one of the camp's few survivors. *Stripes in the Sky,* published in English translation in 1991, is not only an account of the horrors he suffered there, it is a chronicle of Durlacher's personal mission to discover why the fate of European Jews was so persistently ignored. Why were civilian and military targets bombed while the crematoria in the camps were left standing? Why did a quickly constructed model camp so easily fool the German Red Cross and delay further investigation?

Durlacher was one of a group of 89 boys, between the ages of twelve and sixteen, assigned to Auschwitz-Birkenau men's camp B II D in 1944. Their would-be graves—the actual graves of four million others—lay just ahead of them when Dr. Josef Mengele, the mastermind of Nazi pseudo-medical experiments, separated them from nearly 400 others from the same lineup who were sent to the gas chamber. Whatever Mengele intended for them was never known; the war's end eclipsed his experiments. *Stripes in the Sky* describes the so-called "selection" drill, where each boy was made to walk naked in from of Mengele, who stood at the entrance to his barracks in his pristine SS uniform. After each boy told him his name, age, and hometown, he then received a life or death sentence.

The selected people were told lies, if they were told anything, about what awaited them. Also written on neat schedules were *appells,* roll calls at which prisoners stood outside to be counted for hours at a time, often in the rain or snow. At meal calls prisoners received a ladle full of dirty brown water called "tea." Chores included wagon duty, during which the younger boys were made to carry lumber to the crematorium—one log for each body. On one occasion they were forced to pull a wagon full of prisoners who were too old or infirm to walk to the gas chamber under their own power.

The survivors of this group of 89 started renewing their long-dormant ties in 1985, when Durlacher and Yehuda Bacon began a letter-writing and research project to track down the others, more than 20 in number, who were living all over the world.

Durlacher believes his survival in the camp depended on youth, his fitness, and his experience. He was liberated, critically ill, by the Russians, and made his way to Holland, where he married and had a family and ultimately became a sociology professor. It was only in the last ten years of his life that Durlacher began to write about his experiences, of which *Stripes in the Sky* was his initial memoir.

—Martha Sutro

THE STRONGHOLD
Novel by Meyer Levin, 1965

Meyer Levin's *The Stronghold* (1965) is set somewhere in Bavaria, within the walls of a castle functioning as a Nazi prison for the heads of state of a mythically generic country resembling France. At the castle the prisoners have been treated humanely by the baron of the province, a Nazi whose remoteness from the realm of political and military action has left him untouched by fanaticism and also by the reality of the Nazis' genocidal war against the Jews. With the German front collapsing and the Americans rapidly approaching, the prisoners have started planning to resume their duties and, in the process, give voice to the diverse political visions for their homeland that had divided them prior to the Nazi occupation. At the center of their troubled reminiscences is the figure of the former premier Paul Vered, a highly assimilated Jew (perhaps modeled on Leon Blum) whose domestic and military policies, though finally inefficacious against Nazi aggression, are explicitly compared to the democratic socialism of the American president Roosevelt. As it so happens Vered himself arrives at the castle, having been spared the fate of the gas chambers by a Nazi lieutenant colonel named Kraus, who has fled the collapsing front with only a strongbox of jewels, a single Jew as his hostage, and vague and unrealistic hopes for a Nazi retrenchment.

Since Vered has been a witness to Buchenwald and then Auschwitz, where his wife was put to death in the gas chambers, his presence forces the prisoners to encounter the news of the Nazi genocide as more than a rumor or a piece of war propaganda. In the face of this news Levin allegorically traces in the attitude of each character a strain of European politics and the elements of anti-Semitism that reside therein, whether characters represent nationalists and Christian conservatives on the one hand or Marxist leftists on the other. *The Stronghold* is never an especially strong novel, but it is probably best when it addresses itself to the varieties of anti-Semitism that characterized so much of bystanding Europe. Those characters modeled on democratic socialism fare best in the novel's estimation—specifically an ambitious young minister named Remy and his wartime mistress Marianne, each of whom is loyal to Vered, and a "social action" Catholic priest named Frere Luc, who has risked his own well-being in the past to stand for the rights of the working man and now begins to examine the Catholic Church's longstanding anti-Semitism. Although the heroism of Luc's thought and actions is drawn in a sentimental vein, he is in many ways a persuasive character and clearly at the rhetorical center of Levin's novel. For as each of the characters reckons with the legacy of European anti-Semitism, it is Luc alone who has vowed to make the defeat of anti-Semitism his explicit cause. When Luc tries to enlist Vered's help, Vered responds—or is it Levin himself speaking?—that there is little Jews can do to correct Christian anti-Semitism; it is a battle the Christians must fight on their own. Wanting the memory of the Holocaust to fall heavy upon the Christian conscience, Levin also insists—perhaps recalling the politics surrounding the Catholic Church's statement on anti-Semitism at Vatican II—that the emergence of a truer form of Christianity, sensitive to the connotations of Jesus as crucified Jew, is crucial if longstanding prejudices against Jews are to be overthrown.

Most of the second half of *The Stronghold* falls into stock melodrama, with the two poles represented by the survivor Vered and the unapologetic Nazi Kraus. Vered functions less as a character than as ghostly principle of witness. His struggle with survivor guilt, as he wonders whether he had a right to escape "the fate of the Jews," is of little psychological interest. The question seems mostly to be a symbolic one, reminding the reader that Vered carries that other world of Auschwitz with him in his every thought and word. The other person who carries that world with him at all times is Kraus, who is quite clearly a caricature of Adolf Eichmann. Levin had traveled to Israel to cover the Eichmann trial as a freelance journalist, and the character of Kraus becomes slightly more interesting when one reads him as Levin's attempt to reject the position so often, and for the most part wrongly, attributed to Hannah Arendt that Eichmann was an ordinary, not especially hateful villain. When he comes to the castle Kraus offers to release the prisoners if they will sign a statement avowing that he and the baron have treated them well. Fully aware that this statement is intended to protect Kraus and the baron against the Allies' search for war criminals, the prisoners are inclined to accept his offer, imagining that this relatively low-ranking officer and seemingly minor character could hardly be associated with wartime atrocities. It is Vered who assures them that Kraus is none other than the man who planned and administered the Final Solution and so presents them with a moral dilemma in which their own immediate welfare is to be weighed against political conscience. After much deliberation and contention they decide to preempt Kraus and enlist the baron to their cause by making him aware of Kraus's crimes. Thereafter the baron plies Kraus with drink and a woman and soon elicits Kraus's diabolical confession of his responsibilities, as he gleefully utters a version of a statement infamously attributed to Eichmann: "I'll jump into my grave laughing, knowing I pushed six million *Yupen* into theirs!" To spend even two minutes in Eichmann's head is, according to Levin, to hear all of the real hate that lay hidden behind the courtroom demeanor of lies and self-deception, and so Levin makes us venture there to glimpse almost pornographically the perverse sexual fantasies and sadism of a Nazi mind. When the baron sides with his prisoners and puts Kraus under arrest, Levin offers us a fantasy of an Eichmann captured in 1944 rather than in 1961. From his prison cell Kraus imaginatively puts himself on trial and offers a creative defense in which he maintains all of his anti-Semitic zealousness and seeks to be vindicated on those very terms. Levin depicts Kraus much as the Israeli prosecution had tried to portray Eichmann, a view of himself Eichmann explicitly refused in his trial testimony. Whether Levin has imposed the requirements of melodramatic clarity or whether he believed they were to be found in history and in the Nazi mind, all of this makes for pretty clumsy fiction. To make matters worse the baron mysteriously releases Kraus before he can be brought to justice and, for most of the last portion of the novel, Kraus takes a symbolic last stand against Jews and Jew lovers by trying to recapture the castle. If he fails in this battle he also escapes a second capture and so wanders out into the world, representing not only the Eichmann who would be seized in Argentina in 1960 but also the specter of anti-Semitism that remains at large in the world.

—R. Clifton Spargo

THE SUNFLOWER (Die Sonnenblume: Von Schuld und Vergebung)
Memoir by Simon Wiesenthal, 1970

The literature on the Shoah includes anthology, diary, fiction, history, memoir, psychology, reports, and theology, which individually and collectively recount the horrors of the Nazi treatment of Europe's Jews in the historical context of deep-rooted prejudice and ethnocentric behavior. A number of these studies indict the outwardly anti-Semitic actions of church authorities, the inwardly hypocritical humanism of Western democracies, and the inactivity of some influential Jewish leaders as partially responsible for the murder of six million Jews. Few accounts, however, confront the reader directly in a learning process, thereby challenging existing ideas and modes of behavior. Enter Simon Wiesenthal's *The Sunflower,* whose original text and symposium of responses translated from German and French into English (1970) has been reprinted several times and now appears in a new English expanded edition, *The Sunflower: On the Possibilities and Limits of Forgiveness* (1998).

In a sensitive and provocative narrative, Wiesenthal tells the account of being taken one day from his work detail in a Nazi concentration camp to the bedside of a dying Nazi soldier, a participant in the slaughter of innocents, who is terrified of dying with a burden of guilt and asks forgiveness for his actions. Wiesenthal, who knows well that Nazi crimes could never be fully "avenged "(*The Murderers among Us*) but seeks justice for the millions of victims of the most heinous crime of recorded history (*Justice Not Vengeance*), listens with horror and feeling to the German's deathbed confession and walks silently from his presence without granting him absolution. But Wiesenthal is haunted by this memory and invites a distinguished group of respondents (32 in the first edition; 53 in the second edition, including nine reprinted responses) to tell what they would have done in his place.

The contributors reflect a wide variety of behavior and belief, discipline and experience. Their writing is a reciprocal tool: it reveals and at the same time it is revealing. That is, not only do they tackle a moral question from Auschwitz but they also explain and define themselves within and without that world. Though all agree that one cannot forget, there is a divide between commentators whether to forgive. And this speaks of many things: Can one forgive and not forget? Can the living forgive for the murdered dead? Does forgiveness perpetuate the very evil it wants to make easier to bear? Is following orders the same as giving them? Is it right to impose Nazi crimes on a postwar generation in Germany? Can forgiveness confront, not close, the cycle of pain? If forgiveness is not possible, can reconciliation ever be? And so forth.

Wiesenthal reveals his self-dilemma and strength in his narrative of the dying Nazi's bedside plea. He senses in the man's confession a "true repentance," but he answers in silence. But silence has many voices. May not Wiesenthal's silence then be the thread of commonalty of the murdered six million (among them, 89 of his own relatives) as opposed to the voice of heaven and earth? And by telling the story, is he not breaking his oath now for the sake of the living? Sunflowers marked the graves of the German war dead that lord over the unmarked and forgotten mass pits of the Jewish dead. *The Sunflower* serves as a testimony to victims without mark and to be silent no more.

—Zev Garber

SUNRISE OVER HELL (Salamandra)
Novel by Ka-Tzetnik 135633, 1947

After escaping from the death marches in 1945, Ka-Tzetnik 135633, then known as Yehiel Finer, was taken to a hospital in Italy to recover. Compelled to record the unspeakable brutalities of his tormentors and fearing that he might not live long, he feverishly wrote *Salamandra* over a period of two and a half weeks. Close to the bone and swathed in scenes of devastating violence, the work, published in Hebrew in 1947 and in English as *Sunrise over Hell* in 1977, is painful to read. Yet in rendering the seemingly unreal, it is a blow to the solar plexus of indifference, for it leads the reader to ponder the palpable, unforgettable sorrow of the victims and prevents a turning away from the distressing and confronting material.

At the outset it is important to explicate the meaning of the Hebrew title, as it underpins the thematic matrix upon which most of the author's concerns can be mapped out. According to Hebrew lore, the *salamandra* is a phantasmagorical animal that emerges from a fire that has burning in one place for seven years. In essence, the name denotes a being that has been born of fire and out of destruction, one whose threads to the past have been bluntly severed and whose entire being has been crafted out of the flames. (It is interesting to observe that in Israel Ka-Tzetnik changed his family name to Dinur, meaning "of fire.") More broadly, it is this central trope that frames the dramatic backbone of the author's sextet of novels, *Sunrise*

over Hell being the first in the series. Like the *salamandra,* some of the heroes who populate Ka-Tzetnik's literary landscape have survived the total mayhem of concentration camp life but have come through spiritually and physically demolished, re-created from the maelstrom of anarchy into another person. On another level it has been suggested that, since the cycle of six novels is entitled *Salamander,* the ur-message knotted throughout is that without the individual *salamandra,* those brave souls who preserved and endured the mind-numbing assault, the truth would not have been transmitted to future generations.

Cut from a cloth splashed in blood, the nucleus narrative of *Sunrise over Hell* takes place in the ghetto and in Auschwitz and tells the story of Harry Preleshnik, a talented and brilliant musician who is the author's alter ego. (This fact is undisputed; in the book Harry is given the same inmate number—135633—the author adopted for his pseudonym.) The time is just before the war, and the place is Poland. Watching the surfacing of rampant anti-Semitism with dismay, Harry senses the looming danger about to engulf Polish Jewry. In response he decides to emigrate to Palestine, where his future father-in-law, Schmidt, has settled. When the elderly industrialist hears of Harry's plans, however, he informs him through a letter that better he drown his daughter, Sonia, in the sea than bring her to the inhospitable land. Reluctantly, the Zionist Harry agrees.

A few days later the narrative surges headlong into the world of the irrational and the grotesque as the Germans invade Metropoli, rounding up Jews in the street, burning books and prayer shawls, and throwing into the fire beards that have been torn off the men's faces. Before long the Jewish councils are established, followed by the establishment of the ghetto. The author shows the wretched, imprisoned existence of slavery, humiliation, and public executions in the ghetto, as well as the extreme starvation in the work camp to which Harry is transferred. Arriving at a camp in Germany, Harry is struck by the thousands of bony men, their heads shaved and their jawbones protruding, greeting the newcomers with a plea for bread. In a telling moment Harry whispers, "I am in another world." Ultimately Harry is transported to Auschwitz without Sonia, where he is assigned the duty of removing the gold teeth from the mouths of the charred corpses. In addition to the daily savagery there are the *Mussulmen* (living skeletons), those emaciated, half dead prisoners who are the touchstone, the reflexive marker, for the unsettling dehumanization of Auschwitz. Unable to eat or feel hunger, the *Mussulmen* eject any food they ingest because of their ravaged intestines and, once identified by the camp doctor, are immediately dispatched to the gas chambers. Not surprisingly, at one point Harry is reduced to the state of the *Mussulmen,* joining the row of the totally skeletonized group marching toward the crematorium. Yet he is able to draw on his last nugget of internal strength to attempt escape. And although they capture him, the SS men, impressed by his daring act, decide to spare him immediate eradication and send him back to work.

Through the Harry and Sonia dyad the book lays particular emphasis on the notion of love, glaringly absent among the chimneys of Auschwitz. Against incredible odds the couple manages to remain devoted to each other in spite of the fact that they are separated and can communicate only through a fragmented exchange of letters. It is significant that, in complete opposition to the stereotypically erroneous image of the Diaspora Jew held by many Israelis in the 1950s, the author repeatedly underscores Sonia's heroism, painting her as the exemplar of the proud Jew, suffused with pride and dignity, constantly on the guard for her loved ones, and unwilling to bend to Nazi rule. In fact, she is the one who fights in the Warsaw Ghetto Uprising and later joins the partisans. Indeed, throughout the book her fierce determination to fight rather than surrender is on display front and center. For instance, she tells Rabbi Fromkin, who opposes armed resistance, that, while he has chosen for himself and his disciples a shameful death, she and her comrades are sanctifying the name of Israel and that they are the ones acting in accordance with the law of Israel and the name of God.

Lamentably, Sonia is ultimately trapped by a Gestapo operative when she boards a train destined for Auschwitz that she believes is headed for Switzerland. Thrust into the belly of the beast, Sonia quickly becomes like the *Mussulmen* and is discovered by Harry, who recognizes his wife's corpse by the mole on her cheek. Given her construction as a woman of valor and by the fact that throughout the tale she is adumbrated as a woman of action who is able to elude the Nazis time and again and who defies her inevitable fate with all the cunning she can muster, we find Sonia's death all the more shocking because of the state in which she is found and the fact that it is the gentle, passive Harry who endures. Above all, Harry survives the annihilating smokestacks so that he can testify to the truth and tell of the calamity to those who were not there. It is only then that we can truly and tangibly incubate the dead in our memory and in our soul.

—Dvir Abramovich

A SURPLUS OF MEMORY: CHRONICLE OF THE WARSAW GHETTO UPRISING (Sheva' ha-shanim ha-hen: 1939–1946)
Memoir by Yitzhak Zuckerman, 1990

Yitzhak Zuckerman's *A Surplus of Memory: Chronicle of the Warsaw Ghetto Uprising* (1993; *Sheva' ha-shanim ha-hen: 1939–1946,* 1990) is a work that deserves many more accolades than it has received. It is an amazingly detailed chronicle of the bonds of brotherhood against the Nazi machine bent on destroying the Jews of Poland. Zuckerman (whose underground name was "Antek") was a key figure in the organization of the Warsaw Ghetto Uprising and was one

of just a few to survive the ordeal. Given the chances that he and the others in his group took, it is surprising that any of them lived to tell the tale. Zuckerman leaves behind a very clear and detailed chronicle of the events that took place and pays homage to the brave souls who assisted him in the attempt to beat the odds and rise up against Nazi aggression in the ghetto. This work was actually assembled from numerous voice recordings of his recollections of the period and was not released until after his death (at his request). The most striking feature of this work is the ages of those who participated. Most were in their twenties and early thirties. Zuckerman stated that he liked working with young people. "I thought we should start all over with a younger, more ideological generation, who were more willing to sacrifice, that we should start all over and not endanger the generation of activists that I knew," he said.

Zuckerman was a member of the movement *He-Halutz Ha — Tza'ir* (Young Pioneers), a Zionist Socialist movement that later united with *Frayhayt* (Hebrew: *"Dror"*; English: "Freedom") and a member as well of *Żidowska Organizacja Bojowa* (ŻOB; Jewish Fighting Organization). He was dedicated to the education of youth so that appreciation for Jewish life, lore, and history could grow and further foster a movement against those who sought to destroy Europe's Jews. What he could not have foreseen was that he was up against something that he himself could never have imagined. In fact, his most difficult problem was persuading other Jews to believe what was going on outside of the Warsaw Ghetto walls. After having survived a week in a labor camp, which was slowly becoming more of a concentration camp, he realized that the future for the Jews of Poland was very grim. Further reports from other members of his movement, scattered all about Europe, brought further atrocities to light: gassing in Chelmno, mass killings in Vilna (including the annihilation of all of Zuckerman's family, including distant relatives, which almost brought Zuckerman to his knees). With the support of his faithful assistants, including his wife, Zivia Lubetkin (to whom Zuckerman referred as "the backbone of our group"), he began to rise from depression to action. Three factors were present that made the ghetto uprising come together: The various movements involved were very fraternal, consisting of young people who had known one another almost all of their lives, making infiltration nearly impossible to accomplish; the strength and courage of those surrounding Zuckerman; and his ability as an underground figure to move about rather freely, always changing addresses, in order to survive.

The work is divided into fifteen chapters, ending with the pogroms in Kielce. Because it was originally an oral chronicle it can be repetitive in places, and the history of the time is sometimes confused. Zuckerman, however, presents an excellent eyewitness view of ghetto life that haunted him for the rest of his life. "The establishment of the ghetto meant a revolution in our life. Suddenly you saw poverty in a concentrated and harsh form. You got used to it," he said. Zuckerman never got used to the fact that many others seemed to ignore the presence of the ghetto and the cruelty therein. He admonishes those in the know for having done nothing to help, but he is also quick to praise those Poles and others who were sympathetic to his cause and risked their own lives to procure weapons and monetary support for the uprising. Still the world seemed to ignore the plight of the Jews. As Zuckerman stated in *A Surplus of Memory:* "Various people were thinking the same: if the world only knew! Up to now, no one took the initiative or said anything. Then we thought that, as soon as the world hears what is going on, things will change. And the truth was that when the world did find out, it was silent."

Before reading *A Surplus of Memory* it is advised that one study the names of the various movements and their functions as presented in the beginning of the work. The footnotes are also helpful in straightening out any confusion about those involved in the uprising. Barbara Hashav, translator and editor, has done an admirable job of making an oral history come alive in print. This is a work that should be combined with Lubetkin's *In the Days of Destruction and Revolt,* Zuckerman's *The Fighting Ghettos,* and Yisroel Gutman's *The Jews of Warsaw, 1939–43* for a more complete understanding of the Jews of Poland.

—Cynthia A. Klíma

SURVIVAL IN AUSCHWITZ (Se questo è un uomo)
Memoir by Primo Levi, 1947

Survival in Auschwitz (1986), generally understood to be a supreme achievement intellectually, morally, and stylistically, is Primo Levi's first work of witness. It was originally published in Italian in 1947 as *Se questo è un uomo,* and the first English translation appeared in 1959 under the title *If This Is a Man.* Levi committed himself while still in the Lager to communicating the nature of the experience, should he survive. To that end, and at peril of immediate death if found out, he made notes that he intended as an aid in the project. Aside from those notes he could rely on his virtually flawless and detailed memory. He composed the book in the year after the liberation of the camp, but it was refused repeatedly for publication with the excuse that people were tired of the war and would not wish to read it. Published in a small edition in 1947, of which about 600 copies were sold, it gained almost no recognition until it was published by Einaudi in 1958.

The book is composed of a prologue plus 17 chapters . Levi does not aim at a continuous narrative flow covering his period in the Lager. Rather, in each chapter he focuses on an issue or a series of particular events that he supposes bear pondering, if we are at all to understand the nature of the camps and their significance. Scrupulous in restricting his reportage to what he had himself experienced, he focuses with high intensity on

particular people and details of experience in a way perhaps best described as synecdochic: a part stands for and suggests the greater whole. He remarks in his prologue that he does not intend an account of atrocities, and in fact he does not dwell on the details of the horrors he nonetheless gives us to know exist. His writing is lucid, precise, and astonishingly free of rhetorical heightening. His intense focus on significant detail related with taut restraint and the alert moral rigor of his analysis and judgment leave the reader with little room for evasion or indifference. The book exerts an enormous and wholly salutary human pressure on mind and sensibility.

As an epigraph to the book, Levi wrote a version of the Shemà ("Hear, O Israel, the Lord our God, the Lord is one . . .") for the world after Auschwitz. Levi believed that his people had undergone in the twentieth century a new slavery and exodus experience, and he commands all humans, not Israel alone, to listen (*shemà*) and consider that experience. Beginning with his own capture in 1943, the book comes to a close with the Russian liberation of the camp in January 1945. A sustained focus throughout the book is the way in which the camps broke the moral structure of those brought there—broke, that is, their humanity. The dehumanizing nature of life in the Lager is caught in an episode Levi tells of his being desperate with thirst on arrival in camp and of his plucking an icicle to suck to relieve the drive for water. A guard snatches it out of his hand. "Warum?" ("Why?") Levi asks. To which the guard replies, "Hier ist kein Warum" ("Here there is no why"). Levi remarks that for him the most accurate single image of all the evil of his time would be that of the human broken in the Lager: "an emaciated man, with head drooped and shoulders curved, on whose face and in whose eyes not a trace of a thought is to be seen."

Levi weaves through the book signals of that brokenness as the essence of the slaves' experience of camp. Of this, the pervasive response of the prisoners to their captors—"Jawohl!" ("Yes!")—is a verbal example. He notes at the beginning of the book that the prisoners were taught to respond with that word. It recurs as the universal response of the prisoners to a harangue in German at the hanging of a man who had participated in an attempt to blow up the crematoria. "Do you understand?" they are asked. To which they all reply, "Jawohl." "[I]t was as if our cursed resignation took body by itself, as is it turned into a collective voice." And at the end of the book Levi describes the death agony of a Hungarian chemist, Somogyi, in the Infection Ward. His emaciated and disease-racked body taut in a fetal position, he repeats thousands of times without pause, "Jawohl, Jawohl, Jawohl . . ."

The book should not be called a novel. Levi remarks in the prologue to the book that "none of the facts is invented." But the matter goes deeper. Novels characteristically have heroes, and Levi resists utterly casting himself in that role. When he gives testimony (in the episode of the hanging, above) that he was one of those saying "Jawohl," he presents himself as broken too. That there was no achievement or excellence that gave one an increased chance of survival in that world of death he similarly indicates out of his own experience. He survived by the chance fact that as a chemist, he was needed for the Buna and was given just enough extra rations that he lived until the Russians liberated the camp. But being a chemist gave no general advantage in the struggle for survival. Witness Somogyi of the story above.

Levi almost never, in all his writings, addresses the "great why of it all," limiting himself to a description and analysis of the events he experienced and their implications for understanding our possibilities as humans. Nor does he engage in overt and sustained polemic about the implications of Christian anti-Judaism as a precondition for Shoah. In a highly allusive chapter titled "The Canto of Ulysses," in which he reads the experience of Auschwitz through his knowledge of Dante's *Inferno*, he does, however, broach these matters with enormous tact. The point Levi probably wishes to be taken is that through the long history of Christianity there has flowed a stream of understanding that the Christian God would destroy others who did not come to him through the way of Jesus. Levi apparently had an insight that in fact the Germans simply set themselves within this understanding in the position of God and were destroying the "others," the Jews, simply because they were, in German terms, irreducibly "other."

—Ralph G. Williams

SURVIVING THE HOLOCAUST: THE KOVNO GHETTO DIARY (Geto yom-yom: Yoman u-mismakhim mi-Geto Kovnah)
Diary by Avraham Tory, 1988

Surviving the Holocaust by Avraham Tory is one of the most detailed and significant of the ghetto diaries to survive the war, described as "a document of major importance." Buried in a cellar, some of it was lost, but the bulk was recovered shortly after the liberation of Kovno in August 1944. Written in Yiddish, it was first published in Hebrew translation in 1988 and in English in 1990.

The first diary entry is written at midnight 22 June 1941, the day of the German invasion of Soviet Russia. For the remaining months of 1941 the entries are sparse. During 1942 Tory wrote brief entries on a regular basis, most of a paragraph or less in length. The bulk of the diary covers 1943, the last period of the ghetto's existence. The longer diary entries begin in January 1943, providing almost a daily record to August; there are less frequent entries until October, when regular entries cease. Most of the 1943 entries are in the range of 500–1,500 words, some being more than 3,000 words in length. There is one lengthy entry for January 1944 detailing the testimony of an escapee from the Ninth Fort who had been engaged for

months in the task of destroying evidence of Nazi crimes, burning bodies previously left buried.

The English edition, translated by Jerzy Michalowicz, edited by Martin Gilbert, with textual and historical notes by Dina Porat, contains a number of other sources interspersed with diary entries in chronological order. Such additional sources include originals of German orders, council notices, the Last Testament of Dr. Elchanan Elkes, a few memoirs written by Tory during 1944–45 after his liberation, and a brief account written in 1988 detailing the successful attempt to hide the presence of typhus from the Germans. There are also 49 photographs, 12 portraits, facsimile pages of the diary, and nine maps.

The chief feature of the diary is its penetrating insight into daily life covering a period of more than two years, not only within the ghetto but also beyond as Tory exercised a freedom available to few to travel among the non-Jewish population.

The diary provides day-to-day accounts of life in periods of relative quiet and extended accounts of times of crisis. We learn of the thought processes of those trapped, of rumors that spread like wildfire, of rationalizations and denials of those desperate to find reassurance. A detailed memoir written in 1944 recalls the "action" of 28 October 1941. First, the Council of Elders is instructed to order all residents to assemble at 6:00 in the morning. Tortured argument over compliance ensues, ultimately resolved by rabbinical authority. A daylong process of selection, seemingly interminable, follows, to separate 10,000 from the ghetto population of 27,000. The next morning those spared watch the doomed. Isolated overnight, they are formed into columns, from first to last taking six hours to march past the ghetto boundary en route to the killing site in the Ninth Fort.

Detailed conversations and interactions with those placed in authority are recorded, as are German decrees. Religious observance is to cease. Those who die in the ghetto are to be buried without identification names on the graves. Hearses are not to be pulled by horses. The six cows in the ghetto may be kept, but milk produced is to be surrendered. Books are to be handed over to the Organisation for the Confiscation of Jewish Books. Pregnancy—the bearing of Jewish children—is outlawed.

The attempts to make sense of events in the outside world are noted. One source of information is the radio kept by the underground. Other information comes from the Lithuanian population, Jews managing to travel from ghetto to ghetto, survivors of massacres seeking shelter, the engine driver of a trainload of Jews unloaded at Ponar, escapees from the Ninth Fort. And then there is the evidence of the senses: a returning party of Gestapo killers, "their machine guns and combat rifles ... blackened with burned cordite ... bloodstains on their clothing and on their weapons."

We are introduced to individuals numbered in the hundreds—so many that the book calls out for, but does not contain, a biographical guide. They include Dr. Elkes, Oberjude (Chief Jew); Chaim Yellin (Yelin), leader of partisan groups; Joseph Caspi, Zionist, anti-Bolshevik, associate of the Gestapo, exempted from the wearing of the yellow badge, allowed to live in the city and carry firearms; a Christian woman married to a Jew who opts to share his fate, walking through the ghetto with the yellow badge on her clothing, golden crucifix around her neck; Irena Adamovich, Polish Catholic courier who in July 1942 brought news of massacres and of the extermination camps of Belzec, Sobibor, and Majdanek.

In the midst of terrible days the will to live remains undiminished. Tory writes that ''despite the seven chambers of hell that the Jews have gone through, our spirit has not been ended or crushed.'' In July 1943 Zionists celebrated the birthday of Theodor Herzl, rising to their feet to sing the ''Hatikvah,'' hearts filled with joy, tears flowing, crying aloud, ''Our hope is not yet lost.''

—Andrew Markus

T

THE TALE OF THE RING: A KADDISH
Memoir by Frank Stiffel, 1984

The kaddish is the Jewish prayer for the dead, which focuses on praise of God instead of on death. Describing courage, intelligence, and dignity in the face of death is the focus and intention of Frank Stiffel's memoir, *The Tale of the Ring: A Kaddish*. Stiffel was in medical training when World War II came to Poland. With his family he fled to the Warsaw Ghetto, but eventually they were sent to Treblinka. His parents were gassed, but Stiffel and his brother, Martin, survived and escaped the camp, returning to Warsaw where they aided Jews in illegal immigration to Poland.

Martin was not recaptured, but Frank was taken, along with others, to Rabka Gestap Academy, where he was questioned and tortured. His death sentence, which he received for aiding Jews in fleeing to Palestine, was commuted to imprisonment in Auschwitz. His group, so courageous they had impressed their captors at the academy, were the first prisoners to leave there alive.

In *The Tale of the Ring: A Kaddish* Stiffel compares the social structure of Auschwitz to that of a corrupt city. A handful of bigwigs at the top controlled a mass of nonentities at the bottom; if a prisoner survived long enough, it was a hierarchy up which a prisoner might climb a few rungs. Survival was the objective for everyone. Stiffel regarded the struggle as one involving a physical as well as a crucial moral element. "I had the will to survive," he writes, "and in order to achieve it I was prepared to do anything, except one: I would never choose to remain alive at the expense of any of my fellow Haftlinge (prisoners)." Severe illness ultimately led him to seek help at the camp hospital. For most prisoners this constituted a fatal error, because the sick were prime targets for death. Instead, a doctor recognized him as having studied medicine and, after he was well, helped him get a hospital post. For the rest of his time at Auschwitz, he worked in increasingly responsible capacities, gaining a vantage on camp life that infused the memoir he had already started writing on pieces of soap he salvaged.

Stiffel started compiling his secret notes that evolved into *The Tale of the Ring: A Kaddish* immediately after his liberation from Auschwitz in 1945. After coming to New York City, he translated it into English in 1958. A thread of mysticism runs through the book and alludes to the ring mentioned in the title. Stiffel had several prophetic dreams in which a girl spoke to him. In Treblinka he found a ring with a cameo of the face he identified as this woman. He miraculously held onto the ring in spite of many changes in his fortune. After the war he met and married a woman whose face resembled that of the woman on

the ring. Together they immigrated to the United States. Rejected by a dozen publishers, *A Tale of the Ring: A Kaddish* remained unpublished for 30 years. At a Passover seder in 1981 Stiffel met a production editor who volunteered to help him shape the book for publication.

—Martha Sutro

THE TEREZÍN REQUIEM (Terezínské rekviem)
Memoir by Josef Bor, 1963

Music played an important role in concentration camp life, especially in the Theresienstadt (Terezín) ghetto. Musicians often survived much longer than their nonmusical counterparts and had specific functions in the camp that served the Nazis in a twofold fashion: they contributed to the cultural life of the camp, pleasing both the Nazis and the inmates, and they played as the transports left out of Theresienstadt, thereby creating a rather haunting image of culture mixed with the uncertainty of fate. Musicians saw friends, family, and acquaintances to their deaths, and it was for that reason that they also had a rather high suicide rate. The movie *Playing for Time*, starring Vanessa Redgrave, relates the life of musicians in a concentration camp most powerfully, becoming a worthwhile supplement to studies on cultural life during the Holocaust.

In *The Terezín Requiem* (*Terezínské rekviem* in Czech) Josef Bor illustrates the development of a true event in the Theresienstadt ghetto. Raphael Schächter, a first-rate conductor and Theresienstadt inhabitant, decides to take up a study of Giuseppe Verdi's *Requiem*, a multilayered, profoundly difficult piece to play. For this performance he will need at least 500 musicians, no small feat in any normal circumstances; however, in a concentration camp where the configurations were constantly changing with every transport, Schächter needs a near miracle. Bor describes in intimate detail the trials and tribulations of Schächter. The setbacks that befall him are heartbreaking and frustrating. Just when Schächter has found the perfect bass voice, a transport whisks him away. He loses three of his top four performers in one day and must doggedly hunt for replacements. The absence of musical instruments alone is enough to topple the entire proposal. On top of this he meets a wizened old man who pointedly critiques his choice of performance material and calls him a fool for attempting a work in which too much is required, a work that calls for a Catholic, not a Jew, to fully interpret the work to its true potential. It is precisely at this moment that Schächter realizes that his interpretation will have to be something new, something different. His interpretation will incorporate the most vivid and finger-pointing sections toward the Nazis. The one satisfaction Schächter and his artists receive from this is that the Nazis will probably never see themselves in the interpretation.

The artists themselves are no less remarkable. Many have suffered so intensely that music has become their outlet in order to forget their predicament. Several risk their lives to smuggle musical instruments into the camp. One high point in the work is the discovery of a treasure trove of forgotten military instruments in the ramparts of Theresienstadt. Indeed, the work is a testimony to perseverance and the strength of cooperation. Inhabitants of Theresienstadt are also to be thanked for their participation in the entire affair, as Bor states, "A good audience; it wasn't everywhere you'd find one so well-educated musically. And surely nowhere else did the listeners look forward with such hungry longing to the first notes of a *première*."

The final performance of *The Terezín Requiem* takes place with Adolf Eichmann as an audience member. He laughs perversely when he discovers that Jewish artists will be performing a Christian work. He realizes that the Jews will be tolling their own death bell. Only minutes before the performance, Schächter is told that he must shorten the performance to less than an hour. The intense description of the performance of the artists, Schächter's furious conducting, and the audience reaction is beautifully handled by Bor, an eyewitness to the entire event. It is to the credit of fellow survivors who encouraged Bor to write down his observations that this work exists today.

In the spring of 1945, all the musicians were transported out of Theresienstadt en masse, as the German commandant had promised to keep them all together. *The Terezín Requiem* has since been performed numerous times in the United States, most recently by the Santa Clara University Chorale. The emotional intensity of Schächter's artists can, however, never be matched again.

—Cynthia A. Klíma

THE THEORY AND PRACTICE OF HELL: THE GERMAN CONCENTRATION CAMPS AND THE SYSTEM BEHIND THEM (Der SS-Staat: Das System de Deutschen Konzentrationslager)
Memoir and Study by Eugen Kogon, 1946

The Theory and Practice of Hell (1950; originally published in 1946 as *Der SS-Staat: Das System de Deutschen Konzentrationslager*) was one of the most significant sociological studies of the concentration camps to emerge in the first decade after the war. Eugen Kogon's psychosocial portrait of SS and prisoner behavior still stands out for its sophistication, and Kogon did not allow his proximity to the events and persons described to weaken the objectivity of the commentary he provided. As Holocaust historian Harold Marcuse has noted, *The Theory and Practice of Hell* is still in some ways unsurpassed as a firsthand record of life in camps like Buchenwald. Nevertheless, while Kogon's dedication to objectivity and his reliance on other eyewitness accounts make this book more than a straightforward memoir, his experience of life in Buchenwald gives a distinctive shape to the book's description of relations between perpetrators and camp inmates, and personal anecdotes throughout the text suggest his conviction that a level-headed inmate could survive the camp experience without great difficulty. The book sold half a million copies and was translated into eight languages.

Like **Bruno Bettelheim,** Kogon argued that the concentration camp was an extreme example of the state of terror created everywhere in the Reich by the SS state. The book details the main actors in the Nazi machine responsible for the camp system, the categories into which prisoners were forced, and the daily conditions that they faced. Examples are largely taken from his own experience in Buchenwald, and other camps are viewed through short extracts of survivor testimony or by dint of assumptions based on developments in Buchenwald. For Kogon the camps were primarily designed to enable the SS to deal with their "opponents." At the same time, the book gives separate treatment to the attempted liquidation of the Jews, other so-called inferior races, homosexuals, and other undesirables. Aware of the indescribable proportions of the fate of the Jews, Kogon made clear that of all the groups in the camps, their position was the worst. Nevertheless, writing so soon after the liberation, Kogon was only able to give limited coverage to the experience of the vast majority of Jewish victims during the Holocaust. Conditions in the larger death camps, in ghettos, and on shooting grounds often bore little resemblance to Kogon's portrayal of a Buchenwald-style camp system.

The enduring value of *The Theory and Practice of Hell* lies chiefly in the extent to which Kogon cast light on the speedy degeneration of SS and camp inmates into a corrupt, chaotic, and brutal hell. Kogon only used the testimony of inmates and painted the amorality of the SS in the camps with a broad brush rather than seeking to distinguish between individuals or groups in positions of power. Nevertheless, he did succeed in showing that the camps attracted a German elite willing and eager to commit atrocities long before the war years sharpened the camp system into a haven from the front and a bonanza for profiteers and pleasure seekers. Once in the camps, a prisoner was at the whim of guards who often did not care for which category of offense he or she had been condemned. There were some groups of prisoners who were able to work for more favorable treatment from guards and the camp command, particularly by helping to keep order and communication with the prisoners. The primary means for self-preservation described in the book, however, was to take part in or facilitate the corruption and sexual profligacy of the SS.

Kogon was at his best in describing the processes of moral degeneration among camp inmates, the battles that they fought against each other, believing firmly that their survival depended on it, and the intergroup animosities deliberately sharpened by the SS in order to divide and rule. One of the main grounds for criticism of Kogon's work has been his reliance on communist testimony. Thanks to the opening of the archives of the East German Socialist Unity Party, Lutz Niethammer has uncovered testimony that reveals a far more serious level of complicity on the part of the Red *kapos* of Buchenwald than Kogon acknowledged. Nevertheless, *The Theory and Practice of Hell* does not shrink from describing in general terms the principles on which politicals accommodated some of the operations of the SS, particularly with the aim of preventing the camp from being turned over to the control of criminal elements among the inmates. More important to the thesis advanced in the book is Kogon's description of a process of mental hardening in the face of the horrors and challenges of the camp, which he asserted even the most civilized inmates could not avoid. If the camps differed in practice from the theoretical designs of the architects of the Final Solution in Berlin, Kogon suggested that this owed as much to the moral failings of the inmates as it did to the incapacities of the SS who ruled over them.

—George R. Wilkes

THERE IS A PLACE ON EARTH: A WOMAN IN BIRKENAU (Questo povero corpo)
Memoir by Giuliana Tedeschi, 1946

C'é un punto della terra (*There Is a Place on Earth*) was published in Italian in 1988 and in English (translated by Tim Parks) in 1992. An earlier, shorter version of some 125 pages was published in 1946 as *Questo povero corpo* (''This Poor Body'').

Tedeschi was transported to Auschwitz-Birkenau in April 1944. Her book tells of her experiences over the next 12 months, covering a period spent within the Birkenau camp, some months in the Auschwitz barracks, the forced march when the camp was evacuated in January 1945, and brief references to time spent in Ravensbrück and Malchow.

Two different styles of writing are evident in the book. The opening section is little concerned with narrative framework and precise contextualization; the aim is to convey the disorientation of a woman torn from her surroundings and dumped into an environment without understandable reference points. Sentence structure and language eschew a narrow formalism; words flow without immediate context, description is confined to snatches of time and place, the reader left to restructure sequence. There are elements of the lyrical, as in the book's opening words, a description of the death camp: ''There is a place on earth, a desolate heath, where the shadows of the dead are multitudes, where the living are dead, where there is only death, hate, and pain. Surrounding the place and cutting it off from life are thick walls of darkness by night, and by day the infinity of space, the whistle of the wind, the cawing of crows, the stormy sky, the gray of stones.''

Following the introductory section chronology determines sequence, although for the most part the author avoids detailed description of place, focusing on interaction between those of widely divergent national origin and culture—on conversation, tone, accent, and mood.

As the account unfolds, we witness the dawning understanding of the purpose of Birkenau, the shock of discovery that the imagined family camp is located in the crematorium, the recognition of death, the meaning of the flame that burns night and day, refracted through myriad window panes. At night in the crowded barracks Tedeschi hears the ''noise of wheels braking on rails, the confused clamour of the wagons being unloaded in the dark, the echoing of orders and the shouts of Germans.'' Many of the passages are haunting, conveying great depth of meaning with an economy of words. Forced to attend a roll call in pelting rain, the captives return sodden to barracks, their clogs covering the floor with sludge, attempting vainly to dry clothes before the morning and only succeeding in impregnating the bunks with water.

Tedeschi is sent from the Birkenau quarantine block to the work camp, engages in senseless tasks carrying stones, then is assigned to an indoor work detail mercifully sheltered from the elements: her task is to rip apart an endless supply of shoes, separating leather and rubber, to be shipped to an unknown destination. Life becomes less onerous as she is moved to the two-story brick barracks of Auschwitz. After the Birkenau huts the new surroundings are spacious, the bunk beds wide, the lavatories fit for human beings—and the crematoriums are out of sight.

Conditions deteriorate in October when work runs out and she is sent to dig in sand pits—for nine long hours, each day, in the winter cold. The death march on which she embarks, the train journey to Germany, the movement from camp to camp, and her ultimate escape and liberation cover but 23 pages of text but constitute one of the features of Tedeschi's work—a powerful evocation of experience beyond the realms of human understanding.

—Andrew Markus

THIS WAY FOR THE GAS, LADIES AND GENTLEMEN
Short stories by Tadeusz Borowski, 1967

This Way for the Gas, Ladies and Gentlemen is the American title of Tadeusz Borowski's collection of short stories. The edition consists of 12 stories written at different periods of time. The first four were first published in 1946 in Munich in the collection entitled *We Were in Auschwitz*, while the remaining ones, except "The January Offensive," come from *The World of Stone*, published in 1948 in Poland in issues 21 to 24 of *"Nowiny Literackie."*

Collected together Borowski's short stories focusing on the camp not only confirm the significance of his literary testimony but also show the essential changes in his writing. According to the general opinion of critics two of these stories, "This Way for the Gas, Ladies and Gentlemen" and "A Day at Harmenz," belong to the masterpieces of the world camp literature. They include a keen diagnosis of the camp as well as the purest form of Borowski's artistic method. They are the fulfillment of the postulate of the fourth letter to his fiancée, Maria, a prisoner of the women's camp in Birkenau, reconstructed in the story *Auschwitz, Our Home:* "Try to grasp the essence of its pattern of daily events, discarding your sense of horror and loathing and contempt, and find for it all a philosophic formula. For the gas chambers and the gold stolen from the victims, for the roll-call, and for the Puff, for frightened civilians and for the 'old numbers.'"

This philosophic and literary formula lies in the behaviorist narrative, utterly sparse, almost devoid of any emotions, conducted from the point of view of the narrator, whose name is Tadek. In prison he performs a secondary function of a vorarbeiter (a *kapo*'s helper), which in the camp hierarchy, however, puts him above the average prisoner emaciated by starvation and toil. Tadek is an Aryan who simply wants to survive. He is not in danger of immediate extermination or regular selection for gas. He feels quite at home in Auschwitz. He knows the rules of the camp and seems to have accepted them. He sees the camp as an economic enterprise concerned with a maximum profit. That profit is obtained owing to the slave labor of the starving prisoners but above all through the extermination of the Jewish nation, which helps other prisoners to survive while the Germans and civilians make their fortunes on that. Tadek lives in the world in which an inhuman choice between one's own life and someone else's is a daily matter. Under such circumstances asking about morality becomes pointless.

The literary formula for the camp lies also in the principle of contrast. "A Day at Harmenz" begins with a bucolic description of a landscape, of a sunny day, and the soft shadow cast by chestnut trees. In "This Way for the Gas, Ladies and Gentlemen," the Angelus bell from the town of Oswiecim can be heard at noon. This is also a normal day in the camp life. And in this scenery the horrors of the camp and the extermination of the

Jews take place. The narrator talks about terrible things using a common language, typical of the prisoners with "old numbers," devoid of emotions.

The remaining stories included in the American edition of Borowski's camp prose do not present such a consistent artistic method. The narrator in "Auschwitz, Our Home" and in "The People Who Walked On" is close to Borowski. In the former the author included a wide range of formulas evaluating and universalizing the camp experience. It is notably different from the characteristic behaviorist method employed in "A Day at Harmenz."

The short stories from the collection entitled *The World of Stone* are still different. They are much shorter, limited to one motif, revealing a masterly use of contrast and concise form. Their literary character is clearly emphasized in Borowski's foreword, where he stresses the lack of identification of the author with the narrator. By virtue of their subject matter they are connected with the first four stories, but they were taken out of the series of 24 mini-stories carefully arranged by Borowski in such a way that they were to constitute a longer, uniform utterance. According to the unanimous opinion of critics Borowski's pessimistic diagnosis achieves here its furthest extreme. In "The World of Stone" and "A Visit," on the other hand, the narrator is close to the author. Borowski writes about his psychical and emotional condition. Despite the almost cosmic shock caused by evil, he undertakes an attempt to defend the world of primary values.

"The January Offensive" is a story that does not belong to the series in *The World of Stone*. Here Borowski returns to the post-war atmosphere of immigrants' Munich. We can identify the protagonists as **Janusz Nel-Siedlecki** and **Krystyn Olszewski,** the coauthors of *We Were in Auschwitz,* and Anatol Girs, its publisher. In this story Borowski expresses the accusation of the western civilization: " . . . the whole world is really like the concentration camp; the weak work for the strong, and if they have no strength or will to work—then let them steal or let them die." He juxtaposes that image with the story of a Soviet woman-soldier who gives birth to a child during the Soviet January offensive in 1945. Then she takes the baby with her and marches on to Berlin. This was the very offensive that saved the lives of the few remaining Auschwitz prisoners, and this fact is strongly accentuated in the story. "The January Offensive" harbingers Borowski's future ideological choice and commitment to communism.

—Kazimierz Adamczyk

THE TIN DRUM (Die Blechtrommel)
Novel by Günter Grass, 1959

While he was living in poverty in Paris in 1956–60, the German writer Günter Grass received intellectual stimulation from **Paul Celan**, a Jewish poet who had survived the Holocaust but who struggled with horrible memories of the ordeal. Celan supplied valuable advice while Grass was working on the novel *Die Blechtrommel,* which was about to make literary history. Published in 1959, it was issued in an English translation as *The Tin Drum* in 1961. The complexity of *The Tin Drum* may be understood by recognizing the sheer number and variety of critical approaches to Grass's novel. It has been the focal point of numerous sociological, political, historical, philosophical, and psychological interpretations and of genre and symbolism studies. *The Tin Drum* has continued to be regarded as the masterpiece that ultimately led to Grass's highest honor, the Nobel Prize for Literature in 1999.

This picaresque novel addresses the interpretation of history, especially the German past between 1933 and 1945, the period of National Socialism, World War II, and the Holocaust. Oskar Matzerath, the schizophrenic protagonist and narrator of his own story, is in an insane asylum as he writes his ambiguous memoirs and family history covering the first half of the twentieth century. As his story unfolds, it becomes more and more apparent that he has problems with his past, and we cannot believe everything he says. Matzerath lies, displays amoral, even devilish behavior, and is responsible for multiple deaths in his own family. Yet at other times his acts are full of resistance and protest as he reveals the totalitarian and hateful nature of fascism, its appeal to the masses, and its heinous crimes against the Jewish people.

At the age of three Oskar chooses to stop growing by throwing himself down the basement stairs. This act of defiance allows him later to demask the hypocritical nature of adult life in the lower middle class and its complicity in the Third Reich. Oskar's tin drum, a present for his third birthday, is an instrument of protest against the world of adults in a fascist state. As his protest drum wears out every so often, Oskar receives replacements from a Jewish toy store owner named Sigismund Markus. On *Kristallnacht* (Crystal Night, 9–10 November 1938), while synagogues are burning and Jewish stores are being destroyed, Markus becomes the victim of Nazi atrocities: "There once was a toy dealer named Markus, and he took all the toys out of the world with him."

A prime example in the novel of indifference to the plight of the Jews is the behavior of Oskar's father during *Kristallnacht:* "Outside the wrecked synagogue, men in uniform and others in civilian clothes piled up books, ritual objects, and strange kinds of cloth. The mound was set on fire and the grocer took advantage of the opportunity to warm his fingers and his feelings over the blaze." The German shopkeeper serves as a representative of the petite bourgeoisie. When he realizes that it was a mistake to have joined the Nazis, it is too late. In the end he chokes to death on his Nazi Party pin.

A significant part of *The Tin Drum* depicts everyday life in Danzig while the monstrous murder of Europe's Jewry is taking place in the concentration camps, which Oskar learns about from Mr. Fajngold, a Holocaust survivor. Fajngold

remembers the way his relatives had lain "before being taken to the crematoria of Treblinka . . . except for him because he had to strew lime on them." More details about the horrors of Treblinka are revealed later: "I learned about the whole carloads of carbolic acid, lime, and Lysol that he had sprayed, strewn, and sprinkled . . . over the barracks, the shower rooms, the cremating furnaces, the bundles of clothing, over those who were waiting to shower, over those who lay recumbent after their showers, over all that came out of the ovens and all who were about to go in. He listed the names, for he knew them all."

Grass describes his hometown of Danzig (now Gdansk), the main setting of the novel, in a manner that adds historical flavor. Furthermore, he frequently draws parallels between Oskar's life and the course of German history. But Grass is far from historicizing the events. To the contrary, in Grass's view the Nazi past and its victims should continue to play a significant role in people's consciousness. Unless we are not interested in one another's welfare, we cannot afford to forget. What happened yesterday can happen tomorrow. This is the most powerful insight behind Grass's amazing work.

—Mark Gruettner

TO REMEMBER, TO FORGET (Lizkor lishcoah)
Novel by Dahn Ben-Amotz, 1968

In the 1990s, with the rise to prominence of the self-proclaimed New Historians in Israel, many of the country's founding myths were critically analyzed and exposed. While this debate initially was concerned primarily with the 1948 War and the plight of the Palestinian refugees, the Holocaust soon assumed a central role. From the Yishuv's actions during World War II to the treatment of survivors in the hands of the young Jewish state, the instrumetalization of the Holocaust as a means to justify the Zionist enterprise was the target of painful criticism and soul searching by a new generation of scholars.

Set in 1959 and written in 1968, Dahn Ben-Amotz's *To Remember, to Forget* (*Lizkor lishcoah*) can be regarded as a precursor of this debate. The novel tells the story of Uri Lam, a young Israeli architect, and his journey back to Frankfurt, the city of his birth. Lam, who was sent to Italy during the war, is his family's sole survivor, and he returns to Frankfurt to collect reparations from the German government to pay for a new house and car that he purchased in Jerusalem. His trip to Germany confronts this survivor with the country that destroyed his family and forces him to come to terms with his past and with his present as an Israeli Jew visiting a country that has undergone radical changes.

Lam's world is shaped by two seemingly incommensurable poles. He is an Israeli who, like many other Israelis, struggles with the idea of returning to Europe to collect money from the Germans. Lam, born Hirsch Lampel, was recruited in Italy by Zionist emissaries after the war and underwent a typical process of Zionist indoctrination. Upon his arrival in Israel, in an attempt to blend with the local culture that despised everything associated with the Diaspora, he changed his name to Zvi (Hebrew for Hirsch) and then to Uri Lam, and like many young Israelis he went to agricultural school, an integral part of the Zionist *corsus honorum*. At the same time, however, he was a European Jew whose early childhood memories were shaped by the continent's geographical and cultural landscape.

Lam's original plan is to travel in Italy for a month, to rediscover Europe's grand culture, which has turned into a faint memory for him, and then go to Frankfurt to settle his legal affairs. But while in Italy, instead of high culture he is confronted by the violent side of Europe: Customs officers in the port of Genoa interrogate and search him; he spends a night with a Genoes prostitute; his goods are stolen on his way to Milan. Lam is unable to realize his romantic vision of European culture.

In Frankfurt, struggling with the idea of exchanging the death of his family into hard currency, he meets a young German woman, Barbara. Though fluent in German, Lam initially refuses to speak the language, which he considers the mechanism through which the Nazi evil manifested itself. His first encounter with Barbara, who does not speak English, is reduced to a dialogue made out of a few recognizable words and hand signals. This, for him, serves as a sign that their relationship—and the general dialogue between Jews and Germans—can transcend cultural biases. The couple's burgeoning relationship, which is described against the background of post-war Frankfurt, ends up in a wedding in Germany and with the birth of the couple's son, Jonathan, in Jerusalem.

While he did not possess the literary flare of his contemporaries (**Yehuda Amichay, Aharon Applefeld**), and with a style that patches together different story lines into one less-than-cohesive narrative, Ben-Amotz was able to bring to the forefront some issues that were previously regarded as taboos in Israel. Throughout his time in Frankfurt, Lam is constantly faced with reminders of the past (his parents' home, a trip to Dachau) but also a new Germany represented by a younger generation of Germans. In Frankfurt he also contemplates the morality of Jewish nationalism; he goes so far as to wonder whether the Nazi crimes are comparable to the treatment of Palestinian Arabs in Israel—an issue that Israeli historians would only begin to discuss in the 1990s.

Despite the novel's innovative approach to the discussion of the Holocaust in Israel in the 1960s—especially its positive portrayal of German society—ultimately, like most writers of his generation, Ben-Amotz succumbs to the Zionist grand narrative of nationalistic redemption. In the conclusion of the novel, Uri and Barbara move to Israel (make *aliya*), and we learn that on the day that their son is born, Adolf Eichmann is captured by the Israeli secret service. Thus, the Zionist ethos of settlement and the development of Jewish power as a negation of the Diaspora and the memory of the Holocaust prevails.

—Eran Kaplan

TOGBUKH FUN VILNER GETO
Diary by Herman Kruk, 1961

When Nazi Germany attacked the U.S.S.R. on 22 June 1941, Herman Kruk, a Warsaw refugee, vacillated for a moment. He considered if he should flee from the advancing Nazi hordes with the retreating Red Army or remain in Vilna, the Jerusalem of Lithuania, in whose unique Jewish society he had already become an active participant. Kruk cast his lot with that of Vilna Jewry. The first four pages of his diary from this period are missing. The first entry that has come down to us is dated 23 June 1941: "I shall remain [in Vilna]. And immediately I decide definitively: if I have chosen to remain and to become a victim of fascism, I will take my pen in hand and write a chronicle of a city . . . The Jews will be forced into the ghetto—I will record all of this. My chronicle has to see, has to hear and has to become the mirror and the conscience of this great catastrophe and of this difficult time."

From the moment the Germans entered Vilna, Kruk devoted himself without reservation to the dangerous task of secretly recording, on a daily basis, all he heard, saw, and learned of the life, struggle, suffering, and destruction of Vilna Jewry. It required great strength of character to record the most shattering acts of degradation, torture, and slaughter as they were happening. Kruk was empowered by an unflinching sense of historical responsibility to future generations to carry out his mission. He had no illusions. The diary attests to his foreboding of his own imminent death as well as of the imminent destruction of the surviving remnant of Vilna Jewry. At least ten times he writes that in case of his death the diary should be given to his brother, Pinkhos Schwartz in New York City, or to his surviving ideological comrades. Kruk found in his diary his refuge from the Nazi hell, "the hashish of my life in the ghetto."

Kruk's diary provides an authentic, detailed eyewitness account of the history of the Vilna ghetto from its inception until his last surviving entry, dated 14 July 1943, a month before the ghetto's final liquidation. (The succeeding pages of the diary have been lost.) He was particularly well placed to obtain access to the largest number of sources of information. The Vilna ghetto's underground resistance organization, FPO (Fareynikte Partizaner Organizatsye; United Partisan Organization), used the ghetto library, administered by Kruk, as a center of operations and supplied Kruk with information, as did his own party, the Jewish Labor Bund, especially through his friend Grisha Jaszunski, the bund's representative on the

Judenrat. Jaszunski had an illegal, hidden radio in the ghetto. (Kruk himself was the first chairman of the underground bund committee in the ghetto.) At a later date the German-appointed "ghetto head," Jacob Gens, supplied Kruk with information. Kruk also met with Jews who left the Vilna ghetto to visit the smaller ghettos and labor camps in the vicinity, as well as with Jews from such points who entered the Vilna ghetto. He obtained additional information about these places from them. Kruk was sensitive to the changing mood of the ghetto population during the various phases of the Vilna ghetto's existence: during sudden deportations and massacre, in expectation of oncoming threatening events, during the pain and drudgery of daily life, and during the special moments of spiritual exaltation produced by the cultural activity and creativity that flourished in the ghetto. The diary is especially rich in its detailed account of the ghetto's cultural life, since the author played a central role in this area as vice chairman of the Union of Writers and Artists and as head of the ghetto library, art museum, and cultural center.

Kruk was an extremely conscientious chronicler. If he felt that he had insufficient information in a particular entry, he promised to expand it at a later date after culling additional facts. If he learned that he had recorded incorrect information, he returned to the entry and struck out the error. Kruk displayed a high degree of objectivity in his writing. He countered his own subjectivity concerning certain issues by including opposing opinions on the subjects.

When Kruk began his Vilna diary, he wrote it in one copy. About a month after the Vilna Jewry was forced into the ghetto, Kruk reopened the library of the Hevrah Mefitsei Haskalah on Strashun Street as the ghetto library. There he began to dictate his daily entries to his secretary, Rokhl Mendelsund Kowarsky. From that time onward she typed the diary in three copies. The poet **Abraham Sutzkever** says that one copy was kept in the library, a second was sent out of the ghetto to a friend of Kruk who was a Roman Catholic priest, and the third, with its appended documents, was deposited in a metal container in a bunker on Shavl Street. When Sutzkever returned to liberated Vilna in July 1944, he searched for Kruk's hidden ghetto diary. The bunker had been blown up and the metal container was empty, but scattered pages of the diary were strewn throughout the bunker. Sutzkever rescued 380 pages from Soviet Vilna and had them smuggled out to the YIVO Institute for Jewish Research in New York. In 1959, when the YIVO Institute was in the midst of preparing the surviving sections of the diary for publication, an additional 130 pages were found in the archives of Yad Vashem in Jerusalem and were integrated into the text. Documents that Kruk had appended to various pages but that had been lost were found in the YIVO Institute's Vilna Ghetto Archive, known as the Kaczerginski-Sutzkever Collection. The diary was published in Yiddish in 1961 under the title *Togbukh fun Vilner geto* ("Diary of the Vilna Ghetto").

—Eugene Orenstein

TOUCH THE WATER, TOUCH THE WIND (La-ga'at ba-mayim, la-ga'at ba-ruah)
Novel by Amos Oz, 1973

Written in a style that quivers between lyrical surrealism and magical realism, on the one hand, and a casual, even offhanded, journalistic matter-of-factness, on the other, Amos Oz's *Touch the Water, Touch the Wind* (1974; *La-ga'at ba-mayim, la-ga'at ba-ruah,* 1973) like much Holocaust fiction written by non-European nonparticipants, skirts the actual horrors of the camps and ghettos. Instead, it writes on the periphery of the catastrophe and invokes other more contemporary agendas. Like Oz's other, non-Holocaust, fiction, *Touch the Water* is an unflinching and a pained confrontation with the reality of modern-day Israel caught in the Jews' age-old cross fire of group survival and personal fulfillment, now waged as a national rather than a religious struggle.

The protagonist, Elisha Pomeranz, is a Jewish-Polish watchmaker and theoretical mathematician who also takes the alias Dziobak Przywolski, a woodcutter and magician who survives in the woods during the onslaught itself and who is also known as Mieczyslaw, King of New Poland. He skillfully and cleverly makes his way in the company of other survivors through Greece to Palestine. His multiple talents and shifting identities dramatically figure the protean quality of Jewish survival itself, a survival predicated on just this ability of the Jews to absorb, assimilate, and enter into the various landscapes they inhabit. His wife, Stefa (alias Comrade Fedoseyev), who, as a high ranking member of the Communist Party, traces a different trajectory of pre- and post-Holocaust European Jewish history, exemplifies the adaptability of the Jew. But pursued by Nazism on the one hand and communism on the other, even these time-honored Jewish tricks of survival do not prove potent enough to save the Jews. Neither, however, does refuge in the promised land of Israel. This, more than the Holocaust and all of its horrors, is the true locus of torment in Oz's novel.

Not simply orphaned of a past by the Holocaust (two of the younger characters' names are derived from the Hebrew *yatom,* meaning "orphan") but also actively orphaning itself further through its hostility to the past, the Jewish people stand poised in 1967 on the brink of annihilation once more. Against the background of the Holocaust, the threat to Israel's existence is hardly to be dismissed simply as a flaw within the Jewish personality. Nonetheless, given Elisha's and Stefa's extraordinary powers of survival, the rigidity of the kibbutz and its unwillingness to incorporate diasporic Jewish consciousness represent a problem. Thus, we are told, "Ernst, the Secretary of the Kibbutz, thought to himself: It may be that we have a real mathematical genius living with us here. But in fact he is not living among us. He takes no part in the general assemblies, he contributes nothing to the committees, he takes no interest in the great questions like the reform of society or the future of the Movement and the State . . ." Indeed, for

Ernst, Elisha is the "culprit" who seduces his own son Yotam from the ideals of the kibbutz.

Yet it is the "shiftless, withdrawn," and shortsighted Yotam who sets off at the end of the book with his female American counterpart, Audrey, in pursuit of a peace informed less by his father's didactic, pragmatic Zionism than by his spiritual father Elisha's less rooted-at-homeness in the world. Indeed, on his deathbed Ernst himself comes to recognize the role of what he calls "mathemusic," the intangible, ungraspable order of the universe. Denouncing all of the idealisms the book has set up, from the Enlightenment through communism to Israeli collectivism, the high priest of the kibbutz movement testifies, "I, Ernst Cohen, being of sound mind, hereby acknowledge . . . that everything is a delusion which exists for a time only because the whole world . . . is in desperate need of salvation." And yet simultaneously Cohen also becomes a believer: "I, Ernst Cohen, at this moment, tonight . . . hereby testify: here and now, with my very ears, I can hear the stars singing. There is no possible answer to the question, Is this in itself a sufficient proof that the stars are singing. I may add that if I tried to grasp the melody, to repeat it, to reproduce it,— there is no doubt that I should sing it out of tune." Human society, Oz knows, is at best an imperfect replica of a heavenly vision, as Ernst's shortsighted son already seems to know.

In the end the European immigrant Jews Elisha and Stefa Pomeranz are swallowed up to become a part of the earth of Eretz Yisrael, while the new generation of Yotam and Audrey become the new wandering Jews, "roam[ing] from town to town and from land to land, testing the power of words." The old Jew of the Diaspora has sunk down roots in the soil to become a part of its potentially redemptive power, while the new Hebrews, children of the land of Israel, now wander in search of a redemption that only words, the imperfect music of the stars, can bring about.

—Emily Budick

THE TOWN BEYOND THE WALL (La Ville de la chance)
Novel by Elie Wiesel, 1962

In *The Town beyond the Wall* (1964; *La Ville de la chance,* 1962), Elie Wiesel argues that the Communist dictatorships of Eastern Europe have not learned the lessons of the Holocaust in regard to human rights. He describes mistreatment of the mentally ill and of devout Jews in postwar Hungary.

He begins by portraying the sometimes deferential treatment of the mentally ill in the Hasidic milieu of prewar Hungary in the city of Szerencseváros: "Mad Moishe came often to dine with Michael's family; Michael's father was his intimate friend. The young boy had never quite understood what really linked those two men, of whom one believed only in the power of reason while the other resisted all clarity. Michael saw them chatting often: Moishe spoke and Michael's father listened, now amused, now serious."

Wiesel's portrayal of the humane treatment of a mentally ill person is an important cornerstone of his human rights ethic. Michael's father explains why he sees humanity in the personage of the impaired Moishe: "He is far-seeing. He sees worlds that remain inaccessible to us. His madness is only a wall, erected to protect us—*us:* to see what Moishe's bloodshot eyes see would be dangerous."

Michael's Hasidic father believes in the social integration of the mentally ill and views them as valuable members of the larger community. Thereby the degree of suffering inflicted upon the impaired person can be rectified.

Wiesel juxtaposes this approach with that of the postwar Communist Hungarian police, who deliberately attempt to instill mental illness in suspected enemies as a form of torture: " . . . they drive the prisoner crazy. They lock him up in a cell called 'the temple' and keep him standing face-to-the-wall for hours, for days. They call it 'the prayer.'"

The Holocaust survivor Michael finds himself to be a victim of this very procedure when he makes an unlawful but harmless tourist journey to his hometown of Szerencseváros by smuggling himself past the border guards: "'Why don't you open that ugly face of yours and tell us what we want to know?' the officer continued in a bored monotone. '*We* have time, but not you, my boy. You're going mad slowly. You're already showing the first signs. Pretty soon you'll start to talk and shout. You'll spill everything.'" This indictment of Communist cruelty from the pen of a Holocaust survivor came just two years after the publication of Aleksandr Solzhenitsyn's *One Day in the Life of Ivan Denisovich* (1962).

Michael receives unexpected assistance in maintaining his mental balance while in detention from fellow Jew and inmate Menachem, who urges Michael to use his religion as a system of support to survive the ordeal: "'Don't blaspheme,' he chanted. 'All is not madness. God is not madness. What do we know of God or madness? . . . Trust your intelligence to God; he will restore it to you intact, if not purer, more profound.'" Through the figure of Menachem, Wiesel voices the point of view that religion is a pillar of strength and a mainstay of support which cannot be taken from the person who believes in it, even in the darkest crisis.

During his sojourn in the Hungarian prison, Michael learns that Menachem is a victim of Communist religious persecution:

Menachem told him about his own crime against the state: he had organized clandestine classes in religion. At that time anti-Semitism was not only tolerated but encouraged in all countries behind the Iron Curtain. They arrested rabbis and students; they deported them to work camps so they would not "contaminate" the minds of the young. He, Menachem, was neither a rabbi nor a teacher of religion. He was not even very pious. . . . The change occurred one afternoon when his little boy came home from school and asked him, ''Is it true that Jews are the cancer of history? That they live off the past? That they invented God just to humble man and stop progress?'' Menachem went white beneath his beard. After several months of activity he was arrested.

Wiesel is very forthright in this novel about the fact that while he works to keep the memory of the Holocaust, he does not intend to turn a blind eye to Communist persecution of Jews. He posits a oneness between forms of oppression coming from different ideological camps and vows to conquer all of them.

—Peter R. Erspamer

TRACES (Slady)
Short Stories by Ida Fink, 1996

In **Primo Levi**'s famed memoir, *Survival in Auschwitz,* the Italian survivor describes a horrific moment when he breaks off an icicle in order to relieve his parching thirst. When an infuriated guard prevents him from doing so, Levi—understandably and plaintively—asks why. The reply he receives lays bare the essential, irremediable insanity of the Holocaust: ''Here there are no whys.''

Published as *Slady* in 1996 and in English translation in 1997, Ida Fink's second collection of short stories, *Traces* (like her earlier *A Scrap of Time*) gives no rhyme or reason for the savage treatment of Polish Jews by the occupying Germans during World War II. Fink presents story after story— Chekhovian in their economy, precision, and intensity—that chronicle the lives of people caught up in the maniacally conceived and still inconceivable Final Solution. As in her earlier stories, she writes about ordinary men and women living in the small towns and villages of rural Poland; many are young and heartbreakingly eager for life, as in the first story prophetically titled ''The End.''

Here a young man and woman, deeply in love, stand on a balcony ''although it was the middle of the night and only a few hours kept them from the dawn. Down below lay the dark, empty streets; the trees in the square looked like black tousled heads . . . and the asphalt, overheated during the day, exhale[d] its steamy breath.'' The personifications in this opening paragraph are characteristic of Fink's stories. They remind us that everything that is happening is happening to *people*—we are never permitted to forget that critical human dimension. In this case, the young lovers are sharing their last moments together before the invading German forces arrive. In the end the woman tenderly watches over the man; he is asleep and ''lying there defenseless as a child and like a child, unconscious of the evil that had been unleashed.'' Defenseless, innocent, unprepared: he is a perfect and powerful objective correlative (symbol) for Polish Jewry—indeed for European Jewry as a whole.

So too are the three young girls in ''An Afternoon on the Grass,'' in some ways the most affecting story in the collection. ''We were sitting on the grass,'' the narrator tells us, ''Natasha, Masha, and I, beneath a cherry tree heavy with dark, sweet fruit, in a dense sheltered orchard.'' It is another Chekhovian setting ''in a world that has ceased to exist.'' Two of the girls have been living for a year in a nearby city, but they have returned home, hoping to escape capture by the Nazis. The third girl, Masha, who had not been able to afford leaving home, is now lying on the grass with her friends, begging them to tell her what being on their own was like. One of the girls, the narrator, reportedly had a boyfriend. ''Tell me . . . ,'' Masha asks, ''Is it really so beautiful?'' When the narrator, embarrassed, ignores the question, Masha—pathetically— explains: ''Don't be angry. Please understand, I'm just so sad that . . . I'll never know . . . that I'll die without ever . . .'' In this story we are put in excruciating touch with the central horror of the Holocaust, the horror of countless lives destined to end before they have even begun.

Fink's stories have the ring of truth. With rare artistry, she shaped her own experiences (and those of family, friends, and other survivors) into stories that both demonstrate and dramatize how death and daily living proceeded side by side during the dark days of the Holocaust, how normalcy and terror incongruously coexisted, sometimes to humorous effect. For example, in an outlying area of the countryside where the Nazis are slowly but steadily encroaching, a concerned father calls out to his daughter and her friends, sitting outside their cottage on a summer evening: ''Aren't the mosquitoes bothering you girls?'' We cannot help but share the exasperation— and ironic amusement—of the man's wife when she exclaims, ''Mosquitoes, mosquitoes . . . He's worried about mosquitoes.''

Many of the stories in *Traces* deal with the post-Holocaust period when survivors were struggling to survive their survival. So much had been destroyed, swept away. In the title story, for instance (cast in the form of a one-act play), a woman obsessively continues her search for traces of her lost sister. In ''An Address,'' a man who finally locates the woman he thinks is his wife discovers on meeting her face-to-face that she is only a woman who has the same name. And in ''Henry's Sister,'' a woman, anguished by survivor guilt, is unable to face the sister of her husband who did not survive.

Like her first collection of stories, *Traces* is so ably translated that we forget that it was not written in English. It also illuminates aspects of the Holocaust that few writers have dealt with, or even had access to. A *New York Times* reviewer noted, ''Fink's vignettes are not properly read in isolation—from one book to another, they form a single fabric.'' It is the totality of her work—brief but powerful beyond description—that will surely remain a classic and a cornerstone of Holocaust literature as long as Holocaust literature is read, studied, and valued.

—Jacqueline Berke

TRAP WITH A GREEN FENCE: SURVIVAL IN TREBLINKA (Die Falle mit dem grünen Zaun: Überleben in Treblinka)
Memoir by Richard Glazar, 1992

In *Die Falle mit dem grünen Zaun: Überleben in Treblinka* (1992; *Trap with a Green Fence: Survival in Treblinka,* 1995) Richard Glazar recorded his camp experiences as an *Arbeitsjude* (work Jew) in Treblinka, the largest of five Nazi camps devoted exclusively to extermination (some 900,000 Jews were murdered there). Written in Czech immediately after World War II, the memoirs would lie unpublished for more than four decades before the author translated them into German and had them issued in 1992. The title refers to the green leafy fence that greeted the unsuspecting transports as they stepped out of the trains. There, surrounded by such harmless bucolic accoutrements as a tractor and signposts, they would wait in line to be taken directly to the gas chamber: "The narrow strips of grass along the barracks are supposed to have a soothing effect on the passerby. The deep rich green of the fence contrasts with the bright pastel green of the grassy embankment."

Centering around Glazar's 10-month stay as a sorter of the death transports' clothes—from October 1942 until the armed inmate uprising of 2 August—the book is unique for its objectivity. Glazar dispassionately recounts the camp's extermination operations, describes the day-to-day routines of staff and inmates, and reconstructs conversations between prisoners and guards and administrators. A detailed sketch drawn by Esther-Maria Roos, according to the information provided by the author, helps the reader to visualize the layout of the camp. Glazar's spare and economical style reflects the objectivity with which he performed his tasks: "Sorting has become routine for me . . . Most of all I stay alert, and that is how I work: continuously on guard, always sniffing the wind, sensing whence the next danger might come, where the warning sounds."

Comprising 22 chapters ranging in length from two to sixteen pages, the memoir places his account of Treblinka within the context of his experiences during World War II. The early pages describe Glazar's interrupted university studies in Prague and his hiding in a rural Czech village as a farmhand (1939–42). The major portion dealing with Treblinka takes us from his deportation to Theresienstadt (September 1942) through his 10-month incarceration in Treblinka working closely with the fellow prisoners in his unit and then climaxes in the 2 August Treblinka uprising, during which he made his escape.

The remaining quarter of the memoir details his flight across Poland with his closest friend since Theresienstadt, Karel Unger, whom he had been lucky enough to work with throughout the months at Treblinka. Through quick-wittedness and good fortune, Glazar and Unger made it to Mannheim, Germany, with "proper" legal documentation as Vladimir Frysak and Rudolf Masarek, respectively. They lived out the rest of the war in private quarters posing as Czech Gentile workers with the German Todt Organization.

Especially incisive are Glazar's portraits of the SS officials and guards at Treblinka, whose sadistically motivated acts of torture and murder were often provoked by their desire to appear more powerful than their associates vis-à-vis the inmates: a rivalry that made the existence of the worker Jews even more unbearable. Glazar also describes the ongoing black market trading between the inmates and the SS and the Ukrainian guards in goods stolen from the incoming transports. Perceptively he reveals how the welfare of the working Jews depended directly on the number of deportation trains arriving at Treblinka. (Sometimes Glazar could wear new clothes every day and was eating butter, chocolate, and sugar.) Because their very existence depended on extermination, inmates would even pretend not to recognize relatives and friends among the new arrivals and unblinkingly allow them to go to their deaths. Invaluable is Glazar's seventh chapter with its 10-page description of the planning and execution of the Treblinka uprising of 2 August, which for all intents and purposes shut the camp down. Eventually the Nazis attempted to obliterate all traces of the operation, building a farm on the site to house Ukrainians.

The final chapter—a type of epilogue—describes Glazar's appearances as one of only 54 official witnesses of the Treblinka Uprising at the Düsseldorf trials in 1963 and 1971. What gave Glazar the greatest satisfaction he had possibly ever known was that not one of the Treblinka defendants claimed to have acted out of conviction. To Glazar's great disappointment, however, neither the actual architects of the physical death plant at Treblinka nor the bureaucratic pencil pushers in charge of the operation from afar were ever brought forward as defendants.

The candor and succinctness of the memoirs, written as they were immediately following the war, lend them a riveting immanence.

—Steven R. Cerf

TREBLINKA
Memoir by Jean-François Steiner, 1966

Jean-François Steiner's expressed intention in his book *Treblinka*, published in French in 1966 and in English in 1967, was "to reconstruct the history of Treblinka," changing only the names of those survivors who requested it. After introductory chapters describing the events leading up to the destruction of the Vilna ghetto, *Treblinka* tells the story of the death camp from the perspective of its slave prisoners, with a strong emphasis on the planning and execution of the uprising of 2 August 1943. Steiner used both written testimonies and personal interviews with a number of survivors. As Terrence Des Pres has said, "Telling the story from the inside requires novelistic techniques." These include imaginary dialogue, character sketches, and the dramatized montage of fiction. Steiner, however, does not acknowledge this, and the book is presented as a literal representation of real events and is therefore vulnerable to the criticism that it misrepresents the "facts."

James E. Young has used *Treblinka* as an example of what he categorizes as "documentary fiction," which, he argues, creates "the illusion of documentary authority generated by authentic eyewitnesses [which] sustains [its] putative factuality . . . and, by extension [its] power." But Steiner's authority, such as it is, derives not so much from the single instance in the book of direct quotation from the testimony of a survivor, Yankel Wiernik, but from the author's interviews with survivors and his study of witness testimonies combined with his claim about reconstructing the camp's history. Young's analysis of documentary fiction depends on the assumption that the reader of such works is naive: "By allowing himself to be moved to the willing suspension of disbelief by the documentary novel's contrived historical authority, the reader risks becoming ensnared in the encompassing fiction of the discourse itself, mistaking the historical force of this discourse for the historical facts it purports to document."

Sidra DeKoven Ezrahi has described the controversy the book generated as arising from its "being read as [a] historical document" by readers who overlooked works like Wiernik's testimony. Neal Ascherson, too, has worried that "Jean-François Steiner's documentary novel will from now on become the general reference for 'the camps.'" Young, Ezrahi, and Ascherson make the unwarranted assumption that the reader is unable to distinguish between the facts of Treblinka and the, necessarily, fictional elements in the narrative. The presence of dialogue is a clear sign to the reader of reconstruction. Moreover, the English translation includes Des Pres's introduction, which alerts the reader to Steiner's use of novelistic techniques.

Ezrahi believes that Steiner's "failure lies in his imposition of aesthetic forms on historical events rather than transforming those events through the imagination." But Steiner did transform the events using his imagination. What are the reconstructed conversations and events in the book if they are not the product of Steiner's imagination? It is possible that Steiner failed to take the risk of acknowledging the important role played by his imagination. He may have done so because, if he had admitted his function as a creative writer, rather than encouraging the illusion that he was simply a passive conduit of historical truth, this might have led his readers to suspect that whenever actuality impeded aesthetic effect he had succumbed to the temptation to discard the truth, preferring the symmetries of art to the ambiguities of the mundane. Steiner is not alone in this. Many professional historians are similarly disinclined to be open about the way their construction of historical narratives resembles the methods of creative writers.

Steiner interpreted what occurred at Treblinka in terms of a redemptive process. He describes the decision to plan the uprising as "the recovery of [the prisoners'] humanity": "Just when their abdication was total, when all values had ceased to exist, when their humanity had almost left them, the Jews, rousing themselves at the bottom of the abyss, began a slow ascent which death alone would stop." The author does not seriously consider the possibility that for many of the prisoners, rather than being the culmination of a redemptive process, the uprising was simply a desperate act by men with nothing to lose. All hope of surviving the war as a prisoner at Treblinka had, by August 1943, disappeared because new transports had ceased, the cremation of the corpses was almost complete, the Wehrmacht was in retreat on the Eastern Front, and the prisoners were certain that no Jewish witnesses would be allowed to survive the closure of the camp.

Treblinka remains valuable because, as George Steiner has said, "it represents the effort . . . to enter hell by act of imaginative talent," with all the risks this entails.

—Alan Polak

THE TRIUMPH OF LOVE
Poems by Geoffrey Hill, 1998

The Triumph of Love (1998) is Geoffrey Hill's eighth volume of poetry. It is an erudite and brooding poem composed of 150 parts that range from the beautiful single line "Sun-blazed, over Romsley, a livid rain-scarp," which begins the poem, to a 57-line address to *Vergina bella,* the Virgin Mary. The title and content refer variously to Petrarch's *Trionfi* (triumphs), Shelley's "Triumph of Life," and the Jacobean masque. As is true of Hill's earlier poetry, *The Triumph of Love* is driven by his criticism of a culture "with so many memorials but no memory" (LXXVI), criticism complicated by his sense of futility in using poetry to convey history's truths. Although he would take the role of prophets such as Abdiel or Isaiah, there is no guarantee that his message will be heard. Hill uses the rhetorical mode of *laus et vituperatio* (praise and blame) to address a host of historical and contemporary figures ("vassal-lord-puppet strutters"). He takes up his perennial subjects: the corruption of the Church, the violence of wars, and the atrocity of the Holocaust. Hill also returns to his childhood self at numerous points in the poem, thinking back, for instance, to 1939, when he first encountered photos of the Warsaw Ghetto burning, photo negatives forever imprinted on his memory.

The Triumph of Love differs from Hill's earlier work in the bitterness of its humor, a good bit of it self-directed. As Stephen Burt has observed, Hill calls up a series of "antimasquers," voices that take on the roles of a devil's advocate to challenge the poet's angry prophesy. In XXXVII, one of these antimasquers denounces the poet as a

> Shameless old man, bent on committing
> more public nuisance. Incontinent
> fury wetting the air. Impotently
> bereft satire. Charged with erudition,
> put up by the defence
> to be his own accuser.

Another of the detractors is a mischievous and sometimes malicious "editor" who asserts his presence in parenthetical inserts. Various comic errata punctuate the text. For example, in response to the question "What else can I now sell myself, filched / from Lenten *Hebrews*?" the "correction" reads, "Delete: sell myself; filched from. Inert: / Tell myself; fetched from. For inert read insect" (LXIII–LXIV). With typographical errors even in the errata ("inert" instead of "insert"), Hill underscores the slipperiness and impurity of language, which has been a recurring theme in his work.

Much of the tension in the poem derives from Hill's religious beliefs in conflict with the Church's corruption past and present. He wonders "what strange guild is this / that practises daily / synchronized genuflection and takes pride / in hazing my Jewish wife?" (LXVI). Continuing later, he engages in self-irony by employing one of the devil's advocates to refer the reader to "this man's creepy . . . wit— / he fancies himself a token Jew by marriage, / a Jew by token marriage— has buzzed, droned, / round a half-dozen topics (fewer, surely?) / for almost fifty years" (XCVII). One recalls Hill's identification with a concentration camp victim in his early poem "September Song," an identification that entailed risks. Here the tone is sardonic as the speaker declares that "he fancies himself a token Jew by marriage." The line clearly echoes Sylvia Plath's controversial "I think I may well be a Jew." In a poem that ends by defining poetry as "a sad and angry consolation," Hill's increasingly bitter tone seems not only appropriate but also necessary.

The point of recalling the crimes of history, what for Hill have become well-worn topoi, is not simply the recall but the more pressing question of how we might transform historical memory into a moral force that gets beyond guilt: "I am saying (simply) / what is to become of memory? Yes—I know— / I have asked that before" (CXXXVIII). We must remember what we would most forget if we hope to begin to address the injustices of the present. During a moment of self-doubt Hill asks, "Why do I / take as my gift a wounded and wounding /

introspection?" (LXVII). It is precisely this painful yet salvific remembering that is the measure of the poem's triumph: "We shall rise again, clutching our wounds" (XVII).

—Molly Abel Travis

TROST UND ANGST: ERZÄHLUNGEN ÜBER JUDEN UND NAZIS
Memoirs and Poems by Erich Fried, 1983

Erich Fried's tribute to his experiences before the Holocaust is touchingly and sometimes hilariously expressed in his work *Trost und Angst: Erzählungen über Juden und Nazis* ("Consolation and Anxiety: Stories about Jews and Nazis"). It is a collection of short memoirs and poems that expertly relate incidences and emotions leading up to 1938, when Fried was forced to leave Vienna for London as a 17-year-old. In the first story, "Die grüne Garnitur" ("The Green Upholstery") Fried describes the home of his beloved grandmother and the memories he has of her green upholstered furniture. Her house was always clean and in order, and despite the growing restrictions for Jews in 1938, Fried's grandmother was determined to make Erich's life as normal as possible. He was, however, a much more observant child than most and very clever with words, attributes that were much admired by his classmates.

His first glimpses of anti-Semitic flyers are described in "Illegales Material" ("Illegal Material"). Strangely enough, one of Fried's ardent admirers was a member of the illegal (at that time) Hitler Youth named Bertel. As the flyers are distributed, Fried reads the hateful slogans and decides to keep a copy for himself. He bargains with Bertel, allowing him to have one copy as well, while Fried will destroy the rest. Bertel agrees to this and does not beat Fried, as the Hitler Youth were often fond of doing to Jews. Fried manages to assemble a vast collection of Fascist and anti-Semitic material as a young man and expresses his confusion over the hatred against Jews. "Do I also belong to this?" he asks.

Bonds between Fried's classmates ran deep. There were students who belonged to many different parties and movements, ranging from the Hitler Youth to Communists. They may have beaten one another on the playground, but in essence, there is a deep respect that the children have for one another: " . . . that one would have betrayed another was never an issue." When it became too dangerous for Jews to own pro-Fascist material, Fried gave his collection to Bertel. Ironically, it was Bertel who collected money so that a Jewish member of the Hitler Youth could leave Austria and marry his Jewish girlfriend; he even gave them a farewell party at Fried's urging. Although hatred and cruelty were growing in Austria, the children seemed to be less fazed by it than the adults. Bertel never ceased to be amazed by Fried's inability to hate Germany and by Fried's level of tolerance, even after the war and the Holocaust.

Fried's poetry is much more revealing about his internal feelings as a child. In his poem "Kein Kinderspiel" ("No Child's Play"), the last strophe is especially telling:

> That is no longer child's play
> To go to the playground
> As a foreign child,
> It is a dangerous game.
> And you can get taken away for it.
> And also your parents.
> Do you understand?
> Get taken away
> To who knows where?

Fried recognizes those in Austria who had to wear the swastika on their lapels in order to survive. He relates one story where a married couple approaches him while he is in line waiting to give his imprisoned mother some clothing. They apologize to him for wearing the badge and he is touched by the risk they have taken to talk to him. "Not only were my worries alleviated, but I felt like a human being again, at least as good as my neighbors in line with their silver-embossed swastikas." Fried does not place blame on individuals who are drawn into the vacuum of Hitler's movement against their will. He sees the goodness and potential for friendship in most people. He relates his disdain for a beloved teacher who reveals his anti-Semitic slant in class, but praises another Jewish teacher who sends money to a Nazi officer's family in need.

Although Fried outwardly showed a brave front against the growing hatred in Austria, it is indeed *Trost und Angst* that expresses his inner turmoil, his thoughts, and his deep humanism. Yes, there are good and bad people, no matter to what party one belongs. But if there is one lesson Fried teaches us, it is that it is easier to kill those whose faces are unknown to us.

—Cynthia A. Klíma

TWO FORMAL ELEGIES
Poems by Geoffrey Hill, 1959

The dedication of Geoffrey Hill's "Two Formal Elegies" reads "For the Jews in Europe." These paired sonnets, published in his first volume of poetry, *For the Unfallen* (1959), signal Hill's deep concern with the relationship between morality and aesthetics. One of the central questions throughout his life's work has been how one might use art in an act of atonement that gives voice to the victims of the Holocaust and

witnesses to other atrocities of history in a world that has become "witness-proof." As a martyrologist, Hill has written many elegiac poems in various forms. His use here of the sonnet form, with the discipline it requires as well as the questioning and reversal its eight-line/six-line division enables, makes perfect sense in these poems about modern culture's evasions of horrific truths by containing the memories through artifice. We have kept the dead "subdued"; the Germans "disposed" of the Jews, but we who avoid remembering them ensure that they remain buried.

In the first sonnet, which is the most tightly constructed and formal (Shakespearean), Hill uses language to set up a series of double meanings, giving the poem a tension built from the struggle between opposed forces: the dead as restive and threatening; aesthetic fires that merely "play," unlike the crematorium fires; "[f]ierce heart" commanded by "iced brain." Those who died in the Holocaust demand to be remembered. Of course, we cannot "know" these dead; all we can do is "grasp, roughly, the song"—the song being any form of aesthetic atonement that enables the dead to serve as witnesses. Hill offers no ringing endorsement of the power of art to bear witness, however. First of all, we grasp the song imperfectly. Furthermore, the song's effect is ambiguous: "The wilderness revives, / Deceives with sweetness harshness." The phrase "Their best of worlds" alludes to Voltaire's Pangloss, a figure representing misguided optimism in the face of glaring evidence to the contrary. The only way to believe that all things happen for the best in a world set in motion by "Jehovah's hand" (an exacting and vengeful God) is to be guided by the dead's witnessing of the truth as a foundation for future judgment. In a world "[w]ithout the law," a culture bereft of the law of Moses, Hill wonders whether sacrifice and atonement can ever be adequate. Although the song is our last best chance to know the dead and learn from atrocities such as the Holocaust, Hill agonizes over the equivocation of language and the seductive power of poetry to deceive by sweetness and, thus, keep the sins of history buried under cliché and false sentiment.

The second sonnet begins ironically, with the use of ambiguous language. The phrase "For all that must be gone through" can mean both the painful remembering that must be endured and the endless task of exhaustive documentation of the Holocaust. Similarly, "Their long death / Documented and safe" can be interpreted as the historical witnessing that keeps the victims' memory alive or as the kind of documentation that results in a dusty archive or inert museum collection. Hill asks what difference the documentation can make in a world that is "witness-proof." Recalling T.S. Eliot's use of the sea as a symbol of destructive power in "The Dry Salvages," Hill's sea "flickers, roars, in its wide hearth"—an all-consuming fire. His "midlanders" (he is from the English Midlands), who are "brawny with life," warm themselves on seaside holidays at the shores of destruction. The image resonates with the sense of "the fires that [merely] play" in the first sonnet. The midlanders live, love, and "settle on scraped sand," which is the surface of the "sand graves" in the other sonnet.

In the last six lines the poet asks whether it is "good to remind them, on a brief screen, / Of what they have witnessed and not seen?" This question, which emerges repeatedly in Hill's poetry, is never answered; instead, it is the question that drives his self-conscious, fiercely moral project. He concludes "Two Formal Elegies" by again pondering the worth and actual nature of sacrifice. The erecting of historical monuments to the Holocaust "ensures some sacrifice" by "[s]ufficient men [who] carry their weight," but the words "some" and "sufficient" vibrate with doubt. The reader is left with a final question in parentheses, a form of punctuation that Hill has used frequently to brilliant effect for signaling changes of tone and direct addresses to his audience. If Geoffrey Hill's poetry is to reinstill a sense of history in a lost, troubled world, his readers must be pricked by the urgency of this question: "(At whose door does the sacrifice stand or start?)."

—Molly Abel Travis

TYNSET
Novel by Wolfgang Hildesheimer, 1965

The novel *Tynset* is generally regarded as Wolfgang Hildesheimer's crowning achievement in the realm of prose fiction. A year after it was published in 1965, the author received both the prestigious Georg Büchner Prize, specifically for the novel, and the Literature Prize of the City of Bremen. Hildesheimer felt a particular attachment to the work: "I have the feeling that I truly have said something here and I feel a strong kinship to this novel." It is one of the few central European novels written in German during the 1960s that is freighted throughout with Holocaust imagery.

As in two of Hildesheimer's previous literary works, *Nachtstück* (1963; "Nocturne") and *Monolog* (1964; "Monologue"), the anonymous protagonist-narrator of *Tynset* cannot sleep. In fact, it is the melancholy *Nachtstück* that sets up the situation from which the sleepless night in *Tynset* proceeds. As the interior monologue opens, the insomniac narrator is poring over a Norwegian railway schedule, becoming increasingly fascinated by the sound of the eponymous remote town of Tynset. An anchorite living alone with his maid, Celestina, he reveals that he has lived apart from society for 11 years. By imagining himself in Tynset, the narrator fulfills his continuing urge to withdraw ever further into a world of emotions and thoughts, yet at the same time he releases hallucinatory information related to the Holocaust.

The theme of Nazi-related murder appears in a shocking early scene the narrator recalls having heard about in the city of Hamar, not far from Tynset. The German *Kommandant* had ordered 13 Norwegians hanged from lampposts in the street. (The Nazi had originally wanted 17 strung up, but because of time constraints he personally had to shoot the remaining 4 in quick succession.) Even though the narrator has an urge to escape to the pristine sounding Tynset, with this example of World War II Hamar before him he begins to realize that no one area is free of plunder and barbarity.

It is in the middle of the novel that the narrator shares one of his most chilling memories. He not only remembers an object from the Holocaust but also comments on the primitive mentality of those Nazis still living in West Germany in the 1960s: "Where did I see a drum covered with dark human skin that had been made in Zanzibar?—And where did I see lamp shades made of human skin in Germany created by a German amateur craftsman who is alive today as a retiree in Schleswig-Holstein?" Some 15 pages later the narrator reveals that his own father had been murdered in the Holocaust "by Christian family men from possibly Vienna or the region of the Weser river." By underscoring the religion and locale, the narrator indirectly criticizes both Roman Catholic and Protestant authorities for not having protested during the Holocaust, a criticism that also can be found in Hildesheimer's *Nachtstück* when the sleepless protagonist has a vision of cardinals preserving silence as European Jews are being exterminated.

By the novel's final paragraph the sleepless narrator has come to realize that an escape to Tynset is impossible. Just as no single locale can be identified with all of the horrors of the Holocaust, so no geographic location can serve as a refuge from these genocidal events. Hildesheimer himself referred to the novel as a musical rondo, and as such the narrator is once again left alone with his unearthed memories.

The inability to take flight reflects an episode early on when the narrator thinks of a Jewish woman who had tried to conceal her heritage by having a nose job but who, along with her husband, had nevertheless been murdered by the Nazis: "Both actually died. Died, yes that is what one says. She died in a gas chamber . . . and he, his name was Bloch, as far as I remember, he was the only person I ever knew personally who literally dug his own grave, and to be sure while being watched . . . [by an SS man] . . . who shot him . . . using his right hand, that big red and blond hand." The indelible memory of the murderer's hand and references to the Schleswig-Holstein retiree powerfully reemerge in the novel's brief penultimate paragraph to recapitulate the protagonist's harrowing nocturnal memories.

In 1971, 12 years after having translated Djuna Barnes's *Nightwood* (1937) into German, Hildesheimer observed that Barnes's masterpiece shares with his own works of the 1960s the overarching theme of "the night that both surrounds and inhabits us, to which we are delivered." In particular, in the chapterless *Tynset* it is the nocturnal images of deportation and death ("Nacht und Nebel," "night and fog") that hold the protagonist captive in an ongoing nightmare.

—Steven R. Cerf

TZILI: THE STORY OF A LIFE (Ketonet veha-pasim)
Novel by Aharon Appelfeld, 1983

In *Tzili: The Story of a Life,* originally published in Hebrew as *Ketonet veha-pasim,* Aharon Appelfeld weaves the themes of the assimilated yet marginal Jew and the redemptive nature of the physical—both the body and the natural environment—into a tapestry onto which he inscribes Tzili's growth from lonely silence to expressive independence. Unable to write stories when restricted to historical memory, Appelfeld wrote *Tzili* from his own story—but only up to a point. He transformed the boy Erwin Appelfeld into the slightly older Tzili and created an unforgettable, sympathetic victim. Like Erwin, Tzili is alone, left to wander in the forests, where she learns to survive by responding to her physical needs. She learns to eat roots, to wash in cold rivers and streams, to seek other marginal people, particularly the village prostitute, and to move across the East European landscape with other survivors. Finally, she emigrates to Palestine with them. She has learned to expect little and demand nothing. As the critic Inga Clendinnen has succinctly explained, Tzili, like Appelfeld, lost her family and her childhood to the Nazis.

Unlike the young Appelfeld, Tzili, "devoid of charm and almost mute," is neither bright nor ambitious. The youngest in a large family, she is the object of ridicule by her invalid father, shopkeeper mother, brothers, sisters, and schoolmates. She finds amusement by playing alone in the dirt, but her family decides that she needs instruction, so they hire an old tutor whose family abandoned him when they emigrated to America. She absorbs her lessons and recites by rote the teaching that man is but dust and ashes, a being that must follow Torah. Religious training notwithstanding, as a "Jewish girl without any brains," she humiliates the family. Assuming that no one would bother to harm her, they leave her alone to tend the house when the war starts.

However victimized, Tzili is also a survivor. She instinctively resists being raped by a blind old villager who assumes that she is the daughter of a prostitute, overcomes the terror of her first menstruation, and gradually welcomes affection from Mark, an assimilated, urbane Jew who also hides in the forest after escaping from a camp where he left his wife and children. Eventually he is smothered by guilt and unable to endure his isolation and dependence on Tzili, who goes into the plains to barter the clothes of Mark's family for food, cigarettes, and vodka. These are necessities for Mark, who cannot adapt to hiding in the forests. He leaves their bunker for the village, confident that he has overcome his fears and can survive in the plains just as Tzili had. Despite his attempts to assimilate, however, Mark remains identifiably Jewish, while Tzili does not. Her self-sufficiency, trust in her instinct, and guileless interaction with the townspeople enable her to move freely, though cautiously, among them. After Mark leaves, Tzili is bereft and spends the harsh winter searching for him, carrying his haversack and his baby. As he haunts her wanderings, she draws strength and dignity from his oft repeated truth that "A man is not an insect." When she joins a group of survivors, newly liberated by the advancing Red Army, she is no longer marginal; like them, she is homeless. They journey south to Zagreb together, where they board a ship to Palestine, but not before Tzili delivers a stillborn infant and, in so doing, sheds the remnants of her European identity in preparation for a new life.

The Appelfeld scholar Gila Ramras-Rauch has attributed part of Tzili's maturity and independence to her purification by water; she drinks from streams, cleanses herself in rivers, and "above all she had learned the virtues of the wind and the water." A "huge body of water," the sea, will give her "yet another chance for a new start." The character Tzili embodies a past that embraced a non-Jewish European culture that rejected Jews and Jewishness and a future that is centered on Palestine. We are grateful that Appelfeld did not heed the implication of his opening line, "Perhaps it would be better to leave the story of Tzili Kraus' life untold."

—Myrna Goldenberg

U

UNDERGROUND
Play by Joshua Sobol, 1991

Underground (1991) is the third and final play in Joshua Sobol's triptych about the Vilna ghetto during the Holocaust. The play focuses on the secret typhus ward located in the Vilna ghetto. During his research on the Vilna ghetto, Sobol was fascinated to learn that the typhus ward was so secret that even some of the physicians in the hospital did not know that it existed.

Because of the atrocious conditions in which the Jews live, typhus spreads in the ghetto. This deadly disease has to be contained and kept secret in order for the ghetto to survive. If Obersturmführer Hans Kittel and SS Dr. Jaegger discover the outbreak of typhus, they clearly will murder everyone in the hospital and liquidate the ghetto.

Sobol's play, like *Ghetto* and *Adam,* is a dramatic retelling of a historically true story by a character who eyewitnessed the events—narrated in the present by a survivor of the ghetto. In *Underground* a patient is in the hospital in Israel; his nurse finds the diary he possesses and reads about the typhus ward in the ghetto in 1943 (the patient in Israel in the present had been afflicted by typhus and had been saved by Dr. Berka Weiner). Through the anonymous man's diary, Sobol tells the story of how Weiner, his colleague and lover Dr. Sonya Solodova, and Dr. Gottlieb establish the secret typhus ward, with the blessing of Judenrat leader Jacob Gens, in the ghetto hospital, thus saving the lives of the Vilna Jews. These doctors successfully hide the typhus outbreak from the Nazis through a series of deceptive tricks. The doctors provide all of their typhus patients with fake symptoms, which they must rehearse and pretend to be afflicted by when Kittel and Jaegger come to inspect the ward, and the physicians create alternate sets of charts—the actual medical charts that indicate the progression of their disease and the fake charts that inform the Nazi visitors that the patients are afflicted by noncontagious illnesses that do not pose a threat to the community. As Gens points out to Weiner, the Nazis fear the outbreak of contagious diseases and would quickly destroy the ghetto inhabitants to prevent the spread of the illness.

The outbreak of typhus begins with the illness of Judith, who has survived the mass killings in the Ponar forest. Nazi soldiers have murdered thousands of Jewish men, women, and children at Ponar, but a few women, such as Judith, are only wounded and presumed dead by the perpetrators, who then leave the forest. Five of the women have survived and managed to come to the ghetto, where they tell their story to Gens. The survivors tend to be women because the Nazis murder the Jewish men in the morning and the women and children in the afternoon; those men who are wounded but not killed eventually bleed to death because they must feign death for hours while the Nazis are present, but the women who survive the shootings do not have to wait all day to leave the death pits, for they are shot just before the Nazis depart. After Judith returns and tells her story, the doctors discover that she has typhus. She eventually recovers and becomes pregnant by her boyfriend Tana. This pregnancy presents another problem in the ghetto because the Nazis have ordered that all pregnancies must be aborted, yet Judith insists upon keeping her baby. When Nazi soldiers discover that a woman has given birth to a baby, they habitually kill the baby and the entire family.

Dr. Berka Weiner is a caring and humane doctor who reluctantly agrees to head the typhus ward. He is not optimistic about the chances of fooling Kittel and Jaegger, but he agrees to try, partly because he falls in love with Dr. Solodova. Sobol's play dramatizes the personal interests and strong emotions that dictate people's actions in this time of crisis. The playwright also juxtaposes the humanitarians Weiner and Solodova with the selfish and egocentric Professor Lishafsky, who sells drugs for personal profit even though his people, who desperately need the medications, are suffering from disease.

As the play draws to a close, Gens confesses to Kittel that he has been protecting the armed partisans in the ghetto as they flee to the forest. Kittel responds by assassinating the ghetto leader; Gens's death provides closure to the final play in Sobol's triptych. As the play concludes the sounds of machine gun fire are heard, suggesting the liquidation of the Vilna ghetto, which historically occurred only nine days after the murder of Jacob Gens.

—Eric Sterling

THE UNLOVED: FROM THE DIARY OF PERLA S.
(Z deniku sedmnactilete Perly Sch)
Novel by Arnošt Lustig, 1979

The Unloved: From the Diary of Perla S. (1985; *Z deniku sedmnactilete Perly Sch,* 1979) is a 17-year-old girl's testimony of her life in Theresienstadt. What is perhaps most remarkable about this "diary" is Arnošt Lustig's ability to write from a female perspective by observing life through a young prostitute's eyes. Perla S. seeks to survive in a world where there is no more love. Everyone she has loved is gone, and everyone she could love will be taken away from her via transport. Her body is all that she can control, and for her services she receives small bits of bread, candles, or other items that she uses to make her dreary life more pleasant. Her giving of pleasure to others aids her in forgetting the loss of her family and the surroundings of the ghetto. The conversations that she has with both men and women in the camp are detached from any emotion. In fact, it is the cold, undemonstrative manner in which situations and people are handled in everyday contacts that are striking features of this diary. Perla S.'s closest companion is the rat that lives beneath her floorboards, for the rat will never have her name called up for transport. "Rats don't worry about tomorrow," Perla S. writes. "Rats can do without names, without numbers, without return addresses." Perla S. envies the simplicity with which the rat lives, sans concern, sans anguish. In many ways the rat embodies the way Perla S. would like her own life to be.

With her friend Ludmila, Perla S. enjoys walks and partakes in discussions about the factors of life that have come together to bring them to Theresienstadt. They are both emotionally distant from one another as a protective device, for they both know that one of them will wind up going away forever on a transport to the East. Observations of the simpler things in life, such as the moon, stars, darkness, and daylight, are the present highlights of their existence, for these aspects of nature are eternal—they do not disappear as people do. The topics of conversation are also clearly distant from the reality of their world, and the reader perceives the gloomy end for both of them. They are young women who should be going out and having fun, not discussing the philosophical meaning of the miserable circumstances enveloping them. Every day they take a stroll to the insane asylum, which represents another constant in a world where transports change the composition of the camp on a daily basis. The inmates may cease to exist, but the asylum will forever remain standing, long after Perla S. and Ludmila have departed.

The entire structure of the way life goes for the inhabitants of Theresienstadt has been brilliantly construed by Harychek Geduld, a young man who has befriended Ludmila and Perla S. He creates a Monopoly game that no one can ever really win. As transport time approaches for him, his game becomes more and more circular in that every space is always another ending or roadblock to freedom. As Perla S. has written in her diary, "At the same time, we all know that there, where the transports go, things are incomparably worse. And so the choice between what is good and bad has been reduced to the choice between what is worse and worst." In Theresienstadt life is a game with no winner.

Perla S., however, maintains some inner strength to control one aspect of her life, and sex is the tool that she possesses. The men in the camp seem to be strong, especially the Luftwaffe officer who has become one of her most frequent customers. These facades are broken down by Perla S. Even guilt cannot possess her, for there is no one left in her family to feel shame or disgust for what she does to survive. She asks the Luftwaffe officer, "Could you ever think of the female body as a weapon?" She is not allowed elegance—her best effort is to sell herself in the best manner she possibly can. The one item that no one can take from her is her own body. This she can give and take away at will.

Human conditions change, but human nature does not. These are the conclusions that Perla S. draws about life. "In the end, we are all selfish," she writes. Childhood memories are slowly swallowed up by the reality of life. As transport for Perla S. grows nigh, memories of last lines of conversations with friends and family members grow stronger. What will Perla S. leave behind? What will prevent her from being a forgotten utterance or merely a speck on the timeline of humanity? On the eve of transport she hides her diary, leaving it behind as the lone witness to her existence.

—Cynthia A. Klíma

V

VEILCHENFELD
Novel by Gert Hofmann, 1986

In the 1986 novel *Veilchenfeld,* published several years after the critical success of *Die Denunziation,* Gert Hofmann's interpretation of the Holocaust theme took a new turn. For the first time within his work, a Jewish character was not just obliquely referred to in the narrative but placed centrally on the stage of events, even lending his name to the title of the novel. Without lapsing into a sentimental philo-Semitic mood that had sometimes become tempting for West German authors who were writing about Jews, Hofmann managed to reproduce with startling sharpness the mechanisms of ostracism and harassment that marked the period 1936–38, even before the pogrom of *Kristallnacht* and the concentration camps.

The novel begins and ends with the news of the death of Bernhard Israel Veichenfeld. Upon his dismissal from the university in Leipzig, Veilchenfeld, an elderly professor of philosophy, moves to live in a small town in Saxony at the beginning of 1936. After his existence as a Jew in this community becomes unbearable, he puts an end to his life in September 1938. Within this time frame the narrative reveals how Veilchenfeld is gradually deprived of all of his civil and human rights and subjected to various forms of physical and mental abuse. Numerous members of the small town community—his neighbors, his housekeeper, Nazi youth, low-level bureaucrats in the police and other city offices—become culprits in the persecution and humiliation of the old man. Barely anyone speaks to him, and he is afraid to go out during the day, when he might meet people. When he goes out at night, however, he is attacked by Nazi hooligans, and when he attempts to complain about the assault, he is beaten up by the police as well. His apartment is vandalized, while his neighbors silently witness the whole ordeal. After Veilchenfeld has finally decided to move to Switzerland and has waited patiently for days for permission to leave, the police tear up his passport. Veilchenfeld's suicide at the end of the novel implies that there are no solutions left to those "others" who are ostracized by the majority within their home country, especially if they want to retain some measure of dignity and control over their lives. Yet at the same time this individual act of self-destruction serves as a highly symbolic prefiguration of the anonymous mass extermination of Jews that is to start not long after Veilchenfeld's death.

Several features of Hofmann's novel place it among the masterpieces of West German literature on the Holocaust. The work is animated by a highly original narrative voice. The story of Veilchenfeld, who speaks directly only a few lines in the novel, is retold by a young boy named Hans. From his naive but privileged perspective as an alert, curious, and unprejudiced child, Hans combines his immediate observations with his parents' and other adults' accounts of their experiences and thoughts. Thus, the boy tells a story that is very candid in its tone and yet confusing and disjointed because it weaves together diverse pieces of information and various fragmentary, often mutually contradictory, explanations. There is also a striking discrepancy between the dramatic nature of described events, which the reader understands well, and the cool detachment of the child, who obviously comprehends very little or misinterprets what he sees. It is, paradoxically, in these discrepancies and contradictions of the narrative that the reader finds an authentic sense of the atmosphere of lies, fear, and silent complicity reigning in the small German town during the prewar Nazi period. The child who quotes the adults' prejudices about Jews, their lies, and their anti-Semitic language inadvertently pronounces severe indictments on his parents and the townspeople.

Another memorable aspect of the novel is the ambivalence with which the narrator portrays his father. The father, who is a physician and World War I veteran, seems to be a good friend of the persecuted professor. He continues to have him as a patient and to visit him, even after he receives a note from the authorities saying that he should stop because Veilchenfeld suffers from an incurable "hereditary disease." Yet despite his braveness and his dismissal of racism, the father does not see any chance for the professor's survival in Germany and sees suicide as Veilchenfeld's only way out of the situation.

It is noteworthy that Hofmann's *Veilchenfeld* is considered one of the best Holocaust novels in postwar German literature even though it never mentions the word "Jew." The omission of the word does not mean that the author prefers to avoid a direct confrontation with the Holocaust theme but that he has set himself a more ambitious goal. The narrator unmistakably identifies Veilchenfeld as a Jew as he repeats the stereotypic anti-Semitic slurs of the townspeople and explains all of his troubles by the fact that he looks different ("has a large nose"), thinks differently, and, overall, is not "one of us." Yet at the same time, by not using the word "Jew," Hofmann seeks to restitute the sense of personhood of the various Nazi victims by forcing the contemporary reader to respect their humanity regardless of their ethnic or religious background.

—Mila Ganeva

THE VICTORY (Zwyciestow)
Novel by Henryk Grynberg, 1969

The Victory by Henryk Grynberg was published in 1969 by the Paris Literary Institute two years after the writer's emigration to the United States. The novel is a sequel to *Child of the Shadows*, which tells about the author's life until 1947. *The Victory* is divided into two parts. In the first part the protagonist and his mother return to their home village where they learn about the murder of the father. The new owners of Jewish houses are astonished to see the eight-ear-old protagonist and his mother alive. "'Abramkova you're alive?' they say. 'My mother didn't like that question.'" The second part begins after the early success of the Soviet winter offensive. With Warsaw ruined many survivors commence their new lives in Lodz. Among them are but a few Jews who had survived the Holocaust in Poland and some Jewish repatriates from Russia. One of them is the author's stepfather, Asker Usher Powazek, a pre-war Communist, now a survivor of the Mauthausen camp. His wife and the younger daughter died in Treblinka. The older girl got to the Aryan side and was never heard of again.

The book was published after the Polish Communist anti-Semitic campaign of 1968. Because the book was published abroad Grynberg could write freely about the fate of the Polish Jews in the early post-war years, when the Communist dictatorship was being established. Although the authentic and autobiographical character of the book is strongly emphasized by the author, *The Victory* is not a memoir. It is a well-composed novel whose main autobiographical framework is authentic. As in *Child of the Shadows* Grynberg introduces the clash between the narrative conducted form the child's perspective and the actual author's knowledge. The created tension results in paradoxes that define the post-war reality. In the second part of the novel the narrator and the writer are one. Also important are the stories of other characters, which strengthen the authenticity of the presented world. The historical background is widened. Usher's story, as well as the stories of the people coming from Soviet Russia, cast light on the fates of the Jews who fell prey to the other totalitarian state.

The Victory significantly complements the descriptions of the Polish post-war reality as presented in *Ashes and Diamonds* by Jerzy Andrzejewski and *Seizure of Power* by Czeslaw Milosz. Grynberg describes Poland from the perspective of the Jews experiencing anti-Semitism even after the Holocaust. They feel there is no room for them in Poland, where they still fear for their lives. They fear to claim their property back or to have their sons circumcised because they would become recognizable. These Jews think of emigrating. Others, involved in communism, become corrupted by the Soviet terror, and they either seek revenge or pay in the future for being naive.

The word "victory" in the title is empty and meaningless, compromised by the vision of the presented world. This fact is additionally stressed by the last sentence of the novel: "The war was over, but who had won?" The reader is prepared for such a conclusion from the first scene in the novel, when the protagonist and his mother watch the Red Army marching in. The declarative optimism of the woman who promises the boy that people would be good to them is contrasted with his demand not to be a Jew any more.

Thus the war is perceived as won by the evil that exists in human nature. It was anti-Semitism and Nazism that rewarded evil and punished goodness. It was the system that annihilated the Jews and carried out the destruction of human values. Never in Dobre were the Polish inhabitants better off than during the war, when they traded with the starving people in the ghettos of Lodz and Warsaw and when the hiding Jews paid for their lives.

The fear of the few survivors does not end with the war; they become unnecessary witnesses of human wickedness. They seek protection of the Red Army and of the new Communist authorities, who in turn look for supporters. This makes the Jews estranged again. As Communists they are killed by the Polish underground movement and because people "got used to killing the Jews."

Grynberg does not create a one-dimensional world. The Jewish survivors portrayed in his novel are victims of inhuman systems. Their children hunt for Germans while the adults support Communism or carry out provocations against their brothers. But above all the novel focuses on the Holocaust and its effects, on anti-Semitism that can be exploited by any ideology, and on the wrong done to the Jews by other people.

The writer consistently objects to the universalization of the Holocaust experience. He also argues with a stereotype popular among Polish immigrants, according to whom the support of Communism by the Polish Jews was a mass phenomenon. It is notable because immigrants were the first audience of that book.

—Kazimierz Adamczyk

VITTEL DIARY (Pinkas Vitel)
Diary by Yitzhak Katzenelson, 1964

Yitzhak Katzenelson's *Vittel Diary* (1972; *Pinkas Vitel*, 1964) is much more a jeremiad of exceptional power than it is a diary. This work, which was composed in 1943 in Vittel, an internment camp in eastern France, has relatively little to say about life in this comparatively benign place. The greatest horror that Vittel had to offer to the inhabitants was the real and ever-present fear of being declared stateless and deported to a death camp. That is what, in fact, did happen to Katzenelson and his eldest son who was incarcerated in Vittel with him; both were deported to Auschwitz, where they were murdered. In terms of specific and concrete historical information,

Katzenelson's *Vittel Diary* has quite a lot to say about the destruction of the Warsaw Ghetto, to which he was an eyewitness as well as being involved with the resistance. It should be mentioned that by 1942 Katzenelson was well informed and fully aware of what was happening to European Jewry. He also learned that his wife and two younger sons had been deported to a concentration camp where, he assumed with good reason, they had been separated from each other, stripped naked, and gassed. The overarching structure, theme, and style of this work are informed by Katzenelson's need to give voice to the ineffable anguish and devastation he feels at the loss of the two things he loves most dearly: the Jewish people and his family.

Many interesting themes are developed with exceptional passion and originality in *Vittel Diary*. Among them is his assessment of the importance and spiritual beauty of Jews and Judaism. His view of Jews makes it even more agonizing for him to witness their destruction. The essential purity and decency of the Jews contrasts with and intensifies the vileness of their persecutors. In an interesting extended argument, he reclaims Jesus as a Jew. He sees Jesus as just one Jew among many just like him and asserts that Christians stole him for their god and ultimately perverted his true spirit: "Christianity seized hold of one of our Jesuses and used him as if he was their own . . . After seizing one, out of the many Jesuses, they slew him. This dead Jew was converted into a dainty dish, made just as their spirit moved them and to their taste." This brief passage only gives a hint of the argument intended to explain anti-Semitism and Christian iniquity.

As the above passage suggests, Katzenelson, who has witnessed the callous and sadistic murder of large numbers of Jews and who is keenly aware of the nearly completed destruction of European Jewry, seems consumed with a need to identify and condemn all those who are culpable. He refuses to limit the blame to those who are most immediately and conspicuously involved in the murders: "In truth, however, it is the whole wicked German nation which willed and committed the acts of murder and abomination. They ratified all these acts and indeed willed them. The S.S. were the obedient emissaries of the most evil community on earth and they executed their mission most faithfully." Katzenelson's accusations are ultimately leveled against a wide variety of groups and nations, including the Allies, all of whom he sees as either guilty of complicity in or, at best, indifferent to the fate of the Jews. Jews are by no means spared his condemnation. He not only singles out the Jewish police and all those Jews who collaborated with the Nazis but also sees both the Bundists and Aguda as sharing responsibility for the defenselessness and hence the demise of European Jewry. Although these two groups subscribed to antithetical beliefs or ideologies, they were both anti-Zionist, and Katzenelson sees a Jewish homeland as the only means to have escaped the Holocaust. Indeed, had there been a Jewish homeland, no one would have dared to threaten Jews in this way. Katzenelson faults these Jews not only for rejecting a Jewish homeland because it could have served as a safe haven but also because they, and all advocates of assimilation, have alienated Jews from their true culture and being. They have thus made them unable to defend themselves because they lack a knowledge and true appreciation of their identity.

Vittel Diary is unusual, if not unique, in the combination of anguish, knowledge, and insight that the author exhibits in his effort to give voice to and preserve an event of unspeakable horror. Reading this book is an agonizing experience, redeemed only by how successfully Katzenelson captures and preserves his experience of this event. After all, the diary makes quite clear that the author hopes against all hope that somehow some Jews will survive and that the world will remember and care what happened to the rest. Some Jews did survive; and *Vittel Diary* survived to compel all who read it to care.

—Manfred R. Jacobson

W

W, OR THE MEMORY OF CHILDHOOD (W, ou, le souvenir d'enfance)
Novel by Georges Pérec, 1975

Within Georges Pérec's corpus, his book *W, or the Memory of Childhood* (1988; *W, ou, le souvenir d'enfance*, 1975) is both characteristic in its ingenious patterning of different narratives and unique in its gravity. In *W* linguistic play and fragmentation, far from being a hermetic literary game, emerges as the only way in which the events that have shaped Pérec's childhood ("the war, the camps," in his deliberately terse summary in chapter 6, "History with a Capital H") can be attested to without being violated.

W is divided into two distinct narrative strands, one "autobiographical," the other "fictional," that alternate by chapters; if the two terms are placed in quotes it is because the text renders the distinction between autobiography and fiction increasingly tenuous. In the autobiographical strand, printed in standard typesetting, Pérec recounts his fragmentary and faulty memories of his childhood. In the fictional one, printed in italics, a narrator named Gaspard Winckler tells of his voyage to an island off Tierra del Fuego named W, governed by the rules of sport. The W narrative, in fact the fleshing-out of a story Pérec claims to have written as a child, is itself split by an ellipsis (literally three bracketed dots occupying a single page in the middle of the book). On the first side of the ellipsis we learn of how the narrator came to join the voyage; on the other Winckler's story recedes from the narrative, ceding to a coldly impersonal description of the horrors of life for the athlete population of W.

What draws these strands together, apart from their having the same authorial source, is their shared status as traces of a memory that refuses to be told directly. In one of the chapters taking up Pérec's faltering memoir of childhood, he expresses his paradoxical condition as a writer: "I do not know whether I have anything to say, I know that I am saying nothing; I do not know if what I might have to say is unsaid because it is unsayable (the unsayable is not buried inside writing, it is what prompted it in the first place); I know that what I say is blank, is neutral, is a sign, once and for all, of a once-and-for-all annihilation." What does Pérec mean when he speaks of the unsayable prompting writing? The memoir he writes consists of little more than fleeting images of a childhood under the protection of his aunt's non-Jewish family after his parents' deportation to the death camps. So vulnerable to error and distortion are these images that Pérec is consistently appending corrective footnotes (which, implicitly, might themselves be implicitly erroneous) to the original version.

The reason these images of childhood are impossible to set down with any certainty is that their source is, in Pérec's term "the unsayable," the traumatic memory of the camps and his parents' death. The author's fervent desire to clarify these memories is doomed to failure because their meaning consists in their very resistance to clarification or narration; they are the record of an effort to tell what cannot be told, hence Pérec's description of them as "a sign . . . of a once-and-for-all annihilation." Every attempt to tell the story of his childhood "annihilates" itself.

The other sign of this "annihilation" is the W narrative itself. As the vicious and arbitrary brutality of the island's regime comes into focus, so does its similarity to the world of the death camps. The words "FORTIUS ALTIUS CITIUS" emblazoned on the arches of the athletes' villages irresistibly evoke the "ARBEIT MACHT FREI" motto that stood over the gates to the Nazi concentration camps. The sadistic, arbitrary, and unpredictable laws of the competitive events as well as of everyday life on the island provoke further comparisons. Naked women are chased around the track by sprinters and raped publicly once caught. Proper names are discarded not for numbers but for the names of their predecessors in competition. Most redolent of survivor testimony, however, is the relentless and arbitrary changing of the law that disables the athletes' attempts to know and obey it: "The Law must be known by all, but the Law cannot be known." This is why there is no way of explaining life on the island to the novice athlete, for he lacks the fundamental categories to comprehend it; he must learn to absorb horror not as an unpleasant interruption of daily life but as its very texture: "But wherever you turn your eyes, that's what you will see, you will not see anything else, and that is the only thing that will turn out to be true." Pérec as memoirist and Winckler as witness thus share the same dilemma: They tell of what disables their ability to tell.

Indeed, the W narrative and Pérec's memoir perpetually echo one another. Just as the latter seems dispossessed of his power to remember in the very act of remembering, the narrator of the W story, once he shifts from the voyage to the island itself, seems unable any longer to speak in his own name. We lose any hint of Winckler's place in the story—neither the progress of his search for the missing deaf-blind boy nor his personal experience on the island are alluded to. Just as Pérec's attempt to recover the memory of his traumatized childhood only highlights its irrecoverable loss, so Winckler's testimony to the world of W strips him of his ability to speak in anything but an absolutely "blank," "neutral" tone.

Pérec's book, then, is one of the most compelling attempts in Holocaust literature to come to terms with the horror not by direct description or narration but by acknowledging and exploring the impossibility of either.

—Josh Cohen

THE WALL
Novel by John Hersey, 1950

John Hersey's second novel, *The Wall* (1950), represents the Warsaw Ghetto from the construction of its enclosing wall in November 1939 through the April–May 1943 uprising, when the Jewish remnant held the Nazis at bay for more than six weeks. Suffused with history, the novel is one of the earliest fictional works in English to deal comprehensively with the Holocaust. Comprehensive studies of the Holocaust or the Warsaw Ghetto had not yet been written. The available documentation lay primarily in memoirs written in Polish or Yiddish during or after the war. One milk can full of material from the Oneg Shabbat archive, developed under **Emmanuel Ringelblum**, had been uncovered in 1946, but the second buried repository was not discovered until 1950, after *The Wall* was published. Hersey, who was not Jewish and could read neither Polish nor Yiddish, relied on two research assistants (one of them Lucy Davidowicz, later a well-known Holocaust historian) to translate the available works aloud into a wire recorder. These assistants not only translated but also added their own emphases and commentary. It was out of such material that Hersey—a well-known journalist and the author of *A Bell for Adano* and *Hiroshima*—constructed his narrative.

Hersey used a traditional narrative device whereby an ''editor'' announces that he has discovered an archive of more than four million words buried during the years of the ghetto. It has been put together by a historian named Noach Levinson, who died soon after the war, and includes testimony written by others or transcribed by Levinson from conversations. The editor, a fictionalized Hersey, has selected the narrative that becomes *The Wall,* keeping intact Levinson's scrupulous dating of the events and his careful notation of individual voices as well as the dates on which he actually wrote the notes. Levinson bears similarities to the historical Ringelblum, and the hint that the notes might constitute the Oneg Shabbat archives lends authenticity to Hersey's account. Hersey used actual historical events to construct his plot, thereby leaving him free to emphasize characters and their development more than action.

The narrative proper begins in November 1939, a few months after the Nazi occupation and before the actual ghetto was established. We live through the evolution of Jewish life in this setting, including the influx of refugees, the intense overcrowding, the restrictions on Jewish traditions, the completion of the wall, and the ban on Jews leaving the ghetto. We witness the emerging power of the Judenrat and the Jewish police as well as the lost interaction between Jews and Poles. In addition, we experience only a modest Nazi presence, given that the ghetto administration lay mostly in the hands of Jews.

Hersey focuses on a set of families that share cramped living quarters, becoming in effect an extended family centrally involved in the uprising, in which shared responsibility and work create the kinship of comrades. The nuclear families include the religious Mazurs, whose son Stephan joins the ghetto police; the wealthy, secular Apts, especially their two daughters, the plain but caring Rachel and the beautiful, shallow Halinka; and the talented but unambitious Dolek Berson and his sickly wife, Symka. Levinson joins the family later in the book. Earlier, he and Berson had met when the Germans arrested members of the Judenrat and forced them to share a jail cell for several days. The reader watches the characters evolve toward a collective consciousness of their fate as well as of their love and mutual responsibility. We witness the humanization of the cynical Levinson into a key member of the uprising; we watch Rachel Apt move beyond her plainness to become a charismatic leader; and we watch Berson emerge as a man of many talents, particularly after Symka's death, as he moves inevitably into a relationship with Rachel.

The resistance forces develop after the Jews realize that they are being systematically slaughtered at the nearby Treblinka extermination camp. Various Jewish organizations, including Zionists, Socialists, and religious groups, are initially unable to cooperate, but they finally agree to work together as the awareness of their collective fate overrides doctrinal and political differences. They manage to locate minimal weapons and ammunition, achieve some cooperation with Polish partisans, and hold off the Germans while moving from place to place. At the end about 40 escape. Did they resist to save Jewish lives? To show that Jews could actually fight back? To show that Jews were worth saving after all? Is this story of survival about the importance of resistance or the futility of it? Hersey's understated style forces the reader to live through his characters' experiences. Full of effective secondary as well as primary characters and well-imagined scenes, the book neither mystifies nor glorifies the resistance fighters, and its ultimate emphasis is secular rather than either religious or sectarian.

—Michael Hoffman

THE WARSAW DIARY OF ADAM CZERNIAKÓW
Diary by Adam Czerniaków, 1968

The first edition of Adam Czerniaków's notes was published in Hebrew translation, in Jerusalem, in 1968. It was published in English as *The Warsaw Diary of Adam Czerniaków* in 1979. The notes of the chairman of the Jewish Council in occupied Warsaw consist of eight notebooks, with 1,056 pages in total. They cover the period from September 1939 to 23 July 1942—the second day of the great deportations of the Warsaw Jews to Treblinka, when Czerniaków committed suicide. There were originally nine notebooks, but the fifth one (14 December 1940–22 April 1941) was lost.

Czerniaków kept his notes with surprising consistence—day after day, in a laconic, informative style, focusing on his efforts to improve the situation of the Warsaw Jews. This is the only such reliable source informing about the everyday ghetto administration and of the economic, health, and psychical condition of the people condemned to death. His notes reflect all the phases of exploitation of the Jews and present the picture of the ghetto's stratification: people dying of starvation, diseases, poverty, and lice, as well as rich people and those collaborating with the Germans. Czerniaków writes also about the instances of anti-Semitism among the people of Warsaw.

As the critics (Kersz, Zimand, Fuks) agree, the diary seems to be a collection of notes for the future study on the war history of the Warsaw Jews. Hence their briefness and focus on facts, names, and numbers. It looks as if the author wanted to jot down the essential information while preserving in his memory its interpretation and evaluation. It is also argued that the purpose of gathering the notes could have been to secure the material for the future defense against the possible accusations of collaboration, since it should be remembered that the Germans used the Judenrats for executing their extermination policy. Czerniaków's role was equivocally perceived among the Jews. He met not only with respect of his compatriots but also with unfavorable comments and jokes.

But history is not the only dimension of that unique diary. This is also a document of engineer Czerniaków—a man that history entrusted with an unusual mission, which he was trying to fulfill with sacrifice. It consisted in governing the Jewish community condemned to extermination. The author and the protagonist of the diary is a tragic figure. Seven days a week, often risking his life, he was trying to minimize the cruelty of the German ordinances, believing all the time in the purpose of his effort and the chance to save at least some of the Jews. When his illusions were shuttered, he committed suicide. Thus Czerniaków's diary also should be read as the story of his decision. We know that from the first days in the office he had some cyanide prepared. He was ready to face death any day, especially since he was arrested and beaten by the Gestapo and knew that it could happen again.

Publishers term Czerniaków's notes as a diary, which reflects the manner of their writing on a day-to-day basis. Their utterly reduced private aspect and the lack of introspection and wider commentaries, however, require a more precise title. The publisher from Yad Vashem called Czerniaków's work *Joman geto Warsza* ("Warsaw Ghetto Diary"), which may suggest its being synonymous to a chronicle. This association is not unauthorized, since the majority of Czerniaków's notes deal with his activity connected with his social role. And it so happens that the history of the chairman of the Jewish Council's efforts overlaps with that of the ghetto. Although the first sentence, "At night I did not sleep from 12 to 5 a.m.," is typical of an intimate diary, the further notes do not follow that generic pattern. This largely results from the fact that his function determined the nature of that record. He knew that the diary could be confiscated and read by the enemy. That is why Czerniaków's notes are governed by the secrecy rule, which involves the lack of commentaries and omission of entire areas of the ghetto life, such as politics, whose revealing could be dangerous not only for the author but also for the community. Also the incessant work imposes the constraint of briefness. He never knew which note would be the last.

The composition and literary values of Czerniaków's diary are frequently emphasized. The critics notice its literariness in the forms of individual notes, in the concealment rule, in the selection of material, and in the use of literary allusions. There is certainly no answer to the question when a given text becomes a piece of literature. In this case, however, literariness is a secondary feature, which can mostly be identified owing to its being placed within the historical and personal context, since in the face of the menace of history, the laconic style or even the regular occurrence of the notes concerning temperature may be perceived by a contemporary reader as literary devices.

—Kazimierz Adamczyk

WARSAW GHETTO: A DIARY
Diary by Mary Berg, 1945

The diary of a young teenage girl, Mary Berg's *Warsaw Ghetto: A Diary* (1945) was the first full, eyewitness account of life in the Warsaw Ghetto to appear in print in English. It was published before the *Oneg Shabbat* archives and other diaries and memoirs were recovered and is unique for its detail, authenticity, and its poignancy. Like many child diarists, Berg was searching to find meaning in the cruelty she experienced as she struggled to deal with the loss of childhood. Like **Anne Frank** and others, she began her diary as a means to comfort and occupy herself. Later it became an outlet for her and her friends. On her birthday they brought her notebooks, and she often read aloud. Gradually, she began to see that she had a chance to survive but that they had very little. Thus, her diary became a means for her to preserve a record of their torment and of remembering them.

In the ghetto Berg found a mission in recording her diary. After her boyfriend Kowalski said, "Little, girl, it is good that you don't understand too much,'' adding that he was happy she did not have to suffer, Berg wrote: ''Tears choked me, because I do know and understand everything, but I am powerless and cannot help anyone.'' With amazing detail she wrote about daily life in the ghetto. She recorded experiences at school, street scenes in the ghetto, cultural life, and the bits of Aryan life she could see over the wall from their apartment. She explained that she often went outside ''to learn by heart the look of the homeless women wrapped in rags and of the children with chapped and frozen cheeks.'' Berg visited a refugee center and felt shame because she had nothing to give a hungry child. She anguished at the sight of the hungry, greedily looking at bread in a bakery.

Gradually, as with many ghetto youth, Berg began to show a maturity beyond her years. She and other young people from Lodz, Poland, who came from prosperous homes were commonly referred to as ''golden youth'' in Warsaw. She came to realize that she was among the privileged, not among the ''other Jews.'' With honesty, she explained that those without privilege ''have only a ten per cent chance at most [to survive].'' Later, she admitted with equal openness that: ''Only those who have large sums of money are able to save themselves from this terrible life.'' Of course she did not know her fate, but her family's privilege and contacts abroad ultimately did become the key to her survival.

Berg's family still had funds in the ghetto and lived there among the well-fed elite. Her father was a janitor, a much sought-after position because residents who came in late had to pay a fee for the janitor to open the gate, and he got financial support from the Judenrat. Her uncle Abie was a ghetto policeman, a job, she admitted, that required ''pull'' to get. Kowalski was a close relative of Marek Lichtenbaum, the head of the Judenrat after Adam Czerniakow's suicide, so he used connections to get a job as an overseer to the building of the wall. Another suitor, Tadek Szajer, vied for her attention. His family lived a lavish lifestyle as his father was a member of the infamous ''13,'' a group of Gestapo collaborationists in the ghetto. Szajer tried to impress her by joining the red-capped Ambulance Service known in the ghetto for its brutality.

Berg, however, remained sensitive to the growing desperation in the ghetto. In one passage, she wrote about the ''dreamers of bread'' in the streets whose ''eyes are veiled with a mist that belongs to another world.'' She explained that ''usually they sit across from the windows of food stores, but their eyes no longer see the loaves that lie behind the glass, as in some remote inaccessible heaven.'' In the same entry, she also expressed remorse for her privileges, concluding: ''I have become really selfish. For the time being I am still warm and have food, but all around me there is so much misery and starvation that I am beginning to be very unhappy.''

Berg was at an age when young people typically develop their moral codes and a sense of justice. On the one hand, she wanted to keep her prewar values and her faith in a just world in the future. On the other, she enjoyed being with her friends and having a good time as much as possible in the circumstances. At times, she understandably resented feeling guilty for the privileges she had in the ghetto and for the simple desire to survive. Clearly, her models for behavior were both the values of her youth in Lodz and those of the cruel world created by the ghetto.

In her last entry, after the exchange ship had reached its port in the United States, Berg describes the feeling of freedom she had leaving ''the blood-drenched earth of Europe'' behind her. But even as those on the ship saw the first skyscrapers of New York City, she knew forgetting would not prove so easy. She recalled: ''I had thought that on the ship I would forget the nightmare of the ghetto. But, strangely enough, in the infinity of ocean I constantly saw the bloody streets of Warsaw,'' and thus she promised to never forget her young friends in the ghetto. The enduring value of Berg's diary is the fulfillment of her promise.

—Susan Lee Pentlin

WARTIME LIES
Novel by Louis Begley, 1991

Louis Begley's novel *Wartime Lies* is loosely based on the writer's own experiences as a young boy who, with his mother, survived the Holocaust in Poland by passing as a Christian. Begley was just six years old in 1939, when the Germans invaded Poland. His memories would not have sufficed for a full-length novel; neither would they have sufficed for the mature analysis that Maciek, the first-person narrator, engages in. With all its embellishments or inventions, the novel is a compelling and detailed picture of the life of a Jew on the run.

The novel begins with a depiction of prewar life in Poland for Maciek's well-to-do Jewish family. With the war everything changes. New regulations are introduced daily; the family is forced to move and to accept any work that is available. Round-ups become a regular event, and it seems only a matter of time before the family, too, will be caught in an action and deported. To survive requires material resources, which the family possesses (at least initially); a clear but flexible strategy, which requires constant reevaluation and compromise; luck; and, above all, lies. The family is broken up, and some members are killed. Maciek's aunt Tanya cultivates a friendship, which soon becomes a love relationship, with Reinhard, a German who is so sympathetic that he is willing to risk his life to help the family. With Reinhard's help they are able to avoid deportation and relocate from T., their hometown, to Lvov. Betrayed to the Gestapo, Reinhard commits suicide, and Aunt Tanya and Maciek are again on the run.

In Warsaw they pass as Christians, watch the Warsaw Ghetto Uprising with other Poles from a vantage point outside the Ghetto, and then, one year later, are caught in the Warsaw Uprising. Through a clever ruse—and with not a little luck—the two flee Warsaw and find precarious refuge in the country until the end of the war.

Throughout all these experiences they are threatened constantly by discovery, betrayal, and blackmail. Their ever-dwindling resources, constant hunger, and sickness serve to increase their fears. The necessity to lie—especially when Maciek prepares for and takes Communion—preys horribly on his conscience. The novel accordingly underscores much of the survivor experience that readers may know from other accounts of survival in Poland, such as **Nechama Tec**'s *Dry Tears*.

Narrated in the first person by Maciek, the novel is written in a sober style that avoids sensational or lurid description. Violence, atrocities, and death are described plainly and in matter-of-fact language. Dispersed throughout the text are numerous classical passages: Vergil, Catullus, and Dante. These underline just how literary Begley is. They also serve to distance the reader from the text and slow down the action. And finally, they serve to introduce a major preoccupation of Begley's: the role of justice in the human predicament. In an ordered world justice would be an essential element; Maciek would survive because he deserved to survive. But the world that was Poland in World War II was chaotic and irrational, and justice was meted out accordingly.

Wartime Lies is well written and carefully structured and has few weaknesses. There are, for example, no exaggerated descriptions, lurid depictions, or crudely drawn—rather than well-rounded—characters. The reader is provided with an accurate, if often almost unbelievable, account of what life for a Jew on the run in Poland entailed. It ranks with the best of Holocaust literature.

—David Scrase

WE WERE IN AUSCHWITZ (Bylismy w Oswiecimiu) Memoir by Janusz Nel Siedlecki, Krystyn Olszewski, and Tadeusz Borowski, 1946

We Were in Auschwitz (2000) was one of the first publications about Auschwitz. The book was originally published under the title *Bylismy w Oswiecimiu* in Munich in 1946 by the publishing house of Anatol Girs, a Polish prewar publisher, a survivor of Auschwitz and Dachau. The book consists of a foreword, a short informative text about Auschwitz, 14 short stories, and a glossary of Auschwitz terms. In front of the names of each of the three authors their Auschwitz numbers are given: 6643 Janusz Nel Siedlecki, 75817 Krystyn Olszewski, and 119198 Tadeusz Borowski. The idea for the book came

from its publisher, Girs, who signed the foreword with his camp number, 191250. But in its final shape the book stemmed from discussions in which the friends shared their experiences of the concentration camp. The collection is a joint work, and the stories are not signed with their authors' names.

Out of the three writers only Borowski continued his literary activity. Nel Siedlecki chose an immigrant's life and worked in London as an engineer. Olszewski returned to communist Poland and became an architect. The publisher, Girs, emigrated to the United States. Since he did not have enough money to pay for storing the book he had to destroy most of its edition.

The Munich collection includes four famous short stories by Borowski, later published many times. They are "A Day at Harmenz," "This Way for the Gas, Ladies and Gentlemen," "Auschwitz, Our Home," and "The People Who Walked On." According to Tadeusz Drewnowski, Borowski's contribution to the Munich book was by far the largest. Olszewski was the actual author of two stories, "I Fear the Night" and "The Fifth Hundred" while Nel Siedlecki wrote "Between the Sola and the Vistula Rivers," "You'd Better Not Get Ill," and "The Story of a Certain Table." The remaining stories not mentioned here came into being with Borowski's considerable share as a writer. He either wrote down his friends' stories or was responsible for the language and artistic correction. It has to be remembered, however, that Olszewski and in particular Nel Siedlecki were Auschwitz prisoners for much longer than Borowski. Thus Olszewski and Nel Siedlecki to some extent contributed to Borowski's artistic vision of Auschwitz.

The publication of the book corresponded to the demand of readership who expected some authentic reports from concentration camps. This authenticity was confirmed not only by the camp numbers of the editor and authors of the book but also by the entire publication character. The authors intended to say the truth about Auschwitz, and that truth is presented in encyclopedic, personal, and literary dimensions at the same time. Borowski's stories included in this volume later became classic works of the world literature pertaining to the camp life.

The documentary character of the reports is apparent in the book's foreword, which features a short history of the camp in Auschwitz, as well as in the forewords to each story and in the glossary. Borowski's comments on 64 entries in the glossary of the camp jargon not only help with reading the stories but also constitute a separate sociolinguistic study describing and interpreting the phenomenon that the camp was. This lexical analysis of the "Auschwitz language" becomes the last story in the collection. *We Were in Auschwitz* is therefore a carefully composed book, dealing with the history and topography of the camp and also revealing numerous aspects of the camp life and many forms of death.

The reports of the three men who were prisoners of Auschwitz at different phases of its existence allow the audience to observe the changing rules of the camp life in Auschwitz I. Thus the collection illustrates the essential difference between the first camp established in Auschwitz and the extermination camp Auschwitz-Birkenau, built for exterminating the Jews.

The authors, who had just been liberated from camps, were aware that literature required a new language for describing Auschwitz. Borowski's talent and personality became crucial here. The collection is polemic toward the hypothetical and soon materialized, dominating way of writing about Auschwitz in terms of martyrdom, which involved psychological introspection and defined unequivocally the slaughterers and the victims. The book as a whole rejects and opposes such a model employing a grotesque and an ironic distance, which can also be perceived as the need to regain psychical balance after the shock.

The stories written by Olszewski and Nel Siedlecki do not attain the level of literary masterpieces, as is the case of the ones written by Borowski. In spite of some elements of irony, the former present a rather traditional language of literature. They may be classified as memoirs and personal literary documents addressed not so much to a reader but rather to a listener. Their characteristic features include expressions addressed directly to the reader, psychological introspection, naturalistic descriptions of the martyred body, and factographical approach to names and places. Their dominant feature is the concern with the facts, while Borowski's ultimate aim consists in finding a philosophic formula for the camp.

Yet in spite of their lesser literary value, Olszewski's and Nel Siedlecki's stories are a distinct voice within *We Were in Auschwitz,* since beside the encyclopedic and literary discourse, they build up the third dimension of the book, which is that of a personal document.

—Kazimierz Adamczyk

WE'RE ALIVE AND LIFE GOES ON: A THERESIENSTADT DIARY
Diary by Eva Roubíčková, 1998

There is no doubt that Eva Roubíčková has led a most interesting life. She spent her youth skiing and attending dances until the Nazis banned Jews from the ski slopes, dance halls, and schools. At the age of 20 she and her mother were sent with one of the first transports to the Theresienstadt ghetto, where life was much different and much more harsh. Her diary, *We're Alive and Life Goes On: A Theresienstadt Diary* (1998), relates the day-to-day existence of a young woman trapped in a life she did not ask for. She describes circumstances surrounding herself, her friends, and her family, and, although Roubíčková does not possess the literary skills

of other Holocaust writers, this diary contains useful information about life in a concentration camp. Daily existence consisted of seeking work or working, waiting to see who would be next to be transported to the East, and moving from barrack to barrack with little to no notice. Roubíčková's writing style is typical of that of a young person; it is not complicated, yet it is straightforward in its descriptions of daily life in Theresienstadt.

The forward to the diary was written by Virginia Euwer Wolf, who says of the work, "Eva Roubíčková didn't build her diary like a story, with a series of characters and plot developments leading to a climax. Instead, she tried to keep track of the days as they went threateningly by." Roubíčková, who survived the war, has also included an introduction and an afterword to the diary, both of which provide the reader with a good foundation for understanding the before and after of her Theresienstadt life. The diary covers the years 1941 to 1945, and the suspense mounts with every passing day and year. Who will be coming into the camp? Will today be the day for transport to the East, to Poland, the Land of No Return? The reader is left to speculate with Roubíčková each day. As a young person with a magnetic personality, however, Roubíčková amazingly managed to find many non-Aryans who were drawn to her, including her rescuer, Karel Košvanec, who smuggled her supplies and ultimately rescued her from the ghetto during a typhus outbreak in 1945.

At the back of the diary is a list of the family members and friends mentioned within the work. Zaia Alexander, who translated the work from its original German shorthand, has also described Theresienstadt in her translator's note. Maps of the ghetto are included, and Roubíčková's black-and-white photos of her friends, family, and activities lend more personal appeal to the work. Especially interesting are the photos of her prewar life, for they show the great contrast between what was and what will be for the European Jews.

A comparison can be made between *We're Alive and Life Goes On: A Theresienstadt Diary* with the diary of Anne Frank. Granted, Frank was living in Holland in close, cramped quarters with the same people each day, while Roubíčková was forced to deal with change every day. Indeed, it was rare for Roubíčková to live more than just a few days with the same people in the barracks. Frank had more time to study her roommates in depth, but Roubíčková's life was in a constant state of flux. Nevertheless, both diaries capture the essence of young girls living in extraordinary times and experiencing unthinkable circumstances. Like Frank's diary, *We're Alive and Life Goes On: A Theresienstadt Diary* is recommended for high school-age students and beyond for introductory courses on the Holocaust. Both diaries are remarkable in that the authors lived through a horrific time in history, but, unlike Frank, Roubíčková survived to adulthood, married, and had children.

—Cynthia A. Klíma

WHAT A BEAUTIFUL SUNDAY! (Quel beau Dimanche)
Memoir by Jorge Semprun, 1980

The second of Jorge Semprun's books about the Holocaust to be translated, this book, published as *Quel beau Dimanche* in 1980 and in English translation in 1982, picks up and develops many of his key themes and formalistic devices from *The Long Voyage*. Again it is thoughtfully crafted and literary; again it is as much about memory and the retelling of the events as the events themselves.

The basic time frame is one Sunday—in fact, part of one Sunday—in Buchenwald, where Semprun is imprisoned. As a Spanish Communist arrested for being part of the French resistance, Semprun is connected and in part protected by the camp's Communist underground. On this particular Sunday, however, he is assigned to a task outside the camp, and his attention is attracted to a tree. "A tree, just that, in its immediate splendour, in the transparent stillness of the present." As the memoir progresses the tree begins to take on a totemic significance. (Is it Goethe's oak in Weimar and so symbolic of German civilization? No, Goethe's oak is—physically and symbolically—inside the boundaries of the camp.) It is a sign of that which is beautiful outside the universe of the camp and of oppression, a sign of some form of hope. "I felt that with all the strength of my rushing blood that my death would not deprive that tree of its radiant beauty."

As in his other accounts, however, the "beautiful Sunday" is only a starting point, an acknowledged narrative device to bind together a much wider, more comprehensive and contextual memoir of his whole life and political engagements. As in *The Long Voyage* the narrative shifts through time without warning, but unlike that book this account goes into much more detail about his political activities, especially those after the war as a high-ranking member of the (underground) Spanish Communist Party. It covers his activities as a secret agent in Spain, his encounters with European and Russian Communists, various show trials and internal power struggles, his growing intellectual and political disaffection, and his eventual fall from grace. An honest account, the book does not let Semprun escape his own criticisms. A particularly fascinating series of parallels (that do not suggest that they are the same, however) are drawn between the Nazis and the totalitarianism of the Communists. Semprun is moved deeply by Varlam Shalamov's *Kolyma Tales* and is scathing of the hypocrisy of French Communists' attempts to cover up or censor discussions of the gulags. In line with this the book also has a number of more philosophical and political discussions that show not only his growing moral revulsion to Communism as practiced but also his increasing intellectual disagreement with Marxist concepts. That said, he is also aware of the power of Communism to inspire hope and lead people—in the Spanish Civil War, in World War II—to perform acts of resistance and great courage.

This book, then, uses the experiences of a Communist resister in Buchenwald to reflect on the political and intellectual struggles that shaped much of the twentieth century from the perspective of a man deeply involved in these struggles. It is also about the memory and writing of these struggles. When he writes that there "is no such thing as an innocent memory. Not for me anymore," he means both that memories of heroism and defiance in the name of Communism are double-edged (due, not least, to the gulags and the purges) and that their representation is never straightforward; the past is bound up with the present. Both the form and content of this book reveal this.

—Robert Eaglestone

WHAT WE USED TO SAY (Lessico famigliare)
Novel by Natalia Ginzburg, 1963

What We Used to Say (1997; published in Italian in 1963 as *Lessico famigliare* and first translated into English as *Family Sayings*) is Natalia Ginzburg's best-known and, in Italy, most venerated book. It is a memoir-novel about the home she grew up in during the period of ascendant Fascism, the Fascist dictatorship, her eccentric parents, defined to a great extent by her father's weird sayings that molded and characterized life in the household, the difficult life that her Jewish, academic father experienced during Fascism, the activities of her anti-Fascist brothers, the survival of the entire Levi family, and the melancholy that characterized Ginzburg's life and that of her parents—as eccentrics who did not attract a great amount of attention in pre–World War II northern Italy but who were fish out of water in post–World War II Italy. The final part of Ginzburg's novel renders a compelling portrait of the state of mind and soul of an active anti-Fascist and resistance fighter, the important writer Cesare Pavese, a transmitter to Italians of American literature and, with Ginzburg, one of the important editors at the publishing house of Einaudi, which published some of the most important novels of postwar Italian literature.

What We Used to Say is a loving testament to the benign life, in Ginzburg's view, that disappeared with World War II. It is a life that not only millions of Italian readers have identified with and continue to react positively to by buying Ginzburg's novel in high numbers but also one that has appealed so strongly to its readers in the English-speaking world that the first, defective translation, *Familiar Sayings,* was replaced by the second, far better translation in 1997, an event that seldom occurs with foreign literature in English translation. In the book Ginzburg furnishes the reader with a compelling, almost claustrophobic portrait—in spare and simple language, laced with the idiosyncracies of the Italian peculiar to Turin—of the domestic life the Levi household lived during this historically important period in Italian and world history, one particularly instructive about what it was to be a member of upper-middle-class, urban, and intellectual Jewish society during the period of the anti-Semitic, Fascist racial laws that marginalized the Jews of Italy.

Ginzburg's father was a professor of stature at the University of Turin. For his anti-Fascist statements and for refusing to take the oath of allegiance to Benito Mussolini and Fascism after the 1935 promulgation of the racial laws, Ginzburg's father was dismissed, as was Ginzburg's future husband, Leone, from his teaching position at the university. Ginzburg's father subsequently accepted a lesser position at the University of Ghent, in Belgium, in order to support his family. Fleeing the German advance after their invasion of Belgium, he was captured by the Germans and, without making any secret of his name and his being Jewish, fortunately released. Instead of following the suggestion by a German officer to return to Ghent, Ginzburg's father made his long and arduous way back to Italy, thereby surviving the Holocaust.

As was her husband, who paid for his resistance with his life, all Ginzburg's brothers were active anti-Fascists—in contrast to her father's anti-Fascism rants inside the Levi home after the family had hidden an active anti-Fascist Socialist while passage was being arranged for him to Switzerland. One of Ginzburg's brothers escaped capture after bringing anti-Fascist leaflets back from Switzerland. Her other brother returned to clandestine resistance after release from jail in Turin.

This side of life in the Levi family is described alongside the nearly banal events of the family's domestic and social life with their mostly Jewish friends, some of whom would disappear and never be seen again. Ginzburg describes the everyday and the nearly tragic side-by-side in a language that neither sentimentalizes her family nor surrenders to runaway emotionalism. *What We Used to Say* is one of the few pieces of Holocaust literature that tells the story of a family that survives the Holocaust, possibly because of its peculiar characters. Her sober, but not coldhearted, writing style and her dedication to a seemingly contradictory but artistically unique and successfully tempered realism are two of the particular features of *What We Used to Say* but also of her fiction in general that have won Ginzburg an international following and sales success each time her books have come out in Italy and when the ones translated into English have been published.

It is not the big historical events that loom large in Ginzburg's memoir-novel (almost maddeningly, she dedicates only a few lines to her husband's capture and murder shortly before the end of the war); rather, it is the tenacity of her family, the unexpected force that the members of the Levi family carry in themselves, that renders the strong portrait of the Levi family.

Despite the eccentricity of the parents and their relations with everybody outside their home, *What We Used to Say* is an almost didactic novel about the unexpectedly ordered existence of the Levi family amid the disorder and randomness, at least for anti-Fascists, during one of the most momentous and tragic periods in twentieth-century history.

Although her novel proceeds in perfect chronological order, Ginzburg presents the events in her novel, one rife with dialog, in an a-traditional manner, and the power of her deceptively simple language virtually compels the reader's vicarious co-participation in her family's story and their experiences. Readers who find the first part of her novel disappointingly short on action attest that they come to find her seemingly deceptively unassuming narrative fascinating in the end. Ginzburg's novel continues to engage readers and to win her new readers among the young. Whereas the figures in her wartime novel *Tutti i nostri ieri* (''All Our Yesterdays'') are innocent pawns in the momentous historical drama of World War II, Ginzburg's family, these unique Levis—and she includes herself in the cast of strong players, even though she grants herself small space in her memoir-novel—are figures of strength, the opposite of the victims she presents in *Tutti i nostri ieri*. There is much in the way of old-fashioned personal virtues, devotion to family above all else, and compelling realism in *What We Used to Say* to account for its continued success.

—Robert B. Youngblood

WHEN MEMORY COMES (Quand vient le souvenir) Memoir by Saul Friedlander, 1978

The leitmotif of this memoir by one of the leading historians of the Holocaust is taken from the writer Gustav Meyrink: ''When knowledge comes, memory comes too, little by little. Knowledge and memory are the same thing.'' For Friedlander, however, the sequence was inverted: When memory comes, knowledge comes, too. The book describes two things simultaneously: his survival during the Holocaust and the ways in which memory erupts in the present and shapes the self. The memoir is set, as it were, in the Israel of the 1970s and assumes a diary format. Yet his reflections leap from the present to the 1930s, '40s, and '50s as ''memory comes.'' First published as *Quand vient le souvenir* in 1978, the memoir appeared in English translation in 1979.

He writes that before the war ''everyone in our house felt German'': he learned ''*Ich hatt' einen Kameraden*,'' a funeral march often used for the German military, on the piano; his father had been in the Austro-Hungarian army in World War I. As the war loomed, his family moved to France and hoped to emigrate to Canada. The young Paul was placed in a home for Jewish Children near Montmorency. Having been too Jewish for his classmates before, now he was too assimilated and mercilessly bullied. "[B]eaten by Jewish children because they thought I was different from them." He was, he writes, "on my way to becoming doubly Jewish." Finally, however, his parents were unable to escape and tried to take false identities: Paul was, at their request, hidden in a Catholic school. Friedlander writes of this moment of separation: The "extraordinary mechanism of memory: the unbearable is effaced . . . while the banal comes to the fore." He remembers the ugliness of the city and the sun shining on it.

He was baptized and "became someone else: Paul-Henri Ferland, an unequivocally Catholic name." More than this, the "first ten years of my life, the memories of my childhood" had to disappear, "for there was no possible synthesis between the person I had been and the person I was to become." He remained hidden during the war. After the war, however, he began to reclaim his Jewish identity. Discussing a possible vocation in the Catholic church, a priest, Father L., tells him about Auschwitz, which before had remained indistinct to him. "A tie had been re-established, an identity was emerging." This began the long journey of his return to Judaism. Ten years later, in 1956, he read the work of Martin Buber while straying with an uncle near Stockholm, and this too made an impression on him. He is reintroduced to Judaism but not without difficulties. For example at his first Seder he declines the meat—it is Good Friday (a day on which Catholics traditionally abstain from eating meat). But memory is hard. He tries to remember his past—by, for example, drinking a milkshake as he had with his mother—but it avoids him. Yet he presses on, and memory comes slowly, irregularly. Reversing St. Paul's gesture (he changed his name from Saul to Paul on his conversion), Paul-Henri Ferland changes his name to Saul Friedlander. Finally, he settles in Israel.

The book is full of observed details: the white socks of the protesting Sudaten Germans, the texture of French streets. More than this, as one might expect from a book by a historian, it is full of documents: his own diary, letters to the school from his father and mother. It is also full of implicit and occasionally more explicit views about Israel. But the overwhelming quality is that of the attempt of Saul Friedlander to remember, to be true to his memories when they come and to their absences when they do not. The book—like his later historical and theoretical work—is about the constructive interaction between history and memory. On the one hand, he writes (of former Nazis and others) that for "anyone who does not know the facts, the mystical communion with the brownshirt revolution and its martyrs still remains. Thus is evidence transformed over the years, thus do memories crumble away"; on the other hand, this whole book reveals that "history" in itself—dates, facts, evidence—is not enough.

—Robert Eaglestone

WHERE SHE CAME FROM: A DAUGHTER'S SEARCH FOR HER MOTHER'S HISTORY
Memoir by Helen Epstein, 1997

This book breaks new ground in second generation writing. Simultaneously a memoir, a family history, and an exploration of the saga of the Jews in Czech lands, Epstein's book is a search for personal and tribal connections. She wishes to know her foremothers and to understand more about Jewish history. Specifically *Where She Came From* (1997) is a compelling story of the author's great-grandmother, Theresa Furcht, who committed suicide in Vienna after the death of her teenage son; Pepi Rabinek, Theresa's daughter and Epstein's grandmother, murdered by the Nazis; and Franzi, Pepi's daughter and Epstein's mother. The memoir is a secular version of what observant Czech Jews of the seventeenth and eighteenth centuries called *megillot mishpachah* (family scrolls). Epstein notes that she "liked the idea of taking my mother's twelve-page chronicle and bringing three generations of increasingly secular women to life in an old Jewish literary form."

In terms of genre the author hopes that her work will be read not as journalism but as "literary non-fiction." This is a work that integrates many different types of sources, which involved the author becoming an archaeologist of Jewish memory. For instance, in compiling her book Epstein worked in Harvard's Widener Library, where she read communal ledgers from Bohemia. In addition, she utilized historical works in Czech, English, and German and wrote letters of inquiry to various people in Czechoslovakia. Furthermore, Epstein integrated the observations of novelists; the contents of political speeches—especially excerpts from the BBC broadcasts made by Jan Masaryk, son of the founder of the Czech Republic; and her own imagination in weaving the rich tapestry of *Where She Came From*. The result is a work that illuminates the sometimes contradictory interplay between Czech and Jewish history as well as helping Epstein better understand where she came from. Moreover, the memoir offers an intimate portrait of the intense relationship between mothers and daughters.

The two key women in Epstein's work are her grandmother, Pepi, and her mother, Franzi. Epstein views Pepi's life as emblematic of the Jewish experience in central Europe. For example, Pepi was raised by her Orthodox aunt. Consequently the young girl was imbued with normative Jewish teaching (halakah) and its strictures against getting involved in the Gentile world. Yet Pepi moved to Prague, abandoned Jewish ritual, owned her own dress salon, and had a ten-year affair with Emil Rubinek, the man she eventually married. Pepi retains a strong commitment to her fellow Jews, especially the refugees spilling into Prague. Rubinek is Jewish, but baptized, and is not interested in identifying either religiously or ethnically with Judaism. In fact he insists that Franzi be baptized in order not to have any Jewish encumbrance. Epstein notes that both her grandmother and her mother, who was also a dressmaker, were "strong, liberated women who supported the family *and* kept house.'' Thus when the Women's Liberation Movement swept America in the 1970s, the author reports thinking, ''What's the big deal?''

One of the memoir's more poignant moments occurs when Franzi realizes that an action she had taken in defense of her parents led instead to their further suffering. She and her parents had been arrested by the Gestapo in 1942. Franzi returned and discovered a box of poison pills in Emil's desk. Frightened, she went to the pharmacist, who replaced the poison with saccharin. Thus when Pepi and Emil where deported to Riga, Franzi understood that ''Instead of being protective, I had deprived my father of the last possibility to decide his fate as a *free* man.'' Franzi remains guilt ridden and battles suicidal impulses for the rest of her life.

Epstein's relationship with Franzi is intense. Franzi was a Jew who did not practice Judaism. On the one hand, Epstein views her mother as a ''heroine more compelling than any in the Bible, any novel or myth.'' On the other hand, however, Epstein writes, ''I was never sure what belonged to whom, where I ended, and she began.'' Reflecting on the origin of her odyssey of Jewish identity, Epstein observes that it was in her mother's workroom that she ''fell in love with the dead women in my mother's family.'' Utilizing a beautiful metaphor, Epstein differentiates her work from that of the girls who at the end of the day ''swept up and threw out threads and scraps of cloth'' that remained in the workroom. The author's task was different. Rather than throwing things away, she ''collected threads and scraps of stories, hoarding them, mulling them over.'' Reflecting on the distinction between how her mother sewed and how she told Holocaust stories, Epstein notes that Franzi was an expert seamstress. But unlike the clothes that she skillfully made, the story threads contained ''wide gaps in the fabric.'' She ''never fixed the way she told her past.''

Epstein's memoir is itself a type of Holocaust legacy. She reports several rituals that have assumed significance among the second generation—for example, pilgrimage to parental birthplace. In addition, she articulates the contours of the meaning of secular Jewish identity. Finally, *Where She Came From* is an exemplary work for those wishing to connect to the Jewish past and thereby place the Shoah within the context of the continuing panorama of Jewish history.

—Alan L. Berger

THE WHITE HOTEL
Novel by D.M. Thomas, 1981

D.M. Thomas's novel *The White Hotel*, published in 1981, combines an account of the Holocaust, in particular the mass murders at Babi Yar in the Ukraine, with the author's interest in sex, psychoanalysis and its limits, and death. The novel was, and continues to be, a source of great controversy.

The novel's prologue is made up of fictional letters between Freud and other key figures in the birth of psychoanalysis discussing the case of ''Frau Anna''; much of the rest of the book purports to be a case study by Freud. It begins with a poem, ''Don Giovanni,'' followed by ''The Gastein Journal.'' Both tell more or less the same story, of a chance encounter between an opera singer and a recently demobilized soldier and their subsequent affair at a white hotel in the mountains. The accounts are erotically charged and phantasmagoric. They are followed by a longer section, a widely admired pastiche Freudian case study along the model of ''Dora'' or ''The Wolf Man.'' This reveals the earlier sections to be writing submitted as part of the analysis by Freud of one Lisa Erdman, a Jewish singer suffering from neurosis, breathing problems, and severe pains ''in her left breast and pelvic region.'' The origins of her neurosis and her partial cure (the pains continue) are described.

The fourth section continues the singer's story, her small-time operatic successes, her marriage and the birth of her son, and her settling in Kiev. The penultimate section is the story, told in a neutral way, of the massacre of Erdman and her family and (by Thomas's figures) 250,000 others by the Nazis at Babi Yar. She is shot in the breast and later, slowly dying, is raped by official looters of the corpses and has her pelvis broken. (That the rapist is named Demidenko —a Ukrainian, not a German—is not only controversial but was also surely significant for the ''Demidenko affair,'' the dispute that surrounded the publication of Helen Darville's *The Hand That Signed the Paper*.) Some of the symptoms for which Erdman receives analysis foreshadow her death rather than reflect her life, and so for Thomas they indicate the inability of psychoanalysis to come to terms with the traumas of history. This section also incorporates an account of a survivor, Dina Pronicheva, taken from **Anatoli Kuznetsov**'s ''true novel'' *Babi Yar,* a mixture of fact and fiction that was another source of controversy. The novel concludes with a sort of ''heaven,'' where both the traumas from the massacre and from Erdman's early life are resolved.

A number of critics have argued, with some justice, that the book is pornographic, that the violence of Freud's analysis and the portrayal of the hysterical victim-woman and of the Holocaust are all of a piece. The aim of the book, however, seems to be to restore a ''human'' dimension to the numbers murdered in the Holocaust. Thomas writes of the 30,000 killed on the first day of the massacre that ''their lives and histories were as rich and complex as Lisa Erdman-Berenstein's. If a Sigmund Freud had been listening and taking notes from the time of Adam, he would still not have explored even a single group, even a single person. And this was only the first day.'' In this light the psychoanalytically inspired ''pornography,'' if it is seen as such, might be taken to represent the unique and particular complexities, conscious and unconscious, of each victim of the Third Reich.

—Robert Eaglestone

WHO LOVES YOU LIKE THIS (Chi ti ama così)
Memoir by Edith Bruck, 1958

Edith Bruck's memoir, *Who Loves You Like This* (2001; *Chi ti ama così*, 1958), is divided into three loci of struggle: her childhood in Hungary where she lived in abject poverty; her life in the concentration camps of Auschwitz, Dachau, and Bergen-Belsen, which began with her deportation at the age of 12; and her difficult struggle in Hungary, Czechloslavakia, and Israel to resume her life. She generally eschews the kind of philosophical reflections typical of fellow Italian-language Holocaust writer **Primo Levi** in favor of the dramatic flair and swiftness of style typical of compatriot **Elie Wiesel**.

One of the things that makes *Who Loves You Like This* unique among Holocaust narratives is the artful way in which Bruck works the motif of hunger and the threat of starvation into her narrative. In her dedication she alludes to the hunger she had suffered as a child by dedicating the book, "For my mother whose bread had the best taste in the world." She later refers again to her mother's bread, which gave her the trappings of security: "My mother made bread once a weak, on Thursday, and it was the happiest day of my childhood. She sighed with satisfaction when she saw the five large loaves, and she said that we would have another week without worries because when there was bread, there was everything. The first day we could eat as much as we wanted, but then we had to make it last until the next Thursday. It was hard to get enough flour together, and we did not always succeed."

Bruck was born into an impoverished milieu. Before her deportation to the concentration camps, she remembers that she would go to work in exchange "for a bit of food such as apples or spoiled prunes." She would steal eggs and chickens from her neighbors, "but only from the rich ones, because I was too honest to rob the poor." In describing her experiences in Auschwitz, Dachau, and Bergen-Belsen, she recalls suffering from hunger during the excruciating roll calls: "Sometimes the roll call would last all day because people died, or killed themselves, or went insane, and until the missing were found, as punishment we had to kneel in the rain without food for twenty hours." She remembers being assigned to the kitchen commandos in one of the camps: "In this castle, three of us, myself included, worked in the kitchen; eight peeled potatoes; and the others worked for a German family that lived nearby. It was marvelous work because there was food to eat. There was no lack of potato peels."

Although Bruck's positive description of this situation is not without intentional irony, it is in stark contrast to her description of mealtime during one of the Nazi-led death marches from one concentration camp to another: "We stole from each other the little food we had; mothers stole from daughters and daughters from mothers. When one of us was very sick we would say to her, 'Give me your food, you may as well, tomorrow you'll be dead!' But she wouldn't give up hope and saved her piece of bread for tomorrow. Wherever I looked, I saw only selfishness. Someone who had an entire loaf of bread, obtained who knows how, wouldn't give up even a crumb to someone who was dying of hunger." Bruck's remembrances of the distribution of food provide an accurate picture of the grim situational ethics of the Nazi death camps: "Once I ripped a mouthful of bread from a friend's mouth, but after she had done so first." She describes her hunger in heart-wrenching terms: "After a four-day march, they had us in a place where German civilians threw their garbage. What a joy! We ate frozen potato peels and other refuse. Anything we could put in our mouth was good for us: leaves, firewood, dried dung."

Bruck effectively describes how being on the border of starvation dehumanized herself and the other inmates. She also discusses other dehumanizing aspects of concentration camp life, such as excremental assault: "When the alarm sounded, the latrine would be closed for up to two days. Then we had to do our business in the same utensils we ate from and we were beaten." In addition, she recounts how inmates were terrorized by their awareness of the gas chambers: "Once in a while, they sent us to the shower barracks, and we looked at each other in horror, wondering if it would be water that came out or gas." Nonetheless, what makes the strongest impression on the reader is Bruck's manifold description of hunger. That alone makes her work worth remembering.

—Peter R. Erspamer

WINGS OF STONE (Selige Zeiten, brüchige Welt)
Novel by Robert Menasse, 1991

Robert Menasse's most acclaimed novel, *Wings of Stone* (2000; *Selige Zeiten, brüchige Welt*, 1991) is actually the second part of his series *Trilogie der Entgeisterung* ("Trilogy of the Breakdown of Spirit," a reference to G.W.F. Hegel's *Phenomenlogy of Spirit*). Rather than continuing where the first novel *Sinnliche Gewissheit* (1988; "Sense Certainty") ends, namely with the story of the novel's protagonist Roman Gilanian, *Wings of Stone* goes backward in time to narrate the prehistory of two characters who befriend Roman in the first novel, Leo Singer and Judith Katz. Unlike *Sinnliche Gewissheit*, which is written in the first person, Menasse's second novel maintains a more distant narrative perspective with its third-person narration and its use of *style indirecte libre*. In addition, although the story centers around Leo and his life, it cleverly shifts the narrative focus at times to concentrate on Judith, denying Leo the same status of hero that Roman has in the first novel, which is perhaps fitting for a work in which the protagonist is unable to fulfill the responsibilities dictated to him by the genre. Billed by critics as a reverse bildungsroman, *Wings of Stone* tells the story of a character who fails to live up to his own story.

Menasse's novel is not about the Holocaust; indeed, the events in Europe between 1933 and 1945 are not referred to at all, even obliquely. Instead of portraying characters who are overtly affected by the Holocaust, Menasse presents the reader with a world in which the Holocaust, though largely forgotten and somewhat "normalized," continues to figure in the lives of the "second generation," the sons and daughters of those who survived or were forced into exile. In *Wings of Stone* the history of fascism in Austria and the Nazi persecution of the Jews becomes a silent, massive force that informs Leo and Judith's situation and the ways in which they perceive themselves and the world.

Located on two continents and spanning almost 20 years, Menasse's novel begins in Vienna in 1965, when Leo and Judith first meet, and ends in Brazil with Judith's death. At their first meeting in a university cafeteria, the two find that they have much in common—they are both the children of Viennese Jews who fled Austria in 1938 for exile in São Paulo, Brazil. Leo returned to Vienna in 1959 with his parents, who decided to come back home "since everything was back to normal." Yet, having grown up in Brazil, he feels anything but at home in Vienna and longs to return to São Paulo. Judith, on the other hand, has come to Vienna to study against the wishes of her parents, who had no interest in returning to the country that had intended to exterminate them. She is quickly disappointed, however, by the stifling and provincial atmosphere of Viennese cultural life, the Austrians' arrogant ignorance about Brazil, and the remnants of fascism in Austrian politics and society. In the first pages of the novel, the two revel in their luck at finding in each other someone who feels as alienated and homeless as themselves, and Leo quickly falls in love with Judith, believing he sees in her his own "mirror image." This momentary unity, which slowly unravels throughout the course of the novel, butts up against its first obstacle when it becomes clear that, although the two have almost parallel exile experiences, their feelings of alienation are strikingly different from one another. Leo looks back nostalgically to Brazil as his home, but for Judith the ideal image of home has been destroyed, for she has experienced the military takeover in Brazil and the murderous tactics of its totalitarian regime. As she tells Leo, "The exile of the parents means exile for the next generation, too, and they are in exile wherever they are." Leo later discovers this for himself, when he returns to São Paulo after the death of his father and fails to find the home he has idealized in his thoughts. Homeless and without direction, both Leo and Judith are unable to construct their lives in any meaningful way because of the absence of strong roots that would ground their identities.

Intending (but never managing) to write a doctoral dissertation on Hegel's philosophy that will change the world, Leo attempts to retain the original moment of union with Judith by fashioning her into his muse, an ideal antithesis with whom he could attain a synthesis of both love and intellectual production. Judith, however, resists his attempt to co-opt her, and the

novel develops with the slow disintegration of their relationship. At the end, after almost 20 years of struggling with procrastination and literary impotence in which he finds he has written close to nothing, Leo discovers that Judith has secretly recorded his thoughts on Hegel, effectively writing the book that he has spent his life trying to write. In order to claim his life's work, he murders her and assumes the text as his own, publishing it as quickly as possible so that it can begin the hoped-for philosophical revolution. In the end, however, only five copies of the book are sold, and Leo is left with neither home, muse, nor intellectual ambition.

—Erin McGlothlin

A WORLD APART (L'Univers concentrationnaire)
Memoir by David Rousset, 1945

David Rousset's *L'Univers concentrationnaire* (1945; *A World Apart,* 1951) is one of the very first accounts of the German camp system. It won the Prix Renaudot in 1946. The book introduced the phrase and laid out the idea of the "concentration camp universe": "It was a world set apart, utterly segregated, a strange kingdom with its own peculiar fatality." Rousset was a French non-Jewish prisoner, a militant Trotskyite, and a member of the resistance, and he writes from this perspective.

This short book is not a memoir in the straightforward sense: it does not detail Rousset's membership in the resistance, his capture, or his detainment. Rather the book is a report about the camps and the camp system. In a chapter entitled "In My Father's House Are Many Mansions" (taken with savage irony from the New Testament's description of heaven), he offers a tour around the camps, although they are not "all identical or equivalent." The camps have their proletariats, their capitalists who thieve and sell. He describes the labor and—in the "reprisal camps"—the "sports" (walking round and round at the double being whipped, squats in the mud, being thrown into the water tank). He describes the death camps, which are in "utterly different latitudes." These "camps for Jews and Poles were a large scale industry for torture and extermination." Yet, he writes, between these "extermination camps and the 'normal' camps there was no fundamental difference; only a difference in degree."

He also describes, in far from flattering terms—which is odd for a Trotskyite—the different nationalities in the camps: the Russians, "trained to the whip by their masters and with little knowledge of anything but brute force and cunning"; the Poles, "fundamentally conservative, passionately anti-Russian . . . grandly anti-Semitic . . . astonishingly uneducated and chauvinistic"; the Greeks, a few intellectuals but mainly "bandits . . . thieves and debauchees"; the Dutch, "a fair sized core of Protestants . . . active political resistants"; the Czechs, ''men of discipline, for themselves and others, cultures, . . . initiators of action with the structure of the camp''; the Luxembourgers, ''a closed free masonry; in Buchenwald, the police''; the Danes, ''hostages, simple souls''; the French, ''men who do not know how to wash.''

The book also draws on literary and artistic precedents, including Kafka and Céline, to try to understand the experience. Rousset writes, ''I know nothing which reproduces so well . . . the intimate life of the internees as Rodin's *Gates of Hell*.'' There are camp stories: the discovery of cannibalism in 1944 at Neuengamme (''one day he found a human jawbone in his soup''), a fight for bread, and male prostitution in which a *kapo* uses a prisoner.

Yet despite the atrocities and the ''get out'' allowed to some political prisoners who could recant and so escape the camps, Rousset writes that ''a small core remained steadfast'': for example, a German communist named Emil Künder, a block *kapo* who never hit anyone. Rousset is aware, however, that they all lived in ''the Gray Zone'' and that many ''who refused the offers of the SS . . . behaved with great brutality and took part in a number of shady deals.''

The camps, he writes, are the ''gangrene of a whole economic and social system.'' The ''contamination still spreads far beyond the ruined cities.'' The ''positive balance'' of the camps includes a ''dynamic awareness of the strength and beauty of being alive'' (he had just been liberated when writing the book), a confirmation or discovery of the ''dependence of man's condition on economic and social structures and their material relations which determine human behaviour,'' and finally ''the enthralling discovery of humour,'' the black humor, he means, of Kafka and of characters like Ubu, which ''enabled many to survive.''

The book ends with a call to arms. Since, in Rousset's view, the camps ''sprang from the economic and social foundations of capitalism and imperialism,'' they may appear in a new guise tomorrow. ''It is therefore,'' he writes, ''a question of a very specific war to be waged'' in which ''the concentration camp balance sheet provides a marvellous armoury'' and ''German anti-fascists . . . should be our valuable comrades in arms.''

—Robert Eaglestone

THE WORLD OF MY PAST
Memoir by Abraham Biderman, 1995

Abraham Biderman's *The World of My Past* (1995) is a powerful and poignant memoir of the author's experiences during the Holocaust, with the bulk of the details being devoted to his years in the Lodz ghetto, the longest surviving ghetto in Nazi-dominated Europe. The book is more than a memoir, however. Throughout his account Biderman provides information about the broader historical context, based on his own primary research and on his study of secondary sources, which are acknowledged in the footnotes. The inclusion of this broader material is both a strength and a weakness. For the general reader who does not have an in-depth knowledge of the Holocaust, the additional information provides a context, allowing a clearer understanding of Biderman's personal story to emerge. On the other hand, the additional information sometimes interrupts the powerful flow of the narrative.

Without doubt, Biderman's brilliance lies in his ability to create clear, decisive pen sketches both of key historical characters and of various individuals. For example, he draws a forceful picture of Mordechai Chaim Rumkowski, the Jewish leader who ran the Lodz ghetto. In one paragraph Biderman writes as follows: ''The post office printed its own stamps displaying the head of the ghetto emperor, Mordechai Chaim Rumkowski . . . With his long and flowing silver hair he gave the impression of being a member of the nobility. But the proverb, 'Don't judge a man by his appearance', was especially applicable to him. He had the gentle face of an old man which was a mask only, a disguise, and behind it Mephisto was hidden.''

In his chapter on the ghetto in 1942 there are moving descriptions of the German Jews who had been deported to Lodz. One was a member of the distinguished Rothschild family, a Viennese Jew in his mid-60s who tried to use his signature to acquire extra food. As Biderman writes, ''When I saw him for the first time, he was immaculately dressed and cleanly shaven, the image of an upper class, western European gentleman. It was painful to watch the aristocrat become a beggar.'' Rothschild eventually died in the streets of starvation.

Biderman deals with many themes in his memoir. They include issues of good and evil, of man's inhumanity to man, of the strength of the human will, of the anti-Semitism of his native Poland and of the *Volksdeutscher,* and of the indifference of the West. Biderman explores the moral dimensions of ghetto life, especially in terms of the activities of the Judenrat (Jewish Council) and the Sonderkommando, the Jewish police, both through his own personal story and from a broader perspective. In 1942 his older brother, Lipek (or Lipman), is offered the chance of joining the Jewish police, which would have brought special privileges, including additional food, from which the family could have benefited. Biderman's father, Shimon-Dov, stood firm, however. He told his son, ''''So make your choice, Lipman, between your father and the *Sonderkommando*! But make no mistake. Should you decide to join the *Sonderkommando*, you are no longer my son. You will leave my house. I will not live with a *Sonderkommando* policeman under the same roof!''' Biderman writes that at the time he did not understand his father, and it was only with the passage of time that he came to appreciate his father's integrity and moral heroism. Lipek listened to his father; he was later deported from the ghetto and did not survive. The hope of finding his brother after the war was a key factor in providing Biderman with the strength to struggle to survive.

Another important and ongoing theme is the role of the Church and its responsibility for the inbred nature of Christian anti-Semitism, which eventually led to the Holocaust. Biderman believes that the seeds of the Holocaust were planted by the Church with its teaching throughout the generations that Jews had to be punished for shedding the innocent blood of Jesus. Biderman constantly reminds the reader that Jesus was a Jew, or, as he calls him, "Rabbi *Yeshua Hanitzri*."

In his concluding chapter, "Reflections," Biderman writes, "Humanity will have to create a new language, a new vocabulary, that will convey and express the horrors of the Holocaust." For the reader of this compelling but harrowing account of six years of the nightmare, the hell on earth that is called the Holocaust, Biderman has come as close as possible to communicating his "unspeakable pain." He has demonstrated the complexity of the Holocaust in all of its hues, from those who operated at the highest moral level to those who sank to the lowest depravity. For people who wish to gain an understanding of this terrible period from a single work, this is a book to read.

—Suzanne Rutland

THE WORLD OF YESTERDAY: AN AUTOBIOGRAPHY (Welt von gestern)
Memoir by Stefan Zweig, 1941

Stefan Zweig's autobiography, *The World of Yesterday* (1943; *Welt von gestern,* 1941) is a work not so much of his own life but of the world in which he grew up, physically, intellectually, and culturally. *Heimat* for him meant the creations of the artistic and intellectual elite, as well as their creators, including Raoul Auernheimer, Hermann Bahr, Sigmund Freud, Hugo von Hofmannsthal, Karl Kraus, Gustav Mahler, Rainer Maria Rilke, Auguste Rodin, Felix Salten, Arthur Schnitzler, Arnold Schönberg, Richard Strauss, Émile Verhaeren, Bruno Walter, and actors and actresses such as Josef Kainz, Alexander Moissi, and Max Pallenberg, to name but a few Zweig mentioned and who determined the cultural climate of the fin de siècle period until the First World War, a dream-castle era, as Zweig called it. Afterward, between 1919 and 1934, came the Salzburg years for Zweig, followed by the years in exile, first in England and then in South America.

This world of security, as Zweig titled the first chapter, refers primarily to the educated upper middle class in Vienna, specifically the Jewish segment of it. Representatives of this middle-class intellectual group created a refined culture that was more aesthetically inclined than political. Within the framework of Austrian liberalism, they devoted their life to art rather than engaged in politics. There was an emphasis on individualism and an adoration for genius—extraordinary people who were the great movers in the world—the "genius of humanity," as Zweig subtitled his book on Albert Schweitzer.

This hero worship excluded the masses. In retrospect, Zweig admitted to this shortcoming later on in his autobiography: "The masses, which had silently and obediently permitted the liberal middle classes to retain the leadership for decades, suddenly became restless, organized themselves and demanded their rights . . . We did not have the slightest interest in politics and social problems: what did these shrill wranglings mean in our lives? The city was aroused at the elections, and we went to the libraries. The masses rose, and we wrote and discussed poetry. We did not see the fiery signs on the wall . . . And only decades later, when roof and walls fell in upon us, did we realize that the foundations had long since been undermined and that together with the new century the decline of individual freedom in Europe had begun." This mass movement had unwanted political consequences. The result was not foreseen, and in that respect Zweig showed a lack of political acuity and foresight, as did many of his contemporaries. He admitted to this shortsightedness at the beginning of the section titled "Incipit Hitler": "It remains an irrefragable law of history that contemporaries are denied a recognition of the early beginnings of the great movements which determine their lives." It is the tragedy not only of Zweig but also of other great creators in his era that they devoted their life more to their art and the perfection of their own humanistic education than taking part in political events. Zweig, according to Donald Daviau, can be termed an "impressionistic aesthete" who had "no heart for coping with unpleasantness, aggressiveness, and violence, and as a pacifist he refused to fight for any reason: not for his principles, not for his ideals, not for his freedom, not even for his life. His defense was public silence, withdrawal into his work, and when all else failed, flight."

Being silent did not stop the construction of the concentration camps and the Holocaust. Zweig escaped the concentration camp, but it may be said that he was a victim of the Holocaust, according to the definition offered by Ernestine Schlant in her book *The Language of Silence*: "By 'Holocaust' I mean more than the annihilation of millions of human beings under hitherto unimaginable bestiality; I include in this definition the mechanisms, behavior, and attitudes in all of Nazi-occupied Europe for the purposes of hunting down and rounding up Jews to murder them." These attitudes were already present in the aesthetically pleasing pre-Hitler *World of Yesterday*.

—Gerd K. Schneider

Y

YOUNG MOSHE'S DIARY: THE SPIRITUAL TORMENT OF A JEWISH BOY IN NAZI EUROPE
(Hana'ar Moshe: Yoman shel Moshe Flinker)
Diary by Moshe Flinker, 1958

When Moshe Flinker's sisters returned to Brussels after the end of the World War II, they discovered their murdered brother's diary in the basement of their old apartment building. Written in Hebrew, the diary was first published under the title *Hana'ar Moshe: Yoman shel Moshe Flinker* in 1958; it was translated into English and published in 1971 as *Young Moshe's Diary: The Spiritual Torment of a Jewish Boy in Nazi Europe*. Passages in the diary reveal traces of greatness in a young soul engaged in a struggle between hope and despair. The depth of the teenager's ordeal lay not only in his insight into history but also in his compassion, to the point of feeling guilt over the suffering of his fellow Jews. "I see myself as if I were a traitor," he confessed, "who fled from his people at the time of their anguish." Very much aware of the ramifications of the historical events of his time, he was even more aware of what the events meant for the people of Israel and their relation to the God of Israel. As a devout Zionist, he was determined to be a part of his people's return to their homeland, but he could see that their return was becoming more and more impossible. While he said that he could see his homeland in his prayers, around him his eyes saw nothing but ruin.

Writing his diary from November 1942 to September 1943, Moshe Flinker struggled to understand the Holocaust not only in terms of human history but also in terms of sacred history. Indeed, as a religious Jew he believed that God was involved in the design of history, the aim of which is to bring humankind into the messianic age. "It seems to me," he wrote on 26 November 1942, "that the time has come for our redemption." He saw the war as the "birthpang of the Messiah,"
which meant that "not from the English nor the Americans nor the Russians but from the Lord Himself will our redemption come." Whereas some diary writers saw the absence of God in this event, Moshe Flinker tried to see the hand of God. He turned to the prayers and to the Scriptures and incorporated them into his own text, making his diary itself into a kind of prayer.

As the night of the Holocaust grew darker, however, Moshe Flinker felt himself slipping ever deeper into a spiritual void. On 2 February 1943, he wrote, "When I pray I feel as if I am praying to the wall and am not heard at all . . . I think that the holy spark which I always felt with me has been taken from me." Before long the Scriptures, too, were lost on him, as he indicated in an entry dated July 4, 1943: "Formerly, when I took up my Bible and read it, it was as if I had returned to life, as if the Lord had taken pity on me; even in my darkest moments I found consolation in Him. Now even this is denied me." In his movement from prayer to emptiness, from Holy Word to hollow void, one can see an important feature of his Holocaust diary. It begins as a vehicle for God's utterance reverberating in the voice of the diarist and ends as a lamentation over the cessation of that utterance.

Thus, Moshe Flinker saw the content of his diary as a "reflection of [his] spiritual life." If that spiritual life revolved around God's presence and absence, then perhaps his outcry over the silence of God might bear a trace of God's own outcry. Reading his diary, one wonders whether the absent God might be hiding in the question concerning his absence. In any case his diary, written under singular conditions, has universal implications for humanity's ongoing inquiry into the meaning of history.

—David Patterson

Z

ZOG NIT KEYNMOL
Poetry by Hirsh Glik, 1946

With words by Hirsh Glik and music by Dmitri and Daniel Pokrass, ''Zog Nit Keynmol'' became the anthem of the Jewish underground resistance movement in World War II. Inspired by knowledge of the Warsaw Ghetto Uprising in May 1943, Hirsh Glik's lyrics were combined with a march melody from the 1938 Soviet film *Son of the Working People* to create the inspiring song ''Zog Nit Keynmol.'' Following the end of World War II ''Zog Nit Keynmol'' has frequently been sung at Holocaust commemorations worldwide, particularly on Yam Hashoah.

The words to ''Zog Nit Keynmol'' reflect the author's strong belief in Jewish armed resistance to Nazi oppression. Like many other partisan songs, ''Zog Nit Keynmol'' served to reinforce Jewish identity and maintain camaraderie in an environment where heroism was required and death was commonplace. Refusing to admit defeat or accept the possibility that Jewish life in Europe was doomed, the song's lyrics are defiant and optimistic. ''Never say that you have reached the final road'' and ''The hour that we've longed for now draws near, / Our Steps proclaim like drumbeats: We Are Here!'' resound in the first and final stanzas, their repetition emphasizing the strength and determination of Jews in the face of tyranny. The optimistic tone is sustained in the second stanza, where even though Glik recognizes the existence of suffering, ''We come with all our suffering and woe,'' he then continues: ''And wherever any of our blood is shed, / Our courage and our valor rise again!'' Clearly aware of the lyrics' inspirational power, the third stanza proclaims ''But should tomorrow's sun await the dawn too long, / Let this song ring out for ages yet to come.'' Cognizant also of the extremely difficult circumstances facing all Jews in Eastern Europe, Glik's fourth stanza is a clarion call for solidarity in spite of the omnipresent dangers: ''But a people, trapped between collapsing walls, / With weapons held in hand—they sang this song!'' ''Zog Nit Keynmol'' then concludes with a full repetition of the opening stanza, which reinforces the defiant call to resist oppression: ''So, never say that you have reached the final road, / Though lead-grey clouds conceal blue skies above, / The hour that we've longed for now draws near, / Our steps proclaim like drumbeats: Wc Arc Hcrc!''

Knowing that Jewish communities in Eastern Europe were being destroyed all around them, Jewish partisans employed armed resistance to oppose Nazism. Glik's lyrics to ''Zog Nit Keynmol'' helped to sustain the partisans as they risked their lives while forging another link in the long tradition of Jewish poetry dedicated to maintaining unity against hostile outside forces.

—William R. Fernekes

ZUCKERMAN BOUND: A TRILOGY AND EPILOGUE
Story by Philip Roth, 1985

Philip Roth begins and ends *Zuckerman Bound: A Trilogy and Epilogue* (1985) with a story that references the Holocaust. To a large extent the positioning of all four stories is relevant to Nathan Zuckerman's chronological age, and each one describes the problems a writer has to face, but their respective placement also is driven by a broader examination of the relationship between life and art. For example, to what degree does the novelist draw on his own life for thematic material? Although all of the Zuckerman novels respond to that question, *The Ghost Writer* (1979) and *Epilogue: The Prague Orgy* (1985), the stories framing the collection, bring into focus the thematic relevance of the Holocaust and anti-Semitism for a Jewish American writer. They suggest Roth's awareness that although he remained geographically distant from the Holocaust, as a writer he became deeply linked to it in ways that he could never have predicted.

Roth's more solipsistic approach, *The Ghost Writer,* fictionalizes the latent effect of the Holocaust on the negative way some of Roth's Jewish audience read his work. The defensive tone of that earlier work, however, is replaced in *Epilogue: Thc Praguc Orgy.* Here Roth expresses his appreciation of the crucial tie-in between politics and art: in America a Jewish writer gets the chance to be criticized or praised, but in Czechoslovakia a Jew's writing gets imprisoned in layers of anti-Semitic bureaucracy.

Roth has set up the story as three journal entries from Zuckerman's diary, starting with one on 11 January 1976, the day Zuckerman meets Sisovsky, a Czech émigré who fawningly flatters Zuckerman's writing in an effort to persuade Zuckerman to smuggle out his father's Yiddish manuscripts about the Holocaust. According to Sisovsky, his father produced 200 stories about Jewish life in Czechoslovakia. His father, he claims, was the Yiddish Flaubert whose stories, especially the ten little gems relating to life of the Nazis and Jews in 1941, deserve an audience. After Sisovsky tells the tragic circumstances of his father's death at the hands of a drunken Gestapo officer, Zuckerman feels compelled to try and rescue the stories. The remaining journal entries recount what takes place on two days in February of the same year when Zuckerman unsuccessfully attempts to bring the manuscripts to freedom.

As Zuckerman is pursuing the manuscripts, he hears from Sisovsky's alcoholic wife that the authenticity of the stories is suspect. What they describe, she says, did not happen to Sisovsky's father but rather to his friend. She implies that Zuckerman's zealous mission can best be explained as another "shallow, sentimental, American . . . Jew" drawn to a Holocaust story—an analogous accusation to Zuckerman's feelings about the general response of Jews to Anne Frank's diary. This theory particularizes the discussion of the relationship between life and art. To what degree have American Jews considered Anne Frank's story a martyr's tale, a holy book by virtue of its place in the encyclopedia of Jewish suffering? Do Jews immediately elevate and favorably judge any story of the Holocaust without regard to its literary value?

By placing *The Prague Orgy* at the end, Roth can revisit certain issues he began in *The Ghost Writer*. Anne Frank's life takes on a whole other meaning for a non-Jew, Eva Kalinova, Sisovsky's Gentile mistress. As Zuckerman reflects, "They [the Czech regime] have used Anne Frank as a whip to drive her from the stage, . . . Anne Frank as a curse and a stigma!" Kalinova has played so many Jewish parts that she is believed to be Jewish. Like her lover, Sisovsky, she suffers from a strain of anti-Semitism that is reflected in a widespread suffocation of artistic expression. In America she is no longer a Czech actress, and he isn't a Czech writer. Thus, Roth suggests, Anne Frank's story, the story of political, religious, and artistic repression, is metaphorically speaking a legacy from the Holocaust that continues to threaten freedom in ways that Americans often never learn about. Ultimately the story of Anne Frank is not just a Jewish story. The anti-Semitism of the Nazis becomes a symbol of other repressive regimes and the ruin they wreak on the human spirit. Roth implies that to bring these stories to light is a form of resistance.

—Ellen Gerstle and Daniel Walden

ZÜRICH, THE STORK INN (Zürich, Zum Storchen) Poem by Paul Celan, 1960

Paul Celan's eight hundred poems established him as Europe's most significant postwar poet. He wrote in his native German as well as in other languages. He addressed literary traditions as well as theological, philosophical, scientific, historical, and personal material. Celan called his writing of poems an "encounter" where "I went with my very being toward language." His lyric poems often seek what he called "an addressable thou," which registered in a range of forms: the poet, his mother, wife, or sons, a loved one or friend, the

Jewish dead, God, Osip Mandelstam, Rembrandt, Saint Francis, a stone, a word, or something mysterious and unnamable. In the case of "Zürich, Zum Storchen" ("Zürich, the Stork Inn"), Celan's addressee is his beloved friend and poet **Nelly Sachs**. Originally published in German in 1960 (the English translation was published in 1988), it commemorates the first meeting of the two poets in the spring of that year.

Sachs was born in 1891 into an upper–middle class Jewish family in Berlin. In May of 1940, under the threat of Hitler's Third Reich, Sachs took her aging mother and went to live in Sweden. She lived the rest of her life in Stockholm, terminally affected by a persecution anxiety that kept her from ever living in her native Germany again. In 1960 she won Germany's most prestigious honor for women poets, the Droste-Hulshoff Prize. She traveled to Germany to receive the prize, but opted to stay in Switzerland overnight. It was on that visit that she met Paul Celan, with whom she had corresponded since 1954, for the first time. "A fairytale here," she wrote on 26 May from Zürich's Hotel Zum Storchen ("Hotel at the Stork").

Once back in Paris, on 30 May, Celan wrote "Zürich, the Stork Inn" and dedicated it to Sachs. The poem displays their new intimacy and their differing stances within Judaism. It records, on the day marking Christ's ascent into heaven, an epiphany. Looking across the Limmat River toward Zürich's Grossmünster (Great Minster), Celan and Sachs together saw the church mirrored in the water that gleamed with golden sunlight. Both of them knew the force of sunlight in Jewish mysticism; they never forgot the sight.

Celan's opening sentence gives a nod to Margarete Susman, who lived in Zürich and whose 1946 *Book of Job and the Fate of the Jewish People* says that, in light of the Holocaust, "every word is a Too Little and a Too Much." The initial ambivalence in the poem gives way to the heart of the poem—and the encounter—"On the day of an ascension, the/Minster stood over there, it came/with some gold across the water." Although the day Celan and Sachs met was Ascension Day on the Christian calendar, Celan opens the moment to other ascents besides Christ's by speaking of "an" ascension. "Some gold across the water" offers a variation on the miracle of ascension: a particular shining that two survivors witnessed together and which impacted them for the rest of their lives. This vision gives way to a spare hope: "for/his highest, death-rattled, his/wrangling word—." The word *Haderndes* ("wrangling") is used in Exodus 17:2 when the people of Israel struggle with Moses.

Following the certainty of this struggle, the poem moves into meditation and ambiguity. "We/really don't know, you know,/we/really don't know/what counts . . . ." The final line alludes to Sachs's acceptance speech. She had said that "Everything counts" in God's eyes.

Paul Celan drowned himself in the Seine in April 1970. On the day of his funeral, Nelly Sachs died in Stockholm.

—Martha Sutro

CHRONOLOGY

DATE	AUTHOR AND TITLE	EVENT
1933	Feuchtwanger, Lion: *Die Geschwister Oppermann (The Oppermanns)*	Adolf Hitler becomes chancellor of Germany on 30 January. Dachau, the first permanent concentration camp, is opened in a suburb of Munich in March. In April Nazis organize a national boycott of Jewish-owned businesses. The first anti-Jewish laws are also passed, removing all Jews from government jobs, including teaching positions. Further laws follow, and by the end of the year 53,000 Jews have left Germany.
1934		Upon the death of German President Paul von Hindenburg, Hitler combines the offices of chancellor and president, becoming führer, or leader, of the Third Reich, with absolute power. All army officers and soldiers swear allegiance to Hitler.
1935		Germany passes the Nuremberg Laws, which define Jews in racial terms, strip them of German citizenship, and ban marriages and sexual relationships between Jews and non-Jews.
1936		Hitler and the Nazis temporarily ease anti-Jewish actions as the Olympic Games open in Berlin. Germany and Italy enter into agreements that develop into a political and military alliance called the Rome-Berlin Axis.
1937		Buchenwald concentration camp is established on 16 July.
1938		In March the German army moves into Austria, which is annexed by Germany through Anschluss, an agreement that makes the country part of Nazi Germany. Austrian crowds cheer Hitler as he enters Vienna. Anti-Semitic laws rapidly go into effect. An international conference is held in Évian-les-Baines, France, to discuss the plight of Jewish refugees in Europe. No solutions are found to resolve the crisis. In Paris, Herschel Grynszpan, a young Jew, shoots and kills Ernst vom Rath, a German embassy official. Grynszpan's actions spark *Kristallnacht* (''Crystal Night'' or ''Night of Broken Glass''), a series of organized Nazi attacks throughout Germany in which Jews are beaten, synagogues are burned, Jewish homes and businesses are destroyed, and 30,000 Jewish men are arrested and sent to concentration camps. Italian dictator Benito Mussolini adopts the anti-Jewish laws of Hitler.
1939		World War II officially begins when Germany invades Poland on 1 September. Two days later Great Britain and France declare war on Germany. Poland surrenders to Germany on 27 September. The Nazi euthanasia program begins. In time 70,000 mentally and physically disabled Germans, including children, are murdered by Nazi doctors and their staffs. On 21 September Reinhard Heydrich, second in command of the SS, issues a directive to Nazi task forces ordering

DATE	AUTHOR AND TITLE	EVENT
		the ''resettlement'' of Polish Jews to urban centers (specifically, ghettos) near railroad lines. In October Hitler appoints Hans Frank governor-general of certain sections of Poland that later become the resettlement areas for Jews and others the Nazis deem unfit for Reich citizenship. On 23 November Jews in German-occupied Poland are ordered to wear the yellow Star of David on their clothing at all times.
1940		The Lodz ghetto is created in Poland in February and sealed in April. Heinrich Himmler, head of the SS, orders the building of a concentration camp at Auschwitz in occupied Poland. French troops evacuate Paris on 13 June, and German forces take the city the next day. France signs an armistice with Germany on 22 June as German troops occupy the northern part of the country, while a government friendly to Germany (Vichy France) maintains a measure of independence in the south. Anti-Jewish measures soon begin in western European countries controlled by Germany. Field Marshall Philippe Pétain is appointed head of the German-controlled Vichy government in France. He is later convicted of collaborating with the Nazis. The Warsaw Ghetto in Poland is sealed, and nearly 450,000 Jews are confined within its walls.
1941	Brecht, Bertolt: *Furcht und Elend des Dritten Reiches* (*Fear and Misery of the Third Reich*) Zweig, Stefan: *Welt von gestern* (*The World of Yesterday*)	A ghetto in Kraków is decreed, established, and sealed between 3 March and 20 March. On 22 June, in an offensive called Operation Barbarossa, Germany invades the Soviet Union and quickly takes control of much of the country. Special murder squads known as Einsatzgruppen follow the German army into the Soviet Union to eliminate Jews, political dissidents, and others. Hermann Göring, second to Hitler in the Nazi hierarchy, gives Heydrich the authority ''to carry out all necessary preparations . . . for a total solution of the Jewish question'' throughout Nazi-controlled Europe. Rudolph Hoess, commandant of the Auschwitz concentration camp, oversees the first experiments using poisonous gas for the mass extermination of humans. Kiev, the capital of Ukraine, falls to the German army on 19 September. More than 33,000 Jews are murdered at Babi Yar, outside Kiev, on 29 and 30 September. During October construction begins on Birkenau (Auschwitz II) in Poland. The emigration of Jews is banned. In Poland the construction of an extermination camp at Belzec begins on 1 November. The death camp at Chelmno, in the western part of Poland, begins operation. Jews are gassed in sealed vans. In December Germany declares war against the United States.
1942	Zweig, Stefan: *Schachnovelle* (*The Royal Game*)	Heydrich calls the Wannsee Conference, where the Final Solution, a plan to eliminate all European Jews,

DATE	AUTHOR AND TITLE	EVENT

is transmitted to various branches of the German government.

Slovakian Jews become the first Jews from outside Poland to be transported to Auschwitz.

Heydrich dies on 4 June of wounds from an earlier assassination attempt by Czech resistance fighters in Prague.

Anne Frank and her family move into a secret annex constructed in the top stories of her father's office building in Amsterdam.

The Treblinka death camp begins receiving Jews from Warsaw. It is the last of the three camps, along with Belzec and Sobidor, created to exterminate Polish Jews. The Nazis called this plan Operation Reinhard, in honor of the assassinated Heydrich.

In September and October Polish Jews Shimson and Tova Draenger join other Jewish youths in forming the Jewish Fighting Organization to work against the Nazis.

Wladyslaw Bartoszewski, a Roman Catholic Polish resister, helps form a Jewish relief committee called Zegota.

1943

In what came to be known as the Warsaw Ghetto Uprising, small groups of Jews begin attacking German troops on 19 April. They continue fighting for nearly a month, until the Germans have killed almost all of the resisters and completely destroyed the ghetto.

German attempts to deport Danish Jews are defeated when most of the Jewish population of Denmark is safely transported to Sweden.

On 3 November Operation Erntefest begins. The purpose is the extermination of surviving Jews in the labor camps of Trawniki and Poniatowa and in the Majdanek concentration camp. Between 42,000 and 43,000 are killed in the operation.

Operation Reinhard is completed, and after the murder of 1.5 million Jews, Belzec, Sobibor, Treblinka, and Majdanek are closed.

Members of the Jewish community in France establish the Centre de Documentation Juive Contemporaine (Jewish Contemporary Documentation Center) to gather and house documents about the persecution of Jews.

1944   Borges, Jorge Luis: "El milagro secreto" ("The Secret Miracle")
Katzenelson, Yitzhak: *Dos lid funem oysge'harg'etn Yidishn folk* (*The Song of The Murdered Jewish People*)

The Germans occupy Hungary on 19 March and begin large-scale deportations of Jews. By July more than 400,000 Hungarian Jews have been sent to Auschwitz.

On 6 June, later known as D-Day, Allied forces land in Normandy in northern France during the largest sea invasion in history, called Operation Overlord. After heavy fighting the Allies break out of Normandy and sweep eastward across France. By the end of August, France is liberated.

On 20 July a small group of German army officers, eager to end the war, unsuccessfully attempts to assassinate Hitler. Many of the conspirators, along with their families, are tortured and executed.

During the course of October 1944, the industrialist Oskar Schindler is granted permission by the Nazis to establish

DATE	AUTHOR AND TITLE	EVENT

a munitions factory in Czechoslovakia. This allows Schindler to spare Jewish prisoners from death by employing them.

Concentration camp prisoner Roza Robota participates in the inmates' revolt at Auschwitz, which leads to the destruction of one of the crematoria.

On 26 October Himmler orders the destruction of the concentration camps and their inmates.

1945

Asch, Sholem: *One Destiny: An Epistle to the Christians*

Edelman, Marek: *Getto walczy: Udzial Bundu w obronie getta warszawskiego* (*The Ghetto Fights*)

Miłosz, Czesław: *Ocalenie* ("Salvation")

Rousset, David: *L'Univers concentrationnaire* (*A World Apart*)

Berg, Mary: *Warsaw Ghetto: A Diary*

Sutzkever, Abraham: *Di Festung* ("The Fortress")

Wiechert, Ernst: *Der Totenwald: Ein Bericht* (*Forest of the Dead*)

British troops liberate the Bergen-Belsen concentration camp.

The Swedish diplomat Folke Bernadotte negotiates a deal with Himmler that allows 10,000 women to be released from the Ravensbrück concentration camp.

As Soviet troops approach, the Nazis begin the evacuation of the Auschwitz death camp on 18 January, forcing some 66,000 surviving prisoners on a death march. Soviet troops reach the camp on 27 January.

U.S. General George S. Patton and his Third Army liberate the Buchenwald concentration camp in Germany on 11 April.

On 28 April Mussolini is captured by resistance fighters and executed. His body is put on public display in Milan.

American troops liberate the Dachau concentration camp on 29 April.

On 30 April Hitler and Eva Braun commit suicide in his underground bunker in Berlin.

Germany surrenders on 7 May.

Göring is arrested by American troops during May. A year later, after having been condemned to death for war crimes, he commits suicide.

Himmler, the senior Nazi official responsible for overseeing the mass murder of 6 million European Jews, is captured by the Allies on 21 May. Two days later he commits suicide.

Trials for war crimes begin in Nuremberg in November. Justice Robert H. Jackson of the U.S. Supreme Court gives the opening address for the United States before the International Military Tribunal.

1946

Borowski, Tadeusz, Janusz Nel Siedlecki, and Krystyn Olszewski: *Bylismy w Oswiecimiu* (*We Were in Auschwitz*)

Kogon, Eugene: *Der SS-Staat: Das System de Deutschen Konzentrationslager* (*The Theory and Practice of Hell: The German Concentration Camps and the System Behind Them*)

Lengyel, Olga: *Souvenirs de l'au-delà* (*Five Chimneys: The Story of Auschwitz*)

Radnóti, Miklós: *Tatjékos ég* (*Clouded Sky*)

Szpilman, Wladyslaw: *Smierc miasta* (*The Pianist*)

Tedeschi, Giuliana: *Questo povero corpo* (*There Is a Place on Earth: A Woman in Birkenau*)

Tillion, Germaine: *Ravensbrück*

Frankl, Viktor: *Ein Psycholog erlebt das Konzentrationslager* (*Man's Search for Meaning: An Introduction to Logotherapy*)

Glik, Hirsh: *Zog nit keynmol*

Göring, one of the highest Nazi officials to be accused and convicted of war crimes, testifies in his own defense during the Nuremberg trials.

U.S. Brigadier General Telford Taylor becomes the chief counsel for the remaining Nuremberg trials after Jackson resigns.

DATE	AUTHOR AND TITLE	EVENT

1947

Calvino, Italo: *Il sentiero dei nidi di ragno* (*Path to the Spiders' Nest*)
Camus, Albert: *La Peste* (*The Plague*)
Frank, Anne: *Het achterhuis* (*The Diary of a Young Girl*)
Antelme, Robert: *L'Espèce humaine* (*The Human Species*)
Ka-Tzetnik 135633: *Salamandra* (*Sunrise over Hell*)
Levi, Primo: *Se questo è un uomo* (*Survival in Auschwitz*)
Levin, Meyer: *My Father's House*
Millu, Liana: *Il fumo di Birkenau* (*Smoke over Birkenau*)
Nyiszli, Miklos: *Dr. Mengele boncolóorvosa voltam az auschwitzi krematóriumban* (*Auschwitz: A Doctor's Eyewitness Account*)
Sachs, Nelly: ''O the Chimneys!''

Holocaust survivor Simon Wiesenthal forms the Jewish Historical Documentation Center in Austria to track down Nazi war criminals.
The Polish parliament passes an act to establish the Auschwitz-Birkenau State Museum.
The site of the Bergen-Belsen camp serves as an underground training center for Haganah, the Jewish military force in Palestine.

1948

Celan, Paul: ''Todesfuge'' (''Death Fugue'')
Koeppen, Walter: *Jakob Littners Aufzeichnungen aus einem Erdloch*
Aichinger, Ilse: *Die größere Hoffnung* (*Herod's Children*)
Meed, Vladka: *Fun beyde zaytn geto-moyer* (*On Both Sides of the Wall*)
Perl, Gisela: *I Was a Doctor in Auschwitz*
Rudnicki, Adolf: *Wniebowstąpienie* (*Ascent to Heaven*)

On 14 May the State of Israel is established.
The Warsaw Ghetto Monument, a memorial commemorating the Warsaw Ghetto Uprising, is unveiled.

1949

Borges, Jorge Luis: ''Deutsches Requiem''
Weil, Jiří: *Zivot s hvezdou* (*Life with a Star*)

The Federal Republic of Germany (West Germany) is established.
The Ghetto Fighters' House Holocaust and Jewish Resistance Heritage Museum is founded in Israel by Holocaust survivors.

1950

Hersey, John: *The Wall*

The Bergen-Belsen camp is closed.
Former SS official Adolf Eichmann escapes to Argentina.
The Law of Judging Nazi Criminals and Their Helpers is passed in Israel, allowing for the prosecution of former Nazis.

1951

Böll, Heinrich: *Wo warst du, Adam?* (*And Where Were You, Adam?*)
Grade, Chaim: ''Mayn krig mit Hersh Rasseyner'' (''My Fight with Hersh Rasseyner'')
Greenberg, Uri Zvi: *Rehovot hanahar: Sefer ha'iliyot yehakoah* (*Streets of the River: The book of Dirges and Power*)
Klein, A.M.: *The Second Scroll*
Sachs, Nelly: *Eli: Ein Mysterienspiel vom Leiden Israels* (*Eli: A Mystery Play of the Sufferings of Israel*)
Sperber, Manès: *Qu'une larme dans l'ocean* (*Like a Tear in the Ocean*)

The Israeli parliament passes a law establishing Holocaust Remembrance Day (Yom ha-Sho'ah), an annual day of commemoration.
The Conference on Jewish Material Claims against Germany is established by Jewish organizations to discuss restitution for Holocaust survivors.
Following a trial, the former commander of Einsatzgruppe D, Otto Ohlendorf, is hanged at Landsberg Prison. The former SS general Oswald Pohl and the former head of Sonderkommando 1005, Paul Blobel, are also hanged.
The former SS official Jürgen Stroop, who headed the elimination of the Warsaw Ghetto in 1943, is executed after being found guilty of war crimes.
The former Buchenwald guard Hans Schmidt is executed. He is the last war criminal executed by the Allies.
Konrad Adenauer, chancellor of West Germany, issues a formal apology for the Nazi persecution of Jews and offers reparations.

DATE	AUTHOR AND TITLE	EVENT
1952	Bassani, Giorgio: *Una lapide in Via Mazzini* (*A Plaque on Via Mazzini*) Ringelblum, Emmanuel: *Notitsn fun Varshever geto* (*Notes from the Warsaw Ghetto: The Journal of Emmanuel Ringelblum*) Bryks, Rachmil: *Oif kiddush ha-shem un andere dertzeilungen* (*A Cat in the Ghetto*) Cohen, Elie Aron: *Het Duitse concentratiekamp; Een Medische en Psychologische studie* (*Human Behavior in the Concentration Camp*) Remarque, Erich Maria: *Der Funke Leben* (*Spark of Life*)	With the signing of the Luxembourg Treaty, Israel and Germany agree on restitution for the damages done to Jews by the Nazis. A Day of Holocaust Heroism is enacted by the Israeli parliament. Plotzensee Prison in Germany, where many resistance fighters were killed during World War II, is restored as a memorial.
1953	Dürrenmatt, Friedrich: *Der Verdacht* (*The Quarry*) Memmi, Albert: *Statue du sel* (*Pillar of Salt*) Gascar, Pierre: *Le Temps des morts* (*The Season of the Dead*) Ka-Tzetnik 135633: *Beit ha-bubot* (*House of Dolls*)	On 28 August the Israeli parliament passes the Yad Vashem Law, which establishes the Martyrs' and Heroes' Remembrance Authority to commemorate the 6 million Jews killed in the Holocaust, the communities and institutions destroyed, the soldiers and resistance members who fought the Nazis, the dignity of the Jews attacked, and those who risked their lives in order to aid Jews.
1955	Celan, Paul: ''Schibboleth'' (''Shibboleth'') Kolmar, Gertrud: *Das lyrische Werk* (*Dark Soliloquy: The Selected Poems of Gertrud Kolmar*)	Yad Vashem begins an effort to document every Holocaust victim by gathering ''pages of testimony'' about those killed.
1956		After serving 7 years of a 20-year sentence for war crimes, former Einsatzgruppe B commander Franz W. Six is released from prison.
1957	Camus, Albert: *La Chute* (*The Fall*) Goodrich, Frances, and Hackett, Albert: *The Diary of Anne Frank* Brecht, Bertolt: *Der aufhaltsame Aufstieg des Arturo Ui* (*The Resistible Rise of Arturo Ui*) Sylvanus, Erwin: *Korczak und die Kinder* (*Dr. Korczak and the Children*) Klein, Gerda Weissmann: *All but My Life* Minco, Marga: *Het bittere Kruid: Een kleine Kroniek* (*Bitter Herbs: A Little Chronicle*) Presser, Jacques: *De Nacht der Girondijnen* (*Night of the Girondists,* or *Breaking Point*) Różewicz, Tadeusz: *Poezje zebrane* (*Collected Poems*) Sachs, Nelly: ''Landschaft aus Schreien'' (''Landscape of Screams'')	Rabbi Leo Bäck, instrumental in organizing Germany Jewry and helping Jews escape from Germany during World War II, dies in London. Yad Vashem begins publishing the first English-language journals to focus on the study of the Holocaust. The bodies of Jewish forced laborers are exhumed in Hungary. A memorial is established at the Mauthausen concentration camp memorial in Austria. Former SS official Fritz Katzmann dies. He successfully eluded prosecution for 12 years.
1958	Bruck, Edith: *Chi ti ama così* (*Who Loves You Like This*) Grade, Chaim: *Der mames shabosim* (*My Mother's Sabbath Days*) Apitz, Bruno: *Nackt unter Wölfen* (*Naked among Wolves*) Flinker, Moshe: *Hana'ar Moshe: Yoman shel Moshe Flinker* (*Young Moshe's Diary: The Spiritual Torment of a Jewish Boy in Nazi Europe*) Frisch, Max (Rudolph): *Biedermann und die Brandstifter: Eine Lehrstück ohne Lehre, mit einem Nachspiel*	The Buchenwald National Memorial Museum is founded. The Central Office for the Investigation of National Socialist Crimes is established by the West German government.

DATE	AUTHOR AND TITLE	EVENT

(Biedermann and the Firebugs: A Morality without a Moral)
Lustig, Arnošt: *Noc a nadeje* (*Night and Hope*)
Lustig, Arnošt: *Demanty noci* (*Diamonds of the Night*)
Malamud, Bernard: "The Last Mohican"
Malamud, Bernard: "Lady of the Lake"
Megged, Aharon: *Hannah Senesh* (*Hanah Senesh*)
Wiesel, Elie: *La Nuit* (*Night*)

1959

Heimler, Eugene: *Night of the Mist*
Hill, Geoffrey: "Two Formal Elegies"
Grass, Günter: *Die Blechtrommel* (*The Tin Drum*)
Levin, Meyer: *Eva: A Novel of the Holocaust*
Richler, Mordecai: *The Apprenticeship of Duddy Kravitz*
Roth, Philip: "Eli, the Fanatic"
Schwarz-Bart, André: *Le Dernier des justes* (*The Last of the Just*)

The German industrialist Alfred Krupp is made to pay reparations to former concentration camp inmates who were forced to work in his munitions factories.
The former head of Einsatzkommando 3, Karl Jäger, is arrested. He commits suicide before he can be brought to trial.

1960

Celan, Paul: "Zürich, zum Storchen" ("Zürich, the Stork Inn")
Sartre, Jean-Paul: *Les Séquestrés d'Altona* (*The Condemned of Altona*)
Bettelheim, Bruno: *The Informed Heart: Autonomy in a Mass Age*
Sierakowiak, Dawid: *Dziennik* (*Diary of Dawid Sierakowiak: Five Notebooks from the Lodz Ghetto*)
Wiesel, Elie: *L'Aube* (*Dawn*)

In May Eichmann is arrested in Argentina by the Israeli Security Service.
The Anne Frank House in Amsterdam opens its doors as a public museum.

1961

Ka-Tzetnik 135633: *Karu lo Piepel* (*Piepel*) (as *Atrocity,* 1963)
Kruk, Herman: *Togbukh fun Vilner Geto* ("Chronicle of the Vilna Ghetto")
Hart (Moxon), Kitty: *I Am Alive!*
Levertov, Denise: "During the Eichmann Trial"
Manger, Itzik: "My Hate Song"
Rawicz, Piotr: *Le Sang du ciel* (*Blood from the Sky*)
Remarque, Erich Maria: *Die Nacht von Lissabon* (*The Night in Lisbon*)
Uris, Leon: *Mila 18*
Wallant, Edward Lewis: *The Pawnbroker*
Wiesel, Elie: *Le Jour* (*The Accident*)
Yevtushenko, Yevgeny: "Babii Yar"

Eichmann is tried in Israel, found guilty of war crimes, and sentenced to death.
The Hall of Remembrance, a Holocaust memorial, is dedicated in Israel.

1962

Bassani, Giorgio: *Il giardino dei Finzi-Contini* (*The Garden of the Finzi-Contini*)
Frisch, Max (Rudolph): *Andorra: Stück in zwölf Bildern* (*Andorra: A Play in Twelve Scenes*)
Lind, Jakov: "Eine Seele aus Holz" ("Soul of Wood")
Wiesel, Elie: *La Ville de la chance* (*The Town beyond the Wall*)

Eichmann is executed for his part in the murder of hundreds of thousands of Jews.
Israel and Jewish agencies influence the investigation of Swiss bank accounts that may have belonged to Holocaust victims. Claimants receive 9.5 million Swiss francs.
As a result of the Yad Vashem Law, a commission is founded to award and honor "the Righteous among the Nations" who helped save the lives of Jews during World War II.

DATE	AUTHOR AND TITLE	EVENT
1963	Bor, Josef: *Terezínské Rekviem* (*Terezin Requiem*) Amichai, Yehuda: *Lo me-akshav lo mikan* (*Not of This Time, Not of This Place*) Fuks, Ladislav: *Pan Theodor Mundstock* (*Mr. Theodore Mundstock*) Ginzburg, Natalia: *Lessico famigliare* (*Family Sayings; What We Used to Say*) Hochhuth, Rolf: *Der Stellvertreter: Ein christliches Trauerspiel* (*The Deputy*) Jabès, Edmond: *Le Livre des questions* (*The Book of Questions*) Levi, Primo: *La tregua* (*The Reawakening*) Lind, Jakov: *Landschaft in Beton* (*Landscape in Concrete*) Malamud, Bernard: ''The German Refugee'' (''The Refugee'') Semprun, Jorge: *Grand voyage* (*The Long Voyage*) Vrba, Rudolf, with Alan Bestic: *I Cannot Forgive*	Twenty-one SS officers who worked at Auschwitz during World War II are tried in West Germany.
1964	Heyman, Eva: *Yomanah shel Evah Hayman* (*The Diary of Eva Heyman*) Hilsenrath, Edgar: *Nacht* (*Night*) Gouri, Haim: *'Iskat ha-shokolad* (*The Chocolate Deal*) Katzenelson, Yitzhak: *Pinkas Vitel* (*Vittel Diary*) Levin, Meyer: *The Fanatic* Lustig, Arnošt: *Modlitba pro Katerinu Horovitzovou* (*A Prayer for Katerina Horovitzova*) Miller, Arthur: *Incident at Vichy* Schindel, Robert: ''Errinerungen an Prometheus'' (''Memories of Prometheus'') Wiesel, Elie: *Les Portes de la foret* (*The Gates of the Forest*)	The Dachau Concentration Camp Memorial Museum is established on the site of the former camp. A memorial at Treblinka, site of a former death camp, is dedicated.
1965	Ferderber-Salz, Bertha: *Un di zun hot geshaynt* (*And the Sun Kept Shining*) Donat, Alexander: *The Holocaust Kingdom* Grynberg, Henryk: *Zydowska wonja* (*Child of the Shadows*) Habe, Hans: *Die Mission* (*The Mission*) Hildesheimer, Wolfgang: *Tynset* Kaplan, Chaim A.: *Scroll of Agony: The Warsaw Diary of Chaim A. Kaplan* Kipphardt, Heinar: *Joel Brand: Die Geschichte eines Geschäfts* (''Joel Brand: The Story of a Business Deal'') Kosinski, Jerzy: *The Painted Bird* Kosinski, Jerzy: ''Notes of the Author on *The Painted Bird*'' Levin, Meyer: *The Stronghold* Weiss, Peter: *Die Ermittlung* (*The Investigation*) Wiesel, Elie: *Entre deux soleils* (*One Generation After*)	The National Democratic Party of Germany, led primarily by ex-Nazis and espousing nationalist, right-wing doctrines, is founded.
1966	Améry, Jean: *Jenseits von Schuld und Sühne: Bewältigungsversuche eines Überwältigten* (*At the Mind's Limits*) Ka-Tzetnik 135633: *Kokhav ha-efer* (*Star Eternal*) Kuznctsov, Anatoli: *Babii Iar: Roman-dokument* (*Babi Yar: A Documentary Novel*) Senesh, Hannah: *Hanah Senesh: Yomanim, Shirim, Eduyot* (*Hannah Senesh, Her Life and Diary*) Singer, Isaac Bashevis: *Sonim, di Geshichte fun a Liebe* (*Enemies: A Love Story*) Steiner, Jean François: *Treblinka*	The documentation center of the Bergen-Belsen Memorial Museum opens in Germany. Raoul Wallenberg, a Swedish diplomat who saved the lives of some 15,000 Jews during World War II, is honored as one of the Righteous among the Nations by Yad Vashem. Albert Speer, former minister of war production for Nazi Germany, and Baldur von Schirach, the former head of Hitler Youth, are released from Spandau Prison.

DATE	AUTHOR AND TITLE	EVENT
1967	Borowski, Tadeusz: *This Way for the Gas, Ladies and Gentlemen* Bryks, Rachmil: *Geto fabrik 76* (*Ghetto Factory 76*) Birenbaum, Halina: *Nadzieja umiera ostatnia* (*Hope Is the Last to Die*) Gary, Romain: *La Danse de Gengis Cohn* (*The Dance of Genghis Cohn*) Kovner, Abba: *Ahoti ketanah* (*My Little Sister*) Kuper, Jack: *Child of the Holocaust* Potok, Chaim: *The Chosen* Singer, Isaac Bashevis: ''The Lecture'' Zeitlin, Aaron: *Lieder fun churban 'on lieder fun gloybin*	Franz Stangl, former commandant of the Sobidor death camp, who oversaw the gassing of more than 100,000 people in his first two months there, is taken to Germany to stand trial for war crimes. A memorial is built at Birkenau.
1968	Ben-Amotz, Dahn: *Lizkor lishcoah* (*To Remember, to Forget*) Czerniaków, Adam: *The Warsaw Diary of Adam Czerniaków* Hill, Geoffrey: ''September Song'' Kosinski, Jerzy: *Steps* Modiano, Patrick: *Le Place de l'étoile* Rudashevski, Yitskhok: *Yomano shel na'ar mi-Vilnah: Yuni 1941–April 1943* (*The Diary of the Vilna Ghetto*) Singer, Isaac Bashevis: ''The Letter Writer''	
1969	Grynberg, Henryk: *Zwyciestow* (*The Victory*) Kaniuk, Yoram: *Adam ben kelev* (*Adam Resurrected*) Becker, Jurek: *Jakob der Lügner* (*Jacob the Liar*) Lind, Jakov: *Counting My Steps: An Autobiography* Modiano, Patrick: *La Ronde de nuit* (*Night Rounds*)	The text of the German penal code that declared male homosexuality to be illegal and that allowed the Nazi mistreatment of homosexuals is eliminated. A memorial is dedicated at Majdanek, where some 350,000 prisoners were murdered during World War II.
1970	Bellow, Saul: *Mr. Sammler's Planet* Delbo, Charlotte: *Auschwitz et après* (*Auschwitz and After*) Kovner, Abba: *Hupah ba-midbar* (*A Canopy in the Desert*) Wiesenthal, Simon: *Die Sonnenblume: Von Schuld und Vergebung* (*The Sunflower*)	Leonid Brezhnev, the leader of the Soviet Union, orders the exhumation and incineration of Hitler's body. Speer publishes a memoir. Stangl is found guilty of war crimes and sentenced to life in prison.
1971	Hilsenrath, Edgar: *The Nazi and the Barber* Bachmann, Ingeborg: *Malina* Wojdowski, Bogdan: *Chleb rzucony umarlym* (*Bread for the Departed*)	Beate and Serge Klarsfeld discover former SS officer Klaus Barbie in La Paz, Bolivia. He is not extradited until 1983.
1972	Frisch, Max (Rudolph): *Nun singen sie wieder: Versuch eines Requiems* (*Now They Sing Again: Attempt of a Requiem*) Agnon, S. Y.: ''The Sign'' Grass, Günter: *Aus dem Tagebuch einer Schnecke* (*From the Diary of a Snail*) Modiano, Patrick: *Les Boulevards de ceinture* (*Ring Roads*) Potok, Chaim: *My Name Is Asher Lev* Sutzkever, Abraham: *Griner akvarium* (*Green Aquarium*)	Massuah, the Institute for the Study of the Holocaust, is established in Israel.
1973	Cohen, Arthur A.: *In the Days of Simon Stern* Oz, Amos: *La-ga'at ba-mayim, la-ga'at ba-ruah* (*Touch the Water, Touch the Wind*)	As of 1973, only a few American universities and colleges offer courses on Holocaust studies.

DATE	AUTHOR AND TITLE	EVENT
1974	Klein, A.M.: *Collected Poems* Morante, Elsa: *La storia: Romanzo* (*History: A Novel*) Tabori, George: *The Cannibals*	
1975	Kertész, Imre: *Sorstalanság* (*Fateless*) Levi, Primo: *Il sistema periodico* (*The Periodic Table*) Appelfeld, Aharon: *Badenheim 'ir nofesh* (*Badenheim 1939*) Niemöller, Martin: *Martin Niemöller: Briefe aus der Gefangenschaft Moabit* (*Exile in the Fatherland: Martin Niemöller's Letters from Moabit Prison*) Pérec, Georges: *W, ou, le souvenir d'enfance* (*W, or the Memory of Childhood*) Reznikoff, Charles: *Holocaust* Sexton, Anne: *The Awful Rowing toward God*	In memory of the Jews who perished at Theresienstadt, the kibbutz Beit Theresienstadt is opened in Israel. The trial of 16 former officials of the Majdanek concentration camp begins in Düsseldorf.
1976	Fénelon, Fania, with Marcelle Routier: *Sursis pour l'orchestre* (*Playing for Time*) Lustig, Arnošt: *Darkness Casts No Shadows*	Former SS Colonel Joachim Peiper is murdered in his home in France.
1977	Eliach, Yaffa, with Uri Assaf: *The Last Jew: A Play in Four Acts* Abish, Walter: ''The English Garden'' Krall, Hanna: *Zdazyc przed Panem Bogiem* (*Shielding the Flame: An Intimate Conversation with Dr. Marek Edelman, the Last Surviving Leader of the Warsaw Ghetto Uprising*) Moczarski, Kazimierz: *Rozmowy z katem* (*The Conversations with an Executioner*) Szlengel, Wladyslaw: *Co czytalem umarlym* (''What I Read to the Dead'')	Construction of the Simon Wiesenthal Center for Holocaust Studies begins in Los Angeles.
1978	Friedländer, Saul: *Quand vient le souvenir* (*When Memory Comes*) Gurdus, Luba Krugman: *The Death Train: Personal Account of a Holocaust Survivor* Korczak, Janusz: *Pamietnik z getta* (*Ghetto Diary*) Leitner, Isabella: *Fragments of Isabella: A Memoir of Auschwitz* Figes, Eva: *Little Eden: A Child at War* Rybakov, Anatoli: *Tiazhelyi pesok* (*Heavy Sand*)	The Anne Frank Center USA opens in New York City with the purpose of educating the public about the Holocaust and the dangers of discrimination and intolerance. Josef Mengele, a doctor who conducted inhumane medical experiments on Jewish prisoners at Auschwitz, dies a free man in South America.
1979	Epstein, Leslie: *King of the Jews: A Novel of the Holocaust* Ficowski, Jerzy: *Odczytanie popiolów* (*A Reading of Ashes*) Hofmann, Gert: *Die Denunziation* (''The Denunciation'') Lustig, Arnošt: *Z deniku sedmnactilete Perly Sch* (*The Unloved*) Arieti, Silvano: *The Parnas: A Scene from the Holocaust* Müller, Filip: *Sonderbehandlung: Drei Jahre in den Krematorien und Gaskammern von Auschwitz* (*Eyewitness Auschwitz: Three Years in the Gas Chambers*) Roth, Philip: *The Ghost Writer* Sherman, Martin: *Bent* Steiner, George: *The Portage to San Cristóbal of A.H.* Styron, William: *Sophie's Choice* Sutzkever, Abraham: *Di ershte nakht in geto* (''The First Night in the Ghetto'')	The miniseries *Holocaust* is broadcast on U.S. television. It is later credited with breaking the silence about the Holocaust in Germany. The Office of Special Investigations is created by the U.S. Department of Justice. Its purpose is to investigate and bring to justice Nazi war criminals living in the United States. Israel implements a Holocaust curriculum to be taught in its schools. More than 200 American universities offer courses in Holocaust studies.

DATE	AUTHOR AND TITLE	EVENT
1980	Bitton-Jackson, Livia: *Elli: Coming of Age in the Holocaust* Abish, Walter: *How German Is It* Grossman, Vasily: *Zhizn' i sud'ba (Life and Fate)* Lewitt, Maria: *Come Spring* Ozick, Cynthia: "The Shawl" Semprun, Jorge: *Quel beau Dimanche (What a Beautiful Sunday!)*	A law establishing the United States Holocaust Memorial Council, designed to oversee the creation of the United States Holocaust Memorial Museum, is passed by Congress.
1981	Hillesum, Etty: *Het vestoorde leven: Dagboek van Etty Hillesum, 1941–1943 (An Interrupted Life: The Diaries of Etty Hillesum, 1941–43)* Orlev, Uri: *Ha-I bi-rehov ha-tsiporim (The Island on Bird Street)* Hart (Moxon), Kitty: *Return to Auschwitz: The Remarkable Story of a Girl Who Survived the Holocaust* Thomas, D.M.: *The White Hotel*	The Holocaust Memorial Center, the first establishment of its kind in the United States, breaks ground in Michigan. It opens to the public in 1984. A national registry of Holocaust survivors who immigrated to the United States is established.
1982	Dorian, Emil: *The Quality of Witness: A Romanian Diary, 1937–1944 (Jurnal din vremur de prigoanæa)* Eliach, Yaffa: *Hasidic Tales of the Holocaust* Appelfeld, Aharon: *Ha 'pisgah (The Retreat)* Grade, Chaim: "Mayn krig mit Hersh Rasseyner" ("My Quarrel with Hersh Rasseyner") Hillesum, Etty: *Het denkende hart van de barak: Brieven van Etty Hillesum (Letters from Westerbork)* Keneally, Thomas: *Schindler's List (Schindler's Ark)* Levi, Primo: *Se non ora, quando? (If Not Now, When?)*	*Sophie's Choice,* a film version of the novel by William Styron, opens to critical acclaim. Babi Yar Park, a memorial to those who were killed at Babi Yar during World War II, is dedicated in Denver, Colorado.
1983	Appelfeld, Aharon: *Ketonet veha-pasim (Tzili, the Story of a Life)* Fink, Ida: *Skrawek czasu (A Scrap of Time)* Fried, Erich: *Trost und Angst: Erzählungen über Juden und Nazis* ("Consolation and Anxiety: Stories about Jews and Nazis") Kipphardt, Heinar: *Bruder Eichmann* Ozick, Cynthia: "Rosa" Sobol, Joshua: *Geto (Ghetto)*	
1984	Améry, Jean: *Radical Humanism* Tabori, George: *Jubiläum* ("Jubilee") Tec, Nechama: *Dry Tears: The Story of a Lost Childhood* Edvardson, Cordelia: *Bränt barn söker sig till elden (Burned Child Seeks the Fire)* Heyen, William: *Erika: Poems of the Holocaust* Stiffel, Frank: *The Tale of the Ring: A Kaddish*	The Jewish Holocaust Museum and Research Centre opens in Melbourne, Australia. The United States revokes the citizenship of and deports Arthur Rudolph, an engineer and scientist, when his former Nazi ties are discovered. In a controversial move, a Carmelite convent is established by a group of Roman Catholic nuns near and on the grounds of the former concentration camp at Auschwitz. Many Jews object.
1985	Durlacher, Gerhard: *Strepen aus de hemel: Oorlogsherinneringen (Stripes in the Sky: A Wartime Memoir)* Lanzmann, Claude: *Shoah: An Oral History of the Holocaust* Nomberg-Przytyk, Sara: *Auschwitz: True Tales from a Grotesque Land* Roth, Philip: *Zuckerman Bound: A Trilogy and Epilogue*	Human remains found in Brazil are confirmed to be those of the Nazi doctor Mengele.

DATE	AUTHOR AND TITLE	EVENT
1986	Becker, Jurek: *Bronsteins Kinder* (*Bronstein's Children*) Hofmann, Gert: *Veilchenfeld* Levi, Primo: *I sommersi e i salvati* (*The Drowned and the Saved*) Spiegelman, Art: *Maus—A Survivor's Tale*	Elie Wiesel founds the Elie Wiesel Foundation for Humanity, dedicated to promoting human rights. The former Croatian minister of the interior Andrija Artukovic, who was largely responsible for the deaths of Jews in Croatia during World War II, is found guilty of war crimes and sentenced to death. The government of Australia declares its intent to investigate and prosecute former Nazis residing in the country.
1987	Durlacher, Gerhard: *Drenkeling kinderjaren in het derde rijk* (*Drowning: Growing up in the Third Reich*) Kofman, Sara: *Paroles suffoquées* (*Stifled Words*) Ozick, Cynthia: *The Messiah of Stockholm*	On 4 July Barbie is found guilty of crimes against humanity and is sentenced to life in prison. The exhibition *Topography of Terror: Gestapo, SS and Reich Security Main Office on the "Prinz Albrecht Terrain"* opens in celebration of Berlin's 750th anniversary. John Demjanjuk, accused of being the man known as "Ivan the Terrible" in the Treblinka concentration camp, is tried in Israel. He is found guilty of war crimes. The Canadian government enables the investigation and prosecution of former Nazis living in the country.
1988	Bernhard, Thomas: *Heldenplatz* Lebow, Barbara: *A Shayna Maidel* Appelfeld, Aharon: *Bartfus ben ha-almavet* (*The Immortal Bartfuss*) Lewin, Abraham: *A Cup of Tears: A Diary of the Warsaw Ghetto* Orlev, Uri: *Ha-Ish min ha-tsad ha-aher* (*The Man from the Other Side*) Rymkiewicz, Jaroslaw: *Umschlagplatz* (*Final Station: Umschlagplatz*) Tory, Avraham: *Geto yom-yom: Yoman u-mismakhim mi-Geto Kovnah* (*Surviving the Holocaust: The Kovno Ghetto Diary*)	The U.S. Office of Special Investigations continues to research former Nazis living in the United States. Some 600 active files are under investigation. The *Monument against War and Fascism,* a five-piece sculpture installation, is erected in Vienna.
1989	Rich, Adrienne: "Eastern War Time" Nir, Yehuda: *The Lost Childhood: A Memoir* Sobol, Joshua: *Adam* Wiesel, Elie: *L'Oublie* (*The Forgotten*)	The Terezín Memorial is founded on the site of the Theresienstadt ghetto and camp in the Czech Republic.
1990	Fink, Ida: *Podróz* (*The Journey*) Kertész, Imre: *Kaddis a meg nem született gyermekért* (*Kaddish for a Child Not Born*) Klepfisz, Irena: "*Di rayze aheym*/The journey home" Kushner, Tony: *A Bright Room Called Day* Yehoshua, A.B.: *Mar Maniy* (*Mr. Mani*) Zuckerman, Yitzhak (Antek): *Sheva' ha-shanim ha-hen: 1939–1946* (*A Surplus of Memory: Chronicle of the Warsaw Ghetto Uprising*)	The reunification of East and West Germany takes place.
1991	Friedman, Carl: *Tralievader* (*Nightfather*) Menasse, Robert: *Selige Zeiten, brüchige Welt* (*Wings of Stone*) Begley, Louis: *Wartime Lies* Pagis, Dan: *Kol ha-shirim* Sobol, Joshua: *Underground* Zable, Arnold: *Jewels and Ashes*	Kiev, Ukraine, decrees 29 September a memorial day to honor the victims of Babi Yar. Descendants of the Shoah, an organization that assists the children of Holocaust survivors, is established in Melbourne, Australia.

DATE	AUTHOR AND TITLE	EVENT
1992	Glazar, Richard: *Die Falle mit dem grünen Zaun: Überleben in Treblinka* (*Trap with a Green Fence: Survival in Treblinka*) Klüger, Ruth: *weiter leben: Eine Jugend* (*Still Alive: A Holocaust Girlhood Remembered*) Grossman, David: *'Ayen 'erekh-ahavah* (*See Under: Love*) Schindel, Robert: *Gebürtig*	The World Jewish Restitution Organization is formed with the purpose of reclaiming assets and property lost during the Holocaust. The Mechelen Museum of Deportation and the Resistance opens in Belgium. Between 1942 and 1944 the town of Mechelen served as the starting point of a deportation route to Auschwitz. The Sydney Jewish Museum opens in Australia.
1993	Friedman, Carl: *Twee koffers vol* (*The Shovel and the Loom*) Kops, Bernard: *Dreams of Anne Frank: A Play for Young People* Roth, Philip: *Operation Shylock* Sebald, W.G.: *Die Ausgewanderten* (*The Emigrants*)	The United States Holocaust Memorial Museum in Washington, D.C., is dedicated on 27 April. Citing a lack of evidence, the Israeli Supreme Court acquits alleged former Nazi Demjanjuk and overturns his death sentence. The Hollywood film *Schindler's List* is released. The award-winning film succeeds in increasing the public's awareness of the atrocities of the Holocaust. The Roman Catholic nuns who had resided in the Carmelite convent on the Auschwitz grounds relocate as part of an agreement with Jewish organizations.
1994	Kofman, Sara: *Rue Ordener, Rue Labat* Tabori, George: *Mutters Courage* (''My Mother's Courage'') Varga, Susan: *Heddy and Me* Semprun, Jorge: *L'Ecriture ou la vie* (*Literature or Life*)	The Shoah Foundation, dedicated to assembling videotaped testimonies of Holocaust survivors and observers, is established in Los Angeles. The Papal Concert to Commemorate the Holocaust, hosted by Pope John Paul II, marks the Vatican's first attempt to memorialize the Holocaust and the deaths of Jews by Nazi Germany. Britain's war crimes investigation force ceases operation. For the first time France acknowledges the deportation of 76,000 Jews during World War II.
1995	Biderman, Abraham: *The World of My Past* Klemperer, Victor: *Ich will Zeugnis ablegen bis zum letzten: Tagebücher 1933–1941,* and *Tagebücher 1942–1945* (*I Will Bear Witness: A Diary of the Nazi Years*) Schlink, Bernhard: *Der Vorleser* (*The Reader*) Verstandig, Mark: *I Rest My Case* Wilkomirski, Binjamin: *Bruchstücke: Aus einer Kindheit 1939–1948* (*Fragments: Memories of a Wartime Childhood*)	The Topography of Terror Foundation is established in Berlin. The foundation provides historical information about National Socialism (Nazism). The I.G. Farben subsidiary Bayer issues an apology for its participation in the exploitation of Jewish laborers during World War II. The controversial exhibition *Vernichtungskrieg: Verbrechen der Wehrmacht, 1941–1944* (''War of Annihilation: Crimes of the Wehrmacht, 1941–1944'') is shown in German and Austrian institutions. The exhibition provides evidence that the Wehrmacht, the German army during World War II, was involved in the killing of Jews. The C.A.N.D.L.E.S. Holocaust Museum, dedicated to educating the public about the Holocaust and its child survivors, opens in Indiana.
1996	Fink, Ida: *Slady* (*Traces*) Pinter, Harold: *Ashes to Ashes* Sebastian, Mihail: *Jurnal: 1935–1944* (*Journal 1935–1944: The Fascist Years*)	The Swiss Bankers Association completes an investigation of Holocaust-era accounts and determines that approximately $32 million remained unclaimed. Some Jewish organizations believe the amount to be inaccurate. As a result, the Volcker Commission is established by the Swiss Bankers Association and Jewish leaders to investigate both the unclaimed assets of Holocaust victims

DATE	AUTHOR AND TITLE	EVENT
		and charges that assets of Jews were stolen by Nazis and deposited in Swiss banks. Evidence surfaces that former Argentine President Juan Perón and his wife, Eva, had facilitated the clandestine immigration of former Nazis into Argentina.
1997	Baker, Mark: *The Fiftieth Gate: A Journey through Memory* Blatt, Thomas Toivi: *From the Ashes of Sobidor: A Story of Survival* Brett, Lily: *In Full View* Epstein, Helen: *Where She Came From: A Daughter's Search for Her Mother's History* Stollman, Aryeh Lev: *The Far Euphrates*	Riva Shefer, a 75-year-old Latvian Jew who survived a Nazi labor camp, becomes the first recipient of money from a $200 million Swiss fund established to aid Holocaust survivors. Germany offers to pay one-time reparations to Holocaust survivors living in eastern Europe. The World Jewish Congress turns down the offer, requesting instead monthly payments. Evidence arises that in 1951 National City, a U.S. bank, knowingly took looted Nazi gold worth approximately $30 million as collateral for a loan to Spain. The Museum of Jewish Heritage opens in New York City. A memorial museum opens on the site of a former Nazi death camp at Sachsenhausen, Germany. More than 1,600 American universities offer courses on the Holocaust.
1998	Gay, Peter: *My German Question: Growing up in Nazi Berlin* Hill, Geoffrey: *The Triumph of Love* Roubickova, Eva: *We're Alive and Life Goes On: A Theresienstadt Diary*	The Vatican issues a document stating that Pope Pius XII, leader of the Roman Catholic Church during the Holocaust, did all he could to save Jews. Many historians disagree. Maurice Papon, a former official of the Vichy government, is sentenced to 10 years in prison for helping the Germans illegally arrest and deport French Jews. In July the German automaker Volkswagen agrees to pay reparations to those who worked as slave laborers in its factories during the war. UBS and Crédit Suisse agree to pay more than $1.25 billion in reparations to Holocaust survivors and their families in order to end assertions that Swiss banks had knowingly withheld millions of dollars since World War II. In August class-action suits are filed against German and Austrian manufacturers, including Daimler-Benz, BMW, Volkswagen, Audi, Siemens, and Krupp, that used and benefitted from slave labor supplied by the Nazis during World War II.
1999	Epstein, Leslie: *Ice Fire Water: A Leib Goldkorn Cocktail* Molodowsky, Kadya: *Paper Bridges: Selected Poems*	Dinko Sakic, the last commandant of a World War II concentration camp known to be living, is tried for war crimes. The $1.7 billion Remembrance, Responsibility and the Future Fund is established by 12 German corporations to compensate slave laborers whose work benefitted the companies during World War II. The Volcker Commission completes its investigation and determines that 54,000 Swiss bank accounts belonged to Holocaust victims.
2000	Doctorow, E.L.: *City of God*	During the year Germany sets aside $5 billion to provide compensation to slave laborers forced to work for the

DATE	AUTHOR AND TITLE	EVENT
		Nazis during World War II. The money is contributed equally by the German government and German industry. Pope John Paul II makes a historic visit to Israel in March and tours Yad Vashem, the Israeli Holocaust memorial.
2001	Sebald, W.G.: *Austerlitz*	After many years of planning, work begins on a Holocaust memorial in Berlin.

NATIONALITY INDEX

American

Walter Abish
Silvano Arieti
Sholem Asch
Louis Begley
Saul Bellow
Mary Berg
Bruno Bettelheim
Livia E. Bitton-Jackson
Thomas "Toivi" Blatt
Lily Brett
Rachmil Bryks
Arthur A. Cohen
E. L. Doctorow
Alexander Donat
Yaffa Eliach
Helen Epstein
Leslie Epstein
Bertha Ferderber-Salz
Peter Gay
Jacob Glatstein
Frances Goodrich
Luba Gurdus
Albert Hackett
John Hersey
William Heyen
Edgar Hilsenrath
Gerda Weissmann Klein
Irena Klepfisz
Ruth Klüger
Jerzy Kosinski
Tony Kushner
Barbara Lebow
Isabella Leitner
Olga Lengyel
Denise Levertov
Meyer Levin
Arnošt Lustig
Bernard Malamud
Vladka Meed
Arthur Miller
Czesław Miłosz
Kadya Molodowsky
Yehuda Nir
Cynthia Ozick
Gisella Perl
Chaim Potok
Erich Maria Remarque
Charles Reznikoff
Adrienne Rich
Philip Roth
Anne Sexton
Martin Sherman
Isaac Bashevis Singer
Art Spiegelman
George A. Steiner

Frank Stiffel
Aryeh Lev Stollman
William Styron
Nechama Tec
Leon Uris
Edward Lewis Wallant
Elie Wiesel
Aaron Zeitlin

Argentine

Jorge Luis Borges

Australian

Mark Baker
Abraham Biderman
Thomas Keneally
Maria Lewitt
Susan Varga
Mark Verstandig
Arnold Zable

Austrian

Ilse Aichinger
Jean Améry
Ingeborg Bachmann
Thomas Bernhard
Viktor E. Frankl
Eugen Kogon
Jakov Lind
Robert Menasse
Robert Schindel
Simon Wiesenthal

Austro-Hungarian

Emmanuel Ringelblum

British

Eva Figes
Erich Fried
Geoffrey Hill
Bernard Kops
Harold Pinter
W. G. Sebald
Janusz Nel Siedlecki
George Tabori
D. M. Thomas
Rudolf Vrba
Stefan Zweig

Canadian

A. M. Klein
Jack Kuper
Mordecai Richler

Czech

Ladislav Fuks

Jiří Weil

Czechoslovakian
Josef Bor
Filip Müller
Eva Mändlová Roubíčková

Dutch
Elie Aron Cohen
Gerhard Durlacher
Moshe Flinker
Carl Friedman
Etty Hillesum
Marga Minco
Jacques Presser

French
Robert Antelme
Albert Camus
Charlotte Delbo
Fania Fénelon
Romain Gary
Pierre Gascar
Edmond Jabès
Sarah Kofman
Claude Lanzmann
Patrick Modiano
Georges Pérec
Piotr Rawicz
David Rousset
Jean-Paul Sartre
André Schwarz-Bart
Jean-François Steiner
Germaine Tillion

German
Bruno Apitz
Jurek Becker
Heinrich Böll
Bertolt Brecht
Lion Feuchtwanger
Anne Frank
Günter Grass
Wolfgang Hildesheimer
Rolf Hochhuth
Gert Hofmann
Heinar Kipphardt
Victor Klemperer
Wolfgang Koeppen
Gertrud Kolmar
Martin Niemöller
Bernhard Schlink
Erwin Sylvanus
Ernst Wiechert

Hungarian
Hans Habe
Eugene Heimler
Eva Heyman
Imre Kertész

Miklós Radnóti

Israeli
S. Y. Agnon
Yehuda Amichai
Aharon Appelfeld
Dahn Ben-Amotz
Halina Birenbaum
Cordelia Edvardson
Ida Fink
Saul Friedländer
Haim Gouri
David Grossman
Ka-Tzetnik 135633
Yoram Kaniuk
Abba Kovner
Itzik Manger
Aharon Megged
Uri Orlev
Amos Oz
Dan Pagis
Hannah Senesh
Joshua Sobol
Abraham Sutzkever
Avraham Tory
A. B. Yehoshua
Yitzhak ''Antek'' Zuckerman

Italian
Giorgio Bassani
Edith Bruck
Italo Calvino
Natalia Ginzburg
Primo Levi
Liana Millu
Elsa Morante
Giuliana Tedeschi

Polish
Tadeusz Borowski
Adam Czerniaków
Marek Edelman
Jerzy Ficowski
Henryk Grynberg
Kitty Hart
Chaim A. Kaplan
Yitzhak Katzenelson
Janusz Korczak
Hanna Krall
Herman Kruk
Abraham Lewin
Kazimierz Moczarski
Sara Nomberg-Przytyk
Krystyn Olszewski
Tadeusz Różewicz
Adolf Rudnicki
Jaroslaw Rymkiewicz
Dawid Sierakowiak
Wladyslaw Szlengel
Wladyslaw Szpilman

Wisława Szymborska
Bogdan Wojdowski

Romanian
Paul Celan
Emil Dorian
Miklos Nyiszli
Mihail Sebastian

Russian
Hirsh Glik
Chaim Grade
Vasily Grossman
Anatoli Kuznetsov
Yitskhok Rudashevski
Anatolii Rybakov
Manès Sperber
Yevgeny Yevtushenko

Spanish
Jorge Semprun

Swedish
Nelly Sachs
Peter Weiss

Swiss
Friedrich Dürrenmatt
Max Frisch
Richard Glazar
Binjamin Wilkomirski

Tunisian
Albert Memmi

Ukrainian
Uri Zvi Greenberg

TITLE INDEX

25. Stunde (Tabori) 1977
43 Mercy Street (Sexton) 1969
50 opowiadan (Rudnicki) 1966
''53 jours'' (Pérec) 1989
65 Poems (Celan) 1985
99: The New Meaning (Abish) 1990

A. Sutzkever: Selected Poetry and Prose (Sutzkever) 1991
A. M. Klein: Complete Poems (A. Klein) N.d.
A. M. Klein: Literary Essays and Reviews (A. Klein) 1987
A. M. Klein: Short Stories (A. Klein) 1983
A nyomkereso (Kertész) 1977
Abendstunde im Spätherbst (Dürrenmatt) 1959
Abenteur des Ruben Jablonski: Ein autobiographischer Roman
    (Hilsenrath) 1997
Aber auch diese Sonne ist heimatlos: Schwedische Lyric der Gegenwart
    (Sachs) 1957
Aberrations: Le Devenir-femme d'Auguste Comte (Kofman) 1978
Abishag Writes a Letter Home (Manger) 1981
About Schmidt (Begley) 1996
Abraham and the Contemporary Mind (Arieti) 1981
Abruzzo forte e gentile: Impressioni d'occhio e di cuore (Levi) 1976
Abschied von den Eltern (Weiss) 1961
Abschied von Rilke (Zweig) 1927
Absent without Leave and Other Stories (Böll) 1965
Abwägung im Verfassungsrecht (Schlink) 1976
Accident (Wiesel) 1961
Accidentul (Sebastian) 1968
Acc Holc, Midge Detective (Spiegelman) 1974
Ach, Butt, dein Mächen geht böse aus: Gedichte und Radierungen
    (Grass) 1983
Ach chadash l'gamrei (D. Grossman) 1986
Achshav ba-ra'ash (Amichai) 1969
Achshav uve-yamim ha-aharim (Amichai) 1955
Achterloo (Dürrenmatt) 1983
Achtung, die Schweiz: Ein Gespräch über unsere Lage und ein
    Vorschlag zur Tat (Frisch) 1956
Achziv, Keisaria ve-ahava ahat achziv/Akhziv Cesarea and One Love
    (Amichai) 1996
Acrobats (Richler) 1954
Acrophile (Kaniuk) 1961
Acts of Theft (A. Cohen) 1980
Actual (Bellow) 1997
Actuelles 1–3: Chroniques 1944–1948, Chroniques 1948–1953,
    Chronique algérienne 1939–1958 (Camus) 1950–58
'Ad 'alot ha-shahar (Gouri) 1950
'Ad henah (Agnon) 1952
Ad horef 1974: Mivhar (selections) (Yehoshua) 1975
'Ad kav nesher, 1949–1975 (Gouri) 1975
'Ad-lo-or: Po'emah partizanit (Kovner) 1947
'Ad mahar (Orlev) 1958
'Ad mavet (Oz) 1971
Ad nefesh (Appelfeld) 1994
Ad ora incerta (Levi) 1984
'Ad she-ya'aleh 'amud ha-shahar (Appelfeld) 1995
Adam (Sobol) 1989

Adam ben kelev (Kaniuk) 1969
Adam Resurrected (Kaniuk) 1969
Adieu Gary Cooper (Gary) 1969
'Adif melafefon 'al ha-gever mi-pene she (Ben-Amotz) 1985
Admat ha-hol: Po'emah (Kovner) 1961
Admirable Woman (A. Cohen) 1983
Adne ha-nahar (Appelfeld) 1971
Adolf Wilbrandt, eine Studie über seine Werke (Klemperer) 1907
Adrogué (Borges) 1977
Adventures of Augie March (Bellow) 1953
Adventures of Homer McGundy (Lebow) 1985
Aely (Jabès) 1972
Afar ve-teshukah (Kaniuk) 1975
Afn barg (Molodowsky) 1938
Afrique bascule vers l'avenir; L'Algerie en 1957 et autres textes
    (Tillion) 1960
After Babel: Aspects of Language and Translation (G. Steiner) 1975
After the Fall (Miller) 1964
After the Smoke Cleared (Kuper) 1994
After the War: Poems (Brett) 1990
Aftermath (Habe) 1947
Agadat ha-sofer (Agnon) 1929
Against Silence: The Voice and Vision of Elie Wiesel (Wiesel) 1985
Agar (Memmi) 1955
Age of Enlightenment (Gay) 1966
Agnon's Aleph Bet: Poems (Agnon) 1998
Agony (Spiegelman) 1987
Ah boger (Orlev) 1983
Ahad 'asar sipure ahavah: Sheloshim shanah la 'aliyat 11 ha yishuvim
    ba-Negev (Gouri) 1976
Ahashverosh melekh tipesh: Komedyah be-haruzim be-ma'arakhah
    ahat (Katzenelson) 1920
Ahavah bi-lehavot (Ka-Tzetnik 135633) 1976
Ahavat David (Kaniuk) 1990
Ahavat neurim (Megged) 1980
Ahoti ketanah (Kovner) 1967
Airone (Bassani) 1968
Aïssé: Récit (Gascar) 1998
Akt przerwany (Różewicz) 1964
Aktion ''Djungel'': Bericht aus Malaya (Hildesheimer) 1971
'Al 'akhbarim va-anashim (Ben-Amotz) 1990
'Al Berl Kazenelson (Agnon) 1944
Al etzim ve-avanim (Megged) 1973
'Al ha-gesher ha-tsar: masot be-'al peh (essays) (Kovner) 1981
'Al Kapot ha-Man'ul (Agnon) 1922
Al kol hapesha'im (Appelfeld) 1989
'Al Meshulam Tokhner zal: Devarim le-zikhro (Agnon) 1966
'Al nahares Bovel: Biblishe tragedye in fir aktn (Katzenelson) 1967
Al sod hatum: Le-toldot ha-hidah ha-'Ivrit be-Italyah uve-Holand
    (Pagis) 1986
Al tagidi lailah (Oz) 1994
'Al tsad sem'ol (Orlev) 1985
'Al yahase ha-gomlin ben ha-medinah la-golah: (Hartsa'at oreah ba-
    hug li-fe'ile ha-tefutsot) (Zeitlin) 1966
Alan Turing: Erzählung (Hochhuth) 1987
Alba ai vetri: Poesie 1942–1950 (Bassani) 1963

Badener Lehrstück vom Einverständnis (Brecht) 1929

Badenheim 1939 (Appelfeld) 1975

Badenheim 'ir nofesh (Appelfeld) 1975

Ba'et uve'onah achat (Appelfeld) 1985

Bahnhof von Zimpren (Böll) 1959

Bahurim: komedye, eyn akt (Katzenelson) 1900

Baie perdue (Sperber) 1952

Bajedy z augustowskich lasów (Ficowski) 1998

Baket (Rymkiewicz) 1989

Ballad of the Man Who Reached from Grey to Blue (Manger) 1981

Ballad of the Old Soldier (Manger) 1981

Ballade vom Wiener Schnitze (Tabori) 1996

Ballads of Itzik Manger (Manger) 1978

Ballerina (Grass) 1963

Balzac (Zweig) 1946

Bamartef (Sobol) 1990

Banger (Figes) 1968

Bankructwo malego dzeka; Powiesc (Korczak) 1924

Barbarie de l'ignorance: Juste l'ombre d'un certain ennui, with Antoine Spire (G. Steiner) 1998

Bariona; ou, Le Fils du tonnerre (Sartre) 1940

Barney's Version (Richler) 1997

Barre de corail: Suivi de Les aveugles de Saint-Xavier (Gascar) 1958

Barricades in West Hampstead (Kops) 1988

Bartfus ben ha-almavet (Appelfeld) 1988

Bartleby (Borges) 1944

Basement (Pinter) 1968

Bâtir au quotidien (Jabès) 1997

Batterers (Levertov) 1996

Battle Cry (Uris) 1953

Baudelaire (Sartre) 1947

Baym leyenen penimer (Sutzkever) 1993

Baym toyer (Molodowsky) 1967

Be-komat ha-karka (Appelfeld) 1968

Be-merhav shtei tikvot (Amichai) 1958

Be-or ha-tekhelet ha-'azah: ma'amarim u-reshimot (Oz) 1979

Be-reshit (Megged) 1965

Be-shuvah ve-nahat: Sipure 'agadot (Agnon) 1935

Be-sod yesharim (Agnon) 1921

Be-vet ha-mishneh: Mahazeh (Katzenelson) 1919

Beaux présents, belles absentes (Pérec) 1994

Beda sie bili (Różewicz) 1950

Bedingungen der Humanität (Kogon) 1998

Befreiung von der Flucht (Fried) 1968

Begegnung im Balkanexpress (Hildesheimer) 1956

Begegnungen mit Menschen, Buchern, Stadten (Zweig) 1937

Beginning with My Streets: Essays and Recollections (Miłosz) 1992

Beginnings in Jewish Philosophy (Levin) 1971

Begrabene Leuchter (Zweig) 1936

Beine der grösseren Lügen (Fried) 1969

Being There (Kosinski) 1971

Beit ha-bubot (Ka-Tzetnik 135633) 1953

Bekumat hakark'a (Appelfeld) 1968

Bell for Adano (Hersey) 1944

Bellarosa Connection (Bellow) 1989

Belles Lettres (Delbo) 1961

Belling the Cat: Essays, Reports, and Opinions (Richler) 1998

Bellisime avventure di Cateri dalla trecciolina (Morante) 1941

Bells in Winter (Miłosz) 1978

Belorusskaia krovinka: Otryvok iz poemy, stikhi (Yevtushenko) 1990

Ben emunah le-'omanut: Kerekh rishon Mi-dor le-dor: Kerekh sheni Be-'ohole sifrut (Zeitlin) 1980

Ben ha-esh veha-yesha': Po'emah dramatit (Zeitlin) 1957

Beneath the Stone (Tabori) 1944

Bent (Sherman) 1979

Berichte zur Gesinnungslage der Nation (Böll) 1975

Beritten hin und zuruck (Grass) 1959

Berlin-Jewish Spirit, A Dogma in Search of Some Doubts (Gay) 1972

Berliner Antigone: Prosa und Verse (Hochhuth) 1975

Bertolt Brecht, Gesammelte Werke (Brecht) 1971–83

Bertolt Brecht in Selbstzeugnissen und Bilddokumenten (Brecht) 1959

Bertolt Brecht Journals (Brecht) 1993

Berühmten (Bernhard) 1976

Beschreibung des Unglücks: Zur Österreichischen Literatur von Stifter bis Handke (Sebald) 1985

Bessere Welt (Lind) 1966

Besuch der alten Dame (Dürrenmatt) 1956

Besuch um Pfarrhaus: Ein Horspiel, Drei Dialoge (Aichinger) 1961

Bêtes, suivi de le temps des morts (Gascar) 1953

Beton (Bernhard) 1982

Betrachtungen über das Feigenblatt: Ein Handbuch für Verliebte und Verrückte (Tabori) 1991

Betrachtungen über Mozart (Hildesheimer) 1963

Betrayal (Pinter) 1978

Bettany's Book (Keneally) 1998

Bettler oder der tote Hund (Brecht) 1966

Beunruhigungen (Fried) 1984

Beyond Despair: Three Lectures and a Conversation with Philip Roth (Appelfeld) 1994

Beyond Lost Dreams (Siedlecki) 1994

Beyond Sambation: Selected Essays and Editorials, 1928–1955 (A. Klein) 1983

Beyt Kaplan (Sobol) 1978–79

Bi-gevulot Lita, po'emah (Katzenelson) 1908

Bi-levav yamim (Agnon) 1935

Bi-reshut ha-rabim uvi-reshut ha-yahid: Aharon Tseytlin ve-sifrut Yidish: Pirke mavo ve-igrot mu'arot be-livui te'udot le-toldot tarbut Yidish be-Polin ben shete milhamot ha-'olam (Zeitlin) 2000

Biale malzenstwo (Różewicz) 1975

Biale mtilzenstwo i inne utwory sceniczne (Różewicz) 1975

Biblical Names of Literary Jewesses (Bitton-Jackson) 1973

Biblioteca personal: Prólogos (Borges) 1988

Biedermann and the Fire Raisers: A Morality without a Moral (Frisch) 1958

Big As Life (Doctorow) 1966

Big Lie: A True Story (Leitner) 1992

Bilanz (Böll) 1961

Bild-Bonn-Boenish (Böll) 1985

Bild des Sisyphos (Dürrenmatt) 1952

Bilder un humoresken (Asch) 1925

Bile brizy na podzim (Lustig) 1966

Billard um Halbzehn (Böll) 1959

Billigesser (Bernhard) 1980

Billy Bathgate (Doctorow) 1989

Bin; oder, Die Reise nach Peking (Frisch) 1945

Biografie: Ein Spiel (Frisch) 1968

Biosphärenklänge: E. Hörspiel (Hildesheimer) 1977

Birth of the Age of Women (Rich) 1991

Birthday Party: A Play in Three Acts (Pinter) 1958

Birthstone (Thomas) 1980

Furcht und Elend des Dritten Reiches (Brecht) 1938
Fürsorgliche Belagerung (Böll) 1979
Future Is Ours, Comrade: Conversations with the Russians
   (Kosinski) 1960

Ga'aguim le-Olga (Megged) 1994
Gadarene Club (Figes) 1961
Galazka z drzewa slonca (Ficowski) 1961
Gályanapló (Kertész) 1992
Gam ha-egrof haia pa'am yad ptuha ve-etzbaot (Amichai) 1990
Gambling in Sweden: A Sociological Study (Tec) 1962
Gan Riki: Mahazeh bi-shete ma 'arakhot (D. Grossman) 1988
Gan-yeladim: Kovets shalem shel shirim frebeliyim ve-shirei-'am le-
   mishak u- lesha'ashu'im (Katzenelson) 1920
Ganovenfresse: Zwei Erzählungen (Kipphardt) 1966
Garden of the Finzi-Contini (Bassani) 1962
Gascogne (Gascar) 1998
Gasp (Gary) 1973
Gates of November: Chronicles of the Slepak Family (Potok) 1996
Gates of the Forest (Wiesel) 1964
Gathering Evidence: A Memoir (Bernhard) 1983
Gaystike erd (Sutzkever) 1961
Gdzie wschodzi slonce i kedy zapada (Miłosz) 1974
Gdziekolwiek ziemia (Borowski) 1942
Gebärde; Der Fremde (Wiechert) 1947
Geburt der Gegenwart: Gestalten und Gestaltungen der westlichen
   Zivilisation seit Kriegsende (Améry) 1961
Gebürtig (Schindel) 1992
Gedanken in und an Deutschland: Essays und Reden (Fried) 1988
Gedenklider (Glatstein) 1943
Gedichte aus dem Nachlass, 1913–1956 (Brecht) 1982
Gedichte für Städtebewohner (Brecht) 1980
Gefahren von falschen Brüdern: Politische Schriften (Böll) 1980
Gegen die verstreichende Zeit: Reden, Aufsätze, und Gespräche,
   1989–1991 (Grass) 1991
Gegengift (Fried) 1974
Geheimnis der Ottomane: Ein pornographisches Werk
   (Hildesheimer) 1964
Geheimnis des künstlerischen Schaffens (Zweig) 1981
Gehen (Bernhard) 1971
Geheymshtot (Sutzkever) 1948
Gehilfe (Böll) 1960
Geier sind pünktliche Tiere (Schindel) 1987
Geisel (Böll) 1958
Geist und Ungeist in Wien (Sperber) 1978
Gemeiner Kerl: Geschichten (Brecht) 1978
George Steiner: A Reader (G. Steiner) 1984
Georges Perec: Les Choses, espèces d'espaces: Résumé analytique,
   commentaire critique, documents complémentaires (Pérec) 1991
Gérard de Nerval et son temps (Gascar) 1981
Gerhart Hauptmann, der ewige Deutsche (Améry) 1963
German Refugee (Malamud) 1963
Gerushim me'ucharim (Yehoshua) 1982
Gesang vom lusitanischen Popanz (Weiss) 1967
Geschäfte des Herrn Julius Caesar: Romanfragment (Brecht) 1957
Geschichte der französischen Literatur im 19. und 20. Jahrhundert,
   1800–1925 (Klemperer) 1956
Geschichten aus zwölf Jahren (Böll) 1969
Geschichten vom Herrn Keuner (Brecht) 1958
Geschrieben im Grenzdienst 1939 (Frisch) 1940

Geschwister Oppermann (Feuchtwanger) 1933
Gesegnetes Leben: Das Schönste aus den Werken des Dichters
   (Wiechert) 1953
Gesichte der Simone Marcard (Brecht, Feuchtwanger) 1957
Gespräch auf der Probe (Brecht) 1961
Gespräch der drei Gehenden (Weiss) 1962
Gespräch mit Heinz Ludwig Arnold (Dürrenmatt) 1976
Gespräch über Balzacs Pferd (Hofmann) 1988
Gestundete Zeit (Bachmann) 1953
Geteilte Einsamkeit: Der Autor und sein Leser (Sperber) 1985
Geto (Sobol) 1983
Geto yom-yom: Yoman u-mismakhim mi-Geto Kovnah (Tory) 1988
Gewehre der Frau Carrar (Brecht) 1937
Gewiekte wielen: Richard Arkwright (Presser) 1951
Gezang un shpiel: Di ershte shpiel- un lieder-zamlung far Yudishe
   kinder (Katzenelson) 1920
Gezangen fun rekhts tsu links (Glatstein) 1971
Ghetto (Sobol) 1983
Ghetto Diary (Korczak) 1978
Ghetto Factory 76: Chemical Waste Conversion (Bryks) 1967
Ghetto Fights (Edelman) 1945
Ghost Writer (Roth) 1979
Ghosts (Figes) 1988
Gib acht, Genosse Mandelbaum (Hilsenrath) 1979
Gift of Asher Lev (Potok) 1990
Gifts (Singer) 1985
Gilgul: Shirim (Pagis) 1970
Gimpel the Fool and Other Stories (Singer) 1957
Giornata d'uno scrutatore (Calvino) 1963
Girls of Toledo (Sobol) 1992
Giv 'at ha-hol (Agnon) 1919
Gleisdreieck (Grass) 1960
Gli amori difficili (Calvino) 1970
Gli occhiali d'oro (Bassani) 1958
Gli ultimi anni di Clelia Trotti (Bassani) 1955
Gloire à nos illustres pionniers (Gary) 1962
Glos anonima (Różewicz) 1961
Glottal Stop: 101 Poems (Celan) 2000
Glück (Hofmann) 1992
Glück auf (V. Grossman) 1934
Glück: Eine Erzählung (Frisch) 1971
Glühende Rätsel (Sachs) 1964
God and the Story of Judaism (Levin) 1962
God in Ruins: A Novel (Uris) 1999
Godless Jew: Freud, Atheism, and the Making of Psychoanalysis
   (Gay) 1987
God's Grace (Malamud) 1982
Gody voiny (V. Grossman) 1946
Goethes Gedichte: Eine Auswahl (Zweig) 1927
Gog and Magog Show (Sobol) 1977
Going To and Fro and Walking Up and Down (Reznikoff) 1941
Goldberg-Variationen (Tabori) 1991
Golden Cage (Levin) 1959
Golden Egg (Levin) 1957
Golden Mountain (Levin) 1932
Golden Years (Miller) 1990
Goldkorn Tales (L. Epstein) 1985
Goldmäulchen (Grass) 1963
Golem (Singer) 1982

Intervista: Commedia in tre atti (Ginzburg) 1989
Intervista Aziendale, with Carlo Quartucci (Levi) 1968
Intîlniri cu teatrul (Sebastian) 1969
Into the Valley: A Skirmish of the Marines (Hersey) 1943
Intrapsychic Self; Feeling, Cognition, and Creativity in Health and Mental Illness (Arieti) 1967
Introducción a la literatura inglesa (Borges) 1965
Introducción a la literatura nortamericana (Borges) 1967
Inventor (Lind) 1987
Investigation (Weiss) 1965
Invisible Threads (Thomas, Yevtushenko) 1981
Ireland: A Terrible Beauty: The Story of Ireland Today (Uris) 1975
Irisches Tagebuch (Böll) 1957
Irreführung der Behörden (Becker) 1973
Irren; Die Häftlinge (Bernhard) 1962
Irrfahrt der Santa Maria (Böll) 1968
Isaac Bashevis Singer: Conversations (Singer) 1992
Isaac Bashevis Singer on Literature and Life: An Interview (Singer) 1979
Isaac Bashevis Singer Reader (Singer) 1971
Isabella: From Auschwitz to Freedom (Leitner) 1994
'Iskat ha-shokolad (Gouri) 1964
Island On Bird Street (Orlev) 1981
Isola di Arturo (Morante) 1957
Israel (Yehoshua) 1988
Israel haverim (Megged) 1955
Israel, Palestine, and Peace (Oz) 1994
It All Adds Up: From the Dim Past to the Uncertain Future (Bellow) 1994
Italiener (Bernhard) 1971
Itamar metayel 'al kirot (D. Grossman) 1986
Itamar mikhtav (D. Grossman) 1988
Itamar pogesh arnav (D. Grossman) 1988
Itamar ye 'koval ha 'ksamin ha 'shachor (D. Grossman) 1992
Itinerario/Útirány: Poesie scelte (Bruck) 1998
It's a Lovely Day Tomorrow (Kops) 1976
It's a Wonderful Life (Goodrich) 1986
Ivan the Terrible and Ivan the Fool (Yevtushenko) 1979
Izbrannaia proza (Yevtushenko) 1998

Ja (Bernhard) 1978
Jack Cole and Plastic Man: Forms Stretched to Their Limits (Spiegelman) 2001
Jack London, Hemingway, and the Constitution: Selected Essays, 1977–1992 (Doctorow) 1993
Jacko the Great Intruder (Keneally) 1994
Jacob the Liar (Becker) 1969
Jacob Two-Two and the Dinosaur (Richler) 1987
Jacob Two-Two Meets the Hooded Fang (Richler) 1975
Jacob Two-Two's First Spy Case (Richler) 1997
Jacob's Ladder (Levertov) 1961
Jagdgesellschaft (Bernhard) 1974
Jahre und Zeiten: Erinnerungen (Wiechert) 1949
Jak kochac dziecko (Korczak) 1929
Jakob Littners Aufzeichnungen Aus Einem Erdloch (Koeppen) 1948
Jan Palach (Sylvanus) 1972
Jane's Blanket (Miller) 1963
Janusz Korczak: A Tale for Our Time (Bettelheim) 1989
Jardin de curé (Gascar) 1979
Jardín de senderos que se bifurcan (Borges) 1941

Járkálj csak, halálraítélt! (Radnóti) 1936
Jasager (Brecht) 1930
Je batis ma demeure: Poems, 1943–1957 (Jabès) 1959
Je me souviens: Les Choses communes I (Pérec) 1978
Je suis né (Pérec) 1990
Jedermann: Geschichte eines Namenlosen (Wiechert) 1931
Jefta und seine Tochter (Feuchtwanger) 1957
Jegyzokönyv (Kertész) 1993
Jenseits von Schuld und Sühne: Bewältigungsversuche eines Überwältigten (Améry) 1966
Jeremias (Zweig) 1917
Jericho (Gouri) 1983
Jerominkinder (Wiechert) 1946
Jerusalem the Golden (Reznikoff) 1934
Jerusalem, Song of Songs (Uris) 1981
Jerusalems leende (Edvardson) 1991
Jeunesse (Modiano) 1981
Jeux intéressants (Pérec) 1997
Jeux sont faits (Sartre) 1947
Jew: Essays from Martin Buber's Journal ''Der Jude'' (A. Cohen) 1980
Jew Confronts Himself in American Literature (Potok) 1975
Jewels and Ashes (Zable) 1991
Jewess As a Fictional Sex Symbol (Bitton-Jackson) 1973
Jewish Ethics (Potok) 1964–69
Jewish Hasidim, Russian Sectarian Non-conformists in the Ukraine, 1700–1760 (Eliach) 1973
Jewish Resistence (Donat) 1964
Jewish Resistance: Facts, Omissions, and Distortions (Tec) 1997
Jewish Women's Call for Peace: A Handbook for Jewish Women on the Israeli/Palestinian Conflict (Klepfisz) 1990
Jewishness of Mr. Bloom (Hildesheimer) 1984
Jews, Gardens, God, and Gays: Essays in Honour of John Foster (1944–1994) (Baker) 1997
Jews in European History (Friedländer) 1994
Jews of Charleston: A History of an American Jewish Community (Reznikoff) 1950
Jews of Silence: A Personal Report on Soviet Jewry (Wiesel) 1966
Jimbo: Adventures in Paradise (Spiegelman) 1988
Job ou Dieu dans la tempete (Wiesel) 1986
Joe Papp: An American Life (H. Epstein) 1994
Joel Brand: Die Geschichte Eines Geschäfts (Kipphardt) 1965
Joey and the Birthday Present (Sexton) 1971
John Locke on Education (Gay) 1964
Johnnie Cœur (Gary) 1961
Joke (Sobol) 1975
Joseph and Koza; or, The Sacrifice to the Vistula (Singer) 1970
Joseph Fouche (Zweig) 1929
Joshua Then and Now (Richler) 1980
Jossel Wassermanns Heimkehr (Hilsenrath) 1993
Jour (Wiesel) 1961
Journal 1935–1944: The Fascist Years (Sebastian) 1996
Journaux de voyage (Camus) 1978
Journey (Tabori) 1958
Journey (Fink) 1990
Jours de notre mort (Rousset) 1947
Józki, Jaski i Franki (Korczak) 1922
Jubiläum (Tabori) 1983
Jud Süss (Feuchtwanger) 1925
Jud Süss: Schauspiel (Feuchtwanger) 1918
Jüdin von Toledo (Feuchtwanger) 1955

Jüdische Krieg (Feuchtwanger) 1932
Judith (Hochhuth) 1984
Jugend (Koeppen) 1976
Jugend in einer Oesterreichischen Stadt (Bachmann) 1961
Juges (Wiesel) 1999
Juif aujourd'hui: Recits, essais, dialogues (Wiesel) 1977
Juifs et Arabes (Memmi) 1974
Julia Farnese: Ein Trauerspiel in drei Akten (Feuchtwanger) 1915
Julia oder der weg zur macht: Erzeahlung (Hochhuth) 1994
Juliusz Slowacki pyta o gozine (Rymkiewicz) 1982
Junge Lord (Bachmann) 1965
Jürg Reinhart: Eine sommerliche Schicksalsfahrt (Frisch) 1934
Juristen: Drei Akte für sieben Spieler (Hochhuth) 1979
Jurnal: 1935–1944 (Sebastian) 1996
Just Call Me Bob (Lewitt) 1976
Just Like That (Brett) 1994
Justes (Camus) 1949
Justiz (Dürrenmatt) 1985

Ka-hol me-effer (Ka-Tzetnik 135633) 1966
Kaddish For A Child Not Born (Kertész) 1990
Kadisz (Grynberg) 1987
Kafe Kropotkin (Kops) 1988
Kafor al ha'aretz (Appelfeld) 1965
Kaiser in geto (Bryks) 1961
Kaisers Zeiten: Bilder einer Epoche (Hochhuth) 1973
Kaitush ha-mekhashef (Orlev) 1987
Kajtus czarodziej (Korczak) 1960
Kaleidoscope (Zweig) 1934
Kalender für den Frieden 1985 (Fried) 1984
Kalendergeschichten (Brecht) 1948
Kalkwerk (Bernhard) 1970
Kälte: Eine Isolation (Bernhard) 1981
Kamienny swiat (Borowski) 1948
Kampf mit dem Damon: Holerin, Kleist, Nietzsche (Zweig) 1925
Kampf ohne Engel (Fried) 1976
Kanikuly Krosha (Rybakov) 1966
Kantonistn: Vegn der Yidisher rekrutshine in Rusland in di tsaytn fun Tsar Nikolay dem ershtn, 1827–1856 (Lewin) 1934
Kapitlen fun izovn (Zuckerman) 1981
Karikaturen: Drame in dray akten (Katzenelson) 1909
Kärlekens vittne (Edvardson) 1963
Karrieren und Köpfe: Bildnisse berühmter Zeitgenossen (Améry) 1955
Kartenspieler (Bernhard) 1959
Kartki sportowe (Rudnicki) 1956
Kartki z Wegier (Różewicz) 1953
Kartoteka (Różewicz) 1960
Karu lo Piepel (Ka-Tzetnik 135633) 1961
Karunga a holtak ura; néger musék (Radnóti) 1944
Kasheh le-hiyot aryeh (Orlev) 1979
Katastrophen: Über deutsche Literatur (Klüger) 1994
Kater sviazi (Yevtushenko) 1966
Katerinah (Appelfeld) 1989
Kathrine (Habe) 1943
Katz und Maus (Grass) 1961
Kaukasische Kreidekreis (Brecht) 1948
Kazanskii universitet (Yevtushenko) 1971
Kazdy odzyskany dzien: Wspomnienia (Birenbaum) 1998
Ke-hut ha-shani: Shire ahavah 'Ivriyim mi-Sefarad, Italyah, Turkiyah ve-Teman (Pagis) 1978

Kean (Sartre) 1953
Keeper of Accounts (Klepfisz) 1982
Keepers (Lebow) 1988
Kefar: Mahazeh bi-shete ma'arakhot (Sobol) 1996
Kein Name bei den Leuten (Böll) 1953
Ke'ishon h'ayin (Appelfeld) 1972
Kelape tish'im ve-tish'ah (Greenberg) 1928
Kelev bayit (Greenberg) 1929
Kelil tif'eret ha-melitsah (Ben-Amotz) 1986
Keller: Eine Entziehung (Bernhard) 1976
Keme'ah edim: Mivhar (Appelfeld) 1975
Kemo sipurim (Kaniuk) 1983
Keri'ah tamah; Sifrutek (Ben-Amotz) 1974
Kerze von Arras: Ausgewählte Gedichte (Kolmar) 1968
Ketanah-gedolah (Orlev) 1977
Ketavim aharonim: 700–704 (Zuckerman) 1956
Ketavim aharonim: 703–704 (Katzenelson) 1947
Keter ha-drakon (Orlev) 1984
Ketonet veha-pasim (Appelfeld) 1983
Ketov ka-halakhah! Sefer le-h'atakot ule-hakra'ot sistematiyot, kurs-shimushi male ve-shalem shel ha-ortografiyah ha-'ivrit (Kaplan) 1926
Ketsitsah meha-tsohorayim (Orlev) 1995
Key West Tales (Hersey) 1994
Khatzot ha-yom (Megged) 1973
Khaym Lederers Tsurikkumen (Asch) 1927
Kheshvandike nekht (Molodowsky) 1927
Kh'tu dermonen (Glatstein) 1967
Kiddush ha-shem (Asch) 1919
Kiddush Hashem (Bryks) 1952
Kiedy znów bede maly (Korczak) 1961
Kijk 'ns in de la (Minco) 1974
Kilka szczegolow (Rymkiewicz) 1994
Kind (Bernhard) 1982
Kind of Alaska: A Play (Pinter) 1981
Kinder und Narren (Fried) 1965
Kinderbuch (Brecht) 1965
Kinderkreuzzug (Wiechert) 1935
Kinderlied (Grass) 1982
King Log (Hill) 1968
King of the Fields (Singer) 1988
King of the Jews: A Novel of the Holocaust (L. Epstein) 1979
King Solomon and His Magic Ring (Wiesel) 1999
Kinoerzähler (Hofmann) 1990
Kinot le-Tish'ah be-Av (Agnon) 1969
Kishufmakherin fun Kastilien (Asch) 1921
Kitve Profesor Hayim Shirman (1904–1981): Reshimah bibliyografit (Pagis) 1982
Klage und Anklage (Hildesheimer) 1989
Klagenfurter Texte: Ingeborg-Bachmann-Wettbewerb 1999 (Schindel) 1999
Kleine Dramen: Joel; König Saul; Das Weib des Urias; Der arme Heinrich; Donna Bianca; Die Braut von Korinth (Feuchtwanger) 1905–06
Kleine Passion (Wiechert) 1929
Kleine Stechardin (Hofmann) 1994
Kleines Organon für das Theater: Mit einem ''Nachtrag zum Kleinen Organon'' (Brecht) 1960
Kleist, Moos, Fasane (Aichinger) 1987
Klopfzeichen (Böll) 1961

Leben sammeln, nicht fragen wozu und warum: Tagebücher 1918–1924 (Klemperer) 1996

Leben sammeln, nicht fragen wozu und warum: Tagebücher 1925–1932 (Klemperer) 1996

Lebensschatten (Fried) 1981

Lecture (Singer) 1967

Lectures de Derrida (Kofman) 1984

Lefeu, oder, der Abbruch (Améry) 1974

Left Hand Singing (Lebow) 2001

Legende eines Lebens (Zweig) 1919

Legende vom letzten Wald (Wiechert) 1925

Legenden (Zweig) 1945

Legenden und Erzaehlungen (Sachs) 1921

Legendy nowoczesno'sci: eseje okupacyjne (Miłosz) 1996

Legszebb versei (Radnóti) 1972

Leiden am sinnlosen Leben: Psychotherapie für heute (Frankl) 1977

Leiden Israels (Sachs) 1962

Lektury nadobowiazkowe (Szymborska) 1973

Leo Baeck: A Radio Play Based on Authentic Texts (Sylvanus) 1996

Leopoldo Lugones (Borges) 1955

Lesebuch (Bernhard) 1993

Lesebuch (Dürrenmatt) 1978

Lesie, ojcze mój (Ficowski) 1990

Lessico famigliare (Ginzburg) 1963

Lessingscher Geist und die Welt von heute (Améry) 1978

Let, myslenko na zlatych kridlech vanku (Fuks) 1994

Leto v Sosniakakh (Rybakov) 1964

Letsane Purim: Mahazeh (Katzenelson) 1920

Letter to the Alumni (Hersey) 1970

Letter Writer (Singer) 1968

Lettera alla madre (Bruck) 1988

Letters and Drawings of Bruno Schulz (Ficowski) 1990

Letters From Westerbork (Hillesum) 1982

Letters of Denise Levertov and William Carlos Williams (Levertov) 1998

Letting Go (Roth) 1962

Lettre à Bernanos (Camus) 1963

Lettres à un ami allemand (Camus) 1945

Lettres au Castor et à quelques autres (Sartre) 1983

Lettres inedites de O. V. de L. Milosz a Christian Gauss (Miłosz) 1976

Letzte Märchenprinzessin (Menasse) 1997

Letzte Nacht im September (Tabori) 1997

Letzte, unveröffentlichte Gedichte Entwürfe und Fassungen (Bachmann) 1998

Levitation: Five Fictions (Ozick) 1982

Leyl ha'esrim (Sobol) 1976

Lezte Station (Remarque) 1956

Libération d'un Juif (Memmi) 1962

Liberators: Eyewitness Accounts of the Liberation of Concentration Camps: Oral History Testimonies of American Liberators from the Archives of the Center for Holocaust Studies (Eliach) 1981

Libro de arena (Borges) 1975

Libro del cielo y del infierno (Borges) 1960

Libros de sueños (Borges) 1976

Lichtzwang (Celan) 1970

Lid un balade (Manger) 1952

Lider (Glatstein) 1921

Lider (Sutzkever) 1937

Lider fun geto (Sutzkever) 1946

Lider fun hurbn: 700–705 (Molodowsky) 1962

Lider fun togbukh (Sutzkever) 1977

Lider fun yam-hamaves (Sutzkever) 1968

Lider un poemes (Glik) 1953

Lidyah, malkat Erets Yisra'el (Orlev) 1991

Lie Down in Darkness (Styron) 1951

Liebe: Dunkler Erdteil. Gedichte aus den Jahren 1942– 1967 (Bachmann) 1984

Liebe deinen Nächsten (Remarque) 1941

Liebe der Erika Ewald (Zweig) 1904

Liebe gepruft: Sieben Gedichte mit sieben Radierungen (Grass) 1974

Liebe in Deutschland (Hochhuth) 1978

Liebe in unserer Zeit: Sechzehn Erzählungen (Hochhuth) 1961

Liebe und tu, was du willst: Reflexionen eines Christen (Kogon) 1996

Liebesfluchten: Geschichten (Schlink) 2000

Liebesgedichte (Brecht) 1966

Liebesgedichte (Fried) 1979

Lieblose Legenden (Hildesheimer) 1952

Lied vom Weltende (Miłosz) 1967

Lieder Fun Churban 'on Lieder Fun Gloybin (Zeitlin) 1967

Lieder, Gedichte, Chöre (Brecht) 1934

Lieder und Gesänge (Brecht) 1957

Life and Fate (V. Grossman) 1980

Life around Us: Selected Poems on Nature (Levertov) 1997

Life As a Man (Roth) 1974

Life in the Forest (Levertov) 1978

Life Sketches (Hersey) 1989

Life With A Star (Weil) 1949

Light (Figes) 1983

Light up the Cave (Levertov) 1981

Like A Tear In the Ocean (Sperber) 1951

Like You're Nobody: The Letters of Louis Gallo to Bellow, 1961–1962 (Bellow) 1966

Likht fun Dornboym (Molodowsky) 1965

Lilít, e altri racconti (Levi) 1981

Lindberghflug (Brecht) 1929

Lingua, grammatica, stile (Tedeschi) 1971

Link in the Chain (Heimler) 1962

Lionhearted: A Story about the Jews in Medieval England (Reznikoff) 1944

List do Marc Chagalla (Ficowski) 1988

Listy i rozmyslania palestynskie (Korczak) 1999

Literarische Portraits aus dem Frankreich des XVII.–XIX. Jahrhunderts (Zweig) 1923

Literarishe un filosofishe eseyen (Zeitlin) 1980

Literatur und Kunst: Essays, Gedichte und Reden (Dürrenmatt) 1980

Literature Machine (Calvino) 1987

Literature Or Life (Semprun) 1994

Little Boy in Search of God: Mysticism in a Personal Light (Singer) 1976

Little Eden: A Child At War (Figes) 1978

Little Fadette (Figes) 1967

Little Joe Monaghan (Lebow) 1981

Little Lit: Folklore & Fairytale Funnies (Spiegelman) 2000

Little Lit: Strange Stories for Strange Kids (Spiegelman) 2001

Live or Die (Sexton) 1966

Lives of the Poets (Doctorow) 1984

Livre de la mémoire juive: Calendrier d'un martyrologue (Wiesenthal) 1986

Livre de l'hospitalité (Jabès) 1991

Livre de Yukel (Jabès) 1964

Men on Bataan (Hersey) 1942
Menaced World (Levertov) 1984
Mendiant de Jerusalem (Wiesel) 1968
Meneer Frits en andere verhalen uit de vijftiger jaren (Minco) 1974
Mensch erscheint im Holozän: Eine Erzählung (Frisch) 1979
Mensch und seine Meinung (Kogon) 1961
Mensch vor der Frage nach dem Sinn: Eine Auswahl aus dem Gesamtwerk (Frankl) 1979
Mensch zwischen Selbstentfremdung und Selbstverwirklichung (Frisch) 1970
Menschen am Rhein (Böll) 1960
Menschenbild der Seelenheilkunde: Drei Vorlesungen zur Kritik des dynamischen Psychologismus (Frankl) 1959
Mental Illness and Social Work (Heimler) 1967
Mentsh fun fayer (Grade) 1962
Menuhah nekhonah (Oz) 1982
Menzel: Maler des licts (Hochhuth) 1991
Menzogne e sortilegio (Morante) 1948
Mépris des juifs: Nietzsche, les juifs, l'antisémitisme (Kofman) 1994
Mercian Hymns (Hill) 1971
Mercy of Sorrow (Greenberg) 1965
Meredek út (Radnóti) 1938
Meridian (Celan) 1961
Meshaga'at pilim (Orlev) 1977
Meshieh's tsaytn: A kholm fun mayn folk (Asch) 1906
Meshugah (Singer) 1994
Mesilat barzel (Appelfeld) 1991
Messiah (Sherman) 1982
Messiah of Stockholm (Ozick) 1987
Mesure de nos jours (Delbo) 1971
Metafizyka (Rymkiewicz) 1963
Metamorfosis (Borges) 1938
Metaphor and Memory (Ozick) 1989
Metatron: Apokoliptishe poeme (Zeitlin) 1922
Mete Trap (Singer) 1929
Meteor (Dürrenmatt) 1966
Métier impossible: Lecture de ''constructions en analyse'' (Kofman) 1983
Meubles (Gascar) 1949
Mi cernovlasi bratri (Fuks) 1964
Mi-dirah le-dirah: Sipur (Agnon) 1939
Mi itneni malon (Amichai) 1971
Mi-kol 'amali: Shirim u-fo'emot (Glatstein) 1964
Mi-kol ha-ahavot (Kovner) 1965
Mi makir et Yosef G'? (Gouri) 1980
Mi-metulah li-Nyu York (Kaniuk) 1963
Mi-mordot ha-Levanon: ma'amarim u-reshimot (Oz) 1987
Miasto bez imienia (Miłosz) 1969
Michvat ha'or (Appelfeld) 1980
Mickiewicz, czyli, Wszystko: z Jaroslawem Markiem Rymkiewiczem rozmawia Adam Poprawa (Rymkiewicz) 1994
Micromegas (Borges) 1979
Midland in Stilfs: Drei Erzälungen (Bernhard) 1970
Midnight Salvage: Poems, 1995–1998 (Rich) 1999
Mikha'el sheli (Oz) 1968
Mikhreh ha-kerah (Appelfeld) 1997
Miklós Radnóti: The Complete Poetry (Radnóti) 1980
Miklós Radnóti 33 Poems (Radnóti) 1992
Mikreh ha-kssil (Megged) 1960
Mila 18 (Uris) 1961

Milacek (Lustig) 1969
Milhemet ha yetser (Grade) 1970
Milhemet Troyah lo tihyeh (Sobol) 1984
Milim nirdafot: Shirim (Pagis) 1984
Milon olami le-'ivrit miduberet (Ben-Amotz) 1972
Milosz's A B C's (Miłosz) 2001
Min ha-adam va-ma'lah: Shete po'emot dramatit (Zeitlin) 1964
Minds Meet (Abish) 1975
Minetti: ein Portrait des Künstlers als alter Mann (Bernhard) 1976
Minotaure; ou La Halte d'Oran (Camus) 1950
Minotaurus: Eine Ballade (Dürrenmatt) 1985
Mio splendido disastro (Bruck) 1979
Miracle Fair (Szymborska) 2001
Miriam bor i en kibbutz (Edvardson) 1969
Mirliton du ciel (Memmi) 1989
Mirror (Singer) 1973
Misfits (Miller) 1961
Misfits: An Original Screenplay Directed by John Huston (Miller) 1982
Mishak ha-hol (Orlev) 1996
Misheu larutz ito (D. Grossman) 2000
Missa sine nomine (Wiechert) 1950
Missing Persons and Other Essays (Böll) 1977
Mission (Habe) 1965
Misstrauen lernen: Prosa, Lyrik, Aufsätze, Reden (Fried) 1989
Missverständnis (Fried) 1982
Mr. Mani (Yehoshua) 1990
Mr. Peters' Connections (Miller) 1999
Mr. Sammler's Planet (Bellow) 1970
Mr. Theodore Mundstock (Fuks) 1963
Mistler's Exit (Begley) 1998
Mit mayne fartogbikher: In tokh genumen, 1958–1962 (Glatstein) 1963
Mit Sophie in die Pilze gegangen (Grass) 1976
Mit Szigalewa (Wojdowski) 1982
Mitla Pass (Uris) 1988
Mitmacher (Dürrenmatt) 1976
Mitn shtrom (Asch) 1909
Mitteilungen an Max über den Stand der Dinge und anderes (Hildesheimer) 1983
Mitunter sogar Lachen: Zwischenfälle und Erinnerungen (Fried) 1986
Mivhar mi-shirav (Greenberg) 1968
Mivhar sipurim (Megged) 1989
Mizbeyeh (Asch) 1928
Mlode cierpienia (Rudnicki) 1954
Moah: Shirim (Pagis) 1975
Moaus Zur: Ein Chanukkahbuch (Agnon) 1918
Modelo para la muerte (Borges) 1946
Modern Europe (Gay) 1973
Moderne französische Literatur und die deutsche Schule; Drei Vorträge (Klemperer) 1925
Moderne französische Lyrik (Dekadenz, Symbolismus, Neuromantik) Studie und kommentierte Texte (Klemperer) 1957
Moderne französische Lyrik von 1870 bis zur Gegenwart, Studie und erläuterte Texte (Klemperer) 1929
Moderne französische Prosa (1870–1920): Studie und erläuterte Texte (Klemperer) 1923
Moderne joodse verhalen (Minco) 1965
Modlitba pro Katerinu Horovitzovou (Lustig) 1964
Modulations for Solo Voice (Levertov) 1977
Moe samoe-samoe (Yevtushenko) 1995
Mohn und Gedächtnis (Celan) 1952

Moj wiek: Pamietnik nowiony (Miłosz) 1977
Moje dzielo posmiertne (Rymkiewicz) 1993
Moje strony świata (Ficowski) 1957
Moje zrcadlo: Vzpominky, dojmy, ohlednuti (Fuks) 1995
Molcho (Yehoshua) 1987
Momenty wychowawcze (Korczak) 1924
Moneda de hierro (Borges) 1976
Monolog (Hildesheimer) 1964
Monologo (Bruck) 1990
Monologue (Pinter) 1973
Monotonisierung der Welt: Aufsätze und Vorträge (Zweig) 1976
Monsieur Chouchani: L'Enigme d'un Maitre du XX Siecle: Entretiens avec Elie Wiesel, suivis d'une enquete (Wiesel) 1994
Monstervortrag über Gerechtigkeit und Recht nebst einem helvetischen Zwischenspiel: Eine kleine Dramaturgie der Politik (Dürrenmatt) 1966
Montagne Blanche (Semprun) 1986
Montand, la vie continue (Semprun) 1983
Montauk: Eine Erzählung (Frisch) 1975
Montesquieu (Gascar) 1989
Montesquieu (Klemperer) 1914
Moonlight: A Play (Pinter) 1993
Moral Education (Bettelheim) 1970
More Die of Heartbreak (Bellow) 1987
More Eggs of Things (Sexton) 1964
More Out Than In (Kops) 1980
Morgenrot (Koeppen) 1978
Moritz Frohlich-Morris Gay: A German Refugee in the United States (Gay) 1999
Mort dans l'âme (Sartre) 1949
Mort heureuse (Camus) 1971
Morts sans sépulture (Sartre) 1946
Mosby's Memoirs, and Other Stories (Bellow) 1968
Moses the Lawgiver (Keneally) 1975
Mosheh (Asch) 1951
Moskau 1937: Ein Reisebericht für meine Freunde (Feuchtwanger) 1937
Moskauer Orgasmus (Hilsenrath) 1992
Moski, Joski i Srule (Korczak) 1934
Moskva (Asch) 1935
Moskva-hranice (Weil) 1937
Moss (Kops) 1991
Mot ha-avir (Kaniuk) 1973
Mot hazaken (Yehoshua) 1962
Motke ganev (Asch) 1916
Motorbike (Kops) 1962
Mots (Sartre) 1963
Mots croisés (Pérec) 1979
Mots croisés II (Pérec) 1986
Motsets ha-mazal (Orlev) 1980
Mouches (Sartre) 1943
Mountain Language (Pinter) 1988
Moutons de feu (Gascar) 1963
Mozart (Gay) 1999
Mozart (Hildesheimer) 1977
Mozart Briefe (Hildesheimer) 1975
Mud in My Tears (Brett) 1997
Muerte y la brújula (Borges) 1951
Muj znamy Vili Feld (Lustig) 1949
Mul haye'arot (Yehoshua) 1968

Mul ta ha-zekhukhit: Mishpat Yerushalayim (Gouri) 1962
Mulatresse Solitude (Schwarz-Bart) 1972
Mur (Sartre) 1939
Murderers among Us: The Wiesenthal Memoirs (Wiesenthal) 1967
Muschel (Sylvanus) 1947
Muse hat Kanten: Aufsätze und Reden zur Literatur (Fried) 1995
Music Talks: Conversations with Musicians (H. Epstein) 1987
Musicians of Bremen: Retold (Figes) 1967
Mussernikes (Grade) 1939
Muter (Asch) 1919
Mutter (Brecht) 1932
Mutter (Kolmar) 1978
Mutter: Eine Erzählung (Wiechert) 1949
Mutter Courage und ihre Kinder (Brecht) 1941
Mutters Courage (Tabori) 1979
My Bridges of Hope: Searching for Life and Love after Auschwitz (Bitton-Jackson) 1999
My Father's House (Levin) 1947
My First Seventy-Nine Years (Potok) 1999
My German Question: Growing Up In Nazi Berlin (Gay) 1998
My Grandmother's Flowers (Manger) 1981
My Hate Song (Manger) 1961
My Little Sister (Kovner) 1967
My Mother's Sabbath Days (Grade) 1958
My Name Is Asher Lev (Potok) 1972
My Petition for More Space (Hersey) 1974
My Quarrel With Hersh Rasseyner (Grade) 1982
Mysi Natalie Mooshabrove (Fuks) 1970
Mysl pedagogiczna Janusza Korczaka: Nowe zródla (Korczak) 1983
Mysli (Korczak) 1987
Mysli rozne o ogrodach (Rymkiewicz) 1968
Mystery of the Charity of Charles Péguy (Hill) 1983
Myth of the Judeo-Christian Tradition (A. Cohen) 1970
Mythe de Sisyphe (Camus) 1942
Mythus der Zerstörung im Werk Döblins (Sebald) 1980

Na evreiskie temy: Izbrannoe v dvukh tomakh (V. Grossman) 1985
Na koloniach letnich (Korczak) 1946
Na powierzchni poematu i w srodku (Różewicz) 1983
Na przedpolu; artykuly i reportae (Borowski) 1952
Na streše je Mendelssohn (Weil) 1960
Na wchód od Arbatu (Krall) 1972
Nach der ersten Zukunft (Becker) 1980
Nach der Natur: Ein Elementardgedicht (Sebald) 1988
Nach Rußland und anderswohin: Empfindsame Reisen (Koeppen) 1958
Nachlese (Hildesheimer) 1987
Nachricht vom Tag: Erzahlungen (Aichinger) 1970
Nacht (Hilsenrath) 1964
Nacht der Harlekine (Schindel) 1994
Nacht, in der Chef geschlachtet wurde (Kipphardt) 1967
Nacht mit Gästen (Weiss) 1963
Nacht von Lissabon (Remarque) 1961
Nachtgewächs (Hildesheimer) 1959
Nächtliches gespräch mit einem verachteten Menschen: Ein Kurs für Zeitgenossen (Dürrenmatt) 1957
Nachtstück (Hildesheimer) 1963
Nackt unter Wölfen (Apitz) 1958
Nadav ve-imo (Megged) 1988
Nadzieja umiera ostatnia (Birenbaum) 1967

Naftali the Storyteller and His Horse, Sus, and Other Stories (Singer) 1976

Nagelaten dagen (Minco) 1997

Nahe suchen (Fried) 1982

Nakam (Ka-Tzetnik 135633) 1981

Naked Among Wolves (Apitz) 1958

Naked Heart (Gay) 1995

Napoleon: Historie en legende (Presser) 1946

Narod bessmerten (V. Grossman) 1942

Narrative Corpse: A Chain-Story by 69 Artists (Spiegelman) 1995

Narrenweisheit, oder Tod und Verklärung des Jean-Jacques Rousseau (Feuchtwanger) 1952

Narzeczony beaty: Niebieskie kartki (Rudnicki) 1961

Nashim kotvot le-Dan Ben-Amots: Bi-teguvah le-sefer ''Ziyunim zeh lo ha-kol'' (Ben-Amotz) 1980

Nathans Tod (Tabori) 1991

Nationalsozialistische Massentötungen durch Giftgas: Eine Dokumentation (Kogon) 1983

Natural (Malamud) 1952

Natural and the Supernatural Jew: An Historical and Theological Introduction (A. Cohen) 1962

Naufrage du stade Odradek (Pérec) 1989

Nausée (Sartre) 1938

Navrat z zitneho pole (Fuks) 1974

Nawet gdy sie smieje (Birenbaum) 1990

Naye Dramen (Asch) 1930

Naye ertseylungen (Asch) 1928

Nazi and the Barber (Hilsenrath) 1971

Nazi Germany and the Jews: Volume 1, The Years of Persecution, 1933–1939 (Friedländer) 1997

Nazi und der Friseur (Hilsenrath) 1971

Ne umira prezhde smerti (Yevtushenko) 1993

Neboztici na bale (Fuks) 1972

Necessities of Life (Rich) 1966

Ned Kelly and the City of the Bees (Keneally) 1978

Nefesh yehudi (Sobol) 1982

Neither Your Honey nor Your Sting: An Offbeat History of the Jews (Kops) 1985

Neizvestnyi soldat (Rybakov) 1970

Nekrassov (Sartre) 1955

Nelly's Version (Figes) 1977

Neopalimaia kupina: Evreiskie siuzhety v russkoi poezii; antologiia (Donat) 1973

Nerval: Le Charme de la répétition: Lecture de Sylvie (Kofman) 1979

Nerves (Sobol) 1976

Net let: Liubovnaia lirika (Yevtushenko) 1993

Netchaiev est de retour (Semprun) 1987

Netz (Habe) 1969

Neue politische und literarische Schriften (Böll) 1973

Neue Prozeß (Weiss) 1982

Neue Stadt: Beiträge zur Diskussion, with Lucius Burckhardt and Markus Kutter (Frisch) 1956

Neun Erzählungen (Böll) 1966

Nevelot-ha-sipur ha-amiti (Kaniuk) 1997

Nevue fun shvartsaplen (Sutzkever) 1989

New and Collected Poems, 1952–1992 (Hill) 1994

New & Selected Essays (Levertov) 1992

New Art of Color: The Writings of Robert and Sonia Delaunay (A. Cohen) 1978

New Bridge (Levin) 1933

New Dimensions in Psychiatry: A World View (Arieti) 1975

New Life (Malamud) 1961

New Poems 1967: A P.E.N. Anthology (Pinter) 1968

New Year's Garland for My Students, MIT 1969–1970 (Levertov) 1970

New York (Brett) 2001

New York: Mit einem autobiographischen Nachwort (Koeppen) 1959

News from the Front (Thomas) 1983

Next Year in Jerusalem (Sherman) 1967

Nezhnost: Novyii stikhi (Yevtushenko) 1962

Nic w plaszczu Prospera (Różewicz) 1963

Nicht nur zur Weihnachtszeit (Böll) 1952

Nicht verdrängen, nicht gewöhnen: Texte zum Thema Österreich (Fried) 1987

Nie o kwiatach (Birenbaum) 1993

Niebieskie kartki: Przeswity (Rudnicki) 1957

Niebieskie kartki: Slepe lustro tych lat (Rudnicki) 1956

Niekochana (Rudnicki) 1937

Niemandsrose (Celan) 1963

Niepokój (Różewicz) 1947

Niepokoj; Wybor wierszy, 1945–1961 (Różewicz) 1963

Niet verstaan (Durlacher) 1995

Nietzsche et la métaphore (Kofman) 1972

Nietzsche et la scène philosophique (Kofman) 1979

Niggerlovers (Tabori) 1969

Night (Asch) 1920

Night (Hilsenrath) 1964

Night (Pinter) 1969

Night (Wiesel) 1958

Night and Hope (Lustig) 1958

Night before Paris (Sherman) 1969

Night In Lisbon (Remarque) 1961

Night of the Girondists, Or Breaking Point (Presser) 1957

Night of the Mist (Heimler) 1959

Night Out (Pinter) 1961

Night Out, Night School, Revue Sketches: Early Plays (Pinter) 1968

Night Prayer (Manger) 1981

Nightfather (Friedman) 1991

Nigun penimi (Birenbaum) 1985

Nihilist (Dürrenmatt) 1950

Nikoho neponizis (Lustig) 1963

Nine Plays (Reznikoff) 1927

Ninety-Nine Poems in Translation: An Anthology (Pinter) 1994

Nitsanim (Katzenelson) 1900

No Evil Star: Selected Essays, Interviews, and Prose (Sexton) 1985

No Man's Land (Pinter) 1975

No Passion Spent: Essays 1978–1995 (G. Steiner) 1996

No Snow in December: An Autobiographical Novel (Lewitt) 1985

No Third Path: A Study of Collective Behavior (Kosinski) 1962

No Villian: They Too Arise (Miller) 1937

Nobel Lecture (Bellow) 1977

Nobel Lecture (Miłosz) 1981

Nobel Lecture (Singer) 1979

Nobel Prize for Literature (Böll) 1973

Noc a nadeje (Lustig) 1958

Noc bedzie chlodna, niebo w purpurze (Rudnicki) 1977

Noces (Camus) 1939

Noch feiert Tod das Leben (Sachs) 1960

Noch zehn Minuten bis Buffalo (Grass) 1959

Noente geshtaltn (Manger) 1938

Noente geshtaltn un andere shriftn (Manger) 1961

Paulino Lucero, Aniceto y gallo, Santos Vega (Borges) 1960
Pawnbroker (Wallant) 1961
Peepshow (Tabori) 1984
Peletim (Grade) 1947
Pen ishon ha-mavet (Agnon) 1960
Penguin Book of Modern Verse Translation (G. Steiner) 1966
Penguin Modern Poets 8 (Hill) 1966
Penguin Modern Poets 9 (Levertov) 1967
Penitent (Singer) 1983
Penser, classer (Pérec) 1985
People, and Uncollected Short Stories (Malamud) 1990
People Apart: Hasidism in America (A. Cohen) 1970
PEP: J. L. Wetcheeks amerikanisches Liederbuch (Feuchtwanger) 1928
Perchè leggere i classici (Calvino) 1992
Perec/rinations (Pérec) 1997
Peregrinations: Adventures with the Green Parrot (G. Klein) 1986
Peridah meha-darom: Po'emah (Kovner) 1949
Periodic Table (Levi) 1975
Periods of Stress (Klepfisz) 1975
Perser (Feuchtwanger) 1915
Personal and Possessive (Thomas) 1964
Pervoe sobranie sochineniaei v vosmi tomakh (Ycvtushcnko) 1997
Peshitat ha-regel shel g'ek ha-katan (Orlev) 1985
Peste (Camus) 1947
Peter Weiss Werke in sechs Bänden (Weiss) 1991
Peterburg (Asch) 1934
Petit Livre de la subversion hors de soupcon (Jabès) 1982
Petit traité invitant à la découverte de l'art subtil du go (Pérec) 1969
Petites poésies jours de pluie et de soleil (Jabès) 1991
Pewien zolnierz (Borowski) 1947
Pezurai; Mehkarim, reshimot u-felyetonim. 1900–1936 (Kaplan) 1937
Phänomenologie der Entgeisterung: Geschichte des verschwindenden Wissens (Menasse) 1995
Pharaoh (Memmi) 1988
Philosophical Dictionary (Gay) 1962
Philosophie und Naturwissenschaft: Essays, Gedichte und Reden (Dürrenmatt) 1980
Philosophy of Sartre (Sartre) 1966
Physiker (Dürrenmatt) 1962
Pianist: the Extraordinary Story of One Man's Survival In Warsaw, 1939–45 (Szpilman) 1946
Piccole virtu (Ginzburg) 1962
Pictures at an Exhibition (Thomas) 1993
Pictures of Fidelman: An Exhibition (Malamud) 1969
Pie XII et le IIIe Reich Documents (Friedländer) 1964
Piec poematow (Różewicz) 1950
Pierre Corneille (Klemperer) 1933
Pierrots Herrentraum: Eine Pantomine in fünf Bildern (Feuchtwanger) 1916
Piesek przydroczny (Miłosz) 1997
Piesn niepodlegla (Miłosz) 1942
Piesn o zamordowanym zydowskim narodzie (Katzenelson) 1982
Piesni mówione (Ficowski) 1973
Piesni (Papušakre gila); wiersze w jezyku cyganskim (Ficowski) 1956
Pig Dreams: Scenes from the Life of Sylvia (Levertov) 1981
Pig Notes & Dumb Music: Prose on Poetry (Heyen) 1998
Pilatus (Dürrenmatt) 1949
Pillar of Salt (Memmi) 1953
Pinball (Kosinski) 1982
Pinkas Vitel (Katzenelson) 1964

Pinkville (Tabori) 1970
Pinto and Sons (L. Epstein) 1990
Pirhe esh (Gouri) 1949
Pisma wybrane (Korczak) 1978
Pismo obrazkowe (Ficowski) 1962
Pithe devarim (Agnon) 1977
Pitre de Rit Pas (Rousset) 1948
Place at Whitton (Keneally) 1964
Place de l'étoile (Modiano) 1968
Place Where Souls Are Born: A Journey into the Southwest (Keneally) 1992
Plague (Camus) 1947
Plaque On Via Mazzini (Bassini) 1952
Plaskorzezba (Różewicz) 1991
Plat de porc aux bananes vertes (Schwarz-Bart) 1967
Play for the Devil (Singer) 1984
Play Strindberg: Totentanz nach August Strindberg (Dürrenmatt) 1969
Playing for Time (Miller) 1985
Playing For Time (Fénelon) 1976
Playing Sinatra: A Play (Kops) 1992
Playmaker (Keneally) 1987
Plays (Pintcr) 1976–81
Plays and Essays (Dürrenmatt) 1982
Pleasure Wars (Gay) 1998
Plebejer proben den Aufstand: Ein deutsches Trauerspiel (Grass) 1966
Plus profondque l'abime (Sperber) 1950
Po powstaniu (Moczarski) 1980
Pod berlem krola pikowego: Sekrety cyga 'nskich wrozb (Ficowski) 1990
Podróż (Fink) 1990
Poem of the Midway and Other Poems (Thomas) 1974
Poemas (Borges) 1919–1922
Poemat o czasie zastyglym (Miłosz) 1933
Poemat otwarty (Różewicz) 1956
Poems, 1960–1967 (Levertov) 1983
Poems (Glatstein) 1970
Poems (Kops) 1955
Poems (Pagis) 1972
Poems (Pinter) 1968
Poems (Reznikoff) 1920
Poems (Rich) 1952
Poems and Prose (Pinter) 1949–1977
Poems and Songs (Kops) 1958
Poems by Ghalib (Rich) 1969
Poems Chosen by the Author (Yevtushenko) 1966
Poems, New and Collected, 1957–1997 (Szymborska) 1998
Poems of Günter Grass (Grass) 1969
Poems on the Theatre (Brecht) 1961
Poems: Selected and New, 1950–1974 (Rich) 1974
Poems: The Psalter of Avram Haktani (A. Klein) 1944
Poems, with Thomas Kinsella and Douglas Livingstone (Sexton) 1968
Poesía gauchesca (Borges) 1955
Poésie algérienne de 1830 a nos jours: approches socio- historiques (Memmi) 1963
Poesie (Sachs) 1962
Poesie edite e inedite, by Cesare Pavese (Calvino) 1962
Poeszje zebrane (Różewicz) 1957
Poet and His Time: Three Addresses (Wiechert) 1948
Poet in the World (Levertov) 1973
Poetishe verk (Sutzkever) 1963

Pterodactyl Rose: Poems of Ecology (Heyen) 1991
Puberty Tree: New and Selected Poems (Thomas) 1992
Pułapka (Różewicz) 1982
Purgatorium (Tabori) 1999
Purim gvardye (Glatstein) 1930
Putain respectueuse (Sartre) 1946
Puttermesser Papers (Ozick) 1997
Pyl milosny: Niebieskie kartki (Rudnicki) 1964
Pytania zadawane sobie (Szymborska) 1954

QB VII (Uris) 1970
Quality of Witness: A Romanian Diary 1937–1944 (Dorian) 1982
Quand vient le souvenir (Friedländer) 1978
Quarantaine (Durlacher) 1993
Quarrel & Quandary: Essays (Ozick) 2000
Quarry (Dürrenmatt) 1953
Quartier latin (Gascar) 1973
Quartier perdu (Modiano) 1985
Quatre romans analytiques (Kofman) 1974
Qué es el budismo? (Borges) 1976
Quel beau dimanche (Semprun) 1980
Quel petit vélo à guidon chromé au fond de la cour? (Pérec) 1966
Querschnitte: Aus Interviews, Aufsätzen, und Reden (Böll) 1977
Question of Jean Jacques Rousseau (Gay) 1954
Questo povero corpo (Tedeschi) 1946
Qui rapportera ces paroles? (Delbo) 1974
Quiet Moments in a War: The Letters of Jean-Paul Sartre to Simone de Beauvoir, 1940–1963 (Sartre) 1993
Qu'une larme dans l'ocean (Sperber) 1951

Rabbis and Wives (Grade) 1982
Racconti e saggi (Levi) 1986
Racines du ciel (Gary) 1956
Racisme (Memmi) 1982
Radical Humanism: Selected Essays (Améry) 1984
Radical Stage: Theatre in Germany in the 1970s and 1980s (Sebald) 1988
Radnóti Miklós versei (Radnóti) 1948
Ragtime (Doctorow) 1975
Rainer Maria Rilke und Stefan Zweig in Briefen und Dokumenten (Zweig) 1987
Ralph Ellison: A Collection of Critical Essays (Hersey) 1973
Rapporte (Weiss) 1968
Rasskazy (V. Grossman) 1937
Rättin (Grass) 1986
Ratz (D. Grossman) 1983
Rauber-Rede: 3 deutsche Vorwurfe: Schiller/Lessing/Geschwister Scholl (Hochhuth) 1982
Ravelstein (Bellow) 2000
Ravensbrück (Tillion) 1946
Raw: The Graphic Aspirin for War Fever (Spiegelman) 1986
Raw: High Culture for Low Brows (Spiegelman) 1991
Raw: Open Wounds from the Cutting Edge of Commix (Spiegelman) 1989
Raw: Required Reading for the Post-Literate (Spiegelman) 1990
Rayze Aheym/The journey home (Klepfisz) 1990
Razvedchiki gryaduschego (Yevtushenko) 1952
Re in ascolto (Calvino) 1984
Reaches of Heaven: A Story of the Baal Shem Tov (Singer) 1980

Read Yourself Raw: Comix Anthology for Damned Intellectuals (Spiegelman) 1987
Reader (Schlink) 1995
Reading Freud: Explorations & Entertainments (Gay) 1990
Reading Myself and Others (Roth) 1975
Reading of Ashes: Poems (Ficowski) 1981
Reading the Apocalypse in Bed: Selected Plays and Short Pieces (Różewicz) 1998
Real Presences: Is There Anything in What We Say? (G. Steiner) 1989
Reawakening (Levi) 1963
Reb shloyme nogid: A poeme fun Yudishen leben (Asch) 1913
Rebe Doktor Zilber (Asch) 1927
Recht, nicht Rache: Erinnerungen (Wiesenthal) 1988
Recit (Jabès) 1981
Récits d'Ellis Island: Histoires d'errance et d'espoir (Pérec) 1980
Recollections and Reflections (Bettelheim) 1990
Rede an die deutsche Jugend 1945 (Wiechert) 1945
Rede an die Schweizer Freunde (Wiechert) 1947
Rede unter dem Galgen (Aichinger) 1951
Redemption (Uris) 1995
Reden, 1945–1954 (Niemöller) 1958
Reden, 1958–1961 (Niemöller) 1961
Reden, Predigten, Denkanstösse, 1964–1976 (Niemöller) 1977
Reflections on Nazism: An Essay on Death and Kitsch (Friedländer) 1993
Reflections (Rich) 1973
Réflexions sur la guillotine, in Réflexions sur la peine capitale (Camus) 1957
Réflexions sur la question juive (Sartre) 1947
Reflexions sur l'avenir d'Israel (Friedländer) 1969
Reformierte Gesellschaft (Kogon) 1997
Regard (Jabès) 1992
Regenbogen (Apitz) 1976
Regina (L. Epstein) 1982
Regina Amstettin; Veronika; Der einfache Tod; Die Magd: 4 Novellen (Wiechert) 1969
Regio (Różewicz) 1969
Regiony wielkiej herezji; Szkice o zyciu i twórczosci Brunona Schulza (Ficowski) 1967
Règne végétal (Gascar) 1981
Rehoke mishpahah (Orlev) 1996
Reich der Steine (Fried) 1963
Reisen nach Frankreich (Koeppen) 1961
Rekonvaleszenz (Weiss) 1970
Rekviyem le-Terezyenshtadt (Kovner) 1965
Relearning the Alphabet (Levertov) 1970
Rembrandt (Zweig) 1912
Rembrandt's Hat (Malamud) 1973
Remembrance (Rybakov) 1997
Remise de peine (Modiano) 1988
Rendevous mit Margaret: Liebesgeschichten (Böll) 1981
Rendezvous in Oudenaarde (Améry) 1982
Repentance (Sobol) 1977
Reporter (Levin) 1929
Republika marzen: Utwory rozproszone, opowiadania, fragmenty, eseje, rysunki (Ficowski) 1993
Request Stop, Last to Go, Special Offer, Getting Acquainted (Pinter) 1959
Requiem, and Poem without a Hero (Thomas) 1976

Sipure ahavim (Agnon) 1930
Sipurei sof shavua (Kaniuk) 1986
Sipurim poh sipurim sham (Ben-Amotz) 1982
Sipurim ve-agadot (Agnon) 1944
Sistine Madonna (V. Grossman) 1989
Situation (Weiss) 2000
Situation Normal (Miller) 1944
Situations 1–10 (Sartre) 1949
Six Days of Destruction (Wiesel) 1989
Six Memos for the Next Millennium (Calvino) 1988
Sixth Day and Other Tales (Levi) 1990
Sketches (Pinter) 1969
Ski Bum (Gary) 1965
Skin Deep: Tales of Doomed Romance (Spiegelman) 1992
Skrawek czasu (Fink) 1983
Sky of Now (Potok) 1995
Slady (Fink) 1996
Slave (Singer) 1962
Slavs! (Thinking about the Longstanding Problems of Virtue and
    Happiness) (Kushner) 1995
Slawa: Opowiesc (Korczak) 1913
Slight Ache (Pinter) 1961
Slon Ketering: Po'emah (Kovner) 1987
Smierc jednorozca (Ficowski) 1981
Smierc miasta (Szpilman) 1946
Smierc w starych dekoraocjach (Różewicz) 1970
Smieszny staruszek (Różewicz) 1964
Smoke Over Birkenau (Millu) 1947
Smrt morcete (Fuks) 1969
Snapshots of a Daughter-in-Law: Poems, 1954–1962 (Rich) 1963
So kam ich unter die Deutschen (Fried) 1977
So sitze ich denn zwischen allen Stühlen: Tagebücher 1945–1949
    (Klemperer) 1999
So ward Abend und Morgen (Böll) 1955
Soaps (Sherman) 1975
Sobibor: The Forgotten Revolt (Blatt) 1995
Sobranie sochineniy 1981– (Rybakov) 82
Societe eclatee de la premiere la seconde revolution mondiale
    (Rousset) 1973
Socjologia Amerykanska: Wybor Prac, 1950–1960 (Kosinski) 1958
Socrate(s) (Kofman) 1989
Söhne: Roman (Feuchtwanger) 1935
Sol (Szymborska) 1962
Soldat und ein Mädchen (Fried) 1960
Soldaten (Kipphardt) 1968
Soldaten, Nekrolog auf Genf: Tragödie (Hochhuth) 1967
Soleils: Récits (Gascar) 1960
Solitary Thing (Sherman) 1963
Solo (Sobol) 1991
Solomon Gursky Was Here (Richler) 1989
Some Aspects of the Historical Significance of the Holocaust
    (Friedländer) 1977
Some Kind of Love Story (Miller) 1983
Some of These Days (Kops) 1990
Some Sunny Day (Sherman) 1996
Something to Remember Me By: Three Tales (Bellow) 1991
Somewhere a Master (Wiesel) 1982
Somewhere Is Such a Kingdom: Poems 1952–1971 (Hill) 1975
Sommer 14: Ein Totentanz (Hochhuth) 1990
Sommernachtstraum (Fried) 1963

Son of a Smaller Hero (Richler) 1955
Sonderbehandlung: Drei Jahre in den Krematorien und Gaskammern
    von Auschwitz (Müller) 1979
Sonderheft Jean Améry (Améry) 1978
Song of the Murdered Jewish People (Katzenelson) 1944
Songs from the Earth: Selected Poems of John Harris, Cornish Miner,
    1820–84 (Thomas) 1977
Songs in Flight: The Complete Poetry of Ingeborg Bachmann
    (Bachmann) 1994
Songs of Jerusalem and Myself (Amichai) 1973
Sonia Delaunay (A. Cohen) 1975
Sonim, di Geshichte fun a Liebe (Singer) 1966
Sonnenblume: Von Schuld und Vergebung (Wiesenthal) 1970
Sophie's Choice (Styron) 1979
Sorrow Dance (Levertov) 1967
Sorstalanság (Kertész) 1975
Sotn in Gorey (Singer) 1935
Sotto il sole giaguaro (Calvino) 1986
Soul of Wood (Lind) 1962
Soumchi (Oz) 1978
Sounds, Feelings, Thoughts (Szymborska) 1981
Sounds of a Guilty Silence (Birenbaum) 1997
Soupcon, le desert (Jabès) 1978
Sources (Gascar) 1975
Sources (Rich) 1983
Souvenirs de l'au-delà (Lengyel) 1946
Sozialpartnerschaftliche Ästhetik: Essays zum österreichischen Geist
    (Menasse) 1990
Spaete Gedichte (Sachs) 1965
Spaghetti i miecz (Różewicz) 1966
Spalovac mrtvol (Fuks) 1967
Spanish Language in South America: A Literary Problem (Borges) 1964
Spanner (Böll) 1966
Spark of Life (Remarque) 1952
Spazio umano: Problemi in prospettiva: Le dimensioni del raccontare:
    Per il biennio delle Scuole Medie Superiori (Tedeschi) 1972
Species of Spaces and Other Pieces (Pérec) 1997
Spectres, mes compagnons (Delbo) 1977
Spell of Time: A Tale of Love in Jerusalem (Levin) 1974
Sphinx (Thomas) 1986
Spiegelgeschichte: Erzahlungen und Dialoge (Aichinger) 1979
Spiel vom deutschen Bettelmann (Wiechert) 1933
Spiele in denen es dunkel wird (Hildesheimer) 1958
Spinoza of Market Street and Other Stories (Singer) 1961
Spitze des Eisbergs: Ein Reader (Hochhuth) 1982
Sprachgitter (Celan) 1959
Springflut (Böll) 1969
Spurlosen (Böll) 1957
Srebrny klos (Różewicz) 1955
SS-Staat: Das System de Deutschen Konzentrationslager (Kogon) 1946
Stadt: Prosa I–IV (Dürrenmatt) 1952
Städtebauer: Geschichten und Anekdoten 1919–1956 (Brecht) 1978
Stalingrad: Sentyabr' 1942–yanvar' 1943 (V. Grossman) 1943
Stammheim (Tabori) 1986
Stantsiya Zima (Yevtushenko) 1956
Star Eternal (Ka-Tzetnik 135633) 1966
Stara kobieta wysiaduje (Różewicz) 1968
Staryi uchitel' (V. Grossman) 1962
Statue du sel (Memmi) 1953
Status Quo Vadis (Sobol) 1973

Tsviling-bruder (Sutzkever) 1986
Tugend der Kannibalen: Gesammelte Prosa (Kipphardt) 1990
Tui-Roman: Fragment (Brecht) 1973
Tulipe (Gary) 1946
Tunnel (Dürrenmatt) 1952
Turandot; oder, Der Kongress der Weisswäscher (Brecht) 1967
Turm (Weiss) 1949
Turm zu Babel (Zweig) 1964
Tutti i nostri ieri (Ginzburg) 1952
Två rum i Jerusalem (Edvardson) 1978
Twarz (Różewicz) 1964
Twarz trzecia (Różewicz) 1968
Twee koffers (Friedman) 1996
Twentieth Century Russian Poetry: Silver and Steel: An Anthology
     (Yevtushenko) 1993
Twenty-one Love Poems (Rich) 1977
Twenty-One Stories (Agnon) 1970
Two Anglo-Saxon Plays: Oil Islands; Warren Hastings
     (Feuchtwanger) 1928
Two Fables (Malamud) 1978
Two-Fisted Painters Action Adventure (Spiegelman) 1980
Two Formal Elegies (Hill) 1959
Two Plays: A Night in May and Last Treatment (Yehoshua) 1974
Two Voices (Thomas) 1968
Tynset (Hildesheimer) 1965
Tzili: the Story of A Life (Appelfeld) 1983

U sebia doma (Kuznetsov) 1964
Über allen Gipfeln ist Ruh: Ein deutscher Dichtertag um 1980
     (Bernhard) 1981
Über das Altern: Revolte und Resignation (Améry) 1968
Über das Selbsverständliche (Grass) 1968
Über den Beruf des Schauspielers (Brecht) 1970
Über die bildenden Künste (Brecht) 1983
Über die irdische Liebe und andere gewisse Welträtsel in Liedern und
     Balladen (Brecht) 1971
Über die Tugend der Urbanität (Améry) 1969
Über experimentelles Theater (Brecht) 1970
Über Klassiker (Brecht) 1965
Über Kunst und Künstler: Aus einer ungesprochenen Rede
     (Wiechert) 1946
Über Lyrik (Brecht) 1964
Über meinen Lehrer Döblin, und andere Vorträge (Grass) 1968
Über Politik auf dem Theater (Brecht) 1971
Über Politik und Kunst (Brecht) 1971
Über Realismus (Brecht) 1971
Über Theater (Brecht) 1966
Überbau und Underground: Die sozialpartnerschaftliche Ästhetik :
     Essays zum österreichischen Geist (Menasse) 1997
Überflutung: 4 Hörspiele (Hofmann) 1981
Überlegungen (Fried) 1964
Ucieczka z Jasnej Polany (Rudnicki) 1949
Ujhold (Radnóti) 1935
Újmódi pásztorok éneke (Radnóti) 1931
Ulcérations (Pérec) 1986
Ulica Mandelsztama i inne wiersze z lat 1979–1985 (Rymkiewicz) 1992
Ulice ztracenych bratri (Lustig) 1949
Ultimo natale di guerra (Levi) 1984
Ultimo viene il corvo (Calvino) 1949
Um Klarheit (Fried) 1985

Um Winter (Asch) 1910
Umbewusste Gott (Frankl) 1948
Umgang mit Paradiesen: Gesammelte Gedichte (Kipphardt) 1990
Umrisse meiner Liebe: Lyrik, Erzählung (Fried) 1986
Umschlagplatz (Rymkiewicz) 1988
Un di velt hot geshvign (Wiesel) 1956
Un di zun hot geshaynt (Ferderber-Salz) 1965
Un erou al timpului nostru (Celan) 1946
Una citta di pianura (Bassani) 1940
Una lapide in Via Mazzini (Bassani) 1952
Una notte del '43 (Bassani) 1960
Una pietra sopra: Discorsi di letteratura e società (Calvino) 1980
Unattainable Earth (Miłosz) 1986
Unbedingte Mensch: Metaklinische Vorlesungen (Frankl) 1949
Unbefleckte Empfangnis: Ein Kreidekreis (Hochhuth) 1989
Unbekannte Briefe aus der Emigration an eine Freundin (Zweig) 1964
Unbekannte Werk: Fruhe Prosa, Werke aus dem Nachlass, Briefe und
     Tagebucher (Remarque) 1998
Unberechenbare Gäste: Heitere Erzählungen (Böll) 1956
Uncommon Reader (G. Steiner) 1978
Und alle seine Mörder (Fried) 1984
Und Brecht sah das tragische nicht: Pleadoyers, Polimiken, Profile
     (Hochhuth) 1996
Und der Haifisch, der hat Zähne: Die grossen Songs und Kleinen
     Lieder (Brecht) 1977
Und die Moral von der Geschicht (Hochhuth) 1959
Und im Licht mein Herz (Kipphardt) 1971
Und nicht taub und stumpf werden: Unrecht, Widerstand, und Protest
     (Fried) 1984
Und niemand weiss weiter (Sachs) 1957
Und sagte kein einziges Wort (Böll) 1953
Und Vietnam und . . . (Fried) 1966
Under a Cruel Star: A Life in Prague, 1941–1968 (H. Epstein) 1986
Under the Eye of the Storm (Hersey) 1967
Under the Weather (Bellow) 1966
Underground (Sobol) 1991
Understanding and Helping the Schizophrenic: A Guide for Family
     and Friends (Arieti) 1979
Undine geht: Erzählungen (Bachmann) 1973
Undzere oyseyes glien (Greenberg) 1978
Unease (Różewicz) 1980
Unfertig ist der Mensch (Böll) 1967
Ungeduld des Herzens (Zweig) 1939
Ungenach (Bernhard) 1968
Unglückliche Liebe (Koeppen) 1934
Unglückselige Kind (Hildesheimer) 1967
Unheard Cry for Meaning: Psychotherapy and Humanism (Frankl) 1978
Unheimliche Heimat: Essays zur Österreichischen Literatur
     (Sebald) 1991
Unholdes Frankreich: Meine Erlebnisse unter der Regierung Petain
     (Feuchtwanger) 1941
Unintended Consequences (Brett) 1992
Univers concentrationnaire (Rousset) 1945
Unkenrufe (Grass) 1992
Unloved: From the Diary of Perla S. (Lustig) 1979
Unmass aller Dinge (Fried) 1982
Unmeisterliche Wanderjahre (Améry) 1971
Unordentlicher Mensch (Böll) 1955
Unruhige Träume (Tabori) 1992

Voci della sera (Ginzburg) 1961

Voditeli (Rybakov) 1950

Vogel Niemalsmehr: 12 Märchen (Wiechert) 1973

Vogel Scheuchen (Grass) 1970

Vogelfreie (Weiss) 1948

Vogler (Singer) 1928

Voice for the Child: The Inspirational Words of Janusz Korczak (Korczak) 1999

Voice: Translations of Paul Celan (Celan) 1998

Volchiaei pasport (Yevtushenko) 1998

Volkens ibern dakh: Lid un balade (Manger) 1942

Volpone (Zweig) 1926

Voltaire's Politics: The Poet As Realist (Gay) 1959

Volume primo: Se questo è un uomo; La tregua; Il sistema periodico; I sommersi e i salvati (Levi) 1987

Volume secondo: Romanzi e poesie (Levi) 1988

Volume terzo: Racconti e saggi (Levi) 1990

Vom bleibenden Gewinn: Ein Buch der Betrachtung (Wiechert) 1951

Vom deutschen Herbst zum bleichen deutschen Winter: Ein Lesebuch zum Modell Deutschland (Kipphardt) 1981

Vom Geiste neuer Literaturforschung: Festschrift für Oskar Walzel (Klemperer) 1924

Vom Trost der Welt (Wiechert) 1938

Vom U-Boot zur Kanzel (Niemöller) 1933

Von Bis nach Seit: Gedichte aus den Jahren 1945–1958 (Fried) 1985

Von den treuen Begleitern (Wiechert) 1936

Von der Nachfolge dieses jungen Menschen, der nie mehr alt wird, with Herbert Heckmann und Volker Kaukoreit (Fried) 1988

Von hoher und niederer Literatur (Klüger) 1996

Von Schwelle zu Schwelle (Celan) 1955

Von Syrakus aus gesehen, gedacht, erzählt (Hochhuth) 1991

Von Wolle und Granit: Querschnitt durch die schwedische Lyric des 20 (Sachs) 1947

Vor 33 nach 45: Gesammelte Aufsätze (Klemperer) 1956

Vor dem Ruhestand: Eine Komödie von deutscher Seele (Bernhard) 1979

Vor der Regenzeit (Hofmann) 1988

Vorleser (Schlink) 1995

Vorzuge der Windhuhner (Grass) 1956

Vos ikh gloyb (Asch) 1941

Vos zaynen nisht gibliben (Bryks) 1972

Vœux (Pérec) 1989

Voyage chez les vivants (Gascar) 1958

Voyage de noces: Roman (Modiano) 1990

Voyage d'hiver (Pérec) 1993

Voyeur (Tabori) 1982

Vozvrashchenie pushkinskoi Rusalki (Thomas) 1998

Vse techet (V. Grossman) 1970

Vunderlekhe lebnsbashraybung fun Shmuel Aba Abervo: dos bukh fun Ganeydn (Manger) 1939

Vystrel (Rybakov) 1975

Vzmakh ruki (Yevtushenko) 1962

Vzpominky na Julia Fucika (Weil) 1947

W, Or the Memory of Childhood (Pérec) 1975

W, ou, le souvenir d'enfance (Pérec) 1975

Waage der Baleks und andere Erzählungen (Böll) 1958

Wächst das Rettende auch?: Gedichte für den Frieden (Fried) 1986

Waffen für Amerika (Feuchtwanger) 1947

Wahn oder der Teufel in Boston: Ein Stück in drei Akten (Feuchtwanger) 1948

Wahrer Held (Böll) 1960

Wahrhaftige Geschichte (Klemperer) 1954

Wahrheit ist dem Menschen zumutbar: Essays, Reden, kleinere Schriften (Bachmann) 1981

Wakacje Hioba (Wojdowski) 1962

Waking (Figes) 1981

Wald (Wiechert) 1920

Wälder und Menschen (Wiechert) 1936

Walk in Darkness (Habe) 1948

Wall (Hersey) 1950

Walnut Door (Hersey) 1977

Wanderer, kommst du nach Spa (Böll) 1950

Wanderers and Dreamers: Tales of the David Herman Theatre (Zable) 1998

Wanderer's Daysong (Levertov) 1981

Wanderings: Chaim Potok's History of the Jews (Potok) 1978

War Goes On (Asch) 1936

War hier Europa? Reden, Gedichte, Essays (Hochhuth) 1987

War Lover (Hersey) 1959

Warngedichte (Fried) 1964

Warren Hastings, Gouverneur von Indien: Schauspiel in vier Akten und einem Vorspiel (Feuchtwanger) 1927

Wars of the Jews (Sobol) 1981

Warsaw Diary of Adam Czerniaków (Czerniaków) 1968

Warsaw Ghetto: A Diary (Berg) 1945

Warshe (Asch) 1949

Wartime Lies (Begley) 1991

Warts and All (Spiegelman) 1990

Warum haben wir aufeinander geschossen? (Böll) 1981

Was beliebt ist auch erlaubt (Hochhuth) 1960

Was ist eigentlich ein Escoutadou?: Briefe mit Zeichnungen an Julie (Hildesheimer) 1996

Was kostet das Eisen (Brecht) 1939

Was nicht in meinen Büchern steht: Lebenserinnerungen (Frankl) 1995

Was soll aus dem jungen bloss werden? (Böll) 1981

Was Waschbären alles machen (Hildesheimer) 1979

Was würde Jesus dazu sagen?: Reden, Predigten, Aufsätze 1937 bis 1980 (Niemöller) 1980

Wasserman (Kaniuk) 1988

Wassertraeger Gottes: All das Vergangene (Sperber) 1974

Watcher and Other Stories (Calvino) 1971

Waterworks (Doctorow) 1994

Watten: Ein Nachlass (Bernhard) 1969

Way of All the Earth (Thomas) 1979

We Were Children Just Like You (Eliach) 1990

We Were In Auschwitz (Borowski) 1946

Weg zurück (Remarque) 1931

Wegry (Miłosz) 1960

Weib: Roman (Zweig) 1920

Weibliches Bildnis: Sämtliche Gedichte (Kolmar) 1980

Weihnachtsabend in San Cristobal (Böll) 1956

Weil die Stadt so fremd geworden ist (Böll) 1985

Weil unser einziges Nest unsere Flugel sind (Sachs) 1963

Weimar: A Jurisprudence of Crisis (Schlink) 2000

Weimar Culture: The Outsider As Insider (Gay) 1968

Weisman und Rotgesicht: ein jüdischer Western (Tabori) 1990

Weiss wpada do morza: Niebieskie kartki (Rudnicki) 1965

Weisse Büffel; oder, Von der grossen Gerechtigkeit (Wiechert) 1946

NOTES ON ADVISERS AND CONTRIBUTORS

ABRAMOVICH, Dvir. Jan Randa Lecturer in Modern Hebrew Literature and Language, University of Melbourne, Australia; chairperson, Hebrew Culture Department, State Zionist Council, Melbourne; and vice president, Australian Association for Jewish Studies. Editor of *Australian Journal for Jewish Studies.* Author of numerous scholarly articles, including "Israeli Detective Fiction: The Case of Batya-Gur and Shulamit Lapid," "Rape and Violence in Amos Oz's Fiction," and "He Who Rocks the Cradle: The Glorification of Fatherhood and the Attack on Motherhood in the Amos Oz Corpus," all in *Australian Journal for Jewish Studies,* and "The Bipolar Dichotomy in the Representation of Ageing in the Amos Oz Canon," in *Women in Judaism: A Multidisciplinary Journal.* **Essays:** Haim Gouri; Uri Zvi Greenberg; *Atrocity; The Chocolate Deal; House of Dolls; Star Eternal; Streets of the River: The Book of Dirges and Power; Sunrise over Hell.*

ACHBERGER, Karen. Professor of German, St. Olaf College, Northfield, Minnesota. Author of *Understanding Ingeborg Bachmann* and *Literatur als Libretto: Das deutsche Opernbuch seit 1945.* Contributor of articles to numerous journals and reference books, including *New German Critique, Modern Austrian Literature, German Quarterly, Text & Kritik, Monatshafte, East Central Europe,* and *The Dictionary of Literary Biography.* **Essays:** Ingeborg Bachmann; *Malina: A Novel.*

ADAMCZYK, Kazimierz. Assistant professor of Polish literature, Polonia Institute, Jagiellonian University, Kraków, Poland. Author of *Dziennik Jako Wyzwanie: Lechon, Gombrowicz, Herling-Grudzinski.* **Essays:** Tadeusz Borowski; Adam Czerniaków; Henryk Grynberg; Kazimierz Moczarski; Krystyn Olszewski; Janusz Nel Siedlecki; *Child of the Shadows; The Conversations with an Executioner; This Way for the Gas, Ladies and Gentlemen; The Victory; The Warsaw Diary of Adam Czerniaków; We Were in Auschwitz.*

ALFERS, Sandra. Visiting instructor, Department of German Studies, Dartmouth College, Hanover, New Hampshire. **Essays:** Ruth Klüger; *Still Alive: A Holocaust Girlhood Remembered.*

BAER, Gregory. Assistant professor of modern languages and director of honors, Carthage College, Kenosha, Wisconsin. Author of reviews for *GDR Bulletin, msnbc.com,* and *Monatshefte.* **Essays:** Jurek Becker; Edgar Hilsenrath; *Bronstein's Children; Jacob the Liar; The Nazi and the Barber; Night.*

BAER, Ulrich. Associate professor of German, New York University. Author of *Remnants of Song: Trauma and the Experience of Modernity in Charles Baudelaire and Paul Celan* and of numerous articles on trauma theory, photography, and nineteenth- and twentieth-century literature. Editor of *"Niemand Zengt fur den Zengen": Erinnerungskultur nach der Shoah.* **Essays:** Paul Celan; "Death Fugue."

BAHR, Ehrhard. Professor of German, University of California at Los Angeles, and formerly president, German Studies Association and Goethe Society of North America. Author of *The Novel As Archive* as well as books on Goethe, Georg Lukács, Ernst Bloch, and

Nelly Sachs. Editor of three-volume history of German literature and coeditor of *The Internalized Revolution.* **Essays:** Nelly Sachs; *Eli: A Mystery Play of the Sufferings of Israel;* "O the Chimneys!"

BALL, David. Professor of French and comparative literature, Smith College, Northampton, Massachusetts. Translator of *Darkness Moves: An Henri Michaux Anthology.* Contributor to numerous journals, including *Les Temps Modernes, Modern Philology, Revue de Litérature Comparée, Études Anglaises, The Massachusetts Review, The Germanic Review,* and *Translation Review.* Author of six poetry chapbooks. **Essays:** Anne Sexton; *The Awful Rowing toward God.*

BALL, Nicole. Lecturer in French, Smith College, Northampton, Massachusetts. Translator of several books from French into English and English into French, including Maryse Condé's *Pays mêlé* (as *Land of Many Colors*) and Jonathan Kellerman's *Survival of the Fittest* (as *La Sourde*). **Essays:** Patrick Modiano; *Occupation Trilogy: La Place de l'étoile, La Ronde de nuit, Les Boulevards de ceinture.*

BAMMER, Angelika. Associate professor of humanities and comparative literature, Graduate Institute of Liberal Arts, Emory University, Atlanta, Georgia. Author of *Partial Visions: Feminism and Utopianism in the 1970s.* Editor of *Displacements: Cultural Identities in Question.* Contributor to *Medicine and the History of the Body; Borders, Exiles, Diasporas; Encountering the Other(s): Studies in Literature; History and Culture;* and a special issue of *German Quarterly* on "Sites of Memory." **Essays:** Yitzhak Katzenelson; *The Song of the Murdered Jewish People.*

BAUM, Rachel. Lecturer, Departments of English and Hebrew Studies, University of Wisconsin-Milwaukee. Contributor of essays to scholarly publications, including *College Literature* and *Between Hope and Despair: Pedagogy and the Remembrance of Historical Trauma.* **Essays:** Carl Friedman; *Nightfather; The Shovel and the Loom.*

BELLMAN, Samuel I. Professor emeritus, California State Polytechnic University, Pomona. Author of studies of Marjorie Kinnan Rawlings and Constance Mayfield Rourke. Contributor to numerous journals, including *Kansas Review, Southern Quarterly, Saturday Review of Literature, Southwest Review, Arizona Review, The Literary Review, Descant, Short Story, Women and Language,* and *Platt Valley Review,* as well as essays for reference publications, including *Representations of Education in Literature, American Women Writers,* and *Encyclopedia of British Humorists.* **Essays:** E. L. Doctorow; *City of God.*

BENSON, Renate. Professor emerita of German and European studies, University of Guelph, Ontario. Author of *Erich Kästner: Studien zu seinem Werk* and *German Expressionist Drama: Ernst Toller and George Kaiser,* as well as several studies of Anne Hébert's short fiction. Contributor to *The Oxford Companion to Canadian Theater* and *The International Dictionary of Theater.* Translator of French Canadian literary works into German and English. **Essays:**

Ilse Aichinger; Heinrich Böll; *And Where Were You, Adam?*; *Herod's Children.*

BERENBAUM, Michael. Chair, Berenbaum Group, Los Angeles, and adjunct professor of theology, University of Judaism, Los Angeles. Formerly Ida E. King Distinguished Professor of Holocaust Studies, Richard Stockton College; Strassler Family Distinguished Visiting Professor of Holocaust Studies, Clark University; president and chief executive officer, Survivors of the Shoah Visual History Foundation; director, United States Holocaust Research Institute, United States Holocaust Memorial Museum; and Hymen Goldman Adjunct Professor of Theology, Georgetown University. Producer and consultant on Holocaust-related films, including *One Survivor Remembers: The Gerda Weissman Klein Story* and *Desperate Hours.* Author and editor of 12 books, including *After Tragedy and Triumph, The Vision of the Void: Theological Reflections on the Works of Elie Wiesel,* and *Witness to the Holocaust: An Illustrated Documentary History of the Holocaust in the Words of Its Victims, Perpetrators, and Bystanders.*

BERGER, Alan L. Raddock Eminent Scholar Chair of Holocaust Studies, Florida Atlantic University, and formerly Visiting Gumenick Professor of Judaic Studies, College of William and Mary, Williamsburg, Virginia. Author of *Crisis and Covenant* and *Children of Job.* Editor of *Judaism in the Modern World* and coeditor of *Second Generation Voices* and *Encyclopedia of Holocaust Literature.* Contributor to numerous journals, including *Studies in Jewish American Literature, Modern Judaism, Saul Bellow Journal, Modern Language Studies, Literature and Belief,* and *Judaism.* **Essays:** Helen Epstein; *Where She Came From: A Daughter's Search for Her Mother's History.*

BERKE, Jacqueline. Professor emerita of English and codirector of the Center for Holocaust/Genocide Study, Drew University, Madison, New Jersey. Author of *Watch Out for the Weather* (with Vivian Wilson) and *Berke's Twenty Questions for the Writer.* Contributor to numerous journals and anthologies, including *The Oxford Companion to Women's Writing in America* and *New Perspectives on the Holocaust: A Guide for Teachers and Scholars.* **Essays:** Ida Fink; *The Journey; A Scrap of Time and Other Stories; Traces.*

BLAHA, Franz. Associate professor, Department of English, University of Nebraska-Lincoln. Author of numerous essays on comparative popular culture, twentieth-century drama, and German/Austrian poetry and drama. **Essays:** Miklós Radnóti; *Clouded Sky.*

BLOCH, Felicity. Freelance reviewer and writer, Melbourne, Australia. Editor and translator of *I Rest My Case,* a memoir of interwar Polish Jewry by her father, Mark Verstandig. **Essays:** Maria Lewitt; *Come Spring: An Autobiographical Novel.*

BRODSKY, Patricia Pollock. Professor of German and Russian, University of Missouri-Kansas City. Contributor to numerous journals, including *Delos, Poets and Writers, Slavic and East European Journal, Denver Quarterly, Borderlines,* and *Comparative Literature.* Author of *Rainer Maria Rilke* and *Russia in the Works of Rainer Maria Rilke,* as well as a number of scholarly articles, including "The Hidden War: Working-Class Resistance during the Third Reich and the Postwar Suppression of Its History," in *Nature, Society and Thought,* and "Nomen ist Omen: Towards a Definition of Cultural

Identity," in *Germano-Slavica.* **Essays:** Yevgeny Yevtushenko; "Babii Yar."

BROWN, Sharon. Instructor of literature, State University of New York at Stony Brook. Author of *American Travel Narratives as a Literary Genre from 1542–1832: The Art of a Perpetual Journey* and "Alvar Nuñez Cabeza de Vaca," in *The Literature of Travel and Exploration.* **Essay:** *Austerlitz.*

BUDICK, Emily. Professor of American literature, Hebrew University, Jerusalem. Author of *Blacks and Jews in Literary Conversation, Engendering Romance: Women Writers and the Hawthorne Tradition, 1850–1990,* and *Fiction and Historical Consciousness: The American Romance Tradition.* **Essays:** Amos Oz; Aryeh Lev Stollman; *The Far Euphrates; Touch the Water, Touch the Wind.*

BURCH, Steven Dedalus. Visiting assistant professor, Department of Communication Arts, Allegheny College, Meadville, Pennsylvania. Contributor to numerous publications, including *Journal of Dramatic Theory and Criticism, David Mamet Review,* and *Oxford Companion to U.S. Culture.* **Essays:** Tony Kushner; Arthur Miller; Harold Pinter; *Ashes to Ashes; A Bright Room Called Day; Incident at Vichy.*

BUSH, Andrew. Director of Jewish studies and professor of Hispanic studies, Vassar College, Poughkeepsie, New York. Author of *The Routes of Modernity: Spanish-Mexican Poetry from the Early-Eighteenth to the Mid-Nineteenth Century.* Contributor to numerous journals and scholarly publications, including *Diacritics* and *Comparative Literature.* **Essays:** Luba Gurdus; Abraham Lewin; *A Cup of Tears: A Diary of the Warsaw Ghetto; The Death Train: A Personal Account of a Holocaust Survivor;* "My Quarrel with Hersh Rasseyner."

CAMMY, Justin D. Lecturer in Jewish studies and comparative literature, Smith College, Northampton, Massachusetts. Translator of Hinde Bergner's *In the Long Winter Nights: Memoirs of a Jewish Family in Galicia.* Contributor of scholarly articles and reviews to *Polin, The Forward, Midstream,* and *Boston Book Review.* **Essays:** Abraham Sutzkever; *Di Festung.*

CAPORINO, Grace Connolly. Adjunct professor of graduate seminar in Holocaust education, Manhattanville College, Purchase, New York, and visiting lecturer on Holocaust education, Fitchburg State University, Fitchburg, Massachusetts. Contributor to numerous publications, including *Remembering the Future: The Holocaust in the Age of Genocide* and *Teaching for a Tolerant World.* **Essays:** Yehuda Nir; *The Lost Childhood: A Memoir.*

CERF, Steven R. Skolfield Professor of German, Bowdoin College, Brunswick, Maine. Contributor of numerous articles to *Comparative Literature, Comparative Literature Studies, Colloquia Germanica, Revue de la Litérature Comparée,* and *Opera News.* **Essays:** Friedrich Dürrenmatt; Richard Glazar; Wolfgang Hildesheimer; *The Quarry; Trap with a Green Fence: Survival in Treblinka; Tynset.*

COHEN, Josh. Lecturer in English, Goldsmiths College, University of London. Author of *Spectacular Allegories: Postmodern American Writing and the Politics of Seeing* and *Interrupting Auschwitz: Art, Religion, Philosophy.* **Essays:** Georges Pérec; *W, or the Memory of Childhood.*

DACE, Tish. Chancellor Professor of English, University of Massachusetts-Dartmouth; chair, Maharam Foundation/American Theatre Wing/Hewes theatrical design awards, New York; and member, Executive Committee of the American Theatre Critics Association. Author of *Langston Hughes: The Contemporary Reviews,* as well as more than one thousand essays, articles, book chapters, and play reviews. New York critic for *Plays International* in London. **Essays:** Martin Sherman; *Bent.*

EAGLESTONE, Robert. Lecturer in English, Royal Holloway, University of London. Author of *Postmodernism and Holocaust Denial, Ethical Criticism: Reading after Levinas,* and *Doing English,* as well as numerous articles on contemporary European philosophy, historiography, twentieth-century literature, and Holocaust representation. Series editor for Routledge Critical Thinkers. **Essays:** Robert Antelme; Saul Friedlander; Kitty Hart; Sarah Kofman; Olga Lengyel; Filip Müller; David Rousset; Jorge Semprun; D. M. Thomas; Rudolf Vrba; *Eyewitness Auschwitz: Three Years in the Gas Chambers; Five Chimneys; The Human Species; I Am Alive!; I Cannot Forgive; Literature or Life; The Long Voyage; Return to Auschwitz: The Remarkable Story of a Girl Who Survived the Holocaust; Rue Ordener, Rue Labat; Stifled Words; What a Beautiful Sunday!; When Memory Comes; The White Hotel; A World Apart.*

ERSPAMER, Peter R. Adjunct professor of English and history, Mount Senario College, West Allis, Wisconsin. Author of *The Elusiveness of Tolerance: The "Jewish Question" from Lessing to the Napoleonic Wars,* 1997. Contributor to *Yale Companion to Jewish Writing and Thought in German Culture, 1096–1996, Reader's Guide to Judaism,* and *Literature and Ethnic Discrimination.* **Essays:** S.Y. Agnon; Edith Bruck; Etty Hillesum; Piotr Rawicz; Elie Wiesel; *The Accident; Blood from the Sky; Dawn; The Forgotten; The Gates of the Forest; An Interrupted Life: The Diaries of Etty Hillesum, 1941–43; Letters from Westerbork; Night; One Generation After; "The Sign"; The Town Beyond the Wall; Who Loves You like This.*

EZRAHI, Sidra DeKoven. Professor, Institute of Contemporary Jewry, Hebrew University of Jersualem. Author of *By Words Alone: The Holocaust in Literature* and *Booking Passage: Exile and Homecoming in the Modern Jewish Imagination.*

FAYE, Esther. Lecturer, Jewish Studies Program, Department of History, University of Melbourne, Australia. Contributor to numerous historical, literary, and psychoanalytic journals. **Essays:** Lily Brett; *In Full View.*

FERNEKES, William R. Supervisor of social studies, Hunterdon Central Regional High School, Flemington, New Jersey. Author of *The Oryx Holocaust Sourcebook* and coauthor of *Children's Rights: A Reference Handbook.* Contributor to numerous professional journals and reference publications, including *Social Education, The Social Studies, Social Science Record, The Holocaust's Ghost,* and *Teaching Holocaust Literature.* **Essays:** Hirsh Glik; *Zog Nit Keynmol.*

FISCHER, Jaimey. Assistant professor of German, Tulane University, New Orleans, Louisiana. Author of numerous articles on intellectual history and film studies. Coeditor of *Critical Theory: Current State and Future Prospects.* **Essays:** Claude Lanzmann; *Shoah.*

FORAY, Jennifer L. Writing instructor, Columbia University, New York. Coeditor of *Columbia Historical Review,* 2001–2002. **Essays:** Jacques Presser; *Night of the Girondists, or Breaking Point.*

FREADMAN, Richard. Professor of English and director of the Unit for Studies in Biography and Autobiography, La Trobe University, Melbourne, Australia. Author of *Eliot, James, and the Fictional Self: A Study in Character and Narration* and *Threads of Life: Autobiography and the Will,* as well as numerous journal articles. Coeditor of *On Literary Theory and Philosophy: A Cross-disciplinary Encounter* and *Renegotiating Ethics in Literature, Philosophy, and Theory.* Coauthor of *Re-thinking Theory: A Critique of Contemporary Literary Theory and an Alternative Account.* **Essays:** Susan Varga; Arnold Zable; *Heddy and Me; Jewels and Ashes.*

GANEVA, Mila. Visiting assistant professor, Miami University, Oxford, Ohio. Contributor to *Encyclopedia of Contemporary German Culture* and *Chicago Art Journal.* **Essays:** Eugene Heimler; Gert Hofmann; *Die Denunziation; Night of the Mist; Veilchenfeld.*

GARBER, Zev. Professor and chair of Jewish studies, Los Angeles Valley College, Valley Glen, California, and formerly visiting professor of religious studies, University of California at Riverside, and president, National Association of Professors of Hebrew. Editor-in-chief of *Studies in Shoah* and coeditor of *Shofar.* Author of *Methodology in the Academic Teaching of Judaism, Methodology in the Academic Teaching of the Holocaust, Teaching Hebrew Language and Literature at the College Level, Shoah: The Paradigmatic Genocide,* and *Perspectives on Zionism.* Consultant editor to *What Kind of God? Essays in Honor of Richard L. Rubenstein, Peace, In Deed: Essays in Honor of Harry James Cargas,* and *Academic Approaches to Teaching Jewish Studies.* Editorial advisor to *Western States Jewish History.* **Essays:** Jacob Glatstein; William Heyen; Martin Niemöller; Nechama Tec; Simon Wiesenthal; Aaron Zeitlin; *Dry Tears: The Story of a Lost Childhood; Erika: Poems of the Holocaust; Exile in the Fatherland: Martin Niemöller's Letters from Moabit Prison; I Keep Recalling: The Holocaust Poems of Jacob Glatstein; Lieder fun churban 'on lieder fun gloybin; The Sunflower.*

GAROFALO, Piero. Assistant professor of Italian, University of New Hampshire. Coeditor of *Re-viewing Fascism: Italian Cinema 1922–1943.* Contributor to numerous journals, including *Quaderni d'italianistica, Rivista di studi italiani,* and *Italian Culture.* **Essays:** Elsa Morante; *History: A Novel.*

GAWLIŃSKI, Stanisław. Associate professor of Polish studies, Jagiellonian University, Kraków, Poland. Author of *Szkola Poetycka Józefa Czechowicza w Okresie Miedywojennym: Elementy Socjologii i Poetyki* and *Polityczne Obowiazki: Odmiany Powojennej Prozy Politycznej w Latach 1945–1975,* as well as articles on emigrant settlements and modern Polish literature. Coauthor of *Polish Literature 1918–1975.* **Essays:** Tadeusz Różewicz; Bogdan Wojdowski; *Bread for the Departed; Collected Poems.*

GERSTLE, Ellen. Adjunct professor, Farleigh Dickinson University, Teaneck, New Jersey. Coordinator of writing workshops for Holocaust survivors at the Drew University Center for Holocaust/Genocide Study. Contributor to *Studies in American Jewish Literature.* **Essays:** Philip Roth; "Eli, the Fanatic"; *The Ghost Writer;*

Operation Shylock: A Confession; Zuckerman Bound: A Trilogy and Epilogue.

GIGLIOTTI, Simone. Lecturer in history, Victoria University of Wellington, New Zealand, and visiting postdoctoral fellow, United States Holocaust Memorial Museum, Washington, D.C. Formerly instructor of modern European history and the Holocaust, University of Melbourne, Australia. **Essays:** Mark Baker; *The Fiftieth Gate: A Journey Through Memory.*

GILLMAN, Abigail. Assistant professor of German and Hebrew, Boston University. Has published articles on Franz Kafka, Arthur Schnitzler, Hugo von Hofmannsthal, and the history of German-Jewish Bible translation. **Essays:** Yehuda Amichai; *Not of this Time, Not of this Place.*

GLASER, Michael S. Professor of literature and creative writing, as well as founder and director, annual summer literary festival, St. Mary's College of Maryland. Author of three volumes of poetry: *A Lover's Eye, In the Men's Room and Other Poems,* and *Michael Glaser's Greatest Hits, 1975–2000.* Editor of *The Cooke Book: A Seasoning of Poems* and *Weavings 2000.* Contributor of poetry to *Antioch Review, Prairie Schooner, New Letters, American Scholar, Midstream,* and *Jewish Frontier.* **Essays:** Adrienne Rich; "Eastern War Time."

GOLDENBERG, Myrna. Professor of English and director of the Humanities Institute, Montgomery College, Maryland. Contributor to numerous journals and books, including *Feminist Studies, Women in the Holocaust, Holocaust Literature, Remembering for the Future: The Holocaust in an Age of Genocide, Jewish Women: A Comprehensive Encyclopedia, Encyclopedia of Holocaust Literature, Jewish Women in America: An Historical Encyclopedia,* and *Holocaust and Genocide Studies.* **Essays:** Aharon Appelfeld; *Badenheim 1939; The Immortal Bartfuss; The Retreat; Tzili: The Story of a Life.*

GOLDSHLAGER, Alain. Professor of French, University of Western Ontario, London, Ontario, and national director, Canada-Israel Foundation for Academic Exchanges. Formerly president, Canadian Comparative Literature Association and the Canadian Semiotic Association. Has written extensively on nineteenth- and twentieth-century French literature, the philosophy of language, discourse analysis, and anti-Semitic discourse (German, French, and Russian). Author of *Simone Wiel et Spinoza* and *Building History: Art, Memory, and Myth* (with Naomi Kramer). Editor of *Scientific Discourse as prejudice-carrier/Le Discours scientifique comme porteur de préjugés* and *La Shoah: Temoignage impossible?* **Essays:** Edmond Jabès; Albert Memmi; The Book of Questions; Pillar of Salt.

GRUETTNER, Mark. Associate professor of German and chair, Department of Ancient and Modern Languages, Centenary College, Hackettstown, New Jersey. Author of *Intertextualität und Zeitkritik in Günter Grass' "Kopfgeburten" und "Die Rättin."* **Essays:** Günter Grass; *From the Diary of a Snail; The Tin Drum.*

GUINEY, M. Martin. Associate professor of French, Kenyon College, Gambier, Ohio. Contributor to numerous scholarly publications, including *Studies in Twentieth Century Literature, Gide and Politics,*

Selected Proceedings of the 19th-Century French Studies Conference, Masterplots II: American Fiction Series, Masterplots: Twentieth Anniversary Revised Edition, Masterplots II: Women's Literature Series, Dreams in French Literature, and *Bulletin des Amis d'André Gide.* **Essays:** Pierre Gascar; Germaine Tillion; *Ravensbrück; The Season of the Dead.*

GUNTHER, Stefan. Academic program manager, Graduate School, USDA. Author of reviews of *The Stories of David Bergelson* and *Politik mit der Erinnerung.* **Essays:** Walter Abish; Bernhard Schlink; W. G. Sebald; Art Spiegelman; *The Emigrants;* "The English Garden"; *How German Is It; Maus—a Survivor's Tale; The Reader.*

HALIO, Jay L. Professor of English, University of Delaware, Newark. Author of *Angus Wilson* and *Philip Roth Revisited,* as well as several books on Shakespeare's plays in performance. Editor of numerous collections of essays on modern fiction. **Essays:** Bernard Malamud; "The German Refugee"; "The Lady of the Lake"; "The Last Mohican."

HARRAN, Marilyn J. Stern Chair in Holocaust Education, director, Rodgers Center for Holocaust Education, and professor, religious studies and history, Chapman University, Orange, California. Formerly associate, United States Holocaust Museum, and instructor, Barnard College, Columbia University, New York. Author of two books and editor of a book on church history. Contributor to *The Holocaust Chronicle, The Encyclopedia of Religion,* and *The Encyclopedia of the Reformation.* **Essays:** Thomas "Toivi" Blatt; Gerda Weissmann Klein; Miklos Nyiszli; Gisella Perl; *All but My Life; Auschwitz: A Doctor's Eyewitness Account; From the Ashes of Sobibor: A Story of Survival; I Was a Doctor in Auschwitz.*

HATHAWAY, Heather. Associate professor of English and codirector, University Honors Program, Marquette University, Milwaukee, Wisconsin. Author of *Caribbean Waves: Relocating Claude McKay and Paule Marshall,* as well as several book reviews for *African American Review.* Coeditor of *Race and the Modern Artist* and *Conversations with Paule Marshall.* Contributor to numerous publications, including *Beyond the Binary: Reconstructing Cultural Identity in a Multicultural Context, Refiguring the Father: New Feminist Readings of Patriarchy, The Oxford Companion to African American Literature, The Oxford Companion to Women's Writing in the United States,* and *Reader's Guide to Literature in English.* **Essays:** Charles Reznikoff; *Holocaust.*

HAWKINS, Beth. Assistant professor of English, Depauw University, Greencastle, Indiana. Author of *Reluctant Theologians: Kafka, Celan, Jabès,* as well as numerous articles, including "Madness in the Face of Silence," in *Genre,* and "The Washing of the Word/The Washing of the World: Paul Celan and the Language of Sanctification," in *Shofar.* **Essays:** Kadya Molodowsky; *Paper Bridges: Selected Poems of Kadya Molodowsky.*

HOBOT, Joanna. Assistant professor, Jagiellonian University, Kraków, Poland. Author of *Playing Games with Censorship in Polish Poetry (1968–1976).* **Essays:** Marek Edelman; Wladyslaw Szpilman; *The Ghetto Fights; The Pianist: The Extraordinary Story of One Man's Survival in Warsaw, 1939–45.*

HOFFMAN, Michael. Professor of English, University of California at Davis. Author of *The Development of Abstractionism in the Writings of Gertrude Stein, The Buddy System* (a novel), *The Subversive Vision: American Romanticism in Literature,* and *Gertrude Stein.* Editor of *Critical Essays on Gertrude Stein, Essentials of the Theory of Fiction,* and *Critical Essays on American Modernism.* Has contributed numerous essays and book reviews to scholarly journals. **Essays:** John Hersey; Jerzy Kosinski; *Notes of the Author on the Painted Bird; The Painted Bird; Steps; The Wall.*

HOLTSCHNEIDER, K. Hannah. Junior research fellow, Centre for Jewish-Christian Relations, Cambridge University, England. Author of *German Protestants Remember the Holocaust: Theology and the Construction of Collective Memory* and "JüdInnen in Deutschland: Eine Kritische Untersuchung der Theologie Friedrich-Wilhelm Marquardts," in *Von Gott reden im Land der Täter? Theologische Perspektiven der Dritten Generation nach Auschwitz.* **Essays:** Jean Améry; *At the Mind's Limits: Contemplations by a Survivor on Auschwitz and its Realities; Radical Humanism: Selected Essays.*

IOANID, Radu. Director, International Archival Programs Division, United States Holocaust Memorial Museum. Author of *The Holocaust in Romania: The Destruction of Jews and Gypsies under the Antonescu Regime, 1940–1944,* and *The Sword of the Archangel: Fascist Ideology in Romania.* Editor of *Mihail Sebastian, Journal 1935–1944, The Fascist Years.* **Essays:** Mihail Sebastian; *Journal 1935–1944: The Fascist Years.*

JACOBSON, Manfred. Professor, Department of Modern Languages, University of Nebraska-Lincoln. Translator of *The Correspondence of Walter Benjamin 1910–1940* (with Evelyn Jacobson). Author of numerous articles on nineteenth-century German literature. **Essay:** *Vittel Diary.*

KAPLAN, Eran. Postdoctoral fellow, University of Toronto. Contributor to numerous journals, including *Journal of Israeli History.* **Essays:** Dahn Ben-Amotz; *To Remember, to Forget.*

KARCZ, Andrzej. Assistant professor of Polish language and literature, Department of Slavic Languages and Literatures, University of Kansas, Lawrence. Author of *The Polish Formalist School and Russian Formalism.* Contributor to numerous scholarly journals, anthologies, and reference publications, including *Polish Review, Teksty Drugie, Ethos, Zagadnienia Rodzajow Literackich, Sarmatian Review, Postscriptum, Encyclopedia of the Essay, Studia o Stanislawie Vincenzie, Proza Polska w Kregu Religijnych Inspiractji,* and *Encyclopedia of Life Writing.* **Essays:** Adolf Rudnicki; *Ascent to Heaven.*

KAY, Avi. Dean of students and associate professor of psychology, Touro College, Jerusalem. Has served as an educational consultant to the Van Leer Institute in Jerusalem and Poppers-Prins Foundation of Holland. **Essays:** Jack Kuper; *Child of the Holocaust.*

KLÍMA, Cynthia A. Associate professor, State University of New York, Geneseo. Contributor to *Reader's Guide to Judaism* and *History in Dispute: The Holocaust.* Author of "Theater-Zauberworte!: The Prager Kreis and the German Theater," in *Journal of the Kafka Society of America.* Has written numerous book reviews for *Slavic and East European Journal* and *Monatshefle.* **Essays:** Josef Bor; Rachmil Bryks; Yaffa Eliach; Erich Fried; Ladislav Fuks; Bernard

Kops; Arnošt Lustig; Eva Mändlová Roubíčková; Yitzhak "Antek" Zuckerman; *A Cat in the Ghetto: Four Novelettes; Darkness Casts No Shadow; Diamonds of the Night; Dreams of Anne Frank: A Play for Young People; Ghetto Factory 76: Chemical Waste Conversion; Hasidic Tales of the Holocaust; The Last Jew; Mr. Theodore Mundstock; Night and Hope; A Prayer for Katerina Horovitzova; A Surplus of Memory: Chronicle of the Warsaw Ghetto Uprising; The Terezín Requiem; Trost und Angst: Erzählungen über Juden und Nazis; The Unloved: From the Diary of Perla S.; We're Alive and Life Goes On: A Theresienstadt Diary.*

LANGER, Lawrence L. Professor emeritus of English, Simmons College, Boston. Author of numerous books on Holocaust literature, testimony, and art, including *The Holocaust and the Literary Imagination,* 1977, *Holocaust Testimonies: The Ruins of Memory,* 1991, *Admitting the Holocaust: Collected Essays,* 1995, *Art from the Ashes: A Holocaust Anthology,* 1995, *Preempting the Holocaust,* 1998, and *In a Different Light: The Book of Genesis in the Art of Samuel Bak,* 2001.

LEAMAN, Oliver. Professor of philosophy and Zantker Professor of Judaic Studies, University of Kentucky, Lexington. Editor of *Encyclopedia of Asian Philosophy.* Coeditor of *Encyclopedia of Death and Dying.* **Essays:** Charlotte Delbo; Aharon Megged; *Auschwitz and After; Di ershte Nakht in Geto; Green Aquarium; Hannah Senesh.*

LEVINSON, Julian. Assistant professor of English and Judaic studies, University of Michigan, Ann Arbor. Author of numerous articles for professional journals, including "Transmitting Yiddishkeit: Irving Howe and Jewish-American Culture," in *Jewish Culture and History,* Winter 1999, and "Derac(e)inated Jews," in *Postmodern Culture,* Spring 1999. **Essays:** Arthur A. Cohen; Cynthia Ozick; *In the Days of Simon Stern; The Messiah of Stockholm;* "Rosa"; "The Shawl."

LIGĘZA, Wojciech. Associate professor, Jagiellonian University, Kraków, Poland. Author of *Jasniejsze Strony Katastrofy: Szkice o Twórczosci Poetów Emigracyjnych* and *Jerozolima i Babilon: Miasta Poetów Emigracyjnych.* Coauthor and editor of *"Ktokolwiek Jestes bez Ojczyzny—": Topika Polskiej Poezji Emigracyjnej, Wiatr nas nosi po Swiecie: Antologia Polskiej Poezji Zolnierskiej, 1939–1945, Grudki Kadzidla,* and *Pamiec Glosów: o Twórczosci Aleksandra Wata.* Contributor to numerous Polish literary and cultural magazines, including *Pamietnik Literacki, Teksty Drugie, Ruch Literacki, Prace Polonistyczne,* and *Archiwum Emigraczi.* **Essays:** Jerzy Ficowski; Wladyslaw Szlengel; *Co czytalem umarlym; A Reading of Ashes: Poems.*

LINDSAY, Mark R. Lecturer, Department of History, and subdean, Faculty of Arts, University of Western Australia, Crawley. Author of *Covenanted Solidarity: The Theological Basis of Karl Barth's Opposition to Nazi Antisemitism and the Holocaust.* Contributor to numerous scholarly publications, including *Karl Barth: A Future for Postmodern Theology?, Remembering for the Future,* and *Companion to Modern Theology.* **Essays:** André Schwarz-Bart; *The Last of the Just.*

LOENTZ, Elizabeth. Assistant professor of German, University of Illinois at Chicago. Author of *Negotiating Identities: Bertha Pappenheim ('Anna O.') as German-Jewish Feminist, Social Worker,*

Activist and Author, 1999. **Essays:** Irena Klepfisz; Gertrud Kolmar; *Dark Soliloquy: The Selected Poems of Gertrud Kolmar;* "*Di rayze aheym/*The journey home."

McGLOTHLIN, Erin. Assistant professor of German, Washington University, St. Louis, Missouri, and formerly guest lecturer, University of Dortmund, Germany. Author of *Remembering Memory: The Holocaust and the "Second Generation,"* as well as essays on Ruth Klüger and Jean Améry. **Essays:** Robert Menasse; *Wings of Stone.*

McLOUGHLIN, Maryann. Assistant supervisor, Holocaust Resource Center, Richard Stockton College of New Jersey. Contributor to numerous publications, including *Oxford Companion to Crime and Mystery, Clues: A Journal of Detection, Transformations,* and *CEA Forum.* **Essays:** Livia E. Bitton-Jackson; *Elli: Coming of Age in the Holocaust.*

MARKUS, Andrew. Director, Australian Centre for the Study of Jewish Civilisation, Monash University, Victoria. Author of *Race: John Howard and the Remaking of Australia* and *Australian Race Relations.* Coeditor of *The Struggle for Aboriginal Rights: A Documentary History.* **Essays:** Giuliana Tedeschi; Avraham Tory; Mark Verstandig; *I Rest My Case; Surviving the Holocaust: The Kovno Ghetto Diary; There Is a Place on Earth: A Woman in Birkenau.*

MAYOR, Alisa Gayle. Scientific translator and editor, BIOSIS, Philadelphia, and formerly visiting scholar, Department of Slavic Languages, Brown University, Providence, Rhode Island. Contributor to numerous journals and books, including *Modern Czech Studies, Czech Language News, Reader's Guide to Judaism,* 2000, and *Biographical Dictionary of Enlightenment and Revolution,* 2002. **Essays:** Anatoli Kuznetsov; Mordecai Richler; *The Apprenticeship of Duddy Kravitz; Babi Yar: A Documentary Novel.*

METER, Alejandro. Assistant professor of Spanish and Latin American literature, University of San Diego, California. Contributor of articles on Latin American Jewish Writers. **Essays:** Jorge Luis Borges; "Deutsches Requiem"; *The Secret Miracle.*

MEYER, STEPHEN. Associate editor, *Reference Guide to Holocaust Literature.* **Essays:** "Landscape of Screams"; "Shibboleth."

NAKHIMOVSKY, Alice. Professor and chair, Department of Russian, Colgate University, Hamilton, New York. Author of *Russian-Jewish Literature and Identity* and *Witness to History: The Photographs of Yevgeny Khaldei,* as well as other books and essays on Russian twentieth-century literature and Russian-Jewish writers. **Essays:** Dan Pagis; *Kol Ha-shirim: "Aba."*

NEWMAN, Margie. Instructor of English, University of Minnesota, Minneapolis, and lecturer on the experiences of children of Holocaust survivors. Author of the short story "But Does He Speak Yiddish?" in *Outlook,* 2001. **Essays:** Vladka Meed; *On Both Sides of the Wall.*

NEWTON, Adam Zachary. Associate professor of English, University of Texas at Austin. Author of *Narrative Ethics, Facing Black and Jew: Literature as Public Space in 20th Century America, The Fence and the Neighbor: Emmanuel Levinas, Yeshayahu Leibowitz, and*

Israel among the Nations, and *The Elsewhere: On Belonging at a Near Distance.* Contributor to numerous journals, including *ALH, Narrative, SAQ, Prospects,* and *Social Identities.* **Essays:** David Grossman; A. B. Yehoshua; *Mr. Mani; See Under: Love.*

ORENSTEIN, Eugene. Associate professor of Jewish studies, McGill University, Montreal. Contributor to *Leksikon fun der nayer yidisher literatur, Encyclopedia of World Literature in the 20th Century* (Vol. 2), and *The Canadian Jewish Mosaic,* 1981. Co-translator of *Hasidism and the Jewish Enlightenment: Their Confrontation in Galicia and Poland in the First Half of the Nineteenth Century.* **Essays:** Herman Kruk; *Togbukh fun Vilner Geto.*

ORLA-BUKOWSKA, Annamaria. Professor of sociology, Jagiellonian University, Kraków, Poland.

OSBORN, Jan M. Lecturer, Department of English and Comparative Literature, Chapman University, Orange, California; faculty coordinator, Chapman University/Orange High School Literacy Partnership; and co-coordinator, Annual Holocaust Writing Contest, sponsored by the Rodgers Center for Holocaust Education at Chapman University. **Essays:** Chaim Potok; *The Chosen; My Name Is Asher Lev.*

PARTSCH, Cornelius. Assistant professor, Department of German Studies, Mount Holyoke College, South Hadley, Massachusetts. Author of *Schräge Töne: Jazz und Unterhaltungsmusik in der Kultur der Weimarer Republik.* **Essays:** Bertolt Brecht; *The Resistible Rise of Arturo Ui.*

PATTERSON, David. Bornblum Chair in Judaic Studies, University of Memphis, Tennessee. Coeditor of *Encyclopedia of Holocaust Literature.* Author of 20 books, including *Sun Turned to Darkness, Along the Edge of Annihilation,* and *The Shriek of Silence,* as well as 90 articles and book chapters. **Essays:** Silvano Arieti; Alexander Donat; Emil Dorian; Moshe Flinker; Janusz Korczak; Isabella Leitner; Sara Nomberg-Przytyk; Emmanuel Ringelblum; Yitskhok Rudashevski; Hannah Senesh; *Auschwitz: True Tales from a Grotesque Land; The Diary of the Vilna Ghetto: June 1941–April 1943; Fragments of Isabella: A Memoir of Auschwitz; Ghetto Diary; Hannah Senesh: Her Life and Diary; The Holocaust Kingdom; Notes from the Warsaw Ghetto: The Journal of Emmanuel Ringelblum; The Parnas: A Scene from the Holocaust; The Quality of Witness: A Romanian Diary 1937–1944; Young Moshe's Diary: The Spiritual Torment of a Jewish Boy in Nazi Europe.*

PENTLIN, Susan Lee. Professor, Department of Modern Languages, Central Missouri State University, Warrensburg. Author of *Effect of the Third Reich on the Teaching of German in the United States: A Historical Study,* 1977, and *The Holocaust in Memory: Selected Papers,* 1996. **Essays:** Mary Berg; *Warsaw Ghetto: A Diary.*

PIERCE, Peter. Professor of Australian literature, James Cook University, Queensland, Australia. Author of *The Country of Lost Children: An Australian Anxiety, Australian Melodramas: Thomas Keneally's Fiction,* and *From Go to Whoa: A Compendium of the Australian Turf.* Editor of *The Oxford Literary Guide to Australia* and *The Poet's Discovery: 19th Century Australia in Verse.* **Essays:** Thomas Keneally; *Schindler's List.*

PINSKER, Sanford. Professor of English, Franklin and Marshall College, Lancaster, Pennsylvania, and formerly coeditor, Holocaust Studies Annual. Has written extensively on Jewish literature and culture. **Essays:** Leslie Epstein; *Ice Fire Water: A Leib Goldkorn Cocktail; King of the Jews: A Novel of the Holocaust.*

PLOTKIN, Diane. Professor of Holocaust studies and world literature, Brookhaven College, Farmers Branch, Texas. Coauthor and editor of *Sisters in Sorrow: Voices of Care in the Holocaust.* Contributor to a number of scholarly publications, including *Problems Unique to the Holocaust* and *The Pall of the Past: The Holocaust, Genocide, and the 21st Century.* **Essays:** Elie Aron Cohen; *Human Behaviour in the Concentration Camp: A Medical and Psychological Study.*

POLAK, Alan. Member, Department of English Literature, University of Sheffield, England. **Essays:** Chaim A. Kaplan; Jaroslaw Rymkiewicz; Jean-François Steiner; *The Final Station: Umschlagplatz; Scroll of Agony: The Warsaw Diary of Chaim A. Kaplan; Treblinka.*

RAWSON, Judy. Senior lecturer emeritus and formerly chair, Department of Italian, University of Warwick, England. Translator of *The History of Florence* by Niccolo Machievelli. Editor of Manchester University Press edition of Ignazio Silone's *Fontamara.* Contributor to numerous journals, including *Modern Language Review, Italian Studies,* and *Journal of the Association of Teachers of Italian.* **Essays:** Giorgio Bassani; *The Garden of the Finzi-Contini; A Plaque on via Mazzini.*

REID, Allan. Professor and chair, Department of Culture and Language Studies, University of New Brunswick, Canada, and formerly president, Canadian Association of Slavists. Book review editor, *Canadian Slavonic Papers,* and member of the editorial board, *International Fiction Review.* Author of *Literature as Communication and Cognition in Bakhtin and Lotman.* Contributor to numerous scholarly journals, including *The World and I, Russkii iazyk za rubezhom, Linguistica Silesiana, S—European Journal for Semiotic Studies, Canadian Slavonic Papers, Discours social/Social Discourse,* and *Reports on Philosophy.* Coeditor of Isaak Babel issue of *Canadian Slavonic Papers.* Translator of articles by Efim Etkind, Stanislaw Beres, and Stefan Kozak. **Essays:** Halina Birenbaum; Czesław Miłosz; Manès Sperber; Wisława Szymborska; *Hope Is the Last to Die: A Coming of Age under Nazi Terror; Like a Tear in the Ocean; Ocalenie; Poems, New and Collected, 1957–1997.*

REITTER, Paul. Professor of German, Ohio State University. Author of numerous articles, essays, and reviews for scholarly journals and reference publications, including *Germanic Review, The Nation, Shofar, Encyclopedia of German Literature,* and *Internationales Germanistenlexikon, 1800–1950.* **Essays:** Victor Klemperer; George A. Steiner; *I Will Bear Witness: A Diary of the Nazi Years; The Portage to San Cristóbal of A.H.*

ROGACHEVSKII, Andrei. Lecturer in Russian, Department of Slavonic Studies, University of Glasgow. Author of *The Rhetorical Tradition in Pushkin's Oeuvre.* Coeditor of special issues of *Canadian-American Slavic Studies* on East and Central European Émigré Literatures, 1999, "Bribery and Blat in Russia," 2000, "Russian Jews in Great Britain," 2000, and "Russian Writers on Britain," 2001. **Essays:** Anatolii Rybakov; *Heavy Sand.*

ROSENBERG, Edgar. Professor of English and comparative literature, Cornell University, Ithaca, New York, and formerly visiting professor, Stanford University, California, and University of Haifa, Israel. Author of *From Shylock to Svengali,* as well as two monographs on the Jewish figure in Elizabethan and eighteenth-century drama. Editor of Norton Critical Series edition of Charles Dickens's *Great Expectations,* 1999. Contributor of essays, translations, and fiction to a number of magazines and scholarly journals, including *Commentary, Judaism, Esquire,* and *Epoch.* **Essays:** Heinar Kipphardt; Erich Maria Remarque; Ernst Wiechert; *Bruder Eichmann; The Forest of the Dead; Joel Brand: Die Geschichte eines Geschäfts; The Night in Lisbon; Spark of Life.*

ROSENBLUM, Joseph. Independent scholar. Contributor to numerous reference books and journals, including *Dictionary of Literary Biography, Encyclopedia of Romanticism,* and *The Book Collector.* **Essays:** Peter Gay; Isaac Bashevis Singer; *Enemies: A Love Story*; "The Lecture"; "The Letter Writer"; *My German Question: Growing up in Nazi Berlin.*

ROSENFELD, Alvin H. Professor of English and director, Borns Jewish Studies Program, Indiana University, Bloomington. Author of numerous books and articles on Holocaust literature, American Jewish literature, and American poetry, including *A Double Dying: Reflections on Holocaust Literature,* 1980, *Imagining Hitler,* 1985, and *Thinking about the Holocaust: After Half a Century,* 1997.

ROTH, John K. Russell K. Pitzer Professor of Philosophy, Claremont McKenna College, Claremont, California. Author of more than 30 books, including *A Consuming Fire: Encounters with Elie Wiesel and the Holocaust,* 1979, *Approaches to Auschwitz,* with Richard L. Rubenstein, 1979, *Holocaust: Religious and Philosophical Implications,* with Michael Berenbaum, 1989, *Different Voices: Women and the Holocaust,* with Carol Rittner, 1993, *Ethics after the Holocaust: Perspectives, Critiques and Responses,* 1999, and *Holocaust Politics,* 2001.

RUDERMAN, Judith. Vice provost for academic and administrative services and adjunct professor of English, Duke University, Durham, North Carolina. Author of *D.H. Lawrence and the "Devouring Mother,"* as well as books on William Styron and Joseph Heller. Contributor of articles and reviews to *D.H. Lawrence Review, Journal of Modern Literature, Studies in the Novel,* and *English Literature in Transition.* **Essays:** William Styron; *Sophie's Choice.*

RUSSELL, Susan. Assistant professor of theatre arts, Department of Theatre Arts, Gettysburg College, Pennsylvania, and formerly assistant, Empty Space Theatre, Seattle, Oregon Shakespeare Festival, Ashland, and Utah Shakespearean Festival. Directed American premiere of George Tabori's *Jubilee* at Valparaiso University, 1995. Author of "The Possibilities for Brechtian Theory in Contemporary Theatrical Practice: George Tabori's *Jubilee,*" in *Verkörperte Geschichtsentwürfe: George Taboris Theaterarbeit,* 1998. **Essays:** Thomas Bernhard; Erwin Sylvanus; George Tabori; *The Cannibals; Dr. Korczak and the Children; Heldenplatz; Jubiläum; Mutters Courage.*

RUTLAND, Suzanne. Chair, Department of Semitic Studies, University of Sydney, Australia, and president, Australian Jewish Historical Society. Author of *Edge of the Diaspora: Two Centuries of*

Jewish Settlement in Australia and *Pages of History: A Century of the Australian Jewish Press.* Newsletter editor, Australian Association for Jewish Studies. **Essays:** Abraham Biderman; *The World of My Past.*

SACHS, Murray. Professor emeritus of German and comparative literature, Brandeis University, Waltham, Massachusetts. Author of *The Career of Alphonse Daudet: A Critical Study,* 1965, *The French Short Story in the Nineteenth Century: A Critical Anthology,* 1969, and *Anatole France: The Short Stories,* 1974. Contributor to numerous reference works and journals, including *Columbia Dictionary of Modern European Literature* (2nd edition), *St. James Press Guide to Biography, St. James Reference Guide to Short Fiction, PMLA, The French Review, Romanic Review, L'Esprit Créateur, Nineteenth-Century French Studies, ADFL Bulletin, Romance Quarterly,* and *Modern Language Review.* **Essays:** Albert Camus; A.M. Klein; *Collected Poems; The Fall; The Plague; The Second Scroll.*

SANDERS, Ivan. Adjunct professor, Department of Slavic Languages, Columbia University, New York. Translator of works by György Konrád, Péter Nádas, Milá Füst, and Péter Esterházy. Contributor of articles and studies to *New York Times Book Review, New Republic, The Nation, Judaism,* and *Jewish Social Studies.* **Essays:** Imre Kertész; *Fateless; Kaddish for a Child Not Born.*

SCHLANT, Ernestine. Professor emerita and formerly professor of German and comparative literature, Montclair State University, New Jersey. Formerly assistant producer, Cinema Arts Associates, New York; associate professor of German, State University of New York, Stony Brook; and instructor of French, Spelman College, Atlanta. Editor and contributing author of *Legacies and Ambiguities: Postwar Fiction and Culture in West Germany and Japan,* 1991. Translator and author of books, textbooks, articles, and reviews, including *Die Philosophie Hermann Brochs,* 1971, *Hermann Broch,* 1978, and *The Language of Silence: West German Literature and the Holocaust,* 1999. Contributor to *Germanic Review, German Studies Review, Modern Austrian Literature,* and *Modern Fiction Studies,* among others.

SCHMITZ, Walter. Chair, German Literature Department, Technische Universität Dresden, Germany. Coauthor of numerous books, including *Max Frisch, Gesammelte Werke in zeitlicher Folge,* and *Bettine von Arnim: Politische Schriften.* **Essays:** Hans Habe; Wolfgang Koeppen; Hanna Krall; *Jakob Littners Aufzeichnungen aus einem Erdloch: Roman; The Mission; Shielding the Flame: An Intimate Conversation with Dr. Marek Edelman, the Last Surviving Leader of the Warsaw Ghetto Uprising.*

SCHNEIDER, Gerd K. Professor of German, Syracuse University, New York. Author of *Die Rezeption von Arthur Schnitzlers Reigen 1897–1994.* Contributor to numerous journals and encyclopedia, including *Modern Austrian Literature, Jura Soyfer: Internationale Zeitschrift für Kulturwissenschaften, Dictionary of Literary Biography,* and *Encyclopedia of German Literature.* **Essays:** Max Frisch; Stefan Zweig; *Andorra: A Play in Twelve Scenes; Biedermann and the Fire Raisers: A Morality Without a Moral; Now They Sing Again: Attempt of a Requiem; The Royal Game; The World of Yesterday: An Autobiography.*

SCHRECKENBERGER, Helga. Professor of German, director of women's studies, and affiliated faculty member of the Holocaust Program, University of Vermont, Burlington. Author of publications

on Erich Maria Remarque, Gullaume Apollinaire, Gerhard Roth, Felix Mitterer, Henize R. Unger, and others. Translator of works by Gerhard Roth and Elfriede Jelinek. Contributor to *The Feminist Encyclopedia of German Literature* and *Modern Germany: An Encyclopedia of History, People, and Culture, 1871–1990.* **Essays:** Bertha Ferderber-Salz; Eva Figes; Jakov Lind; *And the Sun Kept Shining; Counting My Steps: An Autobiography; Landscape in Concrete; Little Eden: A Child at War;* "Soul of Wood."

SCHRÖER, Olav. Member, Institute for Advanced Theatre Studies, Justus Liebig University, Giessen, Germany, and formerly DAAD-Lecturer in the Division of Foreign Languages, Tel Aviv University. Cowriter of "Shalom Hamlet. Israeli-German Meetings on Stage," a one-hour program for German television, 1998. **Essays:** Peter Weiss; *The Investigation.*

SCRASE, David. Professor of German and director of Holocaust studies, University of Vermont, Burlington. Author and translator of numerous books and articles on modern German literature. **Essays:** Bruno Apitz; Louis Begley; Cordelia Edvardson; Marga Minco; Jiří Weil; *Bitter Herbs: A Little Chronicle; Burned Child Seeks the Fire: Memoir; Life with a Star; Naked among Wolves; Wartime Lies.*

SHAVITSKY, Ziva. Head, Department of Hebrew Studies, University of Melbourne, Australia, and president, Australian Association for Jewish Studies. Contributor of numerous articles to the journals *Abr-Nahrain* and *Australian Journal of Jewish Studies.* **Essays:** Yoram Kaniuk; Abba Kovner; *Adam Resurrected; A Canopy in the Desert; My Little Sister.*

SILVERMAN, Lisa. Member, Department of Germanic Languages and Literatures, Yale University, New Haven, Connecticut. Author of "'Der Richtige Riecher': The Reconfiguration of Jewish and American Identities in the Work of Doron Rabinovici," in *German Quarterly,* 1999. **Essays:** Robert Schindel; "Errinerungen an Prometheus"; *Gebürtig.*

SPARGO, R. Clifton. Assistant professor, Department of English, Marquette University, Milwaukee, Wisconsin, and formerly Paul Resnick Fellow, Center for Advanced Holocaust Studies, United States Holocaust Memorial Museum, 2000–2001. Contributor to numerous journals, including *Studies in Romanticism, Religion and the Arts, Representations,* and *Mosaic.* **Essays:** Meyer Levin; *Eva: A Novel of the Holocaust; The Fanatic; My Father's House; The Stronghold.*

STAHL, J.D. Associate professor of English, Virginia Tech, Blacksburg. Author of *Mark Twain, Culture, and Gender.* Contributor to numerous scholarly journals, including *American Literature, Studies in 20th Century Literature, Mark Twain Journal, The Hollins Critic, Phaedrus,* and *Children's Literature Association Quarterly.* **Essays:** Uri Orlev; *The Island on Bird Street; The Man from the Other Side.*

STANFEL, Rebecca. Freelance writer. **Essays:** Chaim Grade; Jean-Paul Sartre; *The Condemned of Altona; Fear and Misery of the Third Reich.*

STERLING, Eric. Associate professor of English, Auburn University-Montgomery, Alabama. Contributor to numerous journals and scholarly publications, including *European Studies Journal, Denise Levertov: New Perspectives,* and *Moral Problems Unique to the Holocaust.* Author of articles on Janusz Korczark, Rolf Hochhuth, Nelly Sachs, Arthur Miller, Yitzhak Wittenberg, Shimon Wincelberg, and others. **Essays:** Fania Fénelon; Anne Frank; Frances Goodrich and Albert Hackett; Barbara Lebow; Denise Levertov; Joshua Sobol; *Adam; Diary of a Young Girl; The Diary of Anne Frank; During the Eichmann Trial; Ghetto; Playing for Time; A Shayna Maidel; Underground.*

SUTRO, Martha. Freelance writer. **Essays:** Gerhard Durlacher; Itzik Manger; Frank Stiffel; *Drowning: Growing up in the Third Reich; My Hate Song; Stripes in the Sky: A Wartime Memoir; The Tale of the Ring: A Kaddish;* "Zürich, the Stork Inn."

SVENDSEN, Christina. Contributor to *Virginia Quarterly Review* and *Harvard Advocate.* Editor of several travel guides, including *Let's Go: Rome 2000* and *Let's Go: Austria and Switzerland 1999.* **Essays:** Italo Calvino; *The Path to the Nest of Spiders.*

TEJERIZO, Margaret. Lecturer in Russian, Department of Slavonic Studies, University of Glasgow. Editor of the journal *Rusistika.* Author of articles on Unamuno and Russian literature, César Vallejo and Maiakovskii, Zamiatin in the British Press, and Russian language teaching methodologies. **Essays:** Vasily Grossman; *Life and Fate.*

TRAVIS, Molly Abel. Associate professor of English, Tulane University, New Orleans. Author of *Reading Cultures: The Construction of Readers in the Twentieth Century.* Contributor to *Virginia Woolf and Fascism: Resisting the Dictators' Seduction* and to the journals *Narrative, Mosaic,* and *Women's Studies.* **Essays:** Geoffrey Hill; "September Song"; *The Triumph of Love;* "Two Formal Elegies."

TUERK, Richard. Professor of literature and languages, Texas A & M University, Commerce. Author of *Central Still: Circle and Sphere in Thoreau's Prose.* Contributor to many journals, including *MELUS, Modern Jewish Studies, Studies in American Jewish Literature, Prospects, New York Historical Society Quarterly,* and *American Literary Realism.* **Essays:** Saul Bellow; Leon Uris; *Mila 18; Mr. Sammler's Planet.*

TURIM, Maureen. Professor of English and film studies, University of Florida, Gainesville. Author of *Abstraction in Avant-Garde Films, Flashbacks in Film: Memory and History,* and *Oshima Nagisa: Images of a Japanese Iconoclast,* as well as more than 60 essays for anthologies and journals on cinema, video, art, cultural studies, feminist and psychoanalytical theory, and comparative literature. **Essays:** Edward Lewis Wallant; *The Pawnbroker.*

VICE, Sue. Reader, Department of English Literature, University of Sheffield, England. Author of *Psychoanalytic Criticism: A Reader, Introducing Bakhtin,* and *Holocaust Fiction.* **Essays:** Binjamin Wilkomirski; *Fragments: Memories of a Wartime Childhood.*

WAGENER, Hans. Professor of German, University of California at Los Angeles. Author of *The German Baroque Novel,* 1973, *Erich Kästner,* 1973, *Stefan Andres,* 1974, *Siegfried Lenz,* 1976, *Frank Wederkind,* 1979, *Carl Zuckmayer,* 1983, *Gabriele Wohmann,* 1986, *Sarah Kirsch,* 1989, *Understanding Erich Maria Remarque,* 1991, *Understanding Franz Werfel,* 1993, *Carl Zuckmayer Criticism:*

Tracing Endangered Fame, 1995, *Lion Feuchtwanger,* 1996, and *René Schickele: Europäer in neun Monaten,* 2000. **Essays:** Lion Feuchtwanger; *The Oppermans.*

WALDEN, Daniel. Professor emeritus of American studies, English, and comparative literature, Pennsylvania State University, State College. Author of several books, including *On Being Jewish: American Jewish Literature from Cahan to Bellow, Twentieth Century American Jewish Fiction Writers,* and *Conversations with Chaim Potok.* Contributor to numerous journals, including *Studies in American Jewish Literature, Profils Americains,* and *Resources in American Literary Studies.* Editor of *Studies in American Jewish Literature.* **Essays:** Philip Roth; "Eli, the Fanatic"; *The Ghost Writer; Operation Shylock: A Confession; Zuckerman Bound: A Trilogy and Epilogue.*

WEINER, Binyomin. Translator of Yiddish and Hebrew. Contributor to numerous journals, including *The Pakn Trager, Killing the Buddha, The Forward,* and *Di Pen.* **Essay:** *My Mother's Sabbath Days.*

WEITZMAN, Lenore. Clarence J. Robinson Professor of Sociology and Law, George Mason University, Fairfax, Virginia. Author of several books and coauthor of *Women in the Holocaust.*

WILKES, George R. Lecturer, Centre for Jewish-Christian Relations and Cambridge Theological Federation, England. Author of "Changing Attitudes to the 'European-ness' of the Holocaust and Its Victims," in *Remembering for the Future 2000.* **Essays:** Sholem Asch; Romain Gary; Rolf Hochhuth; Eugen Kogon; *The Dance of Genghis Cohn; The Deputy; One Destiny: An Epistle to the Christians; The Theory and Practice of Hell: The German Concentration Camps and the System Behind Them.*

WILLIAMS, Ralph G. Professor and associate chair, Department of English, and formerly director, Program on Studies in Religion, University of Michigan, Ann Arbor. Editor and translator of *Marcus Hieronymus, De Arte Poetica.* Coeditor of *Palimpsest: Editorial Theory in the Humanities.* **Essays:** Primo Levi; *The Drowned and the Saved; If Not Now, When?; The Periodic Table; The Reawakening; Survival in Auschwitz.*

WOOLF, Linda M. Associate professor of psychology and coordinator of the Center for the Study of the Holocaust, Genocide, and Human Rights, Webster University, St. Louis, Missouri. Member, American Psychological Association's Ethnopolitical Task Force Cadre of Experts. **Essays:** Bruno Bettelheim; Viktor E. Frankl; *The Informed Heart: Autonomy in a Mass Age; Man's Search for Meaning: An Introduction to Logotherapy.*

YOUNG, James E. Chair, Judaic and Near Eastern Studies, University of Massachusetts-Amherst. Author of *Writing and Rewriting the Holocaust, The Art of Memory,* and *At Memory's Edge.* Editor of *The Texture of Memory.* **Essay:** Introduction.

YOUNGBLOOD, Robert B. Associate professor of German and Italian, Washington and Lee University, Lexington, Virginia. Author of articles in German and Italian for a number of international publications, including *Atti dell'instituto di cultura venezia, Quaderni di studi sveviani dell'universita' di Trieste,* and *Hochschulschriften der Universität Würzburg.* **Essays:** Natalia Ginzburg; *What We Used to Say.*

ZAPRUDER, Alexandra. Independent scholar and writer. Author of *Young Writers' Diaries of the Holocaust.* Curator of *Private Writings, Public Records: Young People's Diaries of the Holocaust,* Holocaust Museum, Houston, 2002. **Essays:** Eva Heyman; Dawid Sierakowiak; *The Diary of Dawid Sierakowiak: Five Notebooks from the Lodz Ghetto; The Diary of Eva Heyman: Child of the Holocaust.*

ZUCCOTTI, Susan. Independent scholar, New York. Formerly instructor, Holocaust and French history, Barnard and Columbia Colleges, New York, and Trinity College, Hartford, Connecticut. Author of *The Italians and the Holocaust: Persecution, Rescue and Survival,* 1987, *The Holocaust, the French, and the Jews,* 1993, and *Under His Very Windows: The Vatican and the Holocaust in Italy,* 2000. **Essays:** Liana Millu; *Smoke over Birkenau.*

ISBN 1-55862-467-8

90000

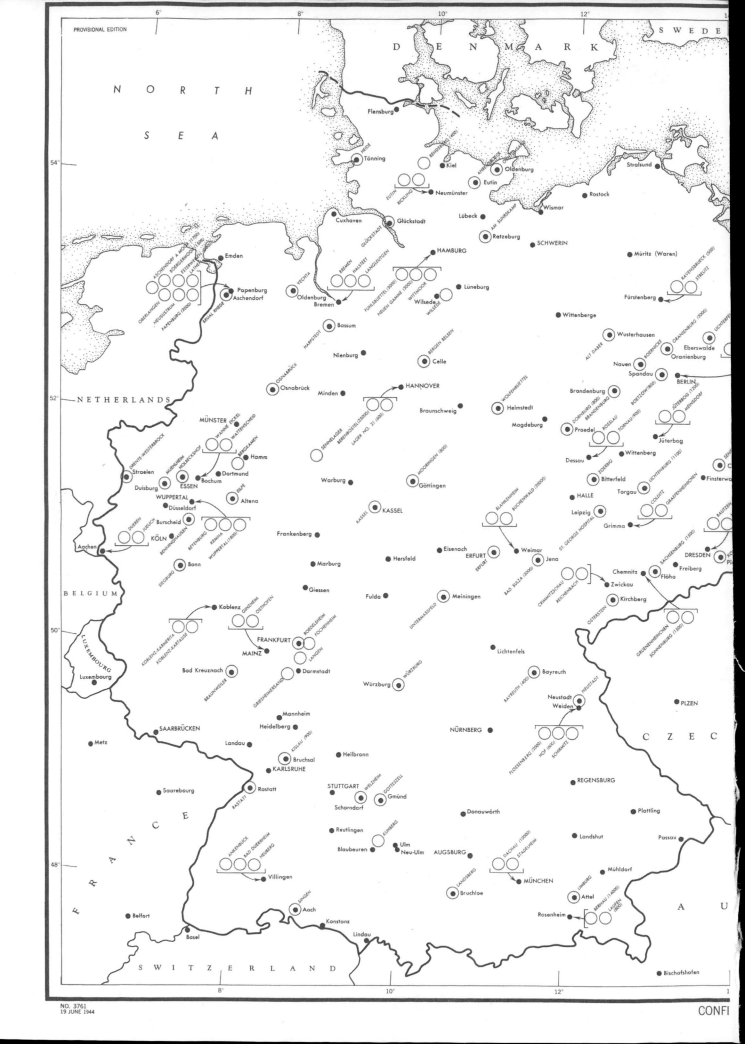

NO. 3761
19 JUNE 1944

CONFI